For Elaine Mills

with best wishes from
your fellow commiserator

John K. Lieberman

Nov. 30, 1992

THE EVOLVING CONSTITUTION

Jethro K. Lieberman

The
EVOLVING
CONSTITUTION

HOW THE SUPREME COURT HAS RULED
ON ISSUES FROM ABORTION TO ZONING

Jethro K. Lieberman

RANDOM HOUSE 1992

All rights reserved under International and Pan-American Copyright Conventions. Published in the United States by Random House, Inc., New York, and simultaneously in Canada by Random House of Canada Limited, Toronto.

Library of Congress Cataloging-in-Publication Data
Lieberman, Jethro Koller.
    The evolving Constitution : how the Supreme Court has ruled on
issues from abortion to zoning / by Jethro K. Lieberman.
        p.   cm.
    Includes bibliographical references.
    ISBN 0-679-40530-5
    1. United States—Constitutional law—Encyclopedias. 2. United
States. Supreme Court.   I. Title.
KF4548.L54 1992
342.73′02—dc20
[347.3022]   92-16590

Manufactured in the United States of America
First Edition

New York   Toronto   London   Sydney   Auckland

For Jo, my s.p.h.p.

Contents

THE EVOLVING CONSTITUTION

How to Use This Book

This is a reference book on the Constitution, not a narrative history. It is an attempt to summarize, in a single volume and in a readable way, what the Constitution means as the United States Supreme Court sees it. This lofty ambition prescribes its own limitations, for although the Constitution is short, its official commentaries are long. No single volume can do justice to the richness of our constitutional history and the sheer profusion of constitutional analysis, even when narrowed to a single court. Since 1803, when Chief Justice John Marshall declared that judges may strike down federal laws that violate the Constitution, the Supreme Court has decided more than 7,500 cases that focus on or somehow deal with the Constitution. Just to list their names is a forbidding exercise.

For that reason, too, this book is not a conventional treatise. It does not dwell on the Court's justifications for its decisions or on the fine, sometimes even gossamer, distinctions that make the doctrinal path so tortuous. There is scarcely room even to list all the issues and controversies that touch on the Constitution. There is certainly no room to tell all their stories in full.

Moreover, because the Constitution is short and old, those who today seek the Constitution's shelter find their problems lying, uncomfortably, in clumps within the protective shadow of a relatively few short sections. Only a few clauses contain the bulk of the cases that come to the courts today: the Due Process Clauses, the Equal Protection Clause, the First Amendment, the Fourth Amendment, the

Sixth Amendment, and a very few others. So diverse are the controversies under these few clauses that a discussion that tracks the Constitution's outline can be compared with the famous Saul Steinberg cartoon of the New Yorker's view of the United States—a swollen Manhattan and very little else.

To overcome these difficulties to the greatest extent possible, this book is arranged by topics. If you want to learn about the abortion controversy, look it up directly under "abortion," not, as you would otherwise have to do, under the more mysterious entry "Fourteenth Amendment."

This arrangement poses its own problems, however. Because so many issues are connected, a discussion by topic risks the Scylla of repetition or the Charybdis of discontinuity. Through a series of cross references and typographical conventions, I hope to have steered between these shoals.

Here is how to use any of the entries in the book.

If you are new to the Constitution and its terminology, first read the short essay entitled "The Constitution: A Guided Tour," beginning on page 6. This essay explains how the Constitution is structured and what it attempts to do. Second, read "Some Thoughts on Interpreting the Constitution" for an overview of why constitutional meaning is so hotly disputed. Turn to "How the Supreme Court Hears and Decides Cases" for a quick look at how the justices grapple with constitutional controversies. Then, look up any topic. For example:

> **abortion** ... In 1973, in *Roe v. Wade*,[1748] the Supreme Court held 7–2 that the FUNDAMENTAL RIGHT TO PRIVACY, protected by the DUE PROCESS Clause of the FOURTEENTH AMENDMENT, is "broad enough to encompass" a qualified right to an abortion.
>
> *Roe* is one of the most notable instances of the use of the Fourteenth Amendment to protect a woman's right to act in her personal life without fear of prosecution. In effect, this line of reasoning, called SUBSTANTIVE DUE PROCESS, says that we retain some personal liberties with which the government may simply not interfere. For ...

The discussion of each topic immediately follows its entry. Words in SMALL CAPITAL LETTERS indicate that a topic under the word or phrase will be found as a separate entry. To avoid cluttering the pages, footnotes have been avoided; all bibliographic information and occasional secondary comments appear in endnotes in the section beginning on page 742. The superscripted note numbers in the text (such as that following *Roe v. Wade* above), whether or not attached to a case name, refer not to the endnotes but to the position of the case in the Table of Cases beginning on page 656. There you will find a brief sketch of the case.

> *See also:* FOURTEENTH AMENDMENT; FUNDAMENTAL RIGHTS; PRIVACY.

This line at the end of a topic tells you where to find related topics that will help round out the discussion. Occasionally the "see also" entry will direct you to topics by concept rather than by name. For example, in the "see also" line under the entry "Bill of Rights" you are directed to "amendments 1 through 10" and to "particular rights guaranteed by the first ten amendments." Such general descriptive terms are necessary to avoid the tedium of listing the dozens of such rights at that point.

> **abridging the freedom of speech,** *see:* **freedom of speech**

The entry on the preceding line is a cross reference. Cross references contain no discussion but enable the reader to look for a topic under a variety of possible labels without having to know in advance what term I or the courts have chosen.

> 1748. Roe v. Wade, 410 U.S. 113 (1973). 7–2, BLACKMUN. (Dissents: White, Rehnquist). 66pp.

Information about major constitutional cases is set out in the alphabetical and numbered Table of Cases beginning on page 656. As in the example above, the initial number corresponds to the number used throughout the text to refer to the particular case. It is followed by the case name and the official citation to the *United States Reports,* available in any law library—410 U.S. 113 means that *Roe v. Wade* can be found in volume 410 of the *United States Reports* beginning on page 113. (Because the Court's own volumes have a production lag of a year or two, some of the most recent cases carry the West Publishing Company citation "S.Ct.") Then comes the Court's vote. The author of the majority opinion is in CAPITALS, and the names of those who concurred or dissented (and occasionally, the names of those not voting) follow. The final number is the total page length of all opinions.

Other sections of this book include:

THE SUPREME COURT'S 1991–92 TERM

For production purposes, the Supreme Court's most recent constitutional rulings are contained in this section beginning on page 583.

THE CONSTITUTION OF THE UNITED STATES

The text of the Constitution and all amendments is set out at page 608.

CONCORDANCE TO THE CONSTITUTION

To find a particular word or phrase used in the Constitution, consult the Concordance, beginning on page 623.

TIME CHART AND BIOGRAPHICAL NOTES ON THE JUSTICES

To see which justices served together, see the TIME CHART OF THE JUSTICES OF THE SUPREME COURT, beginning on page 635. For basic biographical information about each of the justices, see BIOGRAPHICAL NOTES ON THE JUSTICES OF THE SUPREME COURT, beginning on page 645.

FURTHER READING

Finally, for brief descriptions of other reading, consult the section entitled FURTHER READING, on page 739.

A WORD ABOUT WHAT IS *NOT* CONTAINED IN THIS BOOK

Many legal, political, and social issues have constitutional dimensions. But to understand them fully, you must plumb below their constitutional surfaces. The Constitution is not the only law; Congress, the states, their subdivisions, regulatory agencies, and the courts give us plenty of other law to chew on. And since this is not a book about law in general or specific policy issues, inevitably only parts of many stories are told here. The right to vote, for instance, is a constitutional topic; five amendments and several provisions in the main text of the Constitution deal with it. But purely constitutional issues about the right to vote have long since been resolved. Instead, the most difficult questions today arise under such laws as the federal Voting Rights Act. The reader will search in vain here for a narrative on voting and other major policy problems, because this is only a single volume about the Constitution and cases that arise under it, not about policy issues that happen to have constitutional dimensions. The Constitution obviously helps shape the policy debate, but it does not dictate in any detail how we must resolve our pressing problems. Many things are permitted under the Constitution but prohibited by other law. Moreover, constitutional law resides not only in Supreme Court decisions but also in the decisions of many other federal and state courts. For lack of space, not lack of significance, discussion of this vast branch of constitutional law is necessarily omitted. Likewise, the profusion of constitutional theories propounded by many scholars is almost wholly ignored, despite their interest and their habit of turning up years later as the basis of many Supreme Court judgments. Finally, this book does not inquire whether the lower courts and the government abide by the Supreme Court's opinions, even though what happens is often quite different from what the Court says ought to happen. For these limitations I do not so much beg the reader's pardon as ask the reader's understanding—how big a book do you wish to hold in your hands?

Author's Note

References to particular clauses in the Constitution are abbreviated as follows:

Art. I-§8[2] refers to Article I, Section 8, Clause 2. Amendment 14-§1 refers to Section 1 of the Fourteenth Amendment. The full text of the Constitution, subdivided by article, section, and clause, begins on page 608.

To conserve space, many of the discussions

about particular constitutional rights are written as if the Bill of Rights applied directly to the states. Technically, the Bill of Rights limits only the federal government; it does not apply to the states. Beginning in the late nineteenth century, however, the Supreme Court began to apply to the states individual rights contained in the Bill of Rights, by "incorporating" them into the Due Process Clause of the Fourteenth Amendment, which itself applies directly to the states. Through a long process of "selective incorporation" (discussed in detail under INCORPORATION DOCTRINE in this book), the Bill of Rights today has largely been absorbed in the Fourteenth Amendment and hence is equally applicable to the states and the federal government. Because it would be cumbersome in scores of essays to refer to "the Eighth Amendment right against cruel and unusual punishments, as incorporated in the Fourteenth Amendment," the fact of incorporation has largely been omitted.

The Constitution: A Guided Tour

The Constitution was a reaction to the states' unhappy experiences in the decade following the Declaration of Independence. Although loosely bound by the Articles of Confederation, the states were largely autonomous. The Continental Congress had few of the powers of a central government. It had no authority to tax. Though theoretically entrusted with the conduct of foreign relations, it could raise troops only with the greatest difficulty, and it could not control import and export duties. Because all nine states had to agree on national legislation, Congress was largely paralyzed, unable to deal with serious national concerns. There was no executive authority to command troops and no judiciary to enforce any laws that did manage to emerge from Congress. Real power lay in the states, and that meant, mainly, in state legislatures.

To the pained observation of many thoughtful observers, the state legislatures had become omnipotent and despotic: they confiscated property, enacted ex post facto laws, impaired contractual obligations, hindered the repayment of debts, reversed the judgments of courts. Jealous of their prerogatives, the states coexisted uneasily. Trade wars, which sometimes even led to armed conflict, threatened what fellow feeling remained from the revolutionary fervor. Fearing anarchy between the states and despotism within, delegates to a trade convention in Annapolis, Maryland, in 1786 called on their states to send delegates to a new convention to deal with the problems of government in America. Congress endorsed the idea, and the Constitutional Convention was called for May 1787. Four months later the delegates emerged with the present Constitution—"the most wonderful work ever struck off at a given time by the brain and purpose of man," gushed Britain's prime minister William Ewart Gladstone on the Constitution's centennial. (For a history of the Convention, see CONSTITUTIONAL CONVENTION OF 1787 and CONSTITUTION, FRAMERS OF.)

Even with amendments, the Constitution is quite short—about 7,500 words altogether. Those words are divided among seven original articles, ratified in 1788, and twenty-seven amendments, ratified between 1791 and 1992. One of the articles (Article 7) is no longer pertinent, having to do with the original writing and ratification. One of the amendments (the Eighteenth, or Prohibition, Amendment) no longer has any effect either, having been repealed by a later amendment (the Twenty-first).

Broadly speaking, the Constitution establishes the federal government and structures the relationship between the central authority and the states. It does so by both conferring and limiting governmental power. Two fundamental principles lie at the heart of the Constitution: separation and limitation of powers. The principle of separated powers stems from the fear of despotism: to prevent the government from becoming tyrannical, power must be separated and divided among different branches of government.

As usual, James Madison put it best. In *Federalist* 51, he wrote: "If men were angels, no government would be necessary. If angels were to govern men, neither external nor internal controls on government would be necessary. In framing a government which is to be administered by men over men, the great difficulty lies in this: you must first enable the government to control the governed; and in the next place oblige it to control itself. A dependence on the people is, no doubt, the primary control on the government; but experience has taught mankind the necessity of auxiliary precautions." These auxiliary precautions were realized in the Constitution's separation of powers.

SEPARATION OF POWERS

The Constitution separates the powers of government in several different ways.

First, it recognizes three fundamental types of government power—legislative, executive, and judicial—and in Articles I, II, and III vests these powers in three different branches: Congress, the president, and the judiciary.

Second, the Constitution further divides the powers of two of these branches. Congress consists of a Senate and House of Representatives, whose members are elected by different sorts of constituencies. To enact legislation, both houses must agree on the wording of a bill. The federal judiciary is divided also. The Supreme Court has the power to hear appeals, the lower federal courts the power to try cases.

Third, the Constitution prohibits members of the legislative branch from serving simultaneously in the executive branch (and by tradition extending almost to the beginning, members of neither of these branches may simultaneously serve as a federal judge). It also prevents the law from being politicized by giving life tenure to judges on the federal courts and prohibiting Congress from decreasing their salaries.

Fourth, not all power resides in the federal government; the states have significant powers within a sphere closed to the federal government. And they have, through the electoral college and the basis of representation in the Senate (two senators from each state, regardless of population), a substantial influence on the election of the president and the shaping of federal law.

Fifth, the Constitution bars one branch from exercising certain powers that properly belong to another branch. For example, Congress may not pass a "bill of attainder," a law that directs the executive to imprison a particular person. Judgment of guilt may be pronounced only by courts, not by Congress. The president may direct war, but only Congress may declare it.

Sixth and finally, the Constitution reserves the ultimate power to the people, who may, by amending the Constitution itself and by voting for the president and members of Congress, take the public power from one set of leaders and turn it over to another.

Again, Madison best summarized the type of government the Constitution would create: "In the compound republic of America, the power surrendered by the people is first divided between two distinct governments, and then the portion allotted to each subdivided among distinct and separate departments. Hence a double security arises to the rights of the people. The different governments will control each other, at the same time that each will be controlled by itself."

CHECKS AND BALANCES AND THE SHARING OF POWER

Basic as separation of powers is, it is still not enough to foreclose the possibility of tyranny. The problem remains that unless the branches of government have some means of connecting to and dealing with each other, one branch might usurp all power. Madison found (again in *Federalist* 51) that "the great security against a gradual concentration of the several powers in the same department consists in giving to those who administer each department the necessary constitutional means and personal motives to resist the encroachments of the others. . . . Ambition must be made to counteract ambition." It is a "policy of supplying, by opposite and rival interests, the defect of better motives," and it is "particularly displayed in all the subordinate distributions of power, where the constant aim is to divide and arrange the several offices in such a manner as that each may be a check on the other." In short, unless

the branches of government were to *share* power, they could not serve to check and balance each other's powers.

The Constitution achieves this checking and balancing function in several ways. The president, through the veto, has a major share in the legislative power to enact law. Because he may reject its enactments, Congress must pay heed to the president's agenda. In turn, the president's checking power is not uncheckable. Congress may, by a higher vote than originally (i.e., two-thirds instead of a simple majority), overturn the veto. The veto power works in reverse: although the president has the primary power of negotiating treaties and nominating government officials, the Senate may veto treaties and appointments. Likewise, the president has the primary responsibility for carrying out the laws, but Congress has considerable power to influence how government will operate through its power over the budget and its power to establish the various offices of the government.

The courts, too, have a share in the power. They sit to apply the law in particular cases, and through their power to interpret the law and the Constitution itself (although the Constitution is less specific on that point), they can check both Congress's enactments and the president's enforcement policies. But both Congress and the president, in turn, may exert control over the courts. The president names all the federal judges (although the Senate may veto their appointment), and Congress may restrict the types of cases that the courts may hear. Finally, despite the president's power to appoint, Congress may remove any federal official, including members of the Supreme Court, through impeachment. Even this power is divided: the House may impeach, but only the Senate may convict.

Checks and balances are not limited to powers within the federal government. The Constitution provides for a checking and balancing between federal and state governments as well. Article IV declares that the United States must guarantee a "republican form" of government in each state, meaning that the federal government could act against any attempt to establish a dictatorship within any state. Far more important in practice is Article VI, which declares that the Constitution, federal law, and treaties are the "supreme law of the land," superseding any conflicting state law. This article ensures that the states may not act to undermine national law and policy.

LIMITED POWERS AND RIGHTS OF THE PEOPLE

The principle of limited powers stems from the premise that power resides in the people and that the federal government can have only those powers ceded to it by the people. The federal government is, therefore, a government of *enumerated* powers; it can act only through those powers delegated to it. The Constitution limits power in two ways: it specifically delegates only certain powers, and it specifically prohibits the government from acting in certain ways. In general, the Constitution gives the federal government only those powers that ought to reside in a national government—the power to establish uniform regulations of subjects that concern the nation as a whole (for example, a uniform currency, bankruptcy law, internal commerce, a postal system) and the power to govern external relations (for example, defense, treaty making, immigration and naturalization). Legislative powers not delegated to Congress are reserved to the states or are forbidden altogether. Likewise, the federal courts do not have authority to interpret the law whenever they feel like it; they may act only when a case is presented to them. Nor may they hear cases of any description whatever; the Constitution restricts the types of cases that may be brought there.

To secure individual rights, the original Constitution as ratified in 1787 also directly prohibited the government from exercising certain powers. For example, it prohibits Congress from suspending the writ of habeas corpus, without which the government could jail anyone without having to give a reason or press charges; from enacting bills of attainder, through which particular individuals could be sent to prison; from passing ex post facto laws, which would punish a person for doing something that was not unlawful when it was done; and from granting titles of nobility, a provision that prevents the creation of royalty and an official caste system.

The states too are prohibited from enacting many of the same kinds of laws, and others as well, including laws that impair the obligation of contracts and laws that interfere with the national economy and foreign relations. Moreover, the states may not discriminate against citizens of other states, and they are bound to respect each other's laws and judicial rulings.

But the limitation of power was only partly achieved in the original Constitution. It is the role of the Bill of Rights and subsequent amendments to secure other basic rights. The twenty-seven amendments can be grouped, generally, into four categories: rights of the people (usually achieved by limiting further the powers of government), voting, governmental structure, and governmental powers. The Fourteenth Amendment deserves special note because it radically changed the relationship between federal and state power; its ratification in 1868 may truly be called a second constitutional revolution. This amendment prohibits the states from depriving any person of life, liberty, or property without due process of law; and from denying any person the equal protection of the laws. Just as important, the Fourteenth Amendment granted Congress—and by implication, federal courts—the power to enforce these prohibitions, thereby giving the federal government what in time would become a sweeping power over state laws and policies.

In capsule form, the amendments, grouped by subject, established the following constitutional principles and policies:

Rights of the People

The Bill of Rights, comprising the first ten amendments to the Constitution, was ratified in 1791 to overcome the principal objection to the Constitution when it was first submitted to the states in 1788: its failure to guard against the abuse of people's rights. The first nine amendments limit the power of the federal government in many ways—and today through incorporation into the Fourteenth Amendment, they limit the power of the states as well. Among the well-known rights delineated in the Bill of Rights are freedom of speech and press; the right to exercise one's religion, to assemble and petition the government, to be free of arrest or searches without warrant, and to just compensation if private property is taken. It guarantees the right to speedy trial, to confront accusers, to trial by jury, as well as the rights against self-incrimination, double jeopardy, cruel and unusual punishment, and deprivation of life, liberty, or property without due process of law.

Slavery was abolished in 1865 by the Thirteenth Amendment. The Fourteenth Amendment reformed the basic principle of citizenship and, as noted above, limited the power of the states to abuse the rights of the people.

Voting

Several amendments clarified and extended the right to vote to classes of people who had been denied access to voting booths in state and federal elections. The Fifteenth Amendment prohibits both the federal government and the states from denying anyone the right to vote because of race or color. The Nineteenth Amendment likewise prohibits denying women the right to vote. The Twenty-third Amendment grants the vote in presidential elections to residents of the District of Columbia. The Twenty-fourth Amendment abolishes the poll tax. The Twenty-sixth Amendment lowers the voting age to eighteen.

Governmental Structure

The Tenth Amendment, the last of the Bill of Rights, restated the basic principle that a power not given to the federal government remains with the states or with the people. Several amendments altered the plan in the 1787 Constitution for selecting the president and made certain other adjustments. The Twelfth Amendment dramatically altered the way the voting would be counted for president in the electoral college. The Seventeenth Amendment required senators to be elected directly by the people in each state rather than being selected by the state legislatures. The Twentieth Amendment established new dates for the convening of Congress and the inauguration of presidents and provided for the possibility that a president-elect might die before being sworn in. The Twenty-second Amendment limits any president to two terms of office. The Twenty-fifth Amendment deals further with the death and disability of presidents and establishes for the first time the office of acting president. The Twenty-seventh Amendment limits the power of Congress to raise its members' salaries.

Governmental Powers

The trio of Civil War amendments—the Thirteenth, Fourteenth, and Fifteenth—give Congress new national powers not contained in the original Constitution. Congress may act against slavery, peonage, and discriminatory enactments by the states. The Sixteenth Amendment granted Congress the power for the first time to enact a federal income tax. The Eighteenth Amendment, repealed nearly fifteen years after ratification, prohibited the manufacture, sale, or transportation of liquor in the United States "for beverage purposes" and gave Congress and the states the power to enforce it. The Twenty-first Amendment, which repealed Prohibition, continues to give states the power to enforce a ban on liquor if they choose to do so. Various of the voting amendments also give Congress the power to enforce their provisions.

That the United States adheres, in significant ways, to a constitution written more than two centuries ago is quite remarkable. But it has done so in a no less remarkable way, by adroitly bending and twisting and refashioning the constitutional clauses to fit its changing circumstances. No one contemplating the thirteen coastal states with their population of four million in 1787 could have imagined a continental union and then some, with interests and territories in and across oceans, that would govern a population more than sixty times larger through a network of laws and regulations too complex for anyone to fully fathom.

The trials and errors of two centuries have led to several dramatic departures from the spirit of the original Constitution, if not from its text. High on any list must surely rank the growth of bureaucratic, regulatory government. Other features of modern constitutional life that doubtless would have bewildered the passionate people who wrote and ratified the Constitution are standing armies, immense federal and state budgets, powerful presidents, intrusive police presence, and the sweeping array of personal liberties that have been extracted from the few that were originally named.

Five developments, in particular, largely explain the changes.

The first and earliest was Chief Justice Marshall's bold declaration in *Marbury v. Madison* in 1803 that the Supreme Court may declare laws unconstitutional. This ruling created a system of judicial review more powerful than any other in the world.

Second, nearly three-quarters of a century later, was the ratification of the Fourteenth Amendment, which imposed new limits on the states, limits that are subject to further clarification by both Congress and the federal courts. In the twentieth century, and mainly during the past twenty-five years, the Supreme Court has "incorporated" into the Fourteenth Amendment's Due Process Clause most of the rights that once limited only the federal government. This process of incorporation has given the federal courts great power to supervise police and trial procedures once thought to be well outside federal jurisdiction.

Third, the plasticity of the phrase "due process of law" has allowed the courts to control not merely legal procedures but also the substance of laws that both the states and Congress may enact. A doctrine known as "substantive due process" has waxed and waned in different forms for more than a century, and it has permitted the courts, at various times, to overturn the economic and social agendas of state and nation. Once substantive due process condemned wage and hour laws, taxing policies, rate regulation, and other economic controls. Today substantive due process has given rise to a condemnation of laws thought to interfere with personal liberties, giving the courts power to declare, for example, a broad right of personal autonomy and privacy, including a right of abortion.

Fourth, during the past forty years, a newly invigorated Equal Protection Clause has led to a great profusion of cases that have also begun to remake the map of social relations—branding as unconstitutional not only racial discrimination, but laws that discriminate on the basis of sex, ethnicity, and alienage, among other things.

Fifth, invention and industrialization have wholly remade our economy and business relationships, requiring Congress and the federal government to regulate in ways that the Framers could never have imagined.

But all these constitutional developments have been achieved, or been felt necessary, or been tolerated by the Constitution and by a restless population that brings its complaints and legal laments to the United States Supreme Court, demanding yearly that it add to its ever-growing commentaries on this aging but living charter that shapes our lives still.

Some Thoughts on Interpreting the Constitution

The Constitution of the United States is beguilingly—and misleadingly—short, tempting some people to suppose that, unlike sacred texts, it can be read and understood by anyone. This error was most succinctly summed up by George M. Dallas, recognizable today more as the eponym of the Texas town than as vice president of the United States. Dallas wrote his fellow citizens more than 150 years ago: "The Constitution in its words is plain and intelligible, and it is meant for the homebred, unsophisticated understandings of our fellow citizens." He could not have been more mistaken.

The Constitution is elusive, ambiguous, murky, sometimes quite opaque. Many of its phrases were not fresh creations but encrusted with history—for example, "due process of law." Other words and phrases have quite technical meanings accessible only to those schooled in legal arcana—"letters of marque and reprisal," even "common law." Parts of the text are narrow and specific (the age below

which someone may not serve as president); other parts are broad and tantalizingly general ("equal protection of the laws"). In short, even if the Framers had not been practically deified within a generation of their handiwork, the Constitution of the United States inevitably would have come to be just like a sacred text, its meaning knowable only through some human, and fallible, means of interpretation.

In deciding what the Constitution means, we must first grapple with the question, Whose meaning are we seeking? The meaning of the Framers—that is, are we concerned primarily with what those who wrote it had in mind? Or someone else's meaning—our own, for example? This basic question has no ready answer, and so it has remained the fundamental debate for nearly two centuries. It has no clear answer because the Framers themselves didn't supply one in the most obvious place: the Constitution itself.

The Constitution is silent on the question of

how to interpret itself. It does not say, for example, "In resolving disputes over the meaning of this Constitution, choose that meaning intended by the drafters." Likewise, it does not say, "Interpret the words to fit the current situation."

Further difficulties abound. Suppose, for the moment, that we agree we ought to interpret the Constitution according to the original intent—the intent of those who drafted it. Just exactly whose intent must we seek? And how do we uncover what that intent was? One obvious answer to the first question is that we should consult the intent of the Framers. After all, they wrote it. If a word or phrase has any meaning, it must have the meaning of the persons who put it there. But no sooner do we state this obvious proposition than an equally obvious objection arises. There were fifty-five delegates to the Constitutional Convention. The actual words were chosen by a five-member Committee on Style. Did the stylists, by using particular words, alter the meaning of what had been discussed by all, or at least by many others? Did all those voting in favor of particular concepts—ex post facto law, for example—agree not only on what those concepts meant generally but also on how the selected terms used to express those concepts should be interpreted when a difficult case came up? For example, suppose Congress enacts a retroactive tax law. Does requiring a taxpayer to fork over money on income made some months before the law was enacted violate the Ex Post Facto Clause? The answer is by no means obvious.

It is a commonplace that words are frequently chosen as compromises to skirt hard problems; for example, the hard problem of securing unanimity on every part of every proposal being considered. Legislators "fuzz up" their language every day to get votes for their bills. It is precisely because the language is "open," without any specific, hard-and-fast meaning, that legislators are willing to vote for

it. So with the Constitution. Many of its phrases are obscure, we may be reasonably certain, precisely *because* there was no precise meaning on which everyone voting for them agreed. So whose meaning do we select as the *constitutional* meaning—Delegate A's or Delegate B's? The meaning given to the Constitution by this faction of delegates or that one?

Moreover, why settle on the Framers as the people whose intent should govern? They merely proposed the language of the Constitution. Those who ratified it might more properly be supposed to have the crucial intent about its meaning. If they understood by a phrase something different from what the Framers thought, doesn't it make more sense to interpret the Constitution today by their meaning? After all, they were the ones who made it binding law. It is this distinction between Framers' and Ratifiers' intent that explains James Madison's seemingly contradictory statements that, on the one hand, judges should interpret the Constitution by looking "to the sense in which [it] was accepted and ratified by the nation" and on the other hand that the intentions of the Framers "could never be regarded as the oracular guide in expounding the Constitution."

Even continuing to assume we wish to interpret according to the meaning of *somebody* back in 1787, how do we learn what the meaning was? Do we look up these constitutional words and phrases in a late eighteenth-century dictionary? Perhaps we should consult the political treatises, histories, and works of philosophy that the Framers read so that we can learn what words and phrases were current and how they were generally used. Historians must surely look to these sources, but they do not yield the precise meanings that would result in inevitable conclusions.

We do have two more likely sources of meaning to which we can turn. One is *The Federalist Papers*, those enduring brilliant essays by Madison, Alexander Hamilton, and John Jay. But they were writing as partisans, advocates for ratification in New York and Virginia. Furthermore, their purpose was rather more to convince a doubting public of the necessity of a particular kind of federal union than to explore in detail the reaches of every constitutional word. *The Federalist Papers* were, in short, political documents, not legal ones, and they too suffer from the common defect that they express the authors' beliefs, not those of all the delegates, much less the beliefs of those who were shortly to ratify.

The other principal source is the collection of Constitutional Convention notes of James Madison, who exhaustively chronicled most of the debates during that hot 1787 summer in Philadelphia. But they were not published until 1840, four years after his death, and by then much constitutional groundwork had already been laid in the courts. Moreover, Madison's notes, like *The Federalist Papers,* do not ultimately yield the detail we might crave in uncovering the meaning of many elusive phrases, for they cover, at most, only one-fifth of the debates in Philadelphia.

Besides, what we really should wish to know is what the Framers or the Ratifiers thought about the very question of interpretation itself. After all, if we are to be bound by their intent, then how they intended later generations to go about interpreting the text should be the crucial inquiry. Did the Framers or Ratifiers intend us to interpret "broadly" or "narrowly"? Even more to the point, did they wish us to be bound by their intent or not? The drafters might quite wisely have held that they could not possibly resolve all future questions and so they—and we—would have to rely on the good judgment of later generations to work out matters case by case. Unfortunately, we know next to nothing about what the Framers thought of this question of their intent. And we know nothing whatsoever about how the Ratifiers felt.

There are two other, related difficulties over interpreting according to original intent. One is that on many issues of utmost concern to us, the Framers had no intent because they did not conceive—could not have conceived—the problems that would confront this astonishing American people, whose technology and economy would transform the world. The Framers gave Congress the power to regulate interstate, but not local, commerce. In 1985 the Supreme Court ruled that the Commerce Clause gives Congress the power to outlaw arson in a two-story apartment building in Chicago. Is arson of a local apartment building "in" interstate commerce? Can anyone suppose such a problem was on the minds of the Framers? We certainly have no evidence for it.

A second difficulty is that the Framers may have been mistaken in their "intent"—mistaken, that is, in believing that the words they chose embraced their intent. This is not as paradoxical as it may seem. Suppose, as Thomas Jefferson once wrote, "all men are created equal." Suppose, further, that these words had been placed in the Constitution (in fact, of course, they were not put there). Would it have refuted a slave who sought emancipation to say, "Well, Jefferson didn't really *intend* to free the slaves"? Perhaps he personally did not so intend, but it would snap the Constitution beyond repair, or at least utility, to argue that the phrase "all men are created equal" (or some similar set of words) does not apply to slavery. If Jefferson had focused on the gulf between his noble sentiment and his inconsistent behavior in holding slaves, he might have yielded to the inconsistency and either have changed his phrase or manumitted his slaves. If you do not focus on the discrepancy, it is entirely possible to hold inconsistent positions, but one of them must surely be mistaken. We engage in logical inconsistencies all the time—when, for example, we rail against taxes but expect the government to provide us with ever-growing services.

So it is not enough to ask, "What did the Framers intend about Issue X or Problem Y?" We must ultimately ask what they intended by the *phrases* that purport to govern those issues and problems. Jefferson might truly have intended, had he thought grandly about it, that all *persons* are truly created equal and that someday a more humane world would act upon that knowledge, interpreting the phrase for what it *really* means, and not as he, a prisoner of his age, circumscribed it.

By the same token, we ought to be equally suspicious of arguments that the Constitution really does mean anything that people in power, justices of the Supreme Court, wish it to mean. It is no more sensible to permit Justice So-and-So to say that white means black than it is for Framer So-and-So to say that black means white. If we are to have any sort of ordered society, we must live under a Constitution whose words are neither shrunk to an invisible point nor stretched along an infinite line.

How, then, can we go about responsibly interpreting the Constitution? Over the years, the Supreme Court has followed several methods, waxing and waning with shifts in the political mood and the temper of the justices. Because moods and tempers will vary endlessly, the debate over the propriety of interpretation will endure, a hallmark of democratic government. The most significant approaches to interpreting the Constitution are noted briefly here.

INTERPRETATIONS FROM LOGIC

Although constitutional analysis is scarcely an exercise in formal logic, some principles or axioms can fairly be invoked to deduce certain results. The Constitution is largely silent about most of the daily concerns of life. To confine the government strictly to those powers specifically mentioned would make governing impossible; it would defeat the purposes for which the explicit powers were granted. For example, the Constitution does not say that Congress may pass criminal laws or provide penalties for those who violate the laws it does enact. To be sure, the Necessary and Proper Clause gives Congress power to fill in the gaps. But even without it, Chief Justice John Marshall reasoned, no one ever doubted that Congress has the power to "punish any violation of its laws," even though "this is not among the enumerated powers of Congress." Even Thomas Jefferson, a strict constructionist who believed that a power didn't exist if the Constitution didn't name it, overcame his scruples in entering into the Louisiana Purchase, despite the Constitution's silence on the power of the federal government to acquire territory. As Madison said in *Federalist* 44: "Had the Constitution [omitted the Necessary and Proper Clause], there can be no doubt that all the particular powers requisite as means of executing the general powers would have resulted to the government by unavoidable implication. No axiom is more clearly established in law, or in reason, than that wherever the end is required, the means are authorized; wherever a general power to do a thing is given, every particular power necessary for doing it is included."

INTERPRETATIONS FROM PURPOSE

Closely related to interpretation from logic is interpretation from purpose. One of the most heated debates in the nation's early years was whether Congress had the power to create a national bank. When the issue came before the Supreme Court in 1819, Chief Justice Marshall upheld Congress's authority under its power to make all laws necessary and proper to carry into effect its other powers. He declared that the Necessary and Proper Clause must be interpreted in light of the Constitution's purposes: "The subject is the execution of those great powers on which the welfare of a nation essentially depends.... This provision is made in a Constitution intended to endure for ages to come and, consequently, to be adapted to the various crises of human affairs.... We must never forget that it is a *constitution* we are expounding." His decision in *McCulloch v. Maryland* still stands as one of the most eloquent defenses of a broad reading of the Constitution.

INTERPRETATIONS FROM STRUCTURE

The Constitution nowhere uses the phrase "separation of powers." But the structure of its text, placing legislative power in Article I, executive in Article II, and judicial in Article III, is the primary basis for inferring the constitutional doctrine.

INTERPRETATIONS FROM INTENT

The debate over intent, as we have seen, will never be settled because intent itself is so difficult to discern. Still, the Court may adhere to some presumed intent of the Framers if it supposes its obligation to do so. Many of the liveliest constitutional controversies today revolve around the claim that the Framers did or did not intend a certain result. For example, the debate over the separation of church and state centers on what the Framers intended by the words "establishment of religion." Did they really mean to erect a "wall of separation" between church and state, in Jefferson's words, or did they mean only to prevent the state from preferring one church over another?

INTERPRETATIONS FROM CONTEXT

One question in *McCulloch v. Maryland* was what the words in the Necessary and Proper Clause really mean. Does "necessary" mean only that which is "indispensable"? Or could it mean that which is merely "convenient" or "useful"? Chief Justice Marshall noted the am-biguity of the word: "[I]t has not a fixed character peculiar to itself. It admits of all degrees of comparison.... [A] thing may be necessary, very necessary, absolutely or indispensably necessary." The answer, he discovered, lay in another clause, which prohibits a state from imposing certain duties "except what may be *absolutely* necessary for executing its inspection laws." When Congress wanted to use "necessary" in the sense of "indispensable," it knew how to do so. It did not do so in the Necessary and Proper Clause, Marshall noted; the word is used in different senses and its meaning must be discerned from context.

INTERPRETATIONS FROM CANONS OF CONSTRUCTION

In *Marbury v. Madison*, Chief Justice Marshall confronted the question of whether Congress could enlarge the "original jurisdiction" of the Supreme Court. Nothing in the literal language prohibits Congress from doing so. Marshall disagreed, observing that Article III specifically assigns a few types of cases to the Court's original jurisdiction and all others to its appellate jurisdiction. If Congress could override these assignments, then the clause would "have no operation at all." Following a canon of construction—that is, a rule by which courts have historically construed legal instruments—Marshall said: "It cannot be presumed that any clause in the constitution is intended to be without effect, and therefore such a construction [allowing Congress to reassign jurisdiction] is inadmissible." This approach is not always consistently followed. For example, the Court later held that the Counterfeiting Clause (Art. I-§8[6]) is superfluous since Congress could achieve under the Necessary and Proper Clause all that it could achieve under the specific grant of power to punish counterfeiting.

INTERPRETATIONS FROM PLAIN MEANING

Regardless of the Framers' intent, the Court has often insisted that if a constitutional phrase has a "plain meaning" it is to be applied according to that meaning. For example, in abolishing slavery the Framers of the Thirteenth Amendment had in mind black slaves. In 1873, the Court said in the *Slaughter-House Cases* that "[Although] negro slavery alone was in the mind of Congress which proposed the thirteenth article, it forbids any other kind of slavery, now or hereafter. If Mexican peonage or the Chinese coolie labor system shall develop slavery of the Mexican or Chinese race within our territory, this amendment may safely be trusted to make it void."

INTERPRETATIONS FROM HISTORY

The Seventh Amendment guarantees the right to a jury trial in "suits at common law." Does the Seventh Amendment mean to include only suits that were among the types of "common law" cases known in 1789, or does it include suits that are within later extensions of the common law? The historical view would seem to suggest the former. A suit to enjoin a neighbor from playing with dynamite in the basement is not a suit at common law because it would not have been so when the Constitution was ratified. At first glance, such a result may seem to fit nicely with a theory of original intent. Surely the drafters of the Bill of Rights did not mean to include types of suits of which they were unaware or that were not then triable by jury.

But things are not so simple. Historically, the common law has been, and continues to be, variable, evolutionary. For nearly a millennium, it has been a system permitting courts to make law. The common law has changed over time because that is its very nature. Neither history nor original intent can sensibly tell us

to overlook the evolutionary feature of the common law; its capacity for change is as much a part of the historical record as are the cases recognized two hundred years ago.

So when a tenant sues for damages under federal antidiscrimination law, defending against a landlord's attempt to evict him, is a jury necessary? The common law knew no such proceeding. The Court held the Seventh Amendment applicable: "[T]rial by jury [is required] in actions unheard of at common law, provided that the action involves rights and remedies of the sort traditionally enforced in an action at law, rather than in an action at equity or admiralty." But what of a case in which the Occupational Safety and Health Administration seeks to impose monetary fines on a company for violating its regulations? This, too, was unknown to the common law; this, too, sounds like the sort of inquiry "traditionally enforced" in a common law proceeding. The Court held otherwise.

INTERPRETATIONS FROM CONSIDERATIONS OF JUDICIAL ECONOMY

Some decisions may be understood as influenced by the limited resources of the courts. For example, if the Supreme Court had adhered faithfully to the doctrine of separate but equal, by which racially segregated facilities were said to be constitutionally permissible if the facilities were equal, the courts would have been required to examine tens of thousands of schools, restaurants, theaters, and other facilities and would have had to develop a set of criteria for determining the meaning of equality in each instance. In gross, that is an impossible task, and *Brown v. Board of Education* and later decisions may be understood at least in part as the Court's declaration that any rule short of an outright ban on segregation would have been impossible to enforce. For similar reasons, the Court's enunciation of the Sixth

Amendment right to the effective assistance of counsel must strike any fair-minded observer as fanciful or even hypocritical, if viewed solely as a matter of doctrine, since the Court has fashioned a rule permitting defendants to remain behind bars when their lawyers have made all sorts of mistakes. Lacking the stomach to order the states and federal government to fund public defender programs at sufficient levels, the Court has had to rely on a harmless error rule and a rather strained understanding of what constitutes ineffective assistance of counsel, for otherwise court dockets would be overwhelmed with questions of whether lawyers prepared adequately and employed suitable trial strategies.

INTEPRETATIONS FROM NECESSITY AND EXPERIENCE

In a case testing whether the federal government's treaty power could supplant the power of a state to control migratory birds (a question not much on the minds of George Washington, James Madison, and company), Justice Oliver Wendell Holmes wrote in 1920: "When we are dealing with words that also are a constituent act, like the Constitution of the United States, we must realize that they have called into life a being the development of which could not have been foreseen completely by the most gifted of its begetters. It was enough for them to realize or to hope that they had created an organism; it has taken a century and has cost their successors much sweat and blood to prove that they created a nation. The case before us must be considered in the light of our whole experience and not merely in that of what was said a hundred years ago."

INTERPRETATIONS FROM PRECEDENT

Most decisions of the Court rest on precedent, as outgrowths of earlier decided cases. In ruling on whether a new set of circumstances fits within a constitutional provision, the Court will often refer to its earlier cases and reason from them. In certain cases, it will look to what the First Congress did and to whether the precedent set by that Congress has generally been followed. Criticism of particular cases is often mistaken because the critic overlooks the fundamental approach of case-by-case adjudication. Often it is only in hindsight that we can see the Court groping toward a more general solution to a difficult set of problems. The Court's rationale in *Brown v. Board of Education* was attacked initially because it was limited and raised as many problems as it settled. But within the decade it became clear that the Court was settling on a broader rule. Likewise, the Court's initial privacy rulings may be attacked as made up out of whole cloth. Dissenting in *Griswold v. Connecticut*, the 1965 birth control case, Justice Potter Stewart said that he could find no "general right of privacy in the Bill of Rights, in any other part of the Constitution, or in any case ever before decided" by the Supreme Court. But eight years later, in *Roe v. Wade*, Stewart concurred in the judgment that laws against abortion violate a woman's right to privacy, because later cases made it clear that the real basis of *Griswold* was the unconstitutionality of invading a person's liberty, which is protected by the Constitution, not a pure right of privacy, which is not. Though not absolute, the lure of precedent is very strong. Many justices who might not originally have accepted a constitutional doctrine wind up adhering to it because it has become a settled expectation of daily life. The most telling example is, of course, *Roe v. Wade*, adhered to by Courts with justices appointed largely by presidents who have sworn to overturn it.

To discuss any single approach to interpreting the Constitution is to falsify historical reality. Few cases favor one way and exclude others. Nor do the justices often announce that they are following one approach or another. Their interpretive methods are usually implicit, hidden, masked. Moreover, the entire enterprise of interpreting the Constitution is at best ramshackle. Because precedents are collected in books, and now in data banks, we can observe the "evolution" of constitutional thought through a complete fossil record. Every constitutional decision ever published by the United States Supreme Court sits in all but the most modest law libraries, and each is instantaneously retrievable today by anyone with a computer, a modem, and the funds to go on line. This lush growth of the constitutional forest means that the Court must often engage in attempts to reconcile the unreconcilable, fitting together a pattern of cases decided at different times for different reasons by different justices with different agendas. One may legitimately puzzle why inferences drawn in one field are not permitted in another. For example, the Court has said that the Speech and Debate Clause, which immunizes members of Congress from lawsuits, also embraces their staff employees because it is impossible to carry on legislative business today without staff. On the other hand, the Court refused to follow this logic in the search and seizure arena, holding that people have no reasonable expectation in keeping private the telephone numbers they dial, even though, as Justice Thurgood Marshall pointed out in dissent, "unless a person is prepared to forgo use of what for many has become a personal or pro-

fessional necessity, he cannot help but accept the risk of surveillance."

Often a decision will hinge on the severity of the facts and circumstances, forcing the Court to declare a doctrine that it might otherwise have avoided. For example, there is a raging debate on whether the Eighth Amendment prohibits criminal sentences disproportionate to the crime. Justice Antonin Scalia says there is no warrant in the Constitution or in history for a rule of proportionality. But a majority of the Court has decreed otherwise, at least for sentences that are "grossly disproportionate" to the crime. Justice Byron R. White has noted that the Constitution does condemn "excessive fines" and says that it would not be "unreasonable to conclude that it would be both cruel and unusual to punish overtime parking by life imprisonment." Since legislative majorities rarely do grossly disproportionate things, the general rule is that if a legislature has voted for it, it is not grossly disproportionate. But when an aberration occurs, even those who are strict constructionists will find a way to rule against it. Even Scalia agrees that the death penalty may not be used except for murder.

We return, therefore, where we began. There can never be a fixed, unyielding meaning to the Constitution for the same reason that the Constitution endures. It remains a charter of shimmering truths and obscurities that will ever be tailored to our own purposes, no matter how much genius is devoted to proving that the One True Way should yield some other result.

How the Supreme Court Hears and Decides Cases

We associate the Constitution with the United States Supreme Court because for nearly two hundred years the Court has been its authoritative interpreter. But the Supreme Court does not issue rulings willy-nilly. A few years ago, a Washington journalist wrote that "by ninth grade ... I heard about the Constitution of the United States. . . . I thought of the Supreme Court as something like a group of Super Bad guidance counselors who were always there to give an opinion on teen problems. I used to send the Court letters posing 'constitutional questions' that bugged me: 'Should wrestling coaches really be teaching psychology?' " Had one of the justices replied, the ninth-grader would have learned that no pronouncement about the Constitution has any *legal* effect unless it is the ruling of a court in a case that has properly come before it. The justice would not have told the student what he thought about wrestling coaches, because federal judges do not give their opinions to anyone who seeks constitutional enlightenment. You cannot write a letter to procure an opinion, for the Constitution itself dictates that courts remain silent unless they are ruling in an actual case.

Now, it may seem to the bleary-eyed scanner of newspaper headlines that sooner or later everything is hauled into court and branded a constitutional issue. But in fact, relatively few cases ever come before the Supreme Court, and even fewer of those it does hear are constitutional. However, when it does decide constitutional cases, its rulings are often quite momentous. In the 1990–91 term, the last full term with reported statistics before this edition went to press, the Court disposed of 5,412 cases; 904 other cases were held over for the next term. Of the cases dispatched, only 129 were disposed of

by written opinion. In almost all the other cases, the Court either denied or dismissed petitions for review or permitted the parties to withdraw their appeals and petitions. The Court granted review in only 6.5 percent of the cases appealed.

With very few exceptions, the Supreme Court is an appellate court. It hears appeals from cases decided in lower federal and state courts; it does not try cases by hearing witnesses and gathering evidence. Which *types* of cases it may hear are determined by federal law; which *particular cases* the Court ultimately hears it decides for itself. Under the Constitution, Congress may prescribe the kinds of cases to be heard in the federal courts, including the Supreme Court. In the nation's early years, Congress gave the federal courts relatively limited jurisdiction, far less than that allowed by the Constitution itself, so that some types of cases could not get into the courts (for further details, see COURTS, CONGRESSIONAL CREATION AND CONTROL OVER and JURISDICTION). Also, until relatively recently, Congress told the Supreme Court that litigants with certain types of cases were automatically entitled to have their cases reviewed on appeal. But since 1988, the Court has been given complete control over its docket; the justices themselves decide which cases they will hear of the thousands that pour in. The justices generally look for cases that raise important constitutional issues, for cases that have received conflicting treatment in the lower federal courts of appeals, and for cases that raise important questions of statutory or regulatory interpretation. In selecting cases, the Court may hear appeals from both federal courts of appeals and state supreme courts.

The Court traditionally begins its term each

year on the first Monday in October and usually concludes the term's business by the end of June, when a flurry of decisions are often released at the very last moment. Occasionally the Court sits longer or is forced to return for a case of paramount importance. For example, in *United States v. Nixon,* the Court heard oral argument on July 8, 1974, testing whether the president could constitutionally be required to turn over confidential tape recordings in a federal criminal case, and it handed down its extraordinary decision on July 24. Even when the Court is recessed over the summer, a litigant may apply to a particular justice for relief under certain circumstances.

Nothing in the Constitution or federal statutes dictates how the justices go about deciding the cases they have chosen to hear. The procedures they use are set by the Court itself and have evolved over many years. For decades, the Court has followed the "rule of four": if four justices decide to hear a case (in the technical parlance, if they decide to grant a "writ of certiorari," an order to a lower court to send up the record of a case), then the case will be heard.

In every case the justices hear, the arguments are submitted first in written briefs. Each case is then argued orally. Oral arguments are open to the public. In the Court's early years, oral argument in important cases could sometimes last for days. No longer. Today each side is allotted thirty minutes to present its case. In most cases the advocates barely begin to make their arguments when they are peppered with questions from the raised, irregularly shaped bench. (The Supreme Court does not sit in panels, as most other appellate courts do; all the justices sit for each case.) When the advocate has five minutes left, an amber light at the podium winks on. When time has expired, amber turns to red, and the lawyer must stop.

The justices do not decide the case immediately. Each week, at a conference of the justices, every argued case is discussed and tentative votes are taken. The conference discussion is closed to everyone but the nine justices. Indeed the conference of the justices is one of the most secret meetings in a town full of secret meetings. Unlike most other meetings in Washington, however, what occurs there is leakproof.

By long tradition, the senior justice in the majority assigns the task of writing the opinion to one of the justices. If the chief justice is in the majority, he is the senior justice. If the chief justice is in the minority, the senior justice in the majority is the one who has served longest on the bench.

The writer may take one week to several months to circulate the majority opinion, and during that time, in reaction to the opinion itself, or as a result of the persuasion of another justice, votes may change. The Court's decision is never certain until it is printed and announced publicly.

After oral argument the justices may hold a case for as long as they wish, although almost all argued cases are decided by the end of the term. Occasionally the justices may direct the parties to reargue the case. For example, *Brown v. Board of Education,* the seminal school desegregation case, was reargued a year after it first came before the Court. But once the Court publicly announces its ruling, the case is decided. Justices may change their minds often while the opinions are circulating privately between their chambers, but once published, the decisions are final and the case is at an end.

That does not mean, however, that the constitutional or other issues are necessarily settled. Every issue is always open for reargument in later cases; changed parties, changed circumstances, and changed courts often lead to changed conclusions. That is why, for example, abortion has been so active a topic on the Court's calendar for two decades after *Roe v. Wade.* The Supreme Court remains what it has always been—the most powerful constitutional court in the world.

A

---

abortion Historically, control of abortion procedures, and the power to ban abortion, were left to the states. Despite that power, state laws criminalizing abortion date only to the latter part of the nineteenth century; until then it was not a crime to perform or have an abortion. By the mid-twentieth century, however, a majority of states prohibited abortion, although most of them provided an exception when a pregnancy endangered the mother's life.

In 1973, in *Roe v. Wade,*[1748] the Supreme Court held 7–2 that the FUNDAMENTAL RIGHT TO PRIVACY, protected by the DUE PROCESS Clause of the FOURTEENTH AMENDMENT, is "broad enough to encompass" a qualified right to an abortion.

Roe is one of the most notable instances of the use of the Fourteenth Amendment to protect a woman's right to act in her personal life without fear of prosecution. In effect, this line of reasoning, called SUBSTANTIVE DUE PROCESS, says that we retain some personal liberties with which the government may simply not interfere. For sixteen years the Court adhered to this fundamental principle and even strengthened it. Then, in 1989, it cast it in wide doubt without quite casting it aside, in its 5–4 decision in *Webster v. Reproductive Health Services.*

Roe overturned a Texas statute that forbade procuring or attempting to procure an abortion, except to save the mother's life. *Roe* said that the right to an abortion is not absolute; the state's COMPELLING INTEREST in the mother's health and potential life of the fetus permits some regulation. Trisecting pregnancy, Justice Harry A. Blackmun announced a threefold rule: In the first trimester, the decision to abort resides solely with the woman and her physician, apparently because, on the medical evidence, abortion procedures at this stage are safer than childbirth. The ruling did permit the states to specify that only a licensed physician could perform an abortion. In the second trimester, the state may establish further regulations, if they are narrowly drawn to promote the state's interest in the mother's health. In the final trimester, when the fetus is normally considered viable (that is, capable of "meaningful life" outside the womb), the state may assert its interest in the potential fetal life by proscribing abortion, except when necessary to protect the mother's health.

One significant effect of *Roe* was the holding that a fetus is not a "person" within the constitutional use of that term in the Fourteenth Amendment, and hence not entitled to the process due all living persons whenever the government threatens life, liberty, or property.

Roe inflamed public opinion as few modern issues have, and the contentious and anguished debate continues unabated. Critics have charged the 7–2 majority (Justices Byron R. White and William H. Rehnquist dissenting) with exercising, in Justice White's words, "raw judicial power." But until 1989, a wavering majority held firm in numerous decisions against legislative attempts to burden the first trimester right to an abortion.

In a companion case, the Court struck down Georgia requirements that abortions be performed in hospitals accredited by special committees (not applicable to other surgical procedures); that two other physicians and a hospital staff committee approve the abortionist's decision to go ahead; and that the abortion be "necessary."555 The Court ruled that after the first trimester, states may neither ban saline amniocentesis as a means of abortion,1638 nor demand that all abortions be performed in full-service hospitals.25 Similarly, the Court struck down statutes that require women to wait twenty-four hours after consenting to an abortion and doctors to detail to their patients the surgical techniques of abortion and the stages of fetal development.25

In an early case the Court held that states may require women to consent in writing and hospitals to keep records of abortions performed.1638 But in a 1986 case, growing impatient with the blizzard of devices legislators were inventing to burden the woman's choice, a 5–4 majority held that Pennsylvania's informed consent and reporting statute was fatally defective.2043 That law required the attending physician to tell the woman about the possible physical and psychological detriments of abortion and about all medical risks, and to discuss financial benefits available following childbirth, including the father's responsibility. The statute directed the physician also to give the woman material to read that described the anatomical characteristics of the fetus at two-

week intervals and that urged the woman to talk with various public and private agencies that would provide assistance during pregnancy and after childbirth.

Said Justice Blackmun: "All this is, or comes close to being, state medicine imposed upon the woman, not the professional medical guidance she seeks." The hospital reporting requirements were unconstitutionally intrusive in requiring that the woman show her method of payment, personal history, and reasons for deciding to have an abortion—and all these records would be available for public copying.

Many states reacted to *Roe* with laws requiring the woman to obtain consent from her spouse or parents. The Court has voided all spousal consent statutes,1638 but it has upheld parental consent statutes within limits not yet clearly spelled out, on the ground that children do not possess constitutional rights equal to those of adults. The Court has held that an "immature" girl may be refused an abortion unless both parents consent, but the law must permit prompt judicial approval of an abortion even though the parents fail to consent when the abortion is in her best interest.149 A state law may also require a minor pregnant girl to obtain the consent either of a parent or a juvenile court judge.1637 The state may demand that a doctor notify the parents of a minor girl before performing the abortion.833

In a pair of cases in 1990, the Court continued to equivocate on the burden to be imposed on minor daughters. Both cases involved statutes requiring parental notice, as opposed to consent. In a case arising from Minnesota's 1981 abortion statute, the Court held that the state could not constitutionally prohibit a doctor from performing an abortion on a minor girl until at least forty-eight hours after both parents have been notified.929 Speaking for the 5–4 majority, Justice John Paul Stevens said that in the "ideal family setting," a child's "notice to either parent would normally constitute notice to both." The state should not presume that any one parent is incompetent to provide for a daughter's well-being. Moreover, when a family is "dysfunctional" (because of divorce or an abusive parent), the requirement that both parents be notified has been shown to be "positively harmful to the minor and her family." In that same case, however, a different majority of five (Justice Sandra Day O'Connor was the swing vote) upheld a "judicial bypass" of the law, under which a minor daughter can avoid notifying both parents only by obtaining a court order permitting the doctor to proceed.

In the other 1990 case, which arose from a 1985 Ohio abortion statute, a 6–3 majority upheld another limitation on the ability of a minor daughter, unwilling to notify even one parent, to get an abortion. She must prove in juvenile court by "clear and convincing evidence" that: she has sufficient maturity to decide to have an abortion without notifying a parent; or that one of her parents has engaged in a "pattern" of physical, sexual, or emotional abuse against her; or that notice would not be in her best interests.[1519] The court must hold a hearing no later than five days after the girl files her suit and must announce its decision as soon as the hearing concludes; otherwise, the abortion may proceed. The statute contains a limited appeal procedure.

The Court has confined the right to an abortion, whether for a minor or an adult, to a woman's legal freedom to choose. This right does not carry with it any implicit further right to economic resources to carry out the abortion. The Court has consistently held that nothing in the Constitution limits the power of the states and the federal government to decide what medical procedures to fund. As a result, neither the states nor the federal government has to pay for nontherapeutic abortions.[1226, 1644] A state may refuse to pay for an abortion even if it is subsidizing maternity and childbirth costs for the indigent,[1226, 140] and even if the

attending physician has certified that the abortion is necessary to the mother's life or health.[869, 2222] In sustaining the Hyde Amendment the Court explicitly approved a funding cutoff even "in instances where severe and long-lasting physical health damage to the mother would result if the pregnancy were carried to term when so determined by two physicians."[869] And in the 1989 *Webster* case the Court upheld a Missouri statute that prohibits abortions in any public facility.

To the consternation of "pro-choice" advocates (in the lexicon of the 1980s, those who favor a woman's right to abortion) and to the delight of "pro-life" advocates (those who would ban abortion), the Court also upheld in *Webster* a section of the Missouri law that requires physicians to perform a battery of medical tests. Doctors who believe the woman to be twenty or more weeks pregnant must check "gestational age, weight, and lung maturity" to determine whether the fetus is viable. The purpose of the provision is to permit the state to ban abortions at the earliest possible time under *Roe*, except for the most compelling reasons. The Missouri provision appears to contradict *Roe*'s trimester rule.

Under *Roe*, the first twenty-four weeks were beyond the state's control. For that period, only the woman and her doctor could participate in the decision whether or not to abort. But because the Missouri law says the fetus could be viable by the twentieth week, the state now may begin to intrude on the woman's decision at that point, essentially a month earlier than under *Roe*.

While denying that the Court was required to rethink *Roe*, because the state did not claim the power to ban *all* abortions, a plurality of three justices—Rehnquist, White, and Anthony M. Kennedy—did conclude that they saw no reason "the State's interest in protecting potential human life should come into existence only at the point of [fetal] viability, and [no reason] that there should therefore be a rigid line allowing state regulation after viability but prohibiting it before viability." Taken on its face, that language appears to overrule *Roe*, as the dissenting justices, Blackmun, Stevens, William A. Brennan, and Thurgood Marshall, said, and as Justice Antonin Scalia, in concurrence, urged on his colleagues. As Justice Blackmun put it: "If the Constitution permits a State to enact any statute that reasonably furthers its interests in potential life, and if that interest arises as of conception, why would the Texas statute [in *Roe*] fail to pass muster?" But Justice O'Connor, also concurring, saw no conflict between *Webster* and *Roe* because the burden of the tests imposed by law on the woman will be slight (they are simple to administer and relatively cheap) and because the state required the tests at a reasonable time in the pregnancy and only for the purpose of determining whether the fetus is viable, the moment at which even *Roe* said that states could ban abortions.

Because different factions on the Court have been wriggling to perpetuate or repudiate *Roe* against determined opponents, the logic of abortion doctrine today is tortured at best. Whether the Court will follow *Webster* to permit states to dilute to a vanishing point the right to an abortion or ultimately uphold a woman's prerogative, at least in the first half of her pregnancy, may depend in the end not on a doctrine devised by the judiciary but on how the voters speak in elections.

(See THE SUPREME COURT'S 1991–92 TERM for how the Court ruled in its most recent abortion case, *Planned Parenthood of Southeastern Pennsylvania v. Casey.*)

abridging the freedom of speech, *see:* **freedom of speech**

absent members   This term in Art.I-§5[1] refers to members of Congress absent from the House or Senate chambers during formal business. Neither the Constitution nor any law requires members to be present at all times, but each house may penalize members who are absent.

absentee voting   There is no constitutional right to an absentee ballot as such, but a state that makes absentee voting available to some must make it available to all. The Court held unconstitutional a New York State policy denying absentee ballots to suspects awaiting trial and persons serving jail time for misdemeanors. Under New York law, these persons were eligible to vote. The state's denial was an EQUAL PROTECTION violation because it permitted people jailed outside but not inside the county of their residence to register and vote.[1507, 152]

absolute immunity, *see:* **immunity from suit**

absolutism   In constitutional discussion, "absolutism" refers not to dictatorships but to the theory, pressed most vigorously by Justice Hugo L. Black, that the FIRST AMENDMENT absolutely forbids government from interfering with speech or press; that is, no one should be prosecuted or sued for anything said or published. Reading the FREE SPEECH CLAUSE strictly, Black said that the words "Congress shall make no law . . . abridging FREEDOM OF SPEECH" mean exactly what they say: *no* law. Black, who was often joined by Justice William O. Douglas, would have dismissed all prosecutions for obscenity and for incitement to crimes as long as the defendants were engaged only in speaking or publishing. But, especially in his later years, Black distinguished sharply between speech and *conduct* with a speech component, like marching and demonstrations, which he thought could be reasonably regulated. The theory of an absolute right to free speech has never commanded a majority.
See also: BALANCING; SYMBOLIC SPEECH.

abstention doctrine Although it has distinct constitutional overtones, the abstention doctrine is commanded not by the Constitution but by a legal doctrine called "COMITY," the judicial respect for the jurisdiction of other courts. The doctrine itself has no precise definition. In fact, commentators have found different abstention doctrines, each used to permit federal courts to avoid answering constitutional questions.

Justice Frankfurter first announced the doctrine in the *Pullman* case in 1941.[1683] The Railroad Commission of Texas required railroads to put a conductor in charge of sleeping cars, but the Pullman Company routinely used porters when only one sleeping car was involved. In those days in Texas, porters were black, conductors white. The order meant more jobs for whites at the expense of blacks. There were two issues: Pullman asserted that the order violated several constitutional provisions (EQUAL PROTECTION, DUE PROCESS, COMMERCE CLAUSE) if the commission had the authority to issue the order in the first place. If it did not, then the ruling could not be enforced—and the court could avoid ruling on the constitutional questions. The Pullman Company sued in federal DISTRICT COURT, which held that the Texas laws did not in fact allow the commission to issue the order. The Supreme Court reversed, saying that it was not for the federal court to decide that issue. It should have abstained from exercising jurisdiction until the plaintiffs could secure a ruling from the Texas courts.

In practice, the abstention doctrine has many exceptions. For example, the federal courts need not abstain if the state law would be unconstitutional on any interpretation[865] or if the state law is clear in a particular case.[1452]

A major problem with the doctrine is the expensive delays it can cause. Some cases have required the litigants to wait years between the ruling that the court must abstain and the eventual decision on the merits of the case.

Because of such difficulties, the Supreme Court during the 1960s tended to frown on this type of abstention in civil rights and civil liberties cases,[102, 561, 2236] although more recent decisions suggest that even in these cases abstention may sometimes be appropriate.[1789]

A second type of abstention, known as *Younger* abstention, from the 1971 case *Younger v. Harris,* prohibits federal courts from staying state proceedings, a practice first prohibited by Congress in 1793. But federal judicial policy on the issue has wavered.[2063, 1150, 1369, 1768] In *Younger,* the Court held that a federal court may not enjoin state criminal prosecutions. The question of whether the state was acting unconstitutionally could be heard in the state court as part of the prosecution itself (and ultimately on appeal in the Supreme Court). The *Younger* doctrine, however, has grown far beyond the bounds of its original case. It even can result in dismissal of a federal suit filed before the state prosecution has begun, as long as no "proceedings of substance on the merits have taken place in the federal court."[920] In such situations, the federal courts usually dismiss the case.

In administrative, or *Burford,* abstentions, from the 1943 case *Burford v. Sun Oil Company,* the Supreme Court has said that it makes more sense to have the state courts review challenges to state administrative proceedings, since they are usually "an integral part of the regulatory process."[28] A final type of abstention is limited to questions of EMINENT DOMAIN when the underlying state law is unclear.[1192]

See also: ANTI-INJUNCTION ACT; DIVERSITY JURISDICTION; ERIE RULE; JUDICIAL REVIEW; STATE LAW, MEANING OF.

academic freedom "Academic freedom" has several meanings, some of which have received constitutional protection. One sense of the term is freedom of a school or teacher from state control. Another, quite different sense is freedom of a teacher from coercion by the institution itself. Often, constitutional protection depends on whether the school is public or private.

Public and private elementary and secondary schools and public colleges may be regulated in many ways—in employment practices, health policies, accreditation standards, and the like. Private colleges are also subject to state and federal regulation, especially when they accept federal and state funds, which almost all do. However, in *Regents of the University of California v. Bakke,* Justice Lewis F. Powell emphasized the freedom of a university to select its student body, though that freedom does not extend to selecting on strictly racial grounds.

The Constitution supports academic freedom most strongly in the arena of speech and thought. Teachers may not be fired or otherwise punished for expressing their opinions. In 1957 the Supreme Court for the first time gave First Amendment shelter to a teacher's views. A Marxist lecturer had been convicted of contempt for refusing to answer the New Hampshire attorney general's questions about his political opinions and what he had said in college lectures. The Supreme Court reversed, citing the right to "academic freedom and political expression."[1989] In several LOYALTY OATH cases, the Court subsequently emphasized the "transcendent value"[1072] of academic freedom—the freedom of teachers from state censorship and demands for political conformity.

Academic freedom protects against more than state prosecution. In public colleges, at least, it protects against dismissal. For many years, employment in public colleges was characterized as a "privilege," and the states had often conditioned teaching jobs on "proper" opinions and statements by their teachers both in and out of the classroom. But with the demise of the RIGHT-PRIVILEGE DISTINCTION, the Court has said that the state may not fire a teacher for exercising First Amendment rights.[1610] The situation is less clear in private

schools, since without STATE ACTION the First Amendment does not apply.

Academic freedom is generally broader for colleges and universities than secondary schools. Concurring in the 1957 case, Justice Frankfurter noted "four essential freedoms of a university—to determine for itself on academic grounds who may teach, what may be taught, how it shall be taught, and who may be admitted to study."[1989] This sense of academic freedom for the institution does not necessarily protect the individual instructor. A current debate centers on the rights of instructors denied tenure to gain access to secret tenure-review files to see why they were rejected. The Supreme Court rejected a university's claim that it had an absolute privilege against disclosure of these records. If the rejected tenure applicant asserts a valid legal claim (for example, race or sex discrimination), the files must be made available.[2111]

access to ballot   There is no general constitutional right to run for office—at least no one has ever supposed a need for one, since no state has ever banned elections. (Such a ban would presumably run afoul of the REPUBLICAN FORM OF GOVERNMENT clause.) But historically states have severely handicapped minor-party candidates' access to the ballot, despite an obligation under the EQUAL PROTECTION CLAUSE to treat candidates equally. Defining "equal" is the principal problem. The states are entitled to reasonably limit the number of names on a ballot, but not by conditioning access solely on whether a candidate can afford a filing fee.[1202] Nor may the states condition access on race. For example, a Louisiana ballot listing candidates by race was held unconstitutional.[61]

It is more difficult to articulate a satisfactory constitutional theory for sustaining or overturning state laws and policies not related to wealth or race, many of them obviously outrageous, that freeze out some candidates altogether. The requirements for qualifying for local, state, and national ballots are a standing reproach to constitutional principles, even though it is expensive to expose them in court and difficult to attack them all at once.

Some policies, reasonably employed, may be unexceptionable—residency restrictions and party affiliation. The Court has upheld DURATIONAL RESIDENCY REQUIREMENTS of five[1046] and seven[1982] years. But one major impediment to being on a ballot is the requirement that the candidate demonstrate a degree of popular support. Laws that give automatic placement on the ballot to major-party candidates and require lesser-party candidates to file petitions may be upheld if reasonable. For example, the Supreme Court upheld a Georgia law requiring all candidates who wish to run in a general election but who did not win a primary election to file petitions from registered voters equaling five percent of the number who voted in the previous election. Candidates from parties receiving more than twenty percent of the vote in the previous election are excused from having to gather the petitions.[1013]

However, sometimes the legal scheme is so complicated that it keeps all but the two major parties off the ballot. The Supreme Court struck down such an Ohio scheme,[2216] and it voided an Illinois law requiring independent candidates to obtain signatures from twenty-five thousand voters statewide; these petitions had to include at least two hundred voters from fifty of the state's 102 counties.[1383] The Court noted that the effect of this law was that voters in the forty-nine most populous counties, with almost ninety-four percent of the voters, could not form a new party under the law. The Court also struck down another Ohio law that required an independent candidate for president to file public notice of his candidacy eight months before the general election, whereas the major-party candidates did not have to do so for several

more months.[59] The law was aimed at keeping off the ballot third-party candidates such as John Anderson, who ran against Jimmy Carter and Ronald Reagan in 1980. It is also unconstitutional to print the major-party candidates' names on absentee ballots while leaving off the names of independents.[52] On the other hand, the Court upheld a Washington State law that kept from the ballot any minor-party candidate who had not received at least one percent of the primary votes.[1404]

See also: VOTING, RIGHT TO.

access to broadcasting   With limited though important exceptions, the Supreme Court has rejected government orders to broadcasters to grant air time to particular persons seeking access to their vast audiences. In *Red Lion Broadcasting Co. v. Federal Communications Commission,* the Court in 1969 approved the so-called fairness doctrine requiring broadcasters to give free time for replying to personal attacks on the air or for responding to political editorials. The Court did not establish a general constitutional right to access; it said rather that the FCC may impose such a requirement and may revoke it if it chooses. Four years later, in *Columbia Broadcasting System v. Democratic National Committee,* the Court rejected the claim that the Constitution requires radio and television networks to sell political parties time to air dissenting views on controversial social and political matters. But the Court did hold in 1981 that the FCC may revoke the broadcast license of a station that refuses to permit a legally qualified candidate for federal office to buy broadcast time; the Court emphasized that it was upholding this right to access as a narrow exception to the general rule against a right of access.[360]

See also: BROADCASTING, REGULATION OF; EQUAL TIME, BROADCASTERS; FIRST AMENDMENT; FREEDOM OF SPEECH; FREEDOM OF THE PRESS; RIGHT TO REPLY.

access to courts, *see:* **courts, access to**

access to evidence, *see:* evidence, access to

access to government documents, *see:* freedom of information; government documents, confidentiality of

access to press, *see:* freedom of the press; right to reply

access to prisons and prisoners Prisoners retain some but not all constitutional rights. Regulations reasonably necessary to maintain order and security in prison, to prevent escape, to aid in rehabilitation, and to punish offenders will be upheld. But a pervasive system of censoring prisoners' mail may be constitutionally impermissible. In one leading case, the Court prohibited prison authorities from censoring incoming and outgoing letters that "unduly complain[ed]" or "express[ed] inflammatory . . . views or beliefs" or were "otherwise inappropriate."[1668] On the other hand, the Court approved a prison regulation that barred prisoners from soliciting each other to join a prisoners' union or from receiving bulk mailings about unions from outside the prison walls. That regulation, the Court said, was reasonably calculated to avoid disorder.[1031] And whatever a prisoner's right to communicate with others, the Court has said that there is no constitutional right of others, in particular the press, to gain access to prisoners in face-to-face interviews, especially when alternative means are available for prisoners to communicate with the outside world (for example, through mail and visits with family, friends, and clergy).[1583, 1805]

access to private property, *see:* public forum; public function; shopping centers, access to

access to public places, *see:* public forum

access to shopping centers, *see:* shopping centers, access to

account of the receipts and expenditures of all public money Art. I-§9[7] requires the U.S. government to account publicly for receipts and expenditures. Public accounting comes from the Office of Management and Budget, through the annual U.S. budget and a plethora of other documents (although a BUDGET itself is not required under this or any other constitutional provision). The Supreme Court has never interpreted this provision, although questions have arisen about the government's expenditures on the Central Intelligence Agency; the budget of the CIA, as of this writing, is secret and remains unpublished. The Court dismissed a 1974 challenge to the secrecy of the CIA budget by holding, 5–4, that the taxpayer who filed suit lacked STANDING.[1725]

accusation, notice and specificity of Anyone charged with a crime has a SIXTH AMENDMENT right "to be informed of the nature and cause of the accusation." The purpose of this provision is threefold: to permit the defendant to prepare an adequate defense, to protect against the possibility of a second prosecution on the same charge, and to tell the trial court whether the government has stated a legally sufficient case. Usually, the constitutional notice comes in the form of an INDICTMENT or INFORMATION. In a leading nineteenth-century case, the Court invalidated a federal prosecution in which the indictment charged that the defendants intentionally interfered with certain citizens in their "free exercise and enjoyment . . . of the several rights and privileges granted and secured to them by the constitution." In effect, the prosecutors merely repeated the language of the criminal law under which the defendants were charged; the Court said that the prosecutors must give particulars;

that is, they must state which rights and privileges the defendants were accused of interfering with.[495] An indictment also must allege specific facts relating to the crime. If the defendant is accused of burning down a building, the notice must say which one ("a building on the northwest corner of Main and South streets").[343] The requirement of specificity covers any legally relevant circumstance. For example, it is a federal misdemeanor for a congressional witness to refuse to answer "any question pertinent to the . . . [subject] under inquiry." A person may not be indicted for failing to answer a question that does not state the subject of the inquiry because the trial court cannot decide whether the questions asked of the witness were "pertinent."[1776] The Sixth Amendment right to notice applies to both federal and state prosecutions.[1532, 1680]

accusatorial system In the United States, criminal defendants are investigated and brought to trial through an accusatorial criminal justice system. Under this system, familiar to anyone who has watched "Perry Mason," "L.A. Law," or countless other courtroom dramas, the prosecution and defense of a case are in the hands of the lawyers. The judge's role is to keep both the government and the defense to the rules of evidence and trial procedure. The criminal justice system in most other countries is based on the "inquisitorial" principle. The judge plays a much greater role in investigating the case and in shaping the government's trial strategy, and the defendant has fewer opportunities to consult his lawyer or avoid talking to the police and prosecutors.

In our accusatorial system, it is up to the government to prove the defendant guilty, and the government bears a difficult burden: to prove guilt "beyond a reasonable doubt." It is not the defendant's job to prove his innocence. In inquisitorial systems, there is no PRESUMPTION OF INNOCENCE: the defendant bears the burden of proving that he did not commit the crime. The accusatorial system rests as much on centuries-old custom as it does on the Constitution, which does not explicitly create or require it, although many provisions in the Bill of Rights, including the right against SELF-INCRIMINATION the assistance of counsel, the right to a speedy and public trial, and the prohibition against DOUBLE JEOPARDY would stand in the way of any state that wished to adopt an inquisitorial system.

See also: COMPULSORY PROCESS; COUNSEL, ASSISTANCE OF; PROCEDURAL DUE PROCESS; TRIAL BY JURY; TRIAL, PUBLIC; TRIAL, SPEEDY.

accused As used in the SIXTH AMENDMENT, "accused" refers to the person charged with a crime who will be brought to trial. The term is somewhat broader than "defendant," which ordinarily refers to the accused in court. A person suspected of being investigated for a crime is not "accused" until formally arrested or arraigned.

acquisition of citizenship, *see:* **citizenship**

act of state doctrine The act of state doctrine, first formally recognized in 1897,[2089] holds that the courts of the United States may not question the "validity of the public acts a recognized foreign sovereign power commit[s] within its own territory."[117] This doctrine bars private litigants from seeking damages for injuries done to them by the law of another nation. For example, when foreign governments expropriate companies or other privately held property, the owners may not seek compensation in U.S. courts by arguing that the expropriation violates INTERNATIONAL LAW. Likewise, a marriage lawfully contracted in another country may not be attacked in a U.S. court as null and void on the ground that marriage between those two particular people would not be permitted anywhere in the United States.

Strictly speaking, the act of state doctrine is not constitutionally based, although it has, in Justice John M. Harlan's words, "constitutional underpinnings" arising out of the SEPARATION OF POWERS.[117] More realistically, the act of state doctrine is an exercise of the Court's power to declare general law—in this case, international law—for the United States. Congress could presumably repeal the doctrine if it chose to do so. In 1976 a plurality of four justices said that the act of state doctrine should not apply when the challenged foreign acts are "purely commercial" (for example, if a foreign government repudiated a contract to buy or sell a commodity). But a Court majority has not yet been mustered for that proposition.[36]

The act of state doctrine does not apply unless the court is being asked to hold that an official act of a foreign country is unlawful. In a recent case, a U.S. company charged that another U.S. company had bribed Nigerian officials to secure a construction contract. Bribery is a criminal act under Nigerian law. The trial court dismissed the complaint under the act of state doctrine, saying that a U.S. court cannot be asked to determine "the motivation of a sovereign act which would result in embarrassment to the sovereign." The Supreme Court reinstated the lawsuit, holding that the act of state doctrine does not bar lawsuits that may embarrass foreign governments; the question in the case was not whether the bribe was illegal but simply whether it was offered and accepted.[2136]

See also: FEDERAL COMMON LAW.

acting president The term "acting president" is relatively new, having been added to the constitutional lexicon in the TWENTY-FIFTH AMENDMENT in 1967 to deal with presidential disability, although the TWENTIETH AMENDMENT says that a vice president may "act as president" if a president fails to be chosen by the start of a new term. Whenever the president declares that he is unable to discharge the powers and duties of office, the vice president "immediately" assumes the office as acting president. The declaration of inability can be made instead by the vice president and a majority of the cabinet. No president has ever formally invoked this provision, although Vice President George Bush in effect served as acting president for about eight hours in 1986, under the terms of an informal agreement, when President Reagan underwent cancer surgery.

action, *see:* **cause of action; government, affirmative obligations of; state action**

activism, *see:* **judicial activism**

actual malice, *see:* **malice**

ad valorem taxes, *see:* **Import-Export Clause**

addiction Making it a crime to "be addicted to the use of narcotics" violates the Cruel and Unusual Punishment Clause of the EIGHTH AMENDMENT, the Supreme Court ruled in 1962. The Eighth Amendment prohibits punishing someone for "mere status" as an addict, in the absence of showing that the person had bought or sold or used narcotics in the state. In a later case involving alcoholism, the Court said that the meaning of the rule against punishing addictions is that it is cruel and unusual to punish someone for doing what he or she is powerless not to do.[1655]

See also: PUNISHMENT, CRUEL AND UNUSUAL.

adequate state grounds Many appeals to the Supreme Court from state supreme court decisions raise questions of both federal and state law. Since the Supreme Court does not have jurisdiction to hear appeals of cases presenting state issues only, which part of the case, if any, may the Supreme Court review? If the case was decided wholly upon "adequate state grounds"—that is, under state law, without requiring an interpretation of federal law or the Constitution—the Supreme Court may not hear an appeal at all. In 1945 Justice Robert H. Jackson explained the basis of the rule as follows: "Our only power over state judgments is to correct them to the extent that they incorrectly adjudge federal rights. And our power is to correct wrong judgments, not revise opinions. We are not permitted to render an ADVISORY OPINION, and if the same judgment would be rendered by the state court after we corrected its views of federal laws, our review could amount to nothing more than an advisory opinion."[910]

The Supreme Court sometimes looks for ways to avoid exercising federal jurisdiction—cases involving the ABSTENTION DOCTRINE, for example—and the adequate state grounds rule seems like another ideal rationale for that result. But in some recent decisions, the Court has turned the rule on its head to permit it to hear cases it would otherwise be powerless to review. In *Michigan v. Long,* the police had searched the defendant's car, and on appeal the Michigan Supreme Court found that the search violated the defendant's right against unreasonable SEARCH AND SEIZURE. Most of the state court's discussion of the issues centered on the FOURTH AMENDMENT, a federal constitutional question. The Supreme Court has both the constitutional power and the legal authority to review whether the Michigan court had correctly interpreted the federal constitutional rules governing search and seizure. But at the end of its opinion, the Michigan Supreme Court also noted that the search was invalid under the state constitution as well. Said the state court: "We hold, therefore, that the deputies' search of the vehicle was proscribed by the Fourth Amendment to the United States Constitution, *and* Art. 1§11 of the

Michigan Constitution." Did that mean the case rested on adequate state grounds that would preclude a Supreme Court review? The Court said no.

Justice O'Connor announced a new rule: unless the state court unmistakably declares that its decision was based on an adequate and independent state ground, the Supreme Court "will accept as the most reasonable explanation that the state court decided the case the way it did because it believed that federal law required it to do so." In short, unless the state court says something like, "We really mean it," the Supreme Court will feel free to review. In the 1983 *Long* case, the new rule allowed the Supreme Court to use the case as a vehicle for narrowing the scope of the federal constitutional right—the reason, critics charge, that the Burger Court changed the understanding of the adequate state grounds rule. But state courts can avoid the impact of this rule by clearly and plainly stating that the basis of their decision was the *state* law.

The Court has applied this "plain statement" rule to procedural questions as well. The problem here is that a state court might refuse to enforce a litigant's federal rights because the litigant failed to meet a filing deadline or to raise the issue in a certain manner. For example, suppose a defendant in a state prosecution objects to a confession introduced against him at trial on the ground that it was coerced, a violation of the FIFTH AMENDMENT. And suppose the state court rules that it will not consider the defendant's argument because he did not raise soon enough. May the Supreme Court hear an appeal on whether the state violated the Fifth Amendment? Until the 1980s the Court had said that it could not review the case if the state's procedural ground for refusing to consider the federal question was "fair" and "substantial."[2211, 905] This was a hard test for defendants to overcome. In 1985 the Court, following *Long,* said that such cases are reviewable unless the state court "clearly and expressly" says that it is basing its decision on a state procedural requirement.[308, 871]

But even clearly basing a decision on a state procedural rule will not necessarily prevent the Court from reviewing. In a 1991 case, a Georgia murder defendant who had been sentenced to death appealed on the ground that the state prosecutor had unconstitutionally excluded blacks from the jury. The state supreme court said that it could not consider this argument because the defendant did not raise the issue at the appropriate time. But the Georgia Supreme Court announced the rule governing timing after the conviction, and it was now attempting to apply the rule retroactively to bar appeal. Such a retroactive application of a procedural rule, said Justice David Souter for a unanimous Court, "does not even remotely satisfy" the requirement that to be an adequate and independent state ground barring appeal in the Supreme Court, the state rule must have been "firmly established and regularly followed" as of the time it is invoked. Since it had not been established at all before the defendant's trial, the rule could not be invoked to defeat the defendant's federal constitutional rights.[689]

See also: HABEAS CORPUS; JUDICIAL ACTIVISM.

adhering to their enemies, *see:* **treason**

adjournment, effect on legislation, *see:* **pocket veto**

adjournment, time of, *see:* **time of adjournment**

administrative agencies and bureaucratic government The United States government only remotely resembles the structure outlined by the Framers in the Constitution. To have imagined that so much detailed lawmaking could come from a bureaucracy largely in-sulated from the people and even from the executive branch would have been, one supposes, the occasion for some merriment. Not that administrative government was unknown in their time. The Confederation Congress had created a small bureaucracy that carried on the real work of government. The Framers understood that the kind of administration these early civil servants carried out was necessary, but the constitutional reference in Art II-§2[1] to the "principal officer in each of the executive departments" suggests that the Framers considered that the administrative arm would always be subordinate to the central parts of the government. Had they realized that these assistants and deputies, and in time thousands of other administrators, would be wielding considerable legislative, executive, and judicial authority, they surely would have placed some restraints in the Constitution itself. Instead, both a powerful administrative state and a network of legal and political controls have grown up both despite and because of the Constitution's silences.

The agencies over which the president has the most control are the departments that directly constitute the executive branch: the cabinet, or executive departments (State, Treasury, Justice, Defense, and the others). The president nominates the cabinet secretaries and assistant secretaries (subject to Senate confirmation) and may fire them at will. He has considerable power to shape the policies and even the operations of executive departments; he is, after all, the chief executive.

Congress may provide that violation of a regulation be punished exactly as if it were an enactment of Congress,[1092] including criminal penalties.[212, 818] But the penalties must be stated in the congressional statute authorizing the regulation; the administrative agency may not invent a new punishment or enlarge one set out in the law.[1105]

But there is another sort of federal agency,

the "independent" administrative agency, such as the Federal Trade Commission and the Securities and Exchange Commission, which is not mentioned in the Constitution. The president appoints their heads or members but has little if any power to intervene directly in their policies or decisions. And except in rare instances, he has no power to remove agency heads. These agencies, and many others within the traditional executive departments, have an amalgam of powers to make rules (a legislative function), to investigate cases (an executive function), and to hold hearings and assess fines and other penalties (a judicial function). In varying degrees, the independent agencies have, therefore, considerable power to declare, enforce, and interpret law. For example, much detail in the federal tax law comes not from Congress but from regulations written by the Internal Revenue Service and the Treasury Department. The Federal Reserve Board is entrusted with a great deal of power over the economy; the "Fed" and its chief are legally independent from the president. The National Labor Relations Board oversees union elections and collective bargaining, largely under rules of its own making. The Court has held that unless there is evidence of bias in a particular case, legislative, executive, and judicial functions may be constitutionally combined in a single agency.[2241]

Administrative agencies are not limited to issuing rules of general applicability, like gas mileage for automobiles or product labeling requirements. Agencies may issue orders to particular persons, much as a court might issue an injunction. In dozens of cases since the late nineteenth century, the Supreme Court has approved the general principle of administrative government over private persons and entities—railroad rate regulation,[989, 1460, 55] orders of the secretary of war to remove bridges obstructing navigation,[2091] orders of the secretary of labor to deport aliens found to be "undesir-

able residents,"[1227, 2052] and decisions by the Federal Communications Commission to grant or deny licenses to particular applicants for radio and television stations.[1425]

In an important sense, therefore, the independent agencies have become a fourth branch of government. Yet because the Constitution creates, in name, only three branches of government, the administrative bureaucracy must belong somewhere, and so we conventionally locate it in the executive branch. The Constitution provides for a SEPARATION OF POWERS but grants the head of the executive branch, the president, relatively slight *legal* power to direct the workings of independent agencies, though he has considerable *political* control through his power of appointment.

The agencies are subject to both political and legal control by Congress, to the extent that Congress can muster the energy and time to deal with them. Congress creates the agencies, provides operating rules, and funds them. Their power to act comes from congressional DELEGATION of power. Congress oversees agencies in part through annual appropriations hearings and in part through policy hearings. If it can find a majority of its members disposed to doing so, Congress can always override any particular agency rule. If the Internal Revenue Service says, "We interpret the home office deduction to be limited to the following kinds of expenses," Congress may pass a new law overriding the administrative rule. If the Federal Trade Commission says, "Used car dealers must post the mileage of their cars in three-foot-high red letters," Congress may say, "No you don't." (But Congress may not overturn the decision in an administrative case heard by the agency.)

Since it is politically impossible to oversee every rule and every action of all the agencies, for nearly fifty years Congress resorted to a LEGISLATIVE VETO, by which one or the other house could unilaterally overturn an agency rule. In 1983 the Supreme Court said that legislative vetoes are unconstitutional.[979]

Administrative agencies are also subject to JUDICIAL REVIEW. As organs of the government, they must obey constitutional limitations. For example, the Immigration and Naturalization Service may not simply order a person deported without first affording him or her a hearing to determine whether there are grounds to do so.[2251] Likewise, agencies are bound by federal law, so that they may be held to account in the courts for acting outside the scope of the authority given them in federal statutes.

In recent years the notion of an independent administrative power—that is, a fourth branch within the federal government—has come under fierce fire. Although the Court in the 1980s overturned some major policies on that ground,[211, 979] it has consistently rejected the assertions of many presidents that they are constitutionally entitled to supervise every action of every agency or executive official even if Congress has decreed otherwise. With Chief Justice Rehnquist writing the opinion in the 8–1 decision upholding the powers of independent counsels[1389] and joining the 8–1 decision in a case upholding the power of the U.S. Sentencing Commission,[1367] it seems unlikely that the Reagan-Bush Court will seriously reverse or even erode the historical position of administrative agencies and the administrative state.

See also: ADMINISTRATIVE HEARINGS; ADMINISTRATIVE LAW; APPOINTMENT AND REMOVAL POWER; EXECUTIVE BRANCH.

administrative hearings Federal administrative agencies are bound by the PROCEDURAL DUE PROCESS requirements of the FIFTH AMENDMENT that apply to court cases (as state agencies are bound by the procedural due process requirements of the FOURTEENTH AMENDMENT). In general, before an administrative agency can deprive someone of life, liberty, or property, it must hold a fair hearing before an impartial hearing officer.[2251] However, agencies need not hold a hearing at the same stage of each type of proceeding, as long as the aggrieved party can be heard before a final order becomes effective.[1535] In special circumstances, a judicial hearing even after the final order may suffice. For example, the emergency seizure of adulterated foods and drugs[1493] and the suspension of a driver's license for refusing to take a breath test when he or she is suspected of being drunk[1220] may be accomplished before hearings.[209] In rare circumstances, the Court has approved administrative action without any hearing. A controversial instance was the Court's 5–4 1961 decision in *Cafeteria Workers*,[305] permitting the summary exclusion of a cook from a naval base on security grounds without even informing her of the basis of the charges against her and without giving her a chance to rebut.

Although the Constitution controls the outer contours of the administrative process, it is too blunt an instrument to detail the ways in which the many dozens of agencies should best do their jobs. In 1946 Congress enacted the Administrative Procedure Act (APA), the basic law governing how agencies are to issue rules and regulations and to hold hearings. The act provides for impartial hearing officers, termed "administrative law judges," to hear administrative cases involving particular individuals or companies. The act also provides for appeal procedures within the agencies and from the agencies to the federal courts.

Judicial review is not guaranteed in every proceeding. Under the APA, if Congress commits a matter to the discretion of an agency, a court may not review the agency's exercise of that discretion. A simple example is the discretion of the U.S. Postal Service to issue commemorative stamps; the decision to celebrate one person rather than another is for the Postal Service, not the courts. Likewise, decisions about rates, charges, and tolls established by rate-setting agencies are within the administrative discretion of the agency; a court may not recalculate the rates.[1561] An agency's findings of fact are ordinarily unreviewable in court if the findings are supported by "substantial evidence." But courts may review and overturn any administrative action that is "arbitrary, capricious, an abuse of discretion, or otherwise not in accordance with law."

See also: ADMINISTRATIVE AGENCIES AND BUREAUCRATIC GOVERNMENT; ADMINISTRATIVE LAW; ALIENS; DEPORTATION; ENTITLEMENTS; HEARING; IMMIGRATION AND NATURALIZATION; LIBERTY; LOYALTY-SECURITY PROGRAMS; PROPERTY; RIGHT-PRIVILEGE DISTINCTION.

administrative inspections, *see:* **search and seizure**

administrative law "Administrative law" has two distinct meanings. It can refer either to that body of law, including the ADMINISTRATIVE PROCEDURE ACT, that controls the operations and conduct of administrative agencies or to the rules and regulations that the agencies themselves promulgate. In the first sense, although it has constitutional components, administrative law is largely a question of statutory law. Most judicial decisions in the area are concerned with whether agencies followed the requisite legal procedures and acted within the scope of their authority. Constitutional components include issues of DELEGATION and the necessity of JUDICIAL REVIEW.

In the second sense, administrative law is the body of rules and regulations promulgated by administrative agencies and the body of their written decisions in cases they hear. Federal agencies issue thousands of rules yearly under authority from Congress. They are published in the *Code of Federal Regulations,* now hundreds of volumes long. Their outpouring is as often the subject of political bluster as genuine concern. In early 1992 President Bush made a show of ordering federal agencies under presidential control to cease for three months issuing new regulations that might retard economic recovery—even though for nearly twelve years, first as the head of President Reagan's task force on federal regulations and then as chief executive, Mr. Bush had every opportunity to devise a more lasting solution to the problem of regulatory growth.

Once promulgated in final form, federal rules and regulations have the force and effect of law. If they are consistent with the statutory purpose in delegating power to the agency to make them, the courts may not upset them merely because the courts would have written the rule differently.[1825]

See also: HEARING.

Administrative Procedure Act Enacted in 1946, the federal Administrative Procedure Act (APA) was designed to bring order to a field that had become increasingly tangled and confusing, as Congress multiplied the number of federal agencies and the ways in which they operated. Among other things, the APA requires agencies to publish notice of proposed rules in the daily *Federal Register* and to make decisions and other information available to the public. The APA lays out a general scheme for most agencies in making and issuing regulations; they must notify the public of their intention, publish a copy of the proposed regulations, and provide an opportunity for interested persons to comment orally or in writing. Some rule-making procedures require trial-like hearings. Many agencies administer on a case-by-case basis rather than by general rule making. The APA requires independent hearing officers, now called "administrative law judges," to preside over the agencies' dockets; it also requires the agency to provide appeals from these hearings to the agency heads. But so myriad are the ways in which the administrative agencies operate that the APA has not succeeded in bringing uniformity to the field.

Moreover, during the past twenty-five years the courts have been increasingly active in opening agency proceedings, limiting their scope, and ensuring that they adhere to their own rules. Without "constitutional constraints or extremely compelling circumstances," however, the courts may not make up rules but must leave agencies "free to fashion their own rules of procedure and to pursue methods of inquiry capable of permitting them to discharge their multitudinous duties."[2125]

administrative regulations, *see:* **administrative law**

administrative search, *see:* **search and seizure**

admiralty and maritime jurisdiction   Art. III-§2 extends JUDICIAL POWER to federal courts in "all cases of admiralty and maritime jurisdiction." One of the principal purposes of the Constitutional Convention was to eliminate obstacles to a national commerce occasioned by conflicting local rules governing transportation of goods—particularly over the oceans and the nation's waterways. In the Judiciary Act of 1789, the First Congress gave the federal courts exclusive jurisdiction to hear admiralty and maritime cases. That jurisdiction is quite broad,[1450] permitting the federal courts to develop a uniform national law over the whole range of maritime commerce and the shipping industry, including marine insurance, ship charters, collisions, contracts to carry goods, personal injuries while at sea or on navigable waterways, suits by merchant seamen for wages, salvage rights, and many other matters. The Supreme Court has ruled that Congress has the constitutional power to change admiralty and maritime law under the second part of the NECESSARY AND PROPER CLAUSE, which gives Congress the power to make all laws necessary and proper for carrying into execu-

tion "all other powers vested . . . in the government of the United States or in any department or officer thereof."[290] This power is separate from Congress's power to regulate interstate and foreign commerce.[730]

Although the early cases suggested that the admiralty jurisdiction should be limited to the high seas and to "tidal waters,"[2036] eventually the Court concluded[2030] that any navigable body of water is within the jurisdiction,[2033, 2029] even if it is artificial[215] or made navigable only by improvement.[66]

Because admiralty and maritime law is federal, states may not enlarge or decrease it. In the absence of federal law, states may punish crimes on navigable waterways within their jurisdictions.[1234] But a major tension has existed between the states and Congress over the extent to which maritime law covers some types of cases. In *Southern Pacific Co. v. Jensen,* a New York longshoreman was killed after hitting his head as he drove his loading truck out of the cargo hold of a ship and onto the dock. The company and his fellow workers were blameless. Under maritime law, his family had no remedy because the maritime law did not then permit recovery for death without fault. New York State, however, had enacted a workers' compensation system under which an injured worker or his family was entitled to a predetermined payment without having to prove fault. The question was whether the state workers' compensation scheme constitutionally could apply to someone killed working on a ship that sailed in navigable waters. In a 5–4 decision, the Supreme Court said no.

The case prompted Congress to enact the Jones Act in 1920, giving crew members the right to sue for injuries negligently inflicted; it further enacted the Longshoremen's and Harbor Workers' Compensation Act in 1927, giving injured workers and their families compensation for accidents on the job. The interplay between federal and state laws governing accidents and injuries is highly complex and beyond the scope of this book, but in 1970 the Court simplified matters somewhat by reversing a long line of cases and finally holding that family members may sue for wrongful death under the general maritime law, even in the absence of a congressional enactment.[1385]

admission of aliens, *see:* **aliens**

admission to the bar, *see:* **lawyers**

admission to the Union   Art. IV-§3[1] gives Congress the exclusive power to admit new states to the UNION, although states may not be carved up and recombined unless the legislatures of the affected states consent. By long tradition, though not by constitutional command, all states are admitted to the Union on equal footing and can exercise all the powers held by the original states.[1647] In 1911 the Supreme Court struck down an attempt by Congress to force Oklahoma to relocate its state capital as a condition of admission, on the ground that all states retain the exclusive power to decide where their capital cities will be.[482]

adoption and custody of children   The right to adoption and custody and the procedures involved thereby are generally matters of state, not federal, concern. In most cases, the determining issue is the "best interest of the child," and that is a matter of fact for the trial court to determine. But the "best interest" may not be decided on an impermissible constitutional ground, such as race. In *Palmore v. Sidoti*, a custody battle arose when a white mother with custody of her daughter married a black man. The girl's father sued for custody; the judge granted it, revoking the mother's custody because, "despite the strides that had been made in bettering relations between the races in the country, it is inevitable that [the daughter]

will, if allowed to remain [with the interracial couple], suffer from the social stigmatization that is sure to come." The Supreme Court unanimously reversed. While admitting the possibility of such stigma, Chief Justice Warren Burger said: "The Constitution cannot control such prejudices but neither can it tolerate them. Private biases may be outside the reach of the law, but the law cannot, directly or indirectly, give them effect. [The] effects of racial prejudice, however real, cannot justify a racial classification removing an infant child from the custody of its natural mother found to be an appropriate person to have such custody."

In recent years the issue of a natural father's rights has arisen in adoption cases, usually when the mother has remarried and wishes her new husband to adopt her child. In one such case, a closely divided Court struck down a New York State law that permitted the mother of an illegitimate child, but not the father, the right to refuse consent to a child's adoption.[302] The law, said the 5–4 majority, violated unwed fathers' EQUAL PROTECTION right because there was no showing of any substantial relationship between the preference given to the mothers and the state's interest in promoting adoptions of illegitimate children.

But not every impediment to adoption will be upheld on this ground. In a 1983 case, for example, a father who had never made any effort to see or support his out-of-wedlock two-year-old child filed a paternity suit to have himself declared the real father. Unbeknownst to him, the mother in the meantime had remarried and the couple was separately proceeding to adopt the girl. When the father found this out, he sued to overturn the adoption, claiming that the state had violated his right to DUE PROCESS because it was obligated to notify him. The Court rejected his claim and upheld the adoption, pointing out that by simply mailing a postcard he could have listed his name with the state's "putative fathers' registry," which would have notified him whenever an adoption proceeding began.[1148]

See also: DIVORCE; FAMILIES; JUVENILES, RIGHTS OF; LEGITIMACY; RACIAL DISCRIMINATION.

adoption of the Constitution, *see:* **Constitution, ratification of**

adult bookstores and theaters   Municipalities have long struggled with the vexing problem of so-called adult bookstores and movie theaters, establishments that exhibit or sell explicit sexual materials. The question is whether such places may be closed down or, if not, to what degree the municipality may regulate their methods of operation and location. Because it has proved impossible to define OBSCENITY AND PORNOGRAPHY precisely, governments are caught between the desire to rid themselves of what, at a minimum, they hold to be offensive displays that lower the tone of their communities and the command of the FIRST AMENDMENT that government refrain from molesting nonobscene speech, even if offensive.

One approach has been to create certain zones within the community for adult theaters. In *Young v. American Mini Theatres, Inc.,* the Court in 1976 upheld a Detroit ordinance that severely circumscribed the places that theaters showing sexually explicit movies could be located. No adult theater could be located within five hundred feet of any residential area or within a thousand feet of any two other regulated uses, including other adult theaters, adult bookstores, cabarets, any restaurant or other establishment selling liquor on the premises, hotels, motels, pawnshops, pool halls, secondhand stores, shoeshine parlors, and taxi dance halls. The effect of the ordinance was to force adult theaters to disperse throughout the city. The Court reasoned that Detroit was not trying to regulate the content of the performance or to engage in PRIOR RESTRAINT, but

rather to prevent the deterioration of neighborhoods that follows when adult theaters concentrate in a single area.

Ten years later, the Court approved an ordinance of Renton, Washington, that had the opposite effect: to concentrate all adult theaters into a particular section of town. Renton's ordinance prohibited adult theaters from locating within a thousand feet of any residence, church, park, or school. The Court said that the ordinance was not aimed at the content of the movies but was designed primarily to curb the "secondary effects" of such theaters, such as crime, declining property values, and deterioration of the areas in which general retail trade was conducted.[1711]

Another approach to adult theaters has been to license their operation, but licensing tends to present problems of prior restraint. In 1990, in a case whose reasoning was murky because the justices were so divided, the Court invalidated a Dallas ordinance that required all sexually oriented businesses to obtain a license from the chief of police, after first getting approval from the municipal fire, health, and building departments. The ordinance was defective because the public officials had no time limit within which they had to decide whether to grant a license and because there was no provision for judicial review of any denial of a license.[715]

A bookseller may not be convicted of selling an obscene work if he did not actually know its contents. Otherwise, a bookseller would risk criminal prosecution for stocking any of tens of thousands of titles.[1887] For similar reasons, the government may not order the removal of books or films from a seller's inventory on the basis of a prior determination that the works were obscene; sellers are always entitled to relitigate the question of whether the works are obscene and to an independent appeal of any decision against them.[1303]

See also: NUDITY; OFFENSIVE AND INDECENT SPEECH; ZONING.

adultery, *see:* **sexual freedom**

advertising, right to, *see:* **commercial speech; professionals, advertising by**

advice and consent   Art. II-§2[2] conditions the president's power to make treaties and to appoint major federal officials on obtaining the "advice and consent" of the Senate. Treaties require a two-thirds affirmative vote; nominations require a majority vote. The provision today operates solely to give the Senate the power to check the president's actions; the "advice" part of the requirement became moribund very early on. Four months after assuming office, President Washington appeared personally before the Senate to seek its advice in negotiating an Indian treaty. But the Senate referred the discussion to a committee, and Washington departed the Senate in a huff. No president since 1789 has formally sought advice from the Senate on treaty negotiations or nominations, although the political give-and-take surrounding many treaties may substitute in a sense for the constitutional requirement.

For nominations, the advice and consent clause has become almost wholly reversed in meaning. Except for cabinet positions, major diplomatic posts, and Supreme Court seats, the practice today is for senators from the president's party to "nominate"—that is, to give the president a list of people whom they approve for federal jobs and judicial seats in their areas, and to have the president in effect to consent to those names by nominating them. All such nominees must still be formally confirmed by the full Senate.

advisory opinions   The federal courts are not constitutionally permitted to render advice, only to decide cases. Although in the early 1790s several justices responded by letter to legal inquiries from President Washington,[885] Chief Justice John Jay and the associate justices in 1793 declined to answer several questions put by Secretary of State Thomas Jefferson involving the constitutional implications of several delicate foreign policy matters. Jay declared that the federal courts had no power to give advisory opinions; that is, opinions on legal questions not presented formally in the course of a lawsuit. In his letter to Jefferson, Jay cited the "lines of separation" in the Constitution "between the three departments of the government" and noted that "the power given by the Constitution to the President, of calling on the heads of departments for opinions [Art. II-§2], seems to have been *purposely* as well as expressly united to the *executive* departments."

This early extrajudicial comment against extrajudicial commentary served as precedent for the principle that the courts lack power to hear any issue that is not a real CASE OR CONTROVERSY. Three major policy reasons underlie the Court's refusal to render informal advice: (1) The advice may not be taken, hence the finality of the Court's pronouncements will be weakened. (2) An advisory opinion may cause the parties to be lax in briefing and arguing if the issue ultimately is adjudicated formally before the courts. (Chief Justice John Jay's informal advice, in his response to a letter from President Washington in 1790, that it is unconstitutional to require the justices to travel from court to court was rejected by Chief Justice John Marshall when the question came up in a lawsuit thirteen years later.) (3) Advisory opinions would permit the Court to decide constitutional questions that they could conceivably avoid in an actual case, thus creating constitutional precedents for issues that might be both legally and politically unnecessary to decide. Creating unnecessary precedents is bad practice both legally and democratically.
See also: DECLARATORY JUDGMENT.

advocacy, limitations on right of, *see:* **subversive advocacy**

affected with a public interest doctrine
First used by the Supreme Court in the *Granger Cases* in 1877, the phrase "affected [or "clothed"] with a public interest" has to do with government regulation that results in property being taken without JUST COMPENSATION. In the 1877 case, the question was whether Illinois could set the rates charged by the owners of grain silos. In agreeing that the state could, Chief Justice Morrison Waite cited an earlier English case based on the notion that if the business "becomes a practical monopoly, to which the citizen is compelled to resort," the state could regulate.[1402] This doctrine was later used by justices who sought to curb the powers of the early twentieth-century regulation-minded legislatures to permit the Court to strike down state laws that regulated an industry's prices, rates, or conditions of service on the ground that they violated the protesting company's right to DUE PROCESS.[1875]

The Court never succeeded in defining adequately which businesses were and which were not affected with a public interest. In 1923 Chief Justice William Howard Taft listed a classification scheme more puzzling than enlightening. The categories, he said, were three: (1) businesses the legislature had declared must serve the public (such as common carriers and public utilities), (2) businesses that had historically been regulated (keepers of inns, grist mills), and (3) "businesses which though not public at their inception may be fairly said to have risen to be such . . . in consequence to some government regulation." It was never clear which businesses would fit into this last category. The formula led the Court to sustain laws regulating stockyards,[474] tobacco warehouses,[2067] and fire insurance rates,[744, 19] but to strike down laws fixing gasoline prices[2217] and regulating sellers of ice,[1457] as the sentiments of a changing group of justices dictated. Under critical attack that grew fierce as legislatures took to enacting more and more regulatory

policies in the wake of the Depression, the Court finally wrote the doctrine's obituary in 1934 in *Nebbia v. New York,* declaring that price control was thenceforth to be considered nothing other than the state's exercise of its POLICE POWER and that "the courts are both incompetent and unauthorized to deal with the wisdom of the policy adopted or the practicability of the law enacted to forward it." In short, the validity of business regulation now turns on the reasonableness of the regulation, not the nature of the business.

affecting commerce, *see:* **commerce, effects on**

affirmance by an equally divided Supreme Court Occasionally, the vote on a particular case is a tie, either because the Court is not at full strength or because a justice has recused himself from considering the case. The effect of a tie vote is to affirm the decision of the lower court "by an equally divided Court." A case so decided has no precedential value.[2026, 1443]

affirmation, *see:* **oath or affirmation**

affirmative action "Affirmative action" is the name given to a controversial set of policies that at bottom rests on the proposition that government may constitutionally take race or some other SUSPECT CLASSIFICATION into account as long as in so doing it intends to benefit one group rather than harm another. Affirmative action developed first in the courts. Following BROWN V. BOARD OF EDUCATION, which invalidated racial segregation in public schools, the courts were faced with the difficult task of dismantling a deeply entrenched system of dual schools. It became clear that taking the race of schoolchildren into account could not be avoided if states and local school districts were to draw plans to eliminate segregation. When North Carolina passed a law mandating "color-blindness" in drawing school district lines, the Court unanimously overturned the law, because it impeded local efforts to design districts that eliminated dual school systems.[1496] As long as it genuinely sought to redress official discrimination, a government plan in which racial classifications played a part would not be struck down.

By the 1960s, spurred particularly by President Johnson's call for an end to centuries of discrimination, the federal and state governments, and many private businesses, searched for ways to go beyond race-neutral policies of "equal opportunity" to improve the lot of blacks in employment and education. The common belief was that centuries of oppression could not be remedied simply by declaring, finally, that henceforth all were to play on a level field. Programs that gave preference by race—and later by sex, ethnic origin, and other minority attributes—emerged from legislatures and corporate personnel offices, often helped along by government pressure and lawsuits.

The constitutional question that arose was whether, consistent with EQUAL PROTECTION, government, including courts, may consider race in public programs and policies other than to redress past discriminatory acts. Because private employers and schools are not bound by the command of equal protection, the question of "private" affirmative action often turns on the meaning of ANTIDISCRIMINATION laws. Mainly in the Civil Rights Act of 1964, but in other laws as well, Congress has explicitly prohibited discrimination on the basis of race, sex, national origins, and religion, and has also outlawed the use of quotas. These laws apply to both private institutions and to public entities receiving federal funds. Many of the cases arising under the Civil Rights Act do not raise constitutional issues but will be noted here nevertheless because they are integral to the continuing debate on affirmative action (or, as

it is pejoratively put, "reverse discrimination").

The Court first considered affirmative action in the much heralded case of *Regents of the University of California v. Bakke* in 1978. The Medical School of the University of California at Davis set aside sixteen of one hundred places for minority applicants. Minority applicants were eligible to apply for all one hundred places; white applicants for only eighty-four places. Allan Bakke, a white applicant, was refused admission even though his test scores were considerably higher than those of some successful minority applicants. The school justified its policy on four grounds: (1) to reduce the "historic deficit" of groups traditionally disfavored in medical schools and the profession; (2) to counter the effects of past discrimination; (3) to increase the number of doctors who would serve minority communities; and (4) to obtain the "educational benefits that flow from an ethnically diverse student body." Although the Court ordered Bakke admitted, because of an unusual split among the justices it did not reject outright the use of racial criteria. Four justices said that the Equal Protection Clause always bars race from being considered in admitting students to a public school. Another block of four said that race may be considered. Justice Lewis F. Powell was the swing vote. Because he agreed with the first group of four that the medical school's particular program was constitutionally flawed, he made up the fifth vote for admitting Bakke. At the same time, he agreed with the second group of justices that race may be considered as one factor among many in admissions programs.

Justice Powell rejected the school's first justification outright: "Preferring members of any one group for no reason other than race or ethnic origin is discrimination for its own sake. This the Constitution forbids. . . . [The school's] explicit racial classification . . . tells applicants who are not Negro, Asian, or 'Chicano' that they are totally excluded from a specific percentage of the seats in an entering class. No matter how strong their qualifications, quantitative and extracurricular, they are never afforded the chance to compete with applicants from the preferred groups for the special admission seats."

Instead, Justice Powell said, a school may consider race as but one among many elements in deciding whom to admit:

> The file of a particular black applicant may be examined for his potential contribution to diversity without the factor of race being decisive. . . . Such qualities could include exceptional personal talents, unique work or service experience, leadership potential, maturity, demonstrated compassion, a history of overcoming disadvantage, ability to communicate with the poor, or other qualifications deemed important. . . . This kind of program treats each applicant as an individual in the admissions process. The applicant who loses out on the last available seat to another candidate receiving a "plus" on the basis of ethnic background . . . would have no basis to complain of unequal treatment under the 14th Amendment.

Since 1978 the Court has walked a constitutional tightrope in its other affirmative action cases. One that garnered immense public attention in 1979 was *United Steelworkers v. Weber.* The Court held that a private company's voluntary affirmative action plan to recruit more black workers does not violate the 1964 Civil Rights Act. The union and the company had collectively bargained to set aside fifty percent of the openings in a training program for black employees until their numbers were proportional to the number of blacks in the local community. But this ruling did not bear on whether equal protection would permit a similar plan by a public body.

In 1984 and 1986 the Court made it clear that there are constitutional limits to voluntary affirmative action plans when it overturned attempts to favor affirmative action over seniority. In the 1984 case, a lower court had ordered the Memphis Fire Department to retain newly hired minority firefighters over more senior whites in an economic downturn.[665] The 1986 case involved a Michigan school board's layoff policy giving minority teachers preference. In a collective bargaining agreement with a teacher's union, the school board agreed to lay off teachers by seniority, except when necessary to ensure a certain proportion of minority teachers. The plan led to the dismissals of some white teachers with more seniority than the minority teachers who were retained. In *Wygant v. Jackson Board of Education,* Justice Powell's plurality opinion stressed that there had been no showing of past discrimination and that preferring one person to another solely on the basis of race violates equal protection. He also noted that affirmative action in hiring imposed a lesser burden on rejected candidates than race-conscious layoffs, which "impose the entire burden of achieving racial equality on particular individuals."

In two other cases in 1986, the Court rejected the claim of the Reagan administration that race-conscious plans can never be used to benefit people who were not personally discriminated against, at least when it is proven that a union or company was in fact guilty of discriminating against potential employees on the basis of race.[1176, 1175] But these were close cases that hinged on statutory as well as constitutional considerations. And in 1989 the Court suggested that a case is not over merely because a company and a group of employees voluntarily agree to settle it through an affirmative action plan. The Court held that nonminority employees who are affected by the voluntary plan may go back to contest it if they were not parties to the original suit.[1255]

The Court has also appeared recently to distinguish between the power of the federal government and the states to employ affirmative action programs. In 1980 the Supreme

Court sustained the federal Public Works Employment Act, which required contractors to hire minority business for at least ten percent of every public works project.[711] Congress defined a minority business enterprise as one in which a majority of the equity is owned by "citizens of the United States who are Negroes, Spanish-speaking, Orientals, Indians, Eskimos, [or] Aleuts." The justices did not reach consensus on why this "set-aside" is constitutional. Bitterly dissenting, Justice Stevens criticized the "slapdash" features of the program and pointed to the central problem in all such laws: "[O]ur statute books will once again have to contain laws that reflect the odious practice of delineating the qualities that make one person a Negro and make another white."

In a later decision, a Richmond, Virginia, plan to do substantially the same thing in city construction projects was invalidated in 1989. Under Richmond's program, prime contractors were required to subcontract at least thirty percent of the dollar value of any city construction projects to minority businesses, specified, in language plucked straight from the federal law, as "black, Spanish-speaking, Orientals, Indians, Eskimos, or Aleuts." By a 6–3 vote, the Court in *Richmond v. J. A. Croson Company* said that all racial classifications are to be held to the high standard of STRICT SCRUTINY—that it must be established whether the government has a COMPELLING INTEREST that can be served only by classifying on an otherwise forbidden basis. The Court held that Richmond did not. There was no showing of particular discrimination within Richmond against minority contractors. Nor was Richmond's plan "narrowly tailored" to the people who might have been injured by past discrimination; certainly Eskimos and Aleuts were not within that class. Writing for the majority, Justice O'Connor left open affirmative action plans that are aimed at redressing past constitutional wrongs: "[N]othing we say today precludes a state or local entity from taking action to rectify the effects of identified discrimination within its jurisdiction."

A year after *Croson* a closely divided Court reaffirmed the power of Congress to classify by race in licensing broadcasters, suggesting a constitutional difference between the federal government and the states in seeking to improve the lot of groups which by government decree were once generally disadvantaged. The Federal Communications Commission awarded broadcast licenses to minority applicants under a policy that Congress had specifically approved. Under the FCC's policies, minority ownership and management is considered a plus among many factors evaluated in awarding broadcast licenses. Writing for the 5–4 majority, Justice Brennan said that the equal protection component of the FIFTH AMENDMENT does not overcome Congress's COMMERCE POWER to regulate interstate economic activity when the race-conscious classification bears a "substantial relationship" to an "important interest" that Congress has the power to address.[1319] The Court specifically stated that the test for upholding a state affirmative action plan will be tougher than the test for a federal one.

Through the 1990 term the Court remained badly divided on the general issue of affirmative action, except when necessary to remedy specific acts of discrimination. It remains to be seen whether the retirement of both Justices Brennan and Marshall and the addition of the more conservative Justices David Souter and Clarence Thomas will lead to even narrower grounds for upholding affirmative action, or to its outright rejection.

affirmative defenses, *see:* **proof, burden of**

affirmative obligations of government, *see:* **government, affirmative obligations of**

age classifications, *see:* **age discrimination**

age discrimination   Laws that classify by age do not create a SUSPECT CLASSIFICATION and are not subject to STRICT SCRUTINY. For example, the Court upheld a Massachusetts law requiring uniformed state police officers to retire on their fiftieth birthdays.[1265] Even though the law might be imperfect, it nevertheless is rationally related to the state's objective of providing the public with physically fit officers and does not, therefore, unconstitutionally discriminate. Likewise, the Court upheld a federal law retiring Foreign Service personnel when they turn sixty, even though it permits other federal employees covered by the Civil Service system to retire at seventy.[2118] Congress has enacted two major anti–age discrimination laws: the Age Discrimination in Employment Act of 1967, which prohibits employers from discriminating against persons between the ages of forty and seventy, and the Age Discrimination Act of 1975, which prohibits discrimination against people on the basis of age in any program receiving federal financing.

age of majority   The age at which a child becomes an adult depends on state law and is not controlled by the Constitution, except in voting. The TWENTY-SIXTH AMENDMENT prohibits the states and the federal government from raising the voting age above eighteen.

age requirements for holding federal office
The Constitution lists only three age requirements for holding federal office: representatives must be twenty-five, senators must be thirty, and the president and vice president must be thirty-five. Although the Supreme Court has never ruled directly on the point, the weight of precedent is that members of Congress and the president and vice president need not have attained the constitutionally required age on election day but on the day they will be sworn in to office.

age requirements for voting, *see:* **age of majority**

agreement of states, *see:* **Compact Clause**

agriculture, regulation of   Until the 1940s the Court held agricultural production to be beyond the reach of Congress's COMMERCE POWER because, like MANUFACTURING, growing crops and raising livestock were considered local activities. Even then, however, Congress could regulate price fixing and other restraints of trade in the livestock industry or in grain trading, for example, because they constituted a STREAM OF COMMERCE.[1991, 389] But in the middle of the Great Depression, when Congress sought in the Agricultural Adjustment Act of 1933 to boost farm prices by controlling agricultural production through a taxing scheme, the Court in 1936 held that the law violated the TENTH AMENDMENT.[289] Two years later Congress enacted the second Agricultural Adjustment Act, which authorized the secretary of agriculture to set marketing quotas; the Court sustained the law in 1939 on the ground that Congress has the power to regulate interstate sales.[1398] In 1942 the Court upheld the Agricultural Marketing Agreement Act of 1937, which permitted the secretary to set minimum milk prices in various milk marketing areas, even those entirely within a particular city or state.[2264] The Court said that Congress could regulate even intrastate prices as long as they have an effect on interstate commerce. That same year a provision was sustained that permitted the secretary to regulate production of wheat to be consumed entirely on the grower's farm. Against the argument that this was a wholly intrastate activity, the Court responded that the effect on interstate commerce was plain because "home-grown wheat . . . competes with wheat in commerce." [2201]

See also: COMMERCE, EFFECTS ON; TAXING POWER.

aid and comfort, *see:* **treason**

aid to religious institutions, *see:* **religious establishment**

air force, *see:* **armed forces**

airport stops, *see:* **search and seizure: airport stops**

airports, state regulation of, *see:* **preemption**

alcoholic beverages, *see:* **intoxicating liquors**

alcoholism, punishment for, *see:* **addiction**

alibi defense, *see:* **discovery in criminal proceedings**

Alien and Sedition Acts   The Alien and Sedition Acts of 1798 were really four separate acts—the Alien Act, the Alien Enemies Act, the Naturalization Act, and the Sedition Act— all prompted by Federalist fears of war with France and potential subversion by French and Irish citizens living in the United States. Under the Alien Act, the president could deport any alien who was "dangerous to the peace and safety of the United States." Under the Alien Enemies Act, aliens could be jailed or banished during war. The Naturalization Act lengthened the residency required to become a citizen from five to fourteen years. The Sedition Act made it a crime for anyone, including citizens, to write or publish "any false, scandalous, and malicious writing" against the president, Congress, or the government in general. These acts sparked the earliest debate in our history

after ratification of the Constitution about the constitutionality of congressional enactments.

The Federalists, led by President John Adams, defended the Sedition Act by taking a narrow view of the FIRST AMENDMENT. The Republicans, led among others by Vice President Thomas Jefferson, excoriated the administration's prosecution of the Sedition Act. Ten Republican writers were convicted and sent to jail. Jefferson secretly wrote a series of resolutions adopted by the Kentucky legislature, as did Madison for Virginia. These resolutions argued that Congress had acted unconstitutionally by invading the powers of the states and that, in particular, the First Amendment directly prohibited Congress from legislating on matters of speech and press. The outcry affected the presidential election of 1800, hastening the demise of the Federalist party and contributing to Jefferson's election. Jefferson pardoned those convicted, and all but the Alien Enemies Act soon expired. The Supreme Court never heard a case raising the constitutionality of any of these laws, and the issues lay dormant until World War I, when Congress again enacted espionage and sedition laws that finally led to a long line of cases dealing with SUBVERSIVE ADVOCACY.

See also: CRIMES, COMMON LAW; NULLIFICATION, INTERPOSITION, AND SECESSION; SEDITION; SEDITIOUS LIBEL.

aliens   An "alien" is a person who is not a citizen of the United States. Until recently aliens could find very little shelter in the Constitution, even though in formal terms most constitutional rights are guaranteed to "persons," not limited to citizens. Under Art. I-§8[4], Congress has absolute power over admitting aliens into the country; the Constitution imposes no limitations on that power. [1516, 662] Nonresident aliens—those who are not actually residing in the United States—are entitled to none of the protections of the Bill of Rights, including the PROCEDURAL DUE PROCESS right to a hearing.[1085] In one egregious case, a Hungarian national who had lived with his wife and family in upstate New York as a permanent resident alien for twenty-five years left the country to see his ailing mother. On his return, the attorney general barred his entry, citing secret evidence for the exclusion and granting no hearing. The attorney general's decision effectively incarcerated him on Ellis Island, and the Supreme Court denied that his due process rights had been violated.[1851]

Aliens residing in the United States are entitled to the protections of both the FIFTH and the FOURTEENTH AMENDMENTS. For many decades, ignoring the EQUAL PROTECTION CLAUSE, the Court approved state laws that gave citizens greater rights than aliens to pursue jobs and other interests. For example, the Court upheld a Pennsylvania law limiting the right of aliens to develop natural resources[1574] and an Ohio law prohibiting aliens from operating poolrooms. But in 1948, in *Takahashi v. Fish & Game Commission,* the Court began to shift direction. In voiding a California law that denied commercial fishing licenses to resident aliens, the Court gave two reasons: an emerging equal protection rationale that "the power of a state to apply its laws exclusively to its alien inhabitants as a class is confined within narrow limits"; and a FEDERALISM objection that it is for Congress, on admitting aliens to the United States, to determine what limits, if any, to place on their ability to work. Since Congress has done nothing to discourage aliens from working, any state restriction violates the SUPREMACY CLAUSE by conflicting with superior federal policy.

Occasionally since then the Court has struck down laws on supremacy grounds, but generally since the early 1970s, the Court began to overturn restrictive state laws on equal protection grounds,[2055] concluding in *Graham v. Richardson* that alienage, like race, is a SUSPECT CLASSIFICATION requiring STRICT SCRUTINY whenever a state discriminates between aliens and citizens. *Graham* held that states may not deny welfare benefits to aliens. The Court then struck down a Connecticut law prohibiting resident aliens from practicing law,[817] a Puerto Rico law against aliens seeking to become licensed civil engineers,[636] and in *Sugarman v. Dougall* a New York law denying permanent positions to aliens in the state's competitive civil service. But *Sugarman* opened a wide exception to the emerging general rule against classifications by alienage. Justice Blackmun's majority opinion said that in appropriate circumstances, states may require citizenship as a qualification for holding public office, including "elective or important non-elective executive, legislative and judicial positions." The reason, he said, is that "officers who participate directly in the formulation, execution, or review of broad public policy perform functions that go to the heart of representative government." In 1978 the Court approved New York's denial of employment to aliens as state troopers.[686] The next year it agreed that a state may refuse employment as elementary and secondary school teachers to aliens who could be but do not seek to be naturalized.[46] It likewise upheld a California law barring resident aliens from applying for the job of "Deputy Probation Officer, Spanish-speaking."[303] However, the public jobs must have some significant impact on the public. The Court struck down a Texas law barring aliens from becoming notaries public.[156]

If the states may not recklessly discriminate against resident aliens, they might seem to have more room to maneuver against illegal aliens, though any person within a state, whether lawfully present or not, is entitled to a minimum of due process and cannot be jailed or deported without a hearing.[2269, 1103] But the states may not deny all benefits merely because of a person's status as illegal alien. In one celebrated case in 1982, the Court ruled that Texas could not refuse to provide free public education to "undocumented school-age children," minor children of aliens who had unlawfully crossed the border.[1641]

Congress has greater power to discriminate against aliens than the states. Although it struck down a regulation of the federal Civil Service Commission that barred jobs to resident aliens, the Court acknowledged that "overriding national interests may provide a justification for a citizenship requirement in the federal service [though] an identical requirement may not be enforced by a state."[852] In addition, Congress may refuse to let nonpermanent resident aliens receive Medicare benefits and may require resident aliens to have lived continuously in the country for five years before being eligible for benefits.[1268]

See also: CITIZENS AND CITIZENSHIP; DEPORTATION.

alimony Whether to award alimony following divorce and how much to award is a matter for the states and is not governed by the federal Constitution. But the Court did strike down as violating EQUAL PROTECTION an Alabama law that permitted wives to obtain alimony from husbands but forbade the courts to award alimony to husbands in proper cases.[1540]

all deliberate speed The phrase "all deliberate speed" was used at the suggestion of Justice Frankfurter in the second school desegregation case, BROWN V. BOARD OF EDUCATION II in 1955. Frankfurter took it from a much earlier opinion by Justice Holmes on a wholly different issue.[2128] The question in *Brown II* was what remedy the Court would grant the successful litigants seeking an end to enforced SEGREGATION in the public schools. Rather than ordering southern school systems to desegregate immediately, the Court said that they should begin to move toward desegregation "with all deliberate speed," a vague phrase intended to forestall southern states from certain defiance had

they been told to reverse their deeply entrenched policies instantly. Frankfurter's compromise did not work. Massive resistance was the order of the day, enflaming racial politics in the United States for a generation and more. Ten years after the decision, only two percent of southern black children attended integrated schools. Five years after that, in 1969, the Supreme Court finally abandoned its wayward formula, ordering still-resisting school boards to integrate "at once."[34]

alliances of states Art. I-§10 forbids states from entering into "any treaty, alliance, or confederation." The Court recognized this clause in holding that the Civil War confederation of southern states had no legal existence.[2209] Today, because the clause forbids the states from conducting foreign relations, the Court has held that the federal government, not the states, may control offshore resources.[327]

ambassadors, power to appoint and receive A major source of the president's power to conduct U.S. foreign policy is the Art. II-§2[2] power to appoint "ambassadors and other public ministers and consuls" and the Art. II-§3 power to "receive ambassadors and other public ministers." From the power to "receive, etc." has come the understanding that the president alone may determine when to recognize a foreign government and when to break relations with it. The Supreme Court has never pronounced on this long-held principle. When five senators sought to challenge President Carter's termination of a U.S. defense pact with Taiwan, the Court dismissed the case. Dissenting, Justice Brennan thought the Court should have decided the case. He held that the power to abrogate a treaty is "a necessary incident to Executive recognition of the Peking government" and that it is "firmly establish[ed] that the Constitution commits to the President alone the power to recognize, and withdraw recognition from, foreign regimes."[773]

In the early days of the nation, presidents appointed ambassadors, subject to Senate approval, without any legislation creating particular embassies or offices. Ambassadors were paid out of general funds placed at the president's discretion "for the expenses of foreign intercourse." Only in 1855 did Congress specify grades of ambassadorial appointments and qualifications of their holders.

Although Article II expressly requires that the Senate confirm ambassadors and other public ministers and consuls, a policy sanctioned by custom as far back as 1795 permits presidents to name special or personal diplomatic agents without submitting their names to Congress. Modern examples were President Truman's appointment of Averell Harriman as "ambassador at large" and President Nixon's dispatching of Henry Kissinger as a personal representative on a number of delicate diplomatic missions.

amendments to Constitution Of some ten thousand amendments introduced in Congress since 1789, only twenty-seven have ever been ratified to become part of the Constitution. The first twelve were ratified within a few years of the original Constitution: the Bill of Rights (Amendments 1–10) in 1791, the ELEVENTH AMENDMENT in 1795, and the TWELFTH AMENDMENT in 1804. More than sixty years passed before the trio of Civil War amendments were ratified between 1865 and 1870. The FOURTEENTH AMENDMENT (1868), in particular, worked a fundamental change in the relationship between the states and the federal government and empowered courts to expand significantly the range of Americans' personal liberties.

Progressive and Populist reform movements sparked the next wave of amendments nearly half a century later: income tax (SIXTEENTH AMENDMENT, 1913); direct election of senators (SEVENTEENTH AMENDMENT, 1913); PROHIBITION (EIGHTEENTH AMENDMENT, 1919); and women's suffrage (NINETEENTH AMENDMENT, 1920). Three unrelated amendments were ratified during the next forty years: the "lame duck" amendment, shortening the end of the congressional and presidential terms (TWENTIETH AMENDMENT, 1933); repeal of Prohibition (TWENTY-FIRST AMENDMENT, 1933); and presidential term limitation (TWENTY-SECOND AMENDMENT, 1951). A more active period of amending began in 1961, with four amendments ratified during the next ten years: voting rights for District of Columbia residents (TWENTY-THIRD AMENDMENT, 1961); abolition of the poll tax (TWENTY-FOURTH AMENDMENT, 1964); presidential disability (TWENTY-FIFTH AMENDMENT, 1967); and a general lowering of the voting age (TWENTY-SIXTH AMENDMENT, 1971). Finally, after a hiatus of two hundred and three years, the TWENTY-SEVENTH AMENDMENT, limiting the power of Congress to vote itself salary increases, was ratified in 1992.

In more than two centuries, only six other amendments were approved by Congress and sent to the states but not ratified. One was part of the original Bill of Rights, fixing the ratio of representatives to the population. Five later ones also failed: an amendment to deprive of citizenship anyone who accepted a title of nobility from a foreign country (proposed, 1811); an amendment to prohibit Congress from ever abolishing slavery (proposed, 1861); the child labor amendment (proposed, 1924); the equal rights amendment (proposed, 1972; expired, 1982); and an amendment to provide the District of Columbia with representation in Congress and to repeal the Twenty-third Amendment (proposed, 1978; expired, 1985).

Under Article V, by a two-thirds vote in each house, Congress may propose an amendment to the states and may specify whether the states are to ratify it in their legislatures or by special convention. In all but one instance, ratification has been by state legislatures. (The TWENTY-FIRST AMENDMENT, repealing Prohibition, was ratified in special state conventions.) Three-fourths of the states must ratify, meaning that today thirty-eight states are necessary to place an amendment into the Constitution. Another method of amending specified in Article V is for the legislatures of two-thrids of the states to "call a convention for proposing amendments." No such convention has ever been called. However, in the 1970s a convention to propose a balanced-budget amendment came close to fruition; at one time or another thirty-six states supported it.

The states may not demand a special referendum by the people to ratify an amendment sent to the state legislatures.[883] Once the last state necessary to ratification has approved the amendment, no further legal action is required by Congress or the president. Until relatively recently, states notified the U.S. secretary of state, who proclaimed the amendment a part of the Constitution. Today that function is performed by the Archivist of the United States. But the amendment becomes effective on the date of the last ratification, not on the date of the proclamation.[548]

Article V leaves open whether Congress may impose time limits on ratification. In *Coleman v. Miller,* the Court held that questions about ratification are "nonjusticiable" and within the complete control of Congress. Most modern amendments have required the states to ratify within seven years; on average, amendments have been ratified within eighteen months. Ratification of the Twenty-seventh Amendment in 1992 is the major exception to this rule: it was one of the articles of the original Bill of Rights proposed in 1789. Ten of the original twelve articles were ratified by 1791. An eleventh article was presumed dead, but because the Bill of Rights contained no time limit, it was revived in the 1980s and declared

ratified in 1992 when several states suddenly ratified it.

Whether the Court will abstain from all questions involving congressional control is still open. In 1972, Congress sent to the states the Equal Rights Amendment, requiring it to be ratified within seven years. In 1979, the amendment having not gained assent of three-quarters of the states, Congress voted by less than a two-thirds majority to extend the time for ratification by another three and a half years. Because the amendment eventually failed, the issue of Congress's power to extend in such a manner became moot—and the issue remains unsettled. Another unresolved question is whether a state may legally rescind its ratification before an amendment is ratified by the requisite number of states. Congress will probably decide this issue.

Another set of major open issues revolves around conventions called by the legislatures of two-thirds of the states. For example, in the battle over the balanced-budget amendment, some states limited their call for a convention to that single question. Other states have asked in much broader terms for a convention that might consider many other issues. In this situation, may Congress refuse to call a convention on the grounds that the states have not asked for the same thing? And may Congress determine the rules under which such a convention would operate? Most commentators suppose that Congress has considerable power to shape the convention, but so far the issue remains hypothetical.

Only one provision in the Constitution may not be amended: the requirement that each state send two senators to the U.S. Senate. Two other provisions were unamendable until 1808. One, Art. I-§9[1] dealing with importing of slaves, is now moot. The other, Art. I-§9[4] dealing with DIRECT TAXES, was rendered largely irrelevant by the Sixteenth Amendment.

American Civil Liberties Union   Along with the NAACP's Legal Defense Fund, the American Civil Liberties Union (ACLU) is one of the oldest private organizations devoted to litigating on behalf of constitutional rights. Founded in 1920 at a time when the federal government was suppressing free speech and seriously violating the FOURTH AMENDMENT's provision against unreasonable SEARCH AND SEI-ZURE, the ACLU pledged to challenge govern-mental intrusions on the people's civil liber-ties—those rights generally protected by the Bill of Rights and the DUE PROCESS and EQUAL PROTECTION clauses of the FOURTEENTH AMENDMENT. The organization has been active in many celebrated trials, including the suit against the U.S. Customs Bureau for banning James Joyce's masterpiece, *Ulysses;* the prosecu-tion of the SCOTTSBORO BOYS; and the PENTA-GON PAPERS CASE. Headquartered in New York, with affiliated offices in every state, ACLU lawyers appear in thousands of trials and administrative hearings every year. Con-demned over the years as subversive and even as a "criminals' lobby," the ACLU's successes in court, before legislatures, and in popular opinion have spawned a host of "public inter-est" litigation organizations, both liberal and conservative, that promote political and legal agendas through TEST CASES.

American Indians, *see:* **Indians and Indian tribes**

amicus curiae   *Amicus curiae* is a Latin phrase meaning "friend of the court." In important cases on appeal, the outcome of which may affect many different interests beyond those of the immediate parties, particular groups (envi-ronmental organizations, district attorneys, state attorneys general, public interest litiga-tors such as the AMERICAN CIVIL LIBERTIES UNION, and the like) are often permitted to present their own briefs on how the APPELLATE

COURT should rule. No one has the specific right to appear as "amicus"; courts grant the opportunity case by case. The Supreme Court rarely permits any amicus other than the United States (that is, when the United States is not a party to the case) to present ORAL ARGUMENT.

amnesty, *see:* **pardons, reprieves, commutations, and amnesties**

among the several states   The phrase "among the several states" appears four times in the Constitution—in Art. I-§2[3], Art. I-§8[3], Section 2 of the Fourteenth Amend-ment, and the Sixteenth Amendment. In the sense of apportionment of members of Con-gress and federal taxes, it describes how the country is to be divided up. In the sense of Congress's power to regulate commerce, its more modern phrasing is INTERSTATE COM-MERCE.

amplifiers, *see:* **noise regulation**

ancestry, *see:* **racial discrimination**

ancillary jurisdiction   Ancillary jurisdiction is the power of a federal court to hear a claim even though no federal law gives it the author-ity to do so. The courts usually exercise this power under their DIVERSITY JURISDICTION; that is, when two parties in a legal dispute involving state law are citizens of different states. Sup-pose the defendant, who is being sued by a driver from another state for an automobile accident, asserts that the fault was really that of his neighbor. Ordinarily he could not bring a claim against the neighbor in federal court be-cause they are residents of the same state. Under the federal court's ancillary jurisdiction, the defendant may bring a "third-party claim"—that is, sue the neighbor—so that all questions of liability can be resolved in the single case.

See also: JURISDICTION; PENDENT JURISDICTION.

Annapolis Convention   Despite the peace treaty it signed with its former colonies, Great Britain continued to menace American shipping, and the states could not agree on a uniform means of dealing with the British navy. Just as bad, states with natural advantages were penalizing their neighbors. As James Madison put it, some states "having no convenient ports for foreign commerce, were subject to be taxed by their neighbors, through whose ports their commerce was carried on. New Jersey, placed between Philadelphia and New York, was likened to a cask tapped at both ends; and North Carolina, between Virginia and South Carolina, to a patient bleeding at both arms." The solution to the bitter trade wars was national action, but the Confederation Congress was powerless. Maryland and Virginia agreed jointly to navigate the Chesapeake Bay and its tributaries, and they invited Delaware and Pennsylvania to join the pact. In 1786 ten states selected delegates to attend a trade convention in Annapolis, Maryland. In September, for various reasons, delegates from only five states appeared and no quorum ever materialized. The delegates disbanded, but not before recommending to their home legislatures that a new convention be called to begin the second Monday of the following May in Philadelphia to investigate "important defects in the System of the Foederal Government . . . of a nature so serious" that a new constitution might need to be framed. Heeding the call, Congress endorsed the proposal, and the CONSTITUTIONAL CONVENTION received official sanction.

annexation   Although it is no longer a serious concern, the question of constitutional authority to annex foreign territory was a lively issue in the 1840s, following the Texas revolution against Mexico and the establishment of the independent Lone Star Republic in 1836. Some argued that Art. IV-§3 prohibited the United States from entering into an annexation treaty with an independent nation, although the express language of the section says no such thing. Texas was eventually admitted through a joint resolution enacted by a majority vote in both houses.

anonymity, right to   Under a state law prohibiting distribution of any handbill without the name and address of whoever prepared, printed, or sponsored it, a California defendant was convicted for passing out handbills urging shoppers to boycott merchants who discriminated in employment practices. The Court struck down the ordinance, holding that the law went much further than it needed to and that anonymity is protected by the FIRST AMENDMENT: "Anonymous pamphlets, leaflets, brochures and even books have played an important role in the progress of mankind. Persecuted groups and sects from time to time throughout history have been able to criticize oppressive practices and laws either anonymously or not at all. . . . [F]ear of reprisal might deter perfectly peaceful discussion of public matters of importance."[1995]

antidiscrimination legislation   The Constitution contains several prohibitions against discrimination (the two PRIVILEGES AND IMMUNITIES CLAUSES, the EQUAL PROTECTION CLAUSE, the voting amendments), but they are too general to cover every form of discrimination and inequality. Moreover, except for the THIRTEENTH AMENDMENT, they prohibit only governmental, not private, discrimination. To eliminate invidious private discriminations, legislation has been necessary. Federal antidiscrimination laws have been enacted under the several powers given Congress under the Civil War amendments; state antidiscrimination laws fall within the POLICE POWER of the state. Antidiscrimination laws take two forms: some create new substantive rights—for example, forbidding employers to discriminate in hiring and promotion, and barring restaurants, hotels, and theaters from discriminating against patrons; others confer jurisdiction on courts and procedural rights on victims of discrimination to permit them to remedy violations of existing antidiscrimination laws in court. Antidiscrimination policies have also been created in presidential EXECUTIVE ORDERS; for example, President Johnson's executive order in 1965 required all federal contractors to eliminate discriminatory employment practices and to take AFFIRMATIVE ACTION to seek out qualified minorities.

See also: CIVIL RIGHTS CASES; CIVIL RIGHTS LEGISLATION; FREEDOM OF ASSOCIATION; STATE ACTION.

Anti-Federalists   Two warring principles lay at the heart of the debate over ratification of the Constitution. One was the need for a stronger central power; the other was state supremacy. Curiously, both lay claim to the label "FEDERALISM." In its original meaning, the term referred to the principle of state supremacy in a common union. But those who took the name "Federalists" subtly altered the meaning of federalism, identifying it as a method of governing through a central government and the states. The Federalists saw the need for greater central power. They supported the Constitution because it strengthened the power of Congress and created an executive capable of acting on behalf of the entire nation, while at the same time retaining state sovereignty and state control over the central government. Their opponents, now known as the "Anti-Federalists," protested that the real meaning of federalism should be state authority, not national authority, over individuals, and that only the states, not the new central government, should have the power to raise armies and taxes. They were especially alarmed at the lack of state equality in congressional representation. Representation in the House of Representatives would depend on population; they wanted each state to have an equal vote, as in the Senate. The Anti-Federalists insisted that one of the gravest deficiencies in the Constitution submitted to the people for ratification was the absence of a BILL OF RIGHTS. In state after state they pressed their case, deriding the Federalist claim that since the Constitution had not granted Congress the power to interfere with the people's rights, there should be no reason to suppose that it would do so.

Although they were wrong in denying that a large republic could be self-governing, the Anti-Federalists were right to worry about the absence of restraints on government. Their chief contribution to the ratification was their demand for a bill of rights; they forced the Federalists to promise that if the Constitution were ratified, the first order of business in the new Congress would be to draft a set of amendments.

Anti-Injunction Act   State courts have historically possessed the power to issue INJUNCTIONS to prevent certain acts from taking place. Federal courts have not. Although occasionally the federal courts have claimed the INHERENT POWER to issue injunctions,[544] there is little question that Congress can limit the federal courts' power to do so. Beginning as early as 1789, and again in a 1793 enactment, Congress forbade federal courts from issuing stays to state courts in all cases except bankruptcy. That policy, though wavering and somewhat porous with exceptions,[2063, 1369, 2122, 1150, 1768, 1210] remains law to this day. One of the most noted instances of a congressional curtailment of the courts' EQUITY powers (including the power to issue an injunction) was a provision in the Norris-LaGuardia Act of 1932 prohibiting the federal courts from issuing injunctions in labor disputes. In upholding this act[1129, 1453] and others, the Court has pointed to the provision in Art. III-§1[1] entrusting Congress with the authority to "ordain and establish" the lower federal courts: "[N]othing in the Constitution . . . requires Congress to confer equity jurisdiction on any particular inferior federal court."[1178]

See also: ABSTENTION DOCTRINE.

antimajoritarianism, *see:* **majoritarianism**

antitrust law, constitutionality of   Shortly after the first federal antitrust law (the Sherman Antitrust Act) was enacted in 1890, the Court dismissed a major monopolization prosecution of the Sugar Trust. The Court said that MANU-FACTURING is not an activity within interstate commerce; therefore Congress had no authority to attempt to regulate manufacturing activities.[591] But the Court's early hostility toward antitrust was not complete. It upheld the constitutionality of prosecutions of price fixing.[14] By the early years of the twentieth century, the Court developed the CURRENT OF COMMERCE theory[1991] that in time ended any constitutional doubts about the reach of antitrust law to any anticompetitive activity that affects the national market.

The Court has rejected attempts to carve out a FREE SPEECH exception to the restraint-of-trade and monopolization provisions of the antitrust laws. In a case testing whether the antitrust laws could be enforced against anticompetitive combinations of publishers and news agencies: "Freedom to publish is guaranteed by the Constitution, but freedom to combine to keep others from publishing is not."[90] However, the Court rejected an antitrust challenge to a lobbying effort by a group of railroads acting jointly to coax the legislature to enact laws that would have harmed competitors. The Court held that the First Amendment protects such lobbying.[593]

See also: COMMERCE POWER.

appeal   An "appeal" is a request to a higher court to change the decision of a lower court. An appeal is not necessarily final, since in many states, and in the federal system, an intermediate APPELLATE COURT's decision can be appealed further to a supreme court. In 1894 the Supreme Court concluded that there is no general constitutional right to an appeal,[1299] and it has reaffirmed that conclusion much more recently.[1168] But if a state provides an appeal process, it cannot riddle it with irrational exceptions and deny its availability to some groups of people.[1168] The Court's major ruling came in 1956, when it struck down an Illinois rule that required anyone wishing to appeal a criminal conviction to provide a stenographic record of the trial, including indigent prisoners who could not afford to do so.[815] Such a requirement, the Court said, "discriminates against some convicted defendants on account of their poverty," a violation of EQUAL PROTECTION. The Court has reached similar conclusions in a string of transcript cases.[625, 576, 1117, 1185, 726] Likewise, the state may not condition or otherwise burden the very right to appeal a criminal conviction on the defendant's wealth.[569, 1730, 570, 1886]

Even in the absence of a general appellate process, the Constitution may still require that there be some appeal. For example, when a defendant was convicted at a trial in which a mob demanded a guilty verdict, the defendant's federal DUE PROCESS rights were violated and the state had to provide him with some means of vindicating his constitutional rights;[695, 1378, 1377] however, the exact approach to be taken in such cases is within the discretion of the state.[354]

Ordinarily the appellate court may review only the legal sufficiency of the lower court's judgment or decision and may not reconsider the findings of fact. For example, in a simple breach of contract case, an appellate court may not reopen a JURY's verdict or a judge's finding that one of the parties failed to perform his contractual obligations. Instead, the appellate court may consider whether the trial judge committed a particular constitutional or legal error or wrongly instructed the jury about contract law. There is a constitutional exception to this rule, however, for factual determinations by lower courts about circumstances that might have infected the trial in some unconstitutional way. For instance, a trial court could not foreclose an appellate court from reconsidering on its own whether a mob really did dominate the courtroom and force the jury to pronounce a guilty verdict. Such issues are always open to appellate courts to examine anew.[1378, 254] Furthermore, in many First Amendment cases, an appellate court may reconsider a lower court's factual findings; for example, whether a particular book or movie sought to be banned is obscene.

There is one type of case that may not be appealed. Under DOUBLE JEOPARDY, the prosecution may not appeal a jury's or judge's verdict of not guilty.

See also: APPELLATE JURISDICTION; HABEAS CORPUS; JURISDICTIONAL AND CONSTITUTIONAL FACTS.

appellate courts   Most appeals are heard by specialized appellate courts. More than half the states have a two-tier system of appellate courts: an intermediate appellate level court, usually called a "court of appeal," to which a losing party has an absolute right to appeal; and a supreme court to which, in some states, the right is not absolute but within the discretion of the court. (In New York, the state's highest court is called "the New York Court of Appeals"; perversely, that state's trial courts are known as "supreme courts.") In the federal system, appeals from U.S. DISTRICT COURTS and from many decisions of the federal ADMINISTRATIVE AGENCIES may be taken to the U.S. COURTS OF APPEAL, sometimes known as "circuit courts" from the federal circuits in which they sit. In many states and in the federal sys-

tem, there are also specialized appeals courts; for example, the U.S. Court of Appeals for the Federal Circuit, which hears claims against the U.S. government, and the U.S. Court of Customs and Patent Appeals. Atop both the state and federal appellate process is the United States SUPREME COURT, which may hear appeals in appropriate cases from both state supreme courts and U.S. courts of appeals (and occasionally even from lower courts). Appellate courts do not sit as triers of fact; they do not gather new evidence; they do not take testimony. Instead, they hear arguments about the legal validity of the proceedings in the lower court.

See also: APPEAL; APPELLATE JURISDICTION; ORAL ARGUMENT; other types of (named) courts.

appellate jurisdiction   Appellate jurisdiction is the legal authority of a court to review the decision of a lower court or some other governmental body, such as an ADMINISTRATIVE AGENCY. Appellate jurisdiction is not an inherent power of a particular court; the legislature must confer appellate jurisdiction on a court before it is empowered to hear appeals. In the federal system, the appellate jurisdiction is exercised mainly by the U.S. courts of appeals and the Supreme Court.

See also: JUDICIAL POWER; JURISDICTION; SUPREME COURT.

appellate review, *see:* **appeal; appellate jurisdictions; Supreme Court**

application of the legislature   The phrase "application of the legislature" is used twice in the Constitution—in Art. IV-§4 and in Art. V. It refers to a demand by one or more state legislatures that Congress either quell domestic violence within the state or call a constitutional convention.

appointment, Supreme Court justices All federal judges, including the chief justice of the United States and the associate justices of the Supreme Court, must be nominated by the president and confirmed by a majority vote of the Senate. The appointments clause of Art. II-§2[2] specifies no conditions for Supreme Court nominations. Constitutionally, the justices need not even be lawyers—though, in actuality, all have been. Under Art. III-§I, all federal judicial appointments, including the Supreme Court, are for life, as is implied by the phrase "during good behavior." The same clause requires that federal judges be paid a regular salary and that the salary not be lowered as long as they are serving on the bench. Both provisions are intended to secure the independence of the federal judiciary from the legislative and executive branches.

Historical practice and political necessity, not the Constitution, dictate that political, geographical, and to some degree ethnic factors will play a role in any nomination to the Supreme Court. Although most of the Court's 106 justices have been of white, Protestant, Anglo-Saxon stock, there have been some deviations from this "standard" ethnographic makeup. President Andrew Jackson appointed the first of the seven Catholics to serve on the Supreme Court when he named Roger B. Taney in 1836. President Wilson appointed the first of the five Jewish justices to serve in naming Louis D. Brandeis in 1916. It is sometimes said that of the nine places on the Court, at least one must be a "Catholic seat" and another a "Jewish seat," but that is only occasionally true. One or another Jewish justice sat on the Court from 1916 until 1969, when Abe Fortas resigned, but there have been none since then. President Lyndon Johnson appointed the first black justice, Thurgood Marshall, in 1967; and President Bush's ultimately successful nomination of Clarence Thomas to succeed Justice Marshall suggests that Court tradition will probably require a "black seat." President Ronald Reagan appointed the first and so far only woman to the High Bench when he named Sandra Day O'Connor in 1981.

Although most appointees have been in their early fifties, there have been exceptions at either end of the spectrum. The youngest appointee was Joseph Story, appointed in 1812 at the age of thirty-three; the second youngest was William O. Douglas, forty-one, in 1939. Every president except four (William Henry Harrison, Zachary Taylor, Andrew Johnson, and Jimmy Carter) had the opportunity to appoint at least one member of the Court.

The confirmation of most lower federal judges is guaranteed, because politically they are in effect "nominated" by their home state's senators, and senatorial courtesy generally guarantees that the whole Senate will confirm. But Supreme Court nominations are by no means assured. Two of President Nixon's nominees were rejected in a row (Clement Haynsworth, Jr., in 1969 and G. Harrold Carswell in 1970), as was President Reagan's nominee Robert Bork in 1987. And the bruising battle over the confirmation of Clarence Thomas in 1991, which he won by one of the closest votes in history, 51–49, shows that the appointment process is neither a model of decorum nor a nonpartisan search for the soundest constitutional and legal thinkers.

Until relatively recently, Supreme Court nominees did not appear in person before the Senate Judiciary Committee. Personal appearances began with Felix Frankfurter in 1939, who declined to discuss his thoughts about constitutional issues, thereby starting a custom that continues to this day. It is an oddity of American political and constitutional life that it is considered "off limits" to consider the nominee's views on the central reason for which he or she has been nominated. The rationale for refusing to talk about constitutional matters is both that the discussion would be too abstract and would not be relevant to the particular issues that might come before the Court and that a debate on the Constitution during a confirmation hearing might force the nominee into taking an ill-considered position that might prove cumbersome when the justice was confronted with an actual case.

See also: SUPREME COURT.

appointment and removal power   One of the principal means of controlling the federal government is to appoint and to remove its officials. The Constitution gives the president a qualified power to appoint, but the Constitution is silent on the power to remove. Under Art. II-§2[2], the president appoints "ambassadors, other public ministers and consuls, judges of the Supreme Court, and all other officers of the United States" whose positions are established by Congress. All such appointments are subject to approval by a majority vote of the Senate. The president has no power to appoint anyone to an OFFICE that has not been established by Congress, and Congress may determine the qualifications of anyone holding federal office, except for those offices whose qualifications are listed in the Constitution itself.

When Congress created the Federal Election Commission in 1974, it provided that the House would appoint two of its members, the Senate two, and the president two, subject to confirmation by the Congress as a whole. The Court invalidated the law, both because Congress had given itself a direct role in appointing specific members and because the House of Representatives took a role in confirming; neither of these roles is permitted under the Appointments Clause.[270]

The Appointments Clause permits Congress to alter the constitutional method just discussed for appointments of "inferior OFFICERS." Congress may vest the power to appoint in the president alone (meaning that Senate confirmation is unnecessary), in the heads of departments, or in the courts. Congress has occasionally exercised its power to vest the appointing power elsewhere. In 1988 the Court held that an INDEPENDENT COUNSEL is an inferior officer; thus, Congress had acted constitutionally when it vested her appointment in a special division of the U.S. COURT OF APPEALS for the District of Columbia Circuit.[1389]

Constitutionally, appointment has three parts. First is the nomination, which is the president's exclusive prerogative. Second is the confirmation, which is solely the Senate's prerogative. Although the Senate may reject a nominee for any reason, under a long line of opinions of the attorneys general, it may not attach conditions to its consent. Moreover, once the Senate consents to a nominee, it may not revoke its confirmation by a motion to reconsider.[1898] Third, under Art. III-§3, the president commissions the officer. Even after the Senate has confirmed, the president may still decline to commission; that is, to formally invest his nominee in the office. Commissioning is complete when the president signs the commission document and delivers it either to the nominee himself or to another executive branch official with instructions to deliver it to the nominee. In the seminal case MARBURY V. MADISON, Chief Justice Marshall held that an executive branch officer (the secretary of state) may not constitutionally refuse to deliver the commission once the president has signed and sealed it.

When the Senate is recessed, the president may short-circuit the appointment process by making "recess appointments" to any vacant office. Recess appointments expire at the end of the following Senate session.

If appointments provisions are relatively clear, the removal power is positively opaque, because the Constitution is almost entirely silent on the issue. Art. I gives Congress the power of IMPEACHMENT; that is, the power to remove the president, vice president, and all "civil officers" of the United States for "treason, bribery, and other high crimes and misdemeanors." But impeachment is an extraordinary measure and extraordinarily difficult to accomplish—a blunderbuss weapon against noncriminal offenses such as incompetence or bad judgment. The Constitution does not specify a simpler method. It does not state whether the president may simply remove executive officials at his pleasure and, if he can, whether Congress may intervene.

In *Federalist* 77, Alexander Hamilton said that the "consent of [the Senate] would be necessary to displace as well as to appoint" and that such a policy would "contribute to the stability of the administration," since "[a] change of the Chief Magistrate . . . would not occasion so violent or so general a revolution in the officers of the government as might be expected, if he were the sole disposer of offices." But the constitutional policy has not worked out as Hamilton argued. Historically, presidents did remove officials, but Congress and the president came to blows over the issue in 1867, when President Andrew Johnson was impeached over his removal of a cabinet officer in defiance of the Tenure of Office Act, which required approval of a successor before the incumbent could be removed. The Senate failed to convict Johnson by a single vote.

The Supreme Court finally addressed the question of removal in 1926 in *Myers v. United States*. A federal statute said that certain classes of postmasters could be removed by the president only if the Senate agreed. When President Wilson supported his postmaster general's dismissal of a postmaster in Portland, Oregon, the postmaster sued to regain his office, claiming the protection of the statute, since the Senate had not concurred in the removal. Chief Justice Taft, himself a former president, struck down the law, holding that only the president may remove, for without that power he could not be

expected to superintend the government, "tak[ing] care that the laws be faithfully executed."

Taft had hoped to lodge forever the removal power exclusively in the president; but nine years later, in *Humphrey's Executor v. United States*, the Court backtracked significantly. President Franklin D. Roosevelt fired Humphrey, a Hoover appointee, because of significant policy differences, not for malfeasance. But in creating the office of commissioner of the Federal Trade Commission, Congress had said that incumbents could not be removed except "for cause," meaning for some dereliction of duty. Now the Court said: "The Federal Trade Commission is an administrative body created by Congress to carry into effect legislative policies embodied in the statute. . . . Such a body cannot in any proper sense be characterized as an arm or eye of the executive. Its duties are performed without executive leave and . . . must be free of executive control. . . . The President has exclusive authority to remove only " 'purely executive officers.' " In a 1958 decision, the Court further enunciated this doctrine in holding that the president may not unilaterally remove a member of a commission exercising "quasijudicial" authority (in this case, adjudicating war claims) even if the law creating the commission said nothing about limiting the president's power to remove.[2204]

So matters stood until 1988, when the Court seemed to further circumscribe an absolute presidential power to remove executive officials. In *Morrison v. Olson*, a former assistant attorney general of the United States challenged the appointment of an INDEPENDENT COUNSEL who was investigating him for improprieties committed in office. Under the Ethics in Government Act of 1978, the independent counsel, a federal prosecutor, could not be removed except for "good cause." Since a prosecutor is a "purely executive office," the *Myers* rule should have dictated that Congress could not limit the president's power to remove. Against an impassioned dissent by Justice Scalia, Chief Justice Rehnquist held otherwise, saying that "the real question is whether the removal restrictions are of such a nature that they impede the President's ability to perform his constitutional duty." The Court found no impediment to the president's ability from the limited and temporary nature of the independent counsel's job.

See also: EXECUTIVE DEPARTMENTS; HEADS OF DEPARTMENTS; SEPARATION OF POWERS.

apportionment of political districts   To say that voters will elect their representatives is to say little about which groups of them will elect which representatives. If tiny groups of voters elect many more representatives than their number warrants, it is doubtful that the government that results really is representative or "democratic." The Framers were aware of the difficulty, having observed the English "rotten borough" system that kept Parliament from representing the people in any way remotely approaching mathematical equality. In Art. I-§2, the Framers specified the following three rules to ensure equitable representation: (1) "the people" shall elect members of the House of Representatives; (2) the REPRESENTATION of each state's members shall be proportional to the population of the country; and (3) a CENSUS shall be taken each decade to reapportion districts as necessary. Therefore, a state with twice as big a population as another should have twice as many representatives in the House. (Actually, in the Framers' original plan, slaves were counted as THREE-FIFTHS of a person; the THIRTEENTH and FOURTEENTH AMENDMENTS have eliminated this historical barbarism.) These provisions are the only references to districting in the Constitution, since states, rather than people, are represented in the Senate (by Art. I-§3[1] each state, no matter how small or large, has two senators) and the Constitution did not deal with the political structure of the states.

As far as the Constitution is concerned, a state could allow its voters to choose all its representatives in a statewide election. Historically, however, most state constitutions required that representation in state legislatures and the House of Representatives be based on single-member districts of equal, or nearly equal, populations. But substantial population shifts and the blatant refusal of many state legislatures to adhere to new census figures or to their own constitutional requirements led to highly unequal districts. The census requirement at the federal level means only that Congress must reassess and reassign, if necessary, the number of House seats allocated to each state; it says nothing about what size each of the federal House districts within the states must be. At the state level, the constitutional census rule does not apply. From 1901 to 1961, the Tennessee legislature, for instance, ignored the state constitutional requirement that districts be reapportioned every ten years. In Alabama the disparity in population sizes grew to 46:1 in the state senate and 16:1 in the lower house; one-quarter of the population could elect a majority of the legislative seats.

For years, the Court refused to hear challenges to these practices. Violations by states of their own constitutions do not create a federal constitutional question, and malapportionment of federal districts was thought to be a nonjusticiable POLITICAL QUESTION (or, as Justice Frankfurter so pungently put it, courts ought not enter the "political thicket"[424]). But in 1962, in *Baker v. Carr*, the Court for the first time held that the inequality of voting districts was a question that federal courts could entertain. In 1963 the Court took on Georgia's COUNTY UNIT SYSTEM, under which the votes in the least populous county were worth ninety-nine times more than those in the most populous county in statewide primary elections for governor.

Although this was not an apportionment case, for the first time the Supreme Court struck down a voting scheme that weighed populations unequally, saying: "The conception of political equality, from the DECLARATION OF INDEPENDENCE, to Lincoln's Gettysburg Address, to the FIFTEENTH, SEVENTEENTH, and NINETEENTH AMENDMENTS can mean only one thing—ONE PERSON, ONE VOTE."[797] The following year, the Court struck down Georgia's method of apportioning federal House districts, where the disparity was more than 3:1. The Court said the disparities violated Art. I-§2's requirement that representatives be elected "by the people." "To say that a vote is worth more in one district than in another," wrote Justice Hugo L. Black, "would not only run counter to our fundamental ideas of democratic government, it would cast aside the principle of a House of Representatives elected 'by the People,' a principle tenaciously fought for and established at the CONSTITUTIONAL CONVENTION." On June 15, 1964, in six cases challenging districting in Alabama,[1713] Colorado,[1203] Delaware,[1754] Maryland,[1263] New York,[2243] and Virginia,[521] the Court struck down state malapportionment as well.

In the Alabama case, *Reynolds v. Sims*, the Court for the first time articulated the "one person, one vote" rationale. Writing for the majority, Chief Justice Earl Warren said:

Legislators represent people, not trees or acres. Legislators are elected by voters, not farms or cities or economic interests. As long as ours is a representative form of government, and our legislatures are those instruments of government elected directly by and directly representative of the people, the right to elect legislators in a free and unimpaired fashion is a bedrock of our political system. . . . And if [a] state should provide that the votes of citizens in one part of the state should be given two times, or five times, or 10 times the weight of votes of citizens in another part of the state, it

could hardly be contended that the right to vote of those residing in the disfavored areas had not been effectively diluted. . . . The Equal Protection Clause demands no less than substantially equal state legislative representation for all citizens, of all places as well as of all races.

That the Court meant what it said was clear from the Colorado case, decided the same day. The justices rejected an apportionment scheme for Colorado's upper house modeled on election to the U.S. Senate. The unequal size of the U.S. Senate's seats is an explicit command of the Constitution in Art. I-§3 and does not apply to state senates. Moreover, even though Colorado voters had approved the scheme in a referendum in every county, "an individual's constitutionally protected right to cast an equally weighted vote cannot be denied even by a vote of a majority of a state's electorate."[1203] A few years later, Warren said that of all the cases on which he had sat as chief justice of the United States, the reapportionment cases were the most important.

The principle that representation must be apportioned equally is not limited to legislative districts. In a case involving the trustees of a junior college district, the Court ruled that whenever voters are permitted to elect, from districts, members of a public body performing governmental functions, the districts must be composed of substantially equal populations.[835] The only exception seems to be for governmental agencies performing highly specialized functions that affect a relatively narrow class of persons. For example, the Court upheld a policy of limiting the vote for members of a water storage district to landowners and proportioning the votes by the value of the land.[209]

See also: GERRYMANDERING; JUSTICIABILITY; MULTIMEMBER ELECTION DISTRICTS; POLITICAL QUESTION DOCTRINE; VOTING, RIGHT TO.

apportionment of taxes   Art. I-§9[4] limits the otherwise sweeping power of Congress to tax by requiring that any "capitation" or "other direct" tax must be apportioned according to each census. A capitation tax is a tax on a person, like a poll tax; although the meaning of "direct" is far from clear, the consensus is that the Framers used that term to refer to taxes on land. The restriction means that Congress may not impose a tax on the value of land if in so doing it collects more from one state than the proportion of its population to the total national population would allow. In other words, if the population of a large state is twice the population of a small state, the total federal tax collected on the private land in the large state must be only twice as great as the tax collected in the small state, even if the value of the land in the large state is ten, twenty, or even a hundred times greater.

Very early on, the Supreme Court indicated that it would read the clause narrowly. In 1796 the Court sustained a tax on carriages without regard to the census or apportionment, holding that such a tax is an "excise" or "duty," not a direct tax.[971] But nearly a century later, the Supreme Court, against the weight of its precedents, declared that a federal tax on income derived from real estate and personal property was a direct tax and that the Income Tax Act of 1894 was unconstitutional because it did not apportion.[1649] That decision was overruled by the adoption of the SIXTEENTH AMENDMENT, which expressly permits Congress to tax incomes without apportionment. Since then, the Court has not struck down any federal tax as violating the apportionment clause and has upheld several taxes against such a challenge, including the federal estate tax[1474] and the federal gift tax.[243]

appropriate legislation, enforcement of provisions by   The phrase "appropriate legislation" is the term used to confer on Congress power to enforce the provisions of several amendments, beginning with the Thirteenth; it is also used in the Fourteenth, Fifteenth, Eighteenth, Nineteenth, Twenty-third, Twenty-fourth, and Twenty-sixth. In each instance, the grant of power extends the powers delegated to Congress in the original Constitution.

appropriation of money   Art. I-§8[12] restricts appropriations for the military, there referred to as "appropriation of money," to two years. Congress must pass new legislation to continue to fund the armed forces.

appropriations made by law   The federal government may not spend money unless Congress has appropriated the funds; the provision in Art. I-§9[7] barring expenditures from the treasury except "in consequence of appropriations made by law" is a limitation on the powers of the executive branch. It does not restrict Congress's power to appropriate funds. The Court has held that when Congress directs the treasury to pay a particular person a sum of money for any reason, neither the executive nor the courts may question or stop the payment.[1662] Congress need not specify how every penny is to be spent on general federal programs; it may delegate to executive officials the discretion to spend as necessary to accomplish a particular goal, as long as the federal officer is spending from a sum of money specifically appropriated by Congress for that program.[397]

In a recent harsh decision strictly construing the appropriations clause, a disabled civilian employee of the Navy forfeited his pension because he took bad advice from a Navy pension specialist, who told him that it was all right to engage in extra work. However, the law stipulated that any pensioner earning more than a certain amount would be ineligible for some portion of his pension. The employee sued and recovered a judgment equal to his lost pension because the Navy had misled him. The Court reversed, saying the employee could not have the funds, since the law specifically declared him ineligible; therefore the treasury could not write a check even to satisfy the court judgment.[1517]

arbitration, compulsory, *see:* **hearing; trial, right to**

argument, *see:* **oral argument**

arising under   This phrase, extending federal JUDICIAL POWER to cases "arising under this Constitution, the laws of the United States, and treaties," is the key to the Supreme Court's implied power to review the constitutionality of all governmental activity. Found in Art. III-§2[1], it is the basis of "federal question jurisdiction" and says that the federal courts may hear cases that raise a constitutional or other federal legal issue.

See also: FEDERAL QUESTION JURISDICTION; JURISDICTION; MARBURY V. MADISON.

armbands, *see:* **schools, armbands in**

armed forces   Both Congress and the president have constitutional powers permitting them, differently, to govern the armed forces. The president is commander in chief (Art. II-§2[1]). To Congress is committed the power to "raise and support armies" (Art. I-§8[12]), "to provide and maintain a navy" (Art. I-§8[13]), to "make rules for the government and regulation of the land and naval forces" (Art. I-§8[14]), and to call out, organize, arm, discipline, and regulate the MILITIA or National Guard (Art. I-§8[15, 16]. These clauses incorporate the Air Force, Marine Corps, and other military services, such as the Coast Guard during time of war. Congress also has the exclusive and important power to "declare war" (Art. I-§8[11]).

These provisions have sparked intense, longstanding tensions between the legislative and executive branches, as a direct outcome of the SEPARATION OF POWERS. The English monarchs had the power not only to send their armies and navies into WAR but also unilaterally to conscript soldiers and sailors without consent of Parliament. The Framers were insistent that the power to raise a military—that is, call it into being and fund it—be within Congress's powers, not the president's. But once war has been declared, a strong command requires someone who can ultimately decide what to do; that power necessarily rests in the president. Throughout our history, the power to give military orders, including sending troops into battle, has clashed with the power of Congress both to declare war and to regulate the military.

In general, the Court has given Congress broad leeway in governing the armed forces. "The military constitutes a specialized community governed by a separate discipline from that of the civilian.... Congress is permitted to legislate both with greater breadth and with greater flexibility when prescribing the rules by which [military society] shall be governed than it is when prescribing rules for [civilian society]."[1570] Following this general dictum, the Court has approved many regulations that, were they applied to civilians, would be clear violations of CIVIL LIBERTIES guaranteed in the BILL OF RIGHTS. For example, the Court has upheld military base regulations that prohibit demonstrations, speeches, and the distribution of literature not approved by the commanding officer.[808] The Court has also upheld congressional laws over state regulations governing soldiers' life insurance policies[2239, 2223] and state property taxes,[509] as well as the location of bordellos near military bases.[1302] The plenary power of Congress over the military was part of the justification for the Court's holding that it is constitutionally permissible to require men but not women to register for the draft.[1766] Despite Congress's exclusive power to issue disciplinary rules and other regulations that govern the military, the Court has held that during wartime the president has the discretion to alter them as he sees fit.[1677]

See also: COMMANDER IN CHIEF; IMPLIED AND INHERENT POWERS; POSSE COMITATUS; PRESIDENT, POWERS AND DUTIES OF; WAR POWER.

arms, right to keep and bear   The right "to keep and bear arms," which appears in the SECOND AMENDMENT, is one of the most enigmatic rights in the Constitution. By itself, the right might seem to be absolute, since the Second Amendment says that the right "shall not be infringed." But the phrase does not stand on its own; it is qualified as necessary for securing freedom through a "well regulated militia." In the only case it has considered directly under a Second Amendment challenge, the Court upheld the National Firearms Act requiring registration of sawed-off shotguns.[1343] Because there was no evidence that sawed-off shotguns have "some reasonable relationship to the preservation or efficiency of a well-regulated militia, we cannot say that the Second Amendment guarantees the right to keep and bear such an instrument. . . . Certainly it is not within judicial notice that this weapon is any part of the ordinary military equipment or that its use could contribute to the common defense." The Court has also upheld a federal ban on convicted felons' ownership of firearms shipped in interstate commerce.[1160]

No one knows whether some future Court might overturn under the Second Amendment a national ban on possession, sale, or use of some or all firearms, but it seems clear that Congress's hesitation to do something about the gun menace in America has little to do with constitutional doubts. The cases do suggest that whatever its substantive reach, the Second Amendment bars only congressional action, not state bans on firearms or private interference with the ownership or use of guns.[1661, 1742] Although the Court has avoided the issue in recent years, lower courts have held that even

a citywide ban on all handguns does not violate the Second Amendment.

army, *see:* **armed forces**

arraignment   Arraignment is the moment when a defendant is formally notified in court of the criminal charges to be brought against him and when he is required to state how he pleads (guilty, not guilty, not guilty by reason of insanity, or *nolo contendere*). The trial court may not accept a guilty plea if it is not voluntary.[221] An involuntary plea is one induced by a threat, a promise to stop improper harassment, or misrepresentation. The judge must also see to it that defendants pleading guilty understand the charges to which they are pleading. The trial judge must talk to the defendants long enough to assure that they are aware of all the acts and states of mind that the prosecution would have to prove to gain convictions.

In one case, the defendant was sentenced to death for his part in five armed robberies. The trial judge had never discussed anything about his guilty plea with him. The Court reversed, saying that it "was error, plain on the face of the record, for the trial judge to accept petitioner's guilty plea without an affirmative showing that it was intelligent and voluntary."[216] In another case, the defense counsel had failed to tell the defendant that a charge to which he was pleading guilty required an "intent to kill." The Court held that because the defendant was unaware of that element of the offense, acceptance of his guilty plea violated his rights to DUE PROCESS.[899]

arrest, privilege from   Art. I-§6[1] says that members of Congress "shall in all cases, except treason, felony, and breach of the peace, be privileged from arrest during their attendance at the session of the respective houses and in going to and returning from the same." This provision immunizing members from arrests in civil suits was in common use in the 1780s but is rare, if not extinct, today. The clause does not prohibit service of process against members of Congress;[1184, 466] the exception for "treason, felony, and breach of the peace" has been interpreted to mean that they may be arrested for any criminal offense.[2226]

arrest and arrest warrant   An arrest has traditionally been defined as the legally authorized act of depriving a person of liberty. To prevent random detentions at the unfettered whim of the police, the FOURTH AMENDMENT requires any SEARCH AND SEIZURE to be reasonable and ordinarily requires a SEARCH WARRANT. Obtaining a warrant is, of course, impracticable in many situations—specifically, when the police have in sight or are chasing a suspect who would flee if given the opportunity. For many years, it was unclear when the police were required to obtain arrest warrants. Finally, in 1976, in *United States v. Watson*, the Court held that the police may stop and arrest a felony suspect without a warrant, even if there was time to obtain one, as long as the police had PROBABLE CAUSE to believe that a crime had been committed and that the suspect committed it. But this rule is limited to suspects in public places. The Court has explicitly required the police to obtain arrest warrants before entering a person's home without consent to arrest him[1581] (there is no such automatic requirement for arrests in cars[1765]). Whether the police may arrest for all MISDEMEANORS without a warrant is an open question.

The question of what constitutes probable cause is more often considered in cases involving searches; whether an arrest had a proper basis is generally tested by the same rule that determines whether a search was legally justified. However, a GRAND JURY indictment may serve as the basis for an arrest warrant, whereas it will not serve to validate a search warrant.[745]

Not every momentary detention by the police is necessarily an arrest. The Court has upheld, in a variety of circumstances, police stopping and questioning of people even in the absence of probable cause. For example, a police checkpoint along the highway that stops drivers at random to see whether they are intoxicated is permissible,[1333] as is a brief stop at a checkpoint to look for illegal aliens.[1257]

arsenals, *see:* **public buildings**

Article I courts   Since the early days of the United States, Congress has created a variety of "courts" that do not exercise the JUDICIAL POWER of the United States, for example, courts in TERRITORIES outside the states and courts for specialized purposes, such as those for hearing tax, bankruptcy, and military cases. In *American Insurance Co. v. Canter,* Chief Justice John Marshall bestowed the name "legislative courts" on these bodies, because they carry out a purpose enacted under a specific congressional power. Today they are also known as "Article I courts." In practical terms, such courts are essentially administrative agencies. Judges need not serve for life, they may be removed at the whim of the president,[1277] and Congress may even lower their salaries during their terms of office.[2218] Unlike the procedure with judicial branch courts, their work may be reviewed by other branches of government.[660, 783]

Two puzzles that never have been clearly explained are how the Supreme Court may hear appeals from a legislative court and how a legislative court may exercise some aspect of the judicial power. The Court answered the first question by asserting that if the proceedings in the Article I court involve the resolution of legal differences between two parties, the Supreme Court may review as long as its judgment will be final.[535, 1038] The Court answered the second question when it distinguished between matters that historically were heard in court (COMMON LAW suits, suits in EQUITY, and ADMIRALTY AND MARITIME cases) and other matters that traditionally had not been heard there.[1412] Among such nontraditional cases are claims against the United States, questions about Indian tribal membership,[2145, 1956] and customs and internal revenue issues.[1527, 107] After considerable dispute, however, the Court in recent times partially reversed itself and concluded that both the U.S. Court of Claims (now the U.S. COURT OF APPEALS FOR THE FEDERAL CIRCUIT) and the U.S. COURT OF CUSTOMS AND PATENT APPEALS are judiciary rather than legislative courts.[762] The U.S. bankruptcy court is another Article I court; however, Congress had to limit its powers somewhat when the Court declared part of its jurisdiction unconstitutional.[1500]

See also: ARTICLE III COURTS; BANKRUPTCY COURT; FINALITY; JUDICIAL POWER; JURISDICTIONAL AND CONSTITUTIONAL FACTS; PRIVATE RIGHT–PUBLIC RIGHT DISTINCTION.

Article III courts   Article III vests the judicial power of the United States in an independent third branch of government, comprising the Supreme Court and any lower courts created by Congress under the power given in Art. III-§1. Judges of these courts enjoy life tenure (they serve "during good behavior"). Such courts are called Article III, or "constitutional," courts to indicate that they may hear all the cases described in Art. III-§2 as within the federal judicial power. Article III courts today include the U.S. DISTRICT COURTS, the U.S. COURTS OF APPEALS, and some specialized courts such as the U.S. COURT OF APPEALS FOR THE FEDERAL CIRCUIT.

See also: ARTICLE I COURTS; JUDICIAL POWER.

articles for export, *see:* **exports**

Articles of Confederation   "The Articles of Confederation and Perpetual Union" was the name Benjamin Franklin gave to his proposed constitution of the states following the declaration of war in 1775. In 1776 the Continental Congress appointed a committee to draw up a constitution. The effort would consume five years. The debate swirled around such questions as the degree to which the central power should absorb powers of the states, control over western lands, the basis of representation in Congress, and the taxing power. Eventually, the Articles of Confederation accepted the principle of equal representation for each state in Congress and denied to Congress a central power to regulate commerce or to tax. Congress did assume "sole and exclusive" power over foreign and Indian affairs, war and peace, and western lands, with authority to admit new states into the Union on an equal basis with the original states. But the Articles failed to create a federal executive or judiciary, and they required unanimous consent to any amendments. Proclaimed ratified on March 1, 1781, the Articles of Confederation lasted less than eight years. The lack of central power to control commercial and other conflicts among the states led to a call for a new CONSTITUTIONAL CONVENTION in 1787. The new Constitution was ratified on June 17, 1788. On July 2, 1788, Cyrus Griffin, president of the last Confederation Congress, declared that the new Constitution had supplanted the Articles of Confederation.

articles of impeachment   Articles of IMPEACHMENT are the specific counts against a federal official whom the House of Representatives has voted to impeach (akin to indicting). In 1868 the House voted eleven articles against President Andrew Johnson, but the Senate acquitted him by a single vote. In 1974 the House Committee on the Judiciary reported three articles against President Richard Nixon. The full House never voted on them because President Nixon resigned rather than face the overwhelming likelihood that the House would vote to impeach and the Senate to convict. In 1971 then-Congressman Gerald R. Ford initiated unsuccessful impeachment proceedings against Justice William O. Douglas. In recent years, two federal appeals judges have been impeached and removed from office.

arts, *see:* **Patent Clause**

assembly, freedom of, *see:* **freedom of assembly**

assistance, writ of   In seventeenth- and eighteenth-century colonial America, the writ of assistance was the formal authorization by the English Court of the Exchequer to royal customs inspectors to search homes for contraband. In effect, the writ was a general SEARCH WARRANT, a standing invitation to rummage through a person's home looking for whatever the customs inspector could find. So obnoxious was the practice by which writs of assistance were issued that the First Congress outlawed them in the FOURTH AMENDMENT, which requires that a search warrant must be obtained from the appropriate court in each instance and must describe in some detail the specific things being sought and the places to be searched.

assistance of counsel, *see:* **counsel, assistance of**

association, freedom of, *see:* **freedom of association**

association, guilt by, *see:* **guilt by association**

associations, membership in, *see:* **membership in political organizations**

assumption of debt   Art. VI-§1 specifically acknowledged that the United States would stand by its obligation to pay all debts legally owed by the United States under the Articles of Confederation. The change of Constitution would not void the country's ongoing relationships.

attachment of property, *see:* **garnishment and attachment**

attainder, bill of, *see:* **bill of attainder**

attainder of treason   In English law, an attainder of treason was the loss of all legal protection when a person was convicted of treason. Among the rights lost was the right to pass on property either during the traitor's lifetime or to his heirs. The deprivation of a right to inherit was known as "corruption of the blood." It is prohibited by Art. III-§3[2] "except during the life of the person attainted." During the Civil War, Congress enacted the Confiscation Act of 1862, giving the president the power to confiscate the property of rebels. Expressing constitutional doubts, Lincoln insisted that Congress limit the forfeiture of property to the owner's lifetime. Heirs were not entitled to the property while the traitor was living, but after his death they regained absolute ownership. Construing the provision, the Supreme Court said that the Attainder of Treason Clause is intended to benefit heirs in just this situation.[2147]

attendance at legislative sessions, *see:* **arrest, privilege from**

attorney general   Since 1870, the United States attorney general has been the head of the Justice Department and the fourth-ranking official in the cabinet. The job is not listed in the Constitution, but it was among the first established by Congress in the Judiciary Act of 1789, which said that the appointee should be, among other things, "a meet person, learned in the law." Nine attorneys general have later served on the Supreme Court, two of them as chief justices (Roger B. Taney and Harlan F. Stone). Some attorneys general have been prominently identified with the Justice Department's efforts to promote basic CIVIL RIGHTS through the filing of lawsuits, beginning with Attorney General Frank Murphy's creation of the Civil Rights Section (now Division) in 1939. Presidents have often appointed confidants as attorneys general. The political results have ranged from the generally admired stewardship of the Justice Department by President Kennedy's brother Robert to its widely deplored administration by President Nixon's law partner, John N. Mitchell, who went to prison for his role in WATERGATE.

attorney general's list   In 1947, President Truman issued an EXECUTIVE ORDER requiring the attorney general to compile a list of all subversive organizations in the United States. If a federal employee was found to be a member of one of these organizations, his or her loyalty was suspect. Organizations to be listed were described as those being "totalitarian, Fascist, Communist, or subversive . . . or approving the commission of acts of force or violence to deny to others their constitutional rights." Nearly two hundred organizations were eventually listed. Despite serious challenges to the constitutionality of the list or the way in which it was compiled,[1027] the Court never found reason to prohibit its use. It was eventually abandoned in 1974.
See also: BLACKLISTING.

attorneys, *see:* **lawyers**

authority, executive, *see:* **executive authority**

authority of Congress, *see:* **Congress, powers of**

authors and inventors   Art. I-§8[8] empowers Congress to promote "the progress of science and useful arts" by bestowing copyrights and patents on "authors and inventors." The Constitution does not define these terms. It is clear that they are to be read broadly, so that, for example, "author" is not restricted to those who write novels or other books but includes anyone who creates some form of expression, including poets, painters, photographers, screenwriters, playwrights, choreographers, composers, and sculptors. But there are limits to who may be considered an author or inventor. For example, a person who devises an idea—for example, a mathematical formula or a marketing plan—may not copyright it to prevent others from using it, although he or she may copyright a description of the idea.
See also: COPYRIGHT CLAUSE; PATENT CLAUSE.

automobiles, searches of, *see:* **search and seizure: automobiles**

automobiles, stolen, *see:* **interstate commerce**

autonomy, personal, *see:* **dress code; liberty; person and personhood; sexual freedom**

avoidance of constitutional questions, *see:* **constitutional questions, avoidance of**

B

---

bad tendency test In the early years of the twentieth century, the Court sustained criminal convictions against left-wing propagandists for advocating actions that the government feared might eventually lead to its collapse. Though the propagandists did not incite anyone to immediate lawlessness, the Court said that because of its ultimate "bad tendency" such speech was not protected by the FIRST AMENDMENT. In 1925, over the dissents of Justices Louis D. Brandeis and Oliver Wendell Holmes, Justice Edward Sanford declared that "a single revolutionary spark may kindle a fire that, smoldering for a time, may burst into a sweeping and destructive conflagration."[761] This bad tendency test seemed for a time to be undermined by the CLEAR AND PRESENT DANGER test, but it was reincorporated in the Court's 1951 decision in *Dennis v. United States*. This opinion held that even though the likelihood is low that certain propaganda will cause harm, if the danger is great enough it may be suppressed. The test was eventually interred in 1969 in *Brandenburg v. Ohio*.

badges of slavery and servitude Although many slaves were branded, the so-called badges of slavery were not literally physical markings but the legal disabilities under which slaves suffered. The law considered them things rather than persons. Slaves could not vote, serve on juries, speak in public, enter contracts, own property, or even learn to read and write. The THIRTEENTH AMENDMENT, which bans slavery and involuntary servitude, empowered Congress to eliminate these legal disabilities. Immediately after the Civil War, Congress undertook to remedy the situation in several civil rights acts, granting equal rights to the former slaves to enter contracts, own property, and the like. But in 1883, in the *Civil Rights Cases*, the Court struck down the first federal public accommodations law, guaranteeing equal access to restaurants, hotels, and theaters. Justice Joseph P. Bradley said that private "discriminations on account of race or color [cannot be] regarded as badges of slavery" and that therefore Congress had no power under the Thirteenth Amendment to directly ban private acts of racial discrimination. The Court ultimately reversed itself eighty-five years later. In *Jones v. Alfred H. Mayer Co.*, the Court said that Congress can regulate private activity under the Thirteenth Amendment, and it upheld a law barring private acts of racial discrimination in the sale of real estate.

See also: EQUAL PROTECTION; PUBLIC ACCOMMODATIONS; STATE ACTION.

bail and fines   Bail is an amount of money paid to the court as security for a defendant's release from prison before trial. If the defendant does not show up at trial, he or she forfeits the payment. The EIGHTH AMENDMENT provision against excessive bail and fines has a long and tortuous history stretching back to MAGNA CARTA. King and Parliament fought for centuries over the power to keep unconvicted suspects and/or political enemies in prison without trial. In *Darnell's Case* in 1627, the English judges agreed that the king could order anyone to prison without bail before trial. Parliament responded by establishing the right to HABEAS CORPUS, a right that won out against the kings only after a half-century of struggle. But the judges then circumvented habeas corpus by requiring such high bail that as a practical matter, kings could continue to imprison their opponents to silence them. In the 1689 Bill of Rights, Parliament outlawed "excessive bail"; that phrase was carried over by the First Congress into the Eighth Amendment.

Although the provision does not literally guarantee bail to prisoners awaiting trial, the conventional view has been that bail may be denied only if there is a reasonable basis to believe that the defendant will flee the jurisdiction and not stand trial or serve a sentence. In 1951 the Court unanimously declared: "This traditional right to freedom before conviction permits the unhampered preparation of a defense, and serves to prevent the infliction of punishment prior to conviction.... Unless this right to bail is preserved, the presumption of innocence, secured only after centuries of struggle, would lose its meaning."[1937]

Until 1988 the Court had never expressly approved a general power of PREVENTIVE DETENTION—a refusal to set bail because of a fear that the suspect might cause harm if released before trial. But it had suggested that certain kinds of proceedings do not require bail; for example, deportation proceedings of alien communists[345] and juvenile court proceedings.[1810] Finally, in the 1988 case *United States v. Salerno,* the Court rejected the premise that bail may be denied only to prevent flight. Instead, the Court said that judges may allow pretrial detention of "arrestees charged with serious felonies who are found after an adversary hearing to pose a threat to the safety of individuals or to the community which no condition of release can dispel." What appears to be left is the notion that when bail is proper, it may not be excessive. It is not, however, a guarantee of release; a defendant who cannot afford reasonable bail must stay in jail.

The Court has apparently never addressed the issue of what constitutes an "excessive fine" in criminal prosecutions. An attempt to "constitutionalize" PUNITIVE DAMAGE AWARDS in private injury cases failed in 1989. The argument was that large punitive damage awards in particular cases against insurers, manufacturers, and other types of businesses are excessive in relation to the injury and therefore violate the excessive fines provision. The Court said that the clause applies only to fines levied by the government "as punishment for some offense."[263]

balancing   Throughout its history the Supreme Court has insisted on the need to balance state powers and individual rights. Sometimes balancing seems to result from constitutional language. For example, the FOURTH AMENDMENT prohibits "unreasonable" SEARCHES AND SEIZURES, implying that reasonable ones may be conducted and that a court may be called on to determine which are which by "balancing the need to search ... against the invasion which the search entails."[331] Other constitutional phrases may require judicial weighing of interests, though the language does not on its face speak in terms of balancing. The SIXTH AMENDMENT guarantees the right to "a speedy trial," but whether a trial has been convened quickly enough obviously depends on the circumstances. On the other hand, much constitutional language appears absolute—for example, the FIRST AMENDMENT's command that no law shall abridge the FREEDOM OF SPEECH. Nevertheless, in this area as in dozens of others the Court over the years has devised a series of "balancing tests" to determine in individual cases whether the government's interest outweighs an individual's rights. A random listing of various types of cases indicates the extraordinary range of the balancing in which the Court engages:

To determine the validity of a TAKING OF PROPERTY, the Court weighs the "character of governmental action, economic impact, and its interference with reasonable investment-backed decisions."[1669]

To determine the speediness of a trial, the Court looks to the length of and reasons for delays, the extent to which the defendants asserted their right, and the extent to which the delay prejudiced the defendants.[126]

In judging whether to uphold a president's claim of EXECUTIVE PRIVILEGE, the Court will weigh the president's interest in the privacy of executive communications and the state's need for evidence in a criminal prosecution.[1487]

In deciding whether the state may fire public employees for speaking their minds, the Court balances "the interests of the [employee], as a citizen, in commenting on matters of public concern and the interests of the state, as an employer, in promoting the efficiency of the public service it performs through its employees."[1625]

An even-handed state law that incidentally affects INTERSTATE COMMERCE "will be upheld unless the burden imposed on such commerce is clearly excessive in relation to the putative local benefits.[1629]

Political PATRONAGE is not a constitutional basis on which to hire or fire a public employee

unless the government has a "vital interest" in resorting to it.[224]

The Court has announced many other balancing tests in widely disparate areas, including COMMERCIAL SPEECH, SYMBOLIC SPEECH, the PUBLIC FORUM, TAXATION OF INTERSTATE COMMERCE, FREEDOM OF RELIGION, DURATIONAL RESIDENCY REQUIREMENTS, the right to a HEARING, and PREEMPTION. Despite the profusion of balancing tests, the Court appears to resort to balancing for one of four reasons:

(1) To decide whether a rule should be applied in certain types of cases, once and for all, without thereafter having to weigh the interests in the case. For example, balancing the government's interest in securing convictions against the public's interest in being free of unlawful intrusions, the Court conceived the EXCLUSIONARY RULE to preclude unlawfully seized evidence from being used in criminal trials. But in civil trials, the Court found that the balance tilted the other way. Likewise, the MIRANDA RULES were an outgrowth of the Court's growing disinclination to determine in every case whether a confession was coerced.

(2) To weigh claims arising from conflicting constitutional provisions, such as those involved in the debate over FREE TRIAL–FAIR PRESS.

(3) To decide, in a particular case of whatever type, whether the state's interest in avoiding a constitutional provision outweighs the individual's need for constitutional protection.

(4) To weigh competing state and federal interests, as in preemption or DORMANT COMMERCE CLAUSE cases.

Especially in the third and fourth types of judicial balancing, the result will depend on a weighing of such diverse factors that it is anyone's guess whether or not the Constitution has been violated. In a 1988 case involving a state STATUTE OF LIMITATION said to burden interstate commerce, Justice Antonin Scalia complained of the balancing test the Court applied that "since the interests on both sides are incommensurate . . . [it] is more like judging whether a particular line is longer than a particular rock is heavy."[152] This difficulty is apparent whether the Court nakedly balances or resorts to camouflage phrases such as COMPELLING INTEREST, LESS RESTRICTIVE MEANS, or "core function."[1434]

Often the Court engages in a one-sided balancing by mischaracterizing one interest at stake as relatively trivial and the other as relatively strong. This was the nub, for example, of Justice Hugo L. Black's frequent criticism of the Court's use of a balancing test in the arena of free speech: "At most [the Court] balances the right of the Government to preserve itself, against [the defendant's] right to refrain from revealing Communist affiliations. Such a balance, however, mistakes the factors to be weighed. [It] completely leaves out the real interest in [the defendant's] silence, the interest of the people as a whole in being able to join organizations, advocate causes and make political 'mistakes' without later being subjected to governmental penalties for having dared to think for themselves. It is this right, the right to err politically, which keeps us strong as a Nation. [It] is these interests of society, rather than [the defendant's] own right to silence, which I think the Court should put on the balance against the demands of the Government, if any balancing process is to be tolerated."[125]

It is a sign of both the enduring indispensability and the persistent danger of balancing tests that liberals and conservatives alike complain of their misuse. Thus, in 1989 Justice William Brennan protested a decision upholding the constitutionality of random DRUG TESTING with these words: "The majority's Rorschach-like 'balancing test' portends a dangerous weakening of the purpose of the Fourth Amendment to protect the privacy and security of our citizens."[1880] In 1988, Justice Scalia likewise condemned the majority's decision to uphold the constitutionality of the INDEPENDENT COUNSEL law: "The Court has . . . replaced the clear constitutional prescription that the executive power belongs to the President with a 'balancing test.' What are the standards to determine how the balance is to be struck, that is, how much removal of presidential power is too much?"[1389] That Scalia favored a balancing approach in the drug testing case and Brennan favored it in the independent counsel case shows why the Court will not likely abandon its wealth of tests, for to do so would mean that in an important sense the Court would be abandoning its historic task of making informed judgments about the close cases that divide society as much as the justices.

See also: *PROCESS THAT IS DUE; PUBLIC EMPLOYMENT; TRIAL, SPEEDY.*

ballot, *see:* **access to ballot; voting, right to**

bank acts Although Congress has no express power to charter banks, the Court held in 1819 in the celebrated case *McCulloch v. Maryland* that the NECESSARY AND PROPER CLAUSE permitted federal chartering of banks to implement Congress's "great powers, to lay and collect taxes; to borrow money; to regulate commerce; to declare and conduct a war; and to raise and support armies." The power to incorporate banks carries with it the power to authorize them to carry on private banking activities unrelated to any congressional purpose, as long as the private activities are necessary to enable the banks to compete effectively.[1543, 1892, 1636]

See also: *BANK OF THE UNITED STATES; COMMERCE CLAUSE.*

Bank of the United States Congress chartered the first Bank of the United States in 1791, against constitutional objections by James Madison. But Secretary of the Treasury Alexander Hamilton, the bank's prime proponent, prevailed on President Washington to sign a law establishing the bank for a twenty-year term. Hamilton argued that the federal government had ample power to create a financial institution that would serve both private and public purposes, including creating capital for industrial purposes. The first charter expired in 1811, and Congress refused to recharter it until 1816, after federal finances had fallen into disarray as a result of the War of 1812. The bank weathered a serious constitutional attack in 1819 when Chief Justice Marshall ringingly endorsed Congress's power to charter banks[1287] and declared that states could not tax it. The bank again became the center of attack in the 1832 elections, with President Jackson calling for its death. Congress passed a bill to renew its charter, but Jackson vetoed it. In a celebrated message he answered the claims of those who said that he could not veto because the Supreme Court had already proclaimed such laws constitutional: "The opinion of the judges has no more authority over Congress than the opinion of Congress has over the judges, and on that point the President is independent of both." The nation was thereafter without a federal bank until Congress created the Federal Reserve System in 1913.

bankruptcy One of the principal reasons for convening a CONSTITUTIONAL CONVENTION was to prevent the states from forgiving private debts or making it difficult for creditors to recover their loans. In Art. I-§8[4] the Framers gave Congress the authority to enact uniform bankruptcy laws for the whole country, but the requirement of uniformity is not as strict as it might seem. Nearly a century ago the Court approved local variations from state to state;[860] as a result, what a person is entitled to keep after bankruptcy depends on state law.

The national power over bankruptcy is quite broad, extending to every person and business, and even including municipal corporations, such as towns and cities. However, there are limits to how specific a law Congress may fashion. In 1982 the Court rejected a bankruptcy law that applied to only one of many railroads being reorganized.[1688] The fundamental purpose of bankruptcy is to provide a means by which an insolvent person may avoid paying all or a part of his or her debts. Congress, therefore, may affect the rights not merely of creditors and debtors but also of those who purchase the debtors' property.[2261] Congress may establish bankruptcy plans that affect the OBLIGATION OF CONTRACTS. Bankruptcy laws may even nullify contractual obligations undertaken before the bankruptcy law takes effect.[457] Although there have been suggestions that the DUE PROCESS CLAUSE of the FIFTH AMENDMENT imposes some limitations, the Court has rarely voided a bankruptcy provision on this ground. It did so in 1935, invalidating a law that permitted a landowner to stave off foreclosure for five years.[1196] But the Court almost immediately upheld a modified version,[2263] and it remains unclear whether there is any bar to Congress's power to modify the effect of a debtor-creditor agreement when insolvency is looming.

Congress's power over bankruptcy is not exclusive. The states may enact insolvency acts,[1975] as long as they are not preempted by federal bankruptcy law.[985] What constitutes a conflict with federal law for PREEMPTION purposes cannot be reduced to a formula. In one recent case, a state court put a receiver in control of a bankrupt company's property with instructions to clean up a waste disposal site; the Court held that the company's liability to clean up the site could be discharged in bankruptcy, and the state's order was nullified. When there is a federal law, state laws are in effect suspended, but if Congress were to repeal the national law, the state laws would spring back to life.[291] The state law may not, in any event, impair the obligation of an existing contract.

See also: BANKRUPTCY COURT.

bankruptcy court The status of the U.S. bankruptcy courts became an issue in the early 1980s after Congress overhauled the federal bankruptcy laws, creating a special "adjunct" bankruptcy court to the federal DISTRICT COURTS. The bankruptcy judges were given fourteen-year terms and no salary protection. This new federal bankruptcy court was empowered to hear any legal issues arising out of bankruptcy cases. When a bankruptcy court had to rule on breach of contract claims under state law, the Supreme Court said the bankruptcy court as a whole had been unconstitutionally established because its judges were exercising Article III JUDICIAL POWER without Article III protections.[1500] Congress was forced to withdraw ultimate authority over non–"core proceedings" from the bankruptcy court. Now bankruptcy judges may hear nonbankruptcy issues relating to bankruptcy cases, but their decisions may be appealed to the federal district courts.

bar admission and membership, *see:* **lawyers**

baseball In a case long considered an aberration but never overruled, the Supreme Court in 1922 held that professional baseball is not a business in interstate commerce and hence could not be brought within the scope of the federal antitrust laws.[640] By 1953, when the question again came before the Court, it was clear that the legal basis for the earlier ruling had long since been discarded. But the Court declined to reverse itself, saying that in the meantime baseball's antitrust immunity had become the settled expectation because Congress had done nothing to enact new legislation bringing baseball within the antitrust laws.[2057] In effect, the Court changed the basis of the immunity from a constitutional to a legislative one; it was assuming that failure to change the law was Congress's way of saying that it wished

to exempt baseball from antitrust. In 1972 the Court reaffirmed this position, noting that it was up to Congress to change the rule.[679] However, the Court has held that other professional sports—for example, football[1681] and boxing[982]—are subject to antitrust laws.

bear arms, *see:* **arms, right to keep and bear**

begging, *see:* **solicitation; vagrancy**

belief, freedom of, *see:* **freedom of belief**

benign racial and sex classification, *see:* **affirmative action**

Bible reading, *see:* **prayer and Bible reading; schools, religion in**

bicameralism Bicameralism is the division of the legislature into two houses. Both houses must concur on each law to be enacted. As spelled out in Article I, the United States Congress consists of a HOUSE OF REPRESENTATIVES and a SENATE, whose members are elected separately. Bicameralism is an old system, known in ancient Greece and Rome, employed in the British Parliament, and imported into the American colonies in the early seventeenth century. As a political mechanism it allows small and large states to live together in a federal union. It is also one of the central means by which the American system of CHECKS AND BALANCES is assured, since both houses must agree on every bill. The lack of bicameralism was one of the two defects that the Court cited in voiding the LEGISLATIVE VETO, under which one house of Congress reserved for itself the power to veto a regulation promulgated by an executive agency.[979] Bicameralism is a constitutional requirement only for Congress. No federal constitutional rule requires the states to divide their legislatures into two houses, although all but Nebraska do so.

bigamy, *see:* **marriage**

bilingual education, *see:* **education, bilingual**

bill of attainder A bill of attainder is a law enacted by a legislature that punishes an individual without a trial in court. Originally, a bill of attainder was a law condemning someone to death; a "bill of pains and penalties" was a law that directed a lesser penalty. In the Constitution, both are condemned in the single phrase. The bill of attainder is one of the few types of laws that the original Constitution denied to both the federal government and the states, in Art. I-§9[3] and Art. I-§10[1].

The Supreme Court has taken a broad view of the term, refusing to confine the prohibition to laws that name a particular person. After the Civil War, a Missouri law prohibited professionals from practice unless they took an oath that they had never aided the Confederacy; a similar federal law barred lawyers from practicing in federal courts unless they swore likewise. Since a certain number of the professionals and lawyers subject to the law had indeed aided the Confederacy and therefore could not truthfully take the oath, the Court in 1867, in the *Test Oath Cases,* invalidated the Missouri and federal requirements as bills of attainder because they levied a punishment without trial.

The issue did not arise again until 1946, when Congress barred payment of salaries for three federal employees who had been branded as subversives during a congressional committee hearing. The Court voided the law as a bill of attainder.[1199] Finally, in 1965 the Court struck down, 5–4, a provision in the Landrum-Griffin Act making it a crime for a Communist party member to serve as a labor union officer or employee.[261]

On the other hand, a law prohibiting directors of national banks from working for a securities underwriting business is not a bill of attainder because it does not single out a suspect political group or any other identifiable group. Instead, it fashions an objective rule to be applied generally.[186] And in *Nixon v. Administrator of General Services,* the Court sustained a law obviously aimed at a solitary person. The Presidential Recordings and Materials Preservation Act was designed solely to prevent Richard Nixon, who had just narrowly escaped impeachment by resigning, from destroying or hiding a huge number of his White House papers and records. The Court reasoned that under the circumstances Nixon "constituted a legitimate class of one" and that in any event the law's directive to the General Services Administration to assume control of the papers and records did not constitute "punishment."

Bill of Rights The Bill of Rights comprises the first ten amendments to the Constitution. Although Elbridge Gerry had offered a bill of rights to the Constitutional Convention, his motion was defeated ten to one on the grounds that there was no need, for example, to expressly declare a right of free speech because Congress had been given no authority to pass a law abridging the people's right to speak their minds. Whatever power was not delegated to the federal government was reserved to the people or the states.

The absence of such rights was the most substantial argument against ratification of the Constitution in 1787. Many people rightly objected that the opponents of a bill of rights took too legalistic and narrow a viewpoint. Throughout history, governments had encroached on the people's rights; who could assure that this new government would be different? Thomas Jefferson, then in England, wrote to James Madison that "a bill of rights is what the people are entitled to against every government on earth, general or particular, and what no just government should refuse, or rest on inference."

In most states, Federalist proponents of the Constitution succeeded in securing ratification only by promising that they would seek a bill of rights when the new Congress convened after ratification. State ratifying conventions sent Congress suggestions for 210 amendments. Leading the campaign in the first Congress, Madison pared the list to nineteen. The House and Senate eventually agreed on twelve, which Congress sent to the states in September 1789 for ratification. On December 15, 1791, Virginia became the required eleventh state to ratify ten of these amendments, and Secretary of State Thomas Jefferson proclaimed them part of the Constitution. (Connecticut, Georgia, and Massachusetts held out until 1939, when they symbolically ratified the Bill of Rights on the Constitution's sesquicentennial observance.) The two amendments not ratified dealt with the number of representatives in Congress and their salaries. The salary amendment lay dormant for more than two hundred years and was suddenly ratified, as the TWENTY-SEVENTH AMENDMENT, on May 7, 1992.

In form, the Bill of Rights is a limitation on the power of the federal government. That is why the FIRST AMENDMENT says, "Congress shall make no law . . ." rather than "neither Congress nor the states shall make no law. . . ." Madison had pressed for an amendment that would have read: "No state shall violate the equal rights of conscience, or the freedom of the press, or the trial by jury in criminal cases." It was, he proclaimed, "the most valuable amendment in the whole list." But he could not win congressional approval.

In 1833 the Court expressly rejected the argument that the Bill of Rights also applied to the states. The owner of a wharf sued the city of Baltimore for ruining his business by depositing so much sand and gravel along a channel leading to his wharf that ships had to dock elsewhere. The wharfinger argued that in depriving him of his profits, the city's engineering activities amounted to a TAKING OF PROPERTY for which JUST COMPENSATION was due under the FIFTH AMENDMENT. Chief Justice John Marshall dismissed the case because neither the city of Baltimore nor the state of Maryland was bound by the Fifth Amendment.[132]

With the ratification of the FOURTEENTH AMENDMENT, this limitation on the use of the Bill of Rights against the states began to fall. During a fifty-year period (roughly from the 1920s to the 1970s), the Court "incorporated" most, though not all, of the provisions of the Bill of Rights into the DUE PROCESS Clause of the Fourteenth Amendment. Today, for example, neither the federal government nor the states and their political subdivisions may take private property without paying just compensation. Neither Congress nor the states may establish a religion or interfere with the freedom of speech.

See also: amendments 1 through 10; DUE PROCESS; INCORPORATION DOCTRINE; particular rights guaranteed by the first ten amendments.

billboards, *see:* **commercial speech**

bills for raising revenue   Under Art. I-§7[1], all "bills for raising revenues" must originate in the House. The Court has narrowed the phrase's meaning to refer to specific tax measures. If revenue will be raised as an incidental effect of a bill enacted for some other purpose, the Senate may propose it; for example, a bill requiring the District of Columbia to pay a sum of money, raised through taxing, to railroad companies to construct a station.[1337]

bills of credit   A bill of credit is in essence paper money; in form it is a promissory note issued by a government. Art. I-§10[1] prohibits states from issuing bills of credit, and the states have not attempted to print their own currency. However, in 1830 the Court rejected a Missouri scheme to issue interest-bearing certificates to pay state salaries and to be used for payment of taxes.[485, 301] The prohibition against bills of credit does not bar a state from issuing notes for later payment of state indebtedness,[947] nor does it bar bills issued by state banks.[237, 515, 502, 2254]

birth control, *see:* **contraception**

bitter with the sweet   When the state creates certain types of benefits, such as state jobs, the question frequently arises whether the employee or the prospective employee has any legal ENTITLEMENT to the benefit and, therefore, a PROPERTY right, which the state may not revoke without DUE PROCESS of law. In a series of cases beginning in 1970, the Court has wrestled with the degree to which the state may constitutionally limit the procedural right to challenge the withdrawal of a benefit. In 1974, in *Arnett v. Kennedy* Justice William H. Rehnquist said in a plurality opinion that when "the grant of a substantive right is inextricably intertwined with the limitations on the procedures . . . litigant . . . must take the bitter with the sweet." In other words, since the state is creating the entitlement, it should be free to define it as narrowly as possible, including limiting the right to contest the deprivation of the benefit. But six other justices disagreed. Although two years later the Court seemed to flip-flop,[166] the "bitter with the sweet" rationale was expressly rejected in 1985, when the Court ruled that although state law may create a property right, it may not limit the constitutional requirement of a hearing before the right can be taken away.[409]

See also: HEARING; RIGHT-PRIVILEGE DISTINCTION.

black codes   Immediately after the Civil War, the former slave-holding states enacted "black codes" to both spell out and restrict the rights of the newly emancipated slaves. The codes extended to blacks certain incidents of civil status, such as the right to buy, sell, and own property; to make contracts; to marry; to enjoy the status of parents; to travel; to sue and be sued. They also severely restricted blacks in many important respects. For example, the codes barred blacks from some professions; made it unlawful for them to assemble in groups; forbade intermarriage with whites; and created white-only residential areas. In addition, the black codes tailored labor and employment laws in such a way that much of the master-servant relationship of the slave days was retained. In the later 1860s northern response to the codes led to the FOURTEENTH AMENDMENT. Some codes were even repealed, but in time they were reinstituted and formed the basis for the segregated way of life that would last nearly another century.

See also: EQUAL PROTECTION UNDER THE LAWS; MISCEGENATION; PLESSY V. FERGUSON; SEGREGATION.

blacklisting   The extent of the government's power to maintain a registry of dangerous or disloyal people has never been definitively mapped. Under federal law, the ATTORNEY GENERAL'S LIST of subversive organizations was maintained from 1947 to 1974. In 1950 the Supreme Court held that the attorney general could not simply list organizations without giving them the opportunity to demonstrate at a HEARING that they were not disloyal.[1027] Concurring, Justice Hugo L. Black thought the Court should have voided the list altogether, because "officially prepared and proclaimed governmental blacklists possess almost every quality of BILLS OF ATTAINDER." In 1963 the Court did strike down as a PRIOR RESTRAINT a Rhode Island scheme through which the state's Committee on Morality listed "objectionable" books that children ought not to read.[121] But the holding was based on not merely the existence of the list but the agency's practice of notifying distributors that a work had been placed on the list and then sending a police officer to see whether the distributor had withdrawn the work from sale.

In 1987 the Court upheld a provision of the Foreign Agents Registration Act requiring certain materials produced by a foreign government to be labeled as "political propaganda."[1310] In one of those acts of willful blindness to common sense that overcomes the Court on occasion, the majority held that the label "propaganda" has only neutral, not pejorative, connotations and that the labeling requirement poses no FIRST AMENDMENT difficulty because it does not prevent any book or film from being freely distributed. But the Court's decision went beyond the claim that a government "brand" has no CHILLING EFFECT if the book or film merely appears on a list in Washington, for it implicitly upheld the act's requirement that the label be affixed to the book or film itself, making the distributor the agent of the government's opinion. This "Scarlet Letter" approach belies the protestations of the Court's majority that the government was not interfering in any way with the material. Presumably the decision is limited to the government's power over imported products of foreign governments, although it would be consistent with the majority opinion for the government to demand that publishers stamp on the title page of the Bible and the Koran the label "religious propaganda."

See also: RIGHT TO REPLY.

blasphemy   Blasphemy, the vilification of God or the defaming of religion, was long a COMMON LAW offense. It was the basis for several convictions in the nineteenth century, often in cases in which the "blasphemer" had done no more than deny the existence of God. (It was on the ground of blasphemy that the late Ayatollah Khomeini of Iran issued his infa-mous death sentence on British author Salman Rushdie for writing *The Satanic Verses.*) In 1951 the Court struck down a New York law permitting censorship of "sacrilegious" movies[1041] on grounds that it violated FREEDOM OF SPEECH. The Court has never decided a case involving blasphemy itself, but it is difficult to suppose that any of the justices would permit a blasphemy law to stand, both because it would offend free speech and because it would violate the FIRST AMENDMENT's religion clauses.

See also: FREEDOM OF BELIEF; FREEDOM OF RELIGION.

blessings of liberty   By itself, this phrase from the Preamble has no legal force, but it embodies one of the principal purposes of the Constitution. To the Framers, "liberty" meant freedom from a dictatorial monarch rather than license to do whatever we please as individuals.

blood, corruption of, *see:* **corruption of blood**

blood samples   Because samples of a defendant's blood often serve as powerful evidence at trial, the question has arisen whether blood may be obtained and used without violating the FOURTH AMENDMENT's strictures against unreasonable SEARCH AND SEIZURE, the FIFTH AMENDMENT's rule against SELF-INCRIMINATION, the FOURTEENTH AMENDMENT's DUE PROCESS CLAUSE, and the EXCLUSIONARY RULE. The Court has held that none of these constitutional arguments stands in the way of using blood samples at trial in the appropriate case. A routine blood test performed in a hospital while the defendant was unconscious does not violate the PRIVACY interest protected by due process. Even if a defendant suspected, for example, of drunk driving is awake, the taking of blood by a physician "in a hospital environment according to accepted medical practices" does not violate the defendant's right against self-incrimination.[1818]

blood tests　In paternity cases, blood tests are an important source of evidence. Ordinarily, the defendant, a man who has denied fathering the plaintiff's child, must pay for the test. But when a defendant cannot afford to pay, he has a DUE PROCESS right to have the state subsidize it because without the test results, the defendant "lacks a meaningful opportunity to be heard" in the only forum open to him to avoid the large responsibility with which he will be saddled if he is not truly the father and because not only his interests but those of the child are "constitutionally significant."[1172]

See also: FAMILIES.

blue laws, *see:* **Sunday closing laws**

blue sky laws　Blue sky laws, state laws regulating the trading in securities, are constitutionally permissible unless they directly conflict with a federal regulatory scheme.[843, 310, 1316]

bond issues, *see:* **Erie rule; obligation of contract**

book banning, *see:* **censorship**

border search, *see:* **search and seizure, border searches**

born or naturalized in the United States　The phrase "born or naturalized in the United States" appears in Amendment 14-§1. It fundamentally changed the legal basis of American citizenship but is not quite as far-reaching as it might seem. The qualifying phrase "and subject to the jurisdiction thereof" means that certain people born on American soil, such as the children of foreign diplomats, do not become citizens by virtue of their birth.

See also: CITIZENS AND CITIZENSHIP.

borrowing power　Art. I-§8[2] empowers Congress to "borrow money on the credit of the United States." The Framers debated stating that Congress could also issue paper currency, but decided not to. Even so, the Supreme Court in 1871, in the *Legal Tender Cases,*[1142] held that the borrowing-power provision also authorizes Congress to issue treasury notes and to make them legal tender in satisfying preexisting debts. Although the Court has given the government considerable leeway in wriggling out of some of its obligations, the government may not repudiate the debt for which the treasury note stands. In the most noteworthy cases, the *Gold Clause Cases* in 1935, Congress passed a law annulling its obligation to redeem its bonds in gold coin. The Court held that the annulment violated the borrowing clause but refused the creditor relief because he could not show he had suffered any actual damage by being paid in treasury notes rather than gold. The borrowing power can be used in certain circumstances to override state laws. For example, the Court said that a provision in the U.S. savings bonds laws granting survivorship rights overrides a conflicting state law governing ownership on the death of the bondholder.[698]

bound to service　The phrase "bound to service," which appears in Art. I-§2[3], refers to apprentices and indentured servants for a term of years. For purposes of apportionment and taxation, those bound to service were to be counted as FREE PERSONS, in contradistinction to slaves, each of whom counted for only three-fifths of a person. The THIRTEENTH AMENDMENT made the term obsolete.

See also: SLAVERY; THREE-FIFTHS RULE.

boundary disputes between states　Boundary disputes between states are one of the rare classes of cases that the SUPREME COURT is empowered to hear as a trial court, taking evidence and resolving the factual dispute. Under Art. III-§2[2], the Supreme Court exercises ORIGINAL JURISDICTION in cases in which a state is a party. As a practical matter, the Court authorizes special masters to hear such disputes and then, essentially, reviews the masters' findings.

bounties   A bounty is a payment to induce some form of behavior; for example, to turn in scrap metal to a recycling center. Whether a state-paid bounty is constitutional depends on its purpose. The Court has upheld a Maryland policy of paying bounties to induce people in the state to recycle scrapped automobiles. Out-of-state processors charged that by making it more difficult for them to obtain a bounty, the plan violated the DORMANT COMMERCE CLAUSE; the Court rejected their argument because the state was a MARKET PARTICIPANT.[955] But the Court has rejected outright another type of bounty. Alaska determined to pay a dividend from oil revenues to each of its citizens, the amount dependent on how long each person had lived in the state. The Court refused to permit Alaska to apportion benefits according to years of residency, holding in part that Alaska's claim that the bounty was designed to induce certain behaviors was irrational and that, in any event, it is illegitimate for a state to create classes of citizenship by graduating rewards and benefits on the length of time someone has lived in the state.[2287]

See also: RESIDENCY; TRAVEL, RIGHT TO.

boycott   When two or more people agree not to buy from or deal with someone else, they are engaging in a boycott. One of the most common forms is the labor strike, a refusal by employees to work. The right to strike is protected in the federal labor laws but is not constitutional; Congress has the power to outlaw the strike, as it has done by declaring unlawful various forms of "secondary boycotts";[983] for example, a provision in the National Labor Relations Act prohibits PICKETING to persuade potential customers not to

shop in a store that sells goods of a certain manufacturer.[1432] However, noncoercive picketing in a public demonstration is usually a constitutionally protected activity. In one recent case, the Court sharply distinguished between picketing a shopping mall and handing out leaflets at the entrance urging shoppers not to patronize any stores until the mall owner promised to deal only with contractors paying "fair wages." To avoid having to confront a constitutional problem, the Court said that the leafleting was not an unlawful secondary boycott but "only an attempt to persuade customers not to shop in the mall."[530]

An economic boycott may be protected on constitutional grounds if its purpose is primarily political. In 1982, in *NAACP v. Claiborne Hardware Co.,* the Court threw out a million-dollar damage award in a boycott aimed at merchants in Port Gibson, Mississippi, to protest longstanding racial discrimination in local stores, by the police department, and in other public facilities. The protesters gave speeches, picketed white merchants, and announced at meetings the names of blacks who did patronize the stores. Although the boycott was largely peaceful, there were sporadic acts of violence. Without dissent, the Court held "that the nonviolent elements of [the boycotters'] activities are entitled to the protection of the FIRST AMENDMENT." The Court refused to hold the boycotters responsible as conspirators for the occasional acts of violence, most of which were directed against blacks who did not comply with the boycotters' entreaties. However, the Court said that damages could be awarded for provable consequences of the violence.

But the First Amendment does not extend to every boycott with a political purpose. The Court rejected the constitutional claims of a group of trial lawyers who had staged a boycott to force the courts to raise the fees paid to lawyers representing indigent defendants.[651]

See also: CONSPIRACY.

Brady material, *see:* **discovery in criminal proceedings; prosecutorial misconduct**

Brandeis brief   In 1908, in *Muller v. Oregon,* the Supreme Court upheld a law limiting the hours women could work, despite the Court's propensity in those days to disallow wage and hour laws on the grounds of ECONOMIC DUE PROCESS. The Court acknowledged that its decision was based in large part on the brief filed by the lawyer for the state, Louis D. Brandeis. Unlike most such documents of the day, Brandeis's brief was filled with factual data about the conditions facing working women and the extent of social legislation to protect them. Since that time, "Brandeis brief" has come to be the name for a brief designed to demonstrate the rationality of legislation by educating judges to the economic, social, and other conditions that motivated enactment. The Court's willingness to consider the data Brandeis presented amounted to a jurisprudential shift. From then on—though unsteadily at times—the Court has paid heed to the RATIONAL BASIS of legislation. As a rule, it will uphold a law unless it is irrational.

See also: BRIEF.

breach of the peace   Breach of the peace is an age-old offense punishable originally at COMMON LAW and today under state statutes against creating public disturbances or engaging in disorderly conduct. Criminal convictions under these laws for physical disturbances, such as punching someone in a crowd, making loud noises at night, or littering the street with garbage, present no constitutional difficulties. But when the disturbance arises solely or primarily because of what a person says or because of onlookers' reaction to an otherwise peaceful demonstration, the constitutional guarantees of FREEDOM OF SPEECH and FREEDOM OF ASSEMBLY may be invoked. The cases are too numerous to summarize, but a sampling of the decisions since the early 1940s gives a representative picture of the constitutional problems.

In the 1942 case *Chaplinsky v. New Hampshire,* the Court announced the FIGHTING WORDS doctrine, upholding a conviction under a state law banning "face-to-face words plainly likely to cause a breach of the peace by the [speaker]." Seven years later, in *Terminiello v. Chicago,* the Court struck down on grounds of VAGUENESS and OVERBREADTH a municipal ordinance against conduct the trial judge defined as that which "stirs the public to anger, invites dispute, brings about a condition of unrest or creates a disturbance." Speaking to a large group of people in an auditorium, the defendant made a vitriolic speech condemning blacks and Jews; a "howling" mob gathered outside to protest. In overturning the statute, Justice William O. Douglas said that "a function of free speech . . . is to invite dispute. It may indeed best serve its high purpose when it induces a condition of unrest, creates dissatisfaction with conditions as they are, or even stirs people to anger."

In dozens of cases since then, the Court has grappled with the balance between the public's right to order and speakers' rights to express themselves. Sometimes the Court has found the speaker sufficiently inciting the crowd that the breach of peace conviction has been upheld, even though the disturbance came more from the HOSTILE AUDIENCE than from the speaker.[653] At other times the Court has upheld the right of DEMONSTRATORS to march peacefully, even though the crowd surrounding the marchers was growing unruly.[603]

Whether the speech is sufficiently provocative to overcome the freedom of speech or vagueness challenge depends in part on who the audience is. In a trio of cases in 1972, the Court reversed convictions against speakers who had used flagrantly vulgar and offensive language—in one case in front of a school board meeting[1761] and in others in curses directed to policemen.[1159, 256] The majority held that the statutes were overbroad and vague because they permitted convictions for words that were not calculated to cause an immediate physical retaliation. In particular, the Court reasoned that policemen should be trained to avoid taking offense at remarks hurled at them in the heat of an arrest or other confrontation.

In an important free speech case the year before, the Court, speaking through Justice John M. Harlan, reversed the conviction of a young man seen in a corridor of the Los Angeles County courthouse wearing a leather jacket with the words "Fuck the Draft" embroidered on the back. He was convicted of violating a state law that prohibits "maliciously and willfully disturb[ing] the peace or quiet of any neighborhood or person [by] offensive conduct." In *Cohen v. California,* Justice Harlan said that there was no showing that the defendant intended to create a disturbance or that anyone was in fact disturbed and that, in any event, since the words were not directed at anyone in particular his "message" was not within the fighting words doctrine. The reasoning in this case suggests that a breach of the peace conviction for merely speaking is unconstitutional unless the defendant has deliberately egged on a crowd or hurled fighting words at a particular person.

Breathalyzer test   Many states have enacted "implied consent" laws that condition the continued possession of a driver's license on a motorist's willingness to undergo a breath or blood analysis if stopped by the police for drunk driving. The Court has upheld these laws, even in cases where a motorist's refusal to take the test will lead to an automatic ninety-day suspension without a prior hearing on whether the arresting officer had reasonable grounds to suspect intoxication.[1220]

bribery   A United States senator who had been accused of taking a bribe to vote in a certain way challenged the indictment on the ground that he was immune from prosecution under the Speech and Debate Clause of Art. I-§6[1], which says that members of Congress may not be "questioned in any other place" for any speech or debate made in Congress. The Court rejected the challenge, holding that "taking a bribe is, obviously, no part of the legislative process or function; it is not a legislative act."[232] The senator was indicted not for how he voted but for taking the bribe that induced him to vote as he had.

Bricker amendment, *see:* **treaties and treaty power**

bridges and waterways   Federal COMMERCE POWER gives Congress almost limitless authority to regulate the nation's waterways and the bridges spanning them. Congress may judge for itself whether bridges obstructing waterways should be torn down[2091] and may even overturn compacts among the states to permit bridges to stand when the states wish to tear them down.[1595] But if Congress does not forbid it or pass conflicting legislation, the states may exercise considerable control over waterways entirely within their borders; they may even dam up navigable creeks into which the tide flows.[2228] In 1837, in *Charles River Bridge v. Warren Bridge,* the Court held in an important limitation on the CONTRACT CLAUSE that a Massachusetts charter to a private turnpike company to build a toll bridge did not bar the state from later granting a charter to another company to build a competing free bridge.

See also: ADMIRALTY AND MARITIME JURISDICTION; NAVIGATION AND NAVIGABILITY; PREEMPTION.

brief   A "brief" is a lawyer's written argument to a court seeking to prevail on the ultimate merits of the case. The term usually refers to cases on appeal, although briefs are often filed also in trial courts. A written document making an argument on a side issue is usually termed a "memorandum." Because lawyers have departed from the original semantic meaning of the term "brief," many courts today have issued rules limiting the length of briefs that may be submitted.

See also: BRANDEIS BRIEF.

British constitution Unlike the United States Constitution, the British constitution comprises no single document; it is at once a combination of historic texts, such as MAGNA CARTA and the Bill of Rights of 1689, and a deep cultural understanding that Parliament (and earlier, the reigning monarchs) must respect certain individual rights. Unlike the fundamental American principle of JUDICIAL REVIEW, which permits the courts to invalidate laws of Congress on the ground that they conflict with the written Constitution, the British Parliament is supreme, answerable ultimately only to the voters.

See also: SOVEREIGNTY.

broad construction, *see:* **constitutional interpretation, strict construction**

broadcasting, regulation of Because the broadcasting spectrum is limited, the federal government has regulated radio and television and other electronic media in ways it cannot, under the FIRST AMENDMENT, restrict private speakers or newspapers, magazines, books, and other publications. In the Communications Act of 1934, which established the Federal Communications Commission, Congress created a complex plan to regulate the airwaves by granting licenses to applicants who serve, in effect, as public trustees. The congressional DELEGATION to the FCC of the power to license and regulate was accompanied by an extraordinarily loose and vague standard: the agency must act in accordance with "public interest, convenience, and necessity."

In 1943 the Court upheld this basic policy, resting its decision on the scarcity of the airwaves and the need to prevent broadcasters from interfering with each other's signals.[1425] The notion that licensees must act in some sense as public trustees has led the Court to approve such FCC regulations as the FAIRNESS DOCTRINE, requiring radio and television stations to provide ACCESS TO BROADCASTING under certain circumstances. As Justice Byron R. White put it in a later case: "Because of the scarcity of radio frequencies, the Government is permitted to put restraints on licensees in favor of others whose views should be expressed on this unique medium. . . . It is the rights of the viewers and listeners, not the right of the broadcasters, which is paramount."[1700]

The Court has generally held that the FCC does not have the power to base its decision to grant or revoke a license on the content of the political or social views expressed.[1425] In 1984 a closely divided Court struck down an FCC rule prohibiting editorializing by stations that receive public funding. Editorial expression is a "form of speech," which cannot be banned "solely on the basis of . . . content."[641] But some forms of nonpolitical speech may be regulated on the air even on the basis of content. In 1978 the Court declared that radio and television are entitled to lesser First Amendment protection than other media; it held that the FCC may regulate indecent, though not obscene, language that the government could not ban from use in a newspaper, magazine, or book. The case grew out of a radio monologue by comedian George Carlin on the topic of "filthy words." The radio station broadcast the monologue during the afternoon when children might be listening. Speaking for the majority, Justice John Paul Stevens said that "the broadcast media have established a uniquely pervasive presence in the lives of all Americans. Patently offensive, indecent material presented over the airwaves confronts the citizens, not only in public, but also in the privacy of the home, where the individual's right to be left alone plainly outweighs the First Amendment rights of an intruder . . . [and] broadcasting is uniquely accessible to children, even those too young to read."[642]

See also: RIGHT TO REPLY.

Brown v. Board of Education *Brown v. Board of Education* is one of the seminal cases in American history. It held that segregation in the public schools violates the EQUAL PROTECTION CLAUSE of the FOURTEENTH AMENDMENT and paved the way for a powerful judicial assault on all forms of official racism. Linda Brown was a schoolgirl in Topeka, Kansas, whose parents contested her segregated classrooms. Three other similar cases, originating in Delaware, South Carolina, and Virginia, were consolidated with hers for argument in December 1952. After argument, an initial majority favored retaining segregation. When one or two justices changed their minds, the Court asked for reargument because it was hoping to speak with a unanimous or nearly unanimous voice. Before the reargument could be heard, Chief Justice Fred Vinson died, and President Eisenhower appointed Earl Warren to the vacant seat. It was a fateful appointment, for the new chief justice set out to fashion a unanimous Court to overturn the infamous SEPARATE BUT EQUAL doctrine that was the main constitutional prop of segregation, announced originally in PLESSY V. FERGUSON in 1896.

In ordering reargument, the Court directed the lawyers to focus on several questions. Principal among them was whether the framers of the Fourteenth Amendment had intended to ban segregated public schools. Thurgood Marshall, then chief counsel for the schoolchildren, argued that the historical record was unclear. John W. Davis, chief counsel for South Carolina (and the 1924 Democratic candidate for president), urged the Court to uphold the doctrine of "separate but equal" on the ground that it had become an unshakable custom. Siding with Marshall, U.S. Solicitor General J. Lee Rankin, as AMICUS CURIAE, argued that continued segregation was doing the country incalculable harm in its foreign relations with the newly emerging third world.

Although there was ample evidence that the schools black schoolchildren were forced to attend were grossly unequal in budgets, facilities, and quality of teaching, Chief Justice Warren did not rest the unanimous 1954 decision on that ground. He wrote, more sweepingly, of the importance of education and of the damage done: "To separate [elementary school and high school students] from others of similar age and qualifications solely because of their race generates a feeling of inferiority as to their status in the community that may affect their hearts and minds in a way unlikely ever to be undone."

Striking down school segregation as "inherently unequal," *Brown v. Board of Education* unleashed a furious political storm, putting the problem of racism at center stage of national politics, stirring a debate that continues to this day. That *Brown* succeeded in dismantling overt, official segregation was due in no small part to two important features of the case: its unanimity and its rhetorical flatness. The two are directly connected. It was Warren's very blandness that permitted him to secure not merely a majority but unanimity.

In his 1954 opinion, Warren did not say how the states should go about revamping their school systems to eliminate segregation. Instead, the Court ordered further argument. It was not until the following year, in the second *Brown v. Board of Education*, that the Court announced its notoriously vague standard of ALL DELIBERATE SPEED, a rule that was overturned in 1969 when the Court finally ordered an immediate end to segregated school systems.[34]

For years many critics attacked the Court's

decision to overturn the separate-but-equal principle on the ground that the framers of the Fourteenth Amendment never intended that their handiwork be used to integrate schools. That the Court's conclusion is now firmly established is nicely illustrated in an exchange between Justices John Paul Stevens and Antonin Scalia in an unrelated case in 1990. Dissenting in a PATRONAGE case, Scalia said that the Court should not go about overturning long-established political traditions: "When a practice not expressly prohibited by the text of the Bill of Rights bears the endorsement of a long tradition of open, widespread, and unchallenged use that dates back to the beginning of the Republic, we have no proper basis for striking it down."[1778] Stevens responded that "if the age of a pernicious practice were a sufficient reason for its continued acceptance, the constitutional attack on racial discrimination would, of course, have been doomed to failure." Scalia retorted to Stevens that tradition gives content only to *ambiguous* constitutional text." But "no tradition can supersede the Constitution" and both the Thirteenth Amendment and the Equal Protection Clause "leave no room for doubt that laws treating people differently because of their race are invalid." But of course in 1954 when *Brown* was decided, very many people saw a very great ambiguity in the Fourteenth Amendment; indeed, very many saw no ambiguity at all: it did not prohibit segregation. That a tradition-minded justice sees no further ambiguity in the Equal Protection Clause, against the weight of a deadly tradition, suggests the final triumph of the constitutional *principle* of *Brown v. Board of Education.*

See also: RACIAL DISCRIMINATION; SEGREGATION AND INTEGRATION; SOCIOLOGICAL FOOTNOTE AND SOCIAL SCIENCE EVIDENCE.

budget The annual federal budget, released each year from the White House amid much fanfare, is not required by the Constitution. Until the early years of the twentieth century, there was no annual budget; Congress made ad hoc appropriations as necessary. Then, in the 1921 Budget and Accounting Act, Congress regularized federal budgeting by delegating to the president the task of preparing the budget—a major expansion of presidential power. From 1921 until 1969, the responsibility lay with the Bureau of the Budget. This office was situated at first within the Treasury Department and then, in 1939, moved to the Executive Office of the President. In 1969 President Richard M. Nixon renamed the bureau the Office of Management and Budget and increased its authority over executive departments and agencies. Five years later, responding to the president's refusal on several occasions to spend appropriated funds, Congress enacted the Congressional Budget and Impoundment Control Act, giving Congress greater ability to police the executive budget process.

See also: IMPOUNDMENT; SPENDING POWER.

buildings, public, *see:* **public property**

burden of proof, *see:* **proof, burden of**

bureaucracy, *see:* **administrative agencies and bureaucratic government**

business affected with a public interest, *see:* **affected with a public interest doctrine**

business regulation, *see:* **Commerce Clause; economic due process; economic regulation; interstate commerce**

busing Busing first received judicial sanction as a means of redressing school segregation in the 1971 case *Swann v. Charlotte-Mecklenburg Board of Education.* In school districts with many school buildings and segregated neighborhoods, a rule requiring children to attend the closest school might simply perpetuate the effects of the past policies of segregation. The Court therefore approved busing as a means of desegregating the schools; the kind of busing depended on a complex BALANCING of many factors, including the age of the schoolchildren and the time and distance traveled. *Swann*'s condoning of busing created a political uproar. There were many attempts in Congress to curtail the power of courts to require it, mostly unavailing. There was considerable irony in the outcry, since for decades busing of black children to remote schools was a mainstay of many segregated school districts.

Many states moved to curb the authority of school districts to provide or require busing on their own. After the Seattle School Board decided voluntarily to end racial imbalance in the city schools, in part by busing children throughout the city, voters in a statewide initiative enacted a policy that had the effect of prohibiting school districts from busing for racial purposes. The Court voided the initiative[2161] because it discriminated solely on racial grounds: parents who wanted a new kind of academic program could ask the school board to institute one; parents who wanted a busing plan would first have to ask the Washington state legislature to repeal the initiative. The EQUAL PROTECTION CLAUSE was thereby violated.

California amended its state constitution, providing that no state court could order busing unless it would remedy a violation of the federal Equal Protection Clause. Before the amendment, the state courts had been ordering busing in instances not required by the FOURTEENTH AMENDMENT. In this instance, the Court concluded, the state was not discriminating on the basis of race but was holding its courts precisely to the requirements of the Fourteenth Amendment—nothing more and nothing less. It is not a violation of the Equal Protection Clause, Justice Lewis F. Powell said, to require the courts to conform in all respects with equal protection requirements.[490]

Although many busing plans have been drawn up voluntarily by school districts to deal with racial imbalance in the schools, the most fiercely contested busing policies have been those ordered by courts to redress past segregation. Opponents of continuing federal court supervision of school districts have argued that when a court-ordered desegregation plan has finally eliminated "the vestiges of past [official] discrimination," further judicial oversight of the school district should cease. In 1991 the Supreme Court agreed in a 5–3 decision. It held that school districts could discontinue busing, even though the consequence would be in effect to resegregate the schools. Largely black neighborhoods would once again find their children attending mainly black schools, and white neighborhoods would send their children to largely white schools.[184]

See also: RACIAL DISCRIMINATION; SEGREGATION AND INTEGRATION.

butter, *see:* **milk; oleomargarine**

C

cabinet   The Constitution is silent on the subject of the presidential cabinet. It omits any mention of government offices, except for a fleeting reference in Art. II-§2[1] to the "principal officer in each of the EXECUTIVE DEPARTMENTS," from whom the president may require a written opinion about official activities. The cabinet is not an official body; it is essentially a meeting of the secretaries of the executive departments. The cabinet meeting was inaugurated by George Washington and has been maintained, with greater or lesser enthusiasm, by every president since. It could be abolished tomorrow—and some presidents have come close to doing so.

See also: HEADS OF DEPARTMENTS.

cable television   As a medium of expression, cable television is protected at least to some degree by the FIRST AMENDMENT. Whether cable is analogous to broadcast television (because it is television) or to newspapers (because it is not broadcast over scarce public airwaves) has not been settled. But the city of Los Angeles could not use the excuse of "visual blight" to award a cable television monopoly to a single operator when there was room on utility poles for another cable company to string wires; the Court said that unless the city could

show a more important interest than "blight," the other cable operator had a free speech right to operate.[1187] Although the federal government may regulate signal quality, neither the FCC nor the states may regulate the content of programming.[1466] And states may not impose a blanket prohibition against airing OFFENSIVE AND INDECENT SPEECH, beyond pure OBSCENITY, on cable programs; cable television is thus freer than broadcast television to air what it pleases.[2207]

See also: BROADCASTING, REGULATION OF.

campaign financing   The influence of money on politics dates back at least to 1796 in American national elections. As the franchise broadened and more states joined the Union, the cost of appealing to the public mounted apace. No campaign since George Washington's has been free of financial taint. Outright bribery and extortion have always been unlawful, though rampant vote buying and other illegalities have often gone unprosecuted. In 1925 Congress enacted the Federal Corrupt Practices Act, but it was toothless and rarely deterred the bagmen from delivering cash to compliant incumbents and challengers alike. In 1971 Congress passed a somewhat more forceful Federal Election Campaign Act, and it was amended, in the midst of WATERGATE, in 1974. The law was complex and raised significant constitutional difficulties, which the Court addressed in 1976 in *Buckley v. Valeo.* The act prohibits individuals, groups, and campaign committees from contributing more than one thousand dollars to any single candidate and five thousand dollars to any political committee. The law also set ceilings on other expenditures. No one could spend more than one thousand dollars to promote the election of a "clearly identified candidate" independent of that candidate's own efforts, and candidates could spend no more than twenty-five thousand dollars of their own or their families' money. Other provisions require disclosure of contributions and expenditures. Against a FIRST AMENDMENT challenge, the Court upheld the disclosure requirements and the contribution limitations. It held that the giving of money itself has little expressive content and does not outweigh Congress's COMPELLING INTEREST in reducing the "actuality and appearance of corruption" that flows from large contributions.

Congress also wanted to equalize the ability of individuals and groups to influence the outcome of elections, but the Court said that spending money to advocate someone's election or defeat is entitled to no less constitutional protection than "discussion of political policy generally or advocacy of the passage or defeat of legislation." It further added: "[T]he concept that the government may restrict the speech of some elements of our society in order to enhance the relative voice of others is wholly foreign to the First Amendment." Whether you wish to promote your own candidacy or someone else's, you are constitutionally entitled to spend money to do so, as long as the money is not going directly to the candidates themselves.[645]

The Court has looked askance at laws limiting contributions to other political committees and by corporations. It struck down laws that:

(1) limited the amount of money that could be contributed to an association advocating passage of a city referendum to repeal rent control;[400] (2) prohibited corporations from spending money to influence the outcome of a referendum on any proposals other than those directly affecting their business;[667] (3) required that contributions to a corporation organized solely to advocate political positions be made to a separate fund not administered directly by the corporate officers;[644] and (4) criminalized the practice of paying people to circulate petitions that would put an issue on the ballot.[1322] And although in *Buckley* it upheld disclosure of contributions as a general requirement, the Court has recognized that under certain circumstances, when disclosure might subject contributors "to threats, harassment, or reprisals from either Government officials or private parties," it would be unconstitutional to require a political campaign committee to disclose who contributed to it or to whom it disbursed the funds.[257]

The Court has acknowledged that the predominant concern of a campaign finance law is to avoid the actual and apparent corruption of candidates and officials. It upheld the Federal Election Campaign Act's prohibition against corporate solicitation of contributions to political action committees when the corporations solicited funds from nonmember corporations, saying unanimously that "there is no reason why . . . unions, corporations, and similar organizations [may not be] treated differently from individuals."[646] It also upheld a Michigan law that prohibited the state chamber of commerce from using corporate funds but permitted specially segregated funds to be used for campaign purposes unrelated to specific candidates.[98]

See also: ACCESS TO BALLOT; FREEDOM OF SPEECH.

candidacy for public office, *see:* **access to ballot**

canvassers, *see:* **access to ballot**

capital crimes A capital crime is one punishable by death. Because the DEATH PENALTY is the harshest possible punishment, the Court has from time to time imposed special procedural safeguards in the prosecution of capital crimes. It was in such a case, for example, that the Court first declared a state's DUE PROCESS obligation to appoint counsel for indigent defendants.[1652]

See also: DEATH PENALTY; PROPORTIONALITY OF SENTENCE; PUNISHMENT, CRUEL AND UNUSUAL.

capital punishment, *see:* **death penalty**

capitation or other direct tax A capitation tax is a tax on a person, like a poll tax, and although the meaning of "direct" is far from clear, the consensus is that the Framers meant by that term taxes on land. Under Art. I-§9[4], Congress may impose such taxes only by apportioning them among the states according to the census.

See also: APPORTIONMENT OF TAXES; INCOME TAX; POLL TAX.

captive audience The term "captive audience" refers to any group of people who while assembled for a particular purpose are forced by circumstances to listen to or watch a speaker or a commercial message. There is no general constitutional rule governing the conditions under which the government may intervene to regulate what a captive audience may be forced to hear or see. In a 1952 case, the Court refused to overturn a decision by a public utilities commission permitting municipal buses to broadcast radio stations carrying music, news, and commercials. (Justice Felix Frankfurter refused to participate in the case because, he said, "my feelings are so strongly engaged as a victim of the practice.")

In 1974 the Court approved a city's decision to discriminate between types of poster advertisements permitted in mass transit cars. The public rapid transit system sold commercial advertising space to cigarette companies, churches, and liquor manufacturers but refused the space to political candidates or public-issue advertising.[1673] The 5–4 majority agreed that among the city's valid reasons for selling to some and not others was the desire to avoid forcing unwanted political messages on commuters. The Court concluded that the advertising space in the transit cars was not a PUBLIC FORUM.

When people congregate in public forums, however, it is unlikely that the state will be permitted to protect them from unwanted speech. In one of the most vivid cases to raise this issue in recent times, Justice John M. Harlan, writing in 1971 for a 6–3 majority, held that California could not constitutionally prosecute a man for standing in a corridor of the Los Angeles County Courthouse wearing a leather jacket with the words "Fuck the Draft" emblazoned on the back.[417]

captures on land and water, *see:* **war prizes**

Carolene Products **footnote four** In 1938, in *United States v. Carolene Products Co.,* a case dealing with the RATIONAL BASIS standard by which economic legislation would be reviewed when challenged as violating DUE PROCESS, Justice Harlan F. Stone explained that the Court would indulge in a PRESUMPTION OF CONSTITUTIONALITY for most legislation passed by Congress or the state legislatures. To reject an economic regulation the challenger would have to show that it was wholly arbitrary and irrational. But in a celebrated aside, stuck in what was destined to become the famous "footnote four," Stone said that the presumption might not hold for other, noneconomic actions of the government. The suggestion in the short footnote helped launch both a new SUBSTANTIVE DUE PROCESS and EQUAL PROTECTION doctrine by which the Court would closely scrutinize laws affecting political and personal rights. The footnote reads: "There may be narrower scope for operation of the presumption of constitutionality when legislation appears on its face to be within a specific prohibition of the Constitution, such as those of the first ten Amendments, which are deemed equally specific when held to be embraced within the 14th." Stone went on to specifically elucidate that "those political processes ordinarily to be relied upon to protect [DISCRETE AND INSULAR MINORITIES] . . . may call for a correspondingly more searching judicial inquiry."

See also: PRESUMPTION OF CONSTITUTIONALITY; STRICT SCRUTINY.

carriers, *see:* **transportation**

cases of impeachment, *see:* **impeachment**

cases of rebellion or invasion, *see:* **invasion**

cases or controversies The Constitution vests the JUDICIAL POWER in the SUPREME COURT and lower federal courts created by Congress. Several delegates to the CONSTITUTIONAL CONVENTION had suggested that the Supreme Court be part of a COUNCIL OF REVISION to oversee, and veto if necessary, unwise congressional enactments. But following objections by James Madison and others, the Framers said in Art. III-§2[1] that the courts may exercise judicial power only in "cases" or "controversies." The Constitution itself does not spell out the contours of a case or controversy. "These two words," Chief Justice Earl Warren commented in a 1968 case, "have an iceberg quality, containing beneath their surface simplicity submerged complexities."[673] A case or controversy can be any actual dispute between adverse parties over a legal entitlement in which a final judgment is sought. Therefore, federal courts may not issue ADVISORY OPIN-IONS—mere advice as opposed to judicial decisions—to the president or anyone else. Nor may the judges take it upon themselves to distribute press releases condemning laws that they believe to be of doubtful constitutionality. The federal courts may decide issues of legality or constitutionality only when they are actually deciding cases.

A case or controversy must fulfill the following criteria:

First, the parties must be *adverse*—one person pursuing "an honest and actual antagonistic assertion of rights . . . against another."[387] To test the validity of a law allocating Indian lands, Congress once passed a law empowering certain Indians to sue the United States. That is like passing a law authorizing you to sue the United States to test whether a law against flag burning is constitutional, even though you agree that the law is a good idea and you never had any intention of burning a flag. Since there was no controversy between the named Indians and the United States, the Court dismissed the case that the Indians filed.[1413] In order for TEST CASES not to be constitutional the legal interests of the parties must actually be in conflict.

Second, the dispute must also be *ripe:* a presently existing conflict. Ordinarily the courts will not entertain a suit challenging the constitutionality of a criminal law if it has not been enforced against the litigant.[1098, 207] Likewise, ordinarily a case must be dismissed if the dispute has become moot by the time it reaches the courts.[533, 1748]

Third, the party seeking relief must have STANDING: he or she must have suffered an actual injury that can be redressed by a court's judgment. If a driver runs you over while you're walking down the street, I cannot file suit to recover for *your* damages. It does not matter, however, that the actual injury has not yet occurred, if it is likely that it will occur unless the dispute is resolved. For example: I threaten to demolish a building. You say that it is yours. Before the wrecking ball comes down, either of us may sue the other for a DECLARATORY JUDGMENT to establish which of us actually is the legal owner.[18]

Fourth, the case must be about *legal rights.* Suppose you and I are disputing whether Babe Ruth ever played for the Atlanta Braves. A suit to establish which of us is correct is not a case or controversy in the constitutional sense.

Fifth, the courts must be capable of rendering a judgment with FINALITY. In one of its earliest cases, the Supreme Court in 1792 refused to permit lower federal courts to hear "cases" involving pension claims by Revolutionary War veterans because the pension law allowed the Secretary of War to overturn the courts' decisions at his discretion.[885]

See also: JURISDICTION; JUSTICIABILITY; MOOTNESS; POLITICAL QUESTION DOCTRINE; RIPENESS; STANDING.

cause of action To bring an "action"—that is, a lawsuit—in court, you must claim entitlement to some right defined by law. A cause of action is the legal ground or rationale on which a particular claim for damages or other relief may be brought in a lawsuit. Causes of action may be embodied in statutes enacted by the legislature or be part of the COMMON LAW recognized by the courts. Typical examples are negligence claims for injuries in automobile accidents, claims of property damage, trespass, libel, and breach of contract. Occasionally the question arises whether a court or the legislature may constitutionally limit or even abolish a cause of action. For example, until the 1930s, most states permitted suits for "alienation of affection" and breach of promise to marry— often known as "golddigger" suits. During the Depression, most of these causes of action were abolished and appeals to the Supreme Court for their reinstatement were unavailing.[856] Similarly, the Court upheld all challenges to WORKERS' COMPENSATION laws enacted around the turn of the century. These laws abolished the common law action for negligence and substituted a plan under which an employee injured on the job can recover a fixed amount without having to prove fault.[371, 72] As the Court has put it: "A person has no property, no VESTED INTEREST, in any rule of the common law."[1402]

The Court has repeatedly upheld legislative limitations or outright abolition of defenses against particular causes of action—for example, certain defenses in the nineteenth century that made employers practically immune from suit.[1463, 72] In a 1980 case, the Court sustained a California law granting IMMUNITY to parole officials, dismissing a suit brought by the survivors of a young girl killed by a man they paroled. The survivors claimed a due process right to recover for wrongful death. The Court said that the "state's interest in fashioning its own rules of tort law is paramount to any discernible federal interest, except perhaps an interest in protecting the individual citizen from state action that is wholly arbitrary or irrational."[1256] In short, "when state law creates a cause of action, the State is free to define the defenses to that claim."[661]

See also: DAMAGES.

censorship In the ordinary sense of the term, censorship is the banning or suppression of books, films, newspapers, journals, or other forms of expression. For many years, and as recently as the 1960s, censorship was practiced throughout the country by municipal film licensing and certain other government boards that purported to be screening not only movies but also books for OBSCENITY AND PORNOGRAPHY. But much of what was censored had nothing to do with sexual matters, and many works censored on grounds of obscenity were, by today's standards, wholly unobjectionable.

Dissenting in a 1961 case upholding a Chicago film-licensing scheme,[2050] Chief Justice Earl Warren provide a telling glimpse into the world of American censorship. A portion of his dissent follows:

> The Chicago licensors have banned newsreel films of Chicago policemen shooting at labor pickets and have ordered the deletion of a scene depicting the birth of a buffalo in Walt Disney's Vanishing Prairie. . . . Before World War II, the Chicago censor denied licenses to a number of films portraying and criticizing life in Nazi Germany. . . . Recently, Chicago refused to issue a permit for the exhibition of the motion picture Anatomy of a Murder . . . because it found the use of the words "rape" and "contraceptive" to be objectionable. . . . The Memphis censors banned The Southerner which dealt with poverty among tenant farmers because "it reflects on the South." . . . Memphis banned Curley because it contained scenes of white and Negro children in school together. . . . From Joan of Arc the Maryland board eliminated Joan's exclamation as she stood at the stake, "Oh God, why hast thou forsaken me?" . . . Kansas ordered a speech by Senator Wheeler opposing the bill for enlarging the Supreme Court to be cut from the March of Time as "partisan and biased." . . . A particularly frightening illustration is found in the operation of a Detroit book censorship plan. One publisher simply submitted his unprinted manuscripts to the censor and deleted everything "objectionable" before publication. From 1950 to 1952, more than 100 titles of books were disapproved by the censor board.

A major reason for the widespread censorship was the lack of any constitutional definition of obscenity and of any constitutional standards governing the procedures by which censors went after even hard-core pornography. Moreover, until relatively recently, the Court had failed to make it clear both that the FIRST AMENDMENT applies to the states and that it embraces more than merely political speech. Indeed, not until 1952 did the Court hold that films are entitled to First Amendment

protection,[1041] and not until 1965 did it finally find serious constitutional objections to the procedures by which film and other censor boards operated.[699] Today, although film licensing is not dead, it is a shadow of its former self. With exceedingly limited exceptions having to do with vital military secrets and with hard-core obscenity and pornography, censorship by government has been ruled unconstitutional because it violates the First Amendment's ban on PRIOR RESTRAINTS.

See also: FREEDOM OF SPEECH; FREEDOM OF THE PRESS.

census The Constitution does not use the word "census"; it is shorthand for the requirement in Art. I-§2[3] that an "enumeration shall be made" of the "numbers" of persons in the states in a manner chosen by Congress. Congress has assigned the task to the Bureau of the Census. The Constitution's only purpose in requiring a census is to determine the number of representatives to be apportioned to each state. Logically, that requirement should confine the bureau's job to counting people. In fact, the modern census has been accompanied by a growing list of questions to households about all sorts of habits and predilections of interest to businesses as well as government. Presumably this list is constitutionally justifiable under the NECESSARY AND PROPER CLAUSE. The issue has never risen to the Supreme Court. Likewise, although frequently litigated, the question of the bureau's obligation to make an accurate count, and to estimate racial and other subpopulations in each community to avoid undercounting, has never been adjudicated in the Supreme Court.

See also: APPORTIONMENT OF POLITICAL DISTRICTS.

certification of questions When a court asks another court to answer a legal issue, it is said to have certified the question. Federal DISTRICT COURTS sometimes certify questions to state courts for authoritative construction of state law. State courts may answer if state law permits. By this means, the federal courts may abstain from resolving state legal issues.

See also: ABSTENTION DOCTRINE.

certiorari, writ of   Used in England long before the American Revolution, the writ of certiorari is technically an order from a higher court to a lower court to hand up the record of a case. When the Supreme Court grants or denies "cert," it is simply accepting or refusing to hear a case on appeal. In 1988 Congress gave the Court nearly complete discretion over its docket, so that almost all appeals now reaching the Supreme Court come through a writ of certiorari. If the justices do not wish to hear an appeal, they need not. Before 1988, Congress in different judiciary acts at different times established a mandatory docket, designating certain types of cases that the Court was required to hear on "appeal," rather than through certiorari. Even then, though, the Court found ways of refusing to hear cases that it thought inappropriate to consider. Today only cases dealing with reapportionment and the antitrust laws, Civil Rights Acts, Presidential Election Campaign Fund Act, and Voting Rights Acts are mandatory appeals.

See also: SUPREME COURT, JURISDICTION OF.

chaplains   Despite the general command of the ESTABLISHMENT CLAUSE stating that government may not fund religious practices, chaplains have long been paid by Congress and most state legislatures, and for two centuries chaplains have been opening legislative sessions with PRAYER. In 1983 the Court approved the practice,[1246] even though it violated every part of the so-called LEMON TEST, by which the Court determines whether a particular governmental program or policy is an unconstitutional establishment of religion. The 1983 case challenged Nebraska's employment for sixteen years of a Presbyterian chaplain to say prayers "in the Judeo-Christian tradition." In essence, Chief Justice Warren Burger's 6–3 majority opinion pointed to longstanding historical practice to justify what by any other test is a constitutional aberration.

See also: RELIGIOUS ESTABLISHMENT.

checkpoints, *see:* search and seizure: random stops and checkpoints

checks and balances   An eighteenth-century political theory held that liberty is maintained in a democracy through the "virtue" of the people; in other words, the character of the people, rather than institutional arrangements, will keep them free. In *Federalist* 10, James Madison brilliantly disputed this view, building instead a theory of checks and balances. Because it is impossible to eliminate the causes of sectionalism, party rivalries, personal self-interest, and ambition, the Constitution was devised to check its effects; as Madison put it, "to break and control the violence of faction." Madison's great and happy contribution to the Western political tradition was the creation of an extended federal republic: By "tak[ing] in a greater variety of parties and interests . . . you make it less probable that a majority of the whole will have a common motive to invade the rights of other citizens." And to ensure that those who are elected do not easily abuse the public trust, their authority would be fragmented by separating the power given over to each office.

The American system of checks and balances both results from and supports the constitutional rule of SEPARATION OF POWERS. The great powers of government—legislative, executive, and judicial—are disbursed among three branches. But these parcels of power cannot be rigidly separated or there would be no way that one branch could control the other. In *Federalist* 51, Madison found that "the great security against a gradual concentration of the several powers in the same department consists in giving to those who administer each department the necessary constitutional means and personal motives to resist the encroachments of the others. ... Ambition must be made to counteract ambition. ... [I]n all the subordinate distributions of power ... the constant aim is to divide and arrange the several offices in such a manner that each may be a check on the other." By sharing power, each branch can curtail its potential abuse by the others.

The Constitution achieves this checking and balancing function in several ways. To make a law, both houses of Congress, which are elected by different constituencies, must concur on the exact wording of a bill; either can check the other. The president, through the veto, has a major share in the legislative power. Because he may reject its enactments, Congress must heed the president's agenda. The president's checking power may in turn be checked; by a greater plurality than the original vote (two-thirds instead of a majority), Congress may override a veto. The veto power works in reverse too; although the president has the primary power of negotiating treaties and nominating government officials, the Senate may veto treaties and appointments. Likewise, the president has the primary responsibility for carrying out the laws, but Congress has considerable power to influence how government will operate through its power over the budget and its power to establish the various offices of the government. The courts, too, have a share in the power. They sit to apply the law in particular cases; and through their power to interpret the law and the Constitution itself (although the Constitution is less specific on that point), they can check both Congress's enactments and the president's enforcement policies. But both Congress and the president, in turn, may exert control over the courts. The president names all the federal judges (although, again, the Senate may veto), and Congress may restrict the types of cases that the courts may hear. Finally, despite the president's power to appoint, Congress may remove any federal official, including members of the Supreme Court, through impeachment. Even this power is divided: the House may impeach, but only the Senate may convict.

Checks and balances are not limited to powers within the federal government. The Constitution provides for a checking and balancing between federal and state governments as well. Article IV declares that the United States must guarantee a "republican form" of government in each state, meaning that the federal government could act against any attempt to establish a dictatorship within any state. Far more important in practice is Article VI, which declares that the Constitution, federal law, and treaties are the "supreme law of the land," superseding any conflicting state law. This article ensures that the states may not act to undermine national law and policy. But the states are not without power themselves, though their influence has been reduced since the time of the original Constitution, when the state legislatures chose U.S. senators. Still, the ELECTORAL COLLEGE system ensures that presidential candidates must take into account state interests rather than merely individual ones.

Most important of all are the checks and balances that result from elections, which ensure that the government is controlled not merely by its internal parts but by external watchdogs—the people themselves.

chief justice, role of By customary usage, the proper title for the head of the Supreme Court is chief justice of the United States. The words "chief justice" appear only once in the Constitution; Art. I-§3[6] makes the chief justice presiding officer whenever the Senate is trying an impeached president. Because the Constitution is silent about the role, the chief justice's job has evolved through time and occasionally by direction of Congress. Internally, the chief justice is *primus inter pares*—first among equals. Although his vote is but one among many, he can shape debate on cases because he presides at the justices' conferences and has the authority to assign the writing of opinions whenever his vote is with the majority. The influence of the chief justice on the Court's jurisprudence can be small or great, depending on his personal ability and talent as a negotiator and his sense of the possibilities that the Court's caseload presents. When John Marshall came to the Court in 1801, the justices were in the habit of writing individual opinions in most cases; Chief Justice Marshall cultivated a new style in which one justice—the chief justice in important cases—wrote a single opinion for the majority, so that the Court would be seen to be speaking as an institution. In 1954, when Earl Warren came to the office, the justices had been on the verge of rejecting the challenge to the system of segregated education in *Brown v. Board of Education*. His biographers say that as much through his perseverance as anything else, the justices rethought their positions and agreed on a unanimous opinion against SEGREGATION.

Beyond responsibilities as one of the justices, the chief justice by federal law is the chief administrator of the Court, overseeing its budget and directing its employees. As head of the federal judicial system, the chief justice has the legal power to assign judges outside their districts or circuits when emergencies arise. The chief justice also presides over the Judicial Conference of the United States. Established by Congress, the Judicial Conference consists of the chief judge and a district judge from each federal judicial circuit. It compiles statistics and writes reports about the operation and business of the federal courts. The chief justice submits its annual report to Congress. The conference is assisted by the Federal Judicial Center in Washington; the chief justice is chair of the center's board. Congress has assigned other, nonjudicial administrative duties to the chief justice as well; for example, for many years the chief justice has been the chancellor of the Smithsonian Institution.

See also: SUPREME COURT.

child labor A progressive movement to ban children from the workplace succeeded in 1916 in prompting Congress to pass a federal law prohibiting the interstate shipment of any goods or commodities produced in mines employing children under sixteen or in factories employing children under fourteen. Two years later, in *Hammer v. Dagenhart*, the Supreme Court struck the law down, holding that production of goods is not within Congress's power to regulate under the COMMERCE CLAUSE. Although federal laws had previously been upheld that banned shipment across state lines of certain goods, such as lottery tickets and adulterated food, the Court reasoned that those goods were pernicious, whereas the goods produced by children were not themselves harmful. The 5–4 majority also said that the law violated the TENTH AMENDMENT. Seeking a way around direct regulation, Congress responded in 1919 with the Child Labor Tax Law, imposing an excise tax on profits of factories using child labor. Again the Court struck down the law, holding that it exceeded Congress's taxing power.[104] In 1941 a very different Supreme Court expressly overturned *Hammer* in sustaining the Fair Labor Standards Act of 1938, which included provisions banning child labor.[514]

See also: CHILD LABOR AMENDMENT; INTERSTATE COMMERCE.

child labor amendment Stymied in its attempts to abolish child labor from INTERSTATE COMMERCE, Congress in 1924 approved a constitutional amendment that would have empowered it to regulate child labor nationally. By 1938 only twenty-eight states had ratified it. But in that year Congress enacted the Fair Labor Standards Act; and the New Deal Supreme Court upheld it in *United States v. Darby*, expressly overruling its prior conclusion that the COMMERCE CLAUSE did not cover child labor. Thus, the amendment became unnecessary.

See also: AMENDMENTS TO CONSTITUTION; CHILD LABOR.

child pornography, *see:* **obscenity and pornography**

children, *see:* **families; illegitimacy; juveniles, rights of**

chilling effect   Vaguely worded and broadly worded laws dealing with matters of expression may deter the orator, the writer, and the publisher from exercising their FREEDOM OF SPEECH and FREEDOM OF ASSOCIATION. In a metaphor used by the Supreme Court in nearly a hundred cases since 1961, such laws are said to have a "chilling effect" on the right to speak. For example, a law that prohibits membership in an association to which "known subversives" belong is so broad that it would inhibit people from joining all sorts of legitimate organizations for fear that the wrong kind of people belonged to them or that they would be punished for doing so. In other words, to avoid running afoul of the law, people would tend to censor themselves. The metaphor was first used by a Supreme Court justice in 1952, when Felix Frankfurter, concurring in an opinion that struck down a teacher LOYALTY OATH, described the tendency of a subversive-membership law to "chill" freedom of thought and action.[2203] The exact words "chilling effect" first appeared in a Supreme Court opinion in 1961, when Chief Justice Earl Warren quoted an article by Harvard Law School professor Paul Freund.

In 1965 the Court upheld an INJUNCTION against the future enforcement of state criminal laws that were "overly broad and vague regulations of expression" because criminal prosecution would chill the plaintiffs' freedom of speech.[561] However, beginning with *Younger v. Harris* in 1971, the Court has refused relief against pending state court proceedings. Harris was indicted for violating the California criminal SYNDICALISM law, which he said was INVALID ON ITS FACE. A federal court enjoined the state court from proceeding with trial. The Supreme Court reversed the decision, reinstating the prosecution, declaring that concern for "Our Federalism" requires federal courts to abstain in such situations. Harris could raise the constitutional issues in defending against the prosecution itself.

See also: ABSTENTION DOCTRINE; FEDERALISM; OVERBREADTH DOCTRINE; VAGUENESS.

Chinese exclusion   Bowing to a tightly organized opposition in California to Chinese immigration, Congress passed the first of a number of Chinese exclusion acts in 1882. These laws absolutely forbade the entry of Chinese laborers, strictly controlled admission of nonlaboring Chinese, forced the DEPORTATION of many resident aliens, and denied CITIZENSHIP to any Chinese, newly admitted and longtime resident aliens alike. In 1887 Chae Chan Ping, a resident alien of the United States, having lived for twelve years in San Francisco, made the unhappy mistake of taking a short trip to China. Returning with a reentry certificate valid at the time he left, the port inspector refused to admit him into the country because while he had been abroad, Congress had annulled all Chinese reentry certificates. In 1889 the Supreme Court sustained the exclusion,[364] holding that Congress has absolute power "to exclude aliens from the United States and to prescribe the terms and conditions on which they come in"; Chae Chan Ping had no VESTED RIGHT to reenter. The Chinese exclusion acts were finally repealed in 1943.

See also: ALIENS; IMMIGRATION AND NATURALIZATION; JAPANESE-AMERICAN EXCLUSION AND RELOCATION.

choice of law   A recurring dilemma of FEDER-ALISM is determining which law should be applied to a dispute that involves more than one state; for example, an automobile accident or a contract between parties from different states. There is no general formula; each state uses its own "choice of law" principles to decide in any given case whether to use its own law or the law of the other state connected with the incident. Two constitutional provisions limit a state's freedom to choose its own law over laws of other states: the DUE PROCESS Clause of the FOURTEENTH AMENDMENT and Art. IV-§1, the FULL FAITH AND CREDIT Clause.

Under the Due Process Clause, the forum state—the state in whose courts the case is being heard—must have a "significant contact" with the parties and the occurrence that gave rise to the case. To the courts, "significance" means somewhat less than it might to one un-schooled in legal cant. In fact, the word is mostly circular: it means whatever contact a court thinks sufficiently connected to the forum state to warrant the application of that state's law. In the leading modern case, a Wisconsin resident was killed while riding as a passenger on a motorcycle being driven in Wisconsin. The driver of the automobile that hit him was also a Wisconsin resident. Although the deceased was a regular commuter to Minnesota, working in a town a couple of miles over the border from his Wisconsin home, he was not commuting to work when the accident occurred. He owned three automobiles and had purchased three separate fifteen-thousand-dollar insurance policies. His widow, who remarried and moved to Minnesota after her husband's death, sued the insurance companies in Minnesota on behalf of his estate. Under Wisconsin law, the three policies were not "stackable"; that is, she could recover only fifteen thousand dollars. Under Minnesota law, the policies could be stacked or aggregated; thus, she could recover the full forty-five thou-sand dollars. The Minnesota court applied its law, rather than the law of Wisconsin. The question was whether the contacts with Minnesota were significant enough. The man had worked there, and his widow now lived there. The Supreme Court held that these contacts were sufficient to satisfy due process. [42]

Occasionally, the Court has refused to permit a state to apply its own law because the forum state's contacts were insignificant. For example, the Court reversed the application of Texas law to a case involving the "interpretation of an insurance policy issued in Mexico, by a Mexican insurer, to a Mexican citizen, covering a Mexican risk," and assigned to a man domiciled and physically present in Mexico, though nominally a resident of Texas. The Texas court applied its own law to void a limitation in the contract. The Court held that Texas law could not constitutionally be used in the case. [938]

In some cases, the Court has rejected a state court's choice of law under the Full Faith and Credit Clause. In a series of cases involving fraternal benefit societies (associations providing insurance to members), the Court has held that every state must respect the law of the state in which the association was chartered when disputes arise over benefits owed its members. Without a uniform law, inconsistent rulings could make an association's existence untenable. [1536, 1770]

See also: JURISDICTION; LONG-ARM STATUTE.

Christianity, *see:* **religious establishment**

Christmas, *see:* **religious holidays, celebration of**

church and state, *see:* **freedom of religion; religious establishment**

cigarette advertising   The federal Cigarette Labeling and Advertising Act prohibits the advertising of cigarettes and small cigars on radio and television. Partly on the ground that this is COMMERCIAL SPEECH deserving of no particular FIRST AMENDMENT protection, the Court in 1972 affirmed PER CURIAM a federal appeals court ruling upholding the act.[335]

circuit courts of appeals, *see:* **Court of Appeals**

cities, *see:* **political subdivisions**

citizens and citizenship   The Constitution as originally ratified used the word "citizen" eleven times but provided no constitutional anchor for the status of citizenship. In providing that candidates for Congress must have been citizens for a certain number of years (seven for representatives, nine for senators) and in granting Congress the power to provide for naturalization, it was clear that the Framers contemplated foreigners' becoming citizens. But the nature of citizenship and the issue of whether citizenship in a state followed automatically from citizenship in the United States, or vice versa, were questions with no clear answers. On the one hand, a congressional power to naturalize foreigners seems to imply that national citizenship was paramount. Moreover, the PRIVILEGES AND IMMUNITIES Clause of Art. IV-§2 gives to the "citizens of each state" privileges and immunities of "citizens of the several states," implying that the rights of citizens transcend state borders. And in requiring that presidents must be "natural born" citizens, the Constitution implied that anyone born in the United States was a citizen.

All of these propositions sputtered into incoherence when presented with the problem of SLAVERY. For though born in the United States, slaves were not citizens, though the Constitution did not say so. After decades of theoretical debates, the problem suddenly took on explosive urgency when, in 1857, the Supreme Court handed down its fateful decision in DRED SCOTT V. SANDFORD. Among other things, Chief Justice Roger B. Taney said that the only people capable of being citizens of the United States were white people who were citizens of states in 1789, persons naturalized under federal law, and the descendants of each. Blacks, even free blacks who were citizens of their states in 1789 or later, were not and could not become citizens of the United States; Taney reasoned that blacks were not "people of the United States," because they were not members of the political community known to the Framers when the Constitution was written and ratified. This was the strictest of STRICT CONSTRUCTION. Taney said that not even Congress could confer citizenship on free blacks who were born in the United States and thus citizens of their states. Congress's power to naturalize extended only to nonblack foreigners.

This perverse reading of citizenship was finally righted with the ratification of the FOURTEENTH AMENDMENT in 1868. Section 1 declares that "all persons born or naturalized in the United States and subject to the jurisdiction thereof, are citizens of the United States and the state wherein they reside." Reversing Taney's decision, this section makes national citizenship paramount; citizenship in a state now automatically follows a U.S. citizen's residence. Citizenship is vested with birth or upon naturalization; only Congress, not the states, has the power to bestow citizenship. When it does, it may not impose restrictions.

The only qualification to the general rule is that persons claiming citizenship by birth must have been subject to U.S. jurisdiction, meaning that children of foreign diplomats and of alien enemies may not claim citizenship merely by being born within the United States or its territories.[241] Although the question has never come before the Supreme Court, the lower courts have held that children born on the high seas take the citizenship of their parents. Congress has the power to declare citizenship at birth of children born outside the United States to American parents, and it has done so in the Immigration and Nationality Act of 1952. Some citizens born abroad to American parents have dual citizenship because the country in which they are born recognizes them as citizens also. There is nothing in the Constitution to prevent a person from holding two citizenships in this way, since citizenship is a matter of birth, not allegiance. (However, Congress may require naturalized citizens to renounce their original citizenship.)

Today, with three exceptions, there is no SECOND-CLASS CITIZENSHIP; naturalized citizens have the same rights as persons born in the United States. One exception relates to ways in which naturalized citizens can lose their citizenship; a second exception is for convicted criminals, who may lose one or more of their civil rights, such as the right to vote. The third exception is that naturalized citizens may not serve as president. Except for certain political rights, such as voting, constitutional rights are not limited to citizens. The Due Process Clauses and the EQUAL PROTECTION CLAUSE protect all PERSONS, not only citizens.

See also: ALIENS; DEPORTATION; DURATIONAL RESIDENCY REQUIREMENTS; IMMIGRATION AND NATURALIZATION; INDIANS AND INDIAN TRIBES; RESIDENCY.

citizens in each state, *see:* **privileges and immunities**

citizens in the several states, *see:* **privileges and immunities**

civil action   A civil action is any lawsuit other than a criminal prosecution. For discussion of the constitutional power of the states to abolish or limit lawsuits, see CAUSE OF ACTION.

civil commitment   Civil commitment is the nonvoluntary confining of a person to a hospital or other care facility. Unlike prisoners incarcerated for having committed crimes, people may be civilly committed only if a mental illness, retardation, or other extreme handicap might prompt them to hurt themselves or others. In other words, people cannot be removed from home and shut up in a hospital just to get them out of sight, as the Court held in an important 1975 case. Kenneth Donaldson, said to be suffering from delusions, had been committed to a Florida state hospital by his father. After fifteen years of repeated entreaties to be released, Donaldson sued. A jury found abundant evidence that he had never been offered treatment, was not dangerous to himself or anyone else, and could survive on his own with the help of willing friends and family. The Court ordered him released: "A finding of 'mental illness' alone cannot justify a State's locking a person up against his will and keeping him indefinitely in simple custodial confinement... if they are dangerous to no one and can live safely in freedom."[1510]

The larger question, whether mentally ill and other handicapped people are entitled to treatment beyond caring for basic physical needs, has not been resolved. In general, the Court has held that "DUE PROCESS requires that the nature and duration of commitment bear some reasonable relation to the purpose for which the individual is committed."[996] In 1982 the Court held that a state institution may not wholly ignore the needs of a "profoundly retarded" man. The man, who had the mental capacity of an eighteen-month-old child, had been committed at his mother's request. But evidence showed that he had been mistreated once committed, and his mother sued. The Court unanimously concluded that due process required the state to provide "reasonable care and safety, reasonably nonrestrictive confinement conditions [the institution could not

99

simply tie him to a bed or chair], and such training as may be required" to allow him to move around safely. The Court declined to articulate a broader right to treatment and training.[2279]

With one exception, due process requires that before anyone can be committed, the state must first hold a formal HEARING to determine if grounds exist. Since commitment to a hospital or other institution is civil rather than criminal, the state need not prove the need to do so beyond a reasonable doubt, the standard of proof in criminal cases.[1929, 2133] Instead, the state must demonstrate the need for civil commitment by "clear and convincing" evidence.[13, 2133] This remains the standard for committing defendants acquitted of crimes by reason of insanity, who may be confined longer in a mental institution than if they had not been found insane.[1035] The Court noted an apparent exception in ruling that parents (or the government, when acting as guardian of children) may have mentally ill or severely retarded children committed to hospitals or other care facilities without a formal hearing. The Court recognized the possibility of abuse but supposed that parents ordinarily have their children's interests at heart and noted that preadmission interviews by psychiatrists and social workers—"neutral fact finders," the Court termed them—would deter unwarranted commitments.[1565] But no such presumption is indulged in transferring prisoners to mental institutions; a due process hearing is required.[2133]

See also: GOVERNMENT, AFFIRMATIVE OBLIGATIONS OF; LIBERTY.

civil disobedience   Civil disobedience is a political strategy, not a constitutional right. Many times in our history, leaders of political movements have visibly broken the law to call public attention to their moral demands. Law is not synonymous with morality, and the claim that a law is immoral is no defense for breaking a law that is otherwise constitutional. Civil dis-

obedience was a tactic during the long fight against slavery and the struggle for women's suffrage in the nineteenth century, and it was central to Martin Luther King, Jr.'s, fight against SEGREGATION. In his *Letter from Birmingham Jail*, King wrote: "I submit that an individual who breaks a law that his conscience tells him is unjust, and willingly accepts the penalty by staying in jail to arouse the conscience of the community over its injustice, is in reality expressing the very highest respect for law." In its most respected form, civil disobedience is nonviolent; it is indeed "civil," though passions are quickly aroused in matters of great moment and followers, if not leaders, sometimes turn to violence against both established authority and innocent bystanders. Although slavery did not yield to nonviolent protest, the generally nonviolent civil disobedience of the civil rights movement during the 1950s and into the 1960s—marches and sit-ins, in particular—did result in significant constitutional rulings against segregation and overbroad BREACH OF PEACE prosecutions.[1615, 477, 478]

civil liability for illegal search, *see:* **illegal search, liability for**

civil liability of government officials, *see:* **immunity from suit**

civil liberties, *see:* **civil rights and civil liberties**

civil office and civil officers   The terms "civil office" and "civil officer" each appear once in the Constitution. Art. I-§2[2], the INELIGIBILITY CLAUSE, prohibits members of Congress, during their terms, from holding any civil office of the United States if the office was created or the salary or other benefit was increased during the time the member served in Congress. Art. II-§4 says that all civil officers of the United States may be impeached and removed for conviction of treason, bribery, and other crimes. But the Constitution does not define "civil office," and the term has rarely been the subject of litigation. Not every job or function performed for the United States is necessarily a civil office. The term excludes military and congressional office. Although the courts have not ruled, it is the consensus that unpaid trustees of public institutions—such as the Smithsonian Institution—and unpaid members of temporary commissions are not civil officers. And although the president is commander in chief of the ARMED FORCES, he is clearly a civil—that is, a civilian—officer. The Court has never discussed the president's status as an officer of the United States, but it has said that the secretary of war is a civilian, not a military, officer,[283] and has noted that "[t]he supremacy of the civil over the military is one of our great heritages."[581]

See also: CONGRESS; INCOMPATIBILITY CLAUSE; EXECUTIVE DEPARTMENTS; INFERIOR OFFICE AND OFFICERS; SEPARATION OF POWERS.

civil rights, federal protection of, *see:* **civil rights legislation**

civil rights and civil liberties "Civil rights" and "civil liberties" are nonconstitutional terms for related but distinguishable categories of legal rights. "Civil rights" connotes the legal capacity to deal equally with others in society. "Civil liberties" connotes the capacity to act autonomously, free of governmental restraint. Both civil rights and civil liberties issues constitute a significant portion of the Supreme Court's docket each year.

The term "civil rights" encompasses a wide assortment of legal powers without which life would be degraded. Such was the condition of slaves, who had neither political nor civil rights. The most succinct statement of civil rights was given in the first federal civil rights law, the Civil Rights Act of 1866. It was aimed

at the BLACK CODES that sought to reenslave blacks by imposing severe legal disabilities. It declared equal rights under the law and equal rights to enjoy property: "All persons within the jurisdiction of the United States shall have the same right in every State and Territory to make and enforce contracts, to sue, be parties, give evidence, and to the full and equal benefit of all laws and proceedings for the security of persons and property as is enjoyed by white citizens, and shall be subject to like punishment, pains, penalties, taxes, licenses, and exactions of every kind, and to no other." Likewise, all citizens "shall have the same right, in every State and Territory, as is enjoyed by white citizens thereof, to inherit, purchase, lease, sell, hold, and convey real and personal property."

In the 1860s when the Civil War amendments were being drafted, civil rights were distinguished from political rights, on the one hand, and social rights, on the other. Political rights included, primarily, the right to vote, which was later enshrined in the FIFTEENTH and NINETEENTH AMENDMENTS. Social rights, such as the right to equal access to PUBLIC ACCOMMODATIONS and even EDUCATION, were considered of lesser importance and were not thought to be protected in any of the Civil War amendments. The spread of state-mandated SEGREGATION was based largely on that belief.

Civil rights becomes a political issue when minorities challenge their legal status. As a broad generalization, civil liberties is an issue of governmental restraints, not of equality. Battles to broaden the conception of "human rights" have been fought for centuries. In England, the fight goes back at least as far as MAGNA CARTA in 1215. Americans are the beneficiaries of many of those battles, for the drafters of the BILL OF RIGHTS clearly understood the many ways in which governments can oppress those over whom they exercise power. But in spelling out many of the most significant civil liberties, including FREEDOM OF SPEECH and PRESS, FREEDOM OF RELIGION, freedom from arbitrary TAKING OF PROPERTY, procedural fairness in trials, and the right against arbitrary arrest, the Bill of Rights proclaimed liberty far beyond any state document ever written to that time, and beyond most that have been written since. Other civil liberties, including the FREEDOM OF ASSOCIATION and the rights to PRIVACY and TRAVEL, have been inferred from various clauses in the Bill of Rights and from the FOURTEENTH AMENDMENT.

The unequal allocation of civil rights in American society has been due largely to prejudice. Strife over civil liberties is more often a concomitant of fear. Civil liberties are often attacked during times of war, depression, and other calamities. Then, bowing to political exigencies, even normally stalwart proponents of civil liberties have acknowledged the perception that danger lurks in the people's exercise of fundamental freedoms. Jefferson, who pardoned critics imprisoned by President John Adams for violating the Sedition Act, was slow to bar similar prosecutions once he became president. Lincoln suspended the writ of HABEAS CORPUS during the Civil War, Franklin Roosevelt interned Japanese-Americans during World War II, Woodrow Wilson stood by while a presidential candidate was jailed for speaking his mind during World War I. And even in times of lesser strain, there has been a long-running tension between civil libertarians who advocate a generous view of the procedural rights of criminal defendants and strict constructionists who believe that too much deference is paid to defendants and too little to the victims of crime. From all these and from other political battles as well have come the major decisions of the Supreme Court chronicled in hundreds of the entries in this book.

See also: CIVIL RIGHTS CASES; CIVIL RIGHTS JURISDICTION; CIVIL RIGHTS LEGISLATION; EQUAL PROTECTION OF THE LAWS; and see under various freedoms and other rights.

Civil Rights Cases　These cases, decided in 1883, dramatically limited the reach of federal power over civil rights and influenced the course of federal legislation ever since. In the Civil Rights Act of 1875, Congress made it a federal crime to deny equal access to any public accommodation—hotels, restaurants, theaters, and common carriers, such as railroads and ships. The federal law was enacted because the states had failed to curb the spread of RACIAL DISCRIMINATION in private establishments across the country. Several cases soon reached the Supreme Court from California, Kansas, Missouri, New York, and Tennessee. The lead case arose in New York, where Samuel Singleton, doorkeeper of the Grand Opera House, had declined to admit William R. Davis, Jr., and his date, both of whom were black. Other cases concerned refusals to provide food, hotel lodging, seating in the ladies' car of a railroad, and admission to the dress circle of a San Francisco theater.

The question before the Supreme Court was whether Congress had power under the THIRTEENTH and FOURTEENTH AMENDMENTS to enact laws that directly regulated the behavior of private individuals. The 8–1 majority, speaking through Justice Joseph Bradley, found that neither the Thirteenth nor the Fourteenth Amendment conferred such power on Congress. Bradley said that private racial discrimination was not an incident of slavery or involuntary servitude: "It would be running the slavery argument into the ground to make it apply to every act of discrimination which a person may see fit to make as to the guests he will entertain, or as to the people he will take into his coach or cab or car, or admit to his concern or theater, or deal with in other matters of intercourse or business."[1874] And, Bradley continued, although Section 5 of the Fourteenth Amendment empowers Congress to enforce the amendment's provisions, including the EQUAL PROTECTION CLAUSE in Section 1, that clause applies only to discriminatory acts of the states themselves, not to private actions. Dissenting, the first Justice John Marshall Harlan said that the majority had proceeded "upon grounds entirely too narrow and artificial." Noting that the Supreme Court in the 1850s had upheld federal fugitive slave laws, legislation that directly regulated private individuals helping blacks to escape their enslavement, Harlan said: "I insist that the National Legislature may . . . do for human liberty . . . what it did . . . for the protection of slavery and the rights of the masters of fugitive slaves." But Harlan's was the lone dissent, and the case cast a long shadow over federal attempts to deal with racial discrimination.

In PLESSY V. FERGUSON, the Supreme Court seemed to forget its logic altogether in approving state-mandated discrimination. And when, in 1963, Congress once again took up the problem of discrimination in public accommodations, it was still wary of the *Civil Rights Cases,* choosing to rely on the COMMERCE CLAUSE instead. In 1968 the Court implicitly overturned at least part of the *Civil Rights Cases* when it upheld a federal law barring private discrimination in the sale of property.[1028] Congress, the Court ruled, may determine for itself what is a badge or incident of slavery; its decision, unless irrational, must be upheld under the congressional power to enforce the Thirteenth Amendment.

See also: EQUAL PROTECTION OF THE LAWS; STATE ACTION.

civil rights jurisdiction Congress has vested the federal courts with jurisdiction to hear cases, both criminal and civil, involving deprivation of CIVIL RIGHTS, whether guaranteed by the Constitution or federal law. For many years, federal litigants in most types of suits were barred from court unless they could show an injury of ten thousand dollars or more. Because this so-called jurisdictional amount requirement has never been applied to civil

rights cases, they are relatively easy to bring to court. Also, in 1976, in the Civil Rights Attorneys' Fees Award Act, Congress provided that litigants pursuing certain kinds of civil rights cases could recover their attorneys' fees from those charged with discrimination. Congress has also provided that actions charging discrimination under COLOR OF LAW may be brought in state, as well as federal, court.[1229]

See also: CIVIL RIGHTS LEGISLATION; JURISDICTION.

civil rights legislation The first major period of federal legislative activity against discrimination was immediately after the Civil War, when Congress enacted several civil rights laws, including the Civil Rights Acts of 1866, 1871, and 1875, portions of which remain law to this day. However, the national climate changed at the end of Reconstruction following the 1877 election. Rutherford B. Hayes essentially stole the election through a specially constituted electoral commission created to resolve contested southern votes in the ELECTORAL COLLEGE. To secure House ratification of his election, Hayes, a Republican, pledged to southern Democrats that he would abandon the use of force in carrying out the federal civil rights laws. That policy lasted eighty years, until President Eisenhower sent federal troops to enforce desegregation orders in Little Rock, Arkansas. Abetted by Supreme Court decisions, federal concern for civil rights died, and some of the earlier enactments were repealed.[1702, 873, 1001]

The second great period of federal antidiscrimination legislation began in the late 1950s with the Civil Rights Act of 1957, followed by the Civil Rights Acts of 1960, 1964, and 1968, and the Voting Rights Act of 1965. In various ways these laws prohibit discrimination on the basis of race, sex, national origin, and creed in education, employment, housing, and voting. Other federal laws prohibit discrimination on the basis of age, medical condition, and physical handicap. These include the Age Discrimination in Employment Acts, the Equal Pay Act, the Rehabilitation Act of 1973, the Pregnancy Discrimination Act of 1978, and the Americans with Disabilities Act of 1990.

The earliest federal civil rights law, the Civil Rights Act of 1866, was designed to eliminate racially discriminatory state laws. Because doubt was raised about Congress's constitutional power to enact laws dealing with people's personal and private relationships, the FOURTEENTH AMENDMENT was ratified in 1868. It expressly gave Congress the power to enforce its provisions, including the command that the states not deny any persons the EQUAL PROTECTION OF THE LAWS. But by 1883, in the CIVIL RIGHTS CASES, the Supreme Court had emasculated earlier civil rights laws through the STATE ACTION doctrine, which barred Congress from legislating against private acts of discrimination. As a consequence, most of the major modern civil rights laws have been enacted under the COMMERCE POWER and the SPENDING POWER, so that they do not reach every possible form of private discrimination. However, many states have enacted comprehensive state legislation during the past quarter century because the federal laws do not cover all forms of discrimination.

Under the criminal provisions of federal civil rights laws it is unlawful for private individuals to conspire to injure or threaten anyone in the exercise of any rights secured by the Constitution; it is likewise unlawful for anyone to do so or attempt to do so under COLOR OF LAW. These provisions permit federal prosecutions for violent acts against persons. In 1875, the Court ruled that Congress had no power to criminalize private conspiracies that did not affect federal rights.[495] In 1945, the Court began to rethink its position, gradually evolving a doctrine that extends federal prosecutorial power over police brutality and other acts that deprive a person of life, liberty, or property without DUE PROCESS of law. Many of these cases grew out of the extremely violent reaction to the civil rights demonstrations of the 1960s, during which several civil rights activists were murdered.[1831, 2219, 829] In *United States v. Price*, the Court reinstated charges dismissed by the trial court against the sheriff, deputy sheriff, and a policeman in Philadelphia, Mississippi, who had assisted private individuals in murdering the civil rights workers Schwerner, Chaney, and Goodman. Because "state officers participated in every phase of [the crime]: the release from jail, the interception, assault and murder" all three officers could be tried for the deprivation of federally protected civil rights.

The federal rights laws also enable individuals denied constitutional rights to redress their injuries in federal court. Section 1981 of Title 42 guarantees to blacks the same civil rights to make contracts, sue, be parties, give evidence, and to enjoy "the full and equal benefit of all laws and proceedings for the security of persons and property as is enjoyed by white persons." Section 1983 of Title 42 provides a right to sue state officials and others acting under color of state law to deprive "any rights, privileges or immunities secured by the Constitution and laws." Many of the most significant constitutional rulings of the past forty years have been based on violations of this particular section, including the school desegregation case BROWN V. BOARD OF EDUCATION and the legislative reapportionment case *Baker v. Carr*. In 1961, in *Monroe v. Pape*, the Court sustained the use of a civil lawsuit against police officers who had invaded the plaintiff's home, unlawfully seized his possessions, and arrested him. For a time, the Court restricted such suits to the particular police officers or other state officials who intentionally violated a person's rights. But in 1978 the Court interpreted the law to also permit suits against local governments for the actions of their agents.[1372]

In 1951 the Court had narrowly interpreted some of the civil provisions dealing with private persons,[431] but by the late 1960s the Court concluded that Congress had ample power to create such CAUSES OF ACTION under the Thirteenth Amendment and to protect the right to TRAVEL.[812] In 1968 Justice Potter Stewart, for a 7–2 majority, overturned nearly a century of precedent and held, for the first time, that the antislavery Thirteenth Amendment does give Congress power to legislate against private acts of discrimination in the sale of property.[1028] The Court has since sustained related provisions. For example, in 1976 it said that Section 1981's declaration of a right to contract prohibits racially restricted private schools, wherever located, as well as discrimination by private employers.[1774, 1293]

In several VOTING rights cases, the Court appears to have gone even further in sustaining sweeping federal power to root out discriminatory practices. Although the reach of the cases is still not clear, the Court said that at least for some purposes, Congress's enforcement power under the Fourteenth and FIFTEENTH AMENDMENTS extends beyond even those acts of discrimination that the Court has found to be unconstitutional. In other words, Congress has a power independent of the judiciary to declare certain actions unconstitutional.[1053, 1913, 1756]

The civil rights laws are not limited to protecting blacks against discrimination by whites. The Court has read the laws to permit suits charging discrimination on the grounds of national origin or religion;[1847, 1784] they may also permit whites to sue if discriminated against on account of their race.[1293]

See also: PRIVATE RIGHT OF ACTION.

civil service, *see:* **patronage; public employment**

civil trials, *see:* **trial, right to; trial by jury**

civilian-military relations, *see:* **military-civilian relations**

Claims Court, U.S. Because the government may not constitutionally be sued unless it consents, people with such claims were forced to appeal directly to Congress for relief until 1855, when the Court of Claims was created. Through a series of interpretations from 1866 to 1962 the Court of Claims came to be considered not a "legislative," or ARTICLE I, court but a "judicial," or ARTICLE III, court.[2218, 762] In 1982 Congress assigned its judges to the COURT OF APPEALS FOR THE FEDERAL CIRCUIT and created a new Article I court, the United States Claims Court, which continues as before to hear money claims against the United States, except in personal-injury and other tort cases, which can be filed in federal DISTRICT COURT.

class, *see:* **suspect classifications**

class action A class action is a lawsuit brought on behalf of many people who have suffered identical or similar injuries arising out of the same occurrence; for example, RACIAL DISCRIMINATION in segregated schools, abusive treatment in prisons, or losses arising out of fraudulent practices of retailers. The class action is relatively less costly and more efficient than other suits because it resolves legal claims for many, sometimes thousands, of litigants simultaneously. The constitutional difficulty is that the final JUDGMENT of the court binds all members of the class; if the class loses the suit its members cannot later go to court on their own. But the Supreme Court has made it clear that under DUE PROCESS no one can be bound by a decision to which he or she was not a party. In 1940 the Court concluded that a class action can constitutionally bind nonactive class members represented by a lawyer who may never have met them only if the actual parties "adequately represented" the absent members.[862] In many cases, trial judges have concluded that notices must be sent to potential members of the class, allowing them to "opt out" of the class. Potential litigants who opt out cannot share in any recovery, but they are free to file their own lawsuits later on. But if those receiving letters fail to respond, they will be bound by the decision in the case.[1623]

classification of senators, *see:* **senators**

classifications, under- and overinclusive
The question of whether a piece of legislation works an unconstitutional inequality on one or more persons is fundamental to EQUAL PROTECTION. For example, a law against selling alcohol to minors treats minors and adults unequally. Most laws draw lines in this way, and the lines are always to some degree arbitrary. The age at which someone drinks is, abstractly, irrelevant. The true evil is the immaturity and incapacity of certain people, whatever their age, to hold their liquor and not do foolish or dangerous things while intoxicated. Some people under twenty-one are mature and can hold their liquor. Many people over twenty-one are not and cannot. But a law prohibiting liquor sales only to those "too immature or physically unable to avoid causing harm while drinking" would be unenforceable and unconstitutional for a number of reasons, including VAGUENESS. To make most laws workable, the legislature must pick out a characteristic or trait to which the prohibition can be applied. The question then remains whether the trait is connected closely enough to the evil that it does not exclude some people who should be included or include some people who should be excluded. If the law is too "underinclusive" or too "overinclusive" it may be singling out certain people irrationally and treating them unequally.

A law or administrative regulation can be both underinclusive and overinclusive at the same time. One of the most vivid examples was the JAPANESE-AMERICAN EXCLUSION AND RELOCATION during World War II. By military order, tens of thousands of American citizens of Japanese ancestry were excluded from the West Coast and interned in camps to the east. The stated reason was fear of sabotage. This class was overinclusive because most—perhaps all—of its members were loyal citizens or residents not inclined to commit sabotage. It was underinclusive because it excluded Americans of German and Italian extraction who might have been saboteurs on behalf of the Axis powers and who should likewise have been interned to combat the evil. By itself, under- or overinclusivity does not determine whether a classification is unconstitutional. To its shame, the Court upheld the Japanese-American exclusion and relocation orders.[1094] But in many other cases, a lopsided pattern of inclusion or exclusion will doom the classification. For example, the Court held unconstitutional an Oklahoma law using "maleness" as the characteristic for prohibiting sales of certain kinds of beer to people under twenty-one (women over eighteen were permitted to buy the beer).[483]

See also: STRICT SCRUTINY; SUSPECT CLASSIFICATIONS.

clear and present danger   The clear and present danger test, one of the great metaphors of CONSTITUTIONAL INTERPRETATION, was devised by Justice Oliver Wendell Holmes in 1919 to justify CONSPIRACY prosecutions for speech that amounted to espionage. In the case in which he announced it, *Schenck v. United States,* the Court unanimously upheld the convictions of several men for conspiring to violate the Espionage Act of 1917 by printing and circulating a call to draftees to "assert your rights" and refuse to participate in an evil war. The defendants argued that even if the tendency of the circular was to obstruct the draft, it was protected by the FIRST AMENDMENT. Holmes said that no one could have complained about the circular in peacetime. "But the character of every act depends upon the circumstances in which it is done. The most stringent protection of free speech would not protect a man in falsely shouting fire in a theatre and causing a panic. . . . [The] question in every case is whether the words used are used in such circumstances and are of such a nature as to create a clear and present danger that they will bring about the substantive evils that Congress has a right to prevent." Since this was a conspiracy charge, it was not necessary to prove that the defendants succeeded in their project.

In two more cases decided a week later, one of them affirming the conviction of Eugene Debs, the longtime Socialist party candidate for president, Holmes again insisted that advocacy in speeches and pamphlets that "had as their natural tendency and reasonably probable effect to obstruct the recruiting service" could be prosecuted as long as "the defendant had the specific intent to do so in his mind."[53, 704] In essence, Holmes was saying that the law punished the *act* of espionage, and if speech was both the means of espionage and likely to cause the very evil that the espionage law was designed to prevent, then the defendants could be punished for what they urged.

But a few months later, now in dissent, Holmes showed how the Court had misunderstood the import of the test. *Abrams v. United States* involved a new provision of the Espionage Act, which now prohibited not merely actual interference with the war effort but also the "urging" or "inciting" of others. In other words, the previous cases involved prosecutions for directly undermining the American military; this case involved a prosecution for merely speaking out. The defendants were five Bolshevik sympathizers who printed up leaflets attacking President Wilson's decision to send troops to Russia in 1918 and exhorting munitions workers to stop making bullets that "German militarism" and "American capitalism" would use to crush the Russian Revolution.

They threw five thousand of these leaflets from an office building window and distributed others in New York City. They were convicted of writing with intent to incite resistance to the United States and curtailment of war production. Holmes's dissent, one of the most famous and eloquent statements on free speech in our history, sprang from his conviction that the pamphlets presented no danger at all of actually interfering with the conduct of the war and that unless there is real danger that harm will occur right away, the First Amendment prohibits the government from punishing people for what they say.

Holmes began by noting that the majority had completely misread the requirement in the law that the government must prove the defendants intended to obstruct the war effort. He pointed out that a patriot might advocate spending less on making airplanes because he thought they were useless and that the government was wasting money. If Congress agreed with him, but it turned out that he was wrong and that the war actually was hindered by his advocacy, no one would argue that he intended to hinder the military effort. Quite the contrary. Similarly, the real intent of the defendants in this case was to prevent interference with the Russian Revolution, not to impede the army's fight in Germany.

Holmes argued:

The United States constitutionally may punish speech that produces or is intended to produce a clear and imminent danger that it will bring about forthwith certain substantive evils that the United States constitutionally may seek to prevent. . . . [But] it is only the present danger of immediate evil or an intent to bring it about that warrants Congress in setting a limit to the expression of opinion where private rights are concerned. Congress cannot forbid all effort to change the mind of the country. Now nobody can suppose that the surreptitious publishing of a silly leaflet by an unknown man, without more, would present any immediate danger that its opinions would hinder the success of the government arms or have any appreciable tendency to do so.

Holmes went on to present his famous MARKETPLACE OF IDEAS metaphor (quoted in full under that heading), concluding, "[W]e should be eternally vigilant against attempts to check the expression of opinions that we loathe and believe to be fraught with death, unless they so imminently threaten immediate interference with the lawful and pressing purposes of the law that an immediate check is required to save the country.... Only the emergency that makes it immediately dangerous to leave the correction of evil counsels to time warrants making any exception to the sweeping command [of the First Amendment]."

Despite his eloquence, it was many years before the Court accepted the clear and present danger test in reality. In 1925, in *Gitlow v. New York*, the 7–2 majority rejected the clear and present danger test out of hand, turning instead to the BAD TENDENCY TEST. The Court held that when the legislature decides a certain class of speech is dangerous, the courts can only rule on whether a particular speech or pamphlet is within the prohibited class, not on whether it will lead to harm. Not until 1937 did the Court rule that a person may not be prosecuted for participating in a public meeting organized by the Communist party if the meeting itself was orderly and held for a lawful purpose.[536] Although this was not, strictly, a return to Holmes's clear and present danger rationale, it suggested that the Court was finally prepared to bar prosecutions for speech when there was no danger whatsoever.

The problem presented by communism and the Communist party, especially in the aftermath of World War II, again led the Court away from the core of Holmes's thought. In 1951, in *Dennis v. United States*, the Court sustained the convictions of American communists for violating the Smith Act, which made it unlawful to advocate forcible overthrow of the government. Chief Justice Fred Vinson adopted a test formulated by Learned Hand: "In each case [courts] must ask whether the gravity of the 'evil,' discounted by its improbability, justifies such invasion of free speech as is necessary to avoid the danger." This "discounting" test abolishes clear and present danger; in effect, it says that even if the danger is very remote and quite murky, if the evil that might result is huge then the speaker may be punished. That is not what Holmes had in mind. For more than eighteen years thereafter, the Court wrestled with a host of Communist party cases, backing away from the open-endedness of Hand's formulation, but substituting a BALANCING test. Finally, in 1969 the Court seemed to come back to something resembling the clear and present danger test, though it never used those precise words, in holding that speech may not be punished unless it incites to "imminent lawless action."[222]

The clear and present danger test specifically left room for speech to be punished if real dangers might flow from what was being said. But because it gives little guidance to judges—how, after all, can you tell whether a danger is "clear" and "present"?—it was ultimately never more than a metaphor of uncertain utility in frenzied times.

The Court never easily applied the test to the cases dealing with subversion and SUBVERSIVE ADVOCACY for which it was fashioned, but beginning in the 1940s, the justices did use the test to overturn laws prohibiting picketing,[2044] handbilling and solicitations,[1033] and public addresses.[2011] It was also used to reverse CONTEMPT citations for criticism of judges[233, 1586] and convictions for breach of peace by loudmouths on street corners.[334] That it has been pressed into service for which it was never designed suggests the degree to which the test has repeatedly been misunderstood—and the degree to which it is not helpful. As famous as are the words "clear and present danger," they speak to only a part of the struggle for free speech.

See also: FREEDOM OF SPEECH and cross references listed there.

clerks Judges in most of the federal courts employ recent law school graduates as clerks to assist in researching and often writing their opinions. Each clerk serves for a year or two. The practice was begun at the Supreme Court in 1882 by Justice Horace Gray. Today Congress has appropriated funds to pay for four clerks for each Supreme Court justice. Clerkships are prestigious and much sought after. Supreme Court clerks, as well as clerks in other federal courts, often compose drafts of decisions that are too long and are badly written, but that some parts of these drafts are published as the justices' opinions is, of course, not the clerks' fault.

coal regulation, *see: Lochner v. New York*

coastal zones In the mid-nineteenth century, the Court ruled that the states were constitutionally entitled to own and control the shores of navigable waters within their borders.[1647] A century later, in 1947, the Court refused to apply the logic of this rule to coastal zones, the ocean bed up to three miles out from the shore, holding instead that the United States has paramount power over this land and what lies beneath,[328, 1194, 1230] even over the coastal zone of Texas, which as a republic before its annexation owned the seabed.[2025] Although for many years it was supposed that the states could bar outsiders from sharing in the profits of certain natural resources, such as fisheries,[1286] wild game,[736] and even running water,[954] the Court has never permitted the states to bar outsiders from fishing in the three-mile coastal zones. Charging out-of-state fishermen

a much higher license fee than residents was held to violate the privileges and immunities clause.[2058]

Coefficient Clause The NECESSARY AND PROPER CLAUSE in Art. I-§8[18] is sometimes known as the "Coefficient Clause" because it is the constant in the Constitution that allows Congress to carry out its powers in a multitude of directions.

coercion In ordinary usage, "coercion" implies a lack of free will. A showing of coercion against one of the parties to a contract is sufficient to rescind it, and many coercive acts are crimes. It might seem obvious that when the government coerces someone to forgo a legal right it has violated the Constitution. But there is considerable dispute over what makes an act coercive. The Supreme Court has held that coercing a witness to testify by threatening the loss of a public job or a public license to work violates the FIFTH AMENDMENT right against SELF-INCRIMINATION.[725] Likewise, denying a religious person unemployment benefits because she refuses to work on the sabbath is a coercion that violates the FREE EXERCISE CLAUSE.[1857] On the other hand, the Court has held that it is not coercive when the state demands that shops close on Sunday, forcing those who observe the sabbath on Saturday to choose between disobeying religious law and shutting their shops a second day, putting them at an obvious competitive disadvantage.[226,719a]

The Court has also refused to find any unconstitutional coercion when Congress threatens to withhold certain funding unless the states establish programs or pass laws specified by Congress that it could not constitutionally enact directly. In upholding the constitutionality of the unemployment provisions of the federal Social Security system, Justice Benjamin N. Cardozo distinguished between temptation and coercion.[1957] The Social Security Act imposed a tax on employers but rebated most of the tax if the states created ,unemployment funds to which employers would contribute. Cardozo pointed out that the states were not compelled to create unemployment policies, even though the temptation to do so was irresistible. It would be impossible to operate a government in which taxing policy could not be used to induce people to act in certain ways. The Court also sustained Congress's determination to withhold five percent of federal highway funds from any state that did not enact a minimum drinking age of twenty-one. Justice William H. Rehnquist said that the law was "mild encouragement" that the states do as Congress desired and did not come close to the point at which "pressure turns into compulsion."[1915]

The upshot of these cases seems to be that when the rights of an individual are at stake, the legislature may not put someone to a choice by imposing the detriment itself (for example, firing a government employee), but it may take advantage of a detriment that will occur without any government intervention (for example, a marketplace disadvantage). When the choice is imposed on the states, the Court allows Congress even more leeway and presumably would draw the line only at conditions that leave the states no alternative but to do what Congress demands.

See also: PLEADING THE FIFTH; SPENDING POWER; TWO SOVEREIGNTIES DOCTRINE; UNCONSTITUTIONAL CONDITIONS.

coin and coinage, *see:* **currency**

collateral attack A collateral attack is the attempt to relitigate issues already decided in another lawsuit. A direct appeal is not a collateral attack. But after an appeal has failed, the common law has always barred collateral attack. The Constitution does not expressly require this rule, but the FULL FAITH AND CREDIT Clause prohibits a court in one state from

relitigating an issue decided by a court of another state, unless the first court issuing a judgment had no JURISDICTION over the person.[1589] Also, the power of federal courts to issue writs of HABEAS CORPUS in state proceedings when a defendant's constitutional rights have been violated means that often issues raised and decided in state criminal proceedings will be relitigated in collateral cases in federal court.

collective bargaining, *see:* **labor and labor law**

collusive suit When the parties to a lawsuit are not adverse but have manipulated the case to make it seem as though they are on opposite sides, the suit is said to be collusive. In federal litigation, collusive suits are barred by the CASE AND CONTROVERSY requirement of Art. III-§2[1].

color, *see:* **race, color, or previous condition of servitude**

color of law The FOURTEENTH AMENDMENT prohibits the states from depriving any person of life, liberty, or property without DUE PROCESS of law, or from denying any person the EQUAL PROTECTION OF THE LAWS. A state law mandating school SEGREGATION violates the Equal Protection Clause, and the courts will strike it down when a suit is brought by a person injured by the law. But it is not only unconstitutional laws that violate the Fourteenth Amendment; it may also be violated by government officials and employees who are acting in some official capacity, even if the state has not authorized their actions.[939, 1831] For example, a mayor who urges local restauranteurs to maintain segregated lunch counters is acting under color of law;[1182] if the restaurant owners had acted wholly on their own, simply following a community norm, they would not have been acting under color of law.[15] By this same logic, a policeman who helps a mob take a prisoner out of jail and shoot him is acting under color of law;[1663] a policeman who is off-duty and out of uniform, gets drunk, and shoots someone is not acting under color of law. Color of law connotes STATE ACTION or its appearance.

See also: CIVIL RIGHTS LEGISLATION.

comfort to the enemies, *see:* treason

comity Comity is a principle of restraint that steers courts away from cases that might interfere with the authority of other jurisdictions. Federal court ABSTENTION is the most common modern example of this recognition that there is no single governmental authority in the United States. Comity, as Justice Hugo L. Black once put it, is "a proper respect for state functions, a recognition of the fact that the entire community is made up of a Union of separate State governments, and a continuance of the belief that the National Government will fare best if the States and their institutions are left free to perform their separate functions in their separate ways."[2281]

Comity is not specifically mentioned in the Constitution. In fact, under the FULL FAITH AND CREDIT Clause, the courts in one state *must* recognize the judgments of courts in other states. The SUPREMACY CLAUSE demands that when state and federal laws conflict, the states must bow to the supremacy of federal law and judicial decisions. In one striking case where interstate comity did not hold sway, the Supreme Court upheld a decision by the California courts against the state of Nevada when one of its employees injured a California resident.[1444]

See also: ABSTENTION; FULL FAITH AND CREDIT.

Comity Clause, *see:* full faith and credit; privileges and immunities

commander in chief The president is commander in chief of the United States military forces. Granted in Art. II-§2[1], this is one of the few presidential powers made explicit in the Constitution. The Framers made the president military commander both for the sake of efficiency and political accountability. Hamilton, in *Federalist* 69, supposed that the power was limited, amounting "to nothing more than the supreme command and direction of the Military and naval forces, as first general and admiral of the confederacy." In an opinion of the Court, Chief Justice Roger B. Taney said that the president's "duty and power are purely military ... [permitting him only] to direct the movements of the naval and military forces placed by law at his command."[675] In fact, however, the president's power as commander in chief has turned out to be considerably broader.

The true expansion of the military power came with Abraham Lincoln's claim that he possessed a WAR POWER that authorized him to suppress rebellions and to order a naval blockade even though war had not formally been declared. Although Congress ultimately ratified his actions, the Court concluded after the fact that he had acted within constitutional bounds even though he lacked congressional approval.[1667] Since that time, presidents have claimed sweeping power both during and in anticipation of war. They have created executive agencies, authorized military commanders to round up citizens to forestall sabotage, seized factories whose workers were on strike, devised rationing schemes, and ordered sanctions against companies violating rationing orders. In many of these instances, Congress either approved the president's actions after the fact or delegated some power to take the action beforehand. But wartime presidents have insisted that the power was inherently theirs as commander in chief and that congressional authorization was unnecessary.

Few of these claims reached the Supreme Court, but when they did, the Court's decisions seem to fall into two categories: decisions the Court rendered during a war have tended to affirm the president's power; decisions rendered afterward have sometimes proclaimed its limits. Although the Court approved Lincoln's military operations during the Civil War, the postwar Court was dubious about his suspension of HABEAS CORPUS and rejected the argument for an open-ended imposition of MARTIAL LAW that would permit military courts to try civilians.[1345] To its great discredit, the Court in World War II approved President Roosevelt's EXECUTIVE ORDER permitting the JAPANESE-AMERICAN EXCLUSION AND RELOCATION, although the Court characterized it as an action that had later been ratified by Congress.[925] The most significant modern rejection of the claim to open-ended inherent presidential power came in 1952 in the STEEL SEIZURE CASE. Fearing a nationwide strike in the steel industry in the midst of the Korean War, President Truman ordered the secretary of commerce to seize the nation's steel mills. Congress was not consulted and did not ratify his action. In short order the Court held the seizure unconstitutional because the president has no INHERENT POWER, either as commander in chief or as chief executive, to take private property.[2282]

The president's power as commander in chief is at its zenith when actually administering the armed forces themselves. As commander in chief, the president may take actual command of military operations and order when and how battles will be engaged and fought. President Truman's decision to drop atomic bombs on Hiroshima and Nagasaki is the most dramatic evidence of the president's war-making power. Again, few cases have tested the limits of the president's military authority, but the Court has sustained the president's actions in the few that it has heard. The president may create military tribunals in occupied territories and vest them with authority to hold trials.[1224] He may send spies behind

enemy lines.[2062] He may convene COURTS-MARTIAL and in wartime even amend the procedures by which they operate.[1677]

See also: ARMED FORCES; IMPLIED AND INHERENT POWERS; WAR CRIMES.

commerce, effects on In 1824, in *Gibbons v. Ogden,* Chief Justice John Marshall said that under the COMMERCE CLAUSE, Congress may extend its regulations "to those internal concerns which affect the state generally; but not to those which are completely within a particular state, which do not affect other states, and with which it is not necessary to interfere, for the purpose of executing some of the general powers of the government." But it would be more than sixty years before Congress began actively to regulate the national economy, with the Interstate Commerce Act in 1887 and the Sherman Antitrust Act in 1890. When cases challenging these and other laws came to the Court, the justices found two means to block them: they fashioned a doctrine of ECONOMIC DUE PROCESS that would overturn many laws aimed at regulating industrial conditions, and they discovered an inherent limitation on the COMMERCE POWER—that Congress may not regulate local activities unless they directly affect interstate commerce. Chief Justice Melville Fuller announced this rule in the celebrated *Sugar Trust Case* in 1895.[591] The American Sugar Refining Company gained control of ninety-eight percent of the country's sugar-refining capacity by acquiring four other refiners. When the government sued to break up the monopoly, the Court said that the antitrust laws did not apply because production and manufacturing are local activities, not part of interstate commerce. Not until goods "commence their final movement from their state of origin to that of their destination" in some other state have they entered interstate commerce. True, the sugar was sold across the country, but this was only an "incidental" consequence of the refining business. The monopoly's restraint of commerce, as opposed to production, was indirect. In essence, the Court had narrowed the meaning of commerce to "transportation."

When Congress or a federal ADMINISTRATIVE AGENCY regulated transportation, the Court regularly found a direct effect. For instance, in the *Second Employers' Liability Cases,* the Court sustained a law fixing the liability of a railroad carrier toward an injured employee, even if that employee when injured was working on an *intra*state part of the railroad. And in the *Shreveport Rate Case* the Court upheld an Interstate Commerce Commission order regulating the intrastate portion of the railroad's rates because they had an immediate impact on an "instrumentality" of interstate commerce.

The direct-indirect theory was not limited to railroads. As early as 1899 the Court upheld an antitrust prosecution against a group of competing manufacturers who had divided their territories. Now the Court found a "direct" impact on the transportation of goods.[14] In 1905 the Court, speaking through Justice Oliver Wendell Holmes, devised the "current of commerce" theory that would permit the government to reach many more restraints of trade. The defendant meat distributors were charged with rigging the price and number of cattle bought and sold in the Chicago stockyards. Since the cattle had come from out of state and were destined for reshipment out of state, the distributors' activities were not purely local but part of a current or STREAM OF COMMERCE.[991]

Though the Court adhered to this logic in upholding many other federal enactments,[1938, 389] it was unwilling to embrace all of the regulatory power that Marshall had claimed for Congress. The most notable instance of the Court's view was its rejection of a federal CHILD LABOR law.[851]

By the time of the Depression, Congress set about regulating labor and industrial conditions. The Court was hostile, striking the first Agricultural Adjustment Act because it regulated farm production, not commerce, in violation of the TENTH AMENDMENT;[289] it also rejected the Railroad Retirement Act, because even though the railroad employees subject to the act worked on interstate railways, a pension plan "is in no proper sense a regulation of the activity of interstate transportation."[1685]

But President Roosevelt's COURT-PACKING PLAN rattled the justices, and they soon returned full circle to the conception of the commerce power that Marshall had announced more than a century before. In 1937 they sustained the National Labor Relations Act, which extensively regulated the field of labor relations.[1430] The Jones and Laughlin Steel Company said this was no business of Congress. Chief Justice Charles Evans Hughes rejected the earlier "direct-indirect" test: "When industries organize themselves on a national scale, making their relation to interstate commerce the dominant factor in their activities, how can it be maintained that their industrial labor relations constitute a forbidden field into which Congress may not enter when it is necessary to protect interstate commerce from the paralyzing consequences of industrial war?"

By the early 1940s, a wholly reconstituted Court made it clear that the appropriate rule for judging the constitutionality of a commerce law was whether the law had an "effect on commerce." So the Court upheld the Fair Labor Standards Act, regulating the wages of local manufacturing employees.[514] And in a case whose extension of this doctrine is probably still unequaled, the Court upheld a penalty imposed on a farmer under the second Agricultural Adjustment Act for growing more wheat than allotted and consuming it entirely on his farm. The Court said that the allotment scheme was designed both to restrict supply and increase demand. The farmer's effect on the problem may be trivial, but if everyone were free to violate the order then the impact would be large.[2201] This is the conception of the commerce power that has sustained major CIVIL RIGHTS LEGISLATION and antiracketeering laws, among many others.

commerce, foreign   Federal power over foreign commerce springs primarily from the COMMERCE CLAUSE, but other powers in the Constitution, including the WAR POWER, the TAXING POWER, and the TREATY POWER, give both Congress and the president complete authority over the subject. Qualified only by constitutional limitations such as appear in the FIRST AMENDMENT or in the ban on taxing EXPORTS, Congress may ban any product or impose any tariff. The Court sustained an 1897 law setting a standard for tea quality and banning importation of teas "inferior in purity, quality, and fitness for consumption."[297] In 1933 Chief Justice Charles Evans Hughes said that "Congress may determine what articles may be imported in this country and the terms upon which importation is permitted. No one can be said to have a VESTED RIGHT to carry on foreign commerce with the United States."[188] As with regulation of INTERSTATE COMMERCE, the DORMANT COMMERCE CLAUSE operates to restrict the states' capacity to interfere with foreign commerce even when Congress has remained silent. In fact, the foreign commerce clause may even be a broader restraint. In a 1979 case, the Court held that a state property tax on containers of a Japanese shipping company would have been permissible if the containers had come from another state, but since it might interfere with the efforts of the United States to maintain a uniform system of taxing foreign goods, the tax was unconstitutional.[1008]

commerce, interstate, *see:* interstate commerce

commerce, taxation of, *see:* taxation of interstate commerce

commerce among the several states, *see:* interstate commerce

Commerce Clause   Peace with England after the American Revolution disappointed even the optimistic as hopes for a fruitful partnership between equal states faded rapidly. One center of the crisis was Congress's impotence in dealing with spreading trade wars, both domestic and foreign. The Confederation Congress had no authority to regulate commerce with other nations or among the states themselves. England and Spain imposed trade restrictions that kept American goods from European markets, but while Congress could formally negotiate treaties with foreign powers, it could not enact laws to support treaties regulating commerce. Individual states menaced foreign nationals living in America, especially British subjects, and commerce between the states was fraught with peril. The northern ports, New York and Pennsylvania in particular, charged duties on goods imported from Europe. Southern states, without a shipping industry, retaliated by encouraging British and other foreign vessels to carry their crops, to the detriment of northern shipping interests. Hamilton, in *Federalist* 22, compared the states to German principalities whose fine waterways were rendered useless by duties exacted by the petty princes who ruled the states along the riverbeds. In January 1786 the Virginia legislature called for a national convention to "consider how far a uniform system in [the states'] commercial regulations may be necessary for their common interest and permanent harmony." That call led to the ANNAPOLIS CONVENTION, which in turn led to the CONSTITUTIONAL CONVENTION.

What has come to be known as the Commerce Clause appears in Art. I§-8[3]. It empowers Congress "to regulate commerce with foreign nations, and among the several states, and with the Indian tribes." The language was presented to the delegates on August 16, 1787, and was accepted, as Madison's notes record, without debate. This sparse language, together with the NECESSARY AND PROPER CLAUSE, which the delegates also accepted undebated, has become Congress's COMMERCE POWER, a power that in time would overshadow almost all the others, at least in peacetime, and that would eventually give Congress the justification for laws surely undreamed of by the Framers. It would also come to be understood as one of the strongest constitutional limitations on state power. When Congress refrains from regulating, the DORMANT COMMERCE CLAUSE in effect becomes a shield around commercial activity that the states are not permitted to breach.

Both aspects of the Commerce Clause, taken together, have provided the means by which the federal government has forged an immense "common market." The principle of the Commerce Clause, as Justice Robert H. Jackson has described it, is "that our economic unit is the Nation, which alone has the gamut of powers necessary to control of the economy. . . . The material success that has come to inhabitants of the states which make up this federal free trade unit has been the most impressive in the history of commerce. . . . Our system, fostered by the Commerce Clause, is that every farmer and every craftsman shall be encouraged to produce with the certainty that he will have free access to every market in the Nation, that no home embargoes will withhold his exports, and no foreign state will by customs duties or regulations exclude them."[834]

See also: AFFECTED WITH A PUBLIC INTEREST DOCTRINE; AGRICULTURE, REGULATION OF; ANTITRUST LAW, CONSTITUTIONALITY OF; BRIDGES AND WATERWAYS; COMMERCE, EFFECTS ON; COMMERCE, FOREIGN; DELEGATION DOCTRINE; ECONOMIC DUE PROCESS; INTERSTATE COMMERCE; MANUFACTURING; MARKET PARTICIPANT DOCTRINE; POLICE POWER; PREEMPTION; PROHIBITION OF COMMERCE; TAXATION OF INTERSTATE COMMERCE; TRANSPORTATION.

commerce power   Art. I-§8[3], the COMMERCE CLAUSE, empowers Congress to regulate commerce with foreign nations, among the states, and with Indian tribes. Together, this authority is known as the commerce power. It has proven to be not only an affirmative power of sweeping breadth but also a negative power against state interference with INTERSTATE COMMERCE.

In 1824, Chief Justice John Marshall seized the opportunity to describe the federal commerce power "with a breadth never yet exceeded," in the words of Justice Robert H. Jackson.[2201] Marshall's opinion in *Gibbons v. Ogden* firmly established the commerce power as an instrument of national SOVEREIGNTY. New York had granted a monopoly to operate steamboats in the state waters. A competitor, licensed under a federal law regulating the "coastal trade," began a competing ferry service between Elizabethtown, New Jersey, and New York City. The New York licensee succeeded in enjoining the New Jersey ferries from steaming into New York waters. Was navigation commerce? One of the parties argued that only buying and selling, the "interchange of commodities," is commerce.

Speaking for a unanimous Court, Chief Justice John Marshall said that commerce encompasses much more than transportation: "It describes the commercial intercourse between nations, and parts of nations, in all its branches, and is regulated by prescribing rules for carrying on that intercourse." It necessarily follows, Marshall said, that the power to regulate commerce must cross state lines. Where else could commerce "among the several states" exist except at any one moment within one state or another? As for the power itself: "It is the power to regulate; that is, to prescribe the rule by which commerce is to be governed. This power ... is complete in itself, may be exercised to its utmost extent, and acknowledges no limitations, other than are prescribed in the constitution." Marshall's conception has been amply vindicated, though not without considerable backsliding by the Court between the 1890s and the 1930s. Today the commerce power gives Congress carte blanche to regulate any aspect of the economy that even remotely "affects" interstate commerce. Under this single commerce power, Congress has passed laws aimed at such diverse targets as gangsters and racial segregation.

For a discussion of the constitutional extension of the commerce power, see INTERSTATE COMMERCE; for a discussion of how it limits state power, see DORMANT COMMERCE CLAUSE.

See also: COMMERCE CLAUSE and cross references listed there.

commerce with the Indian tribes   The COMMERCE CLAUSE empowers Congress to regulate commerce with the "Indian tribes"; together with the TREATY POWER, it is the source of federal authority over the Indian peoples. This branch of the COMMERCE POWER is as broad as, if not broader than, the power to regulate INTERSTATE COMMERCE, for the Court has construed Congress's power here to give the states even less room in which to exercise their own JURISDICTION.[1690]

See also: INDIANS AND INDIAN TRIBES; PREEMPTION.

commercial speech   "Commercial speech" is the Court's term for advertising, marketing, and promotional literature. In 1942 the Court, in a "casual, almost offhand" manner, as Justice William O. Douglas would later recall it, said that commercial advertising was a LOWER-VALUE SPEECH that did not rate FIRST AMENDMENT protection. In that case, it agreed that New York City could ban a handbill advertising a paid tour of a privately owned submarine.[2115] Not until 1975 did the Court reverse

course. Virginia had outlawed any publication that encouraged or promoted abortion, and a newspaper publisher was convicted for printing an advertisement about abortions available in New York. The Court said that the advertisement "contained factual matter of clear public interest."[164] The following year the Court struck down another Virginia law, this one prohibiting licensed pharmacists from advertising prices of prescription drugs. The Court said that even price advertising contained an idea that was worthy of protection: "I will sell you prescription drug X at price Y."[2131]

In a series of cases during the next ten years, the Court struck down a number of state laws imposing bans on various forms of commercial speech: advertising of straightforward descriptions of legal services,[1679] of nonprescription contraceptives,[341, 192] and of the prices of "routine legal services."[135] It also voided a law against posting "for sale" and "sold" signs on residential property[1170] and against soliciting either by direct mail or advertisement "targeted" audiences for certain kinds of lawsuits.[1665, 2285, 1849]

However, not every form of commercial speech has been upheld. False and misleading advertising may be prohibited, though what constitutes "misleading" is a matter of some looseness. In one instance, the Court upheld a Texas law barring optometrists from practicing under trade names.[702] It also upheld a city's policy of barring signs, including political campaign posters, from municipal utility poles.[401]

In 1980 the Court announced a four-part test to determine whether commercial speech can be prohibited. The case arose when the New York Public Service Commission completely banned promotional advertising by electrical utilities on the ground that it was contrary to the national policy of conserving energy. In *Central Hudson Gas Co. v. Public Service Commission*, the Court reversed the ban, following these steps: (1) the advertisement must be neither false nor misleading; (2) the "asserted governmental interest" must be "substantial"; (3) the regulation must directly advance the government's interest; (4) the regulation must not be more extensive than necessary. The utility won the case under the fourth part of the test, because the ban was so sweeping that it prohibited the utility company from promoting even energy-efficient devices.

In 1986, perhaps signaling retrenchment, the Court approved the ban of advertising that was not misleading for a product that, though possibly harmful, was not illegal. Puerto Rico passed a law against pitching ads for its lawful casino gambling to its residents. Advertising the lures of its gaming tables to outsiders to induce them to fly to the island is permissible. Applying the *Central Hudson* test, the Court by a 5–4 vote said that because ads directed to Puerto Ricans would lead them to the gaming tables, their health, safety, and welfare could be impaired.[1650a] This may seem an odd result, since Puerto Ricans remain legally entitled to gamble in the casinos. If the Puerto Rican legislature was truly concerned about the well-being of its citizenry, it should have banned gambling altogether. Not so, said Justice Rehnquist: "It would . . . be a strange constitutional doctrine which would concede to the legislature the authority to totally ban a product or activity, but deny to the legislature the authority to forbid the stimulation of demand for the product or activity." Perhaps, unless the doctrine has a home somewhere in the First Amendment. The effect of the Puerto Rican gambling case was to weaken the fourth strand of the *Central Hudson* test, for there surely were LESS RESTRICTIVE MEANS of regulating the advertising than a flat ban. In 1989 the Court expressly eliminated the fourth part of the test when it ruled that companies and students had no constitutional right to hold Tupperware parties in dormitories on college campuses.[189] The Court said that as long as a restriction on

commercial speech is "narrowly tailored" to achieve its objective the law may stand.

See also: FREEDOM OF SPEECH.

commission   Art. II-§3 directs the president to commission all officers of the United States. This is the third step of the APPOINTMENT procedure. First, the president nominates someone to fill an office. The appointment is complete when the Senate consents, but appointees may not assume office until the president commissions them in a document attesting to the appointment and formally investing the nominee with the powers of office. Even after the Senate confirms a nomination, the president may withhold the commission. Once the president signs the commission, however, the appointee attains the office. This is the teaching of MARBURY V. MADISON, in which Chief Justice John Marshall said that the failure to deliver the commission does not defeat the appointee's entitlement to the office. But legal entitlement to the office is not the same as occupying it. In that same case, even though he affirmed Marbury's right to a judgeship, Marshall said the Court could not enforce the right. Marbury never took his seat on the bench. Evidently, unless the right can be enforced in some court, an appointee will not be considered commissioned if the president withholds the document.

See also: RECESS APPOINTMENTS.

commitment to other branches   Since the time of MARBURY V. MADISON in 1803, it has been a commonplace that the authoritative interpreter of the Constitution is the Supreme Court. But some provisions in the Constitution, the Court itself has ruled, commit the resolution of constitutional issues to other branches of government. For example, Art. I-§5[1] says that each house of Congress may judge the "elections, returns, and qualifications" of its members. The Court has ruled that the language of the text thus commits to each house, and not to the Court, the power to resolve whether a candidate has been elected. If the question is which candidate for the Senate "received more lawful votes," only the Senate may decide. The losing candidate may not take his case to court claiming that the Senate miscounted the votes.[1768] But the Court has read this "textual commitment" narrowly; in another case, the House refused to seat longtime Harlem Representative Adam Clayton Powell, Jr., after receiving a report that, among other things, Powell had diverted House funds to his personal use. The House asserted its power to exclude Powell for any reason; the Court said the Constitution gives the House discretion to exclude only for certain reasons: if Powell had not been properly elected, was not old enough, or was not a citizen of New York and a resident of his district. None of these conditions applied, so the House could not constitutionally exclude him.[1653]

See also: POLITICAL QUESTION DOCTRINE.

common defence   One of the purposes of the Constitution stated in the Preamble is "to provide for a common defence." This purpose is carried out in Articles I, II, IV, and VI by vesting in the federal government unqualified power to establish, fund, call up, and deploy military forces, to declare and conduct war, to repel invasions, and to conduct foreign affairs.

common law   Long before the Constitution there was the common law, a vast body of legal doctrines fashioned by the courts. Though sometimes said to be "unwritten law," as distinct from laws written in the code books of the legislature, the common law in fact is to be found in thousands of volumes recording the decisions of the courts in cases of every description. For nearly eight hundred years the common law has been developing in the English-speaking courts over myriad subjects brought to the judges by litigants seeking redress of their injuries and a declaration of their rights. Whole bodies of law—tort, contract, property, evidence, and even much of criminal law—were developed by the common law courts. The American Revolution was in large part fought not to throw off the English common law but to regain it against the depredations of the English kings, who had governed through royal prerogative in violation of common law. Every state accepted the common law and the common law process as its birthright. Even the Constitution incorporates several of its principles, including the requirement that the courts operate only in CASES OR CONTROVERSIES, that the government respect the civil liberties of its citizens and the rights of the accused, and that the best rules are those that spring from long usage and custom of the people. The SEVENTH AMENDMENT expressly incorporates the common law, guaranteeing a TRIAL BY JURY for all common law cases tried in federal courts. Today, the common law system prevails in every state, with the partial exception of Louisiana, whose legal system is based on the French Napoleonic Code. Although it is called the "common" law, in fact it is only the method that is truly common; the body of substantive law varies from state to state, according to divergent decisions of their courts and legislative enactments that have modified it.

Although the Constitution assumes the power of state courts to continue to modify the general common law, the Court has held that there is no general FEDERAL COMMON LAW; that is, the federal courts do not have the power to develop substantive bodies of law on their own, apart from their construction of the Constitution and specific federal enactments.[621] This rule was spelled out only in 1938; until then, there had been an extensive development of federal common law in areas now reserved for the states.

See also: CRIMES, COMMON LAW; ERIE RULE.

common law, federal, *see:* **federal common law**

common law, suits at, *see:* **trial by jury**

common law crimes, *see:* **crimes, common law**

commonwealth status, *see:* **territories**

communications industry, regulation of, *see:* **broadcasting**

communism and Communist party   In three major laws, Congress sought to curb and finally eliminate the Communist party of the United States. The Smith Act of 1940 made it a crime to advocate the overthrow of the government by force or violence or to organize any group that promotes such a doctrine. The Internal Security Act of 1950 established a registration scheme for "Communist-action" and "Communist-front" organizations. The Communist party and its members were required to register names, sources of funding, and even printing presses—a striking feature more reminiscent of laws in the Soviet Union at the time than anything in the history of American law. The Communist Control Act of 1954 finally outlawed the Communist party outright. This was the high-water mark of legislative attempts to banish what by then had become a haunted specter in our midst. The Communist Control Act was never really enforced, and the Communist party did not disappear, because by then the Court had pointed to the many constitutional difficulties in the way of dismantling a political organization and harassing its members. The Court sustained, mainly in the 1950s, many features of the 1940 and 1950 acts, even though it occasionally struck down others for going across the line. By the 1960s, most of the major legislative tools designed to dismantle the party had been constitutionally crippled.

Among the techniques that Congress, and many states, employed in the anticommunist laws were: barring party members from holding union and other jobs,[261, 1736] requiring public employees and others to subscribe to LOYALTY OATHS,[487, 102, 609, 1072] making MEMBERSHIP itself a criminal act,[1807, 2272, 1504] forcing members to engage in SELF-INCRIMINATION,[445, 31] withholding pay of subversive public employees,[1199] revoking passports,[67, 2286] seeking CONTEMPT citations for refusing to answer questions about Communist party connections,[125, 2112, 534] dismissing public employees from jobs for refusing to discuss party membership,[1883] banning a person refusing to discuss party membership or activities from becoming a member of the bar,[58, 1130, 105, 1960] deporting alien party members,[1504, 721] terminating Social Security payments and property tax exemptions,[677, 1930] and banning forms of SUBVERSIVE ADVOCACY.[539] The specific doctrines are considered under their appropriate headings.

See also: ATTORNEY GENERAL'S LIST; BILL OF ATTAINDER; DEPORTATION; INVESTIGATORY POWERS OF LEGISLATURE; LOYALTY-SECURITY PROGRAMS; PASSPORTS, RIGHT TO; SEDITION; SEDITIOUS LIBEL.

commuter tax   States may tax nonresident commuters from other states but they may not do so if the burden of the tax falls disproportionately on the out-of-staters. When New Hampshire imposed an income tax exclusively on nonresidents who worked in the state (its own citizens paid none), the Court struck down the tax for violating the PRIVILEGES AND IMMUNITIES Clause of Art. IV-§2[1].

Compact Clause   Under Art. I-§10[2], a state may enter into a "compact or agreement" with any other state as long as Congress consents. Interstate compacts have been used largely to settle boundary disputes; in such matters, the Court has held that Congress need not expressly consent because there is little danger that such agreements threaten federal supremacy. Consequently, boundary and other relatively "minor" compacts are valid unless Congress expressly rejects them.[2127, 2106] Some interstate compacts are more significant and require express congressional approval, such as the New York Port Authority Compact of 1921, creating the Port Authority to oversee and manage the ports and waterways between New York and New Jersey. Once an interstate compact takes effect, it is like a treaty between nations and binds state residents. A provision expressly stating that the states may sue or be sued under the compact permits suits against a state in federal court despite the ELEVENTH AMENDMENT.[1618] Congress has independent power to direct states to comply with their agreements.[2129] Once Congress consents to a compact, a state may not avoid its obligations simply by asserting that it had no power under its own constitution to enter into it.[589] And when one state sues another in the Supreme Court, invoking its ORIGINAL JURISDICTION, the Court may follow general COMMON LAW principles of contract law to resolve the dispute.[2023]

See also: FEDERAL COMMON LAW.

compacts among states, *see:* **Compact Clause**

companion case Companion cases are those with closely related issues decided on the same day. Although one or more justices may write a single opinion to cover all the related cases, each case has its own citation in the court reports and is separate. The companion case is different from a cluster of cases grouped within a single citation and decided by a single opinion. Examples of the latter are BROWN V. BOARD OF EDUCATION, which consisted of cases arising from four states, and the CIVIL RIGHTS CASES, arising from five states.

compelling government interest, *see:* **compelling interest**

compelling interest The "compelling interest" test is a formula that, depending on your political views or degree of cynicism, allows the Court to uphold or reject laws that encroach on constitutional rights. Typically presented with a law that appears to infringe on a constitutional right (FREEDOM OF SPEECH, FREEDOM OF ASSOCIATION, EQUAL PROTECTION, and others), the Court will balance the state's interest in the law against the person's constitutional right to be free of it. If the state has a strong enough reason for the law, then it will be permitted to override a person's asserted constitutional right, at least as long as the interference is only "incidental." But if the state's interest is not compelling enough, then the law, regulation, or administrative practice will flunk the test and be struck down.

The phrase derives from a CONCURRING OPINION of Justice Felix Frankfurter in a 1957 case involving a CONTEMPT citation by the New Hampshire legislature against a university teacher who had refused to answer questions about his lectures. Said Frankfurter: "For a citizen to be made to forego even a part of so basic a liberty as his political autonomy, the subordinating interest of the State must be compelling."[1989] The Court has used different formulations to test the propriety of the laws. As it noted in the 1968 DRAFT CARD BURNING case: "To characterize the quality of the governmental interest which must appear, the Court has employed a variety of descriptive terms: compelling; substantial; subordinating; paramount; cogent; strong."[1508] The notion of "compelling state interest" has surfaced in 163 cases since 1957; "compelling interest" has been invoked in 155 cases; "substantial government interest" in 68.

To determine whether a state has violated equal protection, the Court first inquires whether the disputed law requires STRICT SCRUTINY. If so (as, for example, a law classifying on racial grounds would), then it can be upheld only if it serves a compelling state interest. Usually as soon as the Court announces that it is applying strict scrutiny, it is a foregone conclusion that the state will not be found to have had a compelling enough interest to justify the law.

Beyond the government's interest, the Court will look to the effects of the law and determine whether the means it employs are closely connected to the state's purposes. In the draft card case, the Court said that, among other requirements, the contested regulation must be "unrelated to the suppression of expression" and "the incidental restriction on alleged First Amendment freedoms must be no greater than is essential" to furthering that interest. But the Court rarely overturns a law once it concludes that the government's interest is compelling. For example, the Court upheld the conviction of a man protesting the draft by burning his card because the government was thought to have a vital interest in ensuring that draft-age men had the piece of paper in their possession at all times. In retrospect, this seems plainly silly, and it suggests how easy it is to manipulate the test.

The Court has never been able to state with any precision what makes a state's interest compelling. In *Roe v. Wade,* for example, the Court said that the state does not have a compelling interest to prevent a woman from having an abortion in the first three months of her pregnancy, but that the state's interest in the potential life of the fetus does become compelling in the last three months. Why it is not compelling before that moment is unclear—and that difficulty partly accounts for the heated debate over *Roe* since it was first announced.

Lately the Court seems to have abandoned "compelling interest" analysis in one major

type of constitutional inquiry: whether a law or regulation infringes on someone's FREEDOM OF RELIGION. Many general state laws may prohibit a particular religious practice; for example, state drug laws against peyote use impinge on its use for sacramental purposes by members of the Native American church in Oregon. The Court said the state did not need to demonstrate a compelling interest in the law. To permit religious exceptions to general laws, except when the state has a compelling interest in stopping the ban, would not only make a person "a law unto himself" but would also put the courts "constantly in the business" of determining whether to carve out an exception to an otherwise permissible law. As Justice Antonin Scalia wrote in 1990 for a majority of five, "What [the compelling interest test] produces in . . . other fields—equality of treatment, and an unrestricted flow of contending speech—are constitutional norms; what it would produce here—a private right to ignore generally applicable laws—is a constitutional anomaly."[614]
See also: BALANCING; STRICT SCRUTINY.

compelling state interest, *see:* **compelling interest**

compensation, *see:* **Compensation Clause; just compensation**

Compensation Clause   Art. III-§1 forbids Congress to diminish the compensation of federal judges while in office. This Compensation Clause "has its roots in the longstanding Anglo-American tradition of an independent Judiciary[,] . . . essential if there is a right to have claims decided by judges who are free from potential domination by other branches of government." Although Congress may change its mind about a salary increase and roll it back before it takes effect,[2208] the Court has ruled that once a salary increase takes effect, no part of it may be reduced. In the 1920s the Court went so far as to declare that federal judges—even judges appointed after the tax law took effect[1335]—were exempt from paying income taxes,[632] but the Court soon retreated. Imposing a tax on judges as citizens neither diminishes their compensation in the constitutional sense nor encroaches on their independence.[1514]

Compromise, Great, *see:* **Great Compromise**

compulsory arbitration, *see:* **trial, right to**

compulsory disclosure, *see:* **immunity from prosecution; pleading the Fifth; self-incrimination**

compulsory process   The SIXTH AMENDMENT guarantees every criminal defendant the right to have "compulsory process for obtaining witnesses in his favor." This provision was intended to overturn the rule under English COMMON LAW that defendants in treason and felony cases were not permitted their own witnesses at trial. But because "few rights are more fundamental than the right of an accused to present witnesses in his defense,"[367] the question is, what must the state do to obtain witnesses and to which witnesses does the clause apply? The state must use every reasonable effort, for instance, by issuing subpoenas, to secure the presence at trial of a witness whom the defendant demands to be there. Compulsory process is not a guarantee that witnesses will be found; it is a guarantee that if witnesses can be located the state will bring them to court.

Any witness who genuinely will be helpful to the defendant must be permitted to testify, not merely those whose testimony is admissible under state law. For example, under a Texas rule of evidence, a murder defendant was not permitted to call his accomplice, who had already been convicted and was willing to testify that he alone had committed the crime. In 1967 the Supreme Court reversed the conviction, holding that the compulsory process clause applies to the states as well as the federal government and that federal constitutional standards, not state evidence rules, must be used to determine whom a defendant may call. If a witness is "physically and mentally capable of testifying to events that he had personally observed, and [his] testimony [will be] relevant and material to the defense," the court must let the defendant call him to the stand.[2162]

However, compulsory process does not mean that the defendant may engage in trickery—for instance, by withholding the names of potential witnesses from the prosecution at a pretrial stage and then later demanding that they be called as surprise witnesses.[2000] Nor does compulsory process require the government to disclose the identity of witnesses it has located who might be helpful; whether or not these names should be turned over to the defendant is a general DUE PROCESS consideration, not a compulsory process right.[1592]

See also: CONFRONTATION WITH WITNESSES.

conclusive presumptions, *see:* **presumptions**

concurrent jurisdiction   Under the Constitution, some types of cases may be tried in more than one court. Whether to permit multiple forums or limit the choice to a single court is a question for the legislature. The most obvious example is a case involving citizens of different states. These cases may be heard in one or more state courts and also in federal court under the DIVERSITY JURISDICTION conferred on them by Congress. The initial choice is for the plaintiff, although in many instances the defendant may remove the case to the other forum. Also, depending on the nature of the case, a court may abstain from hearing it because it is more suitable for resolution in a different court.

See also: ABSTENTION DOCTRINE.

concurrent powers FEDERALISM implies that two different SOVEREIGNTIES may each have, or claim to have, the power to legislate over the same subject. This prospect was explicit only once in the Constitution, in the ill-fated EIGHTEENTH, or PROHIBITION, AMENDMENT, which said that "Congress and the several States shall have concurrent power to enforce" its provisions against the sale or possession of INTOXICATING BEVERAGES. The result was a tangle of enforcement difficulties that led to Prohibition's eventual repeal in the TWENTY-FIRST AMENDMENT. For nearly two centuries, too, the question of whether Congress and the states share power to enact regulations that affect INTERSTATE COMMERCE has led to thousands of lawsuits. To resolve this and other conflicts when the states and Congress concurrently exercise power, the Supreme Court has devised BALANCING tests and a doctrine of PREEMPTION, which relies on the SUPREMACY CLAUSE and rules of interpreting statutes.

concurrent resolution A concurrent resolution is a statement agreed to by both houses of Congress that does not require the president's signature. Although a concurrent resolution is not a law, it can have legal consequences, since it is used primarily as a device for spending money on certain of Congress's internal affairs, such as housekeeping. Concurrent resolutions were the vehicle by which Congress exercised the LEGISLATIVE VETO, a device ruled unconstitutional in 1983.[979]

concurring opinion Judges file concurring opinions when they agree on the outcome in a case but disagree with the majority's reasons. Early Supreme Court justices rarely concurred separately, but during the past half century concurring opinions have become much more common, sometimes making it difficult to determine whether there is in fact a majority for any particular proposition in the case. In the first major AFFIRMATIVE ACTION case, *Regents of the University of California v. Bakke,* Justice Powell decided the outcome through a single concurring opinion that differed from the two opposing opinions, supported by four justices each. In rare cases of the very highest importance, all the justices have appended concurring opinions—for example, in 1971, in the PENTAGON PAPERS CASE.

conditioned spending, *see:* **spending power**

conditions, unconstitutional, *see:* **unconstitutional conditions**

condoms, *see:* **contraception**

conduct and speech, *see:* **symbolic speech**

Confederation, Articles of, *see:* **Articles of Confederation**

conference, judicial Supreme Court decisions are tentatively reached at the conference of the justices, a series of closed-door, secret meetings at which they jointly discuss whether to accept cases for review and how to decide cases already argued. Outsiders, including the Court's own secretaries and clerks, are barred. Years ago when the docket was smaller, the conference served as the principal means of negotiating decisions. Today little time is spent at the conference on most cases beyond stating how each justice will vote. The arguments, persuasion, and lobbying take place among the justices outside of the official meeting. From October through April, in the weeks the Court hears ORAL ARGUMENTS, the conference is held on Wednesday and Friday afternoons. In May and June the justices meet all day Thursdays.

The chief justice presides, calling each case and airing his thoughts first; the other justices ordinarily speak by seniority. Once a preliminary vote is taken, the chief justice, if he is in the majority, assigns the case to one of the justices, including himself if he wishes, to write the majority opinion. If the chief justice is in the minority, the senior justice (by length of service on the Court) assigns the opinion. Since votes still can be changed as justices read the draft opinions—majority, concurring, and dissenting—that their fellow members circulate, the Court's decision may also change, and someone else may eventually be assigned to write the final majority opinion.

See also: CHIEF JUSTICE, ROLE OF; SUPREME COURT.

confessions, *see:* **exclusionary rule; Miranda rules; self-incrimination; suppression hearing**

confidential sources, *see:* **reporter's privilege**

confidentiality of government documents, *see:* **government documents, confidentiality of**

confirmation by Senate   Under Art. II-§2[2], before most presidential nominees can take office, the Senate must confirm by a majority vote. In constitutional terms, the Senate must exercise its power to advise and consent, although since George Washington's time, presidents have ceased formally asking the Senate for advice. Senate confirmation is required for all ambassadors and others of ambassadorial rank (including "public ministers and CONSULS"), justices of the Supreme Court and judges of all other federal courts, and all other "officers of the United States," except those (such as the VICE PRESIDENT and members of Congress) whose appointments are otherwise spelled out in the Constitution. INFERIOR OFFI-

CERS need not be confirmed by the Senate unless Congress by law vests their appointment in the president alone, in the courts, or in the heads of EXECUTIVE BRANCH departments.

See also: ADVICE AND CONSENT; APPOINTMENT AND REMOVAL POWER; OFFICE AND OFFICERS.

confiscation   A confiscation, as usually understood, is a TAKING of money or property permitted by law for which JUST COMPENSATION is ordinarily not due. Many criminal laws permit the government to confiscate assets of a criminal enterprise or gain resulting from a criminal act.[339] During wartime, federal laws have permitted confiscations of enemy property. The Supreme Court upheld such laws after the Civil War.[1341]

See also: EMINENT DOMAIN; FORFEITURE; WAR POWER.

conflict of laws, *see:* **choice of law; preemption**

Confrontation Clause, *see:* **confrontation with witnesses**

confrontation with witnesses   The Confrontation Clause of the SIXTH AMENDMENT guarantees every criminal defendant the right "to be confronted with the witnesses against him." Fundamentally favoring cross-examination, the rule gives the accused the opportunity of "testing the recollection and sifting the conscience of the witness" and of permitting the jury to observe the witness's demeanor to see whether his testimony is "worthy of belief."[1272] In 1965 the Court held the Confrontation Clause applicable to the states.[1645] The clause's straightforward application occurs when the witness is available but the prosecution fails to call him, seeking instead to introduce written pretrial statements. In such cases, the pretrial statement is inadmissible.[1393]

The right has bite. In one case the prosecution called a man they said was the defendant's accomplice. He refused to testify on the ground of SELF-INCRIMINATION. The prosecutor then read the accomplice's earlier confession. The Court reversed the conviction, holding that the Confrontation Clause was violated because the defendant could not cross-examine the witness.[568] For the same reason, when a prosecution informant concealed his name and address, the testimony was held to violate the clause.[1891] Even if the witnesses were subject to cross-examination earlier, their presence at trial will be required if there was no opportunity at the prior hearing to cross-examine on the question of the truth or falsity of earlier statements.[1134]

Still, the clause does not bar all out-of-court statements. The Court held that it did not apply to bar pretrial statements of a witness who at trial said that he had been using LSD when the events occurred and could not swear that they happened as he had earlier related. The Court permitted the statements to be introduced because the witness himself was available in court to undergo cross-examination.[319] When witnesses are unavailable, an out-of-court statement may be used under certain circumstances, including a co-conspirator's statements made during the conspiracy and the business records of a company or other enterprise.[588]

A confrontation problem has recently arisen in cases of sex crimes against young children. An Iowa procedure permitted the trial court to place a one-way screen so that the child witness could not see the defendant. Even though everyone could see the child and the right to cross-examination was fully protected, the Court in 1988 in a 6–2 decision held that the procedure violated the clause, because the right to confront includes face-to-face confrontation.[481] The Court modified this absolute view of the clause in 1990, in holding, 5–4, that a similar Maryland procedure was constitutional. The child testified through a one-way closed-circuit television. But the Maryland court had specifically found that this particular child would be traumatized by seeing the defendant. Now the Court said that the clause merely "reflects a *preference* for face-to-face confrontation," and it can be overcome by a "case-specific" showing that the child would suffer "serious emotional distress."[1259] A major unsettled issue is whether the states may excuse child victims altogether and allow their stories to be related to the juries by witnesses testifying to what the children told them out of court.

Congress, lame-duck, *see:* **Twentieth Amendment**

Congress, members of   The Constitution imposes few formal qualifications for election to Congress. Under Art. I-§2[2], members of the House must be at least twenty-five years old, seven years an American citizen, and a resident of the state from which elected. Under Art. I-§3[3], senators must be thirty years old, nine years a citizen, and likewise a resident of the state from which elected. Although the Supreme Court has never had occasion to rule, the consensus is that the first two requirements—age and citizenship—need be met only at the time the member actually takes office. A candidate for the House may therefore be twenty-four or six years a citizen but cannot take office until his or her next birthday or the seventh anniversary of gaining citizenship. By the literal language of Article I, residency is required "when elected," meaning on the day of election. Under Art. I-§3[4], a vacant seat in the House of Representatives may be filled only by a special election. But under the SEVENTEENTH AMENDMENT, the state legislature may by law empower the governor to appoint a temporary replacement to a Senate vacancy. The person appointed serves only until the next regularly scheduled election. Members of the House are elected to two-year terms; members of the Senate, to six-year terms. Congress may neither expand nor diminish the constitutional qualifications for serving in either house.[1653]

See also: IMMUNITY, MEMBERS OF CONGRESS; QUALIFICATIONS FOR OFFICE.

Congress, powers of   Stated abstractly, Congress is empowered to pass laws on all subjects of national import. Congressional enactments may take different forms. They may raise revenues (that is, tax), establish government agencies and prescribe operations and procedures, fund government programs, declare private actions unlawful, and establish public policy over all areas the federal government is permitted to govern. At the CONSTITUTIONAL CONVENTION and in the debates surrounding ratification, there was considerable anxiety over whether Congress was to be a general legislative body, competent to legislate directly over the people. Expressing federalist concerns, the Framers said that it was not, that Congress could legislate only in the areas of its ENUMERATED POWERS. Furthermore, the TENTH AMENDMENT, ratified as part of the BILL OF RIGHTS, expressly states that Congress has only those powers delegated to it; all others belong to the states or the people. This same theme was sounded after the Civil War, when the Court rejected a Reconstruction Congress's law directly barring acts of private RACIAL DISCRIMINATION, such as segregated public accommodations, on the ground that Congress has no general legislative power over the people.[1874]

But in 1819 and 1824, in the celebrated cases *McCulloch v. Maryland* and *Gibbons v. Ogden*, Chief Justice John Marshall laid the foundations for a powerful Congress that can indeed legislate in detail over people's lives. In *Gibbons*, which upheld the federal COMMERCE POWER, Marshall said that Congress may exercise to the fullest whatever powers are enumerated in the Constitution. In *McCulloch*, he said that the NECESSARY AND PROPER CLAUSE gives Congress great latitude in the means used to carry out its policy choices. Today, under the COMMERCE CLAUSE in particular, Congress has sweeping power to enact general legislation that can supplant much of state law. Although the very first sentence of the Constitution, Art. I-§1[1], says that Congress is to have *all* legislative power, a longstanding historical practice, implicitly confirmed by the Supreme Court in hundreds of cases, permits Congress to delegate its powers to executive agencies to fill in the details of most national policies and programs. Congress's principal powers are listed in Art. I-§8, but Articles II–V also grant powers, as do several amendments, most importantly the FOURTEENTH and FIFTEENTH AMENDMENTS.

See also: NATIONAL POLICE POWER; *separate listings for powers given in various constitutional clauses.*

Congress, salaries for, *see:* **Emoluments Clause; Twenty-seventh Amendment**

congressional districting, *see:* **apportionment of political districts**

congressional employees, immunity of, *see:* **immunity from suit**

congressional immunity, *see:* **immunity, members of Congress**

congressional investigations, *see:* **investigatory powers of legislature**

Congressional Record, *see:* **journal of proceedings**

conscience, freedom of, *see:* **freedom of belief; freedom of religion**

conscientious objection   In its most important sense, conscientious objection is the principled refusal to engage in military service, other than as a noncombatant, because of religious or moral scruples against killing. The Constitution itself provides no direct exemption from military CONSCRIPTION, and the Court has never suggested that draft laws must contain an exemption for conscientious objectors. In fact, for most of our wartime history, Congress has provided an exemption for persons whose "religious training and belief" make them conscientiously opposed to participating "in war in any form." Congress has said that the qualifying "belief" must relate to a "Supreme Being" who imposes higher duties than those laid down in a code of law, and that it could not be a belief that springs from philosophical views or "a merely personal moral code." In a 1965 case involving, among others, the folk singer Pete Seeger, the Court avoided the difficulty that this language might discriminate against certain religions by construing the law to mean any belief "that is sincere and meaningful [and that] occupies a place in the life of its possessor parallel to that filled by the orthodox belief in God of one who clearly qualifies for the exemption."[1840] But the Court held firm on the requirement that the conscientious objector must object to all wars. "Selective conscientious objectors" who oppose only "unjust wars" are not constitutionally entitled to an exemption.[755] The Court has also held that Congress may decide to grant educational benefits to veterans but not to conscientious objectors who participated in alternative service.[1021]

See also: FREEDOM OF RELIGION.

conscription Through its power under Art. I-§8[12,13] to raise armies and provide a navy, Congress has broad authority to conscript or draft citizens and even resident aliens for military service, even though it was widely supposed in the 1780s that only the states could actually draft men for their militias. But more than a century of episodic draft laws has con-

firmed the power. In the *Selective Draft Law Cases* in 1918, the Court denied that the military draft in World War I violated the following principles: the antislavery and involuntary servitude provision of the THIRTEENTH AMENDMENT; that only the states could draft; that draftees could not serve in foreign wars; or that draftees could be forced to do no more than what could be required of men called into state militias. Even though the constitutionality of the peacetime draft has never been squarely called into question, the Court has sustained various provisions of the draft law. In the 1968 DRAFT CARD BURNING case Chief Justice Earl Warren said: "The power of Congress to classify and conscript manpower for military service is 'beyond question.' "[1508] So sweeping is Congress's conscription power that the Court could find no constitutional flaw in a peacetime registration scheme that unequally required eighteen-year-old men but not their female counterparts to register for the draft.[1766] Whether Congress or the states may conscript for nonmilitary purposes is an open question. The Court has held that the Thirteenth Amendment does not bar the states from demanding citizenry to serve on juries, or even from requiring all "able-bodied" men between the ages of twenty-one and forty-five to work on public roads near their residences for a reasonable time without being paid.[295]

See also: PROSECUTORIAL DISCRETION.

consent, advice and, *see:* **advice and consent**

consent of governed The Constitution uses the word "consent" eleven times, but "consent of the governed," a phrase from the DECLARATION OF INDEPENDENCE, does not appear. The Declaration says that governments "deriv[e] their just powers from the consent of the governed." In that sense, the Constitution may be seen as the vehicle by which the people of the

United States have consented to their form of government, as the Preamble suggests. But neither the Declaration nor the Constitution requires that the people must consent to every law, regulation, or decision. That would be possible only in a direct democracy, and the Constitution manifestly creates a system of representative government in which the people consent to let specific people hold office for limited terms.

consent search, *see:* **search and seizure: consent searches**

conservation   Congress has broad power to enact conservation and environmental laws to protect and purify the country's natural resources, water supplies, and air. Some constitutional problems arose, however, when the states attempted through the guise of conservation to discriminate against peoples in other states. In 1911 the Court overturned on DORMANT COMMERCE CLAUSE grounds a state law that barred transport of natural gas out of state,[2183] and in 1923 it overturned a law giving preference to residents over outsiders in purchasing natural gas.[1594] Though in 1896 the Court had approved state GAME LAWS that barred shipping wild animals out of state,[736] the modern cases show a marked disinclination by the Court to approve state resource conservation laws that upon closer inspection are simply protectionist. Under the PRIVILEGES AND IMMUNITIES Clause, the Court struck down a South Carolina scheme that charged nonresidents more than residents for licenses to trawl for shrimp.[2058] The game law case was expressly overruled in 1979; the law in question prohibited anyone from shipping to another state any minnows caught in state, even if by a resident.[956]

conspiracy   Conspiracy is a common law offense of such sweeping breadth that if it had been invented in the twentieth century the courts might well have voided it for violating DUE PROCESS. But because of its ancient lineage, and because it has proved so powerful a device for securing convictions in criminal cases, the courts have consistently refused to find constitutional flaw in its central feature. A conspiracy is nothing more than an agreement by two or more people to do something unlawful. Its arresting characteristic is that the conspirators need not actually have done anything unlawful; it is enough to sustain a conviction if, in addition to their agreement, at least one of them has taken a concrete step toward advancing their criminal plan. For example, if two would-be bank robbers pick out a target, agree to invade it at nightfall, and one of them goes to a hardware store to buy a screwdriver with which to pry off the back door, the crime of conspiracy is complete, even if they fall asleep and forget to rob the bank.

Most substantive criminal laws have conspiracy components. Sometimes prosecutors use the conspiracy statutes for the straightforward purpose of bringing to justice conspirators in the true sense, such as members of organized crime. But frequently conspiracy laws have been used to deter the exercise of various CIVIL LIBERTIES, such as the FREEDOM OF ASSOCIATION and the FREEDOM OF SPEECH, as in many of the World War I espionage prosecutions. Conspiracy law also lies at the heart of important provisions in American CIVIL RIGHTS LEGISLATION, permitting the federal government to prosecute individuals for bias attacks and more subtle forms of RACIAL DISCRIMINATION by recalcitrant state officials indifferent to the claims of minorities.

See also: LOYALTY-SECURITY PROGRAMS; MEMBERSHIP IN POLITICAL ORGANIZATIONS; SPEECH, REGULATION OF CONTENT; SYMBOLIC SPEECH.

Constitution, amending, *see:* **amendments to Constitution**

Constitution, as color-blind   Dissenting from the Supreme Court's approval of racial SEGREGATION in its 1896 decision in PLESSY V. FERGUSON, Justice John Marshall Harlan said that the Constitution does not allow a "superior, dominant, ruling class of citizens. There is no caste here. *Our constitution is color-blind,* and neither knows nor tolerates classes among citizens." The phrase was drawn from the brief of Albion W. Tourgee, the New York lawyer, who argued against the SEPARATE BUT EQUAL railroad car law. In his brief to the Supreme Court, Tourgee said: "Justice is pictured blind and her daughter, the Law, ought at least to be color-blind."

Constitution, evolving, *see:* **Constitution, living**

Constitution, following the flag, *see:* **following the flag**

Constitution, Framers of   When Thomas Jefferson heard who had been appointed to attend the CONSTITUTIONAL CONVENTION, he wrote John Adams: "It really is an assembly of demi-gods." The opinion was not universally shared then, but it has now hardened into mythology. Virginia ensured that the convention would not be a routine trade negotiation by choosing George Washington, the leading citizen of state and nation, to head its delegation. That it sent as well James Madison, widely regarded as the intellectual father of the Constitution, and other equally serious leaders, attests to the gravity of the moment. Spurred by Virginia's choices, other states responded accordingly. The host state, Pennsylvania, sent Benjamin Franklin, ailing at eighty-one. Conspicuously absent were Jefferson, then living in Paris as ambassador to France, and Adams, then ambassador to England.

Fifty-five delegates attended the convention. Seventy-four had been appointed (the number is disputed) but nineteen, including Patrick Henry, declined or could not attend. The delegates' average age was forty-two. Franklin was the oldest; the youngest active participant was Charles Pinckney, thirty, of South Carolina. Washington was then fifty-five; Madison, thirty-six. Twenty-one delegates were under forty; fourteen were fifty or over. Eight were foreign-born. Today we call them "delegates," or even more honorifically, "Framers," but some referred to themselves as "commissioners" or "deputies," as George Washington signed himself on the finished document.

Only forty-one of the fifty-five who arrived in Philadelphia stayed to the end; most of the fourteen others attended but briefly. Of course, not every regular was necessarily at every session; the average in attendance was thirty.

Some never spoke a word. Franklin was too feeble to speak personally; James Wilson of Pennsylvania read his remarks. Some spoke more than one hundred times, including Madison, Alexander Hamilton of New York, and George Mason of Virginia, who spoke more than anyone. Hamilton spoke the longest; one of his speeches lasted five hours. Luther Martin had to carry over to the next day his address on equal representation because he had become too exhausted to continue.

Many who were steady deliberators refused to sign, including Edmund Randolph, Elbridge Gerry, and George Mason, all of whom were present on the last day. Randolph protested that the new Constitution did not sufficiently protect civil liberties; however, he later spoke out in favor of ratification at the Virginia convention. Luther Martin, Robert Yates, and John Lansing left in disgust before their brethren finished their labors. Alone of the New York delegation, Hamilton stayed to sign. John Dickinson of Delaware departed before September 17, when the Constitution was completed, but had his colleague George Read sign for him.

Many of the delegates were among the most eminent men of their, or any, era. Others were obscure then and are even more so now. But their credentials were impressive, for that age or any: Twenty-five were college educated, and eighteen had served as officers in Washington's Continental Army. Thirty-four were lawyers, six were planters, eight were merchants, two were ministers, and two were physicians. Forty-six had served or were serving as members of colonial or state legislatures. Eight had signed the DECLARATION OF INDEPENDENCE; six, the ARTICLES OF CONFEDERATION. Sixteen had been or were to become governors.

Their influence on the government they created was no less impressive: Two (Washington and Madison) became president; one (Gerry) became vice president. Five others would run on a national ticket. One (Ellsworth) became chief justice of the United States, and five others served on the Supreme Court. Nineteen became senators; thirteen, congressmen; one (Dayton), Speaker of the House; four, cabinet members; and seven, ambassadors. Perhaps fittingly, the last survivor of that distinguished revolutionary group was James Madison, secretary of state in the Jefferson administration (1801–07), fourth president of the United States (1809–17), and rector of the University of Virginia from 1826 until his death in 1836 at the age of eighty-five.

Constitution, living   The dominant theme of constitutional history, if not constitutional theory, is that the Constitution is "living"—that courts adapt it to changing circumstances, so that the Supreme Court is in effect a permanent CONSTITUTIONAL CONVENTION, amending the Constitution as times change and the need arises. In this spirit this very book is named, though "evolving" may connote a progressive change that is more than the historical facts will bear. Not everyone is happy with this notion. Chief Justice William H. Rehnquist has

written that the idea of a living Constitution "ignores the Supreme Court's disastrous experiences . . . in [embracing] contemporary, fashionable notions of what a living Constitution should contain. . . . [H]owever socially desirable the goals to be advanced, . . . advancing them through a free-wheeling, non-elected judiciary is quite unacceptable in a democratic society." If the Chief's rhetoric overstates the reality a bit—no one has ever argued for a "freewheeling" judiciary—it perhaps matters not that his position is constitutionally sound. For in the end what determines whether we have a living Constitution is what the Court does, not what it says it is doing, what it wishes to do, or what it thinks it has done. "Whatever the Court has said," the noted constitutional analyst Karl N. Llewellyn wrote more than half a century ago, "it has shaped the living Constitution to the needs of the day as it felt them." The justices, after all, are human beings, not disembodied computing constitutional calculators, not, as Justice Oliver Wendell Holmes once commented sarcastically in dissent, oracles of a "brooding omnipresence in the sky."[1920] The justices do not know what the Framers intended. What else can they do but shape the Constitution, as timidly or boldly as they think prudent, to their constitutional vision?

See also: ORIGINAL INTENT.

Constitution, ratification of   Since the Constitution was written in the name of the sovereign people of the United States, the Framers concluded that their work should not simply be dropped on the desks of their respective state legislatures to be debated in the routine course of business. Article VII called for conventions and required the consent of nine states before the Constitution would take effect. The Continental Congress itself could not muster the votes to endorse the Constitution, but its supporters in that body did pass a bill by which they could claim that Congress had voted "unanimously to transmit" it to the states, where the people in turn would elect special conventions to ratify or reject.

In some states ratification was easy: Delaware ratified unanimously on December 7, 1787, and Pennsylvania by a two-to-one majority five days later. But in many states the debate was intense—chiefly, though not exclusively, over the apparently inexplicable failure of the Constitution aborning to protect the people with a BILL OF RIGHTS. To aid the fight, James Madison, Alexander Hamilton, and John Jay penned matchless essays (under the collective pseudonym "Publius"), collected under the title *The Federalist Papers,* to persuade the ratifying delegates in New York and Virginia to vote yes. In the large states, ratification was close: in Massachusetts by nineteen votes, in Virginia by ten, in New York by two. In each state, the issue was almost lost over the lack of a bill of rights, and in each state the pro-ratification forces won only with the promise that they would seek amendments in the very first Congress convened under the authority of the new Constitution. It was a measure of the desire to secure individual rights that in New York, Massachusetts, and Virginia, the Constitution prevailed by a margin of but eighteen votes altogether, what Page Smith called "the greatest act of political prestidigitation in all recorded history." Cyrus Griffin, president of Congress, formally announced on July 2, 1788, that the Constitution had been ratified by the requisite nine states and was in effect. On September 13, Congress named New York the seat of the new national government and took the final steps to putting itself out of business. The states chose electors for president in January 1789, and the electors voted—everyone knew their unanimous choice would be Washington—in early February. The new United States Congress convened in March, and

George Washington was inaugurated in New York City on April 30, 1789.

Constitution, unwritten, *see:* **natural law; Ninth Amendment**

constitutional common law, *see:* **federal common law**

Constitutional Convention of 1787   It had been agreed by the Confederation Congress that a new convention meet in Philadelphia on the second Monday of May 1787 to investigate "important defects in the System of the Foederal Government [and] . . . to devise such further Provisions as shall appear to them necessary to render the Constitution of the Foederal Government adequate to the exigencies of the Union." On May 14, the second Monday, the Virginians and the Pennsylvanians arrived at the Long Room of the Pennsylvania State House, where the DECLARATION OF INDEPENDENCE had been signed nearly eleven years earlier. (The building was shortly renamed Independence Hall.) It took until May 25 to gather a quorum. The delay was attributable in part to muddy roads and high rivers and in part to the values of a bygone culture in which everyone knew that even important events rarely start promptly, so why waste time when others would not likely be there?

From the very start, the importance of the event was marked. The city of Philadelphia even covered the pavement outside the meeting hall with dirt so that the delegates would not be disturbed by the rumblings of traffic passing by the windows. After selecting George Washington president of the convention, the delegates agreed to keep their deliberations secret so that they could speak freely. So strictly did they adhere to their secrecy vows that some Philadelphians speculated that the delegates were conspiring to invite George III's second son to become king of America. Although several delegates took notes, none were published until 1821. The most accurate notes—Madison's—were not published until 1840. One other important preliminary decision was that each state should have but one vote, a decision to which the large states agreed, against their immediate interests, to avoid "beget[ting] fatal altercations between the large & small States," believing that the principle of majority rule would eventually prevail.

In fact, pure majority rule did not prevail. The major issue over which the convention almost foundered was the nature of congressional representation. Through the GREAT COMPROMISE, both small and large states prevailed. The large states' insistence on representation by population prevailed in the House of Representatives. The small states' insistence on representation by state prevailed in the Senate. This debate occupied the delegates between May 29 and July 16 and was settled by a vote of only five states to four. In the next two weeks the delegates hashed out most of the remaining difficult and troubling issues—the powers of Congress, the nature and tenure of the chief executive, the powers of the judiciary, and the relationship between the national government and the states.

The convention delegated to a Committee of Detail the painstaking task of meshing the delegates' general policy decisions into a coherent document. They elected John Rutledge of South Carolina, Edmund Randolph of Virginia, Nathaniel Gorham of Massachusetts, Oliver Ellsworth of Connecticut, and James Wilson of Pennsylvania. On August 6, this committee reported its draft, and for the next month the delegates as a whole debated the form, though not the final wording, of the Constitution. They met every day, five hours a day, for the next five weeks. On September 8, the delegates appointed a new five-man Committee on Style to revise and write the final text: William Johnson of Connecticut, Alexander Hamilton of New York, Gouverneur Morris of Pennsylvania, James Madison of Virginia, and Rufus King of Massachusetts. According to Madison, the final language and style belonged to Morris.

Only now, as the delegates debated the final wording, did they also adopt a preamble. And they did so with a radical change. It had originally been proposed that the Constitution be declared established by the *states*. But Article VII said that unanimity was not required: nine of thirteen states would make it binding. So the delegates ultimately decided that it was "We, the *People*," who had created not merely a new government but a new nation.

The delegates were aware of their historic undertaking. Madison told the delegates they "were now to decide forever the fate of Republican Government." Gouverneur Morris said that "the whole human race will be affected by the proceedings of this Convention." When they had finished, James Wilson declared: "After the lapse of six thousand years since the creation of the world, America now presents the first instance of a people assembled to weigh deliberately and calmly, and to decide leisurely and peaceably, upon the form of government by which they will bind themselves and their posterity."

Madison later recalled that as the delegates rose to sign the Constitution, Benjamin Franklin chanced to be looking at the president's chair, on which a picture of the sun had been painted. Franklin "observed to a few members near him that Painters had found it difficult to distinguish in their art a rising from a setting sun. I have, said he, often . . . looked at that behind the president without being able to tell whether it was rising or setting: But now at length I have the happiness to know that it is a rising and not a setting sun."

See also: ANNAPOLIS CONVENTION; CONSTITUTION, FRAMERS OF; CONSTITUTION, RATIFICATION OF; MADISON'S NOTES ON THE CONSTITUTION; ORIGINAL INTENT.

constitutional conventions, *see:*
**amendments to Constitution; Constitution,
ratification of**

constitutional court, *see:* **Article III courts**

constitutional fact, *see:* **jurisdictional and
constitutional facts**

constitutional interpretation   Alone among
the most contested issues of constitutional interpretation, the question of interpretation itself has almost no constitutional basis. As Judge
Richard Posner has written, "The Constitution
does not say, 'Read me broadly,' 'Read me narrowly.' That decision must be made as a matter
of political theory, and will depend on such
things as one's view of the springs of judicial
legitimacy and of the relative competence of
courts and legislatures in dealing with particular types of issues." Actually, Posner is not
quite accurate. One place, the NINTH AMEND-
MENT, states a rule of construction: that readers
should not construe the Constitution's failure
to list certain rights to mean that unenumerated rights are not retained by the people. Curiously, most proponents of ORIGINAL INTENT
either ignore the Ninth Amendment or else
read it out of the Constitution on grounds that
it is unenforceable, thus undercutting the very
principle they seem to profess. But of course
for STRICT CONSTRUCTIONISTS, the dilemma is
that this single constitutional rule of interpretation appears to call for broad construction. At
any rate, various means, modes, and maybes of
constitutional interpretation have been announced throughout our judicial history.

See also: NATURAL LAW; SUBSTANTIVE DUE PROCESS; SOME
THOUGHTS ON INTERPRETING THE CONSTITUTION, *p. 12.*

constitutional questions, avoidance of   In a
CONCURRING OPINION in 1936,[88] Justice Louis D.
Brandeis summarized seven guidelines that the
Court had used to avoid passing upon a "large
part of all constitutional questions pressed
upon it for decision" in cases "confessedly
within its jurisdiction." The Court will not decide a constitutional question: (1) in a friendly,
nonadversary suit; (2) anticipating that the
issue will someday arise if unnecessary to decide in the particular case; (3) broader than
necessary to decide the case before the Court;
(4) if there is some other ground on which the
case may be decided; (5) unless an injury can be
demonstrated as arising from the operation of
a law the constitutionality of which is being
challenged; (6) if the challenger has benefited
from the statute he is challenging; and (7) if the
challenged statute may be interpreted in some
way to avoid the constitutional difficulty.

In 1803, in MARBURY V. MADISON, the Court
dismissed the suit because the case could not
constitutionally come before it. Nevertheless,
Chief Justice John Marshall went out of his
way to proclaim that President Thomas Jefferson had violated Marbury's right to his commission. Jefferson and others were angered.
"Three questions are reported to have been
decided," one critic said. "The last decision
was that the Court had no jurisdiction to decide the other two, which they nevertheless
decided." Marshall must have been trying to
avoid the constitutional issue, for surely in 1803
the most difficult question was not about the
rights of officeholders but about whether the
Supreme Court could declare a law unconstitutional. In many cases since then, the Court
has ducked constitutional questions, sometimes
by torturing statutes or precedents in the process. For example, in a PASSPORT case in 1958,
the secretary of state refused to issue a passport
to an American citizen because he was suspected of being a communist and had refused
to sign an affidavit disclaiming membership in
the Communist party. The law said that the
secretary could issue passports under such
rules as the president prescribed, but in announcing for a 5–4 majority Justice William O.

Douglas said that the federal passport laws do not delegate the authority exercised by the secretary.[1062] In fact, for many years secretaries had denied passports on national security grounds. Douglas was avoiding getting into the constitutional question of whether citizens could be denied the right to TRAVEL. This case suggests how flexible the Court's avoidance techniques have been, since Douglas devoted most of his opinion to justifying what sounded suspiciously like a constitutional right. Not surprisingly, six years later the Court overturned part of the passport laws on constitutional grounds, citing the very principle of the 1958 case that Douglas said was not being decided.[67] When five justices want to decide a constitutional question, they sometimes do not even pay lip service to the policy of avoidance. In 1991, for example, the Court made new constitutional law by overruling two recent prior cases dealing with VICTIM IMPACT STATEMENTS, even though neither the state courts nor the party seeking review in the Supreme Court had raised the constitutional question that the Court went on to answer.[1580]

constitutional rights, waiver of, *see:* **rights, waiver of**

constitutional rights in wartime, *see:* **rights in wartime**

constitutional torts   A person injured by the unexcused willful conduct or negligence of another may recover DAMAGES in court. But if injuries are caused by government officials acting in an official capacity, recovery is less certain. Damage suits may of course be brought if Congress or the state legislatures specifically authorize them, but in the absence of legislative approval, principles of SOVEREIGN IMMUNITY and the constitutional bar of the ELEVENTH AMENDMENT stand in the way of a court's entertaining a claim. In 1971 the Court carved out a partial exception to the rules against suing government agents personally for damages caused in the line of duty. In *Bivens v. Six Unknown Named Agents of the Federal Bureau of Narcotics,* the Court held that even in the absence of authorizing legislation, the FOURTH AMENDMENT permits federal courts to hear cases charging police and other officials with violating its provisions. In this case, federal agents had broken into the plaintiff's home and done considerable damage before discovering that their tip was bad and they were in the wrong place. Official actions for which redress could be sought in this manner came to be known as "constitutional torts." The Court has extended the constitutional tort doctrine to violations of the FIFTH AMENDMENT (in a sex discrimination suit against a former congressman[523]) and of the EIGHTH AMENDMENT.[344] But during the 1980s the Court seemed to retreat, finding either "special factors counselling hesitation" or an adequate alternative remedy that led it to dismiss several suits seeking to extend the principle—for example, suits charging racial discrimination by a superior military officer[376] and by federal employers[286] and suits charging DUE PROCESS violations in awarding Social Security benefits.[1824]

See also: JURISDICTION.

constructive treason, *see:* **treason**

consuls   Consuls are officials, below the rank of ambassador, sent abroad to represent the government's commercial interests and to assist U.S. citizens living or traveling abroad. Under Art. II-§2[2], all consuls must be nominated by the president and confirmed by the Senate.

contempt   Contempt is the power of courts and legislatures to punish disobedience to their lawful commands. Historically, the contempt power has been quite broad; only relatively recently has the Court imposed constitutional limitations on its exercise. Federal law also authorizes the federal courts to punish misbehavior committed in the presence of the judge "or so near thereto as to obstruct the administration of justice" or behavior that impedes the officers of the courts in their official capacity. Contempt comes in two forms, civil and criminal. Civil contempt is a court sanction, including fine or jail, against a litigant who has failed to comply with a court order. The person against whom the contempt order is sought is entitled to a HEARING, but since civil contempt is not considered PUNISHMENT, the PROCEDURAL DUE PROCESS rights afforded criminal defendants do not apply. The theory is that the individual can avoid the punishment or terminate it at any time by obeying the court's order.[1859]

Criminal contempt sanctions are issued for acts that interfere with or obstruct a court's procedures, such as a defendant's obstreperous behavior in the courtroom or a lawyer's disruptive refusal to accept a judge's ruling during trial. The general rule, upheld as long ago as 1888, is that a trial judge may punish such acts summarily if they were committed in open court and if delay in pronouncing contempt would prejudice the trial.[2014] But in 1974 the Court held that as a matter of DUE PROCESS, constraining both federal and state courts, if a judge does not immediately punish the contempt, then notice must be given of the charges and the individual must have a chance to refute them at a later hearing.[1999] Moreover, if the punishment meted out for criminal contempt is longer than that for a petty offense, interpreted as six months, the defendant is entitled to a jury trial, both in federal and state cases.[381, 174] If the imbroglio leads the defendant to verbally attack a judge or if the judge manifests "marked personal feelings" so as to impair his impartiality, the defendant is constitutionally entitled to have the contempt issue heard by another judge.[1273, 1999] Occasionally criminal contempt

may be issued to maintain existing conditions during a trial. The Supreme Court has upheld criminal contempt when a union disobeyed a court's temporary restraining order, even though it was conceded that the law authorizing the order was itself unconstitutional.[2097]

When the act for which a judge proposes to issue a contempt citation was not done in the judge's presence or in the court, other constitutional limitations come into play—in particular, the FIRST AMENDMENT. Beginning in 1941 with *Bridges v. California*, the Court has considerably restricted the power of judges to cite for contempt newspapers or others who speak out about pending trials. In *Bridges*, a court held the *Los Angeles Times* in contempt when it strongly urged a judge to sentence the defendants, whom it characterized as "thugs," to San Quentin. In a COMPANION CASE, a judge held the labor leader Harry Bridges in contempt for releasing a telegram to the secretary of labor threatening a strike if an "outrageous" court decision was enforced. The Supreme Court reversed the contempt citations, holding that the "tendency" of the editorials and telegram to interfere with the "orderly administration of justice" was not enough to overcome the right to free speech. When a judge convened a grand jury in the midst of a political campaign to look into allegations of vote buying, he held a press conference to announce the investigation. He then ordered contempt against the sheriff, who issued news releases to protest the calling of the grand jury. The judge acted without any explanation of how the releases could interfere with the grand jury investigation. The Court reversed.[2252] The general rule is that "[t]he danger must not be remote or even probable; it must immediately imperil."[484]

Although contempt is both an inherent power of the courts[1745] and also governed by statute, its use in federal courts is governed by the supervisory power of the Supreme Court. In a controversial case in 1990 involving the failure of Yonkers, New York, to move forward on a nondiscriminatory low-income housing plan, the Court ruled that a federal trial judge had abused his discretion in holding four members of the city council in contempt for refusing to vote for the plan.[1926] The judge should have issued contempt sanctions against the city first.

Legislatures, too, may exercise a contempt power to force a recalcitrant witness to appear or to answer questions. As a matter of practice today, contempts of Congress arising in this manner are referred to the U.S. attorney for prosecution in federal court. This power, too, is subject to First Amendment limitations, and will be considered under the heading INVESTIGATORY POWERS OF LEGISLATURES.

content of speech regulation, *see:* **speech, regulation of content**

continuance in office, *see:* **term limitation**

contraception   In 1965, in a major SUBSTANTIVE DUE PROCESS ruling, the Court held that a state has no power to prohibit married couples from using contraceptives or to enjoin doctors from offering medical advice about contraception.[820] In 1972, the year before the Court decided *Roe v. Wade*, the Court took two further steps along the road to constitutionalizing the right to receive and use contraceptives. It squarely overturned the conviction of a doctor who had distributed contraceptives to an unmarried person. Although the Court refrained from expressly saying either that there is an absolute right to distribute contraception or a right to use contraception even if unmarried, that was unmistakably the implication. In a sentence fraught with future importance, Justice William J. Brennan said that "[i]f the right of privacy means anything, it is the right of the *individual*, married or single, to be free from unwarranted governmental intrusion into matters so fundamentally affecting a person as the decision whether to bear or beget a child."[606] In 1977 the Court overturned a New York law permitting only pharmacists to sell or distribute contraceptives to anyone over sixteen years old and barring sale or distribution to anyone under sixteen.[341] A majority agreed that in view of the burden the pharmacist provision imposed on the right to use contraceptives, it was unconstitutional because the state could offer no COMPELLING INTEREST or justification for it. Although there was no majority opinion for the proposition that minors should have equal access to contraceptives, seven justices agreed that that provision should be struck down, in part because it was irrational and scarcely likely to achieve the state's objective of deterring youths from engaging in sex. The justices also voided a provision in the law prohibiting anyone from advertising or displaying nonprescription contraceptives. An emerging question in the new, more sober age of AIDS concerns the right of parents to prohibit their children from receiving contraceptives distributed in schools; this issue is only now just reaching the lower courts.
See also: ABORTION; PRIVACY; REPRODUCTIVE RIGHTS; SEXUAL FREEDOM.

contract, law impairing obligation of, *see:* **obligation of contracts**

contract, liberty of, *see:* **freedom of contract**

contract, right to, *see:* **freedom of contract**

contract, yellow-dog, *see:* **yellow-dog contracts**

Contract Clause   The Contract Clause, set out in Art I-§10[1], is a limitation on the power of states. It prohibits the states, but not the federal government, from enacting any law that impairs the OBLIGATION OF CONTRACTS.

When first discussed at the CONSTITUTIONAL CONVENTION, the clause was to apply only to "private" contracts. During the mid-1780s, to the great consternation of creditors throughout the states, many state legislatures had been enacting debt relief legislation that in some instances relieved debtors of any obligation to repay their debts. That some version of this clause would appear in the Constitution was never in doubt. But the word "private" was soon dropped, and the present version accepted. From the beginning the Court has applied the clause both to laws that impair the obligations of contracts between private persons and to obligations of the state itself under contracts it has entered. The clause does not prohibit the states from making particular types of contracts unlawful, such as wagering or prostitution. Nor does it spell out any general FREEDOM OF CONTRACT. Its focus is more limited and will be discussed in detail under the heading OBLIGATION OF CONTRACTS.

controversies, *see:* **cases or controversies**

controversies between two or more states Under Art. III-§2[2,3], controversies between two or more states are to be tried in the Supreme Court itself, which exercises ORIGINAL JURISDICTION.

conventions of nine states, *see:* **Constitution, ratification of**

Cooley **doctrine** The question of whether Congress has exclusive power under the COMMERCE CLAUSE or shares it with the states found an apparent compromise in 1852 in *Cooley v. Board of Wardens of the Port of Philadelphia.* Pennsylvania required ships above a certain size to employ local pilots when entering or leaving state ports. Cooley, master of the ship, refused to comply because he said the law unconstitutionally interfered with Congress's power to regulate FOREIGN COMMERCE. The Court's Solomonic decision proclaimed what is sometimes called the doctrine of "selective exclusiveness": if the subject to be regulated is *national,* requiring a uniform rule, then only Congress may regulate; if it is *local,* then in the absence of preemptive federal law, the states may regulate as well. Because pilotage is a local concern, the Court sustained the Pennsylvania law. But the distinction between national and local is as easy to state as it is difficult to discern. For nearly a century, the Court adhered uneasily to the *Cooley* doctrine, but it finally recognized the futility of the distinction and in a series of cases between 1925 and 1945 abandoned it in favor of a BALANCING approach.[269, 218, 1919]

cooperative federalism, *see:* **federalism**

Copyright Clause The Copyright Clause is that part of Art. I-§8[8] "securing for limited times . . . to authors . . . the exclusive right to their . . . writings." Since the clause says the right may be secured only for a limited time, it would be unconstitutional for Congress to grant a perpetual copyright. Under the general rule of the 1976 Copyright Act, copyright in WRITINGS, which include many more types of expression than books or articles, lasts for the lifetime of the author plus fifty years. The clause is not exclusive, so that states may protect authors' works to the extent that Congress has left unprotected particular forms of writings.[772] In the 1976 Copyright Act, Congress preempted all state copyright laws, with the exception of tape piracy laws for sound recordings made before early 1972.

Some recent cases have raised the question of whether the FIRST AMENDMENT gives authors the right to quote from unpublished letters and memoirs of public figures. In the only case thus far decided by the Supreme Court, the answer seemed to be no, although the

Court did not say so directly. The *Nation* magazine excerpted a few hundred words from President Gerald Ford's forthcoming memoirs, and his publisher sued for copyright infringement when the *Nation*'s scoop caused *Time* magazine to cancel its serialization of the memoirs. The Court held against the *Nation*'s claim that its word-for-word excerpts were "fair use" under the copyright laws, but it is unlikely that the Court would have reached that conclusion had it acknowledged any murmur from the First Amendment.[868]

See also: AUTHORS AND INVENTORS.

corporal punishment in schools, *see:* schools, corporal punishment in

corporate records, *see:* search and seizure: corporate records

corporations   Like political parties, corporations are a major source of power left untouched in the Constitution. Though thousands of cases have brought corporations before the Supreme Court—they are, after all, the ones with the money to litigate—the Court has rarely had occasion to dwell on their constitutional status. Corporations are given life by the government (they must be chartered either by a state or by Congress), but they are not thereafter the government's plaything. To the contrary, they are PERSONS, Chief Justice Morrison R. Waite said in 1886. The issue was never argued: Waite told the attorneys before ORAL ARGUMENT they needn't argue the point, since the Court had made up its mind.[1799] Defined as persons, corporations gain protection of both DUE PROCESS and EQUAL PROTECTION. This single ruling was the basis on which the Court would build its doctrine of ECONOMIC DUE PROCESS. Corporations are not, however, CITIZENS (except, strangely, for purposes of DIVERSITY JURISDICTION) and are not entitled to the protection of the PRIVILEGES AND IMMUNITIES Clauses.[1579] Neither are they entitled to certain provisions of the BILL OF RIGHTS. For example, the right against SELF-INCRIMINATION does not pertain to corporations, which may be compelled to turn over their books and records in criminal investigations,[2197] even if the records would incriminate the person with custody of them.[2231] They do have FIRST AMENDMENT rights, though, and the states may not prevent them from spending money to influence elections independent of candidates;[667] however, Congress and the states may impose some limitations on their right to spend money directly on candidates themselves.[98] On one occasion, the Court held that because a corporation was a "company town," it was performing a PUBLIC FUNCTION, and the state could not make it a crime for people to hand out religious literature on the company's private property.[1245] But for the most part, the Constitution has served more as a shield for corporations than as a means by which their power may be contested.

See also: JURISDICTION; SHOPPING CENTERS, ACCESS TO.

corruption of blood   In English law, descendants could not inherit property from a person convicted of treason. This legal disability was known as "corruption of blood." It is barred by Art. III-§3[2].

See also: ATTAINDER OF TREASON.

costs, *see:* court costs and fees

Council of Revision   Early in the deliberations of the CONSTITUTIONAL CONVENTION, Edmund Randolph of Virginia proposed that the national executive and some number of federal judges constitute a Council of Revision with authority to veto enactments of both Congress and the state legislatures. Congress and the legislatures would be empowered to override the veto. The delegates defeated Randolph's motion. The idea for a council was revived three more times. James Madison was one of its active proponents. He believed that the national executive would be too weak to resist the legislature. But a majority did not agree. The fatal defect of the plan was that it violated the SEPARATION OF POWERS. As Gouverneur Morris said: "Expositors of laws ought to have no hand in making them." Four times the delegates defeated motions to incorporate a Council of Revision in the Constitution. Madison thought its rejection was one of the convention's biggest mistakes. In hindsight he was unquestionably wrong.

counsel, assistance of   The SIXTH AMENDMENT provides that in all criminal prosecutions, the defendant shall "have the assistance of counsel for his defence." This provision was intended to overturn the English rule that felony defendants could not retain their own lawyers. It did not mean the state must pay for a lawyer for every indigent defendant. But that is what the provision has come to mean. Its modern interpretation began to unfold in 1932, in the SCOTTSBORO BOYS CASE, in which the Court held that a state violated DUE PROCESS when it failed to supply lawyers in a capital case to eight young men who lacked "both the skill and knowledge adequately to prepare" their defense in what amounted to a kangaroo-court atmosphere. Although the logic should have extended to any kind of criminal case, the Court spoke narrowly of the new right it had announced: "[I]n a capital case, where the defendant is unable to employ counsel, and is incapable adequately of making his own defense because of ignorance, feeble mindedness, illiteracy, or the like, it is the duty of the court, whether requested or not, to assign counsel for him as a necessary requisite of due process of law."

Six years later the Court extended this rule under the Sixth Amendment to any federal felony trial,[1024] but in 1942 the Court refused to extend this general Sixth Amendment right to defendants in state prosecutions.[159] For twenty years thereafter, the Court followed a "special circumstances" rule in state cases that gave free counsel only when particular circumstances warranted, including youth and immaturity of the defendant,[1382] the technical nature of the crime charged,[1597] and potential prejudice in the case.[357] Finally, in 1963 the Court recognized the indefensibility of its tortured logic and admitted that all criminal trials are too complicated for a layperson to defend against. In *Gideon v. Wainwright*, the Court held "that in our adversary system of criminal justice, any person haled into court, who is too poor to hire a lawyer, cannot be assured a fair trial unless counsel is provided for him." *Gideon* applied only to felony prosecutions. A decade later the Court declared the same right for misdemeanor prosecutions,[68] at least if the defendant is sentenced to jail.[1829] Likewise, indigent juveniles are entitled to state-supported assistance of counsel.[733] Moreover, the state must provide a lawyer to an indigent defendant seeking his first appeal of a conviction,[569] but there the string runs out. In 1974 the Court held that the state need not provide a lawyer for discretionary appeals beyond the first one or for COLLATERAL ATTACKS on the conviction,[1762] not even for inmates on death row.[1411]

The constitutional right of assistance of counsel is not limited to assistance during the trial itself. It necessarily includes the right to consult with one's lawyer and the obligation of the state not to rush the trial so that the lawyer will have sufficient time to prepare the case.[370] In a criminal proceeding counsel must be provided at ARRAIGNMENT,[846] preliminary hearing,[2193] PROBABLE CAUSE hearing to determine whether a case should go to a GRAND JURY,[425] custodial interrogation,[1927, 624, 1266, 231] LINEUPS,[2139, 754] and SENTENCING.[2065] Even parole and probation hearings may require assistance of counsel, though the right in these instances is not absolute.[2245] Once the accused has invoked the right to counsel, the police may not claim that he waived that right when they later interrogate him in custody.[1329]

Under the right to counsel, the lawyer must have adequate knowledge and experience to defend a criminal case. In short, the right includes "the *effective assistance* of counsel," whether supplied by the state[1305] or privately retained.[506] The Court has said that legal assistance is ineffective if "there is a reasonable probability that, but for counsel's unprofessional errors, the result . . . would have been different."[1970] Precisely how that can be shown remains an open question.

The right to counsel applies only to criminal prosecutions. This is understandable when the rationale is the Sixth Amendment. Under an equal protection rationale, however, the Court for a time had hinted at the possibility that indigents should not be denied a lawyer's assistance in important civil matters. But in 1981 the Court ruled that an indigent mother is not entitled to a lawyer at state expense in a hearing to determine her fitness to retain custody of her children,[1124] because absolute right to assistance of counsel depends on the likelihood of losing one's LIBERTY.

The state may not arbitrarily deny a defendant the right to be represented by a particular lawyer for whom he is willing to pay,[339] although the trial court may prohibit a lawyer from representing a certain defendant for a compelling reason—for example, if there would be a conflict of interest.[2189a] Moreover, the right to counsel does not mean that defendants must have lawyers if they choose not to; the Court has held that defendants have a constitutional right to represent themselves if they knowingly decide to do so.[637a]

Whether lawyers are paid adequately to represent defendants has not been a concern of the Court. In a controversial decision in 1989, the Court upheld a federal law requiring that all proceeds of drug crimes by "continuing crimi-

nal enterprises" be forfeited to the government, even if some of the assets are in the hands of lawyers preparing a defense. Since the law divests the defendant of legal title at the moment of the crime, the assets belong to the government, the Court said. And defendants have "no Sixth Amendment right to spend another person's money for services rendered by an attorney, even if those funds are the only way that that defendant will be able to retain the attorney of his choice."[339]

In civil cases the Court has upheld federal laws sharply limiting the amount that plaintiffs may pay their lawyers—veterans may pay no more than ten dollars to lawyers pressing their claims for service-connected disabilities[2148] and similar limits may be imposed on the fees of attorneys retained to seek redress under the Black Lung Benefits Act.[54]

See also: COURTS, ACCESS TO; INEFFECTIVE ASSISTANCE OF COUNSEL; SELF-INCRIMINATION; WEALTH CLASSIFICATION AND DISCRIMINATION.

counsel, independent, *see:* **independent counsel**

counterfeiting Under Art. I-§8[6], Congress is empowered "to provide for the punishment of counterfeiting the securities and current coin of the United States." This clause is a constitutional oddity, at least in hindsight. In 1850 the Court read the provision narrowly, saying that the clause itself confers no power on Congress to criminalize the act of circulating counterfeit coins or of possessing counterfeiting equipment.[1243] That was a peculiar conclusion, since the counterfeiting clause together with the NECESSARY AND PROPER CLAUSE should surely give Congress almost limitless power to deal with any aspect of counterfeiting. As it turned out, the narrow reading of the clause did not matter, since in the very same case the Court concluded that under its power to "coin money," given in Art.

I-§8[5], Congress has almost limitless power to deal with counterfeiting anyway. Therefore, Congress may indeed criminalize circulation and importation of counterfeit money[1243] and possession of the counterfeiter's tools and dies.[101]

county unit system Until 1963 Georgia had a unique system for nominating its governor and U.S. senators. Every county was assigned a certain number of "units," based on the number of representatives each county sent to the Georgia assembly. The candidates in primaries who won a majority in each county were entitled to the county's units. Whoever received the most units became the party's nominee in the general election. Because smaller counties had proportionately many more representatives in the assembly than large counties, a candidate could win the primary nomination by winning in several small counties, even while losing the total popular vote cast in the statewide primaries. In effect, the votes of people in large counties counted for much less than votes in smaller ones; the disparity between the largest and smallest county was 99:1. In 1963 the Supreme Court declared that the county unit system violated the EQUAL PROTECTION CLAUSE. The Court rejected the argument that the county unit system was permissible because it was modeled on the ELECTORAL COLLEGE system for electing the president; it held that the electoral college is unique and wholly unrelated to questions of voting in the states. Although this was not strictly an APPORTIONMENT case, it was a precursor of what was shortly to follow, since it incorporated a ONE PERSON, ONE VOTE standard.[797]

See also: APPORTIONMENT OF POLITICAL DISTRICTS.

court costs and fees The Court has interpreted various provisions of the Constitution—EQUAL PROTECTION, DUE PROCESS, and the SIXTH AMENDMENT's guarantee of assistance of counsel—to require courts to waive certain costs and fees for indigents. But because the Court has been leery of "opening the floodgates" to all sorts of claims that might be swept into court on the promise of free entry, it is impossible to delineate any logic to the rulings. On the ground that the states may not discriminate against the poor in appeals of criminal convictions, the Court has said that the state must provide free transcripts to indigent defendants seeking nondiscretionary appeals.[815] Likewise, the state may not require indigents to pay filing fees in divorce cases[191] or in state-mandated paternity suits.[1172] However, in most other situations, the Court has refused to waive payments required of all litigants; for example, the state need not waive fees in bankruptcy cases[1098] and in appeals to contest the denial of welfare benefits.[1542] Likewise, although indigents have a broad right to free lawyers in criminal cases, the state need not provide counsel for discretionary appeals[1762] or in state civil proceedings to terminate parental rights.[1124] Under certain circumstances, courts may require litigants to post bonds; for example, in stockholder suits against corporations the Court has upheld state requirements that stockholders pay sizable bonds before permitting their suits to proceed.[416]

The exorbitant cost of litigation, which has drawn vociferous complaints in recent years, has not commended itself to the Court as a general reason for invoking some constitutional protection against the snares of court—unless the defendant can point to a particular constitutional provision. The major example is the Court's treatment of LIBEL law. Beginning in 1964, the Court has promulgated a doctrine aimed at preventing lawsuits against the press, in part because the cost of lawsuits has a CHILLING EFFECT on FIRST AMENDMENT activities.[1472]

See also: COUNSEL, ASSISTANCE OF; COURTS, ACCESS TO; WEALTH CLASSIFICATION AND DISCRIMINATION.

Court of Appeals, U.S. The thirteen United States courts of appeals hear appeals from judgments and orders of the U.S. DISTRICT COURTS and many federal ADMINISTRATIVE AGENCIES. Twelve are located in federal geographic "circuits." Eleven circuits superintend more than one state, but no state is divided among circuits. The twelfth circuit is in Washington, D.C. The formal name of each court is the "U.S. Court of Appeals for the First Circuit (Second Circuit, and so on)." The Washington court is the Court of Appeals for the District of Columbia Circuit. The thirteenth, the COURT OF APPEALS FOR THE FEDERAL CIRCUIT, is not territorial but specialized by types of appeals. The number of judges ranges from six in the first circuit (Maine, New Hampshire, and Massachusetts) to 156 in the ninth circuit (seven western states including California). Judges are appointed for life terms by the president of the United States. The Senate must approve their appointment.

The courts of appeals are "inferior courts," in the words of Art. III-§1, which permits Congress to establish all federal courts below the Supreme Court. Under the JUDICIARY ACT of 1789, trials of certain cases were held before three-judge circuit courts consisting of two Supreme Court justices and the federal trial judge in the district. In addition to their regular duties, Supreme Court justices were required to "ride circuit," traveling from district to district within their assigned circuit, often to quite great distances. Circuit courts tried most federal criminal cases, DIVERSITY cases, and certain of the more significant civil cases. They also heard appeals from district court cases. Congress modified this system in minor ways during the nineteenth century, but as it expanded federal JURISDICTION, more and more cases were overloading the capacity of all the federal courts. The modern courts of appeals were created in 1891, and Supreme Court circuit riding was abolished.

Today the Supreme Court has discretion to review through writ of CERTIORARI the decisions of the courts of appeals, although, in practice, it can hear only a few such appeals. One of the chief reasons for the Supreme Court's decision to review a particular case is to resolve conflict over legal interpretations that develop within the various federal circuits. Precisely because the Supreme Court can hear relatively few appeals, the courts of appeals are the principal means by which the Supreme Court's constitutional rulings are given effect in the cases that later follow.

Court of Appeals for the Federal Circuit Congress created the U.S. Court of Appeals for the Federal Circuit in 1982 to hear appeals formerly heard by the U.S. COURT OF CUSTOMS AND PATENT APPEALS and the U.S. CLAIMS COURT. It is an ARTICLE III court whose judges are entitled to life tenure. Its caseload is defined by subject, not by geography, and includes appeals from decisions by the U.S. Court of International Trade, by the Patent Office in both patent and trademark disputes, and by the U.S. Claims Court.

Court of Claims, *see:* **Claims Court**

Court of Customs and Patent Appeals In 1929 Congress changed the name of the Court of Customs Appeals, established in 1909, to the U.S. Court of Customs and Patent Appeals, giving it JURISDICTION to hear appeals from the U.S. Customs Court and the Patent Office. The court was abolished in 1982 when Congress transferred its jurisdiction to the U.S. COURT OF APPEALS FOR THE FEDERAL CIRCUIT.

Court of International Trade In 1980 Congress changed the name of the U.S. Customs Court, which heard appeals from customs collectors, to the U.S. Court of International Trade and expanded its JURISDICTION to international trade cases. Appeals from this court may be taken to the U.S. COURT OF APPEALS FOR THE FEDERAL CIRCUIT.

Court of Military Appeals The U.S. Court of Military Appeals is a legislative court created by Congress to hear appeals from general courts-martial of people serving in the armed forces. Its three judges are civilians appointed for fifteen-year terms. Its decisions are not automatically appealable; however, the Supreme Court has occasionally reviewed its decisions through CERTIORARI.

See also: ARTICLE I COURTS; MILITARY COURTS AND JUSTICE.

courthouse, picketing of, *see:* **picketing**

court-martial, *see:* **military courts and justice**

court-packing plan In the mid-1930s the Supreme Court struck down, often by 5–4 votes, much of the New Deal program. On a single day in 1935, Black Monday, it declared unconstitutional the National Industrial Recovery Act, rebuked President Franklin D. Roosevelt for attempting to fire a member of the Federal Trade Commission,[958] and invalidated a federal program to relieve farm mortgagors.[1196] At a press conference, Roosevelt blasted the Court for turning the Constitution back to the "horse-and-buggy days." Relentlessly, the conservative majority continued to thwart the New Deal. In 1936 it set aside the first Agricultural Adjustment Act[289] and the Municipal Bankruptcy Act, intended to rescue small towns across the nation from a staggering load of debts.[86] In effect, wrote Justice Robert H. Jackson afterward, the Court *"narrowed* the scope of the great clauses of the Constitution granting powers to Congress. . . . Simultaneously, it *expanded* the scope of clauses which limited the power of the Congress," guided

only by the justices' personal economic predilections.

With the National Labor Relations Act and the Social Security Act yet to be tested, Roosevelt unveiled a plan shortly after his second inauguration to increase the number of judges on the Supreme Court. His proposal, soon dubbed the "court-packing plan," was simple: for every federal judge over the age of seventy, the president could appoint a new judge. The old judges would continue to serve, but the new ones would obviously dilute their voting strength. The plan provided that no more than fifteen justices could sit on the Supreme Court. Roosevelt so far had had no opportunity to appoint any justice to the Supreme Court, and since six of the nine were then over seventy, the plan would have permitted him to fill out the Court to its proposed maximum, giving him more than enough votes to sustain the New Deal legislation. In one of the major blunders of his administration, however, Roosevelt dissembled in presenting his proposal to the public. Instead of forthrightly admitting the need for new thinking on the Court, he said only that he wished to ease the burdens of the increasingly infirm justices. That alienated Justices Harlan F. Stone, Louis D. Brandeis, and Benjamin N. Cardozo, his natural allies on the Court, and prompted Chief Justice Charles Evans Hughes to write the chairman of the Senate Judiciary Committee that "the Supreme Court is fully abreast of its work" and that additions would hinder, not foster, efficiency. Although Roosevelt a month later took to the air to explain his real reasons, it was too late: significant opposition in Congress doomed his plan. But the threat succeeded. Two months after Roosevelt first proposed to pack the Court, the justices upheld four New Deal laws. With Justice Owen J. Roberts switching sides, it rejected its previous understanding of DUE PROCESS and sustained a minimum wage law for women.[2184] It went on to uphold a federal tax on firearms,[1908] the Railway Labor Act designed to promote collective bargaining,[2132] and a new farm mortgagors' relief act.[2263] And in the weeks to come, to the general relief of Roosevelt and congressional New Dealers, it upheld the National Labor Relations Act[143] and the Social Security Act.[1957] By the end of the term, Justice Willis Van Devanter retired, giving Roosevelt his first Supreme Court nominee, the liberal Hugo L. Black. Other retirements were soon announced, and Roosevelt had his Court.

courts, access to   In 1977 prisoners in North Carolina were denied access to legal reference works. For a 6–3 majority, Justice Thurgood Marshall held that the denial violated a "fundamental constitutional right of access to the courts."[204] The remedy, he said, was for the state either to provide an adequate law library or someone with sufficient legal training to assist in preparing legal papers. The right may be fundamental, but it is not as broad as it sounds. It applies mainly to appeals of criminal convictions or to suits to uphold rights while in prison. For example, the Court has held that states may not deny prisoners the right to assist each other in preparing legal papers either to review convictions[1015a] or to file civil rights suits.[2245] In a series of other cases under the EQUAL PROTECTION CLAUSE, the Court has held that defendants and prisoners may not be denied the ability to pursue appeals because of their poverty,[815, 1274] though the rule is riddled with exceptions.

Access to the courts has another constitutional meaning—the right of the press to attend and report on trials. In 1980, in *Richmond Newspapers, Inc. v. Virginia*, the Court for the first time held that there is a "presumption of openness" and that unless there can be shown "an overriding interest" in closing the courthouse doors, the public and the press have a constitutional right to attend. In 1982 the Court struck down a Massachusetts law that directed state judges to banish the public and press from the courtroom when victims of certain sexual crimes are testifying,[763] although it left open the possibility that a COMPELLING INTEREST might be shown for keeping testimony private in a particular case. Some limitations on access are possible for ancillary proceedings; if the prosecutor, defendant, and judge agree, the press and public may be barred from a pretrial hearing to determine whether certain evidence should be suppressed.[723]

See also: ACCESS TO PRISONS AND PRISONERS; COURT COSTS AND FEES; FREEDOM OF THE PRESS; GAG ORDER; PREJUDICIAL PUBLICITY; PRIOR RESTRAINT; WEALTH CLASSIFICATION AND DISCRIMINATION.

courts, congressional creation and control over   Art. III-§1 empowers Congress to create "inferior courts." The First Congress did so in the JUDICIARY ACT of 1789, which limited their JURISDICTION mostly to cases involving private disputes between citizens of different states. Congress did not grant them FEDERAL QUESTION JURISDICTION to consider issues arising under federal law. Early on, the question arose whether federal courts created by Congress may hear all the types of cases set out in Art. III-§2[1] or only those types that Congress says they can hear. The Constitution expressly provides Congress with power to alter the Supreme Court's APPELLATE JURISDICTION but is silent about whether it may limit the lower courts' jurisdiction. In a series of cases beginning as long ago as 1799, the Court has repeatedly said it can.[2078] The definitive holding that Congress has unrestricted power over the lower courts' jurisdiction came in 1850,[1853] and as recently as 1966 the Court reminded South Carolina that Congress could "limit litigation under [any federal law] to a single court in the District of Columbia" when the state argued that it should be able to contest being covered by the VOTING RIGHTS ACT in another federal court.[1913] The Court has also upheld Congress's power to regulate the lower courts' processes and remedies. For example, it sustained a law severely curbing federal DISTRICT COURTS' power to issue INJUNCTIONS in labor cases[1129] and even upheld a provision in the Emergency Price Control Act of 1942 that made it impossible for defendants in federal criminal prosecutions to assert that the regulation they were accused of violating was invalid.[2267]

See also: JUDICIAL POWER; LABOR INJUNCTION; SUPREME COURT, JURISDICTION OF.

courts, federal, *see: specific (named) courts and types*

courts, jurisdiction of, *see:* **jurisdiction**

courts, lawmaking by, *see:* **lawmaking by courts**

courts, powers of, *see:* **judicial power; jurisdiction**

courts, state, *see:* **judicial procedure in state courts; jurisdiction**

creationism, *see:* **evolution, teaching of**

crèche, *see:* **religious symbols, right to display**

credit of the United States, *see:* **borrowing power**

crimes, common law   In England many crimes were defined not by act of Parliament but by the common law courts in case-by-case prosecutions. But in 1812 the Supreme Court ruled that the only kind of federal prosecutions the Constitution permits are those spelled out in laws passed by Congress. No federal common law crimes are allowed.[953] In 1806, at the urging of a federal judge appointed by President Thomas Jefferson, a federal grand jury indicted two Hartford, Connecticut, newspaper editors for the common law crime of SEDITIOUS LIBEL for articles critical of Jefferson, because the Sedition Act of 1798 had lapsed in 1801. The authorities insisted that federal courts could exercise JURISDICTION in such cases. In an odd twist, the issue was appealed to the Supreme Court before the trial. The Court ruled that under Article III, federal courts have only the jurisdiction invested in them by Congress. If Congress has not defined a crime in a statute duly enacted, then there can be nothing for the courts to hear. Otherwise, they could limitlessly expand their jurisdiction simply by plucking "crimes" from the common law ether.

This absolute prohibition against federal common law crimes is a little less clear in the case of state common law crimes. The Court has never squarely ruled in principle against all common law prosecutions—largely, no doubt, because prosecutions for common law crimes are rare, since almost all state criminal law is statutorily defined. But two cases suggest that common law prosecutions would be unlikely to succeed: In a 1940 case, the defendant was charged with common law BREACH OF THE PEACE for proselytizing on a street corner. The Court condemned this conviction as "based on a common law concept of the most general and undefined nature."[334] In other words, the charge suffered from both OVERBREADTH and VAGUENESS. In the other case, a labor organizer was sentenced to six months in prison for common law CRIMINAL LIBEL for publishing a pamphlet condemning the actions of the police during a bitter coal miners' strike in Hazard, Kentucky. Declaring common law criminal libel unconstitutional, the Court in 1966 unanimously agreed that "since the English common law of criminal libel is inconsistent with constitutional provisions, and since no Kentucky case has redefined the crime in understandable terms, and since the law must be made on a case to case basis, the elements of the crime are so indefinite and uncertain that it should not be enforced."[87] Even in the absence of a FIRST AMENDMENT issue, it seems highly unlikely today that the Court would permit any state common law prosecution because by nature the common law is rarely spelled out clearly, and criminal acts "must be defined with appropriate definiteness."[334] Moreover, unless the common law offense somehow clearly spelled out the criminal penalties for violating it, any prosecution would violate DUE PROCESS.[239, 596]

See also: COMMON LAW; FEDERAL COMMON LAW.

crimes, infamous   The Fifth Amendment requires that to be put on trial for a capital or "other infamous crime," a person must first be indicted by a GRAND JURY. What is infamous depends on the punishment that the law permits to be meted out.[2232] In general, if a crime is punishable by imprisonment in a state prison it is infamous.[1222] This provision is applicable only to federal cases; it is one of the rare provisions in the BILL OF RIGHTS that does not apply to the states.[35]

crimes and misdemeanors, *see:* **high crimes and misdemeanors**

crimes of war, *see:* **war crimes**

criminal conspiracy, *see:* **conspiracy**

criminal law   The Constitution expressly grants Congress power to enact criminal law over a tiny list of subjects: TREASON, PIRACY, felonies on the high seas, crimes against the LAW OF NATIONS, and COUNTERFEITING. But it has long been conceded that under the NECESSARY AND PROPER CLAUSE, Congress has broad authority to create a body of federal criminal laws to support every subject over which it has the power to legislate. The states likewise have broad authority under the POLICE POWER to

outlaw antisocial acts, subject only to the constitutional limitations found mainly in Article I and the FIRST AMENDMENT.

See also: CONSPIRACY; CRIMES, COMMON LAW; CRIMES, INFAMOUS; CRIMINAL LIBEL; REGULATORY LAWS; WAR CRIMES.

criminal libel   Criminal libel was a common law crime aimed at defamatory SPEECH. In 1952 the Court upheld an Illinois law criminalizing GROUP LIBEL,[142] defamation of an entire racial or religious class of people. But criminal prosecution for libel of a particular individual as a practical matter has been constitutionally ended. In *Garrison v. Louisiana*, the Court said that criminal libel prosecutions are to be governed by the restrictive rules it had set forth in *New York Times v. Sullivan*, and in 1966 it held that the common law crime could not be prosecuted.[87]

See also: CRIMES, COMMON LAW; FREEDOM OF SPEECH *and cross references there;* LIBEL AND SLANDER.

criminal procedure, states, *see:* **procedural rights of criminal defendants**

criminal sentencing, *see:* **sentencing**

criminal syndicalism, *see:* **syndicalism**

criminal trial, place of, *see:* **trial, place of**

cross, *see:* **religious symbols, right to display**

cruel and unusual punishments, *see:* **punishment, cruel and unusual**

cults   The religion clauses of the FIRST AMENDMENT do not distinguish between old and new religions or between mainstream and "minor" or "deviant" religions. By distinguishing belief from conduct, the Supreme Court in 1879 approved a federal law banning the practice of POLYGAMY, then a tenet of Mormonism—a ruling that ultimately led the church to recant theologically.[1714] But in 1944, in *United States v. Ballard,* the Court made it clear that people were free to proselytize and even tell what the government might regard as outrageous lies. In 1982 the Court struck down a Minnesota law aimed at the Unification Church and other cults considered aberrant. The law required proselytizing sects that receive more than half their income from nonmembers to register and file reports with the state.[1123] However, in *Wisconsin v. Yoder* in 1972 the Court suggested that for some purposes older, established religions might be entitled to an exemption from generally applicable laws that would not be made available to newer sects. The Court upheld the right of the Old Order Amish to remove their children from the public schools in Pennsylvania at the age of fourteen.

See also: FREEDOM OF RELIGION.

currency, federal power over Congress's power over the currency and its power to make paper money valid for all debts derive from a variety of provisions in Art. I-§8, including the power to tax, to borrow, to regulate commerce, and to coin money. The Framers voted against extending Congress power to "emit BILLS OF CREDIT," in effect, paper money. Those with wealth in money, rather than land, feared government power to issue paper currency because the government's temptation to inflate the currency would greatly devalue their wealth. Nevertheless, in *McCulloch v. Maryland,* Chief Justice John Marshall upheld Congress's power to incorporate banks that could issue paper notes. Since that time, with one temporary exception, Congress's power has been forthrightly sustained. It may impose a prohibitory tax on state bank notes to make them unprofitable and assure a stable national currency.[2121] It may establish a federal reserve system to control currency and money supply.[668] In 1869 the court momentarily denied Congress the power to declare treasury notes LEGAL TENDER for all obligations, private or public;[909] but the very next year, in the first *Legal Tender Cases,* the Court reversed itself, and it has upheld the power from that time on.[1142, 1141] In 1935 the Court sustained Congress's ban on private contractual requirements that debts be paid in gold, forcing payment in paper currency that circulated as legal tender.[1490]

See also: BANK ACTS; BORROWING POWER.

current of commerce, *see:* **commerce, effects on; stream of commerce**

custodial interrogations, *see:* **self-incrimination**

custody, *see:* **adoption and custody; families; illegitimacy; juveniles, rights of**

D

---

dairy products, *see:* **milk; oleomargarine**

damages A money recovery in a lawsuit is termed "damages." Damages are "compensatory" when they compensate for financial losses and for intangibles such as pain and suffering. Damages are "punitive" when they are unrelated to the plaintiff's loss but are assessed to punish a defendant for acting in a particularly egregious way. Within occasional limits set by legislatures or between the parties by contract, the amount of damages to be awarded is for the judge or jury to decide; the Court has never rejected a damage award for being unconstitutionally excessive. Nor has the Court yet had to consider the constitutionality of a limitation on damages in particular classes of cases, such as medical malpractice.

But the Court has occasionally considered claims that a damage *action* should be barred or limited. In recent years the Court has fashioned a constitutional law of LIBEL, motivated in large part by the CHILLING EFFECT that damage awards would have on the FREEDOM OF SPEECH and FREEDOM OF THE PRESS. It has also created several IMMUNITY doctrines, barring damage lawsuits against different sorts of government officials. In one case dealing with private property rights, it held that one neighbor could not bring a damage suit against another who sold his property to a black family despite a RESTRICTIVE COVENANT in the deed requiring the sale to whites only. The Court held that permitting such a suit would discourage sales to blacks or force them to pay higher prices in ways that would violate the EQUAL PROTECTION CLAUSE.[133]

See also: CAUSE OF ACTION; CONSTITUTIONAL TORTS; PUNITIVE DAMAGES; REMEDY, RIGHT TO.

dancing, nude, *see:* **nudity**

danger, clear and present, *see:* **clear and present danger**

day on which they shall give their votes, *see:* **electoral college**

de facto–de jure distinction The Latin terms *de facto* and *de jure* mean "in fact" and "in law," signifying the difference between a condition that exists or persists without the law's blessing and that which is legally ratified. For example, a de jure corporation is a company that has been legally incorporated by the state. A de facto corporation is a business not technically incorporated but operating as if it had been. In other words, a de jure corporation is lawful, a de facto one is not, even though the government or courts might treat it as though it were.

The terms are used, with different connotations, in U.S. constitutional law to deal with RACIAL DISCRIMINATION and SEGREGATION. A school system segregated de jure is one in which the law intentionally requires students to be separated by race. If no law commands separation, but residential housing patterns lead to schools largely black or white, they are said to be segregated de facto. De jure segregation is unconstitutional.[249] Whether a de facto segregated school is constitutional depends on how it got that way. As the Court has said, the difference "between *de jure* segregation and so-called *de facto* segregation . . . is *purpose* or *intent* [by the school board] to segregate."[1071] However, the mere fact of racial separation in schools, without any official intent to foster or maintain it, is not sufficient to make out a violation of the EQUAL PROTECTION CLAUSE.[438]

See also: STATE ACTION.

de jure–de facto distinction, *see:* de facto–de jure distinction

death or resignation of the president, *see:* presidential succession

death penalty
In both DUE PROCESS Clauses, the Constitution itself recognizes the death penalty, in saying that a person may be deprived of life as long as in so doing the government acts with due process of law. Capital punishment was common in the colonies and in most of the states through the nineteenth century, where a conviction of murder automatically required execution. Therefore, although the death penalty has been challenged many times, the Court has held that execution, as such, is constitutional. Since nearly three-quarters of the states reenacted death penalty laws in the mid-1970s, there is a broad consensus that a death sentence is neither cruel nor unusual.[809]

But in 1972 the Court in *Furman v. Georgia* declared that the death penalty as imposed in Georgia (and by implication in most other states) was unconstitutional. Although the outcome of *Furman* spared the lives of the prisoners then awaiting execution, the Court was bitterly split 5–4, and its rationale was difficult to decipher, since every justice had an opinion and wrote one. Two justices, William J. Brennan and Thurgood Marshall, thought that capital punishment was unconstitutional under any circumstances. Three other justices, William O. Douglas, Byron R. White, and Potter Stewart—enough to make a majority to stop the executions—said that the constitutional difficulty lay in the lack of guidance to judges and juries on the circumstances under which they could sentence a murderer to death. Absolute discretion often led to discriminatory results that violated the ban on cruel and unusual punishment. But this was a reprieve, not a death knell, for capital punishment itself, and the states took the opportunity to rewrite their capital punishment laws. Beginning in 1976, new cases have appeared regularly in the Court to test the answers to four questions: (1) For what types of crimes may the death penalty be imposed? (2) On whom may it be imposed? (3) By whom may it be imposed? (4) What procedures must be followed and what kind of evidence is sufficient?

The Court has answered those questions as follows:

(1) The death penalty may be imposed only if the defendant deliberately killed another person.[618] It may not be imposed when someone is killed during a robbery or the commission of some other felony if the defendant was not the one who actually did the killing and did not intend anyone to be killed, unless he was a "major participant" in the crime and was "reckless[ly] indifferent to human life."[2053] A rapist

may not be sentenced to death if his victim did not die.[421]

(2) The insane may not be executed,[690] but a mentally retarded murderer may be.[2041] There seems to be a consensus that although children under sixteen years old may not be executed,[1599] those as young as sixteen and seventeen may be.[1942]

(3) The legislature may not make the death penalty mandatory; that is, it may not take the decision whether or not to employ it out of the hands of judge or jury.[2257] That is true no matter how heinous the crime, not even if the defendant was convicted of first-degree murder for killing an on-duty police officer[1739] or if the defendant was serving a life term without possibility of parole when he committed a murder in prison.[1979] The decision need not be for jury; the legislature may saddle the judge alone with that responsibility.[1928] However, whether judge or jury, the sentencing authority must always have the opportunity to consider mitigating circumstances. But the legislature may require the jury to bring back a death sentence if after considering the circumstances the jurors find at least one aggravating and no mitigating circumstances.[176] Likewise, the legislature may make the sentence mandatory whenever the jury concludes that the aggravating circumstances outweigh the mitigating ones.[214] However, neither the prosecutor nor the judge may suggest to the jury that in deliberating on a death sentence the final decision for determining whether such a penalty is appropriate lies with someone else, such as an appeals court.[308]

(4) The death penalty may not be determined by the jury at the same time it is deliberating on the question of guilt. There must be a separate proceeding to consider evidence about the circumstances of the killing and the defendant's character and behavior. The legislature must set out the types of aggravating circumstances that the jury may consider.[809] Permitting the jury to impose death if the de-

fendant has acted in an "especially heinous, atrocious or cruel" manner is unconstitutionally vague,[1275] although not if the state court has interpreted such language to require proof that the defendant inflicted mental distress or physical abuse on his victim.[2149] The jury may consider the future dangerousness of the convicted defendant,[1043] and the defendant must be permitted to bring to the jury's attention "any aspect of [his or her] character or record and any of the circumstances of the offense."[1179] Certain circumstances, like mental retardation, require special instructions to the jury.[1599] Finally, statistical evidence that death sentences are far more likely to be meted out to blacks than whites is not sufficient to overturn a particular death sentence.[1282] The defendant must show that racial animosity was a motive in the jury's decision toward him in particular.

Since 1976 hundreds of death-sentence appeals have come to the Court, most of them through petitions for HABEAS CORPUS. The rules governing such appeals have permitted each defendant to contest over and over again in federal court the constitutionality of state proceedings. The result has been a flood of petitions and considerable delay in the carrying out of death sentences. Determined to limit access to federal courts to renew challenges to death sentences, the Court has been limiting the reach of habeas corpus, which may soon be foreclosed altogether except in rare cases.

See also: COUNSEL, ASSISTANCE OF; HARMLESS ERROR; PROPORTIONALITY OF SENTENCE; PUNISHMENT, CRUEL AND UNUSUAL; RETROACTIVITY; RIGHTS, WAIVER OF; STATISTICAL EVIDENCE, USE OF.

death tax, *see:* **estate tax**

debt of the United States The Constitution imposes no limits on the indebtedness of the United States. For years certain politicians have pleaded for a balanced budget amendment, although most versions would not truly outlaw imbalances but only make slightly more difficult the ability to overspend. Constitutionally, control over U.S. indebtedness remains where it has always been, with Congress and the president, under Art I-§8[1,2]. The one major political attempt in recent years to thwart the irresistible lure of deficit spending foundered on a SEPARATION OF POWERS problem. Under the Gramm-Rudman-Hollings Act, Congress, with considerable presidential encouragement, tried to consign the power to make ultimate budget cuts to the comptroller general of the United States. The Court held that Congress might have entrusted the decision to the president but not to the comptroller general.[211] Since Congress does not trust the president, and vice versa, we shall have to rely on self-restraint.

debtor-creditor relations, *see:* **bankruptcy; repossession**

decision   As in boxing, a decision in court simply means who won, not why. A decision is the outcome of the case from the litigants' perspective, as settled by the votes of the judges. The reasons for the decision are in a court's OPINION. A decision is usually embodied in a JUDGMENT, final order, or decree—a written statement directing a lower court to take some action (for example, dismissing the case); or binding the legal status of the parties (granting an order of adoption); or directing the parties to do or refrain from doing something (pay alimony). The precedential value of a case lies in the HOLDING found in its opinion, not in its decision. For example, in MARBURY V. MADISON, the decision was that William Marbury's case had to be dismissed because it could not be heard by the Supreme Court. The holding in the opinion was that a section of the Judiciary Act of 1789 conflicted with Article III of the Constitution. Because the Court's holding did

not override Marbury's right to his commission, the decision did not prevent Marbury, at least in theory, from going elsewhere for relief.

Declaration of Independence   The Declaration of Independence is the founding document and was the essential act of American union. In Jefferson's masterly and stirring invocation of natural rights and equality, the Declaration persuasively stated a political theory of the social compact on which the drafters and interpreters of the Constitution would later draw. Although its fire has not dimmed, it has no legal force.

declaration of war, *see:* **war, declaration of**

declaratory judgment   A declaratory judgment determines the legal rights in a dispute before one of the parties has suffered an actual injury. Until the 1930s, the Court suggested that a dispute could not be a CASE OR CONTROVERSY unless the plaintiff could claim to have been harmed in some way.[1161] Suppose the holders of a long-term lease on commercial real estate wish to tear down an auditorium on the property and build a new one. In a purely tentative discussion with one of the owners, the lessee broaches the plan and the answer is, "Well, I'm not sure you can do that. You might have to check with all the owners." On the basis of that answer and without formally asking for permission to build a new building, the holders sue the owners for a declaration of their legal right to proceed. In 1927 the Court dismissed such a suit, saying that it did not present a real controversy.[2227] But it seems obvious that if the lessees had formally requested and been denied permission to build, the parties would have had a real controversy. It makes little sense to say that the lessees can determine their legal rights only by bringing in a wrecking ball, thus risking damage and injunction suits.

In 1933 the Court reversed course, agreeing

that actual damage need not be present for a suit to present a justiciable controversy.[1422] In 1934 Congress enacted the Declaratory Judgments Act, empowering federal courts to grant declaratory judgments, and the Court upheld it in 1937.[18] The constitutional requirement of an actual controversy remains. The act may not be used to obtain ADVISORY OPINIONS from federal courts. It merely makes it possible to sue at a more timely moment. But not every future dispute can be resolved with a declaratory judgment. Principles of COMITY may require one court to abstain from interfering with the actions of another. For example, the Court has said that if you are currently being prosecuted in a state court for violating a law, you may not ask a federal court to declare it unconstitutional.[1602] But if state prosecution is not pending, but is merely being threatened, then you may seek declaratory relief in federal court, as long as you can show "a genuine threat of enforcement."[1955]

See also: ABSTENTION DOCTRINE; JUDICIAL POWER; RIPENESS; STANDING.

defamation, *see:* **libel and slander**

defendant's procedural rights, *see:* **procedural rights of criminal defendants**

Defense Department, *see:* **armed forces**

defense in civil actions, *see:* **cause of action**

delegation doctrine   Delegation is the granting to one branch of government a power vested by the Constitution in another branch, an act that seems to violate SEPARATION OF POWERS. The delegation doctrine chiefly limits the bestowal of LEGISLATIVE POWER on the executive branch. Art. I-§1[1] says that "all legislative powers herein granted shall be vested in a Congress." If Congress must have all of them, then it seems inescapable that no one else may have any. "That the legislative power of Con-

gress cannot be delegated is, of course, clear,"[1861] the Court said in 1932, echoing many other such pronouncements, all of them untrue. Legislative power has been continuously delegated throughout American history because Congress has neither the time nor resources to legislate the details of its policies and programs. But the reason Congress so persistently delegates lies deeper than this: in creating agencies to carry out government policy, Congress can scarcely avoid conferring power on them to act and to exercise powers that both the legislative and executive branches can claim.[2168] Moreover, as the Court recognized as early as 1813, not to give the executive leeway in enforcing the laws would leave little room to administer public policy.[2027] Congress frequently tells the executive to carry out a policy only when certain events occur and leaves it to the executive to determine when they have occurred. To take a homely example: a city council may authorize the Public Works Department to post signs requiring cars to be kept off the streets "when heavy snow is likely" and leave it to the department to determine the occasions that merit the posting.

As long as Congress prescribes "an intelligible principle to which [the agencies are] directed to conform"[994] to "fill in the gaps" of general policies, the delegation will be upheld. So understood, the delegation doctrine is the major prop of administrative government, permitting most of the detailed federal law, from the tax code to environmental cleanup policies, to be devised not by Congress but by federal agencies. Despite its frequent mouthings to the contrary, the Court almost always sustains such delegations. In 1897 the Court approved a law permitting the commissioner of Internal Revenue to determine the kind of labels to be placed on packages of oleomargarine,[1092] and tens of thousands of delegations and scores of cases later Congress is still busily delegating its powers.

The Court has been extraordinarily lax in holding Congress to the task of prescribing intelligible principles to guide executive policy makers. It has, for example, upheld the power of the Interstate Commerce Commission to approve railroad mergers that are in the "public interest"[1465] and the power of the Federal Communications Commission to license broadcasters according to "public convenience, interest and necessity."[1425] Other approved verbal formulas with no apparent standards are "just and reasonable,"[1993] "unfair methods of competition,"[650] and "excessive profits."[1163] In short, Congress may delegate even "the need to exercise judgment on matters of policy."[1367] In 1963 the Court upheld a law giving the secretary of the interior absolute discretion in allocating water to southwestern states during shortages.[69]

On two occasions the Court has struck down federal laws when Congress tried to delegate power to private groups. In the SICK CHICKEN CASE the Court in 1935 overturned the National Industrial Recovery Act in part because Congress had given the power to private trade groups to draw up codes of fair competition. Said Justice Benjamin N. Cardozo, "This is delegation running riot." The next year the Court struck down the Bituminous Coal Conservation Act because coal companies were bound to follow wage and hour regulations devised by producers and their employees,[353] even though the Court did not say it was overruling an earlier decision permitting the American Railway Association, a private trade association, to set the height of "draw bars" on freight cars.[1936] In a third case, Congress had given the president power to decide on his own initiative whether and when to ban from INTERSTATE COMMERCE the shipment of any oil that the states had said could not be taken from storage.[1562] Here, the Court said, Congress had failed to guide the president's actions. In dissent, Justice Cardozo said that the majority's reason made no sense, since the only question

was one of timing. In the face of all the other standardless delegations upheld, this case seems, in retrospect, merely one of the many instances of the pre–New Deal Court's tongue-lashing of Franklin D. Roosevelt. Despite the general prohibition against delegation to private groups, the Court has upheld delegation to private entities to carry out the power of EMINENT DOMAIN for a public use.[155]

Although it is hard to imagine any possible broader delegations, the Court has said that in the area of FOREIGN AFFAIRS, in which the president has broad independent powers, Congress may hand over a blank check.[505] Likewise, the Court has approved sweeping delegations during wartime, including the power of the secretary of the treasury to impose a tax[847] and the military to impose a curfew on American citizens.[925] And in 1989, putting an end to speculation that the Court might be ready to get tough, the Court approved the delegation of legislative power to an agency of the federal judiciary, the U.S. Sentencing Commission, to determine a scheme of federal sentences, in the face of an explicit command of the Constitution that the JUDICIAL POWER extends only to CASES OR CONTROVERSIES.[1367]

The supposed ban on delegation is a constitutional problem only among the branches of the federal government. In a 1982 case, though, the Supreme Court invalidated a Massachusetts law empowering churches to block the issuing of liquor licenses to restaurants within five hundred feet of their property. Assigning veto power over municipal affairs to a church runs afoul of the ESTABLISHMENT CLAUSE.[1122]

See also: ADMINISTRATIVE AGENCIES AND BUREAUCRATIC GOVERNMENT; EXECUTIVE POWER.

demonstrators and demonstrations A vexing problem for democratic and constitutional government is the degree to which demonstrators' demands to use public spaces for marches and protests must be permitted to overcome the public's desire for peace and quiet. Since

1939 the Court has insisted that government is not merely an owner of public streets and parks with power to close them at any time. "[T]hey have immemorially been held in trust for the use of the public and, time out of mind, have been used for purposes of assembly, communicating thoughts between citizens, and discussing public questions. . . . The privilege may be regulated in the interest of all; . . . but it must not, in the guise of regulation, be abridged or denied."[838] In the common interest, a city may require marchers to obtain a permit, but the PERMIT SYSTEM must not discriminate among groups on the basis of their views.[479]

The mass demonstrations in the civil rights era of the 1960s led the Court to narrow the government's justifications for forbidding or stopping public marches. In 1963 the Court overturned convictions of 187 black students who marched peacefully along the grounds of the South Carolina State House to protest racial discrimination. A large crowd gathered. The police ordered the students to disperse, and then arrested them when they refused. Justice Potter Stewart said for the Court majority that a state may not "make criminal the peaceful expression of unpopular views."[603] Likewise, when Chicago police ordered a "peaceful and orderly procession" dispersed because "onlookers became unruly," the Court overturned the resulting convictions. The marchers were entitled to press their claims for desegregation of the public schools as long as they themselves were not violent.[811] And in cases stemming from a demonstration by two thousand students in Baton Rouge to protest the jailing of fellow students arrested for picketing segregated lunch counters, the Court said that police may not use BREACH OF PEACE laws to shut down even mass assemblies, on the pretext that violence might occur, if the marchers were peaceful.[477]

These principles applied in full force to the notorious Skokie demonstrations by American Nazis in 1978. Skokie, Illinois, home to many Jewish survivors of the Holocaust, passed several laws designed to block the Nazis from marching. The lower courts invalidated the ordinances, which mandated insurance, forced the marchers to secure permits, prohibited distribution of hate literature, and banned the wearing of "military-style" uniforms. The Supreme Court refused to review a ruling of the U.S. Court of Appeals for the Seventh Circuit that all the ordinances were unconstitutional.[1888] Notwithstanding the wide freedom that political protesters enjoy, municipal authorities retain the power to limit the TIME, PLACE, AND MANNER of demonstrations if they do so in an evenhanded way. They may also curb or even prevent demonstrations in areas not traditionally considered a PUBLIC FORUM.

See also: FREEDOM OF ASSEMBLY; HOSTILE AUDIENCE; PICKETING; VAGUENESS; VAGRANCY.

denaturalization, *see:* **immigration and naturalization**

departments of the federal government, *see:* **executive departments**

deportation Few federal powers that touch on the lives of individuals living in the American community are as immune from JUDICIAL REVIEW as Congress's power over deportation. Aliens—even those who have long resided in the United States—have no constitutional right to remain. Congress has complete discretion over what classes of aliens are deportable and under what conditions.[688] The Court has held that this power even permits Congress to make its grounds for deportation retroactive, so that an alien who committed an act before Congress said that it was impermissible may later be deported for having done it. Because deportation is not considered PUNISHMENT, the EX POST FACTO CLAUSE does not apply.[1145] With one exception, such rights as aliens do possess to contest deportation orders are theirs only by virtue of federal laws that Congress has given and that Congress may take away. The exception is that aliens are entitled to PROCE-DURAL DUE PROCESS, and the government therefore may not order an alien deported without first holding a HEARING before an impartial tribunal,[2251] although it need not be a court.[2269, 1103] However, anyone subjected to a deportation order who claims to be a citizen is entitled to a judicial hearing.[1478]

See also: ALIENS; CITIZENS AND CITIZENSHIP; EXCLUSIONARY RULE; EXILE; EXPATRIATION; IMMIGRATION AND NATURALIZATION.

deprivation   The DUE PROCESS Clauses of the FIFTH and FOURTEENTH AMENDMENTS say that "no person shall be deprived of life, LIB-ERTY, or PROPERTY without due process of law." No other provisions of the Constitution have induced as much judicial commentary as these, but the word "deprivation" has been little discussed until recently. Historically, the Due Process Clauses were understood to bar the state from imprisoning or executing you, or seizing your property, without trial. In addition, some forms of liberty may not be impeded by the state even *with* a trial. All such cases have involved deliberate actions of the state. But a modern state, operating many enterprises and acting through millions of employees and agents, can do many things that diminish the value of your property, interfere with your liberty, or even take your life, without intending to do so—as for example might happen if you chanced to collide with a police car in the middle of a high-speed chase. If the police damage your vehicle, have you been deprived of property without due process of law? Certainly *something* has happened to your property, and no "process of law," due or otherwise, has been followed.

In 1981 the Court held that when a prison employee negligently lost some goods a prisoner had ordered by mail, the state had deprived him of property.[1571] The effect of the holding was small, since the Court went on to say that the loss was not an unconstitutional deprivation: the prisoner's right to file a lawsuit to recover the value of the goods was as much process as was due. But the decision left open the possibility that countless acts of negligence could suddenly become constitutional problems. For example, if a state law barred you from suing the police for wrecking your car, the logic of the Court's ruling would indeed mean that you had been deprived of property without due process, and litigants could clog the federal courts with suits under the CIVIL RIGHTS laws. In 1986 the Court changed its mind. In one case, a prison employee negligently left a pillow on the stairs and a prisoner slipped and fell. In another, prison officials negligently neglected to safeguard a prisoner who had warned them that his life was in danger. In both cases, the Court denied relief.[513, 517] Justice William H. Rehnquist said that negligent injuries are not deprivations in the constitutional sense.

See also: ENTITLEMENTS; GOVERNMENT, AFFIRMATIVE OBLIGATIONS OF; PROCEDURAL DUE PROCESS; PROCESS RIGHTS; PROCESS THAT IS DUE.

desegregation, *see:* **segregation and integration**

design protection   Some but not all types of designs may be patented. The question arose whether state unfair competition laws could be used by designers and manufacturers against pirating competitors, when their designs were not eligible for patent protection under federal law. In 1964 the Court ruled that if Congress fails to grant patentability to something, the states may not do so through laws that in effect give monopoly protection.[447, 1835a]

See also: PREEMPTION.

desuetude, *see:* **prosecutorial discretion**

detention, *see:* **preventive detention**

dictum　From the Latin phrase *obiter dictum,* meaning "that which is said in passing," a dictum is a judge's remark or even a conclusion that is unnecessary to reach the decision in a case. It is unlike a HOLDING, the answer to the precise question raised in the case. Opinions are full of dicta. Over the years, critics and purists have frequently dismissed passages in the Court's lengthy opinions as "mere dictum." But whether a particular chain of reasoning is necessary to reach a conclusion is often difficult to ascertain, and disputation over the point is just as often metaphysical. Many times what appears to be dictum, what may very well be dictum, will become the basis for the Court's holding in a subsequent case. Dictum can be a powerful hint, and readers of decisions ignore it at their peril.

die, right to, *see:* **right to die**

diplomatic immunity　Diplomatic immunity is the federal policy that prohibits civil suits and even many kinds of criminal prosecutions against foreign diplomats residing in the United States. The immunity is granted by congressional enactment and judicial interpretation of international law; nothing in the Constitution requires that the parking ticket of the ambassador's husband be legally unenforceable. To the contrary, Art. III-§2[1,2] empowers federal courts to hear cases affecting ambassadors, public ministers, and consuls. The Supreme Court has ruled that unless Congress prohibits, even state courts may hear such cases.[1523]

See also: IMMUNITY FROM SUIT; ORIGINAL JURISDICTION.

diplomatic recognition　The president alone has the power to recognize a particular government as the lawful government of a foreign nation. This power stems from the grant in Art. III-§2[1] of the power to "receive ambassadors and other public ministers." Presidents have repeatedly exercised the power, and the Court has reaffirmed the power in the occasional challenges that have reached it.[1630] The power to recognize includes the power to refuse to recognize or even to withdraw official recognition. The Supreme Court refused to consider the merits of a suit challenging President Jimmy Carter's decision to recognize the People's Republic of China in Beijing and to withdraw recognition of the government in Taiwan.[773]

See also: EXECUTIVE AGREEMENT; FOREIGN AFFAIRS POWER; TREATIES AND TREATY POWER.

direct taxes　According to Madison, when a delegate asked his colleagues the meaning of direct taxation, "no one answered." History seems to have answered that direct taxes are those imposed on land. Art. I-§10[4] says that Congress may raise revenue through CAPITATION (including, in 1787, taxes on slaves) and other direct taxes only by apportioning them according to each state's population. The provision was included at the insistence of southern states, who feared that northern interests would overtax them. A direct tax raised from a state with ten percent of the American population may be no more than ten percent of the total tax collected. (Under the THREE-FIFTHS RULE, slaves were counted as three-fifths of a person, thus minimizing the total direct taxes that could have been collected from slave states.)

There are many practical difficulties in arriving at formulas for apportioning direct taxation, and the impact of the tax on particular individuals could be quite uneven. To collect a tax on the value of land, for example, Congress could not simply demand that people pay one dollar for every thousand dollars of assessed value, because that would result in a payment bearing no relation to the population of each state. Instead, Congress would first have to establish a formula to raise from each state the appropriate total tax. A further political problem would then arise, since the total value of land is not held equally within or among the states. Relatively few people might hold most of the land in a large state, and they would therefore have to pay a higher valuation than residents of a smaller state in which landholding is more dispersed.

Given these difficulties, the Court as early as 1796 set a precedent limiting "direct" to mean property taxes and allowing Congress to avoid apportioning all other taxes. In the 1796 case, Congress laid a duty on carriages. The Court said it was an indirect tax,[971] as three-quarters of a century later it also called a tax on currency issued by state banks an indirect tax.[2121] For a time beginning in 1895, the Court persisted in the folly of labeling the INCOME TAX a direct tax,[1649] making its collection virtually impossible. This action prompted Congress to propose and the states to ratify the SIXTEENTH AMENDMENT. Today the problem of direct taxes has withered, since Congress imposes no capitation or property taxes, relying instead on income taxes to raise federal revenues. Other federal taxes, like estate taxes and excise taxes on gasoline, are indirect.

See also: ESTATE TAX; TAXATION, CONSTITUTIONAL LIMITATIONS ON.

disability of president and vice president, *see:* presidential succession

disabled, rights of   Rights for the disabled come from enactments of Congress and the state legislatures, not directly from the Constitution. The Court has never read the EQUAL PROTECTION CLAUSE to require STRICT SCRUTINY of laws that have the effect of discriminating against the disabled, nor have the justices seen in the Constitution any affirmative obligation to provide special benefits to the disabled.

See also: CIVIL COMMITMENT; GOVERNMENT, AFFIRMATIVE OBLIGATIONS OF; HANDICAP DISCRIMINATION; MENTAL RETARDATION.

disbarment, *see:* lawyers

discoveries, *see:* writings and discoveries

discovery in civil proceedings   "Discovery" is the name for the procedures by which litigants may gather evidence from each other to present their cases at trial. The Federal Rules of Civil Procedure provide for expansive discovery, including most of their adversaries' documents and answers to questions put orally, if not covered by a rule of EVIDENTIARY PRIVILEGE. Because most evidence is covered by those rules, the Constitution has been little resorted to either for claims that the pretrial process invades some PRIVACY or other interest or that the rules do not permit sweeping enough discovery. When occasional claims arise, the Court has been loathe to interfere. For example, it held that the FIRST AMENDMENT does not foreclose discovery into the state of mind of a television news producer, including his thoughts, opinions, and conversations with colleagues, in producing a documentary that was the basis of a libel suit.[911]

See also: DISCOVERY IN CRIMINAL PROCEEDINGS; REPORTER'S PRIVILEGE.

discovery in criminal proceedings   Unlike civil trials, criminal prosecutions are hedged by specific constitutional limitations, and the sweeping discovery process available in civil trials is therefore considerably more limited in the criminal area. Moreover, the FIFTH AMENDMENT right against SELF-INCRIMINATION means that discovery in criminal cases is mostly a one-way street, from prosecutor to defendant. In 1977 the Court said that "there is no general constitutional right to discovery in a criminal trial."[2170] The Federal Rules of

Criminal Procedure list the types of information the defendant is entitled to see, including statements the defendant has made and reports of health tests and scientific examinations. Aside from these rules, which apply only in federal prosecutions, DUE PROCESS requires the prosecution, on defense request, to disclose evidence favorable to the defendant that bears on guilt or punishment. This type of evidence is known as *Brady* material[220] and, ordinarily, it must be specifically requested. But in 1976, in *United States v. Agurs,* the Court set out a three-part rule for evidence that must be turned over to the defendant: (1) any evidence obviously helpful to the defendant—a witness who says someone else did the crime, for example—even if the defense lawyer has not asked for it; (2) any *Brady* material specifically requested; (3) any knowledge that testimony presented at trial was perjured. A prosecutor refusing or failing to turn over this information risks having the conviction reversed. The main question is whether the evidence is material to the defendant's case, not what the prosecutor's motives were in withholding the information.[1895] Prosecutors may seek certain types of non-incriminating pretrial information from defendants, but they must be evenhanded in doing so. For example, before trial the state may demand a list of the names of witnesses on whom a criminal defendant intends to rely. But the state, in turn, must tell the defense before trial who it might call to rebut them.[2154]

See also: PROCEDURAL RIGHTS OF CRIMINAL DEFENDANTS; PROSECUTORIAL MISCONDUCT.

discrete and insular minorities   In 1938, in *United States v. Carolene Products Company,* Justice Harlan F. Stone in the celebrated footnote four suggested that the Court might have to examine more closely than others the claims of certain "discrete and insular minorities" that they are being treated unconstitutionally. The case itself concerned the constitutionality of a federal law prohibiting companies from shipping "filled milk," skimmed milk mixed with non-milk fats. The Court used it to announce the RATIONAL BASIS test, meaning that the Court would presume state laws valid and overturn them only if shown to be wholly irrational. Stone's footnote was an aside to suggest that the PRESUMPTION of constitutionality might not apply if the law discriminated against certain minorities against whom considerable prejudice exists. In general, the minorities to whom Stone referred are racial and ethnic groups who have been barred from political participation. The idea of strictly scrutinizing laws affecting racial minorities finally bore fruit in 1954 in BROWN V. BOARD OF EDUCATION. In the 1970s the Court began to examine legislation that, it was claimed, discriminated against many other categories of people. In two instances, the Court found a SUSPECT CLASSIFICATION that required STRICT SCRUTINY—alienage and ethnic origins. Laws affecting still other groups of people, the Court has said, are entitled to a heightened, though lesser scrutiny than those affecting people by race.

See also: EQUAL PROTECTION OF THE LAWS.

discrimination   In the nonpejorative sense, discrimination is the purpose of most law. Law is designed to discriminate among good or useful conduct on the one hand and harmful conduct on the other. Often it is necessary to draw a line by pointing to particular sets of persons who will be permitted or not permitted to engage in the conduct. For example, drinking may be harmful if engaged in by certain people; the law says that the young may not drink. Discrimination per se is not unconstitutional. Discrimination against certain people, based on certain characteristics, and for certain reasons, may well be. A major part of the Court's workload during the past forty years has been devoted to sorting all this out.

disease, *see:* **blood samples; medication and surgery, forced; vaccination**

disorderly conduct, *see:* **breach of the peace**

disparaging of rights, *see:* **Ninth Amendment**

dissenting opinion   As its name suggests, a dissenting opinion records the disagreement of a judge with the DECISION in the case. If the judge agrees with the decision but not the reasons for it, he may record his own thinking in a CONCURRING OPINION. Chief Justice Charles Evans Hughes once wrote that dissenting opinions appeal "to the brooding spirit of the law, to the intelligence of a future day, when a later decision may possibly correct the error into which the dissenting judge believes the Court to have been betrayed." The early days of the Supreme Court saw few dissenting opinions: Chief Justice John Marshall wrote only one, in *Sturges v. Crowninshield.* But during the past hundred years, and especially in the modern era, dissenting opinions have been plentiful, at times appearing in nearly three-quarters of all decided cases. Some justices are known to history as Great Dissenters for the acerbity of their disagreements and the acuity of their vision. These include the first John Marshall Harlan at the turn of the century, for his scathing denunciation of the doctrine of SEPARATE BUT EQUAL, and Oliver Wendell Holmes and Louis D. Brandeis for their determined opposition to prosecutions for political advocacy. Mere numbers of dissents are not the basis of the label. In thirty-two years on the bench,

Holmes dissented in seventy-two cases; in only seventeen years on the bench, Chief Justice Warren Burger dissented III times.

district courts   United States district courts are the trial courts of the federal judiciary. Under its Article III power to establish INFERIOR COURTS, Congress divided the United States into ninety-seven federal districts and authorized a total of 575 federal district judges to serve in the courts of those districts. Like all ARTICLE III judges, federal district judges serve for life. Each district is contained within a state; no district overlaps state boundaries. Every state has at least one federal district; some states have more than one—New York has four. Initially, the district courts had extremely modest ORIGINAL JURISDICTION, confined in the main to admiralty and maritime cases. Today the federal district courts are vested with jurisdiction to hear almost every type of federal case allowable; the district courts hear both civil and criminal cases involving federal questions and state issues that arise under DIVERSITY OF CITIZENSHIP. Unlike the U.S. COURTS OF APPEALS, which hear cases in panels of three judges, district court trials are presided over by individual judges who are responsible for moving along every aspect of the cases assigned to them. Also unlike appellate judges, the U.S. district judge is frequently involved in assessing the facts of the cases presented. A district judge's FINDING of fact is ordinarily not appealable, whereas the judge's rulings of law are appealable to the courts of appeals.

District of Columbia, constitutional status of
Under Art. I-§8[17], Congress was given exclusive legislative control over one hundred square miles to be ceded by one or more states for the capital of the United States. George Washington brokered the deal by which Virginia and Maryland ceded land on either side of the Potomac River. Congress assumed con-

trol on February 27, 1801, although in 1846 the Virginia side was returned. Until 1871 Congress was the sole lawmaker. After a disastrous three-year experiment in home rule, Congress turned administration over to a commission of three appointed by the president, a regime that lasted for nearly a century, until 1974, when home rule was instituted anew.

Under the FOURTEENTH AMENDMENT, residents of the District of Columbia are U.S. citizens (the issue was in some doubt until then, since they were not citizens of any state). District residents have no voting representation in Congress and until ratification of the TWENTY-THIRD AMENDMENT in 1961 could not vote for president. A constitutional amendment to give congressional representation to the District of Columbia was proposed in 1978 but was not ratified. District residents are covered by the BILL OF RIGHTS and every other constitutional guarantee.[329] From 1805 until 1949 the District of Columbia was not considered a state for purposes of DIVERSITY OF CITIZENSHIP,[908] although it was considered a state in relation to treaties.[740] But the Court changed its mind after Congress amended the jurisdictional laws, and today residents are considered as though they live in a state for diversity purposes.[1435]

districting, *see:* **apportionment of political districts**

diversity jurisdiction   Art. III-§2[1] permits federal courts to hear cases between citizens of different states or between citizens of a state and foreigners. This is known as diversity of citizenship or, more commonly, diversity jurisdiction. Unlike other types of cases, those arising under diversity jurisdiction depend on the citizenship of the parties and involve claims of state law. The usual rationale for this odd-seeming JURISDICTION is to prevent hostility toward out-of-staters in the home courts of a state citizen. The federal courts have exercised

diversity jurisdiction ever since 1789. Today diversity jurisdiction is lodged in the U.S. DISTRICT COURTS. In 1949 the Supreme Court agreed that diversity jurisdiction covers not only citizens of the states but residents of U.S. territories and the District of Columbia.[1435] In 1806 Chief Justice John Marshall said that when there were more than two parties to litigation, each of the parties must come from a different state to sue in federal court.[1968] But in 1967 the Court ruled that this was not a constitutional requirement; as long as any two adverse parties are citizens of different states, their suit may be heard in federal court.[1950] In 1809 Marshall said also that since corporations cannot be citizens, they cannot sue or be sued in federal courts merely through the diversity jurisdiction.[120] That rationale has undergone several metamorphoses. Today the rule is that a corporation, though not itself a citizen, is treated fictionally as a citizen of the state in which it is incorporated and in which it has its principal place of business, so that it may sue or be sued in federal court except by or against citizens of that state.[2108] The rule for unincorporated organizations, such as partnerships, is different: the citizenship of every partner must be taken into account to determine whether diversity is available.[2108] Not every case theoretically within the jurisdiction is heard; the Court long ago said that federal courts may not hear domestic relations disputes and probate matters.[122, 242]

Diversity jurisdiction cases must be decided under applicable state law, not under a FEDERAL COMMON LAW. Based on an 1842 ruling in *Swift v. Tyson* by Justice Joseph Story, for nearly a century the decisions of federal courts were frequently at odds with the settled law of the states in which they sat. Whether a litigant won or lost a case could depend on which court the case was in. Finally, in 1938 the Supreme Court in *Erie Railroad v. Tompkins* overturned the old rule and declared that federal courts must use applicable state law to decide diversity cases. This common-sense rule masks many difficulties, however. It ends an era of freewheeling lawmaking by federal courts intent on developing their own rules of commercial law, negligence, agency, and the like. But because there may be no settled state law governing issues raised in a particular lawsuit, the federal trial judges must now try to guess at what they think the state law would be. In effect, therefore, the ERIE RULE creates another form of the double-law problem.

Diversity cases constitute a substantial portion of federal caseloads. For years advocates of procedural reform have urged Congress to eliminate the jurisdiction altogether. So far Congress has refused to strip the federal courts of their oldest jurisdiction.

See also: STATE LAW, MEANING OF.

division of powers, *see:* **separation of powers**

divorce   Divorce is a legal concern of the states. Standards and procedures for obtaining or resisting a divorce are solely within the discretion of each state, except that the EQUAL PROTECTION CLAUSE forbids state courts from refusing to hear divorce cases because the applicants cannot afford the filing fees.[191] When both spouses live in the same state, no other constitutional difficulties arise. When one spouse travels to another state to seek an ex parte divorce under the preferential laws of that state, however, serious problems under the FULL FAITH AND CREDIT Clause can create legal havoc. Suppose the wife "moves" to Nevada, which has a six-week residency requirement, secures a divorce, remarries in Nevada, and returns to North Carolina, which promptly prosecutes her for bigamy. Must the North Carolina courts recognize the Nevada decree when she pleads her divorce in defense to the charge?

In such a situation, the Supreme Court in 1942 said that the divorce was binding.[2214] The Court said that it would assume the Nevada domicile was bona fide. Justice Robert H. Jackson vigorously dissented, pointing out that by giving "extra-territorial effect" to any Nevada divorce decree, regardless of whether the other spouse got notice or could respond to the suit, the Court's decision "repeals the divorce laws of all the States and substitutes the law of Nevada" for every divorcing person who can afford the "short trip there." When the question reached it again in 1945, the Supreme Court reversed itself, holding that a divorce decree is subject to COLLATERAL ATTACK in the home state on the ground that there had never been legal domicile in the state granting the divorce.[2215] This was an important ruling because it meant that the deserted spouse would not be left without a remedy when the absent spouse returns home brandishing a decree giving title to all their property. These cases arose in an era when most states made it difficult to obtain a divorce, and Nevada in particular made it easy.

The 1945 case might seem to make every fly-by-night divorce legally shaky, and perhaps it should. The Court somewhat modified the consequences of its ruling later when it held that deserted spouses who actually contest the divorce in Nevada may not later attack it back home.[1858, 414] However, if the deserted spouse never contested an out-of-state divorce, she may collaterally attack it later by proving that the divorcing spouse's domicile was a sham or that the divorce court had no jurisdiction over her.[1720] The Court has also held that even though an out-of-state divorce decree may be valid, it does not necessarily defeat a support or a custody award made to a wife earlier in her home court, before the husband left the state.[629] In short, an ex parte divorce will defeat a bigamy prosecution anywhere, if the domicile was valid in the state granting the divorce;

but it will not defeat the deserted spouse's rights to alimony, support, and custody if she was not served and did not appear in the divorce action.[2120]

Suppose that, unlike Nevada, Iowa wishes to keep newly arrived residents out of its courts for a waiting period of as long as a year before they can file for divorce against a nonresident spouse. In 1975, in a decision running counter to other DURATIONAL RESIDENCY REQUIREMENT cases, Justice William H. Rehnquist observed that "a state such as Iowa may quite reasonably decide that it does not wish to become a divorce mill" and upheld the law.[1909]

See also: JURISDICTION.

domestic tranquillity   In the words of the Preamble, one of the major purposes of the Constitution was "to insure domestic tranquility."

domestic violence   Under the GUARANTEE CLAUSE of Article IV, the federal government may use troops to quell "domestic violence" when asked by the legislature or governor of a state. The meaning of the term has never been tested.

domicile, *see:* **residency**

door-to-door solicitation, *see:* **solicitation**

Dormant Commerce Clause   The COMMERCE CLAUSE empowers Congress to regulate INTERSTATE COMMERCE. As long ago as 1824, in ruling on the constitutionality of state laws in *Gibbons v. Ogden,* Chief Justice John Marshall made clear that when Congress has acted, any conflicting state laws or policies must fall. Under the SUPREMACY CLAUSE, they are preempted. In 1851 the Court intimated that Congress lacks the power to assign to states the power to regulate interstate commerce,[461] but in 1891 the Court ruled that if Congress ex-pressly permits the states to regulate some area of commerce, that itself is congressional regulation.[1682]

The Court has said quite recently that Congress's intent to do so "must be unmistakably clear."[1917] But for long periods of U.S. history, and in many economic areas still, Congress has left commercial activity unregulated. What may the states do? The Constitution is silent. However, the Supreme Court has provided a typical lawyerly answer: it depends. In *Gibbons,* Marshall stated the general rule that if Congress has not acted, neither may the states. In other words, when the Commerce Clause lies dormant, it acts as a shield against interfering state laws. This is the negative power of the Dormant Commerce Clause: a power vested in Congress implies the lack of power in the states. But in the very next breath, Marshall admitted that the states do many things to regulate their "internal affairs," such as imposing "inspection laws, quarantine laws, health laws of every description, as well as laws for regulating the internal commerce of a state." As long as Congress has not superseded these laws, Marshall said, the states may enact them, no matter what the effect on commerce.[2228]

A much stronger version of the Dormant Commerce Clause that the Court gravitated toward only after a century of considerable intellectual struggle holds that otherwise valid health and safety laws must give way if they impinge too much on the free flow of interstate commerce. One incident of this struggle was to transform the Court into an umpire. Since the mid-1850s, a huge number of cases have come to the Supreme Court testing the validity of state economic regulation against a shifting standard by which to measure. In 1851 Chief Justice Roger B. Taney formulated the COOLEY DOCTRINE, which held that the states may validly regulate any "local" subject but that only Congress could regulate a "national" one.[461] No longer was the inquiry supposed to focus on the purpose of the law, so that safety of citizens would be permissible, whereas economic advantage would be impermissible. Now the validity of state laws would turn on whether the nature of the subject regulated was local or national. For nearly half a century the Court purported to follow this local-national distinction, but it followed the policy in an increasingly uneasy fashion: For example, is a ban on discriminatory railroad rates within a state local? No, it is national, said the Court in 1886.[2138] Is a mandatory examination for engineers on interstate trains national? No, it is local, said the Court in 1888.[1884] Gradually the Court shifted its inquiry, approving state laws that only "indirectly" affected interstate commerce and rejecting laws with a "direct" effect.

But these distinctions, too, proved metaphysical. In 1910 the Court upheld a Georgia law that required railroads to post signs every four hundred yards from crossings and to blow their whistles and slow down as they passed them. These safety regulations had only indirect effects on interstate commerce.[1922] Seven years later the Court overturned the same law when the railroad showed that the cumulative effect of the safety law was to stretch a four-hour trip from Atlanta to South Carolina into a ten-hour trip. Now the Court acceded to the railroad's characterization of the law: it directly affected interstate commerce.[1833] If directness or indirectness depends only on how much evidence is amassed at trial, the constitutional utility of the rule is slight. Attacking the whole notion, Justice Harlan F. Stone said "we are doing little more than using labels to describe a result rather than any trustworthy formula by which it is reached."[550]

By the 1940s the Court discarded both the local-national and direct-indirect tests and openly acknowledged that it was BALANCING the states' interests against the interest in unrestricted commerce among the states. In a series of cases dealing with railroads and trucking, the

Court increasingly struck down state requirements that trains be of certain lengths,[1919] that trucks have special gear installed,[161] or that only certain types of trucks may travel over a state's highways.[1049] In a widely quoted definition of the Court's commerce-balancing test, Justice Potter Stewart wrote that an even-handed law designed to protect a local interest is constitutional if its effect on interstate commerce is only incidental, "unless the burden imposed on such commerce is clearly excessive in relation to the putative local benefits."[121] In one instance, an Arizona law required cantaloupe growers to pack their fruit in the state and to label it as having been packed there. A grower accustomed to shipping his cantaloupes to a processing facility in California challenged the law because it would have cost him two hundred thousand dollars to build a packing plant for his seven-hundred-thousand-dollar crop. Arizona, Justice Stewart said, "is not complaining because the company is putting the good name of Arizona on an inferior or deceptively packaged product, but because it is not putting that name on a product that is superior and well packaged." That purpose was too slight to measure up to the burden on interstate commerce. The Court unanimously voided the law.[121]

In adopting a balancing test, the Court has not discarded a purpose test. If a state *intends* to discriminate against out-of-state interests through protectionist laws, either by not letting competitors in or by not letting products out, then the Court more easily has applied the Dormant Commerce Clause to overturn the law. In a 1978 case, for example, the Court struck down a New Jersey law that prohibited anyone from importing solid or liquid waste from outside the state. After all, it had enough of its own. The Court agreed that preventing its landfills from becoming clogged is a legitimate state goal. But New Jersey chose to do so not by regulating the rate at which all garbage may be dumped—New Jersey's as well as others'—but by barring only outside waste. That kind of discrimination "the Commerce Clause [squarely] puts off limits to state regulation."[1621] Similarly, the Court struck down a Madison, Wisconsin, ordinance that refused entry to the markets of the city any milk pasteurized at a plant more than five miles from the center of town, thus protecting local farmers and processors from competing with farmers and processors in Illinois. This ban clearly burdened interstate commerce, without any sound countervailing reason; any health concerns could have been met by inspecting the imported milk and charging the out-of-state companies for the inspection costs.[528] The Court voided as a protectionist measure a North Carolina law prohibiting Washington State apple growers from placing labels on their apples that truthfully showed them to be superior to those grown in North Carolina.[959] Another decision said that states may not try to lock up their natural resources to prevent them from entering the stream of interstate commerce. The Court struck down an Oklahoma statute barring fishermen from shipping out of state any minnows caught in state waters.[956] Summing up in 1986, the Court said that "[w]hen a state statute directly regulates or discriminates against interstate commerce, or when its effect is to favor in-state economic interests over out-of-state interests, we have generally struck down the statute without further inquiry."[262]

But because Dormant Commerce Clause cases require the courts to balance local and interstate interests in the absence of discriminatory intent, not every case is resolved against state concerns. The Court upheld a Maine law that prohibited importing baitfish from across its borders because of legitimate environmental concerns about the ecological effects from parasites and nonnative species.[1228] The Court also upheld a Minnesota law banning milk sold at retail in nonreturnable plastic containers but permitting its sale in paperboard containers, even though plastic containers came from out of state and paperboard is manufactured in-state. The environmental reasons were strong, the Court said, and the burden of using paperboard fell on everyone, not just foreigners.[1356]

Beginning in the mid-1980s, the Court began to carve out an apparent exception to the rule against discriminatory and protectionist state legislation. If the state is a market participant, rather than a regulator of private interests, it may seek its competitive advantage in ways that the Dormant Commerce Clause would otherwise prohibit. Justice Antonin Scalia and some commentators have said that the Court should abandon its reliance on balancing and leave the Dormant Commerce Clause to guard only against discriminatory state laws.[152] But at the moment the Court does not seem inclined to follow him, so the language of relative burdens on the national economy and benefits to the local one will continue to be the language of the Dormant Commerce Clause.

See also: COMMERCE CLAUSE and cross references listed there, especially INTERSTATE COMMERCE; MARKET PARTICIPATION; PREEMPTION; PRIVILEGES AND IMMUNITIES; TAKEOVER LAWS; TAXATION OF INTERSTATE COMMERCE; TRANSPORTATION.

double jeopardy   The FIFTH AMENDMENT says that no person shall "be subject for the same offense to be twice put in jeopardy of life or limb." This is the Double Jeopardy Clause, binding on the federal government and, since 1969, on the states.[153] It says, in essence, that a person may not be put on trial or punished more than once for the same crime—*any* crime, not only those that might lead to capital punishment.[1119] But these simple words mask some complexities. What is the "same crime?" And what constitutes trial?

Many criminal acts violate both federal and state laws. The Court has consistently upheld independent prosecutions by federal and state authorities for the identical criminal act;[1120] for example, robbing a federally insured bank. Likewise, two states may prosecute for the same conduct if the crime was committed in each state—for example, a kidnapping that crossed state lines.[889] A single incident may constitute several different crimes. In one case, the defendant's single sale of narcotics violated three criminal laws, and a trial for violating one of them would not have precluded a separate trial for the others.[784] The test for whether the crimes are different is whether a different fact would have to be proved to establish that each crime had been committed. For example, "joyriding"—driving another person's vehicle without consent—is a "lesser included offense" of the crime of stealing an automobile. A person convicted on the joyriding charge may not later be tried for theft.[255] Similarly, when there are several victims, separate prosecutions do not necessarily constitute double jeopardy since whether the defendant robbed the first victim does not necessarily bear on whether he robbed the second one. But in one such case, the accused robber of several poker players around the poker table was acquitted at the first trial because the prosecution witnesses could not identify him. A second trial for robbery of one of the other players was barred because he had already been acquitted of having committed any robbery.[85]

The question of when during a proceeding double jeopardy takes hold—when it "attaches," in the argot of constitutional lawyers—is equally complicated. "The most fundamental rule" is that a defendant acquitted at trial may not be retried,[1250] "no matter how erroneous" the verdict,[280] even if the defendant stands up in court immediately after the acquittal and shouts, "I did it!" Thus, the prosecutor may not appeal an acquittal,[1067] either in federal or state court.[1557, 805] The rule is the same for an acquittal by a judge as it is for a jury.[687] In one case the judge erroneously excluded evidence and then acquitted because the remaining evidence was insufficient. The Court held that double jeopardy barred retrial.[1795]

Double jeopardy comes into play from the moment the jury is sworn or the first bit of evidence is introduced. If the trial is halted at any time thereafter, the defendant may not be retried,[1604, 493] unless the mistrial is requested by the defendant[1040] or it is granted for a reason not under the prosecutor's control—for example, a deadlocked jury. When an appellate court sets a conviction aside because of errors committed during trial, the defendant under most circumstances may be retried. But if his conviction on a lesser offense is set aside, he may not, at retrial, be found guilty of a greater offense.[802] To borrow the earlier example, if the joyrider's conviction is overturned, at his retrial he may not be prosecuted for the greater crime of theft. And if the appellate court concludes that insufficient evidence had been presented to convict, he may not be retried; the prosecutor gets only one chance to assemble the necessary evidence.[280]

The Double Jeopardy Clause provides less protection in SENTENCING. If a defendant is retried and reconvicted after first winning an appeal, the judge may impose a higher sentence the second time around than the first,[1495] except for the death penalty.[271] The Court has sustained a provision in the Organized Crime Control Act of 1970 permitting federal prosecutors to appeal sentences of "dangerous special offenders" and allowing appeals courts to increase or decrease them.[547]

draft card burning In *United States v. O'Brien,* the Supreme Court in 1968 held that Congress may require draft-age men to carry "draft cards" on their persons and may impose criminal penalties for their failure to do so. Publicly burning a draft card as a symbolic protest against the draft and the Vietnam War was not protected SPEECH, the Court said, and it used the case to enunciate a four-part test to determine when conduct that may be termed SYMBOLIC SPEECH is protected by the FIRST AMENDMENT.

See also: COMPELLING INTEREST; CONSCRIPTION.

draft evasion, *see:* **conscription**

dramatic productions, *see:* **entertainment as protected speech**

Dred Scott v. Sandford   In *Dred Scott v. Sandford,* the Supreme Court declared that blacks could never become citizens of the United States, thereby administering a self-inflicted wound that led to the Civil War. *Dred Scott* was a TEST CASE, its JURISDICTIONAL FACTS rigged to permit the Supreme Court to hear it.

Dred Scott was born in the late eighteenth century, the property of a Virginia family who sold him in 1827 to Dr. John Emerson, an assistant army surgeon. In 1834 Dr. Emerson began a series of fateful travels: first to Illinois (a free state), then to Fort Snelling in the Wisconsin Territory, also free. His health failing, Emerson sent Scott and his family back to St. Louis in 1837 to be hired out. When Emerson died in 1843, his widow Irene Sanford Emerson inherited all his property, including the slaves. Three years later Scott sued for his freedom in a Missouri state court, arguing that he had become irrevocably free by entering Illinois and Minnesota with Emerson. Although a jury found in his favor in 1850, the Missouri Supreme Court overturned the verdict, in the process overruling a precedent that seemed to lie squarely on Scott's side. The Missouri court held that under Missouri law, when Scott reentered the state he again became a slave. That question was not appealable to the Supreme Court, so the issue of Scott's status should have ended there. But fate intervened. Mrs. Emerson

remarried and moved to Massachusetts. Under Missouri law, a married woman could not administer a trust, so administration of her late husband's estate passed to her brother, John F. A. Sanford of New York. Because Sanford was not a citizen of Missouri, he could be sued in federal court under DIVERSITY JURISDICTION, and any decision there could be appealed to the Supreme Court. So a new suit was born— fabricated, more accurately, solely for the purpose of the appeal.

The lawyers alleged on Scott's behalf that Sanford had assaulted Scott and his family. In Scott's name they sued for nine thousand dollars in DAMAGES. The federal trial court in St. Louis ruled that for jurisdictional purposes Scott was a citizen. Sanford (whose name was misspelled with a "d" in the *Supreme Court Reports*) defended on the grounds that he was entitled to lay his hands "gently" on his slaves. In 1854 the federal trial court upheld Sanford's defense, and the case was ready for its rendezvous with Chief Justice Roger Brooke Taney, slaveholder from Maryland.

The Court could have rested its decision on the narrow ground, consistent with its precedents, that the status of a slave is determined by the law of the state to which he returned. Under that rule, Scott would have remained a slave and the case would have been dismissed. But Taney thought to go beyond the question directly raised. On March 6, 1857, two days after President James M. Buchanan was inaugurated, Taney announced a devastating plurality opinion that destroyed the possibility of compromise on the slavery issue. (The justices did not all agree with each other; every justice wrote an opinion. Altogether they consume more than 250 pages in the *Supreme Court Reports*.) First, Taney declared that the Constitution would not permit any black, even a free black, to become a United States citizen. Second, he declared the Missouri Compromise unconstitutional. For more than thirty-five years, the states had lived uneasily with a deal permitting the southern states to retain slavery and Congress to prohibit slavery in northern and western territories. Taney's route to this conclusion was important, because it was the first time the Court relied on a theory of SUBSTANTIVE DUE PROCESS. In barring slavery in the territories, Taney said, Congress violated the DUE PROCESS Clause of the FIFTH AMENDMENT by extinguishing a person's property right in slaves as soon as they crossed the border into the territory. This neither Congress nor the territorial governments could do, Taney said. It never dawned on him to suppose that if anyone's due process rights were violated it was Scott's, since he, after all, was being deprived of liberty by Taney's very decision. *Dred Scott v. Sandford* destroyed the delicate balance among free states and slave, "and the war came." As for Dred Scott, now that his existence as a slave was no longer necessary to a lawsuit, his owners emancipated him. His taste of freedom proved short; he died fifteen months later of tuberculosis.

dress codes   George Mason, Virginia delegate to the CONSTITUTIONAL CONVENTION, suggested that Congress should have the power to enact "sumptuary laws," codes that limit the finery that can be worn and the amount of goods that a person can own. The proposal was defeated seven states to four, Elbridge Gerry of Massachusetts noting that "the law of necessity is the best sumptuary law." In much-attenuated form, dress and grooming codes have reappeared today in the rules of certain public institutions. These include, for obvious reasons, uniformed services of state and nation—police and fire departments, military forces—and for somewhat less obvious reasons, public schools and prisons. In a 1986 case, the Court rejected a claim of FREEDOM OF RELIGION and sustained an Air Force order requiring an Orthodox Jewish officer to refrain from wearing a yarmulke

because it was incompatible with the military dress code.[771] Justice William H. Rehnquist said that "courts must give great deference to the professional judgment of military authorities . . . [that] the traditional outfitting of personnel in standardized uniforms encourages the subordination of personal preferences and identities in favor of the overall group mission." Similarly, the Court upheld a police department grooming code that banned beards.[1058] But an earlier Court rejected a public high school's ban on the wearing of black armbands to protest the war in Vietnam.[2051] The black armband case had more to do with SYMBOLIC SPEECH than with the sort of self-expression that might be associated with the wearing of gold jewelry, extremely short skirts, or no shirts. It would be reading too much into the case to assume that school authorities do not continue to have authority to regulate dress to prevent real distractions in the classroom.

driver's license, privilege of   The Court has held that there is a constitutionally protected property interest in a driver's license. A state may not make an uninsured motorist involved in an automobile accident choose between having his license automatically suspended or posting a bond in the amount of damages claimed by the other party, without first giving the motorist a chance to show that he was not liable for the accident.[145] But the right to a license is not absolute, and failure to take a BREATHALYZER TEST could result in immediate suspension.

drug regulation   The power of both federal and state governments to regulate the sale, use, and possession of drugs both contraband and medicinal is unquestioned. So strong is the government's interest that in 1990 the Court overturned a longstanding FREEDOM OF RELIGION doctrine when it upheld Oregon's ban on the use of peyote, even by members of an acknowledged church who used it for sacramental purposes. The overturned doctrine had appeared to permit religious observers to use peyote as an exercise of religious freedom but, noting that the drug law is constitutional when applied to those who use the drug for nonreligious purposes, the Court ruled that the FREE EXERCISE CLAUSE requires no one to be exempted.[614]

See also: DRUG TESTING.

drug testing   Among the category of searches that police or other officials may conduct without a SEARCH WARRANT are drug tests on certain groups of workers, including railroad and public employees. Noting that drug-impaired train crews "can cause great human loss before any signs of impairment become noticeable," the Court said that the government may require railroad workers involved in train accidents or safety violations to undergo blood, urine, and breath tests even if there is no PROBABLE CAUSE to believe that they had individually been using drugs.[1880] The Court has also sustained mandatory urinalysis for employees being promoted in the Customs Service to jobs in drug enforcement or requiring that they be armed.[1436] Such employees, Justice Anthony Kennedy said for a 5–4 majority, have a "diminished expectation of PRIVACY." The government has a COMPELLING INTEREST in the "fitness and probity" of employees "directly involved in the interdiction of illegal drugs."

See also: BREATHALYZER TEST; SEARCH AND SEIZURE.

Drummer Cases, *see:* **taxation of interstate commerce**

drunkenness, *see:* **addiction**

dual federalism, *see:* **federalism**

dual sovereignty   Dual sovereignty is, in essence, another name for FEDERALISM. It means that both the federal government and the states are sovereign, within the spheres the Constitution has allocated to them. The notion is as old as the Republic. Though at times the sovereignty of the states may seem but a rhetorical flourish, against the centralizing force of national legislation, the Court continues to give it voice. As recently as 1991, Justice Sandra Day O'Connor upheld on the grounds of dual sovereignty a Missouri retirement law for judges, against a claim that it conflicted with the federal Age Discrimination in Employment Act.[810] Dual sovereignty also explains what might otherwise seem the anomaly of state courts that grant broader protections to criminal defendants than the Supreme Court has said to be necessary. Especially during the 1980s, as the Supreme Court gave increasingly shorter shrift to PROCEDURAL RIGHTS claims, many state supreme courts have interpreted provisions in their state constitutions as quite similar or even identical to provisions in the BILL OF RIGHTS and announced a rule opposite to the Supreme Court's. For example, the Supreme Court has said that financing public schools through a local property tax system does not offend the EQUAL PROTECTION CLAUSE of the FOURTEENTH AMENDMENT.[1791] But the California Supreme Court has said that the California constitution prohibits just such a taxing system. In 1984 the Supreme Court said that under the FOURTH AMENDMENT police may search "open fields" even if fenced with no-trespassing signs, and need not first obtain a SEARCH WARRANT.[1531] In 1992 the New York Court of Appeals, the state's highest court, said that New York police may not do so. These rulings are only apparently contradictory. They perfectly illustrate the consequences of dual sovereignty in which two constitutions govern every square inch of the states. Likewise, the Court's consistent refusal to bar as DOUBLE JEOPARDY federal and state prosecutions for the same offense attests to the enduring strength of the concept.

See also: TENTH AMENDMENT.

due process Due process is a protean constitutional concept of rule according to law, fairness in the law's proceedings, and fundamental rights. It has meant many things to many people; if a single phrase can account for the lush variability of constitutional interpretation, it is "due process." The words first appeared in a 1354 act of Parliament restating MAGNA CARTA; they were used to signify that the king might not take a man's property, or jail him, or kill him without following the established forms of the law.

Due process connotes procedure—a person may not be hanged without first having been tried. This concept developed for hundreds of years, and its connotations worked their way into the BILL OF RIGHTS—right to counsel, TRIAL BY JURY, right against SELF-INCRIMINATION. Some other rights became part of our constitutional culture only through the concept of due process itself, such as regularity and fairness of procedure. The state constitutions before 1787 did not use the phrase, but it finally entered U.S. constitutionalism in 1789 when James Madison proposed the language ratified in 1791 as part of the FIFTH AMENDMENT—that no person shall be "deprived of life, liberty, or property without due process of law."

The Due Process Clause was understood to apply only to the federal government, and it was in many ways apparently redundant, since the Bill of Rights did include several of the procedural protections that had so agitated libertarians during the battles to define and enshrine basic civil liberties. The Supreme Court did not hear a case invoking the clause until 1856, when it held that Congress was not at liberty to create just any form of procedure it wished and that the Court would "look to those settled usages and modes of proceedings" known hundreds of years earlier in England.[164] This limiting approach did not last long. The Court would soon turn to the Due Process Clause to check unfair procedures, independent of other constitutional provisions and regardless of English legal history.

That development was largely the consequence in 1868 of the adoption of a second and identical Due Process Clause, which appears in Section 1 of the Fourteenth Amendment and applies to the states. Very early in its history, this second Due Process Clause was pressed into service as a shield against state economic laws. In 1873 a group of butchers in New Orleans asserted that due process prohibited the state of Louisiana from requiring them to give up their slaughterhouses and conduct their business through a monopoly created by state law. In the *Slaughter-House Cases,* the Court said that "under no construction [of due process] that we have ever seen, or that we deem admissible" could Louisiana's law regulating the butchers "be held to be a deprivation of property within the meaning of that provision." Still the appeals poured into Washington by businesses seeking relief from a torrent of economic legislation aimed at problems of the rapid postwar industrialization.[518]

Within the next quarter century, the Court worked a revolution in due process jurisprudence. Beginning in 1884, when it warned that "arbitrary power . . . is not law,"[964] the Court rapidly reinterpreted due process as a *substantive* limitation on the power of both federal and state governments to regulate economic activity. In essence, the Court read into the Due Process Clauses the ancient sense of the words "law of the land"—no new law could be permitted to disturb established customs. That the new due process brakes were being applied to laws governing radically new business relationships was never discussed. This new SUBSTANTIVE DUE PROCESS had one badly battered precedent. In DRED SCOTT V. SANDFORD, the Court had said that a slave could not become free merely by sojourning in a free territory. To free a slave in that manner, the Court said, would be to allow a law of Congress to deprive a person of a property right without due process, because the law itself would have that effect. A law destroying a property right, Chief Justice Roger B. Taney said, violates the Fifth Amendment. For forty years, roughly from the 1890s to the mid-1930s, the Court undertook to gut scores of state and federal laws under the banner of a never fully consistent theory of ECONOMIC DUE PROCESS. The cases that came before the Court were bewildering in their variety, and the Court was prodigious in striking down an extraordinary number.

Beginning in that same period, though, the Court more tentatively acknowledged that due process had other facets as well. First, due process had not lost its earlier meaning of procedural fairness. Second, it protected noneconomic LIBERTY as well as economic and property interests. In time, these principles would produce another revolution in constitutional jurisprudence.

In 1908 the Court said that a law or governmental practice violates due process if it transgresses "a fundamental principle of liberty and justice which inheres in the very idea of a free government and is the inalienable right of a citizen of such government." [2086] In 1937 Justice Benjamin N. Cardozo spoke of due process as "the very essence of a scheme of ordered liberty." [1557] In 1952 Justice Felix Frankfurter spoke of due process as prohibiting practices that "offend those canons of decency and fairness which express the notions of justice of English-speaking peoples even toward those charged with the most heinous offenses." [1746] These conceptions occasionally led the Court to reverse convictions resulting from inherently unfair state prosecutions. For example, the Supreme Court said that it offends due process to let a judge collect part of his salary from the fines he imposed on defendants convicted in his court. [2077] And convictions could not stand when a mob dominated the courtroom, [1378] or when a prosecutor knowingly introduced per-

jured testimony, [1377] or when four illiterate black youths were tried for murder without counsel in a kangaroo-court setting. [1652]

Many state trials were unfair because they refused to grant defendants rights provided for in the Bill of Rights. By their terms, these provisions apply only to the federal government. But the issue of specific procedural protections for state criminal defendants became increasingly insistent. In 1947 Justice Hugo L. Black, echoing the views of the first Justice John M. Harlan in 1892, [1515] asserted that the Fourteenth Amendment's Due Process Clause incorporated the specific provisions of the Bill of Rights, applying them in full force to the states. [11] Although a majority of justices has never accepted Black's INCORPORATION argument, the Court began to "absorb" specific procedural protections into the Due Process Clause of the Fourteenth Amendment. By the end of the 1960s, most of the rights in the Bill of Rights were held to apply to the states.

In fact, this process of selectively incorporating procedural rights had begun much earlier. In 1897 the Court held that due process is violated when a state takes a person's private property without JUST COMPENSATION. [39] The Court recognized in 1925 that FREEDOM OF SPEECH is as much a right against state government as against the federal government. [761] The Court also very occasionally engaged in a noneconomic form of substantive due process, in holding that the states could not infringe on the people's liberty in ways nowhere mentioned in the Constitution. For example, in 1923 the Court said that Nebraska violated a parent's right to liberty in banning the teaching of foreign languages in the schools. [1323] From this initial ruling on the fundamental right to PRIVACY, the Court forty years later would infer a constitutional right to ABORTION—all under the mantle of due process.

Yet another due process arena has been the procedural claims of civil litigants. For a century the Court has been developing a jurisprudence of HEARING rights, the situations in which the government must grant a claimant or civil defendant a right to be heard and the forms which the hearings must take. Beginning in 1970, a major issue has been whether legal ENTITLEMENTS to government benefits—welfare, unemployment, public jobs—are protected by due process so that the government must hold a hearing before revoking a benefit, firing an employee, or otherwise injuring a citizen in some fundamental way.

Today economic due process is almost extinct; substantive due process in the social arena, mainly as a protection of privacy interests, is alive but under attack; and PROCEDURAL DUE PROCESS is a staple of the courts. Each of these issues is discussed under a separate heading.

See also: FREEDOM OF CONTRACT; NATURAL LAW; NINTH AMENDMENT; PROCEDURAL RIGHTS OF CRIMINAL DEFENDANTS; PROCESS RIGHTS; PROCESS THAT IS DUE.

durational residency requirements In 1969 the Supreme Court reaffirmed a FUNDAMENTAL RIGHT of all Americans to travel interstate. The laws prompting this declaration excluded newly arrived residents of Pennsylvania, Connecticut, and the District of Columbia from public welfare programs, which established one-year waiting periods to deter influxes of indigents seeking higher benefits. Applying the STRICT SCRUTINY test, the Court said that deterring migration from one state to another is a constitutionally impermissible purpose. The states sought to justify the distinction between new and old residents by pointing to the tax contribution that old residents had made. This reason was also illegitimate, since it would permit the state to deprive new residents of police and fire protection and deny them access to public parks, libraries, and the like. The states simply may not create classes of citizenship, Justice William Brennan said for the 6–3 majority. Since then the Court has struck down waiting periods, or durational residency requirements, in a number of cases. The states may not impose a one-year wait on the right to vote;[583] a fifty-day period is permissible, however, to permit the states to prepare "accurate voter lists."[1249] The Court has also struck one-year waiting periods for receiving free nonemergency medical care.[1312] However, not all waiting periods have fallen to the judicial axe. To avoid becoming a "divorce mill," Iowa law prohibits anyone newly arriving in the state from filing for divorce against an out-of-state spouse; the Court upheld the one-year waiting requirement.[1909] It also upheld a state law requiring one-year residence to become eligible to receive state college tuition benefits.[1948]

See also: TRAVEL, RIGHT TO.

during good behavior Federal judges hold lifetime appointments by virtue of Art. III-§1, which says that they "shall hold their offices during good behavior." This clause applies to ARTICLE III judges only, not to administrative law judges and others appointed to nonjudicial courts. Judges are subject to IMPEACHMENT should they behave in some "bad" manner. Although the word is not defined, by long historical practice following the Senate's failure to convict Justice Samuel Chase in 1805, judges may be removed only for criminal or corrupt behavior, not for their judicial views.

duty of government to act, see: **government, affirmative obligations of**

duty of tonnage, see: **tonnage duties**

E

economic discrimination   The Court has been almost invariably inhospitable to claims that a law regulating economic or business activity violates the EQUAL PROTECTION CLAUSE simply because it burdens one business or industry more than another. A New York City ordinance banned advertisements on vehicles, except for those advertising the vehicle owner's business. A truck rental company could not rent space on the back of its trucks to advertise beer, but a beer delivery truck could. In 1949 the Court upheld the ordinance, concluding that it was rational for the city to fear greater danger in nonrelated advertising than in the smaller volume of related advertising.[1687] An Oklahoma law regulating eye care forbade opticians from placing old lenses in new frames without a prescription from an ophthalmologist or optometrist, but it exempted sellers of ready-to-wear glasses from this requirement. The Court in 1955 rejected a claim that this protectionist legislation unconstitutionally discriminated against opticians.[2224]

In 1961 the Court rejected a similar challenge to the Maryland SUNDAY CLOSING LAWS, which prohibited certain kinds of retail sales on Sundays but permitted many others. Chief Justice Earl Warren said that the states have wide discretion to enact laws that "affect some groups of citizens differently than others," even if the laws "result in some inequality." The Court declined to set aside any law as long as "any state of facts reasonably may be conceived to justify it."[1297] And in a 1976 case, the Court sustained a New Orleans ordinance expelling pushcart vendors from the French Quarter, except for two companies that had continuously operated their carts from 1963 to 1972. The Court said that the provision "rationally furthers" the city's purpose in preserving the appearance and custom that attract tourists to the French Quarter.[1454] The Court has given no hint that it will alter its less than searching scrutiny of such legislation, although in 1989 it did strike down West Virginia's method of taxing property. The state constitution requires property to be taxed uniformly in proportion to its value. But in the mid-1970s state assessors began to tax recently sold property on the basis of inflated purchase prices without bothering to reassess property that had not been sold. As a result, the Allegheny Pittsburgh Coal Company was taxed at rates up to thirty-five times more than that of comparable neighboring property. The justices unanimously held that "intentional systematic undervaluation" of the surrounding property was constitutionally irrational.[38]

economic due process Economic due process is the now discredited judicial doctrine espoused from the 1890s to the mid-1930s that the DUE PROCESS Clauses of the FIFTH and FOURTEENTH AMENDMENTS permit courts to strike down laws impinging on private property interests and contractual relations. During that period, the Supreme Court itself struck down some two hundred state and federal laws. The concept of economic due process had been soundly rejected in 1873 in the *Slaughter-House Cases,* the Court denying that due process prevented New Orleans from creating a monopoly in the slaughtering business. And in the *Granger Cases* the Court rejected a due process challenge to an Illinois law regulating the rates of grain elevators. To the objection that a state's power over rates may be abused, Chief Justice Morrison R. Waite retorted: "[T]hat is no argument against its existence. For protection against abuses by legislatures the people must resort to the polls, not to the courts." But during the next twenty years, the Court edged closer to a view of itself as the people's protection against abuses by legislatures, as the justices became imbued with laissez-faire economic notions. Although the Court sustained laws involving businesses AFFECTED WITH A PUBLIC INTEREST and laws aimed at known public dangers, such as intoxication,[1397] the justices increasingly took the view that they were entitled to second-guess the legislature's judgment about evils that needed correcting, if the evils affected private property and business enterprise.

Not every law purporting to promote "the public morals, the public health, or the public safety" is necessarily what the legislature makes it out to be, and the Court would be obliged "to look at the substance of things."[1397] In 1898 it sustained a Utah law regulating working conditions of miners because it knew that mining was hazardous,[932] but in 1905 it struck down a New York law similarly regulating working conditions of bakers because it likewise knew that baking was merely an "ordinary" occupation.[1177] Many of the Court's economic due process decisions, like that of the bakers, rested on a FREEDOM OF CONTRACT theory, but economic due process was not confined to laws regulating hours, wages, and working conditions. The Court also struck out at "confiscatory" laws regulating railroad and other rates. The *Granger Cases* had said that the Court did not have the power to assess the reasonableness of rates, and as late as 1888 the Court adhered to that view.[571] But Chief Justice Waite had warned in 1886 that the power to regulate was not unlimited and that "under pretense of regulating fares and freights, the state cannot require a railroad corporation to carry persons or property without reward."[1684] Finally, in 1890 the Court did an about-face, holding that it could review rates.[391] In 1898 it said that rates must not only be reasonable but guarantee the business a "fair return" on its investment.[1899] For more than forty years, the Court was entangled in rate cases, from which it managed to disengage itself only in 1944.[648] A number of other economic regulations also were felled by the due process axe—laws curbing entry of entrepreneurs into an industry,[9, 1457] laws governing corporate ownership,[1164] laws fixing prices of commodities not "affected with a public interest."[2217]

The era of economic due process finally began to wane in 1934, when a 5–4 majority upheld a New York law regulating the price of MILK.[1440] Justice Owen Roberts declared that the states are "free to adopt whatever economic policy may reasonably be deemed to promote public welfare." The courts "are without authority" to override the legislature's policy choices "[i]f the laws passed are seen to have a reasonable relation to a proper legislative purpose, and are neither arbitrary nor discriminatory." In 1937 the Court, overruling prior decisions, sustained a minimum wage law.[2184] The following year, Justice Harlan F. Stone announced the RATIONAL BASIS test: a law is constitutional if there is any rational basis to suppose that it will accomplish permissible legislative goals.[348] Economic due process was dead.

See also: DUE PROCESS *and cross references listed there.*

economic liberties, *see:* **economic due process**

economic regulation   The states and the federal government have broad power to regulate economic affairs. Art. I-§8 grants a cluster of related powers—to tax, borrow, control the currency, and regulate commerce—that together give Congress sweeping control over business and the economy, not merely directly but by creating agencies to administer public policies. To the extent that federal legislation and regulation do not preempt, the states retain independent power to create and govern corporations and to regulate in the interest of public health, safety, and well-being. Until the New Deal, the Court had discerned many constitutional impediments to one or another form of economic legislation. Today those impediments have practically vanished. The power is potent and pervasive. The place to remedy foolhardy economic legislation, as the Court observed long ago, is not the courtroom but the voting booth.

See also: DUE PROCESS; COMMERCE CLAUSE; *and cross references listed under both.*

education, bilingual   The Court has never found a constitutional right of students to be taught in their own language, but it did hold that under federal law a school district may not simply throw non-English-speaking students into regular classrooms, where they could not understand a word being said. Students must be provided with foreign language instruction or be taught to speak English.[1128]

education, compulsory   State compulsory education laws do not generally violate the Constitution. But the states may not force students to enroll in public schools. In *Pierce v. Society of Sisters,* the Court in 1925 struck down an Oregon law that required children between eight and sixteen years of age to attend public school. The Court held that DUE PROCESS bars the states from refusing to permit parents to enroll their children in parochial or other private schools. However, the states may require that to qualify as legal alternatives to public education the private schools meet certain standards and teach certain courses. In *Wisconsin v. Yoder,* the Court held that FREEDOM OF RELIGION for Amish parents requires Pennsylvania to make an exception to its requirement that children attend school beyond the eighth grade. This exception to the general rule is narrow, since it is applicable only to long-established organized groups that can demonstrate commitment to an established and religiously rooted way of life requiring them to withdraw from secular society. An individual child, or an entire family, that announces a newfound conviction against secondary education is unlikely to prevail against the truant officer.

education, foreign languages and, *see:* **schools, foreign languages in**

education, right to   Despite its signal importance, education is not a fundamental constitutional right. In BROWN V. BOARD OF EDUCATION, the Supreme Court said that "education is perhaps the most important function of state and local governments. . . . It is the very foundation of good citizenship. . . . [I]t is doubtful that any child may reasonably be expected to succeed in life if he is denied the opportunity of an education." But the Court did not hold that states *must* offer public education. Rather, the Court said that "[s]uch an opportunity, *where the state* *has undertaken to provide it,* is a right which must be made available to all on equal terms." By "equal," the Court meant free of officially imposed SEGREGATION. But a state is not required to spend equally on each student; the states may constitutionally finance the schools through local property taxes, even though that method of financing results in school districts with greater and lesser amounts to spend per pupil.[1791] But the states may not exclude certain groups of children from the classroom by requiring them to pay tuition, if others need not pay. The Court struck down a Texas law that barred the children of illegal aliens from attending free public schools unless they paid tuition.[1641] Once the states have created a system of compulsory public schooling, the right to attend school is of constitutional significance, the Court has ruled, and a school may not arbitrarily suspend a student. Before schools can suspend or expel any student, they must hold some kind of HEARING to determine whether the reasons for doing so are valid.[785]

See also: BILINGUAL EDUCATION; TUITION GRANTS OR VOUCHERS.

effective assistance of counsel, *see:* **counsel, assistance of**

effects on commerce, *see:* **commerce, effects on**

efficiency   In the *Legislative Veto Case,* Chief Justice Warren E. Burger noted that the "fact that a given law or procedure is efficient, convenient, and useful in facilitating functions of government, standing alone, will not save it if it is contrary to the Constitution. Convenience and efficiency are not the primary objectives— or the hallmarks—of democratic government." Likewise, in one of the early SEX DISCRIMINATION cases, the Court held that a law may not classify on the basis of sex merely to promote "administrative convenience"; for example, to save the time and expense in pension and allowance cases of determining whether a person was truly dependent on his or her spouse.[705] On the other hand, the Court declined to incorporate "jot for jot"[582] all federal guarantees of the BILL OF RIGHTS into the FOURTEENTH AMENDMENT; for reasons of "judicial economy" it approved a system of having nonlawyer clerks issue arrest warrants for violations of municipal ordinances to be tried in local courts, a system that would not be permitted in federal prosecutions.[1848] In various other cases, the Court has paid particular heed to the balance between constitutional rights and the resulting drain on the state's resources. It upheld the trial of misdemeanors before nonlawyer judges in rural areas because of the limited resources available.[1499] For reasons of administrative efficiency it has also upheld police searches of automobiles under certain circumstances without SEARCH WARRANTS.[1916, 304]

See also: ARREST AND ARREST WARRANTS; INCORPORATION DOCTRINE.

Eighteenth Amendment   The Eighteenth, or Prohibition, Amendment was proposed by Congress on June 14, 1919, ratified on January 16, 1919, and repealed by the TWENTY-FIRST AMENDMENT. It was the constitutional basis for the Volstead Act, barring sale or possession of INTOXICATING BEVERAGES. But all prosecutions for violations of the act had to be dismissed on December 5, 1933, the date the Twenty-first Amendment was ratified. Convictions obtained before that date remained valid.[368]

Eighth Amendment   One of the BILL OF RIGHTS, the Eighth Amendment bans cruel and unusual PUNISHMENT and excessive BAIL AND FINES. It was first applied to the states in 1962.[1743] It does not apply to noncriminal penalties, including DEPORTATION and PUNITIVE DAMAGES. It is the primary basis on which the constitutionality of the DEATH PENALTY has been challenged.

elections, choosing time, place, and manner of   Under Art. I-§4[1], Congress has the power to preempt the states in determining the time, place, and manner of elections to Congress. Congress first exercised this power in 1842, when it declared that members of the House of Representatives are to be elected by districts rather than statewide. Modern election regulation includes provisions in the CIVIL RIGHTS laws, the VOTING RIGHTS ACT of 1965 and subsequent amendments, and the Federal Election Campaign Act of 1974. Congress has broad power to establish public funding for campaigns[270] and to protect the right to vote, including making it a crime to stuff ballot boxes[1806] and to commit any acts of violence intended to deter people from voting.[2270]

See also: ACCESS TO BALLOT; ELECTORAL COLLEGE; VOTING, RIGHT TO.

elections, regulation of, *see:* **access to ballot; campaign financing; voting, right to**

electoral college   The Framers provided for direct election by the people of only one federal office—members of the House of Representatives. In the original Constitution, senators were to be elected by state legislatures, and the president and vice president were to be elected by what has come to be known as the "electoral college," a term not found in the Constitution. This electoral system was a compromise, the delegates having defeated plans to elect the president in the Senate and directly by the people. Under Art. II-§1[2-4], each state was to appoint a number of electors equal to the number of senators and representatives that that state has in Congress. Each state legislature has sole discretion on how electors are to be appointed: electors may be appointed directly by the legislature, elected statewide,

elected in districts within each state, or otherwise. The electors were to meet in their states on a day appointed by Congress and vote for both president and vice president. The votes were then to be transmitted to Washington to be counted in the presence of Congress. Whoever received a majority of the votes was to become president; the runner-up was to become vice president. This system "worked" during the first two national elections, because it was clear to everyone that George Washington would receive all the votes. But a major flaw became apparent thereafter. In the 1800 election, Thomas Jefferson and Aaron Burr received an equal number of votes in the electoral college, because there was no mechanism for the electors to specify separate votes for president and vice president. With an equal number of votes cast, the election went to the House of Representatives, which took thirty-seven ballots to settle on Jefferson.

To avoid such confusions, Congress proposed the TWELFTH AMENDMENT, ratified in 1804. Under this amendment, electors must vote separately for president and vice president, and electors in each state must vote for at least one candidate from another state. If no one receives a majority of electoral votes for president, then the election falls to the House of Representatives, which must cast one ballot per state. Only once since 1804 has the House had the opportunity to select the president—in 1824 when it chose John Quincy Adams. If no one receives a majority of electoral votes for vice president, the election falls to the Senate.

The Framers envisioned independent electors, beholden to no one, not even the people, in choosing the president. Their expectations went unfulfilled because they did not foresee the development of political parties and the nominating system, beginning in congressional elections as early as 1796. Although the Framers did not anticipate and could not have planned for it, the electoral college system was key to the development of the two-party system. By the 1830s, all the states but one mandated that the winner in the state of the popular vote for president would receive *all* of that state's electoral vote. The practical consequence of this unit-vote system is to force candidates to seek the middle ground to win. As a result, though the unit-vote is not constitutionally compelled, it has proved useful to the two major parties since it makes it difficult for a third party to garner sufficient votes to win. Winner-take-all seems therefore to be a permanent part of the political system, though it could be changed in each state by the legislature. Since a unit-vote system would not work in the face of independent-minded members of the electoral college, the political parties in most states have adopted rules requiring candidates for presidential elector to pledge support to their party nominees chosen at national conventions. The Supreme Court has upheld such rules,[1696] although it seems clear that the Twelfth Amendment would permit an elector to break such a pledge with legal impunity—as happened, for example, in 1968 when a Republican elector from North Carolina voted for George Wallace rather than for Richard Nixon.

The unit-vote electoral college system permits candidates with less than a popular vote nationwide to become president. This has happened twice—in the elections of Rutherford B. Hayes in 1876 and Benjamin Harrison in 1888. But despite frequent demands that the Constitution be amended to provide for direct election of the president, Congress has resisted every attempt to abolish the electoral college.

electronic eavesdropping and surveillance, *see:* **search and seizure: wiretapping and electronic surveillance**

electronic media, *see:* **access to broadcasting; broadcasting, regulation of**

Eleventh Amendment   In 1793 the Supreme Court accepted ORIGINAL JURISDICTION of a suit against the state of Georgia. The executor of an estate was seeking to recover a sum of money that the state owed for the delivery of supplies years before. Georgia did not deny the debt; but asserting the principle of SOVEREIGN IMMUNITY, it did deny that it could be haled into federal court over a debt. When the Supreme Court took the case, as seemed its duty under Art. III-§2[1-2], and ordered a judgment of default against Georgia,[395] a storm of protest erupted throughout the country. On March 4, 1794, Congress proposed a constitutional amendment, which was ratified on February 7, 1795. The Eleventh Amendment bars suits in federal court "commenced or prosecuted" by citizens of other states or of foreign countries. Despite its simple wording, the Eleventh Amendment has provoked considerable controversy and a confusing set of precedents, which will be considered separately.

See also: STATES, IMMUNITY FROM SUITS IN FEDERAL COURT.

Emancipation Proclamation   On September 22, 1862, acting under the WAR POWER, President Lincoln proclaimed that on January 1, 1863, all slaves in Confederacy states not yet occupied by Union armies would be free if their owners did not publicly renounce the rebellion. Under the Emancipation Proclamation, the Union military was ordered to assist all runaway slaves, a policy that led to a mass northward exodus of blacks, robbing the Confederacy of its labor and contributing two hundred thousand black soldiers to the Union armies. The constitutionality of the proclamation was never tested but it was doubted, and in any event it did not extend to slavery in loyalist states. The consequence of these doubts was the THIRTEENTH AMENDMENT, permanently abolishing all slavery.

Emergency Court of Appeals The Emergency Court of Appeals was established in 1942 during World War II as a temporary ARTICLE III federal court and given exclusive JURISDICTION to hear challenges to the validity of price control orders under the Emergency Price Control Act. The exclusivity meant that a company could not contest the validity of these orders, even as a defense to criminal prosecutions, in federal DISTRICT COURT. The only recourse to an order freezing prices was to obey it and sue in the Emergency Court of Appeals. This forced the courts to enforce price controls, even if unlawful. The Supreme Court upheld the scheme.[2267]

emergency powers In 1866, after the Civil War ended, Justice David Davis, for a 5–4 majority, denied that the federal government could try a civilian for disloyalty in a military court. In words much quoted, but not necessarily taken to heart since, Davis said:

> The Constitution of the United States is a law for rulers and people, equally in war and in peace, and covers with the shield of its protection all classes of men, at all times, and under all circumstances. No doctrine, involving more pernicious consequences, was ever invented by the wit of man than that any of its provisions can be suspended during any of the great exigencies of government. Such a doctrine leads directly to anarchy or despotism, but the theory of necessity on which it is based is false; for the government, within the Constitution, has all the powers granted to it, which are necessary to preserve its existence.[345]

The Constitution does not grant any "emergency" powers as such, although Art. I-§9[2] permits the government to suspend the writ of HABEAS CORPUS "when in cases of rebellion or invasion the public safety may require it." The Constitution provides for no other lifting of constitutional limitations on the government during time of war or other national calamity.

Yet the Court has interpreted the WAR POWER so broadly that, in times of war at least, the federal government has seemed to gather powers that would clearly be denied it in times of peace. The most obvious example is the JAPANESE-AMERICAN EXCLUSION, which the Court upheld as an extension of the war power exercised jointly by the president and Congress.[925] Many acts, denoted as "emergency statutes," have delegated broad powers to the president when he declares a state of national emergency. Such emergency states have been declared in 1933, 1950, 1970, and 1971, triggering more than 450 provisions of federal law vesting military and economic powers in the president. In the National Emergencies Act of 1976, Congress sought to terminate existing emergencies and limit the duration and force of future presidential proclamations. Outside wartime, the Court has occasionally suggested that emergencies will justify laws that might otherwise be unconstitutional. For example, in 1934 the Court upheld a state MORTGAGE MORATORIUM, saying that although "[e]mergency does not create power[,] . . . increase granted power . . . [or] diminish the restrictions imposed upon power [granted, it] may furnish the occasion for the exercise of power."[937] In 1921, the Court held in an opinion by Justice Oliver Wendell Holmes that a "public exigency will justify the legislature in restricting property rights in land to a certain extent without compensation."[173]

See also: EMERGENCY COURT OF APPEALS; PRICE AND WAGE CONTROLS; QUARANTINE LAWS; SEARCH AND SEIZURE: EXIGENT CIRCUMSTANCES.

emigration, right to, *see:* **expatriation**

eminent domain Eminent domain is the power of the government to take private property for public use. The Constitution does not expressly grant Congress the power of eminent domain, but the JUST COMPENSATION Clause of the FIFTH AMENDMENT recognizes it, and the

Court has held that the power preexisted the Fifth Amendment.[346] No property is immune from seizure if it is intended for public use. Congress may take not only private land but also land belonging to the states, with or without state consent, and regardless of the effect that the taking may have on state programs.[1526] States have the power of eminent domain as well, and under the DUE PROCESS Clause of the FOURTEENTH AMENDMENT they are bound by the same requirement of just compensation.[390] Eminent domain is not an exclusive power of legislatures. It may be delegated to public and even private agencies, such as utilities, railroads, and even private housing associations when they are carrying out public purposes.[1488, 155]

The requirement that property be taken only for a "public use" has been interpreted very broadly. The Court upheld a broad program of municipal slum clearance and urban redevelopment under eminent domain, saying that "miserable and disreputable housing conditions may . . . suffocate the spirit by reducing the people who live there to the status of cattle. . . . It is within the power of the legislature to determine that the community should be beautiful as well as healthy, spacious as well as clean, well-balanced as well as carefully-controlled."[155] Although Congress or a state legislature may not simply take land from one person and give it to another solely for that person's private enjoyment, almost any transfer short of that will be upheld, as a 1984 case shows. After a study revealed that nearly half of the land in Hawaii was owned by seventy-two private landowners and nearly all the rest was owned by the state and federal governments, leaving only four percent available to all other state residents, the legislature enacted a sweeping plan that in effect took title from the private landowners and vested it in the current tenants, to avoid injury to the "public tranquility and welfare." The Supreme Court sustained the

scheme as a public use. Justice Sandra Day O'Connor said that whenever a taking is "rationally related to a conceivable public purpose," the use of eminent domain will not be struck down for failing the public use test.[881] This broad view is consistent with the Court's belief that any judicial review of an eminent domain taking must be "an extremely narrow one."[155]

In all cases of takings by eminent domain, the landowner or other property holder must be justly compensated. What constitutes just compensation will be considered separately.

See also: POLICE POWER; TAKING OF PROPERTY; ZONING.

emit bills of credit, see: **bills of credit**

Emoluments Clause   Under Art. I-§6[2], the Emoluments Clause, no member of Congress may be appointed to any federal office during the term for which he or she was elected, if the emoluments—that is, the benefits—of the office were increased or the office itself was created during that time. The extent of this clause has never been tested in the Supreme Court, although President Franklin D. Roosevelt's appointment of Senator Hugo L. Black to the Supreme Court was challenged because Congress had during his term increased the pensions of justices retiring at seventy years of age. The Court declined to consider the case.[1155]

See also: CIVIL OFFICE AND OFFICERS; TWENTY-SEVENTH AMENDMENT.

emotional distress, see: **mental distress**

employee discrimination, see: **employment discrimination**

employee of state, see: **state employees**

employer speech, see: **lower-value speech**

employment, public, see: **public employment**

employment, right to, *see:* **occupation, right to pursue; public employment**

employment discrimination Discrimination by private employers in hiring or promotion on the basis of race, sex, national origins, or religion is not unconstitutional, but it does violate federal law, most importantly Title VII of the Civil Rights Act of 1964. Congress did make an exception for religious groups from its general ban on discriminatory hiring. A church or other religious organization may restrict its hiring to people of the faith. In 1987, the Court upheld this exception in a case in which a janitor at a Mormon-run gymnasium was fired when he refused to become a church member.[471] Discrimination by government employers on the basis of race, sex, national origins, or religion would directly violate several constitutional provisions, including the EQUAL PROTECTION CLAUSE of the FOURTEENTH AMENDMENT and its analogue in the FIFTH AMENDMENT'S DUE PROCESS Clause, as well as the RELIGIOUS TEST of Article VI. In 1972 Congress banned employment discrimination by state and local governments, and the Court sustained provisions mandating back-pay awards and attorneys' fees in suits against state governments. The Court rejected the claim that suits in federal court against states or their agencies violate the ELEVENTH AMENDMENT.[671] The debate in the early 1990s between Congress and President Bush over employment discrimination centered on interpretations of federal law, not on the constitutionality of the legislation.

See also: AFFIRMATIVE ACTION.

employment legislation Until the 1930s, the Supreme Court frequently invalidated state and federal laws regulating wages and hours and other conditions of employment. Under the now-discredited doctrine of ECONOMIC DUE PROCESS, it struck down laws setting maximum hours for bakers in New York[1177] and minimum wages for women in the District of Columbia.[16] Occasionally, employment legislation would survive—for example, laws limiting the work week for women in Oregon[1401] and for interstate railroad workers.[2229] But until the 1930s, the Court's adamant views kept many such laws off the books. In 1941, in upholding the federal Fair Labor Standards Act of 1938, the Court finally declared unequivocally that it was abandoning its long repression of such laws.[514] Just how far the Court moved is clear from a 1952 case in which it upheld a Missouri law giving employees four hours off at full pay to vote on election day.[524]

en banc A court sits *en banc* when all members of the court hear the case. The U.S. COURTS OF APPEALS ordinarily sit in three-judge panels, but litigants may request that they sit to hear or rehear a particularly important case *en banc*, a request rarely granted.

endangered species Congress has full authority under the COMMERCE CLAUSE to enact legislation to protect endangered species.[2008]

enemies The Constitution does not define "enemies," a term used twice: in the TREASON Clause and in Section 3 of the FOURTEENTH AMENDMENT disqualifying from holding any federal office federal officers who have aided enemies of the United States. In each instance, the term by long usage refers to citizens or nationals of an enemy power with whom the United States is at war or with whom war has just been concluded.[1204]

See also: WAR POWER.

entanglement One part of the LEMON TEST for determining if a government program violates the ESTABLISHMENT CLAUSE is whether it leads to an "excessive government entanglement" with religion. In 1982 the Court concluded, 8–1, that Massachusetts could not subject restaurant liquor licenses to the veto of local churches.[1122] Among other things, said Chief Justice Warren E. Burger, the delegation of veto power unconstitutionally "enmeshes churches in the exercise of substantial government powers." In 1988 the Court, 5–4, turned aside an attack on federal grants to various organizations, including religious ones, for counseling unwed pregnant teenagers. The majority found no necessary constitutional difficulty with a religious organization receiving federal money to carry out a secular counseling program; it sent the case back to trial to see whether the funds were used to spread a religious message.[205a] But in a series of cases, the Court struck down public grants of money and materials to religious schools because they would have required too much governmental oversight of the curriculum and classrooms to assure that the funds and materials were being devoted to strictly secular purposes.[2246]

See also: SCHOOLS, RELIGION IN.

enterprise concept   Under the Fair Labor Standards Act of 1938, Congress regulated the wages and hours of workers producing goods to be sold interstate. In 1961 Congress expanded the act to cover all employees of businesses that either produced goods for sale or shipment interstate or that affected INTERSTATE COMMERCE. These employees were said to be part of the interstate "enterprise." The Court unanimously upheld the law as being within the COMMERCE CLAUSE because the law both regulated the competitive position of companies within interstate industries and affected the functioning of the interstate labor market.[1262]

See also: COMMERCE, EFFECTS ON.

entertainment as protected speech   Live theater is entitled to FIRST AMENDMENT protection, and a city may not refuse to permit a dramatic production even in its own auditori-

ums simply because it would not be "in the best interest of the community."[1918] The issue in many such cases is whether on-stage nudity is a constitutionally protected form of expression. The Court has said that nude dancing may be expressive conduct, though only minimally.

See also: NUDITY; PRIOR RESTRAINT; PUBLIC FORUM.

entitlements   Entitlements are legislatively created rights and benefits that the government may not revoke without providing the recipient some kind of a HEARING. Beginning with *Goldberg v. Kelly* in 1970, the Supreme Court has announced that certain types of largesse, such as state welfare benefits, may not be terminated before an evidentiary hearing. The Court has expounded no formula for determining which benefits are a LIBERTY or PROPERTY interest worthy of PROCEDURAL DUE PROCESS, and the cases have described a wandering doctrinal line, depending on majorities of the moment.

See also: BITTER WITH THE SWEET; PROCESS RIGHTS; PROCESS THAT IS DUE; RIGHT-PRIVILEGE DISTINCTION.

entrapment   Nothing in the Constitution bars law enforcement officials from laying a trap for unwary criminals, providing the means for people to violate the law through "sting" operations and the like. For example, the police may pose as buyers of stolen goods or narcotics; if a thief or drug trafficker offers to sell stolen goods or drugs to the poseurs, he may surely be arrested and convicted. However, a defendant has a defense of entrapment if he had no previous disposition to commit the crime and the police have lured him into committing it.[853] The entrapment defense does not arise under the Constitution. The Court has resisted seeing a DUE PROCESS violation even when law enforcement officials aggressively encourage the criminal behavior. The entrapment defense is a "yes-but" defense: "Yes, I did it, but I should be acquitted because I am not a criminal type and the police suckered me into it." Entrapment defenses were raised in the Abscam cases of the early 1980s involving public corruption, but the courts rejected them and the issue never came to the Supreme Court. On one occasion, though, the Court did reverse convictions on a constitutional entrapment theory. Police officials had steered a group of two thousand civil rights protestors to a place across the street from a courthouse and then later arrested their leaders for unlawful picketing near a courthouse. The Court said that convictions under these circumstances constituted "an indefensible sort of entrapment."[478]

enumerated powers　The federal government is said to be one of enumerated powers; it has only those powers actually listed in the Constitution. All other powers, says the TENTH AMENDMENT, are reserved to the states or to the people. The theory of enumerated powers led the Framers to a nearly fatal miscalculation in omitting a BILL OF RIGHTS from the Constitution. As Hamilton argued in *Federalist* 84, the people need no special protection from a government that is not empowered to abridge FREEDOM OF SPEECH or search homes without a warrant. During the ratifying conventions, a consensus emerged that this was sophistry, and so the First Congress drafted a Bill of Rights. Historically, the doctrine of enumerated powers has provided little protection for those who, like Thomas Jefferson, believed in a small sphere for national and a large one for state power. The NECESSARY AND PROPER CLAUSE considerably bolsters Congress in carrying out its enumerated powers. And the EXECUTIVE POWER is not as carefully cabined even as the LEGISLATIVE POWER. Art. I-§1[1] says that the legislative powers "herein granted" are vested in a Congress, implying that the national legislature does not possess other powers that might be considered legislative. But Art. II-§1[1] simply vests the executive power in the president

without any immediate limitation; the Constitution's failure to clarify this distinction has led to two centuries of debate over the limits of presidential power.

See also: PRESIDENT, POWERS AND DUTIES OF.

enumeration of rights, *see:* **Ninth Amendment**

environmental regulation　Environmental regulation poses three constitutional questions: (1) What is the extent of federal power over the environment? (2) What orders may the federal government give to state governments? (3) To what degree are conflicting state environmental protections overridden by federal law?

Constitutional sources for protecting the environment are several: the COMMERCE CLAUSE, the TREATY power, and Congress's power under Art. IV-§3[2] to "make all needful rules and regulations" governing United States property. The National Environmental Policy Act and other major environmental laws have been enacted under the COMMERCE POWER and present no direct difficulties. A migratory bird treaty was the constitutional authority for a federal law protecting birds to which Missouri claimed title; the Court said that Congress may enact a law to enforce a treaty even if it has no direct power to enact the law in the absence of the treaty.[1363] And in upholding the Wild Free-Roaming Horses and Burros Act over the objections of New Mexico that Congress has no power to control wild animals that do not cross state lines, the Court has said that Congress's Article IV power is broad enough to regulate anything that may affect the public lands of the United States.[1083]

Potentially the TENTH AMENDMENT bars the federal government from telling states what laws to write and regulations to issue. But in 1981 the Court upheld an end run around the problem. Congress gave the states a choice—to join a federal program to control surface coal mining or to create their own set of regulations. The choice it did not give the states was to do nothing, and the Court sustained Congress's power under the Commerce Clause to order the states to follow one or the other route.[927]

When federal and state laws conflict, the SUPREMACY CLAUSE requires federal law to pre-empt. So the Court turned down a bid by Burbank, California, to impose a curfew on evening jet flights at its local airport, since Congress in the Noise Control Act had occupied the field of noise regulation.[275] The rule of PREEMPTION likewise forbids the states from imposing their own environmental regulations on federal agencies and facilities, unless Congress clearly authorizes them to do so.[854]

Equal Protection Clause   The Equal Protection Clause is part of the trio of individual rights in Section I of the FOURTEENTH AMENDMENT. It says that no state "shall deny to any person within its jurisdiction the equal protection of the laws." Although by its terms the Fourteenth Amendment applies only to the states, the Supreme Court in a COMPANION CASE to BROWN V. BOARD OF EDUCATION held in 1954 that the DUE PROCESS Clause of the FIFTH AMENDMENT has an equal protection component.[193] Said the Court: "discrimination may be so unjustifiable as to be violative of due process." Since 1954, therefore, the constitutional concept of EQUAL PROTECTION OF THE LAWS applies to all governments in the United States, federal, state, and local.

equal protection of the laws   Despite the egalitarian commitment of the DECLARATION OF INDEPENDENCE that "all men are created equal," the Framers omitted any constitutional rule of equality. Not until 1868, when the FOURTEENTH AMENDMENT was ratified, did the concept of equality have a constitutional base, and not until the modern era did the Court give it enduring constitutional significance.

The Court early concluded that equal protection is not to be confined to an arguably literal reading of the words "equal protection of the laws." That might mean that any law could be upheld, no matter how discriminatory, as long as the exact terms are enforced equally on everyone. For example, if a law said, "No one named Smith may have a driver's license," a literal reading would uphold application of the law as long as the state did not let some people named Smith have a license and deny it to other Smiths. In 1886 the Court gave equal protection much greater breathing room: "[T]he protection of the laws is a pledge of the protection of equal laws."[2276]

Moreover, the clause applies not merely to the laws a legislature enacts but to the ways in which officials carry them out. A San Francisco ordinance required laundries to be operated in stone or brick buildings unless the city's board of supervisors waived the requirement. Most laundries in the city at that time were housed in wooden buildings. The board of supervisors waived the requirement for everyone but the Chinese laundries. In an often-quoted passage, Justice Stanley Matthews said: "Though the law itself be fair on its face and impartial in appearance, yet, if it is applied and administered by public authority with an evil eye and an unequal hand, so as practically to make unjust and illegal discriminations between persons in similar circumstances, material to their rights, the denial of equal justice is still within the prohibition of the Constitution."[2276] In 1948 the Court held that equal protection also applies to the courts themselves. Courts may not enforce private agreements if the result would be to discriminate on the basis of race; for example, by barring the sale of a home to a black family.[854]

But in two late nineteenth-century decisions, the Court managed almost to kill the Equal Protection Clause. In 1883, in the CIVIL RIGHTS CASES, an 8–1 majority announced the

STATE ACTION doctrine: the clause applies only to inequalities enacted or administered by the states—private discrimination does not come within its terms. The immediate result was to invalidate a federal civil rights law, but the cases also meant that it would be impossible to sue in federal court if the states failed to protect their citizens against private discrimination. In 1896, in PLESSY V. FERGUSON, the Court upheld the notion of laws providing SEPARATE BUT EQUAL "treatment" for different races. SEGREGATION became a legal reality throughout the South and much of the rest of the country.

Occasionally the Court found an act of discrimination so blatant that it could not resist the command of the Equal Protection Clause. A West Virginia law excluding blacks from juries was held unconstitutional in 1880.[1967] In 1914 the Court struck down a state policy of barring blacks from white dining cars on railroads without providing comparable dining facilities for blacks.[1279] In 1917 the justices rejected a racial residential zoning law.[267] In the late 1930s the Court began to inch its way toward reinvigorating the Equal Protection Clause in the racial arena, by invalidating certain forms of discrimination in higher education. In 1944 Justice Hugo L. Black announced what would become an important new way of looking at equal protection: all legal restrictions based on race "are immediately suspect. ... [C]ourts must subject them to the most rigid scrutiny."[1094] There was considerable irony in Justice Black's declaration, for it was the last time the Court actually upheld an invidious distinction based solely on race. The Court sustained a military order excluding everyone of Japanese ancestry from major portions of the West Coast. Finally, in BROWN V. BOARD OF EDUCATION in 1954, the Court took the first step in its ambitious constitutional project of outlawing all forms of racial and ethnic segregation (the details of which are considered under separate headings).

In 1927 the Equal Protection Clause was so rarely the basis of a successful challenge to inequality that Justice Oliver Wendell Holmes could remark sardonically that it was "the usual last resort of constitutional argument."[268] Today the clause is a fertile source of constitutional litigation, and the courts, state and federal, have paid serious heed to equal protection claimants.

As it is interpreted today, the Equal Protection Clause seems to measure unequal enactments and governmental policies on a three-part scale. At the high end are laws based on a SUSPECT CLASSIFICATION—laws that classify by race or ethnic origin. The Court has repeatedly reaffirmed that it will subject such laws to STRICT SCRUTINY and will strike them down unless they serve a legitimate and *substantial* or COMPELLING INTEREST and are *necessary* to achieve the legislature's purpose.[817] Other types of laws that must meet this strict scrutiny test are those that affect a FUNDAMENTAL INTEREST, such as the right to VOTE. An intermediate or heightened-scrutiny test has been applied to certain other classifications, such as gender. Under this test, a law will fail unless it serves *"important* governmental objects and [is] *substantially* related to achievement of those objectives."[483] At the low end of judicial scrutiny are all other laws. If a law does not classify on some forbidden basis, it will be upheld unless it is wholly irrational or its means are not *reasonably related* to its ends.[1687] Almost all laws subjected to strict scrutiny flunk, whereas few fail the RATIONAL BASIS test.

In many cases during the 1980s, Justice Thurgood Marshall objected to viewing equal protection claims through this three-part scale. He believed that the Court in fact has engaged in a sliding scale or "spectrum of standards ... [depending] on the constitutional and societal importance of the interest adversely affected and the recognized invidiousness [of the law's classification]."[1791] Although that is what the Court seems to have been doing, no majority has ever agreed to characterize it that way. In any event, it does seem clear that there can be no rigid rule of absolute equality in all laws, since by definition almost all laws classify and draw lines. Complete equality is a meaningless concept. Equal protection is concerned with something considerably narrower and considerably more important: equality that respects the inherent dignity of every human being.

See also: AFFIRMATIVE ACTION; AGE DISCRIMINATION; ALIENS; BUSING; CLASSIFICATIONS, UNDER- AND OVERINCLUSIVE; ECONOMIC DISCRIMINATION; HANDICAP DISCRIMINATION; JURY DISCRIMINATION; PURPOSE-IMPACT DISTINCTION; RACIAL DISCRIMINATION; RELIGIOUS TEST; SEGREGATION AND INTEGRATION; SEX DISCRIMINATION; WEALTH CLASSIFICATION AND DISCRIMINATION.

Equal Rights Amendment   The Equal Rights Amendment was proposed in 1972 to guarantee women equality of treatment with men. The amendment read: "Equality of rights under the law shall not be denied or abridged by the United States or by any State on account of sex." What effect it might have had on military service, marriage, divorce and custody, and labor laws was much debated with no conclusive answers. Congress extended an original seven-year deadline to 1982 to give its supporters extra time to secure approval, but they failed. Thirty-five states ratified, three short of the necessary number, but five of those purported to rescind. By the time the ERA died, many of its potential benefits had already been constitutionalized by Supreme Court rulings extending principles of EQUAL PROTECTION to state and federal programs that discriminated against and in some cases in favor of women.

See also: SEX DISCRIMINATION.

equal suffrage in the Senate   Art. V describes the means by which the Constitution may be amended. It contains one prohibition: no state may be deprived, without its consent, of its equal vote in the Senate. No one has ever

been inclined to do so, but the clause attests to the importance of the GREAT COMPROMISE at the CONSTITUTIONAL CONVENTION.

equal time, broadcasters   A Federal Communications rule required radio and television stations to give equal air time to political candidates. Congress on occasion repealed or blocked the rule to permit nationally broadcast debates between the major party candidates for president. The Court has never held either the rule or its repeal to violate the FIRST AMENDMENT.

See also: FAIRNESS DOCTRINE.

equally divided Supreme Court, *see:* **affirmance by an equally divided Supreme Court**

equity and equitable remedies   Art. III-§2[1] vests in the federal courts judicial power to hear all cases "in law and equity." This is a reference to the double court system that had developed over several centuries in England. The COMMON LAW courts heard cases in which the plaintiffs sought money DAMAGES. Because they were bound by rigid, archaic procedures that dictated dismissal if a single word in a writ was wrongly put, and because the remedy they offered was relatively narrow, a separate judicial system known as "equity" developed. Equity courts, also known as chancery courts because the jurisdiction was originally held by the lord chancellor, were considerably more flexible, open to broader kinds of evidence, and could issue orders such as INJUNCTIONS directing the parties to do or refrain from doing something. Equity courts sat without juries. The Constitution did not create two court systems but combined both in a single federal judiciary, which may issue either common law or equitable remedies as the case requires. The distinction retains current significance only in determining when a TRIAL BY JURY is required in civil cases. It explains why many significant federal cases—those involving school SEGRE-GATION, for example—are heard without juries. These are cases where the plaintiffs sought injunctive relief.

See also: JUDICIAL POWER; SEVENTH AMENDMENT.

Erie rule   The Judiciary Act of 1789 told federal courts to use applicable state law to decide DIVERSITY JURISDICTION cases. In 1842, in *Swift v. Tyson,* Justice Joseph Story declared that state court decisions did not count as "law" under the Judiciary Act. The federal courts could therefore develop their own COMMON LAW, except in certain classes of cases dealing with "local" matters, such as real estate. For the next century, following Story's lead, the federal courts created a vast body of federal law to govern commercial matters alongside often conflicting state law. Whether state or federal law was applied depended entirely on which court the dispute ended up in.

Story had wanted a law that was the same in New York as Des Moines. What resulted, instead, was a law that could differ in Iowa for citizens and noncitizens, as happened in a series of municipal bond cases in the 1860s. The Iowa Supreme Court ruled that private bondholders could not collect principal or interest from Iowa municipalities because the bonds were invalid under the state constitution. Out-of-state bondholders, as noncitizens, could obtain federal rulings that they could collect. The Supreme Court upheld this decision, leaving noncitizens substantially better off than Iowa citizens.[737] Matters came to a head in *Black & White Taxicab & Transfer Co. v. Brown & Yellow Taxicab & Transfer Co.* in 1928. Black and White, a Kentucky company, had a deal with a railroad station to provide exclusive service. Brown and Yellow began competing. Kentucky law prohibited exclusive deals, so Black and White could not take Brown and Yellow to court. Instead, it dissolved its Kentucky corporation and reincorporated in Tennessee. Now

it could go to federal court in Kentucky, which promptly enjoined Brown and Yellow. The Supreme Court upheld the result over strong dissents from Justices Oliver Wendell Holmes and Louis D. Brandeis.

The whole edifice of federal common law built up through diversity finally crumbled in 1938, when in *Erie Railroad v. Tompkins* the Court explicitly reversed Story's HOLDING in *Swift.* Although the question had never been raised in ORAL ARGUMENT or in the lawyers' BRIEFS, Justice Brandeis announced that the crux of the case was "whether the oft-challenged doctrine of Swift v. Tyson shall be disapproved." It was. In confessing hundred-year-old error, *Erie* became the only case in U.S. history in which the Court acknowledged that the Supreme Court itself had acted unconstitutionally in invading rights reserved to the states under the Constitution. Since then, federal courts, where there is diversity, must apply state law, whether declared by state legislatures or state courts. The Erie rule has not ended all conundrums that arise when a CHOICE OF LAW presents itself. For example, in a particular case the law of New York may require the law of Connecticut to be applied. The Court has ruled that when a federal court hears such a case it must apply not Connecticut's law, but New York's *concept* of Connecticut's law.[1081] In other instances, such as a right to TRIAL BY JURY[300] and SERVICE OF PROCESS,[858] the federal courts are bound by federal policy.

See also: FEDERAL COMMON LAW.

error, writ of   Until 1891 the writ of error—a type of appeal—was the principal means of securing Supreme Court review of a case in a lower federal court. In cases to which it applied, the Court was bound to hear an appeal. In 1891 Congress gave the Court power to hear cases by the discretionary writ of CERTIORARI, and in 1925 it changed the name "writ of error" to "appeal."

espionage, *see:* **clear and present danger; sedition**

Establishment Clause   The FIRST AMENDMENT says that "Congress shall make no law respecting an establishment of religion." Together with the FREE EXERCISE CLAUSE, the Establishment Clause is the constitutional basis for SEPARATION OF CHURCH AND STATE. Debate on the meaning of the clause has focused on two questions: Did the Framers mean merely to prevent the establishment of a single national religion, making permissible government aid for all religions as long as one is not preferred over another? Or did the Framers mean to deny all aid to religion, whether preferential or not? As the constitutional historian Leonard W. Levy has persuasively argued, in 1789 when the First Amendment was drafted, six states allowed establishments of religion, and in none were the laws supporting religion restricted to a single church. Massachusetts, for example, had a multiple establishment of Baptist, Episcopalian, Methodist, and Unitarian churches. State taxes were paid to each of them. The other states had similar rules, although in all states the only established churches were Christian. The Framers were well acquainted with these multiple establishments, Levy argues, and in banning establishment, they must have understood the First Amendment to forbid support for any and all religions. For 150 years, there was little controversy because as originally written, the Establishment Clause applied only to the federal government. No one seriously disputed that Madison and the other Framers were opposed to *federal* support for religion. But in 1947 the Supreme Court said that the Establishment Clause applied to the states,[634] prompting a dilemma and debate that continues unabated, since the First Amendment was now being pressed into an area for which it was not originally intended. Religious establishments in the states persisted long after the First Amendment; Massachusetts abolished its established churches only in 1833. The consequence is that the Court has wandered somewhat inconsistently between the two views in the establishment cases that have arisen in ever-greater numbers since then.

See also: FREEDOM OF RELIGION; LEMON TEST; RELIGIOUS ESTABLISHMENT.

establishment of religion, *see:* **religious establishment**

estate tax   Federal estate taxes are not DIRECT TAXES and may therefore be imposed on the value of the property without having to be apportioned.[1474]

See also: APPORTIONMENT OF TAXATION.

euthanasia, *see:* **right to die**

evidence   Evidence is the means by which the parties to a case prove to a judge or jury what really happened. The rules of evidence govern what types of evidence—testimony of witnesses, documents, and physical objects—are admissible for consideration by judge or jury. Rules of evidence are embodied in codes promulgated by courts and legislatures. In only a few instances have these rules been subject to constitutional scrutiny. Relevant evidence may be excluded if: (1) it was unlawfully taken by the police (or, if it was a confession, it was coerced); (2) it is barred by a privilege; or (3) it is inherently unreliable. [See EXCLUSIONARY RULE and SELF-INCRIMINATION for the problems in (1) and EVIDENTIARY PRIVILEGES for the problems in (2).]

Unreliable testimonial evidence is usually controlled by the "hearsay rule." Hearsay evidence is a statement made by someone not at the trial and offered for its truth. For example, if a witness on the stand testifies that a friend told her he saw the defendant commit the crime, that would be hearsay. Because the person making the statement is not available to be cross-examined, hearsay evidence is considered unreliable and is ordinarily excluded. A complex set of "hearsay exceptions" has always permitted some out-of-court statements to be admitted into evidence. For example, "dying declarations" and "statements against interest" are admissible. The constitutional problem is that under the CONFRONTATION CLAUSE of the SIXTH AMENDMENT, a defendant is entitled to cross-examine witnesses against him. In a number of cases during the 1960s,[1645, 265, 123] the Court held that certain out-of-court statements by witnesses no longer available to testify were constitutionally inadmissible, and seemed to be suggesting that all hearsay exceptions were inadmissible. But in 1980 the Court said that "reliable" evidence will be admitted against the defendant if the person making the statement is truly unavailable.[1520]

evidence, access to   In a 1988 case, the Supreme Court noted that a number of constitutional cases had created "what might loosely be called the area of constitutionally-guaranteed access to evidence."[71] As one commentary summed up these rules:

> Although the Court has not provided a comprehensive listing of the constitutional directives that shape this [area of access], the following constitutional obligations and prohibitions would certainly be on any list: (1) the prosecution's duty to disclose evidence within its possession or control that is exculpatory and material; (2) the prohibition against the government's bad faith destruction of such evidence; (3) the state's duty to provide the defense with the power through subpoena to gain the production of witnesses and physical items at trial; (4) the state's duty to provide certain types of assistance or information to the defense that will allow it to use that subpoena power to gain evidence; and (5) the prohibition

against certain governmental actions that interfere with the defense's utilization of its subpoena power.

This access to evidence stems from the Court's 1963 decision in *Brady v. Maryland,* in which a defense lawyer in a murder case had asked the prosecutor for all statements made by a codefendant. The prosecutor neglected, apparently inadvertently, to turn over a statement in which the codefendant had admitted to having actually done the killing. The Court reversed the sentence of death, holding that the defendant was entitled to the evidence, which might have persuaded the jury to a lesser punishment.

See also: DISCOVERY IN CRIMINAL PROCEEDINGS.

evidence, exclusion of, *see:* **exclusionary rule**

evidentiary privileges   Ascertaining the truth at trial, while important, is not paramount. The courts have long recognized other social interests as worthy of protection, and they have provided for these interests through a number of privileges that excuse their holders from testifying. Most of these are familiar—the spousal privilege bars the prosecution in a criminal trial from calling on one spouse to testify against the other; the priest-penitent privilege bars the government from calling a defendant's minister to testify to confidences divulged in the course of religious counseling; the attorney-client privilege bars calling a lawyer to reveal what the client has told him or her in confidence. These are not constitutional rules, although the attorney-client privilege probably is supported at least by the constitutional rights against SELF-INCRIMINATION and to assistance of counsel. Some states have provided by law for a REPORTER'S PRIVILEGE to keep sources confidential, but the Court has refused to recognize this interest as constitutionally protected.[225]

evolution, teaching of Since the notorious Scopes "monkey trial" in 1927, only two states have enacted laws prohibiting the teaching of evolution in public schools. An Arkansas law forbade schools from teaching "the theory or doctrine that mankind ascended or descended from a lower order of animals." The Court invalidated the law in 1968 because the state selected one body of knowledge to ban solely because it conflicted "with a particular interpretation of the Book of Genesis by a particular religion."[619] In 1987 the Court struck down the Louisiana Balanced Treatment for Creation-Science and Evolution-Science in Public School Instruction Act, which forbade teaching evolution unless "creation science" was also taught. Noting the inconsistency of the state's claim that it wanted to advance academic freedom through a law restricting freedom to teach, the Court again concluded that the only purpose of the law was to promote a particular religious doctrine.[600] Defenders of the law asserted the state's power to determine the curriculum of public schools, and several concurring justices agreed that these cases do not lessen that power. The Court did not rely on any general theory of ACADEMIC FREEDOM in dispatching the anti-evolution teaching laws.

ex parte injunction An ex parte INJUNCTION is one that a court issues without first hearing the party to whom it applies. Ex parte (Latin for "one side") orders are rare; they are issued only when the danger is great and action must be taken before a full-scale HEARING can be arranged. Some ex parte injunctions are unconstitutional. For example, an injunction against a protest meeting was held to violate the rule against PRIOR RESTRAINTS.[350]

Ex Post Facto Clause A basic concept of civilized life in a free country is that a person may not be punished for doing that which was not unlawful when he did it. Under Art. I-§9[3]

and Art. I-§10[1], neither the federal government nor the states may enact ex post facto laws, but these clauses do not bar all laws that may have retroactive effect. As early as 1798, the Supreme Court announced an interpretation followed ever since—that the Ex Post Facto Clauses apply only to criminal laws.[307] A law imposing a tax on income made before the law was passed is not barred by the clauses but laws imposing jail terms and other criminal punishment are.

After the Civil War the Supreme Court struck down a law that barred lawyers from practicing in federal courts unless they took an oath that they had not been engaged in the war against the Union. The Court said that the law unconstitutionally imposed a penalty after the fact because it had no bearing on a lawyer's professional duties.[727] Somewhat inconsistently, the Court has ruled that a law passed after a doctor was convicted of a felony stripping him of his license to practice medicine was not a penalty and was therefore permissible.[884, 527] The Court has also upheld retroactive laws denying the vote to former polygamists,[1408] authorizing DEPORTATION for acts not criminal at the time committed,[345] and terminating Social Security benefits when a person was deported for acts not criminal when committed.[677] But when the legislature has enacted a retroactive law imposing a true penalty, there are three circumstances under which it may not be employed:

(1) If the law applies to conduct or behavior not subject to the penalty when committed. People could not be convicted of violating Prohibition laws for purchasing liquor before the laws were passed, although they could be punished for continuing to possess the liquor after the laws took effect.[1790]

(2) If the law would retroactively make more burdensome the punishment for an act. For example, in 1981 the Supreme Court struck down a Florida law that reduced a prisoner's

time off for good behavior after he had earned it.[2171] In 1987 it precluded the use of revised sentencing guidelines that would have resulted in a defendant serving more time than the law would have required when the crime was committed.[1339] However, if a jury improperly sentences a defendant to a fine not allowed by law, the state can then pass a law allowing the judge to reform the sentence without disturbing the conviction.[433]

(3) If the law would deprive the defendant of a defense to which he or she was entitled at the time the act was committed. For example, if a state tightens its drunk driving laws to eliminate the defense of "diminished capacity" to a charge of vehicular manslaughter, the defense must be made available to a drunk driver who caused the accident before the law went into effect.

See also: PUNISHMENT, CRUEL AND UNUSUAL; RETROACTIVITY; WAR CRIMES.

excessive bail, excessive fines, *see:* **bail and fines**

excise tax Art. I-§8[1] empowers Congress to "lay and collect taxes and duties, imposts and excises." An excise tax is a tax on goods manufactured in the United States; an impost or duty is a tax on goods imported from abroad. Congress may impose excise taxes as it pleases, but it must do so uniformly. It may not charge one rate in Maine and another in Arizona.

exclusion, *see:* **immigration and naturalization**

exclusionary rule The exclusionary rule dictates that unlawfully obtained evidence may not be used when a defendant is being prosecuted for a crime; it must be excluded from the trial. The rule rests on the perception that the FOURTH AMENDMENT's provision against unreasonable SEARCH AND SEIZURE would be

meaningless if the police or prosecutor could profit from its violation. Similarly, the FIFTH AMENDMENT's provision against SELF-INCRIMINATION implies that unlawfully obtained confessions must likewise be excluded. The Supreme Court hinted at an exclusionary rule in 1886[213] and imposed it in federal prosecutions in 1914.[2175] Until 1949, however, when the Court finally held that the Fourth Amendment's search and seizure provisions are applicable to the states,[2244] evidence unlawfully seized by state officials could be used in federal prosecutions. This was called the SILVER PLATTER DOCTRINE. Likewise, evidence unlawfully seized by federal officials could be used in state prosecutions. Even after declaring that DUE PROCESS requires states to refrain from violating the Fourth Amendment, the Court held back until 1961 from applying the exclusionary rule to the states. But in *Mapp v. Ohio,* one of the first of the major PROCEDURAL RIGHTS rulings of the Warren Court era, the exclusionary rule was finally made universal in every court. "To hold otherwise," said Justice Tom Clark, "is to grant the right but in reality to withhold its privilege and enjoyment."

The exclusionary rule has been criticized from the start. In *Mapp* itself, the Court alluded to the most famous attack, by Judge Benjamin N. Cardozo when he was on the New York State Court of Appeals: "The criminal is to go free because the constable has blundered." The critics charge that the rule cannot possibly accomplish its major goal—deterrence of unlawful searches and seizures—because it dispenses with perfectly good evidence without deterring the actual behavior of the police, who are motivated more by the culture of the station house and the demands of their chiefs than by whether evidence may or may not be excluded months later at trial. Moreover, many searches turn out to be unlawful not because of anything the police do but because judges or magistrates issued invalid search warrants. It would be more sensible, the critics charge, to provide a disciplinary mechanism for true cases of abuse, while using the evidence to convict the guilty. Pursuing that theory, the Supreme Court in 1971 created a CONSTITUTIONAL TORT—the right to sue law enforcement officials who violate Fourth Amendment rights.[168] Yet few people have availed themselves of the opportunity, despite many hundred unlawful searches yearly, for proof of culpability and DAMAGES in such suits is difficult. To the argument of the rule's proponents that what is ultimately at stake is the integrity of governmental institutions, which must at all costs abide by the law, critics have responded that enforcement of the rule may "generat[e] disrespect for the law and administration of justice."[1963]

In any event, beginning in the 1970s, the Court retrenched. In 1974 it held that the rule does not bar prosecutors from questioning grand jury witnesses about information gained from an illegal search.[306] In 1976 the Court refused a civil defendant use of the rule in a case in which the federal government was suing to recover unpaid income taxes.[1007] In that same year the Court barred state prisoners from seeking independent federal HABEAS CORPUS review of their convictions if they already had the chance in a state appeal to argue that the trial was tainted with unlawfully seized evidence.[1963] In the 1980s the Court carved out even larger exceptions. If the defendant takes the stand, the prosecutor may use illegally seized evidence to impeach his or her testimony,[880] although such evidence may not be used to impeach other witnesses.[1005] If a search warrant was invalid through no fault of the police, and if it was issued by a neutral magistrate, and the police relied objectively and in good faith on it, evidence obtained illegally under the warrant may be used.[1152] Even evidence obtained illegally, without a good-faith justification, may be used if the police can demonstrate that they had independent and lawful

means of finding it[1841] or if the police would eventually have found it anyway—the "inevitable discovery" exception to the exclusionary rule.[1482]

See also: HABEUS CORPUS; HARMLESS ERROR; *MIRANDA* RULES; *MIRANDA v. ARIZONA*; PROBABLE CAUSE; PURPOSE-IMPACT DISTINCTION; SEARCH AND SEIZURE; SEARCH WARRANT; SELF-INCRIMINATION; SILVER PLATTER DOCTRINE; SUPPRESSION HEARING.

exclusive legislation, *see:* **preemption**

execution of warrants, *see:* **no-knock entry**

executive agreement   An executive agreement is an international agreement entered into by the president without submitting it to the Senate for approval, as is required for treaties. Congress often authorizes the executive branch to negotiate such agreements, and many treaties themselves require further detailed agreements to be worked out. But some executive agreements are negotiated solely by the president. Despite the Constitution's silence about this longstanding practice, the Court has approved them on the rare occasions when cases challenging them came before it. In 1937 the Court upheld a complex set of financial agreements that were part of President Roosevelt's diplomatic recognition of the Soviet Union.[109] In 1981 the Court upheld President Jimmy Carter's executive agreement with Iran to settle the hostage crisis. Under the agreement, legal attachments of Iranian property in the United States were "nullified" and claims pending in American courts were "suspended" so that they could be raised anew at a claims tribunal in The Hague. Executive suspension of pending litigation is extremely rare, perhaps unprecedented. Justice William H. Rehnquist said the agreement was constitutional because historically Congress had "acquiesced" in the practice of settling international claims through executive agreements.[510] In the 1950s the Senate came close to passing the Bricker amendment, which in one version would have limited the effect of treaties and executive agreements in the United States. But these and other attempts failed, and presidential power to negotiate legally binding executive agreements remains broad.

See also: TREATY POWER.

executive authority   "Executive authority," as used in Articles I and IV and the Seventeenth Amendment, is the constitutional term for governor, the chief executive of each state.

executive branch   The executive branch, as distinguished from Congress and the judiciary, is that group of departments and agencies that exercise powers granted in Article II. Most but not all federal offices are executive. A few agencies, such as the General Accounting Office and the Congressional Budget Office, are part of the legislative branch; and a few, such as the U.S. Sentencing Commission, are part of the judicial branch. The distinction is important constitutionally for purposes of SEPARATION OF POWERS. The distinction is also important to employees, because employment policies of each branch differ by law.

executive departments   The Constitution mentions the executive departments only once, in Art. II-§2[1], and there as an aside, in saying that the president may request the written opinion of the heads of the departments on subjects relating to their duties. Presumably the president possesses this power anyway, as an attribute of EXECUTIVE POWER. The executive departments constitute the great bulk of what we normally consider the "federal government," including State, Treasury, Defense, and Justice. Except for a dozen or so independent ADMINISTRATIVE AGENCIES, most of the familiar agencies and bureaus are part of the thirteen CABINET-level departments. The Federal Bu-

reau of Investigation, for instance, is a part of the Justice Department. Although the executive departments work for and "report to" the president, who appoints their heads and some of their major officials, they are created and funded by Congress, which dictates both the departments' functions and the powers and means by which their functions are to be carried out. Within uncertain limits, the executive departments are also answerable to Congress. Under SEPARATION OF POWERS, executive departments may not exercise LEGISLATIVE POWER, but Congress has delegated vast authority to each of the departments to engage in regulatory activities that have every hallmark of lawmaking except the name. The political relationship between Congress and the executive departments is much closer and more complex than their constitutional relationship.

See also: DELEGATION DOCTRINE; HEADS OF DEPARTMENTS.

executive immunity, *see:* **immunity from suit**

executive order   Executive orders are orders issued by the president to officials of the executive branch, usually but not always under powers delegated by Congress. Executive orders have reorganized major branches of government, paved the way for removing Japanese-Americans from their homes during World War II, desegregated the ARMED FORCES, and mandated AFFIRMATIVE ACTION in federal hiring. Presidents have issued more than fifteen thousand executive orders since the numbering system began in 1907. Since 1935 they have been published officially.

executive power   Two significant issues have arisen over the executive power vested in the president by Art. II-§1. One is whether the president has a broad inherent power to act in ways not enumerated in Article II. The second is how the executive power can be distinguished from JUDICIAL POWER and LEGISLATIVE POWER. As chief administrator of the government, the president's executive power may be supposed to include those powers necessary to "run things." In the *Legislative Veto Case* in 1983, Chief Justice Warren E. Burger said that "the powers delegated to the three Branches are functionally identifiable." Despite his airy confidence, no one has ever succeeded in doing so. In the very case, the Court held that Congress was engaged in exercising legislative power in determining to override the ATTORNEY GENERAL's decision to suspend DEPORTATION of an alien. But the Court did not find remarkable that the attorney general, an EXECUTIVE BRANCH official, was exercising functionally the very power that the Court had said was legislative. Concurring, Justice Lewis F. Powell thought that Congress was exercising judicial power, not legislative power, in overruling the attorney general. So much for identifying the powers.

In 1986 the Court said that Congress could not constitutionally assign certain functions to the comptroller general of the United States, a legislative branch official.[211] Under the Gramm-Rudman-Hollings Act, the comptroller general had the "ultimate authority to determine the budget cuts to be made" to reduce the federal deficit. This power, the Court said, was executive, not legislative, because "interpreting a law enacted by Congress to implement the legislative mandate is the very essence of 'execution' of the law." This seemingly bizarre conclusion that determining the size of the federal budget is an executive function flows not from anything in the Constitution but from the Court's longstanding approval of the DELEGATION DOCTRINE, under which Congress may transmit legislative power to the executive branch. The executive branch somehow absorbs legislative power and transmutes it into executive power, a feat of prestidigitation explained only by the practical necessity of governing.

See also: IMPLIED AND INHERENT POWERS; PRESIDENT, INHERENT POWER OF; SEPARATION OF POWERS.

executive privilege   Executive privilege is the right of the president to refuse to divulge to Congress or the courts the contents of confidential communications within the EXECUTIVE BRANCH. The issue has historically arisen when Congress has informally requested or subpoenaed documents or demanded testimony about conversations relating to official duties. Information may be kept private because the law prohibits government agencies from releasing, for example, investigative files. Requests for information may also be rebuffed because the information concerns military or diplomatic secrets, internal government affairs, or policy-making matters, such as recommendations of subordinates and working papers.

Until WATERGATE, the Court had occasionally upheld claims of privilege without viewing it as a constitutional prerogative. For example, in a damage action by civilians against the U.S. Air Force for injuries involved in an airplane crash, the Court upheld the government's contention that it need not give the plaintiffs certain records because they contained military secrets.[1715] In 1974, in *United States v. Nixon*, the Court for the first time declared that there is a constitutional basis for executive privilege in the principle of SEPARATION OF POWERS. Said Chief Justice Warren Burger for a unanimous bench, "A President and those who assist him must be free to explore alternatives in the process of shaping policies and making decisions and to do so in a way many would be unwilling to express except privately." This recognition of the doctrine did President Nixon little good, however, for the Court went on to hold that the privilege is not absolute. The president had asserted only a "generalized interest in confidentiality," without specifying particular dangers that might arise from disclosure of the famous tape recordings.

When a prosecutor can demonstrate a particular need for documents, his specific need will outweigh the president's generalized interest. Although the judicial contours of executive privilege remain to be explored, it is unlikely that cases will often arise. Most of the visible controversies are duels between Congress and the executive, and they are resolved politically. The Court did uphold the Presidential Recordings and Materials Preservation Act, a law aimed only at President Nixon after his resignation, against his claim of executive privilege.[1483] The law gave custody of his papers to the General Services Administration to catalogue and maintain, and the Court found justifications for the law comparable to those that compelled disclosure of the tapes to the Watergate special prosecutor.

exhaustion of remedies   Ordinarily, a litigant aggrieved by action of an administrative agency must "exhaust his remedies"—that is, take every avenue of redress through the agency before going to court. The Supreme Court has declared an exception to this rule when a litigant claims that an agency has plainly exceeded its authority under the law or the Constitution,[1881] or when a litigant seeks to uphold a right guaranteed under the federal civil rights laws. The litigant then need not exhaust his remedies either before the agency or in state court.[1575] Otherwise the concept of federal protection would be pointless. There would almost always be a state court to which the litigant would first have to turn; and since it is rare that anyone can appeal a state court case to a federal court other than the Supreme Court, which of course hears very few appeals, the injured party would have no practical means of redress.

exigent circumstances, *see:* **search and seizure: exigent circumstances**

exile   The government may not exile a natural-born citizen by stripping him of citizenship and banishing him from the United States as punishment for crime. In 1958 the Court reversed this penalty imposed on a soldier convicted at a court-martial of desertion during wartime.[2072] To render a person stateless, Chief Justice Earl Warren said, is punishment "more primitive than torture." Likewise, the Court rejected exile as punishment for anyone who leaves or stays out of the country to evade military service during wartime.[1061]

See also: DEPORTATION; EXPATRIATION; IMMIGRATION AND
NATURALIZATION; PUNISHMENT, CRUEL AND UNUSUAL.

expatriation   Expatriation is the decision to voluntarily renounce citizenship.[1605] At COMMON LAW, expatriation required the country's consent because a person was held to owe a perpetual allegiance to the land of birth. In 1868 Congress recognized a right of expatriation, mainly to free noncitizens to give up their foreign citizenship so they could swear allegiance to the United States. But in several later laws, Congress listed a number of actions that it said constituted expatriation by a citizen. Until relatively recently, the Court did not look skeptically at the list. For example, in 1915 the Court upheld a provision in the law putting "in abeyance" the citizenship of any American woman who married a foreigner; citizenship could only be restored if the marriage ended.[1219] In 1958 the Court upheld another provision that divested a dual national of citizenship if he or she voted in an election of his or her other country.[1600] But in 1967, by a slender 5–4 margin, the Court reversed itself and held that Congress has no constitutional power to strip anyone of citizenship. To treat anyone as a noncitizen who was born or naturalized in the United States, the government must prove that the citizen voluntarily renounced his or her citizenship.[21] Although the burden is on the government, Congress need not impose a high standard of proof; proof by a "preponderance of the evidence" is sufficient.[2119]

See also: DEPORTATION; EXILE; IMMIGRATION AND NATURALIZATION.

expel a member   Under Art. I-§5[2], each house of Congress may by a two-thirds vote expel one of its members. Expulsion need not be solely for a criminal offense but may also be for any act that "in the judgment of the [house] is inconsistent with the trust and duty of a member."[375] The power to expel is not the same as the power to *exclude*, which is a much narrower power to judge by majority vote whether a person meets the constitutional qualifications for membership in the House or Senate.[1653]

See also: COMMITMENT TO OTHER BRANCHES.

expenditures, regular statement of, *see:* **account of the receipts and expenditures of all public money**

exports   Art. I-§9[5] prohibits Congress from taxing exported goods. A similar provision in Art. I-§10[2] prohibits the states from taxing either imports or exports without the consent of Congress. The general rule is that whenever a commodity loses its distinctive character as an import or export it may be taxed, but as long as it is still moving within the stream of foreign commerce it may not be.[831, 470] Taxing the income of export companies is not a tax on exports.[1582] But a sales tax on the sale and delivery of goods to a broker for a foreign consignee is impermissible under this clause.[1925] A state's nondiscriminatory property tax on all inventory in a warehouse, including imported goods to be sold in the United States, is constitutional.[1328]

See also: IMPORT-EXPORT CLAUSE; INSPECTION LAWS; ORIGINAL PACKAGE DOCTRINE.

exposure of a person's private life by Congress, *see:* **investigatory powers of Congress**

expropriation, *see:* **eminent domain**

expulsion from Congress, *see:* **expel a member**

extradition   The extradition clause in Art. IV-§2[2] requires the return of fugitives from justice who have fled from one state to another when the state from which they have fled demands their surrender. A state in which a wanted person is serving a jail sentence may have him serve out his term before returning him to the requesting state.[2003] A person living lawfully in one state is subject to extradition if another state indicts him in his absence.[1740] To be extradited, a fugitive must have been formally charged,[1627] but if he was never actually in the state that wants him, he may not be extradited there.[970] In 1987 the Supreme Court overruled an old precedent and held that one state may enforce its demand for extradition in federal court under a federal law regulating extradition procedures.[1674] The fugitive is entitled to contest an extradition order but in a limited fashion only; if he can prove he was not in the state seeking him when the crime was committed, he may not be extradited.[970] He is not entitled to be released because he has an alibi or because the STATUTE OF LIMITATIONS has run. Those questions must be considered at trial.[162] The extradition clause does not bar trial of a fugitive who has been kidnapped in one state and forcibly returned to stand trial in another.[1068, 458] This clause does not control foreign extraditions, which are governed by treaties between the United States and various nations.

extraterritoriality, *see:* **following the flag**

F

facially discriminatory   A law is said to be facially discriminatory if its language specifically draws lines on the basis of a forbidden classification, such as race or ethnic origin. A law segregating schools by race is facially discriminatory. A law may be neutral on its face but nevertheless discriminate, either intentionally or by application. For example, a law that requires candidates for public employment to be a certain height does not overtly discriminate but it may have a differential effect on women, who statistically are shorter. Whether a law neutral on its face is constitutional depends on its PURPOSE.

See also: INVALID ON ITS FACE; PURPOSE-IMPACT DISTINCTION; STATISTICAL EVIDENCE, USE OF; SUSPECT CLASSIFICATIONS.

fair hearing, *see:* **hearing**

fair housing, *see:* **housing discrimination**

fair return, *see:* **fair value fallacy**

fair trial, *see:* **free press–fair trial; trial, fairness of**

fair value fallacy   The fair value fallacy was a characterization of the Court's position in the late nineteenth and early twentieth centuries that railroads were entitled to a fair return on the value of their land.[1899] It was invoked in challenges to railroad rate commissions that demanded railroads cut exorbitant rates. The concept was branded a fallacy because the value of the land depended on the rates railroads could charge. The fair value doctrine was circular, forcing the states to give back to the railroads the value of what the regulation took away. The Court repudiated the doctrine in 1940.[648]

See also: RATE REGULATION.

fairness doctrine   The fairness doctrine was a rule of the Federal Communications Commission, later enacted into law by Congress, that required radio and television broadcasters "to afford reasonable opportunity for the discussion of conflicting views on issues of public importance." The Court upheld the doctrine in 1969,[1700] but Congress has since repealed the law.

See also: ACCESS TO BROADCASTING; FREE PRESS–FAIR TRIAL; GOVERNMENT DOCUMENTS, CONFIDENTIALITY OF; RIGHT TO REPLY.

faith and credit, *see:* **full faith and credit**

families The Constitution does not deal directly with family relations. Family autonomy—the right to live with one's family and to determine what is best for one's family, free of government interference—is only partially protected, mainly through the DUE PROCESS Clause but recently, especially in matters touching on illegitimacy and custodial rights to children, through the EQUAL PROTECTION CLAUSE and FREE EXERCISE CLAUSE. Several related questions have arisen during the past century concerning what limits may be imposed on the right to (1) marry, (2) bear children, (3) raise children according to one's own values, (4) live with or see one's children, (5) live in an "unconventional lifestyle," and (6) be free of the social stigma and legal disabilities stemming from illegitimacy. The answers are seemingly inconsistent, in part because the Court has drawn on different constitutional provisions to ward off state interference or justify state intrusions. MARRIAGE, PARENTAL RIGHTS AND RESPONSIBILITIES, ILLEGITIMACY, ADOPTION AND CUSTODY, and REPRODUCTIVE RIGHTS are discussed separately. As to preserving the family, the Court has written little because the states have generally not sought to interfere with "normal" family relations. Indeed, in 1989 the Court upheld a legal PRESUMPTION that the husband of a woman who has given birth is father of the child, even though the evidence showed that it was almost certain another man was the father.[1325]

In 1977 it did strike down an Ohio town's ordinance that was applied against a woman who lived with her son and two grandsons, one of whom was her son's child. Under the zoning ordinance, the family grouping was illegal. It would have been legal if the grandsons had been brothers rather than cousins. The town justified its ordinance by pointing to overcrowding and traffic congestion and argued that only a nuclear family—a couple and dependent children—has the constitutional right to live together. Disagreeing, Justice Lewis F. Powell pointed to a long tradition of extended families, "of uncles, aunts, cousins, and especially grandparents sharing a household along with parents and children." The Constitution, he said, prevents a town "from standardizing its children—and its adults—by forcing all to live in certain narrowly defined family patterns."[1379] But this right is evidently limited to true relatives. In an earlier case, the Court refused to recognize a constitutional right of groups of unrelated people to live together.[148]

See also: ABORTION; CONTRACEPTION; FREEDOM OF INTIMATE ASSOCIATION; HOMOSEXUALITY; JUVENILES; LEVEL OF GENERALITY; SEXUAL FREEDOM.

farm legislation, *see:* **agriculture, regulation of**

federal appellate courts, *see:* **appellate courts; Court of Appeals, U.S.;** *see also under specific names*

federal budget, *see:* **budget**

federal bureaucracy, *see:* **administrative agencies and bureaucratic government**

federal common law There is a subtle but profound constitutional distinction between the legal system of the states and that of the United States. The states may make law generally on any matter affecting their citizenry. They can determine what sorts of injuries should be redressable through lawsuits, develop the law of contracts, devise rules of inheritance, and enact codes of property law. Federal law, in comparison, is limited to areas enumerated in the Constitution. Today, of course, those areas are far broader than they were conceived in 1787. Nevertheless, Congress has no general authority to enact any law it wishes. Significant facets of life remain entrusted legally to the states.

Historically, many important bodies of law—negligence, contract, property, inheritance, commercial relations—were developed by the courts, not by the legislatures, which only in the late nineteenth century began to enact the codes that are an omnipresent feature of modern law. The state courts continue to develop the law through the case-by-case system of adjudication, or COMMON LAW jurisdiction.

Under the DIVERSITY JURISDICTION, federal courts have the power to hear litigants who have claims under state law. In 1789 Congress instructed federal courts to use state law when deciding these cases. But the question arose what "law" means—is it only an enactment of a legislature, or is it, more broadly, also the decisions of the courts? In 1842 Justice Joseph Story said that "law" means only acts of legislatures.[1990] In the absence of state legislation, he said, the federal courts may decide such cases by making their own law—*federal common law.* So if the question was whether a party to a contract had breached it, a federal court could answer differently from the courts of the state in which the dispute arose. By this audacious ruling, Story gave the federal government a backdoor approach to making general law for the people of the United States. This concept of federal common law lasted ninety-six years, until the Court, in 1938, under the ERIE RULE, finally announced that Story had been profoundly mistaken, proclaiming that "there is no federal general common law." In other words, unless Congress has preempted state commercial laws, a federal court must apply the law of the state in a diversity jurisdiction case, whether that law is expressed in an act of the legislature or in the state's common law.

However, the matter does not neatly end there. For on the very day that Justice Brandeis announced that there is no federal *general* common law, he wrote a majority opinion in another case holding that how waters of an interstate stream are to be divided between two states "is a question of 'federal common law.'"[922] He meant that the common law system of adjudication remains at the heart of federal courts. In hearing cases involving *federal* law, the federal courts will continue to develop a common law—one that envelops the Constitution itself, the enactments of Congress, and the areas of law entrusted to the federal government by the Constitution. Federal common law, in other words, is a large and lively body of law, but it is confined to areas of federal concern. The federal courts do not have the power to intrude on the common law of the states, unless commanded by the Constitution or other federal law.

See also: COMMON LAW; CRIMES, COMMON LAW; FEDERALISM; SUPREMACY CLAUSE.

federal courts, *see: specific (named) courts and types*

federal grants in aid, *see:* **grants in aid**

federal injunction against state proceedings, *see:* **abstention**

federal labor injunction, *see:* **labor injunction**

federal lands, *see:* **public property**

federal number, *see:* **three-fifths rule**

federal powers, *see:* **federalism**

federal protection of civil rights, *see:* **civil rights legislation**

federal question jurisdiction Federal question jurisdiction is the power of federal courts under Art. III §2[1] to hear "cases, in law and equity, arising under this Constitution, the laws of the United States, and treaties made, or which shall be made, under their authority." The First Congress did not confer jurisdiction on the lower federal courts to hear cases raising federal questions, leaving such matters to the state courts, with ultimate though limited review in the Supreme Court. Until after the Civil War, the lower federal courts mainly heard admiralty and maritime claims, patent cases, suits asserting treaty rights, and cases raising state issues through the DIVERSITY JURISDICTION. In 1875 Congress expanded the jurisdiction of the federal courts to include federal questions, so that litigants claiming legal rights or entitlements under the Constitution and all federal laws could take their cases to federal court. From the very first Judiciary Act of 1789, Congress imposed a dollar limitation on federal suits. Litigants could bring diversity cases only if the "amount in controversy" was more than five hundred dollars—the same jurisdictional amount imposed in 1875 when the federal courts gained federal question jurisdiction. Over the years Congress both raised the amount for certain classes of cases (to more than ten thousand dollars in many instances) and abolished the amount for other cases. Finally, in 1980 it abolished the jurisdictional amount requirement altogether. Whether a suit actually "arises under" the Constitution or federal law is a complex, much-litigated question, but the issue largely turns on statutory, not constitutional, interpretation.

See also: JUDICIAL POWER; JURISDICTION; PENDENT JURISDICTION; REMOVAL OF CASES.

Federal Tort Claims Act, *see:* **sovereign immunity**

federal trial courts, *see:* **district courts**

federalism   Federalism is one of the distinctive American contributions to political theory and practice. That it takes practice is evident from the tensions among the sister republics in the former Soviet Union and from the bloody battles in other Eastern European countries. The Framers were concerned to give only those powers to a central government necessary to protect the nation while reserving all other powers to the states.

The Constitution is replete with provisions designed to further this end. For example, in the original Constitution, the people directly elected only members of the House of Representatives. The state legislatures elected senators (direct election was provided for only in the SEVENTEENTH AMENDMENT); and the ELECTORAL COLLEGE system gives the states considerable influence in the election of the president. Within its own sphere, the federal government is supreme. But Congress has only ENUMERATED POWERS, not a general writ to legislate whatever it pleases. And the TENTH AMENDMENT reserves to the states and the people all powers not delegated to the federal government.

The principles are more easily stated than followed. For two hundred years federalism has been a major political and constitutional issue, although the number of cases has been far fewer than the heated debate would suggest. The difficulties that ensue from having two supposedly sovereign authorities governing the same body of people have been resolved more in the political arena than in the courts. Nevertheless, the Court from time to time has had to consider three important and continuing constitutional questions: (1) What power does the federal government have to tell the states what to do, and vice versa? (2) May the federal government impose constitutional restraints on states' activities? (3) What constitutional restraints, if any, block federal commands in matters that affect state lawmaking?

(1) In *McCulloch v. Maryland,* Chief Justice John Marshall in 1819 set the terms of the debate—and answered a good part of it. Maryland imposed a fifteen-thousand-dollar tax on

banks operating but not incorporated in the state. The Bank of the United States, chartered by Congress, had a branch in Baltimore and refused to pay the tax. The state sued to collect it. Marshall agreed that the power of taxation is *concurrent;* both federal and state governments have the power to tax as they please, within constitutional limits. But pointing to the supremacy of federal law, Marshall observed "[t]hat the power to tax involves the power to destroy; [and] that the power to destroy may defeat and render useless the power to create." If Maryland could tax the federal bank it could destroy it. The only control over federal agencies must come from the federal government, not from the states.

Whether the federal government could tax state agencies was a question Marshall left open. The Supreme Court gave its first answer in 1871 in *Collector v. Day,* when it ruled that although a general federal income tax was permissible, it would be unconstitutional to tax a state officer's salary. In 1939 the Court expressly overruled *Collector,*[795] and in 1946 held that the federal government could tax a state-run mineral water business.[1459a] Although the general rule today is less than clear, the Court seems to be saying that the federal government may tax any activity of the states except those thought "to be essential to the preservation of state governments."[893] The rule is not, therefore, reciprocal. As the Court said in 1988, the federal government may directly tax some state activities, but the states may never directly tax federal activities.[1910]

Taxation is not the only means of invading a sovereign's operations. That may be done as well by direct regulation or indirect coercion. The Supremacy Clause clearly prohibits the states from regulating federal activities, and the Court has been alert to attempts by states to do so. In a 1920 case, the Court said that a state may not require a U.S. postal employee to have a state driver's license if he has been licensed

by the federal government to operate a postal truck.[1018] Much more recently, the Court invalidated North Dakota laws aimed at undermining federal policy under the Migratory Bird Conservation Act.[1497]

But there is no reverse Supremacy Clause to enable the states to avoid regulation by the federal government. In 1976, in *National League of Cities v. Usery,* the Supreme Court upheld a challenge to the federal Fair Labor Standards Act under which all state and local government employees were entitled to the act's maximum hour and minimum wage requirements. Justice William H. Rehnquist said that the law would impermissibly interfere with "integral [state] government functions." But in 1985 the Court, 5–4, reversed *National League of Cities.* Justice Harry Blackmun said that the attempt to fence out federal regulation from "traditional governmental functions" is "not only unworkable but is inconsistent with established principles of federalism."[724] The question was whether the minimum wage and overtime requirements of the Fair Labor Standards Act could be applied to the San Antonio, Texas, Metropolitan Transit Authority workers. Unable to decide whether the transit authority was a traditional government function, the Court said that whether or not it is, Congress has sufficient COMMERCE POWER to bring mass transit workers within the law. The dissenters bitterly disagreed, and Justice Rehnquist served warning that "in time" a new majority would uphold an immunity for traditional government functions.

Aside from direct regulation, Congress may attempt to coerce the states into adopting policies that they might not choose on their own. Much of this power derives from federal GRANTS IN AID. In a line of cases, the Court has agreed that Congress has great leeway to use its grants to cajole the states into acting as it wishes. In 1987, for example, the Court sustained a law that said that five percent of a state's allotment of federal highway funds would be withheld unless it enacted a law prohibiting anyone under twenty-one years old from purchasing alcohol. Congress has no direct power to set the drinking age, but the Court said it could act indirectly to accomplish the same end.[1915]

(2) The federal government had only anemic power to restrain state activities when the Constitution was ratified because the BILL OF RIGHTS was understood to confine only federal power.[132] Today, however, the power looms large. The change is attributable almost entirely to the adoption of the Fourteenth Amendment, which during our own era has permitted the federal courts to "incorporate" and apply most of the enumerated rights and many unenumerated ones against the states.

(3) For about fifty years, until the COURT-PACKING PLAN persuaded the justices to rethink constitutional law in the late 1930s, the Court had often interpreted the Tenth Amendment as a direct brake on Congress's power to enact legislation regulating INTERSTATE COMMERCE. The rise and fall of this doctrine is considered under separate headings.

For nearly three-quarters of a century, the fight over SLAVERY engendered another crisis of federalism. A theory of NULLIFICATION, originated by Jefferson and Madison for other reasons, held that the sovereignty of states entitled them to reject unwelcome federal legislation. The Civil War made the issue politically and constitutionally extinct.

See also: ANTI-FEDERALISTS; CONSTITUTIONAL CONVENTION; *FULL FAITH AND CREDIT; INCORPORATION DOCTRINE; NULLIFICATION, INTERPOSITION, AND SECESSION; PRIVILEGES AND IMMUNITIES; SEPARATION OF POWERS; SPENDING POWER.*

Federalist Papers   *The Federalist* is a collection of eighty-five essays written pseudonymously in 1787 and 1788 by James Madison, Alexander Hamilton, and John Jay to promote ratification of the Constitution in New York and Virginia. First published in newspapers under the name "Publius," the essays were collected soon thereafter and published in book form. They are elegant and profound, ranging across the entire proposed Constitution and brilliantly defending its new theory of government. *The Federalist* has endured as a masterwork of political philosophy and as the most comprehensive guide to the ORIGINAL INTENT of the Framers.

feigned cases, *see:* **cases or controversies**

felony   Crimes are usually classified by their seriousness. Misdemeanors are lesser crimes, generally carrying a penalty of no more than a year in jail. Felonies are more serious crimes carrying longer prison terms. Except perhaps in the extreme situation in which a law imposed a heavy sentence for a trivial offense (say, two years for a parking ticket), the Constitution is indifferent to the classification. Under federal law, a felony is any crime punishable by imprisonment for more than a year. State laws vary. Whether misdemeanor or felony, prosecution for any crime punishable by any amount of time in jail requires the state to provide a lawyer for those who cannot afford one.

See also: COUNSEL, ASSISTANCE OF; INDICTMENT; *PROPORTIONALITY OF SENTENCE; TRIAL BY JURY.*

feminism and pornography   Beginning in the 1980s, many feminists have pressed the idea that pornography subordinates women and hence is a form of SEX DISCRIMINATION. In 1984 the Indianapolis City Council adopted an ordinance banning pornography under this theory. The ordinance defined pornography as "the graphic sexually explicit subordination of women in pictures or in words." To be "graphic" within the meaning of the ordinance, the offending work had to present women as sexual objects who enjoy pain or humiliation, experience pleasure in being raped, or who are physically injured, "presented in scenarios of degradation," or depicted for "domination, conquest, violation, exploitation, possession or use." The Supreme Court summarily affirmed a decision by the U.S. Court of Appeals for the Seventh Circuit, striking down the law because it violates the FIRST AMENDMENT.[48] Circuit Judge Frank Easterbrook said that the constitutional problem with the ordinance is that it "discriminates on the ground of the content of the speech." No matter how sexually explicit a work was, it would be permissible if it showed women in an approved manner. No matter how artistic or valuable the work was, it would be impermissible if it showed women in the disapproved way. But "the Constitution forbids the state to declare one perspective right and silence opponents."

See also: FREEDOM OF SPEECH; OBSCENITY AND PORNOGRAPHY; SPEECH, REGULATION OF CONTENT.

Fifteenth Amendment The Fifteenth Amendment was proposed by Congress on February 26, 1869, and was ratified on March 30, 1870. It prohibits federal or state governments from denying the right to vote to anyone on the basis of "race, color, or previous condition of servitude." Section 2 of the FOURTEENTH AMENDMENT appeared to contemplate the right of blacks (though not women) to vote. It provided that if any state denied the right to any "male inhabitants" over twenty-one years old, the state's representation in Congress and its delegates to the ELECTORAL COLLEGE would be proportionately reduced. These reductions never occurred, despite a century-long practice of denying black suffrage. Under the Reconstruction Act the southern states after the Civil War were bound to enfranchise blacks, but the border and northern states were not, and many did not. In 1868 Ulysses S. Grant won election to the White House by a very narrow margin. Without southern black votes he would have lost the popular vote. Democrats were making

a strong comeback, and to remain in control of Congress, the Republicans wrote the Fifteenth Amendment to provide a firmer constitutional basis for black suffrage. Many blacks were immediately elected to state offices across the south. But by the end of the century, various devices, including the POLL TAX and LITERACY TESTS, killed black registration and voting, and the Supreme Court's indifference or outright hostility to black suffrage led it to sustain almost all the tricks. The right to vote began to be vindicated, north and south, only in the late 1960s after enactment of the VOTING RIGHTS ACT OF 1965.

See also: VOTING, RIGHT TO.

Fifth Amendment The Fifth Amendment, part of the BILL OF RIGHTS, contains a cluster of significant rights, including the right to be free of federal prosecution unless indicted by a GRAND JURY, the right against DOUBLE JEOPARDY and SELF-INCRIMINATION, and the right to JUST COMPENSATION if the government takes property for public use. It also contains the federal DUE PROCESS Clause.

See also: EMINENT DOMAIN; INDICTMENT; TAKING OF PROPERTY.

fighting words In 1942 the Supreme Court sustained a New Hampshire law making it a crime to shout offensive or derisive words at anyone on a public street. The state supreme court had narrowed the law to apply only to "face-to-face words" that would likely provoke the hearer to fight. In the case, *Chaplinsky v. New Hampshire,* a Jehovah's Witness had stirred up a crowd by condemning religion as a "racket," and as he was being escorted away he got into a shouting match with a city marshal. Chaplinsky called the marshal a "God damned racketeer" and a "damned Fascist" and was arrested. For a unanimous Court, Justice Frank Murphy said those words were "likely to provoke the average person to retaliation, and thereby cause a breach of the peace." The Court's approval of laws against fighting words, as a limitation of FREEDOM OF SPEECH, has since been considerably watered down. In several cases in the early 1970s, the Court extended FIRST AMENDMENT protection to vulgarisms and "four-letter words" in situations not likely, by the less straitjacketed sensibilities of a later age, to cause particular people to fight. In fact, *Chaplinsky* was the last case in which the Supreme Court upheld a conviction for use of fighting words. In a trio of 1972 cases, the Court reversed the convictions of some unruly people who shouted at police officers among others such things, as the Court rather squeamishly rephrased it, as "m---f--- fascist pig cops." Although the Court's reasons for reversing were a bit mixed, the gist in two of the cases seemed to be that police officers are supposed to be trained to resist retaliating merely because people are shouting vulgarities at them.[1761, 1159, 256] The year before, the Court reversed a breach of peace conviction of a man who wore a leather jacket with the word "fuck" emblazoned on the back. This vulgarity was not within the fighting-words exception to the First Amendment because it was not aimed at anyone in particular.[417]

See also: BREACH OF THE PEACE; DEMONSTRATORS AND DEMONSTRATIONS; OFFENSIVE AND INDECENT SPEECH.

filing fees, *see:* **court costs and fees**

film, censorship of, *see:* **censorship; prior restraint**

final judgment   A final judgment is the end of a case. Under ordinary circumstances, an appeals court may review only the final judgment of trial courts, not their preliminary rulings while the case is still in progress. The rule does not bar the Supreme Court from hearing cases at any stage in the U.S. COURTS OF APPEALS, but it does prohibit review of any case in the state

courts until a final judgment has been issued by the highest court permitted to rule on it. So litigants may not appeal directly to the Supreme Court after losing at trial. In the federal system they must first appeal to a court of appeals; in the state courts they must appeal in whatever manner the state provides. Only when the state appeal process finishes, including a decision by an appeals court not to review, may a case be appealed to the Supreme Court. The rule sounds stricter than it is in practice, since both legislatures and courts have created exceptions.

See also: REVIEW, TIMING OF.

finality   Finality is an important incident of the JUDICIAL POWER granted to the federal courts under Article III. Since 1792 the Court has steadfastly clung to a rule that forbids federal courts from hearing any case over which their FINAL JUDGMENT can be legally disregarded by another branch of government. The issue first arose when Congress directed veterans of the Revolutionary War to file pension claims in federal circuit courts. Under the pension law, the circuit judges were required to certify to the secretary of war the degree of a claimant's war-related disability and what his monthly stipend should be. The secretary was authorized to refuse a pension if he thought that the courts had been defrauded or made a mistake. Today such a task is routinely carried out by administrative boards within the Defense Department without constitutional difficulty.

In 1792 a circuit court refused to take on these administrative duties when a veteran named Hayburn filed a claim. The secretary sought a writ of MANDAMUS in the Supreme Court to order the judge to act. The Supreme Court heard argument but delayed its decision, waiting for Congress to change the law so that the courts' decisions were not subject to the secretary's whim. When Congress did, the

Court dismissed *Hayburn's Case*, but notes of the justices' views were appended to the record, and the Court has followed the logic ever since. In 1948 the Court dismissed an appeal of an airline route award made by the Civil Aeronautics Board. Under the law, the president was empowered to revise or revoke the award after judicial appeals had concluded. The Court concluded that "if the President may completely disregard the judgment of the court, it would be only because it is one the courts were not authorized to render. Judgments within the powers vested in courts [by the Constitution] . . . may not lawfully be revised, overturned or refused faith and credit by another Department of Government."[388] Finality does not bar a legislature from changing the law for later cases. It means only that the government may not change the result in a particular case.

See also: REVIEW, TIMING OF.

finding   When a trial judge, sitting without a jury, determines that a particular version of the facts in a case represents the events as they really happened, the determination is known as a "finding." A judge's findings are not ordinarily reviewable on appeal and may be overturned only if there is no basis in the record to support them.

fines, excessive, *see:* **bail and fines**

fingerprints, *see:* **self-incrimination**

fire, right to shout   "The most stringent protection of free speech would not protect a man in falsely shouting fire in a theatre and causing a panic," said Justice Oliver Wendell Holmes in 1919 in *Schenck v. United States.* This famous line is often misquoted by omitting the word "falsely" and sometimes by adding the word "crowded" before "theatre." Holmes used the image to justify the CLEAR AND PRESENT DANGER formula first announced in the case. Holmes meant that the FIRST AMENDMENT would not bar a law against causing a panic under those circumstances. Holmes's epigram does not say that the state could constitutionally prohibit *truthfully* shouting fire, even if a panic ensued.

See also: FREEDOM OF SPEECH *and cross references listed there.*

firearms inspections, *see:* **search and seizure: administrative inspections**

First Amendment   The First Amendment makes the United States unique among nations by withdrawing from all government the power to dictate what people must feel or believe, how they may worship, what they may say, to whom they may say it, with whom they may mingle, and what they may demand of their government. The power to dictate or control these things is the power to enslave a nation. By freeing the people from government shackles over these fundamental rights of expression, the First Amendment confirms the political theory of the Framers that SOVEREIGNTY lies in the people, not in the government. James Madison, the chief drafter of the First Amendment, had proposed another article also: "The equal rights of conscience, the freedom of speech or of the press, and the right of trial by jury in criminal cases shall not be infringed by any *state.*" Madison thought this to be "the most valuable of the whole list." But Congress rejected it, and as finally drafted, the First Amendment, along with all the other articles of the BILL OF RIGHTS, limited only the federal government. That is why the First Amendment begins: *"Congress* shall make no law. . . ." So understood, many later perplexities simply disappear. The First Amendment says the federal government has no part in establishing a religion, interfering with a person's religious activity, abridging the right to speak or publish, or limiting the right to assemble and

"petition the government for a redress of grievances." But it did not deny that power to the
states. As long as these prohibitions did not
apply to the states, difficult questions could be
avoided. With the piecemeal INCORPORATION
of the First Amendment, however, the questions became more pressing. Once the word
"Congress" is replaced with "any government"
it became necessary to find the limits, if any, of
the rights guaranteed. These topics are explored under the separate headings listed
below.

*See also: FREEDOM OF ASSEMBLY; FREEDOM OF ASSOCIATION;
FREEDOM OF BELIEF; FREEDOM OF INTIMATE ASSOCIATION;
FREEDOM OF PETITION; FREEDOM OF RELIGION; FREEDOM OF
SPEECH; FREEDOM OF THE PRESS; RELIGIOUS ESTABLISHMENT;
and cross references listed under each heading.*

fiscal power of federal government, *see:*
spending power; taxing power

fish and game laws, *see:* **game laws**

flag burning and desecration   For decades,
many state laws have prohibited casting "contempt" on the American flag through various
forms of desecration and misuse—for example,
mutilating, burning, defacing, and trampling
upon it. In several decisions since the late 1960s
the Court has, often by the narrowest margins,
struck down the laws for VAGUENESS, OVER-
BREADTH, or because they were used to constrict constitutionally protected behavior. In a
1969 case, the Court, 5–4, reversed the conviction of a man for "speaking defiant or contemptuous words about the American flag,"[1969] a
decision it followed in 1974 in rejecting a Massachusetts law against contemptuous treatment
of the flag as applied to a man who sewed a
replica of the flag onto the seat of his pants.[1889]
That same year, the Court, 6–3, reversed the
conviction of a man for putting a peace symbol
over a flag which he draped out his apartment
window to protest the U.S. invasion of Cam-

bodia and the shootings at Kent State University in 1970. The state claimed an interest in
preserving the universality of the American
flag as a national symbol. Without deciding
whether such an interest is permissible, the
majority agreed that no conviction could be
sustained for engaging in a peaceful political
protest.[1931]

In 1989 and 1990 two highly controversial
decisions against flag burning laws, both by 5–4
margins, suggest that although the political
storm has abated, a constitutional one may still
be stirring. In the first case, a Texas law prohibited desecration of a "venerated object," including the Texas or American flag, by physically damaging it so as to "seriously offend one
or more persons likely to observe or discover"
the act of desecration. A man protesting the
Republican National Convention in Dallas in
1984 publicly burned the flag, chanting "America, the red, white, and blue, we spit on you."
No one was hurt, but several members of the
crowd testified that they had been "offended."
The Court reversed the conviction. Justice
William Brennan said that there had been no
BREACH OF THE PEACE because the rally remained nonviolent, and no FIGHTING WORDS
had been addressed to anyone. Since Texas
permitted flags to be burned when they were
worn out, the only reason for the prosecution
in this case was to restrict the message that the
protester wished to convey. Punishing advocacy of a political message violates the constitutional right to FREEDOM OF SPEECH.[2021]

In the ensuing uproar over the Court's decision, egged on by the newly elected President
Bush, who urged Congress to propose a constitutional amendment against flag burning, Congress rapidly enacted the Flag Protection Act
of 1989, purporting to cure the problems of the
Texas law. The federal act prohibited anyone
from "knowingly mutilat[ing], defac[ing],
physically defil[ing], burn[ing] . . . or
trampl[ing] upon" any American flag. It was

immediately put to the test, and the Court rejected this law as well.[605] Justice Brennan rejected the government's two major contentions—that flag burning, like obscenity and fighting words, is not protected by the First Amendment, and that the law was not aimed at expression. Justice Brennan noted that each of the banned acts, with the possible exception of burning, "unmistakably connotes disrespectful treatment of the flag" and suggests that the government's real interest was preventing damage to the flag's "symbolic value." That, said Justice Brennan, the government may not do: "Punishing desecration of the flag dilutes the very freedom that makes this emblem so revered, and worth revering."

In essence, the slim majority has held that the First Amendment does not permit the government to put a symbol beyond the reach of its critics. The angry dissenters, however, saw these laws as legitimate under the Court's rule governing SYMBOLIC SPEECH. Said Justice John Paul Stevens in the Texas case: "This case has nothing to do with 'disagreeable ideas.' It involves disagreeable conduct." Chief Justice Rehnquist said that flag burning is not the expression of an idea but "the equivalent of an inarticulate grunt or roar . . . indulged in . . . to antagonize others." The dissenters also argued for a more striking proposition: that the symbolic value of the flag is unique, and alone of all symbols the government may preserve its value as "a symbol of freedom, of equal opportunity, of religious tolerance, and of goodwill for other peoples." A move in Congress for a constitutional amendment giving Congress and the states power to prevent physical desecration of the flag failed in June 1990. Nothing came of many dark vows to inject the issue into the 1990 political campaign, perhaps because by then the country was caught up in guessing whether the United States would declare war on Iraq for its August invasion of Kuwait. So although the issue is dormant, the retirement of two in the majority, Justices Brennan and Thurgood Marshall, suggest that the rule against flag burning laws is not necessarily permanent.

See also: OLYMPICS, USE OF NAME.

flag saluting In 1940 the Supreme Court upheld a West Virginia law permitting children to be expelled from school for refusing to salute the flag and pledge allegiance during classroom exercises. The children, Jehovah's Witnesses, objected that saluting was "forbidden by command of scripture," a verse in Exodus, chapter 20:4–5 ("Thou shalt not make unto thee any graven image"). The Court denied that the children's FREEDOM OF RELIGION had been infringed.[1353] The decision set off a chain reaction against the Witnesses. A week after the decision was announced, the Justice Department received reports of hundreds of serious physical attacks on Witnesses from communities across the country. Three years later, the Court reversed itself, holding on free speech grounds that the states have no power to compel someone to salute a flag or otherwise make a political statement. Said Justice Robert H. Jackson: "[I]f there is any fixed star in our constitutional constellation, it is that no official, high or petty, can prescribe what shall be orthodox in politics, nationalism, religion, or other matters of opinion or force citizens to confess by word or act their faith therein."[2186]

following the flag The question whether the Constitution "follows the flag"—that is, applies to actions by government officials outside the territory of the United States—has occasionally reached the Court with equivocal results. A century ago the Court said: "The Constitution can have no operation in another country,"[1763] and it approved the prosecution of an American citizen, accused of crimes aboard an American ship in Japan, before a consular court with benefit of neither indictment nor jury. In

1901 the Court went further and said that "unincorporated territory" of the United States, such as Puerto Rico and Hawaii when first acquired, were not places where Congress or the courts were restrained by the Constitution; therefore, Congress could enact a nonuniform tax,[572] and a criminal jury could consist of fewer than twelve people.[852] But after World War II, the Court shifted ground and said the Constitution must apply when the government deals with citizens abroad. This new extraterritorial "bite" came in a case in which the dependent wife of an Air Force officer was tried for his murder by court-martial in Germany without a jury; the Court held that the SIXTH AMENDMENT right to trial by a civilian jury was required.[1706] But the World War II experience also confirmed another line of cases holding that the constitutional flag does not follow non-citizens, as the Court declared in denying HABEAS CORPUS to a German national being held as an enemy in a camp outside the United States.[1016] The modern Court seems to have adhered to this distinction, turning down in 1990 the bid of a foreign defendant to suppress evidence that would have been barred by the EXCLUSIONARY RULE if it had been taken in the United States. American agents, without search warrants, rummaged through the Mexican residence of a Mexican citizen. The Court held that the FOURTH AMENDMENT does not apply "when searching the foreign home of a nonresident alien."[2124]

See also: RIGHTS IN WARTIME.

food and drug regulation   The first federal food and drug law, the Pure Food and Drug Act, was enacted in 1906 during a time when the Supreme Court was leery of many economic regulations. But in 1911 the Court sustained the act as clearly falling within Congress's COMMERCE POWER to bar any commodity it wished from INTERSTATE COMMERCE.[920] The act and its revision by the Food, Drug, and Cosmetic Act of 1938, which the Court also upheld,[1978] prohibit the manufacture of misbranded and adulterated food and drugs and give the federal government sweeping enforcement powers. An occasional problem has been the degree to which the states may simultaneously regulate food and drugs. In general, the Court has said that the states have considerable leeway to protect the health and safety of their citizens. In dozens of cases it has upheld state quarantine, inspection, and labeling laws. It has tended to strike down state laws only when they directly conflict with federal regulation—for example, when a state said that certain commodities could carry no label other than those specified in the state law, but federal law required another label;[1289] or when the state laws impede the flow of or discriminate against interstate commerce. The Court invalidated a Virginia law that required out-of-state flour to be inspected upon its arrival but required no locally made flour to be inspected.[2135] It has also struck down a Wisconsin law prohibiting the sale of any pasteurized milk that had not been processed and bottled at certain plants in Wisconsin,[528] and a North Carolina law discriminatorily regulating the labeling of out-of-state apples.[959]

See also: INSPECTION LAWS; QUARANTINE LAWS.

"for sale" signs   An ordinance of Willingboro, New Jersey, prohibited homeowners from posting "for sale" and "sold" signs on their property. Although agreeing that the town had a significant interest in building a stable and racially integrated community, which the ban on real estate signs might serve by preventing "white flight," the Court, 8–0, disagreed that such a ban is within a community's power. The town was not trying to regulate the commercial aspects of a real estate transaction but to restrict the free flow of information, which is an abridgment of FREEDOM OF SPEECH.[1170]

force acts, *see:* **Ku Klux Klan Act**

foreign affairs power   Although power over the foreign affairs of the United States is not clearly defined in the Constitution, no one disputes that it is a power of the federal government, not the states; and a power largely, though not exclusively, vested in the president. Article I vests in Congress the power to regulate foreign commerce, including the authority to ban foreign-made goods and to impose tariffs. Congress has the power to regulate naturalization, to declare war, raise armies, regulate the state militia, and punish crimes at sea and against international law. Under the NECESSARY AND PROPER CLAUSE, it can legislate the admiralty and maritime law and fund and oversee the foreign policy establishment of the United States and fill in the gaps of treaties negotiated by the president. As COMMANDER IN CHIEF, the president is empowered under Article II to conduct war. He alone negotiates treaties, appoints and receives ambassadors, and extends or withdraws DIPLOMATIC RECOGNITION. Under Article III, the federal courts are empowered to hear cases involving foreign diplomats and citizens and cases arising under treaties. Moreover, the states are denied powers to make treaties or foreign alliances, keep troops, make war, tax imports or exports, or regulate the territories of the United States. From these enumerated powers, the federal government has drawn a host of unenumerated ones, such as Congress's power to control immigration and expel aliens and the president's power to enter international agreements even without Senate approval. In 1936 the Supreme Court concluded that even if all these provisions were not in the Constitution, the federal government would still possess exclusive power over the international arena because the states had never possessed them. Without power over foreign affairs, the United States would not be a sovereign nation.[505] Although conflicts between state law and the foreign affairs power rarely reach the Court, when they do the Court has voided any infringing state law. For example, it struck down an Oregon law that barred paying an alien an inheritance unless his country would grant reciprocal rights to any U.S. citizen due to receive an inheritance from that country. This was an unconstitutional attempt to control American foreign policy.[2289]

The more heated debates about the foreign affairs power have centered on the relation between Congress and the president. The presumption has been that under the EXECUTIVE POWER, the president's power is paramount, and the Court has almost always sustained the president's claim to it. Usually the president acts under powers delegated by Congress, and the Court has declared that it will pay extraordinary deference to this kind of DELEGATION. In sustaining the president's embargo on the sale of arms to Bolivia when it was engaged in a battle with Paraguay, the Court said that the constitutional authority to act stemmed not only from a congressional delegation of power but from "the very delicate, plenary and exclusive power of the president as the sole organ of the federal government in the field of international relations."[505]

See also: EXECUTIVE AGREEMENT; PRESIDENT, POWERS AND DUTIES OF; TREATIES AND TREATY POWER; WAR POWER.

foreign commerce, *see:* **commerce, foreign**

foreign languages taught in schools, *see:* **schools, foreign languages in**

forfeiture   Forfeiture is the surrendering of assets to the government. Under the federal Continuing Criminal Enterprise Act, the government may seize all assets, including profits, realized from an accused defendant's drug sales. On a proper showing in court, the government may seize the assets even before an INDICTMENT and even recapture assets given to third parties. An indicted drug defendant paid money to a prominent law firm to represent him at trial, and the United States moved to recapture all the funds the defendant had transferred to the law firm. The lawyers resisted on the ground that an order freezing the assets would violate their client's SIXTH AMENDMENT right to counsel of his choice and would make it impossible to hire other counsel, since he would have no money to pay. The Court upheld the forfeiture provision. The defendant never had the legal right to "his ill-gotten gains," said Justice Byron R. White, and Congress may "lessen the economic power of organized crime and drug enterprises" by negating their "undeserved economic power," especially "the ability to command high priced legal talent."[339] If the forfeiture impoverishes the defendant so that he cannot afford a lawyer, the court will appoint one.

See also: COUNSEL, ASSISTANCE OF.

form of government, *see:* **republican form of government**

formation of new states, *see:* **state, formation of new**

forts, *see:* **public property**

forum, public, *see:* **public forum**

foster families, *see:* **families; parents, foster**

Fourteenth Amendment   The Fourteenth Amendment, proposed by Congress on June 13, 1866, and ratified on July 9, 1868, was drafted in large measure because of doubts that the Reconstruction Congress had the power to enact CIVIL RIGHTS LEGISLATION. But the Republicans then in power, who could muster a two-thirds vote to override President Andrew Johnson's veto of the Civil Rights Act of 1866, feared that they might soon lose political control because

of an unintended constitutional consequence of the THIRTEENTH AMENDMENT. By ending slavery, it automatically repealed the THREE-FIFTHS RULE, under which slaves had been counted as less than a person for purposes of apportioning representation in Congress. For that reason, the 1870 census might soon have shifted House seats to the South. So in early 1866, Congress established the Joint Committee on Reconstruction to try to solve these problems. After many months and drafts, the present text of the Fourteenth Amendment emerged. It sought to minimize the political power of the South by tying representation to voting. If a state stood in the way of black voting, its representation would suffer. Black votes, northern Republicans figured, would mean votes against a Democratic South. The amendment also disqualified from any federal office those who had taken an oath to the Confederacy. These provisions, seemingly important at the time, were either not enforced or are now moot. Far more reaching were the provisions in Section 1 that heralded a second constitutional revolution. First, the amendment put U.S. CITIZENSHIP on its first firm constitutional footing, declaring that citizenship is national and goes with birth. Second, in a single sentence it pronounced a trio of rights that would ultimately alter the constitutional balance between nation and states: "No state shall make or enforce any law which shall abridge the privileges or immunities of citizens of the United States; nor shall any State deprive any person of life, liberty, or property, without due process of law; nor deny to any person within its jurisdiction the equal protection of the laws." Congress was given power to enforce these provisions. Although the Supreme Court killed the privileges or immunities clause within a few years after ratification,[1882] the DUE PROCESS Clause became the basis for applying the BILL OF RIGHTS to the states. The EQUAL PROTECTION CLAUSE, in time, would become the basis for desegregating

American society. These provisions have proved to be the most far-reaching amendments to the Constitution.

See also: DUE PROCESS; EQUAL PROTECTION OF THE LAWS; INCORPORATION DOCTRINE; SEGREGATION AND INTEGRATION; and cross references listed under those headings.

Fourth Amendment   The Fourth Amendment prohibits unreasonable SEARCH AND SEIZURE and requires PROBABLE CAUSE and a particularized description of what is to be searched before a SEARCH WARRANT can be issued. The Fourth Amendment was a response to the use of general warrants by British authorities in colonial days. A general warrant authorized British agents to look anywhere, often for unnamed people, in searching for illegalities, including seditious publications, possession of contraband goods, vagrancy, and many other activities that today would not be illegal. In many colonies the authorities used general warrants or writs of ASSISTANCE to collect taxes and often simply to police the morals of the community. Attacks against general warrants and writs of assistance intensified after 1760 in both England and the colonies, culminating in the Fourth Amendment in 1791. Government invasion of people's homes continues to be a problem, and in 1972 the Court said that the Fourth Amendment itself permits DAMAGE suits when government agents knowingly violate it.[168]

See also: CONSTITUTIONAL TORTS.

fourth branch, *see:* **administrative agencies and bureaucratic government**

Framers of the Constitution, *see:* **Constitution, Framers of**

franchise restrictions, *see:* **voting, right to**

free exercise, *see:* **freedom of religion**

Free Exercise Clause   The Free Exercise Clause is one of three religion clauses in the Constitution. It appears in the FIRST AMENDMENT along with the ESTABLISHMENT CLAUSE. The third clause, the RELIGIOUS TEST clause, appears in Article VI. The Free Exercise Clause provides that the government may not interfere with the people's practice of their religions. In general it has served to protect individual forms of worship and private devotion against laws that might tend to curb religious activity, but it has proved less diligent as a protector of religious ways of life that run counter to widely held social norms. Cases interpreting its reach are discussed under FREEDOM OF RELIGION.

See also: RELIGIOUS ESTABLISHMENT.

free persons   The reference to "free persons" in Art. I-§2[3], a provision no longer operative, was one of the many not so subtle allusions to the original Constitution's sanction of SLAVERY. To determine congressional apportionment, free persons counted for more than slaves.

See also: OTHER PERSONS; THREE-FIFTHS RULE.

free press–fair trial   In 1941 Justice Hugo L. Black observed that "free speech and fair trial are two of the most cherished policies of our civilization, and it would be a trying task to choose between them."[233] The two rights have clashed in two ways: when the press has been thought to be pressuring the courts to reach a particular result in a case, and when reporting about a trial threatens to prejudice the jury. In the 1941 case, the Court sided with the press in overturning CONTEMPT citations against a newspaper and a labor leader for editorials and speeches critical of judicial decisions. Later cases have made it clear that to hold someone in contempt for speaking about judges violates a principle at the core of the FIRST AMENDMENT: the right to discuss and criticize public events and public figures. Judges have "no special perquisite," Justice William O. Douglas said, "to suppress, edit, or censor events which transpire in proceedings before it."[484] The interest in fair trial procedure is weighed more heavily when public reporting seriously prejudices the case against a defendant. No formula can be given for determining whether pretrial publicity is unconstitutionally prejudicial, since the facts of each case are different.

But in several cases starting in 1961, the Court has overturned convictions resulting from PREJUDICIAL PUBLICITY: when the papers in a small town bombarded the community with details about a defendant's confessions and prior record, so that more than sixty percent of the potential jurors said they knew he was guilty;[991] when a television station broadcast a prisoner's confession to the local sheriff;[1728] when the press so blanketed the courtroom in the notorious Sam Sheppard murder case that, in Justice Tom Clark's words, "bedlam reigned at the courthouse," reporters "took over practically the entire courtroom, hounding most of the participants," making the episode a "Roman holiday for the news media."[1856] In that case the Court described a number of stratagems that trial judges must use to avoid journalistic prejudice, including sequestering the jury; directing the jury not to read or listen to news reports; changing VENUE; and ordering trial participants, including witnesses and lawyers, to refrain from talking to the press. In 1976 the Court shut the door on another obvious remedy, enjoining the press itself from publishing prejudicial articles, because this would be a PRIOR RESTRAINT forbidden by the First Amendment.[1441] In 1979 the Court seemed to say that the press could be shut out of courtrooms altogether when it upheld an order clearing the courtroom during a preliminary hearing to consider whether certain evidence should be suppressed.[723] But a year later it largely reversed course, holding for the first time that the press and public have a constitu-

tional right to attend trials and other judicial hearings unless a particularly compelling need for secrecy can be shown—national security, for instance.[1727] Thereafter, the Court struck down a state law requiring the press to be excluded whenever a minor testifies about being being the victim of a sexual attack,[763] rejected a state court's decision to conduct in secret the VOIR DIRE examination of prospective jurors in a rape-murder trial,[1659] and upheld the press's right to a copy of transcripts in a preliminary hearing of a criminal case, even though the judge, prosecutor, and defendant all desired that they be kept confidential.[1660]

See also: FREEDOM OF SPEECH; FREEDOM OF THE PRESS; TRIAL BY JURY.

Free Speech Clause   The Constitution provides for free speech in this phrase in the FIRST AMENDMENT: "Congress shall make no law . . . abridging freedom of speech." The word "Congress" now also means states and local government as well, through INCORPORATION of the First Amendment in the FOURTEENTH AMENDMENT.

See also: FREEDOM OF SPEECH.

freedom of assembly   The "right of the people peaceably to assemble" is one of the core political rights of Americans. Found in the FIRST AMENDMENT, it is of ancient lineage, stemming from the more restrictive right to PETITION the government declared in MAGNA CARTA in 1215. Under the First Amendment, the right to assemble is a distinct right, not dependent on any intention to petition. The first case came to the Supreme Court in 1876, testing the validity of a federal law against interfering with the rights of others to assemble peacefully. A lynch mob was convicted under the statute. They asserted on appeal that there was no constitutional right to assemble and that therefore Congress could not make it a crime to interfere with an assembly. Although it dismissed the indictment for another reason, the Court rejected their main assertion, saying: "The very idea of a government, republican in form, implies a right on the part of its citizens to meet peaceably for consultation in respect to public affairs and to petition for a redress of grievances."[495]

In 1937, in *DeJonge v. Oregon*, the Court struck down state attempts to limit freedom of assembly. DeJonge spoke at a rally in Oregon sponsored by the Communist party. He was convicted under Oregon's criminal SYNDICALISM law outlawing organizations that advocate the violent overthrow of the government. But the rally itself was peaceful, and no one advocated violence or any other crime. DeJonge was charged and convicted solely for assisting with a peaceful meeting under the auspices of an organization some of whose members stood for violence against government. The Court unanimously reversed his conviction. Said Chief Justice Hughes: "[P]eaceable assembly for lawful discussion cannot be made a crime. The holding of meetings for peaceable political action cannot be proscribed. Those who assist in the conduct of such meetings cannot be branded as criminals on that score."

The Court has looked to the freedom of assembly clause to strike down municipal permit schemes that give too much authority to the police or city hall to deny people the opportunity to meet or demonstrate in public places. The mayor of Jersey City in the 1930s had complete discretion to decide whether to let any group meet on the city streets or in the parks, and he rejected a request of a labor union to meet in town. In *Hague v. CIO*, the Court invalidated the permit scheme. Although a city may reasonably regulate the TIME, PLACE, AND MANNER of an assembly, it may not subject the very possibility to the whim of public officials.

In dozens of cases since then (discussed in more detail under PUBLIC FORUM), the Court has wrestled with the problem of balancing the right to assemble against the state's right to regulate the time, place, and manner of the assembly to further important public interests. Government obviously has a legitimate interest in preventing congestion, disorder, and violence in the streets. The government also has an interest in protecting judges from undue pressure or from seeming to bow to undue pressure that could result from picketing—at least more than sporadic picketing—near courthouses.[478] But in the absence of such difficulties, the freedom of assembly is nearly absolute. When a state judge in the late 1970s ordered all reporters and even members of the public out of his courtroom during a murder trial, the Court held that the order violated their First Amendment rights, including the right to assemble.[1727]

See also: DEMONSTRATORS AND DEMONSTRATIONS; FREEDOM OF ASSOCIATION; FREEDOM OF SPEECH; GUILT BY ASSOCIATION; LOYALTY-SECURITY PROGRAMS; MEMBERSHIP IN POLITICAL ORGANIZATIONS.

freedom of association Joining is an American obsession. Throughout our history, we have formed organizations for every conceivable purpose, some noble and elevating, some criminal, some pathetic. Because so many of us belong to organizations it is of some moment whether the Constitution protects us in our memberships. But freedom of association is a slippery concept, for association implies exclusion as well as inclusion. Logically, I am not free to associate either if I *may not* join with a neighbor to my left or *must* join with my neighbor to the right. In fashioning a constitutional right of association from bits and pieces of the FIRST AMENDMENT, the Court has built a doctrine that largely protects the first strand but not the second. That is, freedom of association means that the state may not bar people from joining but it does not preclude the state from ordering me to accept some people with whom I may not wish to associate.

The state obviously may prohibit people from conspiring to commit crimes. But a city may not attempt to prevent people from joining in a common undertaking that was lawful if each had pursued the objective individually. The Court struck down a Berkeley, California, ordinance that prohibited anyone from contributing more than two hundred and fifty dollars to a committee supporting or opposing political referenda, but did not impose any limitation on individual contributions.[400] The Court also has inferred an associational right to engage in disapproved activities that fall within specific constitutional provisions. So laws prohibiting membership in political parties will be closely scrutinized (see MEMBERSHIP IN POLITICAL PARTIES) because the Constitution protects the FREEDOM OF ASSEMBLY, FREEDOM OF PETITION, FREEDOM OF SPEECH, LIBERTY, and PRIVACY. And under the EQUAL PROTECTION CLAUSE a state may not segregate organizations on racial or ethnic lines.

The Court has placed limits on the state's power to regulate or interfere in the internal activities of private associations to the extent that they are engaged in protected activities. In 1958 the Court upheld the right of the National Association for the Advancement of Colored People to operate through local unincorporated affiliates. Alabama sought to enforce its foreign corporation registration law, which, among other things, required lists of the names and addresses of Alabama members. The NAACP refused to turn over this list, fearing official retaliation against the members. Justice John M. Harlan, speaking for a unanimous Court, noted that privacy in groups espousing dissident ideas is "indispensable to preservation of freedom of association."[1416] The Court also struck down a Virginia attack on the NAACP's use of agents to solicit parents of schoolchildren to file desegregation lawsuits, holding that this method of accomplishing political goals is a "mode of expression and asso-

ciation" protected by the First Amendment.[1417] In several later cases, the Court developed the notion that organizations have an associational right to help their members secure legal advice.[246, 2096, 2110]

But if the state may not deprive outsiders of a right to join, it does not follow that insiders have a right to exclude. In several cases during the 1980s, the Court declined to recognize a general freedom of exclusion—or, as it is sometimes called, a freedom *not to associate*. The first case arose in Minnesota in 1984, where a law prohibited any "place of public accommodation" from engaging in sex discrimination. The question was whether Minnesota could force the United States Jaycees chapter to admit women as full voting members. The national Jaycees organization asserted an associational right to restrict voting membership to men between the ages of eighteen and thirty-five. The Court unanimously held that although there may indeed be a right of association for "certain intimate human relationships," this was not one of them. The Jaycees were "neither small nor selective"; many of its members were strangers to each other. Moreover, there was no showing that the admission of women would cause the Jaycees to change its mission or stand for something different.[1741] The Court adhered to its view in 1987, when it sustained a California law prohibiting local Rotary clubs from denying admission to women,[179] and in 1988, when it upheld a New York City law prohibiting clubs and other organizations with more than four hundred members from discriminating on the basis of race, sex, or religion if the club provides regular meals and accepts money for the use of its facilities from nonmembers for business purposes.[1470] The Court reserved the possibility that in some instances a large association might be formed not for commercial but for purely "expressive purposes" that might well be undermined if it could no longer control its admissions. For example, an organization of women formed to advocate and lobby for certain political causes might have an associational right to restrict membership to women. Likewise, there may be a FREEDOM OF INTIMATE ASSOCIATION for small associations—a men's bridge club, a women's bowling team—that would entail freedom to exclude.

Finally, the issue has occasionally arisen whether the state may force people to join an association to which they do not wish to belong. Objections have come from people forced to contribute money to unions, professional organizations, and the like. Throughout the 1960s the Court ducked the issue, viewing the contributions more as a tax than a forced association.[1686, 981, 1127, 247] In 1977 the Court finally held that a group of public employees could be forced to contribute a "service fee equal in amount to union dues" to be used for "collective bargaining in the public sector" but that the dues could not be used for ideological purposes unrelated to collective bargaining.[4] The Court ruled likewise in 1990 that a compulsory state bar may not devote dues of its lawyer members to ideological or political purposes against their wishes.[1057]

See also: GUILT BY ASSOCIATION; PATRONAGE; SPEECH, FREEDOM FROM PAYING FOR OTHERS'; VOTING, RIGHT TO.

freedom of belief   In 1940 the Supreme Court said that the freedom to believe is absolute.[334] But it also said that freedom to act is not, and since only beliefs acted upon are likely to stir people to opposition, cases involving "pure" belief are few. Such a case would present itself only in a culture of fundamentalism, like that of George Orwell's Big Brother, which demands that people refrain from holding improper thoughts. The state would first have to determine what was being thought and then demand that the proper beliefs be affirmed, requirements that raise these questions: (1) May the state inquire into someone's beliefs? (2)

May the state demand that people express certain beliefs?

The Court has answered the first question only in a political context and in a narrow way. During the LOYALTY-SECURITY era of the 1950s, the government asserted its power to refuse licenses and jobs to communists and other security risks. The Court fractured in early cases involving a law requiring labor union officers to file affidavits that they did not believe in violent overthrow of the government.[49] It reached a conclusion only in 1961, when a 6–3 majority held that a state could validly inquire into the political beliefs of a lawyer applying for a license to practice law.[1093] Ten years later, three more decisions thoroughly muddled the issue. Although five justices mustered a majority for continuing government authority to ask about beliefs, one of the five agreed with the four dissenters that the state could never deny a license solely on the grounds that the applicant held wrong beliefs.[105, 1960, 1130]

The Court has answered the second question much less equivocally: the government may not demand that people *express* an approved belief. The RELIGIOUS TEST clause of Art. VI-§2 prohibits the government from inquiring into a person's religious beliefs as a condition of federal office. The Court has apparently never been presented with an instance of a federal religious test, but in 1961 the justices unanimously overturned, under the FIRST AMENDMENT, a Maryland state constitutional requirement that applicants for public office declare their belief in God.[2059] A person's religious beliefs are no business of the government, which may neither ask about nor condition benefits on people's religious feelings. Likewise, the government may not force anyone to make a statement or affirm a belief that is contrary to a personal religious belief. In 1943, overturning a decision to the contrary three years earlier,[1353] the Court in *West Virginia State Board of Education v. Barnette* rejected a school's demand that schoolchildren be forced to salute the flag and pledge allegiance. The Court's decision was grounded in principles of FREEDOM OF SPEECH rather than religious liberty. Justice Robert H. Jackson said that the state's power to compel "affirmation of a belief and an attitude of mind" is strictly limited by the requirement that it prove some CLEAR AND PRESENT DANGER would arise from children standing silently while others muttered their oaths. The *Barnette* case was the basis for another decision more than thirty years later involving Jehovah's Witnesses who objected to New Hampshire's hypocritical demand that they not cover up the state motto, "Live Free or Die," on their license plate. A couple had taped it over because it was repugnant to their religious beliefs. The Court held that a state may not force someone to display an ideological message on private property for the express purpose of having the public see it.[2258]

One narrow exception to the general rule against laws penalizing beliefs is the provision in the military draft laws that historically has provided a combat exemption to draftees with a CONSCIENTIOUS OBJECTION to war. In 1970 the Court seemed to hold that a person whose belief in the wrongness of "war in any form" stems solely from concern for "policy, pragmatism, or expedience" could be refused an exemption from combat status, whereas those whose similar belief stems from religious conviction must be granted the exemption.[2179]

See also: FLAG SALUTING; FREEDOM OF ASSOCIATION; LOYALTY OATH; SPEECH, FREEDOM FROM PAYING FOR OTHERS'.

freedom of conscience, *see:* **freedom of belief; freedom of religion**

freedom of contract In 1873, in the SLAUGHTER-HOUSE CASES, the Supreme Court gave short shrift to the idea that the Constitution protected a person's right to work or to enter into contracts to carry on a business. No construction of the DUE PROCESS Clause of the FOURTEENTH AMENDMENT, said Justice Samuel F. Miller, could ever be devised to embrace such concerns. He proved to be a poor prognosticator. In 1897, after ten years of broad hints, the Court struck down a Louisiana law that forbade insuring property in Louisiana through a marine insurance company not licensed to do business in the state. Justice Rufus W. Peckham said that the law interfered with the liberty to enter into any contract appropriate to carrying on a lawful business.[39]

For the next forty years, the Court embarked on a campaign to limit state laws that either prohibited certain kinds of contracts outright or that in some way limited their terms. The Court followed two general principles. First, a state could regulate the making of contracts only for some well-defined and narrow public purpose, such as protecting public health or safety. A law prohibiting the sale of oleomargarine to protect the public health would be upheld, even though it stood in the way of a consumer's right to buy.[1654] But the Court lashed out at attempts of Congress and state legislatures to develop labor policies by outlawing YELLOW-DOG CONTRACTS, agreements forced on workers not to join unions.[467, 6] As the Court saw it, regulation of labor relations was not part of the traditional POLICE POWER.

Second, even if the state was legislating in a traditional area of public health or safety, the Court might invalidate the law if it thought that the state's concern was unreasonable and that the effect of the law was really to redistribute wealth of employers to employees. In 1898, pointing to the hazardous nature of mining, the Court upheld a Utah law regulating the number of hours that miners could spend underground.[932] It also upheld an Oregon law limiting the hours of female workers because of the perceived need of women for special protec tion.[1401] But in 1905, in LOCHNER v. NEW YORK, a 5–4 majority ruthlessly rejected a New York law regulating the hours and working conditions of bakers. Ignoring voluminous data about health risks, Justice Peckham declared that the Court would not defer to the legislature on whether bakers ought to be regulated and found "no reasonable ground for interfering with the liberty of person or the right of free contract . . . in the occupation of a baker." *Lochner* is emblematic of the Court's doctrine of ECONOMIC DUE PROCESS, used to maintain the Court's laissez-faire philosophy by denying legislatures power to redress imbalances of economic power. This concept of freedom or liberty of contract was finally overthrown in 1937 in a 5–4 decision upholding a state minimum wage law for women and explicitly overruling prior cases to the contrary.[2184] Said Chief Justice Charles Evans Hughes: "What is this freedom [of contract alleged by the challengers]? The Constitution does not speak of freedom of contract. It speaks of liberty and prohibits the deprivation of liberty without due process of law. . . . regulation which is reasonable in relation to its subject and is adopted in the interests of the community is due process." A law against sweatshops is clearly reasonable.

See also: AFFECTED WITH A PUBLIC INTEREST DOCTRINE; OBLIGATION OF CONTRACTS.

freedom of information   "Freedom of information" generally refers to information in the hands of government. There is no general constitutional right to such information. In 1966 Congress enacted the Freedom of Information Act. It amended and supplemented it in later years to open the government to far greater public scrutiny than had been possible before. The act requires the government to provide, on anyone's request, copies of reports and other papers covering a variety of subjects, and it permits federal suits to compel a recalcitrant

government agency to respond. Some categories of information, like investigative reports and business trade secrets, may be kept confidential.

See also: RIGHT TO KNOW.

freedom of intimate association   In 1984 Justice William Brennan noted that over the years the Court had read the Constitution to protect a "freedom of intimate association."[1741] Unlike FREEDOM OF ASSOCIATION cases, most of which arise under the FIRST AMENDMENT, the freedom of intimate association derives from DUE PROCESS, which bars the states from interfering with "certain highly personal relationships." Among the relationships are MARRIAGE, parenthood, and family life. Each of these relationships involves small numbers of people, highly personal selection in forming and maintaining them, and "seclusion from others in critical aspects of the relationship." A pair of lovers or a family is not like a do-good service organization. Government has the power to declare equality in places of public accommodation, but it may not tell anyone whom to marry or not to marry[1200] (as long as the marriage is not polygamous[1714] or homosexual[207]) or with whom to have a child.[341] Nor may the government refuse to permit blood relatives from sharing the same house.[1379]

But so far at least, the recognized class of intimate relationships is small. The Court sustained a municipal zoning law against unrelated people living together.[148] From hints in the cases approving state laws forcing large organizations to accept women,[1741, 179, 1470] it is safe to conclude that the Court might well limit state intrusion on purely private social gatherings of the sort that could meet in someone's home or around a table at a restaurant—a bridge game or a discussion group. Running through all the cases is the notion that the only intimate associations the Court will fully protect from state interference are relatively conventional relationships that already receive social sanction. A full-blown freedom of intimate association is not yet a reality.

See also: CONTRACEPTION; FAMILIES; PRIVACY; REPRODUCTIVE RIGHTS; SEXUAL FREEDOM.

freedom of petition   Before the Glorious Revolution of 1689, petitioning the English government could be hazardous. If more than twenty people signed an appeal to king or Parliament, even respectfully requesting a change in the law, they were guilty of "tumultuous petitioning." But in the United States, the First Amendment fully protects the right to petition the government. The Petition Clause has rarely been singled out, but it was the basis for the Court's ruling in 1963 that the states could not prohibit agents of the National Association for the Advancement of Colored People from soliciting people to serve as litigants in federal court cases challenging SEGREGATION.[1417] The NAACP held meetings to discuss how parents could sign up to become plaintiffs in suits against segregated schools. A staff member would present the parents with a form to sign if they agreed to become involved. Virginia invoked a law against lawyer "ambulance chasing" to ban the staff members and the NAACP from soliciting parents' signatures. Said Justice William Brennan: "Litigation may well be the sole practical avenue open to a minority to petition for redress of grievances."

See also: FREEDOM OF ASSEMBLY; FREEDOM OF SPEECH *and cross references listed there.*

freedom of religion   Religion is the subject of three constitutional provisions. The ESTABLISHMENT CLAUSE of the FIRST AMENDMENT prohibits the government from "establishing"—that is, supporting—religion in certain ways. The FREE EXERCISE CLAUSE of the First Amendment protects a person's right to practice religion. The RELIGIOUS TEST Clause of

Article VI prohibits the state from restricting public office to religious adherents. Together these clauses stand for the principle that the spheres of religion and government are to be kept separate. This proposition is as easy to state as it has proved difficult to apply. If to accommodate a religion's free exercise the state makes an exception to a general law, has it shown a preference for that religion amounting to an "establishment"? RELIGIOUS ESTABLISHMENT is discussed separately. Here the focus is on the degree to which people may conduct themselves according to religious tenets without government interference or handicap.

If religion were solely a matter of PRAYER and inner contemplation, the constitutional issue would be straightforward, for the Court has declared an absolute FREEDOM OF BELIEF,[2186] a right further supported by the Religious Test Clause. But few religions are purely contemplative. Most also prescribe a way of life, and belief shades into conduct when people follow their teachings. Since the state may always regulate harmful conduct, the problem is to determine what forms of socially disapproved conduct are protected from state prohibition or regulation.

The easiest cases would be those in which the state directly attacks a practice because it is religious. "It would doubtless be unconstitutional," Justice Antonin Scalia has written, "to ban the casting of 'statues that are to be used for worship purposes,' or to prohibit bowing down before a golden calf."[614] Easy cases such as these rarely, if ever, arise because the states are not overtly antireligious. The actual cases are those in which a general law, not aimed at a particular religion, has some impact on a religious practice. In all these cases, incidentally, the government may not question the *validity* of the religious belief, as long as it is sincerely held as a religious belief. In a 1944 case, followers of the "I Am" movement were indicted for mail fraud in soliciting funds. Their mailings had said that they were "divine messengers" who had, through "supernatural attainments, the power to [cure] ailments and diseases." The government contested the veracity of their claims. In refusing to allow the jury to consider whether they really were divine messengers or had the power to heal, Justice William O. Douglas said: "Men may believe what they cannot prove. . . . If one could be sent to jail because a jury in a hostile environment found [the miracles of the New Testament, the Divinity of Christ, life after death, the power of prayer] false, little indeed would be left of religious freedom."[113]

In 1878 the Court first distinguished between protected belief and unprotected conduct when it sustained a federal antibigamy law. The Court upheld the conviction of a Mormon in the Utah Territory who insisted that he had a religious duty to practice polygamy. Congress has the power, the Court said, to prohibit actions "in violation of social duties or subversive of good order."[1714] To excuse Mormon polygamy "would be to make the professed doctrines of religious beliefs superior to the law of the land, and in effect to permit every citizen to become a law unto himself." The Court then sustained a series of laws that forced the Mormon church to repudiate theologically its teaching of polygamy. These laws barred polygamists from voting and serving on juries,[1408] required voters to swear they were not polygamists or members of a church that advocated polygamy,[520] and revoked the Mormon church's charter and confiscated its property.[1126] So sweeping were the Court's pronouncements that the Free Exercise Clause would have protected nothing of interest had the Court not resuscitated it in the 1940s.

In *Cantwell v. Connecticut,* the Court dismissed a prosecution against a Jehovah's Witness who had been arrested for proselytizing on a New Haven, Connecticut, street corner. The Court held that religious liberty must include some freedom to act. In regulating to promote some permissible objective, the state may not "unduly infringe" the right to exercise religious beliefs. The Court applied this logic over the years in striking down mandatory FLAG SALUTING laws against religious objections,[2186] in overturning a Tennessee ban on members of the clergy serving as legislators,[1288] and in exempting members of the Old Order Amish from a Pennsylvania requirement that children between the ages of fourteen and sixteen must attend school.[2237] But it upheld Pennsylvania's Sunday closing laws, against the claim of Orthodox Jewish merchants that the law worked a great hardship on them because they were religiously required to close their stores on Saturdays also. The Court said that the law did not prohibit the challengers from practicing their religion; it only indirectly burdened adherence to their faith by making "the practice of their religious beliefs more expensive."[226]

These decisions are not necessarily consistent. In 1963, in *Sherbert v. Verner,* a Seventh-day Adventist whose religious scruples prevented her from working on Saturday had been fired from her job. Other employers required Saturday work also, so she could not find a new job. The state refused to pay her unemployment benefits because it said she had no good reason to decline other suitable work. A 7–2 majority held that the denial of benefits was unconstitutional because it burdened her "free exercise of religion as would a fine imposed against [her] for her Saturday worship" and because South Carolina had no COMPELLING INTEREST in its rule. The state said it was afraid that others might lie about religious precepts to avoid taking jobs; if enough people did lie, the unemployment compensation fund would be depleted. But the state offered no proof that widespread malingering and deceit would follow. In 1989 the Court broadened this principle to require benefits to be paid to a person who refused to work on Sunday not as a member of a particular church but simply "as a Christian."[697]

Sherbert seemed to command that the state must carve out an exception to any general regulation that impinges on a religious practice, unless it can demonstrate a compelling interest in the regulation and show that there is no less onerous way of achieving its purpose. The Court followed this principle in *Wisconsin v. Yoder,* the 1972 decision permitting the Old Order Amish from sending their children to school beyond the age of fourteen. Chief Justice Warren Burger pointed to the Amish "fundamental belief that salvation requires life in a church community separate and apart from the world and worldly influence." The state's interest in the education of all its citizens' children did not outweigh the religious priority of "the Amish community." The Court dismissed the possibility that many groups might try to claim exemption from schooling by noting the unique history of the Amish as a "self-sufficient segment of American society."

But despite these arguments, in several cases the Court found it possible to uphold the state's need to avoid exempting a religious practice from a general law. The Court rejected the claim of an Old Order Amish man that his religion forbade him to pay Social Security taxes for his employees;[1138] sustained the government's denial of tax exemptions to two private schools that practiced RACIAL DISCRIMINATION on religious grounds;[190] upheld an Air Force regulation barring an Orthodox Jewish captain from wearing a yarmulke;[771] refused to recognize a prisoner's right to attend a Friday midday service when prison regulations required him to work;[1513] upheld a requirement that beneficiaries of a federal food stamp program must provide the government with a Social Security number for their child, against the claim that doing so would "rob [the child's] spirit";[206] and permitted the U.S. Forest Ser-

vice to build a road through sacred forestland that Indian tribes used for religious rituals.[1213]

In 1985 the Court invalidated a Connecticut law that prohibited employers from firing workers who refuse to work on whatever day they call sabbath.[2045] Since this law specifically exempted workers for religious reasons and was unconstitutional, it is hard to reconcile it with the Court's earlier rulings that a state must exempt workers for religious reasons.

Finally, in 1990 the Court took a major turn in free exercise doctrine when it ruled that Oregon could constitutionally deny unemployment benefits to someone dismissed from a job because he had used peyote in a sincere religious ritual of the Native American church despite a criminal ban on all drug use. For a 6–3 majority, Justice Scalia said that the logic of *Sherbert* should be confined to unemployment compensation cases, and then only when there is no general criminal law against the practice for which someone is claiming a religious exemption. In the Oregon case, the state outlawed drug use. The law was not aimed at religion. Under these circumstances, Justice Scalia said, the religious person is not entitled to an exemption just because the state has not proved a compelling interest. The state need not prove a compelling interest in its general criminal law every time someone claims a religious exemption, because that would mean, as the Court said in the original polygamy case, that everyone might become "a law unto himself." Oregon could exempt religious users of peyote if it chose to, but nothing in the Constitution commands it to.

The Oregon peyote case has provoked heated controversy. In dissent, Justice Blackmun pointed out that the ruling cuts deeply into the "essential ritual" of the Native American church, since "the peyote plant embodies their deity, and eating it is an act of worship and communion." The effect of the decision, he warned, could devastate the church and more generally permit all sorts of laws to undermine minority religions. The peyote case is surely not the final word.

See also: CONSCIENTIOUS OBJECTION; EVOLUTION, TEACHING OF; MEDICATION AND SURGERY, FORCED; PRAYER AND BIBLE READING; SCHOOLS, RELIGION IN.

freedom of speech   The FIRST AMENDMENT's command that Congress make no law "abridging the freedom of speech" has waylaid an astonishing array of laws, regulations, public programs, and procedures. Next to DUE PROCESS, no other constitutional provision embraces a greater variety of people, events, and concerns. In the seventy-odd years that the Supreme Court has been paying serious attention to the Free Speech Clause, the lines of doctrine have become so multitudinous that no single formula can come close to explaining free speech, and no single summary can possibly fit all the cases.

The impulse to silence people to avoid the perils of anarchy, social disorder, blasphemy, obscenity, and just plain bothersome opinions is worldwide. It has affected all governments at all times in all societies, including ours today. But it was Johannes Gutenberg's remarkable invention of metal type in the late fifteenth century that caused populations to ignite. For one thing, printing led to literacy, the most powerful weapon against oppression ever devised. For another, the printed word endures, unlike the rabble-rouser's muttered imprecations. And so, with the invention of the press came censorship—by popes, monarchs, and ultimately by Victorian citizen groups offended by naughty words in the Bible and Shakespeare and impure thoughts in dime novels.

Political and religious censorship began in England in the 1520s. Until Henry VIII renounced the Church of Rome, sellers of Lutheran Bibles were burned at the stake. In 1538 Henry created a licensing system for all books printed in England, giving official censors the power to punish "seditious opinions." In 1559 Queen Elizabeth I required all new works to be submitted for official approval before being printed. Members of the Stationers Company, the guild to which enforcement of the censorship laws was given, had wide powers to SEARCH anywhere whenever they wished to root out offending publications. The licensing system lasted until 1694.

In the meantime, the COMMON LAW courts developed the crime of SEDITIOUS LIBEL—the "intentional publication . . . of written blame of any public man, or of the law, or of any institution established by law." It did not matter that the writer spoke the truth; indeed, that was worse, for "the greater the truth, the greater the libel." The crime of seditious libel carried over to the colonies, but in 1735 a jury acquitted John Peter Zenger, a newspaper printer, because the critical articles that his newspaper carried about the corrupt royal administration were true. The trial was sensational news throughout the colonies, and as a practical matter, seditious libel was dead though colonial legislatures retained the power to license the press and continued to harass the press until the American Revolution.

In the late 1760s William Blackstone, whose *Commentaries on the Laws of England* greatly impressed colonial lawyers, declared that freedom of the press meant merely that the government could not block publication. Government could always punish later if the publication violated the law. Blackstone's opinion was well known to the drafters of the First Amendment, and ever since then a debate has raged over whether Madison and his colleagues meant to incorporate only Blackstone's crabbed interpretation of free speech or to place the freedom on much more spacious footing. In 1907 Justice Oliver Wendell Holmes thought that the First Amendment prevented only "previous restraint" but left the government free to prosecute for seditious libel or any other criminal utterance.[1576] Holmes would later dramatically change his mind, but in a searching history of the eighteenth-century meaning of freedom of speech and press, the constitutional historian Leonard W. Levy wrote that the Framers "were sharply divided and possessed no distinct understanding" of the phrases they used. On balance, Levy concluded, they meant to receive the Blackstonian definition and perhaps make truth a defense to a charge of seditious libel. Another school, led by Harvard Law School professor Zechariah Chafee, Jr., holds that the Framers meant to abolish seditious libel outright.

In 1798, prodded by President John Adams, Congress enacted the ALIEN AND SEDITION ACTS, which prohibited various types of critical commentaries. Jefferson and Madison railed at these laws as violations of the First Amendment; as president, Jefferson pardoned several people who had been convicted under them. The laws expired in 1801, and no case challenging their constitutionality ever reached the Supreme Court. Because Congress did not enact such laws again until World War I, and because the First Amendment was not held to apply to the states until the 1920s, the Supreme Court only began to consider the First Amendment in 1919. For fifty years the Court mulled over the proposition that the First Amendment bars punishment for SUBVERSIVE ADVOCACY, and in 1969 finally agreed. Along the way, many other important themes have emerged, some of them only after the Supreme Court first said that no such right existed. Gradually, as claims poured in, a broader and deeper understanding of free speech emerged, and the First Amendment's mantle expanded.

It is generally conceded that the First Amendment is at its most absolute in banning PRIOR RESTRAINTS. The government may not enjoin someone from speaking or publishing unless what is about to be uttered will have grave consequences for the very survival of the nation or is illegal for reasons having nothing to do with speech (a false advertisement, for example). The desire to keep government documents secret is rarely a sufficient reason to keep their contents from being aired.

Another major theme was encapsulated in Justice Holmes's famous MARKETPLACE OF IDEAS metaphor: "that the best test of truth is the power of the thought to get itself accepted in the competition of the market."[5] Or, as Justice Louis D. Brandeis put it a few years later, "that without free speech and assembly discussion would be futile; that with them, discussion affords ordinarily adequate protection against the dissemination of noxious doctrine."[2199] The notion that truth will outlast falsehood in an open fight led Holmes to develop and champion the CLEAR AND PRESENT DANGER test. Only those statements or publications that will imminently cause substantial harm to an important interest may be punished. Even talk that many consider subversive must be allowed. Likewise, talk and protests may not be prevented or punished merely because they stir the people to anger. Demonstrations in public places must be given wide leeway. Arrests for BREACH OF THE PEACE may not be based on fanciful or merely anticipated troubles. Since we live in a crowded world, the government may prescribe rules to keep things orderly. A regulation of the TIME, PLACE, AND MANNER of a public demonstration may be permissible, but the scope of the regulation depends on whether the speakers are in a PUBLIC FORUM or some more closely guarded place. In any event, the regulation must be evenhanded toward all comers: a PERMIT SYSTEM is unconstitutional if it hands police absolute discretion to decide who may speak. But a time, place, and manner regulation must be neutral: any law or policy that regulates the *content*, rather than the manner, of speech is unconstitutional.

Not every form of utterance is necessarily "speech" in the constitutional sense. In 1942 the

Court suggested that "there are certain well-defined and narrowly limited classes of speech, the prevention and punishment of which have never been thought to raise any constitutional problem. These include the lewd and obscene, the profane, the libelous, and the insulting or 'fighting' words. . . . It has been well observed that such utterances are no essential part of any exposition of ideas, and are of such slight social value as a step to truth that any benefit that may be derived from them is clearly outweighed by the social interest in order and morality."[372] Since then, however, the Court has steadily backed away from its confident assertion that these classes are "well-defined" and that they "never" raise constitutional problems. The FIGHTING WORDS doctrine has almost vanished. The Court has agonized for decades over the problem of OBSCENITY AND PORNOGRAPHY, and although it continues to maintain that these categories are not protected, it has steadily narrowed the type of publications that fall within those terms. Considerable protection exists for speech that is merely OFFENSIVE AND INDECENT. Since 1964 LIBEL has been "constitutionalized," so that it is much more difficult to sue for false and damaging statements, at least if the injured party is a PUBLIC FIGURE. Freedom of speech is not limited to ideas about politics; it covers as well every manner of social, artistic, religious, and philosophical discussion. Even COMMERCIAL SPEECH, advertisements, commercials, and promotional circulars, are now safe from absolute condemnation by government.

Nor is protected speech limited to conventional categories of speakers—those standing on corner soapboxes or writing in the pages of the daily newspapers. A wide variety of media—movies, radio, television, the live stage—are equally embraced by the First Amendment, as are their ideas. People do not lose their right to free speech because of their employment status, so public employees may not be disciplined for anything they say, on or off the job, or for their memberships and allegiances. Even corporations have free speech rights. And because not every form of communication is limited to words alone, some forms of "expressive conduct" may be protected as SYMBOLIC SPEECH—for example, FLAG BURNING.

The foregoing is but a checklist. A more detailed discussion can be found under each of the headings listed below.

See also: ACCESS TO BROADCASTING; BALANCING; BOYCOTT; BROADCASTING, REGULATION OF; CAMPAIGN FINANCING; CENSORSHIP; CHILLING EFFECT; CONTEMPT; DEMONSTRATORS AND DEMONSTRATIONS; DRAFT CARD BURNING; FAIRNESS DOCTRINE; FLAG SALUTING; FREE PRESS–FAIR TRIAL; FREEDOM OF ASSEMBLY; FREEDOM OF ASSOCIATION; FREEDOM OF PETITION; FREEDOM OF THE PRESS; GAG ORDER; GOVERNMENT SPEECH; GROUP LIBEL; HATE SPEECH; HOSTILE AUDIENCE; LOYALTY OATH; LOYALTY-SECURITY PROGRAMS; MEMBERSHIP IN POLITICAL ORGANIZATIONS; NUDITY; OVERBREADTH DOCTRINE; PATRONAGE; PENTAGON PAPERS CASE; PICKETING; PRIVACY; PUBLIC EMPLOYMENT; RIGHT TO KNOW; RIGHT TO REPLY; SOLICITATION; SPEECH AND CONDUCT; SPEECH, FREEDOM FROM PAYING FOR OTHERS'; SPEECH, REGULATION OF CONTENT; SYNDICALISM; TREASON; VAGUENESS; ZENGER TRIAL.

freedom of the press   The FIRST AMENDMENT protects the expression and communication of ideas twice: in the Free Speech Clause and in a separate Press Clause. The distinction between the two is historically obscure. The Press Clause may have been coupled to the Speech Clause to ensure that speech in any form, spoken or published, fleeting or lasting, is beyond the government's reach. Or it may provide special protection for the institution of the press—the "fourth estate." In 1978 Chief Justice Warren Burger suggested that the Press Clause does not confer any greater protection on the institutional press, in part because of grave difficulties that would arise in determining who or what constitutes the press—established newspapers only? television networks? authors? syndicated columnists? pamphleteers? anyone with access to a laser printer or Xerox machine and a mailing list? Burger concluded that "the First Amendment does not 'belong' to any definable category of persons or entities: it belongs to all who exercise its freedoms."[667] Nevertheless, because of their power and position in American society, the institutional media—newspapers, broadcast stations, film studios, publishing companies—have frequently claimed First Amendment protection that will be applied, if at all, only to them. For example, the major cases involving PRIOR RESTRAINT have arisen when the government has sought to restrain publication of newspaper articles, sale of books, or release of movies. This subject will be considered under its own heading; here suffice it to say that, as the PENTAGON PAPERS CASE shows, the government faces an extraordinarily high hurdle in stopping any publication that is not provably pornographic or that gives away military secrets. The Court has applied the logic of the prior restraint rule as well to bar courts from issuing GAG ORDERS to the press.[1441]

Since 1964 the Court has fashioned a new constitutional law of LIBEL, almost entirely to spare the institutional press from being sued every time it prints stories about PUBLIC FIGURES who take offense at how the news is presented or the criticisms leveled. The rule that the Court announced in the first case, *New York Times v. Sullivan,* is striking, since it bars suits even for false information if the press did not knowingly print falsehoods intending to harm. Similarly, the First Amendment protects the press against lawsuits for publishing accurate versions of information lawfully obtained from court records. A law prohibiting the publication of a rape victim's name is unconstitutional.[480]

Not every claim by the press for constitutional protection has been upheld. The Court has declined to see in the First Amendment a REPORTER'S PRIVILEGE that would permit journalists to decline to answer questions about their sources in an official inquiry.[225] The Court has held that the police may search a newsroom to look for photographs that might help identify criminals, if the police obtain an ex parte SEARCH WARRANT—that is, a warrant issued by a judge without first having heard objections from the newspaper.[2290] A newspaper that promises to keep confidential the name of a source may be sued for DAMAGES for publishing his or her name; the First Amendment does not give reporters or publishers any special exemptions from general rules of law,[418] such as the antitrust laws.[399] The Court has also denied that the press has a general right of access to government information; however, it has said that the government may not shut the press out of certain kinds of proceedings. Newspaper reporters have no constitutional right to interview particular prisoners in jail,[1583, 1805] but they do have the right to attend criminal trials,[1727] preliminary court hearings,[1659] and even to obtain copies of transcripts made in a preliminary hearing of a criminal prosecution.[1660]

The Court has taken a hard look at the TAXATION of the press. In 1936 it invalidated a Louisiana tax that applied only to newspapers with a circulation above twenty thousand. Of the 124 newspapers in the state, only thirteen were subject to the tax, and all but one of these had attacked Senator Huey Long, who with the governor vowed to cut them down to size.[823] In 1983 the Court struck down a Minnesota tax that "singled out the press for special treatment" and targeted a small group of newspapers; only fourteen of 388 paid-circulation newspapers had to pay the special "ink and paper" tax.[1355] The Court followed this decision in 1987 to invalidate an Arkansas tax imposed on all publications except newspapers and religious, professional, trade, and sports journals. Justice Thurgood Marshall held the tax unconstitutional in part because whether it was imposed depended on the *content* of the journal.[76] The dissenters said that only a tax aimed at particular ideas should be disapproved. In a 1989 case, the court rejected a tax exempting only religious publications, viewing the taxing scheme as a RELIGIOUS ESTABLISHMENT rather than a free press violation.[2018] Finally, in 1991, the Court sustained an Arkansas sales tax applicable to cable television providers but not to newspapers, magazines, or satellite broadcasters. Justice Sandra Day O'Connor distinguished the other cases because this tax did not "target a small number of speakers. . . . This is not a tax structure that resembles a penalty for particular speakers or particular ideas."[1133]

See also: CONTEMPT; FREE PRESS–FAIR TRIAL; FREEDOM OF SPEECH; LIBEL.

fruit of the poisonous tree Information that police gain from an unlawful SEARCH AND SEIZURE or illegally obtained confession may not be used directly against a defendant. The information is said to be the "fruit" of the government's illegality, or "poisonous tree." The phrase comes from a 1939 case in which the Court set aside a conviction stemming from evidence gained through an illegal wiretap.[1421] The fruit of the poisonous tree doctrine is not absolute. The government has the burden of showing that the information has been "purged" of its "taint"—by showing, for instance, that the police would have discovered the evidence independently, that the discovery was "inevitable,"[1482] or that an "intervening . . . act of free will" by the defendant has cured the fruit of its poison. For example, even though the defendant had originally been unlawfully arrested, his later confession was not a fruit of the poisonous tree because he had been brought before a magistrate who set BAIL and told him that he had the right not to speak. The decision to confess was not, therefore, attributed to the unlawful arrest.[1017] Similarly, the Court unanimously upheld a victim's LINEUP identification of a suspect who had been unlawfully arrested, because the police had

known his identity all along and the victim's recognition was independent of the arrest.[492]

It is probably impossible to state a general rule, since the circumstances in every case are different, and the issue of whether the tree is poisonous can turn on highly technical grounds. In a 1991 case, the police were chasing a juvenile who threw a small rock onto the ground just before an officer caught him. The rock turned out to be crack cocaine. He claimed that since the state conceded the police originally had no "reasonable suspicion" to chase him, the cocaine was a fruit of an unlawful "seizure" that occurred when he realized he was about to be caught. The Court disagreed, saying that the issue was whether the drugs were dropped before he was seized, in which case they could be used at trial, or after he was seized, in which case they would be tainted. The Court held that since the police neither applied force nor made a "show of authority," like pointing a gun, the suspect was not actually seized at the time he dropped the drugs, so they were not tainted fruit.

See also: ARREST AND ARREST WARRANTS; EXCLUSIONARY RULE; PROBABLE CAUSE.

fugitive from justice, *see:* **extradition**

fugitive slavery Art. IV-§2[3] prohibited so-called free states from freeing runaway slaves. The Constitution required, instead, that the slave "shall be delivered up on claim to the party" asserting ownership. State laws designed to limit the right of recapture were declared unconstitutional.[1664] Because the wording was deliberately obscure—it did not say who must do the delivering up—Congress enacted a number of fugitive slave acts. The Fugitive Slave Act of 1850 was extraordinary in the range of powers it placed in private hands and the manner in which it effectively bribed officials to comply. Owners were authorized to kidnap their slaves, with almost no safeguard against mistake, and federal officials were paid more money to declare that a black was a runaway slave than to declare that he was not. The Court upheld the law a year before the Civil War.[3] The THIRTEENTH AMENDMENT has made the entire clause obsolete.

full faith and credit   An important consequence of FEDERALISM is the ever-present possibility of conflicts among laws of various jurisdictions. The SUPREMACY CLAUSE of Article VI regulates conflicts between state and federal law. The Full Faith and Credit Clause of Article VI regulates conflicts among state laws. It requires each state to treat as legally binding all "public acts, records, and judicial proceedings" of the other states. The most important operation of the Full Faith and Credit Clause has been in the realm of court judgments. Without the clause, a marriage in one state might be easily undone in another; a spouse divorced in one state might go to another state to try to get better terms; a debtor might repudiate a JUDGMENT rendered in another state.

The general rule is that the merits of a controversy may not be reopened in another state once the courts of the first state have rendered a final judgment. A litigant who has won a final money judgment from the courts of one state does not have to re-prove his claims if he goes to another state to enforce it.[1349] That does not mean the successful plaintiff in the first state may go to the other state and, waving his judgment, demand that the sheriff pounce on the debtor's property. The second, or *forum*, state may insist that the creditor follow its own laws in collecting on a judgment.[1878] But the debtor may not resist by asserting that the original CAUSE OF ACTION is contrary to the public policy of the forum state. If a plaintiff wins a judgment against the defendant for causing "mental distress," he may collect on it even if the forum state does not recognize suits for mental distress.[2054]

So strong is this policy of deference to sister states that people can often make end runs around state law. For example, Mississippi prohibited contracts in cotton futures. The defendant, who entered into such a contract, refused to pay the plaintiff when his gamble turned sour. The plaintiff succeeded in obtaining a nonjudicial arbitration award. When the defendant chanced to travel to Missouri, the plaintiff found him there and received a court judgment confirming the arbitration award. When the plaintiff returned to Mississippi the courts refused to let him collect his money because the judgment concerned an illegal contract between two of their own citizens. Justice Oliver Wendell Holmes said that under full faith and credit the Mississippi courts were constitutionally bound to enforce the judgment because it was obtained legitimately in a sister state.[638]

In a 1988 case, owners of mineral rights sued to collect interest payments. Their contracts were governed by Texas law, and under a Texas STATUTE OF LIMITATION, it was too late to sue. But the suit was brought in Kansas, which had a longer statute of limitations for that type of suit. The Supreme Court ruled that the Full Faith and Credit Clause does not require the Kansas courts to follow the Texas statute of limitations.[1980]

A sister state judgment may be challenged in the forum state if the original courts did not have JURISDICTION over the parties, or in special circumstances arising out of DIVORCE and custody decrees.

Beyond court proceedings, the clause says that "public acts" shall be entitled to full faith and credit, but the Court has not read this provision strictly. It relied on a loose reading in DRED SCOTT V. SANDFORD to avoid giving Dred Scott his freedom. Scott had argued that because he had moved to a free state he had gained freedom which he could not lose upon returning to a slave state. The Court said that "no state . . . can enact laws to operate beyond its own dominions." But the Court's absolute pronouncement has been somewhat eroded by the development of a CHOICE OF LAW jurisprudence that sometimes requires one state to follow the law of another. A prime example is the Court's century-old conclusion that a contract must ordinarily be interpreted by the law of the state where it was made, not in the state where a lawsuit is brought.[385] But the rule is fraught with many exceptions; for example, the forum state need not abide by the rule of the contract state to award interest on a judgment.[1081]

The Full Faith and Credit Clause empowers Congress to regulate the manner in which the laws of one state shall be recognized in another. In doing so, Congress has commanded federal courts to be bound by the same general rules, and the Court has upheld the constitutionality of this law.[464] Under the Supremacy Clause, the reverse holds true as well. State courts must respect the laws and judgments not merely of sister states, but of the federal government as well.

See also: COMITY; PRIVILEGES AND IMMUNITIES.

fundamental fairness   In a criminal trial, the Supreme Court has said, "denial of DUE PROCESS is the failure to observe that fundamental fairness essential to the very concept of justice. In order to declare a denial of it we must find that the absence of that fairness fatally infected the trial; the acts complained of must be of such quality as necessarily prevents a fair trial."[1171] The notion of fundamental fairness lies at the heart of the case-by-case consideration of trial procedures used by the federal government and the states. It is not restricted to specific procedural protections in the BILL OF RIGHTS.

See also: INCORPORATION DOCTRINE; PROCEDURAL RIGHTS OF CRIMINAL DEFENDANTS; TRIAL, FAIRNESS OF.

fundamental interests, rights, and privileges   In modern constitutional parlance, a funda-mental interest—sometimes also called a "fundamental right"—is one that triggers STRICT SCRUTINY of a law to see whether it violates the EQUAL PROTECTION CLAUSE. Usually the courts will strictly scrutinize a law that establishes a SUSPECT CLASSIFICATION—that draws a line on the basis of race or ethnic origin for example. If a fundamental interest or right is at stake, the Court may invalidate a law. In 1956 the Court invalidated an Illinois law requiring criminal defendants to supply a costly transcript before their appeals could be heard. Justice Hugo L. Black said that since indigents could not afford the transcripts, the state was in effect determining that only the wealthy could take an appeal.[815] Since then, the Court has said it will look closely at laws that appear to impair three main types of fundamental interests or rights: the right to vote (and to run for office), access to courts, and the right to be free of DURATIONAL RESIDENCY REQUIREMENTS that treat newcomers to a state differently from established residents. Despite the central importance of schooling to American culture and society, the Court has said that it does not recognize a fundamental right to education,[1791] although it did strike down a Texas law requiring the children of illegal aliens to pay tuition to attend the state's free public schools.[1641] For the 5–4 majority, Justice William Brennan said that although education is not a right, "neither is it merely some governmental 'benefit.' . . . [E]ducation has a fundamental role in maintaining the fabric of our society." The substitution of "role" for "right" or "interest" can perhaps be explained by the unique harshness dealt by the state to defenseless children who would ultimately only become a burden to a society that would spurn them.

The term "fundamental rights" is often also used to connote other rights unenumerated in the Constitution but nevertheless worthy of constitutional protection. Probably the most notable example is the right to PRIVACY, derived from the old doctrine of SUBSTANTIVE DUE PROCESS. This line of cases had its beginning in 1923, when one of the most conservative justices in our history, James C. McReynolds, declared a fundamental right to marry and educate one's children[1323] as an outgrowth of the older ECONOMIC DUE PROCESS theories then prevalent. A 1942 case striking down a state Habitual Criminal Sterilization Act on equal protection grounds began the discussion of fundamental interests apart from economic concerns.[1879] As it has emerged, the right to privacy includes several important subsidiary fundamental rights, including the right to marry, to have children, to raise children, to use contraceptives, and to have an ABORTION as well as the right to TRAVEL and FREEDOM OF ASSOCIATION.

In determining which PROCEDURAL RIGHTS OF CRIMINAL DEFENDANTS should be applied to the states as a part of PROCEDURAL DUE PROCESS, the Court has looked, in the words of Justice Benjamin N. Cardozo, to those rights "so rooted in the traditions and conscience of our people as to be ranked as fundamental."[1557]

The Court has also occasionally spoken of fundamental PRIVILEGES OR IMMUNITIES, when defining the rights protected by Art. IV-§2[1] and Section 1 of the FOURTEENTH AMENDMENT. In an early influential case, Justice Bushrod Washington, sitting as a circuit judge, said that privileges and immunities are those "which of right belong to the citizens of all free governments." He identified some of them as protection by the government, HABEAS CORPUS, the right to possess property, freedom from discriminatory TAXATION, and the right to sue.[468]

See also: COMPELLING INTEREST; COURTS, ACCESS TO; INCORPORATION DOCTRINE; NATURAL LAW; NINTH AMENDMENT; SECOND-CLASS CITIZENSHIP; VOTING, RIGHT TO.

fundamental law, *see:* **natural law**

fundamental rights, *see:* **fundamental interests, rights, and privileges**

G

gag order   A gag order is an order from a judge, usually in a criminal case and usually directed to the press, to refrain from discussing the facts. In 1976 the Court unanimously overturned as a PRIOR RESTRAINT a gag order issued in a Nebraska multiple murder trial. The order forbade the press from publishing any information about the defendant's confession or anything else that might implicate the defendant. The Court said the gag was unlikely to affect the trial, that the trial judge had failed to consider other means of protecting the defendant's rights, and that no gag order could be issued without proving a fair trial would be impossible without one.[1441] A gag order is different from an order directing a news organization that is itself a party to a suit to refrain from disclosing any information obtained during pretrial DISCOVERY. The Court unanimously agreed in 1984 that under those circumstances a trial judge may bar disclosure to prevent abuse, without any special FIRST AMENDMENT concern.[1836]

See also: FREE PRESS—FAIR TRIAL; PREJUDICIAL PUBLICITY.

game laws   Until the mid-1970s, the Supreme Court had said that states own animals and natural resources found within their borders and that they could bar shipment beyond them.

For example, in the late nineteenth century the Court upheld a Connecticut law prohibiting anyone from killing game birds and shipping them out of state even though the birds could be freely killed if consumed in state.[736] In 1979 the Court finally overruled this and related cases, holding that the DORMANT COMMERCE CLAUSE prohibits states from engaging in this kind of FACIAL DISCRIMINATION against INTERSTATE COMMERCE.[956] States may engage in genuine conservation efforts but not by discriminating against the interstate flow of goods. However, the Court upheld a Montana elk-hunting licensing program that required out-of-state hunters to pay more than seven times as much as residents for big-game hunting licenses.[109] The Court said that the licensing plan was reasonably related to Montana's conservation efforts, since Montana residents pay for conservation efforts through taxes, and increasing numbers of out-of-state hunters had been stalking Montana elk.

garbage   A state does not have the constitutional authority to ban out-of-state shipments of garbage coming in to landfills if it does not also regulate the dumping of in-state garbage in the landfills. A strict ban on foreign garbage violates the DORMANT COMMERCE CLAUSE because it interferes with INTERSTATE COMMERCE.[1621]

garnishment and attachment   Garnishment is a means by which a creditor can obtain payment on a debt or recover assets by having a court divert some portion of a debtor's wages or other assets directly to the creditor. Garnishment is controlled by state and federal laws. In 1969 the Court held unconstitutional certain kinds of ex parte prejudgment garnishment procedures.[1901] Many states permitted creditors to freeze a debtor's wages or other property, without having to prove that a debt really was owed, by having a clerk of the court fill out a simple form. This system did not give any chance for the debtor to respond before the wages or property were garnished. The Court said that DUE PROCESS entitles debtors to a judicial HEARING before being deprived of wages. The right to a hearing applies to garnishment of other kinds of property—for example, a corporate bank account[1498]—although the Court has said that the standards for a hearing can be relaxed in cases involving property other than wages. A state law may permit garnishment or attachment of property without first holding a hearing, but only if the law requires the creditor to post adequate bond to recompense the debtor in case the court later finds that no debt was owed; the creditor must make some showing before a neutral magistrate, not merely a court clerk, that he or she is likely to prevail in a lawsuit; and the state must hold an adversary hearing on the merits promptly after the garnishment or attachment.[1368]

gays, *see:* **homosexuality**

gender classifications, *see:* **sex discrimination**

general warrant, *see:* **Fourth Amendment**

General Welfare Clause   The General Welfare Clause, Art. I-§8[1], empowers Congress to "collect taxes . . . to pay the debts and provide for the common defence and general welfare of the United States." The clause can be interpreted in three quite different ways. It might mean that Congress may do whatever it pleases to provide for the general welfare, whether or not by taxing. It might be taken as qualifying the power to tax, so that only those taxes raised for the general welfare are constitutional. Or it might be seen as simply shorthand for the other ENUMERATED POWERS listed in Section 8, like the power to regulate commerce or the power to raise armies. James Madison in *Federalist* 41 adhered to this last view. Alexander Hamilton disagreed. He saw the General Welfare Clause as an independent power. In 1936 the Supreme Court agreed with Hamilton's view. Congress has the power to spend tax moneys "for public purposes . . . not limited by the direct grants of legislative power found in the Constitution."[289] This interpretation permitted the Court in 1937 to sustain the Social Security Act, a federal law that provides for the general welfare but that does not easily fit within any of Congress's other enumerated powers.[1957] These rulings give Congress considerable power to regulate through the back door of taxing, as the Court acknowledged in the same year when it upheld an annual federal tax on firearms dealers: "We are not free to speculate as to the motives which moved Congress to impose it, or as to the extent to which it may operate to restrict the activities taxed. . . . [S]ince it operates as a tax, it is within the national taxing power."[1908]

See also: SPENDING POWER; TAXING POWER.

gerrymandering   Gerrymandering is the ancient art of giving a partisan advantage to a candidate or voting bloc by the way election district lines are drawn. The name derives from a Massachusetts master of the art, Elbridge Gerry, who drew the first truly outrageous legislative district in 1812. Except in rare cases, the Supreme Court has avoided the issue, in large part because there are no reliable standards to determine how election districts may fairly be drawn. In 1960 it did strike down under the EQUAL PROTECTION CLAUSE an "uncouth, 28-sided figure" by which Tuskegee, Alabama, excluded most blacks from voting in city elections.[775] But race-conscious redistricting is not unconstitutional per se. To comply with the VOTING RIGHTS ACT, New York redistricted Brooklyn seats in the state legislature to create black majorities in several districts rather than in the one in which they had been situated. In so doing, a district in which thirty thousand Hasidic Jews had considerable voting clout was splintered into several districts. The Hasidic community challenged the reapportionment on equal protection grounds, but the Court upheld the plan, giving short shrift to the Hasidim's claim to a separate voting identity, holding that the new districts provided them with "fair representation" as whites and that in any event the discrimination was not "purposeful."[2094]

Today gerrymandering is practiced probably far more often for partisan than racial reasons, and in 1986 the Court declared that claims of partisanship in legislative apportionment are justiciable—that is, proper for a court to hear. The Indiana Democratic party charged that Indiana's 1981 reapportionment was rigged against Democrats by a complicated scheme of multi-member and single-member districts. In the 1982 elections, Democratic candidates got 51.9 percent of the state votes but only forty-three of one hundred seats in the state house of representatives. But the Court set a high threshold for showing "vote dilution," holding that data from a single election is insufficient to provide "evidence of continued frustration of the will of a majority of the voters or effective denial to a minority of voters of a fair chance to influence the political process."[519]

See also: APPORTIONMENT OF POLITICAL DISTRICTS.

God, references to in public documents The United States motto, "In God We Trust," is imprinted on all paper currency. Occasionally, the constitutionality of the motto and other references to God in public documents is questioned under the ESTABLISHMENT CLAUSE. The Court has shrugged off the issue, noting in passing the motto's historical longevity. In a 1983 case, Justice William Brennan confessed that he did not know how to view references to God in constitutional terms but that perhaps there is no problem because time has drained the motto of all religious significance.[1246]

gold regulation　In 1933, when Congress took the United States off the gold standard, it outlawed "gold clauses" in all private and public contracts, existing as well as future ones. Gold clauses required payment of debts in gold rather than paper currency. The Supreme Court sustained the invalidation of the private clauses,[1490] but not the public ones. The Court said that Congress may not annul obligations incurred when it sells treasury bonds.[1611] But the ruling made no practical difference, because the Court said that bondholders were entitled to no more than the face amount of the bonds in dollars, not gold.

good behavior, *see:* **during good behavior**

good-faith exception, *see:* **exclusionary rule**

government, affirmative obligations of The Constitution has been called a negative, not a positive, charter. It generally constrains government *from* acting. Rarely does it command government *to* act, and in those instances it is almost always to ensure fair treatment of someone in custody or otherwise disadvantaged by the government itself. The Court has held that DUE PROCESS requires prisons to ensure adequate medical care for inmates [626] and hospitals to provide a safe environment for involuntarily committed mental patients. [2279] For the same reason, when the government intends to deprive a person of LIBERTY, several constitutional clauses require it to provide a speedy trial by jury, to pay for the indigent defendant's lawyer, and to make witnesses available so that the defendant can confront them in open court. But these are affirmative obligations only in a very narrow sense. A broader sense in which government would be obliged to help the needy and suffering, providing adequate shelter for the homeless, food for the starving, and care for the sick and infirm, is not a requirement of the Constitution. [1168] The Constitution does not command government to *refrain* from assistance—welfare laws, after all, are constitutional—but there is "no affirmative right to governmental aid" [542] if the government chooses not to act.

In a particularly gruesome case, neighbors reported to Winnebago County officials in Wisconsin that a man was physically abusing his three-year-old son. Calls were referred to the local office of the Department of Social Services, which began to investigate. A few months later when the son was hospitalized with suspicious injuries, a court temporarily removed him from home, but within days a department team found insufficient evidence of abuse and sent the child home. Certain conditions were imposed on the child's return. The father was to seek counseling, move his girlfriend out of the house, and accept visits from the department's caseworker. For fourteen months, the caseworker diligently recorded in her notebook growing signs of continuing abuse and the father's evident refusal to undertake counseling or evict his girlfriend. But the caseworker said nothing. Several months later, the father viciously battered his son, leaving

the child permanently brain-damaged and institutionalized for the rest of his life. The child's mother, divorced years earlier from the father, sued the county for violating her son's due process rights by failing to protect him. She sought DAMAGES on his behalf to pay for long-term custodial care. In 1989 the Supreme Court held that the county had not violated the Constitution because the father, not government officials, had done the beating. Said Chief Justice William H. Rehnquist for the 6–3 majority, the government has no constitutional obligation "to protect an individual against private violence." [542] Because the government constitutionally could have done nothing at all, it does not matter that the county intervened in some way. The caseworker and other government officials did not make the boy worse off for what they failed to do; they simply didn't make him better off.

The case has excited considerably controversy. The difficulty lies in the meaning of "action." In Rehnquist's view, the state did not act unconstitutionally because it did not act at all. Only action, not inaction, can violate due process. But consider: under this case, Winnebago County has no constitutional duty to maintain a fire department. Does that mean that the fire chief can constitutionally refuse to send the engines to your burning house? Does the fire chief *act* when he fails to respond to the alarm, or does his refusal to move the trucks indicate *inaction*? The Court provides no way out of this muddle. Rehnquist said that although the state, through its local agency, may have been aware of the dangers facing the boy, "it played no part in their creation, nor did it do anything to render him any more vulnerable to them." Dissenting, Justice William Brennan pointed out that the state did indeed render him more vulnerable. By creating the Department of Social Services, it aroused in the entire community the expectation that real threats would be dealt with, making the neighbors less likely to intervene. The state had acted, just as it acts in supporting fire stations with trained firefighters to come to your rescue as necessary. To *decide not to act* when there is every institutional requirement to do so is not inaction—it is very real action.

Nevertheless, it is unlikely that the Court will change its mind, for the confusion over action and inaction is deeply enmeshed in constitutional thinking. In the CIVIL RIGHTS CASES in 1883, the Court caused a century of misery by refusing to conceive of EQUAL PROTECTION OF THE LAWS affirmatively rather than negatively. It ruled that under equal protection the state itself is obliged not to actively discriminate. The state may not refuse fire protection for blacks while providing it for whites. But the state need not outlaw private acts of discrimination—when a restaurant refuses service to blacks, the state has not acted and so there is no violation of equal protection. There is much in politics, but little in logic, that sees a state's refusal to protect its citizens against discrimination as something other than a denial of equal protection of the laws. But so matters stand.

See also: STATE ACTION.

government, republican form, *see:* **republican form of government**

government aid to religious institutions, *see:* **religious establishment; schools, religion in**

government contractors, *see:* **affirmative action; set-asides**

government documents, confidentiality of
Whether the government has the constitutional right to insist on the confidentiality of its papers, documents, and information depends largely on whether the information remains in its possession or has leaked out. In the PENTA-

GON PAPERS CASE, the Supreme Court reaffirmed the FIRST AMENDMENT prohibition against PRIOR RESTRAINT—except in the rarest cases, a court may not enjoin publication even of purloined government documents. States may enact laws prohibiting government employees from releasing the names of crime victims, but the law may not bar the press from accurately publishing information obtained from official documents, including victims' names.[480, 685] The Court has held unconstitutional GAG ORDERS prohibiting pretrial publication of information about a defendant[1441] and a criminal law prohibiting disclosure of confidential information gleaned from a state commission secretly investigating a judge.[1115] Presumably the Court would reach the same result over publication of GRAND JURY information, although it has not ruled on the issue. In 1990 it did strike down a Florida law prohibiting grand jury witnesses from disclosing their testimony even after the grand jury's term had ended.[296] With some important exceptions, however, the press has no general right of access to information still in the government's hands. The federal Freedom of Information Act establishes a federal policy of making available government information and provides a judicial enforcement mechanism if government agencies prove recalcitrant, but the law is not constitutionally compelled. For example, the Court has held that the press is not constitutionally entitled to interview prisoners.[1583, 1805] However, a splintered Court in 1978 ruled that if a prison grants access to members of the public it may not exclude the press and it must, moreover, permit the press *effective* access. Prison authorities may not, for example, bar press photographers under these circumstances.[945] The Court has also declared a right of press access to trials and pretrial proceedings.[1727, 763, 1659, 1660]

See also: FREE PRESS—FAIR TRIAL; PREJUDICIAL PUBLICITY; REPORTER'S PRIVILEGE.

government speech   The problem of government speech turns the usual FREEDOM OF SPEECH case around. Instead of the government trying to regulate the speech of private citizens, here it is private citizens trying to regulate the speech of government officials. The question is whether the FIRST AMENDMENT requires that when government talks or spends money to advance political and social positions, it do so in a content-neutral manner. Stated so broadly, the answer must be no, for by what standard would a court measure the degree of neutrality required in controversial matters? Is the president barred from taking a position on ABORTION because it is unconstitutional to spend public money on partisan matters? The ESTABLISHMENT CLAUSE says the government may not prefer one religion to another, but the Free Speech Clause has no comparable guarantee of neutrality when the government is not the regulator but the speaker itself. For that reason, there is no First Amendment bar to using public funds for political campaigning.[270] In 1991, in a case whose implications remain unclear, the Court upheld a federal Department of Health and Human Services regulation that bars recipients of federal funding for family planning services from receiving counseling about ABORTION or referring a client to an abortion clinic. Under the regulation, even doctors are forbidden to discuss abortion as an alternative to childbirth. The Court said that the regulation does not discriminate "on the basis of viewpoint; [rather, the government] has merely chosen to fund one activity to the exclusion of the other."[1777]

Nevertheless, in certain instances, the Court has hinted at the possibility that there may be some First Amendment restrictions on what the government can do with what it owns.

In 1982 the question posed was whether a school board could "censor" books by removing from the school library certain books, including Kurt Vonnegut's *Slaughterhouse Five,* Desmond Morris's *The Naked Ape,* Bernard Malamud's *The Fixer,* and Richard Wright's *Black Boy.* The board issued a press release saying that the listed books were "anti-American, anti-Christian, anti-Semitic, and just plain filthy. . . . It is our duty, our moral obligation, to protect the children in our schools from this moral danger." Acknowledging the broad, perhaps unfettered, discretion that school boards have in fixing the classroom curriculum, Justice William Brennan said for a Court plurality that boards do not have absolute discretion over libraries, a place to which students voluntarily go or refrain from going. Students have a right to receive ideas; and control over ideas "may not be exercised in a narrowly partisan or political manner." A Democratic school board could not order all books written by Republicans to be removed, nor could an all-white school board order the removal of all books by or about blacks. So whether a school board may remove library books depends on its motivation. A board may remove vulgar books, but it may not remove books solely to deny children access to ideas with which board members disagree.[182] The Court has not revisited this theme in ten years, so it is likely that a more sophisticated attempt to remove books from school libraries will survive.

See also: RIGHT TO KNOW.

Gramm-Rudman-Hollings Act, *see:* **budget**

grand jury   A grand jury sits to determine whether there is PROBABLE CAUSE to indict— that is, to formally accuse—someone of a crime. The FIFTH AMENDMENT requires INDICTMENT by grand jury for federal prosecutions of all serious crimes, except military courts martial. This provision is one of the few that has not been incorporated in the DUE PROCESS Clause of the FOURTEENTH AMENDMENT, so states are not obliged to use grand juries,[964] and about half do not. The grand jury serves not merely to indict but to gather information. Grand jury testimony is usually secret, although this is not a constitutional requirement, and Congress has authorized grand juries to issue certain types of reports, for example, in cases involving organized crime and public officials. In a number of cases, the Court has ruled that the grand jury is not constitutionally bound to observe various safeguards that apply at trial. Grand juries operate under loose rules of procedure and are not required to consider the accused's side of the story. They may summon witnesses without telling the witness what they are investigating or that he or she might be indicted as a result of the jury's inquiry,[2163] and they may exclude a witness's lawyer during testimony.[1236] The EXCLUSIONARY RULE does not apply; a grand jury may draw on any information gleaned from an unlawful SEARCH AND SEIZURE.[306] Still, witnesses haled before grand juries retain some constitutional rights, including the right against SELF-INCRIMINATION.[172] Under federal rules, grand jury indictments do not require unanimity; twelve votes are sufficient for any federal grand jury of between sixteen and twenty-three jurors.

See also: INDICTMENT; INFAMOUS CRIME; INFORMATION.

grandfather clause　When a legislature or regulatory agency outlaws an activity, it sometimes exempts some or all people who have been engaging in the activity for a period of time. For example, a new building code that requires fire escapes to be installed on all three-story residences might be applied only to newly constructed homes. The exemption for existing homeowners is known as a "grandfather clause." In these circumstances, a grandfather clause poses no constitutional difficulty, even though it burdens some more than others. But several states used grandfather clauses to deter and prevent black voting at the turn of the century, by imposing onerous burdens on registration and then exempting whites who

had been eligible to vote before a certain date. The Supreme Court invalidated these laws in 1915[830] and 1939.[1118] More recently, in a nonracial case, the Court upheld a grandfather clause that permitted two pushcart vendors in the French Quarter of New Orleans to continue to sell their wares because they had been operating eight years, even though all other vendors were told to leave.[1454]

See also: ECONOMIC DISCRIMINATION; VOTING, RIGHT TO.

grants in aid　Once the New Deal Court freed the federal government to spend federal revenues on any program that it considered in the GENERAL WELFARE, Congress established hundreds of programs to be operated by the states with federal funding known as "grants in aid." Most grant-in-aid funding comes with tough strings attached, and the Court has shown no inclination to upset federal conditions on constitutional grounds. In 1987 the Court sustained a law that permits the secretary of transportation to withhold five percent of any state's highway grants unless it passed a law raising the drinking age to twenty-one.[1915] Since the STANDING requirement makes it difficult for ordinary citizens to contest any federal spending program, few such suits can be brought to challenge these programs.

See also: SPENDING POWER.

Great Compromise　The major hurdle facing the delegates to the CONSTITUTIONAL CONVENTION in 1787 was the method of federal REPRESENTATION. Large states wanted some form of representation proportional to population; small states wanted to be represented equally in the national legislature. Early in the proceedings, Edmund Randolph of Virginia presented the Virginia Plan: Congress would consist of two houses, and the states would be represented in each house according to population. In the lower house, representatives would be elected directly by the people. Members of the upper house would be chosen by the lower house from lists of candidates supplied by state legislatures. Since three states alone—Virginia, Pennsylvania, and Massachusetts—held nearly half the population of the country, Randolph's plan seriously disturbed the other states' delegates. William Paterson of New Jersey countered with a radically different idea. Under the New Jersey Plan, each state would be represented equally in a one-house Congress. For a month the debate raged, nearly tearing the convention apart.

Finally, the delegates turned to a proposal of Roger Sherman of Connecticut. Why not have it both ways? Give the states an equal voice in the upper house and a proportional voice in the lower. This was the Great Compromise. Members of the House of Representatives would be elected directly by the people, each state to have a share proportional to their population, slaves to count for three-fifths of a person. Each state would have two senators, elected by the state legislatures. Because large states would get larger representation, they would be required to pay more for the privilege: DIRECT TAXATION by the states would also be in proportion to population, so that a state with twice as many people could be taxed twice as heavily as another. On July 16, 1787, the delegates adopted this compromise by a vote of five to four. New Jersey, Delaware, Maryland, and North Carolina sided with Connecticut. Pennsylvania, Virginia, South Carolina, and Georgia were opposed. The New York delegates had walked out and did not participate; the Massachusetts delegates were divided and did not vote. Rhode Island did not attend the convention. The losers acceded to the compromise, and the convention—and the Constitution—were saved.

group libel Group libel is the defaming of a class of citizens because of their race, color, creed, religion, origin, or sex. In 1952 a 5–4 majority sustained an Illinois law that made group libel a criminal offense.[142] Although the

case has never been overruled, its authority has probably been seriously eroded by later cases suggesting that a hate-filled message not aimed at anyone in particular is constitutionally immune from attack unless it immediately incites its listeners to unlawful violence.[222]

See also: HATE SPEECH; LIBEL AND SLANDER.

Guarantee Clause The Guarantee Clause, located in Art. IV-§4, says that "the United States shall guarantee to every state in this union a REPUBLICAN FORM OF GOVERNMENT." In 1849 Chief Justice Roger B. Taney said that Congress alone has the constitutional authority to decide whether a state government is republican. The issue may not be raised in court.[1208]

See also: COMMITMENT TO OTHER BRANCHES; JUSTICIABILITY; POLITICAL QUESTION DOCTRINE.

guilt by association It is a commonplace that one ought not to be condemned for the company one keeps. Guilt is individual. In striking down an Arizona law requiring state employees to take a LOYALTY OATH, Justice William O. Douglas said that such a law "infringes unnecessarily on protected freedoms. It rests on the doctrine of 'guilt by association' which has no place here."[609] The Arizona law said in effect that if you were a member of the Communist party or any other organization that espoused as "one of its purposes" overthrow of the government, you could be convicted for taking the oath, even if you did not personally subscribe to the organization's goals and went to their meetings simply because you liked the milk and cookies served. Similarly, a law prohibiting members of a "Communist-action organization" from working in a defense facility "quite literally established guilt by association alone," the Court said in 1967.[1736] In *DeJonge v. Oregon*, the Court in 1937 overturned the conviction of a speaker at a peaceful meeting of a radical organization. To hold otherwise would have defeated FREEDOM OF ASSOCIATION. But despite the usual protestations that guilt by association has no place in American society, it is a principle that lies at the heart of the criminal justice system. In CONSPIRACY cases, one conspirator may be convicted for actions undertaken by the co-conspirators. And in a few egregious instances, the Supreme Court has upheld the idea in different forms. For example, in permitting Japanese-Americans to be removed from their homes during World War II, it explicitly endorsed the proposition that the government could infringe basic rights because of one's ancestry.[925] In 1950 the Court sustained a provision of the federal labor laws that prohibited the National Labor Relations Board from enforcing a union's rights if its officers did not swear they were not communists.[444] In the end, whether one is guilty of association depends on how closely one is perceived as associating with people who, at the time, are considered to be up to no good.

See also: MEMBERSHIP IN POLITICAL ORGANIZATIONS.

guilty mind, *see:* **regulatory law**

guilty plea   The Constitution does not compel a trial if a criminal defendant wishes to plead guilty, but the plea must be entered knowingly and voluntarily. A guilty plea may be revoked if offered by a lawyer without the defendant's knowledge or because the lawyer was incompetent.[2056] It may also be withdrawn if the defendant did not understand all the elements of the crime to which he had pleaded guilty. The Court reversed one conviction because the defendant did not understand that in pleading guilty to second-degree murder he was acknowledging that he intended to kill the victim.[899] But the prosecutor is entitled to drive a hard PLEA BARGAIN. For example, a prosecutor told a forgery suspect that he would recommend a five-year sentence if the forger pleaded guilty. If he did not, the prosecutor said he would seek a further indictment under the state's "habitual criminal statute," which

could lead to a life sentence if this defendant was convicted at trial. The defendant refused the deal, went to trial under the new indictment, and drew a life sentence. The Court dismissed the defendant's challenge to the prosecutor's hardball tactics.[200] If a prosecutor withdraws an offer of leniency before a defendant accepts a plea bargain and the defendant later pleads guilty in a less beneficial second deal, he has no right to enforce the first offer.[1216] But the prosecution may not renege on an accepted offer and recommend that the judge impose a harsher sentence.[1801] Judges are not required to hand down the sentences bargained for because they are not party to the deal. A prosecutor, an executive branch official, cannot constitutionally bind judicial officers. But a prosecutor who promises to dismiss certain charges as part of the deal may be held to his promise.

Gulf of Tonkin Resolution   In 1964 President Lyndon B. Johnson told Congress that North Vietnamese patrol boats had attacked U.S. Navy destroyers in the Gulf of Tonkin. He asked for authority "to take all necessary steps, including the use of armed force, to assist any member or protocol state of the Southeast Asia Collective Defense Treaty requesting defense of its freedom." Congress passed the Southeast Asia Resolution, or Gulf of Tonkin Resolution, as it was more popularly called, by votes of 88–2 in the Senate and 416–0 in the House. It was this authority that Johnson relied on to commit ground troops that essentially began the Vietnam War. Despite many attempts to challenge the war on the constitutional ground that Congress had not declared it, the Supreme Court steadfastly refused to hear such cases.[1205] Congress repealed the Gulf of Tonkin Resolution in 1971.

guns, *see:* **arms, right to keep and bear**

H

habeas corpus Habeas corpus (Latin for "have the body") has long been celebrated as the "Great Writ," the chief mechanism for preventing kings from simply ordering their enemies to jail. Established in England well before the American Revolution, habeas corpus is technically an order to a jailkeeper to "have the body" of a prisoner brought before the court to justify continued detention. But for centuries habeas corpus has required the jailer to do more than simply recite orders from the executive authority that the prisoner be clapped in jail. Judges hearing habeas petitions require legal justification, meaning that the state must prove the prisoner was confined according to a law duly enacted and duly enforced in the courts.

Habeas corpus is one of the few individual rights included in the original Constitution. Art. I-§9[1] says that "the privilege of the writ of habeas corpus shall not be suspended, unless when in cases of rebellion or invasion the public safety may require it." This provision was included to prevent the federal government from suspending the writ in *state* cases since the Constitution did not directly establish a federal court system. Since 1807, it has been assumed that this clause does not automatically give *federal* prisoners a right to habeas corpus.[194] However, since 1789 Congress has provided federal courts with JURISDICTION to issue writs of habeas corpus and so the issue has never been put to the test. The Constitution leaves open the question of *who* may suspend the writ, the president or Congress. Abraham Lincoln did so on his own in 1863, arousing a storm of opposition, and Congress eventually approved the suspension retroactively. After the Civil War ended, the Supreme Court held in *Ex parte Milligan* that only Congress may suspend, and it denied even Congress the power to suspend as long as civilian courts remain open. After World War II, the Court rejected Congress's suspension of habeas corpus and the declaration of martial law in Hawaii because the public safety did not genuinely require it, since the civilian government and courts continued to function and months after Pearl Harbor there was no longer threat of invasion.[581]

Before the Civil War, state courts issued writs of habeas corpus to federal prisoners, often to free antislavery advocates jailed for violating the draconian Fugitive Slave Act. The Court declared this use of the writ unconstitutional in 1859,[3] as it had earlier declared that federal courts did not have inherent constitutional authority to issue writs on behalf of state prisoners. To undo the effect of this ruling, Congress in the Habeas Corpus Act of 1867 said federal courts could hear state prisoners' claims through habeas corpus. Any claim that a prisoner was unconstitutionally imprisoned could now be brought to federal court. However, there were only narrow grounds for concluding that someone was being unconstitutionally detained. At COMMON LAW, habeas corpus was available only when the defendant was detained by executive order, not when a prisoner had been jailed after conviction at trial. The Court adopted that rule until 1867,[2166] when it began to consider cases in which the prisoner charged that he had been convicted under an unconstitutional statute. The theory was that such a conviction deprived the trial court of its jurisdiction.[1865, 2276]

The true breadth of the Habeas Corpus Act only became apparent in 1915, when the Court for the first time overturned a conviction because the mob-dominated state trial violated the prisoner's right to due process.[695] Although a defendant could always protest the unconstitutionality of his conviction by appealing directly to a higher court, the Supreme Court had now made it possible for a prisoner later to bring a *separate* habeas corpus suit. In other words, a prisoner could get a second bite of the apple. This was important for two reasons. A defendant's theoretical right to have the Supreme Court review an unconstitutional conviction was usually unavailing, since the Court obviously had neither the time nor resources to hear every such case. So a defendant with no means to challenge the state proceedings independently had no chance of federal review. Because state judges are not always insulated from political pressures, as are life-tenured federal judges, many commentators have argued that federal habeas corpus is essential. Moreover, unless a defendant could bring a separate habeas case, constitutional rights that the Supreme Court announced *after* the defendant's direct appeals ended could never be applied to his case.

Much of this reasoning remained theoretical until the 1950s. For one thing, the Court adhered to an EXHAUSTION OF REMEDIES rule. A prisoner could not simply ask for habeas corpus separately if he still had a chance to appeal his conviction. But if the state appeals court "adequately" considered and then rejected his constitutional claims, the Court was disinclined to permit separate habeas review. In 1953, however, the Court announced in *Brown v. Allen* that under the Habeas Corpus Act, *any* constitutional claim could be raised in a separate habeas corpus hearing in federal court, even if the state court had fairly considered the claim and rejected it. In the 1960s, as the Warren Court began furiously requiring the states to abide by most of the provisions of the BILL OF RIGHTS, many state courts resisted and more and more claims were pressed on the federal courts.

In 1963 the Court further broadened its interpretation of the Habeas Corpus Act: First, it declared that the federal courts could inquire into the *facts* of the matter; they were not bound by the state courts' FINDINGS.[2066] Second, the Court made it much easier than before to file successive habeas petitions, either to raise questions not previously considered or to reconsider questions already presented.[1797]

The third case was the most dramatic. The usual rule in appeals is that if a defendant makes a procedural mistake, such as failing to object to evidence, or filing the appeal papers late, the appeals court need not entertain the question. Thereafter, the Supreme Court may not review because the state appeals court had an "independent and adequate state ground" to deny the appeal. In other words, the defendant lost not because he had been denied his federal constitutional rights but because he had made procedural errors. But now in *Fay v. Noia* the Court changed all that, opening habeas cases to all sorts of issues that the defendant had procedurally failed to raise in state court. The Court said that the "independent and adequate state ground" simply did not apply to habeas cases, only to direct appeals.

These three cases were immediately put to the use. In 1961 state prisoners filed 1,020 habeas cases in all federal courts. In 1965 the number jumped to 4,845, and in 1970, 9,063, although very few prisoners were actually released. By the 1970s, there was considerable discontent from many quarters about the growing caseloads and the second-guessing of state courts, and a new Supreme Court began to cut back on its liberal interpretation of the Habeas Corpus Act. In 1976 the Court said that habeas corpus would no longer be available to contest violations of the FOURTH AMENDMENT, such as the use of evidence gained from an unlawful SEARCH.[1963] Only in a direct appeal may a defendant argue that the EXCLUSIONARY RULE should apply in his case. In 1977 the Court further undercut *Fay v. Noia* in holding that if a defendant fails to raise a claim in accordance with state procedures, federal courts may review on habeas corpus only if he had a "good cause" for not doing so and if failure to consider the claim would demonstrably prejudice him.[2140] This "cause and prejudice" test is more difficult to meet but not impossible. In one case the defendant found out only after trial that the county had racially discriminated in picking the jury, a cause sufficiently prejudicial to permit a reversal of the conviction through habeas corpus.[44]

During the 1980s, as more and more multiple habeas cases were filed, especially in DEATH PENALTY cases that delayed executions by years, the Court grew increasingly impatient and began vigorously to constrict the previous generous reading of the Habeas Corpus Act. In 1986, for example, it extended the "cause and prejudice" test to appeals; a lawyer's failure to raise the constitutional issues on appeal now will ordinarily preclude separate habeas review.[1410] In 1989 the Court said that federal habeas courts "need only apply the constitu-

tional standards that prevailed at the time the original proceedings took place."[2004, 1599] A new Supreme Court ruling need not be applied retroactively. This may prove to be a highly restrictive doctrine, since often it is highly unclear what the prevailing constitutional standards were. Only if the state court misinterpreted a prevailing constitutional requirement may the federal habeas court reverse the conviction. In recent years, the Court has announced a number of highly metaphysical guidelines for determining when a constitutional rule was or was not "dictated" by a prior case.[1781, 1804]

In 1991 the Court finally all but buried *Fay v. Noia*. If a state prisoner fails to raise federal claims in a state appeal, even if only because his lawyer missed a filing deadline, the federal courts may not hear an attack on the conviction in a habeas corpus proceeding unless the defendant can demonstrate that a "fundamental miscarriage of justice" will result. Also in 1991 the Court sharply undercut a defendant's ability to file successive habeas petitions. The rule had been that if the defendant lost one habeas case, he was always free to raise another. Henceforth, the defendant will not be permitted to raise at a subsequent habeas hearing any matter he could have raised at a previous one, unless he had good cause and can demonstrate substantial prejudice—for example, newly discovered evidence that might prove the defendant was actually innocent.[1283]

Congress could at any time redirect the debate and reverse the Court's recent concerted narrowing of the Great Writ. Whether Congress will be able to muster sufficient votes to override a veto remains to be seen.

See also: HARMLESS ERROR; RETROACTIVITY.

habitual offenders, *see:* **proportionality of sentence**

hairstyle, right to, *see:* **dress codes**

handicap discrimination   Discrimination against handicapped or disabled persons has never been held to violate the EQUAL PROTECTION CLAUSE. No doubt if a state were to enact a law prohibiting the handicapped as a class from attending public schools or patronizing restaurants, the Court would have little difficulty applying STRICT SCRUTINY to the classification. But states have not done so. The real complaint has been, rather, that in failing to accommodate facilities to the special needs of the handicapped, the state is discriminating. Again, the Court has found no such right, but Congress and many states have enacted several laws requiring various forms of public assistance for the handicapped, including easier access to public and private buildings, prohibitions against discrimination in hiring, affirmative action in federal hiring, and richer educational programs.

See also: EQUAL PROTECTION OF THE LAWS; GOVERNMENT, AFFIRMATIVE OBLIGATIONS OF; SUSPECT CLASSIFICATIONS.

happiness, pursuit of   In 1986, reacting to the Supreme Court's declaration that the federal government had overstepped its legal authority in telling hospitals how to deal with newborn handicapped babies, President Reagan said: "If our Constitution means anything, it means that we, the Federal Government, are entrusted with preserving life, liberty, and the pursuit of happiness." Of course the Constitution says no such thing. The phrase "life, liberty, and the pursuit of happiness" is Thomas Jefferson's, from the Declaration of Independence. In the 1970s, a constitutional "happiness amendment" was proposed that would have permitted federal courts to hear cases in which the happiness of a significant number of people was disturbed by the conduct of anyone. For obvious reasons, the proposal went nowhere.

hard-core pornography, *see:* **obscenity and pornography**

harm, types of, *see:* **psychic harm**

harmless error   A trial can be a magnificently complicated performance—the intersection of different intelligence and personalities, time pressures, and knowledge or lack of it about hundreds of often only dimly articulated rules. The chances for foulup are large. So all appellate courts in the United States, state as well as federal, are commanded by law to ignore "harmless errors," mistakes that do not have a significant bearing on the outcome of the case. In 1967, in *Chapman v. California,* the Supreme Court announced a constitutional harmless-error rule for criminal prosecutions. Certain constitutional errors, the Court said, can never be harmless: the use of a coerced confession at trial, the presence of a biased judge, or the failure to provide the defendant with a lawyer. If these errors occur, the conviction must automatically be reversed. To avoid reversing for other kinds of constitutional errors, the reviewing court must determine beyond a reasonable doubt that the error did not change the outcome of the case. During the past quarter century, the Court has been confronted with a wide range of errors that defendants have asserted cannot constitutionally be considered harmless. The Court has rejected most of these claims—for example, an erroneous jury instruction about the nature of the offense,[1650] improper comment on the defendant's refusal to take the stand,[878] unconstitutionally seized evidence,[366] mistaken restriction of a defendant's right to cross-examine a witness for evidence of bias,[537] and failure to instruct the jury on the constitutional presumption of innocence.[1065] The effect of these rulings was to subject each of these, and many other, errors to the harmless-error rule: could the appellate court say beyond a reasonable doubt that they would not have affected the outcome of the case? If it could, the error was harmless, and the conviction must stand. In 1991 the Court distinguished between mere "trial errors" and "structural defects" in the trial process. Reversing part of *Chapman*, a badly fractured Court held that involuntary confessions are no longer beyond the pale of the harmless-error rule and no longer require automatic reversal if used at trial.[70] Henceforth they must be tested against the reasonable-doubt standard. If the other evidence is sufficient to ensure that the jury would not possibly have acquitted even without the confession, the guilty verdict may stand.

See also: PROCEDURAL RIGHTS OF CRIMINAL DEFENDANTS *and cross references listed there.*

hat, *see:* **dress codes**

Hatch Act, *see:* **public employees**

hate speech   A mood of "political correctness" in the 1990s and a heightened sensitivity to a growing incivility on college campuses and in other institutions have led many to deny the old adage, "Sticks and stones may break my bones but names will never hurt me." Paradoxically, in aiming at hate speech, many articulate defenders of the freedom of speech have been searching for a way to define and regulate a form of expression. The constitutional precedents point in different directions. A forty-year-old criminal GROUP LIBEL case, never formally overruled, seems to stand for the proposition that the state may criminalize expression that demeans a "class of citizens" by race or religion.[142] But the courts' unwillingness to deny parade permits to Nazi marchers in Skokie, Illinois, in 1978 bespoke a ripening consensus that the government simply may not silence speakers because of their message.

One way around these precedents, perhaps, is to prohibit *conduct,* rather than "pure speech." In 1988 the University of Michigan adopted disciplinary rules prohibiting forms of "behavior" that demean or vilify a person because of his personal characteristics. The Michigan rule permitted suspension or expulsion for "behavior, verbal or physical, that stigmatizes or victimizes an individual on the basis of race, ethnicity, religion, sex, sexual orientation, creed, national origin, ancestry, age, marital status, handicap or Viet-Nam era veteran status," if the speaker intended to interfere or the speech had the "reasonably foreseeable effect of interfering with an individual's academic efforts, employment, participation in University sponsored extra-curricular activities or personal safety." This rule was struck down by a Michigan federal DISTRICT COURT. The court said the rule suffered from VAGUENESS and OVERBREADTH.

Private universities, not legally bound by the First Amendment, have experimented with similar rules and have similarly been caught between their abhorrence of the highly charged campus incivility and their distaste of censorship. To limit the focus of the prohibition, Stanford University proposed barring speakers who have targeted particular individuals, engaging in "harassment by vilification." An open question is whether this rule will be limited to situations in which one person hounds another around the campus or will be applied more broadly to any crank making a general speech. Another approach has been to view racist and other forms of hate speech as attempts to cause mental distress. But this approach, too, has a constitutional pitfall. In a case involving the Reverend Jerry Falwell, the Court ruled that PUBLIC FIGURES may not recover DAMAGES for publications causing mental distress without demonstrating "actual MALICE."[965] Whether malice in the constitutional sense needs to be shown when hate speech is directed by one private individual toward another remains another open question, as does the question of whether there is a constitutional difference between a damage suit in a particular case and a law broadly prohibiting a class of speech. The problem remains that of the CHILLING EFFECT: we should be chary of regulations against even the most obnoxious and hate-filled speech because they become a trap that can force people into costly and time-consuming defenses or into refraining from saying what's on their mind, even if the thought does not cross into forbidden territory. In any event, the debate is intense and continuing, and the clarifying case has not yet reached the Supreme Court.

See also: FREEDOM OF SPEECH and cross references listed there.

head coverings, *see:* **dress codes**

heads of departments   The Court has ruled that "heads of departments" in Art. II-§2[2] means cabinet members only. So the chief judge of the United States Tax Court, an ARTICLE I COURT, is not the head of a department in the constitutional sense. However, the chief judge may nevertheless be vested with the power to appoint INFERIOR OFFICERS because the Tax Court is a "court of law" within the meaning of the appointments clause.[701]

See also: APPOINTMENT AND REMOVAL POWER; CIVIL OFFICE AND OFFICERS; INFERIOR OFFICE AND OFFICERS.

health, *see:* **abortion; medication and surgery, forced; right to die**

health insurance, *see:* **General Welfare Clause**

hearing   By explicit command of the FIFTH and FOURTEENTH AMENDMENTS, neither the states nor the federal government may deprive any person of "life, LIBERTY, or PROPERTY without due process of law." The most fundamental notion of DUE PROCESS is the right to NOTICE of a claim or charge and the right to defend against it. The right to a hearing raises four questions: (1) For what deprivations must a hearing be held? (2) When must it be held? (3)

Who must hold the hearing? (4) What procedures make it fair?

(1) Any criminal proceeding requires a TRIAL. Less certain is the formula for determining when civil deprivations require a hearing and whether they must be in court or before some other agency. The state may demand payment of taxes, condemn property, outlaw a method of doing business, garnish wages, seize tainted food, fire an employee, injure someone on the road, deport an alien, or confiscate a driver's license. In general, the Court has said that a hearing is required only when the deprivation is aimed at a particular person. A legislature or administrative agency drafting a rule aimed at large numbers of unnamed, unknown persons need not hold a hearing.[160] As far as due process is concerned, in other words, Congress could enact the Internal Revenue Code entirely in secret, without even hearing from lobbyists. But when the state proposes to do something to a particular individual, it usually must provide a forum in which objections can be heard. There are two major exceptions to this rule. One is that aliens may be excluded at the border without any sort of hearing[1042, 2269, 1085] even if the alien had long resided in the United States and was returning from a brief vacation abroad.[1851] But anyone claiming U.S. citizenship may neither be excluded[1102] nor deported[1478] without a hearing though not necessarily in court.

The other major exception stems from the difficulty of defining with precision what constitutes liberty or property. A modern welfare state that distributes benefits, licenses, and jobs may seriously disadvantage someone if it can terminate an allowance or boon without permitting the beneficiary to show why it is mistaken. An elderly pensioner will surely be harmed if the Social Security Administration decides without notice or hearing to cut off his or her monthly check. But is an employee of the public recreation department entitled to a hearing when his or her boss cancels a day off because someone else called in sick? Since almost any state action could be seen as having some impact on a liberty or property interest, a broad reading of the due process clauses would require vast numbers of hearings, to the point of paralysis. Beginning in 1970, the Court has been stepping gingerly through this terrain (see PROCESS RIGHTS).

(2) The Court has said that a hearing "must be granted at a meaningful time and in a meaningful manner."[78] What is meaningful depends on the situation, and the Court has never demanded that every hearing be heard *before* a deprivation. When an individual would suffer particularly severe harm, the state must hold a hearing first—before terminating welfare benefits,[766] permitting wages to be garnished,[1901] or summarily suspending a driver's license following an accident,[145] although the Court did uphold an Illinois summary procedure for revoking the licenses of drivers repeatedly involved in traffic accidents.[554] But in rare situations when the public would be seriously harmed by delay, the state may act first and listen later; it may, for example, seize adulterated food and drugs without notice.[1493, 635] In some instances, the Court has also approved the use of two separate hearings to consider all aspects of the deprivation. During World War II the Court upheld a scheme in which defendants charged with violating price control orders were denied the opportunity to defend by showing that the orders were illegal. Congress had created an EMERGENCY COURT OF APPEALS for litigants to separately contest the legality of the orders, and that was sufficient to satisfy the right to a hearing.[1178] Likewise, the Court upheld an Oregon summary eviction procedure that barred tenants from defending on any ground other than payment of rent. To enforce their right under the lease to have the premises adequately maintained, the state may tell them to file a separate lawsuit.[1168]

(3) The Constitution does not require that every hearing be in court. Any number of significant government policies with direct impact on particular people are carried out by administrative agencies. For example, parole boards rule directly on whether to restore liberty to particular prisoners. Many deprivations may be contested in front of the administrative agencies about to take the disputed action. A principal need not obtain a court order to permit the suspension of a student from school. It is enough to hold an informal hearing with the student to learn whether the school authorities are mistaken about the facts that warrant the suspension.[785] On the other hand, the hearing need not be administrative. The Court upheld a federal law during World War II sustaining the power of the price administrator to set maximum rents without hearing from those affected by his orders. The Court said that the right to a hearing was satisfied because the claimant could challenge the order afterward in court.[209] Likewise, the Court has said that a person's right to protest a government employee's unauthorized intentional destruction of property is satisfied if the state permits the person to sue after the damage is done.[952]

(4) What constitutes a fair hearing can be succinctly stated only in a highly abstract way. In criminal trials, the BILL OF RIGHTS conditions the trial process in many ways (see PROCEDURAL RIGHTS OF CRIMINAL DEFENDANTS). Civil trials require an adversary procedure before a neutral decision maker, and must include the opportunity to appear before the judge with the party's own lawyer to present a case. Judges must explain their decisions and base them on the record in the case (see TRIAL, FAIRNESS OF). Administrative hearings, likewise, must be before unbiased decision makers, but the definition of bias is somewhat relaxed. A judge who has a personal stake in the outcome is constitutionally disqualified from hearing a case.[749, 2077] But an administrative agency is

allowed to have some monetary stake in the recovery of fines (to pay its expenses), as long as the particular hearing officer was not personally biased or responsible for the agency's funding.[1248] In recent years, the most frequently debated issue is the kind of procedures that the government must provide when threatening to terminate someone's benefit or job. The Court has said that there can be no fixed answer and has announced a BALANCING test to determine what process is due when a hearing is constitutionally required[1269] (see PROCESS THAT IS DUE).

See also: ADMINISTRATIVE HEARING; DEPRIVATION; EMINENT DOMAIN; JUDICIAL REVIEW; TAKING OF PROPERTY.

hearsay   Hearsay is evidence offered at trial by someone who has no direct knowledge of its truth. Hearsay comes in the form of a statement by one person about what another person said he saw or knows. For example, the prosecutor calls Mrs. Smith to the stand to testify that Mr. Jones told her he saw you rob the bank. Her testimony is hearsay, because she can only say that she heard Mr. Jones say it. Mrs. Smith cannot affirm the truth of it, and no amount of cross-examination of Mrs. Smith can test whether Mr. Jones was mistaken or lying. For that reason, this kind of hearsay testimony is inadmissible in every state and in federal trials. However, the hearsay rule is riddled with exceptions. Many types of out-of-court statements are held to be sufficiently reliable that they can be introduced at trial; for example, records kept in the ordinary course of business and the declaration of a person who knows he or she is dying. The "hearsay rule" is not a constitutional doctrine, although the Confrontation Clause often requires the same result. In administrative proceedings, hearsay may be introduced unless it is "wholly unreliable."[1723]

See also: CONFRONTATION WITH WITNESSES; EVIDENCE.

heresy, *see:* **religious belief, sincerity and truth of**

high crimes and misdemeanors   Art. II-§4 says that TREASON, bribery, and "other high crimes and misdemeanors" constitute the reasons for which the president, vice president, and all other CIVIL OFFICERS of the United States shall be removed from office after impeachment and conviction. Treason is separately defined in the Constitution, and bribery is outlawed in many criminal laws. But the meaning of "high crimes and misdemeanors" is obscure. There are two schools of thought, and each can muster evidence for its position from remarks at the CONSTITUTIONAL CONVENTION, the ratifying conventions, and in the First Congress. One school—that of James Madison, among others—holds that the president may be removed from office for "maladministration" as well as for committing a crime. The other school holds that impeachment is permissible only for the commission of an indictable offense. This latter view was strongly affirmed in the botched impeachment trial of Justice Samuel Chase in 1805. The Jefferson administration wanted Chase off the Supreme Court. Chase was impeached. In the Senate it was argued that Congress had the power to remove a judge for holding "dangerous opinions" that might "work the destruction of the nation." But the Senate failed to convict, and the Chase trial has long been considered precedent for the narrow view of the phrase. The same themes played out at the trial of President Andrew Johnson, who was impeached for removing a cabinet officer in violation of the Tenure of Office Act. Johnson asserted absolute constitutional discretion to remove his department heads without Senate approval, a power later confirmed by the Supreme Court.[1415] Johnson's opponents said he could be removed from office for subverting "some fundamental or essential principle of government" or for abusing "discretionary powers." His defenders said the Constitution could only be referring to "high criminal offences against the United States." Johnson was acquitted by a single vote. In 1974, when the House of Representatives earnestly debated the impeachment of Richard Nixon, the question was again raised but left unresolved.

See also: IMPEACHMENT.

higher law, *see:* **natural law**

highways, *see:* **spending power; transportation**

historic sites, *see:* **taking of property**

holding   A holding is the precise ground on which a court decides a case—the reason for its DECISION. Any conclusions of law necessary to decide the case are part of its holding. Judicial PRECEDENT derives from the holdings of cases, not from incidental statements unnecessary to decide the case. These other statements are known as "obiter dicta."

See also: DICTUM; STARE DECISIS.

holidays, *see:* **religious holidays, government celebration of**

home visits by welfare case workers, *see:* **search and seizure**

homelessness, *see:* **housing, right to**

homosexuality   Constitutional law has not yet fully ratified the reality of a sexually permissive America, and it will not likely do so in the near future. By 1990 about half the states repealed their laws against homosexual relations or passed laws permitting sexual behavior between consenting adults. But in the other states, homosexual conduct is criminal and in nine states can be punished by jail terms of more than a year. In 1986, in *Bowers v. Hardwick,* the Court declined the opportunity to extend its PRIVACY rulings to homosexuals. A policeman arrived at the Atlanta home of Michael Hardwick to serve an arrest warrant for public drinking, found him in bed with another man, and arrested him on a charge of violating the Georgia sodomy statute, which prohibited both heterosexual and homosexual sodomy. The prosecutor refused to prosecute, but Hardwick, seeing the opportunity for a test case, sued.

In the Supreme Court, four justices solidly voted to uphold the law and four voted to invalidate it. Justice Lewis F. Powell provided the fifth vote to uphold. Justice Byron R. White's majority opinion said that the Court was "quite unwilling" to "announce . . . a fundamental right to engage in homosexual sodomy." Reciting the long history of its moral and legal condemnation, White said that it "is, at best, facetious" to claim that the right to commit sodomy is "deeply rooted in this Nation's history and tradition," as Hardwick had contended. Justice Powell agreed with the majority that Hardwick could claim no substantive right, but he was troubled by the penalties that Georgia might impose in some other case. Noting that the state code provided for a prison sentence of up to twenty years for a "single private, consensual act of sodomy," Powell suggested that such a sentence might be unconstitutional as a cruel and unusual PUNISHMENT.

In a blistering dissent, Justice Harry Blackmun quoted the Court's language in *Wisconsin v. Yoder,* a 1972 case dealing with the rights of Pennsylvania Amish to maintain their clannish way of life: "A way of life that is odd or even erratic but interferes with no rights or interests of others is not to be condemned because it is different." The Court was refusing, Blackmun said, to recognize "the fundamental interest all individuals have in controlling the nature of their intimate associations with others." In an equally telling dissent, Justice John Paul Stevens noted that the weight of the Court's precedents would make it impossible for a state to outlaw sodomy between consenting heterosexuals. That being the case, some showing must be made to explain the difference in treatment between heterosexuals and homosexuals. The state gave none and, Stevens said, could give none. But these were dissents.

See also: SEXUAL FREEDOM.

hostile audience The hostility of an audience has sometimes been said to justify stopping the speaker addressing it. In *Feiner v. New York* in 1951, the Supreme Court affirmed the conviction of a speaker for disorderly conduct. He had been speaking to—or, perhaps more accurately, hectoring—a crowd in Syracuse, New York. He denounced President Harry S. Truman and the mayor of Syracuse, called the American Legion "a Nazi Gestapo," and said: "The Negroes don't have equal rights; they should rise up in arms and fight for them." Observers said his speech "stirred up a little excitement. . . . [There was] some pushing, shoving and milling around." Two policemen arrived and after about twenty minutes someone in the crowd said to one of them: "If you don't get that son of a bitch off, I will go over and get him off there myself." The police ordered Feiner to stop speaking and then arrested him for refusing to heed "reasonable police orders" aimed at preventing a breach of the peace. Chief Justice Fred M. Vinson said that there was no evidence the police ordered him to stop because they disliked his message; their sole concern was with preserving order. Dissenting, Justice Hugo L. Black said that the defendant, a "young college student," was being sent to the penitentiary simply for his unpopular views, there being no showing of "any threat of riot or uncontrollable disorder." An isolated threat to assault the speaker does not prove the likelihood of disorder. In any event, Black said, the first duty of the police should be to protect the speaker from the crowd, not the crowd from the speaker.

Although *Feiner* has never been directly overruled, Justice Black's views are now closer to the majority view. Police may not arrest unless they can point to objective evidence that violence will occur; their good-faith subjective view is insufficient to stop a speaker because he's stirred up a crowd. In 1963 the Court overturned breach of peace convictions of 187 black students demonstrating against segregation in South Carolina. The police had ordered them to disperse when a large crowd gathered. Said Justice Potter Stewart: "The FOURTEENTH AMENDMENT does not permit a state to make criminal the peaceful expression of unpopular views."

See also: DEMONSTRATORS AND DEMONSTRATIONS.

hours of labor, *see:* **labor and labor laws**

House of Representatives, *see:* **Congress**

housing, right to The Court has held that there is no "fundamental interest" in "decent shelter" and "possession of one's home." Tenants objected to Oregon's procedures for eviction for failure to pay rent. Among other things, the tenants were legally barred during the summary eviction procedure to defend by pointing to the landlord's failure to maintain the premises adequately. Said Justice Byron R. White: "We do not denigrate the importance of decent, safe, and sanitary housing. But the Constitution does not provide judicial remedies for every social and economic ill. We are unable to perceive . . . any constitutional guarantee of access to dwellings of a particular quality or any recognition of the right of a tenant to occupy the real property of his landlord beyond the term of his lease, without the payment of . . . rent."[1168]

housing discrimination Discrimination on the basis of race in the sale of private housing is not directly barred by the Constitution. But in 1948, the Supreme Court in an adroit twist declared that to enforce racially RESTRICTIVE COVENANTS would involve the courts themselves in violating the EQUAL PROTECTION CLAUSE.[1854] Private agreements not to sell to disfavored minorities, including blacks and Jews, were no longer enforceable, but a purely private decision not to sell on the basis of race or religion remained legal until the 1960s. Then, at least three federal laws—the Civil Rights Act of 1964, the Civil Rights Act of 1968, and the revived Civil Rights Act of 1866—and many state acts outlawed discrimination on the basis of race, color, religion, sex, and national origin in selling, leasing, and financing of homes and apartments.

See also: CIVIL RIGHTS LEGISLATION; STATE ACTION.

I

ideas The FIRST AMENDMENT protects ideas absolutely. As Justice Lewis F. Powell said in a 1974 LIBEL case, constitutionally "there is no such thing as a false idea."[746] The state has no power to prevent or discourage the expression or discussion of ideas, no matter how immoral[1078] or repugnant.[2011] Although the state may ban certain forms of expression in public, such as OBSCENITY AND PORNOGRAPHY, it may not regulate at all what people may read or watch in the privacy of their homes.[1944] And since the line between the statement and the advocacy of an idea is extremely thin, the state may not ban every advocacy unless it is intended to produce imminent lawless action and likely to do so.[222]

See also: FREEDOM OF BELIEF; OFFENSIVE AND INDECENT SPEECH; SPEECH, REGULATION OF CONTENT; SUBVERSIVE ADVOCACY; WRITINGS AND DISCOVERIES.

illegal search, liability for, *see:* search and seizure: liability for illegal search

illegitimacy The concept of illegitimacy is based not merely on a theological view that the sins of the parents should be visited upon the children. It is also an intensely practical doctrine designed to preserve a man's estate against claims of interlopers. Common law prohibited children born out of wedlock, and the unmarried mother, from claiming against the father's estate on his death. Until 1968 most states similarly put significant legal impediments between parents and their illegitimate children, without a murmur from the Supreme Court. Then the Court confronted a Louisiana law that barred illegitimate children who had not been formally acknowledged by their natural parents from suing to recover for the wrongful death of their mothers. In discriminating between legitimate and illegitimate children, the law violated EQUAL PROTECTION, said Justice William O. Douglas, adding that the Court was "extremely sensitive" to denials of "basic civil rights."[1156] No matter what the history and tradition of a custom enshrined in law, the Court would not hesitate "to strike down an invidious classification." It made no sense, Douglas said, that the wrongdoer could escape solely because the child was illegitimate. The dissenters said that since no one has a basic right to recover for the death of another, the states could define however they wished the extent of the right to sue.

Although the Court had now recognized a difficulty in classifications based on legitimacy, its succeeding cases did not trace a straight line. In 1971 a different majority upheld a New York

State law that gave other relatives a stronger claim on the estate of someone dying without a will than his illegitimate children, even if he had acknowledged them.[1107] The next year, however, the Court invalidated a Louisiana law discriminating in the payment of workers' compensation benefits.[2172] In 1976 the Court did an about-face again, upholding as a reasonable requirement a provision in the Social Security law that makes it more difficult for some illegitimate children to obtain survivors' benefits.[1270] The federal law says that acknowledged nonmarital children are entitled to survivors' benefits, but unacknowledged children must prove that they were actually living with or being supported by the deceased parent. Zigzagging the next year, the Court, 5–4, struck down an Illinois law absolutely barring illegitimate children from inheriting if their father left no will, even if paternity had been proved in the father's lifetime. The majority said that although the state properly had an interest in avoiding spurious claims, the law was too draconian.[2071] In 1978 the Court seemed to limit the force of this principle to the exact situation, by upholding a New York law prohibiting inheritance by illegitimate children unless paternity had been proven before the father died.[1112]

The Court has been somewhat more consistent in striking down state attempts to limit the right of nonmarital children to prove paternity. In 1973 the Court nullified a Texas law absolutely denying the right of illegitimate children to support.[774] Texas responded to the decision by requiring illegitimates to prove paternity within one year of their birth; the Court struck down the law in 1982.[1350] Thereafter it invalidated Tennessee and Pennsylvania laws requiring, respectively, paternity suits within two years[1626] and six years[404] of birth. In the Pennsylvania case, the Court finally held that the status of illegitimacy requires the Court to employ a "heightened scrutiny" for laws that

classify on the basis of a parent's marital status.

See also: STRICT SCRUTINY.

immigration and naturalization   From its Art. I-§8[4] power to enact naturalization policies, Congress derives the power also to regulate immigration. The scope of the power was not much debated during the first century, but in 1875, as states began to limit the flow of new peoples, the Court said that the power was exclusive in Congress, an attribute of national sovereignty, and that any state limitations are void.[900] Just how sweeping a power it is the Court demonstrated in 1889 in upholding the Chinese Exclusion Act of 1882, banning all Chinese immigration for ten years and denying citizenship to any Chinese resident aliens.[364] In many cases thereafter, the Court, without discussing constitutional issues, upheld federal laws barring naturalization for Japanese[1548] and Hindus.[2037] The Court did recognize that the FOURTEENTH AMENDMENT made citizens of children born in the United States to aliens ineligible for citizenship,[2249] with the curious exception of the only true American natives, the INDIANS, whom the Court in 1884 declared ineligible on constitutional grounds.[610] Although in 1965 Congress overhauled the thoroughly racist "national origins" laws of 1890 and 1920, the Court has never applied to the immigration laws any of the modern constitutional jurisprudence directed against RACIAL DISCRIMINATION and other invidious classifications.

In 1976 the Court said that the power to exclude is a "fundamental sovereign attribute" possessing a "political character" that permits the Court only "narrow judicial review,"[852] and the next year the Court upheld restrictions based on sex and legitimacy that would have been struck down in any area other than immigration.[662] Congress has decreed other, nonracial reasons to exclude immigrants, beginning in 1875 when it proscribed prostitutes and convicts, and it has steadily added to its list of undesirable attributes and behaviors. Among the categories: idiots, lunatics, persons likely to become public charges, persons convicted of crimes involving "moral turpitude," paupers, polygamists, adulterers, epileptics and those suffering from tuberculosis, the insane, anarchists, professional beggars. None of these categories has ever been struck down on constitutional grounds.

Although Congress has absolute power to exclude from the United States a newly arriving immigrant,[1085] and there is precedent for the proposition that the government has complete discretion to bar even a permanent resident from reentering the country after a lengthy sojourn abroad,[1851] the Court in 1982 said that a resident alien who has departed only briefly may not be excluded without being granted a HEARING to contest the exclusion.[1116]

See also: ALIENS; DEPORTATION; EQUAL PROTECTION OF THE LAWS.

imminent danger, *see:* **clear and present danger; subversive advocacy**

imminent lawlessness, *see:* **clear and present danger; subversive advocacy**

immunity, intergovernmental Within certain spheres, neither the federal government nor the states may intrude on the other. This is the doctrine of intergovernmental immunity. It is not explicit in the Constitution but inferred from its structure, from the SUPREMACY CLAUSE, and from the purposes of the federal union. The doctrine was first enunciated by Chief Justice John Marshall in *McCulloch v. Maryland* in 1819. He held that "the states have no power, by taxation or otherwise, to retard, impede, burden, or in any manner control, the operations" of federal law. Marshall specifically left open the question whether the immunity is

reciprocal. The Court finally said that it was in 1871, when it held that the federal government could not tax the salary of a state judge.[430] For six decades the Court applied this logic to exclude from federal taxes earnings derived in some way from state revenues, most notably the interest earned on state bonds.[1649] This position lasted until 1988, when the Court finally overruled itself.[1910] In 1937 the justices finally began to shrink the area of intergovernmental immunities, by concluding that a tax on income derived from state or federal activities is not a tax on the government itself. The Court upheld a state tax on a contractor's gross receipts from doing business with the federal government[1003] and income taxes by both states and the federal government on the salaries of the other's employees.[893, 795] As long as neither the states nor the federal government attempt to tax an actual agency or other instrumentality of the other, a nondiscriminatory tax is constitutional.[1622]

Intergovernmental immunity doctrine for a time operated to discourage attempts by the federal government to regulate certain "core" functions of state government. (The Supremacy Clause independently operates to prevent the states from regulating in any manner that conflicts with federal law or policy.) In 1936 the Court, reversing a trend of many decades, ruled that under the COMMERCE POWER Congress could extend the Federal Safety Appliance Act to state-owned railroads.[327] For forty years the Court held unwaveringly to the principle that there was no effective limit on Congress's power to regulate INTERSTATE COMMERCE as long as those activities in some way affected commerce. In 1976 the Court by a 5–4 vote concluded that Congress could not apply the Fair Labor Standards Act to employees of state and local governments.[1434] Justice William H. Rehnquist said that to do so would "impermissibly interfere . . . with integral governmental functions." But after several cases in which it refused to fault other extensions of federal law to state employees, the Court in 1985 again executed an abrupt about-face and overruled the 1976 case, saying that it could not figure out how to recognize federal laws that regulate the "states as states" and could not identify what exactly constitutes a "traditional," "integral," or "necessary" state function.[724] Rehnquist, now dissenting, warned that sooner or later the Court would reverse yet again because, as another dissenter, Justice Sandra Day O'Connor, said, "the states *as states* have legitimate interests which the National Government is bound to respect even though its laws are supreme."

In 1991 the Court signaled that it would continue to take intergovernmental immunities seriously when it read the federal Age Discrimination Employment Act narrowly to exclude state judges from a federal ban on mandatory retirement. The Missouri state constitution requires all judges to step down at age seventy; the federal ban does not apply to elected and "policy-making" officials. Justice Sandra Day O'Connor applied a "plain statement" rule to hold that because an extension of the federal ban to judges would "upset the usual constitutional balance of federal and state powers," the Court would read the language of the federal exemption to include judges in the absence of a plain statement from Congress that it meant to prevent them from being retired because of age.[810]

See also: FEDERALISM; PREEMPTION; STATES, IMMUNITY FROM SUITS IN FEDERAL COURT.

immunity, members of Congress The Constitution provides members of Congress with two immunities: an exceedingly narrow immunity against a practically extinct form of arrest and a broader immunity from libel and other suits. Art. I-§6[1] says that members are "privileged from arrest" while attending, going to, or returning from the current session of Congress.

Because the privilege does not extend to any case of "treason, felony and breach of the peace," the Court has construed the immunity to cover only arrests for debt in civil suits,[1184] a practice common in the 1780s but now dead. In any event, the privilege extended only to the arrest; it would not operate to stave off suit indefinitely. Members have no privilege against arrest or prosecution in any criminal case.[2226] The clause also expressly provides immunity from civil libel suits, and the Court has expanded that immunity so that if they are conducting legislative business, members may not be sued civilly. This immunity is discussed under SPEECH AND DEBATE CLAUSE.

See also: IMMUNITY FROM PROSECUTION; IMMUNITY FROM SUIT.

immunity from prosecution The FIFTH AMENDMENT privilege against SELF-INCRIMINATION prohibits the government from compelling testimony, either in court or before a legislature, of anyone whose admissions might lead to criminal prosecution. But federal and state laws provide that the government may grant immunity from prosecution to witnesses whose answers it requires. The Court has consistently held that as long as a grant of immunity precludes any possibility of criminal prosecution, a witness may be compelled to testify and punished for contempt if he or she refuses. The Fifth Amendment privilege is intended to protect against prosecution, not personal humiliation or other wounds.[260, 2088] In 1892 the Court struck down a so-called *use* immunity law, which permitted prosecutors to use independent evidence and evidence to which they were led by the testimony.[475] Some difficulty has arisen, though, over attempts to narrow the scope of immunity. So Congress rewrote the law, requiring a grant of *transactional* immunity, meaning that a witness could not be prosecuted for any part of the matter or transaction to which he has testified, even if the government has entirely independent evidence of his complicity.

But when the Supreme Court in 1964 applied the rule against self-incrimination to the states,[1233] the question arose whether a witness granted immunity by a state could later be prosecuted by the federal government for the same matter, since the states have no legal authority to grant immunity to a federal witness. The Court ruled that the Fifth Amendment requires that immunity given by one governmental authority be respected by another.[1409] If the states grant immunity, neither the testimony nor any evidence deriving from it may be used in a federal prosecution, and vice versa. But the Court did not say that the federal government was barred from using evidence to prosecute if it was wholly independent of the compelled testimony. Taking the hint, Congress reenacted and in 1972 the Court upheld a grant of use immunity[1050] under which the government may not use compelled testimony or anything deriving from it for any reason. For example, the state may not impeach a witness at a later trial by referring to testimony he gave earlier under a grant of immunity.[1447] But the government may prosecute if it has wholly independent evidence. Of course, proving that evidence did not derive from immunized testimony can be difficult. The case against Oliver North for his involvement in the Iran-contra affair was largely dismissed because of doubts that the prosecution had learned and used nothing from North's immunized testimony before a congressional investigating committee.

The Constitution grants no general official immunity from prosecution. Members of Congress may be prosecuted for any crime (see IMMUNITY, MEMBERS OF CONGRESS). From time to time the argument has been made that the president, as a unique constitutional officer, is immune from prosecution as long as he is in office. The issue has never been resolved—largely because it has, thankfully, remained almost wholly academic (see PRESIDENT, IMMUNITY OF). There is no federal immunity from federal prosecution for state officials.

See also: IMMUNITY FROM SUIT *and cross references there.*

immunity from suit Under the doctrine of SOVEREIGN IMMUNITY, the government may be sued only if it consents. In the Federal Tort Claims Act, Congress has waived much, but not all, of the sovereign immunity of the United States, consenting to many types of DAMAGE suits against the federal government. Scores of other federal laws permit litigants to take the federal government to court to challenge a broad array of actions, from rules issued by federal agencies to refusals of officials to carry out the law. State legislatures and many state supreme courts also have gradually eroded state sovereign immunity. Under the ELEVENTH AMENDMENT the states do retain a certain measure of immunity from suits in federal courts, but the immunity is far from complete.

The Supreme Court has fashioned for federal officials a doctrine of "official immunity" from civil suit. The extent depends both on what the official did and the nature of the office held. Official immunity does not rest on constitutional grounds but stems, rather, from COMMON LAW. Officials are not immune from civil suits involving their private lives; they may always be sued for divorce, for causing an accident, or for breach of contract. But they do enjoy an absolute immunity from suits that do not arise from violations of constitutional rights. For example, the Court has held that neither cabinet officers[1924] nor lower-ranking administrative officials[130] may be sued for libel for statements connected to their official duties. The theory of official immunity is that it is unfair to subject to liability an official legally required to exercise discretion in carrying out his office, and that if officials could be sued they might well hesitate to use the powers of office for the public good.

In 1971 the Court for the first time held that the Constitution directly gives private citizens the right to sue federal officials for damages for committing CONSTITUTIONAL TORTS. In the particular case, federal narcotics agents had allegedly broken into the wrong home without a warrant, violating the FOURTH AMENDMENT'S SEARCH AND SEIZURE provision.[168] Suits may be filed against not merely lower-ranking federal officials but also members of Congress,[523] cabinet secretaries,[298] and even the president's personal assistants.[864] In all these situations, the Court has held that federal officials are entitled to a "qualified immunity" only. Qualified immunity extends only to actions taken in good faith. If an official knows, or reasonably should know, that he or she is violating someone's constitutional rights, he or she may be sued. The doctrines of absolute and qualified immunity are judicially created. Congress could overturn them, expanding or contracting the immunity as it wished.

The president[1485] and federal judges[217] are absolutely immune from suit. Federal prosecutors are absolutely immune from civil suits for malicious prosecution.[2271]

The immunity of state officials is based on a different principle, although the result is often the same. Under federal CIVIL RIGHTS laws, state officials may be sued for violating people's federal constitutional rights; the extent of the immunity depends on interpretation of the federal statute, not the Constitution. In general, state judges,[1974] prosecutors,[978] and legislators[1110] are absolutely immune from suits for either common law or constitutional torts. But governors and other high-level state executive officials have only a qualified immunity.[1813]

See also: GOVERNMENT, AFFIRMATIVE OBLIGATIONS OF; IMMUNITY FROM PROSECUTION; IMMUNITY, INTERGOVERNMENTAL; IMMUNITY, MEMBERS OF CONGRESS; JUDICIAL IMMUNITY; PRESIDENT, IMMUNITY OF; SPEECH AND DEBATE CLAUSE; STATES, IMMUNITY FROM SUIT IN FEDERAL COURT.

immunity of states from federal suit, *see:* **states, immunity from suit in federal court**

impairing the obligation of contracts, *see:* **obligation of contracts**

impartial jury, *see:* **jury and jurors, impartiality of**

impartiality of judges and hearing officers
Impartiality of judges and hearing officers is a fundamental prerequisite of DUE PROCESS. Any decision maker with a financial stake in the outcome of a case or proceeding is constitutionally ineligible to serve. The classic case was that of Ohio mayors who sat as municipal judges and pocketed a percentage of fines collected for violations of the liquor laws, a practice the Court struck down in 1927.[2077] Curiously, the Court revisited Ohio mayors in 1972, this time reversing a conviction handed down by a mayor who sat as a traffic court judge and collected funds that constituted a substantial proportion of village funds.[2152] In 1973 the Court overturned a decision by the Alabama State Board of Optometry to revoke the licenses of optometrists employed by business corporations—about half the optometrists in the state. The board consisted entirely of optometrists in private practice, the natural competitors of those whose licenses they had revoked.[749] Likewise, the Court upset a ruling of the Connecticut state supreme court in an insurance case because one of the justices had his own, similar insurance case pending in a lower court, and the ruling of the supreme court, for which he voted, would advance his case as well.[20]

The neutrality principle extends to nonpecuniary issues. When a judge issued a CONTEMPT citation to a defendant who had slandered him in court, the Supreme Court ruled that a contempt trial would have to be conducted before another judge: "No one so cruelly slandered is likely to maintain that calm detachment necessary for fair adjudication."[1273] In administrative hearings, however, the Court has been less receptive to arguments that institutional bias, even though not directly shared by the hearing officer, should be grounds for reversal. For example, the Court unanimously rejected a challenge to a system of Medicare reimbursements under which insurance carriers were hired by the secretary of health and human resources to screen claims and reject those it found unmerited. The secretary had warned the carriers against paying doctors who overbilled, but the Court said that that was no proof that the actual insurance agents hearing the claims were biased.[1826]

impeachment of government officials   Impeachment is the means by which federal officials may be removed from office for misbehavior. Six constitutional provisions establish and define the mechanism. Art. I-§2[5] gives the House of Representatives the sole power to impeach. Impeachment is like an accusation or indictment; for an official to be removed the impeachment must be tried and the official found guilty. By Art. I-§3[6], the Senate has the sole power to try all cases of impeachment; two-thirds of the senators present, sitting as jurors, are necessary to convict. Procedures in impeachment and trial are for the House and Senate to devise, except that when the president is on trial, the chief justice presides in the Senate. An impeachment trial is not a criminal prosecution. Under Art. I-§3[7], the sole penalties are removal from office and disqualification from ever again holding federal office. Conviction after impeachment is final; the president may not pardon anyone removed from office after being impeached. But impeachment is not

an exclusive proceeding. The disgraced officer may be tried separately for criminal offenses. Finally, under Art. II-§2[4], the impeachment procedure is available for any CIVIL OFFICER of the United States, including the president, vice president, other executive officials, and judges, but not members of Congress.

The major constitutional question is the grounds that the House and Senate may use to justify impeachment and conviction. Art. II-§4 specifies that federal officers may be removed for "treason, bribery, and other HIGH CRIMES AND MISDEMEANORS." Treason and bribery are well defined; "other high crimes and misdemeanors" is a much more obscure phrase, derived from ancient English legal practice. From the Senate's failure by one vote to convict President Andrew Johnson, the consensus has developed that neither the president nor any other officer should be removed merely over policy differences with Congress. Whether the officer may be removed only for committing an indictable criminal offense, rather than also for serious ethical lapses or abuse of office not amounting to crimes, has never been authoritatively settled. The issue might have been tested had President Richard Nixon not resigned in 1974, because the House was ready to impeach for offenses that were not solely criminal in the narrow sense.

impeachment of witnesses, *see:* **exclusionary rule**

implied and inherent powers   The federal government is said to be one of ENUMERATED POWERS. Because the language of the Constitution is often vague and elliptical, a narrow reading of the powers granted to the federal government could considerably constrict its field of operation. So from the earliest days, the Supreme Court has heeded Chief Justice John

Marshall's declaration that the Constitution itself does not specify a rule of STRICT CONSTRUCTION.[1287] Construing the Constitution broadly, Marshall found implicit in the COMMERCE POWER authority for Congress to regulate more than merely transportation. Today the commerce power, through implication, has become an exceedingly broad congressional tool. Likewise, Marshall saw every reason to infer from the NECESSARY AND PROPER CLAUSE an intention not to limit Congress to only those means that are *absolutely* necessary to get the job done but any *appropriate* means that Congress chooses. Other examples spring readily to mind: the power to "establish" post offices must surely carry with it an implied power to punish those who rob the mail. The power over naturalization has been taken to imply an absolute power over IMMIGRATION. Implied powers of this sort—powers fairly included within the spirit of the constitutional text—are not limited to Congress. The president, for example, has the power to fire subordinates, implied from the grant of EXECUTIVE POWER, though the precise authority to fire is nowhere stated.[1415]

Of a very different sort are powers sometimes also called "implied" but often called "inherent": power that supposedly inheres in the office by its very nature, quite apart from what the Constitution says. In 1936 Justice George Sutherland said that FOREIGN AFFAIRS powers inherently reside in the president and in the federal government simply because the United States is a nation with "powers of external sovereignty."[505] Sutherland was not speaking of a power implied from an enumerated power, but rather presupposing a whole range of powers that simply followed from the nature of things. This theory of inherent power sits uneasily in the constitutional tradition, although the Supreme Court has generally approved presidential assertions of sweeping power over foreign affairs. But in 1952, in the STEEL SEIZURE CASE, the Supreme Court declared that there were limits, and that the president had no inherent authority to seize private property without the sanction of Congress.

implied constitutional right of action When you are injured without legal right by a private person, you may sue for DAMAGES to recover for your losses. The right to bring suit is found in both COMMON LAW principles and in specific laws creating CAUSES OF ACTION and vesting the courts with JURISDICTION to hear such cases. When a federal official causes injury by violating your constitutional rights, the possibility of suing for damages is less clear because Congress has enacted no general law permitting such claims to be filed. In 1971 the Supreme Court inferred from the FOURTH AMENDMENT a right to sue when rights such as freedom from unreasonable SEARCH AND SEIZURE are violated.[168] The right to sue for damages for constitutional violations in the absence of express congressional authorization is known as an implied constitutional right of action.

See also: CONSTITUTIONAL TORTS.

Import-Export Clauses Art. I-§10[2] prohibits the states from levying "imposts or duties on imports or exports," except whatever is "absolutely necessary" to fund their inspection laws. By "imposts or duties," the Framers meant simply taxes. Today the common meaning is a tax on imports. A partially parallel provision in Art. I-§8[5] prohibits the federal government from taxing exports. The clauses do not apply to state taxation of goods imported from sister states.[2253] The Import-Export Clauses were designed to put tariff policy in the hands of Congress and to prevent either the states or the federal government from taxing agriculture or manufacture bound for foreign countries.

The clauses leave unsettled whether the states are forever precluded from taxing foreign-made goods. If a state imposes a use tax on automobiles, must it restrict the levy to Cadillacs and refrain from taxing Rolls Royces? In 1827 Chief Justice John Marshall announced the ORIGINAL PACKAGE DOCTRINE.[253] A state could not tax imports as they are unloaded at the docks or even in a domestic company's warehouse, so long as they remain in the "original package."[1328] But once they are incorporated into the rest of a company's inventory for manufacture or resale, they become domestic goods and may be taxed like any other. This doctrine held sway for almost 150 years, until in 1976 the Court said that as long as the tax is not discriminatory—that is, one that singles out imports—foreign goods may be taxed once they are received at a company's warehouse, even if they remain in their original package.

The Court seems disposed to grant the states the broadest possible power to tax. In 1986 it upheld an ad valorem or value tax on all property in a company's warehouse on January 1 of each year. The company had argued that the particular imported commodity (tobacco) was sitting in a customs-bonded warehouse, where it would remain for two years while it aged. Only after aging two years and the payment of customs duties would it be mingled with the rest of its inventory; and only then, the company argued, could the state tax it. The Court disagreed, holding that since the tobacco would eventually be used for domestic consumption, it was no longer "in transit."[1678] The export limitation on the federal government applies to goods in transit, broadly defined. Once an article begins its journey abroad—for example, by being delivered to the warehouse of a carrier that would ultimately ship to a commission merchant for a foreign consignee—the federal government may not tax it.[1925] But a tax on the income of an export company is permissible.[1582]

imposts, *see:* **Import-Export Clauses**

impoundment Presidents since Franklin D. Roosevelt have from time to time refused to spend sums of money legally required to be spent. Although Congress has authorized the spending and appropriated the funds, and the president has signed the bill to make it law, the president may nevertheless disagree with some parts of a program. Because presidents do not have a LINE-ITEM VETO, they have taken it upon themselves to *impound* the funds. There is no constitutional authority for impoundment. To the contrary, Art. II-§3 requires the president to "take care that the laws be faithfully executed." In 1974 President Richard Nixon impounded billions of dollars of appropriated funds for programs he disapproved, essentially claiming a line-item veto over all spending programs. Congress then enacted the Congressional Budget and Impoundment Control Act, requiring the president to tell Congress in advance of funds he proposes to impound. The act gave Congress a LEGISLATIVE VETO to stop the impoundment, but in 1983 the Supreme Court said that legislative vetoes are unconstitutional.[979] The problem so far remains a political one. The Supreme Court has never ruled directly on the constitutionality of the practice.

in forma pauperis **petitions** The Supreme Court charges a fee of two hundred dollars to file petitions for a writ of CERTIORARI. Those who cannot afford to pay the fee may file a petition *in forma pauperis* (in the manner of a pauper) attesting their inability to pay. Many *in forma pauperis* petitions are filed; few are granted.

incitement to unlawful conduct, *see:* **clear and present danger; subversive advocacy**

income tax Although expressed in technical language, the SIXTEENTH AMENDMENT as a practical matter granted Congress the power to tax income. Most tax law is statutory, not constitutional. The Constitution sets no limit on the income tax rate nor compels either a progressive or a "flat" tax. These questions are for Congress. The only significant constitutional issue is what "income" means. For the most part, the Court has interpreted "income" broadly, so that provisions of the tax law are rarely overturned on constitutional grounds. In 1920 the Court did rule that a stock dividend—that is, a dividend in the form of stock rather than cash—is not income to the stockholder. It is capital and cannot be taxed until its value is received when sold.[607] This decision, never overruled, has sparked a large literature in the tax field, too technical to relate here, concerning the types of stock dividends and the purposes for which they are issued, all of which may bear on whether the increase in value may be taxed as income.

In the 1930s the Court turned back a strong challenge to the taxation of undistributed corporate profits. Corporations thought to prevent a tax on stockholder dividends by keeping the money in the corporation. The Court held that earnings, whether or not distributed, are taxable if Congress says so, even if the tax is a surcharge, payable only on undistributed corporate profits.[896, 897] The Court also approved the taxing of gifts of stock. The argument was that stock received as a gift is a capital asset, and when it is sold, the money realized is a return to capital, not income. The Court said that Congress was fully empowered to tax as income the difference between the selling price and the value of the stock when received.[1992] In fact, Congress may impose a tax even if no money is received at all. A bondholder gave the interest coupons to his son before the date on which the interest was due and argued that since his son received the actual payment of interest, only the son could be taxed. The Court again disagreed, saying that the income

tax may not be avoided by assigning in advance income that is due. To avoid the tax, the father would have had to give the bond itself to his son.[894] Income from unlawful transactions and businesses[1977] may be taxed; for example, money received through extortion[1779] and embezzlement,[1005] even though the embezzled funds must legally be returned, is taxable in the year it is received by the crook. Since there is no constitutional requirement that the income tax be "fair," Congress may allow taxpayers to offset their income by whatever sorts of deductions it chooses, and it may also exempt types of businesses from the tax as it chooses.[895]

See also: APPORTIONMENT OF TAXES; RETROACTIVITY; TAXATION OF INTERSTATE COMMERCE; TAXATION BY STATES.

Incompatibility Clause   Art. I-§6[2] says that "no person holding any office under the United States shall be a member of either house during his continuance in office." This is one of the core provisions of SEPARATION OF POWERS. It means that, unlike British parliamentary practice, a member of Congress may not serve in the executive or judicial branches. Violations of the clause are rare because the prohibition is all-encompassing and the general principle has always been accepted. However, ambiguity over the term "office" has led to at least one question: may members of Congress hold reserve commmissions in the ARMED FORCES? The Court has never ruled, holding in the one modern case to raise the issue that the plaintiffs lacked STANDING.[1816]

See also: CIVIL OFFICER AND OFFICERS; INELIGIBILITY CLAUSE; OFFICE AND OFFICERS.

incorporation doctrine   In the course of proposing amendments that would become the BILL OF RIGHTS, James Madison offered a provision that would have required the states to respect "the equal rights of conscience, the freedom of speech or of the press, and the right of trial by jury in criminal cases." Madison declared this amendment to be "the most valuable of the whole list." But the Senate rejected it, and the first ten amendments as ratified were intended to restrain only the federal government from abusing the people's rights. In 1833, ruling against the owner of a wharf who asserted that he was entitled to JUST COMPENSATION under the FIFTH AMENDMENT because the city of Baltimore destroyed his property, Chief Justice John Marshall confirmed what had long been assumed when, in dismissing the suit, he said that the Fifth Amendment, like all of the others, applies only to the federal government, not to the states.[132] If a state wished to execute heretics, or shut down newspapers, or confiscate a person's property without compensation, nothing in the federal Constitution would stop it. Many state constitutions had provisions similar to those in the Bill of Rights, but many others did not. And if a state chose to ignore its own constitutional limitations, the federal judiciary could do nothing.

So matters stood until 1868 when the FOURTEENTH AMENDMENT was ratified. Three clauses of Section 1 enjoined the states from enforcing any law that abridges the "PRIVILEGES OR IMMUNITIES of the citizens of the United States," from depriving any person of "life, LIBERTY, or PROPERTY without DUE PROCESS of law," and from denying "the EQUAL PROTECTION OF THE LAWS." Although the major purpose of the Fourteenth Amendment was to give Congress a firm constitutional basis on which to enact protective legislation for the former slaves, the clauses themselves are broad and open-ended. The question was what types of rights they secured against state depredations.

In 1873 the Supreme Court killed the first clause. In the *Slaughter-House Cases,* the Court ruled that the Privileges or Immunities Clause protected certain narrow federal rights only, such as the right to travel to Washington, D.C. But, as Justice Stephen J. Field said in dissent, the majority's view made the clause redundant,

for federal rights were already protected by the Constitution. Another, more plausible reading of the clause was that privileges or immunities of citizens of the United States were precisely those rights guaranteed in the Bill of Rights, and that the clause therefore made them applicable to the states. But that meaning terrified the majority, which denied that either due process or the Equal Protection Clause had any similar effect.

In 1892 the first Justice John M. Harlan insisted that the Fourteenth Amendment prohibits the states from denying or abridging any "of the fundamental rights of life, liberty or property, recognized and guaranteed by the Constitution of the United States."[1515] In other words, the Fourteenth Amendment *incorporates* every provision in the Bill of Rights. Harlan's was a minority voice. But in 1897 the Court for the first time declared that a state violates due process when it takes property without paying just compensation.[390] The Court did not say that the Fourteenth Amendment obligates states to abide by the Fifth Amendment's Just Compensation Clause. It applied only to this one right, not all of the Bill of Rights. But this ruling that due process protects certain fundamental rights might eventually lead to the protection of even more rights against the state than are enumerated in the Bill of Rights.

For the next fifty years the Court pressed due process into service to strike down, piecemeal, many state actions that would have violated the Bill of Rights had the federal government undertaken them. As Justice Benjamin N. Cardozo explained in 1937, the Court was "selectively incorporating" the Due Process Clause of the Fourteenth Amendment certain rights "so rooted in the traditions and conscience of our people as to be ranked as fundamental." Not all rights would be incorporated, only those "implicit in the concept of ordered liberty."[1557] In this particular case, Justice Cardozo spoke for a majority that found no fundamental right against DOUBLE JEOPARDY. The problem with Justice Cardozo's formulation was that there could be no guide to what was fundamental except the justices' own consciences, as both Justices Hugo L. Black and Felix Frankfurter would later declare, to opposite effect.

In 1947, in *Adamson v. California,* Justice Black corralled three other justices to proclaim, in dissent, that the Fourteenth Amendment, taken as a whole, was intended to incorporate *all* of the Bill of Rights and *only* the Bill of Rights. For Black, the only sensible incorporation was *total incorporation,* for that avoided the problem of judicial discretion to pick and choose rights to apply to the states. Two of the justices who joined Black's opinion, Frank Murphy and Wiley Rutledge, accepted only half his theory. They believed the Fourteenth Amendment incorporated the Bill of Rights but that incorporation is not limited to those rights.[11] Justice Black steadfastly resisted this idea as a form of NATURAL LAW jurisprudence that has no place in a constitutional system in which judges are subservient to elected legislators.

Justice Frankfurter vehemently objected to the idea of total incorporation. In fact, he objected to the very word "incorporation." He saw the Court as engaged in a slow process of "absorbing" certain fundamental rights. In 1952, in *Rochin v. California,* he proclaimed that the Court should strike down only official abuses of rights that "shock the conscience," as in the forced stomach-pumping the police had employed in the case to find narcotics that their suspect had swallowed.[1746] Judicial interpretation, Frankfurter said, "requires an evaluation based on a disinterested inquiry pursued in the spirit of science, on a balanced order of facts exactly and fairly stated, on the detached consideration of conflicting claims, on a judgment not *ad hoc* and episodic but duly mindful of reconciling the needs both of continuity and of change in a progressive society." The reader

may be forgiven for being more bemused by the solemnity of Frankfurter's rhetoric than confident of his claims. To Black, the "accordion-like qualities" of Frankfurter's philosophy "must inevitably imperil all the individual liberty safeguards" specifically enumerated in the Bill of Rights. The oddity of all this was that the best evidence of those rights long considered fundamental were the very ones that the First Congress had placed in the Bill of Rights, and which the "absorptionists" wanted to reacquire case by case.

The Black-Frankfurter debate prompted a large literature. On balance, the historians seem to have concluded that while Black very well may have been wrong about the intentions of the immediate framers of the Fourteenth Amendment in the Thirty-ninth Congress in 1866, no one can really say for sure. But the debate itself pushed the Court to take ever more seriously the claims of state criminal defendants that the Bill of Rights should curb police and prosecutors' conduct. Although a majority of the Court has never subscribed to Black's view, the Warren Court during the 1960s selectively "absorbed" or "incorporated" almost all of the Bill of Rights into the Fourteenth Amendment, thus largely accomplishing what Black set out to do. Of all the provisions in the Bill of Rights, only these have not been held to apply to the states: the SECOND AMENDMENT right to keep and bear ARMS,[1661] the THIRD AMENDMENT provision against quartering of soldiers in private homes, the Fifth Amendment right to grand jury indictment,[964] the SEVENTH AMENDMENT right to a jury trial in civil cases,[11] and the EIGHTH AMENDMENT prohibition of excessive BAIL OR FINES.[263] The Court has also held that although the SIXTH AMENDMENT prohibits federal convictions except by twelve-member unanimous juries, states may provide juries of as few as six,[2210, 114] and juries of twelve need not reach a guilty verdict unanimously.[65]

The following table shows when each provision in the Bill of Rights was incorporated in the Fourteenth Amendment.

Amendment	Right Incorporated	Year Incorporated
	FREEDOM OF SPEECH [761, 670]	1925 (DICTUM), 1927 (HOLDING)
	FREEDOM OF THE PRESS [1439]	1931
	FREEDOM OF ASSEMBLY [536]	1937
	FREE EXERCISE OF RELIGION [334]	1940
	Ban on RELIGIOUS ESTABLISHMENT [634]	1947
	FREEDOM OF ASSOCIATION [1416]	1958
	Right against unreasonable SEARCH AND SEIZURE [2244]	1949
	EXCLUSIONARY RULE [1238]	1961
	Right to JUST COMPENSATION [390]	1897
	Right against SELF-INCRIMINATION [1233]	1964
	Right against DOUBLE JEOPARDY [153]	1969
	Assistance of COUNSEL in capital case [1615]	1932
	Right to public TRIAL [1532]	1948
	Assistance of counsel in all felony cases [752]	1963
	Right to confront adverse witnesses [1645]	1965

Amendment	Right Incorporated	Year Incorporated
6	Right to impartial jury [1569]	1966
6	Right to COMPULSORY PROCESS to obtain witnesses [2162]	1967
6	Right to SPEEDY TRIAL [1084]	1967
6	Right to JURY in nonpetty criminal cases [582]	1968
6	Right to counsel in imprisonable misdemeanor cases [68]	1972
6	Right to notice of accusation [1680]	1972
6	Right to unanimous verdict if only six jurors [276]	1979
8	Ban on cruel and unusual PUNISHMENT [1743]	1962

It was this generally wholesale incorporation of the Bill of Rights into the Due Process Clause of the Fourteenth Amendment that during the 1960s put the Court into the business of overseeing police and prosecution practices in the states, prompting a steady flow of cases that continues unabated.

See also: EFFICIENCY; LEVEL OF GENERALITY; PROCEDURAL DUE PROCESS; PROCEDURAL RIGHTS OF CRIMINAL DEFENDANTS; *specific provisions of the Bill of Rights.*

incrimination, *see:* **self-incrimination**

indecency, *see:* **offensive and indecent speech**

independent and adequate state grounds, *see:* **adequate state grounds**

independent counsel In 1973 the ATTORNEY GENERAL named Archibald Cox WATERGATE special prosecutor to investigate and prosecute all Watergate-related offenses. Under regulations establishing the office, the attorney general specified that Cox would "not be removed from his duties except for extraordinary improprieties on his part." Later that year, President Nixon fired Cox and dissolved the office but was pressured almost immediately into re-creating the office and appointing a new special prosecutor, Leon Jaworski, who was even more insulated from being discharged than was Cox. Jaworski was given the power to review all evidence and to contest the president's assertion of EXECUTIVE PRIVILEGE.

During ORAL ARGUMENT in *United States v. Nixon,* the president's lawyers insisted that Jaworski could not sue the president for documents because Jaworski was an executive branch official. This was an *intrabranch* dispute. Their interests were not legally adverse and could not be heard in Court. The Supreme Court disagreed, holding that the president retained the power to amend or revoke the regulation that established the special prosecutor's authority but that he had not done so, and as long as it was in force the president was bound by it. The courts could hear the case, for it concerned "the kind of controversy courts traditionally resolve."

In 1978 Congress, via the Ethics in Government Act, authorized the appointment of an independent counsel when there are "reasonable grounds" to suspect that a high-ranking executive official may have committed a crime. The appointment is made by the Special Division of the U.S. COURT OF APPEALS for the District of Columbia Circuit. The independent counsel has "full power and independent authority to exercise all investigative and prosecutorial functions and powers" of the Justice Department necessary to prosecute the particular case. The independent counsel may

be removed only for "good cause." In *Morrison v. Olson,* the Court upheld the act, rejecting a challenge that the Special Division could not constitutionally appoint a special prosecutor. The independent counsel, the Court said, is an INFERIOR OFFICER, and under Art. II-§2[2] Congress may vest the appointment in the courts. The Court also rebuffed the argument that the appointment violates SEPARATION OF POWERS. Although agreeing that the independent counsel exercises EXECUTIVE POWER, Chief Justice William H. Rehnquist held that the president's need to control the counsel's discretion is not "so central to the functioning of the EXECUTIVE BRANCH" as to require that the president have absolute power to fire. Moreover, because the independent counsel's duties are limited to particular cases, the grant of largely unsupervised prosecutorial power does not "impermissibly undermine" the powers of the executive branch. In a lengthy dissent, Justice Antonin Scalia insisted that in the face of Art. II-§1[1], vesting all executive power in the president, the Court's upholding of the independent counsel law means that the "concept of a government of separate and coordinate powers no longer has meaning."

See also: APPOINTMENT AND REMOVAL POWER.

Indians and Indian tribes The existence of the native peoples of the continent is mentioned only twice in the work of the Framers. Art. I-§8[3] gives Congress the power to regulate commerce with the Indian tribes; and Art. I-§2[3] says that Indians not taxed are not to be counted in apportioning seats in the House of Representatives among the states, a provision repeated in the FOURTEENTH AMENDMENT. The Framers saw the Indians as independent peoples and their tribes as independent nations, not as citizens, slaves, or dependents. The Framers therefore did not purport to be making rules for governing the Indians any more than for governing French and Spanish colonists on the American continent. Instead, the United States would deal with the tribes through treaties, as it would deal with any foreign nation.

But it would not take long for the United States to breach the spirit of the Constitution because there were no corresponding rights to be enforced. Quite early the federal government asserted plenary power over all lands within the United States, and by 1823 the Supreme Court concurred, holding that with the white man's "discovery" and "conquest" of America went control.[1019] In 1831 the Cherokee nation sued the state of Georgia in the Supreme Court, seeking to prevent the state from meddling in its internal affairs. Chief Justice John Marshall dismissed the suit because the Cherokees were not a foreign nation, which would have given the Court JURISDICTION, but rather a "domestic dependent nation" under U.S. "protection."[382] "Protection" was a euphemism, and it was wholly unbounded by the Constitution. Although many of the Indian treaties predated the Constitution and were, under Art. VI-§1[2], declared to be the supreme law of the land, the Court conceded to Congress the absolute power to break treaties as it wished. Moreover, many Indian treaties were fraudulent. For example, the 1835 treaty that sent thousands of Cherokees to their deaths and the entire Cherokee nation west to Oklahoma was a brazen sham. It was known to everyone that the treaty was neither negotiated with nor signed by any Cherokee leader. Nevertheless, the Supreme Court held that courts may not inquire into whether an Indian treaty was legitimately negotiated or ratified.[656]

In 1871 Congress gave up all pretense and forbade the United States from entering into any further Indian treaties. From then on, all dealings with the Indians would be through unilateral federal legislation under Congress's power to regulate commerce with the Indians, including the power to "limit, modify or elimi-nate the powers of local self-government the tribes otherwise possess."[1800] In fact, Congress may terminate a tribe's very existence, distribute tribal property to its members, and cease providing any benefits made available to other Indian tribes still recognized by the government.[1315] These broad powers are limited by the BILL OF RIGHTS, and in particular the JUST COMPENSATION Clause of the FIFTH AMENDMENT. During the 1980s especially, the Court has been vigilant in requiring the government to pay for what it takes, including dispossession of tribal lands and property rights, even those taken as long ago as 1795.[926, 1876, 1534] Because Indians are viewed as members of political, not racial, groups, the Court has held that Congress may single out Indians without running afoul of EQUAL PROTECTION. The Court upheld the Indian Preference Act of 1934, giving Indians preference in hiring by the Bureau of Indian Affairs, against a challenge that the preference amounted to racial discrimination against other groups.[1391]

In 1868 the Fourteenth Amendment automatically made all former slaves citizens of the United States, but Indians were not included in the rule extending citizenship to people born in the United States. The citizenship clause limits the birth right only to those people "subject to the jurisdiction" of the United States. In 1884 the Court ruled that because the Indian tribe is "an alien though dependent power," children born to members of a tribe on tribal lands were not subject to U.S. jurisdiction at birth and therefore were not citizens under the Constitution.[610] Congress thereafter conferred citizenship on selected tribes and members of tribes by treaty and legislation and finally, in 1924, declared that all Indians are citizens at birth. American citizenship does not extinguish tribal citizenship; all tribal Indians are entitled to dual citizenship.[1479]

Today the Constitution's significance for the Indian tribes lies in its prohibition against interference by the states, not as a brake against federal power. The principle was stated as early as 1832 by Chief Justice Marshall, in striking down a Georgia law requiring state residents to obtain a license before moving onto lands of the Cherokee nation. In *Worcester v. State of Georgia,* Marshall said that the Indian nations were "distinct, independent political communities, retaining their original natural rights, as the undisputed possessors of the soil . . . in which the laws of Georgia can have no force." It was this decision that prompted President Andrew Jackson, according to legend, to say, "John Marshall has made his decision, now let him enforce it." The principle retains some vitality, for the grant of power to Congress withdraws jurisdiction from the states, including their power to regulate internal commercial matters.[2192, 1690] Many cases have held that the states may not generally tax commercial activities undertaken on reservations or tax the land itself.[1317] Tribes may tax non-Indians who conduct business in tribal territory;[2158] subject even non-Indians to the jurisdiction of tribal courts in civil cases;[990] and regulate gambling,[317] though not liquor,[1719] free of state interference. Unless Congress has withdrawn criminal jurisdiction, tribes have exclusive jurisdiction to prosecute their members for committing offenses under tribal law, and state criminal laws do not apply.[2191] Tribes do not have criminal jurisdiction over non-Indians[1530] or even Indians from different tribes[586] unless Congress has conferred it, and so far it has not. The Court has ruled that only the federal government may prosecute crimes by non-Indians against Indians[1530] and that states may prosecute crimes committed on a reservation by a non-Indian against a non-Indian.[1278] Off the reservation, Indians are subject to all state and federal criminal laws.

The Supreme Court has said that "the United States undoubtedly owes a strong fiduciary duty" to Indians,[1445] and the modern Court has shown that it is inclined to hold the United States to its "special trust relationship" with the Indians. But the Court also has held unequivocally that the United States may terminate a trust relationship with a tribe whenever it wishes, even without the tribe's consent.[1315] That is the precarious realm within which the Constitution still applies to Indian relations.

See also: TREATIES AND TREATY POWER.

indictment An indictment is a formal written accusation of crime. In the federal system, an indictment may be issued only by a GRAND JURY, and under the SIXTH AMENDMENT no one may be prosecuted for any federal felonies without being indicted. Indictments are not constitutionally required in state cases.[964] Since the proceeding before a grand jury is not a trial, an indictment may be based on HEARSAY evidence, which is insufficient to convict, and even on evidence unlawfully obtained.[306] The defendant's constitutional right to object to these forms of evidence has not yet been asserted at trial.

See also: EXCLUSIONARY RULE; INFAMOUS CRIME; INFORMATION.

indigents, rights of, *see:* **wealth classification and discrimination**

indirect taxes, *see:* **apportionment of taxes; direct taxes**

individual liberty, *see:* **liberty**

ineffective assistance of counsel The SIXTH AMENDMENT right to assistance of counsel has been held to imply the "right to the effective assistance of counsel."[1305] The Court has often said that the converse—ineffective assistance of counsel—is a constitutional denial of the Sixth Amendment right, even if the lawyer has been retained by rather than appointed for the defendant.[506] "Ineffective" does not necessarily mean incompetent or unprepared; it means an inability to perform as an independent lawyer devoted to the defendant. When a public defender told a trial judge that in representing three particular defendants certain conflicts of interest might arise, the judge was constitutionally required either to assign new counsel or to ensure that there were in fact no real conflicts.[934]

However, counsel's assistance is not necessarily ineffective because the lawyer made mistakes. Only very serious errors, such as would likely have produced an entirely different outcome at trial, will suffice to require a new trial.[1970] In 1991 the Court ruled that if a person is not constitutionally entitled to a lawyer, then the lawyer's mistakes, no matter what they are, do not amount to constitutionally ineffective assistance of counsel. A death-row convict's lawyers misunderstood a state procedural rule and filed a petition for HABEAS CORPUS three days late. The result was that the appeal was dismissed, and the Court refused to consider the underlying merits of the appeal because the dismissal rested on an independent and ADEQUATE STATE GROUNDS. But because the convict had no constitutional right to file the habeas petition, his lawyer's misreading of the rules would be held against him.[427]

See also: COUNSEL, ASSISTANCE OF; HARMLESS ERROR.

Ineligibility Clause The Ineligibility Clause, Art. I-§6[2], bars members of Congress from simultaneously holding federal executive or judicial office. It also prohibits their appointment to federal office during the time for which they were elected if the office was either created or its salary or benefits were increased during that same time. The second part of the clause is sometimes also known as the EMOLUMENTS CLAUSE.

See also: CIVIL OFFICE AND OFFICERS.

infamous crime The FIFTH AMENDMENT requires indictment by a GRAND JURY before anyone can be prosecuted federally for a capital or "otherwise infamous crime." An infamous crime, the Court has said, is defined entirely by the degree of punishment that it carries and may change as public opinion changes. Imprisonment in a federal penitentiary makes a crime infamous, and this punishment applies to all federal felonies.[2232] But a crime punishable by federal imprisonment for no more than six months is not.[578] Whether an indictment is necessary depends on the maximum sentence allowable for the offense with which the accused is charged; it makes no difference whether the sentence is ultimately the maximum term or nothing.

inferior court An inferior court is any lower court, one from which appeals may be made to a higher court. Trial courts are inferior courts. The term "inferior" does not refer to competence.

inferior office and officers There are four classes of people serving the EXECUTIVE BRANCH. Three are provided for in the Constitution: (1) the president and vice president, who are elected; (2) OFFICERS, sometimes referred to as "principal officers," who must be appointed by the president and confirmed by the Senate; and (3) inferior officers, whose appointment Congress may vest in the president alone (thereby dispensing with Senate confirmation), in the heads of EXECUTIVE DEPARTMENTS, or in the courts. The fourth category consists of all other employees, and the Constitution is silent about their appointment.

The Court has said that "any appointee exercising significant authority" under federal law is an "officer of the United States."[270] At the extremes, it is easy to see that the head of a federal department is a principal officer, whereas a postal truck driver is not an officer at all but an employee. But as the Court itself has confessed, the line between inferior and principal officers is "far from clear."[1389] In 1987, in *Morrison v. Olson,* the Court determined that an INDEPENDENT COUNSEL is an inferior officer, for several reasons. First, she was removable by a higher federal official, the attorney general. Second, her duties were limited to investigating and prosecuting certain federal crimes, unlike the much more open-ended power possessed by United States attorneys. Third, she had limited jurisdiction over certain people only. Fourth, even though her appointment lasted for an indefinite time, it was temporary in the sense that once she accomplished the specific task for which she was appointed, her office terminated. In earlier cases, the Court concluded that Department of State vice consuls were inferior officers,[597] as were election supervisors;[1865] U.S. commissioners with authority to arrest, imprison, and initiate prosecutions for violations of civil and voting rights;[764] and the Watergate special prosecutor.[1487]

In 1991, in a case at the other extreme testing the distinction between employees and inferior officers, the commissioner of Internal Revenue argued that "special trial judges" appointed by the chief judge of the United States Tax Court were employees, not inferior officers, because they had no authority to decide cases but only to hear cases and prepare proposed findings and opinions. The Court disagreed, holding that the office of special trial judge was established by law, which spelled out the duties, salary, and means of appointment. Moreover, they exercise significant discretion in taking testimony, conducting trials, and enforcing DISCOVERY orders.[701] The difference between inferior officers and employees is significant in this respect: employees may be hired by any delegate or subdelegate of an executive department or agency, whereas an inferior officer may be appointed only in the manner spelled out in Art. II-§2[2]; that is, they may be appointed by the president without Senate approval.

See also: APPOINTMENT AND REMOVAL POWER; EXECUTIVE DEPARTMENTS.

informant's tip, *see:* **probable cause**

information　Like an INDICTMENT, an information is a formal written charge that someone has committed a crime, but it may be filed by a prosecutor on oath without seeking the vote of a GRAND JURY. In the federal system, prosecutors may use informations for misdemeanor charges only; all felony prosecutions may be initiated only by indictment. Many states also require indictments for both misdemeanor and felony charges, but DUE PROCESS does not require that states use indictments.

information, right to, *see:* **freedom of information; right to know**

inherent powers, *see:* **implied and inherent powers**

initiative　Citizens may bypass their legislatures and vote directly for legislation through an initiative, a measure on a ballot asking voters to register a yes or no. Initiatives do not violate the GUARANTEE CLAUSE[1554] but they are subject to constitutional limitations, for an initiative is as much STATE ACTION as a legislative enactment.[1708] When the voters of Akron, Ohio, amended their city charter to provide that a majority of voters must approve any enactment by the city council regulating real estate transactions on the basis of "race, color, religion, national origin or ancestry," the Court held that the initiative violated EQUAL PROTECTION because the city charter amendment made it more difficult, on racial lines, to enact some kinds of real estate policies than others.[960]

injunction An injunction is a court order directing a party to do or refrain from doing something, like running a dangerous business in the neighborhood or holding an unlawful strike. It is one of the remedies available to a federal court in exercising its power of EQUITY. Only judges, not juries, may issue injunctions. Because an injunction has no fixed form, it is a malleable weapon that can be tailored to provide exact relief against the legal wrong for which the defendant is held liable. Early in the century, federal injunctions were directed largely against LABOR UNIONS and unionizing activities, until Congress called a halt in the Norris-LaGuardia Act of 1932. Despite the ELEVENTH AMENDMENT bar to federal suits against states, the Court has held since 1908 that federal courts may issue injunctions against state officials who act unconstitutionally,[2278] permitting the federal injunction to be put to use in SEGREGATION and other civil rights cases. The power to redress particular types of injuries through injunction is quite broad. In 1990 the Supreme Court said that a federal court may even order a local school district to raise taxes to pay its share of the cost of undoing a segregated school system and may enjoin enforcement of state laws that prohibit local taxes from being raised.[1364] An injunction has considerable bite: the Court has held that a person may not simply disregard a court order. Even if unconstitutionally issued, a court order must be obeyed, on pain of CONTEMPT, until it is overturned on appeal.[2142]

See also: ANTI-INJUNCTION ACT; STATES, IMMUNITY FROM SUIT IN FEDERAL COURT.

injunction, labor, *see:* **labor injunction**

innocence, presumption of, *see:* **presumption of innocence**

insanity defense A defendant who pleads insanity asserts that he was not mentally responsible for his criminal act. The BURDEN OF PROOF is on the defendant to show that he was insane; the state does not bear any constitutional burden of disproving insanity.[1577] DUE PROCESS forbids prosecuting someone who is insane at the time of trial, because it would be impossible for the defendant to assist in his own defense.[165] An insane defendant may not be held in jail indefinitely; he may be held only as long as necessary to determine whether he will become well enough to stand trial. If not, he must be committed to a hospital or other mental institution through civil commitment proceedings.[996] It likewise offends due process to execute someone who is insane, and the question of whether an inmate awaiting execution is insane may not be left to the standardless discretion of a governor. The issue must be presented to an impartial hearing officer or agency.[690] A defendant acquitted at trial by reason of insanity may not be imprisoned, but he may be civilly committed, if necessary for a time shorter or longer than the sentence he could have received, since the purpose of the commitment is medical, not penal.[1035]

inspection laws The IMPORT-EXPORT CLAUSE prohibits states from taxing imports or exports except to the extent "absolutely necessary" to carry out their "inspection laws." Inspection laws aim at protecting the public health and safety and against fraud. States may impose on exporters or importers the cost of storing, actually inspecting, and labeling goods for quality, weight, and size.[2080] The Court has found no fault with general inspection laws designed for these purposes[1573] and has always agreed that inspection taxes were "absolutely necessary." But the Court has struck down inspection laws that were a pretext for keeping goods out of the state altogether.[210] Similarly, [nontax] inspection laws that apply equally to domestic and foreign goods are generally upheld, but inspection laws that discriminate between domestic and INTERSTATE COMMERCE are unconstitutional.[2135, 840]

See also: DORMANT COMMERCE CLAUSE; QUARANTINE LAWS; TAXATION OF INTERSTATE COMMERCE.

institutional litigation   "Institutional litigation" is the name for a type of federal lawsuit that began to be filed in some numbers in the 1960s and 1970s against various institutions, usually state prisons, hospitals, and schools, alleging continuing violations of prisoners', patients', and students' constitutional rights. What made these suits different from the ordinary DAMAGE suit is that the plaintiffs sought broad injunctive relief against a pattern of ongoing abusive official conduct. In many such cases, federal DISTRICT COURTS issued INJUNCTIONS so detailed that the judges, in essence, became prison, hospital, and school administrators. Despite criticism that they permit courts to interfere with government, institutional lawsuits as a class have raised no particular constitutional issues with which the Supreme Court has felt compelled to grapple. Many comprehensive orders against state institutions have often been negotiated between the parties and consented to, so that no appeal followed.

See also: EQUITY AND EQUITABLE REMEDIES; GOVERNMENT, AFFIRMATIVE OBLIGATIONS OF.

insular minorities, *see:* **discrete and insular minorities**

insurrection   Insurrection is revolt against constituted authority. Under the WAR POWER and Congress's power to call the MILITIA to suppress insurrection (Art. I-§8[15]), the federal government may constitutionally wage civil war. Section 3 of the Fourteenth Amendment disqualifies any federal or state officer who participated in insurrection against the United States from holding any future federal or state OFFICE.

integrated bar, *see:* **lawyers**

integration, *see:* **segregation and integration**

intent, *see:* **motive, intent, and purpose**

intent of the Framers, *see:* **constitutional interpretation; original intent**

intergovernmental immunity, *see:* **immunity, intergovernmental**

intermediate scrutiny, *see:* **strict scrutiny**

internal revenue, *see:* **income tax**

international affairs, *see:* **foreign affairs**

international agreements, *see:* **executive agreement; treaties and treaty power**

international law   International law governs the relations between nations and between the subjects and citizens of those nations. Because there is no universally recognized final authority for adjudicating international legal disputes, international law sometimes seems to be a particularly obscure blend of diplomacy and politics. But the Supreme Court has said that "[i]nternational law is a part of our law and must be ascertained and administered by the courts of justice."[2034] The body of international law is not spelled out in or dictated by the Constitution. It is a composite of international customs and practice, judicial decisions, and treaty obligations. One of the principal modern sources of international law is the United Nations Charter, a multilateral treaty that the United States ratified in 1945. The Court has never ruled on whether its provisions are automatically binding on the United States and the states in the absence of implementing congressional legislation. But as with all treaties, Congress is constitutionally empowered to abrogate it when it wishes.

See also: TREATIES AND TREATY POWER.

international travel, *see:* **travel, right to**

interposition, *see:* **nullification, interposition, and secession**

interpreting the Constitution, *see:* **constitutional interpretation**

interpretivism   During the past two decades, constitutional scholars have waged a fierce debate over the power of judges to impose norms or values on society in the name of the Constitution. On one side of the argument are "interpretivists"—those such as Justices Hugo L. Black and Antonin Scalia who believe that the only valid norms are those deriving from the intent of the Framers as expressed in the text of the Constitution itself or reasonably to be inferred from the text. Noninterpretivists, in comparison, are those who such as Justices William O. Douglas and William Brennan, believe that judges may look to evolving social norms and "fundamental values" of society as the basis for constitutional judgments. Interpretivism does not turn on whether one believes in broad or STRICT CONSTRUCTION, for in either case the reader is interpreting a text. The comparison is between those who believe that a final judgment about whether or not something is constitutional depends on actual constitutional words and phrases and those who believe that the Constitution permits judges to give effect to values—such as, perhaps, PRIVACY—that lie entirely outside the text. Although the interpretivist-noninterpretivist debate is in some form as old as the Constitution, it gained amplitude as the Court began to look to FUNDAMENTAL INTERESTS to overturn certain laws on DUE PROCESS and EQUAL PROTECTION grounds. It became extraordinarily heated when the Court's decision in *Roe v. Wade* struck down laws against ABORTION, a subject mentioned nowhere in the Constitution and arguably far beyond any intentions of the Framers. The debate played out in public in the Supreme Court confirmation hearings of Robert Bork in 1987, and it continues to this day.

See also: CONSTITUTION, LIVING; CONSTITUTIONAL INTERPRETATION; NATURAL LAW; ORIGINAL INTENT; PENUMBRA THEORY; SUBSTANTIVE DUE PROCESS.

interrogation, *see:* **self-incrimination**

interstate comity, *see:* **comity; full faith and credit**

interstate commerce   Congress has no power more sweeping than that of regulating commerce. The cornerstone is its power, under Art. I-§8[3], to regulate commerce "among the several states." In 1824 Chief Justice John Marshall gave an expansive reading to this power, holding in *Gibbons v. Ogden* that "commerce" encompasses more than buying and selling—the interchange of commodities. It also includes navigation and gives Congress authority to regulate the manner by which the commerce is undertaken. In so doing, Congress may regulate any "commerce which concerns more states than one." This open-ended invitation to regulate matters *concerning* more than one state was qualified only by the requirement, in Marshall's opinion, that there be some commercial or monetary connection with the thing regulated.

Until the late nineteenth century, most interstate commerce cases reaching the Court dealt with the DORMANT COMMERCE CLAUSE—the power of the states to enact commercial regulations in the absence of federal law. But beginning in 1895 and continuing for more than forty years, the Court embarked on an inconsistent mission to limit the reach of the power by redefining the things that are *in* commerce. The Court dismissed a federal antitrust suit against monopolization of the refined sugar industry because it was a monopoly of manufacturing, not commerce.[591] "Manufacture," said Chief Justice Melville Fuller, "is transformation—the fashioning of raw materials into a change of form for use." Commerce, on the other hand, is simply buying, selling, and incidental transportation. Likewise, agriculture, mining, and other industries are local activities within the jurisdiction of the states only. True, the local business activity might affect commerce external to the state in which it is located; but if the Court were to permit Congress to regulate whenever some business practice affects commerce, then Congress could swallow the whole thing, and comparatively little would be left of state power. Whether Congress has the power to regulate depends, therefore, on the nature of the activity, not its effects. Fuller's theory sounded more logical than it proved capable of being, because measuring "direct" and "indirect" effect was ultimately a subjective exercise without standards to which anyone could point.

Almost immediately, in fact, the Court developed seeming exceptions to its rule. An agreement to fix prices was held to have a direct effect on commerce and could therefore be prosecuted under the federal ANTITRUST LAWS.[14] The Court upheld the power of the federal Interstate Commerce Commission to regulate *intrastate* railroad rates to curb discrimination against *interstate* rates,[948] and it also approved federal safety regulations applied to intrastate railroads because they were tied inextricably to the interstate aspect of the business.[1923] Federal regulations of other local activities were upheld if the activities were part of a current, or STREAM OF COMMERCE. For example, stockyards could be regulated because they were but a "throat" through which cattle flowed from the farms to the ultimate consumers.[1938] This same theory led the Court to sustain the National Motor Vehicle Theft Act, even though the stealing itself is done locally.[245] The act was aimed at rings of car thieves who transported and sold stolen vehicles out of state.

The Court also almost always upheld congressional bans on shipment of goods across state lines. It first sustained, by a narrow margin, the Federal Lottery Act, which prohibited importing, mailing, or carrying lottery tickets across state lines.[369] Thereafter the Court upheld federal bans on interstate shipment of adulterated eggs[924] and the "white slave traffic," the transportation of women across state lines for prostitution, outlawed in the Mann Act.[931] In 1917 the Court held that the Mann Act could be invoked against a simple sexual dalliance if the couple crossed a state line—an activity having nothing to do with commerce in the sense in which Chief Justice Marshall had first conceived it.[332] It seemed as though Congress could crack down as it pleased on immoral and harmful interstate activities.

But in 1918 the Court drew the line at Congress's attempts to control CHILD LABOR, striking down laws that forbade shipping goods across state lines if they were made by children in factories, even though the commercial effects were far more obvious than those in some of the Mann Act cases.[851] Through the 1920s and into the 1930s, the Court persisted in viewing with great suspicion congressional intrusion into the workplace, denying a federal power over wages, hours, and conditions of workers not engaged in an activity that the Court would concede was, in the nature of things, interstate. Then, in 1935, the Court struck down the Railroad Retirement Act, which established a compulsory retirement plan for interstate railroad workers, whom the Court had long regarded as amenable to federal regulation.[1685] When the Court then proceeded to void the National Industrial Recovery Act,[1] the Bituminous Coal Conservation Act,[353] and the Agricultural Adjustment Act,[289] President Franklin D. Roosevelt proposed his COURT-PACKING PLAN. Although the plan failed, the Court in 1937 sustained the National Labor Relations Act in a decision that heralded a revolution in the constitutional understanding of the interstate commerce power.

The National Labor Relations Act protected union organizing and delegated to the National Labor Relations Board power to issue orders against unfair labor practices. The Jones and Laughlin Steel Corporation resisted the NLRB's orders. A national labor law was beyond the range of federal power. Not so, said the Court, emphasizing the size and complexity of the company, spread out in many states, summoning materials from many more, and shipping three-quarters of its product out of state. Bowing to the reality of national markets, the Court finally dismissed its old distinctions between manufacturing and commerce, direct and indirect, and held that "interstate commerce itself is a practical conception . . . [that cannot] ignore actual experience."[1430]

Finally, in 1942 the Court signaled that it was abandoning any further pretense that there were commercial activities Congress could not reach. The secretary of agriculture penalized a farmer for growing more wheat than allotted under the Agricultural Adjustment Act of 1938. The farmer intended to consume the excess wheat wholly on his own farm and contended, therefore, that it could not possibly be in interstate commerce. The Court unanimously disagreed. Considered alone, the farmer's small amount of excess wheat may be trivial, but "his contribution, taken together with that of many other similarly situated, is far from trivial."[2201] As Justice Robert H. Jackson aptly put the rule in 1949: "If it is interstate commerce that feels the pinch, it does not matter how local the operation that applies the squeeze."[2248]

For the past half century, Congress has used its interstate commerce power as a general PO- LICE POWER over harmful activities far removed from the traditional understanding of commerce. It was the means by which Congress overcame old constitutional obstacles to enacting national CIVIL RIGHTS LEGISLATION. In the Civil Rights Act of 1964, Congress outlawed discrimination on the basis of race, color, religion, or national origin in any PUBLIC ACCOM- MODATION, including hotels, restaurants, and theaters. In the CIVIL RIGHTS CASES in 1883, the Court had said Congress had no such power under the FOURTEENTH AMENDMENT. Now Congress claimed it could enact similar legislation under the interstate commerce power, and the Court unanimously agreed. These facilities may appear to be local, but they inevitably have a profound effect, as a class, on interstate travel. It is unnecessary, therefore, to prove that any particular instance of a refusal to serve someone on the basis of race had an effect on commerce. Congress has constitutional authority to apply the law as much to a resident refused service by a local diner in the town in which he or she lives as to an interstate traveler.[888, 1052]

Congress has also enacted many general criminal laws under the interstate commerce power. In the Consumer Credit Protection Act, it outlawed loan sharking, defined as credit transactions in which violence or threats of violence are used in collecting debts. Congress said it wanted to go after organized crime, which is often engaged in loan sharking and operates on a national scale. The Court upheld the law, observing that Congress had outlawed a class of activities that in the aggregate affect interstate commerce. Whether a particular loan shark had any effect on that commerce is irrelevant.[1603]

The practical import of the Court's interstate commerce jurisprudence is this: Congress's belief that it must legislate provides the constitutional justification for doing so.

See also: COMMERCE CLAUSE; COMMERCE, EFFECTS ON; COMMERCE POWER *and cross references listed there;* FEDERALISM; PROHIBITIONS ON COMMERCE; TAXATION OF INTERSTATE COMMERCE; TENTH AMENDMENT.

interstate compacts, *see:* **Compact Clause**

interstate taxation, *see:* **taxation by states; taxation of interstate commerce**

interstate travel, *see:* **travel, right to**

intimacy, *see:* **freedom of intimate association**

intoxicating beverages The national experiment with Prohibition, placed into the Constitution in the EIGHTEENTH AMENDMENT, lasted just short of fifteen years, from January 1919 to December 1933. The amendment banned the manufacture, sale, transportation, importing, and exporting of "intoxicating liquors . . . for beverage purposes." When the TWENTY-FIRST AMENDMENT repealed general Prohibition, it left a limited form in place, prohibiting anyone from transporting or importing any intoxicating liquors into a state against its laws. This provision, the Court held until recently, overcame the usual presumption against discriminatory economic legislation; it permitted a state to impose fees and other conditions that burden the importation and sale of liquor made out of state[1949] and to regulate prices in virtually any manner the state chooses.[1834]

In the 1980s, however, the Court restored much of the vitality of its COMMERCE CLAUSE jurisprudence in holding that the states do not have carte blanche to regulate liquor. The Twenty-first Amendment confines state regulations to certain purposes: "control over whether to permit importation or sale of liquor and how to structure the liquor distribution system."[326] The Commerce Clause continues to prohibit "mere economic protectionism," so

a purely discriminatory law not "designed to promote temperance or to carry out any other purpose" of the amendment will be struck down.[100] The Court has not read the Twenty-first Amendment to have repealed any part of the FOURTEENTH AMENDMENT, so it struck down an Oklahoma law on EQUAL PROTECTION grounds that discriminated between males and females in the type of beer that each could drink before the age of twenty-one.[483] The power to regulate liquor sales does not overcome an ESTABLISHMENT CLAUSE prohibition against delegating power to a church to veto liquor licenses for nearby bars.[1122] On the other hand, the Twenty-first Amendment overcomes FIRST AMENDMENT concerns over some forms of expressive conduct, as the Court held in sustaining a statewide ban on topless dancing in bars.[1471] The Twenty-first Amendment does not defeat otherwise valid federal legislation and programs simply because they relate to liquor. The Court struck down a state attempt to regulate liquor advertising on cable television, viewing the entire field as preempted by federal policy.[336] The Court also upheld a federal plan to coerce the states into raising the drinking age through forced highway spending cuts for states that refuse to raise the age limit on their own.[1915]

See also: DORMANT COMMERCE CLAUSE; NUDITY; POLICE POWER.

intrastate commerce, *see:* **interstate commerce**

invalid on its face A law is facially invalid if it overtly prohibits activity protected by the Constitution. For example, the Court has held that a law prohibiting anyone from casting "contempt" on an American flag is facially invalid under the FIRST AMENDMENT[1969] because it directly infringes FREEDOM OF SPEECH. But a law prohibiting setting fires on public streets is not facially invalid, though it may still be unconstitutional if applied under certain circumstances to a protester burning a flag.[605]

invasion   The Constitution speaks of invasion in three clauses: Art. I-§8[15], giving Congress the power to call out the MILITIA to repel invasions; Art. I-§9[2], providing that HABEAS CORPUS may be suspended during invasions when the public safety requires; and Art. IV-§4, requiring the United States government to protect each state against invasion. The word "invasion" is used unexceptionably, and the Court has never been called on to give it a meaning.

See also: REBELLION; WAR POWER.

inventions, *see:* **writings and discoveries**

inventors, *see:* **authors and inventors**

inverse condemnation   Under its EMINENT DOMAIN power, the government may seize private property for public use and pay JUST COMPENSATION. Often, however, without exercising eminent domain, the government may take some action that either destroys private property or interferes with it to such a degree that it becomes relatively useless. To recover for the loss, the owner may file a so-called inverse condemnation suit—inverse, because the government has not in fact condemned the property. The plaintiff is asserting that the government's actions should be treated as though it had for purposes of compensation.

See also: TAKING OF PROPERTY.

investigatory powers of legislature   The Constitution is silent about the power of Congress to summon witnesses or subpoena documents. But Congress has long been known as the "grand inquest of the Nation," and from the very earliest days, the power to investigate has been widely regarded as a necessary adjunct of the LEGISLATIVE POWER. Until 1881 the Court

had not been presented with any serious question about the extent of the power. But in that year it concluded that a select committee of the House of Representatives had overstepped its constitutional authority in putting questions to a witness connected to the bankruptcy of a private banking firm that held federal funds. The Court held that the inquiry violated SEPARATION OF POWERS because the matter could properly be investigated only by the courts. Congress has no "general power of making inquiry into the private affairs of the citizen."[1075] Since then, the Court has never invoked this principle to quash a legislative investigation. In 1927 the Court upheld a Senate investigation of corruption in the federal government,[1298] and it seems highly unlikely that the Court would fault a legislative inquiry into any subject on which Congress may validly decide to legislate or appropriate funds. As Chief Justice Earl Warren said in 1957, the investigative power "includes surveys of defects in our social, economic or political system" so that Congress can remedy them, and it permits Congress to probe any federal agency "to expose corruption, inefficiency or waste."[2165]

The Court has, however, occasionally been sensitive to claims that the legislative purpose violated the FIRST AMENDMENT. These claims surfaced during the post–World War II days of McCarthyism, when both houses of Congress launched investigations aimed at uncovering the extent of communist infiltration of American society. In two cases in 1957, the Court reversed CONTEMPT convictions against a congressional witness and a witness before a state investigating commission. Both refused to testify on the ground that the questions about their affiliations violated their First Amendment rights. Declaring that "[t]here is no congressional power to expose for the sake of exposure," Chief Justice Warren struck down the congressional contempt citation on the narrow DUE PROCESS ground that the witnesses could not tell whether the questions put were pertinent to the investigation, and the state contempt on the ground that it had not been proved that the state investigation had been authorized.[2165, 1989]

But in 1959 the Court rejected a First Amendment attack against both congressional and state investigations. The witnesses had refused to answer questions about their membership in the Communist party. For a 5–4 majority, Justice John M. Harlan, applying a BALANCING test, said that Congress has "wide power to legislate in the field of Communist activity," and concluded that the questions were pertinent and not beyond the scope of the inquiry.[125] In the state case, the Court concluded that the request for a list of all guests who attended a summer camp thought to be subversive was valid and in aid of an investigation into state subversive activities.[2112] Said Justice Tom Clark for a 5–4 majority, "[E]xposure—in the sense of disclosure—is an inescapable incident of investigation." The dissenters saw the record quite differently, arguing that "the investigatory objective was the impermissible one of exposure for exposure's sake."

In 1963 the Court weighed the investigative power and the interest in FREEDOM OF ASSOCIATION and came out the other way. A committee of the Florida legislature was seeking membership lists of the National Association of Colored People to determine whether any were members of the Communist party. The president of the NAACP's Miami branch refused to bring the lists but agreed to testify personally. He was asked about fourteen persons, and he said he had no knowledge of any of them. He was sentenced to six months in prison for failing to bring the lists. Another 5–4 majority reversed, holding that the state had failed to show a "substantial relation" between the NAACP's information and subversive activities. In the other cases, Justice Arthur Goldberg

said, witnesses were asked about their own membership. This inquiry was directed not to the Communist party but to a nonsubversive organization. That was insufficient to overcome an organization's right to privacy of membership lists.[750] In 1966 the Court reversed a state contempt conviction based on a witness's refusal to answer a question about events that had occurred seven years earlier.[534] Since that time, no further cases have arisen. Because the Court has not repudiated its reliance on balancing, the outcome in a future case probably depends more on the weight new justices will give to conflicting values than on any clearly articulated constitutional principle.

Witnesses may refuse to answer questions put during legislative investigations on the ground that the answer might be incriminating. "Taking the Fifth" has never seriously been questioned in this context, although the Court has held that the right against self-incrimination does not cover officers of organizations asked to turn over records of their organizations.[1307]

See also: EXECUTIVE PRIVILEGE; FREEDOM OF SPEECH *and cross references listed there;* PLEADING THE FIFTH.

invidious discrimination   An "invidious discrimination" is one that seems on its face to be palpably unfair, prejudiced, or otherwise unjustified. The term was first used by Justice William O. Douglas in a case involving compulsory sterilization, to explain why the Court would not adhere to its usual relaxed standard of RATIONAL BASIS review but instead subject the law's classification to STRICT SCRUTINY.[1879] Considerable debate surrounds the nature of the discrimination practiced in laws that classify by race, ethnicity, and sex. The Court always strikes down invidious discriminations—those it views as harming or intended to harm. But the Court has been more equivocal about noninvidious classifications of that type, such as those intended to work a good for an oppressed group through AFFIRMATIVE ACTION. Opponents of affirmative action see racial classifications for any purpose equally invidious. But the Court so far has distinguished between the two types. Although it applies strict scrutiny to both types, only the invidious discriminations are invariably struck down.

See also: EQUAL PROTECTION OF THE LAWS.

involuntary servitude   Prohibited along with SLAVERY by the THIRTEENTH AMENDMENT, involuntary servitude is in essence forced labor or peonage. Its two major forms are labor forced upon someone at gunpoint, essentially as private prisoners; and labor exacted against one's will to pay off a debt. After the Civil War, a form of legalized work slavery developed in many states. The employer would advance a small sum of money; the worker would be obligated to work off the debt and could not quit until it was paid. If he attempted to quit, he would be arrested, jailed, and ultimately returned to the employer's custody. In the 1867 Peonage Act, Congress prohibited all such systems and abolished all laws and "usages" that established and maintained the peonage system. In 1905 the Supreme Court upheld the act against a constitutional challenge that Congress could not outlaw private employment arrangements or nullify state laws. The Court said that Congress had the power directly under the Thirteenth Amendment.[410] In 1911 the Court struck down an Alabama law under which a person who defaulted on an employment contract could be sent to jail if he did not repay sums advanced under the contract. "The state may impose involuntary servitude as a punishment for crime, but it may not compel one man to labor for another in payment of a debt, by punishing him as a criminal if he does not perform the service or pay the debt."[103] For that reason, courts may not enforce employment contracts by ordering a person whose services were engaged to perform the work. In other words, everyone has a constitutional right to quit. Lawfully imprisoned people may be required to work; and the Court has refused to extend the idea of involuntary servitude beyond the purpose for which the provision was enacted. The military draft and compulsory jury service do not run afoul of the provision.[295, 81]

irrebuttable presumption doctrine, *see:* **presumption, irrebuttable**

item veto, *see:* **line-item veto**

J

jails, picketing of   Despite a broad right of DEMONSTRATORS to march and picket in public places, the Supreme Court held in 1966 that the state may deny access to the grounds of a municipal jail. Students protesting the incarceration of fellow students demonstrating against segregation and racial discrimination were ordered to clear the entrance to a Florida jail and to move behind the perimeter of the property or they would be arrested for trespassing. For a 5–4 majority, Justice Hugo L. Black sustained the convictions because there was no evidence that the sheriff had arrested the students for what they were saying. The arrests were attributable solely to their refusal to leave "that part of the jail grounds reserved for jail uses," a rule enforced against all, not just these demonstrators. People do not have the constitutional right to "propagandize . . . whenever and however and wherever they please. . . . The Constitution does not forbid a state to control the use of its own property for its own lawful nondiscriminatory purposes."[12] Dissenting, Justice William O. Douglas said that a jailhouse, like a legislative chamber or an executive mansion, is one of the seats of government, and assembling there may have been the only way to exercise the FREEDOM OF PETITION.

See also: PICKETING; PUBLIC FORUM.

Japanese-American exclusion and relocation   In February 1942, shortly after the bombing of Pearl Harbor, President Franklin D. Roosevelt issued Executive Order 9066, later partly ratified by Congress, granting certain military commanders absolute discretion to designate "military areas" within the United States from which anyone could be excluded. By March 1942 Lieutenant General John L. DeWitt, commanding general of the Western Military Command, declared large portions of the West Coast, from California to Washington, to be military areas from which Japanese-Americans, citizens as well as aliens, were to be excluded, ostensibly to prevent espionage and sabotage. The pretext was the threat of invasion, but in fact, DeWitt was simply heeding the cries of local bigots, including California's congressional delegation and California attorney general Earl Warren, who later repented his position. Perhaps the most telling private comment was that of John J. McCloy, an aide to Roosevelt: "If it's a question of safety of the country, [or] the Constitution of the United States, why, the Constitution is just a scrap of paper to me."

Within the next two years, 120,000 Japanese-Americans, 70,000 of them American citizens, were subjected first to curfews, forcing them to remain at home between 8 P.M. and 6 A.M., and then to forcible removal from their homes. They were "relocated" to internment camps in several states to the east, even though not a single person was accused of disloyalty, much less convicted of an act of espionage or sabotage. Most lost their homes and other property; many of them were never adequately reimbursed, and some were not reimbursed at all.

Three cases, each involving an American citizen, reached the Supreme Court. Gordon Hirabayashi was convicted of violating the curfew and of resisting "evacuation" from his home in Seattle. Fred Korematsu was convicted of refusing to leave his home in San Leandro, California. Mitsuye Endo was removed from her home in Sacramento and sent to a "relocation center" elsewhere in California and eventually to Utah, where she sued for release. In 1943, in *Hirabayashi v. United States*, the Supreme Court upheld the curfew order; and in 1944, in *Korematsu v. United States*, the general exclusion. It is now known that the Army deliberately lied to the Supreme Court, asserting military justification for the orders when it knew there was none. The strategy worked, because the 6–3 Court majority's ultimate rationale was the deference a court must pay to military operations during war. Said Justice Hugo L. Black, otherwise a noted civil libertarian, "exclusion of the whole group is a military imperative. Outside of *Dred Scott v. Sandford* and *Plessy v. Ferguson*, it was the Court's worst hour, since a *claim* of military necessity should not have survived the Court's announced test for racially discriminatory legislation. In *Korematsu*, Black said that "all legal restrictions which curtail the civil rights of a single racial group are immediately suspect. ... [C]ourts must subject them to the most rigid scrutiny." This was the first time the Court said that race is a SUSPECT CLASSIFICATION and that a law discriminating on a racial basis may be upheld only after scrutinizing it far more searchingly than other kinds of legislative classifications. As it turned out, *Korematsu* was also the last case in which the Court upheld such INVIDIOUS DISCRIMINATION.

In a withering dissent, Justice Frank Murphy condemned "this legalization of racism." Murphy said that the "exclusion goes over 'the very brink of constitutional power' and falls into the ugly abyss of racism" because the orders applied to people solely on the basis of their ancestry. It is wholly unreasonable to assume that *"all* persons of Japanese ancestry may have a dangerous tendency to commit sabotage and espionage." Although the Supreme Court must give "great respect" to the military for matters within its competence, the military here had acted far outside its competence. The army's exclusion order was based on "questionable racial and sociological" theories grounded in "misinformation, half-truths and insinuations that for years have been directed against Japanese Americans by people with racial and economic prejudices."

Justice Robert H. Jackson, also dissenting, accused the Supreme Court of delivering "a far more subtle blow to liberty than the promulgation of the [exclusion] order itself. A military order, however unconstitutional, is not apt to last longer than the military emergency. But once [the Court holds] that the Constitution sanctions such an order, the Court for all time has validated the principle of racial discrimination. ... The principle then lies about like a loaded weapon. ... A military commander may overstep the bounds of constitutionality, and it is an incident. But if we review and approve, that passing incident becomes a doctrine of the Constitution."

The Court has never formally overruled *Hirabayashi* and *Korematsu*; however, it seems exceedingly doubtful after the constitutional transformation of racial relations during the half century since the exclusion cases that anyone could fire the "loaded weapon." In part that is because the Court itself limited their range. On the same day it decided *Korematsu,* the Supreme Court unanimously ordered Mitsuye Endo freed on her petition for a writ of HABEAS CORPUS.[615] The government acknowledged Endo to be a loyal citizen. "Loyalty is a matter of the heart and mind not of race, creed, or color. He who is loyal is by definition not a spy or a saboteur." Since the government could detain only potentially disloyal people, it had no reason to hold Endo.

In 1984, citing manifest evidence that the Army had lied to the Supreme Court forty years earlier, a federal DISTRICT COURT vacated Fred Korematsu's conviction. One of the charges on which Gordon Hirabayashi was convicted was also vacated. In 1988, acknowledging "the fundamental injustice of the evacuation, relocation, and internment," Congress apologized and offered reparations of twenty thousand dollars for each living survivor of what the government, in internal memoranda, called "concentration camps."

See also: EQUAL PROTECTION OF THE LAWS; RACIAL DISCRIMINATION.

jeopardy, *see:* **double jeopardy**

job, *see:* **occupation, right to pursue**

journal of proceedings   Art. I-§5[3] requires Congress to publish a journal of its proceedings, including how members voted on particular bills, on demand of one-fifth of the members. Proceedings that in the judgment of Congress require secrecy may be withheld. The journal, today known as the *Congressional Record,* is published daily. It is notoriously unreliable, since House and Senate rules permit members to edit their remarks. Nevertheless, the Court has ruled that the journal's recording of quorums and votes is conclusive and cannot later be contradicted in court.[115] However, if the language in the journal differs from the

language of a bill actually signed by the president, the final version of the law, and not the journal's version, is controlling.[664]

See also: YEAS AND NAYS.

journalist's privilege, *see:* **reporter's privilege**

judges   The Constitution is silent about qualifications for federal judges. By custom as old as the nation, judges have always been LAWYERS. Judges of higher courts are not required to have served on lower courts. Federal DISTRICT COURT judges have usually had experience as trial lawyers or prosecutors. Appellate judges have often pursued other forms of law practice or have served in political office. Justices of the SUPREME COURT frequently are appointed from the federal COURTS OF APPEALS, from state supreme courts, or from high political office. Federal judges on the district courts, courts of appeals, and Supreme Court are appointed for life. Federal administrative judges serve for a period of years. Qualifications of state judges depend on the constitutions and laws of the states; they usually serve for a period of years, not for life.

See also: CHIEF JUSTICE; DURING GOOD BEHAVIOR.

judgment   A judgment is the DECISION of the court, fixing the rights of the parties. If upheld on appeal, or if the parties fail to appeal within the prescribed time, the judgment is final, and the particular issue between the parties may not be relitigated.

See also: FINALITY; HOLDING; RES JUDICATA.

judgment, finality of, *see:* **final judgment; finality**

judicial activism   "Judicial activism" is a political, sociological, or pejorative term, not a constitutional one. An activist court answers questions its critics believe it need never have considered; it imposes its policy views not merely on the parties before it but on the citizenry generally; and, its critics charge, it usurps the legislature's functions. Throughout the 1960s, the Warren Court was branded as the epitome of activism because of its long line of PROCEDURAL DUE PROCESS cases, extending the BILL OF RIGHTS to the states, and its EQUAL PROTECTION antisegregation cases, beginning with BROWN V. BOARD OF EDUCATION. Such decisions have been cited as the hallmark of liberal judicial "result-oriented" activism.

But judicial activism is not restricted to liberal judges. In many ways, the Burger Court that followed was no less active. Four of its members were appointed by President Richard M. Nixon, who declared that his aim was to foster a "conservative philosophy" on the high bench. Yet it was this court that decided one of the most activist decisions in our history, *Roe v. Wade*, the abortion case. The Burger Court also largely created the constitutional doctrine of SEX DISCRIMINATION, despite the failure of the states to ratify the EQUAL RIGHTS AMENDMENT. And the Rehnquist Court, the most politically conservative court since the early 1930s, has scarcely forsworn activism. Its decisions overturning twenty years of settled law by limiting the reach of federal EMPLOYMENT DISCRIMINATION laws had to be reversed by Congress, with a reluctant President Bush signing the bill in 1991.

In any era, the Court's decisions suggest how difficult it is for most judges to adhere to the austere judicial restraint advocated by Justice Felix Frankfurter. He believed that judges should engage in "rigorous self-restraint" against writing their policy views into law because invalidating even socially undesirable laws "deflects responsibility from those on whom in a democratic society it ultimately rests—the people."[50] Frankfurter, a political liberal, became one of the fiercest judicial conservatives.

In sixteen years the liberal Warren Court overturned twenty-five federal and 150 state laws. The nominally conservative Burger Court in seventeen years overturned thirty-four federal and 192 state laws. Judges are no less human for wearing black robes and sitting high up behind benches; like most people, they find it hard to abstain from exercising whatever power they may have to right the world's manifold wrongs. A 1983 Burger Court decision illustrates this tendency: a well-established rule requires federal courts, including the Supreme Court, to refrain from reviewing state court decisions that rest on an "independent and ADEQUATE STATE GROUND." In this case, the Michigan Supreme Court ruled that the police had subjected the defendant to an unconstitutional SEARCH AND SEIZURE, under the rules of both the state constitution and the U.S. Constitution. The U.S. Supreme Court disagreed. It said that the U.S. Constitution permitted the search. But under the Court's established rule, it should not have intervened, because regardless of the Michigan court's error about federal constitutional law, what the state court says about its own constitution is off limits to the U.S. Supreme Court. But that did not deter the justices. They simply changed their rule. The Court's new rule allows it to reverse unless the state court offers a "plain statement" that its decision rests solely on state law. Since there is ample room to argue over how plain a "plain statement" need be, the Court thus took on considerable power to conform state Bill of Rights decisions to its own notions. This was no less an activist decision for its perhaps laudable desire to unfetter the police to do their jobs.

See also: ABSTENTION DOCTRINE; COUNCIL OF REVISION; JUDICIAL POWER; STARE DECISIS; STRICT CONSTRUCTION.

judicial immunity In 1871 the Court held that federal judges may not be sued personally for DAMAGES for injuries caused by decisions rendered in cases before them or for any other exercise of JUDICIAL POWER, unless a judge "clearly" had no JURISDICTION to hear the particular case.[217] The rule is necessary, the Court said, because a judge must be "free to act upon his own convictions, without apprehension of personal consequences to himself."

Similarly, though on a nonconstitutional basis, the Court declared in 1978 that state judges are immune from tort suits when acting within their jurisdiction.[1974] But the Court construed "jurisdiction" so broadly that it is doubtful any damage suit could ever succeed. The case concerned an Indiana woman who presented a state judge with a "petition" to sterilize her teenage daughter. No Indiana law permits such a petition to be filed in its courts. Nevertheless, a state judge granted the petition the day he received it, without holding a hearing. The daughter was unrepresented, had no notice, and could not appeal. The mother told her daughter she was having an appendectomy. Two years later when the daughter had married and discovered from a doctor why she could not conceive, she sued her mother, the doctor, and the judge in federal court under a civil rights law providing redress for violation of constitutional and federal legal rights. The Supreme Court held that the Indiana judge had acted within his jurisdiction because approving a petition is a judicial act. Dissenting, Justice Potter Stewart insisted that "a judge is not free, like a loose cannon, to inflict indiscriminate damage whenever he announces that he is acting in his judicial capacity. . . . A judge's approval of a mother's petition to lock her daughter in the attic would hardly be a judicial act simply because the mother had submitted her petition to the judge in his official capacity."

judicial legislation and policy making, *see:* **lawmaking by courts**

judicial power of the United States Before the Constitution, there was no way to bring most questions of federal law to federal courts. The ARTICLES OF CONFEDERATION allowed only certain types of ADMIRALTY AND MARITIME cases to be heard in courts established by Congress. The Constitution radically departed from that crabbed view of federal cases. In establishing the SUPREME COURT and authorizing Congress to establish lower federal courts, Article III created a third branch of the federal government—the judiciary—to which is committed the "judicial power of the United States." Judicial power is the power to decide cases—that is, to resolve a legal dispute between adverse parties. Under SEPARATION OF POWERS it is a power reserved to the courts. Congress may declare the laws to be applied, and the EXECUTIVE BRANCH may enforce the laws through criminal prosecutions or CIVIL ACTIONS, but they may not declare the rights of the parties in an actual controversy. Judicial power is therefore the power to interpret the law and to say what it means and how it applies to a concrete dispute. Although the grant of judicial power does not empower the federal courts to create a federal "general COMMON LAW"[621] or common law crimes,[953] it does confer considerable authority on the courts to develop bodies of judge-made law in areas of established federal law, such as admiralty and maritime law, INTERNATIONAL LAW, and the DORMANT COMMERCE CLAUSE. Unlike LEGISLATIVE POWER and EXECUTIVE POWER, judicial power does not permit courts to *initiate* action. They must wait until litigants bring cases to them, and the cases must concern a current despite. Courts may not issue advisory opinions, and the Supreme Court may reconsider only those cases not subject to reconsideration by other governmental bodies.

The Constitution seems to command that the judicial power be vested in the courts, but certain types of cases may be heard in *administrative,* rather than *judicial,* courts. In contrast to ARTICLE III COURTS established under the judicial power, federal ADMINISTRATIVE AGENCIES may hear many important types of cases arising under federal law, including bankruptcy, environmental, securities, and trade regulation laws.

Despite the language of Article III, that the judicial power *shall be vested* in the federal courts and *shall extend* to specified classes of cases (see JURISDICTION), it has long been held that the federal courts may not exercise the judicial power unless Congress has authorized the courts to hear that class or type of case. Congress need not confer jurisdiction to hear each class or even any jurisdiction at all.[2078] But when it does, the courts may exercise all judicial power, including, most significantly, the power to declare a law unconstitutional. No less significantly, judicial power includes power to review decisions of the state courts and to reverse whenever those decisions conflict with the Constitution or federal law, whether the case is civil[1251] or criminal.[420]

The judicial power includes the power to hold trial and issue a final and binding JUDGMENT. It also includes the power of an appellate court to review the legality of the judgment in the lower court. The courts also have ancillary powers to issue remedies, to deter or punish misconduct by CONTEMPT,[1745] to make rules of procedure governing practice before the courts,[2164] to appoint referees and investigators of various sorts,[1616] and even to determine which lawyers will be permitted to practice.[727] The Supreme Court has declared that it has supervisory power over the lower federal courts and that it and the lower federal courts have supervisory powers over court personnel and others, including parties, witnesses, and jurors, who participate in judicial matters.[1292] Supervisory power can sometimes have a substantial effect on the outcome of a case. For example, in 1943, in *McNabb v. United States,* the Court was confronted with convictions stemming from the murder confessions of several uneducated southern moonshiners. Federal authorities had held the accused for questioning for several days without bringing them before a judge promptly, as required by federal law. To avoid "making the courts themselves accomplices in wilful disobedience of law," the Court said that it was exercising "its supervisory authority over the administration of criminal justice in the federal courts" to bar the confessions from being heard, even though no law required the evidence to be excluded.

Many of these powers are subject to congressional control.[2168, 1352] Congress may prohibit the application of certain remedies, such as INJUNCTIONS, in particular classes of cases.[1129] Although the Court has said that the contempt power is "inherent in all courts,"[1745, 1926] since 1789 Congress has enacted laws governing the exercise of that power, and the Court has, somewhat ambiguously, upheld its authority to do so.[1327] Congress has also spelled out the use of and the kinds of writs that the federal courts may issue, including the writ of HABEAS CORPUS, and the Court has sustained these laws.[194]

An important attribute of judicial power is the FINALITY of a court's decisions. If some other governmental body may reconsider the outcome of a particular case, then the case is not properly one on which the judicial power of the United States may be exercised.[885]

See also: ABSTENTION DOCTRINE; ADVISORY OPINIONS; ARTICLE I COURTS; BILL OF ATTAINDER; CASES OR CONTROVERSIES; CONSTITUTIONAL QUESTIONS, AVOIDANCE OF; DECLARATORY JUDGMENT; DIVERSITY JURISDICTION; ELEVENTH AMENDMENT; FEDERAL QUESTION JURISDICTION; HOLDING; JUDICIAL REVIEW; JUSTICIABILITY; LAWMAKING BY COURTS; MOOTNESS; NULLIFICATION, INTERPOSITION, AND SECESSION; POLITICAL QUESTION DOCTRINE; RETROACTIVITY; RIPENESS; SOVEREIGN IMMUNITY; STANDING; STATES, IMMUNITY FROM SUIT IN FEDERAL COURT.

judicial procedure in state courts   Since the 1960s, state criminal prosecutions must abide by most procedures in the BILL OF RIGHTS. But the Constitution imposes no general requirement that state civil procedures mimic federal procedures or adhere to some abstract notion of fairness. A state may abolish certain defenses once available to defendants.[208] Likewise, the states may establish STATUTES OF LIMITATION to bar lawsuits once a certain amount of time has passed after an injury has occurred. Although states ordinarily may establish whatever BURDEN OF PROOF they please in civil cases, DUE PROCESS requires states to meet the standard of "clear and convincing evidence" when the state proposes to commit someone indefinitely to a mental institution[13] or to deprive parents of custody of their children.[1802] Unlike the requirement imposed by the SEVENTH AMENDMENT, the states are not constitutionally bound to grant civil litigants the right to a jury trial.[2144]

See also: EVIDENCE; PRESUMPTIONS; PROCESS RIGHTS; PROCEDURAL RIGHTS OF CRIMINAL DEFENDANTS; TRIAL BY JURY.

judicial review Judicial review is America's novel contribution to political theory and the practice of constitutional government. In its usual meaning, it is the power of courts to declare laws and acts of government unconstitutional. Despite occasional remarks of seventeenth-century British judges that the courts could control acts of Parliament when they violate NATURAL LAW, the colonists inherited a tradition of absolute parliamentary supremacy. As one English judge said in 1701, "an act of parliament can do no wrong, though it may do several things that look pretty odd." But in 1761 James Otis attacked the royal governors' use of writs of ASSISTANCE to search the colonists' homes, declaring that an "act against the Constitution is void: an act against natural equity is void: and if an act of Parliament should be made [authorizing the writs], it would be void." Of Otis's speech, John Adams later wrote: "Then and there the child independence was born."

At the CONSTITUTIONAL CONVENTION, the Framers rejected several motions to create a COUNCIL OF REVISION, in which both judges and the president could veto a congressional enactment. Most of the delegates believed that judges should consider the constitutionality of laws only when hearing cases, and many believed that courts could void only those laws aimed at the judiciary itself. Other delegates insisted that courts could never invalidate laws. John Francis Mercer of Maryland said that "laws ought to be well and cautiously made, and then to be uncontroulable."

In *Federalist* 78, Alexander Hamilton seemed to advance forthrightly a broad power of judicial review. The duty of courts, he said, "must be to declare all acts contrary to the manifest tenor of the Constitution void. Without this, all the reservations of particular rights or privileges would amount to nothing." But Hamilton's argument may be narrower than it appears. The constitutional historian Leonard W. Levy suggests that Hamilton was writing to assuage fears of the ANTI-FEDERALISTS that Congress would usurp state powers and that he was not necessarily arguing that the courts could invalidate federal laws that did not concern the states. Scholars have concluded that the evidence that the Framers intended judicial review is inconclusive.

Whatever the Framers intended, Chief Justice John Marshall claimed the power of judicial review in 1803, in the most celebrated case in American history, MARBURY V. MADISON. "It is emphatically the province and duty of the judicial department to say what the law is," Marshall wrote. So when the Constitution and a law conflict, "the court must determine which of these conflicting rules governs the case. This is the very essence of judicial duty." Since the Constitution is paramount law—for if it may simply be altered by the legislature, what is its purpose?—the Constitution must control. Otherwise, the "courts must close their eyes on the constitution." And judicial blindness "would subvert the very foundation of all written constitutions." It would mean that even though the Constitution says an act "is entirely void," it would be "in practice, completely obligatory."

Since *Marbury,* judicial review has been an accomplished political fact, no matter how often Congress and presidents have reproved it. Despite a long-running debate over the legitimacy of its actions, in two centuries the Court has overturned 125 acts of Congress, struck down nearly 1,200 state and municipal laws and ordinances, and repudiated many more acts of federal and state officials. The principal objection is the seeming paradox in a democracy of nonelected officials overruling policy judgments of the people's elected representatives.

The theoretical debate will never be settled, for the palpable tension between representative institutions and the people's rights is at the heart of the Constitution. But on a practical level, judicial review *is* the solution: it is one of the principal CHECKS AND BALANCES in a complex system of separated powers. Just as the Court checks unconstitutional legislation, so the Court's constitutional rulings can be altered over time by presidential appointments, as Roosevelt demonstrated in the late 1930s and as Presidents Ronald Reagan and George Bush have been demonstrating more recently. Moreover, as explored under a separate heading (see SUPREME COURT, JURISDICTION OF), Congress potentially has a powerful check of its own—the power to curb the kinds of cases the Court may hear.

See also: JUDICIAL POWER; JUDICIAL SUPREMACY; JURISDICTION; SEPARATION OF POWERS.

judicial supremacy   By long convention, though not without continued debate, the Supreme Court, rather than Congress or the president, is held to be the final arbiter of constitutional questions, short of constitutional amendment. "We are under a Constitution, but the Constitution is what the judges say it is," declared Justice Charles Evans Hughes, in an often-quoted speech in 1907. Judicial supremacy stems from the Court's function, not from any inherent superiority. As Justice Robert H. Jackson once put it: "We are not final because we are infallible, but we are infallible only because we are final."[248]

The claim is not merely that the Court has the final word in a particular case, but that the other branches of government, and the states, must follow the spirit of the Court's decisions in matters in which they may not be parties in court. The Court's most dramatic assertion of judicial supremacy came in 1958 when Governor Orville Faubus and other Arkansas state officials declared that they were not bound by *Brown v. Board of Education,* which outlawed segregated schools. The school board sought to postpone a plan to desegregate the schools because of the "chaos, bedlam and turmoil" that followed in the wake of the governor's violent opposition to integrated schools. The Supreme Court denied the postponement and in *Cooper v. Aaron,* a decision signed by each of the nine justices, told Governor Faubus that he and all other state officials were indeed bound by *Brown.* The Court said that judicial supremacy dates back to MARBURY V. MADISON, which "declared the basic principle that the federal judiciary is supreme in the exposition of the law of the Constitution, and that principle has ever since been respected by this Court and the Country as a permanent and indispensable feature of our constitutional system." Since then the Court has reiterated the principle in cases involving APPORTIONMENT of legislative districts,[108] the power of Congress to exclude a duly elected member,[1653] and President Nixon's claim of EXECUTVE PRIVILEGE to refuse to surrender papers required by a criminal court subpoena.[1487]

At its broadest, the claim of absolute judicial

supremacy does not hold. For one thing, the Court's decision that Congress *may* enact a certain bill does not mean that the president *must* sign it. In other words, the Constitution commits to the president, not the courts, the decision whether to veto. Other decisions, too, are committed to other branches. For another thing, there is a difference between constitutional rulings that bind the states and constitutional decisions directed to Congress and the president, the Court's co-equals. Had he been politically popular rather than politically wounded, President Nixon might well have defied the justices' instruction that he hand over secret tapes.

By and large, Congress and the presidents have abided by the Court's rulings, even if sometimes unenthusiastically. But the potential for a larger conflict is always present because of the constitutional command that the president "take care that the laws be faithfully executed." In 1985 Attorney General Edwin Meese III "declared" that the federal Competition in Contracting Act was unconstitutional, even though President Ronald Reagan had signed the bill. The U.S. budget director instructed government agencies to ignore provisions requiring the Pentagon to withhold funds from federal contractors while the U.S. comptroller general investigated claims of rigged bids.

Presidents have sometimes refused to enforce laws they claim are unconstitutional for the same reason that the Court strikes down unconstitutional laws: fidelity to the Constitution outweighs a duty to enforce a congressional enactment. If the president's opposition is confined to arguing against the law in court when a test case arises, judicial supremacy is not undermined. But Meese went further. A case did go to court, and the court, holding the act constitutional, ruled against the administration's position. In testimony before Congress, Meese denied the authority of a federal DIS-TRICT COURT to pass on the constitutionality of the law. This was a direct challenge to judicial supremacy. In Meese's view, court rulings *about* the Constitution and the Constitution *itself* are two different things. The administration, Meese said, had independent authority to interpret the Constitution on its own and to ignore the courts. Meese eventually backed down for purely practical reasons: Congress threatened to terminate funding for his office, including his salary.

But the Meese defiance was an aberration. The Court may always rule on the constitutionality of laws in the appropriate cases, and there is wide political consensus that these constitutional rulings are definitive unless they are overruled or the Constitution is amended.
See also: COMMITMENT TO OTHER BRANCHES; JUDICIAL REVIEW.

judicial system, *see: articles listed at courts*

judicially manageable standards, *see:* **justiciability**

judiciary acts　Article III extends the JUDICIAL POWER OF THE UNITED STATES to the Supreme Court and to any inferior federal courts that Congress establishes. It also declares the categories of cases that the courts may hear. But with the exception of the Supreme Court's ORIGINAL JURISDICTION, the federal courts may not automatically hear cases within those categories—in other words, the judicial power is not self-executing. The federal courts may hear only those cases over which Congress has vested them with JURISDICTION. In 1789 the First Congress gave form to the Supreme Court, established the first lower federal courts, and vested them with limited forms of federal jurisdiction—that is, it authorized them to hear certain kinds of cases. The Judiciary Act of 1789 survived in its original form for nearly a century, and some parts endure to this day. Since 1789 Congress has enacted thirty-seven other laws, the most recent in 1988, affecting the jurisdiction and business of the Supreme Court.

See also: CASES OR CONTROVERSIES; COURT OF APPEALS, U.S.; DISTRICT COURTS; SUPREME COURT.

jurisdiction   The federal courts may not exercise JUDICIAL POWER unless Congress has vested them with jurisdiction. The distinction between judicial power and jurisdiction is subtle but important. Judicial power is the power to decide a case. Jurisdiction is the authority to decide a *particular* case. Art. III-§2[1] limits the federal courts in exercising judicial power to seven classes of cases: (1) cases raising questions under the Constitution, federal law, or treaties; (2) cases affecting ambassadors and related officials; (3) ADMIRALTY AND MARITIME cases; (4) controversies to which the United States is a party; (5) controversies in which the states themselves are parties; (6) disputes between citizens from different states; and (7) controversies "between citizens of the same state claiming lands under grants of different states."

Federal jurisdiction falls into two general classes: jurisdiction over the subject and over the parties. For example, if a dispute is an issue ARISING UNDER THE CONSTITUTION, federal law, or a treaty, the Court may hear the case regardless of who the parties are. Likewise, if the dispute concerns one of the many types of parties—ambassadors, citizens from different states—it does not matter what the issue is; the federal courts may hear the case. In two far-reaching early decisions, the Court relied on the distinction between issues and parties to proclaim the jurisdiction of the Supreme Court to hear appeals from state as well as federal cases. The Judiciary Act of 1789 grants appellate jurisdiction to the Court to review final decisions from state courts whenever the state court rejects a claim based on federal law. Virginia argued that if a case arose in the state court, it must end there. For the Court to hear an appeal of the federal issue, the case must

have originated in the federal courts. In 1816, in *Martin v. Hunter's Lessee,* Justice Joseph Story rejected Virginia's argument: "It is the *case,* then, and not the *court,* that gives the jurisdiction." In 1821, in *Cohens v. Virginia,* the defendants were convicted in a Virginia state court for violating an antilottery law. They asserted that the state law was void because it conflicted with a federal lottery law. Virginia argued that the Supreme Court could have no jurisdiction over a criminal prosecution because the state was a party. Chief Justice John Marshall rejected the state's argument because jurisdiction did not depend on who the *parties* were but on what the *issues* were.

In controlling the jurisdiction of federal courts, Congress may determine not only what types of jurisdiction to allocate but also whether to confer *exclusive* jurisdiction. Jurisdiction to hear cases arising under a particular federal law may be assigned exclusively to the federal courts—as Congress has done, for instance, in the copyright and patent laws. If jurisdiction is nonexclusive, litigants may raise federal claims in state courts.

Jurisdiction of state courts is determined by state law, but state jurisdiction has a constitutional dimension. In *Pennoyer v. Neff* in 1878, the Court announced the basic rule required by DUE PROCESS under the FOURTEENTH AMENDMENT. Every state has exclusive jurisdiction over people and things within its borders; a state has no jurisdiction over people and things outside.

Jurisdiction is different from NOTICE. For a court to hear a case, it not only must have jurisdiction over the person but the defendant must receive notice of the suit through SERVICE OF PROCESS or must consent to jurisdiction of the court. In other words, a JUDGMENT has no legal effect if the person whom it purports to bind has not been served or voluntarily appeared in court to defend against the plaintiff's claims.

A court cannot have jurisdiction over a person who is a legal resident of another state, has no ties to the forum state, and who is outside the state when the suit is filed. But temporary absence will not defeat jurisdiction if the potential defendant is a legal resident. A person may be sued in the state in which he or she lives, even if he or she is vacationing out of state when the suit is filed.[1347] Residence is not necessary to invoke a court's jurisdiction. In 1990 the Court ruled that a nonresident who is physically present in a state, even if in transit to somewhere else, may be sued there.[281]

Between 1878 and 1945, the Court began to water down the seemingly hard-and-fast requirement that the defendant must be in state for the courts to exercise jurisdiction. One approach was to create a legal fiction. If an out-of-state defendant heard about the suit and hired a lawyer to defend against it, the court would assume he or she had consented if any issue other than lack of jurisdiction was raised.[1195] Another legal fiction was the "consent" to jurisdiction of an automobile owner or driver for the "privilege" of driving on the state's roads. In other words, an accident victim could sue a driver from out of state who had returned home. All the plaintiff had to do was serve the secretary of state or some other such official, as long as the official in turn notified the defendant, usually by mail, of the suit.[915] The Supreme Court also approved the practice of many states to require a nonresident as a condition of "doing business" in the state to consent to being served by an agent within the state.[907]

The rules governing jurisdiction over corporations were much more complex and murky. If a corporation was doing "sufficient" business in a state, its salespeople could be served for suits relating to its business activities.[1598] But what constituted sufficient business was unclear.[800, 984] But if a company stopped doing business before the suit was filed, it could avoid jurisdiction,[1737] as it could if the suit concerned something other than the business it was actually carrying on in the state.[1528] If it was not doing business in the state, a corporate officer or stockholder who happened to be there could not be served.[768]

Finally, in 1945, in *International Shoe Co. v. Washington,* the Court announced a new "minimum contacts" test. The case arose when the state of Washington sued the International Shoe Company to collect unpaid unemployment compensation taxes for its in-state salesmen. International Shoe was a Missouri corporation and had not obtained a license to do business in Washington. It employed resident salespeople to make sales; they sent their orders to the company in Missouri for fulfillment. The state served notice on the salespeople and sent a registered letter to the company's Missouri headquarters. The Court held that this method satisfied the due process requirement of "presence" in the state and adequate notice. "Presence," Chief Justice Harlan Fiske Stone said, was a question-begging term. The real issue was whether the company had sufficient contacts to "make it reasonable, in the context of our federal system ... to require the corporation to defend the particular suit ... brought there." In a series of cases thereafter, the Court held that foreign mail-order insurance companies with no offices or agents in the state could be sued there simply because they solicited business and sent policies through the mail.[1295] In a recent case, the Court upheld jurisdiction over an out-of-state publisher sued for libel because the magazine circulated in the forum state.[1055]

Building on these cases, the states have all enacted LONG-ARM STATUTES, permitting service of process by mail against out-of-state defendants. If the defendant fails to respond, the plaintiff can obtain a default judgment, and under the FULL FAITH AND CREDIT Clause the judgment will be binding in the defendant's home state.

Despite *International Shoe*'s liberal test, however, the Court has not upheld every assertion of jurisdiction. For example, a divorced mother living in California could not sue her former husband in California to alter their support and custody agreement merely because he bought his daughter a plane ticket to fly from New York to live with her mother. The father was a New York resident, the couple had lived in New York when married, and he continued to live in New York with his children after the divorce, under a separation agreement signed in New York and awarding him custody. Buying a plane ticket for his daughter gave him no contact with California.[1099]

The rules are somewhat different when the suit concerns land. Jurisdiction is then based on the presence of the property in state, and it therefore does not matter that the owner lives out of state, as long as the defendant actually receives notice of the suit.[1399] Likewise, when an estate is being probated, the probate court has jurisdiction over the deceased's property located in the state and may determine ownership rights that will bind every interested party, no matter where they are living.[779]

However, when a suit is filed against property purely for the sake of obtaining jurisdiction over a foreign defendant, more difficult questions arise. The Court has said that the minimum-contacts requirement still applies. For example, a plaintiff was injured in an automobile accident while a passenger in the defendant's car in Indiana. The plaintiff moved to Minnesota and sued the defendant there. The defendant continued to live in Indiana and had no contacts with Minnesota. The plaintiff claimed that jurisdiction could be based on the fact that the defendant's insurance policy covered an accident in Minnesota. In other words, the contract between the insurance company and the defendant was said to be "property" located in Minnesota because the contract obligated the insurer to defend its policyholders in

lawsuits anywhere. The Supreme Court dismissed the case, holding that the defendant must have done something purposeful that connects to the state. Doing business in Indiana with a company that is also present in Minnesota is simply not enough.[1775]

One other major set of problems arises when spouses living or moving to different states seek divorces or alterations of their DIVORCE decrees. In general, a state court may grant a divorce on behalf of the spouse living there, even if the other spouse is not present, but no decree affecting custody or support payments will be valid without jurisdiction based on something more substantive than the mere existence of the "marriage" in the state.

See also: ABSTENTION DOCTRINE; AMBASSADORS, POWER TO APPOINT AND RECEIVE; ANCILLARY JURISDICTION; CASES OR CONTROVERSIES; COURT OF APPEALS, U.S.; DIPLOMATIC IMMUNITY; DISTRICT COURTS; DIVERSITY JURISDICTION; FEDERAL QUESTION JURISDICTION; GARNISHMENT AND ATTACHMENT; ORIGINAL JURISDICTION; PENDENT JURISDICTION; REMOVAL OF CASES; SOVEREIGN IMMUNITY; STATES, IMMUNITY FROM SUITS IN FEDERAL COURT; SUPREME COURT, JURISDICTION OF.

jurisdictional and constitutional facts   Congress and state legislatures often empower ADMINISTRATIVE AGENCIES to hear cases and take actions involving rights of private claimants; these include cases involving DEPORTATION, utility rate making, workers' compensation, and other benefits. In determining the rights of claimants, the agency frequently must decide whether certain fundamental facts exist that may determine a person's constitutional rights. For example, citizens may not be deported, so if a person whom the Immigration and Naturalization Service wishes to deport claims to be a citizen, it will have to determine the validity of the claim. The question then arises whether the agency's conclusion is final, or whether the courts have an independent constitutional power to look into the facts anew. The Supreme Court has held that if constitutional rights are at stake, Congress may not leave fact-finding to agencies.[494] On appeal of the agency's decision, a court has the constitutional duty to reexamine the factual premise. These are known as "jurisdictional" facts, because if the agency was wrong it lacked JURISDICTION to hear the matter—the Immigration Service has no authority over citizens.[1478]

The jurisdictional fact doctrine has been heavily criticized, and when the question involves PRIVATE RIGHTS—a claim by one individual against another, not involving governmental penalties or benefits—it is used only in maritime workers' compensation cases.[71] When significant personal rights are at stake, however, the Court has been more hesitant to let agencies and sometimes even trial courts or juries have the final word on the facts. Facts that the courts may reassess are known as "constitutional facts." The doctrine has particular vitality in cases involving FIRST AMENDMENT freedom of expression and in criminal prosecutions involving coerced confessions. The Court has held that it may substitute its own judgment about the facts for those of the lower courts in cases involving the LIBEL OF PUBLIC FIGURES,[746] OBSCENITY,[1338] and the admissibility into evidence at a criminal trial of a confession that the defendant claims was involuntary.[84]

In 1920 the Court held in *Ohio Valley Water Co. v. Ben Avon Borough* that the constitutional fact doctrine applies to state administrative agencies empowered to set utility rates. When a utility company asserts that the rate was set so low as to be confiscatory, DUE PROCESS requires a court, not an agency, to determine whether it constituted a TAKING OF PROPERTY without JUST COMPENSATION. If a state could commit to an agency the final decision about the "fairness" of the rate, the constitutional question would be unreviewable in court. This doctrine was considerably undercut in 1944 when the Supreme Court ruled that courts may not upset an agency's rate determinations

unless that the rate is "unjust and unreasonable in its consequences."[648]

See also: ARTICLE I COURTS; ARTICLE III COURTS; JUDICIAL POWER; PRIVATE RIGHT–PUBLIC RIGHT DISTINCTION.

jury and jurors, impartiality of The right to TRIAL BY JURY means the right to an impartial jury. Impartiality has two components. First, the jury must be a "representative cross section of the community,"[2002] meaning that JURY DISCRIMINATION is unconstitutional. Second, the jurors must individually be free of bias against particular defendants and their characteristics. Bias of this sort is not confined to obvious examples of racial bigotry, although such bias has prompted the Court to require potential jurors to be asked about any racial prejudice, when it is likely that such prejudice would taint the trial.[845] Prejudicial pretrial publicity has been held to deprive a defendant of the right to an impartial jury,[1856] and if the community as a whole has been tainted, the defendant is entitled to a change of VENUE, both in felony[991] and misdemeanor[822] cases. Jury tampering is likewise unconstitutional, whether or not it was meant to influence the jury's vote. For example, the Court reversed a conviction when two deputy sheriffs who were principal prosecution witnesses were assigned to take care of the jurors during trial.[2079] When a mob dominates or threatens to dominate a trial, the jury's lack of partiality is presumed and the conviction must be reversed.[695] The requirement of impartiality is the basis for the rule that the judge must consider whether a confession is voluntary; it may not be introduced into evidence with instructions to the jury to disregard it if it proves to be inadmissible.[995]

In 1968 the Court ruled that people conscientiously opposed to the DEATH PENALTY may not automatically be excluded from a jury. Potential jurors must be allowed to state whether they might be willing to consider imposing capital punishment in an appropriate case.[2240] However, a person may be excluded from the jury if his opposition to the death penalty would "prevent or substantially impair the performance of his duties as a juror in accordance with his instructions and his oath." Whether the person is so impaired need not be proved with "unmistakable clarity."[2141] A conviction must be reversed if a potential juror was wrongly excluded on this ground; the rule of HARMLESS ERROR does not apply.[796] The judge must exclude from the jury anyone who is biased in favor of the death penalty.[1764]

See also: JURY SIZE; JURY UNANIMITY; PREJUDICIAL
PUBLICITY.

jury discrimination   Two provisions of the Constitution prohibit INVIDIOUS DISCRIMINATION in selecting juries. Explicit RACIAL DISCRIMINATION is barred by EQUAL PROTECTION. As early as 1880, the Supreme Court reversed a conviction obtained in West Virginia against a black defendant because state law required blacks to be excluded from all juries.[1967] The same rule applies to discrimination based on national origin.[913] Unconstitutional jury discrimination also may be shown to exist if the selection process can easily be manipulated by those in charge or if, statistically, the jurors of the excluded group are substantially underrepresented in the total of all jurors called.[358]

Jury discrimination also violates the command of the SIXTH AMENDMENT that juries be impartial. On this ground, the Court has reversed convictions of a white defendant because blacks had been systematically excluded[1614] and of a male defendant because women had been excluded.[2002] A state may not grant women an automatic exemption from jury service merely because they ask[584] nor require that women first submit a written request to serve in order to be called.[2002]

A somewhat more subtle method of discrimination has been employed through peremptory challenges. During jury selection, the parties are entitled to "strike," or exclude, biased persons from the jury. In addition to these exclusions "for cause," most state courts and the federal courts permit the parties a certain number of peremptory challenges—that is, the right to strike a potential juror for any reason or for no reason at all. In 1965 the Supreme Court for the first time addressed the problem of peremptory challenges against jurors of a certain race. It held that if a prosecutor uses peremptory challenges to exclude blacks "in case after case, whatever the circumstances, whatever the crime and whoever the defendant or the victim may be," the practice violates equal protection.[1986] But the Court refused to find a constitutional problem in striking blacks in a particular case. As a consequence, it was nearly impossible to show racial bias in a prosecutor's use of peremptory challenges. In 1986 the Court overruled itself. In *Batson v. Kentucky*, the Court said that prosecutors may not, even in a particular case, "challenge potential jurors solely on account of their race or on the assumption that black jurors as a group will be unable impartially to consider the state's case against a black defendant." In 1991 the Court went further, holding that a person of another race may challenge racially motivated peremptory challenges; that is, the prosecutor may not challenge blacks even if a white is being tried.[1656] Also in 1991 the Court forbad racially based peremptory challenges even in civil trials in which the government is not one of the parties, on the ground that exercising peremptory challenges is STATE ACTION because the state created the challenge system.[599]

However, the Court has not invalidated discrimination on any basis other than race, sex, or national origins. Though there was no clear majority, it refused to reverse the conviction of a Hispanic defendant whose prosecutor struck several Hispanic jurors because their ability to speak Spanish might lead them to disregard the official English translations of the testimony of

Spanish-speaking witnesses. A plurality opinion held that peremptory challenges under these circumstances do not constitute racial discrimination.[912]

See also: JURY AND JURORS, IMPARTIALITY OF; JURY SIZE; JURY UNANIMITY; TRIAL BY JURY.

jury size The SIXTH AMENDMENT requires that federal criminal juries consist of twelve persons.[2042] But state criminal juries need not satisfy this requirement. In 1970 the Court held that juries composed of as few as six jurors may be used to try felonies.[2210] In 1978 the Court struck down a conviction rendered by a five-person jury, saying that six was the minimum.[114] In federal civil trials under the SEVENTH AMENDMENT, the Court has held that six-person juries are permissible.[429] No minimum number of jurors is imposed on state civil trials, since the Seventh Amendment does not apply to the states.[1354]

See also: JURY UNANIMITY.

jury trial, right to, *see:* **trial by jury**

jury unanimity Under the SIXTH AMENDMENT's right to TRIAL BY JURY, guilty verdicts in federal prosecutions must be unanimous.[62] A single vote against conviction results in a hung jury. But state jury verdicts need not be unanimous if twelve jurors have been empaneled. In 1972 the Court upheld a 10–2 guilty verdict under the Sixth Amendment[65] and a 9–3 verdict under the DUE PROCESS Clause of the FOURTEENTH AMENDMENT.[1017] However, when the state criminal jury consists of as few as six persons, their verdict must be unanimous; a 5–1 verdict violates the right to trial by jury.[276] In 1979 the Court said it was reserving judgment on whether other combinations of votes, such as 8–4 or 7–5, would be constitutional.[276] Under

the SEVENTH AMENDMENT, the Court once said that federal civil juries must also be unanimous.[54, 1934] Whether this rule remains good law is an open question in view of the Court's decision in 1973 that federal civil juries may consist of as few as six persons.[429]

See also: JURY SIZE.

just compensation The FIFTH AMENDMENT requires the government to provide "just compensation" when it exercises its power of EMINENT DOMAIN to take someone's property. The Court has ruled that the compensation to be paid must be measured by the value of the property to the owner—that is, the amount of the loss suffered—not by the value of the gain realized by the government.[1374] Generally, the owner's loss is calculated as market value—what a seller would pay in an arm's length transaction in a functioning market. But when markets are not functioning, or market value cannot otherwise be calculated, the owner is entitled to a payment that is fair.[1344]

Each case is decided on its unique facts. In one post–World War II case, the Court held that market value at the time of taking was not the test for a tugboat, since the government's need for the tug during the war inflated its value far above what it would ordinarily be worth.[472] If some part of the value of the property is attributable to actions of the government, just compensation need not include the incremental value created by the government.[710] Sometimes only part of a tract of land may be condemned. Then the government owes in proportion to the value of the total, except that if the government uses the condemned property in such a way as to increase the value of the property remaining in the owner's hands, the increase in value may be used to offset the compensation that must be paid.[137] Ordinarily, the government must pay only for what is actually taken; incidental losses, such as the loss of customers and future business, are not compensable. But the Court has carved out an exception for temporary takings. When the government seized for the duration of the war a leased plant in which a laundry was housed, forcing the business to cease until it could regain its facilities, the Court awarded payment to cover for the loss of patronage.[1076] Legal costs, such as a lawyer's fee, of determining fair market value need not be included.[558]

See also: TAKING OF PROPERTY.

justiciability Justiciability is the suitability of a dispute for judicial resolution. In various cases, the Court has discerned a number of doctrines that require the courts to dismiss claims presented for decision. These doctrines are not all of the same order. Some are premised on the belief that particular cases do not present a sufficiently sharp conflict between the parties to ensure that the courts will hear the best arguments that could be made. By serving to keep the Court from deciding cases prematurely, the political system is kept freer than it would be if anyone could ask the Court to determine abstract rights at any time. The Court has interpreted the religion clauses in the FIRST AMENDMENT to prohibit courts from deciding religious disputes.[1054] A somewhat different rationale is based on the POLITICAL QUESTION DOCTRINE under which some suits may be nonjusticiable because the Constitution has committed their resolution to other branches of government. A broader version of this doctrine holds that some issues are so inherently political that the courts have no standard by which to judge. It was to this notion that Justice Felix Frankfurter was referring when he admonished the federal courts to refrain from entering the "political thicket" in cases calling into question the constitutionality of legislative APPORTIONMENT.[424] Despite the

names of its subcategories, the doctrine of justiciability remains hazy, and the Court has not consistently followed any one of its strands, suggesting that the doctrine is itself more political than legal.

See also: COMMITMENT TO OTHER BRANCHES; CONSTITUTIONAL QUESTIONS, AVOIDANCE OF; FREEDOM OF RELIGION; MOOTNESS; RELIGIOUS ESTABLISHMENT; RIPENESS; STANDING.

juveniles, rights of Because the Constitution is silent about children, there is no coherent theory about the rights of juveniles. On the one hand, a child is a PERSON within the meaning of the FOURTEENTH AMENDMENT and therefore entitled to DUE PROCESS and EQUAL PROTECTION OF THE LAWS if the state acts against him. On the other hand, children who have not attained the age of majority are answerable to their parents, and so are subject to a nonconsensual subordinate relationship that, in legal terms, would violate the THIRTEENTH AMENDMENT if enforced against an adult.

In general, the law views children through the eyes of their parents. The rights of juveniles, with some narrow exceptions, are the rights of parents, who may determine the child's living conditions, quality and quantity of education, and moral and religious upbringing. These rights spring from a parent's LIBERTY interest under a concept of SUBSTANTIVE DUE PROCESS. Because the state has no "general power . . . to standardize its children,"[1628] the parent's legal power to determine how the child will live is substantial. In *Wisconsin v. Yoder,* the Supreme Court held that Old Order Amish parents may remove their children from the public schools after the eighth grade to keep them from being "exposed to worldly values" and lured into a secular way of life. The Court made no provision for Amish children who might wish a larger education to depart the closed society of their parents.

A child has rights against parents only if the

parents are abusive. The state may remove the child from home, but only on showing "clear and convincing" evidence at a HEARING that the parent is unfit.[1802] On the other hand, parents may commit their children to mental institutions without any formal hearing at all.[1565] The state has no constitutional obligation to prevent parental abuse, even if it has good reason to believe that a parent is physically torturing a child.[542]

Juveniles do have some rights of personal autonomy, even against their parents. The Court has held, to this writing, that minor girls have certain rights to an ABORTION free of parental veto.[149, 1519] It has also struck down laws prohibiting children from access to contraceptives,[341] but it has sustained laws that prohibit children from obtaining indecent but not legally pornographic material.[759]

Outside the family, the Court has very occasionally given constitutional protection to minors' activities against the claim of the public schools to act *in loco parentis*. In 1969 the Court rejected a school's demand that one junior high school student and two high school students remove black armbands they wore as a silent protest against the Vietnam War.[2051] Justice Abe Fortas said that the school was not regulating "the length of skirts or the type of clothing, . . . hair style, or deportment." Nor did the ban on armbands "concern aggressive, disruptive action or even group demonstrations." The Court has studiously refrained from hearing appeals in many cases challenging grooming and dress codes, including one in which Pawnee Indian children challenged a short-hair rule, claiming the right to wear long braids as part of their religious heritage.[1456] In 1986 the Court upheld the power of a school to discipline a high school student for giving a lewd speech at a school assembly. The Court sharply distinguished between the political message in silently wearing an armband and sexual innuendo, even though the speaker was endorsing a student running for school office.[158] In 1988 the Court permitted a school to censor the contents of a high school newspaper, distinguishing a student's expression "that happens to occur on the school premises" from "school-sponsored publications . . . supervised by faculty members" for educational purposes.[886] The irony of an educational system that teaches democratic values by censoring newspapers escaped the Court majority entirely.

Similarly confused are the rules governing juveniles accused of crime. Since the early part of the century, states had conducted relatively informal hearings before sending juvenile delinquents to long stretches in reformatories. But in 1967 the Court ruled that juveniles are constitutionally entitled to be represented by counsel and to due process procedural protection in juvenile proceedings. In *In re Gault*, the Court overturned a six-year commitment of a fifteen-year-old boy to an "industrial school" for making an obscene phone call, following a hearing at which he had no lawyer, was given no notice of the charges, and was not permitted to cross-examine witnesses against him. Justice Fortas said that "it is of no constitutional consequence" that the receiving institutions are not called "jails." The practical reality is that they are "peopled by guards, custodians, state employees, and 'delinquents' confined . . . for anything from waywardness to rape and homicide. . . . Under our Constitution, the condition of being a boy does not justify a kangaroo court." Moreover, the Court said three years later, the charges must be proved beyond a reasonable doubt.[2234]

Children are also entitled to the benefit of the DOUBLE JEOPARDY Clause.[228] But there is no right to TRIAL BY JURY in juvenile proceedings.[1300] The Court has upheld PREVENTIVE DETENTION for juveniles accused of crime if there is a "serious risk" that the juvenile will continue to break the law before trial and if an adversary hearing is promptly held to determine the probability of the risk.[1810] It is not clear whether there is an absolute rule against imposing the DEATH PENALTY on children under sixteen years of age,[2041] but in 1989 the Court apparently ruled that sixteen- and seventeen-year-old children may be executed for capital crimes.[1942]

See also: CONTRACEPTION; FAMILIES; GOVERNMENT, AFFIRMATIVE OBLIGATIONS OF; PARENTAL RIGHTS AND RESPONSIBILITIES.

K

Ku Klux Klan Act   Beginning in 1866, Congress enacted a series of laws to protect the civil rights of the newly emancipated slaves. One of these, the Civil Rights Act of 1871, commonly known as the Ku Klux Klan Act, was designed to enforce the FOURTEENTH AMENDMENT, which had been ratified three years earlier. Among other things, it allowed anyone deprived of federal rights by persons acting under COLOR OF LAW to file a civil suit for redress. It also provided for federal prosecution of private conspiracies to deprive people of their federal rights. In 1883 the Court struck down the criminal conspiracy provision on the ground that Congress could legislate only against STATE ACTION. It had no authority under the Fourteenth Amendment to reach private actions.[873] But the civil provision has survived. Today it is codified in Section 1983 of Title 42 of the United States Code, and it is the principal basis for suits against state officials in federal court for violating individuals' constitutional and other federal rights. Section 1983 came into widespread use after 1961, when the Court ruled that police officers could be sued for DAMAGES for unlawfully breaking into a person's home without PROBABLE CAUSE or a SEARCH WARRANT.[1375] In 1978 and 1980, the Court dramatically widened the scope of liability by holding that local governments could also be sued for damages for the unlawful actions of their officials.[1372, 1545]

See also: CIVIL RIGHTS CASES; CIVIL RIGHTS LEGISLATION; RACIAL DISCRIMINATION; STATES, IMMUNITY FROM SUITS IN FEDERAL COURT.

L

labor and labor laws   Until the New Deal, both COMMON LAW courts and the Supreme Court were hostile to the interests of laborers. The courts regularly struck down laws designed to protect labor organization and concerted activities. In the early part of the century, the Court's *"Allgeyer-Lochner-Adair-Coppage* doctrine," as Justice Black dubbed it,[1167] overturned state and federal laws that restrained and regulated certain working conditions and relationships. In 1918 the Court struck down a federal law against child labor,[857] in 1921 a state law prohibiting courts from stopping labor strikes and PICKETING,[2073] in 1925 a state law requiring arbitration of wage and hour disputes,[565] and as late as 1936 a federal law regulating wages and hours in the coal industry.[353] But in 1937 the Court overturned forty years of constitutional jurisprudence. Abolishing the old distinction between "direct" and "indirect" commerce, the Court sustained the National Labor Relations Act, which established the National Labor Relations Board and empowered it to regulate collective bargaining and to enforce new rules against unfair labor practices.[1430] That same year, the Court signaled that the overthrow of ECONOMIC DUE PROCESS would be deep and lasting. It upheld one law barring the use of INJUNCTIONS to stop peaceful strikes and picketing[1843] and also reversed its earlier stance against minimum wages, upholding a state minimum wage for female employees.[2184] Finally, in 1941 the Court sustained the Fair Labor Standards Act of 1938, broadly extending federal control over minimum wages and maximum hours in business generally.[514] Although in constitutional theory Congress may not regulate working conditions in businesses that are not in INTERSTATE COMMERCE, the Court has made it clear that little connection is necessary. As long as some interstate commerce is affected, the volume is not germane,[1429] and even an indirect connection is sufficient. For example, a retail oil distributor that sold only within its home state but purchased its supply from a wholesaler that in turn bought oil out of state was held to be sufficient interstate contact to be covered by federal law.[1431] In 1976 the Court rejected a congressional attempt to cover certain state employees under the Fair Labor Standards Act,[1434] but in 1985 the Court reversed itself,[724] so that, at the moment at least, Congress has broad power to regulate labor conditions in both the private and public sectors throughout the United States.

See also: BOYCOTT; CHILD LABOR; FREEDOM OF CONTRACT; LABOR INJUNCTION; LABOR UNIONS; LOCHNER V. NEW YORK; PUBLIC EMPLOYMENT; YELLOW-DOG CONTRACT.

labor injunction From the earliest years of the nineteenth century, the courts issued IN-JUNCTIONS to prohibit workers from engaging in concerted activity, such as strikes and PICK-ETING, to force employers to provide better working conditions and higher wages. Courts enjoined even peaceful activity, viewing it as mere prelude to violence. By the early twentieth century, state legislatures began to pass laws providing some protection for collective activities of workers. To counter judicial hostility toward laborers, the Arizona legislature enacted an anti-injunction law, prohibiting the courts from enjoining strikes, picketing, and advertisements and leaflets about strikes. In 1921 the Supreme Court invalidated this law, holding that by barring a judicial remedy to protect businesses from the effects of strikes, intimidation, and even LIBEL, employers were denied DUE PROCESS of law.[2073] But in 1937 the Court upheld a very similar state ban on injunctions against picketing.[1843] In 1938 the Court choked off the employers' alternative of seeking a federal injunction, by sustaining the Norris-La-Guardia Act. Enacted six years earlier, the law prohibited federal courts from issuing labor injunctions except under rare circumstances in which the employer can demonstrate that unions or workers will cause irreparable harm through unlawful, not merely economically harmful, actions.[1129]

See also: LABOR AND LABOR LAWS *and cross references listed there.*

labor unions Until 1937, the power of state legislatures and Congress to fashion and support a basic right to unionize was highly suspect in the courts, which relied on a now-discredited theory of FREEDOM OF CONTRACT. Summing up judicial attitudes before the New Deal, Justice Felix Frankfurter wrote in 1949: "[U]nionization encountered the shibboleths of a premachine age. . . . Basic human rights expressed by the constitutional conception of 'liberty' were equated with theories of *laissez faire.* The result was that economic views of confined validity were treated by lawyers and judges as though the Framers had enshrined them in the Constitution. . . ."[50] The watershed year was 1937, when the Court upheld the National Labor Relations Act, which created the modern system of collective bargaining, protected the right of workers to form and join unions, and required employers to deal with them.[1430] During the next several years, the Court swept away laws that hampered workers from meeting and PICKETING. It overturned a municipal policy against assembling to discuss labor issues,[838] a law barring picketing intended to hinder a business,[2044] and a law requiring union organizers to register with authorities before talking to workers.[2038] However, the right to organize and picket is far from absolute. The Court has upheld restrictions in the federal labor laws against many forms of picketing, including secondary boycotts. Recently, serious questions have arisen over whether workers can be compelled to join unions or pay dues for activities with which they disagree. The Court has held that although employees may often be required to join or to pay dues to unions as though they were members, the unions may not spend compulsory dues on political activities, either candidates or causes, that are not relevant to the union's primary activity as a collective bargaining representative for its members.[4]

See also: FREEDOM OF ASSOCIATION; LOWER-VALUE SPEECH; SPEECH, FREEDOM FROM PAYING FOR OTHERS'.

lame-duck Congress, *see:* **Twentieth Amendment**

landmark preservation, *see:* **taking of property**

law, *see:* **administrative regulations; common law; legislation; state law, meaning of**

law of nations Art. I-§8[10] authorizes Congress to punish offenses against the law of nations. This is constitutional language for what we know today as INTERNATIONAL LAW.

law of the land The phrase "law of the land" originated in MAGNA CARTA in 1215, where it signified that the king could no longer do whatever he pleased but would, instead, be bound by a mystical fundamental law that surpassed even the sovereign in power. In the mid-fourteenth century, the phrase "DUE PROCESS" appeared, and for centuries thereafter the phrases were used interchangeably—for example, in the English Petition of Right in 1628. In the earliest state constitutions in this country, as in the NORTHWEST ORDINANCE of 1787, "law of the land" was used exclusively to connote government fidelity to law. In the FIFTH AMENDMENT and later the FOURTEENTH AMENDMENT, the U.S. Constitution used the due process terminology exclusively, though that language carried with it strong overtones of the more ancient phrase. By the late nineteenth century, the Supreme Court was reading the Due Process Clauses substantively, finding in them a faint residue of the old "law of the land" concept, even though the Due Process Clauses seemed to be purely procedural. The Constitution uses the phrase "law of the land" only once, in the SUPREMACY CLAUSE, which says that the Constitution, federal laws, and treaties are the "supreme law of the land," at least suggesting, therefore, that there can be no anterior, free-floating law to which even the Constitution may be subordinated.

See also: NATURAL LAW.

lawmaking by courts The textbook view that legislatures make law and courts interpret it is not only naive but ahistorical. Over the centuries, the basic principles of contracts, torts, property relations, wills, and trusts, among other branches of the COMMON LAW, were largely an invention of the judges, not the legislatures. Judicial lawmaking aroused no general cries of illegitimacy because, on the one hand, voting and representative institutions were only weakly developed, and, on the other hand, no one supposed that the courts were *making* the law at all. Legal thinkers believed, rather, that judges "discovered" or "found" the law and then merely "declared" it in announcing how they were resolving disputes of the parties before them. This notion was part of a larger belief that law was found, not made. Centuries ago, even the occasional legislative enactment was thought to be not new law but a restatement of ancient, existing law. But even when people became realistic enough to admit that legislatures could make law, they continued to assert the myth that judges could not. Alexander Hamilton, in *Federalist* 78, wrote that the Supreme Court "may truly be said to have neither FORCE nor WILL but merely judgment."

Throughout the nineteenth century, jurists clung to the notion at the same time that Congress and state legislatures began to discover their powers after the Civil War. Into the twentieth century, many courts sharply limited the reach of legislation on the ground that common law must prevail. In 1917 Justice Oliver Wendell Holmes began an assault on this misconception: "The common law is not a brooding omnipresence in the sky, but the articulate voice of some sovereign." [1920] But if the law is made, not discovered, who is to make it—legislatures, or also courts? Holmes said that "judges do and must legislate, but they can do so only interstitially." Or, as Justice Felix Frankfurter more accessibly phrased the idea: "I used to say to my students that legislatures make law wholesale, judges retail." The growing understanding that judges do indeed make law undercut the assertions of Supreme Court justices, especially in their SUBSTANTIVE DUE PROCESS decisions, that they were only interpreting the

Constitution—that is, discovering constitutional law—not writing their own policy preferences into the Constitution. In 1936 Justice Owen J. Roberts struck down the Agricultural Adjustment Act of 1933, saying: "When an act of Congress is appropriately challenged in the courts as not conforming to the constitutional mandate, the judicial branch of the Government has only one duty,—to lay the article of the Constitution which is invoked beside the statute which is challenged and to decide whether the latter squares with the former."[289] But this was the last gasp of "mechanical jurisprudence," the idea that the courts are just neutral calculating machines. Within a year, Justice Roberts switched sides, and the Court withdrew from imposing its own economic views on legislation. A generation later, however, it began a new era of broad policy making, this time in the field of social relations, an era which the Court in the 1990s may be trying to close.

See also: DUE PROCESS; MAJORITARIANISM; PRIVACY; STRICT CONSTRUCTION.

lawyers Despite the prominent role of lawyers in the American political and legal systems, the Constitution does not mention them. There is no constitutional requirement that judges be lawyers, although it has always been assumed that the federal judiciary would be staffed by lawyers. Alexander Hamilton noted in *Federalist* 78 that "a voluminous code of laws is one of the inconveniences necessarily connected with the advantages of a free government.... [I]t will readily be conceived from the variety of controversies which grow out of the folly and wickedness of mankind that the records of those precedents must unavoidably swell to a very considerable bulk and must demand long and laborious study to acquire a competent knowledge of them."

Unlike other professionals, lawyers have, at least in theory, been held up to special scrutiny by the courts. Though it is a commonplace to say that lawyers are "officers of the court," the phrase is relatively meaningless, serving only as a reminder that some aspects of their behavior are subject to judicial discipline within constitutional limits. Most states prohibit lawyers from making out-of-court statements about their pending cases if they know, or should know, that the statements will "have a substantial likelihood of materially prejudicing" the proceeding. In a 1991 case, a Nevada criminal defense lawyer held a press conference after his client was indicted and said the police had made the defendant into a scapegoat for their own crimes. The Nevada State Bar reprimanded the lawyer, who appealed to the Supreme Court on the ground that the reprimand violated his FREEDOM OF SPEECH. A five-justice majority agreed, although all the justices agreed that there may be times when the state may prohibit discussion of pending cases.[739]

The special relationship of lawyer to court has not stopped the Supreme Court from striking down a rule that only American citizens could be admitted to law practice,[817] or that only the citizens of a state could be permitted to practice in its courts.[1984, 1985, 127] However, the Court has sustained state-mandated lawyer-protectionist policies forcing litigants to hire local attorneys when going to court. A particularly egregious example was a Kansas rule that required a lawyer who was a citizen of Kansas, admitted to practice in Kansas, and who maintained an office in Kansas to hire another Kansas attorney as "associate counsel" every time he went to court, solely because he also happened to have an office in Missouri in which he spent the majority of his working time.[1254]

In the late 1950s and early 1960s, a deeply divided Court held that lawyers could be denied admission to the bar for refusing to answer questions about membership in the Communist party, even if they disavowed any belief in the legitimacy of violence or the overthrow of the government.[1093] In 1971, however, a still-divided Court veered sharply away from this position, holding that since mere membership in an organization may not be punished, refusals to answer questions about membership may not be the basis for prohibiting someone from practicing a profession.[105, 1960]

Membership in lawyers' organizations has also raised constitutional difficulties. In 1961 the Court declined to consider whether lawyers may be compelled to join an "integrated" bar.[1127] The term refers not to racial integration but to a statewide organization that all lawyers admitted to practice in the state must join, or at least to which they must pay dues. But in 1990, after several rulings against improper use of union dues, the Court held that the State Bar of California would violate the FIRST AMENDMENT if it spent part of members' compulsory dues on ideological or political activities unrelated to the bar's twin mission of regulating the profession and "improving the quality of legal service available to the people of the state."[1057]

The Court has also dealt extensively with problems of lawyer advertising and solicitation of clients.

See also: ALIENS; COUNSEL, ASSISTANCE OF; GAG ORDER; INEFFECTIVE ASSISTANCE OF COUNSEL; MEMBERSHIP IN POLITICAL PARTIES; PROFESSIONALS, ADVERTISING BY; SOLICITATION; SPEECH, FREEDOM FROM PAYING FOR OTHERS'.

lawyers' advertising, *see:* **professionals, advertising by**

lawyers' fees   The Court has upheld a variety of legislative schemes limiting the amount that lawyers may collect from their clients and even effectively prohibiting lawyers from being paid, against challenges that such limitations violate FREEDOM OF CONTRACT or DUE PROCESS. In 1925, for example, the Court held that Nebraska could prohibit a lawyer from charging a

client whatever fee they negotiated for representation in a workers' compensation case. Speaking for a unanimous Court, Justice Oliver Wendell Holmes said that the state court could set the fee because "a large proportion" of injured workers "need to be protected against improvident contracts, in the interest not only of themselves and their families but of the public."[2274] In 1985 the Court sustained a federal limitation of ten dollars on the fees that lawyers can collect for representing members of the armed forces who seek disability benefits from the Veterans Administration.[2148] Disability claims should be reviewed in a nonadversary forum "designed to function throughout with a high degree of informality and solicitude for the claimant" and to minimize extensive litigation that would deplete the resources available for claims. In 1990 the Court sustained a law permitting the secretary of labor to set fees for lawyers representing black lung disease claimants in administrative hearings and to bar any fees except when the claimant wins an award.[2101] The Court held that the contingency fee arrangement and lengthy delays in paying lawyers did not deprive claimants from obtaining the effective assistance of counsel. Had Congress barred fees altogether, however, the Court conceivably would have reached a different result. As Justice Thurgood Marshall noted in a CONCURRING OPINION, the claim procedures are "highly" adversary. Lawyers for the Labor Department and mine operators "actively oppose the award of benefits to a claimant at all levels of the black lung system" and the claim process is therefore "qualitatively different from the Veterans' Administration system." The Court has also upheld a federal FORFEITURE law permitting the government to seize a defendant's assets, even if paid as a lawyer's fee, if the assets constituted or derived from the proceeds of drug violations.[339]

See also: COUNSEL, ASSISTANCE OF.

leaflets, distribution of, *see:* **permit system; solicitation**

leaks Leaks are unauthorized disclosures of information, usually, though not necessarily, from the government. Leaking is a high art form in Washington, practiced by all sides, to doom some policy proposal or to embarrass a political enemy by airing secrets to the press. In a recent sensational leak, law professor Anita Hill accused Supreme Court nominee Clarence Thomas of sexual harassment. Once leaked, the charges led to the dramatic televised hearings that came close to derailing the nomination. Since in the nature of things a leak will upset someone in the government, the question often arises whether the government has legal authority to stop the press from publishing leaked information or to punish the leakers afterward. In the PENTAGON PAPERS CASE, the Court in 1971 held, 6–3, that except in an extraordinary case, PRIOR RESTRAINT against publication is unconstitutional.[1473] Whether the government may demand that publishers or reporters reveal the names of those who supplied secret information is less clear. There is no general REPORTER'S PRIVILEGE against disclosing the names of sources,[225] but the Court has never decided whether a general subpoena to obtain the names of sources is enforceable to permit the leakers to be prosecuted. After the journalists who first reported Professor Hill's charges refused to tell a Senate committee who their sources were, a Senate lawyer threatened to issue a subpoena. Defiance of the subpoena could have led to CONTEMPT citations and jailing. But the Senate committee refused to authorize the subpoenas, and the issue was not tested.

See also: RIGHT TO KNOW.

least restrictive means, *see:* **less restrictive alternative or means**

legal procedure, *see:* **judicial procedure in state courts**

legal tender Legal tender is the form of payment that courts recognize as legal satisfaction of debt—that is, the type of payment tendered to the creditor. Congress has exclusive authority to determine what tender shall be legal—gold, silver, or paper currency. Under Art. I-§10[1], the states are denied power to fix legal tender in anything other than gold or silver, but Congress may supersede this rule, and it has done so.

See also: BILLS OF CREDIT; BORROWING POWER.

legislation Legislation is law enacted by a legislature. A particular enactment is known as a "statute," as distinct from rules and regulations promulgated by ADMINISTRATIVE AGENCIES or HOLDINGS of courts that have legal effects beyond the immediate parties. For Congress to enact a law, a majority of each house must approve an identically worded bill; then, the president must sign it, or refrain from vetoing it, or Congress must override the presidential veto by reenacting the bill by a two-thirds vote. To be constitutional, legislation must be within the LEGISLATIVE POWER of the legislature and not overstep any constitutional limitations imposed on the legislature, such as the prohibitions against EX POST FACTO laws and BILLS OF ATTAINDER.

See also: ADMINISTRATIVE LAW; COMMON LAW; CONGRESS, POWERS OF; LEGISLATIVE VETO; MOTIVE, INTENT, AND PURPOSE; PRESUMPTION OF CONSTITUTIONALITY; SEPARATION OF POWERS; STATE LAW, MEANING OF.

legislative apportionment, *see:* **apportionment of political districts**

legislative courts, *see:* **Article I courts**

legislative fact In general, legislative facts are facts used by courts and legislatures that permit a court to uphold a particular law as constitutional. DUE PROCESS prohibits an arbitrary or irrational law, as in the obviously silly example that a law against wearing clothes with pockets out of doors could not be constitutionally justified by asserting that it would minimize the number of people who carry concealed weapons. So irrational a law could be saved only if it could be shown that the legislature knew that most concealed weapons are carried in pockets and that pockets are used for almost no other purpose. In other words, to prove the rationality of a law, its defenders must be able to point to some reality that justifies it. That reality is legislative fact.

Legislative facts are usually assumed and are rarely introduced into evidence at trial. For example, a law against carrying concealed weapons would withstand constitutional challenge since there is an obvious connection between concealment and the danger that the legislature has every right to legislate against. Legislative facts are often noted in a legislative committee's report on a bill, and sometimes are recited in the preamble to the bill itself. Unless the legislature's assertions are irrational, as sometimes happens when the legislature is motivated by extraneous purposes, the courts defer to its judgment.

A well-known exception occurred in *Southern Pacific Co. v. Arizona* in 1945. The Arizona Train Limit Law of 1912 outlawed trains longer than fourteen passenger cars or seventy freight cars. In a suit to collect penalties against a railroad for violating the law, the state answered charges that the law unconstitutionally burdened INTERSTATE COMMERCE by pointing to its strong interest in safety. The trial judge spent more than five months hearing evidence that after thirty years the law no longer served its purpose and actually was more likely to cause accidents than deter them. The hearing record was 3,000 pages long, and the judge's FINDINGS covered nearly 150 pages, only five of which were devoted to the law of the case. The Supreme Court sustained the trial judge's approach, holding that the legislative facts demonstrated that the "law had no reasonable relation to safety" and did not outweigh the national interest in an "economical and efficient railway transportation system."

See also: BRANDEIS BRIEF; MOTIVE, INTENT, AND PURPOSE; PRESUMPTION OF CONSTITUTIONALITY.

legislative intent When a law's language is unclear, the courts inquire into what the legislature intended in order to help understand what a law really means. Judges also use legislative intent to gauge whether the legislature had a constitutionally valid purpose in enacting the law. The justices have different philosophies about whether legislative intent is a valid means of construing statutes, but at one time or another the courts, and the Supreme Court in particular, have been forced to consider the legislature's intent. The question comes up frequently in PREEMPTION questions—whether Congress intended that state laws should be disregarded when they overlap but do not directly conflict with federal laws.

Often the quest for legislative intent is a fig leaf for judicial policy making. For example, the Court sometimes infers from a federal law that private litigants have a right to sue for DAMAGES or other relief, even though Congress has expressed no intent for them to be able to do so. The question then arises what remedies the courts may afford in such suits. The answer can only dubiously be found in legislative intent. As Justice Antonin Scalia has observed: "Quite obviously, the search for what was Congress's remedial intent as to a right whose very existence Congress did not expressly acknowledge is unlikely to succeed."[696]

Another issue is whether judges may, or can, determine intent solely from the language of the statute or can look, as well, at evidence such as committee reports or speeches by members on the floor of Congress. Many of the same difficulties that attend the deciphering of the ORIGINAL INTENT of the Framers apply to the search for the legislature's meaning. Is the "collective intent" of Congress a meaningful concept? If not, whose intent governs—a majority of the members? the floor managers of the bill? the chair of the committee reporting the bill? the actual drafters, who are hired staff lawyers? And how can their intent be discerned? from the committee reports? from floor speeches? These may or may not be useful or reveal the true intent of those who voted for the measure. The Court has given no definitive answers to these questions.

See also: MOTIVE, INTENT, AND PURPOSE; PRIVATE RIGHT OF ACTION.

legislative investigation, *see:* **investigatory powers of legislature**

legislative power   Legislative power is the power to make law. The Constitution grants this power to Congress and limits it to enumerated subjects. These subjects are found mainly in Art. I-§8, but other congressional powers are contained in Articles II, III, IV, and V, and in several amendments, including, most importantly, the Civil War amendments. That Congress is not confined to legislating narrowly is due in part to the latitude conveyed in the NECESSARY AND PROPER CLAUSE. Unlike the JUDICIAL POWER, Congress's legislative power is self-executing; that is, it may initiate laws on its own and for any reason, within the bounds of the Constitution. The Constitution requires Congress to exercise its legislative power in a certain way—a bill becomes a law only after both houses, by majority vote, have separately agreed to its exact wording and the president has signed it, or at least refrained from vetoing it. Congress may override a presidential veto by a vote of two-thirds of the members present. Despite the clear command of Art. I-§1[1] that

"all legislative power herein granted shall be vested in a Congress," the Court has held that Congress has broad leeway to delegate its power to the EXECUTIVE BRANCH.

See also: BICAMERALISM; CONGRESS, POWERS OF; DELEGATION DOCTRINE; ENUMERATED POWERS; EXECUTIVE POWER; LAWMAKING BY COURTS; LEGISLATIVE VETO; ORDER, RESOLUTION, OR VOTE; PRESENTMENT; SEPARATION OF POWERS; VETO POWER.

legislative veto   When Congress delegates LEGISLATIVE POWER to federal agencies, it cannot directly control the details of resulting regulations or other actions of the president and EXECUTIVE BRANCH officials. Beginning in the 1930s, Congress sought a veto power over the rules promulgated or actions taken by the executive under a congressional delegation of authority. Legislative veto provisions in such laws permitted either house of Congress to pass a resolution of disapproval of executive action. Some legislative vetoes required both houses to disapprove by passing a concurrent resolution. By 1983, when the Supreme Court struck them down, Congress had enacted at least two hundred laws providing for legislative vetoes. In *Immigration and Naturalization Service v. Chadha*, the Court invalidated a legislative veto in the Immigration and Naturalization Act. The act authorizes the attorney general to suspend a decision by the Immigration and Naturalization Service to deport an ALIEN. Using a legislative veto, either house of Congress could set aside the attorney general's suspension. In other words, either house could restore the original DEPORTATION order. The Court reasoned that the legislative veto was an exercise of legislative power and that Congress may exercise this power only in the manner provided in Art. I-§7[2,3]. First, by majority vote, each house must approve a bill or resolution. But since many legislative vetoes could be accomplished by a single house, they violated this requirement of BICAMERALISM. Second, each bill that Congress passes must be presented to the president. But since the whole point of a legislative veto was to disapprove an executive action, they all failed this requirement because they took effect without being submitted to the president.

In essence, *Chadha* says that Congress may delegate its powers to executive agencies but not to one of its own houses. This constitutional mutation arises because when legislative power is delegated to the executive, it suddenly becomes EXECUTIVE POWER[211] unless it is reclaimed by Congress, whereupon it miraculously becomes legislative once more.

In any event, the consequence of *Chadha* was to kill all legislative vetoes, though not necessarily to stymie Congress in its attempts to shape administrative regulations and executive action. By the Court's reasoning, the only way Congress can disapprove an ensuing regulation is to pass a law repealing it. Such a law requires the president's signature, or a two-thirds majority willing to override his veto. But in fact Congress has other means to impose its will on the executive besides simply legislating anew. For example, a delegation may provide that the ensuing executive rule or action will *not* become law unless both houses pass a joint resolution. Because Congress has almost complete power over federal spending, it may refuse to appropriate moneys for the operation of programs or rules that either house dislikes. Moreover, federal agencies pay attention to congressional oversight committees, so expressions of disapproval even from a committee may be sufficient to derail or change many rules and executive actions.

See also: DELEGATION DOCTRINE.

legislatures, state, *see:* **state legislatures**

Lemon test In 1971, in *Lemon v. Kurtzman,* the Supreme Court announced a three-pronged test for determining whether a law or govern-

ment expenditure violates the FIRST AMENDMENT by creating an establishment of religion: "First, the statute must have a secular legislative purpose; second, its principal or primary effect must be one that neither advances nor inhibits religion; finally, the statute must not foster an excessive government entanglement with religion." Under this test, a state law that violates any one of the prongs must be struck down. For over twenty years, critics have sharply debated whether the *Lemon* test is useful in determining how far the state may go in aiding a religious institution or religion generally. The Court has been close to schizophrenic on the issue of state subsidies. In *Lemon* itself, the Court unanimously held that Pennsylvania could not use public funds to provide textbooks for parochial school students or to pay their teachers' salaries. In 1968 the Court held that states may lend textbooks to parochial schools.[46] In 1977 it held that states may not lend maps or magazines.[2246] The inconsistencies are a reflection of precarious majorities and a changing Court membership. Dissatisfaction with the *Lemon* test may lead the Court to abandon it. For many years, Justice Sandra Day O'Connor has been promoting an "endorsement" test: any law or governmental practice is unconstitutional if it endorses a religion or religion generally. In 1989 a majority of five spoke in favor of this test.[37] But since the four dissenters remain on the Court and two members of the majority, Justices William Brennan and Thurgood Marshall have since retired, it is unclear at this writing whether or to what degree *Lemon* has been or will be supplanted.

See also: CHAPLAINS; ESTABLISHMENT CLAUSE; RELIGIOUS ESTABLISHMENT.

lesbians, *see:* **homosexuality**

less restrictive alternative or means The Supreme Court sometimes strikes down laws that interfere with constitutional rights because the legislature could have achieved its purposes in a less blunderbuss fashion. When the state has a legitimate objective, the Court may insist that it use means that least restrict the exercise of constitutional rights. This insistence allows the Court to stop short of invalidating the government's objectives altogether and permits the state to achieve its purposes in some manner. For example, the Court struck down a law that required state judges to clear the courtroom whenever an underage witness testified about sexual offenses.[763] The law was much too broad, said the Court; the state could have found less restrictive means to shelter a particular witness from the embarrassment of public testimony. Similarly, a scheme that barred dairy farmers from selling their milk unless it had been pasteurized in certain plants within the state was voided because it was far too intrusive a regulation of INTERSTATE COMMERCE; to ensure safe milk the state could have relied on a less restrictive inspection system.[528] The requirement of a least or a less restrictive means is often used in FREEDOM OF SPEECH cases. In an important statement of this principle, the Court said in 1968 that a governmental regulation "unrelated to the suppression of free expression" would be upheld if "the incidental restriction on alleged FIRST AMENDMENT freedoms is not greater than" essential to carrying out an "important" or "substantial" governmental interest.[1508] Although the least restrictive alternative is often cited, its enduring vitality is open to question. In 1980, for example, the Court devised a four-part test to determine when a state could regulate COMMERCIAL SPEECH. The fourth prong of the test was whether "the governmental interest could be served as well by a more limited restriction."[361] But in 1989 the Court did away with the least restrictive means test, holding that it imposed too heavy a burden on the state. The Court substituted a "reasonableness" test—whether

the "fit between the legislature's ends and the means chosen . . . is [not necessarily perfect] but . . . narrowly tailored to achieve the desired objective."[189]

See also: COMPELLING INTEREST; STRICT SCRUTINY; SYMBOLIC SPEECH.

letters of marque and reprisal Under Art. I-§8[11], Congress may authorize private shipowners to interdict and seize the ships and property of U.S. enemies on the high seas. The authority is known as a "letter of marque and reprisal." Art. I-§10[1] prohibits states from granting such letters. The clause is now archaic; Congress has not commissioned privateers in a century and a half.

level of generality When the Court uses SUBSTANTIVE DUE PROCESS to decide a case, the central issue is whether the law or government practice at issue invades a fundamental LIBERTY or PROPERTY interest. The justices cannot look to the language of the Constitution to determine what is fundamental because substantive due process, by definition, involves a search for rights that lie outside the Constitution's text. So the justices must look to something else— for example, a venerable custom or tradition, or a deeply rooted value of the American people. The Court's PRIVACY rulings rest on the assumption that privacy is a fundamental liberty interest. But because privacy itself is a general term, the question remains in each case whether a particular sort of privacy is entitled to constitutional protection. In the first major privacy case, *Griswold v. Connecticut,* the Court struck down a law against the sale or distribution of contraceptives, even to a married couple. The Court stressed the intimacy of the MARRIAGE relationship to reach its decision. But the privacy right the Court announced could have been expressed in a more general way— for instance, the right to intimacy between any two people, or a right to procreate, or even a right to determine one's own lifestyle. The higher or broader the level of generality, the more kinds of cases will be encompassed and the easier it will be for judges to make policy.

Beginning in the late 1980s, Justices William Brennan and Antonin Scalia engaged in a debate about the appropriate level of generality to be used in characterizing certain rights to be protected.[1325] This debate is perhaps a more sophisticated version of the debate between Justices Hugo L. Black and Felix Frankfurter over the incorporation of rights in DUE PROCESS. Justice Scalia's position is twofold: under due process, the Court may shield only those interests "traditionally protected by our society" and then, only if the tradition is characterized at the most "specific" level of generality. Justice Brennan disagreed that tradition "places a discernible border around the Constitution." Other values besides those that can be fathomed from a tradition may be protected, he urged, and in any event, the concept of tradition itself is elusive.

The case in which this debate arose makes the issues clearer. Under California law, there is a legal PRESUMPTION that a woman's husband is the father of children born during their marriage. This presumption may be rebutted only in limited ways—for instance, by showing that the husband is sterile. The case arose when Michael H. claimed to be the father of Victoria, the child of Carole D. and Gerald D., and sued for visitation rights. A blood test confirmed that he was the father by a probability of 98.07 percent. The state courts held that Michael had not overcome the presumption and denied him visitation. The Supreme Court agreed, although without majority opinion.[1325] Justice Scalia said that California's unforgiving rule was intended to preserve "the relationships that develop within the unitary [or "marital"] family." Brennan said that the Court should have looked more generally to "parenthood" as an interest that due process protects. Scalia

responded that the Court must look to "the most specific level [of generality] at which a relevant tradition protecting, or denying protection to, the asserted right can be identified." Otherwise, he said, there is no stopping point, for someone else could argue that not only parenthood but "family relationships," "personal relationships," or even "emotional attachments in general" should be protected. Because general traditions are imprecise, "they permit judges to dictate rather than discern the society's views." Brennan retorted in turn that Scalia's PLURALITY OPINION "squashes [the freedom not to conform] by requiring specific approval from history before protecting anything in the name of liberty," which would make the Constitution a "stagnant, archaic, hidebound document."

The debate continues.[789, 281] Just before Brennan retired in 1991, a majority rejected Scalia's view that tradition and historical practice limit the search for rights protected by due process.[1552] Whether the Court will continue to reject it is an open question.

See also: INCORPORATION DOCTRINE.

libel and slander   Under common law, critical comments about the king or his government constituted SEDITIOUS LIBEL and were punishable by death or imprisonment. It was irrelevant if the critic was speaking the truth, for "the greater the truth, the greater the libel." The question of whether the FIRST AMENDMENT made unconstitutional the ALIEN AND SEDITION ACTS of 1798 never reached the Supreme Court because the laws expired in 1801. Sedition prosecutions disappeared for over a century, resurfacing only in the aftermath of World War I when defendants were accused not merely of criticizing the government but of directly inciting others to interfere with the war effort.

State common law also recognized a CAUSE OF ACTION for false statements that damage someone's reputation or bring a person into public contempt. The law of defamation of character boasted odd inconsistencies between the written (libel) and oral (slander) versions. Rules also varied from state to state for what constituted libel or slander, how it could be proved, who bore the burden of proof, and how to measure damages. Whatever bearing the First Amendment had on seditious libel, no one supposed that nongovernmental libels were entitled to constitutional protection. In 1942 Justice Frank Murphy, speaking for a unanimous Court, said that "the prevention and punishment" of "certain well-defined and narrowly limited classes of speech . . . have never been thought to raise any Constitutional problem [including] . . . the libelous."[372] But in 1964, in *New York Times v. Sullivan*, the Court inaugurated a constitutional revolution in libel.

The case arose in 1960 when colleagues of Martin Luther King, Jr., took out a full-page fund-raising advertisement in the *New York Times,* decrying "an unprecedented wave of terror" against peaceful black demonstrators in the South. One paragraph told of "truckloads of police armed with shotguns and tear-gas [who] ringed the Alabama State College Campus." L. B. Sullivan, the elected police commissioner of Montgomery, Alabama, sued the *Times* for libel. Although the ad had not named him, he contended that everyone in Montgomery understood the word "police" to refer to him and that they would suppose him responsible for the acts referred to in the ad. The ad misstated some minor events: for example, Martin Luther King was arrested four times, not seven. Sullivan's witnesses told the jury that they would not want to be associated with someone party to the events described in the ad, even though none testified that he had in fact shunned Sullivan on account of it. With no evidence of any actual harm, the jury awarded Sullivan five hundred thousand dollars—one thousand times more than the maximum sum

(five hundred dollars) allowed by the Alabama code for the crime of falsely and maliciously calling someone a criminal. The Alabama Supreme Court upheld the award, saying that the jury was entitled to consider that the *Times* had acted irresponsibly by failing to review its own prior account of the events in question. The Supreme Court unanimously reversed. The ad was protected by the First Amendment because it concerned "one of the major public issues of our time." Requiring proof of every assertion would have a CHILLING EFFECT on speech about public issues. Said Justice William Brennan: "A rule compelling the critic of official conduct to guarantee the truth of all his factual assertions—and to do so on pain of libel judgments virtually unlimited in amount—leads to . . . self-censorship. . . . Under such a rule, would-be critics of official conduct may be deterred from voicing their criticism, even though it is believed to be true and even though it is in fact true, because of doubt whether it can be proved in court or fear of the expense of having to do so. . . . The rule thus dampens the vigor and limits the variety of public debate."

Under the *New York Times v. Sullivan* rule, public officials may not recover DAMAGES for a "defamatory falsehood" unless the public official can prove that the false statement was made with "actual MALICE"—that is, "with knowledge that it was false or with reckless disregard of whether it was false or not." This rule applies not only to criticism of official conduct but also to attacks on the honesty and integrity of public officials, whether elected or appointed.[1373] It applies equally to civil libel suits and CRIMINAL LIBEL prosecutions,[731] as the Court ruled the same year in dismissing an indictment against New Orleans district attorney James Garrison.

The Court extended the actual-malice rule to PUBLIC FIGURES in 1967.[504, 91] If the plaintiff is a public figure, the subject of the libel need not be political to qualify for the actual-malice rule. In 1984 the Court held that the magazine *Consumer Reports* could not be held liable for a false statement in a review of audio speakers unless the manufacturer could show that the editors had acted with actual malice.[202] Otherwise, reviewers of all sorts would be constant targets of suits for inadvertent misstatements.

In 1971 the Court seemed to announce a sweeping extension of the rule to anyone caught up in a matter of public controversy, even if the person would otherwise have remained obscure.[1760] But the Court soon backed away, holding instead that private figures—people who have not thrust themselves into the limelight and have achieved no "general fame or notoriety in the community"—may recover damages for false defamatory statements by showing that the defendant was merely negligent. However, there must still be a showing of carelessness. A libel judgment may not stand if there is no showing of fault. Unless a private-figure plaintiff can demonstrate actual malice, there can be no PUNITIVE DAMAGES. The plaintiff may recover only "compensation for actual injury."[746] Moreover, the burden is on the plaintiff to prove that the statement over which he is suing is actually false; the defendant need not prove it to be true.[1620]

"Falsity" is not limited to direct contradictions of fact. False statements may appear in a more innocent guise. In 1991 the Court grappled with the problem of misquotation. In two articles in the *New Yorker* and later in a book, author Janet Malcolm wrote about a controversy surrounding the firing of Dr. Jeffrey Masson, a psychiatrist, as director of the Freud Archives. Masson charged that Malcolm falsely attributed to him several statements, placed in quotation marks in the articles and book, that he never said—including, for example, the statement that if he had continued as director, the archives "would have been a center of scholarship, but it would also have been a place of sex, women, and fun." Conceding that he was a public figure, Masson argued that actual malice could be shown simply by proving that Malcolm knew he had not said what she put inside quotation marks. He argued that only corrections of grammar and syntax could escape the actual-malice test. Malcolm countered that as long as what she quoted was a "rational interpretation" of what Masson actually said, there could be no actual malice. Justice Anthony M. Kennedy disagreed with both positions, holding that a concocted quotation can be the basis of a libel judgment against a public figure, but only if it constitutes a "material change in meaning."[1267]

Most of the post-*Sullivan* cases have been against media defendants—newspapers, magazines, book publishers, and radio and television stations. Some commentators have suggested that when a private figure sues a nonmedia defendant, the *Sullivan* rules should not apply. Although the Court has rejected the media-nonmedia distinction, it has held that punitive damage awards are permissible without proof of actual malice when both parties were private and the false statement was of no public concern. The case concerned a credit report issued by Dun and Bradstreet to a bank with a false statement that a contractor seeking credit had voluntarily entered bankruptcy proceedings. This was a matter "of purely private concern," said Justice Powell.[580]

See also: GROUP LIBEL; LOWER-VALUE SPEECH; MENTAL DISTRESS; OPINION-FACT DISTINCTION; PROOF, BURDEN OF.

liberty   The FIFTH and FOURTEENTH AMENDMENTS prohibit the government from denying liberty to any person without DUE PROCESS of law. This protection can mean that the government may ultimately deprive a person of liberty but only after fair procedures to determine that there is a sound reason to do so. It can also mean that the government is altogether forbidden from interfering with a person's freedom of action.

When the government proposes to deprive a person of liberty by locking him or her behind bars, due process requires that it abide by a battery of essential rights before, during, and after an impartial TRIAL BY JURY. The restraints on government action in the BILL OF RIGHTS are largely procedural, but many of them have a substantive effect on a person's liberty. For instance, under the EIGHTH AMENDMENT's ban on cruel and unusual PUNISHMENT, the state may not imprison a person at all if the offense was wholly involuntary,[1743] nor for a length of time grossly disproportionate to the offense committed.[1905] But for the most part, as long as the state abides by the procedural restraints in the Constitution, it is constitutionally permitted, after a guilty verdict, to strip the defendant of liberty, sometimes for life.

Beginning in the late nineteenth century, the Supreme Court, extending the concept of liberty protected by due process, devised the doctrine of FREEDOM OF CONTRACT—the notion that the government may not regulate hours or wages or working conditions, for instance, because to do so is to interfere with the inalienable right of one person to make a deal with another. In 1923 Justice James McReynolds declared that "without doubt," liberty "denotes not merely freedom from bodily restraint but also the right of the individual to contract, to engage in any of the common occupations of life, to acquire useful knowledge, to marry, establish a home and bring up children, to worship God according to the dictates of his own conscience, and generally to enjoy those privileges long recognized at common law as essential to the orderly pursuit of happiness by free men."[1323] This liberty interest was broad enough in the 1920s to invalidate state laws dictating the kinds of schools that children must attend[1628] and to apply FREEDOM OF SPEECH principles to the states.[670] In time, lib-

erty would assume an even broader meaning. The principal modern outgrowth of the Court's developing doctrine of SUBSTANTIVE DUE PROCESS is the right to PRIVACY, which confers on everyone a zone of autonomy from state regulation in matters including ABORTION, procreation, family relations, and even the RIGHT TO DIE.

In 1970 the Court advanced a new conception of liberty, though changes on the Court halted development far short of its potential. The problem the Court addressed was the government's denial of ENTITLEMENTS provided by legislation, such as welfare payments, unemployment compensation, jobs, and similar benefits, to particular recipients. Because these entitlement programs are not constitutionally required, the benefits had long been considered "privileges" that the government could unilaterally refuse to provide. A one-time Court majority saw that the Due Process Clauses protected a recipient from suffering a "grievous loss," because the loss would impair a liberty or property interest. This conception of liberty and property as freedom from grievous loss was procedural only. The constitutional difficulty is not that the government was refusing, reducing, or ending someone's benefits, but that it was doing so without first affording the recipient a fair HEARING.

The Court first announced this new "civil procedural due process" right in *Goldberg v. Kelly*, in which a 6–3 majority, speaking through Justice William Brennan, said that New York State could not withdraw welfare benefits without giving the recipient a chance to contest the state's decision to do so. To terminate before a hearing "may deprive an *eligible* recipient of the very means by which to live while he waits." The hearing need not be in court, but the administrative body must afford the recipient a panoply of procedural rights, including the right to present evidence orally before an impartial decision maker, to confront and cross-examine adverse witnesses, to be represented by a lawyer, and to have a statement from the hearing officer about what evidence was relied on and what the basis for the decision was.

Goldberg did not bar the government from terminating an entitlement in an appropriate case. It held, rather, that like criminal due process, the state may burden liberty only by following proper procedures. For several years after *Goldberg*, the Court found liberty interests in an assortment of government benefits or actions: driver's licenses,[145] the public posting of a person's name as an alcoholic,[2236] the status of parolees,[1390] the conditions under which pretrial detainees are held,[147] the transfer of a prisoner to a mental hospital,[2133] a student's desire to remain in school,[785] a prisoner's refusal of antipsychotic drugs,[2160] and corporal punishment in schools.[980] But the Court's majority wavered and shifted as different claims were pressed. In many other cases, the Court did not find a liberty interest: loss of reputation because the police erroneously labeled someone an "active shoplifter,"[1578] the practice of a state pardons board in reducing life sentences of some but not all applicants,[451] and the mistaken discharge of a public employee.[166]

By the 1980s, new Court majorities made it clear that they would examine separately a litigant's claim to have been deprived of a liberty or property interest, rather than lumping the two interests together to find a generalized "loss." As a result, the new procedural due process revolution has been contained to certain relatively narrow kinds of interests, explored in somewhat more detail under the heading PROCESS RIGHTS. The Court has also made it clear that discerning a claimant's liberty interest is only half the case. Not every interest is entitled to the same kind of hearing. The question of what the state must do when it proposes to invade or terminate an entitlement is explored under the entry PROCESS THAT IS DUE.

See also: BITTER WITH THE SWEET; CIVIL COMMITMENT; GOVERNMENT, AFFIRMATIVE OBLIGATIONS OF; PREVENTIVE DETENTION; PRISONERS' RIGHTS; PROCEDURAL DUE PROCESS; RIGHT-PRIVILEGE DISTINCTION; REPRODUCTIVE RIGHTS.

liberty of contract, *see:* **contract, right to**

libraries, *see:* **readers' rights**

licensing laws, *see:* **occupational licensing; right-privilege distinction**

life, *see:* **abortion; death penalty; punishment, cruel and unusual**

limited government, *see:* **checks and balances; enumerated powers**

line-item veto It is a firmly established political convention that a presidential veto kills an entire bill, no matter how extensive it is or how many different provisions it contains. Pork-barrel and log-rolling politics often stuffs widely disparate subjects into enacted bills, forcing presidents to agree to some unwanted policies or appropriations to gain those they do find acceptable. Since Ulysses S. Grant, many presidents have pressed Congress to grant them a line-item veto—that is, authority to veto selectively those provisions they do not wish to see enshrined in law. Whether Congress could do so is doubtful, but in any event it has never wanted to do so, nor has any president unilaterally assumed the power. The question has never reached the Supreme Court.

See also: ORDER, RESOLUTION, OR VOTE; VETO POWER.

lineup A lineup is a proceeding in which witnesses to a crime attempt to identify the suspect as the perpetrator by picking him out from a group of people. In 1967 the Supreme Court held that because a lineup is a "critical stage in a criminal proceeding" the defendant is entitled to counsel under the SIXTH AMENDMENT. A lineup identification of a defendant whose lawyer was not present during the proceeding is inadmissible at trial.[2139, 754] In 1972 the Court limited the reach of this rule to lineups conducted after the "initiation of adversary criminal proceedings, whether by way of formal charge, preliminary hearing, INDICTMENT, INFORMATION, or ARRAIGNMENT."[1080]

When the police rig a lineup or other identification procedure to lead the witness to identify the person in custody, it may violate DUE PROCESS, depending on the "totality of circumstances."

In the case in which the Court announced this rule, the suspect was handcuffed to a policeman and brought to the victim's hospital room, where he was recovering from a stabbing. Asked whether the prisoner was "the man," the patient identified him. The suspect was the only black person among seven white police officers in the hospital room. The Court disallowed the identification testimony.[1966] Another doubtful procedure is having the victim first observe and identify the suspect immediately following a formal preliminary hearing in court, rather than having an independent lineup out of court at a later time. Seeing a suspect formally identified by the justice system may lead a witness to suppress her doubts.[1381] The Court has found less objectionable the use of pictures for identification, holding that the defendant's lawyer need not be present when the victim or witness is shown pictures and asked whether he or she can identify the perpetrator, even if the defendant has already been indicted, and even though the risk is as great as at a lineup of signaling to a witness who the police think the perpetrator is.[83]

See also: COUNSEL, ASSISTANCE OF; PROCEDURAL RIGHTS OF CRIMINAL DEFENDANTS.

liquor, *see:* **intoxicating beverages**

listeners' rights, *see:* **readers' rights**

literacy tests   Beginning in 1890, many southern states made the ability to read and write a condition for registering to vote. Statistics showed that two-thirds of black citizens were illiterate, as compared to only one-quarter of whites, so literacy was a useful device for states bent on circumventing the FIFTEENTH AMENDMENT right to vote. Despite these laws, various devices were used to allow illiterate whites to register, including GRANDFATHER CLAUSES and highly selective and discriminatory enforcement of the literacy test requirement. Often whites were simply excused from the test. Often blacks were required to satisfactorily "interpret" certain passages from the Constitution or laws according to the wholly subjective judgment of state election officials. In 1949 the Court invalidated such subjective literacy tests;[1821] but in 1959 the justices unanimously rejected the contention that literacy tests as such are unconstitutional, holding that the ability to read and write is related to "intelligent use of the ballot."[1125]

Literacy tests were finally abolished by Congress, in four steps. First, in the original VOTING RIGHTS ACT OF 1965, Congress banned literacy tests in certain states and counties for five years; the Court upheld the law as a constitutional exercise of Congress's power to enforce the equal voting provision of the Fifteenth Amendment.[1913] Second, Congress also required states to enfranchise Puerto Ricans literate in Spanish, even if they could not read English; the Court upheld that provision as well.[1053] Third, in 1970 Congress temporarily suspended literacy tests nationwide, and the Court unanimously affirmed its power to do so.[1537] Finally, in 1975 Congress permanently banned literacy tests. The ban has not been challenged in the Supreme Court.

See also: VOTING, RIGHT TO.

litigation, right to Although there is no general constitutional right to file a lawsuit, the Supreme Court has discerned in the FIRST AMENDMENT a constitutional interest against state interference with activities designed to make it easier for a litigant to sue. Historically, the state courts have prohibited lawyers from engaging in a range of supposedly unethical activities, including "ambulance chasing," SOLICITATION, aiding the "unauthorized practice of law" by nonlawyers, and the use of "lay intermediaries"—nonlawyer agents who assist in or help pay for litigation in which they have no legal interest. Virginia used these ethical restrictions to bar the National Association for the Advancement of Colored People from soliciting plaintiffs in suits against racially discriminatory public schools and to make it more difficult for lawyers to cooperate with the NAACP in those suits. In a 6–3 decision in 1963, Justice William Brennan said that the NAACP's activities, "vigorous advocacy of . . . lawful ends, against governmental intrusion, . . . are modes of expression and association" protected by the First Amendment.[1417] Litigation is "a form of political expression" because it "may well be the sole practicable avenue open to a minority to petition for redress of grievances." The Court broadened this principle throughout the 1960s, striking down various lawyer referral and fee arrangements negotiated by unions on behalf of their memberships. The Court held, for example, that states may not prohibit unions from advising their members to seek legal advice before settling personal injury claims or from referring workers to particular lawyers,[246] from employing a salaried lawyer to help with workers' compensation claims,[2096] or from pressing selected lawyers to agree that they would not charge members more than twenty-five percent of whatever recovery they won in federal workers' compensation cases in return for the union's recommendation that members seek their assistance.[2110]

See also: LAWYERS and cross references listed there.

live performances, *see:* **entertainment as protected speech**

livestock, commerce in, *see:* **stream of commerce**

loan-sharking, *see:* **interstate commerce**

lobbying "Lobbying" is writing and speaking designed to influence legislators to vote, act, or refrain from acting in certain ways. In 1946 Congress enacted a detailed registration and reporting requirement for professional congressional lobbyists. Because the FREEDOM OF PETITION protects an individual's right to write or speak to elected officials, the question arose whether the FIRST AMENDMENT permits such regulations. Construing the law narrowly to avoid constitutional difficulties, the Court held that the law is constitutional if read to apply only to those who receive money for lobbying on behalf of others directly with members of Congress.[875] However, the government may not constitutionally prosecute business enterprises under the antitrust laws for joining hands in lobbying the legislature to enact, or the executive to enforce, laws that would hurt their competitors.[593] Likewise, the First Amendment protects the concerted efforts of business interests to deter competition and even to injure their competitors by costly and time-consuming resistance to their competitors' petitions to ADMINISTRATIVE AGENCIES and courts.[325]

local government, *see:* **political subdivisions**

local taxes, *see:* **property taxes; taxation by states; taxation of interstate commerce**

Lochner v. New York   More than any other case, *Lochner v. New York* is the symbol of the Supreme Court's forty-year odyssey of ECO-NOMIC DUE PROCESS, during which the justices wrote their economic predilections into the Constitution. New York passed a law prohibiting bakeries from working their bakers more than ten hours a day and sixty hours a week. Fined for a greater than sixty-hour work week in his bakery in Utica, New York, Lochner appealed his conviction, asserting that the DUE PROCESS Clause of the FOUR-TEENTH AMENDMENT protected the employee's liberty of contract. In 1905 a bare majority of the Court agreed. Justice Rufus Peckham conceded that the state has broad POLICE POWER to protect "the safety, health, morals and general welfare of the public." But the police power has a limit, and the question in every case, he said, is whether its exercise was "an unreasonable, unnecessary and arbitrary interference" with the right of the individual to contract for work. Peckham could find no reason to limit the hours of a baker. No one claimed that "bakers as a class are not equal in intelligence and capacity to men in other trades or manual occupations," or that they could not care for themselves. Restricting the numbers of hours would lead to neither more wholesome bread nor healthier employees. Betraying the central fallacy of the case, Peckham said that "[t]o the common understanding the trade of a baker has never been regarded as an unhealthy one."

In fact, it long had been. The legislature had a wealth of data and studies available, which Justice John M. Harlan, dissenting, reviewed in some detail. In the words of one student of industrial diseases, the baker's work life is "among the hardest and most laborious imaginable," leading to many physical infirmities and a shortened lifespan. Peckham and the other four majority justices simply refused to consider the actual evidence. They substituted

their own judgment for that of the legislators about whether bakers should be protected, using an artificial historical characterization of baking as a safe occupation, compared to mining, which the Court seven years earlier had characterized as "ultrahazardous."[932]

Just as the majority refused to credit the rationality of the legislature's means, so it also rejected the reasonableness of the legislature's ends. The Court refused to concede to the legislature the authority to alter the balance of economic power between bakery owners and unorganized workers who were powerless to resist the sweatshops. The majority saw the hours law as an unconstitutional redistribution of wealth, extracting from the employers' pockets a higher than market wage.

In one of his most famous dissents, Justice Oliver Wendell Holmes lambasted the majority for assuming the power to decide what was best for the people of New York. Holmes pointed out that the Court had sustained state laws that "regulate life in many ways which we as legislators might think as injudicious or if you like as tyrannical as this, and which equally interfere with the liberty to contract," including SUNDAY CLOSING, usury, and antilottery laws. "The 14th Amendment does not enact Mr. Herbert Spencer's Social Statics. . . . [A] constitution is not intended to embody a particular economic theory, whether of paternalism and the organic relation of the citizen to the State or of laissez faire. It is made for people of fundamentally differing views." It does not matter that a judge finds a law "natural and familiar or novel and even shocking." Shibboleths such as liberty of contract are not helpful, for "general propositions do not decide concrete cases." Judges must uphold a law unless a "rational and fair man" would be compelled to conclude that it "would infringe fundamental principles as they have been understood by the traditions of our people and our law." But it was impossible to call the New

York State legislature unreasonable in believing that the law would benefit the bakers' health. Holmes's dissent eventually became the majority view. The Court killed *Lochner* silently in 1917,[274] effectively in 1937,[2184] and in name in 1949.[1167]

See also: AFFECTED WITH A PUBLIC INTEREST DOCTRINE; BRANDEIS BRIEF; INTERSTATE COMMERCE; LAWYERS' FEES; PLESSY V. FERGUSON.

loitering, *see:* **vagrancy**

long-arm statute A long-arm statute gives courts in the state JURISDICTION over a defendant who is neither physically present in, nor a legal resident of, the state. The state in effect is stretching the "long arm" of the law to reach beyond the state's power to govern. Because the Court has held that long-arm statutes are constitutional only if the state has had at least a "minimum contact" with the out-of-state defendant, the laws generally specify the kinds of contacts that will confer jurisdiction—for example, soliciting business in the state by mail or even merely driving through it.

See also: SERVICE OF PROCESS.

lotteries, commerce in In 1903 the Court upheld Congress's power to regulate INTERSTATE COMMERCE by prohibiting outright anyone from importing a lottery ticket into the United States or from carrying a lottery ticket "from one state to another." This affirmation of what today is taken almost for granted troubled the Court greatly. *The Lottery Case* was argued three times and finally decided by the slimmest majority. The dissenters argued that letting Congress suppress lotteries is to concede to Congress a sweeping POLICE POWER reserved to the states under the TENTH AMENDMENT. Moreover, carrying a lottery ticket is not commerce, they said. But Justice John Marshall Harlan brushed these objections aside, saying he saw nothing in the Constitution that gave a right to carry across state lines something that will harm the public morals.

Louisiana Purchase, constitutionality of In 1802 the King of Spain transferred the Louisiana territory to Napoleon, who envisioned a French empire in the new world. Americans had lived peacefully next to Spanish territory because the Spanish had granted Americans the right to navigate the Mississippi and to use the port of New Orleans. Napoleon's imperial plans were worrisome because U.S. interests might be seriously disrupted. So President Thomas Jefferson sought to negotiate navigation rights from the French, only to learn in the summer of 1803, quite to his and the country's amazement, that Napoleon would cede the entire territory for eleven million dollars. The Louisiana Purchase would double the size of the country and provide security from foreign ambitions. But Jefferson was troubled by a constitutional doubt. He had long expressed his belief in STRICT CONSTRUCTION; that is, he believed that it was improper to construe powers not explicitly set out in the text. Since the Constitution says nothing about any power to acquire foreign territory, or to admit any part of it into the UNION as a state or states, he thought it would be necessary to amend the Constitution. He even drafted an amendment to submit to Congress. However, he yielded to the pleas of many in Congress who feared that Napoleon would reconsider if Jefferson delayed the purchase to secure an amendment and agreed to keep his constitutional doubts to himself. The Louisiana Purchase was his most popular act as president. Twenty-five years later, in an unrelated case, the Supreme Court held that the treaty power and the WAR POWER include the power to acquire territory from other nations.[51]

lower federal courts, *see:* **Court of Appeals, U.S.; district courts**

lower-value speech Whatever the political philosophies of individual justices, there is now near unanimity on the Supreme Court that certain types of speech lie at the "core" of the FIRST AMENDMENT. As Justice Lewis F. Powell put it in 1974, under the First Amendment "there is no such thing as a false idea."[746] Speech advocating political, social, artistic, religious, moral, scientific, or economic ideas may not be outlawed. But the Court has never taken an absolutist view of the FREEDOM OF SPEECH. At various times, the Court has said that certain categories of speech lie outside the First Amendment's core and simply do not qualify for constitutional protection. These categories are said to be of a "lesser" or "lower value of speech." In 1942 Justice Frank Murphy said for a unanimous Court:

> There are certain well-defined and narrowly limited classes of speech, the prevention and punishment of which have never been thought to raise any Constitutional problem. These include the lewd and obscene, the profane, the libelous, and the insulting or "fighting" words—those which by their very utterance inflict injury or tend to incite an immediate breach of the peace. It has been well observed that such utterances are no essential part of any exposition of ideas, and are of such slight social value as a step to truth that any benefit that may be derived from them is clearly outweighed by the social interest in order and morality.[372]

Under the BALANCING approach in speech cases, the Court weighs the harm of the particular expression against its value, measured by its distance from the core of the First Amendment. But to define the category of speech, the Court does not weigh the particular expression. It examines its *nature*. If the speech in question fits within a particular category of lower-value speech, the Court permits the government to regulate or even to ban it. For most of this century, there have been major

clashes over which categories lie within the First Amendment core. In 1925 a 7–2 majority held in *Gitlow v. New York* that "utterances advocating the overthrow of organized government by force" may be banned by the legislature, even if there was not even a remote danger that the particular advocacy would lead to violence. In 1969 the Court repudiated the Court's conclusion in *Gitlow* that SUBVERSIVE ADVOCACY is a category of speech not shielded by the First Amendment.[222] Likewise, the Court has narrowed the 1942 categories considerably. In later rulings in the areas of LIBEL AND SLANDER, OBSCENITY AND PORNOGRAPHY, and FIGHTING WORDS the Court has limited the kinds of speech that can be considered to be within those categories, and hence are subject to governmental restriction. Other categories, including COMMERCIAL SPEECH and OFFENSIVE AND INDECENT SPEECH, have likewise been shrunk. The Court has also rejected the claim that *employer speech* may be absolutely banned; an employer's antiunion speeches and literature may be restrained only if they are coercive.[1433]

Some categories of lower-value, or even no-value, speech do remain. For example, false advertising and other untrue commercial messages are not entitled to constitutional protection,[361] nor are advertisements for unlawful goods and services or ads that encourage illegal activities.[1635] Likewise, speech that is an integral part of an illegal activity, such as blackmail, may obviously be outlawed.

See also: SOLICITATION; SPEECH, REGULATION OF CONTENT; SYMBOLIC SPEECH.

loyalty oath Beginning in the 1940s, the federal government and the states attempted to weed out disloyal employees—mainly those thought to be members of the Communist party or sympathetic to COMMUNISM—by requiring applicants for public employment to subscribe to loyalty oaths. Typically, loyalty oaths required applicants and employees to swear that they were not engaged in efforts to overthrow the government by force or violence, that they did not advocate such a subversive doctrine, or that they were not members of an organization that engaged in such efforts or taught the necessity of doing so. In the 1950s, the Supreme Court upheld many such oaths against FIRST AMENDMENT challenges—for example, as applied to a candidate for public office,[742] to nonelected public employees,[728] and to teachers.[7] However, by the 1960s the Court began to strike down many such oaths on the grounds of VAGUENESS and OVERBREADTH.

In 1961 it struck down as unconstitutionally vague a Florida requirement that every teacher swear, "I have not and will not lend my aid, support, advice, counsel or influence to the Communist Party." Justice Potter Stewart said that the oath smacked of "extraordinary ambiguity" and lacked any "terms susceptible of objective measurement."[487] In 1964 the Court voided two oaths, one requiring teachers to swear that they "will by precept and example promote respect for the flag and the institutions of the United States of America and the State of Washington, reverence for law and order and undivided allegiance to the government" and the other requiring all state employees to swear that they would refrain from aiding "in the commission of any act intended to overthrow, destroy, or alter or assist in the overthrow, destruction, or alteration" of the government.[102] In 1966 a 5–4 majority struck down an Arizona oath requiring teachers to swear that they were not knowingly members of an organization that had for one of its purposes the unlawful overthrow of the state government. The problem, said Justice William O. Douglas, was that the oath forced teachers to avoid organizations even though they did not personally agree with the organization's objectives—for example, a "seminar group predom-

inantly Communist"—thus violating the FREEDOM OF ASSOCIATION.[609]

In 1967, a 5–4 majority struck down a New York teacher oath that it had affirmed in 1952, holding as overbroad the requirement that teachers swear they were not members of the Communist party or other subversive organizations.[1072] But the Court has approved more limited oaths unrelated to an employee's memberships. In 1972 in its last major loyalty oath case, a 4–3 majority upheld a Massachusetts requirement that employees swear both that they will "uphold and defend" the Constitution and that they will "oppose the overthrow of the [government] by force, violence or by any illegal or unconstitutional method."[422] The majority read the word "oppose" to mean simply a "commitment not to use illegal . . . force."

Loyalty oath laws were originally enacted as part of a broad antisubversive movement. The Court's rulings have deprived them of any such use and render the truncated oaths that remain relatively meaningless. "I support and will defend the Constitution" cannot constitutionally mean what that oath seems to say. It is inconceivable that someone who believes that the income tax is unconstitutional, and would dearly love to see the Sixteenth Amendment repealed, could be precluded from holding a government job, as long as she pays the tax. Moreover, since conspirators will scarcely entertain a scruple against lying, and many nonconspirators are deeply offended by oaths on purely moral grounds, the loyalty oath serves but one purpose: to give the righteous the psychic satisfaction of forcing all those whom they can reach to subscribe to their own views. "No passion is stronger in the breast of man," wrote Virginia Woolf, "than the desire to make others believe as he believes. Nothing so cuts at the root of his happiness and fills him with rage as the sense that another rates low what he prizes high." Evidently it remains constitutional for a state to require this limited intrusion on FREE-DOM OF BELIEF.

See also: FLAG BURNING; MEMBERSHIP IN POLITICAL PARTIES; OATH OF OFFICE; TEST OATH.

loyalty-security programs   After World War II, fear of a worldwide communist conspiracy led President Harry S. Truman to issue the first of several EXECUTIVE ORDERS establishing federal loyalty-security programs to screen out subversives from sensitive public employment. In 1950 Congress enacted the Internal Security Act over Truman's veto. In 1953 President Dwight D. Eisenhower issued an executive order shifting emphasis from loyalty to security risk, enabling loyalty-review boards to consider such things as homosexuality and alcoholism, as well as political affiliations. Most states enacted their own loyalty-security laws. The loyalty-security programs used several devices to combat the perceived threat. On suspicion of disloyalty, administrative boards could bar employment or recommend dismissal. Membership in the Communist party or other subversive organizations included in the ATTORNEY GENERAL'S LIST was made the basis for discharge. Applicants for jobs were required to subscribe to LOYALTY OATHS, and false swearing was subject to perjury penalties.

As a whole, the loyalty-security programs posed several constitutional difficulties. There were repeated challenges on grounds of FREE-DOM OF ASSOCIATION, FREEDOM OF SPEECH, and the DUE PROCESS right to CONFRONTATION with witnesses. But a majority of the justices were as skittish about the communist threat as the rest of the nation, and so the Court skirted many of these constitutional problems until the late 1950s, when the excesses of Senator Joseph McCarthy and others were unmasked. In hindsight, much of the evidence amassed against particular employees was flimsy to nonexistent. But because the loyalty-security boards often refused to tell employees the names of their accusers or the nature of the accusation, it was impossible to establish the reliability of the evidence. In many cases the Court avoided ruling on whether unsupported dismissals violated due process. Instead, it held through narrow interpretations of the law that an employee could not be fired because the boards lacked power to act or because they failed to conform to their own procedural requirements.[1613, 423, 1845, 806]

Beginning in the early 1960s, the Court did confront many of the speech and associational aspects of the loyalty-security programs and severely restricted the power of the government to criminalize SUBVERSIVE ADVOCACY and mere MEMBERSHIP IN POLITICAL ORGANIZATIONS. The power of Congress and the president to provide for national security by barring employment to people who pose a genuine security risk remains unquestioned, but the means by which the risks are assessed must conform to constitutional standards.

See also: BLACKLISTING; CONSTITUTIONAL QUESTIONS, AVOIDANCE OF; GUILT BY ASSOCIATION; INVESTIGATORY POWERS OF LEGISLATURE; PASSPORTS, RIGHT TO; PLEADING THE *FIFTH*; PREVENTIVE DETENTION; SELF-INCRIMINATION; UNCONSTITUTIONAL CONDITIONS.

M

Madison's notes on the Constitution After electing George Washington president of the CONSTITUTIONAL CONVENTION on May 25, 1787, the delegates adopted a rule requiring strict secrecy of their proceedings. Several delegates kept notes. William Jackson, a close friend of Washington, was elected secretary and kept the official journal. First published in 1819, it contained neither transcription nor summary of debate, only motions and votes. The first substantive set of notes published was that of Robert Yates of New York. Yates refused to sign the Constitution and worked against its ratification in New York. His notes are almost wholly unreliable, because Edmond C. Genet, into whose hands they had passed before publication in 1821, altered them for partisan political advantage.

The most complete record was that of James Madison. Madison took notes daily, a task he later declared almost killed him. His colleagues regarded him as a semi-official reporter, and many entrusted to his keeping copies of their speeches. Madison refused to publish his notes before his death. When he died in 1836, the last surviving delegate, his widow sold the collection to the federal government, which arranged for its publication in 1840. "At once, all other records paled into insignificance," wrote Max Farrand, who meticulously edited the notes of Madison and others in four volumes published by Yale University Press between 1923 and 1937. Historians later uncovered additional records.

The question remains how accurate and comprehensive Madison's notes are. The answer concerns any constitutional interpreter, but it especially concerns those who believe that the Constitution should be understood only by the ORIGINAL INTENT of the Framers. Ever since 1840, anti-Madisonians have suspected that Madison altered or distorted the record. In 1953 Professor William W. Crosskey of the University of Chicago Law School published a two-volume work asserting that Madison's notes were corrupt. Some modern historians have followed Crosskey's lead; but in an important article in 1986, James H. Hutson, chief of the Manuscript Division of the Library of Congress, took careful aim at the naysayers. After an extensive review of the evidence, including chemical analysis of the papers on which Madison wrote, Hutson concluded that "Madison's notes are a faithful account of what he recorded at the convention in 1787—augmented by motions, resolutions, and votes that he believed to be, and in the vast majority of cases were, accurately recorded." However, the completeness of the record is another matter.

At most, Madison managed to record only seven to ten percent of the proceedings. Moreover, there is some reason to believe that in his notes Madison fleshed out his own remarks at the convention. As Hutson concludes, "Madison's notes are not a forgery, but they are far from a verbatim record of what was said in the Convention, [omitting] much of what happened in Philadelphia."

See also: CONSTITUTION, FRAMERS OF.

magazines   In the constitutional sense, "magazines" are places where ammunition and other provisions are stored. Art. I-§8[17] rather redundantly empowers Congress to erect magazines, forts, and other buildings in the nation's capital.

See also: PUBLIC BUILDINGS.

Magna Carta   In 1215, the barons of England refused to swear allegiance to King John until he acceded to their demands that he renounce his abusive and lawless ways. John's agreement at Runnymede to redress their grievances was incorporated in a charter known as Magna Carta (Latin for "great charter"). Magna Carta is justly renowned for its fundamental proposition that not even the king is above the law. Its most well-known provision is Chapter 39, in which John pledged that "no freed man shall be taken, imprisoned, disseised, outlawed, banished, or in any way destroyed, nor will We proceed against him, except by the lawful judgment of his peers and by the LAW OF THE LAND." Magna Carta also promises that justice will not be sold, denied, or delayed, and it contains precursors of many provisions in the BILL OF RIGHTS, including the concept of JUST COMPENSATION for property taken by the state. In 1297 Magna Carta was reconfirmed by the king in Parliament, in effect enacting Magna Carta as a fundamental law and decreeing that thereafter any law contrary to Magna Carta should be treated as void. In the late seventeenth century, William Penn drew on Magna Carta in drafting the charter of the Pennsylvania colonial government, and after the American Revolution many state constitutions borrowed liberally from Magna Carta. Even in our own time, Magna Carta is occasionally referred to as a source for understanding constitutional provisions. In 1983, for example, Justice Lewis F. Powell looked to Magna Carta in concluding that a punishment disproportionate to the magnitude of the crime violates the EIGHTH AMENDMENT's provision against cruel and unusual PUNISHMENT.[1905]

mail, *see:* **post office**

mail order taxes, *see:* **taxation of interstate commercee**

majoritarianism   For nearly two centuries, a debate has raged over the legitimacy of JUDICIAL REVIEW. Those who find judicial rejection of legislative enactments problematic point to its antimajoritarian nature: unelected judges overturn policies of elected legislators and chief executives in apparent contradiction to the sovereignty of the people. It is hard to justify the antimajoritarian argument when the courts interpret ordinary statutes, for legislatures may simply pass new laws to reverse the courts' misunderstanding. When a court declares a statute unconstitutional, however, the legislature's only recourse is a politically difficult constitutional amendment.

Why for two centuries have we preferred unelected judges to elected officials to decide constitutional issues? The answer is at once profoundly simple and complex. The simple answer is that otherwise the partisan passions of the moment would quickly erode fundamental constitutional constraints. The Constitution, in other words, serves precisely to prevent popular majorities from working their will whenever and however they please. The complex answer ranges far beyond the scope of constitutional law itself, although Yale Law

School Professor Charles L. Black, Jr., has suggested that the scheme of CHECKS AND BALANCES does provide a constitutional answer. Because Congress is empowered to modify or perhaps even abolish the Supreme Court's APPELLATE JURISDICTION, the ultimate authority to determine what kinds of questions are open to judicial review remains in the people's hands. The people's perception and acceptance of results has further weight: though unelected, judges are not beyond the popular will; they just follow it more slowly. Judges do not mysteriously appear on the bench. They are put there by elected officials, and despite the wildly disingenuous assertion of judicial candidates that it would be improper to discuss judicial philosophy, their constitutional perspective, insofar as it can be discerned, is the reason they are nominated and confirmed, or not confirmed. The 1987 rejection of Robert Bork's nomination to the Supreme Court can be viewed also as a popular rejection of at least his most severe view that there is no constitutional right to PRIVACY. Likewise, the confirmation of several relatively conservative jurists beginning in the 1980s can be taken as a popular acceptance of a desire to halt the presumably leftward movement of the Court into the 1970s. And if strict majoritarianism were truly a requirement of the American political system, then much of the current regime must be considered illegitimate: congressional committee rules, filibusters, and voting registration impediments all conspire as significantly as judicial review, but on a far less principled basis, to keep majority rule from working in practice. Even more important, most of our law is made by nonelected officials far more obscure than the Supreme Court and almost as unreviewable—the bureaucrats to whom Congress has delegated vast amounts of legislative power.

See also: JUDICIAL SUPREMACY; SEPARATION OF POWERS; SUPREME COURT, JURISDICTION OF.

majority   The Constitution provides for voting by varying majorities, depending on the issue, as follows:

One-fifth vote

Art. I-§5[3]   Each house may determine by a one-fifth vote whether its members' votes must be publicly recorded.

Simple majority

Art. I-§5[1]   A majority of each house of Congress constitutes a quorum.

Art. I-§7[2]   All legislation is enacted by a majority of members present in each house of Congress.

Amendment 12   A majority of votes cast in the ELECTORAL COLLEGE is necessary to elect the president and vice president. If no candidate receives a majority the election is thrown into the House of Representatives, and the House elects the president by a majority vote of all states, each state casting one vote. If no candidate for vice president receives a majority of the votes of all electors appointed, then the Senate elects the vice president by a majority vote of all senators, not merely of those present.

Amendment 25-§2   A majority of both houses is necessary to confirm a vice president nominated by the president. §4-[1,2] If a majority of the principal officers of the EXECUTIVE DEPARTMENTS side with the vice president in declaring that the president is incapacitated, the vice president becomes ACTING PRESIDENT. Similarly, a majority vote of the cabinet is necessary to send to Congress the question whether the president may resume his office.

Two-thirds vote

Art. I-§3[6]   The Senate may convict an impeached federal official.

Art. I-§5[2]   Either house may expel a member.

Art. I-§7[2]   Both houses may override a presidential VETO.

Art. II-§2[2]   The Senate may consent to treaties and presidential appointments.

Art. V   Congress may propose amendments to the Constitution.

Amendment 14   Congress may remove a disability against serving in state or federal office because of participation in a rebellion against the Constitution.

Amendment 25   Both houses may declare a president unfit to continue the duties of office, when a temporarily incapacitated president declares that no inability exists any longer.

Three-quarters vote

Art. V   Three-quarters of the states are necessary to ratify proposed constitutional amendments.

Nine-thirteenths vote

Art. VII   The Constitution was required to be ratified by nine of the original thirteen states.

malice   In ordinary parlance, malice is the desire to cause harm to others or see them suffer. At COMMON LAW, malice is an act done with such intent. In the constitutional law of LIBEL, however, the Supreme Court has used the term in a different, more refined way. A person who maliciously defames an official or other PUBLIC FIGURE is not answerable unless the utterance was made with what the Court has termed "actual malice." A statement is made with actual malice when the speaker knows that what he said was false or he recklessly disregarded whether or not the statement was false.[1472] This means that a speaker can vow to destroy the reputation of a public official whom he profoundly hates and hence speak maliciously in the ordinary sense but still be immune from liability, as long as he genuinely believes that he is speaking the truth. The contrary also follows. A speaker may genuinely admire and respect a person about whom a false statement is made, desiring to do no harm

at all. But if the statement was known to be false and does injury, the speaker has acted with actual malice.

mandamus, writ of   A writ of mandamus (Latin for "we command") is a court order to a government officer, including a lower court, to carry out a particular nondiscretionary task required to be performed by law. Congress has vested the federal courts with the power to issue mandamus in appropriate cases.
See also: MARBURY V. MADISON.

mandatory retirement   Nothing in the Constitution bars the federal government, the states, or private employers from mandating retirement at a certain age, although it certainly permits the states and the federal government to pass laws against mandatory retirement. In 1991 the Court narrowly read the federal Age Discrimination in Employment Act to sidestep the constitutional difficulties of applying it to state judges.[810]
See also: AGE DISCRIMINATION.

Mann Act, *see:* interstate commerce; national police power

manufacturing   In 1888 the Supreme Court upheld an Iowa law that forbade the manufacture of INTOXICATING BEVERAGES in the state, even as applied to a company all of whose production was intended for shipment and sale out of state.[1074] Because the states may not constitutionally impede INTERSTATE COMMERCE, to sustain the law the Court had to proclaim that manufacturing as an activity is not itself a part of commerce. This decision led to several others barring Congress from regulating business activities, such as working conditions in factories, on the ground that the production of goods and services was not commerce in the constitutional sense. The Court eventually overturned this line of cases in the constitutional revolution of the late 1930s.[1430]

See also: ANTITRUST LAW, CONSTITUTIONALITY OF; DORMANT COMMERCE CLAUSE; STREAM OF COMMERCE DOCTRINE.

Marbury v. Madison *Marbury v. Madison* is the seminal case in U.S. constitutional law that firmly established the principle of JUDICIAL REVIEW by the Supreme Court over acts of Congress. In February 1801, eighteen days before President John Adams, a Federalist, was due to leave office, the lame-duck Congress passed a judiciary act that among other things created sixteen new judgeships. Thomas Jefferson, the newly elected president, saw the act as an attempt by the Federalists to maintain control over the judiciary. Adams set about appointing judges and submitting their names to the Senate for confirmation. Then, on February 28, just five days before Jefferson was to be inaugurated, Congress passed another judgeship bill establishing justice of the peace courts in the District of Columbia. On March 2, Adams submitted forty-two names to the Senate for confirmation as justices of the peace; the Senate obliged him on March 3, his very last day in office. Official commissioning papers were hurriedly drawn up by John Marshall, who continued to serve as secretary of state even though he had been confirmed as CHIEF JUSTICE of the United States on January 27. During the day and into the night of March 3, the commissions were prepared in Marshall's office, forwarded to Adams for his signature, and then returned to the secretary of state's office, where clerks affixed the official seal and undertook to deliver the documents to the new judges.

That, at least, was the official story. Adams's opponents later claimed that he had signed the commissions in blank even before he forwarded the names of his appointees to the Senate. But whatever the exact sequence of signatures, by midnight of March 3, the last moment of Adams's presidency, four of the commissions

had not been delivered to the "midnight judges." The following day, as Jefferson recounted, he "found them on the table of the department of State, on my entrance into office, and I forbade their delivery." Jefferson's position was that since they had not been delivered, the commissions were "mere nullities." Jefferson appointed new justices, many of them the same men whom Adams had named. But four he refused to reappoint.

The following December, William Marbury and the other three disappointed judges filed suit in the Supreme Court, asking it to issue a writ of MANDAMUS to James Madison, the new secretary of state, ordering him to deliver the commissions. So threatening did this suit seem to the Jeffersonians that the new Republican Congress abolished the 1802 term of the Supreme Court, so that the case could not be heard for an entire year. On February 9, 1803, the proceeding began with a runaround. The one person who could personally testify to the facts, John Marshall, was now on the other side of the bench as chief justice. Marshall's immediate successor as secretary of state, Levi Lincoln, could not "recollect" to whom the commissions belonged. Finally a state department clerk signed an affidavit attesting to the facts. James Madison, the nominal defendant, refused to cooperate and did not appear in court.

On February 24, Marshall issued the Court's decision. Significantly, he announced it as the "OPINION of the Court," not merely as his own opinion. There were no dissents and no separate opinions, as had been the custom. Marshall said that three questions were to be decided: (1) Was Marbury entitled to the commission? (2) If he had a right to it, did the laws provide him with a remedy? (3) Was mandamus the proper remedy?

(1) In eight pages, Marshall showed that Marbury had a legal right to the commission. The president had nominated him, the Senate had confirmed him, and the president had then

commissioned him by signing the official commission. Under the Constitution, this was the "last act" required to appoint. At that point the president's power over a judge must cease, or else a judge would always serve at the whim of the president. Once the commission is signed, the appointment is irrevocable, and the secretary of state is bound by law to affix the seal and record the appointment. To the argument that the last required act of appointment is not signing but delivery of the commission, Marshall responded that the president never personally delivered commissions to officeholders. He delivered them instead to the secretary of state, just as happened here. Moreover, it makes no sense to assume that a judge cannot hold his office unless he physically possesses the parchment on which the president's signature is affixed, for then "accident or fraud, fire or theft might deprive an individual of his office." No government could operate on that basis.

(2) Marbury not only had a right to the commission but a remedy. In this part of his opinion, Marshall essentially spelled out the notion that in a government of laws, to say that a person has a right is to say that the courts may uphold it. Marshall was careful to say that the Court was not asserting any power by judges to look into acts that the Constitution committed to the president's discretion, such as the conduct of foreign affairs. But when "a specific duty is assigned by law, and individual rights depend upon the performance of that duty, . . . the individual who considers himself injured, has a right to resort to the laws of his country for a remedy."

(3) The only thing now standing between Marbury and his judgeship was whether a writ of mandamus was the proper remedy. In form, it surely was, as Marshall demonstrated by reviewing the history of the writ. Mandamus was designed for exactly such a case, when an administrative official refuses to follow the law. But one problem remained. The remedy Mar-

bury sought was not merely mandamus—it was mandamus *to be issued by the Supreme Court.* It was on this point that Marbury would lose.

Marbury sought mandamus in the Supreme Court because of a provision in the Judiciary Act of 1789, authorizing the Court to issue the writ "in cases warranted by the principles and usages of law." Since Congress had authorized the Court to do so, the Court could refuse only if the law itself was unconstitutional. And so, Marshall said, it was. This was an astonishing turn of events, for in all the excitement over the case, no one had supposed that it would turn on some constitutional defect in the technical statute authorizing certain remedies. The issue was barely touched on in ORAL ARGUMENT, and none of the newspaper accounts had even hinted at it. Nevertheless, said Marshall, the law was unconstitutional because Article III of the Constitution does not permit the Court as a trial court to hear cases other than those involving states or ambassadors. Even though the Constitution does not say Congress is forbidden to expand the Court's ORIGINAL JURISDICTION, Marshall said that it would be absurd to permit it to do so, for otherwise the provision narrowly delineating the Court's original jurisdiction would have been pointless.

And so, Marshall concluded, since the law is unconstitutional, it must be struck down. To give it effect in the face of a written Constitution "would subvert the very foundation of all written constitutions." It would mean that Congress could disregard constitutional limits at its pleasure, the very antithesis of the limited government that the Framers had worked so hard to create. Marshall's HOLDING in *Marbury v. Madison* was a masterstroke, for not only did it establish the principle of judicial review but it was irresistible. No matter how much Jefferson fumed he could do nothing, since he had won the case.

As for William Marbury and the other judges, the decision did them no good. Although Marshall had said they undoubtedly had a remedy in some other court, in fact it appears that the Judiciary Act did not give the circuit courts the power to issue mandamus. There was also no way to sue the United States for money claims, so Marbury could not recover even back salary. Marbury let his claim to office lapse.

marines, *see:* **armed forces**

maritime law, *see:* **admiralty and maritime jurisdiction**

market participant doctrine   In a few cases decided in the late 1970s and early 1980s, the Court relaxed its strict rule against state interference with INTERSTATE COMMERCE when the state is acting as a *participant* rather than as a *regulator* of the market. To reduce the number of abandoned automobiles, Maryland authorized the payment of a bounty from public funds to processors that would scrap cars registered in the state. Because of paperwork requirements, the bounty policy favored in-state processors; out-of-state processors found it difficult to collect the bounty for Maryland-titled cars junked in some other state. The out-of-state processors argued that the policy burdened interstate commerce, but the Court held that Maryland could constitutionally enter into the market to induce processors to recycle the cars. The state was not prohibiting anyone from recycling junked vehicles in or out of the state; it was merely making it economically worthwhile for in-state processors to do so. The Court reasoned that it made economic sense for the state to spend its money to clear out cars abandoned in the state, rather than sending money out to scrap cars abandoned elsewhere. The state was acting as a participant in the market, bidding up the price so that suppliers of abandoned cars would be motivated to turn cars over to in-state processors.[955]

The Court also approved a South Dakota policy of limiting cement sales from a state-owned plant to South Dakota residents[1703] and a requirement by the city of Boston that whenever the city funds any construction project, at least half the employees must be city residents.[2194] But the market participant doctrine has sharp limits. In a 1984 case, Alaska refused to sell state-owned timber to any buyer who would not promise to process part of the lumber in-state. The Court held that Alaska was not acting as a market participant because a seller ordinarily does not attempt to tell buyers how to use the purchased goods. By imposing conditions on commerce outside the market in which it was participating—the market for processing timber rather than the market for timber itself—the state was violating the DORMANT COMMERCE CLAUSE.[1917]

See also: PRIVILEGES AND IMMUNITIES.

marketplace of ideas   In 1919, in *Abrams v. United States,* Justice Oliver Wendell Holmes, writing in dissent, proclaimed an arresting metaphor to explain FREEDOM OF SPEECH. It has been much quoted, even if not wholly followed, ever since: "[W]hen men have realized that time has upset many fighting faiths, they may come to believe even more than they believe the very foundations of their own conduct that the ultimate good desired is better reached by free trade in ideas—that the best test of truth is the power of thought to get itself accepted in the competition of the market, and that truth is the only ground upon which their wishes safely can be carried out. That at any rate is the theory of our Constitution. It is an experiment, as all life is an experiment."

His point was that the expression of opinion should compete openly in the marketplace of ideas, even "opinions that we loathe and believe to be fraught with death," unless there is no time to combat expression that imminently threatens the very existence of the country. Or, as Chief Justice Fred Vinson later put it, the "basis of the First Amendment is the hypothesis that speech can rebut speech, propaganda will answer propaganda, free debate of ideas will result in the wisest governmental policies." [539] Holmes was writing at a time when a majority of the Court believed that the Constitution imposed significant restraints on the government's ability to regulate the *commercial* marketplace, so his metaphor may be seen in part as an ironic reminder to his brethren of the paradox in which they were engaging: economic activity was being protected against state infringement even though there was no explicit constitutional text; expressive activities were not protected even though there was.

Holmes did not purport to guarantee anyone the economic means to enter the marketplace; the marketplace metaphor means simply that without an extremely cogent reason the government may not silence those who speak. As long as there is time for "bad" speech to be overcome by "better" speech, the government may not intrude. In 1969 the Supreme Court adopted a version of this notion in *Brandenburg v. Ohio*, which held that the state may not punish speech advocating unlawful action unless it incites and is likely to prompt imminent lawless action. Because the marketplace metaphor speaks only in terms of truth, it does not protect certain other forms of expression that today have received at least limited constitutional protection on other theories, including LIBEL and SEXUALLY EXPLICIT EXPRESSION.

See also: CLEAR AND PRESENT DANGER; ECONOMIC DUE PROCESS; RIGHT TO REPLY; SUBVERSIVE ADVOCACY.

marque, *see:* **letters of marque and reprisal**

marriage The Supreme Court has firmly recognized a fundamental constitutional right to enter into a "normal" marriage. It has just as firmly rejected the contention that the Constitution guarantees a right to an unconventional one. In 1942 Justice William O. Douglas noted in a criminal sterilization case that marriage is "one of the basic civil rights of man . . . fundamental to the very existence and survival of the race." [1879] Douglas returned to this theme twenty-three years later in *Griswold v. Connecticut*, which voided the state CONTRACEPTION law: "We deal with a right of PRIVACY older than the BILL OF RIGHTS. . . . Marriage is a coming together for better or for worse, hopefully enduring, and intimate to the degree of being sacred. It is an association that promotes a way of life, not causes; a harmony in living, not political faiths; a bilateral loyalty, not commercial or social projects. Yet it is an association for as noble a purpose as any involved in our prior decisions [upholding FREEDOM OF ASSOCIATION]."

State impediments to marriage are unlikely to survive the STRICT SCRUTINY required by DUE PROCESS. In 1978 the Court struck down a Wisconsin law that prohibited a man from marrying because he could not meet his support payments to children from an earlier marriage and with whom he did not live. The law's asserted purpose was to give noncustodial parents an incentive to provide for their children. Justice Thurgood Marshall said that the law's means were not necessary to its goals and that the state could have used such LESS RESTRICTIVE ALTERNATIVES as wage assignments, criminal penalties, and civil contempt proceedings. [2283] In 1987 the Court unanimously invalidated a Missouri prison rule that forbade inmates from marrying except for a compelling reason, such as pregnancy or birth of a child, since no interference with valid penal regulations or concerns could be shown. [2082]

However, there is no fundamental right to marry anyone you please. Of course, under EQUAL PROTECTION, the state may not bar marriages because the couple are of different races, religions, or national origins. [1200] But, as Justice Potter Stewart noted, "a state may legitimately say that no one can marry his or her sibling, that no one can marry who is not at least 14 years old, that no one can marry without first passing an examination for venereal disease, or that no one can marry who has a living husband or wife."[2283] More than a century ago, the Court upheld an 1882 anti-Mormon law against bigamy and polygamy, calling them "crimes by the laws of all civilized and Christian countries."[520] And the Court's holding in *Bowers v. Hardwick,* the 1986 HOMOSEXUALITY case, makes it abundantly clear that there is no constitutional right to homosexual marriage.

See also: MISCEGENATION.

martial law   Martial law is government by the military. In 1849 the Supreme Court held that the question of whether martial law had been validly declared in Rhode Island during severe disturbances, permitting the legislature to govern as if under siege, was exclusively for the political authorities of the state to determine.[1208] But after the Civil War the question arose whether President Abraham Lincoln was constitutionally entitled to order the Army to try spies and those who had aided the Confederacy. The Court backtracked, declaring in 1866 that the courts could determine whether martial law had been a necessity. In a 5–4 decision, the Court held that martial law is unconstitutional when the civil courts are open and functioning. Only when the courts are "actually closed and it is impossible to administer criminal justice according to law" may military tribunals, in the war zone itself, try civilians according to their own rules and the law of war. Moreover, martial law may be declared only by Congress and only during wartime.[1345] After World War II, the Court interpreted narrowly the governing law of the territory of Hawaii to reject the substitution of military tribunals for civil courts until late 1944, again because the civil courts had been functioning and no military necessity had been proved.[581]

masters, *see:* **special master**

McNabb-Mallory rule   The McNabb-Mallory rule was named for two cases, *McNabb v. United States* in 1943 and *Mallory v. United States* in 1957, in which the Supreme Court declared that in federal prosecutions confessions were inadmissible if obtained during unnecessary delays in arraigning the defendant. The rule depended on the Court's power to supervise the lower federal courts, not on the Constitution, and was based on the premise that it would deter federal law enforcement officials from overbearing interrogations before suspects could be advised of their rights. But it operated to exclude some voluntary confessions because of unavoidable delays in AR-RAIGNMENT. Congress abolished the rule in 1968, which by then had been superseded anyway by MIRANDA V. ARIZONA and other cases dealing explicitly with the voluntariness of confessions on constitutional grounds.

See also: SELF-INCRIMINATION.

measures, *see:* **weights and measures**

medication and surgery, forced   Until the mid-1970s, few cases involving a right to refuse medical treatment found their way to the courts. Most of them involved people with religious scruples against blood transfusions and other medical procedures for their children. The lower courts have uniformly held in favor of the state's interest in treating the children. The Supreme Court has never squarely decided whether a parent's FREEDOM OF RELIGION can ever outweigh a child's need for medical care. In 1968 the Court indirectly decided that religious objections do not outweigh a child's right to live, by affirming without opinion a ruling upholding a law that allowed sick children to become wards of trial courts when their parents refused life-saving blood transfusions.[1010] In 1985 the Court held that surgery to which a patient does not consent is unconstitutional, even if undertaken to extract evidence for use in a criminal prosecution; in the case reviewed the police forced a suspect to undergo general anesthesia to remove a bullet from his chest.[2235] In 1990 the Court refrained from recognizing any absolute right of a person to refuse medicine on his or her own behalf when the state has a strong interest in administering it, but it did hold that a prison inmate has a LIBERTY interest in avoiding the injection of antipsychotic drugs. The Court said that a prison must give an inmate an opportunity to persuade an administrative board that he is not dangerous and therefore may refuse medication. But the inmate bears the burden of proof.[2160]

The issue of forced medical care has taken on new urgency and difficulty since the mid-1970s, when the relatives of comatose patients in "persistent vegetative states" began to ask that hospitals turn off new technologies capable of prolonging their lives. Two separate issues are presented in these RIGHT TO DIE cases. One is whether people may constitutionally choose for themselves to reject medical treatment without which they will die. In 1990, in the *Cruzan* case, the Court suggested that they may, without conclusively deciding the matter.[497] The other issue is how much evidence it takes to prove that people want to die when they are comatose and no longer able to speak for themselves. The Court said that the state may refuse a relative's entreaties to pull a patient off a life-support system unless "clear and convincing" evidence can be offered that the patient would have spurned the continuing treatment. The *Cruzan* case may prompt the states to enact laws regulating "living wills" by which people may make their wishes known.

See also: ABORTION; BLOOD SAMPLES; VACCINATION.

members of Congress, *see:* **Congress, members of**

membership in political organizations   For more than forty years, the Supreme Court wrestled with the problem of whether the government may outlaw membership in dangerous political organizations, such as the Communist party or other radical political parties. In 1927, in *Whitney v. California,* the Court upheld the state's power to criminalize membership in any organization that proposed some day to preach "criminal SYNDICALISM," the doctrine of violent change in industrial ownership, even if the organization was not currently advocating that people immediately undertake any unlawful activity. In a CONCURRING OPINION, Justice Louis D. Brandeis eloquently objected to the basis of the Court's opinion. "Fear of serious injury cannot alone justify suppression of free speech and assembly. Men feared witches and burned women. It is the function of speech to free men from the bondage of irrational fears." The state ought not be permitted to ban advocacy of ideas that fall short of incitement, especially when there is no evidence that anyone would act on the ideas advocated.

In 1951 the Court upheld the conviction under the Smith Act of several leaders of the Communist party. The Smith Act prohibited teaching the necessity of violently overthrowing the government, organizing any group to advocate such a doctrine, or becoming a member of any such group, knowing its purposes. The defendants did not arm themselves or others for violent struggle, nor even exhort any particular persons to take to the barricades. Rather, they advocated the *idea* of armed rebellion, and for those acts the Court sustained their convictions.[539] Ten years later, the Court specifically upheld the membership provision of the Smith Act, though construing it to require proof that the member not only understood the party's purposes but also shared in its intent to overthrow the government "as speedily as circumstances would permit."[1807] Under the Subversive Activities Control Act,

"Communist-action organizations" were required to register with the attorney general and supply lists of their members. The Court upheld this requirement against the Communist party of the United States.[445]

But thereafter the Court began to narrow the apparent sweep of its decisions permitting membership to be outlawed or burdened. The Communist party never actually registered with the attorney general because a later decision made it clear that forcing members to register violated their FIFTH AMENDMENT right against SELF-INCRIMINATION.[31] The Court invalidated as violating the right to travel a provision prohibiting members of communist organizations from using their passports.[67] The Court likewise struck down a law prohibiting anyone from working in a defense facility who was a member of a communist-action organization, having knowledge or notice that it was required to be registered with the attorney general.[1736]

The Court also narrowed the ground for discharging public employees for failing to take or falsely subscribing to LOYALTY OATHS, which were really a means of penalizing certain memberships. On grounds of VAGUENESS, the Court voided a law that in effect barred membership in undefined "subversive organizations." Moreover, public employees may not be fired for failing to affirm that they did not belong to specifically listed subversive organizations, whether because they innocently belonged to an illicit group but were unaware of its unlawful purposes[2203] or even whether they knew its purposes. The flaw, said Justice Douglas, was that the oath requirement impaired the membership right of one who did not personally subscribe to the organization's illegal purposes.[609] The Court also refused to countenance a law that made inactive membership in an unlawful organization grounds for discharge.[1072] The rule today, therefore, appears to be that the government may refuse to hire or

may fire a person for his political views only if he is a knowing member of an organization devoted to the unlawful overthrow of the government, if he subscribes to those purposes, and if he is actively engaged in the group's efforts toward that goal.

The Court also has limited the power of the state to inquire into a person's memberships. In 1960 a 5–4 majority held that a state could not demand that public school teachers list annually every organization to which they belonged for the past five years. The requirement, said Justice Potter Stewart, impairs the teacher's FREEDOM OF ASSOCIATION, in part because the state had failed to demonstrate that it would keep the records confidential. Even if the membership list was kept confidential, "the pressure upon a teacher to avoid any ties which might displease those who control his professional destiny would be constant and heavy." The law was also overbroad because, instead of asking teachers about certain organizational activities, the law sought to know about all, many of no conceivable relevance. The state could have achieved its purposes with means less restrictive of personal liberties.[1855]

See also: ACCESS TO BALLOT; CLEAR AND PRESENT DANGER; FREEDOM OF SPEECH; INVESTIGATORY POWERS OF LEGISLATURE; LESS RESTRICTIVE ALTERNATIVE OR MEANS; POLITICAL CONVENTIONS; POLITICAL PARTIES; SUBVERSIVE ADVOCACY; TRAVEL, RIGHT TO; VOTING, RIGHT TO.

memorandum order A memorandum order is an order of a court without an accompanying OPINION to explain the reason that the court issued it. Most orders of the Supreme Court are memorandum orders, since it is in this manner that the Court grants or denies motions for cases to be reviewed, for briefs to be filed AMICUS CURIAE, and for indigent appeals to be heard IN FORMA PAUPERIS. Most such memorandum orders are purely procedural, but when the Court denies a petition for CERTIORARI, the memorandum order ends the case and gives effect to the lower court's HOLDING.

menorah, *see:* **religious symbols, right to display**

mental distress   In *Hustler Magazine v. Falwell*, the Supreme Court in 1988 extended the actual-MALICE rule to cases charging the defendant with intentionally inflicting mental or emotional distress on the plaintiff. *Hustler* magazine ran a parody of the Campari "First Time" advertisements depicting Jerry Falwell, the well-known minister and political activist, committing incest while drunk with his mother in an outhouse. The bottom of the page carried a disclaimer that said "Ad parody—not to be taken seriously." Falwell sued for LIBEL, invasion of PRIVACY, and intentional infliction of emotional distress, but the lower court found against him on the first two claims. On appeal, Falwell asserted that a PUBLIC FIGURE may recover DAMAGES for any "outrageous" utterance intended to inflict and actually causing emotional distress, regardless of whether the utterance is true or false or an expression of opinion.

The Court disagreed. Even though private acts intended to cause mental anguish are actionable, the FIRST AMENDMENT bars recovery in this case. Our political history is replete with attacks on political and public figures by political cartoonists, caricaturists, and satirists who have explored "unfortunate physical traits or politically embarrassing events—an exploration often calculated to injure the feelings" of the person satirized. The Court was unimpressed with Falwell's argument that ordinary satire was protected but not "outrageous" comment. There simply is no way to lay down "a principled standard to separate" permissible from impermissible satire, and "the pejorative description 'outrageous' does not supply one." As a consequence, subjects of caricature may not recover for their emotional distress unless they can show that the satirist made a false

statement of fact with knowledge that the statement was false or with reckless indifference to whether or not it was true.

mental illness, *see:* **civil commitment; insanity defense**

mental retardation   The Supreme Court has advanced somewhat from its 1927 decision that the state may sterilize "mental defectives" in institutions because, as Justice Oliver Wendell Holmes so cavalierly remarked, "three generations of imbeciles are enough." [268] Not until 1982 did the Court declare that the state owes at least a minimal duty of care toward those it has confined in institutions. The state must maintain a safe environment and permit institutionalized patients freedom of movement; they may not be arbitrarily tied to bed or chair. [279]

In 1985 the Court declined to hold that mental retardation was a "quasi-suspect" class requiring a heightened scrutiny of laws that discriminate on that basis. A municipal ZONING ordinance of Cleburne, Texas, barred group homes for the "feeble minded" in areas permitted to sorority and fraternity houses, college dormitories, and nursing homes for the ill and the aged. Although agreeing that the retarded have an immutable characteristic distinguishing them from all others, the Court asserted that they are not politically powerless because they have attracted the "attention of the lawmakers" and that it could find no simple way to distinguish the retarded as a class from others who might attack legislation aimed at them, including "the aging, the disabled, the mentally ill, and the infirm." To recognize each of these groups as needing special constitutional protection would force courts into making judgments about legislative policies that they are ill-equipped to do. Nevertheless, the Court rejected the zoning ban on group homes for the retarded because it was irrational. The city could offer no sound reason for distinguishing between group homes for the retarded and people who are otherwise infirm, except "vague, undifferentiated fears." The Court refused to sanction a law resting "on an irrational prejudice against the mentally retarded."[407]

The Court has refused to see in the EIGHTH AMENDMENT's ban on cruel and unusual PUNISHMENT an absolute prohibition against executing mentally retarded killers. Saying in 1989 that the Eighth Amendment might indeed ban executing those who are "profoundly and severely retarded and wholly lacking the capacity to appreciate the wrongfulness of their actions," the Court held that a jury may sentence to death a retarded person who is competent to stand trial and who failed to prove insanity, but only if the judge instructed it to consider evidence that the defendant was retarded as a potentially mitigating circumstance.[1599]

See also: RATIONAL BASIS OR RELATIONSHIP TEST; REPRODUCTIVE RIGHTS; STRICT SCRUTINY; SUSPECT CLASSIFICATIONS.

mere evidence rule   In 1921 the Supreme Court held that a SEARCH WARRANT could not authorize law enforcement officers to search and seize "mere evidence" of a crime, such as incriminating documents. A search warrant must be confined, it said, to the instrumentalities of the crime (the gun, the burglar's tools) and the fruits of the crime (the jewels stolen, the drugs traded).[786] The Court reasoned that the public had a property interest in fruits and instrumentalities of crime but not in evidence. In 1932 the Court extended this mere evidence rule to warrantless searches.[1139] But in 1967, the Court reversed itself, holding that the distinction between types of "property" is "wholly irrational": the same "papers and effects" might be mere evidence in one case and an instrumentality of the crime in another. For example, clothing that in one case might merely identify

the suspect in another might have been used as a uniform to help commit the crime.[2153] There continued to be some question whether under the FIFTH AMENDMENT's right against SELF-INCRIMINATION papers and effects could be seized as evidence, but in 1976 the Court held that the seizure of business records was permissible because the seizure did not compel the defendant to say or do anything. He had not been forced to create the documents or to authenticate them at trial.[50]

message, right to receive, *see:* **readers' rights**

military courts and justice   Under Art. I-§8[14] Congress has authority to "make rules for the government and regulation" of the ARMED FORCES. The principal modern military code is the Uniform Code of Military Justice, enacted in 1950. The UCMJ continues the old tradition of trial by COURT-MARTIAL under a law common to all uniformed members of the military services, whether in war or peacetime. Although courts-martial use trial-like procedures, they are convened by military authority and are not ARTICLE III courts.[1100] The UCMJ provides for several stages of review within the military system, including an appeal in some instances to the Court of Military Justice, an ARTICLE I court consisting of three civilian judges appointed by the president and subject to Senate confirmation. Court-martial verdicts may not be appealed directly to civil courts.[590] There is at least a limited indirect route to appeal some cases through HABEAS CORPUS,[1345],[2275] but the only issues that may be raised are whether the military had jurisdiction over the defendant and the offense charged and whether it acted within its powers.[918],[282] Many of the PROCEDURAL DUE PROCESS issues that arise in state court proceedings are absent in the military setting because the UCMJ provides for most of the rights contained in the BILL OF

MILITARY-CIVILIAN RELATIONS

RIGHTS, including the right against DOUBLE JEOPARDY, the right against SELF-INCRIMINATION, the right to MIRANDA-type warnings, and the right to appointed or retained counsel in the more serious types of court-martial. However, the FIFTH AMENDMENT specifically states that INDICTMENT by GRAND JURY is not applicable to "cases arising in the land and naval forces," and there is no right to TRIAL BY JURY. The UCMJ provides for trial before a panel of military personnel appointed by the commanding officer convening the court-martial or before a military judge sitting alone.

The Supreme Court has held that there is no right to counsel in "summary courts-martial," the lowest level of criminal trial for essentially petty offenses.[1334] Many of the offenses for which members of the armed forces may be tried are peculiar to the military; there simply is no analogue to "absent without leave" in civilian life. Because the military is a largely closed society with traditions and necessities far different from those of society at large, the Court has been willing to relax many constitutional rules that would apply to prosecutions in civil courts. For example, the Court saw no problem of VAGUENESS in provisions of the UCMJ outlawing "conduct unbecoming an officer and a gentleman" and "all disorders and neglects to the prejudice of good order and discipline in the armed forces."[1570] The UCMJ also provides for trial of many crimes that are not military in nature; for example, rape and other assaults of civilians and robberies committed off-base.

In 1969 the Court held in *O'Callahan v. Parker* that military personnel may not be tried by court-martial for crimes that are not "service connected," but in 1987 the Court overruled *O'Callahan* because "the service connection approach . . . has proved confusing and difficult for military courts to apply."[1907] Military personnel have no right, in the absence of express congressional authorization, to sue for DAM-AGES for injuries inflicted on them, whether physical or otherwise, "aris[ing] out of or . . . in the course of activity incident to service." The Court refused to entertain the claim of an enlisted man that his superiors were racially discriminating in awarding assignments and performance evaluations.[376] It also dismissed the suit by a master sergeant charging that the Army had given him LSD without his knowledge or consent as part of an experiment to test human reactions to the drug.[1947]

See also: FOLLOWING THE FLAG; IMMUNITY FROM SUIT; MILITARY-CIVILIAN RELATIONS; SOVEREIGN IMMUNITY.

military-civilian relations The American tradition that civilians must control the military is older than the Constitution. The DECLARATION OF INDEPENDENCE condemned King George III for "affect[ing] to render the Military independent of and superior to the Civil Power." Under Art. II-§2[1] the president is the COMMANDER IN CHIEF of the ARMED FORCES, and the WAR POWER is divided between Congress and the president. Civil authorities in the states, too, have a role, although it is more limited, with power to appoint the officers of the MILITIA. Moreover, from the very beginning, CONSCRIPTION of civilians into the army for a limited time was a well-understood and accepted practice. The tradition of civilian control extends beyond leadership of the military. It applies as well to the general governance of civil society. Except in the most extreme and rare circumstances, when MARTIAL LAW is necessary during wartime to maintain order in the community, civil judicial authority is paramount to military tribunals for everyone except uniformed members of the armed forces. In *Ex parte Milligan* after the Civil War and again in *Duncan v. Kahanamoku* after World War II, the Supreme Court affirmed the principle that as long as the civil courts are open, military tribunals may neither supplant them nor try civilians accused of disloyalty or any other crime. The armed forces may govern civilians by military law only in the actual theater of operations, and it is for the civilian courts, and ultimately the Supreme Court, to determine the validity of the claim of necessity to operate by military law.

Military law is a creature of Congress; it is not self-imposed. But Congress may apply it only to the military itself. The Court denied the Army power to try by court-martial a former soldier who was charged, after he received an honorable discharge, with committing murder in Korea while in uniform. The murder charge could be tried only in federal court.[2061] Nor may the Army try the civilian dependents of military personnel, even if the crimes were committed outside the United States[1079] and even if the civilian was accused of murdering a member of the armed forces.[1706] Likewise, the military may not try its civilian employees by court-martial.[819, 1294]

militia Although the power to declare and conduct war lies with the United States, the states possess the independent power to arm and train their citizens for defensive purposes. Citizens armed by the states are known as the "militia." Until early in the twentieth century, Congress left the militia entirely up to the states, even though Art. I-§8[15,16] grants Congress the power to call forth the militia; to organize, arm, and discipline the militia; and to govern the militia when it is employed in the service of the United States. But in 1916 Congress defined the militia as all "able-bodied" males between eighteen and forty-five years of age who are citizens of the United States or who have declared their intention to become citizens. The National Guard, troops whose officers are appointed by the states and whose training is conducted by the states, is part of the militia and may be drafted into the United States military. The 1916 act largely preempted local control of the militia, and the Supreme

Court upheld Congress's power to do so.[1842] In 1991, the Court held that Congress may order the National Guard to train outside the United States without the consent of the governor of the state in which they are stationed and without any declaration of national emergency.[1608]

See also: CONSCRIPTION; POSSE COMITATUS; WAR POWER.

milk Even during the period in which the Supreme Court struck down many state laws for violating ECONOMIC DUE PROCESS, the Court consistently upheld laws regulating the processing and sale of milk, including laws requiring impure milk to be confiscated,[8] ice cream to contain a certain proportion of butter fat,[967] condensed milk to be made from whole rather than skimmed milk,[890] and "filled milk" to contain only milk fats, not nonmilk fats or other oils.[1782] Two of the major turning points from economic due process came in milk cases. In one case, the Court upheld a federal ban on the shipment in INTERSTATE COMMERCE of skimmed milk mixed with nonmilk fats;[348] in the other, it sustained a state law fixing the selling price of milk, rejecting the assertion that milk is not AFFECTED WITH A PUBLIC INTEREST and that due process denies legislatures the power to control market prices.[1440] This same law was the battleground over a key DORMANT COMMERCE CLAUSE case in 1935, in which the Court refused to condone a state law prohibiting milk dealers from selling milk in state if they bought it out of state for below the in-state minimum price. The destination state may not use its POLICE POWER to establish "an economic barrier against competition with the products of another state or the labor of its residents."[110] Similarly, a state may not demand that out-of-state producers pasteurize their milk in state as long as it is clear that there is a LESS RESTRICTIVE ALTERNATIVE to ensuring wholesomeness, such as inspecting it at the border.[528] But a state may require milk to be sold in nonplastic, rather than plastic, nonreturnable containers, even though plastic containers were manufactured out of state and the nonplastic ones in the state.[1356]

See also: OLEOMARGARINE.

minimum contact test, *see:* **jurisdiction; property tax**

minimum wage laws   In 1918 the Supreme Court declared that minimum wage laws violate FREEDOM OF CONTRACT by barring employers and workers from negotiating any wages they please.[16] But in 1937 the Court overruled itself, declaring that there is no general freedom of contract and that legislatures may enact minimum wage laws to bolster the bargaining power of economically weak classes of workers and to prevent them from being victimized by circumstances.[2184]

See also: ECONOMIC DUE PROCESS.

mining regulation, *see: Lochner v. New York*

minorities, *see:* **discrete and insular minorities; equal protection of the laws; racial discrimination; sex discrimination; suspect classifications**

Miranda **rules**   In *Miranda v. Arizona,* the Supreme Court announced a multipart constitutional rule governing the use of confessions. The *Miranda* rules amount to a code of police conduct. They are familiar to anyone who has ever seen a police drama on television, where the arresting officer tells the suspect, "I'm going to read you your rights." After being arrested, and before being questioned, a suspect must be told that (1) he has a right to remain silent, (2) any statement he makes may be used as evidence against him, (3) he has a right to a lawyer, either retained or appointed. The defendant may waive these rights if he does so voluntarily, knowingly, and intelligently. But if he indicates in any manner and at any stage that he

does not wish to be interrogated or wishes to consult with a lawyer before giving answers, there can be no questioning. Even if he has answered some questions or volunteered some statements, he retains the right not to answer further questions until he consults with a lawyer and thereafter consents to be questioned. No statements obtained by the police in violation of these rules may be admitted into evidence at the trial.

See also: MIRANDA V. ARIZONA; SELF-INCRIMINATION.

Miranda v. Arizona   In March 1963 Ernesto Miranda was arrested for the kidnapping and rape of an eighteen-year-old woman employed by a Phoenix, Arizona, theater. An indigent twenty-three-year-old with only an eighth-grade education, Miranda was placed in a LINEUP, and the victim identified him as her assailant. He was then taken for questioning directly to a separate room, where two police interrogators persuaded him after two hours to confess. He wrote out his confession in longhand. There was no indication then or later that the police had used physical force, threatened him, or promised leniency in return for the confession. Miranda was convicted. His case wended its way to an appeal in the Supreme Court during the 1965–1966 term, along with three other convictions resulting from confessions made during police interrogations.

Michael Vignera confessed to the New York police that he had robbed a dress shop. Carl Calvin Westover was arrested by the Kansas City (Missouri) police for committing two local robberies. Fourteen hours later, after a lengthy interrogation, agents of the Federal Bureau of Investigation questioned him still further about an unrelated California robbery. Three hours later they had his confession. Roy Allen Stewart was arrested in Los Angeles for a series of purse-snatchings. One of his victims had been injured and later died. Stewart let the police search his home, where they discovered objects taken from each of the victims. During eight interrogation sessions over the next five days, Stewart refused to confess. Finally, during the ninth session, he admitted robbing the dead victim, and for the first time police brought him before a magistrate for ARRAIGN-MENT.

With the exception of Westover's interrogation by the FBI, none of the suspects had been advised of any constitutional rights, including the right to a lawyer. Of course, the police had no reason to believe that they were required to do so. But during the previous three years, the Court had incorporated through the Due Process Clause of the FOURTEENTH AMENDMENT the FIFTH AMENDMENT right against self-incrimination[1233] and applied the EXCLUSIONARY RULE to confessions made under certain circumstances when the suspect had not been permitted to consult with a lawyer.[1266, 624] On June 13, 1966, in a decision consolidating the appeals of Miranda, Vignera, Westover, and Stewart, the Supreme Court announced a dramatic set of rules that were quickly dubbed *Miranda* rights, warnings, or rules, requiring the police to warn suspects that they have a right to remain silent, that what they do say may be used against them, and that they are entitled to a lawyer before being questioned. The decision in *Miranda v. Arizona* was greeted with fury by police officials who predicted, against the weight of the evidence, that law enforcement would be seriously crippled. Since 1966, a steadily more conservative Court has made significant inroads into the requirements of the case, without ever overruling it. (The exceptions are discussed under the heading SELF-INCRIMINATION.)

Ernesto Miranda himself came to no good end. He was reconvicted on the original charges through other evidence and served four years in jail before being paroled. In 1976 he was stabbed to death in a skid-row bar in Phoenix during a quarrel over a card game. In his pocket were two "Miranda cards," on which the *Miranda* warnings were printed. He had been printing and selling them for two dollars each near the Maricopa County Superior Court. The Phoenix police read from one of the cards in his pocket to warn his suspected killer of his rights.

See also: COUNSEL, ASSISTANCE OF; INCORPORATION DOCTRINE; PROCEDURAL RIGHTS OF CRIMINAL DEFENDANTS.

miscegenation   Miscegenation is interracial MARRIAGE or interbreeding. Antimiscegenation laws, which were common in colonial America, were intended to prevent the estate of a white man from passing to his mulatto children; however, there was no enforcement against interracial sexual relations as such. In 1883, fifteen years after the FOURTEENTH AMENDMENT was ratified, the Supreme Court missed the opportunity to strike down miscegenation laws under the EQUAL PROTECTION CLAUSE. The Court grossly misread the clause when it sustained an Alabama law that imposed a heavier penalty on the commission of adultery by an interracial couple than by a couple of the same race. The Court justified this result by noting that the punishment was the same for black as well as white.[1549] The HOLDING amounted to the conclusion that equality was for groups, not for individuals. If equality applies to individuals, then a black woman could not be punished more heavily than a white woman for having sexual relations with a white man. After 1883, the issue disappeared for eighty years. In 1956 the Court dismissed a challenge to Virginia's antimiscegenation law, ducking the chance of invalidating these laws under the authority of *Brown v. Board of Education,* apparently because the justices were worried about what southern politicians would do if presented with an issue even more emotional than school SEGREGA-TION.[1419] In 1964 the Court finally gathered the confidence to overturn the 1883 Alabama case by striking down Virginia's criminalization of interracial cohabitation.[1304]

The final blow came in 1967, when in *Loving v. Virginia* the Court definitively overturned all laws against interracial marriage. A Virginia couple, a black woman and white man, married in the District of Columbia. They were sentenced to one year in jail under the state's antimiscegenation law, but the sentence was suspended on condition that they leave the state and not return as a couple for twenty-five years. The Court unanimously reversed the conviction, holding that the state had offered no "legitimate overriding purpose independent of invidious discrimination" to justify the law. Virginia claimed the law was designed to "preserve racial integrity." In fact, the law prevented only whites from intermarrying with other races (except with descendants of Pochantas!); it did not bar nonwhites from intermarrying. But the Court did not rest its decision on this obvious discrimination. Chief Justice Earl Warren said that even if the law had evenhandedly sought to keep all races from intermarrying, the Equal Protection Clause prohibits restrictions on "the freedom to marry solely because of racial classifications."

misdemeanor   A misdemeanor is a minor criminal offense, usually distinguished from a FELONY by the term and place of confinement. Offenses punishable by less than a year's imprisonment are misdemeanors, as are those for which a person may be sent to a local jail rather than a state or federal penitentiary. The Supreme Court has ruled that under the SIXTH AMENDMENT persons accused of misdemeanor are entitled to be represented by lawyers if a jail term results,[68] although not if a jail sentence was theoretically possible but not actually imposed.[1829] In other words, indigent defendants who are not provided with lawyers at a misdemeanor trial may not be sentenced to jail time. Defendants are entitled to a jury in any misdemeanor trial in which the possible sentence is more than six months' imprisonment.[111]

Missouri Compromise   The Missouri Compromise was a deal cooked up in 1820 that resolved for a generation the debate over the spread of SLAVERY into the territories of the United States. Slavery opponents contended that Congress had ample power to attach restrictions on slavery on admitting new states into the UNION. Proslavery forces denied Congress any power to abolish slavery in any state, new or old. Under the compromise, Missouri was admitted as a slave state, Maine as a free state. Moreover, all new states carved out of the Louisiana Purchase north of Missouri's southern border were to be free states. For thirty years, Congress followed the practice of admitting free and slave states in pairs to maintain the balance. But in 1857 in DRED SCOTT V. SANDFORD, the Supreme Court declared the Missouri Compromise constitutionally invalid, a decision that led directly to the Civil War.

mistrial, *see:* **double jeopardy**

mobility, *see:* **travel, right to**

moment of silence, *see:* **prayer and Bible reading**

monetary power, *see:* **currency**

money, *see:* **currency**

monopoly, *see:* **antitrust law; interstate commerce**

Monroe Doctrine   President James Monroe, following the advice of his secretary of state, John Quincy Adams, proclaimed in his 1823 STATE OF THE UNION address that the United

States would resist with military force any attempt by European powers to assume power or restore political control over any country or region in the western hemisphere. The Monroe Doctrine, as it came to be known, was the earliest major assertion of unilateral presidential war-making power.

See also: PRESIDENT, POWERS OF; WAR POWER.

mootness   Because the federal courts may exercise JUDICIAL POWER only over CASES AND CONTROVERSIES, the Supreme Court has developed a constitutional doctrine requiring that a case be dismissed whenever it becomes moot— that is, whenever the controversy is no longer live. It is not enough that the controversy was real when the case was initiated; it must continue to be a case capable of being legally resolved by a court, either at trial or on appeal.[1405] A case can become moot for many reasons. The law may have been changed while the case was pending.[29, 279] The defendant in a criminal prosecution may have died.[585] The lapse of time during the pendency of the case may have changed the status of the parties. For example, a case involving a minor child may become moot if the child becomes an adult before the case is decided;[93] or a student complaining about discrimination in a school's admissions policy may have graduated before the case could be fully appealed.[533] However, one party may not cause an appeal to be dismissed by voluntarily stopping the conduct for which he or she is being sued. He or she must show that "there is no reasonable expectation that the wrong will be repeated."[2137]

The general constitutional rule against hearing moot cases has several exceptions. Some cases concern short-lived controversies that expire long before the judicial process can be exhausted. The Court has said that disputes "capable of repetition, yet evading review" may be heard even if the particular controversy is moot, as long as the same thing could happen again to the particular party. Examples are short sentences in criminal cases,[1864] short-term administrative orders[1838] and INJUNCTIONS that expire before review is possible,[1441, 350] ACCESS TO BALLOT and other election disputes,[1965], [1759] and cases involving ABORTION rights.[1748] If part of the relief requested has become moot, the case may still be heard as long as some part of the claimed injury remains unredressed, no matter how small.[665] For example, Adam Clayton Powell, Jr., could still maintain his suit against the House of Representatives for excluding him, even though he had been reelected and was again in the House when the appeal was heard, because he still had a claim for back pay.[1653] If there are multiple plaintiffs, as in a class action, the case will not be moot if the named plaintiff's claim is moot (for example, if he or she has died) because the controversy still exists for other members of the class.[1909]

See also: JUSTICIABILITY.

moral turpitude   Some laws provide for greater sanctions if the defendant's act involved "moral turpitude." An Oklahoma law provided for sterilization of habitual criminals if convicted three times for a felony involving moral turpitude. A provision in the Alabama constitution disfranchised anyone convicted even once of a crime of moral turpitude. The federal immigration laws have long provided for DEPORTATION of resident ALIENS similarly convicted. But despite repeated attempts, the Court has been unable to define the term with any precision. The dictionaries define "turpitude" as baseness, vileness, or depravity. "Moral turpitude," as Justice Robert H. Jackson once said, therefore "seems to mean little more than morally immoral."[1039]

Nevertheless, against a VAGUENESS challenge, the Court upheld a deportation order against an alien who had been convicted of defrauding the United States for evading taxes on the sale of liquor. Whatever else moral turpitude might mean, the 6–3 majority said, it includes crimes invovling fraud. Dissenting, Jackson said "there appears to be universal recognition that we have here an undefined and undefinable standard." The government suggested that crimes of moral turpitude can be determined by measuring them against "the moral standards that prevail in contemporary society." Jackson concluded that doing so was a hopeless task. Pointing to several circuit court decisions with wildly inconsistent results, Jackson said the "chief impression" from attempts to define the term "is the caprice of the judgments." Evading a tax, Jackson said, is far from being universally condemned as immoral: "I have never discovered that disregard of the Nation's liquor taxes excluded a citizen from our best society and I see no reason why it should banish an alien from our worst." [1039]

In the Oklahoma sterilization and Alabama disfranchisement cases, the Court never reached the issue of what "moral turpitude" means because it found the laws fatally defective under the EQUAL PROTECTION CLAUSE. The Oklahoma law required that burglars be sterilized but exempted embezzlers, presumably because embezzlement is more likely to be a white-collar crime committed by a "better class" of people. [1879] The Alabama law was stricken because the Court concluded that the moral turpitude provision was intended to discriminate against blacks when enacted in 1901. [962]

morality, *see:* **public morals**

mortgage moratorium In the midst of the Depression, Minnesota passed a relief act for homeowners. In effect it permitted homeowners to stave off foreclosure sales by two years in return for paying "all or a reasonable part" of the fair rental value of the property, rather than the full amount of principal and interest owed. A building and loan association challenged the law under the CONTRACT CLAUSE on the ground that it impaired the mortgagor's OBLIGATION OF CONTRACT. The Court held, 5–4, that the Minnesota's mortgage moratorium did not abolish a homeowner's ultimate obligation under the mortgage contract, since it did not repudiate the debt. Rather, the moratorium was a "temporary relief from the enforcement of contracts in the presence of disasters . . . produced [by] economic causes." [937]

motive, intent, and purpose One of the earliest maxims of JUDICIAL REVIEW is that in determining whether a statute is constitutional, the courts will not inquire into the motives of the legislators in enacting it. This principle was established in 1810 in *Fletcher v. Peck*, the case growing out of the YAZOO LAND SCANDAL, in which members of the Georgia legislature had been bribed to make land grants. When the voters swept the corrupt legislators out of office and the new legislature revoked the grants, Chief Justice John Marshall declared that a court could not pronounce the original grant void because "impure motives" had contributed to its passage.

There are many problems with inquiring into legislators' personal motives. One problem is that of proof: ordinary civil litigation might have to be interrupted while the court required legislators to take the stand and defend themselves. Such a rule would expose the legislature to potentially endless interruptions, and it would require the courts to determine what kinds of incentives or inducements, short of outright donations of cash, constitute corrupt motives. Since there can be no clear rule, it would make the courts perpetual censors over legislation whenever enough legislators could not satisfactorily explain *why* they passed a law.

Another problem is that since people rarely act solely from a single motivation, the court would be required to determine not only that a corrupt motive existed but that without it the legislator would have voted differently. To compound these difficulties still further, the court would necessarily have to inquire into the motives of every legislator for every law so challenged, since laws are enacted by majority vote. How many legislators would need to be corrupt to overturn the law? All? A majority? A substantial minority? If courts were permitted to assess legislators' motives, no law would ever be secure. "So long as Congress acts in pursuance of its constitutional power," the Court has summed up, "the Judiciary lacks authority to intervene on the basis of the motives which spurred the exercise of that power."[125]

The judiciary can, however, hold an inquiry into two closely related matters: what is the *purpose* of the law and what is the *intent* of the law? Suppose, in a partially hypothetical case, that people are resisting an unpopular war, loudly demonstrating against the president's policies, and that many young men are burning their draft cards. Fearful that these demonstrations will weaken political support for the war, the president privately tells every member of Congress that the administration will make campaign funds available to anyone who votes for a new draft-resister bill. The bill says that "any male between the ages of eighteen and twenty-seven must carry a draft card on his person at all times." The bill passes, and federal law enforcement officials, carrying a SEARCH WARRANT, arrest a noisy opponent of the draft for taking a shower without carrying his draft card. In a case testing the constitutionality of the draft card law, we can ask: (1) What was the purpose of passing the law? (2) What is its intent?

The *motive* of the individual legislators might have been solely to get their hands on campaign funds; or they might also have believed it was a patriotic thing to do; or they might have wanted the funds, believed it was their patriotic duty, and supposed that the law might "help with the problem." In assessing the

constitutionality of the law, a court could not inquire into any of these personal motives.

But in trying to understand what the law in fact means, the court could inquire into legislative intent. On its face, the law says that a draft card must be carried "at all times." Did the legislature really intend that the law apply to what a person does in the privacy of his home? Presumably not. The court might also look to "legislative history"—what the congressional committee said in its report on the bill, for example—to determine what conduct is fairly embraced by the words of the act. If the legislature did intend such a result, the law presumably would be struck down as unconstitutional. More likely, since it is doubtful that the legislature contemplated such a case, the court would construe the law narrowly to avoid the constitutional problem. But a further problem remains. Assume the intent of the law is simply that a draft-eligible man must carry his draft card with him whenever he is outside his home. Suppose that one man burns his card in front of television cameras to demonstrate his contempt for the president's war policies. Is the burning protected as an act of SYMBOLIC SPEECH under the FIRST AMENDMENT? That depends on the purpose of the law. If the only reason for the law was to prevent people from vocally expressing their opinions of the president's policies, it would indeed be unconstitutional, for Congress has no permissible interest in doing so. But Congress does have a substantial or even COMPELLING INTEREST in enacting a draft law, and it certainly may require that the draft be administered through a system that includes registration cards. So inevitably in cases such as this, the courts will be forced to consider purpose even if they may not consider motive.[508]

Inquiry into legislative purpose arises in many types of cases. The Supreme Court has said that a law is an unconstitutional BILL OF ATTAINDER if its purpose is to oust labor leaders from union positions for their political activity.[261] The Court has held that although the legislature has broad power to hold hearings, it may not ask certain questions if its purpose is merely to expose a person's affairs to the public.[2165]

Often the words "motive," "purpose," and "intent" are used loosely and interchangeably. The Court said that whether school authorities may remove books from library shelves depends upon their "motivation. . . . If [they] *intended . . .* to deny [students] access to ideas with which they disagreed, and if this intent was the decisive factor" in the decision, then the removal was unconstitutional.[182] Presumably the Court meant "purpose."

Probably in no area are the courts more often concerned with legislative purpose than in cases involving claims of RACIAL DISCRIMINATION and other forms of discrimination unconstitutional under the EQUAL PROTECTION CLAUSE. As the Court has said: "Because legislators and administrators are properly concerned with balancing numerous competing considerations . . . courts refrain from reviewing the merits of their decisions, absent a showing of arbitrariness or irrationality. But racial discrimination is not just another competing consideration. When there is proof that a discriminatory purpose has been a motivating factor in [a governmental] decision, . . . judicial deference is no longer justified."[77]

And sometimes, despite rhetoric to the contrary, the Court even looks to legislators' motives—for example, in religion cases raising the question of whether the state legislature was aiming at creating a RELIGIOUS ESTABLISHMENT.[600, 2146]

A law is not unconstitutional if Congress fails to state what its purpose was in enacting it or to recite what provision in the Constitution empowers it to enact the law.[2255] "This Court," said Justice Rehnquist in a 1980 case, "has never insisted that a legislative body articulate its reasons for enacting a statute." It is enough when "there are plausible reasons for Congress' action."[2105, 620]

See also: DE FACTO-DE JURE DISTINCTION; INVESTIGATORY POWERS OF LEGISLATURE; LEMON TEST; NATIONAL POLICE POWER; PUBLIC MORALS; PURPOSE-IMPACT DISTINCTION; TRANSPORTATION.

motor vehicles   States may license the operation and regulate the use of motor vehicles, including those coming from other states,[902] unless the regulation conflicts with federal law or discriminates against INTERSTATE COMMERCE.[1914] The Court has said the states retain broad and pervasive power to regulate their highways and that safety measures "carry a strong presumption of validity." However, when the effect of a highway safety measure is slight and its burden on interstate commerce is great, the law violates the DORMANT COMMERCE CLAUSE.[161] The states may constitutionally demand drivers to carry adequate insurance against injuries they might cause.[456]

See also: TAXATION OF MOTOR VEHICLES; TRANSPORTATION.

movies, censorship of, *see:* **censorship; prior restraint**

multimember election districts   The Supreme Court has held that with the exception of the United States Senate, representation for most elected public bodies must be chosen on the basis of equal populations. But the Constitution does not require that representatives be chosen from "single-member districts"; that is, that a single representative be chosen from each geographic constituency. In a multimember district, the same group of electors chooses more than one representative. This would happen, for example, if a city were entitled to three representatives in the state assembly and instead of being divided into three districts, the city was a single district whose residents could vote for three representatives. The Court has held that multimember districts as such are constitutional[691] as long as they were not constituted to discriminate on the basis of race or some other forbidden ground.[2195] Ordinarily the courts should defer to the legislature's decision on how representatives are to be elected. But if the legislature refuses to apportion in a constitutional manner, and a lower court is forced to order reapportionment, it "should prefer single member districts over multimember districts, absent persuasive justification to the contrary."[2238]

See also: APPORTIONMENT OF POLITICAL DISTRICTS.

multiple taxation, *see:* **taxation, multiple domiciles**

municipal bond cases, *see:* **Erie rule; obligation of contract**

municipalities, *see:* **political subdivisions**

murder   The crime of murder is generally defined by state law. However, under the NECESSARY AND PROPER CLAUSE, Congress may define and punish murder on federal territory, at high sea, and against federal officials.

See also: DEATH PENALTY.

N

narrow construction, *see:* strict
construction

National Industrial Recovery Act, *see:* Sick
Chicken Case

National Labor Relations Act, *see:*
interstate commerce; labor and labor laws

national police power   Considerable doubt
that Congress has constitutional authority to
legislate in matters of public health, safety, and
morals was finally resolved more than a half a
century ago. The general power to regulate
such matters, dubbed the POLICE POWER by
Chief Justice John Marshall in 1827,[253] was originally thought to be exclusive to the states. But
nothing in the Constitution precludes Congress from enacting a law that regulates the
public welfare, as long as the law falls within
one of its ENUMERATED POWERS. Since 1842,
when it banned the importation of obscene
books and pictures from abroad, Congress has
prohibited the flow of many goods into the
country on the ground of public morals and
health, and the Court has upheld these laws.[2173]
Since Congress's power over INTERSTATE COM-
MERCE is in constitutional terms exactly the
same as its power over foreign commerce,

there seems to be no logical reason that Congress may not prohibit anything from being
shipped among the states. But such domestic
PROHIBITION OF COMMERCE raised many judicial
eyebrows.

In 1892 the Court upheld Congress's power
to prohibit the mailing of lottery tickets, lotteries in those days being considered one of the
major national evils. The Court's rationale was
that because Congress had established the
postal system, Congress could control its
use.[1694] By only the slimmest majority the
Court in 1903 approved a similar federal ban on
all shipments of lottery tickets in interstate
commerce.[369] Thereafter the Court approved a
federal law against the interstate "white slave
traffic."[931] But the Court drew a line in 1918,
striking down a law banning the shipment
across state lines of goods made by child labor.
The majority reasoned that in the other cases
the goods or services themselves were harmful
or immoral, whereas the goods made by children were not.[851] The Court finally repudiated
this distinction in 1941, revitalizing Congress's
power to ban whatever it wants from interstate
shipments,[514] as long as there is no independent constitutional limitation on its doing so.
For example, it would violate the FIRST
AMENDMENT to prohibit the shipment of news-

papers from state to state. During the past half century, the Court has approved extensive congressional use of its national police power, including banning RACIAL DISCRIMINATION in public accommodations;[888], [1052] outlawing the kidnapping of people across state lines;[777] prohibiting anyone ever convicted of a felony from receiving or possessing firearms transported at any time in interstate commerce, even if the felony was committed long after the person came into possession of the gun;[131], [1808] and criminalizing loan sharking, even if the extortionate act was performed entirely within one state.[1603] The Court has also approved Congress's use of its SPENDING POWER to coerce states into enacting public safety and welfare laws. For example, the Court upheld the conditioning of federal highway grants on the states' enactment of laws raising the drinking age to twenty-one years.[1915]

See also: STATE ACTION.

national security   Under the WAR POWER, the power to make TREATIES, the COMMERCE POWER, and the FOREIGN AFFAIRS POWER, Congress and the president have considerable authority to provide for the national security. But all these powers have limits. The Supreme Court has ruled that the president does not have an inherent power to conduct electronic surveillance of domestic groups or individual citizens without obtaining a SEARCH WARRANT. To wiretap or bug the premises in the United States of suspected subversives, the Court unanimously ruled, the administration must seek a warrant from a neutral magistrate.[2102] Whether the president, solely on his own initiatives, may authorize wiretaps and bugs on the premises of foreign nationals, such as embassies, has not been decided.

See also: LOYALTY-SECURITY PROGRAMS; SEARCH AND SEIZURE; SEDITION.

national supremacy, *see:* **Supremacy Clause**

nationality, people classified by   Laws that classify people by race are rarely likely to survive the Supreme Court's STRICT SCRUTINY test under the EQUAL PROTECTION CLAUSE. Even though the FOURTEENTH AMENDMENT was originally proposed and ratified as protection for the former black slaves, the Court held as long ago as 1880 in a jury discrimination case that any INVIDIOUS DISCRIMINATION based on color or national origins is unconstitutional: "If a law should be passed excluding all naturalized Celtic Irishmen, [there would be no] doubt of its inconsistency with the spirit of the amendment."[1967] Since then the Court has repeatedly reaffirmed this principle, extending it to discriminations based on a person's religion or status as an alien.[791], [1847], [1784]

nations, law of, *see:* **international law**

Native Americans, *see:* **Indians and Indian tribes**

nativity scene, *see:* **religious symbols, right to display**

natural born citizen, *see:* **citizens and citizenship**

natural law   During the Senate confirmation battle over Justice Clarence Thomas in the fall of 1991, talk of "natural law" was much in the air. Natural law is an ancient philosophical concept. In constitutional terms, natural law assumes there is a "higher" or "fundamental" law anterior or superior to the Constitution and given by God or nature. It is also referred to as "right reason," the "nature of things," or "fundamental values" that inhere in an "unwritten Constitution." The claim of such a law has deep roots in American history. The DECLARATION OF INDEPENDENCE appeals to "self-evident truths" and "inalienable rights." Alexander Hamilton asserted in 1774 that "[t]he sacred rights of mankind are not to be rummaged for, among old parchments, or musty records. They are written, as with a sun beam, in the whole *volume* of human nature, . . . and can never be erased or obscured."

Some justices expressed a belief in the natural law tradition in the earliest days of the Court. The most often cited example is the opinion of Justice Samuel Chase in 1798 that the Court could void a state legislative enactment even though the Constitution permits it: "An ACT of the Legislature (for I cannot call it a *law*) contrary to the *great first principles of the social compact,* cannot be considered a *rightful exercise of legislative authority.*"[307] In 1810, in *Fletcher v. Peck,* Chief Justice John Marshall said that the Court's decision was justified "either by general principles which are common to our free institutions, or by the particular provisions of the constitution of the United States." But in the 1798 case, Justice Thomas Iredell vigorously opposed the idea "that a legislative act against natural justice must, in itself be void . . . [because] the ideas of natural justice are regulated by no fixed standard: the ablest and the purest men have differed upon the subject." Only if a law violates a constitutional provision, said Iredell, may it be declared void. Natural rights talk largely disappeared until after the Civil War and the ratification of the FOURTEENTH AMENDMENT.

In the *Slaughter-House Cases* in 1873, the Court saw no reason to disapprove a legislated monopoly as a violation of natural law. But just two years later, an 8–1 majority overturned a state tax law, saying: "It must be conceded that there are . . . rights in every free government beyond the control of the State. . . . There are limitations on [governmental] power which grow out of the essential nature of all free governments. Implied reservations of individual rights, without which the social compact could not exist, and which are respected by all governments entitled to the name."[1174]

By the turn of the century, the Court had forgotten *Slaughter-House* and thereafter due process, rather than free-floating principles of natural right and justice, was used as a constitutional tool to stike down laws of which a majority disapproved. It was on the basis of SUBSTANTIVE DUE PROCESS that the Court struck down state ABORTION laws in *Roe v. Wade* in 1973. Occasionally, the Court dispenses with the Constitution altogether in confirming a right. For example, in reiterating the right to TRAVEL, the Court said that it had "no occasion to ascribe the source of this right to . . . a particular constitutional provision."[1850]

The only modern justice continuously—and strenuously—objecting to these developments was Hugo L. Black, who repeatedly chastised his judicial brethren for using the " 'natural law' formula," saying that it "should be abandoned as an incongruous excrescence on our Constitution."[11] In *Griswold v. Connecticut,* he noted that "a collection of the catchwords and catch phrases invoked by judges who would strike down under the Fourteenth Amendment laws which offend their notions of natural justice would fill many pages," including conduct that "shocks the conscience"[1746] or that "shock[s] itself into the protective arms of the Constitution."[992] All of these verbal formulations,[1231, 842] he said, suffer from the same defect. "If the judges, in deciding whether laws are constitutional, are to be left only to the admonitions of their own consciences, why was it that the Founders gave us a written Constitution at all?"[1901] But Black's was a decidedly minority view; in 1991 a majority on the most conservative Court in sixty years indicated that it would not relinquish the natural law power, even if it has abandoned the nomenclature.[1552]

See also: CONSTITUTIONAL INTERPRETATION; FUNDAMENTAL INTERESTS, RIGHTS, AND PRIVILEGES; INTERPRETIVISM; NINTH AMENDMENT; PRIVACY.

natural resources, *see:* **environmental regulation; game laws**

naturalization, *see:* **immigration and naturalization**

navigation and navigability In 1824, in *Gibbons v. Ogden,* Chief Justice John Marshall declared that navigation is an aspect of commerce and that Congress therefore has the power to regulate it under the COMMERCE CLAUSE. Since that time, the Court has recognized a sweeping power in Congress to regulate not merely the act of navigation but everything incidental to it along the nation's navigable waterways, which are the "public property of the nation."[757] Congress may delegate to the secretary of the navy the power to determine whether a bridge is obstructing any navigable waterway and to order it altered or even removed.[2091] The federal government may demand that owners of obstructions remove them at their own cost,[1712] and in declaring a bridge, dock, or other property as an obstruction, the government incurs no constitutional obligation to pay JUST COMPENSATION.[751, 1692] Congress may also permit an obstructing bridge to remain in place, even one that a court has previously required to be torn down.[1595] Congress's power extends to navigable waters lying entirely within one state, when the regulations it enacts apply to ships used to carry goods in INTERSTATE COMMERCE.[2028] It also extends to waters that are not naturally navigable but have been[1731] or can be[66] made so by artificial improvements. The power to regulate navigation extends to control of rates charged by interstate shippers[1464] and to practices of those who own docks, warehouses, and other facilities related to interstate shipping.[324] Federal control over waterways is not limited to navigation. Its authority, the Court has said, "is as broad as the needs of commerce.... Flood protection, watershed development,"[66] and

even the development of hydroelectric power[371] are all within the domain of Congress. *See also:* ADMIRALTY AND MARITIME JURISDICTION.

navy, *see:* **armed forces**

Necessary and Proper Clause The Constitution sets out only the thinnest skeleton of federal power. For instance, Art. I-§8[7] says that Congress may establish POST OFFICES and POST ROADS, but it says nothing about the power to hire letter carriers, issue stamps, regulate their prices, or make laws against stealing the mail. To put flesh on the skeletal powers, Art. I-§8[18] says that Congress may "make all laws which shall be necessary and proper for carrying into execution" its ENUMERATED POWERS. The ANTI-FEDERALISTS condemned the Necessary and Proper Clause as the "sweeping" or "elastic" clause because it potentially could swallow up any limitations on federal power. In 1791, arguing against a bill to create a national bank, Thomas Jefferson insisted that the clause empowered Congress to use only those means that are *absolutely* necessary to carry out an enumerated power. Alexander Hamilton disagreed, maintaining that the clause empowers Congress to do whatever is useful in accomplishing its purposes. President George Washington sided with Hamilton and signed the bank bill. The issue came to the Supreme Court in 1819, when Maryland challenged the Second Bank of the United States, asserting that the Constitution gave Congress no authority to charter banks.

In *McCulloch v. Maryland,* Chief Justice John Marshall gave the Necessary and Proper Clause the broadest interpretation, which it retains to this day. The word "necessary," Marshall said, is not confined to "indispensable" means to an end, but embraces any means that are "convenient, or useful, or essential." The Necessary and Proper Clause "is made in a constitution intended to endure for ages to come, and, consequently, to be adapted to the various *crises* of human affairs." In one of the most celebrated lines of constitutional interpretation, Marshall concluded: "Let the end be legitimate, let it be within the scope of the constitution, and all means which are appropriate, which are plainly adapted to that end, which are not prohibited, but consist with the letter and spirit of the constitution, are constitutional." From that time forward, the Necessary and Proper Clause has been indispensable to the steady expansion of federal power. With minor exceptions, the entire body of federal criminal law owes its existence to this clause. The clause has also been instrumental in giving Congress powers over entire areas of American life, including the sweeping monetary and fiscal powers by which it regulates the national economy.[1141]

The Necessary and Proper Clause is not limited to supplementing the enumerated powers of Congress. It also enables Congress to enact laws implementing "all other powers vested by this Constitution in the government of the United States or in any Department or Officer thereof." This means that Congress has power to legislate in many areas other than those specifically delegated to it. It may establish all the offices and agencies of the federal government, create and regulate the entire federal court system,[1716] modify admiralty and maritime laws,[2032, 290] and enact laws to implement treaties that it would have no constitutional authority to enact in the absence of the treaty.[1363]

Despite its extreme plasticity, the Necessary and Proper Clause is not of itself a grant of independent power to accomplish ends not permitted by the Constitution. To the argument that the clause permits Congress to authorize military COURTS-MARTIAL to try crimes committed by dependents of members of the ARMED FORCES, the Court responded that Art. I-§8[14] empowers Congress to regulate "the

land and naval forces" only. People who are not members of those forces cannot be brought within those regulations on the ground that doing so is a means to regulating the military. Moreover, the clause cannot overcome the FIFTH and SIXTH AMENDMENTS, which act as separate prohibitions against trying a citizen without an INDICTMENT or a jury.[1079]

See also: ADMIRALTY AND MARITIME JURISDICTION; CURRENCY, FEDERAL POWER OVER; MILITARY-CIVILIAN RELATIONS; TREATIES AND TREATY POWER.

necessities of life, *see:* **wealth classification and discrimination**

needful buildings, *see:* **public property**

neutral magistrate, *see:* **search and seizure: neutral magistrate**

neutral principles   In an often-quoted speech at Harvard Law School in 1959, Professor Herbert Wechsler chastised those who applaud or condemn a court's constitutional ruling by "whether its result seems to hinder or advance the interests or the values they support." For instance, a critic of communist prosecutions is scarcely being consistent in advocating prosecution of racial hatemongers. According to Wechsler, "The courts [have a special duty] to judge by neutral principles."

As his hardest test of neutral principles, Wechsler examined the Court's school desegregation decision, *Brown v. Board of Education,* and found it wanting—not because of its result but because Chief Justice Earl Warren's stated conclusion, that segregated schools have deleterious effects on black school children, could not have "really turned on the facts." Wechsler noted the many situations in which integration in an extremely hostile atmosphere might be more deleterious. By Warren's reasoning, in such a case the school should *not* be desegregated. Only if the Court had declared "that the FOURTEENTH AMENDMENT forbids all racial lines in legislation," would the decision have rested on a neutral principle.

The argument about *Brown* seems somewhat myopic. By the time Wechsler gave his address, five years after *Brown*, the Court had moved quite far toward the neutral principle that Wechsler suggested. At least one implication of this history, therefore, is that in interpreting the Constitution case by case, the courts are groping toward neutral principles. But nothing in the concept of neutrality tells the courts which of two opposing neutral principles to prefer. Wechsler thought that the "heart of the issue" in *Brown* was not discrimination but a conflict between two ways of seeing FREEDOM OF ASSOCIATION: denying the association to parents of black schoolchildren who wish their children not to be barred from white schools or imposing it on white parents who want their children to associate only with other white children. A second difficulty is that nothing in the concept of neutrality tells us which of two unrelated neutral principles should be selected: a ban on racial lines in legislation or support for freedom of association. A critic of the Supreme Court could probably make a better case for the proposition that the Court is more often wrong because it chooses the wrong neutral principles than because it is not neutral at all.

The Supreme Court has used the concept of neutral principles in a slightly different sense in a rare class of cases in which judges are called on to determine which of two competing groups is entitled to possession of church property. When a congregation is ruptured by doctrinal schism, the ousted group sometimes sues to regain control, claiming that under the "laws and regulations" of the church they are the rightful governors. The Court has said that under the ESTABLISHMENT CLAUSE judges may not interpret church doctrine to see which group has been faithful to the church's princi-

ples. The courts may decide such disputes only if the state has enacted a "neutral principle of law," such as a majority vote of all church members, by which to determine the outcome.[1036]

See also: LEVEL OF GENERALITY; RELIGIOUS ESTABLISHMENT.

neutrality proclamation   In 1793 President George Washington proclaimed neutrality in the war between France and Great Britain. The Proclamation of Neutrality was undertaken unilaterally under a claimed independent presidential power over FOREIGN AFFAIRS, without congressional authorization, which many thought constitutionally required, in view of Congress's power to declare or to refrain from declaring war. In effect, this was the earliest recorded example of ADMINISTRATIVE LAW-making. To assuage the cabinet's doubts, Secretary of State Thomas Jefferson wrote the justices of the Supreme Court, asking their advice about the constitutionality of the proclamation. The Court advised Jefferson that it was constitutionally forbidden from offering ADVISORY OPINIONS.

New Jersey Plan, *see:* **Great Compromise**

new states, *see:* **state, formation of new**

newsgathering   Under the FIRST AMENDMENT's guarantee of FREEDOM OF SPEECH and FREEDOM OF THE PRESS, anyone is free to ask questions and conduct investigations to report the news. The Constitution does not shield someone who commits crimes to uncover information—there is no constitutional right, for example, to break into an office in the search for news—but there is a constitutional right to publish or broadcast information about public affairs that the government prefers to remain secret.[1473] The right to gather news does not mean that the government must cooperate or provide access to whatever official documents or other newsworthy information the press desires, although the Supreme Court has held that except in the rarest circumstances, the trial of a criminal case must be open to the public, including the press.[1727]

See also: ACCESS TO PRISONS AND PRISONERS; GAG ORDER; PENTAGON PAPERS CASE; PRIOR RESTRAINT; RIGHT TO KNOW.

newsman's privilege, see: **reporter's privilege**

newspapers, see: **contempt; freedom of the press**

Nineteenth Amendment   Until 1838 no state permitted women to vote in any elections. In that year, Kentucky approved female voting in school elections, and that limited right spread to some other states. But a comprehensive right to vote did not develop. In 1875 the Supreme Court foreclosed one potential avenue to women's suffrage, holding that the right to vote is not one of the PRIVILEGES OR IMMUNITIES guaranteed by the FOURTEENTH AMENDMENT.[1358] The first state in which women gained the right to vote was Wyoming, in 1869, but during the next forty-five years only ten other states followed suit. Finally, after an intense political campaign following World War I, Congress proposed the Nineteenth Amendment, the women's suffrage amendment, on June 4, 1919, and by August 18, 1920, it was ratified. By its terms the Nineteenth Amendment applies to both men and women, denying the United States and all states the power to discriminate in voting on the basis of sex. The Court has heard only one case touching on the Nineteenth Amendment, holding in 1937 that a Georgia POLL TAX law did not discriminate against men by giving women a partial exemption.[229]

See also: VOTING, RIGHT TO.

Ninth Amendment   The Ninth Amendment is the great paradox of the Constitution. The most telling argument against the Constitution during the ratification debates was that it did not contain a BILL OF RIGHTS. The Constitution's proponents disingenuously argued that for two reasons no listing of rights was necessary: first, since the new federal government was one of limited and ENUMERATED POWERS only, it would lack the authority to enact laws that violate people's rights; and second, since it would be impossible to list all rights, the omission of some from a Bill of Rights might be interpreted as conferring a power on Congress to enact laws invading the unlisted rights. These arguments were weak, as the ANTI-FEDERALISTS quickly pointed out. The NECESSARY AND PROPER CLAUSE, to which the Anti-Federalists also objected, could well bestow on Congress ample power to invade the people's rights. Moreover, the proposed Constitution *did* list some rights anyway—for example, the right to be free of EX POST FACTO laws and BILLS OF ATTAINDER. But by the Federalists' very own argument, that demonstrated the necessity for a Bill of Rights, since the Constitution omitted most other rights that everyone agreed the people ought to retain. Recalling these debates a year later, James Madison introduced in the First Congress as part of the proposed Bill of Rights a rule of interpretation that became the Ninth Amendment: "The enumeration in the Constitution of certain rights shall not be construed to deny or disparage others retained by the people." In other words, do not conclude from the way the Constitution is written that there are no rights beyond those listed.

For those who fear the antimajoritarian tendency of JUDICIAL REVIEW, the Ninth Amendment potentially poses a severe problem. For despite all the palaver about broad or STRICT CONSTRUCTION and the wisdom of abiding by the ORIGINAL INTENT of the Framers, it is clear that the Constitution itself contemplates rights that lie wholly outside its text. Even worse, historians of the period have shown that the rights the Framers contemplated were "natural rights," those "created in us by the decrees of Providence, which establish the laws of our nature. They are born with us; exist with us; and cannot be taken from us by any human power without taking our lives. In short, they are founded on the immutable maxims of reason and justice." These are the broad rights of NATURAL LAW. Madison believed that natural law embraced even FREEDOM OF SPEECH, and it was the one significant right that eventually found its way into the Bill of Rights that Madison omitted. In short, the Ninth Amendment is an invitation to the judicial declaration of unenumerated rights, "the repository for natural rights, including the right to pursue happiness and the right to equality of treatment before the law."

For 175 years, the Ninth Amendment lay dormant, if not forgotten. Although a few justices referred to it in passing,[2098] no one ever remotely suggested it as the basis for upholding a claim to an unenumerated right. For the first century, it was unnecessary to do so, since the Bill of Rights did not apply to the states and Congress enacted few laws that violated the kinds of rights that might be sheltered in the Ninth Amendment. Thereafter, the Court found other avenues—primarily through DUE PROCESS—to unenumerated rights. Then in 1965 the Court in *Griswold v. Connecticut* proclaimed a right of marital PRIVACY, a right not explicitly listed in the Constitution. In his majority opinion, Justice William O. Douglas referred to the Ninth Amendment, among others, to justify the Court's striking down an anti-CONTRACEPTION law. But it was the CONCURRING OPINION of Justice Arthur Goldberg, joined by Chief Justice Earl Warren and Justice William Brennan, that put the Ninth Amendment into constitutional discourse. Goldberg's point was that the Ninth Amendment strongly supports the view that the LIBERTY protected by due process "is not restricted to rights specifically mentioned in the first eight amendments."

Griswold unleashed a torrent of discussion. In the next fifteen years alone, more than 1,200 cases in the lower courts raised Ninth Amendment issues. Except for a solitary glancing reference in 1980, the Supreme Court has not returned to it.[1727] However, Professor Charles L. Black has suggested that the Court should not hesitate to discern and protect unnamed rights "closely analogous or functionally similar to a named right." For example, the FIFTH AMENDMENT says that no person may "be twice put in jeopardy of life or limb." It does not say that a person may be tried but once if the only penalty is a jail sentence. Yet the Court has interpreted the DOUBLE JEOPARDY provision to apply under these circumstances—a result, Black concludes, entirely consistent with the Ninth Amendment.

no religious test, *see:* **religious test**

nobility, titles of, *see:* **title of nobility**

noise regulation   Legislatures possess the undoubted power to regulate noise levels in factories and other workplaces in the interests of worker health and safety. Although it is limited in some cases by the FIRST AMENDMENT, the same power exists to regulate noise in the community at large. In 1943 the Court struck down a municipal ordinance prohibiting anyone from knocking on the doors of people's homes to distribute literature. The city said the ordinance was a means of protecting night-shift workers from being awakened during the day. The Court said the ban was a "naked restriction of the dissemination of ideas."[1253] Five years later the Court struck down an ordinance requiring anyone operating a sound truck to obtain permission from the chief of police, because the ordinance provided no limit on the chief's discretion to deny a permit.[1783] But in 1949 the Court upheld an ordinance banning sound trucks or other amplified vehicles that "emit . . . loud and raucous noises." Although there was no majority opinion, the Court seemed to say that to protect the public streets all amplifiers capable of loud noises could be banned even though on a particular occasion the loudspeaker was neither raucous nor loud.[1096]

See also: PERMIT SYSTEM; SOLICITATION.

no-knock entry   A no-knock entry occurs when police enter a suspect's home without first announcing their intention to enter, either to ARREST the suspect or to search the premises. The Federal Code of Criminal Procedure requires federal law enforcement officials to announce themselves before entering. The Court has not laid down any such requirement for the states, although a law authorizing or requiring police in every instance to enter without first announcing their presence would presumably violate the FOURTH AMENDMENT.

See also: SEARCH AND SEIZURE; SEARCH WARRANT.

nominations, *see:* **appointments**

nondelegation doctrine, *see:* **delegation doctrine**

nonobscene but sexually explicit expression, *see:* **offensive and indecent speech**

nonresidents, *see:* **residency**

Northwest Ordinance   The Northwest Ordinance of 1787 was enacted by the Confederation Congress, before the Constitution was ratified, to govern territory constituting the eventual states of Illinois, Indiana, Michigan, Ohio, and Wisconsin. The ordinance established the fundamental precedent that the continental territories of the United States would eventually be admitted into the UNION as full-

fledged STATES. It included a plan by which the territories could apply for statehood if they reached a certain population size and adopted a constitution providing for a REPUBLICAN FORM OF GOVERNMENT. The Northwest Ordinance was the first national law to contain specific rights as limitations on the powers of government, including many of the familiar provisions of the BILL OF RIGHTS, such as TRIAL BY JURY, JUST COMPENSATION for property taken by EMINENT DOMAIN, a ban on cruel and unusual PUNISHMENT, and the requirement of procedural regularity known in the Bill of Rights as DUE PROCESS. The ordinance also included the forerunner of the CONTRACT CLAUSE and barred SLAVERY and involuntary servitude from the territory and from any states later formed from it.

notice   Notice is a fundamental requirement of DUE PROCESS. A law enacted in secret or a regulation unpublished by an ADMINISTRATIVE AGENCY would clearly be unconstitutional. Reacting in part to just such a concern, Congress in 1935 enacted the Federal Register Act, requiring all executive orders, rules, and regulations having legal effect to be published in the daily *Federal Register.* In 1986 the Supreme Court dismissed the request that a disaster relief program be reopened because the government's news releases did not adequately inform potential beneficiaries of its terms and duration. Since the proper information was published in the *Federal Register,* the beneficiaries had no constitutional grounds to complain of the lack of notice.[1213a]

Notice is also required of any proceeding undertaken by the government in which an individual's life, LIBERTY, or PROPERTY may be adversely affected. When prosecutions are brought or lawsuits filed, notice is rarely an issue because the INDICTMENT or legal complaint will notify the defendant that a case is pending. The Court struck down a New York law that permitted trust companies to manage individual trusts jointly and to advertise in newspapers when making periodic payments to individual beneficiaries. The right to receive earnings was extinguished for each beneficiary who did not make a claim. The Court said that a newspaper ad is sufficient notice to beneficiaries whose names and addresses the trustee did not have. But notice must be sent by mail to each individual beneficiary whose name and address was known to the trustee.[1399]

See also: ACCUSATION, NOTICE AND SPECIFICITY OF; SERVICE OF PROCESS.

notice of accusation, *see:* **accusation, notice and specificity of**

noxious products   In 1903 the Supreme Court held that Congress could constitutionally ban from INTERSTATE COMMERCE any noxious product—that is, a product that would harm the public in any way.[369] In 1918 the Court interpreted this doctrine as a restraint on federal power, holding that if a product itself was not inherently harmful Congress could not prohibit commerce in it.[851] In 1941 the Court finally abandoned the notion that Congress was limited to banning only noxious products, holding that the question of who may engage in what kind of interstate commerce is solely for Congress to determine.[514]

See also: NATIONAL POLICE POWER; POLICE POWER; PROHIBITION OF COMMERCE.

nudity   Whether nudity can be banned depends on whether it is a form of expression protected by the FIRST AMENDMENT. Depictions of the nude body are constitutionally protected as long as they are not obscene. Therefore, the state may not ban books and magazines with nonobscene photographs of nudes. Likewise, a city may not prohibit drive-in movie theaters from showing films with nonobscene nudity, even if the screen is visible to a passerby on the street.[622] But because certain types of films may have a deleterious effect on the neighborhood, the Supreme Court has upheld ZONING ordinances that disperse "adult" theaters around town[2277] or that force them into particular areas in town.[1711] "Live" nudity poses somewhat different problems because it is less clear that it is a form of expression. Public indecency laws prohibiting public nudity are constitutional because they are aimed at conduct, not expression, reflecting "moral disapproval of people appearing in the nude among strangers in public places."[128]

But since some forms of conduct are themselves expression—for example, dancing—the question has frequently arisen to what degree the states may ban public nudity when it is "expressive conduct." The rule for nudity on stage in a dramatic performance is the same for photographs and movies: it may not be banned unless it is obscene.[1918] But the rule for nude dancing is not the same. The battle is usually fought over nude dancing in bars. In 1975 the Court said that under certain circumstances, the "customary 'barroom' type of nude dancing" is entitled to constitutional protection.[564] Nevertheless, the Court has ruled, the TWENTY-FIRST AMENDMENT permits the states to prohibit simulated sexual activities or movies of them and live topless dancing in bars and other establishments licensed to sell liquor, even if none of the pictures or dances are obscene in the constitutional sense.[322, 564, 1471] In a 1991 case, the Court in a 5–4 decision, with no majority opinion, held that the states may ban nude dancing in places other than bars under a general law barring nudity in public places. A plurality of three justices said that "nude dancing . . . is expressive conduct within the outer perimeters of the First Amendment, though . . . only marginally so."[128] Even so, they and two concurring justices voted to uphold an Indiana requirement that a dancer may not dance wholly nude for customers of an adult entertainment theater, but must wear "pasties" and a G-string.[128]

See also: OBSCENITY AND PORNOGRAPHY; OFFENSIVE AND INDECENT SPEECH; SYMBOLIC SPEECH.

nullification, interposition, and secession

Nullification and interposition are the discredited theories that the states may declare laws enacted by Congress unconstitutional. The term "nullification" was first introduced by Thomas Jefferson, who secretly drafted the Kentucky Resolution condemning the Federalists for enacting the ALIEN AND SEDITION ACTS in 1798. "Interposition" was the word James Madison used in the Virginia Resolution to the same effect. Jefferson and Madison's point was that the states must act to quash unconstitutional enactments since at the time there was no institution that could authoritatively interpret the Constitution. Five years later Chief Justice Marshall assigned the task of JUDICIAL REVIEW to the SUPREME COURT in MARBURY V. MADISON. The Alien and Sedition Acts expired in 1801, so their constitutionality was never tested. But the theory that the states could legitimately defy federal law did not die.

In 1828 John C. Calhoun of South Carolina advanced the thesis of a "concurrent majority": a majority within a state could veto federal actions, thereby avoiding tyranny by the national majority. In 1832 South Carolina protested two national tariffs by enacting a Nullification Ordinance prohibiting on pain of CONTEMPT certain appeals to the Supreme Court and an enforcement act providing a DAMAGE remedy against federal officials who arrested South Carolinians for failing to pay the tariffs. President Andrew Jackson met the crisis head on, branding the Nullification Act as treason and pushing through a Force Act that authorized him to send in troops to put down open disobedience. South Carolina backed down. Calhoun continued agitating for his interpositionist views, advocating statewide

quarantines against mail carrying antislavery propaganda. For several years, some states did actively interfere with the delivery of the U.S. mail.

Though southern states were the more persistent proponents of nullification and put the theory to its ultimate test during their attempted secession, resolved only by the Civil War, northern states too presumed to override federal law. The most notable instance occurred when an abolitionist editor, Sherman M. Booth, helped rescue a fugitive slave in Wisconsin and was promptly arrested for violating the federal Fugitive Slave Act. The Wisconsin courts took the position that the act was unconstitutional. Twice they released Booth in HABEAS CORPUS proceedings, the second time even though Booth had been convicted in federal court of violating the act. In 1859, speaking through Chief Justice Roger B. Taney, the Supreme Court reaffirmed the supremacy of federal law, and the Wisconsin Supreme Court ultimately backed down.[3]

In announcing their secession, southern states in 1860 and 1861 relied on the "compact theory" of the UNION, which held that the United States was in effect a contract among states from which a state could withdraw whenever it chose. President Abraham Lincoln set the constitutional tone for the Civil War and the Reconstruction that followed in his assessment that secession was simply "the essence of anarchy." The states, he said, "have their *status* in the Union, and they have no other *legal status*." Congress and the Supreme Court relied on this premise in later legislation and cases that treated the states not as having seceded but as having had rebellious and corrupt governments.

Echoes of nullification and interposition reappeared in the 1950s, when southern states reacted to *Brown v. Board of Education* with the SOUTHERN MANIFESTO. Segregationist politicians raced to the microphones to proclaim an absolutist state SOVEREIGNTY. Senator James O. Eastland of Mississippi said: "On May 17, 1954, the Constitution of the United States was destroyed because the Supreme Court disregarded the law and decided integration was right. . . . You are not required to obey any court which passes out such a ruling. In fact, you are obligated to defy it." The Court responded in 1958[463] and 1960[287] with the declaration that "interposition is not a *constitutional* doctrine. If taken seriously, it is illegal defiance of constitutional authority."

See also: REPUBLICAN FORM OF GOVERNMENT; STATES AND STATEHOOD; SUPREMACY CLAUSE.

number of free persons, *see:* **free persons**

number of justices on the Supreme Court, *see:* **Supreme Court, number of justices**

O

oath, loyalty, *see:* **loyalty oath**

oath of office   Art. VI-§3 requires all members of Congress and state legislatures, executive officers of both the United States and the states, and all judges, state and federal, to take an oath to support, or to affirm their support of, the Constitution. According to Alexander Hamilton in *Federalist* 27, the oath was intended to incorporate all state officials "into the operations of the national government *as far as its just and constitutional authority extends*" to render them "auxiliary to the enforcement" of federal law.

The clause figured in a 1966 case overturning the exclusion of Julian Bond from the Georgia House of Representatives.[195] Bond had criticized the war in Vietnam. The Georgia House excluded Bond on the ground that his remarks showed he could not conscientiously take an oath to support the Constitution. The Supreme Court said that Bond's remarks were protected under his FREEDOM OF SPEECH and that they did not conflict with any assertion of fidelity to the Constitution. Exclusion from an elected position for remarks that the candidate is constitutionally entitled to make violates the FIRST AMENDMENT.

The only American official required to take a different oath is the president. Art. II-§1[8] requires that every president take the following oath or affirmation: "I do solemnly swear [or affirm] that I will faithfully execute the Office of President of the United States and will to the best of my Ability, preserve, protect and defend the Constitution of the United States." Although by its terms this clause says that every president must swear the oath *before* entering OFFICE, it has never been assumed to be legally binding. Historically, presidents-elect take the oath of office at an inauguration ceremony and do not presume to exercise the powers of office until then. But when a president dies in office, the vice president succeeds to and is invested with the powers of the office from that moment, even before he has arranged officially to take the oath.

The OATH OR AFFIRMATION Clause applies only to holders of state or federal office. Congress and the states have sometimes imposed an oath requirement on their employees and on people seeking licenses from the government. After the Civil War, the Supreme Court struck down both federal and state requirements that lawyers swear a TEST OATH that they had not participated in the REBELLION against the UNION on the grounds that such requirements amounted to an unconstitutional BILL OF AT-

TAINDER.[727, 500] After World War II, the federal government and many states required as a condition of holding a public job that their employees take a LOYALTY OATH. Although for a time the Court sustained some of these oaths, eventually it held that most of them violated the First Amendment or were void because of VAGUENESS.

One odd case, never overruled but questionable in view of the Court's position on loyalty oaths, was handed down in 1890. A territorial government required every prospective voter to swear that he was neither a polygamist nor a member of any organization that advocated polygamy and that he would not "in any manner whatever" advocate that anyone commit polygamy. The Court upheld this anti-Mormon law as a means of stamping out the practice.[520] Since simple MEMBERSHIP IN POLITICAL ORGANIZATIONS may not be prohibited[609] and advocacy that does not amount to incitement of an imminent lawless act may not be punished,[222] it is unlikely that such a voter's oath would be upheld today.

oath or affirmation   The requirement that officials take an OATH OF OFFICE is tempered by the alternative that they *affirm* their support of the Constitution. The word "affirmation" was added to Art. VI-§3 to respect the sensibilities of Quakers, who are bound by religious belief to refrain from swearing any oath.

obiter dictum, *see:* **dictum**

obligation of contracts   Under the CONTRACT CLAUSE of Art. I-§10[1], no state may pass any "law impairing the obligation of contracts." The policy underlying this clause was a principal impetus of the CONSTITUTIONAL CONVENTION. Many state legislatures had enacted laws abrogating the rights of creditors to collect their debts. SHAYS'S REBELLION in 1786 and 1787, which aimed at stopping the courts from fore-closing on farmers' mortgages, alarmed many state leaders and convinced them that both constitutional and military power were necessary to protect the rights of creditors. But the constitutional clause protecting their rights was obscurely worded. Although the Framers may have supposed its meaning was clear, the history of the clause at the hands of the Court suggests otherwise. The Framers chiefly meant to bar states from nullifying contracts between private parties, but the clause first came to the Court's attention in cases dealing with grants or contracts made by the states themselves.

In 1810, in *Fletcher v. Peck,* Chief Justice John Marshall held that the Georgia legislature could not revoke grants of land that it had made to several land companies. In 1812 the Court used the clause to strike down the repeal of a New Jersey land tax exemption.[1449] And in the famous *Dartmouth College Case,* the Court prohibited New Hampshire from enlarging Dartmouth's board of trustees, holding that the 1769 royal charter was a contract that delegated exclusive power to the trustees to fill board vacancies. Shortly after deciding *Dartmouth,* the Court gave the clause the meaning that the Framers probably intended when it struck down a New York BANKRUPTCY law that discharged debtors of any further existing debt on surrendering their property to their creditors.[1975]

However, over Marshall's dissent, the Court in 1827 held that states could pass prospective bankruptcy legislation, since parties who enter into contracts always do so with the tacit understanding that they will be bound by existing contract law.[1518] In other words, the Contract Clause bars the state from impairing the obligation of existing contracts, not from barring the making of contracts in the future or from subjecting them to rules governing remedies for breaches that will occur after the law is passed.

By the 1830s the Court made it clear that a state may regulate or even revoke grants and charters as long as it reserved the right to do so in the original grant. In the *Charles River Bridge Case* in 1837, one bridge company with a charter from Massachusetts protested the state's granting of a charter to another company to build a competing bridge, claiming that it had been granted a monopoly. Chief Justice Roger B. Taney said that no grant of a monopoly appeared in the original charter and that the Court would not only refrain from inferring one but would hold any ambiguity in a charter against the company "and in favor of the public."[377] From this case the Court fashioned a general rule that the Contract Clause does not override "the [POLICE POWER] of the state to establish all regulations that are reasonably necessary to secure the health, safety, good order, comfort, or general welfare of the community; [and] this power can neither be abdicated nor bargained away, and is inalienable even by express grant."[94]

Even if a corporate charter promised that a state would refrain from exercising its power of EMINENT DOMAIN to take corporate property, the state always remains constitutionally free to do so, as long as it pays JUST COMPENSATION.[2185] A company chartered to operate a lottery cannot complain under the Contract Clause when the state later outlaws lotteries.[1962] Similarly, private parties may not prevent a state from enacting a law in the interests of healthy, safety, or welfare simply by making a contract to do that which the later regulation prohibits. To regulate or ban harmful activities, a state may always prohibit people from entering into certain kinds of private contracts—for example, gambling, prostitution, and consumption of INTOXICATING BEVERAGES. Just because the original contracts for the sale of beer were lawful does not bar the state later from prohibiting beer sales.[203]

The question remains what constitutes an "obligation." In the 1934 *Mortgage Moratorium Case*,[937] the Court distinguished between the obligation and the remedy. To forestall a wave of farm foreclosure sales at the height of the Depression, Minnesota passed a law permitting farmers to stay on their farms, even if they could not pay the mortgage, as long as they paid a "reasonable part" of the fair rental value of the property. The moratorium was limited to two years. Then a farmer would have to pay what was owed under the mortgage. In upholding the law, Chief Justice Charles Evans Hughes for a 5–4 majority said that the law did not repudiate the debt or destroy the contract but rather temporarily relieved the debtor from full enforcement. The bank or other creditor was entitled to take title if the farmer failed to redeem during the two-year period.

For four decades the Court rejected all Contract Clause claims. Then in 1977 it upheld such a challenge to an attempt by New Jersey to repudiate a state covenant to bondholders that it would not use Port Authority revenues to subsidize rail passengers. The Court held that the state's repeal of its covenant was neither "reasonable" nor "necessary." For a 6–3 majority, Justice Harry Blackmun said that "a state cannot refuse to meet its legitimate financial obligations simply because it would prefer to spend the money to promote [another public interest]."[2107] In 1978 the Court applied the Contract Clause to invalidate a Minnesota law that retroactively altered the terms of a private pension agreement.[41]

But in the 1980s the Court once again relaxed its scrutiny of regulatory laws that interfered with contractual obligations. In 1983 it announced a three-part test in determining whether to uphold a challenge under the Contract Clause. (1) First, a court must determine whether the law substantially impairs a contractual relationship. If so, (2) the state "must have a significant and legitimate public purpose" to regulate. If so, (3) the state's adjustment of the contractual obligations must be based on "reasonable conditions" and be "of a character appropriate to the public purpose."[616] But that test may be dispensed with if an asserted impairment really results only incidentally from "a generally applicable rule of conduct." Alabama increased its tax on oil and natural gas taken from wells in the state and forbade producers from passing the increase on to purchasers. The Exxon Corporation sued to bar enforcement of the law, because it had existing contracts permitting tax increases to be passed along. The Court rejected Exxon's argument, since the Alabama law was not aimed at Exxon's or anyone else's contracts but was a rule generally applicable to everyone and was "designed to advance a broad societal interest."[637]

The Contract Clause is a limitation against only the states. Congress has explicit power to enact uniform bankruptcy legislation under Art. I-§8[4]. Nevertheless, in 1935 the Court read the Contract Clause into the DUE PROCESS Clause of the FIFTH AMENDMENT. Under a federal farm mortgage act similar to Minnesota's, federal bankruptcy courts could hold off creditors for five years, allowing bankrupt farmers to stay in possession and to pay a reasonable rent set by a court, and then to redeem the farm at an appraised value. Despite its holding in the *Mortgage Moratorium Case,* the Supreme Court unanimously struck down this law, because the interference with the farmers' existing obligations was too drastic.[1196] But in 1937 the Court largely recanted, upholding a modified version of the law that the Court deemed less restrictive of the creditors' rights.[2263]

See also: RETROACTIVITY; YAZOO LAND SCANDAL.

obligations of government, *see:*
government, affirmative obligations of

obscenity and pornography   In 1957 the Court held 7–2, speaking through Justice William Brennan, that obscenity is a form of LOWER-VALUE SPEECH that the FIRST AMEND-MENT does not protect.[1767] That generalization is practically useless, however, since the question in that case, as in almost every other such case, is whether the condemned work really is obscene; for if it is not, then of course it *is* entitled to First Amendment protection. The excruciating constitutional difficulty with obscenity, therefore, is not whether it is protected but how to recognize it.

Until the 1930s, American courts judged a work to be obscene if it had a tendency "to deprave or corrupt those whose minds are open to such immoral influences." This test permitted the states to censor all sorts of literary works, including those of nineteenth- and twentieth-century authors such as Stephen Crane, Walt Whitman, Theodore Dreiser, and Mark Twain; classical writers, such as Rabelais and Voltaire; straightforward sex hygiene books; and works of scientific thinkers such as Sigmund Freud. The test for obscenity permitted censorship of an entire work because of a single suggestive passage, regardless of the author's intent or the effect of the work as a whole. This rule was finally toppled by a decision of federal district judge John Munro Woolsey in 1933 to allow James Joyce's *Ulysses* to be imported and sold in America. But there was still no general constitutional rule, and in the name of obscenity, censorship boards could ban almost anything they disliked. The Police Board of Censorship in Chicago once held obscene a Walt Disney movie on the vanishing prairie because it showed a buffalo giving birth, and the censorship board of a southern town banned a movie as obscene because it depicted black and white schoolchildren playing together.

In the 1957 case, the Court held that whether a work may be banned as obscene depends on "whether to the average person, applying contemporary community standards, the dominant theme of the material, taken as a whole, appeals to prurient interests." This definition meant that scenes of racially mixed schoolchildren could never be banned as obscene, and presumably meant that nature films were likewise protected. But it solved few real problems, since what the Court meant by "appealing to a prurient interest" was highly obscure. "Prurient" refers to "lustful desire." How does a work "appeal" to a lustful desire? And what is a contemporary community standard? What a jury thinks or what any five of the nine justices of the Supreme Court think? One thing became certain: whatever a state might ban as obscene, it assuredly may not censor a work simply because it deals with a sexual theme.[1078] In 1962 the Court said that the work must be "patently offensive,"[1237] and in 1964 it added that censors must prove it lacks "redeeming social importance."[999]

In the 1960s the Warren Court greatly narrowed the definition, requiring the censor to pass a three-pronged test. To be legally obscene, a plurality said in a case involving the eighteenth-century novel *Fanny Hill*, the dominant theme of the work taken as a whole must (1) appeal to prurient interest in sex, (2) be "patently offensive because it affronts contemporary community standards relating to the description or representation of sexual matters," and (3) be "utterly without redeeming social value."[1311] Although this was not wholly a majority view, the practical effect was that only hard-core pornography could be stopped. And not even hard-core pornography can be banned in the privacy of one's home. In *Stanley v. Georgia*, the Court rejected a Georgia law criminalizing the knowing "possession of obscene matter."[1944] What was once shocking and by common consent could surely have been banned became by the 1970s almost passé.

However, in the 1970s a changing Court retrenched somewhat. In 1971 and 1973 the Court limited the reach of the private possession case, holding that the right to view concededly obscene materials at home is not a bar to federal laws against mailing obscene works[1707] or to purchasing them.[2085] In 1973, in *Miller v. California*, the Burger Court undertook to reshape obscenity law by announcing a new test of whether a work is obscene: (1) the average person, applying contemporary community standards, would find that the work, taken as a whole, appeals to the prurient interest; (2) the work depicts or describes, in a patently offensive way, sexual conduct specifically defined by the applicable law; (3) the work, taken as a whole, lacks serious literary, artistic, political, or scientific value. For any work to be judged obscene, the state must first have enacted an obscenity law that spells out what may not be depicted. It may not rely on vague standards such as "conduct that is vile, base, lewd, and offensive." Each state must specify in detail what body parts and specific acts may not be shown. Moreover, only "ultimate sexual acts" may be forbidden. A state could not outlaw depictions of people kissing, and NUDITY alone does not make a work obscene.[622]

As with most Supreme Court tests, the *Miller* rules raised more questions than they answered. One major issue is whether the jury has absolute discretion to determine whether every part of the test has been met. The jury may determine for itself whether the work appeals to the "prurient interest."[1650] But, said the Court in a moment of notable opaqueness, "prurient" does not refer to "material that provoked only normal healthy sexual desires" but only to "sexual responses over and beyond those that would be characterized as normal."[241] The jury has great but not "unbridled discretion" to determine whether a work is "patently offensive." In a case just one year after *Miller*, a Georgia jury found the movie *Carnal Knowledge* patently offensive and obscene; but Justice William H. Rehnquist reversed, holding that there are "substantive constitutional limitations" on what a jury may find patently offensive and that courts may review a jury's findings. That a work deals with sex is not enough to make it patently offensive. Since the camera never focused on the actors' bodies during what the audience understood to be sexual moments, it did not "depict or describe" ultimate sexual acts and hence could not constitutionally be found obscene.[1012]

The jury may apply its own notions of "contemporary community standards" and may rely on standards of its local community; jurors need not try to ascertain a single national community standard.[849] However, the "average person" applying those community standards must be drawn solely from the adult population. The jury may not apply a standard of what is suitable for children.[1631] The Court has refused to allow the jury to determine under a local community standard whether a work has serious "value." Otherwise, a single local community anywhere in the United States could translate its disapproval into a judgment of literary worthlessness that could censor the book throughout the country.[1650] Despite every attempt to fashion and refine a tool to separate sexual trash from the permissibly erotic, the Court has probably never been more perspicuous than Justice Potter Stewart, who in a celebrated line in 1964 said that he doubted he could ever "succeed in intelligibly" defining hard-core pornography, "[b]ut I know it when I see it."[999] And that, of course, is just the problem.

If a work *is* obscene, the state may ban it even if it is sold or shown only to consenting adults. In a case decided along with *Miller*, the Court held 5–4 that the state may outlaw the showing of hard-core pornographic films, even if the "adult theatre" is clearly labeled and warns viewers of what kinds of movies it shows.[1566] Why a person should have a constitutional right to watch hard-core pornography in his or her home but not in a local movie theater has never been explained.

Despite the confusion over adult obscenity, the Court has forged a much greater consensus on the problem of child pornography. In 1982 the justices unanimously agreed in *New York v. Ferber* that there is no free speech protection for depictions of children engaged in sexual activities, even if the pictures are not obscene under *Miller*. Works that may be banned under *Ferber* need not be patently offensive and need not appeal to the prurient interest of the average person. Nor must the work be considered as a whole; the whole work may be banned even if only a portion involves child pornography. The *Ferber* rule is limited to works that visually depict children—photographs and movies—and may not be used to ban merely verbal descriptions. Even though the law would bar some depictions that the state presumably has no interest in preventing—for example, a *National Geographic* photograph of children in a foreign culture—the Court would not overturn the law when used against a real child pornographer. In 1990 the Court held that the state may outlaw the mere possession of child pornography even in the privacy of one's home.

Since truly obscene works are not constitutionally protected, not only may the state criminally punish those who traffic in them, it may also confiscate the works to prevent further showing or distribution. Seizure of books and films, which presents a different set of difficult problems, is discussed under PRIOR RESTRAINT.

See also: ADULT BOOKSTORES AND THEATERS; FEMINISM AND PORNOGRAPHY; OFFENSIVE AND INDECENT SPEECH; PANDERING; RES JUDICATA.

occupation, right to pursue From time to time, the Supreme Court has declared in passing that "the right of the individual to . . . engage in any of the common occupations of life" is protected by the DUE PROCESS Clause of the FOURTEENTH AMENDMENT [1323] and that qualifications for employment "must have a rational connection with the applicant's fitness or capacity" to do the job.[1823] But the Court has rarely paused to invalidate many of the burdens that the states often saddle on people seeking to practice even common occupations. In the SLAUGHTER-HOUSE CASES in 1873 the Court dismissed out of hand the notion that a law forcing butchers in New Orleans to shut down their slaughterhouses and to work for a state-chartered private monopoly was an interference with the right to work. In 1947 the Court upheld another Louisiana law that had the practical effect of permitting riverboat pilots to deny a license to anyone other than their relatives and friends.[1095]

When the Court has upset restrictions on the right to work at certain jobs, the reason has almost always been that the state has deprived the job seeker of some *other* constitutional right, such as FREEDOM OF SPEECH or FREEDOM OF ASSOCIATION,[1823] EQUAL PROTECTION OF THE LAWS,[2074] or PRIVILEGES AND IMMUNITIES under Art. IV-§2[1].[1984, 2093] On rare occasions, the Court has upset a scheme permitting an organization to prevent competitors from working,[749] but more often it upholds laws that impose absolute prohibitions against doing certain work by all but people specially licensed to do so, even when the licensing requirements are irrational, as when a lawyer-dominated legislature passed a law barring anyone but lawyers from engaging in the business of debt adjuster.[658]

See also: OCCUPATIONAL LICENSING; PUBLIC EMPLOYMENT.

occupation tax Congress has enacted various tax laws aimed at occupations that it wishes to outlaw. In 1935 the Court struck down a special federal excise payable by anyone who conducts a business in violation of a state law, because the excise was intended as a prohibition rather than a real tax.[455] But in 1937 the Court reversed course and upheld such taxes, even though it seemed plain that the real purpose was not to raise revenue but to stamp out

intrastate commerce.[1908] In the 1950s the Court upheld excise tax laws aimed at gambling and the narcotics business.[1045, 1796] However, in 1968 and 1971 the Court ruled as a violation of the FIFTH AMENDMENT right against SELF-INCRIMINATION certain provisions of occupational tax laws requiring the gambler or seller of narcotics to register and make admissions that could lead to state prosecution.[1240, 2100]

See also: TAXATION OF INTERSTATE COMMERCE; TAXATION-REGULATION DISTINCTION.

occupational licensing The states control entry into all fields of professional endeavor and many nonprofessional ones. Only journalism and the ministry are protected by the FIRST AMENDMENT. The usual method of control is to require practitioners to obtain a license. Some forms of licensing require the applicant to demonstrate practical competence; others require registration and the payment of a fee. Though the Court occasionally struck down a licensing law during the period in which it upheld ECONOMIC DUE PROCESS,[1457] even then it would often uphold such laws on the ground that the occupation was AFFECTED WITH A PUBLIC INTEREST. When the Court withdrew from the business of second-guessing the economic decisions of legislatures, it ignored the widespread abuse of licensing laws by which one occupational group makes it more difficult for competitors to operate.

In an important 1955 case, the Court upheld an Oklahoma law regulating the business of opticians, forbidding them, among other things, to duplicate or even replace lenses into frames unless their customers had prescriptions from an optometrist or ophthalmologist. Reciting the many inconsistencies and even "needless, wasteful requirement[s]" of the law, the Court nevertheless upheld it because "it is for the legislature, not the courts, to balance the advantages and disadvantages" of particular policies that regulate business and industrial conditions.[2224] In 1963 it upheld a Kansas law that prohibited anyone but lawyers from engaging in the "business of debt adjusting."[658] Only when the state actually delegates its power to one group of professionals to regulate its competitors does the regulatory scheme violate DUE PROCESS.[749]

Attacking protectionist occupational licensing laws under the DORMANT COMMERCE CLAUSE would probably be equally unavailing. Beginning roughly around the time of Andrew Jackson's presidency, the states abandoned the field of occupational licensing. When at the turn of the century they began to impose competency requirements on certain professionals, such as doctors and related practitioners, the obvious purpose was to protect the public health and safety. A doctor licensed in one state had no legal standing to practice medicine in another state, despite the FULL FAITH AND CREDIT Clause and the obvious effect that such requirements had on INTERSTATE COMMERCE, in part because what these practitioners did appeared to be professional services, not commerce. By careless analogy, the health and safety rationale was extended to all sorts of fields far removed from the professional services of the "learned professions." Even though the Supreme Court has since held that professionals are subject to the antitrust laws, and hence are engaged in interstate commerce,[769] the Court has not even hinted that states have anything less than carte blanche to license occupations as they wish.

offenses against the law of nations, *see:* **piracy**

offenses against the United States Art. II-§2[1] empowers the president to grant PARDONS for all "offenses against the United States" except in cases of impeachment. This provision refers to any act made criminal by federal law, including criminal CONTEMPT,[824] regardless of the penalty that may be imposed.

offensive and indecent speech The FIRST AMENDMENT, the Supreme Court once said, protects speech that "may strike at prejudices and preconceptions and have profound unsettling effects as it presses for acceptance of an idea."[2011] Despite the wide berth that the government must give to speech that most of the community may think dangerous, the Court has also said that certain categories of LOWER-VALUE SPEECH may be regulated. The state may not prohibit the expression of offensive, indecent, or even immoral *ideas,* but it may certainly outlaw some forms of offensive, indecent, and immoral *conduct.* The trick, therefore, is to distinguish between advocacy and a grunt.

That many or even most people are repulsed by an idea, that an idea may profoundly offend a significant group in the community, is not grounds for CENSORSHIP. When New York State refused to license the movie *Lady Chatterley's Lover* because it advocated adultery, a proposition the censors found immoral, the Court held that the state's refusal was unconstitutional.[1078] Likewise, when the New York courts held that a movie may be banned as "sacrilegious," because it supposedly "treated [a particular religion] with contempt, mockery, scorn and ridicule," the Supreme Court reversed, holding that "the state has no legitimate interest in protecting any or all religions from views distasteful to them."[1041] Although in 1952 the Court did uphold a GROUP LIBEL law prohibiting any publication that "exposes the citizens of any race, color, creed or religion to contempt, derision, or obloquy,"[142] the decision has probably been repudiated by a host of later cases, making the task of regulating offensive HATE SPEECH a difficult one.

Offensive and indecent speech often has the narrower connotation of vulgar language. During the past two decades, the Court has greatly broadened the scope of constitutional protection for common vulgarities. In 1971 Justice John M. Harlan, speaking for a 6–3 majority, held that California could not constitutionally punish a young man for walking in the corridors of the Los Angeles County Courthouse wearing a jacket emblazoned with the words "Fuck the Draft."[417] In essence, said Harlan, the state, acting as the guardian of public morality, wished to "excise . . . one particular scurrilous epithet from the public discourse." People who did not want to look at the jacket could avert their eyes. True, the immediate consequence of free speech "may often appear to be only verbal tumult, discord, and even offensive utterance." But the realm of public discourse is broad, and protects "linguistic expression [that] . . . conveys not only ideas capable of relatively precise, detached explication, but otherwise inexpressible emotions as well." In short, said Harlan, since "the state has no right to cleanse public debate to the point where it is grammatically palatable to the most squeamish among us," it may not pick and choose words to suppress, for there is no "ascertainable general principle" to dictate a stopping point short of ultimate purity. It is "often true that one man's vulgarity is another's lyric."

In 1972 the Court summarily vacated the convictions of three people in incidents involving the use of common street vulgarities. In the first case, the defendant had spoken heatedly at a school board meeting.[1761] In the second, the defendant shouted at policemen who were arresting her son;[1159] and in the third, the defendant had ranted about certain policemen in highly unflattering terms.[256] The laws under which they were convicted prohibited, among other things, "indecent" and "offensive" language in public and "obscene or lascivious language or word in any public place, or in the presence of females." Although there was no majority opinion, it seems clear from these cases, and from a decision the following year

overriding a university's expulsion of a graduate student for publishing a pamphlet using coarse language,[1564] that vulgarity as such does not amount to the kind of FIGHTING WORDS that may be the basis for an arrest.

Notwithstanding the general principle against censoring vulgarity, the Court in a 5–4 decision upheld the power of the Federal Communications Commission to regulate indecent radio broadcasts.[642] A New York radio station aired comedian George Carlin's twelve-minute monologue entitled "Filthy Words," in which he repeatedly used seven common "curse words and swear words" that, he said, "you definitely wouldn't say ever." Carlin was attempting to make a serious point about the use of language, but the FCC said the monologue was indecent because it was broadcast on a Wednesday afternoon when children might be listening. In upholding the FCC's authority to sanction radio stations for such programs, the majority emphasized that the case depended entirely on the "context." It refused to rule out the use of the words during a late night broadcast. Dissenting, Justice William Brennan lamented the "acute ethnocentric myopia that enables the Court to approve the censorship of communications solely because of the words they contain."

Context was significant also in a school case in which a principal suspended a high school student for nominating a fellow student before a schoolwide assembly in a speech laced with sexually suggestive euphemisms, even though the words themselves were not coarse. The Court upheld the suspension 7–2. This time Brennan concurred, saying that school officials were simply attempting to "prevent disruption of school educational activities."[158]

In 1989 the Court indicated that it continues to recognize a significant constitutional distinction between obscene and merely indecent expression. The Court unanimously rejected a provision in the Communications Act that bars indecent telephone messages. Congress had acted against "dial-a-porn" telephone services, through which a caller could listen to a "sexually-oriented pre-recorded telephone message." Justice Byron R. White noted the difference between a public radio broadcast and a message confined to a willing caller. The desire to protect children from such messages, he said, does not justify a total ban on nonobscene communications.[1780]

See also: ADULT BOOKSTORES AND THEATERS; OBSCENITY AND PORNOGRAPHY; SYMBOLIC SPEECH.

office and officers   The Constitution uses the terms "office" and "officers" fifty-four times, in most cases referring to particular offices, such as those of the president, Congress, or the judiciary. But in certain clauses, the Constitution uses the terms generically and opaquely to refer to different classes of federal officials. Art. I-§6[2] distinguishes without defining CIVIL OFFICE and *any office.* Art. I-§9[8] refers to an "office of profit or trust"; Art. I-§3[7] to an OFFICE OF HONOR, TRUST OR PROFIT; Art. II-§2[2] to INFERIOR OFFICERS; Art. II-§3 to "all the officers of the United States"; Art. II-§4 to civil officers; Art. VI-§3 to "all executive and judicial officers" and to "any office or public trust"; Amendment 14-§2 to "executive and judicial officers of a state"; Amendment 14-§3 distinguishes between "civil" and "military" office; and Art. II-§2[1] and Amendment 25-§4[1,2] to "principal officers of the EXECUTIVE DEPARTMENTS." The Supreme Court has rarely been called on to construe the main term or explore the differences among its variations. In general, the Court has said that "[t]he term embraces the ideas of tenure, duration, emolument, and duties."[877] Whether a particular person holds an office in the constitutional sense depends on the purpose in asking. For purposes of the EMOLUMENTS CLAUSE the term "office" may mean something different from the term when used in connection with the APPOINTMENT AND REMOVAL POWER of the president or the IMPEACHMENT power of Congress. Officers in the constitutional sense do not exhaust the category of people who may be on the federal payroll. *Employees* who are not *officers* are those people appointed by inferior officers.[743]

Regardless of the nature of the office, Congress has constitutional authority under the NECESSARY AND PROPER CLAUSE to create all federal offices and establish the qualifications for all officers other than those of Congress itself, the president, vice president, and the federal judiciary. Even these officers are subject to some congressional control, since salaries and perquisites of office must always be established by federal law. Congress may regulate the conduct of all federal offices, except to the extent that autonomy is granted in the Constitution itself. Congress does not violate the appointment power when it saddles someone already holding office with additional duties, since Congress has not created a new office but merely regulated an existing one.[1860] Under the Hatch Act, Congress has barred all federal employees except a narrow group of "policy determining" officers from being actively involved in political campaigns. The Supreme Court upheld the act, rejecting the assertion that it violates the FIRST, FIFTH, NINTH, and TENTH AMENDMENTS.[2098, 402]

See also: PATRONAGE; PUBLIC EMPLOYMENT.

office of honor, trust or profit   The phrase "office of honor, trust or profit" appears in Art. I-§3[7] as a description of the offices an impeached federal official is disqualified from holding in the future. The term has never been judicially defined but presumably refers not only to political appointment but to any federal government employment. The phrase compares to the ones in Art. I-§9[8] and II-§1[2] prohibiting the holder of an "office of profit or trust" from accepting any gift, title, or office of any kind from a foreign country or from serving in the ELECTORAL COLLEGE. Again, this phrase has not been construed, but presumably the omission of the word "honor" in the latter clause would permit someone holding a purely honorary office, such as a former president, to accept a gift or title from a foreign monarch, as President Ronald Reagan did in receiving an honorary knighthood from Queen Elizabeth in 1989.

office of trust or profit, *see:* **office of honor, trust or profit**

officeholding, *see:* **office and officers; term limitation**

oleomargarine   At the turn of the century, the states had a difficult time understanding the purpose of nonfat butter and enacted many laws against various forms of margarine, or oleomargarine as it was then called. Despite many decisions under the doctrine of ECONOMIC DUE PROCESS voiding state laws regulating business, the Court sustained an Ohio ban on oleomargarine colored yellow[337] on the ground that the law was aimed at preventing fraud. The same principle applied to imported butter substitutes. The Court upheld a Massachusetts law banning shipment of yellow oleomargarine from other states, even if the oleomargarine was still in the ORIGINAL PACKAGE.[1640] But the Court did not permit states to ban outright the sale of interstate oleomargarine, no matter how it was colored,[1822] and it struck down a New Hampshire law banning the sale of all oleomargarine unless colored pink.[432] Today these cases are curiosities.
See also: DORMANT COMMERCE CLAUSE; INTERSTATE COMMERCE; MILK.

Olympics, use of name   The Supreme Court upheld a federal law giving the U.S. Olympic Committee the exclusive right to use the word "Olympics" and related symbols, sustaining an INJUNCTION against the Gay Olympic Games from using the word in their name or advertising.[1794]

one man, one vote, *see:* **one person, one vote**

one person, one vote   "The conception of political equality from the DECLARATION OF INDEPENDENCE to Lincoln's Gettysburg Address, to the FIFTEENTH, SEVENTEENTH, and NINETEENTH AMENDMENTS can mean only one thing—one person, one vote."[797] So said the Court in 1963, overturning Georgia's COUNTY UNIT SYSTEM. The following year the Court adopted one person, one vote as the test for determining the constitutionality of legislative apportionment.[1713] Since then, the Supreme Court and lower federal courts have remade political geography by applying the test in hundreds of cases from around the country. The courts have been toughest on disparities in federal legislative districts, invalidating in one case a reapportionment plan in which the largest district exceeded the mathematically precisely equal district by only 2.43 percent; the Court accepted a plan requiring a difference of only 0.086 percent between the largest district and the ideal district.[2196] In districting for state legislatures, the courts have been a bit more lenient, permitting disparities to allow legislative districts to conform to some existing political boundaries, such as counties.[1225] The reapportionment cases continue, as the Court demonstrated when in 1989 it unanimously struck down the time-honored New York City Board of Estimate in which the population range was 78 percent between the most and least populous boroughs.[185]
See also: APPORTIONMENT OF POLITICAL DISTRICTS.

one step at a time   Laws are sometimes challenged under the EQUAL PROTECTION CLAUSE for criminalizing certain activities while permitting closely related activities to continue. For example, an Oklahoma law forbade opticians from selling eyeglasses, including a plain frame without lenses, unless the customer had a prescription from an opthalmologist or optometrist. The law made an exception for sellers of ready-to-wear glasses, such as sunglasses. Thus, a department store could sell nonprescription sunglasses but opticians could not. In 1955, speaking for a unanimous Court, Justice William O. Douglas upheld the discrimination, saying that the legislature may "take one step at a time" in reforming evils in a particular field.[2224]

open fields doctrine, *see:* **search and seizure: open fields doctrine**

opinion of the court A court's opinion is a statement of the reasons for the decision. Without judicial opinions our legal system would be wholly different, for cases would have no value as PRECEDENT and there would be no body of constitutional or any other type of law. Opinion writing is an ancient tradition in the COMMON LAW system, but it is not explicitly commanded by the Constitution or by statute. On occasion the Supreme Court issues PER CURIAM decisions without opinion, affirming or reversing the decision of the lower court or dismissing the case. Until John Marshall was appointed Chief Justice, it was a common practice for each justice of the Supreme Court to write an opinion in each case. Marshall amplified the institutional voice of the Court by writing, or assigning to another justice the task of writing, a single majority opinion of the Court. Justices are not bound to keep silent if they disagree with the opinion of the Court. They may agree with the outcome but disagree with the reasons and therefore write a CONCURRING OPINION. They may disagree with the outcome and write a DISSENTING OPINION. Or they may disagree and merely record their vote as

dissenting. When there is no single majority opinion, but enough justices agree on an outcome to resolve the case, the largest bloc of justices to agree on a common reason files a PLURALITY OPINION.

opinion of the principal officer, *see:* **executive branch; office and officers**

opinion-fact distinction In 1974 in an important LIBEL case, Justice Lewis F. Powell said: "Under the FIRST AMENDMENT there is no such thing as a false idea."[746] He meant that no one may be prosecuted or sued for expression of political, social, scientific, artistic, religious, moral, or economic ideas. The expression of mere *opinion* is protected by the First Amendment. However, false factual statements are not protected simply by being couched in the language of opinion. A daily newspaper sports columnist said that a high school wrestling coach had lied under oath during an investigation into a disturbance at the school gym. Defending against the coach's libel suit, the newspaper's parent company said that the columnist had merely been stating his opinion. The Court rejected the contention that a libel court must always first inquire into whether a statement was opinion or fact and dismiss any suit involving opinions. When a speaker says, "[I]n my opinion, Mayor Jones is a liar," Chief Justice William H. Rehnquist said, "he implies a knowledge of facts which lead to the conclusion that Jones told an untruth." Rehnquist distinguished this "false" kind of opinion from a true form of opinion that would not be actionable: "In my opinion Mayor Jones shows abysmal ignorance by accepting the teaching of Marx and Lenin."[1336]

oral argument Oral argument is the colloquy between judges and lawyers in a CASE OR CONTROVERSY. Although lawyers argue motions before trial judges, oral argument is usually before an APPELLATE COURT. It is the lawyer's only opportunity to discuss the case directly with the judges who will decide it. Since argument occurs after the judges have had an opportunity to read the BRIEFS, the lawyer is usually peppered with questions and has little time to make a direct, uninterrupted presentation. Skilled advocates welcome questions, because through them the lawyers can learn how and why the issues are troubling the judges and can explain how the position they are advocating will resolve the judges' doubts. In the early days, oral argument in the Supreme Court could go on for days and was a high form of entertainment for the fashionable, upper-class audience that would attend carefully to the rhetorical flourishes of the nation's leading advocates. Today, because of its crowded docket, the Court allots each side only thirty minutes. The Court hears oral argument in four cases on certain Mondays, Tuesdays, and Wednesdays during fourteen weeks between October and April. The justices hold a conference within a day or two after hearing argument to take a preliminary vote, which often decides the case. *See also: CONFERENCE, JUDICIAL.*

order, resolution, or vote   The Constitution decrees that a bill can become law only when both houses of Congress have passed it and it has been presented to the president for signature. But what is a bill? Suppose Congress labels a piece of legislation by some other name, passes it, and announces that it is law without PRESENTMENT. Anticipating this dodge, Art. I-§7[3] says that in addition to bills, "every order, resolution, or vote" must also be presented to the president before it can take effect, just as in the case of a bill. But in a bit of ambiguous wording, the clause says that the president is to receive all orders, resolutions, and votes "to which the concurrence of the Senate and House of Representatives may be necessary," except a vote on adjournment.

Taken literally, the language would mean that whenever a member of Congress moves to amend a pending bill, the president must have the opportunity to approve it before it could take effect. To give this clause its literal meaning would quickly paralyze the government. The Court has read the language to mean that the president must be presented only with legislative "output" intended to become law, however it was originally labeled. In 1798 the Court held that congressional voting on resolutions proposing amendments to the Constitution need not be presented to the president,[933] because under Article V, approval of constitutional amendments is for the states, not the president. However, the Court has held that resolutions authorizing congressional vetoes of administrative action are subject to this provision; a unilateral LEGISLATIVE VETO is unconstitutional.[979]

ordered liberty   In 1937 the Court rejected the argument for total INCORPORATION—that every right enumerated in the BILL OF RIGHTS as a prohibition against conduct by the federal government applies equally to conduct by the states. But, said the Court, some *essential* rights are equally applicable. Justice Louis D. Brandeis coined the paradoxical phrase "ordered liberty" to describe the principle of balance by which the Supreme Court could decide whether or not to require the states to be bound by these rights. He wrote that only if a right is "of the very essence of a scheme of ordered liberty" does the DUE PROCESS Clause of the FOURTEENTH AMENDMENT require the states to respect it. Among such rights, he said, were "freedom of thought and speech," because they are "the matrix, the indispensable condition, of nearly every other form of freedom." But some rights, he said for the Court, were not of the essence of ordered liberty; for example, the right to be free of DOUBLE JEOPARDY.[1557] Although Justice Hugo L. Black agreed with

Brandeis's formulation in 1937, a decade later he began a bitter war against the phrase and the method of analysis that Brandeis proposed. The Court overruled Brandeis's conclusion about double jeopardy in 1969,[153] but it has never wavered from his conclusion that the Fourteenth Amendment does not require total incorporation, and the Court continues to refer to "ordered liberty."

See also: NATURAL LAW.

original intent In 1985 in a speech to the American Bar Association, Attorney General Edwin Meese III called for "a jurisprudence of original intention." It was time, he said, for the justices of the Supreme Court to return to "the [Framers'] original meaning of constitutional provisions," which are "the only reliable guide for judgment." Meese's speech raised a storm that has not yet abated, rousing dozens of historians, judges, constitutional scholars, and others to ponder whether original intent is a meaningful concept and how it might be ascertained. Deciding constitutional cases according to the Framers' intent has a surface appeal, for if it is possible it saves us from unelected judges wandering around looking for values to impose on us. That the Court has almost never in its history founded any large part of its decisions on original intent should, however, give pause to those in search of it.

Two problems, one conceptual and one practical, immediately stand in the way: Did the Framers themselves *intend* that the judges be bound by their intent? The Constitution does not say so. If the Framers did not intend it, then a jurisprudence of original intention is not a constitutional doctrine at all but a political predilection and, at that, only one among many. Meese himself offered no proof that the Framers believed in original intent, and it is safe to say that the historians disagree. Then *whose* intent should guide us? The intent of the delegates to the CONSTITUTIONAL CONVENTION or the intent of the Ratifiers? There is striking evidence that James Madison, the undisputed intellectual father of the Constitution, believed that if later interpreters were to look at someone's intent, it was not to his or his colleagues' in Philadelphia but to the intent of those who ratified in the thirteen state conventions. One reason Madison decided to leave his notes on the convention unpublished until after his death was to avoid judicial attempts to plumb the Framers' minds.

The practical problem is how to go about uncovering the intent of people who lived in an age now separated from ours by the gulf of two centuries. The most detailed records we have, Madison's notes, are not a verbatim record of the Convention proceedings. *The Federalist Papers* were essentially advocacy pieces by only three of the delegates, whose job was to persuade the people to ratify. Moreover, uncovering the "intent" of even one person is a difficult job for a highly skilled historian. Trying to uncover what the hundreds of delegates to the ratifying conventions thought each constitutional clause meant is impossible, both because good records no longer exist, if they ever did, and for the more important reason that on many of the major controversies of our age, we can be reasonably sure that the "Original Intenders" had no intent at all. They contemplated neither a modern technology nor a modern bureaucracy, with all their opportunities for good and ill.

Furthermore, judges are not historians, and the "law office histories" which they often construct from snippets of diaries and essays are far from the subtle reconstructions that would yield true history. In short, judges simply are not equipped to act also as historians, and the record is fairly clear that they do not accept the conclusions of constitutional historians when the conclusions contradict judicial prejudices.

Still greater difficulties might ensue if we ever could discover the original intentions of the Original Intenders. That is because the Constitution speaks in short phrases, and the intent of its makers may have had little to do with the phrase actually chosen. Take this simple example. The SEVENTH AMENDMENT says that in all federal COMMON LAW suits, the parties shall have the right to a jury "where the value in controversy shall exceed twenty dollars." Of course the dollar amount is so clear that judges would say there is no reason to look beneath the words for the intent. But the amount is also so inherently arbitrary that we might well wonder what the intent could possibly have been. Suppose we could conclude that the Original Intenders intended by twenty dollars a rather high threshold, rather than the ludicrously low threshold it appears to be today. Suppose twenty dollars in 1787 was the equivalent of one thousand or even five thousand dollars in our money. What, then, does "intent" tell us? That the words "twenty dollars" do not really mean twenty dollars? That the Original Intenders meant to make it difficult, not easy, to get a jury? A jurisprudence of original intentions might well tell us to ignore the plain words of the Constitution, a result with which no Supreme Court justice today would agree.

So despite the continued agitations over original intent, it seems likely that the Court will continue, as it has through the past two centuries, to decide cases with only an occasional nod to the Original Intenders when convenient, but otherwise to reach results that accord with its philosophical predilections and the reigning culture of the moment.

See also: CONSTITUTION, LIVING; CONSTITUTIONAL INTERPRETATION; INTERPRETIVISM; MADISON'S NOTES ON THE CONSTITUTION; NATURAL LAW; NINTH AMENDMENT; STRICT CONSTRUCTION.

original jurisdiction Courts have two types of JURISDICTION, original and appellate. Original jurisdiction is the power of a court to try a case, to hear testimony and review evidence offered to uncover the facts of the matter. In the federal system, the trial courts are the United States DISTRICT COURTS. Article III-§2[1] limits federal jurisdiction to certain kinds of cases, and under Art. III-§1 Congress may determine which of these types of cases may be heard by trial courts. Art. III-§2[2] confers original jurisdiction on the Supreme Court in a narrow range of cases affecting foreign ambassadors and diplomats and cases in which a state is a party, although this clause does not bar Congress from vesting CONCURRENT JURISDICTION in the lower federal courts to hear suits involving diplomats.[201] Since ambassadors have DIPLOMATIC IMMUNITY they may not be sued at all in their official capacities, nor for political and historical reasons do they file suits as plaintiffs. Because the ELEVENTH AMENDMENT bars suits in federal court against states when brought by individuals, the only remaining classes of cases that can be tried in the Supreme Court are those in which one state is sued by another state or by the United States. The Court occasionally hears such cases, although it has often said that "our original jurisdiction should be invoked sparingly."[2114]

When a case is to be tried in the Supreme Court, the justices do not sit as a panel of trial judges with jury. Instead, they appoint a SPECIAL MASTER to hear the evidence and write a report. They then consider objections to the report on questions of law, just as they do in hearing cases under their APPELLATE JURISDICTION. Under Art. III-§2[2], Congress may diminish the types of appellate but not original cases the Supreme Court may hear. Under MARBURY V. MADISON Congress may not expand the Court's original jurisdiction. Congress may, however, grant CONCURRENT JURISDICTION to the federal district courts to hear cases that fall within the Supreme Court's original jurisdiction.[201] The Court has declined to try many recent environmental cases involving disputes between cities and states because the technical facts and issues could be sorted out more expeditiously in the district courts.[973] State courts may also have concurrent original jurisdiction over cases that could be heard in the Supreme Court.[1523]

original package doctrine   The IMPORT-EXPORT CLAUSE bars states from taxing goods imported from abroad. If the clause meant literally what it says, the states would confront intractable difficulties in determining to what degree commodities made from imported goods could be taxed. In 1827 Chief Justice John Marshall announced the original package doctrine, which he thought would resolve these difficulties. Imported goods remain exempt from state taxation, he held, as long as they remain unsold and kept in a warehouse in the original package in which they were imported.[253] But when the imported goods are mixed with "the mass of property in the country" they lose their "distinctive character as an import." The original package doctrine remained good law for nearly 150 years. Its principal utility to importers lay in their being able to avoid general property taxes laid on the assessed value of a company's property on a fixed day of each year. As long as the imported goods remained in the original package, their value could not be taxed.[1201]

For a time, the Court also used the original package doctrine to bar one state from regulating goods imported from a sister state. For example, notwithstanding a PROHIBITION law a state could not prohibit a company from importing from another state and then selling liquor in its original package.[1149] The Court overruled this aspect of the original package doctrine in 1935,[110] and in 1976 finally dispatched the rest of it, holding that states may tax goods imported from abroad, even though the goods remain in their original packages, as long as the tax is nondiscriminatory.[1328]

other persons   One of the ways by which the delegates to the CONSTITUTIONAL CONVENTION papered over their deep disagreement over the issue of SLAVERY was to sidestep the word in the Constitution itself. In Art. I-§2[3], the euphemism employed was "other persons," stating who counted, and by how much, in apportioning DIRECT TAXES and representation in Congress. The clause was superseded by Section 2 of the FOURTEENTH AMENDMENT.
See also: THREE-FIFTHS RULE.

other public ministers   The term "other public ministers" is coupled with AMBASSADORS in Articles II and III and by historical convention, though not by any decision of the Supreme Court. The term has been assumed to mean "all officers having diplomatic functions, whatever their title or designation."

overbreadth doctrine   Suppose that a state law prohibits "all picketing" and that the police have arrested a group of antiwar protesters for beating bystanders over the head with placards. May the protesters challenge their arrests and convictions under this law? It is clear that their conduct could be punished and that they would have no basis to challenge convictions under a more narrowly drawn law that outlawed "physical assault during any demonstration." But because the law under which they were charged is *overbroad*—that is, because it condemns activities protected by the Constitution—the Court will strike it down because of its CHILLING EFFECT.

The overbreadth doctrine says that "the very existence of some broadly written statutes may have such a deterrent effect on free expression that they should be subject to challenge even by a party whose own conduct may be unprotected."[401] It has been used to strike down a range of laws, including prohibitions of peaceful picketing[2044] and promotional advertising by an electric utility;[361] LOYALTY OATHS requiring public employees to swear that they were not members of certain political organizations;[1072] denials of passports[67] or public jobs[1736] to members of organizations listed as subversive by the attorney general; and bans on the use of "abusive language,"[778] anonymous handbilling,[2291] and live entertainment.[1809] Ordinarily, an overbroad law will be struck down "on its face," meaning that it may not be used again. If the legislature wishes to punish the bad conduct, it must enact a new and narrower law. This result contrasts with the more usual practice of reversing a conviction, because the law was applied unconstitutionally in the particular case, without striking down the law altogether. But an overbroad statute need not necessarily be wholly invalidated. In a 1985 case, for example, the Court found a Washington State OBSCENITY law overbroad but refused to invalidate it because the activity of the person challenging it was constitutionally protected. Therefore, said the Court, it would simply reverse the conviction. In effect, the Court's decision carved the unconstitutional feature out of the law, while leaving the constitutional parts intact.[241]

In 1973 the Court announced what appeared to be a major limitation of the overbreadth doctrine. Laws that sweep more broadly than the Constitution allows will be upheld unless they are "substantially" overbroad, in cases in which the person may constitutionally be convicted for, or barred from undertaking, his particular conduct.[240] For example, the Court upheld a Los Angeles ordinance prohibiting anyone from posting a sign on public property.[401] The Court said that the challengers, a political group that wished to affix campaign posters on utility poles, could not show how the law prohibited any other expression entitled to First Amendment protection. Nevertheless, the new "substantial overbreadth doctrine" continues to have vitality. On this ground the Court struck down a law prohibiting films with nudity from being shown in public drive-in theaters,[622] a law barring charities from soliciting contributions unless they devoted three-quarters of their receipts to charitable purposes,[1811] a law permitting police to arrest citizens for annoying them,[946] and a municipal ordinance prohibiting anyone from engaging in all "First Amendment activities" in the Los Angeles International Airport terminal.[124]

See also: STANDING.

overinclusivity, *see:* **classifications, under- and overinclusive**

overruling   When the Supreme Court declines to follow the reasons that led it to decide an earlier case in a particular way it is said to *overrule* its prior decision. By doing so, it is announcing that it is deciding a similar case in a different way, According to one count, the Court has overruled two hundred of its decisions since 1790. The power to overrule is an inherent part of the JUDICIAL POWER. In overruling a precedent, the Court does not actually disturb the result in the particular case overruled. It simply announces that it wrongly decided the case and henceforth will not follow the disapproved reasoning.

See also: STARE DECISIS.

overt acts   Under the TREASON clause, Art. III-§3[1], no one may be convicted of treason unless at least two witnesses testify "to the same overt act," defined as going to war against the United States or giving "aid and comfort" to enemies of the country. This provision ensures that people cannot be convicted of treason merely for speaking out in opposition to national policy.

P

Palmer raids For about six months beginning in November 1919, U.S. Attorney General A. Mitchell Palmer, prompted by the post–World War I "Red Scare," ordered federal law enforcement officials to raid the homes and offices of thousands of presumed radicals, most of them ALIENS whom Palmer wanted to deport. The searches were fundamentally lawless, conducted without ARREST or SEARCH WARRANTS and without PROBABLE CAUSE to suspect the detainees of having committed any crime. A raid on January 2, 1920, netted five thousand arrested people in thirty-three cities, two thousand of whom were subsequently released without charges. Federal officials committed many other flagrant violations of the Constitution, even as it was then construed: defendants were denied the right to consult with their own lawyers, convictions were obtained without witnesses. One indirect constitutional consequence of these raids was a decision in early 1920 that federal prosecutors may not make copies of unlawfully seized books and papers and use the copies to obtain an INDICTMENT from a GRAND JURY.[1869]

See also: FRUIT OF THE POISONOUS TREE; SEARCH AND SEIZURE.

pamphleteering, right to, *see:* **permit system; picketing; prior restraint; solicitation**

pandering In 1966, in *Ginzburg v. United States,* an uncommonly silly decision that ran counter to the permissive trend of the day, the Court upheld a pornography conviction of Ralph Ginzburg, publisher of *Eros* magazine and other publications, in large part because he "pandered" to the "erotic interests" of customers by giving his magazine and books "salacious appeal," including mailing them from Middlesex, New Jersey; Blue Balls, Montana; and Intercourse, Pennsylvania. The Court's theory was that in a close case, evidence that sellers of sexually explicit materials intended to engage the libidinous instincts of their buyers may be used to persuade a jury that the works really are obscene. Justice Hugo L. Black dissented, stating that the result of the newly concocted pandering rule is that a jury may find guilty a person who mails nonobscene material because it "may not find him or his business agreeable." The concept of pandering was mentioned in only five subsequent obscenity cases, the last in 1978.[1631]

See also: OBSCENITY AND PORNOGRAPHY.

paper money, *see:* **currency**

pardons, reprieves, commutations, and amnesties Under Art. II-§2[1], the president has the power to grant "reprieves and pardons for offenses against the United States, except in cases of impeachment." When the pardon power first came before the Supreme Court, Chief Justice Marshall followed English doctrine, declaring that a pardon is an "act of grace," a private though official act of the president. The person to whom a pardon is offered must agree to accept it for it to take effect.[2233] The Court seemed to affirm this view in 1915 when a witness before a federal GRAND JURY refused to testify on the ground that so doing might tend to incriminate him. President Woodrow Wilson offered the witness a full pardon, but the witness still declined to testify, asserting that accepting the pardon would imply guilt. The Supreme Court unanimously agreed that the witness could not be forced to accept the pardon or testify.[277]

The pardon power extends to all federal offenses, including criminal, but not civil, CONTEMPT.[824] Neither the president nor Congress may pardon the commission of state crimes. The effect of a pardon is to annul all punishments—jail sentences, fines, forfeitures, and other penalties, including disqualifications from holding OFFICE[727]—and to restore all civil rights,[213a] except that a fine already paid into the U.S. treasury may not be returned unless Congress separately appropriates the funds to do so.[1086] A pardon does not necessarily wipe out all record of the offense. If the pardon was issued before conviction, then "in the eye of the law the offender is as innocent as if he had never committed the offense."[727] But if the pardon was bestowed after conviction, a court may take into account the pardoned felon's record when sentencing for a later conviction.[342]

The president may *commute* a defendant's sentence, substituting a lighter for a heavier penalty, without requiring the defendant's consent.[163] The president's power to commute is constitutionally based, and Congress may not limit it by general legislation. The president may impose an independent condition in commuting the new sentence, as long as the condition does not itself violate the Constitution.[1814] For example, the Court approved the president's commutation of a military death sentence to life imprisonment without possibility of parole, even though the Uniform Code of Military Justice provides that that possibility may never be foreclosed.

Only the president may pardon a particular person;[2103] but both the president, through proclamations,[1082] and Congress, by law, may issue general *amnesties* to entire classes of people.[260] A congressional amnesty may provide for all fines to be excused.[2031] Both pardons and amnesties may be bestowed any time after the offense is committed, even before indictments are issued,[727] and possibly without identifying or even fully knowing what the crimes were. President Gerald R. Ford in his notorious pardon of his predecessor asserted the authority to exonerate Richard M. Nixon for all crimes that "may have been committed." But no pardon may be issued before a crime is committed because such authority would confer the power to ignore law altogether.

Blanket amnesties have a long lineage in American history. George Washington issued the first in 1795, followed by others in 1800 (John Adams), 1801 (Thomas Jefferson), 1815 (James Madison), 1863 (Abraham Lincoln), 1865, 1867, and 1868 (Andrew Johnson), and 1902 (Theodore Roosevelt). In 1974 President Ford proclaimed a conditional amnesty for Vietnam War deserters and draft evaders, requiring them to perform alternative public service in return for the pardon.

See also: IMMUNITY FROM PROSECUTION; TEST OATH.

parental rights and responsibilities In a pair of cases in the mid-1920s, the Court first announced a SUBSTANTIVE DUE PROCESS right for parents to raise a family in accordance with their values. The Court struck down a Nebraska law forbidding children from being taught foreign languages[1323] and an Oregon law requiring children to attend public school and prohibiting parochial and private schools.[1628] At least in the absence of some emergency, the state has no power to interfere "with the LIBERTY of parents and guardians to direct the upbringing and education of children under their control. . . . The child is not the mere creature of the State; those who nurture him and direct his destiny have the right, coupled with the high duty, to recognize and prepare him for additional obligations."

The power of parents over their children's upbringing and welfare is broad but not absolute. For example, in certain states they have a QUALIFIED RIGHT to have mentally disturbed children committed to institutions,[1565] to withdraw children from school after a certain age if the parents adhere to an established and religious way of life,[2237] and to be provided with notice if a minor daughter plans to have an ABORTION.[833, 1637, 929, 1519] But the state retains a COMPELLING INTEREST in the welfare of children and may terminate the rights of natural parents if the state demonstrates, by "clear and convincing evidence," that they are mistreating their child or are unfit because they have exhibited "permanent neglect."[1802] Despite the seriousness of a termination proceeding, the state need not in every instance provide indigent parents with a lawyer to represent them.[1124] Although the Court has not had occasion to rule directly on the issue, the state presumably could not constitutionally remove a child from the natural parents in the absence of abuse simply because it would be "in the best interests of the child" to be placed elsewhere.[1894]

See also: ADOPTION AND CUSTODY OF CHILDREN; FAMILIES; ILLEGITIMACY; JUVENILES, RIGHTS OF; MEDICATION AND SURGERY, FORCED; PARENTS, FOSTER; PATERNITY.

parents, foster   Foster parents have a lesser right than natural parents to retain custody of their children. In 1977 the Supreme Court unanimously upheld a state procedure providing that for children who have been in foster care for less than eighteen months, the state need give only ten days' advance notice that it intends to remove the children. As long as the foster parents may confer with the social services agency before the removal, the child may be taken from their home, provided that the agency thereafter holds a full-scale adversary HEARING and that judicial review is available.[1894] The rights of natural parents may not be terminated without a preremoval judicial hearing.

See also: PARENTAL RIGHTS AND RESPONSIBILITIES.

parks, right to speak in, see: **public forum**

parole   There is no general constitutional right to parole—that is, to release from imprisonment before the prisoner has served out the full sentence—even if a state has established a general parole system.[807] Many states have a system of *indeterminate sentencing* under which judges sentence defendants to a range of time to be served, leaving it up to administrative parole boards to determine when, if at all, the prisoners may be released. Because this system in effect entrusts a considerable power over sentences to administrators, the Court has held that under some circumstances DUE PROCESS entitles prisoners to a HEARING on whether they are entitled to be paroled. When the law requires a parole board to order a prisoner to be released unless he has violated disciplinary rules, then the prisoner has a "protectable expectation of parole" entitling him at least to a meeting with the parole board and to be informed of the reasons for denial of parole.[807] Likewise, a prisoner may not be denied "good time credit," which would permit him to be released early, unless the prison authorities give him advance notice of the charges, the opportunity to call witnesses and present evidence (except when prison discipline will be undermined), and a written statement of the facts and reasons for the decision to reduce good time credit.[2245] However, when an individual has already been paroled and is living in society, then the parole board may not revoke his parole without both a preliminary hearing and a formal adversary hearing, including appointed counsel in some instances.[1390] When parole is to be revoked because the defendant has been convicted of a second crime, the revocation is usually automatic and no lawyer need be appointed to represent the defendant at the revocation proceeding. On the other hand, when the facts that would legitimate revocation are sharply disputed, a lawyer is necessary.[717]

See also: COUNSEL, ASSISTANCE OF; PROBATION.

particularity in warrants, *see:* search warrant

party A party to a lawsuit is a person, corporation, political entity, or other body whose legal rights will be directly affected by the outcome. The party bringing a lawsuit is the *plaintiff;* the party against whom the suit is filed is the *defendant.* Depending on the circumstances, there can be many plaintiffs and defendants in any case.

See also: JURISDICTION; POLITICAL PARTY; SERVICE OF PROCESS.

passports, right to There is no absolute constitutional right to a passport, but on two occasions the Supreme Court has ruled against the U.S. government when it refused to issue passports to individual citizens. In the first case, in 1958, the Passport Office denied a passport because the applicant failed to submit an affidavit saying that he had never been a member of the Communist party. The Court ordered the office to issue a passport. To avoid dealing with the constitutional issue, the Court read the passport law narrowly, holding that Congress had not delegated the secretary of state authority to require such affidavits. But along the way the 5–4 majority declared a fundamental right to travel as part of the LIBERTY protected by the FIFTH AMENDMENT.[1062]

In 1964 the Court struck down on constitutional grounds a provision in the Subversive Activities Control Act of 1950 that automatically denied passports to any MEMBER OF A POLITICAL ORGANIZATION listed as subversive by the attorney general.[67] However, the next year the Court upheld a State Department rule drastically restricting travel to Cuba on an American passport.[2286] And when the State Department revoked the passport of Philip Agee, a former CIA agent, because he was noisily revealing the names of active American intelligence agents in cities throughout Europe, the Court upheld another regulation permitting the secretary of state to revoke a passport if the activities of someone traveling abroad are causing serious damage to national security or foreign policy, distinguishing a broad freedom to travel within the United States from a more restricted right to travel abroad.[839]

See also: ATTORNEY GENERAL'S LIST; CONSTITUTIONAL QUESTIONS, AVOIDANCE OF; TRAVEL, RIGHT TO.

Patent Clause Art. I-§8[8] empowers Congress to establish a national patent system to give inventors an exclusive right for a limited time to exploit their inventions. Under the 1952 Patent Act, inventors may obtain a seventeen-year monopoly over their inventions. The Constitution provides only one standard for the issuance of patents—that they "promote the progress of science and the useful arts." Most patent questions arise under the federal act, but the Supreme Court has found that two constitutional consequences flow from the standard given in Clause 8. One is that patents may be issued only for new and useful inventions.[944] Under the present law, the invention must be "nonobvious" to a person skilled in the field in which the invention was made. Otherwise, a patent would have the effect of removing "existent knowledge from the public do-main," and doing so would scarcely promote any sort of progress.[790] The other constitutional consequence is that a researcher may not patent the discovery of a law of nature and thereby gain exclusive right to all devices that take advantage of it. To be patentable, a discovery must be embodied in some invention.[712] Once a patent is granted, the government may not itself use the invention or revoke the patent without paying JUST COMPENSATION.[1002] If an invention or manufacturing process is not patentable under federal law, the states may not use their "unfair competition" laws to prevent other manufacturers from making or using it.[196]

See also: AUTHORS AND INVENTORS; PREEMPTION; TRADE SECRETS; WRITINGS AND DISCOVERIES.

paternity   When the state files a paternity suit, DUE PROCESS requires it to pay for blood tests if the putative father is too poor to afford them, because the tests might help establish that he is not the father and should not be ordered to support the child.[1172] The Supreme Court has not had occasion to say whether this rule applies also in private suits filed by a child's mother. In such private suits, paternity may be established by a "preponderance of the evidence."[1733]

See also: ILLEGITIMACY; PROOF, STANDARD OF.

patronage   The Supreme Court decided in 1976 that under the FIRST AMENDMENT non–civil service employees may not be fired solely for reasons of patronage. The case involved the dismissals of holdover Republican employees of an Illinois county sheriff's office by a newly elected Democratic sheriff.[612] Only "policy-making" officials may be dismissed because of their party affiliation, a 5–4 majority agreed. In 1980, in rejecting the attempt of a Democratic county public defender to fire Republican assistant public defenders, a 6–3 majority said that whether a public employee may be fired

for patronage reasons depends on "whether the hiring authority can demonstrate that party affiliation is an appropriate requirement for the effective performance of the public office involved."[224] In dissent, Justice Lewis F. Powell stressed longstanding patronage practices that "helped build stable political parties." In 1990 a 5–4 majority extended the patronage cases still further, holding that the patronage limitations apply also to most other employment-related decisions, including transfers, promotions, and hiring.[1778] But since that time, two of the majority, Justices William Brennan and Thurgood Marshall, have retired, and the rule against patronage therefore may be in some doubt.

See also: FREEDOM OF ASSOCIATION; PUBLIC EMPLOYMENT.

peace, breach of, see: **breach of peace**

peaceably to assemble, see: **freedom of assembly**

penalty-subsidy distinction   The federal income tax code bars tax-exempt status to charitable organizations that engage in lobbying or political activities. Taxation with Representation of Washington, a taxpayer's public interest group, was denied charitable status because it actively lobbied for changes to the tax laws. It asserted that the denial violated its FIRST AMENDMENT rights because Congress was conditioning a government benefit on the organization's surrendering a constitutional right to lobby. In an opinion by Justice William H. Rehnquist, the Supreme Court held that the government had not imposed a penalty on but rather had merely denied a SUBSIDY to lobbying organizations. Tax exemptions and tax deductibility are forms of subsidy, in effect cash grants to particular taxpayers. There is no constitutional right to a subsidy, and the government may select among recipients as long as it does not "discriminate invidiously" so as to "aim at the suppression of dangerous ideas."[1704]

The Court did find such suppression in 1984, when it overturned a federal law prohibiting any public broadcasting station using public funds from airing political editorials or endorsing candidates. The effect of the law was to force the stations to forgo a core First Amendment right to voice their opinions in order to obtain public funding for any of their programs.[641] The Court also overturned as a violation of FREEDOM OF THE PRESS an Arkansas sales tax law that taxed general interest magazines but exempted newspapers and various types of journals.[76]

See also: FREEDOM TO PETITION; GOVERNMENT SPEECH; LOBBYING; PUNISHMENT, CRIMINAL AND CIVIL; SPENDING POWER; SPEECH, REGULATION OF CONTENT; UNCONSTITUTIONAL CONDITIONS.

pendent jurisdiction   Sometimes a federal case involves a closely related claim under state law. A federal court is permitted to decide the state claims on a theory of *pendent jurisdiction* appropriate, according to the Supreme Court, whenever both claims "derive from a common nucleus of operative fact."[2095] By deciding both claims, the court can achieve judicial economy and spare the parties the need for "bifurcated proceedings." Pendent jurisdiction is not an absolute. The Court has held that under the Federal Arbitration Act, some claims must be arbitrated and may not be heard by courts.[1392, 529] And in an important case in 1984, the Court overturned on ELEVENTH AMENDMENT grounds the extension of pendent jurisdiction to suits in federal courts against state officials asserting violations of rights under state law.[1588]

Pentagon Papers Case   In June 1971, the *New York Times* and the *Washington Post* began to publish excerpts from a classified Defense Department study, officially titled "History of U.S. Decision-Making Process on Viet Nam Policy," but popularly known as the Pentagon Papers. The newspapers obtained these documents from a former Defense Department official, Daniel Ellsberg. A day after publication began, Attorney General John N. Mitchell ordered government lawyers to take the newspapers to court to restrain further articles, claiming grave national harm. By undermining peace negotiations, the government asserted, publication of the excerpts would prolong the war and risk the death of many soldiers. Federal district courts decided against the government, but two U.S. COURTS OF APPEALS issued temporary restraining orders against further publication pending appeal.

The Supreme Court agreed to hear the cases less than two weeks after the first article appeared, heard argument the next day, and decided against the government four days after that. In a 6–3 PER CURIAM decision in *New York Times Co. v. United States*, the Court held that the government had not met its "heavy burden of showing justification for the enforcement" of a PRIOR RESTRAINT against the press. Each of the justices wrote separate CONCURRING or DISSENTING OPINIONS.

Justice Hugo L. Black said that "every moment's continuance of the INJUNCTIONS" amounted to "a flagrant, indefensible, and continuing violation of the FIRST AMENDMENT." Justice William O. Douglas agreed, adding that no law prohibited the newspapers from publishing the articles and that the government has NO IMPLIED OR INHERENT POWER to obtain injunctions against the press. Justice William Brennan, also concurring, said that the only exceptions to the rule against prior restraint occur when the disclosure would immediately imperil the security of troops engaged in or about to be engaged in battle. Justice Potter Stewart said that the responsibility for maintaining secrecy "must be where the power is"—the president, not the courts, must keep classified information secret. If it LEAKS out, the courts may not stop the presses. Justice Byron

R. White agreed with Brennan and Douglas that no law authorized injunction and that the government had not met its burden, and he added that the government had gone down the wrong route. Instead of seeking injunctions, it should have sought INDICTMENTS against those who leaked the information. Justice Thurgood Marshall espied a SEPARATION OF POWERS problem "for this Court to use its power of CONTEMPT to prevent behavior that Congress has specifically declined to prohibit."

Dissenting, Justice John Marshall Harlan, pointing to the "almost irresponsibly feverish" attitude of the Court in deciding the cases so hurriedly, said that the president is entitled to much greater leeway in seeking to block matters dealing with FOREIGN AFFAIRS. The Court may independently review whether the material against which an injunction is sought deals with foreign affairs and whether the secretary of defense had personally assessed the risks; if so, the courts should refrain from redetermining "the probably impact of disclosure on the national security." Also dissenting, Justice Harry Blackmun wanted the Court to remand the cases to the lower courts to develop standards through a BALANCING that would say when the press could be enjoined because, the "First Amendment, after all, is only one part of an entire Constitution." Chief Justice Warren E. Burger dissented solely because "we literally do not know what we are acting on"; he contended that the Court should have extended the temporary restraining orders until the lower courts could conduct a full trial on the merits.

penumbra theory   In *Griswold v. Connecticut*, the controversial 1965 PRIVACY case striking down Connecticut's CONTRACEPTION law, Justice William O. Douglas was faced with the problem of finding a distinct right to marital intimacy in the face of a constitutional silence. Nowhere does the Constitution use the word "privacy." So Douglas cobbled a privacy right out of several constitutional doctrines under the First, Third, Fourth, Fifth, Ninth, and Fourteenth Amendments that, he said, amount to "zones of privacy," including FREEDOM OF ASSOCIATION, PARENTAL RIGHTS, the ban on the quartering of soldiers, and the right against unreasonable SEARCHES AND SEIZURES and SELF-INCRIMINATION, among many others.

The specific guarantees in the BILL OF RIGHTS, Douglas said, "have penumbras, formed by emanations from those guarantees that help give them life and substance," which establish a right of privacy protected generally from government intrusion. Douglas took this tack to avoid being criticized for making an open-ended SUBSTANTIVE DUE PROCESS decision that he and other justices had long condemned earlier courts for making in cases involving economic regulation, including LOCHNER V. NEW YORK. By pointing to penumbras, Douglas was trying to show that there are *specific* constitutional provisions, not the vague DUE PROCESS Clause, that shelter the right of married couples to use birth control. *Griswold* was one of the rare instances in which Justice Hugo L. Black parted company with Douglas in a CIVIL LIBERTIES case. Black denounced Douglas's technique of substituting "for the crucial word or words of a constitutional guarantee another word or words, more or less flexible and more or less restricted in [meaning]," thereby "diluting or expanding a constitutionally guaranteed right."

See also: NATURAL LAW; NINTH AMENDMENT; STRICT CONSTRUCTION.

peonage, *see:* **involuntary servitude**

people, rights retained by, *see:* **Ninth Amendment**

people of the several states   Art. I-§2[1] says that the "people of the several states" shall elect members of the House of Representatives. By this phrase the Framers meant that representatives from each state are to be elected by the people in that state. In 1964 the Supreme Court read the phrase to mean "that as nearly as is practicable one man's vote in a congressional election is to be worth as much as another's."[2182]

See also: APPORTIONMENT OF POLITICAL DISTRICTS; ONE PERSON, ONE VOTE.

per curiam A per curiam opinion (Latin for "by the court") is a very brief unsigned opinion that simply declares in whose favor the case is decided; for example, affirming the lower court's decision for the appellant, or reversing and remanding the case to the lower court to reconsider its decision in light of the Court's opinion in some other recently decided case. Per curiam opinions are usually reserved for cases in which the law is settled and there is no reason for an extended discussion. Sometimes, as in the PENTAGON PAPERS CASE, it is used because none of the justices can agree on a reason for the decision, even though there is a majority for a certain result. Justices occasionally file concurring and dissenting opinions.

See also: HOLDING.

peremptory challenge, *see:* **jury discrimination**

perjured testimony Perjured testimony is unlawful but not unconstitutional, unless the prosecutor in a criminal trial knows that the evidence offered through a prosecution witness is false.[1377] The prosecutor is constitutionally obligated under DUE PROCESS to correct false statements. The falsehood need not bear directly on the guilt of the defendant. For example, a conviction must be overturned when the prosecutor does not correct the false statement of an accomplice of the defendant that he had been promised nothing for his testimony when

in fact the prosecutor had promised him consideration in his own case to follow.[1420, 753] In another case, a witness had been sexually involved with a woman whose husband murdered her because of her infidelities. The prosecutor knew of the relationship but told the witness not to volunteer the information, so at trial the witness claimed the relationship was wholly casual. Even though the false testimony at most impeached the credibility of the witness, the conviction was contaminated by the perjury and could not stand.[32] In 1986 the Court held that the SIXTH AMENDMENT right to effective assistance of counsel in a criminal prosecution was not violated when an appointed lawyer refused to cooperate with his client's desire to commit perjury on the witness stand.[1481] The lawyer told the defendant that if he committed perjury the lawyer would tell the judge about it and then seek to withdraw from the case. Chief Justice Warren E. Burger said that since the lawyer had not breached but had abided by the code of professional responsibility, his actions in deterring the defendant from committing perjury did not violate the defendant's Sixth Amendment rights.

See also: PROCEDURAL RIGHTS OF CRIMINAL DEFENDANTS; PROSECUTORIAL MISCONDUCT *and cross references listed there.*

permit system Beginning in 1938, the Supreme Court has decided a series of cases involving the efforts of municipalities to ban or regulate the use of public streets and parks by groups of people for demonstrations, picketing, meetings, and distribution of pamphlets and other literature. Because the public has an interest in the use of its streets and other public places, the Court has long recognized that municipalities may impose TIME, PLACE, AND MANNER RESTRICTIONS on demonstrators' access, despite the FREEDOM OF ASSEMBLY. But those restrictions must be evenhanded and may not be based on the message of the particular group. One common method of regulation is to require DEMONSTRATORS to obtain a permit from the chief of police, mayor, or other municipal agency authorizing each particular use of the public spaces. A permit system without standards to guide the administrative official violates the right against PRIOR RESTRAINT implicit in the FIRST AMENDMENT.

In the 1938 case, a Griffin, Georgia, ordinance prohibited anyone from distributing "circulars, handbooks, advertising, or literature of any kind . . . without first obtaining written permission from the City Managers." A Jehovah's Witness passed out religious pamphlets without a permit. The Court unanimously reversed her conviction, holding the ordinance INVALID ON ITS FACE because it gave the city manager unbridled discretion to withhold permits for any reason or no reason at all.[1198] But in a 1941 Jehovah's Witness case involving eighty-eight marchers, the Court upheld convictions resulting from a parade down a city street in the absence of a required permit because the permit system required the licensing authority to grant or deny permits in a nondiscriminatory manner, taking into account only such things as overlapping parades, the risks of disorder, and the time of the demonstration.[479]

The Court has adhered to this distinction. In 1969 the Court unanimously struck down a Birmingham, Alabama, permit law that authorized the city to deny parade permits if in the city's "judgment the public welfare, peace, safety, health, decency, good order, morals, or convenience require that [the permit] be refused."[1862] Birmingham officials had pointed to the ordinance to deny permits to a civil rights protest march led by Martin Luther King, Jr., and other ministers. Summing up the constitutional rule, Justice Potter Stewart said that "a law subjecting the exercise of First Amendment freedoms to the prior restraint of a license without narrow, objective, and definite standards to guide the licensing authority is unconstitutional."

Permit systems often raise two related questions: (1) When demonstrators parade without first requesting a permit, does their failure to ask for one preclude them from challenging the system itself? If they are being prosecuted for violating the ordinance, they may raise as a defense that the ordinance is invalid on its face.[1198] On the other hand, if demonstrators have been enjoined from marching, they may not violate the INJUNCTION with impunity but must contest it in court.[2142] And a 1953 case suggests that when demonstrators have actually applied for and been denied a permit, they may not avoid a conviction for then going ahead and marching anyway. They should first contest the denial in court, even if the denial was wholly arbitrary.[1651] However, this principle may not have survived a series of later cases that make timeliness an important factor in any licensing scheme involving expressive activities.[699] (2) Do those affected by a standardless permit system have STANDING to contest the system, even if they have not yet asked for a permit or the agency has not yet denied them one? In 1988 in a suit involving permits for newspaper vending machines on city streets, the Court held 6–3 that a newspaper could challenge the law "on its face," even though the publisher had not yet suffered any injury by it.[1111]

See also: FREEDOM OF SPEECH *and cross references listed there;* PUBLIC FORUM.

person and personhood   The Constitution uses the word "person" or "persons" forty-six times and the word "people" nine times. "Person" usually refers to an OFFICEholder, but sometimes it has more particular meanings. In several instances, it means any individual human being; for example, in the TREASON Clause of Art. III-§3[1], the EXTRADITION Clause of Art. IV-§2[2], and the Citizenship Clause of the FOURTEENTH AMENDMENT. The Constitution distinguishes between person and a "natural born citizen" in Art. II-§1[5]. The references to "other persons" in Art. I-§2[3] and "such persons" and "each person" in Art. I-§9[1] are allusions to slaves; the Framers were too delicate or too embarrassed to use the term SLAVERY in the Constitution. In three clauses "people" means those eligible to vote; in the others it refers generally to the whole population of a state or of the nation. But the Constitution's failure to state a general theory of personhood has allowed the Supreme Court in three vastly different historical epochs to develop the term in possibly contradictory ways.

In 1857, in *Dred Scott v. Sandford*, Chief Justice Roger B. Taney gratuitously and disastrously said that the "people of the United States" could never constitutionally comprise blacks as a race, meaning that blacks could be neither citizens nor holders of constitutional rights. The first sentence of the Fourteenth Amendment was written and ratified precisely to overrule Taney's wretched conclusion. For purposes of citizenship at birth, therefore, person means *any* human being, not those of a particular race or national ancestry. Under the Fourteenth Amendment, constitutional protections for "persons" are not limited to citizens. DUE PROCESS and EQUAL PROTECTION apply to all persons, "without regard to any differences of race, of color, or of nationality." [2276] Constitutionally, in other words, we are one common humanity.

Somewhat astonishingly, for these same purposes, the Court has not confined "person" to human beings. One of the most far-reaching constitutional pronouncements the Court ever made was that "person" encompasses CORPORATIONS and other legal entities, so that the constitutional protections of the Fourteenth Amendment apply to ordinary businesses as well as to people. The issue was never truly explored, and the reasons for the conclusion were never set forth in an OPINION OF THE COURT. Instead, during ORAL ARGUMENT in an 1886 case, Chief Justice Morrison R. Waite told the lawyers that they need not debate whether the Equal Protection Clause applies to corporations because, he said for his colleagues, "We are all of the opinion that it does." [1799] Perhaps the only corporate entities not considered persons under the Fourteenth Amendment are municipal corporations—towns, cities, counties, and the like—which have neither due process nor equal protection rights against their states. [1475]

The question of personhood lies also at the center of the most divisive modern social issue in the country—ABORTION. In *Roe v. Wade*, the Supreme Court expressly declined to hold that a fetus is a person, for such a conclusion would of course have led the Court to uphold state abortion laws, since the decision to take another's life is always subject to state control. Instead, the 7–2 majority developed a different theory of personhood—that of the autonomy each woman has over her body. What the steady erosion of *Roe* bodes for the constitutional conception of personhood can be expected to occupy center stage for many years to come.

See also: DRESS CODES; PSYCHIC HARM; SLAVERY; THREE-FIFTHS RULE.

personal mobility, *see:* **travel, right to**

personhood, *see:* **person and personhood**

petit jury A petit jury is a trial jury, historically consisting of twelve jurors, as distinct from the GRAND JURY, usually consisting of twenty-three members.
See also: JURY AND JURORS.

petition, freedom of, *see:* **freedom of petition**

picketing Picketing is a form of protest, usually but not necessarily in labor disputes, in which people hold placards with messages intended to influence the opinion and actions of passersby on the streets. In the labor context, pickets often hope to deter passersby from patronizing the stores or offices of those they are picketing. In 1940, after years of constitutional hostility toward labor picketing, the Supreme Court for the first time struck down a state antipicketing law that prohibited all forms of peaceful picketing.[2044] Disseminating information about a labor dispute, said the Court, is "within that area of free discussion" guaranteed by the FIRST AMENDMENT. But the Court soon reassessed the breadth of its ruling and eventually concluded that even peaceful labor picketing may be enjoined or regulated as a CLEAR AND PRESENT DANGER if it has a "sole, unlawful immediate objective" to violate the labor laws.[748]

In 1980 the Court showed that it was prepared to interpret the unlawful objective test broadly, in holding that the National Labor Relations Board could prohibit a peaceful picket urging consumers to refrain from buying nonunion products sold by someone not a party to the dispute.[1432] The Court held that the picketers were "coercing" or "signaling" neutrals to engage in practices that violate the labor laws. The picketers said they were only peacefully asking individual consumers not to make purchases, decisions that each individual is lawfully entitled to make. However, in 1988 the Court distinguished "handbilling" from picketing and upheld the right of construction union members, in a dispute over wages, to pass out leaflets at the entrance to a mall in "an attempt to persuade customers not to shop" in any of the stores there.[530]

Although even peaceful labor picketing is now subject to sharp limitations, "public issues" picketing has been given broader constitutional protection. In 1982 the Court unanimously upheld the right of black citizens in Mississippi to BOYCOTT white merchants, even though there were sporadic outbursts of violence, because the principal purpose of the picketing was "to change the social, political, and economic structure of a local environment" that had long violated blacks' CIVIL RIGHTS.[1418] In the right circumstances, the states may regulate political picketing under narrowly drawn laws, for unlike the publication of IDEAS, which may not be regulated, picketing is "speech plus"—that is, speech mixed with conduct. But the states may not discriminate among types of picketing on the basis of the political views expressed or the content of the message.

In 1972 the Court unanimously struck down a Chicago ordinance prohibiting anyone from picketing within 150 feet of a school but permitting "peaceful picketing of any school involved in a labor dispute." The Court said Chicago could have banned all picketing near schools, but it may not select certain kinds of messages for official approval.[1646] In 1988, the Court invalidated a District of Columbia ordinance that barred picketing within 500 feet of a foreign embassy if the "sign tends to bring the foreign government into 'public odium' or 'public disrepute.'"[197] Protesting the policies of foreign nations by carrying signs near their embassies is "classically political speech" that may not be banned outright when there is a LESS RESTRICTIVE ALTERNATIVE available, such as a law against intimidating and harassing foreign officials.

But also in 1988 the Court approved a restriction on "focused picketing" of a private residence. After protesters, in a group of as many as forty, had picketed the residence of an abortion doctor several times within a few weeks, a Milwaukee suburb adopted an ordinance barring picketing of homes. Justice Sandra Day O'Connor said that the ordinance was narrowly drawn to get at the exact evil—harassing people where they live—and that the protesters had many other channels of communication open to them.[703] The dissenters agreed that the town could regulate the time and manner of the picketing but thought that picketers carrying a political or social message on a public street could not be barred from ever doing so.

See also: DEMONSTRATORS AND DEMONSTRATIONS; LABOR AND LABOR LAWS; PUBLIC FORUM; SOLICITATION; SYMBOLIC SPEECH; TIME, PLACE, AND MANNER RESTRICTIONS.

piracy   Art. I-§8[10] empowers Congress to "define and punish piracies and felonies committed on the high seas, and offenses against the LAW OF NATIONS." This is one of the few express grants of congressional power to write criminal laws. The Framers generally accepted the principle that the United States as an independent nation was bound by INTERNATIONAL LAW, and so the national legislature, not the states, should be the competent authority over these matters. Although Congress may define with particularity what constitutes piracy or offenses against the law of nations, the Court in 1820 upheld a law punishing "the act of piracy, as defined by the law of nations."[1897] During World War II, the Court maintained this position, approving a law that subjected to military trials "offenders or offenses that . . . by the law of war may be triable by . . . military commissions," without spelling out in any clearer detail what those offenses are.[1677] Under this clause, "high seas" is interpreted quite broadly, so that Congress can reach offenses committed on U.S. ships even when they are anchored in foreign ports.[713] Congress need not say that it is acting under this clause to enact a valid law punishing crimes under international law, as long as the law does deal with an international offense. On this ground, the Court upheld a federal law punishing the counterfeiting in the United States of foreign government securities.[73]

plain view doctrine, *see:* **search and seizure: plain view**

platter, silver, *see:* **silver platter doctrine**

plea, *see:* **arraignment; guilty plea; plea bargaining**

plea bargaining   Most criminal cases in the United States never go to trial. Instead, the defendant and prosecutor bargain over the plea: the defendant agrees to plead guilty to a charge less serious than that with which the prosecutor actually charged him, and the prosecutor agrees to recommend a less serious sentence. In 1970 the Supreme Court upheld the basic constitutional authority of the state to engage in plea bargaining,[221] and in several cases since then it has underscored the importance of the practice for keeping the criminal justice system afloat. On the one hand, if the state agrees to a plea bargain, the prosecutor's office must abide by it; a new prosecutor may not refuse to accept the defendant's agreement to plead to a lesser charge.[1801] On the other hand, since the practice results from *bargaining,* the prosecutor is entitled to drive a *hard* bargain. It is constitutional for the prosecutor to threaten the ACCUSED with the maximum possible charges, unless the accused relinquishes his or her right to a trial and pleads to a lesser charge.[1773] Likewise, the prosecutor may threaten to and actually reindict the accused on even more serious charges unless the accused pleads guilty to the original charge.[200] At the same time, the Court has insisted that a GUILTY PLEA must be voluntary; a defendant who does not understand the charge may later insist on the right to trial.[899]

See also: ARRAIGNMENT; TRIAL, RIGHT TO.

pleading the Fifth   "Pleading the Fifth" refers to the refusal of a defendant or witness to testify at a trial or other public hearing, including one before a legislative committee, on the ground that the answers to the questions may tend to incriminate him or her, in violation of the right against SELF-INCRIMINATION found in the FIFTH AMENDMENT. A witness may refuse to testify only if to answer risks criminal prosecution. A witness granted IMMUNITY[260] or who has accepted a PARDON is in no legal danger of prosecution and so may not plead the Fifth.

Whether a witness pleading the Fifth may be retaliated against depends on the circumstances. In 1956 the Court overturned the dismissal of a public college teacher who pleaded the Fifth before a congressional investigating committee.[1883] However, if the questions that the witness refuses to answer are relevant to assessing whether he or she continues to be qualified to hold a job, refusal to answer at an investigation by the employing agency may constitute grounds for firing.[1153] A licensing agency may not revoke a license solely because a person being investigated by the agency—for example, a lawyer haled before a disciplinary committee of the bar—refuses to cooperate with the investigation.[1932] Nor may a police department fire an officer who refuses to waive his right against self-incrimination during an official investigation, although the department could insist that he forfeit his job for refusing to answer "questions specifically, directly, and narrowly relating to the performance of his official duties."[725] In other words, public employees may be forced to testify about their own duties, but if they answer from fear of being fired, they may not later be criminally prosecuted.[732]

Plessy v. Ferguson In 1883, in the CIVIL RIGHTS CASES, the Supreme Court struck down a federal law barring RACIAL DISCRIMINATION in PUBLIC ACCOMMODATIONS. Although the law was aimed at discriminatory acts by *private* individuals, the Court's apparent retreat from the purposes that animated the FOURTEENTH AMENDMENT emboldened the states to place a *public* imprimatur on racial SEGREGATION.

In 1887 Florida passed the first of many "Jim Crow" laws (the name derived from a line in an 1820s minstrel song), establishing SEPARATE BUT EQUAL railroad passenger cars for blacks and whites. Jim Crow laws spread quickly through the South. In 1891 a group of black citizens organized a Citizens' Committee to Test the Constitutionality of the Separate Car Law and solicited funds for a lawsuit. In 1892 they set in motion an elaborate plot to bring a TEST CASE to court. Homer Adolph Plessy, a man who was one-eighth black (one of his eight great-grandparents was black) and who could easily have passed for white, climbed aboard the East Louisiana Railroad in New Orleans and sat in the whites-only coach. Alerted to the scheme, the conductor requested that he move to the black car. When Plessy refused, a train detective arrested him. Thus a case was instigated that would reach the Supreme Court in 1896.

Plessy's lawyer, Albion W. Tourgee of New York, argued that the question was not whether the facilities were in fact equal, as the Louisiana Supreme Court had justified its ruling against Plessy, but whether a state may "label one citizen as white and another as colored in the common enjoyment" of daily activities. Tourgee insisted that in prohibiting SLAVERY, the THIRTEENTH AMENDMENT bans not merely ownership of people but also "a caste, a legal condition of subjection to the dominant class." That the railroad law imposed just that, Tourgee said, was amply demonstrated by the exemption for black nurses attending white children: dependent blacks could sit in white cars but nonservile blacks could not. This law reeked of dominance and oppression. "Justice is pictured blind and her daughter, the Law, ought at least to be color-blind," Tourgee said.

The Court did not agree. In *Plessy v. Ferguson,* a 7–1 majority held that under the EQUAL PROTECTION CLAUSE, states may make classifications as long as they are reasonable, and what is reasonable depends on the "established usages, customs, and traditions of the people, and with a view to the promotion of their comfort, and preservation of the public peace and good order." In other words, the people may do just as they please, since they will never deviate from their own usages, customs, and traditions. The railroad law, said Justice Henry B. Brown, promoted racial peace. Those who drafted the Fourteenth Amendment, he concluded, "could not have intended to abolish distinctions based on color." It was not the law that "stamps the colored race with the badge of inferiority," said Brown, *but their own feelings about it.*

To Justice Brown's abject surrender to racial fear in an opinion full of sociological nonsense, Justice John Marshall Harlan responded with one of the great dissents in American constitutional history. Plainly the law was designed to put the state's seal of supremacy on the white race. But "in view of the constitution, in the eye of the law, there is in this country no superior, dominant, ruling class of citizens. There is no caste here. *Our constitution is color-blind,* and neither knows nor tolerates classes among citizens. In respect of civil rights, all citizens are equal before the law. . . . It is difficult to reconcile [the boast that we are the freest society] with a state of law which, practically, puts the brand of servitude and degradation upon a large class of our fellow citizens. . . . The thin disguise of 'equal accommodations' . . . will not . . . atone for the wrong this day done. In my opinion, the judgment this day rendered will, in time, prove to be quite as pernicious as the decision made by this tribunal in the Dred Scott case."

Harlan was undoubtedly correct. *Plessy* paved the way for rigid racial segregation in almost every facet of life in many southern states. Not until BROWN v. BOARD OF EDUCATION in 1954 did the Court begin the formal OVERRULING of *Plessy,* an effort that today is largely constitutionally complete.

See also: AFFIRMATIVE ACTION; CONSTITUTION, AS COLOR-BLIND; SEGREGATION AND INTEGRATION; SOCIOLOGICAL FOOTNOTE AND SOCIAL SCIENCE EVIDENCE.

plurality opinion For a judicial opinion to be an OPINION OF THE COURT, a majority of justices must agree with the reasons given for the HOLDING. When a majority agrees on the result but not on the reasons, several different opinions may be written. The opinion with which the largest number of justices concur is known as the plurality opinion. Although it has precedential value, it is considerably weaker than a majority opinion, since a later Court may be less disposed to be bound by it under STARE DECISIS.

pocket veto The president's power to veto legislation is ordinarily not absolute: Congress may override a veto by a two-thirds vote in each house. But in one instance, the president has an absolute veto, called a "pocket veto." Under Art. I-§7[2], the president has ten days (not counting Sunday) to decide whether to veto a bill passed by Congress and presented to him for signature. If he does not sign it within ten days, the bill becomes law, unless Congress has adjourned, thereby making it impossible for the president to return the bill. When a bill dies in this manner, the president is said to keep it in his pocket. The pocket veto provision was adopted to prevent Congress from manipulating its recesses so that a president could never return a bill while Congress was in session. The question is what constitutes an adjournment—a two-day recess? the end of the first session of a Congress? the end of a Congress? (A Congress lasts two years—the length of the terms of members of the House; a session of Congress lasts one year.)

In the *Pocket Veto Case,* Congress had adjourned its first session fewer than ten days after passing a bill. The Court said that the word "adjournment" is not limited to a final adjournment at the end of a particular Congress; it means any adjournment that prevents the president from returning the bill within the allotted time. In the only other Supreme Court case on this clause, the Court said that the pocket veto clause applies only when Congress as a whole has adjourned, not when one house only has done so, so that a bill can be returned during a three-day recess of the Senate.[2262] These days, the clause serves little practical function, since regardless of official recesses or adjournments between sessions, congressional committees may meet and congressional employees may be delegated the duty of receiving presidential veto messages. Incidentally, Congress need not be in session for a bill signed by the president to become law, as long as it is signed within ten days after the adjournment.[1106, 604]

See also: VETO POWER.

poisonous tree, *see:* **fruit of the poisonous tree**

police, regulation of   In scores of situations, the Court has held that the BILL OF RIGHTS imposes substantive limitations on police actions, especially those involving SEARCH AND SEIZURE and confessions obtained in violation of the right against SELF-INCRIMINATION. Individual police officers may be sued for DAMAGES in federal court for violation of a person's constitutional rights.[1375] But the Court has shied away from blanket attacks on police departments as a whole. In a key 1976 case, *Rizzo v. Goode,* the Court overturned a federal trial court's order to city officials to draft a "comprehensive program for dealing adequately with civilian complaints" against an asserted city-wide practice of mistreatment and even brutality in law enforcement. The Court held that the case presented no CASE OR CONTROVERSY because there were no allegations of misconduct against specific plaintiffs.

In 1983, in a case that was to have chilling implications a decade later, the Court similarly refused to hear a case involving the use of "chokeholds" by the Los Angeles Police Department. The plaintiff had been subjected to a chokehold when stopped for a motor vehicle infraction. He sued both for damages and to restrain the department from using chokeholds in such circumstances thereafter. Justice Byron R. White, for a 6–3 majority, held that the plaintiff lacked STANDING because it was unlikely that he would "suffer future injury from the use of chokeholds by police officers." Such a case could be heard only if someone could plead and show that the police *always* used chokeholds unnecessarily or that the department ordered them to do so.[1188]

police interrogation, *see:* **self-incrimination**

police power   Unlike the LEGISLATIVE POWERS of Congress, those of the states are not limited by the principle of ENUMERATED POWERS. Under the Constitution, the states retain full authority to legislate in any field and to achieve any objective, subject only to the limitations imposed in the Constitution itself. In 1824, in *Gibbons v. Ogden,* Chief Justice John Marshall referred to "that immense mass of legislation, which embraces every thing within the territory of a state, not surrendered to the general government; all of which can be most advantageously exercised by the states themselves. INSPECTION LAWS, QUARANTINE LAWS, health laws of every description, as well as laws for regulating the internal commerce of a state . . . are component parts of this mass." In 1827 Marshall dubbed the totality of state legislative power the "police power."[253] "The traditional police power of the States," the Supreme Court has said as recently as 1991, "is defined as the authority to provide for the public health, safety, and morals."[128] In fact, as the Court has held at various times, it is even broader: it permits the states to enact regulations that foster "public convenience or the general welfare and prosperity," so that, for example, a law requiring railroads to drain their roadbeds to avoid water damage to adjacent privately owned land is well within the police power.[386]

While the interests encompassed by the police power are numerous, there are restraints on state legislative activity in the CONTRACT CLAUSE, the COMMERCE CLAUSE, and the DUE PROCESS Clause of the FOURTEENTH AMENDMENT. Until after the Civil War, the Court relied chiefly on the concept of the DORMANT COMMERCE CLAUSE to prevent the states from enforcing regulations that interfered with INTERSTATE COMMERCE. With the rapid rise of industrialization after the Civil War, the Court significantly undercut the Contract Clause as it upheld state legislation and regulation that acted to impair the OBLIGATION OF CONTRACTS. By 1878 the Court had announced a general principle that the states may not bargain away their police power; in other words, a contract with a corporation granting a monopoly or promising not to regulate is not binding.[203]

This understanding of the police power was both boon and bane to American business. Because the Court viewed the police power as adaptable to changing times, states could "legislate so as to increase [their] industries, . . . develop [their] resources, and . . . add to [their] wealth and prosperity."[124] At the same time, the increasing bulk of regulations impinged in one way or another on the autonomy of business to operate outside the watchful eye of the state. The question was whether such exercises of the police power unconstitutionally interfered with private PROPERTY rights. The JUST COMPENSATION CLAUSE of the FIFTH AMENDMENT barred the federal government from "taking" property without paying for it, but the Court had said in 1833 that the Fifth Amendment did not apply to the states.[132] With the ratification of the Fourteenth Amendment in 1868, the possibility arose that a similar restric-

tion would limit the states. At first the Court specifically denied, in the SLAUGHTER-HOUSE CASES in 1873, that the new amendment was intended to have any such effect. But changing attitudes and a changing bench eventually led the Court to a radical new theory: a SUBSTANTIVE DUE PROCESS limitation on the states' police powers. In 1897 the Court formally "incorporated" the Just Compensation Clause into the Fourteenth Amendment.[390] This brake on legislation was not limited to the classic form of outright appropriation of property but to every form of regulation that interfered in some way with business not AFFECTED WITH A PUBLIC INTEREST. As a consequence, the Court took upon itself the power to strike down exercises of the police power that seemed to it to invade property interests, defeat VESTED RIGHTS, or interfere with FREEDOM OF CONTRACT.

Eventually the Supreme Court reversed course, holding in *Nebbia v. New York* in 1934 that state economic laws are presumptively valid and that the courts may not invalidate them as long as they have "a reasonable relation to a proper legislative purpose and are neither arbitrary nor discriminatory." But as it has turned out, the Court has not accorded a PRESUMPTION OF CONSTITUTIONALITY to every kind of state law enacted in the interests of public health, safety, welfare, and morals. Under the PREFERRED POSITION doctrine set out in the famous CAROLENE PRODUCTS FOOTNOTE FOUR, the Court has scrutinized especially closely police power enactments that seem to infringe on rights enumerated in the BILL OF RIGHTS.

See also: ECONOMIC DUE PROCESS; INCORPORATION DOCTRINE; NATIONAL POLICE POWER; PREEMPTION; PUBLIC MORALS; TAKING OF PROPERTY; ZONING.

political activity The right to engage in political activities lies at the core of the Constitution. The Constitution establishes a representative democracy, which means both that the people must be free to elect their representatives and that the people's voices may not be stilled when their representatives are deliberating on policy. The right to vote necessarily implies the right to form POLITICAL PARTIES, to participate in political campaigns, and to run for office. All these rights find shelter in the voting provisions and amendments and in the FIRST AMENDMENT's protection of the FREEDOM OF SPEECH, FREEDOM OF ASSEMBLY and PETITION, and FREEDOM OF ASSOCIATION. From these same provisions derive the rights to editorialize and to comment freely on candidates and elected officials and to engage in LOBBYING.

These rights are nearly absolute for the citizenry generally, but less so for public employees, some of whose political interests may be subordinated to the requirements of PUBLIC EMPLOYMENT. For example, under the Hatch Act, federal employees are forbidden to "take any active part in political management or in political campaigns." The Supreme Court upheld the act and regulations banning employees from running for office, serving as a member of a party nominating convention, soliciting votes by mail, distributing campaign literature, and otherwise engaging in any active role on behalf of candidates or parties in an election.[2098] But public employees do not forfeit all political rights. The Court has struck down most forms of political PATRONAGE hiring and firing, and in the LOYALTY OATH cases has made clear that except in extreme cases employees may retain MEMBERSHIP IN POLITICAL ORGANIZATIONS without being fired.

See also: ACCESS TO BALLOT; CAMPAIGN FINANCING; LIBEL AND SLANDER; VOTING, RIGHT TO.

political conventions   Saying that "the states themselves have no constitutionally mandated role" to play in choosing political party nominees for public OFFICE, the Supreme Court has held in several cases that political party con-

ventions, not the courts, are the appropriate forums for resolving disputes arising over whether a delegate has been properly elected to cast a vote at a political convention.[476] Only the convention may determine whom to seat, even if the delegates choose to unseat other delegates properly elected under a state winner-take-all primary.[1506] "A political party's choice among the various ways of determining the makeup of a State's delegation to the party's national convention is protected by the Constitution," the Court has held, pointing to the FREEDOM OF ASSOCIATION. At the core of this freedom is the right to advocate political views and candidates, which "necessarily presupposes the freedom to identify the people who constitute the association, and to limit the association to those people only."[538]

See also: ACCESS TO BALLOT; POLITICAL PRIMARIES; VOTING, RIGHT TO.

political expenditures   In 1976 the Court recognized for the first time that political expenditures—money spent to promote candidates—constitute a form of FREEDOM OF SPEECH protected by the FIRST AMENDMENT.[270] Congress may not curb a person's expenditure of money on candidates independent of the candidate's own efforts or those of the candidate's party. But the Court did uphold general restrictions on how much candidates or parties may spend.

See also: CAMPAIGN FINANCING.

political parties   One major political development that the Framers missed but should have anticipated was the rise of the political party. Perhaps because everyone assumed George Washington's election as the first president, the factions that very shortly became active had not yet been fully organized as discrete partisan organizations. In any event, the Framers were extremely chary of acknowledging the role of partisan politics, and the Constitution says nothing about political parties. Madison extolled the Constitution because of it, saying in *Federalist* 10 that it was designed chiefly to avoid the "mischiefs of faction." In his farewell address in 1797, Washington warned specifically of the dangers of "the spirit of party." But by then political parties were already forming, and in due course they would create a political system for nominating and electing the president and other officials about which the Constitution was wholly silent.

The constitutional question throughout our history, therefore, has been the degree to which the party system may be regulated. Of the most profound importance was the development of a fairly stable two-party system. This came about largely independently of the law. Although the Constitution does not require that two parties dominate the political scene at any one time, the virtual lack of governmental authority over the election process helped ensure the rise of the two-party system. Because of the constitutional role of the states in the ELECTORAL COLLEGE, the states recognized the advantage of a winner-take-all system under which a candidate for president receives all of a state's electoral votes. This system politically encouraged a two-party system, since splinter parties would find it almost impossible ever to secure the electoral votes of a single state, much less the votes of the many states necessary to elect a president. And since so much even of local politics turns on ties to the national party system, the United States for the most part has sustained a centrist government. So rooted has the two-party system become that the Supreme Court has exalted to the status of a COMPELLING INTEREST a state's interest in the stability secured through a two-party system. It upheld a state law prohibiting any candidate from running independently if affiliated with any party during the previous twelve months, although the state may not impose a longer time limit than that on the right

of party renegades to run independently.[1965] Following this position, the Court also said that states could not set early deadlines for independent candidates to put their names on the ballots, because otherwise those dissatisfied with what happens at a political convention would be barred from running in opposition.[59]

The Court upheld a Washington State law that requires each major party to establish a statewide committee consisting of two committee members from each county. The state committee has the power to call conventions, provide for the election of delegates to national conventions, and fill vacancies on the party ticket. In 1976 the state Democratic party decided to add new members to the legally required state committee that had served for years as the central governing body of the state party. When a challenge arose to the composition of the expanded state committee, the Court upheld the original state law, saying that the states have a legitimate interest in ensuring that the nomination process is fair and orderly. The Court recognized that a political party has the constitutional right to conduct its purely internal affairs as it sees fit, but it noted that the state did not compel the Democratic party of Washington to use the state-mandated committee as its central governing arm. It could choose another institutional mechanism, but it could not transfer the legal authority of the state committee to another body not established as the law requires.[1241]

Nevertheless, because political parties lie at the heart of the POLITICAL ACTIVITIES protected by the FIRST AMENDMENT, the Court has been extremely deferential to party activities at POLITICAL CONVENTIONS that involve the actual selection of nominees. However, under the FIFTEENTH and NINETEENTH AMENDMENTS, the right to equal voting means that the parties may not deny access to POLITICAL PRIMARIES on the basis of race, national origins, or sex. And for the obvious reasons that political parties are about *politics* and the expression of political beliefs is protected under FREEDOM OF SPEECH, the states may not bar political parties from permitting non–party members to vote in the party's primary[1997] or from endorsing a particular candidate running in a party primary.[630] In 1991 the Court refused to decide a controversy arising under a provision in the California state constitution prohibiting parties from endorsing, supporting, or opposing candidates for elected nonpartisan local offices. The Republican County Central Committee sued for a DECLARATORY JUDGMENT that the ban violated its First Amendment rights. But the Court held 6–3 that the case was not justiciable because there was no showing of a "live dispute," since the party could not point to any threat by a state official to enforce the prohibition on endorsements.[1710]

See also: ACCESS TO BALLOT; CAMAPIGN FINANCING; JUSTICIABILITY; PATRONAGE; RIPENESS.

political primaries   The Supreme Court has repeatedly made sweeping pronouncements about the constitutional rights of POLITICAL PARTIES as private organizations to be free of state supervision under a general FREEDOM OF ASSOCIATION. Since the Constitution limits governmental, not private, activities, the Court faced a certain difficulty in dealing with whites-only primaries. In 1935 it even held that a party primary is a private affair from which blacks could be constitutionally excluded by the party itself,[826] though not by state law.[1486] But in cases in 1944 and 1953 it reversed course, overruling its earlier decision and holding that primary elections, no matter how constituted or organized, are so intimately enmeshed with STATE ACTION that any exclusion of participation by race, no matter how sanctioned, violates the FIFTEENTH AMENDMENT.[1885, 2012]

See also: ACCESS TO BALLOT; VOTING, RIGHT TO.

political question doctrine   In 1803, in MARBURY V. MADISON, the very case in which the Supreme Court first claimed for itself the power to determine the constitutionality of federal legislation, Chief Justice John Marshall said that "[t]he province of the [Supreme Court] is, solely, to decide on the rights of individuals, not to inquire how the executive, or executive officers, perform duties in which they have a discretion. Questions in their nature political, or which are, by the constitution and laws, submitted to the executive can never be made in this court." This is the premise of the political question doctrine, that the Supreme Court has no constitutional basis to hear cases involving the exercise of discretionary powers by other branches of government. A simple example is the PARDON power of the president. The Court may not review the president's refusal to pardon a convicted criminal, since the decision is solely for the president. The Court actually first applied the doctrine, though not by name, seven years before *Marbury* when it refused to decide whether the government had violated a treaty obligation.[2155] In 1827 it held that the president and Congress had unreviewable discretion over when the militia should be called into service.[1252] Largely because few controversies not involving people's rights are ever brought to court, the Court has had relatively few occasions to dismiss claims on the ground that they present an unreviewable political question. In recent years it has even overruled itself and held that some formerly unreviewable questions were within its reach.

The major political question committed to other branches is the Art. IV-§4 guarantee of a REPUBLICAN FORM OF GOVERNMENT for each state. The Court has also come close to saying that the president's conduct of FOREIGN AFFAIRS is beyond review. Certainly the questions of which foreign governments to recognize[1559] and who is the actual ruler of a foreign nation[1034] are exclusively for the president. So too are the issues of whether a nation has the authority to enter into a treaty obligation with the United States[556] and whether a treaty has lapsed because the foreign nation has lost its independence.[2010] Congress, not the Court, has the final say on whether a constitutional amendment has been ratified.[426] Congress and the president are the final authorities on whether a war has begun or concluded.[439, 2255, 1204, 1135] Most issues relating to federal control over INDIANS AND INDIAN TRIBES are political questions beyond the scope of the Court's constitutional authority.

Until the 1960s, the Court consistently held that questions of APPORTIONMENT OF POLITICAL DISTRICTS were political. Even grotesquely malapportioned legislatures were beyond constitutional reach in the courts. But in 1962 the Court overruled previous decisions, holding in *Baker v. Carr* that apportionment is a justiciable issue that may be heard in the courts. This decision signaled a narrowing of the political question doctrine, and the Court soon began to order the reapportionment of Congress and state legislatures. The doctrine, Justice William Brennan said, arises out of the Supreme Court's relationship to the other federal branches, not to the state governments. Summing it up, Brennan said the political question doctrine would be applied in one of the following six circumstances: (1) when there is a "textually demonstrable commitment to another branch"; (2) when the courts have no standards they can discover and use to resolve the dispute; (3) when the courts cannot decide without a policy determination that properly belongs to the political branches; (4) when the courts would have to show great disrespect for coordinate branches of government; (5) when there is "an unusual need" to adhere to a "political decision already made"; or (6) when considerable embarrassment might result if different

branches of government pronounced different views on the same issue.[108]

The Court found no political question bar to its decision that a state legislature may not exclude a duly elected member because of his or her expression of political views.[195] And in 1969, despite Brennan's conclusion that the doctrine limits the Court's power to hear disputes involving other federal branches, the Court held that it did not apply when Congress sought to exclude Representative Adam Clayton Powell, Jr., for financial misdealings, because the Constitution expressly states only narrow grounds under which Congress may do so.[1653] In 1973 the Court applied the doctrine to bar courts from inquiring into how National Guard troops are trained and disciplined, both because this is about the clearest example of a governmental action intended to be left to the political branches and also because the courts are probably less competent to judge in this area than any other branch.[756] In 1990 the Court refused to defer to Congress in judging whether a revenue bill was unconstitutional because it was enacted first by the Senate, in violation of Art. I-§7[1], which requires all bills raising revenue to originate in the House.[1403]

See also: COMMITMENT TO OTHER BRANCHES; JUSTICIABILITY.

political subdivisions   The Constitution does not speak about cities, towns, counties, or other forms of municipal government, such as school and water boards. The only governmental units mentioned in the Constitution are the United States itself, the states, foreign nations, and the Indian tribes. Cities and other local units of government are political subdivisions of the state, and the distinction is constitutionally significant. "We are a nation not of city-states but of States," the Court said in 1982 in holding cities, but not states, subject to federal antitrust laws.[446]

Because municipalities are creatures of the state, for most purposes, actions of a political subdivision are like actions of a state—constitutionally valid if they are legitimate for a state, but unconstitutional otherwise.[2093] Although private CORPORATIONS enjoy certain constitutional protections from state and federal legislation, MUNICIPALITIES do not. Cities, the Supreme Court said in 1907, are "created as convenient agencies for exercising such of the governmental powers of the State as may be entrusted to them. . . . The state, therefore, at its pleasure may modify or withdraw all such powers, may take without compensation such property, hold it itself, or vest it in other agencies, expand or contract the territorial area, unite the whole or part with another municipality, repeat the charter and destroy the corporation."[961]

Attempts to press the CONTRACT CLAUSE into service to prevent the state from reassigning one municipality's property and contractual obligations to another have been unavailing. A state may move a county seat, even if the residents of the old seat had donated land and obligated themselves through bonds to erect public buildings.[1477] On the same ground, no municipal officerholder has a constitutional right to the office if the state chooses to repeal the office, revoke or change its duties, or lower its salary.[294, 1361] States entirely at their whim may change the duties of local officials and determine whether they are to be elected or appointed.[1906] And although the ELEVENTH AMENDMENT bars federal courts from entertaining suits against the states, it does not prohibit federal suits against municipalities.[1372] Likewise, the FOURTEENTH AMENDMENT provides cities no constitutional protection from state direction. For example, the state may direct that cities recompense property owners for destruction resulting from riots, even though the city was not responsible for the damage.[384]

Notwithstanding the general discretion of the states over its political subdivisions, the Constitution does impose some restraints. A city may not be mapped geographically to deny certain people the right to vote.[775] In a line of decisions since 1964 involving APPORTIONMENT OF POLITICAL DISTRICTS, the Court has held that elections to most political offices be by districts of equal populations.[1713] For a time, the Court suggested that cities were immune under the TENTH AMENDMENT from federal control over their hiring and wage practices, holding in *National League of Cities v. Usery* that Congress may not "directly [impair] their ability to structure integral operations in areas of traditional governmental functions." But in 1985 the Court overruled *National League of Cities,* holding in *Garcia v. San Antonio Metropolitan Transit Authority* that it is impossible to define "traditional" governmental functions and so it would leave the issue to Congress.

See also: DORMANT COMMERCE CLAUSE; INTERSTATE COMMERCE; VOTING; RIGHT TO.

poll tax   The poll tax was a "head tax" imposed as a condition in many states on the "privilege" of voting. Although nominally a nondiscriminatory tax, in modern parlance it was regressive and discouraged the poorest people from registering. In 1937 the Supreme Court upheld the poll tax against an EQUAL PROTECTION challenge.[229] After a struggle in Congress that lasted more than a quarter century, the battle against the poll tax was partly won by ratification of the TWENTY-FOURTH AMENDMENT, which bars any state from conditioning voting in federal elections on payment of a tax. Two years later, the Court struck down all remaining poll taxes in state and municipal elections by ruling that the poll tax denies the class of impoverished voters the equal protection of the laws.[867]

See also: VOTING, RIGHT TO.

polygamy   Polygamy, the practice of having multiple spouses, was never permitted under American law. Because it was a tenet of Mormonism, a federal law against polygamy in U.S. TERRITORIES was attacked as violating the FIRST AMENDMENT right of FREEDOM OF RELIGION. The Court distinguished *beliefs* from *practices*, holding that Congress, and therefore the states as well, have the power to regulate antisocial practices.[1714] "Crime is not the less odious because sanctioned by what any particular sect may designate as 'religion,'" the Court said in a decision upholding a federal law requiring voters to forswear membership in any order that advocates polygamy.[520] The Mormon church underwent a doctrinal change abjuring polygamy, which remains unlawful to this day in every state.

See also: FREEDOM OF BELIEF; OATH OF OFFICE.

pornography, *see:* feminism and pornography; obscenity and pornography

ports Art. I-§9[6] prohibits Congress from giving preferences to the ports of one state over those of another, either by enacting tougher regulations or imposing higher taxes. But the Court has held that this clause does not prohibit Congress from conferring benefits or detriments on particular ports or a class of ports, as long as the benefits and burdens do not depend on the states in which they are located. For example, Congress may appropriate funds to build lighthouses and docks in certain ports only and to improve only particular harbors.[1595, 1912] The Court upheld an Interstate Commerce Commission tariff that established a higher rate for ferry services traveling east across the Mississippi than for those traveling west. Because the charges depended on economic factors, and not the geographic location of the ports, it did not matter that a port in one state was benefited more than a port in another state.[1193] The clause applies only to Congress. It does not bar the states from imposing differential regulations on their ports,[1387] and Congress may constitutionally empower the states to regulate harbor pilots, even though the pilot regulations may burden out-of-state ports more heavily.[2040]

See also: DORMANT COMMERCE CLAUSE; INTERSTATE COMMERCE.

posse comitatus A posse comitatus is a group of citizens summoned to aid in law enforcement, usually to round up a suspect. In constitutional terms, the question has been whether the president may order the use of federal troops to quell domestic violence, whether as a posse comitatus or not. In 1792 Congress authorized the president to use either the MILITIA or the ARMED FORCES to put down rebellions that could not be suppressed through ordinary judicial proceedings. In 1827 the Supreme Court held that the question of necessity was the president's alone.[1252] Thereafter, in disturbances surrounding enforcement of the Fugitive Slave Act, President Franklin Pierce asserted the authority to entrust military forces to the command of U.S. marshals for use as part of the posse comitatus. In 1878 Congress enacted the Posse Comitatus Act, barring the use of soldiers as any part of the posse comitatus, unless Congress has specifically authorized their use. The act has since been extended to the other military services and is legislative recognition of the fundamental principle that civilian affairs are off limits to U.S. military services. However, in the 1871 Force Act, portions of which continue to this day, Congress expressly authorized the president to call up military forces when state authorities are powerless or refuse to put down violence that interferes with the exercise of the people's constitutional rights. It was this provision that President Dwight D. Eisenhower invoked during the Little Rock, Arkansas, school DESEGREGATION crisis in 1958, and that presidents have used since to restore order after urban rioting.

post office   Art. I-§8[7] grants Congress the power to establish post offices and post roads. For nearly a century a minor debate ensued over the breadth of the postal power. Does the clause limit Congress merely to *designating* existing buildings and roads as post offices and roads, or may Congress appropriate funds to *build* roads and office buildings? In 1876 the Supreme Court finally opted for the broader construction, holding that the federal government could exercise its power of EMINENT DOMAIN to acquire land on which to build a post office.[1089] The postal power includes the power to prevent any interference with the carrying of the mail,[998] a power broad enough, the Court held in 1981, to sustain a federal law prohibiting anyone from depositing circulars without postage into anyone's mailbox.[2104] Because the postal power is federal, the states may not directly abridge it. In 1845 the Court held that the states may not tax vehicles carrying the mail on its roads,[1835] nor may a state convict a mail truck operator for driving in the state without a state driver's license.[1018]

The major constitutional difficulty that has arisen under the Postal Clause is the extent of federal power to bar the mail to those who would use it for harmful purposes. The Court held in 1878 that Congress could bar the mailing of literature on lotteries,[998] and in 1902 that Congress could likewise prohibit the mailing of any fraudulent solicitations or advertisements,[1671] a line of decisions that it has followed to the present day in upholding laws against many forms of business fraud conducted in part through the mail. But "Congress may not exercise its control over the mails to enforce a requirement which lies outside its constitutional province."[608] Thus federal power over the mail is subject to the FIRST AMENDMENT prohibition against general CENSORSHIP. As Justice Oliver Wendell Holmes said in a DISSENTING OPINION in 1921 that has now largely been adopted: "The United States

may give up the Post Office when it sees fit, but while it carries it on the use of the mails is almost as much a part of free speech as the right to use our tongues." So in 1946 the Court rejected a Post Office contention that it could exclude *Esquire* from the mail on the grounds that the magazine's articles were vulgar and in poor taste.[859] And in 1965 the Court invalidated a law permitting the Post Office to hold up "communist political propaganda" and forward it only when the addressee specifically notified the department that he or she wished to receive it.[1114] This was the first time the Supreme Court ever struck down a *federal* law for violating the First Amendment. However, Congress may legitimately allow recipients to tell the Postal Service not to forward a certain type of mail, so that under federal law the Postal Service constitutionally maintains a list of recipients who do not wish to receive obscene or sexually oriented mail.[1769]

post roads, *see:* **post office**

poverty, *see:* **wealth classification and discrimination**

powers, separation of, *see:* **separation of powers**

practice of law, *see:* **lawyers**

prayer and Bible reading   In 1962 the Supreme Court for the first time encountered the issue of a prayer written by a state agency to be recited in the public schools. The case arose in New York, where the state Board of Regents wrote the following "nondenominational" prayer: "Almighty God, we acknowledge our dependence upon Thee, and we beg Thy blessings upon us, our parents, our teachers and our Country." A local school board ordered that the Regents prayer be used daily in each classroom. The New York courts upheld the prayer as long as the school respected a parent's desire that the child not say it. The Supreme Court held 6–1 that any prayer, even a nondenominational voluntary prayer, is unconstitutional because it is "wholly inconsistent with the ESTABLISHMENT CLAUSE."[617] Praying is a religious activity, and the Establishment Clause says that it "is no part of the business of government to compose official prayers for any group of the American people to recite as a part of a religious program carried on by government."

In 1963 the Court struck down a Pennsylvania requirement that the public school day open with the reading of "at least ten verses from the Holy Bible." A local school interpreted the law by mandating that students read in unison from the Bible and recite the Lord's Prayer, although a written note from a parent could excuse any child from the Bible reading or from attending the session. In *Abington School District v. Schempp* Justice Tom Clark for an 8–1 majority held that whether a law is valid under the Establishment Clause depends on whether there is "a secular legislative purpose and a primary effect that neither advances nor inhibits religion." The Bible reading and prayer failed both parts of the test. The Bible reading (the King James version was used) was not undertaken as a course of study in history or the sociology of religion; it was undertaken as a religious exercise, and it obviously was intended to further religion itself. Justice Clark emphasized that the decision did not prohibit "the study of the Bible or of religion, when presented objectively as part of a secular program of education." The Court was saying, rather, that a state may not require or permit a public school itself to engage in religious activities, which is what every demand for school participation in prayer amounts to. Since schoolchildren remain free to this day to pray independently during any free moment in school, the many constitutional amendments introduced (but not passed) in Congress since

the early 1960s reflect a clear contempt for the principle that government not involve itself in religious undertakings.

In 1985 the Court struck down an Alabama "voluntary prayer" law authorizing schools to set aside a minute for private meditation or prayer.[2146] The Alabama legislature had amended a previous law allowing a minute simply for meditation. The Court held that the new law, specifically adding the prayer provision, had no secular purpose at all, and noted that the law's sponsor had declared his proposal was an "effort to return voluntary prayer" to the schools. Since the earlier law already provided students that right, by setting aside a minute of silence, the new law was intended "to convey a message of State endorsement and promotion of prayer." But a neutral moment-of-silence law, in the absence of a suggestion from teachers that students use it to pray, would probably be constitutional and could be used for prayer by teachers and children alike.

In a related vein, the Court struck down PER CURIAM a Kentucky law ordering public schools to post a copy of the Ten Commandments on the walls of each classroom, even though the state insisted that its purpose was secular and not religious. The 5–4 majority disagreed, finding no secular legislative purpose, since the Ten Commandments are "undeniably a sacred text in the Jewish and Christian faits."[1961]

The Court did uphold the practice of the Nebraska legislature of starting each legislative day with a prayer conducted by a Presbyterian chaplain on the legislative payroll. Even though this practice is clearly inconsistent with the LEMON TEST for determining whether state conduct violates the Establishment Clause, the Court did not overrule the test but made an exception because of the long historical tradition of legislative prayers.[1246]

See also: RELIGIOUS ESTABLISHMENT; SCHOOLS, RELIGION IN.

Preamble The Constitution's Preamble neither confers nor limits governmental power.[1000] Adopted in September 1787, after the delegates to the CONSTITUTIONAL CONVENTION had agreed on the substantive provisions, the Preamble states three important tenets. The first is that the Constitution derives ultimately from the people in their entirety, not from the states.[1287, 395, 1251] An early version of the Preamble began, "We, the people of the states of . . . ," followed by a list of the thirteen states. The draftsman, Gouverneur Morris, changed it to read, "We, the people of the United States." A second tenet, shown in the Preamble's recitation of purposes, is that government is established to serve human ends. In many cases the Court has referred to the Preamble as a guide to interpreting the scope of a power granted. The third tenet is perhaps more a faith expressed in the present tense: "We the people *do* ordain and establish the Constitution"—a reminder, if we choose to make something of it, that the Constitution is not simply a document that was established by a collection of people remote from us in time but one that is continually ordained and established by the people.

precedent This book is about precedent, the previous judicial rulings that serve as a guide to resolving future constitutional and legal disputes. The COMMON LAW legal system is fundamentally based on precedent, the notion that the law develops through the slow accretion of HOLDINGS that constitute authoritative interpretations of constitutional provisions and other laws. Whether the courts are *bound* by their precedents is another question, discussed separately under STARE DECISIS.

preemption Under the SUPREMACY CLAUSE federal law preempts—that is, supersedes—inconsistent state law. In preemption cases the courts must determine whether the federal law was intended to supplant state law, not whether

Congress has the power to do so. As long as Congress has enacted a law under one of its ENUMERATED POWERS, inconsistent state laws are invalid. If Congress expressly states that it is preempting a field, the courts will give effect to that declaration. Likewise, as Chief Justice John Marshall noted in *Gibbons v. Ogden* in 1824, if federal law permits an action that state law prohibits, the Court must disregard the state law. But when federal law does not explicitly say that it supersedes state law and there is no obvious conflict, the Court follows certain general principles in deciding whether to give federal law preemptive effect.

The Court usually begins with a presumption that "Congress did not intend to displace state laws."[1261, 1451] Tests for whether Congress intended to preempt include (1) how pervasive the scheme of federal regulation is, (2) whether the federal law touches "a field in which the federal interest is so dominant" that it would make no sense to let state laws on the same subject stand, and (3) whether the state policy would produce a result inconsistent with the objective of the federal law.[1721] Even if Congress has not intended to fully displace state regulation of a specific area, state law is preempted to the extent that it actually conflicts with the federal law.[684, 923]

These tests are so general that it is impossible to fit the cases into clear patterns, but some random examples give the flavor of the Court's preemption jurisprudence. Although the federal Atomic Energy Act preempts state laws governing safety standards in building nuclear reactors and was intended to promote nuclear power, the Court held that it does not preempt state power to regulate the sale and transmission of electricity generated by nuclear facilities licensed by the Atomic Energy Commission. The states may even impose a moratorium on building new nuclear plants.[1551] Federal antitrust laws do not preempt state laws requiring businesses to engage in restraints of trade,[1568] but similar municipal ordinances are preempted.[1108] In another case, the Court struck down a local noise ordinance prohibiting jet flights from leaving the Burbank, California, airport between 11 P.M. and 7 A.M.[275] Even though the federal Aeronautics Act did not specifically state that it was preempting all local noise rules, the Court held that the safety policies of the federal law required the Federal Aviation Administration to have complete authority over takeoffs and landings, leaving nothing for states or municipalities to regulate. Likewise, the Court has held that the federal labor laws preempt state DAMAGE suits for harms caused by organizational PICKETING.[1792]

Federal policies as disparate as those dealing with espionage, bankruptcy, and patents and copyrights[1835a, 447] may lead to preemption. The Court invalidated a Pennsylvania law prohibiting SEDITION against the United States, because the Smith Act, the federal antisubversion law, preempts state espionage laws.[1591] It also struck down a provision in the Uniform Motor Vehicle Safety Responsibility Act, a law enacted in several states, that permits a state to suspend the license of any driver who fails to pay a monetary judgment for causing a traffic accident, even if the failure to pay stems from the driver's bankruptcy. The Court held, 5–4, that the license suspension unconstitutionally defeats the purpose of the bankruptcy law—to let debtors start fresh.[185]

preferred freedoms, *see:* **preferred position**

preferred position   When the Supreme Court in the late 1930s repudiated the ECONOMIC DUE PROCESS dogma, it said that the constitutionality of legislation involving economic interests would be tested by a rationality standard: unless the law was arbitrary and irrational it would be upheld. But even as the Court was withdrawing from close scrutiny of economic and social policy making by the legislatures, it signaled that it would examine a different set of laws more closely—namely, those that interfered with fundamental rights. In 1938 in the CAROLENE PRODUCTS FOOTNOTE FOUR, Justice Harlan Fiske Stone declared that the Court might thenceforth be less willing to indulge in the presumption that laws are constitutional when they appear on the surface to fall "within a specific prohibition of the Constitution," in particular the prohibitions in the BILL OF RIGHTS. In 1942 Stone, then chief justice, first used the phrase in a case involving a municipal tax imposed on itinerant peddlars, including sellers of religious literature. Stone said that the FIRST AMENDMENT does not prohibit only laws that discriminate against speech. Rather, the Constitution puts the FREEDOM OF SPEECH and FREEDOM OF RELIGION in a preferred position and bars taxes that interfere with those freedoms.[1032]

In several cases throughout the 1940s a majority of the Court persisted in declaring a preferred position for First Amendment freedoms. In 1949 Justice Felix Frankfurter condemned the concept, saying that the preferred position of freedom of speech is a "mischievous phrase" that "has uncritically crept into some recent opinions." To Frankfurter "preferred position" was a "deceptive formula," because the constitutionality of a law ought not to be doubted simply because in some way it touches on communications.[1096] By the 1950s, with new justices on the Court, the preferred position doctrine was invoked far less frequently, and by the 1960s it was obviously no longer true that the Court was preferring First Amendment freedoms above others. Without depreciating the high place of the First Amendment in the constitutional scheme, the activist Warren Court also began invigorating many other provisions in the Bill of Rights by incorporating them into the FOURTEENTH AMENDMENT. Today, although the phrase is not often heard, it remains true that laws trenching on basic issues of CIVIL

RIGHTS AND CIVIL LIBERTIES are scrutinized far more closely than laws that regulate economic relationships.

See also: FUNDAMENTAL INTERESTS, RIGHTS, AND PRIVILEGES; INCORPORATION DOCTRINE; PRESUMPTION OF CONSTITUTIONALITY.

pregnancy, *see:* **abortion**

prejudicial publicity   Prejudicial publicity about a criminal defendant may violate the DUE PROCESS right to a fair trial. The Court first confronted the issue in a 1961 case in which so much publicity about the defendant had been published that ninety percent of the potential jurors had formed some opinion of the defendant's guilt, and two-thirds of the actual jurors began the trial believing the defendant guilty. Under those circumstances, the Court said, it would override the trial judge's finding that the jurors were to be believed in saying that they could render an impartial verdict.[991] In 1963 the Supreme Court overturned a DEATH SENTENCE and conviction because the judge refused to change trial VENUE in a case in which a local Louisiana television station three times broadcast the defendant's filmed confession to an audience consisting of more than a third of the parish population.[1728] In 1964 the Supreme Court reversed the conviction of the Texas commodities swindler Billy Sol Estes because the pretrial hearings were televised and seen by people who became jurors in the very case.[628] And in 1966 it reversed the conviction of Dr. Sam Sheppard because the judge had permitted the trial to become a "media circus" in which Sheppard was subjected to "massive, pervasive, and prejudicial publicity" that grossly interfered with his right to a fair trial.[1856]

What emerged from these cases is a general rule that when a significant portion of potential jurors are exposed to highly prejudicial information inadmissible at trial, the trial judge must reject potential jurors' assurances that they can be impartial. Whether the degree of prejudice reaches that level depends on the "totality of circumstances," including the heinousness of the crime and the community's reaction to it. If the prejudice is not so overwhelming, then a reviewing court should accept the judge's determination that the jurors' assertions of impartiality were believable except for "manifest error"—for example, if the trial judge failed to ask any of the jurors about the possibility of prejudice. But the number and type of questions to be asked lie within the trial judge's discretion.[1396] Notwithstanding the unconstitutionality of prejudicial publicity, criminal defendants have no absolute right against the televising of their trials. In 1981 the Court upheld a Florida policy of televising that was carefully worked out to respect the defendants' rights.[369a]

See also: FREE PRESS–FAIR TRIAL; GAG ORDER; TRIAL, FAIRNESS OF; VOIR DIRE.

prerogative   The British crown had numerous powers, known as "prerogatives," that were exercisable unilaterally and without Parliament's consent. In his *Second Treatise on Civil Government,* John Locke wrote that prerogative is the power "to act according to discretion without the prescription of the law and sometimes against it." This leading English liberal, from whom the American revolutionaries learned the fundamental lesson that governments derive their just powers from the consent of the governed, believed that kings should have this unbounded prerogative, since it was "impossible to foresee and so by laws to provide for all accidents and necessities that may concern the public." The delegates to the CONSTITUTIONAL CONVENTION declined to invest the president with prerogative powers, instead distributing to Congress many of the powers exercised by the kings. Although presidents have repeatedly pressed the claim that the grant of EXECUTIVE POWER in essence convers an *inherent* power to act in the public interest, the Court has rebuffed the claim when put that starkly, as it showed in rejecting President Harry S. Truman's assertion that he could seize the nation's steel mills without congressional authorization.[2282] However, on many occasions it has quite broadly construed the president's *implied* powers under the vague language of Article II.

See also: IMPLIED AND INHERENT POWERS; PRESIDENT, INHERENT POWER OF.

presentment   Under Art. I-§7[2,3], every bill or other ORDER, RESOLUTION, OR VOTE that Congress has enacted to become law must be *presented* to the president for signature or veto. Congress's failure to comply with the Presentment Clauses was a partial basis for the Court's decision in 1983 striking down the LEGISLATIVE VETO. In criminal law, a presentment is in effect an INDICTMENT, brought at the initiative of the GRAND JURY rather than of the prosecutor.

president, death, resignation, or disability of, *see:* **presidential succession**

president, election and term of   The Constitution as ratified in 1788 provided for the indirect election of the president through the ELECTORAL COLLEGE. Unlike the present system, though, Art. II-§1[3] provided that the electors, appointed as the state legislatures determined, would vote for *two* people, without specifying which one of the two was to be president. The one with a majority would become president. The one with the next highest number of votes would become vice president. This system was wholly unsuitable to a system of partisan POLITICAL PARTY nominations and worked well only twice: to confirm the election of George Washington as president in 1788 and 1792. By the 1796 elections it was already beginning to break down; in 1800 it led to near paralysis

when Thomas Jefferson and Aaron Burr won an equal number of electoral votes. The election was thrown to the House of Representatives, still in Federalist hands, where it took thirty-seven ballots to select Jefferson, the Republican.

A major problem was apparent. If parties continued to nominate only one set of candidates without specifying which was the candidate for president, the election was almost certain to be thrown each time to the House of Representatives. And if the opposing party controlled the House, chaos might ensue. Dissatisfaction with the impasse was so widespread that in 1804 the states ratified the TWELFTH AMENDMENT, which requires electors to specify the persons for whom they are voting for president and vice president. This change essentially established the system by which presidential elections operate, at least formally, to this day. If no one has a majority, then the House, one vote per state, chooses from among the top three vote-getters in the electoral college. Twenty-six votes (that is, one more than half) are necessary for election. This procedure has been invoked only once, in the 1824 election, when four candidates were nominated after the two-party system broke down. John Quincy Adams, son of the first Federalist president, was elected, even though he had received fewer electoral votes than Andrew Jackson. Only if there were a serious enough third-party bid for president to keep the electoral vote for each candidate below a majority would the House again be the agent for choosing the president.

Art. II-§1[1] specifies a four-year term for president and vice president, but the Constitution originally set no limit on how many terms a person could serve. George Washington set an important precedent in deciding against running for a third term in 1796. The tradition lasted until 1940, when Franklin D. Roosevelt, in the face of an impending war, announced for and won a third term and followed that by a fourth-term victory in 1944. Determined to avoid domination of the White House by a popular Democratic president, the Republican-controlled Congress proposed the TWENTY-SECOND AMENDMENT, ratified in 1951, which barred more than two full terms for anyone elected in his own right or two and one-half terms for anyone first succeeding to the office as vice president on the death or resignation of the president. Ironically, the amendment arrived just in time to prevent a still popular President Dwight D. Eisenhower from making a third run for the White House in 1960. In the mid-1980s there was some talk of repealing the Twenty-second Amendment to let President Ronald Reagan run again, but nothing came of it and the two-term tradition now seems firmly ensconced in the Constitution.

president, immunity of   The issue of whether the president is immune from judicial process has a long history but until recently had relatively few answers. Thomas Jefferson insisted that not only was the president immune but so were EXECUTIVE BRANCH officials, such as the secretary of state. Jefferson denounced Chief Justice John Marshall's conclusion in MARBURY V. MADISON that executive officials could not only be sued but could be ordered to perform ministerial acts. Historically, cabinet officers have been sued in their official capacities. In 1867 the Supreme Court declared that the president himself was immune from judicial process. Without hearing the merits, it dismissed a lawsuit seeking to enjoin President Andrew Johnson from enforcing the post–Civil War Reconstruction Acts.[1360] From time to time, executive officials have also maintained that they cannot be criminally prosecuted as long as they remain in office, or that they must first be impeached before they can be tried. The argument was pressed, for example, by Vice President Spiro

T. Agnew before he resigned in disgrace in 1973.

But the constitutional position of subordinate officers may be different from that of the president. To date, the Court has given two definitive, and possibly contradictory, answers. In a suit against President Richard M. Nixon for firing an Air Force civilian "whistleblower," the Court held that presidents are absolutely immune from liability for civil DAMAGES in connection with official acts.[1485] In other words, the courts are legally obliged to dismiss any damage suit filed against the president in his capacity as president, without considering the merits of the allegations. However, in *United States v. Nixon* the Court also held that the president is not above the law, in the sense that a court may legally order him to produce necessary documents in a criminal prosecution. Whether the president may be tried, before being impeached, for crimes committed in the course of official duties remains an open question.

See also: EXECUTIVE PRIVILEGE.

president, inherent power of   Article II vests in the president the executive power, without defining its scope. As exercised by kings, executive power was vast and virtually unconfined by law, often known as royal PREROGATIVE. Given the rich history of royal prerogative, it is remarkable that the Framers devoted almost no time to discussing EXECUTIVE POWER. The opening sentence of Article II established, rather, that the office of chief executive would be filled by one person, not several people, as had been suggested; it also settled on the title "president." Succeeding sections of Article II enumerate specific powers of the president, and the question is whether the executive power is restricted to the powers enumerated or is the source of a much broader, unconfined power. Unlike Article I, which specifies that only certain LEGISLATIVE POWERS are vested in Congress, Article II vests in the president "the" executive power—that is, *all*, not a part of it.

In 1793 Hamilton defended Washington's PROCLAMATION OF NEUTRALITY in the war between France and England on the ground that it was within the president's executive power. Madison charged that Hamilton's position amounted to reestablishing royal prerogative. The argument has been repeated many times in our history, especially at moments of crisis. Lincoln asserted sweeping power to conduct a war, including the power to suspend HABEAS CORPUS. Later war presidents—especially Woodrow Wilson, Franklin D. Roosevelt, Harry S. Truman, and Richard Nixon—claimed similarly sweeping powers. Thomas Jefferson swallowed his own STRICT CONSTRUCTIONIST doubts and agreed to the Louisiana Purchase, believing that it was good to double the size of the country even though it might have been unconstitutional. Theodore Roosevelt, summing up the idea of inherent power, said that "I declined to adopt the view that what was imperatively necessary for the Nation could not be done by the President unless he could find some specific authorization to do it. My belief was that it was not only his right but his duty to do anything that the needs of the Nation demanded unless such action was forbidden by the Constitution or by the laws."

The extent of the executive power has waxed and waned in cases before the Supreme Court. Chief Justice John Marshall in MARBURY V. MADISON said that "the President is invested with certain important political powers, in the exercise of which he is to use his own discretion, and is accountable only to this country in his political character, and to his own conscience." The Civil War Supreme Court concurred in Lincoln's conception of the WAR POWER,[1667] and although after the war it rejected military trials of civilians,[1345] it also refused to permit injunctions to be issued against the

president, a doctrine that has blossomed into a full-scale IMMUNITY of the president today from civil suits for any official actions.[1485] In 1890 the Court upheld the president's inherent authority to assign bodyguards to federal judges,[1437] and in 1895, the power of the president to seek injunctions in railroad strikes, even though in each case no law of Congress gave him any authority to do so.[532] The Court also upheld the EXECUTIVE ORDER imposing a curfew on American citizens of Japanese ancestry during World War II, although the Court said that its constitutionality rested on joint action of Congress and president.[925]

But in 1952 the Court drew a line in the STEEL SEIZURE CASE. President Truman claimed the inherent power to seize the nation's steel mills on the eve of a national steelworkers' strike. The Supreme Court, 6–3, denied the power. In a famous CONCURRING OPINION, Justice Robert H. Jackson said that an "emergency" power inherent in the president without congressional approval "either has no beginning or it has no end. If it exists, it need submit to no legal restraint. I am not alarmed that it would plunge us straightway into dictatorship, but it is at least a step in that wrong direction." In 1971 President Nixon claimed the power, even without a federal law authorizing it, to seek an injunction against the publication of secret war papers. In the PENTAGON PAPERS CASE, the Supreme Court, again 6–3, held that to do so would be an unconstitutional PRIOR RESTRAINT. Although the PER CURIAM decision was maddeningly terse, several of the concurring justices made it clear that no prior restraint could ever be justified without a carefully drafted law authorizing the executive to seek injunctions under narrow circumstances. The following year the Court, this time unanimously, disapproved Nixon's argument that he had inherent authority to place wiretaps in the offices of domestic organizations on national security grounds.[2102]

The most that can be gleaned from the episodic nature of the cases that reach the Supreme Court is that under the loose, vague powers specifically listed in Article II, the president will be given wide constitutional berth in the area of FOREIGN AFFAIRS and relatively less room to govern on his own in the domestic sphere. But whatever else it is, the executive power is not limitless, as Richard Nixon explicitly acknowledged when he bowed to the Supreme Court's decision in *United States v. Nixon* that he must turn over the tapes that would destroy his presidency.

See also: JAPANESE-AMERICAN EXCLUSION AND RELOCATION; LEGISLATIVE VETO; PRESIDENT, IMMUNITY OF; PRESIDENT, POWERS AND DUTIES OF; SEPARATION OF POWERS; VETO POWER; WAR POWER.

president, powers and duties of When George Washington assumed office in New York on April 30, 1789, he had so little to do that he took to advertising in the newspapers "visits of compliment" between two o'clock and three o'clock on Tuesday and Thursday afternoons. He hosted dinners at four on Thursdays for government officials and their families, "levees" for men of the general public on Tuesdays at three, and tea on Friday evenings for anyone "properly attired." It has been considerably more than a century since any president could legitimately lavish his time on nonofficial duties, so demanding has the job become. The change is the consequence of political, historical, and economic forces, not constitutional ones.

As the possessor of the EXECUTIVE POWER, the APPOINTMENT AND REMOVAL POWER, and the power to require the written opinion of the principal OFFICERS of the government, the president is the head of the United States government, a small role when the government was small and an immense role as the government has become ever larger. As COMMANDER IN CHIEF, the president is in charge of the ARMED FORCES. The president has the chief (though not the sole) role in conducting foreign affairs, through the appointment and removal power, the power to receive AMBASSADORS, and the power to make treaties. The appointment and removal power gives the president the political clout to staff the government and the courts and thereby to effect major policy changes. The president's power to "recommend" legislation to Congress permits strong presidents to dominate even the shaping of legislation, presumably a task for Congress. For all the hollow assertions by recent presidents that Congress is to blame for large deficits, for the better part of the twentieth century it has been the president, not Congress, who proposed the national budget. The president is of course constitutionally entitled to propose a deficit-free budget whenever he pleases.

Finally, Art. II-§3 commands the president to "take care that the laws be faithfully executed." Though written in the form of a *duty*, presidents have derived from these eight words considerable *power*. They imply that the president may delegate duties imposed on the executive and act through administrative officers.[2205] However, the Faithful Execution Clause does not vest the power to act exclusively in the president. In the 1830s, Andrew Jackson insisted that Congress could never impose specific legal duties on subordinate executive officials but must look only to the president to carry out the law. The Supreme Court strongly disagreed, holding that Congress may direct government officials to carry out the law in certain ways, not subject to any presumed power in the president to veto their actions or to direct that they act in ways other than required by law.[1060] The requirement to carry out the laws inescapably carries with it the power to interpret the law, and it helps underwrite the massive delegation of LEGISLATIVE POWER to the executive.

In one notorious case a century ago, the

Supreme Court even held that the clause confers on the president the power to enforce law other than that which has expressly been declared by Congress. The question was whether the president, through the attorney general, could order a U.S. marshal to protect a justice of the Supreme Court against a death threat and whether the marshal could lawfully kill the potential assassin. The Court agreed that the order was valid and that the shooting could not be prosecuted under state murder laws.[1437] It has long been assumed, though never definitively adjudicated, that the president may supervise enforcement of the federal criminal laws, directing federal prosecutors to seek IN-DICTMENTS or to refrain from doing so, although the power is not unlimited. Both in *United States v. Nixon* in 1974 and in *Morrison v. Olson* in 1988 the Court held that under certain circumstances Congress may vest in special federal prosecutors authority to prosecute that is unreviewable on the merits by the president.

See also: DELEGATION DOCTRINE; FOREIGN AFFAIRS POWER; IMPLIED AND INHERENT POWERS; IMPOUNDMENT; PRESIDENT, INHERENT POWER OF; TREATIES AND TREATY POWER; WAR POWER.

presidential succession   Art. II-§1[6] says that if the president leaves office other than at the expiration of his term, the "powers and duties" of the office "shall devolve" on the vice president. Whether the vice president could assume the higher office as president, or simply as some sort of ACTING PRESIDENT, was unsettled until the death of William Henry Harrison in 1841, one month into his term. Harrison's vice president, John Tyler, insisted that the Constitution made him president, not acting president, and the precedent stuck. More than a century later, the tradition was incorporated in the TWENTY-FIFTH AMENDMENT. Still other gaps remained, and these were plugged by the TWENTIETH AMENDMENT and Twenty-fifth Amendment.

The Twentieth Amendment, ratified in 1933, specifies that if the president-elect dies before assuming office, the vice president–elect shall become president. If for some reason the president has not been chosen, the vice president–elect is to "act as president" until a president is chosen. Congress may specify in a general law who shall act as president if neither president nor vice president has been chosen, or if both the sitting president and vice president have died, resigned, been removed, or become unable to serve before the constitutionally elected president takes office. Congress enacted a presidential succession act in 1948, specifying that the next in line to the presidency is the Speaker of the House of Representatives, followed by the president pro tem of the Senate, and then through the list of CABINET officers.

The Twenty-fifth Amendment, ratified in 1967, provided that the vice president becomes the president if the president resigns rather than dies. It also permits Congress by a majority vote to confirm the president's nomination of a vice president when a vacancy occurs in that office, as has happened during forty of the past two hundred years. Finally, it establishes a mechanism to determine how to proceed should a president be disabled, as also has happened several times during our history. For example, James Garfield was in a coma for eighty days after his assassination until he died; Woodrow Wilson was almost wholly incapacitated from a stroke for eighteen months at the end of his second term, and his duties were apparently largely assumed by his wife, Edith Wilson. Under the Twenty-fifth Amendment, the president may either declare his inability in writing or the vice president and a majority of cabinet officers may declare that the president is unable to discharge the duties of office. The vice president then becomes acting president, until the president declares, again in writing, that he is no longer disabled. But the vice president and a majority of the cabinet may override that declaration by notifying Congress that the disability continues. Congress then has twenty-one days to decide the issue. It takes a vote of two-thirds in each house to maintain the vice president as acting president. Otherwise the president will regain his office.

press, freedom of, *see:* **free press–fair trial; freedom of the press**

press, taxation of, *see:* **freedom of the press**

presumption, irrebuttable   A law may declare a presumption that any gift of property a person makes within six years of his death was really made "in contemplation of death" to avoid an estate tax. If the law refuses to permit the person against whom the presumption applies to show that it is false—that the gift of property really was freely intended as a gift— then the presumption is said to be *irrebuttable*. The Court occasionally has held irrebuttable presumptions unconstitutional as a violation of PROCEDURAL DUE PROCESS, because in effect they forbid a litigant from proving an ultimate fact that will determine the outcome of the case. In 1931 the Court held the gift presumption unconstitutional,[1817] and in the 1970s it struck down a number of presumptions used to limit the conferring of government benefits or other rights. For example, it invalidated an irrebuttable presumption that an illegitimate father is unfit and may not gain custody of his child.[1945] It also overturned a rule that conclusively presumed that a student is a nonresident of the state and must pay higher tuition if at the time of application for admission his address was out of state.[2134] The Court said that the student must be allowed to show that he is a bona fide resident of the state. The Court also struck down an irrebuttable presumption that

every pregnant school teacher is unfit to continue teaching and must take unpaid maternity leave four or five months before delivering;[408] and one that barred food stamps to any household containing someone eighteen years or older who was claimed as a dependent on a federal income tax return the year before by someone ineligible for food stamps.[540]

But in 1975 the Court refused to overturn a federal requirement that to obtain Social Security survivors' benefits a spouse must have been married more than nine months to a covered worker. Not to allow the government to insist on such presumptions, said Justice William H. Rehnquist, "would turn the doctrine . . . into a virtual engine of destruction for countless legislative judgments" which had long been thought constitutional.[2177] For the future, the question is whether Congress or state legislatures could rationally conclude that a particular limitation would protect against a corruption of the system; for example, by someone marrying a dying person just to collect government benefits. Not to allow such conditions or presumptions would require a vastly complicated and expensive system of HEARINGS to determine case by case whether abuse of a standard had occurred. The Court concluded that due process does not require the government to hold individualized hearings in such cases. So although the six-year presumption in the estate tax might continue to be unconstitutional, the legislature may surely make nonrebuttable some shorter period to avoid the difficult issue of proving the intent of someone who is dead at the time of the hearing.

See also: PRESUMPTIONS.

presumption of constitutionality   In 1976 in one of its many DEATH PENALTY cases, the Court said that capital punishment laws come to the Supreme Court with a presumption of validity.[809] Generally, though not consistently, the Court has accorded the benefit of the doubt to any law attacked as unconstitutional. Often when the justices have strong doubts about the constitutionality of a particular measure, they will interpret the law in such a way as to avoid the constitutional issues. However, during some eras, the Court while perhaps paying lip service to the presumption, behaved as if certain classes of laws were presumptively unconstitutional; for example, economic laws felled during the era of ECONOMIC DUE PROCESS. Only occasionally would such a law escape the Court's constitutional axe, and then only because of some highly particularized showing of need, as through a BRANDEIS BRIEF.[1401] In 1938 the Court reversed course, holding that it would not pronounce an economic regulation unconstitutional unless there was a showing that it could not rest "upon some rational basis within the knowledge and experience of the legislators,"[348] a showing almost impossible to make. But at the same time, the Court began to speak of the PREFERRED POSITION of FIRST AMENDMENT rights, and although it did not say that laws merely touching on freedom of expression or religion would be overruled, it did suggest that they would be examined more searchingly than other kinds of legislation claimed to be unconstitutional. As the Court said in a 1963 case: "Any system of PRIOR RESTRAINT of expression comes to this Court bearing a heavy presumption against its constitutional validity."[121] In 1944, in *Korematsu v. United States*, the Court declared that it would subject to STRICT SCRUTINY laws that classified on the basis of race. Since then laws characterized as invidiously discriminating on the basis of race, sex, national origins, and alienage have been pressed for greater justification than other types of laws. Likewise, under a conception of SUBSTANTIVE DUE PROCESS, the Court has also held laws interfering with people's LIBERTY and PRIVACY to higher standards or justification than other laws, leading to the inescapable conclusion that although the Court may begin by presuming laws constitutional, it does not presume that they must all meet the same burden of justification.

See also: CAROLENE PRODUCTS FOOTNOTE FOUR; CONSTITUTIONAL QUESTIONS, AVOIDANCE OF; INVIDIOUS DISCRIMINATION; RATIONAL BASIS OR RELATIONSHIP TEST.

presumption of innocence The presumption of innocence has deep roots in the COMMON LAW. As commonly understood, the presumption means that the burden is on the government to prove at trial that the ACCUSED is guilty; the accused has no burden to prove innocence. In 1979 the Supreme Court said that the presumption of innocence is required by DUE PROCESS and requires the judge or jury "to judge an accused's guilt or innocence solely on the evidence adduced at trial and not on the basis of suspicions that may arise from the fact of his arrest, indictment, or custody or from other matters not introduced as proof at trial."[147] The presumption of innocence obviously does not preclude the state from taking a suspect into custody, nor even, the Supreme Court has ruled, from holding the suspect in PREVENTIVE DETENTION pending trial.[1785] The Supreme Court has held that at trial the presumption of innocence bars the state from keeping a defendant in prison clothing, since "the constant reminder of the accused's condition" in identifiable attire might unfairly affect a juror's judgment about the defendant's guilt.[627]

See also: PROOF, BURDEN OF; REASONABLE DOUBT.

presumptions Much of the legal system operates by presumptions; because one fact can be more easily proven than another, the provable fact is *presumed* to demonstrate the existence of the less easily proven fact. A simple example is contained in drinking age laws. The law presumes that people under a certain age cannot hold their liquor. A prosecutor need show only that the person the bartender served was under the legal age. The prosecutor need not show that the underage drinker was an irresponsible drinker, and the bartender may not defend by showing that the person he served really could hold her liquor.

The Court has held that *statutory presumptions*—the legislature's declaration that a prosecutor may prove an element of a crime by proving some other fact with which it is closely connected—are consistent with DUE PROCESS as long as it can "be said with substantial assurance that the presumed fact is more likely than not to flow from the proved fact on which it is made to depend." In so saying the Court upset a conviction obtained when the jury was permitted to infer knowledge that marijuana was unlawfully imported from proof that the defendant possessed it.[1132]

What constitutes a strong enough connection between provable and presumed fact cannot be summed up in a formula. For example, the Court upheld an inference that a moonshiner was "carrying on" or helping to carry on the illegal manufacture of liquor simply because he was found on the site of an illegal still,[719] but it struck down the presumption that a person found at the site had possession, custody, or control of the still.[1755] To convict someone of the more serious charge of controlling the still, the prosecutors must actually prove the fact. Similarly, the Court distinguished between presumptions of knowledge concerning the importation of heroin and cocaine, upholding a presumption that a possessor of heroin knew it was imported but rejecting the same presumption for cocaine, since much cocaine is processed domestically.[2083] The Court also upheld presumptions that the possessor of recently stolen goods must know they were stolen if he could not satisfactorily explain how he obtained them[129] and that a person who failed to return a rental car intended to steal it.[340]

Presumptions are important ingredients in civil cases as well, and the Court has judged them by a due process standard of essential fairness that varies with the importance of the interest at stake. Presumptions that deal with economic and business relationships will be upheld as long as they are reasonable and do not absolutely foreclose the person against whom they are invoked from proving the case.[118] When important constitutional interests are at stake, however, the Court will look more closely into whether the presumption is arbitrary and whether the defendant has a fair chance to present a defense against it. For example, the unfitness of natural parents to retain custody of their children may not be presumed by making generalizations about the parents' behavior; instead, they must be shown to be actually unfit in the circumstances.[1802] On the other hand, in 1989 the Court upheld a California presumption that the child born to a married couple was sired by the husband. The law refused to permit the trial court to be swayed by blood tests showing a probability of 98.07 percent that someone else was the father.[1325]

See also: PRESUMPTION, IRREBUTTABLE

pretrial disclosure, *see:* **gag order; prejudicial publicity**

preventive detention   Preventive detention is the locking up of people suspected of being dangerous and likely to commit harmful criminal acts. Stated that starkly, preventive detention is undoubtedly unconstitutional, since people may be deprived of their LIBERTY only after *committing* criminal acts, except for those who are mentally deranged and thus subject to commitment to mental institutions. The government rarely has enacted a general policy of imprisoning dangerous people, although in the Internal Security Act of 1950, Congress did provide for preventive detention of people likely to engage in espionage or sabotage. The provision was repealed in 1971 without being tested.

However, since people arrested are often jailed before being prosecuted, the question has arisen to what degree dangerous defendants may be kept in jail before trial. Read literally, the BAIL Clause of the EIGHTH AMENDMENT might seem to require that every person held in jail be offered the opportunity to make bail, since the clause says that "excessive bail shall not be required." In 1951 the Court observed that the "right to freedom before conviction permits the unhampered preparation of a defense, and serves to prevent the infliction of punishment prior to conviction. . . . [Otherwise] the PRESUMPTION OF INNOCENCE, secured only after centuries of struggle, would lose its meaning."[1937] Nevertheless, the Court concluded in 1952 that the Eighth Amendment does not require that bail be set in every instance. Rather, the courts may not set excessively high bail in certain cases specified by the legislature.[345] Still, the consensus seemed to be that bail could be denied only to prevent a suspect either from fleeing the jurisdiction to avoid standing trial or from interfering with a potential witness or juror.

In 1987, however, in *United States v. Salerno*, the Court upheld the federal Bail Reform Act of 1984, permitting people accused of certain violent federal crimes to be held in jail without bail upon a showing that there is no other way to assure the safety of the community. The Court said that this kind of pretrial detention is not "PUNISHMENT for dangerous individuals" but a means of "preventing danger to the community[,] . . . a legitimate regulatory goal." The Court justified its conclusion by noting that (1) the act applies only to the most dangerous types of crimes, (2) the detainee is entitled to a prompt hearing at which the government must convince the judge by "clear and convincing evidence" that there is no other way to assure the community's safety, (3) the length of detention is limited by the requirements of the Speedy Trial Act that the trial itself begin

promptly, and (4) the detainee must be housed separately from convicted defendants.

See also: PAROLE; PROBATION.

previous condition of servitude   Section 1 of the FIFTEENTH AMENDMENT prohibits the United States or any state from denying or abridging the right to vote "on account of race, color, or previous condition of servitude." The phrase refers to SLAVERY, abolished four years earlier in the THIRTEENTH AMENDMENT.

price and wage controls   During the ascendancy of ECONOMIC DUE PROCESS, the Supreme Court struck down many state and federal policies designed to boost wages and control prices, although it upheld some price controls under an EMERGENCY theory of the WAR POWERS[173] and federal railroad rate regulation, even of intrastate rates, under Congress's COMMERCE POWER.[948] In 1934 the Court began to back away from its previous stern refusal to recognize broad constitutional authority in the legislatures to deal with economic problems by constructing both floors for and ceilings on prices and wages. Like any other form of regulation, the Court said in *Nebbia v. New York*, price control "is unconstitutional only if arbitrary, discriminatory, or demonstrably irrelevant to the policy the legislature is free to adopt."[1440] In 1937 the Court upheld minimum wage laws.[2184] Just how sweeping a power the Court finally conceded to the legislatures was shown in the World War II price control cases. In early 1942 Congress enacted the Emergency Price Control Act, establishing a federal Office of Price Administration and empowering it to fix maximum prices and rents that were "generally fair and equitable." In 1944, in *Yakus v. United States,* the Court upheld the law, despite a lone dissent by Justice Owen J. Roberts arguing that the decision effectively overruled the DELEGATION DOCTRINE set forth only nine years earlier in the SICK CHICKEN CASE. Not only did it uphold the raw power of an administrative official to limit prices, the Court also approved a novel limitation on an affected person's right to appeal a price or rent ceiling. Only the EMERGENCY COURT OF APPEALS could hear challenges to the price administrator's decisions, and the Court agreed that Congress could strip the federal DISTRICT COURTS of the power to hear this kind of case.[1178] Moreover, said the Court, Congress could constitutionally bar a defendant accused of violating a rent order from arguing at trial that it was unlawful, since the only permissible means of challenging an order was to file an independent suit in the Emergency Court.[2267]

See also: RENT CONTROL.

primary elections, see: **voting, right to**

principal officers, see: **office and officers**

prior restraint   Beginning in the sixteenth century, the British press could publish only if licensed to do so. The government could thereby control the press by censoring what it disapproved before publication. The freedom from licensing was what William Blackstone meant in the 1760s when he said in his famous *Commentaries on the Law of England* that FREEDOM OF THE PRESS "consists in laying no *previous* restraints upon publication." Today FREEDOM OF SPEECH and the press are understood far more broadly, but the Court regards *prior restraints* as constitutionally more objectionable than many other forms of government interference with freedom of expression.

The Court's first major pronouncement came in 1931 in *Near v. Minnesota,* when it overturned a state law permitting the courts to "abate"—that is, close down—as a public nuisance any "malicious, scandalous and defamatory newspaper or other periodical." The law had been used to enjoin the publishers of a Minneapolis newspaper that carried inflammatory articles linking the police chief and other public officials to local gangsters. The injunction was against any future publication of such articles. A 5–4 majority held that the Minnesota law constituted a prior restraint, and therefore violated the FIRST AMENDMENT, because to avoid prosecution thereafter the publishers would either have to go out of business or in essence submit articles to the court for clearance or risk punishment for CONTEMPT. Said Chief Justice Charles Evans Hughes, "This is the essence of censorship." Not prior restraint but "subsequent punishment for such abuses as may exist is the appropriate remedy," he said. However, in the intervening sixty years the Court has considerably narrowed the possibility of subsequent punishments as well. The *Near* decision left open the possibility of restraining the press in "exceptional cases": "a government might prevent actual obstruction to its recruiting service or the publication of the sailing dates of transports or the number and location of troops." That these circumstances are narrow indeed was demonstrated forty years later when a 6–3 majority in the PENTAGON PAPERS CASE refused to permit the Court to consider an injunction against the *New York Times* and the *Washington Post* for publishing excerpts from a secret history of the Vietnam War, despite the government's claim that publication would endanger national security, lead to soldiers' deaths, and prolong the war.

The strong constitutional presumption against prior restraints is not limited to publications that deal with public officials or pressing political issues. The Court has overturned an injunction against a community organization's distribution of literature attacking a real estate broker for block-busting activities,[1538] a GAG ORDER against publication of an accused person's confession before trial,[1441] and a ban on the placing of "for sale" and "sold" signs on a person's front lawn.[1170] The rule against prior restraints is central to the decisions involving municipal PERMIT SYSTEMS, through which mayors, police chiefs, and licensing agencies exercise uncontrolled discretion to decide who may hold a public meeting or distribute literature in public places.[1198, 1862] Likewise, an EX PARTE INJUNCTION against a protest meeting was held to constitute an unconstitutional prior restraint.[350] In 1988 the Court struck down an ordinance giving a mayor complete discretion to decide annually whether to renew a license to place newsstands on city sidewalks.[1111]

Despite the broad condemnation of prior restraints, the Court has repeatedly held that one type of publication, obscene writings and films, may be restrained beforehand. Because OBSCENITY AND PORNOGRAPHY are not constitutionally protected, the government need not wait until they are circulated to punish their purveyors.[2050] But the doctrine of no prior restraints has had a significant impact on the *means* by which the government may restrain such publications through censorship boards. In 1965 the Court struck down a Maryland licensing scheme that essentially put the burden on the movie exhibitor to prove that a work was nonobjectionable and that had no time limit within which a court had to review a decision against issuing a license. The Court held that the censor, not the exhibitor, must bear the burden of proving obscenity; that only a court, not an administrative agency, may issue a final order against exhibition; and that the decision to issue a license or to go to court to seek an order against the film must be undertaken within a very brief period.[699] Fifty days is too long, especially when the law imposes no requirement that the courts decide promptly.[2006] The Court has applied these principles to a variety of circumstances, striking down, because it provided no "rigorous procedural safeguards," a Chattanooga, Tennessee, ordinance that permitted a city auditorium board to refuse to license a production of the musical *Hair*,[1918] and a Dallas licensing ordinance for sexually oriented businesses because the licensor had an unlimited time in which to decide whether or not to issue the license.[715]

See also: ADULT THEATERS AND BOOKSTORES; BLACKLISTING; SOLICITATION.

prisoners' rights In 1871 the Virginia Supreme Court declared that a prisoner has no constitutional rights but is "for the time being the slave of the state." As overblown as the statement may have been in theory, it perhaps approached truth in practice. Today, however, although the constitutional rights of prisoners are relatively restricted, as the Court has said, "[t]here is no iron curtain drawn between the Constitution and the prisons of this country."[2245] The justices have ruled repeatedly that the courts should defer to the judgment of prison officials in making and enforcing prison routines and discipline.[496] For example, prisoners have no FOURTH AMENDMENT right to be free of unreasonable SEARCHES AND SEIZURES, so prison authorities may conduct shakedown searches for weapons and drugs whenever they please.[952] Prisoners have no constitutional right to be incarcerated in a particular prison. Prison officials have absolute discretion to order a prisoner transferred, without any sort of HEARING, to another prison, either within the state[1308] or in another state,[1529] even though the new prison has worse conditions. The Court also overturned decisions of lower courts ordering an end to "double-celling"—putting two prisoners in a cell designated for one—because the practice is not overly harsh in a world of limited resources and "cannot be said to be cruel and unusual under contemporary standards."[147, 1718]

On the other hand, the EIGHTH AMENDMENT's ban on cruel and unusual punishment prohibits prison authorities from maintaining conditions that "involve the wanton and unnecessary infliction of pain."[969] In 1978 the

Court upheld a lower court's conclusion that the Arkansas prison system as a whole was "a dark and evil world completely alien to the free world"—including mass starvation, sadistic discipline, ruthless overcrowding in punitive isolation cells, sickening working conditions, toleration of vicious attacks by prisoners on each other, and even murder. The decade-long litigation finally ended when the Court sustained an order prohibiting prison authorities from sending anyone into an isolation cells for longer than thirty days. Arkansas prison officials did not even bother to appeal other parts of the lower court's order, agreeing that the other conditions were constitutionally repulsive.[969] The Court has also ruled that it is cruel and unusual to ignore a prisoner's need for medical attention.[626]

Even though prisoners' rights may be diminished by the needs of the prison, DUE PROCESS prohibits arbitrary discipline unrelated to institutional requirements. For example, prison regulations may not deny inmates the right to marry.[2082] A prisoner may not be deprived of credit for good behavior without notice of the violation with which he is being charged and an opportunity to defend against it, including the right to call witnesses and present documentary evidence, but not to confront or cross-examine adverse witnesses.[2245] Somewhat contradictorily, the Court has held that the state may deny good time credits on the basis of quite meager evidence[1983] and that despite the right to a hearing the prisoner is not entitled to be represented by a lawyer.[138] Hearings required for other types of deprivation can be quite "skeletal." For example, a prisoner may be sent to solitary confinement with only a very informal opportunity to rebut the charges,[917] and no hearing at all is required for denial of parole[807] or commutation of sentence.[451] Prisoners are not constitutionally entitled to lawyers to pursue discretionary appeals,[787] but they do have a constitutional right of ACCESS TO COURTS to contest their convictions, including a reasonable right of access to law libraries[2280] or to consult with someone trained in law.[204]

Although prison authorities may transfer an inmate at will to another penal institution, they do not have an unrestricted right to transfer to a mental institution. The inmate must be given the opportunity to demonstrate at a trial-type hearing that he or she is not suffering from the mental illness that the law requires as a condition for transfer.[2133] Prisoners also have a constitutional interest in not being forced to take antipsychotic drugs, but the hearing need not be adversary and may be held before independent medical professionals to determine whether the prisoner is suffering from a mental condition for which the drugs would be effective.[2160]

Prisoners have FIRST AMENDMENT rights consistent with the need for institutional order, but a regulation may restrict the FREEDOM OF RELIGION and FREEDOM OF SPEECH "if it is reasonably related to legitimate penological interests." So a prison may prohibit inmates from corresponding with each other[2082] and limit visits and correspondence by outsiders.[1668, 1805] But the prison may not grant religious privileges to one denomination and deny them to another.[465, 496] There is an EQUAL PROTECTION right not to be segregated by race, though that right can be overcome on a showing that institutional security and discipline make racial segregation necessary.[1136]

Prisoners have a right against guards' unauthorized and intentional taking of their property, although the remedy need be only the right to file a civil lawsuit for the value of the property.[952] There is no due process right to a remedy if prison officials are merely negligent in depriving a prisoner of life, liberty, or property, though the state at its discretion may grant prisoners a right to file a civil suit against the state for such losses.[513, 517]

privacy The Supreme Court's idea of privacy is one of the oddest conceptions in all constitutional law, although the Constitution nowhere uses the word itself. The one provision that deals with privacy, the FOURTH AMENDMENT, prohibits the government from engaging in "unreasonable searches and seizures," but the Court has inexplicably concluded, for example, that people do not have a "reasonable expectation of privacy" in the telephone numbers they dial, and therefore the police need not obtain a SEARCH WARRANT in asking the telephone company to record those numbers.[1893] A vastly different conception of privacy—personal autonomy to act in ways unconstrained by government intrusion—is nowhere mentioned in the Constitution, yet the Court has blessed ABORTION, for example, as a privacy interest partly beyond the power of government to control.

In constitutional law, privacy has three independent strands: (1) the government's interest in the private, secret, and intimate details of a person's life; (2) the government's interest in protecting people from invasions of privacy by news media and other individuals; and (3) the individual's interest in personal autonomy.

(1) The first strand is discussed under SEARCH AND SEIZURE, as well as INVESTIGATORY POWERS OF LEGISLATURES and FREEDOM OF ASSOCIATION. It also concerns compilations of information about an individual's personal life. In 1977 the Court declined to see any constitutional difficulty in a New York law requiring doctors to supply and the state to maintain in a central computer file the names and addresses of all patients receiving prescriptions for hazardous but legal drugs, including amphetamines and opium derivatives. Patients sued to bar the data bank from listing their names, charging that their vulnerability to being identified invaded a constitutional "zone of privacy." Observing that the law prohibited disclosing patients' identities, Justice John Paul Stevens said for a unanimous Court that the data bank does not, on its face, "pose a sufficiently grievous threat" to an individual's interest "in avoiding disclosure of personal matters" or "in independence in making certain kinds of important decisions."[2189]

(2) Beginning about a century ago, and sparked by a famous article co-authored by Louis D. Brandeis, states began to recognize a CAUSE OF ACTION against invasions of privacy by the press. Invasion of privacy laws take different forms. Some are limited to the right not to have one's picture used to advertise products without consent; others more broadly protect against the publication of private facts about oneself. But following its decision in the libel case *New York Times v. Sullivan,* the Court extended its logic to the privacy arena, holding that under the FIRST AMENDMENT nondefamatory factual inaccuracies in a news story about a person's involvement in a matter of serious public interest may not be the basis for a DAMAGE award,[2048] at least if the reporter acted without actual MALICE.[333] Whether this principle applies only to PUBLIC FIGURES AND OFFICIALS or more broadly to anyone caught up in a public event remains an open question. But the Court held that the state may not permit a rape victim to recover damages when a television station reported her name, after having ascertained her identity from public court records and open court proceedings;[480] nor may a sexual assault victim recover damages from a newspaper for publishing her name, obtained from a press release issued by the sheriff's department.[685]

The Court has been little more patient with claims that a person's privacy has been invaded by subjecting him to unwanted and offensive information. In 1952 the Court upheld a decision of a District of Columbia agency permitting radios on municipal buses, despite the argument that the music and news would invade the privacy of the CAPTIVE AUDIENCE of riders.[1673] In 1969 in *Cohen v. California*, the Court rejected a claim that a person sporting a vulgar motto on the back of his jacket in the Los Angeles County Courthouse could be convicted for BREACH OF THE PEACE. To the argument that the vulgar word would disturb the tranquility of the passersby, the Court said that onlookers could simply avert their eyes. Similarly, the Court struck down a New York Public Service Commission order to a private utility company to refrain from enclosing leaflets discussing controversial topics with customers' utility bills. Again the Court rejected the rationale that the state could spare the sensibilities of customers who might not want to read what the utility wrote.[454] On the same grounds, the Court invalidated a federal ban on the mailing of unsolicited contraception advertisements.[192] However, the Court did uphold a federal law permitting the recipient of unsolicited sexually oriented literature to have the U.S. Postal Service force the mailer to remove the recipient's name from his mailing list.[1769] And despite a general right to engage in peaceful PICKETING, the Court upheld a municipal ordinance barring "focused picketing" that targeted a particular person's residence.[703]

(3) The third and most paradoxical strand of the privacy doctrine has provoked the greatest controversy largely because the term "privacy" is a misnomer for what is really being protected.

In *Griswold v. Connecticut* in 1965, the Court struck down the state's anticontraception law. In this major SUBSTANTIVE DUE PROCESS ruling, Justice William O. Douglas held that the law, which prohibited the use of CONTRACEPTION even by married couples, "concerns a relationship lying within the zone of privacy created by several fundamental constitutional guarantees." The zone of privacy is included in the LIBERTY protected by the DUE PROCESS Clauses of the FIFTH and FOURTEENTH AMENDMENTS. The interest protected in *Griswold* was, in a sense, privacy, since the immediate concern was the fear of police intrusion into the intimacy of the marital bedroom, but the decision was in fact much broader.

In striking down a law against the use of contraceptives, the Court was really declaring a right to personal autonomy over one's body and a liberty to act in certain ways, as became abundantly clear when in *Roe v. Wade* the Court recognized a constitutional right to abortion and in other decisions developed a general right to procreation. In the name of privacy the Court also upheld the right to possess and read obscene materials in the privacy of one's home, even though there is no right to buy or mail obscenity. Although these cases seemed to add up to a general constitutional right to SEXUAL FREEDOM, the Court has not gone quite that far, as it demonstrated in 1986 in upholding a state ban on homosexual relations.[207] If these cases were really about privacy, the Court would not have let the state dictate what consenting adults can in fact do in the privacy of their homes.

See also: FAMILIES; FREEDOM OF BELIEF; OBSCENITY AND PORNOGRAPHY; OFFENSIVE AND INDECENT SPEECH; PENUMBRA THEORY; PUBLIC MORALS; PUBLICITY, RIGHT TO PERSONAL; REPRODUCTIVE RIGHTS.

privacy expectation in automobiles, *see:* **search and seizure: automobiles**

private property, *see:* **eminent domain; just compensation; property; taking of property**

private right of action   Ordinarily, a person harmed when someone violates the law may sue the lawbreaker. But that is not a constitutional requirement and the law does not always permit such suits. The question arises frequently when Congress or a federal ADMINISTRATIVE AGENCY creates legal duties without specifically stating who may sue for their violations. For example, the Federal Trade Commission Act prohibits businesses from engaging in deceptive acts or practices, but only the Federal Trade Commission may sue to enforce the act. A deceived consumer has no private right of action against the lawbreaker. In 1964 the Supreme Court began to liberally infer private rights of actions in federal statutes.[993] But in 1979 the Court retrenched, saying it would infer private rights to sue only when Congress had fairly clearly manifested such an intent.[2064] The Court has occasionally inferred a direct right to sue by those who have been injured by unconstitutional actions of government officials; this is the doctrine of CONSTITUTIONAL TORTS.

See also: IMMUNITY FROM SUIT; STANDING.

private right–public right distinction The private right–public right distinction is the Supreme Court's arcane attempt to explain how ADMINISTRATIVE AGENCIES may constitutionally adjudicate legal disputes. The Constitution seems to say that CASES OR CONTROVERSIES must be decided by courts that conform to the requirements of Article III, such as life tenure for judges. But Congress has frequently empowered administrative courts—those that do not conform to Article III—to resolve legal controversies. The Court has upheld the power of administrative agencies to decide workers' compensation claims[494] but rejected the power of BANKRUPTCY COURTS to hear claims involving breaches of contract.[1500] The difference, according to a plurality opinion in 1982, is that workers' compensation claims are *public* rights created by Congress, whereas breach of contract claims are *private* rights created by state law. An Article I administrative court may be assigned to adjudicate public rights but not private rights.

See also: ARTICLE I COURTS; ARTICLE III COURTS; JUDICIAL POWER; JURISDICTION; JURISDICTIONAL AND CONSTITUTIONAL FACTS.

private schools, right to attend In 1928 the Supreme Court struck down an Oregon law requiring all children between eight and sixteen years of age to attend a public school. The Court held that in barring parents from sending their children to private schools the law violates SUBSTANTIVE DUE PROCESS by "unreasonably interfer[ing] with the LIBERTY of parents and guardians to direct the upbringing and education of children under their control."[1628]

privilege against self-incrimination, *see:* **self-incrimination**

privilege vs. right, *see:* **right-privilege distinction**

privileged from arrest, *see:* **immunity, members of Congress**

privileges and immunities Art. IV-§2[1] says that the "citizens of each state shall be entitled to all privileges and immunities of citizens in the several states." Sometimes known as the Comity Clause, this murky language has four possible meanings—that (1) Congress must treat everyone equally; (2) every state must treat its own citizens equally;[1299] (3) citizens carry the citizenship rights of their own state when they go to another state;[545] or (4) a state may not favor its own citizens by discriminating against nonresidents who come within its borders. This last view is the one that has stuck.[1579] This clause, the Supreme Court said in 1948, "was designed to insure to a citizen of State A who ventures into State B the same privileges which the citizens of State B enjoy."[2058] (The clause encompasses the rights of citizens, not corporations[119] or other business entities.[1579]) The clause does not say what rights a state must guarantee to its own citizens;[219] it simply says that a state may not deny *fundamental* rights to citizens from other states if it grants them to its own.

In the leading pronouncement on what was fundamental, Justice Bushrod Washington, in a case he heard while riding circuit and not in the Supreme Court, said in 1823 that these rights include "protection by the government; the enjoyment of life and liberty, with the right to acquire and possess property of every kind, and to pursue and obtain happiness and safety. . . . The right of a citizen of one state to pass through, or to reside in any other state, for purposes of trade, agriculture, professional pursuits, or otherwise . . . and an exemption from higher taxes or impositions than are paid by the other citizens of the state." Justice Washington denied that the clause prohibited the states from enacting GAME LAWS to preserve the natural resources of a state, and the Supreme Court followed his lead until the late 1970s, when the protectionist position was overthrown under the DORMANT COMMERCE CLAUSE theory.[956]

The Court has looked to the Privileges and Immunities Clause in several modern cases to strike down legislation discriminating between residents and nonresidents in matters of fundamental right. In 1973 the Supreme Court invalidated a law prohibiting non-Georgians from obtaining ABORTIONS in Georgia because the state could not prove that the law would conserve scarce public hospital resources.[555] An Alaska law that preferred residents to nonresidents in working on the oil pipelines was struck down because the state could not demonstrate that nonresident pipeline workers were a "peculiar source of evil" or that the law was closely tailored to deal with it.[919] Nonresidents may be taxed on the income they make within the state, but they may not be denied exemptions allowed to state residents.[2069] Holding that the right to practice law is a fundamental right, the Court has voided state rules prohibiting nonresidents from being admitted to the bar[1984, 1985, 127] and a city from limiting a certain percentage of city construc-

tion jobs to city residents, at least not without proof that grave economic problems of the inner city would be corrected by the hiring rule.[2093] However, not every discrimination touches on a fundamental right. The Court upheld a Montana elk-hunting tax that was higher for nonresidents than residents. Whatever may be fundamental, said Justice Harry Blackmun, "elk hunting by nonresidents in Montana is not one of them."[109] And some discriminations can be justified. For example, nonresidents doing business in the state[559] or driving on the state highways[915] can be served with a summons via a state official even though residents must be served directly.

A second and related "Privileges or Immunities" Clause in the FOURTEENTH AMENDMENT says that "no state shall make or enforce any law which shall abridge the privileges or immunities of citizens of the United States." However, five years after the Fourteenth Amendment was ratified, the Supreme Court killed the clause with a single blow. In the SLAUGHTER-HOUSE CASES, a 5–4 majority said that the clause refers only to privileges of *national*, not state, citizenship. These rights, as the Court later listed them, are very narrow, including, for example, the right to travel across the country, to petition Congress, and to vote in national elections.[2086] Justice Hugo L. Black's view eighty years later was that the Privileges or Immunities Clause was intended to make the first eight amendments to the Constitution applicable to the states. Black's view has considerable cogency, but only once has this clause had any constitutional effect: in 1948 the Court apparently struck down a law prohibiting a native-born minor from having his parent, a Japanese resident alien who was ineligible to become a citizen, purchase property in his name.[1546] (On one earlier occasion the Court had used the clause to invalidate a law, but it overruled itself five years later.[428, 1223])

See also: IMMUNITY FROM SUIT; INCORPORATION DOCTRINE.

probable cause The FOURTH AMENDMENT says that neither arrest warrants nor SEARCH WARRANTS may be issued except on a showing of "probable cause." In essence, a judge may not issue a warrant unless the police have adequate grounds for believing that a person has committed the crime for which they are seeking to arrest him[906] or that the places they wish to search contain specific items connected to the crime.[874] In many situations, police may proceed without a warrant, but even so they still need probable cause to arrest, search, or seize possessions.[366] Without it, any resulting evidence will be excluded from trial, with one significant exception: if a warrant is ultimately found to be defective because the police lacked probable cause in obtaining it, the evidence may be admitted if the police in good faith reasonably believed the warrant was valid.[1152]

What constitutes *probable* cause depends, as the word suggests, on what, under the circumstances, the police may reasonably deduce from knowledge of certain facts. There is no formula for determining *how* probable the cause for suspicion must be: the Court has said that the rule calls for "more than bare suspicion" and "less than evidence which would justify . . . conviction."[235] In one case the Court said that the police did not have probable cause when an informant told them that a man named Toy who operated a laundry on a certain street had heroin, because many laundry operators named Toy worked on the block and the informer gave no reason to single out the man the police arrested.[2250] A mere conclusion, in the absence of facts, cannot amount to probable cause,[22] so that the statement that a person has a general criminal reputation (that is, he is "known" as a gambler) cannot serve either as the basis for obtaining a warrant or arrest.[1933] Unlawfully seized evidence may not serve as the basis for probable cause. For example, the police may not arrest someone without probable cause, seize evidence that then establishes the crime, and justify the arrest on the basis of the evidence.[1864] Likewise, probable cause does not arise on either the mere refusal of a person to identify himself[258] or his failure to claim innocence when found in the presence of a suspect whom the police do have probable cause to arrest.[546] Probable cause to search or arrest must be particularized: a valid tip that drugs are being sold in a bar does not entitle the police, without further cause, to search everyone in the bar.[2273]

Frequently at issue is the reliability of an informant's tip. The inquiry is twofold: whether the information itself is adequate to support a reasonable suspicion and whether the police have sufficient reason to believe that the informant himself is credible. A wholly anonymous tip without much detail is likely to be unreliable. At one time, the Court required the reliability of both the evidence and the informer to be independently shown,[22, 1933] but in 1983 the Court replaced this "two-pronged" test with a "totality of the circumstances" test.[974] When the police are dealing with a known informant whose information has been highly accurate in the past, probable cause is clearly established.[1284] And when the informant provides details of sufficient quantity and quality about the criminal activity, there can be reasonable confidence that the information was reliable when at least part of the informant's story is corroborated before the arrest or search.[575] The Court has said that one particularly credible source of information is that stemming from observations of fellow police officers; no independent corroboration is necessary.[2123] Probable cause is also established when an arrest is based on a request from police in other cities for assistance in arresting a suspect.[2198] Another factor contributing to probable cause is a "deliberately furtive gesture": if the police see a person holding a "highly suspicious object" who then attempts to hide it from their view, probable cause for arrest is established.[1864] In search cases probable cause frequently depends on the time that has elapsed between the commission of the crime and the moment of the search. The Court held that there was no probable cause to search a hotel for alcohol when the report of an illegal sale was three weeks old.[1846]

When the police have arrested someone without first obtaining a warrant, the suspect is entitled to a prompt HEARING to determine whether the police had probable cause to make the arrest.[745] But if the report on which the police relied turns out to be false, the resulting search or arrest is not unlawful if the police had probable cause to accept the report as truthful when they received it.[906]

See also: SEARCH AND SEIZURE.

probation   There is no constitutional right to be placed on probation. But when SENTENCING is deferred and a convicted defendant is put on probation, DUE PROCESS entitles that person to a HEARING and to be represented by counsel if he is charged with violating probation.[1313] However, when sentence has already been imposed but suspended and the violation of probation consists of a conviction for a second offense, no lawyer or hearing is necessary. But if the probationer denies having violated a condition of probation or if he can offer reasons that might justify continuing probation, a lawyer might be required.[717] If he violates probation by failing to pay a fine, which, through no fault of his own, he cannot pay, the sentencing court must consider alternatives to jail.[141] Since probation is a form of criminal punishment, the probation department may search the probationer's home without a SEARCH WARRANT and even without PROBABLE CAUSE, as long as there are reasonable grounds for believing that the home contained something violating the terms of probation.[952]

See also: COUNSEL, ASSISTANCE OF; PAROLE.

procedural due process   Procedural due process is the central constitutional idea that government must act according to regular and known procedures—that is, that government, no less than the citizenry, must be law-abiding. Both the FIFTH and FOURTEENTH AMENDMENTS command the federal government and the states to refrain from arbitrary and capricious behavior that might deprive a particular person of life, LIBERTY, or PROPERTY. This requirement, enforced through procedural due process, prevents "unjustified or mistaken deprivations" and promotes "participation and dialogue by affected individuals in the decision-making process."[1248]

Procedural due process entitles you to a day in court (or a HEARING before some official tribunal) to argue that you should not be dealt with in a certain way or that you deserve a remedy for harm already done, but it does not guarantee you a positive outcome. Indeed, even when your case is a sure loser, you are still entitled to be heard.

Procedural due process is not just about any procedures but about *fair* ones, designed to arrive at an impartial and just resolution of the controversy. A court that decided cases by tossing a coin would clearly be violating procedural due process, no matter how much the government publicizes the coin-tossing rule or how rigorously it adheres to it. Because fairness depends on circumstances, procedural due process is a flexible concept ranging from the stringent requirements of an adversary hearing in criminal prosecutions to the highly informal procedures permitted when a public school principal decides to suspend a student for making trouble in the playground. But in all cases the two chief requirements are NOTICE of the claim and an opportunity to be heard.[2086]

The government need not offer a due process hearing whenever it acts, and legislatures are not bound to observe procedural due process. As the Supreme Court observed in 1915, general statutes, such as tax laws, may "affect the person or property of individuals, sometimes to the point of ruin, without giving them a chance to be heard."[160] Likewise, an ADMINISTRATIVE AGENCY promulgating a general regulation is not constitutionally required to afford a hearing unless the regulation is really an order directed at a particular person or small group of people.[683, 1183]

Fair procedures are due, rather, only when the government action threatens a particular person's life, liberty, or property. Criminal prosecutions obviously implicate these interests, because the penalty could be death (deprivation of life), imprisonment (deprivation of liberty), or a fine (deprivation of property). Procedural fairness in prosecutions is a large issue because the defendant's interests are protected not only by the Due Process Clause but also by many provisions in the FOURTH, FIFTH, SIXTH, and EIGHTH AMENDMENTS. Procedural due process is as significant in a civil courtroom as in the criminal trial. So, for example, a state may not authorize an administrative official to garnish wages or attach property unless there has first been a judicial hearing.[1901] In recent years, a third category of procedural due process concerns has arisen in connection with the termination of government benefits or the imposition of burdens by the government in a noncriminal trial setting. The procedural question in these cases is twofold: has the government harmed or interfered with a liberty or property interest and if so, what procedures must it afford the complaining party? These issues are dealt with under the separate headings PROCESS RIGHTS and PROCESS THAT IS DUE.

See also: ADMINISTRATIVE HEARINGS; GARNISHMENT AND ATTACHMENT; GOVERNMENT, AFFIRMATIVE OBLIGATIONS OF; PROCEDURAL RIGHTS OF CRIMINAL DEFENDANTS; PROOF, STANDARD OF; STANDING; STATE ACTION; TRIAL, RIGHT TO.

procedural rights of criminal defendants

Four articles of the BILL OF RIGHTS—the FOURTH, FIFTH, SIXTH, and EIGHTH AMENDMENTS—and the FOURTEENTH AMENDMENT provide criminal defendants with a significant battery of procedural rights unlike those of any other criminal justice system in the world. Taken together, the rights spelled out in these various constitutional provisions establish an ACCUSATORIAL SYSTEM of justice, which puts the burden of proving guilt on the government. Often when the government fails to observe these constitutional limitations, the defendant's conviction will be reversed, and sometimes the defendant will even be let go. Critics of police procedures fall into two philosophical camps. One, following Justice Oliver Wendell Holmes, would saddle the government with the burden of its official lawlessness, in particular in the form of the EXCLUSIONARY RULE. "We have to choose," Holmes said in 1928, "and for my part I think it is a lesser evil that some criminals should escape than that the Government should play an ignoble part."[1533] On the other hand, Benjamin N. Cardozo, when he was chief judge of the New York Court of Appeals in 1926, said that the exclusionary rule means that "the criminal is to go free because the constable has blundered."

Until the 1960s the issue of the criminal defendant's procedural rights excited relatively little public notice because the Constitution had a small role to play in local police operations, although the Court occasionally denounced some state trials as so fundamentally unfair as to amount to a violation of DUE PROCESS, independent of the specific guarantees in the Bill of Rights. But when the Court began to "incorporate" the many procedural rights into the Fourteenth Amendment, it stirred a lively public debate that continues unabated. Critics of the Court's solicitude for criminal defendants should consider that in a very real sense the constitutional restraints on police and judicial actions protect the innocent far more than the guilty. A moment's thought about the criminal justice systems in communist nations should suggest that the central evil was the pervasive power of the government to lock up its enemies without the rudiments of a fair trial as we understand the term. The procedural rights guaranteed in the U.S. Constitution ensure that the innocent, whether or not social malcontents and enemies of the state, will not likely even be brought to trial, much less convicted, for crimes they did not commit or for conduct that is not criminal.

See also: ACCUSATION, NOTICE AND SPECIFICITY OF; ADDICTION; ARRAIGNMENT; ARREST AND ARREST WARRANT; BAIL AND FINES; BILL OF ATTAINDER; BREATHALYZER TEST; CORRUPTION OF BLOOD; COUNSEL, ASSISTANCE OF; CRIMES, COMMON LAW; DEATH PENALTY; DISCOVERY IN CRIMINAL PROCEEDINGS; DOUBLE JEOPARDY; DRUG TESTING; ENTRAPMENT; EVIDENCE; EVIDENCE, ACCESS TO; EX POST FACTO CLAUSE; EXTRADITION; FREE PRESS–FAIR TRIAL; FRUIT OF THE POISONOUS TREE; FUNDAMENTAL FAIRNESS; GRAND JURY; GUILT BY ASSOCIATION; GUILTY PLEA; HABEAS CORPUS; HARMLESS ERROR; IMMUNITY FROM PROSECUTION; INCORPORATION DOCTRINE; INEFFECTIVE ASSISTANCE OF COUNSEL; INSANITY DEFENSE; JURY AND JURORS, IMPARTIALITY OF; JURY DISCRIMINATION; JURY SIZE; JURY UNANIMITY; LINEUP; MCNABB-MALLORY RULE; MERE EVIDENCE RULE; MIRANDA RULES; MIRANDA V. ARIZONA; NO-KNOCK ENTRY; PARDONS, REPRIEVES, COMMUTATIONS, AND AMNESTIES; PAROLE; PERJURED TESTIMONY; PLEA BARGAINING; PLEADING THE FIFTH; PREJUDICIAL PUBLICITY; PRESUMPTION OF INNOCENCE; PREVENTIVE DETENTION; PRISONERS' RIGHTS; PROBABLE CAUSE; PROBATION; PROCEDURAL DUE PROCESS; PROOF, BURDEN OF; PROOF, STANDARD OF; PROPORTIONALITY OF SENTENCE; PROSECUTORIAL DISCRETION; PROSECUTORIAL MISCONDUCT; PUNISHMENT, CRIMINAL AND CIVIL; PUNISHMENT, CRUEL AND UNUSUAL; REASONABLE DOUBT; REGULATORY LAWS; SEARCH AND SEIZURE; SEARCH WARRANT; SELF-INCRIMINATION; SENTENCING; SHOCK THE CONSCIENCE TEST; SILVER PLATTER DOCTRINE; SUPPRESSION HEARING; TRANSCRIPTS, RIGHT TO; TRIAL, FAIRNESS OF; TRIAL, PLACE OF; TRIAL, PUBLIC; TRIAL, RIGHT TO; TRIAL, SPEEDY; TWO-SOVEREIGNTIES DOCTRINE; VAGUENESS; VICTIM IMPACT STATEMENTS.

procedural rules   Central to the idea of DUE PROCESS is that governmental institutions must operate under procedures known to those who deal with them. All courts have rules of procedure, setting forth such things as timetables, the means of invoking JURISDICTION, and permissible types of pretrial DISCOVERY. For the federal courts, the task of devising these rules is within the LEGISLATIVE POWER, but as long ago as 1825 Chief Justice John Marshall held that Congress may delegate to the courts themselves the power to write the rules.[2168] The Federal Rules of Civil Procedure, originally promulgated in 1938, were devised by a committee of federal judges, subject to a LEGISLATIVE VETO, and the Court upheld the judges' power to do so.[1863] States are free to devise their own procedural rules as long as they do not offend "some principle of justice so rooted in the traditions and conscience of our people as to be ranked as fundamental."[1903] For example, they may not by imposing fees deny indigents access to courts in certain kinds of cases.[191]

See also: COURTS, ACCESS TO; ERIE RULE; PRESUMPTIONS; PROCEDURAL DUE PROCESS; SERVICE OF PROCESS; STATUTE OF LIMITATION.

process rights   In a CONCURRING OPINION, Justice Felix Frankfurter once wrote that PROCEDURAL DUE PROCESS consists of the "right to be heard before being condemned [by the government] to suffer grievous loss of any kind."[1027] The thought is as philosophically noble as it is constitutionally wrong. Though it is certainly true that a person may not be convicted of a crime without a trial, historically without asking permission of a court, the government has deprived people of many benefits whose loss would indeed be felt as "grievous"—for example, the loss of a driver's license, a government job, or a welfare check. But the license, job, and check were considered privileges to which no one was constitutionally entitled. Many governmental omissions or failures to act might also lead some people to conclude that they had suffered grievous losses—perhaps the U.S. Postal Service's failure to pick the "right" likeness of Elvis Presley on a postage stamp. In a simpler age of few government benefits, the issue might seem academic, but in a "welfare state" era, when the government is the dispenser of largess without which our lives would be wholly transformed, how to ascertain what is a constitutionally protected interest is a large problem.

The Due Process Clauses themselves refer to life, LIBERTY, and PROPERTY. In a celebrated law review article in 1964, Charles Reich, then a professor at Yale Law School, suggested that many forms of government benefits, which he termed ENTITLEMENTS, were embraced by the terms "life," "liberty," and "property" and should therefore receive at least enough constitutional recognition to require the government to hold a HEARING before terminating them. In 1970, in *Goldberg v. Kelly,* the Supreme Court, referring to Reich's article, for the first time said that one type of government benefit—welfare payments—was a form of property that could not be terminated without a "due process hearing." The case was heralded as a "due process revolution," but in fact, with some perhaps surprising exceptions, the Court has fairly narrowly limited the kinds of interests included within the terms "life," "liberty," and "property."

Only those acts or omissions through which the government *intends* to infringe life, liberty, or property are constitutional deprivations. If a prison guard unintentionally but negligently injures a prisoner, no constitutional right has been infringed, and the state need provide the prisoner neither hearing nor remedy, not even the remedy of a DAMAGE lawsuit after the fact.[513, 517]

Whether an interest is constitutionally protected depends not on how important it is to the individual but on its nature: is it a liberty or property interest?[187] The "right" Elvis stamp may be very important to some people, but they have neither a liberty nor a property interest in the government's choosing correctly. Liberty interests have been held to be implicated when, in addition to physical restraint, such as imprisonment, the government seeks to

commit an adult to a mental institution[13] or to permit a parent to commit a child over the child's objection;[1565] withdraw early-release credits from a prisoner;[2245] revoke parole[1390] or probation;[717] transfer a prisoner involuntarily to a mental institution;[2133] administer antipsychotic drugs to a prisoner;[2160] spank a schoolchild;[980] fire an employee because he or she has exercised FIRST AMENDMENT rights to express an opinion;[1610] fire an employee in such a way as to seriously foreclose future employment opportunities—for example, by announcing publicly the person's incompetence;[413] terminate the rights of natural parents to custody of their children;[1802] suspend or revoke a driver's license;[145] deport a resident alien;[1478] and suspend a student from school.[785] A considerable debate has raged over whether a liberty interest is infringed when the government libels an individual. The Court seems to have said that when a defamation triggers some other injury, such as the loss of a job or a legal incapacity to buy liquor, then a liberty interest is involved; otherwise not.[1578] The Court has also held that no liberty interest is involved when a state prison refuses to permit inmates to receive visitors, as long as no state law specifically granted the right.[1066]

In all but the last of these cases, the Court has determined the meaning of liberty directly from the Constitution. In determining what constitutes a *property* interest, however, the Court has generally supposed that courts must look to see whether Congress or the states have created some sort of entitlement. Again, the issue is troublesome only in connection with government jobs or benefits, since ordinary forms of property—land, homes, automobiles, and other personalty—are well understood to be included within the term "entitlement." There does appear to be an understanding of what is a constitutionally protected interest: a government benefit, such as a payment or a job, is a property interest only if the law creating it establishes criteria that the claimant appears to meet for continuing to receive the benefit.[766,166] So, for example, a teacher hired on a one-year contract expressly stating that it confers no tenure has no constitutionally protected entitlement to renewal,[187] but when a teacher has worked many years on contracts constantly renewed so that there is a "de facto" tenure system, he or she has a property interest in further renewals.[1610] Among other types of property interests, the Court has discerned welfare benefits,[766] certifications and licenses to run a business[1505] and practice a profession,[1772] and government jobs that expressly grant some form of security.[79] But if the government job is declared to be "at the will and pleasure" of the supervising authority, then there is no property interest.[166]

In declaring these various interests to be aspects of liberty or property, the Court has declared nothing more than that some form of procedural due process is necessary to take it away.

See also: BITTER WITH THE SWEET; PROCESS THAT IS DUE; REPUTATION; RIGHT-PRIVILEGE DISTINCTION; VESTED RIGHTS; UNCONSTITUTIONAL CONDITIONS.

process that is due   The nature and timing of the HEARING required when the government has invaded or threatens to invade an interest protected by DUE PROCESS is a constitutional question. The courts are not bound by state or federal law declaring the procedures to be used unless they protect the individual more than the constitutional minimum. Even though the states or Congress may define a PROPERTY interest, they may not attempt to limit the procedural safeguards in terminating it.[409] For example, when the state hires an employee to work at the "will" of his supervisor, the employee has no property interest in the job and can be fired without explanation. But if the state hires someone on a contract that says he or she may be fired only for cause, the state

may not then refuse to give the reasons for the firing or to forbid anyone to contest it.

When a PROCESS RIGHT is affected, the appropriate procedure must be determined. Despite the profusion of cases involving government benefits, the Court has been relatively stingy in requiring the full-blown adversary trial necessary in criminal prosecutions or ordinary civil litigation. Rather, the Court has employed a BALANCING test, weighing three factors: the private interest affected by what the government does; the risk that a particular procedure will erroneously deprive the individual of his or her interest, and the value of any additional procedures in minimizing that risk; and the government's interest, including the administrative burden and cost, in having to comply with additional procedures.[1269] Among the procedural questions weighed in this balance are whether a hearing must be held before the deprivation or may be held afterward; and whether the claimant is entitled to prior notice, DISCOVERY, the right to confront and cross-examine witnesses, to be heard in person, to be represented by a lawyer, and the like.

Among the rights, benefits, or statuses that may not be terminated without a prior hearing are: welfare benefits,[766] a natural parent's custody of children,[1802] and involuntary transfer of a prison inmate to a mental institution.[2133] In these situations, the administrative hearing must be full and formal, with advance notice; an opportunity to appear, present evidence, and make oral argument; a right to confront and cross-examine witnesses; full disclosure of the evidence; a right to an attorney; a decision based on the evidence that states the reasons for its conclusions and is made by an impartial decision maker. In other cases, the hearing held before the deprivation may be quite informal. For example, to suspend a student from school for up to ten days, a principal need only notify the student of the pending decision and give the student a chance to tell his or her story.[785]

Suspension of a driver's license also requires a prerevocation hearing, but the procedures may be far less formal than when the state wishes to terminate welfare benefits.[145]

In some instances, the government may dispense with the requirement of a hearing altogether, though not without some informal "procedure." For example, the Court said that the only process due a public medical school student on the verge of being dismissed was notice to her of her academic difficulties and a fair set of oral and written examinations administered by the faculty from which they could conclude that she had failed.[178] A government utility must devise procedures, but not necessarily a hearing, to determine whether a customer's service may rightly be terminated.[1314] In many other types of cases, the Court has held that the only process due is an after-the-fact or postdeprivation hearing—for example, in withdrawals of Social Security disability and welfare benefits,[1269] public employment dismissals,[79] and the seizure of ships thought to be carrying contraband.[311] In still other situations, the Court has even determined that procedural due process is satisfied without any special hearing, before or after the loss, as long as the aggrieved person may file an ordinary civil DAMAGE suit in court; for example, when a prisoner alleges that his property was intentionally destroyed by a guard,[952] and when a student is spanked in school.[980]

See also: ACCESS TO COURTS; COUNSEL, ASSISTANCE OF; GARNISHMENT AND ATTACHMENT; PROCEDURAL RIGHTS OF CRIMINAL DEFENDANTS; SEVENTH AMENDMENT; TRIAL, RIGHT TO.

proclamation of neutrality, *see:* **neutrality proclamation**

procreation, *see:* **reproductive rights**

production, *see:* **interstate commerce; manufacturing**

profanity, *see:* **offensive and indecent speech**

professionals, advertising by   Until the 1970s, the Court had never indicated any constitutional objection to state regulation of advertising for professional services. Court rules in every state, however, forbade advertising by lawyers, and the semi-official codes of ethics of doctors and other professionals also barred them from using commercial messages to attract patients or clients. In 1955 the Court expressly approved an Oklahoma law barring eye-care professionals from advertising the sale of lenses and frames.[2224] But in 1976 the Court struck down a Virginia law prohibiting pharmacists from advertising the prices of prescription drugs;[2131] the following year it voided an Arizona law against the advertising of "routine legal services."[135] Since then the Court has struck down other laws that prohibit professional advertising that is neither actually nor inherently misleading,[1679] but it has upheld restrictions on the use of trade names by professionals—for example, Texas State Optometrists or TSO—because they might mislead the public by suggesting that a doctor in one office works in another.[702]

See also: COMMERCIAL SPEECH; LAWYERS; OCCUPATIONAL LICENSING; SOLICITATION.

Prohibition, *see:* **intoxicating beverages**

prohibition, writ of   A writ of prohibition is an order from a higher court to stop hearing a case that lies beyond the lower court's JURISDICTION. Congress has granted the Supreme Court the power to issue writs of prohibition to both lower federal courts and to state courts. The U.S. COURTS OF APPEALS may issue the writ to U.S. DISTRICT COURTS. The writ of prohibition is not a substitute for an appeal, and the courts issue them sparingly at their discretion in appropriate cases.

prohibition of commerce The COMMERCE POWER authorizes Congress to *regulate* commerce between the states. But may Congress *prohibit* the shipment of particular goods across state lines? The power to prohibit was debated for exactly one century, beginning in 1841, when Henry Clay warned that if Congress had this power, it could do away with the interstate slave trade by the simple expedient of outlawing the shipment of slaves from state to state.[825] Those who opposed the power saw lurking in it the means by which Congress could move beyond economic regulation and impose its moral vision on the country. Strict federalists believed that the authority to regulate morals was not an attribute of the national LEGISLATIVE POWER but was reserved to the states in the exercise of their POLICE POWER. But in 1903, in *The Lottery Case,* after two rearguments, the Court held, 5–4, that Congress could ban the carrying of lottery tickets for sale or distribution from one state to another. Justice John Marshall Harlan found that nothing in the Constitution gives anyone the right to carry from one state to another "that which will harm the public morals." In 1913 the Court sustained the Mann Act, sometimes called the White Slave Act, prohibiting the transportation of a woman across state lines for prostitution or any other immoral purpose.[931] However, the Court drew the line in the *Child Labor Case* in 1918, denying that Congress had the power to prohibit goods from shipping in INTERSTATE COMMERCE if produced by children under sixteen who were forced to work more than a specified number of hours or at certain times of the day. The Court said that the critical difference between child labor and the other forms of commerce was that the goods children produced were not themselves harmful. The Court finally overruled the *Child Labor Case* in 1941, expressly and definitively holding that Congress may prohibit whatever it pleases from being shipped in interstate commerce.[514]

See also: CHILD LABOR; NATIONAL POLICE POWER; TENTH AMENDMENT.

proof, burden of In criminal trials, DUE PROCESS requires that the government prove the guilt of the ACCUSED.[2234, 627, 1798] The defendant need offer no proof at all and is entitled to an acquittal if the government fails to prove beyond a REASONABLE DOUBT all elements of a crime—that is, every fact required to show that the defendant committed the crime charged.[1400] But this stringent burden of proof does not mean that the government must prove the absence of mitigating factors, for example, insanity or "extreme emotional disturbance" of the defendant. The state need not prove the defendant sane; it may require the defendant, if he wishes to escape conviction, to bear the burden of proving that he was insane when he committed the crime.[1577] In civil cases, the plaintiff has the burden of proof, although the plaintiff's standard of proof is less than a prosecutor's; in most civil cases the burden is on the plaintiff to show that his case is more probable than not.

proof, standard of The standard of proof refers to the weight of the evidence required to rule in favor of one party at trial or an administrative hearing. Just as in everyday life, people require different sorts of proof for different sorts of actions, so different kinds of legal interests require higher or lower standards of proof. For example, it doesn't take much evidence to persuade most people to carry an umbrella in case of rain—perhaps the meteorologist's brief report on the morning news. It takes considerably more proof to persuade most people to put snow chains on their tires. The highest standard of proof is constitutionally required in criminal prosecutions, in which the prosecutor must prove the state's case beyond a REASONABLE DOUBT.[2234] The state must prove every element of the crime by that standard.[1400] In ordinary civil cases, the standard is no more than a "preponderance" of the evidence; the plaintiff must show that his or her contention is more probable than not. The constitutional battleground is over the third, middle standard, usually expressed as the "clear and convincing proof" standard. The Court has held that the clear-and-convincing standard is required in CIVIL COMMITMENT proceedings[13] and in proceedings to permanently terminate a natural parent's custody of children.[1802] But a mother seeking support payments need not prove paternity of the father by anything more than preponderance of the evidence.[1733] In 1990, in *Cruzan v. Director, Missouri Dept. of Health*, the RIGHT TO DIE case, the Court held that a state may require proof by clear and convincing evidence that a person in a persistent vegetative state wished to die rather than to be maintained on life support systems. Without such proof the state need not constitutionally accede to a parental request that the support be terminated.

property   The Constitution uses the word "property" four times. Art. IV-§3[2] refers to property belonging to the United States and gives Congress the power to regulate and dispose of federal possessions. The JUST COMPENSATION Clause of the FIFTH AMENDMENT requires that the government compensate owners for any property taken under the power of EMINENT DOMAIN or otherwise. The DUE PROCESS Clauses of both the Fifth and FOURTEENTH AMENDMENTS prohibit both the federal government and the states from depriving any person of property without due process of law. But the Constitution is silent about what constitutes property. In a definition with which the Framers were conversant, Sir William Blackstone said that the "right of property is that sole and despotic dominion which one man claims and exercises over the external things of the world." For Blackstone, property was that

which a person could use to the complete exclusion of anyone else, "save only by the laws of the land." This last condition suggests a circularity that often infects constitutional considerations of property rights. For if owners may do as they please with their property, except to the extent that the law limits their right to do so, property appears to be wholly subject to the state. The Supreme Court has come close to this position in interpreting the Just Compensation Clause, holding in the main that only if an owner has been wholly deprived of the use of property must the government compensate. A law or regulation that merely interferes with one aspect of property is not a constitutional TAKING OF PROPERTY.

The meaning of property under the Due Process Clauses has varied. During the reign of ECONOMIC DUE PROCESS, the Court construed property to mean not merely a thing itself but the capacity of the thing to earn money. For example, states were not permitted to regulate the rates of businesses not AFFECTED WITH A PUBLIC INTEREST. But by the late 1930s, the Court backed away from this interpretation, freeing government to regulate property as it chooses, short of depriving the owner of its use altogether.

Beginning in the 1970s, the Court took a renewed interest in the meaning of property as it tried to sort out what kinds of interests the states could deprive individuals of without affording them some sort of HEARING. In general, the Court has indicated that beyond the obvious—a person's rights to land and other real property, tangible personal property, and certain rights to intangibles, such as corporate dividends that accrue from ownership of stock—a "property interest" is an interest recognized by law. If a state law or regulation gives someone an expectation to continue holding the interest—for example, a public job or a welfare benefit—then it is property that the state may not take away or terminate without giving the possessor an opportunity to be heard.

See also: LIBERTY; PROCESS RIGHTS; PROCESS THAT IS DUE; PUBLIC PROPERTY; VESTED RIGHTS.

property, abandoned   Most states have laws requiring property unclaimed for a long time to "escheat" (that is, to be turned over) to the state or to previous owners. The Supreme Court has upheld these laws, many of which give very little protection to people about to lose their property, against attacks that they violate the owners' DUE PROCESS rights. For example, New York was permitted to take life insurance proceeds if private beneficiaries failed within seven years to claim any money due, even though the life insurance company and the actual funds were located outside New York.[452] Likewise, states may seize unclaimed shares of a corporation and unpaid dividends, even though the last owners lived out of state and the dividends were held out of state.[1939] The Court has also approved an Indiana law that returned to their original owners interests in coal, oil, gas, or other minerals if they had not been used in twenty years. The law required neither the state nor the person about to regain the rights to notify those whose rights were about to expire.[2016]

property qualifications for voters   From the very beginning of nationhood, most states imposed a property qualification on voters. Only white male adults who owned a certain value of land could vote in local, state, and even federal elections. Nothing in the Constitution barred the states from conditioning voting on ownership, nor did express language in the three Civil War amendments change the constitutional understanding. However, in 1966 the Court struck down the POLL TAX and in so doing swept away property qualifications as well. The Court held that under the EQUAL PROTECTION CLAUSE the states may not condi-

tion voting on "wealth or affluence or payment of a fee" because "wealth, like race, creed, or color, is not germane to one's ability to participate intelligently in the electoral process."[867] Since then, the Court has struck down laws limiting voting in school elections to people who own property in the district or have children in the schools,[1097] as well as laws limiting to property owners the right to vote on referenda involving revenue bonds[398] and general obligation bonds.[1624] However, states may use property qualifications when the impact of the election will fall predominantly on property owners. If, for example, an election is held to decide whether to create local water storage districts[89] and to elect their boards of directors,[1788] the state may allocate votes proportionate to the number of acres owned.[112]

See also: VOTING, RIGHT TO.

property tax   States have broad but not absolute constitutional discretion to impose property taxes, but that power is limited by the EQUAL PROTECTION CLAUSE, the DUE PROCESS Clause of the FOURTEENTH AMENDMENT, and the COMMERCE CLAUSE. Under the Equal Protection Clause the Supreme Court has conceded to the states considerable leeway in granting exemptions in a variety of property tax schemes. For example, the Court upheld against a SEX DISCRIMINATION challenge a Florida law granting a five-hundred-dollar property tax exemption to widows but not to widowers.[1044] The Court also upheld an Ohio law exempting nonresidents who store property in local warehouses from a tax imposed on residents storing property there.[40] The Court reasoned that the state was permitted to attract out-of-state business to its warehouses and that the tax exemption was a rational means of doing so. Property taxes may be used as the basis for providing public education, even if the amounts provided differ among school districts because of the difference in property values between the districts.[1791] But gross disparities in the taxes paid by residents of the state can violate equal protection. In 1989 the Court overturned a Pennsylvania practice of taxing owners on assessments made at the time of sale but of failing to reappraise neighboring unsold property.[38] In an age of inflation, the result was that purchasers of property were being taxed at rates between eight and thirty-five times higher than those who had held their property for ten years.

Due process limitations on the power of states to tax property center on the issue of where the property is located. If the property, whether land or tangible personal property, is wholly located within the state, it may be taxed even if the owner lives out of state.[352] If the property is wholly out of state, the legislature may not tax it.[2092] The hard questions arise, usually in connection with business assets, when property occasionally moves through a state and when it is partly located in many states. For example, states may not tax the value of ships owned by foreign corporations merely because they arrive in ports of the state. Only the state in which the business is incorporated may tax, at least if the ships are not regularly enough in one place to constitute its "tax home."[1921] On the other hand, a state may tax an airline's entire fleet, even though the planes are not continuously present in the state, if the state is their "home port" and the company maintains its headquarters there.[1502] When part of an out-of-state business's property is regularly in a state, such as railroad cars that travel on tracks traversing the state, the state may tax the cars proportionately to the whole.[1633] Different methods of apportioning the property value are allowed,[1015, 749] but in every case it must be established that the property has sufficient connection with the taxing state.[1544] When the property moves, the Court assesses each case on its facts, holding in one instance that an airline could be taxed on the propor-tionate value of the planes that land in the state when the company makes eighteen scheduled stops per day. It presumably could not be taxed if it occasionally stopped in a state to refuel but not as a part of scheduled service.[223]

A closely related issue is the power to tax *intangible* property: corporate securities, dividends, mortgages, bank deposits, and the like. In a sense taxability turns on location, since it is always debatable where an intangible essence, like a share of ownership in a foreign corporation, actually exists. The Court has given different answers in a number of cases difficult to reduce to a single generalization. For example, it has approved a state's taxing a mortgage on land within the state, even though the mortgage instrument was held by a nonresident out of state.[1803] It has also upheld a tax on bank deposits owned personally by a resident, even though the bank was out of state and the funds derived from a business conducted entirely out of state.[663] It struck down a tax on property held in trust in another state, the income of which was paid to a resident.[244]

But in a significant ruling that has endured, the Court in 1897 upheld state taxes on intangible property of corporations, including "all corporate franchises and all contracts, privileges, and goodwill of the concern."[10] This principle has permitted states to impose a proportionate tax on the total value of foreign companies doing business in the state. In another significant decision upholding state taxing authority, the Court sustained a North Dakota tax on the intangible property of the Cream of Wheat Company. Cream of Wheat was incorporated in North Dakota but all its property, tangible and intangible, was located elsewhere. The company protested that upholding the tax would subject it to double taxation, since the state in which its property was located obviously could tax it as well. The Court retorted that the Fourteenth Amendment does not prohibit double taxation.[491]

However, double taxation may be barred under the Commerce Clause. The due process question is whether the property has sufficient connection with the state. The interstate taxation question is whether a state property tax interferes with INTERSTATE COMMERCE. If it does, the Court will invalidate the tax even if the state has sufficient contacts with the property to tax it under due process. For example, a company may not be taxed by its incorporating state on all its property if most of it is rarely in the state and is subject to being taxed proportionately by other states. "Otherwise," the Court said, "there would be multiple taxation of interstate operations and the tax would have no relation to the opportunities, benefits, or protection which the taxing state gives those operations."[1940]

See also: EDUCATION, RIGHT TO; IMPORT-EXPORT CLAUSES; ORIGINAL PACKAGE DOCTRINE; TAXATION OF INTERSTATE COMMERCE; WEALTH CLASSIFICATION AND DISCRIMINATION.

proportionality of sentence   The idea that the punishment should fit the crime has a lineage as old as MAGNA CARTA. A century ago Justice Stephen J. Field argued that the EIGHTH AMENDMENT condemns "all punishments which by their excessive length or severity are greatly disproportionate to the offenses charged."[1515] A majority accepted Field's view in 1910 in overturning a fifteen-year hard-labor sentence of a defendant convicted of falsifying minor public documents. The hard labor was to be served with chains on the ankles in a brutal Philippine prison. After release the convicted man was to be subjected to perpetual surveillance and a permanent loss of all civil and political rights.[2176] Until recently, most of the debate over proportionality centered on capital punishment. Although the DEATH PENALTY as such is not disproportionate when imposed on a murderer, the Court has ruled that

capital punishment is unconstitutionally disproportionate when meted out for rape that did not lead to death[421] and for felony murderers when the defendant himself neither intended that anyone be killed nor did the killing.[618] Most states permit the judge or jury to weigh the circumstances before imposing capital punishment. The Court has mandated certain procedural safeguards, so that some degree of proportionality is built into even the death penalty, but it has said that "comparative proportionality reviews" are not constitutionally required. Courts reviewing death penalty sentences need not assess whether a death sentence handed down in one case was proportionate to sentences handed down in other murder cases.[1675]

When the sentence is imprisonment or a monetary fine, the Court has been much less open to the claim that the punishment is disproportionate to the crime, although Justice Lewis F. Powell did suggest in a CONCURRING OPINION in 1986 in *Bowers v. Hardwick* that a long prison sentence for a "private, consensual act of sodomy" might well be cruel and unusual because disproportionate to the crime. The Court has declined to find recidivist statutes generally unconstitutional. Recidivist laws impose stiffer sentences on a person convicted of a felony if he or she has a record than on a person convicted of the identical crime for the first time. In 1980, in *Rummel v. Estelle,* the Court upheld, 5–4, a mandatory sentence of lifetime imprisonment for a Texas defendant convicted of obtaining $120.75 by false pretenses, a crime Texas regards as a felony because the amount obtained exceeded fifty dollars. He had been convicted twice before of similar felonies, the first time of fraudulently using a credit card to obtain groceries worth eighty dollars and the second time of passing a forged check in the amount of $28.36. Justice William H. Rehnquist for the majority declined to view the sentence as disproportionate to the crime since society is entitled to determine how harsh a sentence is necessary to deter repeat offenders.

In 1982 the Court similarly upheld a sentence of forty years for possessing and distributing nine ounces of marijuana valued at about two hundred dollars.[968] However, in 1983, in *Solem v. Helm,* a different 5–4 majority did invoke the principle of proportionality to strike down a lifetime prison sentence for a defendant who had been convicted of minor nonviolent crimes, including passing a bad check in the amount of a hundred dollars. The difference in result hinged on the reality of the lifetime sentence. In *Rummel* the defendant was eligible for parole in twelve years. In *Solem* there was no possibility of parole, so the reality of a life sentence led the Court to reject the principle that proportionality can never apply to felony prison sentences. The criteria used for determining whether a sentence is disproportionate were: the gravity of the offense and the harshness of the penalty; the sentences imposed on other criminals in the same jurisdiction; and the sentences imposed for commission of the same crime in other jurisdictions. In 1991 a new 5–4 majority upheld a mandatory lifetime prison sentence without possibility of parole for the crime of possessing 650 grams of cocaine.[866] In his majority opinion, Justice Antonin Scalia declared that the proportionality of a sentence should never be a constitutional consideration, but only Chief Justice Rehnquist agreed. The other seven justices said that even in noncapital cases, a sentence grossly disproportionate to the offense is unconstitutional.

See also: PUNISHMENT, CRUEL AND UNUSUAL.

prosecution, selective, *see:* **prosecutorial discretion**

prosecutorial discretion   It has long been assumed that prosecutors have wide discretion to decide which cases to prosecute, and the Supreme Court has been generally unreceptive to the claim that the prosecutor's office violates the EQUAL PROTECTION CLAUSE in selecting certain defendants or types of crimes to prosecute: "unequal application" of a law fair on its face is permissible "unless there is shown an element of intentional or purposeful discrimination."[1902] Discretion is necessary for several reasons: lack of resources to prosecute every crime that is committed, acts that by consensus are criminalized for symbolic value only (like adultery), and the need to take into account all the circumstances in particular cases. Prosecution might do more damage than good in some situations; for example, when the victim declines to press charges, when a grant of IMMUNITY would make an offender into an informant, and when the crime is minor and the offender offers full restitution. Nevertheless, selective prosecution "deliberately based upon an unjustifiable standard such as race, religion, or other arbitrary classification"[1547] would violate the Equal Protection Clause, although no such case has ever reached the Court. But selecting particular cases to prosecute is not in itself a constitutional violation, the Court ruled, in upholding the government's policy of prosecuting as draft evaders only those people who advised the Selective Service that they had failed to register.[2169]

Prosecutors may not, however, act vindictively. For example, when the defendant after conviction has the right to retrial, the prosecutor may not retaliate "by substituting a more serious charge for the original one," since the knowledge that the prosecutor could do so would seriously deter the defendant from exercising his legal rights.[170, 780] Another possible attack on prosecutorial discretion stems from the long nonenforcement of particular criminal laws. Many such laws lie dormant and are commonly understood to be "dead," or in legal parlance, to have fallen into *desuetude,* even though the legislature has not repealed them. The question is whether a prosecutor may revive such a law by prosecuting a case under it. The Court has said that the prosecutor may do so because laws remain laws until repealed by the legislature.[553]

See also: DOUBLE JEOPARDY; RIGHTS, WAIVER OF; SENTENCING.

prosecutorial misconduct Public prosecutors are bound by DUE PROCESS to observe certain standards of conduct in the prosecution of their cases. They may not knowingly present PERJURED TESTIMONY; nor may they suppress evidence favorable to the defendant when requested,[220] and even if not requested, evidence that is obviously exculpatory.[23] Prosecutors are permitted to act tough in negotiating a PLEA BARGAIN with the defendant. Although every state has rules governing out-of-court statements that would "have a substantial likelihood of materially prejudicing" a trial, prosecutors routinely hold press conferences but are almost never called to task, whereas now and then defense lawyers who talk about their clients are.[739] Both federal[2279] and state[978] prosecutors are immune from private DAMAGE suits for their misconduct. Although they may in theory be disciplined by state authorities, they rarely are.

See also: PROSECUTORIAL DISCRETION.

prostitution, *see:* **national police power; prohibition of commerce**

protection of the laws, *see:* **equal protection of the laws**

psychic harm The Supreme Court has occasionally declared that under DUE PROCESS and FIRST AMENDMENT principles the state may not lock up or otherwise punish people simply because their appearance or behavior offends others. In holding in 1975 that the state may not "fence in the harmless mentally ill solely to save its citizens from exposure to those whose ways are different," a unanimous Court said that "[o]ne might as well ask if the State, to avoid public unease, could incarcerate all who are physically unattractive or socially eccentric. Mere public intolerance or animosity cannot constitutionally justify the deprivation of a person's physical liberty."[1510] The Court expressed similar sentiments in striking down VAGRANCY laws[412] and a BREACH OF THE PEACE conviction of a man wearing a vulgarity on the back of his jacket, saying that those who take offense may "avoid further bombardment of their sensibilities simply by averting their eyes."[417]

Despite these rulings, there is no general principle that bars the state from outlawing acts that give merely psychic offense. Perhaps the most noteworthy example of the Court's reluctance to create a broad principle was its holding in *Bowers v. Hardwick* in 1986 that there is no constitutional bar to a state law criminalizing homosexual relations between consenting adults in the privacy of their homes. The 5–4 majority was unable to point to any concrete harm against which the state was legislating except a general sense that the conduct was "immoral"—in other words, that it offended most people deeply. The Court has also sustained ordinances banning public displays of signs and other messages in the "esthetic interest" of avoiding "visual clutter."[401] The disparity between the Court's occasionally broad statements condemning laws against psychic harm and its deviant holdings stems in large part from the Court's (and everyone else's) inability to define "harm" in any general way.

See also: DRESS CODES; MENTAL DISTRESS; PERSON AND PERSONHOOD; PRIVACY; PUBLIC MORALS; SEXUAL FREEDOM.

public accommodations A public accommodation is a privately owned restaurant, hotel, theater, or other establishment open to the public generally. Historically, the concept of public accommodations has been the source of power to ensure that owners do not discriminate on a forbidden basis, such as race or religion. In 1883, in the CIVIL RIGHTS CASES, the Supreme Court struck down a federal law that prohibited owners from engaging in RACIAL DISCRIMINATION in public accommodations. Congress enacted the law under its power to enforce the FOURTEENTH AMENDMENT, which prohibits the states from denying EQUAL PROTECTION OF THE LAWS. But the Equal Protection Clause applies only to STATE ACTION, the Court ruled, not to private acts of discrimination; therefore Congress had no authority to tell owners they could not discriminate. Ninety years later in the Civil Rights Act of 1964 Congress tried a new approach, this time meeting success in the Court, by using its COMMERCE POWER to prohibit discrimination in public accommodations connected to INTERSTATE COMMERCE. The Court upheld the act's public accommodations provisions in two major cases, one involving an Atlanta hotel that catered to out-of-state travelers[888] and the other, a local Birmingham restaurant that spent a considerable sum on meat imported from other states.[1052]

See also: SEGREGATION AND INTEGRATION.

public acts, records, and judicial proceedings, *see:* **full faith and credit**

public buildings, *see:* **public property**

public debt, *see:* **debt of the United States**

public employment In 1892, Justice Oliver Wendell Holmes, then sitting on the Massachusetts Supreme Judicial Court, insisted that the constitutional rights of public employees could be suspended simply because they worked for the federal or state governments: "The petitioner may have a constitutional right to talk politics," Holmes said, "but he has no constitutional right to be a policeman." Holmes's position has not stood the test of time. In two major areas, the Court has declared that the Constitution may not be ig-

nored when an individual takes a government job. The FIRST AMENDMENT shields many, though not all, associations and expressions of opinions by government workers. DUE PROCESS provides a limited right to challenge a discharge at a HEARING.

In a series of decisions during the late 1950s and 1960s, the Court narrowly limited the government's authority to use LOYALTY OATHS as the basis for hiring or firing. In 1972 it declared that individuals may not be refused government jobs because of how they have exercised their constitutional rights.[1610] This principle does not deprive the government of all authority to deal with speech or activities of employees that may interfere with efficient performance of the job. In such cases, the problem "is to arrive at a balance between the interests of the [employee], as a citizen, in commenting upon matters of public concern and the interest of the state, as an employer, in promoting the efficiency of the public services it performs through its employees."[1625] Employing this BALANCING test in 1968, the Court concluded that a public school teacher could not be fired for sending to the local newspaper a letter critical of the school board's financial dealings.[1625] In 1979 the Court unanimously agreed that a teacher could not be fired for making critical statements to her principal in private.[761a] In 1983 the Court distinguished speech about matters of public concern from matters of concern only within the employee's office. In the particular case, an assistant district attorney in New Orleans was upset when her boss, District Attorney Harry Connick, transferred her to a new position. She circulated a questionnaire to various members of the staff "concerning office transfer policy, office morale, the need for a grievance committee, the level of confidence in supervisors, and whether employees felt pressured to work in political campaigns." Fired for insubordination, she claimed that the discharge was due solely to her circulation of the survey, which involved matters of public concern. In a 5–4 decision, Justice Byron R. White disagreed, holding that the entire episode "reflect[ed] one employee's dissatisfaction with a transfer and an attempt to turn that displeasure into a cause célèbre. . . . The First Amendment does not require a public office to be run as a roundtable for employee complaints over internal office affairs."[453] On the other hand, in 1987 the Court held, also 5–4, that a clerk in a county sheriff's office, hearing that President Ronald Reagan had been shot, could not constitutionally be fired for saying: "If they go for him again, I hope they get him."[1693] Because the employee played no "confidential, policymaking, or public contact role," it did not matter that the remark was controversial. It dealt with a matter of public concern, and the sheriff had not shown that the clerk's statement "had interfered with the public functioning of the office." Dissenting, Justice Antonin Scalia said that "no law enforcement agency is required by the First Amendment to permit one of its employees to 'ride with the cops and cheer for the robbers.' "

The Court has delivered a mixed message about the rights of employees to belong to organizations. In the 1960s, it said that an employee could not be fired for MEMBERSHIP IN POLITICAL ORGANIZATIONS presumed to be subversive except under very limited circumstances. Likewise, in a series of PATRONAGE cases beginning in 1976, the Court has held that applicants may not be denied public jobs and public employees may not be fired on the basis of their political party affiliations, again except under narrow circumstances. But the Court has sustained the Hatch Act, which prohibits federal employees from actively participating in political campaigns.[2098] In a unanimous opinion, Justice White said the Court would not disturb Congress's judgment that the government could not operate "effectively and fairly" unless partisan activities by its employees were

curbed. Since the limitations were not aimed at any particular party and do not limit the right of employees to express their opinions or to vote, the act does not offend the First Amendment.[402]

Whether an applicant or an employee is entitled to a public job, or at least to challenge the decision not to hire or to fire, is a difficult question that turns on the particular circumstances in each case. In 1972, the Court held that a jobholder has no right to a hearing when the job is terminated if he had no "legitimate claim of entitlement to it."[187] A public school may decline to rehire a teacher serving on a one-year contract because nothing in the contract gave him any sort of tenure right. The school need neither give reason nor hold a hearing under these circumstances. The Court also held that a police officer is not entitled to a hearing before being terminated for insubordination, "causing low morale," and "conduct unsuited to an officer," even though classified as a nonprobationary "permanent employee," if the state law permits him to be fired at the will of a responsible municipal supervisor.[166] However, a hearing would have been required before discharge if there had been a claim that the employee was fired for exercising a constitutional right. Even though an employee may have a legitimate claim of entitlement to a public job—and hence a property interest in it—there is nevertheless no constitutional right to a full-scale adversary hearing before termination. The employee is "entitled to oral or written notice of the charges against him, an explanation of the employer's evidence, and an opportunity to present his side of the story." But nothing more.[409]

See also: PROCESS RIGHTS; PROCESS THAT IS DUE; RIGHT–PRIVILEGE DISTINCTION; UNCONSTITUTIONAL CONDITIONS.

public figures and officials In 1964, in *New York Times v. Sullivan*, the Supreme Court ruled that public officials could not recover DAMAGES for libel unless they could show that the defendant had published a falsehood with "actual MALICE." The plaintiff in *Sullivan* was a chief of police. What other public officials come within the rule? In several cases during the succeeding decade, the Court essentially said that the term embraces anyone elected or appointed to public OFFICE, including municipal judges,[731] county attorneys,[904] deputy sheriffs,[1935] state legislators,[803] police captains,[2049] and even candidates for public office.[1373] But not all public employees are public officials. For example, the actual-malice rule does not apply in the case of a public university professor.[966]

In 1967 the Court extended the logic of *Sullivan* to public figures, private individuals who are "intimately involved in the resolution of important public questions or, by reason of their fame, shape events in areas of concern to society at large."[504] By this definition, said the Court, a well-known university football coach and a retired Army general who was politically active are public figures.[91] The Court seemed at first to be suggesting that anyone thrust into the limelight by public events, however unwillingly, is a public figure.[1760] But in 1974 the Court drew back a bit, holding that public figures are only those people who by dint of their own efforts and intentions "have assumed roles of especial prominence in the affairs of society." A lawyer is not a public figure simply because the newspapers report on one or even many of his clients,[746] and neither are a socialite involved in a highly publicized divorce,[2047] a person convicted of CONTEMPT for failing to testify years earlier at a GRAND JURY hearing,[2247] or a scientist who published the results of publicly funded research.[966]

See also: LIBEL AND SLANDER; OFFICE AND OFFICERS.

public finance, *see:* **borrowing power; spending power**

public forum   Public forum is the Supreme Court's name for the public places where people may congregate to exchange views and speak their minds. In 1895, Justice Oliver Wendell Holmes, then serving on the Massachusetts Supreme Judicial Court, discerned no constitutional objection to laws banning or limiting public speaking in a highway or public park. Such a law "is no more an infringement of the rights of a member of the public than for the owner of a private house to forbid it in his house." The Supreme Court affirmed.[521a] Not until 1939 did the Court reconsider, and then it struck down a PERMIT SYSTEM that gave unbridled discretion to city officials over the streets and parks, which "time out of mind have been used for purposes of assembly, communicating thoughts between citizens, and discussing public questions."[838]

Since then, the Court has frequently been called on to determine which places qualify as part of the public forum. That does not mean that members of the public are then free to speak however and whenever they please. The government may impose reasonable TIME, PLACE, AND MANNER RESTRICTIONS on the assembly or speech. Otherwise, unbearable and unending noise, massive demonstrations that would tie up traffic, and general rowdiness would be unstoppable. But in the guise of regulating the manner of using the public forum, the government may not bar the public from it altogether. In addition to streets and public parks, the Court has held that the sidewalks in general are part of the public forum.[808] For example, the Court overturned a District of Columbia ordinance banning the display of flags and political placards on the sidewalk in front of the Supreme Court building[788] and another ordinance banning certain political signs within five hundred feet of an embassy.[197] In these "quintessential public forums," Justice Byron R. White summarized, the government may not ban public communication. Any time, place, or manner restriction must be "content-neutral, . . . narrowly tailored to serve a significant government interest, and leave open ample alternative channels of communication."[1609]

Beyond the traditional public forum, the Court has considered two other categories:

(1) Public property that the government has "opened for use by the public as a place for expressive activity," even though not constitutionally required to do so. These so-called "limited public forums" include public theaters,[1918] public fair grounds,[891] and school facilities that are opened generally to student group activities.[2202] The government may close these forums, but until it does, it may not discriminate among viewpoints or the content of expression by those who wish to use the space to communicate.

(2) Public property that the government has not opened for public use. Beyond the ordinary time, place, and manner restrictions on public gatherings, the government may prohibit communications in these "nonpublic forums" altogether, as long as the expression is not suppressed merely because the public officials oppose the speaker's viewpoint. Among the places held to be nonpublic forums: jailhouse grounds;[12] advertising space on municipally owned buses;[1144] military bases,[808] including their public streets, as long as the base commander does not selectively permit members of the public to speak there;[685a] home mail boxes;[2104] grounds adjacent to any school building;[797a] the interoffice mail system within a school system;[1609] public utility poles;[401] and even certain sidewalks, depending on their location. In a 1990 case, the Court held that the sidewalks in front of a U.S. Post Office in Maryland are a nonpublic forum, even though sidewalks generally are public forums, because the sidewalk in question was part of Postal Service property leading from a parking lot to the front door and because the Post Office had not

"dedicated" the sidewalk to public uses, although the public could of course use the sidewalk to enter the building.[1090] The Court also upheld a federal EXECUTIVE ORDER limiting the types of charities that may participate in a charitable fund-raising campaign within federal office buildings, holding that the forum in question was not federal office buildings but the right to be part of a charitable solicitation.[469]

See also: DEMONSTRATORS AND DEMONSTRATIONS; SOLICITATION; SPEECH, REGULATION OF CONTENT.

public function By longstanding consensus, constitutional limitations apply only to STATE ACTION—that is, to enactments of legislatures, decisions of courts, or acts of administrative agencies and public officials. The police may not search through your desk without a SEARCH WARRANT, but a visiting guest may do so with constitutional impunity. Notwithstanding the general rule, the Supreme Court has carved out a narrow exception. When a private party is exercising a public function, then the Constitution applies as if the actor were a public entity. The public function rationale has been applied clearly in only two situations: political primaries, though conducted by private POLITICAL PARTIES, may not exclude voters on the basis of race;[2012] and a "company town" may not prohibit people from distributing literature on its streets.[507]

In *Marsh v. Alabama*, the company town case, the Gulf Shipbuilding Corporation owned all the land that constituted Chickasaw, Alabama, a suburb of Mobile. A deputy county sheriff served as the town's policeman and was paid by Gulf. Other businesses rented stores on a "business block," and the United States used one of the buildings as a post office from which six postal employees delivered the mail. A Jehovah's Witness came onto the public shopping street, stood near the post office to distribute religious literature, and was warned that the street was private. She was convicted of TRES-PASS. The Court reversed, holding that the "more an owner, for his advantage, opens up his property for use by the public in general, the more do his rights become circumscribed by the . . . constitutional rights of those who use it." The state may not permit a private town to govern its residents free of constitutional limitations.

In 1968 a 5–4 majority extended the rationale of *Marsh* to private shopping centers, holding that union members may not be convicted of trespass for peacefully PICKETING a supermarket in a privately owned mall.[45] But in 1976 the Court overruled the 1968 shopping center case, holding that a shopping center is not like a company town and the owners may exclude picketing and distribution of literature at their discretion.[950] Despite many other attempts, the Court has consistently declined to extend the public function doctrine. In rejecting the claim that a public utility company may not terminate service without providing the customer a HEARING, the Court said that providing electrical service is not a public function because such services are not "traditionally *exclusively reserved to the State*."[997] The Court similarly declined to find a public function in a state law permitting a warehouse to sell off the goods of an owner who had failed to pay a storage fee.[672]

See also: PROCEDURAL DUE PROCESS; PROCESS RIGHTS; PROCESS THAT IS DUE; SHOPPING CENTERS, ACCESS TO; SOLICITATION.

public interest litigation, *see:* **interest group litigation**

public morals Populist reform couched in the name of public morality is a political force as old as the country. SLAVERY, Prohibition, CHILD LABOR, ABORTION, OBSCENITY AND PORNOGRAPHY, CONTRACEPTION, and DIVORCE have been among their targets. The *United States Reports* are replete with statements by the Supreme Court that the states' POLICE POWER includes the power to regulate conduct injurious to public morals. "The traditional police power of the States," the Supreme Court said in 1991 in its most recent recapitulation of this theme, "is defined as the authority to provide for the public health, safety, and morals."[128] If an offense against morality also causes a more palpable harm, there can be no constitutional difficulty in regulating or outlawing it.

In the PUBLIC ACCOMMODATION cases, the Court said Congress may regulate on the basis of moral judgments as long as it exercises a power given it by the Constitution. For example, it may deal with the disruptive effect of racial discrimination on commerce under the COMMERCE CLAUSE.[888] Conversely, if an act is deemed immoral *solely* because it offends a tenet of someone's religion, the religion clauses of the FIRST AMENDMENT forbid the state from prohibiting it; for example, the state may not punish someone who refuses to worship on the Sabbath.

More equivocal are cases in which the activity is widely believed to "corrupt" society in general but is not provably harmful to one person in particular. The primary example is in the area of sexual activity and expression. In upholding a Georgia law against homosexual sodomy, the Court said that the law "is constantly based on notions of morality, and if all laws representing essentially moral choices are to be invalidated under the DUE PROCESS Clause, the courts will be very busy indeed."[207] In explaining why a state may prevent consenting adults from watching obscene films, the Court said that it "accepted that a legislature could legitimately act on [the conclusion there is a connection between antisocial behavior and obscene material] to protect *'the social interest in order and morality.'* "[1566] Whatever the philosophical merits of the Court's rationale, these offenses did not suffer from the vice of VAGUENESS—the offenses were enacted under a power to protect public morals but were specifically defined. However, when a state purports to outlaw "any act injurious to public morals," without further definition, the law violates due process.[1414]

See also: RELIGIOUS ESTABLISHMENT; SEXUAL FREEDOM; SUNDAY CLOSING LAWS.

public officers, *see:* **office and officers**

public property   Congress has power under Art. IV-§2[3] to "make all needful regulations" and to "dispose" of United States property. In 1840, in a challenge to Congress's power to lease mines on federal property, the argument was raised that leasing is not the same as disposing. The Court disagreed, holding that the form of disposal, whether temporary or permanent, is entirely in Congress's hands.[793] Since then the clause has been broadly construed to give Congress plenary power over federal lands and buildings. Congress may eject settlers and withdraw grazing rights on public lands,[1165] transfer public lands to Indian tribes and delegate to the president the authority to do so,[1877] and block state policies in order to protect wild animals on federal lands.[1083] In the *Tennessee Valley Authority* case, the Court held that Congress has power to authorize TVA to sell electricity because to "dispose" of potential electrical energy it could construct dams and build generating and transmitting equipment.[88] The states may not tax federal lands.[2117] In 1982 the Court relied on this clause to permit the Department of Health, Education, and Welfare to donate a building that had housed a U.S. military hospital to a private religious college. When a group of taxpayers sued, charging that the giveaway violated the ESTABLISHMENT CLAUSE, the Court dismissed the case, saying that the taxpayers had no STANDING to contest any disposal under this clause since they were not personally harmed.[2116]

public purpose doctrine, *see:* **eminent domain**

public safety, *see:* **police power**

public schools, *see:* **schools**

public trial, *see:* **trial, public**

public use, *see:* **eminent domain**

public utility regulation   Under the Public Utility Holding Company Act of 1935, the parent holding companies of most of the nation's gas and electric utilities were required to register with the Securities and Exchange Commission. In 1938 the Court upheld the registration requirements and a provision barring utility companies from using the mails for any purpose if they failed to register.[608] Thereafter the Court sustained as an exercise of Congress's COMMERCE POWER the "death sentence" provision of the act, which essentially permits the government to terminate utility companies not properly serving local communities.[1492, 53]

See also: RATE REGULATION; UTILITIES, REGULATION OF.

publicity, prejudice in criminal trials, *see:* **gag order; prejudicial publicity**

publicity, right to personal   A circus performer whose act consisted of shooting himself out of a cannon sued a television station for broadcasting a tape of his entire act. The station asserted a FIRST AMENDMENT right to show its tape as a news event. The Supreme Court held that there is no protected free speech interest under these circumstances. The states may protect a person's right to be paid for his performances by authorizing suits against those who invade what was termed a right to personal publicity. This was not an instance in which a DAMAGE suit would prevent the public from gaining access to expression; rather, the right to personal publicity simply determines "who gets to do the publishing."[2284]

Puerto Rico, constitutional status of Puerto Rico is a constitutional anomaly, neither state nor territory. Its inhabitants are citizens of the United States under a 1917 federal law. The Puerto Rican Federal Relations Act of 1950, ratified in a Puerto Rican REFERENDUM in 1952, vests the power of local self-government in Puerto Ricans. The Supreme Court has concluded that for most purposes Puerto Rico should be accorded "the degree of autonomy and independence normally associated with a State of the Union,"[636] but it has no voting representation in Congress. Ruling case by case, the Court has made the major constitutional restraints against government power applicable to Puerto Rico—EQUAL PROTECTION,[636] PROCEDURAL DUE PROCESS,[311] SEARCH AND SEIZURE,[2060] and the freedoms guaranteed by the FIRST AMENDMENT.[116] Nevertheless, under its power over U.S. TERRITORIES, Congress may "treat Puerto Rico differently from States so long as there is a rational basis for its actions."[872]

See also: STATES AND STATEHOOD.

punishment, criminal and civil Whether the government may inflict a burden or detriment on a particular individual may depend on whether it has imposed a *punishment.* Both the EIGHTH AMENDMENT ban on cruel and unusual punishments and the EX POST FACTO CLAUSES apply only to punishments meted out following conviction in a criminal prosecution. For example, neither preventive detention of an ACCUSED before trial[1785] nor the deportation of an alien for acts not unlawful at the time they were done[863] are punishments.

In situations involving other constitutional limitations, the Court has distinguished between criminal and civil penalties. A law imposing a burden on a named person or small class of people is not an unconstitutional BILL OF ATTAINDER unless the burden is a punishment. In addition to death, imprisonment, EXPATRIATION, forfeitures, and punitive fines, the

Court has held that a legislative ban on a particular person's holding a job is a punishment. But a law depriving former President Richard M. Nixon of his official papers was held not to be a punishment and hence not a bill of attainder,[1483] nor is a law stripping deported aliens of their right to old-age benefits because of membership in the Communist party.[677] A jail term imposed for CONTEMPT is punishment if it is imposed for contumacious behavior in court, but a jail term imposed for *civil* contempt—for example, when a person refuses to testify though required to do so by law—is not a punishment and therefore not subject to the constitutional provisions dealing with punishment. For instance, the president may PARDON criminal but not civil contempts. Even though Congress has classified a fine as a civil penalty, unless it directly relates to the government's loss and is not simply retributive or deterrent, it is actually a criminal punishment. If a person has already been convicted and sentenced for filing $16,000 in inflated Medicare claims, a later $130,000 civil fine is really a punishment and constitutes an unconstitutional DOUBLE JEOPARDY.[844]

See also: PLEADING THE FIFTH; PROCESS THAT IS DUE; PUNISHMENT, CRUEL AND UNUSUAL.

punishment, cruel and unusual The EIGHTH AMENDMENT prohibits the infliction of "cruel and unusual punishments." Issues arising under this clause fall into four categories: (1) what constitutes a punishment; (2) what punishments by nature are cruel and unusual; (3) whether some punishments are allowable only in certain cases; and (4) whether actual prison practices or only judicial sentences are governed by the clause.

(1) The Supreme Court has ruled that the clause applies only to punishments of those convicted in state[1743] or federal court of having committed crimes. It is not applicable to other penalties, forfeitures, or losses inflicted on people by government, not even corporal punish-

ment of schoolchildren by teachers[980] or deportation of aliens.[863] Nor is it applicable to conditions facing people committed to mental institutions[2279] or to jails awaiting trial.[147]

(2) Until early in the twentieth century, the Court judged whether a punishment was unconstitutionally cruel and unusual by looking to see how closely it resembled the punishments of which the Framers disapproved: tortures such as drawing and quartering, emboweling and burning alive, and beheading. The Court therefore upheld death by firing squad[2206] and by electrocution,[1059] since these forms of capital punishment do not resemble the barbarisms that the Framers wished to eliminate. In 1910 the Court reinterpreted the Eighth Amendment, holding that it has an "expansive and vital character" from which can be drawn meanings more attuned to modern sensibilities.[2176] In 1958 the Court reversed the sentence of a military COURT-MARTIAL stripping a World War II deserter of his American citizenship. The condition of statelessness represents "the total destruction of the individual's status in organized society [and] is a form of punishment more primitive than torture."[2078] The Court also struck down as cruel and unusual a criminal conviction and penalties for the mere status of being a drug addict.[1743] But despite many challenges, the Court has never held that capital punishment is in itself cruel and unusual.

(3) Punishments that by their nature are not cruel and unusual may become so because they are grossly disproportionate to the acts they are meant to punish or because of the ways in which they are administered. In a few cases the Court has applied a rule of PROPORTIONALITY to bar serious punishments for relatively minor crimes; for example, hard labor with chains on the ankles for fifteen years for the crime of falsying public documents,[2176] or life imprisonment with no possibility of parole for minor, nonviolent offenses such as passing bad checks

for small amounts.[1905] In 1972 the Court held that capital punishment was cruel and unusual as applied in several states because of the arbitrary and even "freakish" manner in which juries imposed it.[714] Many years earlier, however, the Court had upheld as not cruel and unusual a state's decision to hold a second electrocution when the electric chair malfunctioned the first time, injuring but not killing the prisoner.[1191]

(4) In 1978 the Court held that "confinement in a prison . . . is a form of punishment subject to scrutiny under the Eighth Amendment standards."[969] For a more detailed discussion, see PRISONERS' RIGHTS.

See also: DEATH PENALTY; PUNISHMENT, CRIMINAL AND CIVIL.

punitive damages   In civil lawsuits, the plaintiff normally seeks to recover an award of money, known as DAMAGES, to compensate for the injury suffered. The damage remedy is not intended to punish the defendant but to recompense the plaintiff. However, in certain civil cases, usually those in which "gross negligence" is involved, the jury may award the plaintiff *punitive damages* as a means of punishing the defendant for wanton misconduct. Because the law leaves to the judge and jury the size of punitive damages awards in any case, the question has arisen whether the lack of a guiding standard violates constitutional limitations. In 1989 the Supreme Court held that the Excessive Fines Clause of the EIGHTH AMENDMENT does not bar punitive damage awards as long as "the government neither has prosecuted the action nor has any right to receive a share of the damages awarded."[263] In 1990 the Court held, 7–1, that the COMMON LAW method of assessing punitive damage awards has been so uniformly upheld that it cannot be considered "so inherently unfair as to deny due process and be *per se* unconstitutional." However, punitive damages are not wholly immune from due process attack. Expressing concern about punitive damages that "run wild," the Court said in 1991 that if a jury has unlimited discretion to impose punitive damages, an award disproportionate to the magnitude of the offense might be unconstitutional. In the case, the Court upheld an award by a jury instructed that it had discretion to take into account the "character and the degree of the wrong," especially because the award was subject to state court review to ensure that it did "not exceed an amount that will accomplish society's goals of punishment and deterrence."[1552]

See also: BAIL AND FINES; PUNISHMENT, CRUEL AND UNUSUAL.

pure food and drug laws, see: **food and drug regulation**

purpose of law, see: **motive, intent, and purpose**

purpose-impact distinction   The Constitution manifests distrust of government in several significant ways, among them the doctrine of SEPARATION OF POWERS and the principle that the LEGISLATIVE POWER is limited and that Congress may act only under its ENUMERATED POWERS. But those powers are so broad that the question repeatedly has been raised whether the Constitution prohibits Congress or state legislatures from passing laws with an illegitimate purpose. In 1810, in *Fletcher v. Peck,* Chief Justice John Marshall said that the Court could not constitutionally be concerned with legislators' motives. But in 1819, in *McCulloch v. Maryland,* he said that Congress could not pass a law to accomplish an unconstitutional purpose under the "pretext" of exercising one of its powers.

Historically, the Court has applied Marshall's pretext rationale quite selectively. For example, in striking down a congressional ban on interstate shipments of goods produced by child labor,[851] the Court said that Congress's purpose was to invade the powers of states (over regulations of the workplace), even though the law was written in the form of a PROHIBITION OF COMMERCE that was entirely within Congress's power.[369] But the very next year the Court upheld Congress's power to tax narcotics sales, even though the clear purpose of the tax was to regulate drug usage in the states, just the kind of regulatory power the Court had said Congress did not possess.[566]

In the arena of CIVIL RIGHTS, however, the Court has held for more than a century that when a law or a government action on its face is nondiscriminatory, the courts must look to its underlying purpose to determine its constitutionality. In *Yick Wo v. Hopkins* in 1886, the Court confronted a San Francisco ordinance requiring a commercial laundry to be housed only in a stone or brick building unless the Board of Supervisors granted an exception. On its face, the law did not discriminate against any class of people. In practice, however, the board granted exceptions for wooden buildings only to non-Chinese laundry operators. The Court held that the board's exceptions policy violated the EQUAL PROTECTION CLAUSE, because the discriminatory effect of the policy was manifest and the board had offered no reason for the disparity in result. Therefore, said the Court, the inescapable conclusion was that the board's purpose was "hostility to the race and nationality to which the [Chinese laundry operators] belong." A purpose to discriminate on racial grounds is unconstitutional.

Since then the Court has often, though not always, found an unconstitutional purpose underlying neutral laws when the state can give no plausible explanation for the discriminatory impact. In 1915 the Court struck down an Oklahoma voter registration requirement that all persons must pass a literacy test except those whose ancestors had been eligible to vote in 1866, before the FIFTEENTH AMENDMENT, the equal voting rights amendment, was ratified.[830] The law had the effect of permitting all illiterate whites and no illiterate blacks to vote. The

Court saw plainly that the only purpose of the law was to evade the commandment of the Fifteenth Amendment. In 1964 the Court struck down a Prince Edward County, Virginia, scheme under which all public schools were closed and all-white private schools were supported with public tax dollars.[814] Although the state could decide to let a county abandon its public schools and help fund private ones, it could not do so when the only reason was to avoid desegregation.

However, when a law has a discriminatory *impact* but a nondiscriminatory *purpose,* the Court is unlikely to find a constitutional violation. In 1976, in *Washington v. Davis,* a District of Columbia qualifying test for police officers resulted in the failure of many more black than white applicants. The exam tested verbal and reading facility and was developed by the U.S. Civil Service Commission for nationwide use. The Court held that because the test was "reasonably related to the requirements of the police recruit training program" and was not designed or operated "to discriminate against otherwise qualified blacks," the department could constitutionally continue to use it.

The question, then, is what will suffice as proof that a law neutral on its face but with a disproportionate impact on a racial group had INVIDIOUS DISCRIMINATION as its purpose. The Court has said the answer depends on the circumstances. In some cases—for example, that of the Chinese laundry operators and the systematic exclusion of blacks from all juries[1967]— the answer is that *impact* alone makes the inference statistically indisputable. But in other, more equivocal, cases the Court has refused to draw the inference. In 1971, for instance, it allowed Jackson, Mississippi, to close down its municipal swimming pools after being ordered to desegregate them, because the city had no

affirmative duty to operate pools and there was evidence that the closing was motivated, at least in part, by the fear of violence and the loss of revenues—constitutional, nondiscriminatory purposes.[1558] Justice Lewis F. Powell said in a 1977 case that to determine whether the legislature or administrator has intended to discriminate the courts might look to the "historical background of the decision," the "specific sequence of events leading up to the challenged decision," including sudden departures from normal procedures, and the statements made by legislators or administrators when the decision was made.[77] Applying these principles in 1979, the Court refused to disturb a Massachusetts law that "overwhelmingly" favors male applicants to civil service jobs because of an absolute lifetime VETERANS' PREFERENCE. Although few female applicants were veterans, the Court concluded that the state acted nondiscriminatorily to favor veterans, not men.[1612]

In contexts other than equal protection, the Court has held to the principle that neutral laws are valid unless a purpose to discriminate can be shown. For example, voting laws do not violate the Fifteenth Amendment solely because they have a disproportionate impact.[1370] But the Court has also concluded that even though the courts may not void neutral laws without proof of discrimination, under its power to enforce equal voting rights, Congress may require states to amend their voting laws and policies solely because of the impact that they have on minority groups.[1756]

See also: DE FACTO–DE JURE DISTINCTION; MOTIVE, INTENT, AND PURPOSE; RACIAL DISCRIMINATION; SEGREGATION AND INTEGRATION; STATISTICS, USE OF; VOTING, RIGHT TO.

pursuit of happiness, *see:* **happiness, pursuit of**

Q

qualifications for office The Constitution prescribes few formal qualifications for holding federal office and none for holding state office. Under Art. I-§2[2], members of the House of Representatives must be at least twenty-five years of age and have been CITIZENS of the United States for no less than seven years on the day they take the OATH OF OFFICE. A similar rule for senators in Art. I-§3[3] requires that members-elect be at least thirty years of age and citizens for nine years. These clauses also provide that all members of Congress must have been residents of the states from which they were chosen on the day elected. Under Art. II-§1[5], the president of the United States must be a "natural-born citizen," with the exception of early presidents born before the United States was created; they were required to be citizens. Presidents must be at least thirty-five years old and have resided at least fourteen years in the United States. Under the TWELFTH AMENDMENT the vice president must meet the same qualifications.

Although these are the only formal qualifications, the Constitution prescribes a few disqualifications. Under the TWENTY-SECOND AMENDMENT, presidents may serve only two full terms of their own. The maximum any president may serve is ten years; a vice president who succeeded to the office on the death or resignation of the president and then served less than two years may be reelected to two full terms. Under Art. I-§6[2], no sitting member of Congress may serve in the EXECUTIVE BRANCH. Under Art. II-§1[2], no member of Congress or of the executive branch may serve in the ELECTORAL COLLEGE. Section 3 of the FOURTEENTH AMENDMENT disqualifies from any federal or state office any person who having taken an oath of either federal or state office thereafter "engaged in insurrection or rebellion" against the United States; however, Congress may remove this disability by a two-thirds vote. *See also:* COMMITMENT TO OTHER BRANCHES.

qualified immunity, *see:* **immunity from suit**

qualified rights A right that may be limited under certain circumstances is known as a "qualified right." It is not a constitutional term, although it has had constitutional recognition, most famously in *Roe v. Wade,* the ABORTION case in 1973. The Court held that a woman has a qualified right to terminate her pregnancy. The right is nearly absolute during the first trimester, but the state may regulate the abortion procedure after the end of the first trimester. In the third trimester, there is no constitutional right to abortion at all. Similarly, the Court has held that the press has a qualified right to be present during the VOIR DIRE examination of jurors for a criminal trial.[1659] The press may be barred from the hearing on a showing "that closure is essential to preserve higher values and is narrowly tailored to serve that interest." Other rights generally stated to be absolute are often in fact qualified by circumstances. For example, the right to TRAVEL is obviously qualified by a prison sentence, and the state may also burden the right to travel by imposing penalties on parents who flee to escape paying support obligations for their children.[1030]

quarantine laws   To prevent the spread of disease, states may enact quarantine laws that prevent certain crops, animals, or goods from being exported or imported, even though the laws will interfere with INTERSTATE COMMERCE. The Court has sustained a ruling of a state sanitation commission barring anyone from bringing cattle, horses, or mules into the state during an anthrax epidemic.[1077] Similarly, it upheld a law prohibiting the sale of condensed milk not made from unadulterated milk,[890] a ban on cattle imported without a health certificate from the state of origin,[1359] and a law requiring cosmetics to be registered with state health officials to determine their safety.[205] However, health laws may not exclude products "beyond what is necessary for any proper quarantine."[1896] In 1978 the Court struck down a New Jersey law that forbade landfill operators from importing solid and liquid garbage into the state. The usual quarantine laws require the destruction of all toxic products, whether imported or homemade, because the danger to health lies in the product itself. But the New Jersey law was not concerned with the health hazards from domestic wastes, which could be dumped without limit in domestic landfills. The law therefore discriminated against interstate commerce.[1621]

See also: GAME LAWS.

quartering of soldiers   The THIRD AMENDMENT provides that during peacetime soldiers may not be quartered in anyone's home without the owner's consent. In time of war, the United States could presumably requisition homes for the use of military personnel, but only if Congress has first enacted a law prescribing whose homes are to be requisitioned and in what manner. This is the only right in the BILL OF RIGHTS that has apparently never been violated. The Supreme Court has never heard a case testing the meaning of the Third Amendment.

quasi-suspect classification, *see:* **suspect classification**

quorum   A quorum is the minimum number of people legally sufficient to transact official business. Art. I-§5[1] provides that for Congress to enact laws and conduct other business a quorum is a simple majority. Under the TWELFTH AMENDMENT, when the election of the president has been thrown into the House of Representatives, a quorum of two-thirds of the states is necessary; representatives from at least thirty-four states must be present. When the Senate selects a vice president, a quorum is two-thirds of all senators, or sixty-seven. The Court has occasionally been called on to determine whether a congressional investigating committee can validly issue a subpoena without a quorum (yes[266]) or perjury can be committed before a committee lacking a quorum (no[396]), but its answers were not based on constitutional interpretation.

quotas, racial, *see:* **racial discrimination**

R

race, classification by Until the ratification of the FOURTEENTH AMENDMENT in 1868, the Constitution did not even theoretically bar laws that classified people by their race. Although the EQUAL PROTECTION CLAUSE was clearly intended to prohibit racially discriminatory classifications, its purpose was not realized until decades later. The Court's most grievous failure to bar racial classifications came in 1896 in *Plessy v. Ferguson* when it announced the SEPARATE BUT EQUAL doctrine, approving legally enforceable segregation of the races. This acquiescence in laws embodying racial classifications was foreshadowed in several opinions of the Court and buttressed in several later ones.[1549] With the declaration in BROWN V. BOARD OF EDUCATION that segregated schooling was unconstitutional, the Court signaled a larger development: that any law invidiously classifying on racial ground would be struck down. The Court actually had announced this constitutional conclusion a decade earlier in *Korematsu v. United States*, ironically upholding JAPANESE-AMERICAN EXCLUSION AND RELOCATION while announcing that racial classifications are suspect and requiring courts to subject them to "rigid scrutiny."

By the 1960s the Court was firmly committed to the task of rooting out most racial classifications in laws and the administration of public policy, including laws prohibiting MISCEGENATION[1200] and cohabitation by interracial married couples,[1304] child custody awards based solely on the race of the parent,[1560] laws requiring a candidate's race to be listed on the ballot,[61] and laws requiring separate listings by race on various types of public records, like tax rolls.[1996] In short, any racial classification enacted for an invidious purpose or that cannot be justified by the most COMPELLING INTEREST is invalid. Few racial classifications aside from the supposedly benign use of race for AFFIRMATIVE ACTION will ever be sustained. A rare example is the racial segregation of prisoners when it becomes overwhelmingly necessary to maintain order.[1136]

See also: INVIDIOUS DISCRIMINATION; PURPOSE-IMPACT DISTINCTION; RACIAL DISCRIMINATION; SEGREGATION AND INTEGRATION.

race, color, or previous condition of servitude This descriptive phrase is located in the FIFTEENTH AMENDMENT, which denies the states and the federal government power to abridge the right to vote on any of these bases. The phrase covers a person's national origins as well.

See also: VOTING, RIGHT TO.

racial balance, *see:* affirmative action;
racial discrimination; segregation and
integration

racial discrimination   Ratified in 1868, the
EQUAL PROTECTION CLAUSE of the FOUR-
TEENTH AMENDMENT soon proved no deterrent
to blatantly discriminatory acts directed
against former slaves. When, however, a law
strictly enacted a glaring inequality, the Court
dutifully struck it down—for example, in 1880
a West Virginia law excluding all blacks from
criminal juries,[1967] in 1914 a law forbidding
blacks from using the only dining car on a
railroad,[1279] and in 1917 a law that forbade blacks
from moving onto a block more than half of
whose residents were white.[267] But these were
feeble straws in a very gentle wind. In 1896, in
PLESSY V. FERGUSON, the Court engrafted onto
the Equal Protection Clause the doctrine of
SEPARATE BUT EQUAL, which would leave large
sections of the country wholly segregated for
more than half a century.

Following its decision to end segregated
schools in BROWN V. BOARD OF EDUCATION in
1954 the Court began to strike down not only
official segregation but also diverse sorts of
laws that classified by race and racial laws and
practices that discriminated in a wide spectrum
of political and legal activities, including voting, jury service, political candidacy, and MAR-
RIAGE. No less important, the Court undertook
a dramatic rereading of federal power—congressional, executive, and judicial—to enact
laws and carry out policies designed to end
racial discrimination. Particularly noteworthy
were the Court's decisions that the courts may
not enforce racially RESTRICTIVE COVENANTS,
that through the COMMERCE POWER Congress
may prohibit discrimination in PUBLIC ACCOM-
MODATIONS, that the THIRTEENTH AMENDMENT
gives Congress the direct power to outlaw private refusals to deal with members of another
race, and that the FIFTEENTH AMENDMENT

gives Congress sweeping power to eliminate
racial discrimination in voting. Much more
heatedly debated is the doctrine of AFFIRMA-
TIVE ACTION, which grew out of the unexceptionable observation that it would be necessary
for the courts to take race into account to remedy a past act of purposeful discrimination.
Whether the "benign" use of race may be used
for purposes other than a judicial remedy remains very much an open question. If preferences could be granted on a racial basis simply
to improve the lot of a particular group, then
the command of the Equal Protection
Clause—that states may not deny to "any person" the equal protection of the laws—would
be thwarted. As the Court has repeatedly said,
equal protection is for individual persons, not
for abstract groups.[1705]

Along the way, certain enduring principles
have been fashioned that seem relatively im-
pervious to the considerable shifts of political
values and temperament on the Supreme
Court during the past four decades. Invidious
explicit racial discrimination is unconstitutional. A statute is also unconstitutional if
though it appears neutral, it was enacted to
discriminate. But a law not intended to discriminate is not unconstitutional merely because it has a disparate impact on different
races.[2159] Finally, the Equal Protection Clause
bars discrimination against a person of any
race, not only blacks. Though the Fourteenth
Amendment was ratified as a primary means of
protecting those who had been slaves, the
Court has long recognized that "if a law should
be passed [discriminating against] all naturalized Celtic Irishmen" the Equal Protection
Clause would be no less violated.[1967] Moreover,
Congress has power under the Thirteenth
Amendment to prohibit discrimination not
only against blacks[1028] but also against whites in
general[1293] and nonblack minorities.[1847, 1784]

See also: ACCESS TO BALLOT; CIVIL RIGHTS AND CIVIL
LIBERTIES; CIVIL RIGHTS CASES; DE FACTO–DE JURE

radio, *see:* **access to broadcasting; broadcasting, regulation of**

random stops, *see:* **search and seizure: random stops and checkpoints**

rape, *see:* **death penalty; statutory rape**

rate regulation In 1877 the Supreme Court declared in *Munn v. Illinois* that the states' PO-LICE POWER includes the power to regulate the rates of PUBLIC UTILITIES—in that case, the rates of grain elevators. With the reasonableness of the rates, said Chief Justice Morrison Waite, the courts are not concerned. That the power "may be abused . . . is no argument against it. For protection against abuses by legislatures the people must resort to the polls." But as the legislatures increasingly turned to regulating railroad rates, the Court's resolve to avoid rate cases weakened. In 1886 Waite himself said that a state may not set a rate that is confiscatory— that is, so low that it amounts to a TAKING OF PROPERTY without JUST COMPENSATION.[1684] By 1890 Waite had died and a new Court was ready to retreat wholesale from the confident assertion in *Munn.* "The reasonablenes of rates . . . is eminently a question for judicial investi- gation," the Court now said.[391] By 1898 it had launched the FAIR-VALUE FALLACY, holding that a utility is entitled to a fair return on the value of its property, determined ultimately by the courts.[1899] At the same time, the cases were not uniformly hostile to the rate setters. The Court declared that it was not the business of the courts to set rates or to revise the orders of rate-setting ADMINISTRATIVE AGENCIES, as long as the rates set are fair and reasonable under the circumstances;[1699, 988] nor were the courts

generally entitled to "reexamine and weigh all the evidence" considered by the rate author- ity.[1793]

However, in 1920 the Court flip-flopped. In the *Ben Avon* case,[1524] it said that DUE PROCESS requires a court independently to reassess any evidence presented to an agency to support a rate claimed by the railroad or other utility to be confiscatory. Not until 1944 did the Court finally return almost to the point where it began, holding that the method of rate setting was for the legislatures and the agencies they create, not for the courts, although it did not recant the power to set aside a wholly unrea- sonable rate.[648] Swept away were cases de- cided over more than forty years in which the Court attempted to pluck from the Con- stitution particular formulas for setting fair rates.

See also: AFFECTED WITH A PUBLIC INTEREST DOCTRINE; ECONOMIC DUE PROCESS.

ratification, *see:* **amendments to Constitution; Constitution, ratification of**

Ratifiers' intent, *see:* **constitutional interpretation; original intent**

ratio of representation Art. I-§2[3] specifies that each member of Congress should repre- sent no fewer than thirty thousand constitu- ents. In 1789, in what would have been the First Amendment had it been ratified, Congress sent to the states along with the BILL OF RIGHTS an amendment that required a change in the mini- mum ratio when the population grew suffi- ciently that the House of Representatives would consist of more than one hundred mem- bers. The ratio would go to 1:40,000 until the House grew to two hundred members, when the ratio would become 1:50,000. Under this proposed amendment, there could never there- after be fewer than two hundred members in the House of Representatives nor a larger ratio than 1:50,000. The states failed to ratify the proposed amendment, leaving Congress free to decide for itself how many House seats there should be, as long as the 1:30,000 ratio is observed. In 1929 Congress set the number of representatives at 435. As a consequence, House seats are reallocated every ten years following the CENSUS. The current ratio of representation is about 1:575,000.

rational basis or relationship test   When the Supreme Court repudiated the doctrine of ECONOMIC DUE PROCESS in the 1930s, it advanced a new test for determining whether a law runs afoul of the Due Process Clause. In 1934 Justice Owen J. Roberts, speaking for a 5–4 majority upholding a law regulating the price of milk, said that due process demands "only that the law shall not be unreasonable, arbitrary or capricious, and that the means selected shall have a real and substantial relation to the object sought to be attained."[1440] In 1938 Justice Harlan Fiske Stone said in *United States v. Carolene Products* that "regulatory legislation affecting ordinary commercial transactions" is constitutional unless it fails to rest "upon some rational basis within the knowledge and experience of the legislators."

Since then, the Court has never invalidated a state economic or business regulation on the ground that it was irrational or lacked a substantial relationship to its purpose. The rational basis test is used also for determining the validity of legislative classifications under EQUAL PROTECTION. The Court has said that a "statutory discrimination will not be set aside if any state of facts reasonably may be conceived to justify it."[1297] In judging legislation under this test, the Court refuses even to let the law's opponent offer proof that it does not serve its intended purpose, as long as the legislature *"could rationally have decided"* that the law would promote its objective.[1356] Moreover, "rational distinctions may be made with substantially

less than mathematical exactitude."[1454] The Court has been almost, but not quite, as deferential to economic legislation under equal protection as under due process. It has upheld MANDATORY RETIREMENT laws,[1265] apparently discriminatory OCCUPATIONAL LICENSING laws,[2224, 658] discriminatory SUNDAY CLOSING LAWS,[1297] distinctions among types of aged needy people receiving federal "comfort allowances,"[1827] laws limiting the amount a family can receive in child welfare benefits,[511] distinctions for purposes of receiving federal food stamps between households with closely related people and those containing distantly related or unrelated people,[1212] laws barring former drug users from holding nonsafety public jobs,[1467] laws making it politically difficult to build low-rent housing,[1006] and filing fees required to be paid by indigents to seek bankruptcy protection[1098] and to contest the denial of welfare benefits.[1542]

On the other hand, purporting to apply the rational basis test, the Court has occasionally struck down laws because the burdens placed on certain groups of people were discriminatory and irrational. But the Court's reasoning in many of these cases seems to be closer to the STRICT SCRUTINY that it reserves for laws classifying on the basis of race or some other SUSPECT CLASSIFICATION. For example, it struck down as irrational a law distinguishing among types of illegitmate children for purposes of receiving Society Security disability benefits,[1014] a state property tax system that disproportionately taxed property on the basis of when it was sold rather than on its true value,[38] and a zoning ordinance that forbade the construction of a group home for the mentally retarded but that permitted the operation, among other things, of hospitals, sanitariums, and nursing homes for convalescents or the aged.[407]

See also: CLASSIFICATIONS, UNDER- AND OVERINCLUSIVE; ECONOMIC DISCRIMINATION; ILLEGITIMACY; ONE STEP AT A TIME; WEALTH CLASSIFICATION AND DISCRIMINATION.

readers' rights The FIRST AMENDMENT is ordinarily viewed as protecting the rights of those who speak and publish, as FREEDOM OF SPEECH and FREEDOM OF THE PRESS seem clearly to imply. Is there a correlative right of listeners and readers to *receive* information? In a sense, the right to speak and the right to hear may be opposite sides of the same coin, or even opposite edges of the same side. If the government tells a newspaper "You have the right to publish but no one has the right to read what you print, so the police are going to impound your edition to keep anyone from seeing it," a classic PRIOR RESTRAINT would be the result. But it often makes sense as well to talk of an independent right of readers and listeners.

For example, in 1965 the Court struck down a federal law requiring the post office to refrain from delivering "communist political propaganda" unless the addressee specifically requested each piece of mail after being notified of its arrival.[1114] In one of the first COMMERCIAL SPEECH cases, the Court permitted consumers to challenge a law prohibiting pharmacists from advertising prices of prescription drugs.[2131] The Court spoke of the consumers' right to receive the information, even though the law did not bar any particular consumer from calling up a drugstore to inquire. And in a case the dimensions of which remain to be seen, the Court tentatively concluded that the right of public school students to read books in the school library means that school authorities may not remove books claimed to be offensive if they intended by doing so to deny students "access to ideas" with which the authorities disagreed.[182] The right of readers and listeners to *receive* information unfiltered by the government is different from their right to *obtain* information that others wish to withhold.

See also: RIGHT TO KNOW.

reapportionment, *see:* **apportionment of political districts**

reason of state Reason of state or, as it is sometimes known, *raison d'état,* is the political doctrine that the state may do whatever it must to ensure its survival. Derived from Machiavelli and long used by totalitarian governments, the reason-of-state doctrine is fraught with peril to democratic institutions. It has no constitutional basis, but neither has the Court rejected it altogether, at various times allowing considerations of NATIONAL SECURITY to lead it to narrow interpretations of constitutional limitations.

Concurring in *Dennis v. United States,* the 1951 Communist conspiracy case, Justice Felix Frankfurter suggested that one reason to uphold convictions under the SMITH ACT was that the courts must forswear upsetting political decisions about the "outcome of [contending] forces," since the government, not the courts, has "knowledge of the topmost secrets of nations." On the other hand, the Court rejected President Harry S. Truman's assertion that in the national interest he had the inherent EXECUTIVE POWER to seize the nation's steel mills because of a threatened strike[2282] and President Richard M. Nixon's insistence that the president may order foreign intelligence wiretaps free of constitutional restraints.[2102]

See also: IMPLIED AND INHERENT POWERS; SEARCH AND SEIZURE: WIRETAPPING AND ELECTRONIC SURVEILLANCE; STEEL SEIZURE CASE.

reasonable doubt Guilt in a criminal prosecution must be proven in every element of the crime beyond a "reasonable doubt."[2234] This highest standard of proof in the legal system does not mean absolute certainty but the certainty that comes from excluding unreasonable, fanciful doubts. In assessing the voluntariness of a confession, a mere preponderance-of-the-evidence standard will do, although the states may require a higher standard if they wish.[1143] Likewise, the Court has ruled that the reasonable doubt standard is unnecessary to determine whether evidence seized by the police must be excluded from trial,[1271] whether MIRANDA RULES have been violated,[436] and whether leads that derived from an unlawfully obtained confession turned up evidence that would inevitably have been discovered and therefore be admissible at trial even though the confession must be excluded.[1482]

However, the Court has held that when a witness identifies a suspect at an unconstitutional LINEUP, the prosecutor must prove with "clear and convincing" evidence, a standard higher than preponderance of the evidence, that the witness's in-court identification of the suspect was not tainted by having picked the suspect out at the lineup.[2139] Although the reasonable doubt standard is ordinarily used to benefit the defendant, it sometimes favors the prosecution. For example, in a HABEAS CORPUS proceeding, a federal court may not overturn a DEATH PENALTY unless no judge or jury could have found beyond a reasonable doubt that the evidence was sufficient to warrant it.[1158]

See also: COUNSEL, ASSISTANCE OF; EXCLUSIONARY RULE; HARMLESS ERROR; PROOF, STANDARD OF.

reasonableness of search, *see:* **search and seizure: reasonableness of**

rebellion   Section 3 of the FOURTEENTH AMENDMENT disqualifies federal, state, and military officeholders who have sworn an oath to support the Constitution from ever holding any civil or military OFFICE of the United States or of any state or from serving in the ELECTORAL COLLEGE if they engaged in insurrection or rebellion against the United States or aided an enemy of the United States. This section was intended to exclude Confederates who fought against the Union in the Civil War from Congress and all state and federal offices. The Supreme Court has never been called on to interpret this section, but the lower courts concluded that it is not self-executing and Congress must enact legislation to give it effect. Because the framers of the Fourteenth Amendment did not intend disqualification necessarily to be permanent or universal, but rather to ensure the immediate security of the nation, Section 3 empowers Congress to remove the disability by a two-thirds vote in each house. Congress exempted many people from the disqualification even before the Fourteenth Amendment was ratified, and in 1869 Congress enacted amnesty bills restoring officeholding rights to more than one thousand former Confederates. At the urging of President Ulysses S. Grant, Congress in 1872 exempted everyone covered by Section 3 except senators and representatives of the Thirty-sixth and Thirty-seventh Congresses, federal judges, U.S. military officers, heads of EXECUTIVE DEPARTMENTS, and foreign ministers who had engaged in rebellion. Disqualification against even these people was removed in 1898. Section 3 has not been resorted to since then.

rebuttable presumption, *see:* **presumption, irrebuttable; presumptions**

recall   Recall is a procedure used in many states through which voters may remove elected or even appointed public officials from OFFICE. Unlike IMPEACHMENT, through which the legislature may remove public officials, there is no implication in a recall that the officeholder has engaged in criminal wrongdoing. Because the Constitution specifies the duration of terms for elected federal officials, it presumably would be unconstitutional for Congress or the states to pass a law permitting recall elections for themselves, the president, or the vice president. Likewise, the APPOINTMENT AND REMOVAL POWER would preclude a recall procedure for federally appointed officials; federal judges serve "during good behavior" and may be removed only by impeachment. The issue of recall for federal officials has never arisen in the Court.

See also: TERM LIMITATION.

recess appointments   Under Art. II-§2[3], the president is empowered to "fill up all vacancies" in federal OFFICES that may "happen" when the Senate is recessed. A person named under a "recess appointment" takes office immediately, but the tenure of office lasts only until the next session of Congress ends. Although the clause seems to say that a recess appointment may be made only if the vacancy occurred *during* the recess, the Supreme Court has never quarreled with an understanding since the 1820s that presidents may fill up any vacancies that "happen to exist," even if the office was actually vacated while the Senate was in session. If the person is to remain in office beyond the end of the next session, he or she must win Senate confirmation.

Recess appointees do not always succeed. For example, in 1795 President George Washington named John Rutledge chief justice of the United States under a recess appointment. Rutledge took his seat immediately, but the Senate failed to confirm him, and so he was forced to leave the Supreme Court in 1796. The recess appointment power is sometimes adroitly used to circumvent the constitutional confirmation procedure.

See also: APPOINTMENT AND REMOVAL POWER.

recess of Congress   The decision to recess or adjourn sessions of Congress is for Congress alone to make, except that under Art. I-§5[4] both houses must agree to a recess of more than three days, and under Art. II-§3 the president may determine the adjournment if the houses disagree. This power has never been exercised. Under this same clause, the president may convene special sessions of the whole Congress or either house, and on many momentous occasions, presidents have done so. For example,

President Franklin D. Roosevelt convened Congress the day after the attack on Pearl Harbor on December 7, 1941.

recidivist statutes, *see:* **proportionality of sentence**

recognition of nations, *see:* **diplomatic recognition**

redistribution of wealth and income   The constitutionality of government policies that redistribute wealth and income was once seriously doubted. The Supreme Court's many ECONOMIC DUE PROCESS cases rested in part on the proposition that it was illegitimate for the states to transfer wealth in the guise of laws regulating rates that could be charged or conditions under which labor could be employed. By limiting the number of hours an employee could work, the law was said to unconstitutionally skew the actual or natural price of wages in favor of the employee. In essence, the proponents of this view held that the law effected a TAKING OF PROPERTY without JUST COMPENSATION. It was this theory that Justice Oliver Wendell Holmes lambasted in his famous dissent in LOCHNER V. NEW YORK, insisting that the Constitution does not embody any particular economic theory. With the death of economic due process in the late 1930s, constitutional restraints on redistribution policies came to an end.

See also: INCOME TAX; SPENDING POWER; TAXING POWER; WEALTH CLASSIFICATION AND DISCRIMINATION.

redistricting, *see:* **apportionment of political districts**

redress of grievances, *see:* **freedom of petition**

referendum   Early in the 1992 presidential campaign, nonparty candidate Ross Perot suggested that through some form of electronic linkup the people might be consulted directly about laws to be enacted. Perot even hinted at a constitutional amendment barring Congress from passing tax laws, leaving taxation to the people directly. Direct lawmaking of that sort is known as a "referendum."

The child of the Progressive movement, the referendum and its sibling, the INITIATIVE, were born near the turn of the century to provide a direct-democracy alternative to hidebound legislatures. In 1912 the Supreme Court turned aside a constitutional challenge under the GUARANTEE CLAUSE.[1554] Since then, many states have established referenda for many issues, submitting to the voters, for example, whether to authorize bonds for construction projects and whether to restructure municipal governments. In general, the Court has upheld the use of the referendum at the state and municipal level as a device for deciding issues of particular concern to those permitted to vote in them, even when the outcome does not depend on a bare majority or even on a single majority vote.

For example, the Court sustained a law requiring a sixty percent majority to approve the incurring of bond debt within a POLITICAL SUBDIVISION.[781] Distinguishing the principle of ONE PERSON, ONE VOTE, the Court noted that the requirement of a supermajority to decide a particular issue is not the same as weighted voting to choose legislative representatives. The Court also upheld a New York procedure by which a county charter can be adopted only if separate majorities of city and noncity residents within the county agree.[1180] Voters may approve or veto ZONING changes through a referendum, as long as the general electorate as a whole is polled on whether a particular change should take effect.[594] But the Court has rejected a system by which neighbors as a whole were empowered to vote on a particular zoning variance by someone with an interest adverse

to theirs.[2156] The latter decision resembles the Court's rulings under different constitutional provisions that a state may not delegate power to a church to determine whether liquor licenses should be allocated[1122] or to one group of professionals to determine whether to license competitors.[749]

A referendum constitutes STATE ACTION. The people are collectively bound by the same constitutional restraints that bind the representative institutions of government, including DUE PROCESS and EQUAL PROTECTION.[1708] The Court saw no equal protection difficulty in a referendum procedure to approve or reject decisions of local authorities to build low-income housing.[1006] A referendum procedure at the federal level would be unconstitutional, because BICAMERALISM and PRESENTMENT would be lacking if the people were asked to approve a law directly. Art. I-§7[2,3] explicitly requires both houses of Congress to enact a bill, which must be submitted directly to the president, not to the people, for approval.[979]

See also: LEGISLATIVE VETO; REPRESENTATION; VETO POWER; VOTING, RIGHT TO.

registration, compelled, *see:* **conscription; war power**

regulation, *see:* **administrative agencies and bureaucratic goverment; administrative law; Dormant Commerce Clause; economic regulation; interstate commerce**

regulatory agencies, *see:* **administrative agencies and bureaucratic government**

regulatory laws Although not strictly on a constitutional basis, the Supreme Court has distinguished among ordinary criminal laws and laws aimed at regulating and ameliorating the conditions of an interdependent industrial society. Convictions under ordinary criminal laws, such as those against murder and theft, generally require that the defendant have knowledge of wrongdoing, or, as it is called, a "guilty mind."

Interpreting a federal law against theft of government property, the Supreme Court reversed the conviction of a man who took spent bomb casings from an uninhabited site in Michigan that the Air Force used as a target range and that local hunters used to shoot deer. Believing the property abandoned and of no use to anyone, the defendant salvaged the casings for their scrap value, but the trial court refused to let the jury consider his state of mind. In effect, the trial judge said that anyone would be guilty of theft for picking up and taking home something belonging to someone else, even though reasonably believing the thing abandoned. In reversing, Justice Robert H. Jackson explained that, as usually understood, an act is a crime only when constituted "from concurrence of an evil-meaning mind with an evil-doing hand." [1388]

However, some kinds of "public welfare offenses"—actions that endanger people in the use of such things as food, drugs, highways, and the machinery of production—have been dealt with more harshly in various administrative regulations. The Court has upheld the application of these laws under certain circumstances to people who neither intended to violate the laws nor had any awareness of wrongdoing. In a leading case, the Court in 1975 upheld the conviction of the chief executive officer of a national retail food chain for failing to supervise his subordinates, to whom he had delegated the responsibility of ensuring that foodstuffs stored in the company's warehouses were safe from contamination by rodents. The U.S. Food and Drug Administration notified the company that its food was being contaminated in violation of the Federal Food, Drug, and Cosmetic Act. The CEO was aware of the FDA's letter but mistakenly relied on subordinates to deal with the problem. Chief Justice E. Warren Burger said that even though the CEO had no personal knowledge of his subordinates' failure to remedy the unsanitary conditions, he could be held criminally responsible for it. "In the interest of the larger good it puts the burden of acting at hazard upon a person otherwise innocent but standing in responsible relation to a public danger." [1567]

The requirement of a guilty mind has a constitutional dimension when a particular constitutional guarantee is implicated. For example, in 1959 the Court said that under the FIRST AMENDMENT it is unconstitutional to convict a bookseller for possessing an obscene book without showing that he knew the contents to be obscene. [1887]

See also: ADMINISTRATIVE LAW; ECONOMIC REGULATION; POLICE POWER.

rehearing   On rare occasions, an appellate court may agree at a party's urging to reconsider its decision. Under its rules, the Supreme Court will accept a petition to rehear a case only when a majority of justices votes to do so, and that rarely happens. A case is sometimes reheard when there was an AFFIRMANCE BY AN EQUALLY DIVIDED SUPREME COURT. Since a 4–4 vote has no precedential value but simply leaves the lower court's decision undisturbed, the return of an ill justice or the arrival of a newly appointed one may lead to a more satisfactory resolution of the case.

released time   The phrase "released time" refers to the practice in many schools of permitting students to attend religious instruction during school hours. In 1948 the Court struck down, under the ESTABLISHMENT CLAUSE, an Illinois law allowing religious teachers to come into public schools to give religious instruction during regular school hours. The program was unconstitutional, said Justice Hugo L. Black, because tax-supported property was used for religious purposes and because students compelled by law to attend school were released from their secular classes on condition that they attend religious classes and not for other purposes.[977]

But four years later, in an opinion by Justice William O. Douglas, the Court sustained a New York City policy of releasing public school students during the school day to go to religious centers for religious instruction.[2288] Douglas denied that there was any evidence of "coercion to get public school students into religious classrooms" and suggested it would be unconstitutional for a public school teacher to coerce a student into taking religious instruction. Dissenting, Justice Felix Frankfurter sardonically noted that there was no proof of coercion because the lower courts had refused to let those who objected to the practice offer any. Also dissenting, Justice Robert H. Jackson noted that rather than shortening the school day, school authorities were suspending school time for one purpose only—religious exercises. Those who did not wish to participate in religious activities were forced to remain in school. The program, said Jackson, was thus palpably a preference for religion: "The day that this country ceases to be free for irreligion it will cease to be free for religion—except for the sect that can win political power."

See also: RELIGIOUS ESTABLISHMENT; SCHOOLS, RELIGION IN.

religion, definition of   The ESTABLISHMENT CLAUSE prohibits public schools from teaching the divinity of Christ or Allah. It does not stand in the way of teaching the theory of quantum physics or evolution. Why the schools may teach scientific but not religious dogma depends on the constitutional meaning of religion. The short answer is that there is none, or at least that the Court has never given a satisfactory one. Religious claims are pressed in many contexts—SOLICITATION of funds, CONSCIENTIOUS OBJECTION to military combat, ritual practices, living arrangements, and educa-

tional curricula, to name just a few. In practice, whether a particular claim is religious depends entirely on the circumstances. In the conscientious objector cases, the Court avoided constitutional decisions by interpreting federal law broadly enough to cover many sorts of religious convictions, both theistic and nontheistic.[1840] In *Wisconsin v. Yoder,* the Court held that an entire way of life may constitute a religion for some purposes. In the evolution cases, the Court held that unconstitutional religious proselytizing in the schools cannot be avoided simply by labeling a doctrine "Creation Science."[600]

See also: LEMON TEST; RELIGIOUS ESTABLISHMENT.

religion, freedom of, *see:* **freedom of religion; religious establishment; schools, religion in**

religious belief, sincerity and truth of   The truth of religious belief or doctrine is not constitutionally open to question. In the leading case, adherents of the "I Am" cult were indicted for fraudulently soliciting funds by mail. Their SOLICITATION letters asserted that they were "divine messengers" and attained a "supernatural . . . power to heal." The Supreme Court refused to let the jury consider the truth of falsity of the beliefs they preached. Justice William O. Douglas said that "heresy trials are foreign to our Constitution": people "may believe what they cannot prove. They may not be put to the proof of their religious doctrines or beliefs."[113] In other words, whether a *belief* is true may not constitutionally be questioned, but whether it *is believed* is subject to proof. For example, under CONSCIENTIOUS OBJECTION laws, a draftee could escape combat service if his "religious training and belief" led him conscientiously to oppose "war in any form."[1840] Whether the religious teaching is true may not be raised, but whether the draftee actually was convinced that war is wrong may obviously be an issue. Without a test for sincerity, anyone could claim conscientious objector status, just as anyone could escape a fraud conviction by insisting that his claims are religiously based. Dissenting in the mail fraud case, Justice Robert H. Jackson would not have permitted an inquiry into either sincerity or belief because they cannot realistically be separated: "How can the government prove these persons knew something to be false which it cannot prove to be false?" Moreover, faith itself is often held in the face of considerable doubt. The deepest religious conviction is often of this sort: "I admit that the proposition I am advancing sounds crazy, but I believe it anyway." Nevertheless, the constitutional distinction between truth *of* the belief and sincerity *in* the belief seems well established.

The principle that belief is not open to judicial investigation has led the Supreme Court to deny courts the power to adjudicate fights for control of church property on the basis of which warring faction represents the "true" church. To do so would require the courts to make judgments about doctrine, and that they are constitutionally forbidden to do.[1054] Instead, courts must look to church rules. If the church has a governing body, then its decision is determinative; if the church operates congregationally by majority vote, then the majority may determine who is to control.[1658] Courts may not set aside a church's defrocking of its bishop despite his claim that the church violated its own rules.[1844] Despite this general conclusion, the Court said in 1979 that in the absence of proof to the contrary, the state may apply a PRESUMPTION that the majority of the congregation is entitled to decide the issue.[1036]

See also: NEUTRAL PRINCIPLES.

religious establishment   The most obvious purpose of the ESTABLISHMENT CLAUSE was to prevent the government from declaring an official church in which people must worship and to which they must tithe, either privately or through tax subsidies. Today, there is no danger that the government will decree a religious establishment. The question is what more the Establishment Clause accomplishes. The Framers meant to sever religion and government, believing that the people could better achieve their secular purposes through the state and their religious purposes through independent churches. Writing to the Danbury (Connecticut) Baptist Association in 1802, President Thomas Jefferson said that the First Amendment built "a wall of separation between church and state." His statement remains the central metaphor for interpreting the clause, but it suggests as many questions as answers.

In 1947, in a case approving public funds for bus transportation to and from all elementary schools, both public and parochial, speaking for a sharply divided Court, Justice Hugo L. Black said the Establishment Clause "means at least this: Neither a state nor the Federal Government can set up a church. Neither can pass laws which aid one religion, aid all religions, or prefer one religion over another. Neither can force nor influence a person to go to or to remain away from church against his will or force him to profess a belief or disbelief in any religion. No person can be punished for entertaining or professing religious beliefs or disbeliefs, for church attendance or non-attendance. No tax in any amount, large or small, can be levied to support any religious activities or institutions. ... Neither a state nor the Federal Government can, openly or secretly, participate in the affairs of any religious organizations or groups and vice versa." Despite the clarity and vigor of Black's summary, the dissenters heatedly replied "exactly so"—and came to the opposite conclusion about the constitutionality of paying for parochial school transportation.

Since then, in determining whether laws or government programs are consistent with the

Establishment Clause, the Court has followed the three-pronged LEMON TEST, which says that a law or program does not violate the Establishment Clause if its primary purpose is secular, if its principal effect neither aids nor inhibits religion, and if government and religion are not excessively entangled. Establishment cases have come to the Court in cases involving public and government aid to parochial schools, RELEASED TIME programs in schools, PRAYER AND BIBLE READING in public institutions, controls over school curricula, government celebration of holidays and display of RELIGIOUS SYMBOLS, and government accommodation of certain religious preferences.

In recent years, Justice Sandra Day O'Connor has proposed asking, instead of whether the law has a primarily secular purpose, "whether the government intends to convey a message of endorsement or disapproval of religion."[1209] The endorsement test has sparked considerable discussion, especially in cases dealing with religious symbols. The Court has also apparently carved out an exception to the *Lemon* test when a practice has had long historical acceptance. For example, the Court has approved the practice of the Nebraska legislature to pay a chaplain of a single denomination to offer prayers at the start of legislative days.[1246] The justices have also approved the custom of celebrating Christmas with certain symbols,[1209] though the historical evidence is somewhat shaky and the Court's position may be better understood as a refusal to upset millions of people by reversing such longstanding traditions as the United States motto ("In God We Trust") for purely symbolic gains.

In the 1990s, new conservative voices are pushing for changes to traditional Establishment Clause doctrine. Perhaps the most hotly contested battleground will be over whether the Establishment Clause bars state policies that benefit any or all religions or only those programs that discriminate among religions.

Some years ago, William F. Buckley declared that the First Amendment "was not designed to secularize American life" but to guard against a national preference for one religion. Buckley's sentiment suggests the trap into which the Court might walk. The Establishment Clause has nothing to do with "secularizing" American life. To the contrary, it makes the government impotent to do so by denying the government any role in religion at all, leaving Americans free individually and within their churches to live lives as religious as they please—and on their own terms.

See also: CHAPLAINS; DELEGATION DOCTRINE; EVOLUTION, TEACHING OF; FREEDOM OF RELIGION; GOD, REFERENCES TO IN PUBLIC DOCUMENTS; RELIGION, DEFINITION OF; RELIGIOUS BELIEF, SINCERITY AND TRUTH OF; RELIGIOUS HOLIDAYS, GOVERNMENT CELEBRATION OF; SCHOOLS, RELIGION IN; SUNDAY CLOSING LAWS.

religious holidays, government celebration of   In 1984 the Supreme Court approved, 5–4, a municipal "observance of the Christmas holiday season" without a single word of constitutional justification. Rather, Chief Justice Warren E. Burger's majority opinion simply stated the conclusion that towns around the country, in common with "Congress and Presidents," have "taken note of a significant historical religious event long celebrated in the Western World" and that to celebrate Christmas is a "legitimate secular purpose."[1209] The majority was concerned with the display of RELIGIOUS SYMBOLS but the question that might have been asked is whether, under the ESTABLISHMENT CLAUSE, government has any business celebrating religious holidays, even one "acknowledged in the Western World for 20 centuries." Justice Sandra Day O'Connor said that even though they may have "religious aspects," public holidays have "cultural significance" and celebrating them is a "legitimate secular purpose." As presidents, the two men most responsible for the Establishment Clause, Thomas Jefferson and James Madison, refused to proclaim even such secular national holidays as Thanksgiving because they believed that so doing unconstitutionally entangled state and church.

religious liberty, *see:* **freedom of religion**

religious schools, *see:* **schools, religion in**

religious symbols, right to display   That the United States was founded by deeply religious people is indisputable. But the consequence of the tradition on which their devotion was based has led to difficult problems at the intersection of church and state—particularly in the symbolism that religious adherents have successfully affixed to the secular arms of the government. For two centuries the motto of the United States has been "In God We Trust." Most presidents, but not Thomas Jefferson or James Madison, proclaimed Thanksgiving as a specifically religious holiday, asking Americans to give thanks to God for the bounty of the land. Both the Senate and the House have long employed religious chaplains, paid for out of public funds. In recent times the Pledge of Allegiance acquired the words "under God" to describe the presumed belief of the nation.

In view of these latent and blatant symbols, the Court was understandably reluctant in 1984 to declare unconstitutional a municipal display of a crèche in a Christmas display in downtown Pawtucket, Rhode Island. Speaking for a 5–4 majority, Chief Justice Warren E. Burger in *Lynch v. Donnelly* held that there is a *secular* purpose for the crèche—a nativity scene depicting the infant Jesus, Mary, Joseph, angels, shepherds, kings, and animals, ranging in height from five inches to five feet—namely, a depiction of the "historical origins" of Christmas. Burger denied that the primary effect of the display was to benefit religion, though he acknowledged that there was an "indirect, remote, and incidental benefit." In a sentence

devoid of self-awareness, Burger said that displaying this palpably religious symbol "is no more an advancement or endorsement of religion than the Congressional and Executive recognition of the origins of the Holiday itself as 'Christ's Mass.' " Throughout his opinion, Burger refers to Christmas as "the Holiday," in a perhaps unconscious imitation of the Framers' strategy of avoiding using the word SLAVERY in the Constitution. To outlaw the crèche, Burger said, would be a "stilted overreaction to our history," and would require the Court to acknowledge that a "host of other forms of taking official note of Christmas" violate the Establishment Clause. This the majority was unwilling to do.

Concurring, Justice Sandra Day O'Connor said that the government's celebration of the holiday "generally is not understood to endorse" its religious content. She begs the question. Only in a society acculturated by the constant and overwhelming cultivation of the holiday could its religious significance be presumed secular. So common an event is difficult for a majority to view as an endorsement precisely because it is so familiar. The majority overlooked the trial testimony of the town's mayor, who said that the purpose of displaying the crèche was to "keep 'Christ in Christmas.' " Dissenting, Justice William Brennan lamented that the majority's superficial conclusion that the symbols at the heart of Christianity are no different from Santa Claus or his reindeer "is not only offensive to those for whom the crèche has profound significance, but insulting to those who insist . . . that the story of Christ is in no sense a part of 'history.' "

Lynch was precursor. In 1989 Justice Harry Blackmun was a swing vote between two sets of four justices who produced two different 5–4 conclusions about religious symbols. This time the Court rejected the display of a crèche because it stood by itself on the Grand Staircase of the Allegheny County (Pennsylvania)

Courthouse, but upheld the display of a menorah next to a Christmas tree and a sign "saluting liberty" near the City-County Building.[37] The crèche was held to violate the Establishment Clause because it was donated by a Catholic organization and sat in a prominent public space unadorned by jolly Santas or other decorations. Beginning in 1982, the city displayed a menorah, symbol of the Jewish holiday Chanukah, which usually falls near Christmas, alongside the annual Christmas tree display. The joint display was held to be nothing more than the celebration of two holidays, hence under *Lynch* secular and constitutional.

The Court, or some segment of it, has developed a theory of secular religiosity. In a sentence of near spooflike quality, Blackmun said: "Although the Christmas tree represents the secular celebration of Christmas, its very association with Christmas (a holiday with religious dimensions) makes it conceivable that the tree might be seen as representing religion when displayed next to an object associated with Jewish religion." Only a Christian could consider a Christmas tree only conceivably religious or perhaps only secularly religious.

Dissenting, Justice John Paul Stevens noted that, among other things, many Christians profoundly abhorred the use of the crèche "as an aid to commercialization of Christ's birthday," and many Jews equally deplored the use of the menorah. Quite aside from whether the municipality was endorsing any religion or religion in general, Stevens said that the Establishment Clause was meant to prevent public bodies from fomenting disagreements over the use of religious symbols. Moreover, Justice Stevens noted, the net effect of the Court's decision must seem very odd to people unversed in the "intricacies of Establishment Clause jurisprudence," for the Court must seem clearly to be preferring a Jewish symbol to a Christian one.

Speaking for himself and three others, Justice Anthony M. Kennedy disagreed that the crèche display was unconstitutional. He worried that the decision would lead the Court to act as a censor, condemning the "orthodox" in favor of the secular in celebrating religious holidays and leaving "the only Christmas the state can acknowledge" as one "in which references to religion have been held to a minimum," a result he branded "Orwellian." Kennedy did agree that certain kinds of symbols used in certain ways would clearly be unconstitutional—for example, "the permanent erection of a large Latin cross on the roof of city hall."

Where the Court will go with its perplexing analysis of religious symbols remains a mystery.

See also: LEMON TEST; RELIGIOUS ESTABLISHMENT.

religious test   The eighteenth-century British claim to religious toleration was hypocritical. The Toleration Act of 1696 provided toleration only for Protestants, and any Christian who renounced the faith was rendered incapable of holding public OFFICE. In the colonies, only Rhode Island was open to all. Pennsylvania, the most liberal of the other colonies, denied citizenship or civil rights to those who refused to "acknowledge the being of a God . . . [who is] the rewarder of the good and punisher of the wicked." The state required officeholders to swear an oath that they believed the whole of the Bible was divinely inspired. North Carolina denied office to any who would not swear belief in the truth of Protestantism.

Under the moral and political leadership of Thomas Jefferson and James Madison, the states after the Revolution began to rethink the link between church and state. Jefferson's Virginia Statute of Religious Liberty in 1786 explicitly broke the link, declaring public office open to all, independent of religious belief. The Framers embodied this principle in Art. VI-[3], prohibiting the federal government from requiring any "religious test" as a qualification for any "office or public trust under the United States." No cases have ever arisen under this clause, which applies only to federal officeholding, although the Court did consider a related question when it struck down a provision in the Maryland state constitution in 1961 that required a prospective notary public to swear a belief in the existence of God. The Court invalidated this last of the state religious test clauses under the First Amendment.[2059] In 1978 the Court struck down under the Free Exercise Clause a Tennessee law barring the clergy from holding state office, a reverse form of a religious test.[1288]

See also: FREEDOM OF RELIGION; RELIGIOUS ESTABLISHMENT.

remand When a higher court's ruling in a case requires further action, it *remands* the case to the lower court; for example, when a conviction is reversed because of an inadequate jury instruction. The lower court's further disposition of the case may then, under appropriate circumstances, be appealed anew.

remedy, right to There is no general constitutional right to a remedy for injuries caused either by other individuals or by the government. Of course, much of the law is concerned with providing remedies for harms, and so the question does not often arise whether the failure to provide a remedy is unconstitutional. The longstanding doctrine of SOVEREIGN IMMUNITY bars suits against the government for official acts unless the government consents. Federal civil rights laws contain a major exception to this nonconstitutional but nevertheless firmly entrenched policy by providing for suits in federal court against *state* officials who deprive a person of federal constitutional rights. Through the doctrine of CONSTITUTIONAL TORTS the Court has also inferred a limited right to sue *federal* officials for DAMAGES when they violate someone's constitutional rights.

But not every harm committed by public officials is compensable under these theories. In 1986 the Court held that it is not a constitutional violation for a state to act negligently, and any resulting harms may be redressed only through state lawsuits. But the Constitution does not require that the state allow such suits. So if the injury was caused by a state official who is immune from suit, the injured party will have no remedy at all.[513, 517]

See also: CIVIL RIGHTS AND CIVIL LIBERTIES; EQUITY AND EQUITABLE REMEDIES; GOVERNMENT, AFFIRMATIVE OBLIGATIONS OF; IMMUNITY FROM SUIT; PROCEDURAL DUE PROCESS; PROCESS RIGHTS; STATE ACTION.

removal of cases Some types of cases fall within the CONCURRENT JURISDICTION of both federal and state courts. Congress has provided that many such cases brought initially in state courts may be *removed*—that is, transferred—to federal court. For example, when a citizen of one state sues a citizen of another in state court, the defendant may invoke the DIVERSITY JURISDICTION of the federal courts and have the case removed there. Both civil and criminal cases may be removed under appropriate circumstances. When a state prosecuted a federal internal revenue agent who had killed a man in the course of his official duties, the Court held removal proper to permit the agent to assert federal justification for the killing and to block the state's attempt to hinder the enforcement of federal law.[2007]

See also: JURISDICTION.

removal power, *see:* appointment and removal power

rent control The Supreme Court has upheld many different types of rent control laws, beginning after World War I, when it sustained under the WAR POWER a federal law limiting the amount by which landlords could raise rents and conferring on tenants the right to remain in possession as long as they paid the rent.[173] During[2267] and after[1163] World War II, the Court sustained similar national rent control regulations, dismissing the case of one landlord who complained that the rent ceiling prevented him from obtaining a fair return on the value of his property.[209] The end of the war did not terminate Congress's war power over rents.[2255, 674] However, a law that prohibited making "any unjust or unreasonable rate or charge" was invalidated for violating DUE PROCESS under the FIFTH AMENDMENT because it was too vague about what rates would violate it.[1104] Retroactive rent regulations have been upheld to bar eviction of a tenant against whom an eviction judgment had been rendered before the rent control law was enacted.[676] A federal rent control agency may order a landlord to refund rents already collected if the increase in rent has not been officially approved.[2256]

In 1988 the Court signaled that it might be willing to rethink the basic constitutionality of rent control laws because they constitute a TAKING OF PROPERTY without JUST COMPENSATION. A San Jose, California, ordinance permitted an annual rent increase to be rolled back if, among other things, it was an "economic and financial hardship" on the present tenant. Although finding no due process or EQUAL PROTECTION difficulty, the Court speculated that such a law might be an unconstitutional taking. It declined to consider the issue because the law had never actually been enforced against any landlord.[1587] Dissenting, Justice Antonin Scalia insisted that the law is unconstitutional because the hardship of a tenant is not the landlord's fault, and if the town wishes to aid poor tenants it should not put the burden solely on landlords.

See also: PRICE AND WAGE CONTROLS; RATE REGULATION; RETROACTIVITY; VAGUENESS.

repel invasions, *see:* **invasion**

reporter's privilege　Most witnesses to events that become the subject of government investigations or legal proceedings are obliged to tell what they saw or what they know when appearing before a GRAND JURY or in court. The COMMON LAW recognizes "testimonial privileges," so that, for example, spouses may not be compelled to testify against each other, and doctors, lawyers, and the clergy may not be required to reveal the confidences they receive. Under the FIFTH AMENDMENT, an ACCUSED has a constitutional right against SELF-INCRIMINATION, and so may not be compelled to testify at all when being investigated or prosecuted. The Court has also recognized limited FREEDOM OF ASSOCIATION and FREEDOM OF SPEECH privileges against revealing certain kinds of information to government investigators. But the Court has never agreed that FREEDOM OF THE PRESS confers on reporters a privilege to withhold the identity of their sources.

In 1972 it specifically rejected the claims of three journalists that they had a FIRST AMENDMENT right to withhold information from a grand jury.[225] For a 5–4 majority, Justice Byron R. White conceded that compulsory testimony might tend to dry up certain sources who would fear their names leaking out. But White said that the public interest in pursuing and prosecuting crimes must take precedence over the public interest in "possible future news about crime from undisclosed, unverified sources." To cries of alarm that the press would be undermined, White noted that no such privilege has ever been conceded and yet for two centuries "the press has flourished." White was careful to note that NEWSGATHERING is entitled to some First Amendment protection and that bad-faith investigations, such as official harassment "undertaken not for purposes of law enforcement but to disrupt a reporter's relationship with his news sources would have no justification." He also made clear that the Court's decision did not prevent Congress or the states from enacting "shield laws" that give reporters a legal right to refuse to answer certain questions. In 1978 the Court refused to accord journalists and editors any special privilege against a police search of the newsroom for evidence that the reporters and photographers had gathered of crimes committed by others.[2290] And in 1979 the Court held that journalists are not privileged in LIBEL AND SLANDER suits from answering questions about their state of mind while writing their stories.[911]

See also: INVESTIGATORY POWERS OF LEGISLATURE.

repossession   In 1972 the Supreme Court ruled that whenever a state law gives a creditor the right to repossess any "significant property interest," the debtor is entitled to notice and a HEARING before being deprived of the property's use.[708] But in 1974 the Court held that as long as certain procedural protections are guaranteed, a court may order property to be seized without first giving the debtor a hearing. Prehearing seizure orders are valid, the Court said, if (1) the creditor demonstrates before a neutral magistrate, not a court clerk, that there are reasonable grounds to believe the property may be repossessed; (2) the creditor supplies adequate security to recompense the debtor should the creditor be mistaken; and (3) a prompt postrepossession adversary hearing is held, at which the creditor must bear the burden of proof.[1368] In 1991 the Court seemed to backtrack, holding in a case in which a man's house was attached as part of a civil suit for assault and battery that the states may not permit real estate to be attached without a prior hearing, except in rare circumstances.[450]

Property stored in a warehouse may be sold without a court order for failure to pay storage charges.[672] It is only when state officials such as sheriffs are used to attach a debtor's property and when the attachment procedures are constitutionally deficient that the private creditor may be sued in federal court.[1206]

See also: GARNISHMENT AND ATTACHMENT.

representation   The Constitution established representation as the fundamental political principle, but it says next to nothing about the type of representation or the responsibilities of representatives to their constituents. Members of the House of Representatives are chosen by state and allocated by population, but the Constitution is silent about how individual members are to be chosen, beyond the requirement in Art. I-§2[1] that people qualified to vote in elections for the state legislature are entitled to vote for members of the House. Each state may determine for itself whether to require a single representative to be elected from separate districts or permit the statewide electorate to vote for multiple members. Likewise, whether to have winner-take-all elections or some form of proportional representation is a political issue for the states as long as the method does not discriminate against voters on a basis forbidden by EQUAL PROTECTION or by the FIFTEENTH or NINETEENTH AMENDMENTS. Art. I-§3[1] originally gave the choice of senators to the state legislatures, but in 1913 the SEVENTEENTH AMENDMENT established popular voting within each state. Because elected, the president is said to be a representative of the people, but the ELECTORAL COLLEGE is a fundamentally different representative system.

The Constitution is even more opaque about the requirement of representation at the state level. Art. I-§2[1] implies that the state legislatures must consist of elected representatives. Since all state houses are elected bodies, the issue has never been tested. In 1966 the Court upheld a Georgia election law permitting the state legislature to elect the governor when no candidate got a majority of the vote. The logic of the decision seems to suggest that elections, as such, are not a prerequisite for every major political OFFICE.[692] The Court also upheld a Puerto Rican procedure permitting a political party to fill a vacant seat in the legislature caused by the departure of one of its members.[1747]

Because representation is fundamental, decisions made by nonrepresentative institutions are often thought to be suspect: decisions by unelected judges are said to be anti- or countermajoritarian, even though they may sometimes seek to protect those whom "political processes ordinarily to be relied upon"[348] fail to protect. Moreover, "representative" often cannot be equated with "legitimate," since many of the actual operations of Congress and the executive branch are far from representative. The platitude that voters may, after all, always "throw the rascals out" when representatives vote unwisely is naive, since much of what gets enacted is effectively insulated from electoral wrath.

See also: APPORTIONMENT OF POLITICAL DISTRICTS; CHECKS AND BALANCES; MAJORITARIANISM; MULTIMEMBER ELECTION DISTRICTS; RATIO OF REPRESENTATION; REPUBLICAN FORM OF GOVERNMENT; SEPARATION OF POWERS; VOTING, RIGHT TO.

representation, District of Columbia, *see:* **District of Columbia, constitutional status of**

representatives in Congress, *see:* **Congress, members of; qualifications for office**

reprieves, *see:* **pardons, reprieves, commutations, and amnesties**

reprisal, *see:* **letters of marque and reprisal**

reproductive rights The right to reproduce implies the right both to beget and bear children and to refrain from doing so. Though this right is not mentioned in the Constitution, the Supreme Court has declared procreation a fundamental right under SUBSTANTIVE DUE PROCESS. It was not always so. In 1927 the Court upheld a Virginia law requiring sterilization of mentally defective institutionalized persons. In a widely quoted—and deplored—sentence, Justice Oliver Wendell Holmes said that "three

generations of imbeciles are enough."[268] But in 1944, in an opinion by Justice William O. Douglas, the Court struck down an Oklahoma law requiring sterilization of persons convicted of three felonies comprising MORAL TURPITUDE, except for embezzlement. Douglas noted that the sterilization law "involves one of the basic civil rights" and said the law was a "clear, pointed, unmistakable discrimination" that violated EQUAL PROTECTION.[1879] Then in *Griswold v. Connecticut* in 1965, the Court announced a broad right to PRIVACY, which soon led in two directions: to an almost absolute right to CONTRACEPTION for anyone, whether or not an adult and whether or not married, and to a broad right to ABORTION. As presently construed, the fundamental right to procreation clearly prohibits compulsory limitation of family size, a policy encouraged or enforced by some other countries.

See also: FAMILIES; FUNDAMENTAL INTERESTS, RIGHTS, AND PRIVILEGES; ILLEGITIMACY; SEXUAL FREEDOM.

republican form of government Art. IV-§4 says that the "United States shall guarantee to every state in this union a republican form of government." The Supreme Court has consistently declared that issues arising under this clause are to be settled politically, not judicially. The leading case is *Luther v. Borden,* which arose when in the 1840s a popular and violent uprising in Rhode Island for a time claimed to have replaced the legally elected government. The question was whether the head of a government posse, which raided the home of an opponent of the original government, could be sued for trespass. The posse asserted that the raid was authorized by the lawful government and hence not trespass. The homeowner asserted that the popular uprising had ousted the original government; hence the raid was not legally authorized and therefore was trespass. Chief Justice Roger B. Taney said that the issue was a POLITICAL QUESTION, and that it was constitutionally up to Congress to decide whether to intervene. Since Congress had done so by an act of 1795 that gave the president authority to call out the MILITIA to suppress an insurrection in any state, it was therefore for the president to decide whether an insurrection had actually occurred and whether it should be quelled by force.

After the Civil War, Georgia asserted that Reconstruction legislation was unconstitutional because the state already had a republican form of government and that Congress was therefore powerless to deal with its government structure. The Court responded that the clause did not act as a restriction on Congress but rather gave it power to act.[741] In 1912 the Court rejected the contention that political devices such as the INITIATIVE and REFERENDUM, by which people can make law directly, violate the clause.[1554]

See also: COMMITMENT TO OTHER BRANCHES; JUSTICIABILITY; POSSE COMITATUS; STATES AND STATEHOOD.

reputation When a person's reputation is wrongly sullied, the constitutional ramification depends on whether the defamation was caused by a private individual or the government. When the LIBEL AND SLANDER results from erroneous statements of a private person, including newspapers and the broadcast media, the actual-MALICE rules first enunciated in *New York Times v. Sullivan* apply: unless the defendant knew that the statement was false, or acted in reckless disregard of whether or not it was false, a PUBLIC FIGURE OR OFFICIAL may not recover DAMAGES. When the government defames, a different issue arises. State officials may be sued in federal court for violating a person's federal rights. In 1971 the Court considered a suit in which a police chief, acting under a Wisconsin habitual drunkard law, posted a notice in all the town's liquor stores that a particular woman was not permitted to buy or receive liquor for one year. The chief acted unilaterally, without first giving the putative drunkard an opportunity to be heard. The Supreme Court held that an interest in one's "good name, reputation, honor, or integrity" is an aspect of LIBERTY protected by the FOURTEENTH AMENDMENT and that the failure to provide notice and hold a hearing violated the woman's right to PROCEDURAL DUE PROCESS. She could therefore sue in federal court for damages.[2236]

However, in 1976 the Court significantly backtracked in *Paul v. Davis,* a case arising when a police chief, without first providing notice or holding a hearing, distributed to local merchants a man's name and photograph in a sheaf of "active shoplifter" materials. The man had been arrested but the charges were dismissed. This time the Supreme Court dismissed the lawsuit, holding that the government invades no constitutional liberty interest when the only consequence of its action is injury to reputation. The Court distinguished the Wisconsin and other earlier cases on the ground that in those cases the government had infringed or extinguished an additional right of the injured persons; for example, by depriving the woman of her common right to obtain liquor. The upshot of *Paul v. Davis* is that the government need not provide a hearing before releasing stigmatizing information about a person, although state law may (but need not) independently permit a damage suit for libel against the government official. In 1991 the Court extended *Paul,* holding that the government may release information about a person's job performance without a hearing even when the result may well be that he or she will be denied credentials required to continue working for the federal government.[1866]

See also: PROCESS RIGHTS; REMEDY, RIGHT TO.

res judicata Res judicata (Latin for "the thing has been decided") is an old COMMON

LAW principle that bars further litigation of an issue about which a court has rendered a final decision in a dispute between the parties. Although it is not a constitutional term, the Court has accorded it nearly constitutional status, akin to the DOUBLE JEOPARDY rule barring reprosecution of a defendant for the same offense. The Court has held that " 'principles of public policy and of private peace' dictate that the matter not be open to relitigation every time there is a change in the law,"[56, 652, 876] so res judicata applies even when a new constitutional interpretation would have changed the result in an earlier case.[393]

An issue is not res judicata if it was decided in a case not involving one of the parties. The Court reversed an Alabama procedure under which a bookseller could be *criminally* convicted of selling obscene materials if caught with any book or magazine in inventory that had been adjudged obscene at a prior *civil* hearing unrelated to the defendant. The Alabama law prohibited the bookseller from relitigating the issue of the work's obscenity, since there was another party to "represent" the work at the earlier obscenity determination. In an opinion by Justice William H. Rehnquist, the Court unanimously concluded that under the FIRST AMENDMENT a later court and jury in an unrelated proceeding must decide the issue fresh.[1303] But the Court pointed to res judicata to prohibit the federal government and an Indian tribe from relitigating the issue of water allocation when the government had previously represented the tribe and other people with an interest in the water allocation.[1445]

See also: RETROACTIVITY; STARE DECISIS.

reserved powers, *see:* **spending power; Tenth Amendment**

reserved rights, *see:* **Ninth Amendment**

residence The concept of residence is pliable. It takes its meaning from the legal benefit or burden sought to be gained or avoided. For purposes of voting, residence is determined by the law of the state in which the person seeks to vote. Most states look to whether a person maintains a permanent home there to which he or she returns after a temporary absence. This form of residence is often known as "domicile." But not every state has so commonsensical a policy. Under Texas law President George Bush could call the Lone Star State his legal residence simply by renting a hotel room and declaring an "intention" to make it his home someday, even though the president actually lived in the District of Columbia and Maine.

Under the PRIVILEGES AND IMMUNITIES CLAUSE, residence and citizenship are practical equivalents. To determine DIVERSITY JURISDICTION, the Court has distinguished between permanent domicile and temporary residence. A person temporarily residing in one state is not a citizen[1981] but can become one merely by moving to a different state and declaring an intention to remain there indefinitely.[2225] In recent years, the Court has found constitutional limitations on state authority to deny residency status to newcomers through DURATIONAL RESIDENCY REQUIREMENTS.

See also: CITIZENS AND CITIZENSHIP; TRAVEL, RIGHT TO; VOTING, RIGHT TO.

residential picketing, *see:* **picketing**

resignation of the president, *see:* **presidential succession**

resolution, *see:* **order, resolution, and vote**

responsibility of government, *see:* **government, affirmative obligations of**

restrictive covenant A restrictive covenant is an agreement in a deed prohibiting the landowner from using the property in a certain way. For example, restrictive covenants in the deeds of neighbors may bar each of them from maintaining a certain kind of business on the premises or from erecting more than two floors on a dwelling. Restrictive covenants of this type are enforceable and present no constitutional difficulty. But until 1948 the courts also upheld *racially* restrictive covenants barring owners from selling to buyers of a certain race or religion. The racial covenant became widespread after 1917 when the Court invalidated racially exclusionary ZONING laws that segregated blacks into certain neighborhoods.[267] The courts enforced the covenants by permitting homeowners to sue to enjoin neighbors from voluntarily selling to black buyers.

In 1948, in *Shelley v. Kraemer,* the Court killed all racially restrictive covenants by ruling that they are judicially unenforceable under EQUAL PROTECTION, since an INJUNCTION against the sale of a home to enforce a racial covenant amounts to STATE ACTION that unconstitutionally discriminates solely on the basis of race. Even though the Equal Protection Clause does not apply to the federal government, the Court held in a COMPANION CASE that the courts may not enforce racial covenants in the District of Columbia on the ground that it would violate "public policy of the United States" to permit federal courts to enforce agreements constitutionally unenforceable in state courts.[963] In 1953 the Court extended the principle to bar a homeowner's suit for DAMAGES against a neighbor who violated a racially restrictive covenant. Otherwise, the majority said, a damage suit would be an indirect means of blocking sales to blacks on purely discriminatory grounds.[133] Many deeds still contain racially restrictive covenants, but as a consequence of these cases, the covenants are legally meaningless.

result-oriented jurisprudence, *see:* **neutral principles**

retardation, *see:* **mental retardation**

retirement, *see:* **mandatory retirement**

retroactivity   Whether a retroactive law or rule can constitutionally have legal effect depends almost entirely on the particular circumstances in which it is to be applied. Despite some popular misconceptions, the Constitution precludes legal retroactivity in only one area—criminal punishment. The EX POST FACTO CLAUSES of Article I bar the federal government and the states from punishing conduct that was not unlawful when it was undertaken. But as early as 1798, the Supreme Court upheld retroactive laws that do not have penal effect.[307] The court has frequently upheld Congress's custom of giving tax laws retroactive effect by, for example, making their effective date the beginning of the year in which they were enacted.[264, 516a] The Court has distinguished retroactive gift taxes, though, striking down a law imposing a tax on recipients in whom the property had wholly vested before the tax was enacted.[2111a] Laws that limit a person's enjoyment of property or other legal rights acquired before the law was enacted are constitutional. In 1976, for example, the Court upheld a federal law requiring coal mining companies to pay disability benefits to workers suffering from black lung disease, even though they had quit their jobs before the law was passed.[2113] BANKRUPTCY laws frequently operate to extinguish prior contractual commitments, and the Court has upheld them.[860] In 1989 the Court upheld a federal law imposing a user fee on claimants who won awards from the Iran–United States Claims Tribunal, including those whose awards were rendered before the fee law was enacted.[1931a]

Judicial decisions also frequently operate retroactively. They may apply new rules in pending cases, and the new rules may affect similar cases decided earlier. Ordinarily a court's announcement of a new rule that applies to the parties before it has no constitutional consequences, but is the essence of the

COMMON LAW. State courts occasionally refuse to apply such rules to the parties in the case in order to avoid the unfairness of retroactivity. But federal courts are generally precluded from following this policy, since the effect of announcing a rule change only for the future is in essence an unconstitutional ADVISORY OPINION.[1966]

In rare cases, the Court has found that the consequences of a court's retroactive decision violates DUE PROCESS. For example, in a leading 1930 case a bank had sued to enjoin enforcement of a Missouri county tax that it said was being assessed in an unconstitutionally discriminatory manner. The Missouri Supreme Court dismissed the suit, holding that because the bank failed to pursue an appeal before the state tax commission in a timely fashion, it was therefore barred from complaining in a later lawsuit. In an earlier case, the state supreme court had ruled that the tax commission could not consider the type of case it was now declaring the bank should have presented. The state court's second decision retroactively barred the bank from obtaining any legal relief, saying in effect, "you waited too long to take advantage of a remedy that we are just now announcing you had." For a unanimous Court, Justice Louis D. Brandeis declared that the consequence of the state court's ruling was unconstitutionally to deny to the bank "the only remedy ever available for the enforcement of its right to prevent the seizure of its property."[236]

Retroactivity of criminal procedure decisions became a major problem for the Court in the mid-1960s. Until 1965, the Court had generally concluded that any constitutional ruling should be applied retroactively.[1744] But as it began applying the BILL OF RIGHTS to the states, the question frequently arose whether a "new" constitutional rule or a new interpretation of an old one should apply to prisoners and criminal defendants whose convictions had become final before the rule was announced. The problem is that if every new constitutional rule must be given retroactive effect, thousands of state prisoners across the country could be released from penitentiaries on HABEAS CORPUS appeals for "mistakes" that prosecutors could not have known they were committing. For many years, the Court's search for a doctrine became, in Justice John Marshall Harlan's words, "almost as difficult to follow as the tracks made by a beast of prey in search of its intended victim."[1221] In 1989, after many shifts produced by changing coalitions of justices, the Court announced that it would adhere to the position Harlan had advocated: a "new" constitutional rule will be applied to any cases still on direct appeal, but not to habeas corpus appeals of final state court decisions, with two limited exceptions.[2004] One exception is for a new rule that says that the particular defendant or what he did is constitutionally beyond the reach of criminal law. The second exception is a new rule recognizing a procedural right "without which the likelihood of an accurate conviction is seriously diminished." A rule that merely makes it *more* likely that a conviction will be accurate is not within this exception.[1804]

Determining what constitutes a "new" rule calls for an exceedingly fine judgment. The Court has said that even though a rule is a logical consequence of a prior rule, it is nevertheless "new" unless it was "dictated" by the prior rule.[1599] A rule is new if it is a proposition that "was susceptible to debate among reasonable minds."[292] Following these flexible standards, the Court ruled in 1990 that a 1981 decision requiring police to cease questioning a suspect in custody who demands to see a lawyer did not "dictate" the rule announced in 1988 that the police must also cease interrogation of a suspect who has requested a lawyer in connection with a separate, unrelated investigation.[292] Therefore the Court refused to apply the 1988 rule retroactively. It upheld the conviction of a defendant who was questioned despite his request for a lawyer on an unrelated charge.

See also: ADEQUATE STATE GROUNDS; EXHAUSTION OF REMEDIES; OBLIGATION OF CONTRACTS; VESTED RIGHTS.

revenue, *see:* **General Welfare Clause; income tax; spending power; taxing power**

revenue sharing, *see:* **grants in aid; spending power**

reverse discrimination, *see:* **affirmative action; racial discrimination; segregation and integration**

review, timing of   A party unhappy with the course of a trial may not suddenly ask the Supreme Court to review the proceedings. Under federal law, the Supreme Court may hear an appeal from lower court decisions only at certain times and under certain circumstances. The most important rule is that the court may hear state appeals only from the highest court in which a decision may legally be rendered. If there is a higher state court that has legal authority to consider an appeal, the litigant must first appeal to that court, even if it is extremely unlikely that the court will hear the case. Even then, the Court may review only "final judgments," meaning that the state court case must have come to an end.

However, the Court has carved out several general exceptions to this final judgment rule. For example, the Alabama State Supreme Court upheld the constitutionality of a state law prohibiting newspapers from printing an editorial about a proposition on the ballot on election day. It then sent the case back to trial, so technically the case was not at an end. But the newspaper conceded that it had written the editorial, so it was clear that it would be convicted and would then appeal the constitutional question. Under those circumstances, the Court held that the state court's ruling on the

constitutional issue was final and could be appealed. The Court then held that the Alabama court was wrong on the constitutional issue, thus ending the need for a trial.[1348]

Even if the litigant would not necessarily lose at trial, a state court's ruling on a federal question can be appealed before the case has ended. The Mississippi Supreme Court upheld a state law against printing the names of rape victims in newspapers and remanded the case to trial. Since the newspaper might win on other, nonfederal grounds at trial, it could be argued that there was no need for an appeal in the U.S. Supreme Court until the jury rendered its verdict. The Court held, however, that since under those circumstances there could be no appeal at all in the U.S. Supreme Court, a faulty constitutional ruling would be left intact. The Court ruled that it could review immediately the state court's final judgment about the constitutional question. In so doing, it reversed the state court, holding that the FIRST AMENDMENT prohibits an absolute ban on printing a crime victim's name.[480]

See also: ABSTENTION DOCTRINE; ADEQUATE STATE GROUNDS; FINALITY; MOOTNESS; PRIVACY; RIPENESS; SPEECH, REGULATION OF CONTENT.

Revision, Council of, *see:* **Council of Revision**

revolution, right of   Although it was a necessary antecedent *to* the Constitution, revolution is understandably not a right protected *by* the Constitution, even though the DECLARATION OF INDEPENDENCE says that the people have a right and duty to "throw off" any government that seeks "to reduce them under absolute despotism." Because the Constitution itself is a better answer to tyranny than revolution, there is no need for a constitutional right of revolution, which would surely turn the Constitution into a "suicide pact," as Justice Robert H. Jackson once lamented might be the tendency of the

Court's "doctrinaire logic" in free speech cases.[2011] Through SEPARATION OF POWERS, equal voting rights, and widespread CIVIL RIGHTS AND CIVIL LIBERTIES, including the FIRST AMENDMENT freedoms of expression and FREEDOM OF ASSOCIATION, the Constitution is designed to check the "long train of abuses and usurpations" to which despots are prone.

right against self-incrimination, *see:* **self-incrimination**

right of revolution, *see:* **revolution, right of**

right of the people to keep and bear arms, *see:* **arms, right to keep and bear**

right to a speedy and public trial, *see:* **trial, public; trial, speedy**

right to assemble, *see:* **freedom of assembly**

right to be informed, *see:* **accusation, notice and specificity of; government documents, confidentiality of; readers' rights; right to know; right to reply**

right to contract, *see:* **freedom of contract**

right to counsel, *see:* **counsel, assistance of**

right to die Whether there is a constitutional right to die has never been squarely decided. In the much discussed case *Cruzan v. Director, Missouri Dept. of Health,* the Supreme Court said in 1990 that "for purposes of this case, we assume that . . . a competent person [has] a constitutionally protected right to refuse lifesaving hydration and nutrition." The issue in *Cruzan* was not whether a hospital must honor a patient's unequivocally expressed desire to die. The problem was that the patient herself was in a persistent vegetative state and unable to express any desire. The issue was how much

evidence it would take to prove that, when competent to do so, the patient had stated her wish that the hospital should "pull the plug" under these circumstances. The Supreme Court upheld Missouri's requirement that her wish to be refused treatment be shown by "clear and convincing evidence." *Cruzan* did not discuss a hypothetical right of a conscious and functioning person to commit suicide, and it is extremely dubious that the Court's right-to-die DICTUM will be held to encompass such a situation.

See also: MEDICATION AND SURGERY, FORCED; PROOF, STANDARD OF; VACCINATION.

right to education, *see:* **education, right to**

right to employment, *see:* **occupation, right to pursue; public employment**

right to know As it is conventionally viewed, the freedoms of expression guaranteed by the FIRST AMENDMENT protect the right of speakers to have their say and the right of readers and listeners to read and hear what's being said. A third possible right, only weakly developed and potentially destructive of the other two rights, is the *right to know*—that is, the right to the knowledge that someone else possesses. In 1980, for the first time, the Court held that there is a constitutional right to attend a criminal TRIAL, in essence upholding a right of access to certain government information.[1727] But there is no such general right, although Congress has the power to order government files opened and to some degree has done so in the Freedom of Information Act. There have also been scattered decisions that imply a right to know. For example, the Court spoke of a right to acquire knowledge when it struck down a law prohibiting the teaching of foreign languages to children[1323] and when it invalidated a law criminalizing the mere possession of pornographic literature in the home.[1944] But a right-to-know doctrine would be treacherous if held to embrace an enforceable right or power to demand certain kinds of information.

In a 1961 case, there was a fleeting suggestion that a Wisconsin law requiring every lawyer in the state to join and pay dues to the state bar was permissible because, among other reasons, people of the state have the right to know where their lawyers stand on certain issues.[1127] The Court made little of the suggestion; but broadly extended, such a notion would seriously infringe fundamental notions of PRIVACY. It might also seriously impinge on FREEDOM OF THE PRESS. If people have the right to know what candidates for political office are thinking on certain issues, then perhaps the state has the power to order newspapers to publish interviews or even articles by the candidates. In 1974 the Court said that a Florida RIGHT TO REPLY law that had such an effect clearly violated the First Amendment.[1324]

In 1978 the Court hinted at a right to obtain information superior to the right of broadcasters to deliver it. In an astounding statement in the Case of the Seven Dirty Words, the Court said that "the broadcast media have established a uniquely pervasive presence in the lives of all Americans. Patently offensive, indecent material presented over the airwaves confronts the citizens, not only in public, but also in the privacy of the home, where the individual's right to be left alone plainly outweighs the First Amendment rights of an intruder."[642] Who here is the intruder? The Court seems to conceive of radio broadcasts as a fixed natural resource like water that the state may purify before it comes into the home, rather than the active product of a speaker constitutionally entitled to talk. In effect, the Court is saying that the public has a *right* to certain kinds of programming. The people's right is to turn off the radio.

See also: FREE PRESS—FAIR TRIAL; FREEDOM OF SPEECH; FREEDOM OF THE PRESS; OFFENSIVE AND INDECENT SPEECH; READERS' RIGHTS; RIGHT TO REPLY.

right to petition, *see:* **freedom of petition**

right to privacy, *see:* **privacy**

right to procreate, *see:* **reproductive rights**

right to publicity, *see:* **publicity, right to personal**

right to reply   Although the FIRST AMENDMENT permits the government to provide a right of ACCESS TO BROADCASTING media, the Supreme Court has taken a dim view of state laws granting access to newspapers and private mailings. In 1974 the Court unanimously struck down a Florida right-to-reply law that required newspapers to provide political candidates attacked in their pages with equal space to respond to criticism.[1324] Florida argued that its law was justified by the need to ensure the "free flow of information." But since no law prevented political candidates from saying whatever they wanted, the real purpose of the law was to enable candidates to reach the newspaper's audience and to foster a "responsible press." The Florida law was a subtle attempt to legislate a RIGHT TO KNOW. Chief Justice Warren E. Burger noted that while a responsible press is a desirable goal, the Constitution does not require it, and the First Amendment bars any attempt by the government to guarantee it. FREEDOM OF THE PRESS means freedom from any attempt by government to tell editors how to do their jobs. Among other things, the requirement of equal space would limit the freedom of the newspaper to determine how to make up its pages and would multiply lawsuits in determining what in fact is "equal" and what constitutes an attack sufficient to warrant compulsory space.

In 1986 the Court held, 5–3, that a state public service commission could not constitutionally order a privately owned utility company to include in the envelope containing its monthly customer newsletter a mailing from an advocacy group opposing the utility's position on public issues. The commission's order unconstitutionally discriminated on the basis of "viewpoint": only those groups seeking to raise funds to oppose the utility's position in rate-making proceedings before the commission were permitted access to the customers via the envelopes.[1550]

See also: SPEECH, REGULATION OF CONTENT.

right to travel, *see:* **travel, right to**

right to trial, *see:* **trial, right to**

right to vote, *see:* **voting, right to**

right to welfare benefits, *see:* **welfare benefits, right to**

right to work, *see:* **occupation, right to pursue**

right-privilege distinction   Until the 1970s, it was generally assumed that what the government gave in jobs or benefits it could take away, free of constitutional restraints. The government benefit was a "privilege," not a right. Justice Oliver Wendell Holmes declared this distinction in his epigram in 1892 while still on the Massachusetts Supreme Judicial Court: "The petitioner may have a constitutional right to talk politics, but he has no constitutional right to be a policeman," meaning that the policeman could be fired for expressing his views. Beginning in the 1950s, in several LOYALTY OATH cases, the Court blunted the government's blanket power to fire employees for exercising political rights. By the 1970s, the distinction had collapsed. As Justice Potter Stewart put it in a 1972 case: "[E]ven though a person has no 'right' to a valuable governmental benefit and even though the government may deny him the benefit for any number of reasons, there are some reasons upon which the government may not rely."[1610] These reasons include a desire by the government to infringe an employee's or beneficiary's FREEDOM OF SPEECH.

See also: PENALTY-SUBSIDY DISTINCTION; PROCESS RIGHTS; PROCESS THAT IS DUE; PUBLIC EMPLOYMENT; UNCONSTITUTIONAL CONDITIONS; VESTED RIGHTS.

rights, waiver of   The Constitution's guarantee of a right does not mean that you are bound to take advantage of it. You have a right to speak but may keep quiet. When accused of a crime, you have the right to a TRIAL BY JURY and proof beyond a REASONABLE DOUBT, but you may waive those rights by pleading guilty. Waiver questions frequently occur in criminal cases, and the Court has made it clear that although waiver is permissible, an ACCUSED may not be held to have waived rights inadvertently. Waiver must be voluntary and "knowing, intelligent [and] done with sufficient awareness of the relevant circumstances and likely consequences."[221] As long as the waiver is knowing and voluntary, a person may even waive a right to contest a death sentence under a law not yet shown to be constitutional, as the Court ruled in upholding Gary Gilmore's desire to be executed.[758]

A person may waive a constitutional right by deed as well as by word. When a judge said in open court that he intended to talk in private to a juror seated in a criminal case to determine whether the juror's objectivity had been undermined, the Court treated the defendants' failure to object or to demand to be present as a waiver of their DUE PROCESS right.[718] The Court also treated a woman's failure to appear at a custody hearing or to discuss the case with a lawyer assigned to represent her in a separate criminal case as a waiver of her right to a lawyer in a proceeding to terminate her parental rights.[1124] The Court said that a defendant who pleads not guilty by reason of insanity has waived his right to insist that the government use a high standard of proof at a CIVIL COMMITMENT proceeding that he was mentally ill.[1035]

Before determining whether the waiver was voluntary and knowing, there must be a showing that there was a waiver at all. For example, signing a contract permitting a seller to "take back" goods if the buyer defaults is not a waiver of a right to notice and a hearing.[708] But if a contract is the product of negotiation "carried on by corporate parties with the advice of competent counsel" and if it explicitly states that no notice or hearing is necessary for REPOSSESSION, then waiver has been demonstrated.[507] Cases sometimes arise in which the police unlawfully arrest a suspect, who then sues for DAMAGES under federal CIVIL RIGHTS laws. Should the courts enforce an agreement between prosecutor and defendant dropping both the pending criminal charges and the damages case—in essence, a waiver of the defendant's right to sue under the civil rights laws? In 1987 the Court said that it depends on the circumstances. The problem is that the situation may be inherently coercive: the threat of criminal charges will often prompt a defendant to avoid them by dropping the civil case. But if the prosecutor can demonstrate that the agreement was voluntary and not the "product of an abuse of the criminal process," it can be enforced.[1476]

See also: PLEADING THE FIFTH.

rights in wartime   The Supreme Court has broadly adhered to the principle that citizens and residents of the United States, except for enemies, are entitled to all constitutional rights during wartime except when caught in the actual theater of military operations.[1345, 581] With the exception of the Civil War, the United States has been almost wholly free of such conditions, so the Court has had almost no opportunity to put flesh on the bones of this constitutional doctrine. However, the courts are less likely to uphold the principle under the stress of war itself; thus the Court approved JAPANESE-AMERICAN EXCLUSION AND RELOCATION in 1944,[1094] a ruling considered dubious to the point of worthlessness today. After World War I, the Court affirmed convictions for speeches and publications held to violate the Espionage Act. Said Justice Oliver Wendell Holmes: "When a nation is at war, many things that might be said in time of peace are such a hindrance to its effort that their utterance will not be endured so long as men fight and that no Court could regard them as protected by any constitutional right."[1812] But the sweeping nature of Holmes's interdiction of speech has not stood the test of time.[222] Enemies are entitled to little constitutional protection. Enemy property, even if owned by a citizen, may be seized free of the JUST COMPENSATION requirement of the FIFTH AMENDMENT.[1867] Enemies themselves are not entitled to the trial protections of the SIXTH AMENDMENT and may be tried independently by military tribunals.[1677]

See also: WAR POWER.

rights retained by the people, *see:* **Ninth Amendment**

ripeness   Although a constitutional issue might be within a court's JURISDICTION, the Supreme Court will refrain from hearing it until the dispute between the parties has advanced, or *ripened,* sufficiently to present a concrete CASE OR CONTROVERSY. Concerns about ripeness usually surface when people wish to challenge a law before it is applied to them. In 1947 the Court declined to consider the claims of federal civil servants that the Hatch Act was unconstitutional. The act prohibited them from engaging in certain political activities; but the

Court said that since the employees were only considering doing so, their claim would not be ripe until they actually engaged in the forbidden activities and the government then actually prosecuted one of them.[2098] Without waiting for ripeness the courts might frequently be called upon to issue unconstitutional ADVISORY OPINIONS about hypothetical occurrences.

However, legal ripeness cannot be determined as a farmer would examine fruit. Since the courts may issue DECLARATORY JUDGMENTS when a particular action is threatened, the ripeness doctrine ultimately gives the Court discretion to select among the many types of cases that present claims of potential harm. In a 1961 birth control case, the Court declined to resolve the issue because it was not shown that the physician who had been consulted by a married couple about CONTRACEPTION had any real fear of prosecution.[1643] But in a 1973 Georgia ABORTION case, the Court heard and decided a case favoring a constitutional right of doctors to perform abortions on the ground that the law "chilled and deterred" them from practicing medicine, even though none of them had been threatened with prosecution.[555] In 1991 the Court declined to consider an attack on a provision in the California constitution prohibiting POLITICAL PARTIES from endorsing candidates in certain nonpartisan elections because, Justice Anthony M. Kennedy said, there was no "live dispute," since there was evidence that some parties had violated the provision and not suffered for it.[1710] However, the Court decided *Bowers v. Hardwick,* the homosexual sodomy case, even though the prosecutor declined to seek an INDICTMENT. The Court declined to rule on whether the Army's surveillance of politically active civilian groups violated their FIRST AMENDMENT rights because, Chief Justice Warren E. Burger said, the protesters alleged only a "subjective chill" and did not claim "specific present objective harm or a threat of specific future harm."[1109]

On the other hand, it heard an appeal in a case challenging a law limiting liability should a nuclear power plant explode, even though none had done so and the likelihood was remote.[579] Refusing to hear the case until claims were riper, the Court said, might forever deter the development of nuclear power because unless the Court could rule one way or the other right away, operators would fear that they might lose the protection of the liability-limiting law.

See also: JUSTICIABILITY; MOOTNESS.

Rule of Four Under a well-established custom of the Supreme Court, whenever four justices think that a writ of CERTIORARI should be granted, the Court will agree to review the case, even though the majority thinks appeal is unsuitable.[1751] But the Rule of Four does not require the Court to decide the case in any particular way or even to decide it at all, if after ORAL ARGUMENT a majority thinks otherwise.[1461] The rule does not prohibit one or more of the four from changing their minds, permitting the Court to dismiss the appeal without hearing argument,[284] and occasionally the Court appears to have deviated from its tradition in dismissing, on a 5–4 vote, a writ of certiorari as "improvidently granted."[2070] Sometimes the rule is disregarded altogether; in 1980, four justices dissented to the denial of certiorari in two DEATH PENALTY cases, indicating that the majority refused to consider the appeals despite the rule.[574, 2187]

rule of law In the revolutionary year 1776, Thomas Paine wrote in his *Common Sense* "that in America, *the law is king.* For as in absolute governments the King is law, so in free countries the law *ought* to be king; and there ought to be no other." In Paine's sense, the *rule of law* means that the government, no less than the citizenry, must be law-abiding, a constitutional concept encapsulated in many constitutional principles, including PROCEDURAL DUE PROCESS, SEPARATION OF POWERS, and JUDICIAL REVIEW. In *United States v. Nixon,* the Supreme Court upheld not merely the rule of law but the *principle* of the rule of law, against President Richard M. Nixon's claim that the Constitution grants the chief executive plenary power to do as he wills and that he can be challenged in only two ways: at the ballot box or by IMPEACHMENT. The Court answered that the president was bound by the law.

See also: ENUMERATED POWERS; IMPLIED AND INHERENT POWERS; STARE DECISIS.

rule-making power, *see:* **delegation doctrine**

rules of its proceedings Under Art. I-§5[2], each house of Congress "may determine the rules of its proceedings." Except in rare circumstances, this clause commits to the houses of Congress power beyond judicial scrutiny to adopt whatever "parliamentary rules" they choose, as long as they do not "ignore constitutional restraints or violate fundamental rights." [115] Because the Senate is a "continuing body," its rules remain in force until the Senate changes them, whereas the House is reconstituted every two years and must therefore readopt its rules at the beginning of each new Congress. [1298] When the impact of a rule or congressional procedure affects a private right, the Supreme Court has held that the courts may intervene. For example, the Court interpreted the Senate's confirmation rules, concluding that they did not permit the Senate to reconsider a vote to confirm an appointment to a federal ADMINISTRATIVE AGENCY, and so the confirmed nominee was entitled to hold the OFFICE. [1898] On the other hand, the Court reversed a perjury conviction for testimony before a House committee on the ground that no QUORUM was present, even though, as four dissenting justices noted, House rules say that once a committee quorum has been established, its continuance is presumed until someone calls attention to its absence. [396]

S

safety regulations, *see:* police power

sailors, rights of, *see:* military courts and justice

salaries, taxation of, *see:* income tax; taxing power

salary protection of federal judges, *see:* Compensation Clause; income tax

sales taxes, *see:* taxation of interstate commerce

Santa Claus, *see:* religious symbols, right to display

schools, armbands in, *see:* juveniles, rights of; symbolic speech

schools, busing to, *see:* busing

schools, compulsory attendance, *see:* education, compulsory

schools, corporal punishment in   In 1977 the Supreme Court turned aside a challenge to the established custom in many school systems of permitting teachers or school disciplinarians to spank students for violations of school rules. Although the child has a "LIBERTY interest" in avoiding a beating, the Court held that DUE PROCESS does not require the school to hold a HEARING before inflicting corporal punishment since any excessive force or punishment wrongly imposed can be dealt with by an after-the-fact lawsuit.[980]

schools, discrimination by, *see:* tuition grants or vouchers

schools, foreign languages in   To express its disapproval of American peace negotiations with Germany after World War I, Oregon enacted a law prohibiting the teaching of German and all other modern languages except English in all its public and private schools. In a 1923 opinion that represented a linchpin in the series of modern SUBSTANTIVE DUE PROCESS cases, Justice James McReynolds invalidated the law, holding that the concept of LIBERTY includes "not merely freedom from bodily restraint" but also the right to carry on many commonplace activities, including the acquisition of "useful knowledge."[1323]

schools, free speech in, *see:* students' rights

schools, religion in   One of the major arenas of contention under the ESTABLISHMENT CLAUSE is the extent to which the states may provide money or other forms of aid that benefit religion, either in public or private schools. Litigation over these issues dates back to 1947, when the Court upheld a New Jersey law that permitted school districts to reimburse parents of children attending public and parochial schools for bus transportation to and from the schools. A sharply divided Court upheld the law, discerning in the transportation program a legitimate purpose that would extend benefits to all citizens regardless of religious belief.[634] Justice Hugo L. Black compared free busing to other services to which religious institutions are entitled, such as police and fire protection. Justice Robert H. Jackson's strongly worded dissent noted that the law provided reimbursements only for public and Catholic parochial schools and specifically excluded other schools, making the payment a benefit for a particular religion.

The Court did not reconsider the question of state aid for twenty years, when it sustained a New York program under which public school districts were required to lend secular textbooks to all schoolchildren, including those attending religious and nonreligious private schools.[183] This time Justice Black dissented, declaring the law to be "a flat, flagrant, open violation" of the Establishment Clause because it was a step down the road to having the government pick up the tab for a religious school's total budget. In addition, as Justice William O. Douglas forcefully pointed out, the system was operated in such a way that religious educators had considerable freedom to choose textbooks that bore definite religious messages. "There is nothing ideological about a bus," Douglas said, or "about a school lunch, or a public nurse, or a scholarship," but a textbook "is the chief . . . instrumentality for propagating a particular religious creed."

In 1971, in *Lemon v. Kurtzman,* the Court struck down a Pennsylvania law reimbursing religious schools for the cost of teachers' salaries, textbooks, and instructional materials in secular subjects. It also struck down a Rhode Island policy of paying nonpublic elementary school teachers a fifteen percent salary supplement. The "cumulative impact" of these programs, Chief Justice Warren E. Burger concluded, "involves excessive entanglement between government and religion" because the state would have to undertake a general and enduring "surveillance" of what is taught in the secular subjects in the parochial schools to prevent public money from being used to propagate religious faith. However, in that same year, the Court upheld federal grants available to all public colleges, including religious colleges, for constructing buildings and facilities to be used exclusively for secular purposes.[2046]

Although it approved the lending of textbooks to religious schools, the Court drew the line in 1977 at lending maps, tape recorders, and many other instructional devices and materials. In that same case, it rejected a policy of reimbursing transportation expenses for religious students taking field trips, distinguishing them from buses to and from home.[2246] Other distinctions seem equally baffling. If a religious school prepares state-mandated tests, the state may not reimburse the school for the costs of administering them.[1154] But if the state prepares the examination, it may reimburse the school for costs of its administration.[442] The Court upheld PROPERTY TAX exemptions for religious institutions,[2150] but refused to permit states to rebate tuition payments and provide income tax deductions or credits for the cost of religious schooling.[441] States may provide speech and hearing diagnostic services in religious schools,[2246] but they may not provide remedial services to these same schools.[1309]

These apparently inconsistent conclusions could be explained by the amorphous LEMON

TEST that the Court employs to sort out constitutional from unconstitutional extensions of aid: does the program have a secular purpose, is its primary effect secular, and does it excessively entangle church and state? On these questions, the most fair-minded people may differ, perhaps much to their own chagrin. The Court did manage to agree unanimously that a program providing financial aid for vocational rehabilitation to the handicapped is constitutional when the recipient has sole discretion of how to use the tuition funds, including attending a Christian college to become a "pastor, missionary, or youth director."[2242]

A different issue is whether school authorities may bar religious groups from meeting in public schools. In 1948 the Court voided a RELEASED TIME program under which secondary schoolchildren were permitted to leave classes early to attend religious worship in the schools during school hours.[977] But in 1981 the Court said that public colleges could constitutionally grant facilities to students wishing to meet voluntarily for religious purposes as long as the school provides access to its buildings to all sorts of other voluntary student groups.[2202] In 1990 the Court upheld the federal Equal Access Act, requiring public secondary schools receiving federal funds to let student religious groups use school premises to the same extent that it permits other "noncurriculum" groups, such as a scuba diving club, to use them.[2188]

See also: EVOLUTION, TEACHING OF; PRAYER AND BIBLE READING.

schools, right to attend private, *see:* **private schools, right to attend**

schools, search in, *see:* **search and seizure: schools**

schools, single-sex The Supreme Court has never squarely decided whether the states may operate single-sex schools. In 1982, though, it held that the School of Nursing at the Mississippi University for Women could not constitutionally exclude men.[1362] The majority concluded that the state failed to advance an "exceedingly persuasive justification" for its decision to exclude a male registered nurse working in Columbus, Mississippi, where the school is located. The question was whether the state had an "important governmental objective." It is not permissible, said Justice Sandra Day O'Connor, simply to separate men and women or to exclude one as innately inferior. Mississippi asserted that its admissions policy was designed to compensate for previous discrimination against women. But of course there was no discrimination against women in the field of nursing; to the contrary, the single-sex policy simply perpetuates the old stereotype that only women are fit for nursing. Moreover, because the school was prepared to admit the male nurse as an auditor, it admitted that having a man in the classroom was not a distraction. Excluding men therefore would serve no educational goal. Justice Lewis F. Powell dissented, saying that this was not properly a SEX DISCRIMINATION case. There were other nursing schools in the state that admitted men. Mississippi was simply providing women "with a traditionally popular and respected choice of educational environment." Other dissenters noted that because the case dealt only with a professional school, it would not represent a precedent for other cases involving single-sex business schools or even college programs.

science and useful arts, *see:* **Patent Clause**

Scottsboro Boys Case In 1931 a fight broke out between nine black youths and a group of whites, including two girls, on a freight train traveling through northeastern Alabama. A posse stopped the train and took the nine black boys into custody. One of the white girls told the sheriff that her companion had been raped by each of the blacks. The boys were held in a jail in Scottsboro (hence the name that has stuck ever since), and a lynching was prevented only because the Alabama National Guard was called out. Two weeks later, in a trial that started and finished in a single day, eight of the nine were convicted in this small town while nearly ten thousand people waited in the streets outside the courthouse. As the "trial" began, the judge refused to appoint counsel but "jawboned" two lawyers, one not a member of the Alabama bar, to nominally assist the defendants. The Scottsboro Boys were sentenced to death.

An appeal reached the Supreme Court, which reversed. The trial, said Justice George Sutherland in *Powell v. Alabama,* was utterly lacking in DUE PROCESS because ignorant, illiterate youths, surrounded by a mob, could not possibly have a fair HEARING without the assistance of counsel. This was the first time that the Court had reversed a criminal conviction because of the state's failure to provide a basic procedural necessity. In a capital case, everyone is entitled to a lawyer, whether one is requested or not. At the retrial, the court appointed a New York lawyer, Samuel S. Leibowitz, for the boys. He discovered that the girl who claimed to have been raped was in fact a well-known prostitute apparently traveling on the train with a customer. She had fabricated the rape story to cover up her crossing a state line illegally. Nevertheless, an Alabama jury reconvicted the Scottsboro Boys, and they were imprisoned, ultimately to be pardoned decades later.

See also: COUNSEL, ASSISTANCE OF; PROCEDURAL RIGHTS OF CRIMINAL DEFENDANTS.

search and seizure   The FOURTH AMENDMENT's prohibition against "unreasonable searches and seizures" has ancient roots, summed up in the English maxim "Every man's house is his castle." But in the 1760s the British government disdained the right against unreasonable searches and authorized "writs of assistance," under which a British agent could enter any home or building to search for smuggled goods on which customs duties had not been paid. The writs were issued even though the agents offered no reasonable grounds for believing that the goods were in any particular place. The writs did not state what was being searched for, did not name the people suspected of having contraband, and were valid indefinitely. Abuse of these writs was a primary goad to the Revolutionary War, and at the ratifying conventions in 1787 and 1788, the people did not forget. The Fourth Amendment was the result.

Unfortunately, the Fourth Amendment's two clauses are far from clear. The first clause says that the people have the right to be secure "in their persons, houses, papers, and effects" against *unreasonable* searches and seizures. The second clause says that a SEARCH WARRANT may not be issued without probable cause and without "particularly describing the place to be searched, and the persons or things to be seized." Whether the two clauses must be read together or are independent has been at the crux of the debate. If they are read together, then any search conducted without a warrant is by that very reason unreasonable. If read separately, some reasonable searches may be conducted without warrants, and the warrant restrictions apply only to those searches requiring warrants. At one time the Court connected the clauses closely, so that all but a few warrantless searches were considered unreasonable. That connection is now severed, and exceptions to the warrant requirement have multiplied.

Cases involving the law of search and seizure are numerous and wondrously variegated. Doctrine has changed as justices come and go. The Burger Court (1969–86) wrote opinions in 130 search and seizure cases. Since the issue first arose in 1925, the Court has considered the problem of automobile searches in ninety cases. The profusion of cases arises largely because differences in circumstance dictate differences in outcome, since the question is almost always whether the search or seizure was "reasonable."

The Court first considered the Fourth Amendment in 1886. Comparing an order to give up private papers to SELF-INCRIMINATION, the Court held that the Fourth Amendment precluded a court from enforcing an order to turn over physical evidence.[213] In 1914 the Court announced the exclusionary rule: in federal prosecutions, unlawfully seized evidence must be excluded from trial.[2175] Until 1949 the Fourth Amendment was assumed not to apply to the states, but in that year the Court unanimously concluded that freedom from unreasonable searches and seizures is a fundamental right that the DUE PROCESS Clause of the FOURTEENTH AMENDMENT makes applicable to the states.[2244] The Court declined to apply the exclusionary rule to the states, holding that they had other methods of enforcing the right, but the Court reversed itself in 1961.[1238] As a result, most of the Court's search and seizure rulings have come in the last three decades.

The constitutional problem of search and seizure has four parts: (1) What does probable cause mean? (2) What constitutes a "search" or a "seizure"? (3) Under what circumstances must warrants be obtained? (4) What are the legal consequences of an unconstitutional search or seizure? Questions 1 and 4 are discussed under the headings PROBABLE CAUSE and EXCLUSIONARY RULE. Question 3 is discussed in the various search and seizure subheadings that follow.

As to Question 2, to determine whether the police have made a search or seizure, the Court looks to the interest protected by the Fourth Amendment. In 1928 it suggested that the interest was a person's private property: a warrant would be necessary to search a person's home but not to tap his phone, since no property interest is invaded when the police listen in on a telephone call.[1533] Since then the Court has substantially modified its views. Today the premise is that the Fourth Amendment protects a person's PRIVACY.[2153] Because the Fourth Amendment protects "people, not places," the root question is whether a person has an "expectation of privacy" on which he may reasonably rely.[1051] That expectation does not depend on having a property interest in the space that the police invade. For example, an office worker has a privacy right in an office shared with others, even though he owns neither office nor papers.[1235] "Expectation of privacy" is not an artificial judicial rule but a reflection of life: what areas of their lives do people in fact expect to remain private? The highest expectation is in the privacy of one's home.[33, 1351, 1581] People have a much lesser expectation of privacy in, say, their automobiles.[74, 1765] They have an intermediate expectation of privacy in their luggage.[363] An overnight guest has a constitutionally protected interest in the privacy of a friend's home[1357] but not in a friend's car.[1689] Ultimately, almost every case turns on its own facts. About the most that can be said in summary is that people's homes remain their castles, but otherwise the Court has largely concluded that we live in goldfish bowls.

See also: ARREST AND ARREST WARRANT; ASSISTANCE, WRIT OF; DRUG TESTING; HABEAS CORPUS; MERE EVIDENCE RULE; NO-KNOCK ENTRY; *various search and seizure listings below.*

search and seizure: administrative inspections   Until the 1960s it was generally assumed that if administrative officials were conducting routine inspections and not investigating a particular crime, the FOURTH AMENDMENT did not apply. In 1967 the Court reversed itself, holding that building code inspectors must obtain SEARCH WARRANTS to inspect homes[331] and commercial buildings[1839] for code violations. The rule was extended in 1978 to workplace inspections by agents of the Occupational Safety and Health Act.[1247] The occupational law was so open-ended, permitting inspections of almost every workplace, that it would be unreasonable to leave inspections to the complete discretion of the agency. But building on earlier cases permitting warrantless inspections of particular industries, such as liquor[434] and firearms,[167] the Court ruled in 1982 that some kinds of warrantless administrative inspections are permissible when the property is subject to close federal regulation, as in mining.[562] Entry into buildings to fight fires is permissible without warrants of any kind, since the fire itself makes the entry reasonable, and if firefighters discover evidence of arson, the PLAIN VIEW doctrine permits them lawfully to seize it. However, to return to the scene to check for further evidence requires a warrant.[1332] A public employee's office may be searched without a warrant or probable cause as long as the purpose of the search was work-related rather than "investigatory."[1511] In 1987 the Court said that inspectors need not obtain warrants to inspect automobile junkyards. The inspections were part of an administrative scheme to combat automobile theft. The Court ruled that even though evidence of criminality may turn up in the course of such inspections, they were valid because this was a civil inspection system; the state need not address every social problem exclusively through the criminal law.[1458] The Court has also upheld random boarding of vessels either at sea or in port by customs inspectors to check documentation, even without suspicion of illegalities.[2126]

search and seizure: airport stops   To stop and frisk, the police ordinarily must be able to articulate a reason to suspect wrongdoing. But the Court has approved police stops of suspected drug couriers at airports based on a profile consisting of factors each of which, taken separately, may be innocent.[1904]

search and seizure: automobiles   Search of automobiles was an early exception to the usual requirement of a SEARCH WARRANT. In 1925 the Court ruled that as long as a law enforcement official has probable cause to believe an automobile contains evidence that can constitutionally be seized, he can dispense with a warrant because an automobile, unlike a home, can move.[351] Since then, the Court has decided ninety automobile search cases, and the resulting rules are accessible only to the specialist. In general, the Court has concluded that the public has a reduced expectation of privacy in automobiles; therefore, many types of searches that would require warrants if the police were searching a home are not required for automobiles. As long as the police have probable cause, they may, without warrants, search interior areas of cars, including glove compartments and spaces under the seats;[1689] however, they may not search the passengers unless there is independent probable cause to arrest them.[546, 2273] Warrantless searches of closed containers may not be conducted just because the police find them in automobiles,[363] but if there is probable cause to search the automobile, police may also search the container without a warrant.[1765] Likewise, if the police have probable cause to search a closed container in the car, they may do so even if they have no warrant to search the car itself.[315] When police impound a car, they may inventory its contents, including closed containers, and any incriminating evidence found may constitutionally be used at trial.[435] Mobile homes placed in a parking lot may be searched as though they were automobiles.[318]

search and seizure: border searches   It has been accepted since 1789 that customs and other law enforcement officials may stop people at the border to inspect their persons and possessions without probable cause or any reasonable grounds to suspect wrongdoing.[1691] But the search must be at or near the border. A roving patrol looking for illegal aliens may not stop an automobile twenty miles from the border without probable cause to believe that their prey is in the car.[43] Border inspectors may stop cars just to ask a few questions or check papers if they have some rational basis to suspect that illegal aliens are inside; however, the ethnic appearance of the passengers is not a sufficient reason.[234] If the border guards have a reasonable suspicion based on objective facts that a person crossing the border has committed a crime, they may stop him for more than a few minutes even without a warrant. In one case, the Court upheld a day-long detention of a person suspected of having swallowed the narcotics he was smuggling across the border.[1376]

search and seizure: consent searches The FOURTH AMENDMENT right to be free from unreasonable searches and seizures may be waived. If the police show up at your door and ask to search your quarters, you may consent to their doing so. But the consent must be freely given; the prosecution has the burden of showing that consent was voluntary.[273] A third party may consent to the search if he has some authority over the place or thing to be searched; you may validly authorize the police to search for evidence pinning a crime on your roommate, for instance.[1271] The search will be upheld even if the police are mistaken about the authority of the third party to consent, as long as the belief was reasonable.[976] But neither a hotel night clerk[1964] nor a landlord[374] may validly consent to the search of a suspect's hotel room or apartment.

In 1991 the Court declined to hold that a police request to search through a bus passenger's luggage is always coercive. As a means of interdicting drug traffic, the Broward County (Florida) police department randomly boards buses and asks permission to search luggage. In this case, even though the police had no reason to believe that a particular passenger had drugs, they asked permission to search after advising him that he could refuse. He consented; they searched and found cocaine. On appeal the Florida Supreme Court concluded that a person in his situation would never really feel free to refuse permission because of the close quarters of the bus. The Supreme Court rejected this notion, holding that whether or not there was coercion depends on the particular circumstances in each case. The Fourth Amendment does not require a flat rule that consent may never be freely given by passengers on a bus.[680]

search and seizure: corporate records Seizure of papers is fraught with constitutional difficulties, not only under the FOURTH AMENDMENT but also under the FIFTH AMENDMENT's ban on SELF-INCRIMINATION. Nevertheless, the Court permits papers to be seized under a warrant issued with probable cause to believe that they contain evidence of a crime—for example, fraudulent land transactions.[63]

search and seizure: electronic surveillance, *see:* **search and seizure: wiretapping and electronic surveillance**

search and seizure: execution of warrants, *see:* **no-knock entry**

search and seizure: exigent circumstances "Exigent circumstances" are exceptional circumstances that permit the police to search without a warrant. The Court has identified several types of exigent circumstances: search incident to arrest,[2175] searches of automobiles on the roadways,[351] "hot pursuit" of suspects who flee into buildings,[2153] BLOOD TESTS to determine whether a driver was intoxicated,[1818] and stop and frisk detention of suspicious individuals.[2013] The concept of exigent circumstances is open-ended; such searches may proceed whenever the police reasonably believe that they may "protect or preserve life or avoid serious injury."[1354]

search and seizure: fingerprints and other objective evidence In 1967 the Court overturned the MERE EVIDENCE RULE, which had prohibited police from seizing evidence connecting the suspect to the crime, other than actual contraband, weapons or tools used to commit the crime, or the "fruits" of the crime, such as stolen goods.[2153] Since then the Court has ruled in a number of cases that fingerprints,[522] blood,[1818] skin and fingernail scrapings,[501] may all be taken, as may voice and handwriting samples.[549] However, not every type of useful evidence may be seized. The Court said that police may not force a suspect to undergo surgery with general anesthesia in a hospital to remove a bullet from his chest.[2235]

search and seizure: home visits In 1971 the Court approved a welfare inspection system under which welfare recipients forfeit their benefits if they refuse to admit caseworkers who appear at the door to conduct a home visit. The Court suggested that this was not a search in the constitutional sense, even though evidence that might cause recipients to lose benefits could be used against them in later proceedings.[2266]

search and seizure: incident to arrest
There has always been an exception to the FOURTH AMENDMENT's warrant requirement for searches "incident to an arrest." If the police have valid grounds to arrest, then they may search. The controversy turns on *what* they may search. Through the 1980s the Court allowed the police to search through anything within the arrestee's "immediate control." For example, they could search his person and the room in which he is located, including drawers and the like, to prevent him from using weapons. But police could not intrude into other rooms without a valid search warrant.[394] The Court rejected a warrantless search that lasted four days and combed through an arrestee's entire house.[1351] In 1990, however, the Court held that the police may undertake a "protective sweep" of the premises where the arrest was made, as long as they have a "reasonable belief" that a dangerous person might be lurking there.[1258] Since an arrestee has an expectation of privacy in luggage, the police may take it but may not search it without a warrant.[363] But a seemingly broad exception to this rule permits the police to inventory an arrestee's effects, including a shoulder bag, without a warrant; if criminal evidence is uncovered, it may be used at trial.[975]

In a 1991 case, Alameda County (California) police in a patrol car rounded a corner and saw several youths "huddled around" a parked car. When the youths saw the police they started to run. The police gave chase. One of the youths ran down an alley and did not notice an officer in pursuit. At the last moment, seeing the officer almost on top of him, the youth threw something onto the pavement. The officer tackled the youth, handcuffed him, and on radioing for help discovered that the object was crack cocaine. At a juvenile proceeding, the youth claimed that the cocaine had been unlawfully seized because it was the fruit of an unreasonable "seizure" of the youth himself. His theory was that the officer was exhibiting a show of force by chasing him, and that that amounted to a seizure. The Court held, 7–2, that the chase was not a seizure, that the cocaine was abandoned by the fleeing youth, and that it could therefore be used in evidence.[321]

search and seizure: liability for illegal search
Under federal civil rights laws, municipal police[1375] and even the city itself[1372] may be sued

for violating an individual's FOURTH AMEND-
MENT rights. This law is not applicable to federal law enforcement officials, but in 1971, in
*Bivens v. Six Unknown Named Agents of the Federal
Bureau of Narcotics,* the Supreme Court held
that the Fourth Amendment itself permits individuals injured by unconstitutional searches
to file DAMAGE suits against the officials who
carried out the search.[168] There was some suggestion that such suits might provide a reasonable deterrent to police lawlessness so that
the EXCLUSIONARY RULE could be abolished.
Though weakened, the exclusionary rule still
applies in both state and federal court for violations of the Fourth Amendment. The Court
has partially limited the Fourth Amendment
right to sue. A federal law enforcement official
may have a suit against him dismissed on
showing that it was objectively reasonable for
him to believe there was probable cause or an
exigent circumstance to search, even if the
warrantless search is later held unconstitutional.[60]

See also: CIVIL RIGHTS AND CIVIL LIBERTIES; CONSTITUTIONAL
TORTS; IMMUNITY FROM SUIT.

search and seizure: neutral magistrate   The
FOURTH AMENDMENT does not say who is empowered to issue warrants. The Supreme
Court has repeatedly said that when warrants
are required, they are to be issued only by a
"judicial officer."[1139, 1051, 2102] There would be no
point at all in having a warrant if the police
could search whenever in their own judgment
they have evidence that would lead a judicial
officer to issue one. The evidence must be presented to a "neutral and detached magistrate."[1022] The magistrate need not be a judge
with the independence of a federal judge appointed under Article III. For example, city
clerks supervised by judges may issue warrants.[1848] But the issuer cannot be a person
engaged in law enforcement, such as the attorney general, for then he cannot be neutral;[462]

nor may he be paid for each warrant issued, for
then he is not detached.[449]

search and seizure: open fields doctrine   In
1924 the Court held that certain "open fields,"
such as vacant lots and pastures, are not protected by the FOURTH AMENDMENT and that the
police may search them without obtaining a
warrant or even having probable cause.[916] Even
fenced fields fall within the open fields doctrine, except for areas immediately adjacent to
a person's home.[1531] This rule has been applied
to garbage left on the street; police may rummage through it without a warrant or probable
cause.[320] Likewise, police may inspect an open
field from low-flying helicopters and whatever
they see may be admitted at trial.[682]

search and seizure: plain view   If the police
are lawfully in a place where evidence of criminal wrongdoing is in "plain view," they may
seize it without a search warrant; for example,
marijuana lying exposed in a college dormitory
in which the police were lawfully standing.[2157]
The discovery of objects in plain view need not
be inadvertent; that is, they need not be things
the police did not expect to find. In a case
where the warrant only authorized the police
to search for stolen goods but the officers saw
the robbery weapons in plain sight, the Court
upheld the seizure.[943]

search and seizure: prisons   The FOURTH
AMENDMENT does not apply to prison cells.
Prison authorities may search inmates' cells at
will. Random "shakedown" searches may be
conducted without setting forth any policy by
which guards will undertake them.[952] Similarly, probation authorities need neither warrant nor probable cause to conduct administrative searches of a probationer's home.[816]

**search and seizure: random stops and check-
points**   The FOURTH AMENDMENT provides

practically no protection to drivers caught in a roadblock. In 1990 the Court upheld sobriety checkpoints at which police may stop any car passing along the road at a fixed point to check for signs of intoxication, without any reasonable grounds to believe that any particular driver is drunk.[1333] If the police have a reasonable belief that weapons may be present, they may stop and frisk and seize any weapons found in the places where weapons would ordinarily be placed.[1330] They may also seize any evidence found in plain view.[2019] The Court has also upheld fixed checkpoint stops of automobiles at the border to question passengers, even though the authorities have no reason to believe that illegal aliens are in the car.[1257]

search and seizure: schools School officials need neither warrants nor probable cause to search school grounds, as long as they have reasonable grounds to believe that a student has violated the law or school rules. In one case a student was accused of violating a no-smoking rule. The Court held that a search of her purse was valid, and the illegal drugs found there were admissible in juvenile proceedings.[1448]

search and seizure: standing to contest Suppose that, fearing detection, a drug dealer hurriedly stuffs drugs into his companion's purse and that without probable cause or a warrant the police search it. There they find the drugs. May the prosecutor offer into evidence the drugs so seized? Even though the search of the companion was unconstitutional, the Court ruled that the drug dealer has no constitutional grounds for complaint, since he had no expectation of privacy in her purse.[1695] In general, therefore, the FOURTH AMENDMENT rules will be applied only if the search violates an interest of the person against whom the evidence will be used.[1689]

search and seizure: stop and frisk When a police officer's suspicion about someone's behavior falls short of the constitutional requirement of probable cause to arrest, the Court has permitted a lesser form of search and seizure. For example, an experienced police officer may see suspicious characters "casing" a store as if they were planning to rob it. The FOURTH AMENDMENT, said Chief Justice Earl Warren in 1968, permits the officer to "stop and frisk" these not-quite-suspects if they cannot give an immediate and reasonable account of themselves. Any weapons discovered in the frisk may be seized and the suspect arrested.[2013] But the officer may not rely on generalized suspicions; he must be able to specifically articulate the circumstances that gave rise to his suspicions.[473] So, for example, a person's mere appearance in a high crime area is not a reasonable ground to stop and frisk,[258] nor is a person's ethnic appearance.[234]

See also: SEARCH AND SEIZURE: AIRPORT STOPS.

search and seizure: wiretapping and electronic surveillance Wiretapping is eavesdropping on telephone conversations. The constitutional question is whether evidence gathered by wiretapping (or other forms of electronic surveillance) is subject to the FOURTH AMENDMENT's prohibition against unreasonable search and seizure, requiring the government to obtain a search warrant after first showing probable cause to believe that a crime has been committed. When the issue first came before the Supreme Court in 1928 in *Olmstead v. United States,* Chief Justice William Howard Taft held for the 5–4 majority that the police did not need a warrant because intercepting a phone conversation was neither a physical trespass of a person's home nor a seizure of tangible property. In a bitter dissent that has since become the basic constitutional rule, Justice Louis D. Brandeis said: "The makers of our Constitution . . . conferred, as against the government, the right to be let alone. . . . Every unjustifiable intrusion upon the privacy of the individual, by whatever means employed, must be deemed a violation of the Fourth Amendment."

Is placing a "bug" in someone's home or office subject to the Fourth Amendment if bugging the premises requires a physical trespass? In a 1942 case, the Court said there was no trespass because the bug was placed on one side of a party wall and in no way intruded into the room from which it plucked out conversations.[770] But when officials, without a warrant, pushed a "spike mike" into the wall to make contact with a heating duct so that it could broadcast conversations, there was an unconstitutional trespass.[1868] By the late 1960s, the Court reconsidered, holding that the Fourth Amendment protects people, not places; therefore the relevant issue is not whether there has been some intrusion into a wall but whether there is some expectation of privacy. Overruling *Olmstead*, the Court held that people do expect that their telephone conversations and conversations in a room will be private.[1051] The result is that wiretapping and other forms of electronic surveillance are now subject to the Fourth Amendment's warrant requirement (and are also regulated by federal statutes).

New technologies pose related issues. For example, the police may, without a warrant, install a beeper on a car to follow it along the public roads,[1087] but they need a warrant to install a beeper in a private residence to know whether a particular object is continuously present.[1048] Somewhat mysteriously, the Court held that since there is no expectation of privacy in the phone numbers that a person dials, the police may surreptitiously install a device to record those numbers without obtaining a warrant.[1893]

See also: NATIONAL SECURITY.

search and seizure: with and without warrants Whenever practicable, the police must obtain "advance judicial approval of searches and seizures through a warrant procedure," the Court said in the 1960s.[2013] In essence, its view of the FOURTH AMENDMENT then was that only in exceptional cases could the probable cause and warrant requirements be dispensed with. In the 1990s that general outlook seems greatly altered. The Court has determined that in a wide variety of circumstances it is not practicable to obtain a warrant. With the exception of searches of a person's home, the warrant rule today has more exceptions than inclusions. Among other circumstances now excepted from the rule are random DRUG TESTING, random stops and checkpoints, administrative searches in many industries, factories, and offices, schools, and automobiles on the road.

search incident to arrest, *see:* **search and seizure: incident to arrest**

search warrant When a search warrant is required under the FOURTH AMENDMENT, it must describe with particularity "the place to be searched, and the persons or things to be seized." Police may not lawfully seize something not specifically listed in the warrant, unless they are lawfully on the premises and spot evidence of a crime that is in plain view.[462] A warrant to search for and seize obscene materials may not simply authorize police to look for "obscene" books. The items must be particularized so that the magistrate issuing the warrant can be certain that the police have probable cause to believe they will find the materials and so that it can be determined later whether what they find squares with what they said they would find.[1242] The Court invalidated a seizure of two thousand books and pamphlets under a warrant that broadly authorized the taking of writings "concerning the Communist Party of Texas."[1943] A good-faith mistake in a warrant may sometimes be excused. The Court upheld a search of an apartment mistakenly listed as the only one on the third floor of the building when it turned out that there were two.[1260]

See also: EFFICIENCY.

seat of the government of the United States, *see:* **District of Columbia, constitutional status of**

secession, *see:* **nullification, interposition, and secession**

Second Amendment The Second Amendment was ratified in 1791 as part of the BILL OF RIGHTS. Despite the seemingly broad language protecting the "right of the people to keep and bear arms," the Supreme Court in its rare constructions of the amendment has narrowly confined it so that Congress has been free to impose restrictions on gun ownership and sale. The Second Amendment applies only to the federal government and does not prevent the states from enacting any gun control legislation they please.[1661]

See also: ARMS, RIGHT TO KEEP AND BEAR.

second-class citizenship In theory, a person either is or is not an American citizen—the Constitution formally recognizes only one class of citizenship. Said Chief Justice John Marshall in 1824: "A naturalized citizen . . . becomes a member of the society, possessing all the rights of a native citizen, and standing . . . on the [constitutional] footing of a native."[1543] Before the Citizenship Clause of the FOURTEENTH AMENDMENT was ratified in 1868, this sentiment was never entirely true: free blacks were denied equal benefits of citizenship in many northern states. (Under DRED SCOTT V. SANDFORD, this discrimination was formally justified by the anomaly that free blacks were not entitled to citizenship at all.)

Today there are three ways in which some citizens differ, two because of explicit constitutional provisions and one because of a constitutional obscurity. (1) Under Art. II-§1[5] only "natural born" citizens may be president. Naturalized citizens, then, may not serve as president. The Constitution does not define "natural born," and the issue sometimes surfaces when a potential candidate turns out to have been born abroad to American parents. Under federal law, such a person is a citizen from birth. But it is unclear whether the citizenship derives from birth or naturalization. Section 1 of the Fourteenth Amendment says that any person "born or naturalized in" the United States is a citizen. A person born abroad was, of course, not "born in" the United States, so it is possible that such a person is naturalized, by virtue of the law conferring citizenship at birth and hence ineligible to run for president. The issue has never reached the Supreme Court. (2) Persons convicted of crimes may suffer the loss of important incidents of citizenship, such as the right to vote. The THIRTEENTH AMENDMENT explicitly exempts prisoners from the abolition of INVOLUNTARY SERVITUDE. (3) Naturalized citizens may lose their citizenship in ways not applicable to citizens born in the United States. Under federal law, a person born abroad to one parent who was an American citizen becomes an American citizen at birth but forfeits that citizenship if he or she fails to live continuously in the United States during any five-year period between his or her fourteenth and twenty-eighth birthday. The Supreme Court upheld Congress's power to create such a conditional citizenship: "[W]hile it lasts, [his citizenship] although conditional, is not 'second-class.'"[1749]

However, the Court struck down laws divesting a naturalized citizen of citizenship for voting in foreign elections[21] and for living continuously for three years in his former country. Native-born citizens may not be deprived of their citizenship in this manner, the Court said: "[T]he rights of citizenship of the native born and of the naturalized person are of the same dignity and co-extensive." [1819] The Court has adhered to this notion in striking down under the EQUAL PROTECTION CLAUSE several state DURATIONAL RESIDENCY laws that provide greater benefits to longtime residents than to those who have newly arrived. In 1982, for example, the Court invalidated as irrational an Alaska law that doled out dividends to residents from its sale of oil and other natural resources, the amount varying with the length of residence. The states are not permitted, said Chief Justice Warren E. Burger, "to divide citizens into expanding numbers of permanent classes." [2287] The Court similarly voided laws granting tax exemptions and a VETERANS' PREFERENCE to only those Vietnam veterans who were residents of the states before a certain date. [940, 97]

See also: ALIENS; CITIZENS AND CITIZENSHIP; DEPORTATION; EXPATRIATION; IMMIGRATION AND NATURALIZATION.

secrecy, *see:* free press–fair trial; gag order; leaks

Section 1983, *see:* civil rights legislation; immunity from suit; Ku Klux Klan Act

securities laws, *see:* takeover laws

security programs, *see:* loyalty-security programs

sedition Sedition is a lesser form of TREASON. It encompasses subversive activities that tend to undermine the government or the authority of the state. Since the espionage and sedition trials after World War I, the crucial difficulty has been to distinguish between seditious actions and constitutionally protected speech. Most sedition laws, including the original Sedition Act of 1798, criminalized the advocacy of sedition, as well as sedition itself. For half a century, between 1919 and 1969, the Supreme Court struggled to draw a line, at first rejecting Justice Oliver Wendell Holmes's CLEAR AND PRESENT DANGER test in favor of the theory that if a particular speech or publication has a tendency, even if not immediate, to lead to lawless violence, the speaker may be punished. These doctrines were aired chiefly in cases involving criminal SYNDICALISM and COMMUNISM AND COMMUNIST PARTY, until the Court in 1969 in *Brandenburg v. Ohio* declared that mere advocacy, unless directed to inciting and likely to produce "imminent lawless action," is protected under the FIRST AMENDMENT. Laws against seditious actions, such as actual physical violence, remain constitutional. However, in 1956 the Supreme Court declared that the anti-communist Smith Act, which criminalized seditious advocacy, preempted all state sedition laws, so that only federal enforcement is allowed. [1591]

See also: SEDITIOUS LIBEL; SUBVERSIVE ADVOCACY.

seditious libel Seditious libel was defined at COMMON LAW as any oral or written attack on the king or his government. Centuries ago, seditious libel was considered the equivalent of TREASON and was punishable by torture and death. When treason came to be understood as some OVERT ACT to produce a consequence inimical to the realm, punishment for seditious libel was limited to fines and imprisonment. In 1735 the ZENGER trial in New York established the fundamental principle that a true statement could not be punished as a seditious libel, no matter how vociferous the criticism of the government. In 1791, with the ratification of the BILL OF RIGHTS, the constitutional issue was whether any form of seditious libel survived the FIRST AMENDMENT. In 1798 the Federalists pushed the Sedition Act through Congress to silence criticism of President John Adams's policies. The act forbade publication of any false, scandalous, and malicious statements about Congress or the president. The act was denounced by Adams's opponents, and when Thomas Jefferson became president he pardoned several editors convicted under it. The law lapsed in 1801 and never was put to the test in the Supreme Court.

The question of seditious libel did not arise again until after World War I, when several federal convictions were obtained under the Espionage Act for speeches and publications that at bottom were nothing more than what we might today consider relatively mild criticism of the government. The Supreme Court upheld the government, provoking the classic dissent of Justice Oliver Wendell Holmes in 1919 in *Abrams v. United States:* "I wholly disagree with the argument of the government that the First Amendment left the common law as to seditious libel in force." Inventing the CLEAR AND PRESENT DANGER test, Holmes insisted that no one could be punished for words alone unless they were likely to cause people imminently to act lawlessly. In 1964, in *New York Times v. Sullivan,* the Court said that actual MALICE must be shown in ordinary defamation lawsuits and noted that although the Sedition Act was never tested, "the attack upon its validity has carried the day in the court of history." In 1964, in *Garrison v. Louisiana,* the Court reversed a conviction of the New Orleans district attorney, James Garrison, for "criminal libel," the practical equivalent of seditious libel. Garrison, who gained fame for investigating President Kennedy's assassination, denounced local judges as lazy and corrupt. Although the *Garrison* case does not necessarily preclude seditious libel suits if the speaker knowingly and falsely defames a public official, as a practical matter the crime of seditious libel is dead.

See also: CRIMINAL LIBEL; SEDITION; SUBVERSIVE ADVOCACY.

segregation and integration   In the CIVIL RIGHTS CASES in 1883, the Supreme Court denied that Congress had the constitutional authority to prohibit private acts of RACIAL DISCRIMINATION. Nevertheless, the Court agreed that such acts were legally wrong and that the states should provide a remedy. But in 1896, in PLESSY V. FERGUSON, the Court turned its back on its own prior statements and on the central meaning of the FOURTEENTH AMENDMENT and officially approved racial segregation. The Court's primary justification was that the EQUAL PROTECTION CLAUSE required absolute equality only for political and civil rights, such as voting and the right to enter contracts. It did not require equality for "social rights," such as riding on railroads, the central issue in the case. Instead, as long as the state provided SEPARATE BUT EQUAL facilities, the Constitution was satisfied. One conundrum was why, if equal protection did not embrace social rights, facilities needed to be equal at all. Why not just deny blacks the right altogether to ride on railroads? Another mystery is how the Court could square separate but equal with FREEDOM OF CONTRACT. For example, in 1908 the Court upheld a law that prohibited *voluntary* interracial education. Justice Rufus Peckham, the author of LOCHNER V. NEW YORK, the archetypical decision upholding a liberty to contract, saw no inconsistency in holding that a law merely *regulating* the terms of an employment agreement between a worker and his employer is unconstitutional, whereas a law *prohibiting* blacks from entering contracts for admission to colleges that also enroll whites was perfectly constitutional.[154]

Plessy created a segregated America, from schools and neighborhoods down to black and white telephone booths, cemeteries, brothels, and even, in some states, Bibles to swear in witnesses in court. In 1927 the Supreme Court extended *Plessy* to formally uphold school segregation.[776] In 1938, however, the Court was presented with a different kind of case: the segregated University of Missouri Law School, the only law school in the state, refused to admit a black but offered him funds to attend a law school out of state. He insisted on his right to attend a Missouri law school equally with whites, and the Supreme Court now agreed. Since no out-of-state school taught Missouri law, the education he was offered was clearly separate and *un*equal.[1365] The Court's decision ordering Missouri to provide the black student with a legal education helped prompt the NAACP to found its Legal Defense and Education Fund and to name Thurgood Marshall its general counsel. Marshall became the chief architect of the litigation strategy that dismantled America's official apartheid. Marshall brought a series of education cases, each designed to point out the futility of the separate but equal dogma. For example, in 1950 the Court agreed that a hastily established black law school in Texas was scarcely the equal of the venerable University of Texas Law School. Marshall shrewdly chose to challenge segregation in a law school, because the justices would know firsthand the difference between a quality education and an inferior one there.[1988]

In 1954 the Court reached beyond the task of sorting out case by case whether a particular school was the equal of another and held in the epochal BROWN V. BOARD OF EDUCATION that separate is *inherently* unequal. Though *Brown* purported to rest its conclusion only in the context of education, it quickly became clear that the Court was embarked on the far more ambitious project of striking down every facet of official segregation. Between 1954 and 1963, with almost no discussion, the Court struck down laws requiring segregation of beaches,[1276] buses,[734] golf courses,[935] public parks,[1455] and municipal restaurants.[2081] Finally, in 1963, in a case involving a segregated public courtroom, the Court declared that it "is no longer open to question that a state may not constitutionally require segregation of public facilities."[1023]

Having pronounced legally mandated segregation unconstitutional, the more difficult question was how to desegregate. Clearly it was not sufficient simply to nullify state laws requiring segregation, for that would simply leave segregated schools and other institutions in place. In 1955 the Court declared that the states should proceed with ALL DELIBERATE SPEED toward dismantling the discriminatory dual school systems.[250] For fifteen years the Court left the process to the lower courts. The major constitutional theme was that the courts had power to oversee desegregation plans for school systems that had deliberately engaged in segregation in the past. But that did not necessarily mean they should order schools integrated merely because there was racial imbalance. The key question was whether a discriminatory purpose accounted for the school systems as they then existed.

In 1968 the Court presaged a major shift, holding that "freedom of choice" had not worked and that the lower courts should begin exercising their power to achieve results.[801] In 1969 a unanimous Court rejected its own "all deliberate speed" timetable, holding that this much-abused guideline was no longer constitutionally permissible.[34] In 1971 the Court went even further, for the first time speaking of the need to achieve better racial balance and discussing the kinds of remedial steps, including BUSING, to which the courts might need to resort to end segregated school systems.[1987] The Court also turned its attention to northern segregation, declaring that when it can be shown that one part of a school district had been deliberately segregated, a desegregation order might be appropriate for the entire district,[1071] though the Court refused to permit *inter*district remedies if only one of the districts had been shown to have deliberately segregated its schools.[1346] Proving deliberate segregation in the North was more difficult than in the South, since racial discrimination was a result of segregated housing rather than statutory enactments. In 1979 the Court said that a showing that the schools were intentionally segregated in 1954 would serve as prima facie evidence that a dual system twenty-five years later was an outgrowth of those policies, permitting the courts to order sweeping changes.[525]

As recently as 1990 the Court affirmed broad power in the lower courts to continue to devise plans that would end the legacy of separate but equal school systems, holding that the federal courts have the power to order school districts to raise the necessary taxes to accomplish an ambitious plan and to enjoin state authorities from enforcing laws that prohibit taxes from being raised.[1364] The Court also upheld remedial power to hold the city of Yonkers, New York, in CONTEMPT for failing to abide by a decree addressing segregated housing, but it struck down a portion of the trial judge's contempt order against individual city council members who had refused to vote for the necessary implementing legislation.[1926] In 1991 the Court said that a federal court INJUNCTION directing compliance with a desegregation plan does not last forever. If it can be shown that a school district has lived up to the plan for a reasonable period of time, and the "vestiges of past discrimination" have been eliminated, the court's JURISDICTION over the school system must come to an end.[184]

See also: AFFIRMATIVE ACTION; BUSING; DE FACTO–DE JURE DISTINCTION; MISCEGENATION; PURPOSE-IMPACT DISTINCTION; SOCIOLOGICAL FOOTNOTE AND SOCIAL SCIENCE EVIDENCE; STATE ACTION; VOTING, RIGHT TO.

seizure, *see:* **search and seizure**

selective exclusiveness, *see:* **Cooley doctrine**

selective incorporation, *see:* **incorporation doctrine**

selective prosecution, *see:* **prosecutorial discretion**

Selective Service Act, *see:* **conscription**

self-executing treaties, *see:* **treaties and treaty power**

self-help remedies, *see:* **repossession**

self-incrimination   The right against self-incrimination, protected by the FIFTH AMENDMENT, is central to the ACCUSATORIAL SYSTEM of criminal justice: together with the PRESUMPTION OF INNOCENCE, the right against self-incrimination ensures that the state must bear the burden of prosecution. The Fifth Amendment says that no person "shall be compelled in any criminal case to be a witness against himself." The surface meaning is relatively limited: the state may not force a defendant to testify in a criminal prosecution against his will. The clause seems to allow the possibility that the state could force a suspect to confess before trial, but that unduly harsh reading has never been accepted. PLEADING THE FIFTH has come to mean that no official organ of the state may exact a statement from anyone, whether or not formally ACCUSED, that might ultimately lead to criminal penalties in the same or some other legal proceeding. A witness may decline to testify on the grounds of self-incrimination in a civil proceeding,[1281] before a GRAND JURY,[475] or when called by a legislative committee[2165] or an administrative agency.[821] The Fifth Amendment applies to both federal and state prosecutions.[1233]

This "privilege," as it is often called, confers a right that is at once both broader and narrower than its text seems to suggest. On the one hand, the word "compel" has been read broadly. A witness may not be held in CONTEMPT for refusing to testify and must be free as well of other official sanctions, including loss of public employment,[732, 725, 2090] of a public license,[1932] or of the right to do business with the state.[1140] But if the only "penalty" that might occur is loss of face, humiliation, or disgrace, and not an actual prosecution, the witness may not be excused from testifying. Therefore a witness who receives IMMUNITY FROM PROSECUTION may be compelled to testify. [260]

On the other hand, the phrase "witness against himself" has been read relatively narrowly. During the past quarter century, the Supreme Court has underscored many times that the Fifth Amendment protects only what it terms "testimonial" evidence—knowledge possessed by the person himself, whether locked in his head or among his private papers. But it does not prevent the police from putting a person in a LINEUP, making him speak certain words to hear the sound of the voice, or demanding fingerprints or handwriting and blood samples. [1818, 2139, 936] Nor does it exempt a person's accountant from releasing incriminating tax records. [669] Determining what is testimonial can involve fine lines: a driver stopped by the police for involvement in an accident may not refuse to give his name and address, [316] but in a 1990 case the Court said that when police stopped an apparently drunk driver on the road, they could demand that he answer routine booking questions, including his age, but that they could not demand that he state the date of his sixth birthday. [1590]

The right against self-incrimination is personal. It may be claimed only by a person who himself might be at risk for testifying. It may not be claimed on behalf of another, including a corporation, so that a custodian of corporate records may not resist a subpoena directed to the corporation on the ground that the records might incriminate him, nor may a corporation plead the Fifth. [2197, 841] The privilege must be claimed. A person who begins to testify without indicating that he fears incrimination may not suddenly refuse to testify further. [1753] A defendant who takes the stand in his own behalf may not claim the right against self-incrimina-

tion and refuse to answer particular questions on cross-examination that bear on his direct testimony. [260] But if the defendant refuses to take the stand, the prosecutor may not comment to the jury about the defendant's refusal to do so. [813] Indeed, to avoid any adverse effect that might arise from the exercise of the Fifth Amendment right, the Court has said that a prosecutor may not even tell the jury that a defendant who has offered an alibi at trial refused to say anything when originally questioned by the police. [573] And if the defense asks, the judge must instruct the jury to give no weight whatsoever to the defendant's failure to take the stand. [355]

Considerable confusion has arisen over the connection between the Fifth Amendment and the tax laws, which require taxpayers to file informational returns. The Court has made it clear that those engaged in unlawful business activities have no right to refrain from filing tax returns on the ground that doing so would call to the government's attention the illegal nature of their earnings. [1977, 729] Nevertheless, laws that require particular people suspected of criminal activity to file registration statements do violate the privilege. The Court struck down on this ground a federal law requiring members of the Communist party to register with federal authorities, because the answer to any of the many questions on the form might lead to prosecution. [31] It also voided on the same ground a number of tax laws requiring people engaged in certain illegal activities to file special forms and pay a special tax. [1240]

These same principles underlie the Court's controversial rulings governing police interrogation of suspects and confessions. Until its decision in 1965 holding the Fifth Amendment applicable to the states, [1233] the Court measured the admissibility of confessions in prosecutions under DUE PROCESS standards. The general rule was that confessions were admissible only if voluntary, meaning that coerced confessions must be excluded.[942] In 1936 the Court for the first time held this rule applicable to the states, in a case in which Mississippi authorities beat a confession out of suspects with ropes and studded belts.[254] But until the 1960s, a confession was not considered coerced or involuntary merely because the suspect was not warned of his right to remain silent.[1657] Instead, the Court engaged in a BALANCING test, in which it judged from the "totality of circumstances" in scores of cases whether the police had overreached and thus coerced the suspect or had merely encouraged him to speak the truth. Coercion was not limited to physical torture; prolonged questioning and isolation in jail could be just as coercive.[365] So could threats to take a woman's children from her[1214] or to bring an invalid wife into the station house[1752] if the suspect did not cooperate and sign confessions.

By the 1960s, it was becoming clear that something more was needed: once the Court began to think about a more useful means of determining voluntariness, the path to the MIRANDA RULES was relatively quick. In 1964, in *Escobedo v. Illinois,* the Court for the first time held that a confession was involuntary solely because the police refused to let a suspect speak with his lawyer, despite repeated requests and despite the lawyer's presence at the police station. Finally, in 1966, in MIRANDA V. ARIZONA, the Court arrived at the rule, familiar from countless police dramas, that a confession is constitutionally involuntary and hence inadmissible at trial unless the police have advised the suspect that he has the right to remain silent (this is the Fifth Amendment right), that any statement may be used against him, that he has the right to a lawyer, appointed for him if he cannot afford his own.

Miranda provoked both a political storm and a vast body of further interpretations. If *Miranda* eliminated the tedious and often impossible task of discerning whether a confession was coerced in the constitutional sense, it imposed a new burden on the Court: to ascertain under what circumstances *Miranda* would apply. For example, one line of cases has now made clear that the *Miranda* rules are applicable only when the suspect is "in custody." If he is under arrest, even if not formally, the Miranda rules apply.[1539] But questioning a suspect in his own home, when he is not charged and will not be arrested, is not custodial.[143] Another set of questions is raised when the suspect asserts his rights. If he refuses to speak until he has consulted with a lawyer, the police must thereafter refrain from questioning him until the lawyer has arrived.[601] But if the suspect at first says he wishes not to speak, without asking for a lawyer, the police may warn him anew of his rights and attempt to question him again.[1331] The suspect may waive his rights, but whether the waiver itself was voluntary is a separate constitutional question that has prompted numerous cases.[1494, 1386]

Involuntary confessions are inadmissible in court, but confessions that violate the *Miranda* rules may be used for certain limited purposes. For example, if the defendant takes the stand and denies committing the crime, his station house confession, inadmissible because he had not been read his rights, may nevertheless be used to show that he was lying on the stand.[870] But a confession can still be involuntary for reasons other than failure to follow the *Miranda* rules (one obtained by torture, for example) and this other type of involuntary confession may not be used to impeach.[1351]

The Court has fashioned a "public safety" exception to *Miranda.* If the police have arrested a suspect and ask about the location of a weapon that the suspect may have just discarded, the failure to warn does not preclude the use at trial of the defendant's statement or the weapon itself. The police should not be put in the position of having to make split-second decisions about whether the suspect will cooperate with the police after being warned.[1459]

See also: COUNSEL, ASSISTANCE OF; EXCLUSIONARY RULE; HARMLESS ERROR RULE; IMMUNITY FROM PROSECUTION; McNABB-MALLORY RULE; MERE EVIDENCE RULE; SEARCH AND SEIZURE: FINGERPRINTS AND OTHER OBJECTIVE EVIDENCE; SUPPRESSION HEARING; TWO SOVEREIGNTIES RULE.

Senate, *see:* **Congress; Great Compromise; Seventeenth Amendment**

senatorial courtesy, *see:* **advice and consent**

senators, *see:* **Congress, members of; qualifications for office**

sentencing   Judges and juries have unusually wide discretion to impose sentences. Many sentencing laws specifically provide for indeterminate sentences (for example, fifteen years to life), and many others allow the judge to determine the term of imprisonment or amount of the fine from a range prescribed by the legislature. A judge cannot with absolute discretion pluck a sentence from thin air; the legislature must prescribe at least a range. The Supreme Court has said that DUE PROCESS imposes few restrictions on what the judge may consider in passing sentence. Presentence reports may contain much information that would have been inadmissible at trial.[2213] But the information must be "materially true," and a mistake of "constitutional magnitude"—for example, a statement in a presentence report that a defendant had been convicted of an earlier crime when in fact the prior proceeding was constitutionally flawed—entitles the defendant to resentencing.[2075] A judge may also consider his or her own belief that the defendant had lied during the trial and therefore impose a harsher sentence.[798] But the race of the defendant may never be considered.[1282]

A series of cases have dealt with the issue of judicial vindictiveness for exercising the right to retrial. A judge may not punish a defendant who insists on his right to a new trial by handing down a harsher sentence at the second trial than he received after the first one.[1495] This rule, not surprisingly, has developed many twists and turns so that, for example, if the defendant was originally sentenced after a GUILTY PLEA, which he then withdraws, the judge may award a heavier sentence at a later trial.[27] If a defendant has served time following conviction and then is retried because of errors in his first trial, he must receive credit for time already served in the new sentence to avoid the possibility that he would have to serve more than the maximum time allowed by law; the second sentence, however, may be heavier than the first.[1495] The usual rule is that sentences are not appealable,[567] but the legislature may constitutionally permit prosecutors to appeal in most instances.[547]

See also: DEATH PENALTY; DOUBLE JEOPARDY; PAROLE; PROBATION; PROPORTIONALITY OF SENTENCE; STATISTICAL EVIDENCE, USE OF; VICTIM IMPACT STATEMENT.

separate but equal   In PLESSY v. FERGUSON, the Supreme Court gave a constitutional imprimatur to official segregation of the races by upholding a Louisiana law requiring "separate but equal" railroad cars for blacks and whites. The separate but equal doctrine originated in an opinion of Massachusetts Chief Justice Lemuel Shaw in an 1849 case holding that Boston school segregation was constitutional, despite a provision in the Massachusetts state constitution declaring that "all men are born free and equal." Shaw agreed that "all persons without distinction of age or sex, birth or color, origin or condition, are equal before the law." But he shrank at the implications of his statement, and concluded mysteriously that the rights to which any person is entitled "depend on laws adapted to their respective relations and conditions." A law decreeing separate schools did not offend the state constitution, as long as the schools were equal. Shaw did not trouble to inquire whether the schools were in fact equal or even how that equality could be measured. Neither did the *Plessy* Court. Not until the 1930s did the Supreme Court begin to consider the actual equality of conditions. Long before any constitutional standard could emerge—and perhaps because no such standard is possible—the Court struck the doctrine a fatal blow in BROWN V. BOARD OF EDUCATION by concluding that "separate" itself can never be "equal."

See also: MISCEGENATION; RACIAL DISCRIMINATION; SEGREGATION AND INTEGRATION.

separation of church and state, *see:* **religious establishment**

separation of powers   Separation of powers is one of the deepest political principles of the Constitution, the core protection against tyranny. Safety lies in power divided, ambition checking ambition. The Constitution secures the separation of powers in two ways. Under Art. I-§6[2], no sitting member of Congress may hold any post in the executive branch. This single clause differentiates the American national government from the British, where cabinet ministers are all members of Parliament. This clause separates only Congress and the executive branch. Formally it does not preclude a member of the executive from simultaneously holding judicial office, and there is a fleeting precedent for such an occurrence: John Marshall continued to serve as John Adams's secretary of state after having been confirmed as chief justice of the United States, and even served a single day into the Jefferson administration. The Constitution is silent on whether members of state government may simultaneously serve in the federal government, and here too there is odd precedent: in the 1790s Roger Sherman served as both U.S. senator and mayor of New Haven, Connecticut; in the 1930s Louisiana Governor Huey Long was, for a brief time, simultaneously a U.S. senator.

The Constitution also requires that the legislative, executive, and judicial branches of the federal government exercise different powers. This rule derives partly from the text of the Constitution and partly from its structure. Art. I places the LEGISLATIVE POWER exclusively in Congress. Article II bestows the EXECUTIVE POWER on the president, and Article III confers the JUDICIAL POWER on the Supreme Court and whatever lower federal courts Congress creates. But because the Constitution does not define these powers, nor mark their boundaries with any precision, the doctrine of separation of powers is porous and difficult to define. The issue of separation of powers usually arises in two situations: encroachment of one branch's power by another branch or delegation of one type of power to another branch. The 1952 STEEL SEIZURE CASE illustrates encroachment. The Court said that President Harry S. Truman had overstepped his powers because in seizing the nation's steel mills he was exercising a legislative power. *Bowsher v. Synar,* which in 1986 struck down the Balanced Budget and Emergency Deficit Control Act (popularly known as Gramm-Rudman-Hollings), illustrates the delegation problem. The Court said that separation of powers was violated because Congress attempted to assign an executive power to a legislative branch official. Under the law, the comptroller general of the United States was given the power to reconcile budget deficit estimates by the Office of Management and Budget, an executive branch agency, and the Congressional Budget Office. The comptroller general's recommendations on what budget items to slash would be transmitted to the president, who was obligated to reduce the budget by those amounts. The Court reached two conclusions. Determining how to cut the budget under the act is an executive function. The comptroller general is not an executive official, even though appointed by the president, because Congress retains the power to fire him. Since the comptroller general is therefore a creature of Congress, he cannot carry out an executive function.

In a somewhat different vein, the Court in 1983 voided the LEGISLATIVE VETO, a device by which one or both houses of Congress could unilaterally veto a rule, regulation, or decision of an executive branch agency or department. The Court held that in so doing Congress was acting legislatively, which requires BICAMERAL-ISM and PRESENTMENT to the president, features absent in the usual legislative veto.[979] The case excited considerable comment for its very oddity. The power to issue a rule or regulation is a legislative power delegated to an agency. The Court was saying, in essence, that in the name of separation of powers, Congress is free to delegate to the executive but not to itself. This case, therefore, was really about the *ways* a branch may exercise its power.

On the other hand, in an opinion that in some ways contradicts the Legislative Veto Case, the Court upheld the power of Congress to create the office of INDEPENDENT COUNSEL, a special prosecutor appointed by the federal courts who is largely independent of the president. The case means that the executive power presumably vested by the Constitution wholly in the president may be delegated elsewhere.[1389] In 1989 the Court also upheld a congressional delegation of rule-making authority to the U.S. Sentencing Commission, an agency located in the judicial branch and consisting partly of federal judges.[1367] The commission has the authority to issue mandatory sentencing guidelines for use in federal prosecutions. The Court concluded that separation of powers permits one branch to share in the power of another, and that the danger of presidential interference in this judicial agency—the president has the power to remove the judges from the commission "for good cause"—is too remote to pose any constitutional difficulty, even though, of course, it was precisely this difficulty

in the comptroller general's case that led the Court to strike the budget balancing law. Separation of powers is a vital constitutional doctrine, greatly in need of clarification.

See also: APPOINTMENT AND REMOVAL POWER; CHECKS AND BALANCES; DELEGATION DOCTRINE; IMPOUNDMENT; INHERENT AND IMPLIED POWERS; LINE-ITEM VETO; PRESIDENT, POWERS AND DUTIES OF; WAR POWER.

service of process   For a court to determine the legal rights of the parties, it must have JURISDICTION both over the particular subject of the dispute and over the parties themselves. Under DUE PROCESS, no person is subject to a court's jurisdiction unless he or she has been made a party to the suit. Jurisdiction depends, in part, on NOTICE, and notice is usually provided through "service of process." Personal service is the best way to notify a potential defendant because it provides actual notice through the official papers handed to him that he is being sued. Under the usual circumstances, personal service is constitutionally required.[1291] Since a court usually has no jurisdiction over parties outside the state in which it sits, personal service ordinarily is effective only when the defendant is in the state. But personal service is not the only constitutional means of obtaining personal jurisdiction. Under some circumstances, service may be obtained through the mail[716] or even by posting. However, service that does not reasonably guarantee actual notice is constitutionally defective. For example, the Court held invalid the practice of posting notices on the doors in an apartment complex because the evidence showed that children often removed them before the occupant could find them.[804] Service may be made on agents appointed for that purpose, and all states require as a condition of doing business that out-of-state companies designate an agent to receive process. In 1988 the Court held that a state may not deny the protection of a STATUTE OF LIMITATION to a company not doing or registered to do business in the state. The state wanted to deny the company the statute of limitations to coerce it into designating an agent so that it would be subject to suits in the state's courts.[152]

When a federal court is hearing a case within its DIVERSITY JURISDICTION, it is not constitutionally bound by a state's strict rules governing service of process but must apply the federal rules instead, even though they make it easier for the plaintiff to serve the defendant.[858]

See also: LONG-ARM STATUTE.

service or labor   Under Art. IV-§2[3], the owner of a slave, euphemistically referred to as a person "held to service or labor," was constitutionally empowered to go anywhere to seize a runaway. The law of the state to which the slave had fled provided no protection, since the slaveowner was entitled to do in the other state whatever the laws of his own state permitted him to do to recapture his possessions. The Supreme Court held that state laws that interfered with such seizures violated this clause,[1664] although a state law that penalized people harboring fugitive slaves was permissible.[1379a] This clause was abolished by the THIRTEENTH AMENDMENT.

See also: SLAVERY.

servitude, *see:* **involuntary servitude; slavery**

session of Congress   Congress is in session when it assembles to conduct business. Under the TWENTIETH AMENDMENT, it must assemble on January 3rd each year, unless it changes the date by law. Historically, a particular Congress lasts for two years, between each election for the House of Representatives, and is numbered sequentially since the First Congress in 1789. Each Congress has two sessions, denoted the First and Second. Under Art. I-§5[4], a session lasts until Congress officially adjourns.

Whether Congress is in session has a bearing on the president's VETO POWER and on his power to make RECESS APPOINTMENTS.

See also: RECESS OF CONGRESS.

set-asides   In the Public Works Employment Act of 1977, Congress required that ten percent of grants for certain public construction projects be set aside for "minority business enterprises." A minority business is defined as a business at least fifty percent of which is owned by minorities, defined in turn as "citizens of the United States who are Negroes, Spanish-speaking, Orientals, Indians, Eskimos, and Aleuts." The Supreme Court upheld the set-aside provision in 1980 against a challenge that it violated EQUAL PROTECTION. Chief Justice Warren E. Burger's PLURALITY OPINION said that Section 5 of the FOURTEENTH AMENDMENT empowers Congress to enforce the amendment's equal protection guarantee and that Congress had "abundant historical basis" to conclude that "traditional procurement practices" perpetuated the effects of longstanding discrimination against minorities in the construction trades. Burger said that the means Congress chose were constitutional because the use of racial and ethnic criteria were no broader than necessary to accomplish Congress's mission of eliminating the vestiges of discrimination.[711]

In 1989 the Court ruled, 6–3, that a similar plan adopted by Richmond, Virginia, failed the STRICT SCRUTINY test.[1726] Municipalities do not enjoy Congress's Fourteenth Amendment power to redress societywide discrimination. Richmond failed to identify the extent of discrimination in the construction industry or to show that its plan was aimed at remedying that discrimination. Moreover, in using the same definition as Congress, Richmond had put onto its legislative books the desire to set aside funds for Eskimos and Aleuts, who it could hardly be claimed had been discriminated against in

Richmond, Virginia. The Court left open the possibility of set-asides on a proper showing that actual discrimination was taking or had taken place. In 1990 the Court approved another congressional set-aside program, this one permitting some radio and television broadcast stations to be transferred from their present owners to minority-controlled firms only. The sharply divided Court concluded that Congress has power to promote broadcast "diversity."[1319]

See also: AFFIRMATIVE ACTION; PURPOSE-IMPACT DISTINCTION.

Seventeenth Amendment The Seventeenth Amendment, proposed by Congress on May 13, 1912, and ratified on April 8, 1913, provides for the direct election of SENATORS. Under Art. I-§3[1], senators were not popularly elected but were chosen by the state legislatures. To the Framers this was an important ingredient of FEDERALISM, providing the states with a check on Congress. But by the late nineteenth century, numerous scandals involving the buying and selling of Senate seats and political delays in filling seats had led many states to devise nominating systems that informally amounted to direct elections. By the time the Seventeenth Amendment was proposed, twenty-nine states, as a practical matter, had left the election of senators to the people anyway, not to the legislatures. The amendment simply ratified the practice.

Seventh Amendment The Seventh Amendment provides for jury trials in certain federal civil cases. Late in the CONSTITUTIONAL CONVENTION, the delegates noted that they had made no such provision but an attempt to add it to Article III failed. The state ratifying conventions particularly recommended such a right be added, and it was among James Madison's original proposals in Congress in 1789. The right does not extend to every civil matter but only to those traditionally denominated as suits at COMMON LAW. It is noteworthy as one of only two places in the Constitution to mention a dollar amount—the right to a civil jury is guaranteed whenever the amount in controversy exceeds twenty dollars. (Art. I-§9[1] allowed Congress to tax up to ten dollars for every slave imported into the country.)

See also: TRIAL BY JURY.

sex discrimination In 1873, five years after the FOURTEENTH AMENDMENT was ratified, Justice Joseph P. Bradley, in a case denying women the right to practice law, said that "[t]he natural and proper timidity and delicacy which belongs to the female sex evidently unfits it for many of the occupations of civil life. . . . This is the law of the Creator."[219] As late as 1961 the Court upheld a law making jury service mandatory for men and optional for women.[949]

In 1948 the Supreme Court sustained a law barring women from serving as bartenders unless they were wives or daughters of male owners. The states, said Justice Felix Frankfurter, may certainly draw "a sharp line between the sexes. . . . The Constitution does not require legislatures to reflect sociological insight."[765] By the early 1970s, however, a vast sociological upheaval finally reached the Court, with the EQUAL RIGHTS AMENDMENT hovering in the background. In 1971 the Court struck down an Idaho law that required probate courts to choose male family members over females in the administration of estates. The Court concluded that mere admininistrative convenience does not justify a sex-based distinction (the rule eliminated hearings in the probate courts to select the administrator[1701]). Two years later the Court struck down a federal law automatically giving male members of the ARMED FORCES an allowance for wives but requiring female members to prove the dependency of their husbands.[705] A plurality led by Justice William Brennan said that classifications based on sex are "inherently suspect" and must pass the STRICT SCRUTINY test. However, that position did not gain a majority; the concurring judges reached the same result under the weaker test.

In 1976 the Court declared a new *intermediate scrutiny* test: "To withstand constitutional challenge . . . classifications by gender must serve important governmental objectives and must be substantially related to achievement of those objectives."[483] This was the first case in which the victim of the discrimination was male. The Court then struck down an Oklahoma law prohibiting the sale of 3.2% beer to males under twenty-one years of age but permitting females eighteen years or older to purchase it. The purpose of the law was to deter drunk driving, surely an important objective, but as Justice Brennan noted, the law let males *drink* the beer; they just could not legally buy it. This strange disparity was surely not "substantially related" to eliminating accidents caused by intoxication.

Since then, the Court has considered a number of challenges to sex classifications, striking many but upholding some. For example, it upheld the limitation of draft registration to males,[1766] laws granting VETERANS' PREFERENCES in ways that benefited mostly men,[1612] STATUTORY RAPE laws that punished underage males but not females,[1326] PROPERTY TAX exemption laws that discriminated between widows and widowers,[1044] a Navy personnel policy that allowed female officers more time to avoid mandatory discharge,[1815] a law that permitted pregnancy disability to be excluded from a state's disability insurance system,[735] and federal Social Security old-age benefits programs that slightly favor women.[314]

On the other hand, the Court struck down jury exclusion laws that permit women to avoid mandatory service,[2002, 584] a single-sex public nursing school,[1362] a law requiring males but not females to pay alimony,[1540] a law forcing widowers but not widows to prove dependence on the deceased spouse to receive death benefits,[2181] a law requiring pregnant schoolteachers to leave their classrooms four and five months before delivery regardless of their ability to work,[408] and a host of ILLEGITIMACY laws dealing unequally with the mothers and fathers of the children. The seeming difference in result stems from the open-endedness of the scrutiny test that is applied: what is "important" and "substantially related" is always a question of judgment about the particular circumstances.

See also: ABORTION; AGE OF MAJORITY; CUSTODY AND ADOPTION OF CHILDREN; FAMILIES; SUSPECT CLASSIFICATIONS.

sexual freedom The sexual permissiveness of modern times is almost entirely a result of changing social mores and hardly at all of any constitutional conclusions about personal LIBERTY. Although the Supreme Court has established a fundamental right to marital intimacy, PROCREATION, ABORTION, and access to CONTRACEPTION, it has never squarely held that the Constitution protects the right of consenting adults to engage in sexual activity. The Court may have indirectly held that the state may not punish sexual relations between unmarried heterosexuals. In *Eisenstadt v. Baird* in 1972 the Court struck down a law prohibiting the distribution of contraceptives to unmarried couples, reasoning that the law interferes with a right to PRIVACY. Presumably a constitutional right to use contraceptives necessarily includes the right to use them in a certain way.

Nevertheless, the Court has shied away from the central issue. Most states once did, and many states still do, outlaw adultery, fornication, and what were once quaintly termed "unnatural" sexual acts. The question of a person's freedom to engage in sex, whether married or not, rarely comes before the Court, largely because the states do not enforce these laws. But in its most recent pronouncement on the issue, the Court upheld, 5–4, the Georgia antisodomy law as applied to a homosexual couple. Although the statute expressly condemned sodomy even if committed by a heterosexual married couple, the Court stressed that it was deciding only that homosexuals have no constitutional right to engage in sexual relations.[207] The upshot is that the states remain free, within some limits, to define the boundaries of sexual behavior. Since 1961, half the states have repealed their antisodomy laws, and it is clear that if they choose, the states may extend specific protection against discrimination on the basis of sexual preference or orientation.

See also: MARRIAGE; STATUTORY RAPE.

sexual orientation, *see:* **homosexuality; sexual freedom**

sexual preference, *see:* **homosexuality; sexual freedom**

sexually explicit expression, *see:* **obscenity and pornography; offensive and indecent speech**

Shays's Rebellion   After the Revolutionary War, a depression threatened the very lives of many small farmers. Foreclosures mounted, and in many states popular movements prompted the legislatures to enact relief measures, including laws staying foreclosures and excusing debt. The Massachusetts legislature refused every entreaty to do so, and in 1786 farmers besieged the local courts to prevent foreclosures from being carried out. In September Daniel Shays, a farmer and former army captain, organized a military force bent on seizing a military arsenal. Shays's Rebellion failed, but the attempt frightened many members of the establishment, leading to insistent demands for legal reform and remedies. Three weeks after Shays's movement collapsed, Congress passed a resolution calling for the CONSTITUTIONAL CONVENTION.

shield laws, *see:* **reporter's privilege**

ships, *see:* **admiralty and maritime jurisdiction; transportation**

shock the conscience test   Beginning in 1947, a debate in the Supreme Court erupted over the extent to which the FOURTEENTH AMENDMENT "incorporated" the BILL OF RIGHTS. Justice Hugo L. Black insisted that Section 1 of the Fourteenth Amendment was intended to do just that and that judges ought not be free to consult their personal predilections to determine whether DUE PROCESS might require the states to observe other, unenumerated rights. Countering Black's thesis, Justice Felix Frankfurter said that the Court must determine in each case whether a right is "implicit in the concept of ORDERED LIBERTY" so that its violation by the state would be unconstitutional. In a 1952 case, *Rochin v. California,* the Court was presented with a conviction based on evidence taken when the suspect's stomach was pumped. Acting on a tip, police broke into the suspect's room and saw capsules on a nightstand by the bed. The suspect swallowed them. The police handcuffed their man and took him to a local hospital, where doctors forced a tube down his throat, forcing him to vomit up what turned out to be capsules containing morphine. Did the forced stomach-pumping violate due process? Frankfurter said that it did but that the conclusion did not rest on "our merely personal and private notions." Instead, he said that the police did "more than offend some fastidious squeamishness or private sentimentalism about combating crime too energetically. It is conduct that shocks the conscience." Justice Black concurred in the Court's reversal of the conviction, but protested the conscience-shocking "test" as permitting wholly open-ended discretion by judges to nullify whatever they personally abhor.

See also: INCORPORATION DOCTRINE; NATURAL LAW; PROCEDURAL RIGHTS OF CRIMINAL DEFENDANTS.

shopping centers, access to   In 1968 a sharply divided Supreme Court held that states may not employ trespass laws to bar peaceful labor union picketing of a store in a private shopping center.⁴⁵ The shopping center was performing a PUBLIC FUNCTION and in so doing was in effect an arm of the state, which under the FIRST AMENDMENT may not limit anyone's right to express an opinion. The decision created a right of access to private shopping centers and other such quasi-public places. But in 1972 the Court retrenched, distinguishing the labor union's picketing from that of a protest group that wanted to distribute antiwar leaflets in a shopping center. The union's picketing was related to one of the stores in the first shopping center. The stores in the antiwar case were wholly unrelated to the subject of the protest, and therefore the protesters could be barred by the shopping center owners.¹¹⁷³ In 1976 the Court came full circle and overruled its 1968 decision. Employees of a warehouse located elsewhere but owned by a store in a shopping center picketed the store in a labor dispute and were ousted. The Court now held that the shopping center is not performing a public function and the owners therefore have no constitutional obligation to let anyone distribute anything.⁹⁵⁰ However, in 1980 the Court ruled that although the federal Constitution does not require it, neither does it prohibit such distribution if a state independently by law says that private shopping malls must allow members of the public to distribute literature on the shopping center grounds.¹⁶⁶⁹

See also: PUBLIC FORUM.

Sick Chicken Case   In 1933 President Franklin D. Roosevelt signed into law the National Industrial Recovery Act, terming it "the most important and far-reaching legislation ever enacted by the American Congress." At the heart of the act was a congressional delegation of power to the president to establish codes of fair competition for any trade or industry in INTERSTATE COMMERCE. Between August 1933 and February 1935, the National Recovery Administration, the president's agent in formalizing the codes, drew up more than seven hundred industrial codes and issued more than eleven thousand administrative orders. Critics charged that the NRA was a cover for industry to engage in wholesale violations of the antitrust laws. Challenges to the act came to court, and one of them quickly reached the Supreme Court. It involved the Live Poultry Code, which applied only to the New York metropolitan area and covered solely the sale of kosher chicken. Under Jewish religious law, chickens had to be purchased live and slaughtered following a religious ritual. The poultry code required "straight killing": a wholesale customer purchasing at the slaughterhouse could not pick out the best birds for slaughter but was required instead to take the contents of a coop or half-coop. The straight killing rule was designed to prevent the widespread practice of selling diseased chickens: if a favored customer could not select the healthy chickens, the wholesaler would have no incentive to buy sick birds. Four brothers operating the A.L.A. Schechter Live Poultry Market were convicted of violating the code by selling several tons of tubercular chickens below market price and ignoring the straight killing requirement. For selling a single sick chicken, they faced a three-month jail term and a seven-thousand-dollar fine.

Their appeal raised two points: (1) the National Industrial Recovery Act, as applied to them, was beyond the COMMERCE POWER because their sales of chickens occurred wholly within a single state. The STREAM OF COMMERCE in the chickens had come to rest in Brooklyn. (2) Congress's delegation to the president to establish the code was unconstitutional because it was a wholesale grant of the LEGISLATIVE POWER, reserved by Art. I-§1[1] to Congress. In *A.L.A. Schechter Poultry Corp. v. United States,* the Court agreed with both contentions. As a result, the National Recovery Administration died. The *Schechter* case was an important factor in Roosevelt's decision to move forward with his ill-fated COURT-PACKING PLAN. The commerce part of the decision has long since been overruled.

See also: DELEGATION DOCTRINE.

silence of defendant, *see:* **self-incrimination**

silences of the Constitution   The Constitution says that Congress has the power to regulate commerce but is mum on what the states may do if Congress has not acted. Justice Robert H. Jackson once noted the judicial consequence of this gap in widely quoted words: "Perhaps even more than by interpretation of its written word, this Court has advanced the solidarity and prosperity of this Nation by the meaning it has given to these great silences of the Constitution."[834]

silver coin, *see:* **currency**

silver platter doctrine   In 1914 the Supreme Court announced the EXCLUSIONARY RULE, forbidding courts from considering evidence that federal law enforcement officials obtained unlawfully.[2175] But if *state* officials obtained evidence in a manner that violated the SEARCH AND SEIZURE provisions of the FOURTH AMENDMENT and turned it over to federal prosecutors, the Court permitted the evidence to be used, as long as *federal* officials did not participate in the search[299] or press state officials to conduct the search on their behalf.[722] Surveying the cases in 1949, Justice Felix Frankfurter dubbed this

loophole in the exclusionary rule the "silver platter" doctrine: the rules prohibited evidence to be used if federal officials "had a hand" in an unlawful search but permitted it to be used if it had been handed to the federal government "on a silver platter."[1207]

When the doctrine was fashioned in the 1920s, the Fourth Amendment did not apply to the states, so the police were not violating the Constitution no matter how lawless their searches. Since any kind of unlawfully seized evidence could be admitted at state trials, the states could also use evidence unconstitutionally seized by the federal government,[2230] unless it had been suppressed in a federal proceeding.[1697] But in 1949 the Fourth Amendment was finally held to apply to the states, even though the Court did not at the same time extend the exclusionary rule to state proceedings.[2244] That ruling made the silver platter doctrine untenable, because it meant that the federal government could profit from constitutional violations by state officials. The Court finally abolished the doctrine in 1960.[611] In 1976, however, the Court resurrected it for civil cases, holding that under certain circumstances, evidence unlawfully seized by state officials may be used in federal civil proceedings such as tax assessments, as long as federal officials were not involved in the seizure.[1007]

sincerity of religious belief, *see:* **religious belief, sincerity and truth of**

sit-in, *see:* **trespass**

Sixteenth Amendment   The Sixteenth Amendment, proposed by Congress on July 12, 1909, and ratified on February 3, 1913, removed the constitutional obstacle to the federal INCOME TAX that the Supreme Court had decreed in 1895[1649] in holding that such a tax is a DIRECT TAX required under Art. I-§9[4] to be apportioned by states. The practical effect of the 1895 decision was to make it legislatively impossible to raise an income tax. The Sixteenth Amendment simply lifts from the laying of a federal income tax the insuperable burden of the apportionment and enumeration requirements.

See also: APPORTIONMENT OF TAXES.

Sixth Amendment The Sixth Amendment provides several important rights to the accused in criminal prosecutions. These include the right to a speedy and public trial by an impartial jury, to be informed of the nature of the accusation, to confront adverse witnesses in open court, to obtain favorable witnesses to testify in defense, and to have the assistance of counsel. Some of these rights were well established under British law at the time of the American Revolution; others were accepted only grudgingly. All are crucial bulwarks against tyranny. The Sixth Amendment is now applicable to the states as well as the federal government, having been incorporated right by right into the DUE PROCESS Clause of the FOURTEENTH AMENDMENT.

See also: ACCUSATION, NOTICE AND SPECIFICITY OF; COMPULSORY PROCESS; CONFRONTATION WITH WITNESSES; COUNSEL, ASSISTANCE OF; INEFFECTIVE ASSISTANCE OF COUNSEL; JURY AND JURORS, IMPARTIALITY OF; JURY DISCRIMINATION; JURY SIZE; JURY UNANIMITY; TRIAL, PUBLIC; TRIAL, SPEEDY; TRIAL BY JURY.

slander, *see:* **libel and slander**

Slaughter-House Cases In 1869 the Louisiana legislature was bribed into giving the Crescent City Live-Stock Landing and Slaughter-House Company a monopoly of the slaughtering business in New Orleans. A thousand butchers were forbidden to slaughter animals on their own premises. Instead, all such business had to be done on the premises of the Crescent City Company. The butchers went to court, arguing that the company's legal monopoly violated the FOURTEENTH AMENDMENT by depriving each butcher of the right "to purchase products, or to carry on trade, or to

maintain himself and his family by free industry." In 1873 the Supreme Court rejected the butchers' every argument, dealing a death blow to the new PRIVILEGES AND IMMUNITIES clause of the amendment and denying that DUE PROCESS or EQUAL PROTECTION have any connection with economic matters beyond protecting those who were once slaves. The Fourteenth Amendment, the Court declared, was not to become "a perpetual censor upon all legislation of the states on the civil rights of their own citizens."

This was a famous wrong prediction. Within thirty years the Court would be doing precisely what it denied it had the power to do in the *Slaughter-House Cases.* But for the moment it refused to find any due process prohibition on a state's economic legislation, a position it affirmed eleven years later when a new Louisiana legislature turned the tables on the Crescent City monopoly. Ten years after the *Slaughter-House Cases,* the legislature repealed the monopoly law, and Crescent City argued that it had been deprived of its due process right to the exclusive slaughtering trade in New Orleans. In 1884 the Court unanimously upheld the law's repeal.[288]

See also: ECONOMIC DUE PROCESS.

slavery Slavery was a big problem for the Constitution makers. Those who profited by it insisted on protecting it; those who loathed it dreaded even more the prospect that to insist on abolition would mean that the Constitution would die aborning. So the Framers reached a compromise, of sorts. The words "slave" and "slavery" would never be mentioned, but the Constitution would safeguard the "peculiar institution" from the abolitionists. The document that emerged from the CONSTITUTIONAL CONVENTION contained ten separate provisions dealing with slavery, an indication of how significant the Framers perceived the problem to be:

1. Art. I-§2[3]: the "federal number" clause apportioning House seats by population, counting "other persons" (that is, those who were not "free persons") as three-fifths of a person.
2. Art. I-§2[3]: apportioning direct taxes the same as representatives, so that the total slave population could not be taxed.
3. Art. I-§8[15]: granting Congress power to call up the MILITIA to suppress insurrections, including slave rebellions.
4. Art. I-§9[1]: prohibiting Congress from banning the slave trade before 1808 and permitting a head tax on slaves of up to ten dollars.
5. Art. I-§9[4]: redundantly prohibiting a direct tax not based on the federal census as provided for in Art. I-§2[3].
6. Art. I-§9[5]: prohibiting Congress from taxing exports from any state, a provision included in part to prevent Congress from taxing the slave trade out of existence.
7. Art. I-§10[2]: prohibiting the states from taxing exports, and thus from taxing the products of slave labor.
8. Art. IV-§2[3]: prohibiting states from emancipating fugitive slaves.
9. Art. IV-§4: requiring the federal government to protect the states against domestic violence, including slave insurrections.
10. Art. V: making the slave trade and direct tax provisions unamendable.

Unlike any other issue in American history, the slavery question dominated political and constitutional thinking for decades; never since has any single issue so exercised the population at large or for so long a time—not SEGREGATION, not ABORTION, not WATERGATE. Constitutional disputation was the stuff of pamphleteering, street argument, vigilantism, and occasional rioting—day after day, year after year, until finally, in 1865, the defeated southern states joined the Union in ratifying the THIRTEENTH AMENDMENT. The sprawling body of constitutional law governing slavery and in this one instance, the general supremacy of state over federal law, was relegated to the history books.

See also: BADGES OF SLAVERY AND SERVITUDE; CITIZENS AND CITIZENSHIP; CIVIL RIGHTS AND CIVIL LIBERTIES; DRED SCOTT V. SANDFORD; INVOLUNTARY SERVITUDE; MISSOURI COMPROMISE; NULLIFICATION, INTERPOSITION, AND SECESSION; RACIAL DISCRIMINATION; SERVICE OF LABOR.

smoking, *see:* **cigarette advertising**

social Darwinism   The most explicit adoption of social Darwinism as a constitutional requirement was in *Coppage v. Kansas,* in which the Court insisted that it is "impossible to uphold freedom of contract and the right of private property without at the same time recognizing as legitimate those inequalities of fortune that are the necessary result of the exercise of those rights." It was this sentiment that Justice Oliver Wendell Holmes had earlier denounced in his famous epigram in LOCHNER V. NEW YORK: "The Fourteenth Amendment does not enact Mr. Herbert Spencer's *Social Statics.*" Spencer, a well-known sociologist, was the creator of the concept of social Darwinism. *See also: ECONOMIC DUE PROCESS.*

Social Security, *see:* **spending power**

sociological footnote and social science evidence   One of the criticisms of Chief Justice Earl Warren's opinion in BROWN V. BOARD OF EDUCATION was a footnote to contemporary sociological and psychological studies that, said Warren, demonstrated the harm that segregation causes to the discriminated class. Segregationists charged that the studies were simply wrong. Integrationists fretted about the same thing: suppose the studies were wrong? Or suppose someone could demonstrate worse harm from desegregating? The legitimacy of the Court's apparent reliance on controversial studies did not begin with Warren and *Brown.*

Indeed, *Brown*'s antithesis, PLESSY v. FERGUSON, was awash with bogus sociological blather. Sociological assumptions undoubtedly underlie much of the law, especially when large changes are begged of the Court in the name of the Constitution. In 1948 Justice Felix Frankfurter justified a law against women working as barmaids by noting that despite changing mores, the "Constitution does not require legislatures to reflect sociological insight, or shifting social standards."[765] But that is simply to say that the Constitution will then be interpreted according to someone else's sociological insight, as indeed Frankfurter's very opinion betrays.

In any event, the Court continues to cite social science evidence to buttress its opinions in a variety of cases. In the 1973 school property tax case, Justice Lewis F. Powell discussed sociological research into the impact of spending on the quality of education to show that differences in spending on school districts within a state do not necessarily violate the Equal Protection Clause.[1791] In 1990, in a case involving the Confrontation Clause of the SIXTH AMENDMENT, the 5–4 majority cited "the growing body of academic literature documenting the psychological trauma suffered by child abuse victims," to soften the meaning of the clause from mandatory face-to-face confrontation to merely a preference for face-to-face confrontation.[1259]

See also: STATISTICAL EVIDENCE, USE OF.

soldiers, quartering of, *see:* **quartering of soldiers**

soldiers, rights of, *see:* **military courts and justice**

solicitation   Face-to-face or direct-mail solicitation is a principal means of communication. In a variety of contexts, the Supreme Court has held that most forms of solicitation enjoy FIRST AMENDMENT protection. The con-

stitutional doctrine had its origins in cases dealing with the rights of the people to gather and distribute literature in the PUBLIC FORUM— public parks and the streets. The solicitation cases began with the Court's holding in 1943 that a town may not prohibit people from ringing doorbells and handing out pamphlets door to door.[1253] The town had argued that the ordinance was necessary to prevent disturbances to people on night shifts who wished to sleep and had used the ordinance to prosecute a Jehovah's Witness who had handed out religious tracts. The Court said that a flat ban was impermissible because LESS RESTRICTIVE ALTERNATIVES were available to solve the problem. For example, the town could criminalize repeated visits by a solicitor who had been advised by the homeowner that the intrusion was unwelcome.

The right to ring doorbells is not absolute. In 1951 the Court sustained an ordinance prohibiting magazine salesmen from calling on people at home unless the homeowner had consented in advance.[227] The difference in outcome turned largely on the difference between handing out religious literature and trying to make a commercial sale. But even certain commercial solicitation was protected when the Court overturned an ordinance that required a city permit before asking people to join dues-paying organizations.[1952]

The Court has also struck down antisolicitation ordinances on the ground of VAGUENESS. For example, it is unconstitutional to require advance police permission to go from house to house on behalf of a "recognized charitable [or] political campaign or cause" because it is impossible to say with certainty what is "recognized."[972] In 1980 the Court in an 8–1 decision broadly upheld the right of solicitors both to go door to door and to ask for contributions of people on the streets. The ordinance barred any solicitation by charities that did not devote at least three-quarters of their receipts to "charitable purposes," not including administration expenses. Few charitable organizations could meet that test, including most "public interest" groups. The Court held that the town's asserted interests were not strong enough to justify the intrusion on the First Amendment rights of organizations to talk to people and raise funds to spread their messages.[1811, 1837, 1729] The Court struck down another ordinance under the ESTABLISHMENT CLAUSE. The law required religious organizations to register with city officials before soliciting funds, unless they received more than half their funding from members. In a challenge by the Reunification Church (headed by the Reverend Moon), the Court said that by favoring older, more established churches, this law clearly discriminated among religions, a direct violation of the prohibition against RELIGIOUS ESTABLISHMENT.[1123]

The Court has also found constitutional limitations on the power of states to regulate the extent to which LAWYERS may solicit legal business. In *NAACP v. Button*, the Court struck down a Virginia rule of court that precluded NAACP lawyers and staff members from holding public meetings about desegregation cases and inviting members of the public to serve as plaintiffs. Although the rules against general forms of "ambulance chasing" are still valid, the Court has struck down some court rules that prohibited lawyers from conducting a direct-mail campaign targeted to potential plaintiffs in specific classes of cases.[1849]

See also: ANONYMITY, RIGHT TO; PERMIT SYSTEM; TIME, PLACE, AND MANNER RESTRICTIONS.

solicitor general   The U.S. solicitor general represents the federal government in the Supreme Court, overseeing the briefs, arguing the most important cases himself on behalf of the United States, and assigning other cases to his staff or to other government lawyers across the country. The office was established in 1870 and until 1953 the solicitor general was the second-ranking official of the Department of Justice. Since then, with the addition of deputies to the ATTORNEY GENERAL, the solicitor general is fourth-ranking. Because he is empowered to decide whether to appeal a ruling adverse to the United States in the lower courts, the solicitor general is the principal federal litigation strategist.

sound trucks, *see:* **noise regulation**

Southern Manifesto   In 1956 ninety-six southern members of Congress issued an impassioned statement denouncing the Supreme Court for its decision in BROWN V. BOARD OF EDUCATION, decreeing an eventual end to school desegregation. This Southern Manifesto proclaimed that the southern states were not constitutionally bound to abide by the Court's decision and bid the citizens to "resist forced integration by any lawful means." The Southern Manifesto summarized, rather than activated, the deep wellspring of loathing for the Court's decision to end the long reign of SEPARATE BUT EQUAL, though the clarity of the manifesto's argument doubtless contributed to the southern strategy of massive resistance and the long delays in taking even the first tentative steps toward restoring civil rights to a people long disenfranchised.

See also: JUDICIAL REVIEW; NULLIFICATION, INTERPOSITION, AND SECESSION.

sovereign immunity   Sovereign immunity is the doctrine that the government may not be sued in its own courts unless it consents. This doctrine is not found in the Constitution but has been upheld as inherent in the legal system and was first enunciated by the Supreme Court in 1793.[395] Since at least 1882, the Court has held that a suit against a federal officer is a suit against the United States and is barred under sovereign immunity if the remedy sought would affect the legal relations of the United States or its property.[1137, 1946] But if the officer is acting unlawfully or beyond the scope of his authority, the suit may be maintained.[1619] When the government establishes a corporation to carry out a program, the government does not pass on its immunity to the corporation, which therefore may be sued.[1056]

In the Federal Tort Claims Act of 1946, Congress waived the sovereign immunity of the United States so that people injured by federal employees—in driving accidents and the like—could recover DAMAGES in federal court. The act permits recovery to the extent that the law of the state where the injury occurred would hold a private person liable for the injury. In the Intentional Tort Amendment Act of 1974, Congress waived sovereign immunity for such matters as false arrest and assault, but still excluded are common law deceit, defamation, interference with contractual relations, and misrepresentation. In 1950 the Court ruled that members of the ARMED FORCES may not sue the government for injuries occurring in the course of their service,[657] an absolute rule to which the Court has adhered as recently as 1987,[1026] despite protests from some members of the Court that the result has been a heap of inconsistencies that has not really kept the government out of court.

Although the constitutional text does not seem hospitable to a claim of sovereign immunity by the states, the Court has read such a requirement into the ELEVENTH AMENDMENT, barring suits in federal court by citizens against their own states, thereby mirroring the rule for the federal government.[861]

See also: CONSTITUTIONAL TORT; IMMUNITY FROM SUIT; STATES, IMMUNITY FROM SUIT IN FEDERAL COURT.

sovereignty At the CONSTITUTIONAL CONVENTION and afterward at the ratifying conventions, the ANTI-FEDERALISTS had a special worry: how to preserve the sovereignty of the states against the encroachments of a new central government. Federalists thought the Constitution answered this question through its careful enumeration of powers granted to the federal government and the various political controls the states could exercise in the selection of national leaders. But the issue was worrisome enough that the TENTH AMENDMENT, the final article of the BILL OF RIGHTS, redundantly reminded the nation that whatever powers the federal government did not have the states retained. Still, deeper thinkers saw a profound paradox in all this: how could two separate and supposedly "sovereign" legislatures—Congress and the state legislatures—govern the same geographic territories? Everyone knew, because all the philosophers said so, that sovereignty ultimately could reside in but one place—that was its very nature. James Wilson provided the answer at the Philadelphia ratifying convention: in the United States, only the *people* are sovereign, and the people may delegate portions of their sovereign power to whatever sets of governments they choose to create. It was for this reason that the Preamble begins "We the People." And it was for this reason, too, that the Constitution in Article V provides for a means of amending itself.

See also: AMENDMENTS TO CONSTITUTION; CHECKS AND BALANCES; FEDERALISM; SEPARATION OF POWERS; SOVEREIGN IMMUNITY; STATES, IMMUNITY FROM SUIT IN FEDERAL COURT.

special master Because of severe time demands or the extraordinary number of documents that must be sifted to uncover the facts in some cases, courts sometimes appoint a special master to assist in duties that would overwhelm the judges. The Supreme Court uses special masters in cases invoking its ORIGINAL JURISDICTION, such as boundary and water disputes between the states. The special master assembles the evidence and writes an advisory opinion or decree, which the Court at its discretion may adopt, modify, or reject.

special prosecutor, *see:* **independent counsel**

speech, freedom from paying for others'
Despite the general FREEDOM OF ASSOCIATION, some associations between people are legally compelled—compulsory education, the draft, and memberships in certain kinds of organizations. For example, under labor laws that operate in many states, employees must pay dues to unions. Lawyers must belong—that is, pay dues—to "integrated bars," statewide bar associations. The question arises whether the organizations to which the dues are paid may advocate political positions contrary to those of dissenting members. The question was first presented in the mid-1950s but the Court ducked it,[1686, 981, 1127] finally squarely reaching the constitutional issue in 1977 in a case involving a school union. The Court held that the union could not require dissenting members to subsidize the union's "ideological activities" unrelated to collective bargaining. Compulsory contributions to someone else's political activities violate FREEDOM OF BELIEF.[4] In 1990 the Court unanimously ruled that the State Bar of California may not spend money of unconsenting members on ideological or political activities unrelated "to the purpose of regulating the legal profession or improving the quality of legal service available to the people of the state."[1057]

In 1991 the Court returned to the union setting and was divided only on the issue of whether the union was limited to spending its dissenters' money on duties imposed on it by law. A plurality held that the union could compel dues to be spent on "legislative lobbying or other union political activities," even though not required to do so by law, but only to the extent that those activities related to "contract ratification and implementation."[1146] Eight of the justices were clear that unions may not spend money against their members' wishes on

political campaigns and the like. An open question is the system by which a portion of the dues will be returned to the dissenting union member. Neither a proportionate refund nor an unexplained advance reduction is constitutionally sufficient, the Court has said. Instead, the organization must provide a "prompt decision by an impartial decisionmaker" to determine how much money the member may deduct from dues.[392]

See also: CONSCRIPTION; EDUCATION, COMPULSORY.

speech, freedom of, *see:* **freedom of speech**

speech, regulation of content   At the core of FREEDOM OF SPEECH and FREEDOM OF THE PRESS is the principle that the government may not criminalize or interfere with expression on the basis of its content or viewpoint. A law that banned the expression of views about environmentalism or the philosophies of political leaders would clearly be unconstitutional, as would a law permitting only kind things to be said about the president. But the simplicity of this generalization belies two major difficulties. One difficulty stems from the proposition that the FIRST AMENDMENT favors only certain kinds of speech. The kinds that it favors it protects absolutely, but the kinds that it disfavors are entitled to little or no protection. The second difficulty is that laws enacted for reasons other than regulating what a person says may have an unintended or unavoidable side effect on speech. At what point must a law not aimed *at* speech be voided because of its impact *on* speech?

Over the years, the Supreme Court has suggested that certain kinds of LOWER-VALUE SPEECH are unworthy of full First Amendment protection. One of the major free speech battlegrounds has been over whether this proposition is true and, if so, which kinds of speech fall within the disfavored category. From time to time, this lesser-breed category has included

SUBVERSIVE ADVOCACY, LIBEL AND SLANDER, OB-
SCENITY AND PORNOGRAPHY, HATE SPEECH,
FIGHTING WORDS, OFFENSIVE AND INDECENT
SPEECH, COMMERCIAL SPEECH, and speech
amounting to BREACH OF THE PEACE. With the
exception of obscenity and pornography, during the past quarter century it has developed
that even regulations aimed at these types of
speech will not be sustained. The Court has
held that in striking at them as types of speech,
the government is aiming at content. This conclusion is largely true even for obscenity and
pornography. Although the Court continues to
assert that the First Amendment provides no
shield for the obscene and pornographic, its
insistence seems mainly a fig leaf, for it has
consistently whittled away at what may constitutionally be so labeled.

An Indianapolis ordinance banned pornography that showed the subordination of women
but did not apply to sexually graphic material
that dealt with women as equals of men. This
is *viewpoint* discrimination. In a PER CURIAM decision the Court struck the ordinance.[48] An
example of impermissible *content* regulation
was a Michigan law that prohibited the sale of
any book to the general reading public because
it might have a deleterious effect on the state's
youth. The Court unanimously invalidated the
law because a state may not reduce the level of
reading matter to that which is suitable only for
children.[293] Likewise, a state may not make it a
crime for a newspaper to publish an editorial
on election day urging its readers to vote a
certain way on the issues.[1348]

The problem of the regulation with incidental effects on speech is more intractable because the situations are so various that it is
impossible to articulate a general formula for
resolving the conflict between the government
and speech interests. Nevertheless, when a law
or regulation has the effect of discriminating
against expression on the basis of its content or
the viewpoint expressed, the Court is likely to
strike it down. For example, Chicago banned
all PICKETING within 150 feet of any school except for "peaceful picketing of any school involved in a labor dispute." The Court unanimously struck down this ordinance because
"above all else, the First Amendment means
that government has no power to restrict expression because of its message, its ideas, its
subject matter, or its content."[1646] Unlike a permissible TIME, PLACE, AND MANNER RESTRIC-
TION, which might constitutionally have prohibited *any* picketing near the school during
school hours, the Chicago ordinance discriminatorily banned certain kinds of ideas altogether—that is, picketing dealing with anything other than school disputes. In the interest
of eliminating "visual pollution," a San Diego
ordinance severely limited the kinds of displays that could be mounted on outdoor billboards. Most types of messages were forbidden,
but among the exceptions were advertisements
for products sold on the premises, "for sale"
signs, signs telling the time and temperature,
historical markers, and religious symbols. Two
difficulties lurk in this list of exceptions: they
generally elevate commercial over noncommercial messages, and they pick and choose
even among noncommercial messages. A picture of a crèche could legally be displayed; a
political message from a concerned citizen
could not. This was unconstitutional content
discrimination, said a PLURALITY OPINION.[1320]

In a 1988 case, a District of Columbia regulation prohibited anyone from displaying a sign
within five hundred feet of a foreign embassy
that would tend to cast the foreign government
into "public disrepute." This was not viewpoint discrimination because it was not aimed
at a particular set of politics—for example,
against this kind of country or that one. But it
was content-based because, said Justice Sandra
Day O'Connor, "the government has determined that an entire category of speech—
[signs] critical of foreign governments—is not

permitted."[197] Although the government does have genuine interests in protecting foreign embassies, it has no COMPELLING INTEREST in sheltering foreign diplomats from politically distressing signs; in any event, the means chosen were not "narrowly tailored" to accomplish its purposes. An existing law would presumably work just as well—namely, a federal law against intimidating or harassing foreign officials. A final example is a federal law that prohibited any broadcast station from airing editorials if it received funds from the Corporation for Public Broadcasting. This, too, the Court held to be impermissible content regulation.[641]

See also: PENALTY-SUBSIDY DISTINCTION; SEDITIOUS LIBEL; SPENDING POWER; SYMBOLIC SPEECH.

speech and conduct, *see:* **symbolic speech**

Speech and Debate Clause   Art. I-§6[1] says that members of Congress may "not be questioned in any other place" for any speech or debate delivered in either house of Congress. On its face, the Speech and Debate Clause seems to immunize members of Congress from LIBEL AND SLANDER suits. This was certainly the intention of the Framers, who knew well the long history of royal attempts to silence their parliamentary critics. The clause requires dismissal of any suit for injuries caused by "legitimate legislative activity," not merely formal debate, because its purpose is to protect members "not only from the consequence of litigation's results but also from the burden of defending themselves."[2009]

The Court has interpreted the meaning of "legislative activity" broadly. Members voting to hold a witness in CONTEMPT could not be sued because their erroneous vote led to the witness's false imprisonment, since voting is integral to the legislative function.[1075] The courts may not enjoin a congressional committee from subpoenaing bank records as part of an investigation, no matter what the motive for

the investigation was.[595] Not even allegations that a Senate committee chairman was conspiring with state officials to violate people's civil rights may be heard in court.[560] When a congressional committee issued a libelous report that the superintendent of documents printed and offered for sale, a suit was dismissed against the committee and staff members, but the Court permitted it to go forward against the superintendent because, as an EXECUTIVE BRANCH official, he was not covered under the clause.[557] Distinguishing the dissemination of materials within Congress and circulation of materials outside, the Court permitted a libel suit against a senator for defamatory statements in a constituent newsletter. Even though press releases and newsletters are valuable tools for communicating with the public, they are not essential to the legislative function.[966]

When general criminal laws are at issue, the Court reads the clause considerably more narrowly, holding in one leading case that the clause does not immunize from prosecution a senator who was bribed to vote in a certain way, since taking a bribe is "no part of the legislative process or function."[232] Likewise, a GRAND JURY may inquire into how a senator acquired classified military documents and what arrangements he made to have them published.[794] Until the early 1970s, the Court had held that the clause immunizes only the members themselves, not employees of Congress.[1653] But in 1972 it held that in view of the "complexities of the modern legislative process" it is "literally impossible" to carry on legislative functions without the help of aides and that therefore the clause will be interpreted to immunize aides as long as their conduct is of the type protected by the clause.[794]

speed, *see:* **all deliberate speed**

speedy trial, *see:* **trial, speedy**

spending power The power of the federal government to spend public money has never been questioned as long as the expenditures have been made to further one of Congress's ENUMERATED POWERS, either express or implied. But for nearly a century and a half the question was left open whether under Art. I-§8[1] Congress could appropriate money for the general welfare, unconnected to any particular grant of power listed in Section 8. On one side of the debate was James Madison, who in *Federalist* 41 said that the authority of the GENERAL WELFARE CLAUSE, "to pay the debts and provide for the common defence and general welfare of the United States," was a redundancy, amounting to nothing more than the power to pay for the programs that Congress could otherwise establish. On the other side of the debate was the staunch nationalist, Alexander Hamilton, who said in *Federalist* 30 and 34 that the General Welfare Clause was a separate grant of power, entitling Congress to spend money for any purpose as long as it was in the general welfare of the nation. With such a power, Congress could spend money on roads and other "internal improvements," a practice that it began early without significant opposition.

Since many of its expenditures could doubtless be justified under its other powers, especially its power over INTERSTATE COMMERCE, the issue did not loom large until the New Deal, when Congress enacted a number of programs using federal money to induce people to act in certain ways. For example, under the Agricultural Adjustment Act, which established a crop support program, the government paid farmers to reduce their planting to boost farm prices. In 1936 the Court reviewed this act and determined, first, that Hamilton had been correct—the General Welfare Clause grants Congress independent power to spend; and, second, that the act was unconstitutional for another reason: it "invades the RESERVED RIGHTS of the states" because the TENTH AMENDMENT prohibits Congress from regulating agricultural production.[289] That Tenth Amendment theory was shortly to be discredited and overruled, but its conclusion about the spending power has remained intact.

In 1937, in two COMPANION CASES, the Court upheld the Social Security Act on the ground that it is in the general welfare of the nation, despite the novelty of its features. The act taxed payrolls of businesses with eight or more employees. But if the employer's state enacted an unemployment fund, subject to specific criteria specified by Congress, then the employer was entitled to a credit of ninety percent of the payroll tax. In effect, Congress was pressuring businesses all across the country to pressure the states to create unemployment compensation schemes that would raise money to be paid into a fund held by the secretary of the treasury. The act was challenged as unconstitutionally coercing the states, but Justice Benjamin N. Cardozo, for a 5–4 majority, said that there was no coercion in the constitutional sense: the states were free not to establish any unemployment program. The consequence then would simply be that the U.S. treasury would collect a tax, and the tax itself was entirely within Congress's power.[1957] In the second case, Cardozo spoke for a 7–2 majority that upheld the old-age benefits aspect of Social Security, under which the federal government taxes both employers and employees, holds the money in trust, and pays it out when the employees retire. This program is unquestionably for the general welfare, Cardozo said, and it was manifestly clear that such a program could be sensibly undertaken only by the federal government, since each state might fear putting itself at a disadvantage if it alone were to impose a payroll tax.[892]

These cases provide the constitutional justification for the vast profusion of federal GRANTS IN AID and revenue-sharing programs of the past half century. Moreover, the Court has confirmed the power of Congress to condition a grant on the state's performing certain acts, including the enactment of laws that Congress could not pass directly. In 1947 the Court upheld a provision in the Hatch Act that conditioned Oklahoma's receipt of federal highway money on its willingness to remove from office a member of the state highway commission.[1525] In 1987 the Court sustained a federal law requiring the secretary of transportation to withhold highway funds from any state that failed to raise its minimum drinking age to twenty-one years. South Dakota protested that since Congress clearly had no power directly to raise the drinking age in the state, it should not be permitted to accomplish the same thing indirectly. The Court disagreed, holding that the only limitation on the spending power is coercing the states to do something that is in itself unconstitutional. Since it is clearly constitutional to raise the drinking age, Congress's method is legitimate under the Spending Clause.[1915]

In 1991 a sharply divided Court concluded for the first time that this same principle permits a federal agency to restrict the speech of recipients of federal funds.[1777] Under a regulation of the Department of Health and Human Services, family planning centers that received federal funds were prohibited from "encourag[ing], promot[ing] or advocat[ing] ABORTION as a method of family planning." In effect, the regulation said that doctors and staff at family planning centers receiving federal funds could neither talk about abortions with their patients nor refer them to abortion counselors who would talk to them about an abortion option. For the majority, Chief Justice William H. Rehnquist said that this was not an abridgment of speech because the government was merely declining to spend its money in a certain way. It is choosing to subsidize one form of family planning rather than another. To the argument that the ban on talking about abortion penalizes doctors for their opinions, Rehnquist responded that the government was not denying a benefit to doctors because of what they would say; rather, the government is "simply insisting that public funds be spent for the purposes for which they were authorized." The dissenters saw the matter quite another way, arguing that the regulation discriminates against the *content* of speech because it prohibits a particular subject from being discussed. It also discriminates against the doctors' *viewpoint* because they remain free to talk against abortion; they just may not speak in favor.

See also: GENERAL WELFARE CLAUSE; GOVERNMENT SPEECH; PENALTY-SUBSIDY DISTINCTION; SPEECH, REGULATION OF CONTENT; TAXING POWER.

sports, *see:* **baseball**

standard of proof, *see:* **proof, standard of**

standard of weights and measures, *see:* **weights and measures**

standards, judicially manageable, *see:* **justiciability**

standing   A lawsuit may not be filed by anyone to sue for anything. For example, your dislike of the colors on postage stamps does not give you standing to sue the U.S. Postal Service. The standing doctrine is one aspect of the CASE OR CONTROVERSY requirement of Art. III-§2[1] that determines whether the federal courts may exercise the JUDICIAL POWER OF THE UNITED STATES. As the Court has interpreted this provision, a plaintiff must demonstrate that he (a) suffered an actual injury of the type for which a court may give relief (b) by some action of the defendant and that (c) the court will be able to redress the injury. Complicating the search for standing is a set of "prudential" standing rules, not rooted in the Constitution, that Congress may alter if it chooses. These rules require that (a) the defendant violated the plaintiff's legal right, not someone else's; (b) the plaintiff's injury is somehow differentiated from those of all other people in the country; and (c) the injury is of a type that the law or constitutional provision in question was designed to protect.

In the typical lawsuit, these conditions are always satisfied. For one thing, most people do not go out of their way to sue unless they are being injured by someone they can identify, and they are not likely to press on if they learn that there is no law to provide them with a remedy. But in certain classes of cases filed by taxpayers grousing about government expenditures or by public interest groups challenging government policies, the standing issue can pose difficult problems. Unfortunately, as the Supreme Court itself has said: "Generalizations about standing to sue are largely worthless as such."[92]

Ordinarily, a taxpayer has no standing to sue the government for carrying out an arguably unconstitutional program that she claims is wasting the public's money. The classic case was that of a taxpayer in the early 1920s who wanted to enjoin the federal government from providing funds for a maternity welfare program. The Court dismissed the suit, saying the taxpayer had failed to show any "direct injury."[707] The consequence of this "taxpayer standing" doctrine is to put beyond judicial reach most direct constitutional challenges to the exercise of the government's SPENDING POWER and to leave the allocation of federal funds in the political realm. Similarly, a "citizen suit" lacks standing if the injury asserted is simply the plaintiff's interest in having the government act constitutionally—for example, a citizen may not maintain a suit charging a violation of the INCOMPATIBILITY CLAUSE by members of Congress who hold military commissions.[1816] In 1968, however, the Court opened a small hole in the closed door of taxpayer and citizen suits, holding that a suit may proceed if the plaintiff alleges that the government is spending federal money unconstitutionally to support a program that violates the ESTABLISHMENT CLAUSE.[673]

The Court has denied standing in cases in which a plaintiff challenges the government's decision to give benefits to someone else. For example, a group of indigent patients were denied treatment at certain hospitals that were receiving federal tax benefits. They sued the Internal Revenue Service to stop the hospitals from receiving the benefits. The Court said the indigents had no standing to sue since they could not show that a loss of tax benefits would prompt the hospitals suddenly to begin treating them.[1872] Organizations as such ordinarily do not have standing on behalf of an undifferentiated public interest. For example, Citizens for Better Postage Stamps, Inc., has no standing to sue the Postal Service to change stamp designs. But an organization may sue on behalf of its members if they individually have standing, if the suit concerns a matter in which it is interested as an organization, and if the participation of individual members in the suit is not necessary.[959]

The Court usually recognizes the right of a state to sue on behalf of its citizens for economic or other injuries caused by other states or private parties.[1261] Recently, many members of Congress have sued the executive branch, alleging that a government policy injured them as members of Congress. Some lower courts have found standing, but the Supreme Court has not yet ruled. Ordinarily, a plaintiff may not challenge a government action that is violating another person's rights, but in certain instances the Court permits a plaintiff to do so. The injury need not be solely economic. The Court allowed a suit to go forward in which the plaintiffs alleged that as users of the outdoors in the Northwest, their enjoyment of nature would be seriously injured by railroad rates set by a federal agency, since the rates would deter the use of recycled goods, which in turn would have a baneful effect on the environment.[1830]

See also: JUSTICIABILITY; OVERBREADTH; VAGUENESS.

stare decisis   Stare decisis (Latin for "stand by what is decided") is a general principle of COMMON LAW courts that later judges are bound by the decisions of their predecessors. It is one of the principal reasons that the Supreme Court's opinions are so long, so forbidding, and usually so daunting to the lay reader. Stare decisis saddles judges with historical baggage that they must take along on every constitutional trip. Judges may not come to each case fresh and say: "How should I decide this one?" Rather, stare decisis commands judges to say: "What does the past tell me about how I should decide this one?"

Stare decisis is not a rule of the Constitution and is not itself even a law; it is a deeply entrenched policy that judges breach when necessary. In the Supreme Court, at least, stare decisis is a misleading account of how cases are decided. To be sure, to a great degree the Court does respect its precedents. For example, MIRANDA V. ARIZONA persists, despite a long campaign by presidents who have appointed justices who might have been supposed antagonistic to it. But like many seminal cases, *Miranda* has not survived unscathed. The Court has reinterpreted it and hedged it with qualifications. Over the long haul, in other words, the Court may evolve a doctrine quite different from what went before without ever explicitly OVERRULING a previous case.

On the other hand, the Court has on many celebrated occasions dramatically overruled its precedents. The school desegregation case, BROWN V. BOARD OF EDUCATION, for instance, essentially overruled a fifty-eight-year-old precedent, PLESSY V. FERGUSON. The stated ground for doing so was not just that it was now fifty-eight years later or that there were differ-

ent justices on the Court but that social and economic conditions themselves had greatly changed in the interim, so that what was once considered a legally unimportant interest— schooling—had been transformed into one of the most important interests. In *Erie Railroad v. Tompkins,* the Court overruled a ninety-six-year-old precedent because it was convinced that the Court had made a fundamental error that was especially hurtful to a modern economy. In its constitutional jurisprudence, the Supreme Court possesses the only realistic power to correct its own errors or to adjust for changing conditions.

Slow change has always been accepted. What has excited considerable controversy is the practice of a Court, infused with new justices, suddenly overruling precedents of only a few years' standing. In 1944 Justice Owen J. Roberts lamented in a case reversing the Court's nine-year-old holding in a "white primary" case that the Court's recent decisions were akin to "the same class as a restricted railroad ticket, good for this day and train only."[1885] In 1991 the Court overruled two precedents, less than four years old, concerned with VICTIM IMPACT STATEMENTS. "Power, not reason, is the new currency of this Court's decisionmaking," charged Justice Thurgood Marshall in his final term.[1580] But as Chief Justice William H. Rehnquist answered him, the overruled cases were "decided by the narrowest of margins, over spirited dissents challenging the basic underpinnings of those decisions. . . . [T]hey were wrongly decided."

See also: ERIE RULE; VOTING, RIGHT TO.

state, admission to the Union, *see:* **admission to the Union**

state, as market participant, *see:* **market participation doctrine**

state, authority of, *see:* **executive authority**

state, compelling interest of, *see:* **compelling interest**

state, formation of new   Art. IV-§3[1] empowers Congress to admit new states into the UNION. The Constitution is silent about any conditions that Congress may exact in return for admitting a territory to statehood. At the CONSTITUTIONAL CONVENTION the Framers refused to adopt provisions that would have required all states to be admitted on the basis of exact equality. Nevertheless, that is the settled interpretation: "Equality of constitutional right and power is the condition of all the states of the union, old and new" [623] regardless of how the territory came to be acquired or who settled the region. In 1911 the Supreme Court struck down a congressional directive to the newly admitted state of Oklahoma that it refrain from moving the location of its capital city. Where a state chooses to situate its capital is a matter of SOVEREIGNTY possessed equally by all states, said Justice Horace Lurton, and Congress may not interfere. [482] Congress may not admit states with powers less than those enjoyed by the original thirteen. [1647] As soon as a state is admitted, congressional enactments that applied to the area when it was a territory lapse altogether unless the state readopts them. [1606] However, on the eve of its admission to the Union, a state may make binding contracts with the federal government. For example, a promise not to tax certain lands held by the United States and later granted to a railroad was held not to infringe state sovereignty. [1954]

state, injunction against, *see:* **states, immunity from suit in federal court**

state, instrumentalities of   An instrumentality of a state is an activity owned and operated by the state or one of its political subdivisions, such as a municipal transit system or a public utility. In the days when the TENTH AMENDMENT was seen as a barrier against Congress's exercise of the COMMERCE POWER, whether a particular activity was an instrumentality of the state and hence immune from certain federal taxes or regulations was an important question. With the demise of the Tenth Amendment as an effective shield against Congress, the issue is less important. Whether an entity is a state instrumentality continues to be an issue when someone attempts to sue in federal court, for under the ELEVENTH AMENDMENT states are immune from federal suit under certain circumstances.

See also: IMMUNITY, INTERGOVERNMENTAL; STATES, IMMUNITY FROM SUIT IN FEDERAL COURT.

state, not to impair contract, *see:* **obligation of contract**

state, suits against, *see:* **states, immunity from suit in federal court**

state action   State action is the requirement that constitutional restraints and limitations may be applied only to things that the government does, not to actions of private individuals. If you eat a piece of your sister's Halloween candy, that is not a TAKING OF PROPERTY for which she is entitled to JUST COMPENSATION (although she might have you prosecuted for theft). The sometimes baffling problem is how to detect whether the state had a constitutionally significant hand in whatever injury is being sued for in a particular case.

The state action doctrine has had its greatest impact in the area of race relations, beginning with the CIVIL RIGHTS CASES in 1883. In the Civil Rights Act of 1875, Congress outlawed "private" acts of discrimination in places of PUBLIC ACCOMMODATION—theaters, restaurants, hotels, railroads, and the like. The question confronting the Supreme Court was whether Congress had the power to enact such civil rights laws. The law was defended under Congress's power to enforce the FOURTEENTH AMENDMENT's command that the states not deny any person the EQUAL PROTECTION OF THE LAWS. Justice Joseph P. Bradley explained that this argument was flawed because in all these cases it was not the state that was denying admission to black patrons; it was private owners and their agents. Congress could pass corrective laws only against actions that the state took. Bradley's central point, and one that has plagued constitutional law ever since, is that the Constitution does not care about state *inaction*. This seminal decision was grievously flawed and has caused doctrinal confusion ever since. If a city provides fire and police protection for white residents and refuses to provide these services for black residents, it may not have "acted," since a refusal to lift a finger is not an action in Bradley's sense, but it is surely denying blacks the equal protection of the laws. Just so, as Justice John Marshall Harlan noted in his eloquent dissent, the states had long required places of public accommodation to provide their services to all comers. By failing to insist that these places refrain from racial discrimination, the states were denying equal protection. Nevertheless, the distinction between action and inaction stuck. Among other things, this perverse reading made it constitutionally difficult, for a very long time, to hold state officials responsible for their acquiescence in mob lynchings.

Though narrowing the meaning of "action," a word not contained in the Constitution at all, the Court has expanded the meaning of "state." In the easiest cases—when a law actually requires segregated facilities—the state has clearly acted. State action applies also to administrative regulations and practices,[2276] to state officials acting in an official capacity,[2130] to courts,[1854] and even to referendum votes of the entire people in a community.[1708] The Court has also held that Congress has the power to

outlaw the actions of even private individuals for violating others' constitutional rights, if the private individuals were conspiring with state officials in doing so.[1663]

The difficult cases are those in which the state encourages or cooperates in some manner with private individuals. Under its PUBLIC FUNCTION analysis, the Court held that a company town was equivalent to the state when the manager of a town owned entirely by a private company ejected a Jehovah's Witness from the main street and refused to permit her to distribute literature.[1245] By this finding, the Court could apply the FIRST AMENDMENT to the case. If the property had been considered wholly private, the First Amendment would have been irrelevant, since it does not offend the Constitution for you to tell your neighbor not to say certain things on your land. But the Court has sharply limited the public function doctrine to situations in which the private actor is carrying out all of the functions that would normally be carried on by the state. The Court refused, for example, to find that a private shopping mall is a state actor.[950] On the other hand, a municipality may not avoid the Constitution's strictures by handing part of itself over to private managers. The Court refused to view as private a public park in Macon, Georgia, originally created for whites only, that the city turned over to private owners so that it could remain segregated.[633] The Court also found constitutionally objectionable white primary elections in which blacks were not permitted to vote, even primaries conducted under entirely private auspices.[2012]

Another form of state action is state involvement in or connection with an otherwise private activity. The clearest example was shown in *Shelley v. Kraemer*, in which the Court struck down racially RESTRICTIVE COVENANTS because the only means of enforcing them would be through the courts, which then would involve a branch of government in an action based solely on RACIAL DISCRIMINATION. The Court also found state action when a private restaurant that leased space from a public parking authority refused to serve black patrons. Although the parking authority had no rule requiring the restaurant to discriminate, it was enough that it tolerated the discrimination and profited to some degree from the restaurant's activities.[285] But the mere fact of state regulation or licensing is not necessarily sufficient to transform the regulated industry or the licensee into a state actor. The Court said that merely holding a state liquor license does not make a private club an arm of the state,[1384] nor does the state's regulation of an electrical utility subject the utility to the procedural requirements of the Due Process Clause, even though the state is extensively involved in setting the utility's tariffs and rules of operation.[997] If the state authorizes a warehouse to sell its customers' private property when they fail to pay storage costs, the warehouse does not become a state actor by disposing of the property legally under the law.[672]

The receipt of government money from the state does not make a private entity into a public one. The Court refused to view a private nursing home as a state actor because it received Medicaid reimbursements, even though the law extensively regulated the manner in which the homes could operate.[175] An institution, such as a private school, that obtains almost all its funding from public sources does not thereby become an arm of the state, any more than a government contractor would be.[1709] But the Constitution does not prohibit a state from refusing to award a construction contract unless the contractor promises to refrain from engaging in discriminatory acts.

In 1988 the Court was presented with an interesting twist on the usual state action case: could the National Collegiate Athletic Association (NCAA) be considered a state actor in imposing sanctions or calling for sanctions on

Jerry Tarkanian, longtime basketball coach at the University of Nevada at Las Vegas? Under pressure from the NCAA, the public university suspended Tarkanian for improprieties. Tarkanian sued, alleging that the NCAA was sufficiently enmeshed in the university's decision to suspend him that the NCAA should be considered a state actor. If it was a state actor, then it violated his PROCEDURAL DUE PROCESS rights by failing to give him a hearing. The Court, 5–4, disagreed, holding that the NCAA's policing of its rules governing the conduct of sporting events does not make it a state actor, nor was its involvement with the university sufficient, since far from active cooperation, the university had for the most part resisted the NCAA's demands that Tarkanian be disciplined.[1426]

See also: CIVIL RIGHTS LEGISLATION; GARNISHMENT AND ATTACHMENT; GOVERNMENT, AFFIRMATIVE OBLIGATIONS OF; PROCESS THAT IS DUE; SEGREGATION AND INTEGRATION; SHOPPING CENTERS, ACCESS TO; TRESPASS.

state apportionment, *see:* **apportionment of political districts**

state citizenship, *see:* **citizens and citizenship**

state compacts, *see:* **Compact Clause**

state constitutional law, *see:* **Supremacy Clause**

state courts, *see:* **judicial procedure in state courts**

state employees, federal law applied to, *see:* **federalism; interstate commerce; Tenth Amendment**

state grounds, independent and adequate, *see:* **adequate state grounds**

state law, meaning of   In the 1789 Judiciary Act, Congress told federal courts that in DIVERSITY JURISDICTION cases they must look to state law to decide the case. But what does "law" mean? In 1842, in *Swift v. Tyson,* Justice Joseph Story answered that only a *statute* counted. A court decision was not a law and the federal courts were not bound by it. The Supreme Court reversed this notion nearly a hundred years later in *Erie Railroad v. Tompkins.* In hearing diversity cases, federal judges may not ignore the rulings of state courts either about the meaning of a legislative enactment or about a COMMON LAW rule. But suppose the law is unclear or that neither the state legislature nor the state supreme court has spoken. In 1991 the Supreme Court said that when that happens a federal COURT OF APPEALS is not bound by the decision of the federal trial judge on what the law of the state probably is. Appeals courts have independent authority to determine for themselves what the state courts probably would say if presented with the question.[1787]

See also: ERIE RULE.

state legislatures   State legislatures are bound by many constitutional limitations, such as the EX POST FACTO CLAUSE in Art. I-§10[1] and the DUE PROCESS and EQUAL PROTECTION CLAUSES of the FOURTEENTH AMENDMENT. But state legislatures are not clones of Congress and do not have to use the legislative procedures set forth in Article I. They are governed, instead, by their state constitutions, most of which do in fact contain SEPARATION OF POWERS and other federal constitutional principles. In one respect state legislatures are bound *not* to resemble Congress. The Supreme Court has ruled that representation in each house of the state legislatures must be by population. The principle of Senate representation—two senators per state—may not be translated to an equal number of state senators per county or

other geographic region unless the populations in those regions are equal.

See also: APPORTIONMENT OF POLITICAL DISTRICTS.

State of the Union   The president is bidden by Art. II-§3 "from time to time [to] give Congress information of the state of the Union." In modern times the explicit requirement has become a moment of high ceremony, the president appearing before a joint session of Congress in late January every year to give the State of the Union address in prime time. Placed in a clause dealing with the president's relations with Congress, the State of the Union is a useful reminder that presidents and Congress are expected to work together.

See also: PRESIDENT, POWERS AND DUTIES OF.

state of war, *see:* **war, state of**

state police power, *see:* **police power**

state regulation of commerce, *see:* **Dormant Commerce Clause**

state sovereignty, *see:* **states' rights**

state taxation of commerce, *see:* **taxation of interstate commerce**

statehood, *see:* **states and statehood**

Statement and Account Clause, *see:* **account of the receipts and expenditures of all public money**

states, disputes between   Under Art. III-§2[1,2] the Supreme Court has ORIGINAL JURISDICTION to hear cases involving "controversies between two or more states." From their earliest days, states brought the Court their boundary disputes. In 1838 the Court held that determining boundaries is not a POLITICAL QUESTION but a legal issue.[1716] Construing the word "controversy" liberally, the Court has determined that many other types of disputes between states are justiciable and that the clause permits the Court to determine the rule for decision in the absence of any settled principle, congressional enactment, or multistate COMPACT; for example, disputes over control and use of common waterways,[1047] breach of contract claims,[1064] claims to the inheritance tax on a deceased person's estate,[2020] and the collection of unclaimed intangible property.[2022] On occasion the Court has declined to hear cases on the ground that the issues were not justiciable. For example, it refused to consider Alabama's suit to enjoin nineteen other states from enacting laws prohibiting the sale of goods made by convicts,[26] or Louisiana's suit against Texas to reform the administration of its quarantine laws.[1190] Also, the Court will not hear original suits filed by a state on behalf of individual citizens.[1264] Many such suits may be heard in state courts or the lower federal courts and then appealed to the Supreme Court.

states, immunity from suit in federal court
As ratified, Art. III-§2[1] extended the JUDICIAL POWER OF THE UNITED STATES to suits between a state and a citizen of another state. In 1793 the Supreme Court accepted such a suit under its ORIGINAL JURISDICTION,[395] exciting immense fears throughout the country, for it had not occurred to the states that their SOVEREIGN IMMUNITY against suit could be overcome by the simple expedient of suing in the courts of a different sovereign—the United States. Within less than two years, the states had ratified the ELEVENTH AMENDMENT, which appears to withdraw from federal judicial power suits "commenced or prosecuted" between states and citizens. But the amendment ultimately accomplished far less than what many had hoped, for it has scarcely kept states and state officials out of federal court. For one thing, said Chief Justice John Marshall in an appeal arising from a state court, the Eleventh Amend-

ment does not bar federal review of a state case, since it was a continuing case that the state had instituted, not one that had been "commenced or prosecuted" originally in federal court.[420] This was a fateful decision, for without it the Supreme Court might have been unable to enforce the commands of the SUPREMACY CLAUSE and bind the states into a single nation. In 1824 Marshall discovered an essential loophole in the amendment, finding a way to restore considerable federal judicial power over state acts. His theory was simple: a state *officer* is not a state, and so in the appropriate circumstances, a suit against state officials rather than states may be brought to federal court.[1543]

By the late nineteenth century, the JURISDICTION of the federal courts had been greatly expanded, including, for the first time, power to hear claims of unconstitutional actions by the states against their own citizens. The Eleventh Amendment says nothing about such suits; by its terms only suits brought by citizens of other states or countries are barred. Yet in *Hans v. Louisiana,* in a feat of some prestidigitation, Justice Joseph P. Bradley said that even though the amendment does not say that a state is immune from suit by its own citizens in federal court, it should mean that. The drafters did not include that happenstance in the Eleventh Amendment because they never supposed that anyone would ever try it. The Court also held that states may not be sued in ADMIRALTY AND MARITIME cases, even though the amendment seems to permit it.[1468] Rather perplexingly, in view of this apparent policy judgment, the Court in 1979 upheld the constitutional power of the California courts to entertain a suit by a California citizen against the state of Nevada.[1444] Notwithstanding the Eleventh Amendment, the states may waive their immunity and consent to be sued in federal courts if they choose.[832]

But the largest loophole in the Eleventh Amendment is Marshall's notion about suits against state officials. In 1908, in *Ex parte Young*, the Court held that the attorney general of Alabama could be sued in federal court to enjoin him from enforcing an unconstitutional law or violating a federal law. The fiction on which this decision rested was that if the act was found to be unconstitutional, it was no act of the state, so the suit must therefore be against the state official as an individual committing an illegal act. However, in 1984 the Court held, 5–4, that suits may not be heard in federal court against state officials who it is alleged have violated *state* law.[1588] The word "state" does not extend to POLITICAL SUBDIVISIONS, so that counties[1166] and school boards,[1395] among others, may be sued in federal court regardless of the amendment.

The amendment is more porous still, for the Court has sustained the power of Congress by statute to supersede the Eleventh Amendment under its later-created power to enforce the FOURTEENTH AMENDMENT. Congress may subject states, even in their official capacity, to suits in federal court for violating the fundamental rights protected in the Fourteenth Amendment.[671] Moreover, under the COMMERCE POWER, under certain conditions, Congress may even rescind the Eleventh Amendment altogether and subject states to federal DAMAGE suits.[1593]

states, taxation by, *see:* **taxation by states**

states and statehood   After the Revolutionary War, the former colonies became states, independent SOVEREIGNTIES. The very word "state" was chosen not only to connote their coequal status in the family of nations, but also to mark them as republics and distinguish them from monarchies. Though the states thought of themselves as legally independent, not merely from England but from each other, in fact they were bound by too many ties to maintain separate existences. From the very beginning, they

were closely allied through the Continental Congress and then in the ARTICLES OF CONFEDERATION. Even so, real governmental power lay with each state. The national government was an agent of the states, created by compact and alterable at the will of the states.

By defining the meaning of UNION, the Constitution gave the states a distinctively different juridical status. They were no longer independent or sovereign, even in theory, but meshed into a distinctively new federal system, in which governmental power is assigned to the state or federal government by function, and in which a system of CHECKS AND BALANCES gives each some measure of control over the other. The SUPREMACY CLAUSE awards the final say to the federal government if the exercise of state and federal power conflicts, but federal power is limited and the states have a sizable hand in forming the federal government (more so originally than after the ratification of the SEVENTEENTH AMENDMENT).

The states are not linked solely through their relationship with the federal government. The FULL FAITH AND CREDIT and PRIVILEGES AND IMMUNITIES requirements of Article IV link the states directly and obligate them to act toward all Americans as part of a common nation.

The Constitution assumes stability of the states as juridical entities. A state's borders are not transient lines but fixed; under Art. IV-§3[1] they are unalterable unless both the state and Congress consent to a change. Once Congress admits a new state to the Union, it assumes full legal equality with all other states and its statehood is perpetual. Congress may not rescind its vote or repeal the admission. Though the Constitution does not explicitly declare any principle of equality, the Supreme Court has consistently assumed one.[1606] During the Civil War, President Abraham Lincoln was careful to maintain that the Confederate states had not dissolved or reverted to territorial status but had maintained their status as states. When, at war's end, provisional governments were established in the defeated Confederate states, it was not because they had lost their capacity to govern but because their governments were held to have been corrupted, a decision that Congress may make under the GUARANTEE CLAUSE.[2024]

Time has worn away a degree of constitutional independence that the Court once conceded to the states under the TENTH AMENDMENT. Under a theory of "reserved powers," the Court held in many cases from the end of the Civil War until the beginning of World War II that the Tenth Amendment imposed constitutional limitations on the power of Congress to interfere with certain state functions and powers. That theory died in 1941,[514] and except for a brief and limited resurrection in the mid-1970s, remains dead. While the change in relationship between the states and the federal government is related to changing constitutional doctrines, it is more sensibly explained by reflecting on the immense changes to the economy and technology of the nation, awakening Congress to its COMMERCE POWER in ways undreamed of by the Framers but in accord with the control they provided for from the very beginning.

See also: COMPACT CLAUSE; DORMANT COMMERCE CLAUSE; EXECUTIVE AUTHORITY; FEDERALISM; IMMUNITY, INTERGOVERNMENTAL; MARKET PARTICIPANT DOCTRINE; OBLIGATION OF CONTRACTS; STATE LAW, MEANING OF; STATE LEGISLATURES; STATE, FORMATION OF NEW; STATE, INSTRUMENTALITIES OF; STATES, DISPUTES BETWEEN; TAXATION OF INTERSTATE COMMERCE; TRAVEL, RIGHT TO.

states' rights "States' rights" is not a constitutional term but a political slogan, employed in various forms throughout American history to suggest that the states possess SOVEREIGNTY over certain matters—mostly having to do with SLAVERY, race relations, and police procedures—and that in those areas the states are superior even to federal law and the decisions

of the Supreme Court. In its more extreme forms, the doctrine of states' rights has always been a doctrine advocating the power of an entrenched group to repress less favored groups. Under the SUPREMACY CLAUSE, the position of ardent states' rightists simply collapses, as it has historically, though not without bitter struggle and wistful hopes even to this day.

See also: SOUTHERN MANIFESTO; FEDERALISM; JUDICIAL REVIEW; TENTH AMENDMENT.

statistical evidence, use of A statute or administrative policy, neutral on its face, does not necessarily violate the EQUAL PROTECTION CLAUSE because it affects racial groups differently. To show a constitutional violation, there must be proof that the legislation or policy has a discriminatory purpose. Proving legislative or administrative intent is often difficult, and so the question arises whether statistical evidence is sufficient to prove discrimination. The answer is: sometimes.

In the classic 1886 case *Yick Wo v. Hopkins,* Chinese laundry operators in San Francisco were arrested for operating their businesses in wooden buildings. A city ordinance required that all laundries be situated in brick or stone buildings unless the board of supervisors consented to a variance. The board consented to variances for non-Chinese laundry owners but refused consent to hundreds of Chinese laundrymen. The Supreme Court held that from these facts alone it could infer a policy "applied and administered by public authority with an evil eye and an unequal hand."

In 1935 overturning the conviction of one of the SCOTTSBORO BOYS because blacks were excluded from the jury, the Court looked at the history of jury selection in the state and held that the evidence that for more than a generation no black person had ever been called, even though a substantial number were legally qualified, was evidence of RACIAL DISCRIMINATION in jury selection.[1491]

And in more recent JURY DISCRIMINATION cases, the Court has been willing to entertain statistics to shift the burden of proof: once a significant disparity has been shown between the numbers of a particular group who could be called and who were actually called, the state must then demonstrate that it was not discriminating.[358] In the 1989 SET-ASIDE case, the Court, while striking down the minority construction law, said that an inference of discriminatory exclusion from government contracting business might be drawn if there is shown "a significant statistical disparity between the number of qualified minority contractors willing and able to perform a particular service and the number of such contractors actually [so] engaged."[1727] On the other hand, the Court rejected a massive statistical study purportedly demonstrating racial discrimination in DEATH SENTENCES in Georgia, saying that the study did not demonstrate racial bias in the particular case.[1282] In legislative apportionment cases, the Court has sometimes accepted statistical evidence[2195] and sometimes not.[1370] In general, as Justice William Brennan said in a SEX DISCRIMINATION case, "proving broad sociological propositions by statistics is a dubious business,"[483] though it is sometimes the only evidence possible.

See also: DE FACTO–DE JURE DISCRIMINATION; PURPOSE-IMPACT DISTINCTION.

statute of limitation   A statute of limitation is a legal deadline for filing lawsuits. Plaintiffs who fail to file within the time period forfeit the right to do so thereafter. The Supreme Court has rarely struck down a statute of limitation for being unreasonably short under DUE PROCESS, nor found any problem if a state decides to shorten an existing statute.[2190] But the statute must operate reasonably. A state may not use a statute of limitation to bar legal relief when the state itself was the cause of delay. In a 1982 case, an Illinois administrative agency dismissed an employment discrimination claim because it had failed to schedule a required HEARING within the legally mandated period, thus depriving the claimant of any remedy. The Supreme Court unanimously held that a state may not deprive a person of a legal claim in such a manner.[1181] The Court has also occasionally found fault with statutes of limitation in ILLEGITIMACY cases. In 1982 it voided a Texas law requiring illegitimate children seeking child support from fathers to file suits before their first birthday;[1350] in 1983, a Tennessee two-year statute of limitation;[1626] and in 1988, a Pennsylvania six-year statute,[404] all on the EQUAL PROTECTION ground that there was no corresponding statute of limitation for marital children.

See also: ERIE RULE; JUDICIAL PROCEDURE IN STATE COURTS; RETROACTIVITY.

statutory rape   In 1981 the Supreme Court upheld statutory rape laws against a SEX DISCRIMINATION challenge.[1326] Statutory rape is the crime of having sexual relations with a minor girl, even if she consents. The California law in question set the age of consent at eighteen. A seventeen-year-old boy was convicted of having intercourse with a girl under the age of eighteen. The question was whether the law violated EQUAL PROTECTION in providing punishment for the boy only. A sharply divided Court said that there was no constitutional violation. The purpose of the law, to prevent teenage pregnancy, was a legitimate one and the law was a rational way of accomplishing that end. Even though the law places a burden on males not shared by females, there was no suggestion that males because of past discrimination needed special protection from the courts, that the gender classification was made for administrative convenience, or that the law rested on any sexual stereotypes. Instead, the law simply reflected the common understanding that females were already far more burdened with the consequences of sexual intercourse and pregnancy and therefore the deterrent effect of the law could be limited to males.

stay of execution   A stay of execution is an order from a higher court to a lower court to postpone enforcing its judgment pending an appeal. Stays may be granted by all federal courts in appropriate circumstances. Under federal law, stay applications to the Supreme Court are made to the individual justice assigned to supervise the particular judicial circuit in which the case is pending. In controversial cases, the individual justice will frequently poll his colleagues to see whether at least four justices think the stay should be issued. A litigant may appeal to the entire Court if an individual justice denies a stay. "Stay of execution" also refers to an executive decision to delay a DEATH SENTENCE. In recent years, the Supreme Court has been extremely reluctant to grant stays of execution to permit the condemned prisoners to make further HABEAS CORPUS appeals.
See also: RULE OF FOUR.

steamboats, *see:* **transportation**

Steel Seizure Case   In April 1952 steel unions were poised to call a strike against the nation's steel mills. Afraid that the strike would cripple the national security in the midst of the war in Korea, President Harry S. Truman ordered Charles Sawyer, secretary of commerce, to "seize" the steel mills, operate them as government property, and negotiate new contracts with the union. The president claimed the power to seize and operate the mills under his inherent power as chief executive, including his power as COMMANDER IN CHIEF. He could point to no clause in the Constitution specifi-

cally granting seizure power, nor to any law authorizing him to do so. In less than two months, the time it took to get the case to the Supreme Court, the steel companies regained their mills.

In *Youngstown Sheet & Tube Co. v. Sawyer*, the Court declared, 6–3, that the president has no inherent authority to seize private property. In a famous concurring opinion, Justice Robert H. Jackson explained that the president's power fluctuates and depends on how much Congress has underwritten it. If Congress complies or expressly authorizes the president to act, then his power is at its zenith. Had Congress authorized the seizure, then the Court would have presumed Truman's actions to have been constitutional and the steel companies would have had a difficult burden of proof to overcome. However, when Congress has been silent, then there is a "zone of twilight" in which the president and Congress may have concurrent power to act. Finally, when the president acts against the expressed or implied will of Congress, his power is at its "lowest ebb," for then all that exists is an inherent power, minus whatever power Congress could give him. In the Steel Seizure Case, the Court noted that Congress had debated giving the president seizure power in an earlier labor law but decided against it.
See also: EMINENT DOMAIN; IMPLIED AND INHERENT POWERS; PRESIDENT, INHERENT POWER OF.

sterilization, *see:* **reproductive rights**

stop and frisk, *see:* **search and seizure: stop and frisk**

stream of commerce doctrine   In the late nineteenth century, the Supreme Court took a narrow view of Congress's COMMERCE POWER, holding that certain antitrust laws and regulations of working conditions were unconstitutional because Congress had no power to regulate local activities. But it found an exception for activities that, while local if considered in isolation, were actually part of a "stream" or "current" of commerce carried on between the states. In 1905 Justice Oliver Wendell Holmes upheld the power of the government to enjoin price fixing by meat dealers because, although the prices were fixed in a single location, the commodity in fact began its journey in one state and almost always ended it in another, by way of the stockyard where brokers arranged its sale and transit. This typical "constantly recurring course" is a "current of commerce," and the purchase of cattle is a part of that current.[199] Congress followed up Holmes's metaphor in the Packers and Stockyards Act of 1921, regulating working conditions, charges, and fraudulent practices by meat packers. The Court upheld the law, finding that the packers were engaged in INTERSTATE COMMERCE since the stockyards "are but a throat through which the current flows" and the packers' work is "only incident to this current from the west to the east." The sales of meat do not stop the flow but facilitate the current.[1938]

See also: ANTITRUST LAWS, CONSTITUTIONALITY OF; COMMERCE, EFFECTS ON; ECONOMIC REGULATION; INTERSTATE COMMERCE.

strict construction   Those who advocate strict construction of the Constitution believe that the words of the text should be given no broader meaning than they will bear and that no meaning outside the words themselves is responsible or appropriate. Broad or liberal constructionists, by contrast, suppose that the meaning of the words cannot fully determine the outcome of cases, because in so many instances the words themselves provide no guide. What is an "unreasonable" SEARCH AND SEIZURE? What is an "establishment of religion"? At a minimum, the interpreter must look to history, and that already implies an interpretation beyond the four corners of the document. The debate between strict and broad con-

structionists is as old as the Republic. In the first years of the Washington administration, Thomas Jefferson (strict) and Alexander Hamilton (broad) battled over the basic powers of the government, Jefferson holding that the Constitution gave the federal government relatively little room in which to maneuver, Hamilton finding ample constitutional legitimacy for a far-reaching national government. Yet when Thomas Jefferson, as president, was presented with the land deal of a lifetime, the LOUISIANA PURCHASE, he overcame doubts that he lacked constitutional authority to make it.

In recent political discourse, "strict construction" is often a synonym for "conservative." But there is no sound correlation between constitutional interpreters who would stick to the text and political views about what the text means. Liberals can read closely, conservatives broadly. Justice Hugo L. Black, generally regarded as a leading liberal politician and jurist, believed himself to be a strict constructionist; he scorned the idea that judges were competent or authorized to draw new rights out of the DUE PROCESS Clauses. Conservative justices at the end of the last century read wildly between the lines to create constitutional theories that were certainly no part of the constitutional text.

As descriptive terms, "strict" and "broad" construction do not define how a justice will or ought to approach the interpretive task. Perhaps they could be refashioned as descriptors of a problem far less discussed: to what degree should judges confine their opinions to the specific facts of the case at hand? "The Court sustains this legislation by assuming two deviations from the facts of this particular case," stormed Justice Robert H. Jackson in the *School Bus Transportation Case;* "first, it assumes a state of facts the record does not support, and secondly, it refuses to consider facts which are inescapable on the record."[634] The Supreme Court *Reports* are strewn with laments and tongue-lashings like Jackson's about the failure of the majority or the dissenters to think through the facts of the case to be decided.

See also: CONSTITUTION, LIVING; CONSTITUTIONAL INTERPRETATION; INCORPORATION DOCTRINE; NEUTRAL PRINCIPLES; ORIGINAL INTENT; SHOCK THE CONSCIENCE TEST; SUBSTANTIVE DUE PROCESS.

strict scrutiny   In determining whether a SUSPECT CLASSIFICATION violates the EQUAL PROTECTION CLAUSE, the courts probe the law or policy far more closely than when an ordinary classification is at stake. This more searching inquiry into the justification for the law is called "strict scrutiny," a term first used by Justice William O. Douglas in 1942 in a case calling for the sterilization of certain convicted felons.[1879] The strict scrutiny test has been variously stated, but in recent form the Supreme Court has said that a law that classifies on the basis of race or ethnic origins must be *"necessary* to promote a *compelling state interest."*[583] In cases involving "quasi-suspect" classifications, such as laws based on sex, the Court requires an "intermediate" or "heightened" scrutiny test. To withstand invalidation, a sex classification must "serve *important* governmental objectives and must be *substantially related* to achievement of those objectives."[483] Since it is impossible to quantify the difference between "necessary" and "important" or "compelling" and "substantially related," the cases must be consulted to gain a sense of what kinds of classifications will survive each type of scrutiny. Indeed, the tests may simply be taken as convenient labels for the Court's ultimate decision to strike down a law or not. Classifications subjected to strict scrutiny do not survive. The Court has rejected all laws invidiously discriminating on the basis of race or ethnic origin. Some classifications based on sex have survived. When neither a suspect nor a quasi-suspect classification is at issue, the Court uses the RATIONAL BASIS OR RELATIONSHIP TEST, which most statutory classifications pass.

See also: AFFIRMATIVE ACTION; ALIENS; INVIDIOUS DISCRIMINATION; MENTAL RETARDATION; PURPOSE-IMPACT DISTINCTION; RACIAL DISCRIMINATION; SEX DISCRIMINATION.

students' rights   Students have a mixed bag of constitutional rights. The Supreme Court has held that the FIRST AMENDMENT protects high school students who peacefully wear black armbands to protest a war.[2051] But students do not have absolute freedom to speak as they please. The Court upheld a school's disciplining of a student who gave a "lewd" school election speech to a high school audience.[158] The Court also upheld the right of public school authorities to censor student newspapers,[886] although it recognized a higher degree of constitutional protection for student speech in colleges, holding in 1973 that a public university may not expel a student for using "indecent language" in the student newspaper.[1564] Students in public high schools and colleges have the right to meet for religious purposes if the schools open their campuses to other outside groups.[2202, 181] Students also have a right to prevent school authorities from depleting school libraries of materials the authorities consider "offensive," if the motivation for removing the books was to censor ideas.[182] Students have limited procedural rights when school authorities wish to discipline them for infractions of school rules. A student may not be suspended, even for a brief time, without at least an informal HEARING at which the student is notified of the charge and offered the opportunity to rebut it.[785] Students have a LIBERTY interest in being free of undeserved corporal punishment, but the Court refused to require schools to hold any kind of hearing *before* students are physically beaten, because, the Court said, after-the-fact lawsuits are sufficient remedies for any wrongs done.[980]

See also: ACADEMIC FREEDOM; EDUCATION, COMPULSORY; JUVENILES, RIGHTS OF; PROCESS RIGHTS; PROCESS THAT IS DUE.

subject of commerce, *see:* **prohibition of commerce**

subpoena power A subpoena is a court order requiring a witness to come forward to testify or to produce documentary or other tangible evidence for inspection in court, either before or during trial. Subpoenas are issued at the behest of parties, though the court has discretion to refuse to issue the subpoena if the subpoenaed witness can show why he should not be called—for example, the irrelevance of his testimony, the existence of an EVIDENTIARY PRIVILEGE, or the constitutional right against SELF-INCRIMINATION. Failure to comply with a lawful subpoena is punishable by CONTEMPT. The SIXTH AMENDMENT affords criminal defendants COMPULSORY PROCESS—that is, power to subpoena favorable witnesses. The Sixth Amendment's right to CONFRONTATION WITH WITNESSES may require the government to subpoena other witnesses for trial.

subsidy There is no general constitutional obligation for the government to spend money on behalf of individuals, even if the funds are necessary to further the exercise of a constitutional right. The Supreme Court has held, for example, that neither DUE PROCESS nor EQUAL PROTECTION requires the government to subsidize ABORTIONS of indigent women through the Medicaid program, even though it pays for other medical services.[869] The only major exception to this general policy is that when the government has restricted a person's LIBERTY, by confining him in a penal or other institution, it must meet certain due process standards of maintenance and treatment.[2279]

See also: GOVERNMENT, AFFIRMATIVE OBLIGATIONS OF; PENALTY-SUBSIDY DISTINCTION; SPENDING POWER; UNCONSTITUTIONAL CONDITIONS.

subsidy-penalty distinction, *see:* **penalty-subsidy distinction**

substantial relationship test, *see:* **rational basis or relationship test**

substantive due process The Constitution spells out certain rights of the people and certain restraints on government power. Most of the rights and most of the restraints are procedural: you are entitled to a fair trial before being locked up; you may not be compelled to be a witness against yourself; your home may not be searched unless the police first obtain a SEARCH WARRANT. The Constitution does not say that the government may not lock you up or search your home, only that they must do so in a certain way. A very few rights are more substantive—for example, the government may not prohibit you from speaking your mind or worshipping as you choose. But most important features of life—the right to marry and raise a family, the right to work and pursue a calling—are not enumerated in the Constitution.

The Framers had fought a revolution to secure fundamental human rights. Because they believed that a government of ENUMERATED POWERS would not abuse the people's NATURAL RIGHTS if it was not given the power to do so, the document prepared at the CONSTITUTIONAL CONVENTION listed scarcely any rights at all. The ratifying conventions showed that this was a serious error and the BILL OF RIGHTS was the result, including the rarely invoked NINTH AMENDMENT, which says that government should not assume that the people have forfeited rights just because the Constitution does not list them.

In the early years of the Supreme Court, the justices occasionally talked as if the government could be restrained on "general [natural law] principles which are common to our free institutions," without pinning the restraint to any language in the Constitution.[678] But so free-floating a theory was inconsistent with the meaning of a written Constitution. Instead, the Court pressed into service the DUE PROCESS

Clauses of the FIFTH and FOURTEENTH AMEND-MENTS. These clauses were intended to brake the power of government to carry out certain acts without following the law; in other words, they acted as *procedural* reins on government. But then, beginning perhaps with DRED SCOTT v. SANDFORD, in which Chief Justice Roger B. Taney said that a person's property right in his slaves cannot be extinguished simply by the act of moving to a free state, the Court began to see that due process might involve more than procedure. Not only could the Court tell the government, "You may not do this unless you do it in the proper way"; it could tell the government, "You may not do this at all." This latter proposition is the doctrine of substantive due process.

The Court began to use this line of reasoning in the late nineteenth century, mostly in cases concerning the power of government to regulate business, economic activities, and property rights. This use of substantive due process was roundly criticized as giving judges carte blanche to impose their policy views on the people. Economic due process had exhausted itself by the time of the later New Deal, when President Franklin D. Roosevelt's COURT-PACKING PLAN dealt it a deathblow.

But substantive due process itself did not die. In the early years of this century, the Court cautiously discerned other, noneconomic rights that it held to be fundamental and beyond the power of government. Many of these are constitutionally familiar, because the Court took substantive limitations in the Bill of Rights—for example, FREEDOM OF SPEECH—and held that they restrain the states no less than the federal government. But some substantive rights had no anchor in the text. In 1923 the arch-conservative Justice James McReynolds declared for the Court that Nebraska could not forbid the teaching of foreign languages to children.[1323] The acquisition of knowledge is part of the LIBERTY possessed by every person and the state may not constitu-

tionally interfere with it. Until the 1960s, there were few substantive due process decisions of this type, partly because the post–New Deal justices were uncomfortable with the thought of judges declaring what amounted to natural rights. Occasionally a case would crop up—notably, Justice William O. Douglas's decision striking down an Oklahoma law permitting the sterilization of some but not all three-time losers.[1879] Although he based his decision on the EQUAL PROTECTION CLAUSE, he spoke of basic liberty, fundamental rights, and basic civil rights.

In 1965, again speaking through Douglas, the Court revived substantive due process in a significant way, striking down Connecticut's birth-control law and announcing, in *Griswold v. Connecticut,* a fundamental right to PRIVACY. Douglas strained to show that the right to privacy could actually be found in the Constitution, and he cited PENUMBRAS, offshoots or tendrils of other constitutional rights. The somewhat surreal quality of *Griswold* can be explained by Douglas's resistance to being seen as an advocate of a theory of substantive due process, for he was one of Roosevelt's original appointees and a sworn enemy of economic due process. Eight years and many privacy decisions later, the Court handed down *Roe v. Wade,* the most inflammatory substantive due process decision of the century. Whether or not ABORTION remains a recognized constitutional right, substantive due process is not likely to disappear. Perhaps mindful of the public outcry during the Senate hearings into Robert Bork's nomination to the Supreme Court, the most recent justices have said that they cannot conceive of a Constitution without some notion of a right to privacy.

Even so, substantive due process is a relatively limited doctrine. It does not, under any understanding so far expressed, permit the courts to strike down in the name of constitutional freedom anything they suppose fundamentally unfair. The debate over whether the space program or anti-poverty spending is a higher national priority remains a political issue. The only due process for decisions such as these is the ballot box.

See also: CONTRACEPTION; ECONOMIC DUE PROCESS; PROCEDURAL RIGHTS OF CRIMINAL DEFENDANTS; PROCESS RIGHTS; PROCESS THAT IS DUE; PROPORTIONALITY OF SENTENCE; REPRODUCTIVE RIGHTS; SEXUAL FREEDOM.

subversive activities, *see:* **sedition**

subversive advocacy   Advocating one's ideas and beliefs is the central concern of the Free Speech and Press Clauses of the FIRST AMENDMENT. It is also one of the most politically contentious arenas of constitutional debate, because advocacy is not confined to ideas with which most of us agree. Society would be anemic indeed if it allowed us to minister only to the believing or preach only to the converted. Ultimately, the right to advocate our beliefs is the heart of a free society. "If there is any principle of the Constitution," said Justice Oliver Wendell Holmes, "that more imperatively calls for attachment than any other it is the principle of free thought—not free thought for those who agree with us but freedom for the thought that we hate."[1828] But precisely because passionate advocacy can stir so many to hatred, the right to advocate positions that frighten or disgust the community has long been a constitutional battleground.

The issue centers on the right to advocate unlawful conduct, to incite people to act unlawfully, and to promote highly unpopular ideas that might promote radical political and social change. The problem is as old as the Republic. In 1798 Congress enacted the Sedition Act, which outlawed statements or publications critical of the government. The law soon expired and it would be over a century before the constitutionality of SEDITION laws reached the Supreme Court.

The federal Espionage Act of 1917 prohibited interference with military recruitment and outlawed attempts to cause insubordination in the ranks. Agitators were prosecuted for speeches and pamphlets that were said to violate the act. The Court heard several appeals in 1919. In one of them, the conviction rested on a leaflet that argued against conscription, urged people to assert their constitutional rights, and blamed the war on Wall Street. In *Schenck v. United States,* Justice Oliver Wendell Holmes affirmed the conviction for a unanimous Court. In ordinary times, Holmes said, the defendant may have been within his constitutional rights to say what he did, but not in wartime. Holmes said that the test was whether the words were of such a nature and used in such a way as to "create a CLEAR AND PRESENT DANGER that they will bring about the substantive evils that Congress has a right to prevent."

Holmes affirmed similar convictions in other cases decided at the same time,[704, 531] but several months later he was suddenly in dissent. In *Abrams v. United States,* the Court was presented with a conviction under an amendment to the Espionage Act. Whereas the original act prohibited certain *actions,* the law now prohibited certain kinds of *speech*—anything that would incite resistance to the United States during the war. The majority again affirmed, but Holmes wrote one of his most celebrated dissents. Setting forth his MARKETPLACE OF IDEAS metaphor, Holmes said that now the government was punishing the expression of opinion, and opinion that stood no chance of being acted upon. Moreover, there was no showing that by the publication "of a silly leaflet" this "unknown man" had any *intention* of causing the injuries at which the law was aimed.

For the next fifty years, the issue of subversive advocacy was whether it was consistent with FREEDOM OF SPEECH to prohibit any statement, no matter how unbelievable or unlikely to cause harm, that just *might* tend to incite someone into carrying out an unlawful and violent act that could harm the security of the nation or state. In a series of criminal SYNDICAL-ISM cases, the Court declined to follow even the clear and present danger test. In *Gitlow v. New York*, it held instead that certain kinds of subversive advocacy could be punished regardless of whether they could conceivably cause any harm. In 1927, in *Whitney v. California*, the Court essentially sustained the notion of GUILT BY ASSOCIATION. It was in this case that Justice Louis D. Brandeis penned the most powerful plea for expressive freedom in the annals of judicial opinions, condemning laws that punish the expression of any thought that was not *imminently likely* to cause *serious* harm.

During the Smith Act prosecutions of COM-MUNISM AND THE COMMUNIST PARTY in the early 1950s, the Court adopted a watered-down version of the clear and present danger test, holding essentially that even speech highly unlikely to realize its objective, or unlikely to reach it anytime in the near future, may be punished if the harm that might be caused is great enough.[539] By the late 1950s the Court took a more subtle look at the subversive advocacy laws and the evidence used to sustain convictions, and it began to qualify its earlier broad pronouncements. For example, it held unconstitutional laws that penalized mere MEMBERSHIP IN POLITICAL ORGANIZATIONS; only "knowing" and "active" membership in an organization devoted to lawlessness could expose the member to conviction.[1807] As late as 1961, though, the Court insisted that "present advocacy of *future* action for violent overthrow," as well as "advocacy of *immediate* action to that end" could constitutionally be punished.[2272] But in the 1960s the Court struck down a number of subversive conspiracy convictions on a variety of nonconstitutional and occasionally constitutional grounds.

Finally, in 1969, the Court adopted a strong version of Holmes's clear and present danger test. The leader of a motley Ku Klux Klan "rally" on a farm in Ohio was convicted under the state criminal syndicalism law for advocating the "duty . . . of violence or unlawful methods of terrorism as a means of accomplishing industrial or political reform." The rally consisted of twelve hooded figures and several television camera operators. There were no spectators. The speaker rather laconically notified his television audience that the Klan intended to march on Washington to demand rights for the "Caucasian race" and that if Washington did not respond, "it's possible that there might have to be some revengeance [sic] taken." In a PER CURIAM opinion, the Court unanimously overruled *Whitney* and reversed the conviction, announcing the following rule: A state may not forbid "advocacy of the use of force or of law violation except where such advocacy is directed to inciting or producing imminent lawless action and is likely to incite or produce such action."[222] A speaker urging a mob to attack a government building "right now" or to storm a jail cell to lynch the prisoner may be prosecuted for his speech. But ugly, detestable "advocacy of illegal action at some indefinite future time"[914] is constitutionally protected. "Let's take back America!" or "Your time will come!" is not a prosecutable utterance. For the moment at least, the law of subversive advocacy has been constitutionally settled.

See also: BLACKLISTING; FREEDOM OF ASSOCIATION; LIBEL AND SLANDER; LOYALTY-SECURITY PROGRAMS; MEMBERSHIP IN POLITICAL ORGANIZATIONS.

succession to office of president, *see:* **presidential succession**

suffrage, *see:* **voting, right to**

suicide, *see:* **right to die**

suits at common law, *see:* **trial by jury**

summary opinion   The Supreme Court does not always decide every case with a full opinion or even after having heard ORAL ARGUMENT. Sometimes it issues a summary opinion, a short PER CURIAM decision or order with little explanation of the reasons for its conclusion. Although a case decided summarily is not entitled to as great a precedential value as cases decided with full opinions, it is nevertheless binding "until such time as the Court informs [the lower courts] that [it is] not."[920] Individual justices frequently dissent from the Court's refusal to hear oral argument and to dispose of cases summarily. For example, four justices objected to the Court's "indefensible" determination to dismiss Senator Barry Goldwater's suit against President Jimmy Carter when Carter decided to recognize mainland China and break off diplomatic relations with Taiwan. Five justices thought the case was nonjusticiable because it raised a POLITICAL QUESTION or was not yet ripe for resolution, but the dissenters thought the case was so obviously important that oral argument should have been heard.

See also: JUSTICIABILITY.

Sunday closing laws   Laws compelling Sunday worship and prohibiting certain activities on that day were enacted during the colonial era. Although compulsory worship laws today would unquestionably violate the ESTABLISHMENT CLAUSE, the Court has been much more charitable toward laws regulating commercial and other activities on Sunday. In 1900 the Court refused to strike as a violation of DUE PROCESS a state law that prohibited barbering on Sundays.[1617] At that time, the religion clauses of the FIRST AMENDMENT were not thought to be applicable to the states; but by 1961, when the Court heard challenges to three Sunday "blue laws," the First Amendment had been "incorporated" into the FOURTEENTH AMENDMENT and so the question was primarily whether such laws represent a RELIGIOUS ESTABLISHMENT or interfere with the FREEDOM OF RELIGION.

The cases concerned discount stores in shopping malls open seven days a week and stores owned by Orthodox Jews who for religious reasons could not open their stores on Saturday. Even though the Sunday laws were motivated by religious concerns, their current use was secular, said Chief Justice Earl Warren. They "provide a uniform day of rest for all citizens." That the day chosen, Sunday, has particular significance for Christians does not defeat the state's secular interest, since the fact remains that "Sunday is a day apart from all others."[1297] Moreover, the closing laws do not force a religious belief on anyone; they merely make the practice of certain religious beliefs more expensive. The FREE EXERCISE CLAUSE does not invalidate laws that indirectly burden the practice of a person's religion. To provide an exemption for people who observe the Sabbath on a different day would be to defeat the purpose of providing a uniform day of quiet in the community, although a state could provide an exemption if it chose for people who worship on a different day.[226] But a state may not give a person an absolute right against dismissal from a job for refusing to work on the Sabbath. Connecticut reformed its Sunday laws, permitting a wide variety of businesses to remain open. The revised law said that an employer could not fire a worker who refused to work on Sunday or any other day claimed as the Sabbath. In 1985 the Supreme Court invalidated this law as an impermissible religious establishment.[2045]

The Sunday closing laws were also challenged on EQUAL PROTECTION grounds, since they defined commonsense understanding of what could and could not be sold. In one state, fish could be sold wholesale but not retail on Sundays. In another state, the sale of all merchandise was banned except retail sales of tobacco products, confectioneries, milk, bread, fruits, gasoline, greases, drugs and medicines, and newspapers and periodicals—there goes the neighborhood. But the Court said that the states have wide discretion to determine how much quiet they wish to provide and that the distinctions were not wholly irrational.

See also: LEMON TEST.

suppression hearing A suppression hearing is a judicial HEARING before trial to consider whether a confession to be used in a criminal prosecution was voluntarily made. In 1964 the Supreme Court held that a suppression hearing is a constitutional necessity, striking down the New York procedure in which the voluntariness of a confession was left to the jury.[995] Instead, the Court held, the state must permit the judge to make a preliminary determination, and if he finds the confession involuntary, then it may not be presented to the jury. If he finds it voluntary, the jury may hear it; but the defendant is entitled to present evidence of coercion, either to impeach the confession's credibility or to raise before the jury the question of its voluntariness.[489] The judge need not find the confession voluntary beyond a REASONABLE DOUBT at the suppression hearing; a preponderance of the evidence is a sufficient standard of proof.[1143] Suppression hearings are also used to determine the constitutionality of a SEARCH AND SEIZURE. Sometimes the defendant will take the stand at a suppression hearing, and the Court has ruled that in so doing he does not forfeit his right against SELF-INCRIMINATION. Any testimony he gives at the suppression hearing may not be used at trial, and he may not be compelled to take the stand before the jury.[1870]

See also: EXCLUSIONARY RULE.

Supremacy Clause At the CONSTITUTIONAL CONVENTION, James Madison wanted Congress to have the power to negate state laws. The delegates rejected his proposal, and instead adopted the Supremacy Clause of Art. VI-[1]: "This Constitution, and the laws of the United States which shall be made in pursuance thereof; and all treaties made, or which shall be made, under the authority of the United States, shall be the supreme law of the land." Without this clause, the nation might have fallen apart long ago, squabbling over the effects of conflicting laws and policies emanating from Congress and the states. The scope of the Supremacy Clause was set, as in so many other instances, by Chief Justice John Marshall. In *McCulloch v. Maryland,* he established that the Supremacy Clause bars the states from taxing the United States or any of its instrumentalities. In *Gibbons v. Ogden,* he established that although a state may have the power to pass a certain law, the law has no legal effect if it conflicts in some way with a law that Congress is likewise empowered to enact. The rule that federal law is paramount to state law applies to all levels of state law, including not only legislative enactments but also state constitutions and judicial opinions.

The concept of federal legal supremacy raises two different sorts of questions: what constitutes federal "law," and what constitutes a "conflict"?

Plainly, federal statutes are law in this sense, as are treaties to which the Senate has consented. State laws that conflict with federal treaties or federal laws implementing those treaties are void.[1363] Regulations promulgated by federal ADMINISTRATIVE AGENCIES are likewise supreme, and the Court has said that the very existence of a federal agency's power to regulate, even though unexercised, may indicate that the states must refrain from acting. In other words, if a federal agency decides *not* to regulate, the courts will take that as a decision that there should be no regulation by states either.[75] A difficult question has occasionally arisen over what weight a local state court must give to a lower federal court's pronouncement when confronting similar issues. The Court has never resolved the issue. But it is central to the Supremacy Clause that the Supreme Court's construction of federal law or the Constitution is binding on the states.[463]

In regard to the second question, many laws may conflict below the surface. In sorting out whether a state law actually conflicts with federal law, the federal courts have served as the primary umpires.

Art. VI-[3] requires not merely federal officers but all state officers as well, including judges at every level, to take an OATH to support the federal Constitution. This clause was intended to be more than merely ceremonial. The Framers assumed that many federal laws and programs would have to be carried out by state officials, and the Judiciary Act of 1789 so empowered state courts. In adjudicating cases, however, state judges are not free to disregard relevant federal laws on the ground that they are "foreign" to the state, in the same way that the law of Mexico or Canada is foreign to the United States.

In 1947 the Court confirmed that the relationship between the federal government and the states is not the same as between nations in the international arena. Under a wartime federal price control act, a buyer who was overcharged could recover DAMAGES equal to three times the overcharge. The law permitted suit in federal or state court. A Rhode Island court confronted with such a suit refused to award the triple damages because, it said, under rules of international law, a court is not obligated to enforce a "penal" statute, which it held the federal price control act to be. Said Justice Hugo L. Black for a unanimous Court: "We cannot accept the basic premise [of] the Rhode Island Supreme Court . . . that it has no more obligation to enforce a valid penal law of the United States than it has to enforce a penal law of . . . another country." Federal law is also the law of Rhode Island, and the state courts must enforce it when required to in particular cases. [2015]

See also: FEDERALISM; IMMUNITY, INTERGOVERNMENTAL; PREEMPTION; TENTH AMENDMENT.

Supreme Court   The United States Supreme Court is the only court established by the Constitution. Art. III-§1 vests the JUDICIAL POWER OF THE UNITED STATES "in one Supreme Court." In *Federalist* 78, Alexander Hamilton said that the judiciary, having neither sword nor purse, "will always be the least dangerous" branch. It seemed, instead, to be the invisible branch.

When the federal government moved to Washington from Philadelphia in 1800, it developed that no provision had been made for housing the justices. Indeed, the architects had forgotten about the Supreme Court altogether. So an east basement room of the Capitol was hurriedly prepared. During the next decade, because of renovations and other exigencies, the Court found itself in the library once occupied by the House of Representatives and then, to avoid the library's draft on winter days, in Long's Tavern. Finally, in 1810, the Court convened in a basement room, designed especially for it, under the Senate chamber. The war of 1812 interrupted proceedings, and the Court again moved, this time with Congress, and even settled into a rented house, until it finally returned to the restored basement chamber in 1819. Chief Justice Marshall announced the opinion in the *Dartmouth College* case on the day he and his brethren returned to the Capitol. There the Court stayed until 1860. During the Civil War, the Court moved to the old Senate chamber on the Capitol's first floor. In these quarters it remained for seventy-five years. The courtroom itself was capacious, but the justices' adjacent space was miserably cramped, and none of them had individual office space.

The Court did not get a permanent home until 1935, when a huge marble building at One First Street, Northeast, in Washington, D.C., opened for business. Its elaborate facades and monumental interior spaces have led critics to label it a "marble palace" and a "marble mausoleum." Chief Justice Harlan Fiske Stone called it "almost bombastically pretentious." It was, he said, "wholly inappropriate for a quiet group of old boys such as the Supreme Court." The justices would be, said one of them, "nine black beetles in the Temple of Karnak."

The Supreme Court building provides each justice with a three-room office suite, and it also contains many ornate rooms for library, conference, staff offices, and other private and public functions. The courthouse was built at a cost of less than ten million dollars, probably fifteen times less than what it would cost to build today. Indeed, so efficient were its contractors that they actually returned to the treasury ninety-four thousand dollars of the funds appropriated for its construction and furnishings—an astonishing feat, at least to a modern era accustomed to the inexorable law of "cost overruns."

See also: CONFERENCE, JUDICIAL; DURING GOOD BEHAVIOR; JUDICIAL REVIEW; JURISDICTION; SUPREME COURT, JURISDICTION OF; SUPREME COURT, NUMBER OF JUSTICES; see also Time Chart of the Justices of the Supreme Court; Biographical Notes on the Justices of the Supreme Court; and How the Supreme Court Hears and Decides Cases.

Supreme Court, jurisdiction of   Under Art. III-§2[2], the Supreme Court has ORIGINAL JURISDICTION over cases affecting diplomats and cases in which a state is a party. This provision is the only self-executing grant of jurisdiction in the Constitution—that is to say, the Supreme Court is empowered to hear such cases whether or not Congress approves.[1063] That was the essential point of MARBURY V. MADISON: Congress may neither enlarge nor diminish the class of cases that the Supreme Court may hear as a trial court. The Court's original jurisdiction is not exclusive, however; Congress may assign these cases to other courts as well.

The Supreme Court has APPELLATE JURISDICTION over all categories to which the JUDICIAL POWER extends but "with such exceptions and under such regulations as Congress shall make." Because Art. III-§1 grants Congress complete discretion over whether or not to establish the lower federal courts, Congress's power to bestow them with only limited jurisdiction has always been assumed. The Court has explicitly ratified this view, as long ago as 1812,[953] again in the mid-nineteenth century,[356, 1853] and as recently as 1966.[1913] From 1789, when the lower federal courts were established, Congress has in fact refrained from conferring all permissible jurisdiction. For instance, the first federal courts had no FEDERAL QUESTION JURISDICTION. Congress assumed that cases raising claims under federal law would be heard in state courts.

A larger debate has arisen over the breadth of Congress's power to control the Supreme Court's appellate jurisdiction. Could Congress, for example, divest the Court of jurisdiction to hear appeals in abortion or school prayer cases? Initially, in 1810, Chief Justice John Marshall said that the Supreme Court has complete constitutional jurisdiction unless Congress limits it[587]; but by mid-century the Court had taken the opposite view: it has no appellate jurisdiction except what Congress decides to confer, within the limits of Article III.[134] If Congress decides to choke off jurisdiction, the Court is powerless to hear the case. That, at least, was the Court's conclusion in 1868 in *Ex parte McCardle.* Following the Civil War, army courts were busily trying civilians accused of antiwar activism. In 1866 the Supreme Court ruled one such trial unconstitutional.[1345] In 1868 a similar case arose against William McCardle, an antiblack Mississippi publisher who preached violent opposition to Reconstruction. The publisher sought his release from military confinement through a writ of HABEAS CORPUS, and the case was argued in the Court. But angered at the 1866 decision and alarmed that the Court might take the opportunity to curb other Reconstruction policies, Congress withdrew jurisdiction from the Court in all habeas corpus cases, including cases then pending. The Court upheld Congress's control over its appellate jurisdiction and dismissed McCardle's appeal. Congress later restored the Court's jurisdiction in habeas cases.

Since that time, the issue of whether Congress may simply cut off the Court's jurisdiction in any particular class of cases has never been squarely presented, and the Court has expressed occasional doubts that *McCardle* remains good law.[762] But the Court has held that Congress may not, in the guise of limiting jurisdiction, dictate how a case is to be decided. In an 1872 case, Congress attempted to deny jurisdiction to hear cases involving enemy property captured during the Civil War. The courts had ruled that a presidential PARDON entitled a former Confederate claimant to indemnification. Congress decreed that a presidential pardon had the opposite effect and that the courts must dismiss such cases. The Supreme Court held, in effect, that Congress was unconstitutionally violating the SEPARATION OF POWERS by prescribing how the courts must rule in pending cases.[1082]

During the past several decades, Congress has periodically confronted bills abolishing the Court's appellate jurisdiction in controversial topics of the day, including DESEGREGATION, ABORTION, APPORTIONMENT of state legislatures, and school prayer. Popular sentiment for High Court review of all constitutional questions has so far kept these bills from passing. How the Court would rule if Congress attempted to limit its jurisdiction probably depends on exactly what Congress would say. A law repealing the Court's jurisdiction to review PATENT CLAUSE cases would undoubtedly be upheld, but a law repealing the Court's right to hear cases involving the rights of blacks, or women, or ALIENS might well fail as a violation of EQUAL PROTECTION. But it is this direct congressional power over the Supreme Court's jurisdiction, a leading commentator has argued, that gives legitimacy to the Court's rulings. It cannot be charged that unelected judges act undemocratically in making constitutional rulings, because Congress implicitly permits them to do so and may terminate their power at its will.

If the Court has jurisdiction to *hear* a case, must it *decide* the case? In 1821 Chief Justice John Marshall said, "It is most true that this Court will not take jurisdiction if it should not: but it is equally true, that it must take jurisdiction if it should. . . . *We have no more right to decline the exercise of jurisdiction which is given, than to usurp that which is not given.* The one or the other would be treason to the Constitution."[420] Despite Marshall's bold words, the Court ducks many more cases than it accepts, largely by refusing to grant a writ of CERTIORARI. In one often-cited MISCEGENATION case, the Court refused to hear an appeal by a person convicted of having entered an interracial marriage, not because there could be any doubt of how the Court should rule, but presumably because it was wary of further fanning the political firestorm that had greeted its decision in BROWN V. BOARD OF EDUCATION the year before.[1419]

See also: ABSTENTION DOCTRINE; ADEQUATE STATE GROUNDS; CONSTITUTIONAL QUESTIONS, AVOIDANCE OF; FINAL JUDGMENT; FINALITY; JURISDICTION; MAJORITARIANISM; STARE DECISIS.

Supreme Court, number of justices   The Constitution does not say how many justices must serve on the Supreme Court. The number is for Congress to decide. In the Judiciary Act of 1789, Congress decreed that the Supreme Court should consist of the CHIEF JUSTICE of the United States and five associate justices. In 1801 Congress provided that one of those seats should lapse when the next vacancy occurred, but that law was repealed the following year. In 1807 Congress increased the number of associate justices to six; in 1837, to eight; and in 1864, to nine. This was the largest number ever to sit on the Court. In 1866, to bar President Andrew

Johnson from making appointments to the Court, Congress reduced the number to six and forbade Johnson from appointing any replacements until retirements or death brought the number of sitting justices to that number. When Ulysses S. Grant became president in 1869, Congress raised the number of associate justices again to eight, where it has stood ever since, producing a nine-member Supreme Court (the chief justice and eight associate justices). In his COURT-PACKING PLAN, President Franklin D. Roosevelt urged Congress to increase the number of associate justices to a maximum of fourteen, but Congress rejected the idea.

supreme law of the land, *see:* **Supremacy Clause**

surgery, *see:* **medication and surgery, forced**

surveillance When the government undertakes surveillance of particular people suspected of criminal activity, the FOURTH AMENDMENT provisions governing SEARCH AND SEIZURE regulate the lengths to which law enforcement officials can go. It is less clear constitutionally how far the government may go simply to "keep a watch" on various organizations, gathering generalized data about groups thought to threaten public order. Direct interference with political activities would clearly violate the FIRST AMENDMENT, but there is no general rule against government investigation. In 1972 the Supreme Court turned aside a challenge to the Army's surveillance of "lawful and peaceful civilian activities." The plaintiffs asserted that the very fact of intelligence-gathering about legal domestic groups was unconstitutional because of the CHILLING EFFECT. The Court held, 5–4, that the case was not ripe and therefore had to be dismissed. The mere fear that the Army might at some unknown future date misuse the information it was gathering was insufficient to demonstrate "specific present objective harm" or a "threat of specific future harm."[1109]

See also: JUSTICIABILITY; RIPENESS.

suspect classifications When laws are challenged under the EQUAL PROTECTION CLAUSE, the Supreme Court scrutinizes their purpose and operation by different tests, according to the type of classification laid out in the law. The Court pays the closest attention and subjects the law to the most searching scrutiny when it encounters what it has termed a "suspect classification." A classification is suspect if the legislature or administrative agency has fastened on an innate or immutable characteristic that a person has no power to change, such as race or ethnic origin. The concept of suspect classification was enunciated in 1944 in the JAPANESE-AMERICAN RELOCATION AND EXCLUSION case. As Justice Hugo L. Black put it, "all legal restrictions which curtail the civil rights of a single racial group are immediately suspect."[1094] Since the 1950s, the Court has held that legal classifications based on race, national or ethnic origins, or alienage are suspect and are subject to STRICT SCRUTINY. With the exception of AFFIRMATIVE ACTION cases, no classification based on race or national origins has been upheld in nearly half a century. Many classifications based on a person's status as an ALIEN have been stricken as well. The Court has refused to view sex classifications as suspect, somewhat surprisingly since sex is no less immutable than race. Instead, since the early 1970s it has seen sex-based classifications as "quasi-suspect" and tested their constitutional validity by a "heightened scrutiny" standard. Another classification accepted as quasi-suspect is ILLEGITIMACY. But the Court has refused to find MENTAL RETARDATION, age, or poverty classifications to be quasi-suspect. Critics of these labels point out that there is only one

Equal Protection Clause, not three, and that the tests employed for each of these classifications are highly manipulable.

See also: AGE DISCRIMINATION; ECONOMIC DISCRIMINATION; WEALTH CLASSIFICATION AND DISCRIMINATION.

sweeping clause, *see:* **Necessary and Proper Clause**

symbolic speech   Not every communication is made through "pure" speech—words spoken or written. Conveying messages effectively often requires something more. Heckling a speaker from the back of a crowd is much less noticeable than holding up a huge placard that can be seen on nightly television. Demonstrating contempt for a political regime often takes the form of a hunger strike. Outrage at some public policy is often much better expressed by displaying a popular symbol, defaced in a pertinent way. Many people marching sends a message far more effectively, one may suppose, then writing a letter to the editor. The question in each case is the degree to which the FIRST AMENDMENT shelters this symbolic speech— the use of symbols and even certain behavior or conduct. The Supreme Court first recognized a constitutional right to symbolic speech in 1931 in the *Red Flag Case.*[1971] California outlawed the displaying of a red flag to symbolize "opposition to organized government." The Court struck down the law because it interfered with "the opportunity for free political discussion."

In 1968, in *United States v. O'Brien,* the Draft Card Burning Case, the Court established a test for determining when a law regulating conduct is constitutionally deficient because it interferes with the "communicative aspect" of the conduct. The defendants stood on the steps of a Boston courthouse and burned their draft cards before live television cameras and a sizable audience. "Knowingly" mutilating or destroying a draft card was a federal offense. O'Brien asserted that burning his card was the only real way to get people to listen to his antiwar message and that the First Amendment protected his "communication of ideas by conduct." He was arrested and convicted.

The Supreme Court affirmed his conviction. Chief Justice Earl Warren rejected the notion that "an apparently limitless variety of conduct can be labeled 'speech' whenever the person engaging in the conduct intends thereby to express an idea." But even if it is speech, in some sense, Warren said, a government regulation will be upheld if (1) it deals with an area in which the government has constitutional power to act; (2) it furthers an "important or substantial governmental interest"; (3) the governmental interest is unrelated to suppressing ideas or expression; and (4) the incidental restriction on the expression is no greater than is essential to further the government's interest. Applying the analysis, Warren said that Congress clearly had power to create and regulate a military draft, that the law regulating draft cards furthered the operation of the military registration system, and that the law was no broader than it had to be. Finally, Warren rejected O'Brien's contention that the law was specifically aimed at suppressing protest. Unlike the Red Flag Case, the draft card law on its face dealt "with conduct having no connection with speech." The Court will not strike down an "otherwise constitutional statute" because the legislators may have had an "illicit" motive. It does not matter what the purpose of the legislators was if the purpose of the law is not related to suppressing speech.

In 1969 the Court did reject a government ban on symbolic conduct, holding that a Des Moines, Iowa, public school could not constitutionally prohibit high school students from wearing black armbands to symbolize their protest of the war. This time the Court saw the policy as aimed directly at conduct "akin to pure speech."[2051] In a series of highly controversial FLAG BURNING AND DESECRATION cases, the Court has also upheld the symbolic speech claims of people who burned American flags on the streets or used them in ways that many people found offensive. In cases decided between the early 1970s and 1990, the Court consistently determined that the government's only interest was in deterring the ideas being communicated and that government has no constitutional interest in deterring or punishing messages, no matter how offensive.

The Court refused to upset a National Parks Service regulation prohibiting sleeping in public parks in a case in which a large group of people protesting the plight of homeless people sought permission to camp in public spaces in Washington, D.C.[403] The Park Service authorized the demonstrators to use the park space and even to construct tents to symbolize the desperate living conditions of the homeless. But it refused to permit the demonstrators to sleep overnight in the tents. The service said they could pretend to sleep but they could not actually sleep. The Court assumed that sleeping was expressive conduct but even so, it held that under *O'Brien* the regulation was justifiable. The Park Service applied the regulation to everyone; there were other ways the homeless demonstrators could deliver their message; and the regulation was no broader than it had to be to preserve park spaces. People who sleep in the parks in tents will inevitably do more damage than people who use them merely to make a political point.

Conduct that is properly labeled "symbolic speech" should be distinguished from conduct that merely accompanies speech, although sometimes the two are difficult to differentiate. A writer has every right to deliver his manuscript to a publisher, no matter what it says, but he has no constitutional right to deliver it by driving his car to the publisher's office at one hundred miles an hour. Demonstrators have rights to gather in public places, and even to march, and the very fact of their massing to-

gether may be part of their message, just as PICKETING is entitled to constitutional protection. But as some justices have from time to time observed, speech mingled with conduct is "speech plus,"[1417] and the government may regulate the noncommunicative aspects of that conduct under reasonable TIME, PLACE, AND MANNER RESTRICTIONS.

See also: COMPELLING INTEREST; DEMONSTRATORS AND DEMONSTRATIONS; NUDITY; SPEECH, REGULATION OF CONTENT; SYMBOLS, REGULATION OF.

symbols, regulation of   There is no general constitutional rule governing the use and regulation of symbols. The right to use a symbol depends on the symbol and the purpose to which it is put. If the symbol is being used for political purposes, the FIRST AMENDMENT prohibits the government from interfering. For example, in the FLAG BURNING AND DESECRATION cases, the Court has denied Congress or the states power to block SYMBOLIC SPEECH. But the Court upheld an act of Congress bestowing on the U.S. Olympic Committee the exclusive rights to use the word "Olympic," essentially on the theory that under the COMMERCE POWER Congress may secure rights to TRADEMARKS.[1794] Under the COPYRIGHT CLAUSE, Congress may provide copyright protection to artists and designers who create and sell original symbols. Under the ESTABLISHMENT CLAUSE, the government itself may be precluded from using or displaying certain symbols if they tend to create a RELIGIOUS ESTABLISHMENT.

syndicalism   In the aftermath of World War I, thirty-three states enacted "criminal syndicalism" laws, aimed at those who advocated "crime, sabotage, violence or other unlawful methods of terrorism as a means of accomplishing industrial or political reform." Many of the criminal syndicalism laws were broad, prohibiting not merely direct advocacy but cooperation with syndicalists by joining their organizations, attending their meetings, printing their literature, or even speaking up in favor of acts of criminal syndicalism. Many of these laws survived constitutional attack.

When the California Criminal Syndicalism Act was upheld in *Whitney v. California,* Justice Louis D. Brandeis attacked laws that violated the CLEAR AND PRESENT DANGER test: "Fear of serious injury cannot alone justify suppression of free speech and assembly. Men feared witches and burned women. . . . Even advocacy of [lawbreaking], however reprehensible morally, is not a justification for denying free speech where the advocacy falls short of incitement and there is nothing to indicate that the advocacy would be immediately acted on." In 1927 the Court overturned a conviction under the Kansas syndicalism law because the prosecutor failed to show that the defendant had advocated anything illegal.[670] In 1937 the Court held that no one may be convicted under a syndicalism law for attending a peaceful meeting of the Communist party.[536] Finally, in 1969, the Court overruled the *Whitney* case, holding the Ohio criminal syndicalism law unconstitutional and ending a half century of prosecutions against rabble-rousers and purveyors of hateful speech.[222]

See also: COMMUNISM AND COMMUNIST PARTY; MARKETPLACE *OF IDEAS; SEDITION; SUBVERSIVE ADVOCACY.*

T

takeover laws During the 1980s, many states amended their corporation laws to stem the wave of mergers and acquisitions of locally incorporated businesses by out-of-state companies. In 1980 the Supreme Court unanimously rejected a Florida law that prohibited out-of-state banks and bank holding companies from owning Florida investment advisory businesses on the grounds that it violated the DORMANT COMMERCE CLAUSE because it intended to "protect [local] citizens from outside competition." [1157] In 1982 the Court also struck down portions of the Illinois Business Take-Over Act, which severely curbed the ability of an out-of-state business to tender for the stock of Illinois corporations, because the burden on INTERSTATE COMMERCE outweighed any local benefits. [598] But in 1987 it sustained an Indiana law making the acquisition of voting rights dependent on the majority vote of disinterested stockholders. The Court discerned no discrimination against interstate commerce since the law applies whether or not the purchasers reside in Indiana. Since the Indiana target companies are regulated solely by the Indiana law, there is no danger of inconsistent regulations burdening interstate commerce. [498]

See also: BALANCING.

taking of property Under its power of EMINENT DOMAIN, the government may take a person's private property, as long as it pays JUST COMPENSATION. In constitutional terms, property has been "taken" when the government takes over a parcel of land, ousting the owner and claiming title, or when it destroys the property or severely impairs its utility. For example, when the noise from U.S. military aircraft flying low over a farm next to the airport made farming impossible, the Court held that the government had effected a taking, even though it laid no claim to the land itself. [359] Similarly, in a rare case in which Justice Oliver Wendell Holmes and Louis D. Brandeis were on opposite sides, the Court held in 1920, in an opinion by Holmes, that a Pennsylvania law banning subsurface coal mining was an unconstitutional taking. [1596] The mining company sold land to homeowners while reserving the right to mine below the surface. The homeowners agreed not to sue the mining company for any resulting damages. To prevent collapse of the homes, the state legislature then barred all mining, depriving the company of the fruits of its bargain. This law rendered useless the company's only property interest. As laudable as the legislature's objective was, such a burden should be placed on society at large, by requiring the government to reimburse the company for the loss of its rights, rather than on the company alone.

But not every exercise of the POLICE POWER to benefit the public can be regarded as a taking for which just compensation must be paid. Almost every regulation interferes to some extent with someone's property interests, and if every effect must be compensated, harm-doers could charge the public for refraining from causing injuries. Therefore, regulations that merely diminish the value of property or interfere with its full enjoyment are rarely invalidated. For example, the Court upheld a Virginia law requiring the destruction of a certain type of red cedar because it was diseased and threatened the state's apple orchards, even though the tree owners were not compensated for their losses.[1340] Other impairments to property held not to be unconstitutional include the destruction of property by armies retreating from the Philippines during World War II,[330] damage to buildings occupied by federal troops to quell a local riot,[1424] a regulation prohibiting further use of a profitable dumpsite to protect the neighborhood,[767] destruction of fishnets to prevent the extinction of certain fisheries,[1131] and a ban on the sale of eagle feathers already in a commercial inventory.[64] In 1987, in another coal mining case, the Court sustained a regulation under which the companies were not barred from mining all their coal. Instead, they were required to leave in place half the coal, or two percent of their total supply, under certain structures to prevent them from subsiding. This was not comparable to the deprivation that would result from a taking, and the law was obviously designed to protect the "public interest in health, the environment, and the fiscal integrity of the area."[1073] In a decision of particular importance to real estate developers and municipalities, the Court upheld New York City's landmark preservation law, which prohibits owners, without the city's consent, from altering the exterior of buildings designated as landmarks. The law was applied to prevent the construction of a multistory office tower on top of Grand Central Station in midtown Manhattan.[1585]

In 1982 the Court held that when the government authorizes "permanent physical occupation" of private property, just compensation is required—for example, when a municipal ordinance permits a cable television company to install cable in privately owned rental buildings.[1186] The Court also held that a state may not demand that beachfront property owners allow the public to walk across their property in return for permission to build a larger home on the beach unless the state is willing to pay for the intrusion on the property. It said that there was no connection between the purpose to be served by the zoning ordinance—control over structures near the water—and the interests of beachcombers to walk where they please.[1489] When a regulation is so severe that it constitutes a taking, the state must pay for the loss, even if it is only temporary. Nor may the state avoid the requirement of just compensation simply by repealing the regulation.[666]

See also: RENT CONTROL; ZONING.

Tax Court The United States Tax Court is an ARTICLE I, or legislative, court. Its judges do not have life tenure but serve for fifteen years. It hears challenges to Internal Revenue Service determinations that individual taxpayers owe additional taxes. Its decisions may be appealed to U.S. courts of appeals.

taxation, *see:* **apportionment of taxes; commuter tax; direct tax; estate tax; excise tax; freedom of the press; General Welfare Clause; immunity, intergovernmental; Import-Export Clause; income tax; occupation tax; poll tax; property tax; spending power; standing;**

taxation, constitutional limitations on; taxation by states; taxation of interstate commerce; taxation of motor vehicles; taxation-regulation distinction; taxation without representation; taxing power; use taxes

taxation, constitutional limitations on Art. I-§8[1] says that all indirect federal taxes must be "uniform throughout the United States." The clause does not seem to mean what it says. The Supreme Court has held that "uniform" does not mean that each person must pay at the same rate. The clause does not bar the progressive income tax; those earning higher incomes may be required to pay at a higher rate, as long as all millionaires in a particular bracket pay the same higher rate throughout the country. [1088] The federal government may impose an estate tax on community property, even though relatively few states have community property. As long as the tax is the same in states that do have community property, the tax is uniform. [659] In 1983 the Court even upheld an exemption from a windfall profit tax on crude oil limited only to oil produced in Alaska. The Court rationalized the seeming lack of uniformity by reasoning that Congress was using "Alaskan oil" as a descriptive term for oil that was costly to extract; an exemption related to excessive costs does not lack uniformity. [1670]

See also: DIRECT TAXES.

taxation by states The states have broad but not absolute power to tax residents and non-residents with property or business interests in the state. Both the DUE PROCESS and EQUAL PROTECTION CLAUSES of the FOURTEENTH AMENDMENT bar wholly arbitrary taxes or taxes that arbitrarily discriminate. The courts may not invalidate a tax solely on the grounds that it is "excessive." [1958, 1634] A tax may provide benefits for people other than those paying it, so that residents of a town that receives from the state less revenue than it paid out in INCOME TAX is constitutional. [512] Nineteenth-century cases held that a state may not raise a tax to put to private uses. For example, the Court struck down a municipal tax because the proceeds were used to induce a bridge manufacturer to relocate its factory in the city. [1174] But the definition of "public purpose" has long since been expanded. The Court has repudiated the notion that taxing for such programs as unemployment compensation is private because the money goes to particular individuals. [347] Today it is extremely unlikely that a court would strike down a tax because it was not levied for a public purpose. In 1976, for instance, the Supreme Court upheld a tax on mining companies for payment to employees who contracted black lung disease, including workers who fell ill before the tax law was passed. [2113]

Because taxation depends on an infinite variety of factors, tax laws invariably depend on classifications. The Court has been exceedingly generous to the states in upholding classifications, usually through exemptions, claimed to be discriminatory: "[The state] may, if it chooses, exempt certain classes of property from any taxation at all, such as churches, libraries, and the property of charitable institutions. It may impose different specific taxes upon various trades and professions, and may vary the rates of excise upon various products; it may tax real estate and personal property in a different manner." [150] The Court today is even more lenient than the Court of decades ago. For example, in 1928 the Court rejected a state policy of taxing taxicabs owned by corporations but not by individuals. [1676] The Court overruled that conclusion in 1973. [1147] However, the state may not discriminate among corporations solely on the basis of their state of incorporation. For example, states may not deny foreign corporations licensed to do business in the state an exemption from certain taxes that similar domestic corporations enjoy. [2200, 1321]

Taxpayers have no right to be heard about the fairness of any general tax, fixed in amount or rate, enacted by the state legislature or municipal council, and applicable throughout the state or city.[2084] But if the tax depends on an assessment, the taxpayer has a right at some point to contest the fairness of the assessment.[836] Special assessments made by particular taxing boards for particular benefits may not be made without first granting the taxpayer a right to present evidence and arguments before the assessment is made.[1183] Because it is a general principle that late payments of a tax may be penalized, many states require a taxpayer to assert any constitutional challenges after the tax is paid. In 1990 the Court upheld state power to deny legal relief before a tax is paid, but it held that a state must then provide a forum in which the tax may be contested; if the tax turns out to be invalid, the state must not only refrain from collecting it but must refund the amounts unconstitutionally received.[1301]

See also: COMMUTER TAX; ESTATE TAX; FREEDOM OF THE PRESS; OCCUPATIONAL TAX; POLL TAX; PROPERTY TAX; TAXATION OF INTERSTATE COMMERCE; USE TAX.

taxation of interstate commerce The constitutionality of state taxes that affect INTERSTATE COMMERCE has a long and tangled history; hundreds of cases have reached the Supreme Court, beginning in the 1820s. In 1873, in the *State Freight Tax Case*, the Court struck down a Pennsylvania tax assessed on all the freight carried through the state. Since TRANSPORTATION is an act of commerce, when the commerce travels from state to state, it is not under state control. This principle held up in varying degrees until well into the twentieth century, but it was riddled with a host of subprinciples and exceptions. For example, a tax on the production of a commodity, even if ultimately destined for interstate shipment, is not a tax on interstate commerce.[941] Goods stopped in transit so that work could be per-

formed on them lost their interstate character,[738] unless they were unavoidably detained through no fault of the shipper.[415] Once goods are offered for sale in the destination state, they may be taxed there,[592] but not if imposed on goods made out of state when competing home-state goods are not taxed.[2180]

For many years, the Court applied a special rule in the so-called Drummer Cases: goods brought into the state following a contract of sale with an out-of-state vendor. Typically, a company's agent would "drum up" business by traveling throughout his sales territory with samples, take the customer's order, and send the sales contract to the out-of-state seller, which would then ship the purchased goods to the buyer. Such sales were held to be entirely in interstate commerce and thus could not be taxed.[1735, 957] The rule of the Drummer Cases was gradually extended, so that even products that had to be assembled in the taxing state were held to be beyond its taxing power.[309] But with one significant exception, the rule was weakened to the vanishing point during the Depression.

The true principle, the Court said in 1937, is "equality." The Court sustained a Washington State law that taxed goods imported from other states but exempted all goods on which a like tax had already been paid. This did not burden interstate commerce, said Justice Benjamin N. Cardozo, because "the stranger from afar is subject to no greater burdens as a consequence of ownership than the dweller within the gates."[903] There is no rational distinction between goods sold after they arrived in the state, which could be taxed, and goods that arrived after having first been sold by contract with an out-of-state company. The Court therefore upheld general taxes on purchases of consumption goods, regardless of where the goods originated.[1296]

The one significant exception concerns taxation of purchases from out-of-state mail order houses. If the customer orders through catalogues by telephone or the mails and the company maintains no offices or agents in the taxing state, the state may not require the mail order house to collect a sales tax.[1423]

In 1959, wearied after decades of intensely scrutinizing a taxing scheme to determine whether it had a "direct" or "indirect" impact on interstate commerce, the Court announced a new principle: a nondiscriminatory tax proportioned to the actual business done in the state may be assessed against a company whose business is solely in interstate commerce.[1501] In 1977 the Court listed four factors that are essential in determining the validity of such taxes. First, the activity to be taxed must have at least a minimal connection with the taxing state. An out-of-state seller has such a connection, for example, if it has retail outlets, property, or a sales agent in the state.[1428, 1941] Second, the tax must be apportioned to the business done in the state. The Dormant Commerce Clause does not dictate any particular formula, as long as it is rational.[82, 47] Third, the tax must not discriminate, meaning that it may not impose a heavier burden on out-of-state goods or activities than on those of local competitors.[1446] Fourth and finally, a tax that affects interstate commerce is valid only if the taxing state "has given anything for which it can ask return"[1423] (that is, provides some benefits to the interstate commerce).

See also: COMMUTER TAX; INCOME TAX; OCCUPATION TAX; PROPERTY TAX; USE TAX.

taxation of motor vehicles Because motor vehicles pose a constant threat to others on the highways and even to the highways themselves, the states may constitutionally impose a tax on vehicles passing through the state in the course of INTERSTATE COMMERCE, as long as the tax is based on some reasonable measure of their highway use, such as truck capacity,[405]

mileage driven in the state,[987] or even fair market value of the vehicle.[338]

See also: TAXATION OF INTERSTATE COMMERCE.

taxation-regulation distinction In 1922 the Supreme Court struck down the Child Labor Tax Law, which imposed a tax on the net profits of businesses employing child labor.[104] Although disguised as a pure tax measure, the law was really a regulation that secured obedience through the penalty of a tax. Among other things, the Court noted, the tax had to be paid on total net profits even if only one child worked for the employer on one day of the whole year, regardless of the size of the business. Moreover, the tax was payable only if the employer "knowingly" employed a child. An earnings tax ordinarily does not depend on the taxpayer's state of mind. Knowledge requirements are, however, common to the criminal law. This tax law, the Court ruled, was nothing more than a subterfuge to get around its earlier ruling that Congress could not regulate child labor.[851] The Court distinguished the *Child Labor Tax Case* from cases that claim that a tax is excessive. As long as Congress is empowered to tax a particular thing or activity, the Court said that the tax will not be invalidated even if it is so onerous that it effectively discourages or prohibits the activity.[2121, 1285, 566]

In 1935 the Court did void a federal excise tax on conducting a retail liquor business in violation of state laws. The tax was a penalty, not a means of raising revenue.[455] But the Court quickly backed away from this approach, upholding a tax on firearms dealers and saying that the justices would not speculate on the motives that led Congress to enact the law, as long as the measure was aimed at producing revenue.[1908] In 1953 the Court upheld a tax on professional gamblers who conduct their operations in violation of state laws.[1045] Among other things, the law required those subject to the act to register with the Internal Revenue

Service. The Court also held that the compulsory provisions did not violate the gamblers' right against SELF-INCRIMINATION, a holding overruled in 1968.[1240]

See also: TAXING POWER.

taxation without representation The colonists' loathing of taxes imposed by a Parliament whose members they could not choose was a root cause of the American Revolution. A central principle of the Constitution is that there can be no federal taxation that has not been approved by a body of representatives elected by the people. Art. I-§7[1] expresses this principle by requiring that all federal tax laws originate in the House of Representatives. In 1990 the Supreme Court held that a bill creating a "special assessment" for a Crime Victims Fund need not originate in the House because it was not intended to raise revenue for the general treasury.[1403] Either house of Congress may originate a bill that establishes a particular governmental program and that incidentally raises money to support it.

The principle of no taxation without representation does not apply to the states and has not prevented them from taxing the income of nonresidents who have no say in the scope or amount of the taxes assessed.[2069] But the states may not impose taxes on nonresidents if the state does not also impose a like tax on residents. In 1975 the Court held that a New Hampshire commuter income tax assessed against out-of-state commuters, with no corresponding income tax on New Hampshire residents, violated the PRIVILEGES AND IMMUNITIES Clause.[99]

taxing power Under Art. I-§8[1], Congress is empowered to "lay and collect taxes, duties, imposts, and excises." This clause was designed to overcome a chief weakness of the Confederation—its inability to raise taxes. The taxing power conferred under this clause is sweeping.

Except for a prohibition against taxing goods exported from the states and a mostly moribund requirement that DIRECT TAXES be apportioned according to population, the taxing power "reaches every subject"[1162] and "embraces every conceivable power of taxation."[264] Congress's objective in assessing a tax may be to regulate, but as long as the tax raises revenues, its regulatory effect will almost never be unconstitutional. For example, under the taxing power, Congress may enact protective tariffs on goods imported from abroad.[994]

Nevertheless, the Supreme Court has from time to time set certain constitutional limitations. Before the late 1930s, the Court rejected congressional attempts to tax the salaries of state officials[430] and even the salaries of federal judges,[632] but it eventually repudiated this line of cases.[795, 1514] The federal government may not tax state interests so as to impair state SOVEREIGNTY, even though the Court rarely finds an impairment. For example, it upheld a federal tax on a state's sale of its mineral waters.[1459a] A century ago, the Court objected to federal taxation of the interest on state or municipal bonds,[1649] but over the years the Court has relaxed its hold on this principle and in 1988 overruled it outright.[1910] Constitutional objections to a federal INCOME TAX were withdrawn when the SIXTEENTH AMENDMENT was ratified in 1913.

See also: TAXATION-REGULATION DISTINCTION.

taxpayers' suit, *see:* standing

teaching, *see:* academic freedom; evolution, teaching of

televising of trials, *see:* prejudicial publicity

television, *see:* access to broadcasting; broadcasting, regulation of; cable television

temporary appointment, *see: * recess appointment

Tennessee Valley Authority, *see: * public property

Tenth Amendment   Sometimes known as the Reserved Powers amendment, this final article of the BILL OF RIGHTS reserves to the states or the people any "powers not delegated to the United States by the Constitution, nor prohibited by it to the states." It was added to quiet fears that the federal government would soon swallow the states. However, the Tenth Amendment does not really draw a sharp line between federal and state powers. Congress rejected a proposal to reserve for the states all powers not *expressly* delegated to the United States. Had the word "expressly" been added, the Tenth Amendment might have had a lasting importance. But in *McCulloch v. Maryland,* Chief Justice John Marshall said that the Constitution delegates more than narrow, expressly stated powers to Congress. It also entrusts to the federal government powers fairly implied from the ENUMERATED POWERS and powers NECESSARY AND PROPER to carry out federal objectives. Marshall's theory was that the Tenth Amendment blocks only those laws designed to invade state concerns and enacted under the pretext of an enumerated federal power.

From roughly the end of the Civil War until the late 1930s, the Supreme Court developed a doctrine that led it to strike down certain laws for unconstitutionally invading the reserved powers of the states. In 1871 the Court held that even though a federal income tax was valid, Congress could not tax the official salaries of state officers,[430] a holding not overruled until 1939.[795] In 1908, in the *Employers' Liability Cases,* a sharply divided Court nullified a federal law making all employers engaged in interstate commerce liable for negligence to employees, including those carrying out purely intrastate activities. The reserved powers theory reached its apogee in 1918 when the Court expressly relied on the Tenth Amendment to invalidate the federal CHILD LABOR law. It said that Congress was attempting to regulate the conditions of employment, a power reserved to the states,[851] even though by prohibiting the shipment in INTERSTATE COMMERCE of certain goods Congress was doing nothing more than the Court had previously approved.[369] Between 1918 and 1941 the Court struck down several other congressional enactments on the same ground, including taxes on child labor,[104] the sale of grain futures,[921] the sale of coal by certain producers,[353] and some agricultural products.[289] But the Court began to back away from its reserved powers thesis in 1937 when it upheld the Social Security Act[1957] and the National Labor Relations Act,[1430] noting that Congress could regulate activities that affected interstate commerce, regardless of whether the states might do so in the absence of federal regulations. Finally, in 1941, Chief Justice Harlan Fiske Stone, on behalf of a unanimous Court, said the COMMERCE POWER is "complete in itself" and no state power may be invoked to limit it. The Tenth Amendment, Stone said, "states but a truism that all is retained which has not been surrendered."[514]

Not until 1976 did the Court again invoke the Tenth Amendment. In *National League of Cities v. Usery* the Court struck down a federal law regulating the hours and wages of certain state employees, based on a principle that it drew from the Tenth Amendment, even though the Tenth Amendment itself was not violated by the law. But in several cases in the early 1980s, it backed away[647, 620], and in 1985 a 5–4 majority overruled *Usery,* with the result that for the moment, the Tenth Amendment is once again "but a truism" that Congress may exercise all those powers bestowed on it by the Constitution, but only those powers.[724]

See also: FEDERALISM; TAXATION-REGULATION DISTINCTION.

term limitation   Disgust with incumbents began to translate in the 1990s into a political movement to impose a limit on the number of terms elected politicians may serve. The Constitution's only term limitation is contained in the TWENTY-SECOND AMENDMENT, barring presidents from running for more than two full terms. Term limitations imposed by states on their own offices is presumably constitutional. Many states have long restricted the length of time their governors may serve, and restrictions on the length of legislators' terms seem no different. A potential obstacle lies in the path of term limitations for Congress, however, since the age, residency, and citizenship qualifications for U.S. representatives in Art. I-§1[3] and U.S. senators in Art. I-§3[3] may be taken as exclusive, meaning that neither the states nor Congress may add qualifications to the list. No test case has reached the Supreme Court, but there is at least indirect authority for the proposition that any law adding to the qualifications for federal office would be unconstitutional. In 1969 the Court rejected an attempt by the House of Representatives to exclude an elected congressman for fraudulent acts on the ground that Art. I-§5[1], authorizing each house to be the judge of the qualifications of its own members, restricts any inquiry into constitutional fitness to serve to the specific qualifications listed in Art. I.[1653]

See also: QUALIFICATIONS FOR OFFICE.

term of court   The Supreme Court's term begins on the first Monday in October and runs through the following June. Under extraordinary circumstances the Court may reconvene to hold ORAL ARGUMENT and render decisions between July and October. *United States v. Nixon,* the decision requiring President Richard M. Nixon to turn over the WATERGATE tapes in a federal prosecution, was heard and decided in July 1974, after the end of the Court's 1973–74 term. The Court's term is set

by Congress, but not since it delayed the decision in MARBURY V. MADISON by postponing the term for a year has Congress manipulated the Supreme Court's term for political purposes. Requests for STAYS OF EXECUTION can be made to individual justices at any time.
See also: SUPREME COURT.

term of office, *see:* **Congress, members of; president, election and term of; term limitation**

territorial courts   Territorial courts are ARTICLE I legislative courts. They operate in Guam, the Virgin Islands, and other U.S. TERRITORIES. The constitutionality of territorial courts was resolved in 1828 when Chief Justice John Marshall explained that under its Art. IV-§3[2] authority to "make all needful rules and regulations" for U.S. territories, Congress could create non-ARTICLE III courts to hear cases arising in them.[51] Because judges of territorial courts need not be given life tenure, Marshall's decision enabled Congress to phase out the courts when the territories gained statehood and replace them with their own court systems.

territorial expansion, *see:* **Louisiana Purchase, constitutionality of; territories**

territories   Before the Constitution, in the early 1780s, the Continental Congress embarked on an ambitious plan to obtain for the United States as a whole the vast western lands claimed by several states. Congress's plan was to ready this territory for statehood; the Constitution carried it forward in Art. IV-§3[1], permitting new states to join the Union. Until U.S. territories become states, however, Congress has complete legislative authority over them under Art. IV-§3[2].[1871] Congress may exercise its authority directly, just as though it were a state legislature, or it may delegate its authority to a territorial legislature.[2143] Although the Constitution does not explicitly empower the federal government to acquire new territory, the LOUISIANA PURCHASE settled all political doubts. Chief Justice John Marshall many years later observed that territorial acquisition was undoubtedly constitutional under the treaty power and the WAR POWER.[51] When in the late nineteenth century the United States began to acquire overseas territories that were not likely to become states, the question arose whether Congress was bound by constitutional restrictions in legislation affecting them. In a series of decisions dubbed the *Insular Cases,*[572, 526, 563] the Court held in 1901 that Congress may declare whether it wishes to "incorporate" a particular territory into the United States. If it does, the Constitution applies; otherwise, not. Incorporated territories are those that Congress intends some day to become states. The United States presently has no incorporated territory. Territories may also be organized or unorganized—that is, Congress may impose direct federal rule or permit territorial inhabitants to exercise a large measure of self-rule. Such is the case with PUERTO RICO, which Congress has declared to be a "commonwealth" of the United States—an unincorporated organized territory that shares many of the attributes of statehood except that it does not send representatives to Congress.

See also: FOLLOWING THE FLAG; STATES AND STATEHOOD; TERRITORIAL COURTS.

test case A test case is a dispute arranged with an eye to litigating specific issues. Unlike those in a COLLUSIVE SUIT, the parties in a legitimate test case have adverse interests. For example, *Dred Scott v. Sandford,* the famous case testing the limits of slavery before the Civil War, was a "rigged" case. The parties arranged the facts in a certain way to present the constitutional issue to the courts. Nevertheless, the legal claims of each party were adverse—had

the Court ruled Dred Scott free, his owner could not have claimed that they had a side agreement not to be bound by the court ruling. Many well-known constitutional decisions in the Supreme Court have resulted from carefully managed test cases, including the Supreme Court's first decision overturning a state law, in 1810 in *Fletcher v. Peck;* the invalidation of the federal CHILD LABOR law, in 1918 in *Hammer v. Dagenhart;* the upholding of the Social Security Act in 1937, in *National Labor Relations Board v. Jones & Laughlin Steel Corp.;* and the great school desegregation case in 1954, BROWN V. BOARD OF EDUCATION. The major business of several national public policy groups, including the AMERICAN CIVIL LIBERTIES UNION and the NAACP Legal Defense Fund, has been to develop, sponsor, and litigate test cases.

See also: CASES OR CONTROVERSIES; JUSTICIABILITY.

test oath After the Civil War, Congress and several states enacted laws conditioning the practice of certain professions on the taking of an oath that the practitioner had not acted in any way against the United States during the war. The Supreme Court struck down these test oaths as BILLS OF ATTAINDER.[727, 500]

See also: LOYALTY OATH; OATH OF OFFICE.

testimonial compulsion, *see:*
self-incrimination

textbooks, *see:* **schools, religion in**

Third Amendment The Third Amendment bars the QUARTERING OF SOLDIERS except during wartime when necessary for military reasons. The British government directed troops to take over the colonists' homes as necessary so that they would be on hand to enforce the tax laws. Quartering of soldiers was one of many justifications in the DECLARATION OF INDEPENDENCE for the colonists' rebellion against the crown. The amendment has apparently never been violated; no cases have ever reached the Supreme Court.

Thirteenth Amendment   The Thirteenth Amendment, proposed by Congress on January 31, 1865, and ratified on December 6, 1865, abolished SLAVERY and INVOLUNTARY SERVITUDE throughout the country. The Thirteenth Amendment is self-executing, requiring no supporting legislation from Congress. It is the only amendment to act directly on the people and the states, prohibiting private acts of peonage as well as laws permitting and enforcing the subjugation of one human being by another, except for punishment of crime. The amendment also gave Congress the power to enforce its terms, the first addition to congressional powers since the original Constitution was ratified in 1787. Congress quickly passed the Civil Rights Act of 1866, extending citizenship to the former slaves and prohibiting RACIAL DISCRIMINATION of the kind embodied in the burgeoning BLACK CODES. Doubts that discriminatory acts amounted to slavery or involuntary servitude prompted the Reconstruction Congress to propose the FOURTEENTH and FIFTEENTH AMENDMENTS, also extending enforcement power to Congress.

But the fervor of the late 1860s had cooled by the time the constitutional issues reached the Supreme Court in the 1870s. Against a furious dissent by the first Justice John Marshall Harlan, the Court held in 1883 in the CIVIL RIGHTS CASES that the federal government had no power under the Thirteenth or the Fourteenth Amendment to bar *private* acts of discrimination in places of PUBLIC ACCOMMODATION. Harlan said that racial animosities translated into discriminatory acts were precisely the BADGES OF SLAVERY AND SERVITUDE that the amendment was intended to prevent. In PLESSY V. FERGUSON in 1896 the Court saw no Thirteenth Amendment obstacle to a SEPARATE BUT EQUAL railroad car law. Legally enforced SEGREGATION

of the races was held not to be a badge of slavery. In 1906 the Court struck down a federal law prohibiting conspiracies to deprive people of their employment on racial grounds.[928]

This crabbed reading of the Thirteenth Amendment lasted until 1968. In that year the Court overruled these earlier cases and upheld a provision in the century-old Civil Rights Act of 1866 that outlaws racial discrimination in the sale of property.[1028] The Thirteenth Amendment is not limited to human subjugation, the Court said. It embraces also the incidents of slavery, especially including civil disabilities and incapacities founded on race. No less important, the Court conceded to Congress the authority to determine what constitutes a "relic of slavery" and to eliminate any such injustice.

See also: CITIZENS AND CITIZENSHIP; STATE ACTION.

three-fifths rule   In deciding how many seats each state was entitled to in Congress and what proportion of taxation could be assessed against the residents of each state, the Framers had to face up to how to categorize slaves. If they were "persons," they should count. If they were merely property, they should not. In arguing over tax issues in the Continental Congress, the southern states refused to concede that slaves were people, both to preserve their legal right to hold slaves and to keep their taxes down. Northern states sought full enumeration to make the tax burden square with reality. Slaveholding states objected that since property such as land, sheep, cattle, and horses did not count, why should their other property— slaves? Benjamin Franklin retorted: "Sheep will never make any insurrections." In 1783 a committee of the Continental Congress proposed as a compromise that slaves be counted as three-fifths of a free person. The number, which became known as the "federal number," worked itself into Art. I-§2[3] four years later. "All other persons"—slaves—were to count as three-fifths of a free person for purposes of apportioning representation in Congress and direct federal taxation. "Free persons," including indentured servants, counted as whole persons. "Indians not taxed" were not counted at all. The rule became moot with the ratification of the THIRTEENTH AMENDMENT.

tie vote   Under Art. I-§3[4], the vice president is president of the Senate but has power to vote only in the event of a tie. There is no constitutional provision for tie votes in the House of Representatives; the House may provide by rule for that rare occurrence. By the Supreme Court's own rule, when the justices are evenly split the result is said to be an AFFIRMANCE BY AN EQUALLY DIVIDED COURT; the decision of the lower court stands.

time, place, and manner restrictions   The public has a FIRST AMENDMENT right to gather in public places like city streets, parks, and sidewalks to promote their views. But obviously the right cannot be absolute. Thousands of protesters do not have an unfettered right to march down Main Street whenever they please, nor to erect tents in a public park to facilitate an extended stay there, nor to cluster on a person's doorstep. To preserve the public peace and maintain the public spaces for their primary uses, the Supreme Court has upheld "time, place, and manner" restrictions on the right to assemble and broadcast messages, as long as the regulations are not aimed at the *content* of a message but reasonably control the *manner* in which it is delivered.

Of course, what is reasonable necessarily depends on the circumstances in each case. Some types of regulations are void because they are unreasonable—for example, PERMIT SYSTEMS that give municipal authorities unbridled discretion to decide whether or not to let anyone gather at all. Other types of regulations depend on where they are employed. A ban on loud noises obviously functions differently when the speakers are attending a public carnival or sitting in a public library. In a string of disparate cases over the years, the contours of the power to regulate free speech activities in the PUBLIC FORUM have emerged. The desire to avoid littering the city streets does not justify a flat ban on the distribution of leaflets and handbills, since the city may always penalize the litterers directly.[1820] But a ban on amplified sound trucks driving through the city streets is constitutional.[1096] In 1988 the Court upheld an absolute ban on "focused PICKETING"—the targeting of a particular person's home for demonstrations. The Court stressed the various alternatives open to the picketers to propagate their message.[703]

The Court also upheld a regulation curtailing the distribution at the Minnesota State Fair of any wares, including printed literature, except from rented booths on the fair grounds.[891] The International Society for Krishna Consciousness challenged the regulation on the ground that by limiting its ability to spread its message, the state was interfering with its FREEDOM OF SPEECH. But, said Justice Byron R. White, the First Amendment "does not guarantee the right to communicate one's views at all times and places or in any manner that may be desired." The restriction was upheld because it was content-neutral (it applied to everyone at the fair), served a significant government interest (to prevent disorder in a crowded and confined space), and left open "ample alternative channels for communication" (the society's members could mingle with the crowd and could hand out whatever they liked from their booth). For similar reasons, the Court sustained a Los Angeles ordinance barring the posting of signs on public property, against the challenge of a political candidate who wished to affix campaign signs to public utility poles.[401] As long as the time, place, or manner restriction is "narrowly tailored" to achieve the government's content-neutral interests, the Court said in 1989, the regulation need not be the least restrictive means of doing so.[2151]

See also: DEMONSTRATORS AND DEMONSTRATIONS; LESS RESTRICTIVE ALTERNATIVE OR MEANS; SOLICITATION; SYMBOLIC SPEECH; VAGUENESS.

time of adjournment   Under Art. I-§5[4], either house of Congress may adjourn for up to three days without the consent of the other house. Beyond three days, both houses must agree to the same adjournment. If they do not agree when or how long to adjourn, Art. II-§3 gives the president the extraordinary power to adjourn the houses "to such time as he shall think proper." This power has never been exercised.

See also: RECESS OF CONGRESS.

title of nobility   Art. I-§9[8] prohibits the United States government from conferring titles of nobility, such as knighthood. The clause stands today as a symbolic recognition that there are to be no degrees of citizenship or legal privilege among the people. The clause also prohibits any federal officeholder, without the consent of Congress, from accepting a title from a foreign government. This clause does not apply to state officeholders or people not holding government office. An amendment in 1812 proposed by Congress would have barred every citizen from accepting a title, but the states failed to ratify it.

See also: OFFICE OF HONOR, TRUST, OR PROFIT.

Tonkin Gulf Resolution, *see:* **Gulf of Tonkin Resolution**

tonnage duties   A tonnage duty is a charge on the privilege of bringing a ship into port or keeping it there. Art. I-§10[3] prohibits the states from charging any tonnage duties, regardless of whether or not the charge is measured by the actual weight of the ship.[411] But a charge for rendering services, such as piloting

and towing, is not a tonnage duty,[461] even if measured by the ship's tonnage.[1555] Harbor fees may be charged only for services actually rendered;[1953] an annual tax on boats measured by their tonnage is unconstitutional.[1951]

See also: IMPORT-EXPORT CLAUSE.

topless dancing, *see:* **nudity**

total incorporation, *see:* **incorporation doctrine**

trade names   State regulations of professional trade names, aimed at eliminating deception of the public, are consistent with the FIRST AMENDMENT.[702]

See also: PROFESSIONALS, ADVERTISING BY.

trade secrets   Ordinarily, under the PREEMPTION doctrine, the states may not grant legal protection to an invention or process that is patentable under the federal Patent Act but that, for some reason, was not patented. But the Supreme Court allowed an exception for a chemical process that its inventor, in the interest of keeping it secret, had not patented. A competitor discovered the inventor's trade secret from former employees, who had agreed in writing not to reveal it. The Court held that state trade secret laws are compatible with the Patent Act because they serve different interests. Failure to enforce the contracts not to divulge trade secrets might lead to a reduction of useful research, at least in areas in which certain industrial processes are only doubtfully patentable.[1070] The Court also upheld a state law that makes enforceable a licensee's royalty payment to an inventor, even if the invention ultimately failed to gain a patent, since the law neither induced anyone to refrain from seeking a patent nor caused anyone to withdraw a useful idea from the public domain.[80]

See also: PATENT CLAUSE; WRITINGS AND DISCOVERIES.

trademarks   In 1879 the Supreme Court held in the *Trade-Mark Cases* that commercial trademarks are not constitutionally entitled to patent protection since they are not WRITINGS AND DISCOVERIES and do not "depend upon novelty, invention, discovery, or any work of the brain." This neurologically astonishing conclusion had no practical long-term consequence, since Congress has obvious power under the COMMERCE CLAUSE to enact federal laws protecting and regulating the use of trademarks used in INTERSTATE COMMERCE, as it has done in the Lanham Act. In 1987 the Court upheld an act of Congress granting the U.S. Olympic Committee the exclusive use of the word "Olympic," in a challenge by a group wishing to stage the "Gay Olympic Games."[81]

tradition, *see:* **level of generality**

transaction immunity, *see:* **immunity from prosecution**

transcripts, right to   In 1956 the Supreme Court held on EQUAL PROTECTION grounds that the states may not refuse to provide an appeal of a criminal conviction merely because the defendant cannot afford to pay for the necessary trial transcript.[815] Nor may the states refuse to pay for transcripts unless a trial judge certifies that "justice will thereby be promoted"[625] or that the claim of errors are not "frivolous,"[576] or if a public defender attests that the appeal is in vain.[1117] Indigent defendants are entitled to free transcripts in certain HABEAS CORPUS proceedings.[1185, 726] The Court also overturned a New Jersey law requiring prisoners who are unsuccessful in their appeals to pay back the cost of transcripts provided them because the law was unequal: it did not require persons who received fines or suspended sentences in lieu of jail to reimburse the state if they lost their appeals.[1730]

However, the right to a free transcript is not absolute. In a habeas corpus hearing, unlike in direct appeals, the right may be conditioned on the judge's certification that the appeal is not frivolous and that the transcript is necessary to decide the case.[1217] The Court also upheld North Carolina's refusal to provide a free trial transcript following a mistrial in a small town. The defendant was retried before the same judge, and the court reporter in the first trial was available to read back his notes well in advance of the new trial, thus permitting the defendant's lawyer to prepare for it.[238]

See also: WEALTH CLASSIFICATION AND DISCRIMINATION.

transportation   In *Gibbons v. Ogden* in 1824, Chief Justice John Marshall held that INTERSTATE COMMERCE is not limited to buying and selling but includes navigation and transportation from state to state. Because various forms of transport are subject to overlapping state and federal powers of regulation, the Supreme Court since the late nineteenth century has issued scores of rulings in cases pitting state safety regulations against the federal interest in the unimpeded flow of interstate commerce. In some of the early cases, the Court sustained state regulations that seem dubious even by the DORMANT COMMERCE CLAUSE doctrines of the times. For example, Georgia was permitted to require engineers serving entirely on interstate railroads to take a licensing examination.[1884] The Court also sustained another Georgia law commanding railroads to construct posts near every railroad crossing and to blow their whistles and slow down as they passed the posts.[1922] The impact on interstate commerce, the Court said, was indirect.

The Court soon reversed itself when an interstate railroad managed to demonstrate that abiding by the law would turn a four-hour train ride into a ten-hour train ride from Atlanta to the South Carolina border. The facts plainly demonstrated a direct effect. By the 1920s, the Court was moving away from the "direct-indirect" analysis, looking instead to see whether the purpose of the law was safety or interference with competition. When the state of Washington denied a carrier a license to operate between Seattle and Portland because there was sufficient competition, the Court ordered the license to be issued, since this was parochial protectionism.[269] The Court also sustained a similar refusal by Ohio to license a carrier between Cleveland and Flint, Michigan, because the roads were so congested that additional traffic would create a safety hazard.[218]

These cases turned on how the law's purpose was characterized, but the Court soon turned to a very different BALANCING approach. In 1938 the Court sustained a South Carolina law limiting the size of trucks on its highways, even though nearly ninety percent of all trucks in the United States exceeded the maximum size. The Court was willing to grant the state considerable leeway in its judgment about safety hazards.[1914] But by 1945 the Court's perception was changing. It overturned an Arizona law enacted in 1912 limiting the length of trains passing through the state. The Court noted that enforcement of the old law was a serious encumbrance to interstate commerce, since trains pulling into Arizona had to stop and remove cars. Moreover, the evidence suggested that the law might promote rather than reduce accidents, since whatever safety was achieved through smaller trains was offset by the greater number of trains passing through the state.[1919] To preserve an "efficient and economical" national railway system, Congress alone could prescribe necessary uniform standards. The states must let the trains roll. In 1959 the Court underscored this approach in striking down an Illinois law requiring interstate trucks to install a certain kind of mudguard, the use of which conflicted with regulations of forty-five other states. The effect of the law was to force truckers to abandon their vehicles and shift their cargoes when they reached the Illi-

nois border.[161] The Court continued to take a dim view of state regulations. In 1981 it voided an Iowa law limiting freight truck length.[1049] The evidence of the state's safety interest was slight, but the impact on interstate commerce was great; the purpose—at least in part—was to keep some traffic out of the state. Laurence Tribe says that this case "stands for the rule that under the commerce clause a state may not reduce the risks posed to its own citizens by the stream of commerce by diverting that stream out-of-state, thereby increasing the hazards to non-residents." Eventually, Congress preempted the entire field by expressly authorizing larger trucks on all national highways.

See also: NAVIGATION AND NAVIGABILITY; PREEMPTION; TAXATION OF MOTOR VEHICLES.

travel, right to   The right to travel has long had constitutional protection, even though no specific clause says it does. In the 1860s, the Supreme Court declared that the PRIVILEGES AND IMMUNITIES Clause of Art. IV guarantees everyone the right to come and go from state to state[1579] and that there is an inherent constitutional right to travel to the nation's capital.[488] The Court followed these precedents in 1941 when it struck down California's "anti-Okie" law, forbidding anyone from bringing a nonresident into the state knowing that the other person was indigent.[602] The Court majority said that the COMMERCE CLAUSE bars any one state from attempting to "isolate itself from difficulties" common to all the states.

The Court has adhered to the principle of interstate migration in several recent cases, striking down various DURATIONAL RESIDENCY REQUIREMENTS on the ground that imposing waiting periods on newcomers for the receipt of benefits impairs the right to travel. In essence these cases largely stand for the proposition that the states may not erect barriers to migration. However, they do not bestow an absolute right on anyone to travel wherever they wish under any circumstances. The Court upheld a State Department restriction on travel to Cuba during the early 1960s;[2286] and in 1981, distinguishing the right to travel in America from a lesser right to travel abroad, it upheld the revocation of the passport of a former Central Intelligence Agency operative who was barnstorming through Europe exposing his former colleagues.[839] The Court also struck down a State Department regulation permitting the revocation of a passport if the bearer was a member of a group that he knew to be a "Communist organization" on the ATTORNEY GENERAL'S LIST.[67]

treason   Art. III-§3[1] confines the crime of treason to "levying war" against the United States or to "adhering to the enemies, giving them aid and comfort." No one accused of treason may be convicted unless two witnesses testify to the same OVERT ACT or the ACCUSED confesses in open court. This extraordinary concern for limiting the reach of treason prosecutions, when the Constitution is silent about other crimes, is the fruit of the Framers' fear of the centuries-old abuse of the law of treason by British authorities. Under the English Statute of Treason, a person could be executed for "compass[ing] or imagin[ing] the death of our lord the King." This came to be known as "constructive treason" because a case could be constructed entirely by pointing to writings that merely questioned the king's authority rather than to actual traitorous acts intended to overthrow the king or the government. The Treason Clause was designed to prevent U.S. officials from prosecuting political disagreements as disloyalties to the nation.

From the earliest days, the Supreme Court has been guided by the desire to keep treason prosecutions within narrow bounds. In 1807, in a case growing out of some mischief by Aaron Burr, Chief Justice John Marshall said that "levying war" did not mean the mere laying of plans to go to war "but the actual assembling of men for the treasonable purpose."[194] In 1945 the meaning of the second part of the clause came before the Court, which concluded that "adhering to" means that the accused has an intent to aid the enemy. Thus, merely criticizing the government, even out of sympathy for the enemy, is not treason if the speaker did not intend to betray the nation.[486] Moreover, the two-witness requirement means that both witnesses must testify to an overt act that amounts to treason, not merely to circumstantial evidence. However, two years later the Court muddled the issue in upholding a conviction of treason for the first time. The witnesses testified that the defendant had sheltered an enemy, his own son, and helped him purchase an automobile and obtain a job in a defense factory. In themselves, these were innocent acts, but the Court held that they gave aid and comfort to the enemy because other facts showed that the father knew his son was engaged in treasonous acts.[879] The Treason Clause does not bar Congress from providing punishment for acts dangerous to the national security that fall short of treason, but it does stand in the way of prosecutions for hostile thoughts, words, and even plans—so long as they remain on the drawing board.[194]

See also: ATTAINDER OF TREASON; CORRUPTION OF BLOOD.

treasury   The treasury is the EXECUTIVE BRANCH department that holds the funds of the United States. Under Art. I-§9[7], no disbursement may be made from the treasury unless it has been authorized by Congress, either specifically or as part of a general program.

See also: APPROPRIATIONS MADE BY LAW.

treaties and treaty power   Under Art. II-§2[2], the president may negotiate treaties with foreign governments. To have legal effect, the Senate must consent by a two-thirds vote. Final approval depends on the president, who may still decline to ratify.[1366] Once ratified, treaties are the law of the land, and under the SUPREMACY CLAUSE any contrary state laws are preempted.[2155] The treaty power is quite broad, permitting the federal government to accomplish what Congress might not have constitutional authority to do directly. In 1920, in *Missouri v. Holland,* the Supreme Court upheld a federal migratory bird law, enacted under the authority of a treaty negotiated with Canada. At that time, the TENTH AMENDMENT was thought to bar Congress from regulating the hunting season of birds within the states, but Justice Oliver Wendell Holmes said that the Tenth Amendment does not limit the treaty power. The bird treaty was aimed at preserving a valuable species, a result quite beyond the power of the states to achieve. Since the treaty was valid, so was any legislation enacted to implement it.

Thirty years later, *Missouri v. Holland* alarmed isolationists who feared that if the United States signed the U.N. Charter and other international agreements, many constitutional limitations might be overridden. In the early 1950s Congress toyed with the so-called Bricker amendment, which would have denied any effect to a treaty that conflicts with the Constitution itself. The amendment failed by one vote in the Senate. Later, in 1957, the Supreme Court ruled in *Reid v. Covert* that "no agreement with a foreign nation can confer power on Congress, or on any other branch of government, which is free from the restraints of the Constitution."

Treaties are not necessarily self-executing. They may depend for their legal effect on implementing legislation, and a long-established tradition, never denied by the Court, allows Congress to decide whether or not to appropriate funds or pass any other laws necessary to fulfilling treaty obligations.[693] In giving its consent, the Senate may attach conditions or reservations to the treaty. The president may decline to ratify in the face of the Senate's reservations. But if the president does ratify the treaty, the Senate's limitations bind the United States, though not the other signatories.[694] Moreover, Congress has absolute constitutional discretion to decide to abrogate a treaty simply by enacting a later law that conflicts with the treaty requirements.[887, 1106] Conversely, a self-executing treaty supersedes any conflicting early federal or state laws.[693, 460]

The power to negotiate treaties resides exclusively with the president.[505] The president may also have the power to abrogate treaties, but the Court has never squarely decided it. In 1979 Senator Barry Goldwater sued President Jimmy Carter, asserting that the president had no power to withdraw DIPLOMATIC RECOGNITION of the Republic of China (Taiwan) in order to recognize the People's Republic of China (Beijing). The Court refused to decide the merits of the controversy.[773] Four justices said that the case presented a nonjusticiable POLITICAL QUESTION. A crucial fifth vote for dismissing Goldwater's complaint was based on the view that the case was not ripe for review. As a result, the president's decision to recognize mainland China was left intact. But whether it resides exclusively with Congress or the president or is shared jointly, the power to determine that a treaty has lapsed is not for the courts.[378]

See also: EXECUTIVE AGREEMENT; INDIANS AND INDIAN TRIBES; JUSTICIABILITY; PREEMPTION; RIPENESS.

treatment, right to   There is no general constitutional right to health care. Only in one restricted setting has the Supreme Court gingerly announced a limited right to treatment. When a mentally handicapped person has been committed to an institution, the Court has tentatively recognized a right to "minimally adequate or reasonable training to ensure safety and freedom from undue restraint."[2279]

See also: CIVIL COMMITMENT; MENTAL RETARDATION.

trespass A trespass is an unauthorized intrusion onto a person's property. Trespass laws ordinarily excite no constitutional attention. But they occasionally pose constitutional difficulties when used to infringe a FIRST AMENDMENT right. Under the PUBLIC FORUM doctrine, a municipality may not constitutionally use trespass laws against otherwise law-abiding people gathered in the public streets or parks. In one rare case, the Court reversed a trespass conviction against a religious proselytizer for handing out leaflets in a town owned entirely by a private corporation. It held that because the corporation was performing a PUBLIC FUNCTION, passersby had a free speech right to be there.[1245] There is no such right to distribute literature or to picket in a private shopping mall,[950] but the states may enact laws requiring private shopping centers to let people circulate political petitions or pamphlets, in effect repealing trespass laws to that extent.[1669]

A troublesome application of trespass laws arose in the 1960s when civil rights protesters staged sit-ins in private restaurants and other PUBLIC ACCOMMODATIONS. The Court reversed a number of trespass convictions on narrow grounds, in general suggesting that official policies of segregation lay behind the owners' exclusionary practices, including the use of trespass laws to enforce those policies.[1615, 1182, 146] The issue became moot after the enactment of the Civil Rights Act of 1964. The Court held that it required dismissal of prosecutions against those who would have been entitled to be served if the law had been in force at the time of the arrest.[850]

See also: PICKETING; SEGREGATION AND INTEGRATION; SHOPPING CENTERS, ACCESS TO.

trial, fairness of Quite aside from specific guarantees in the BILL OF RIGHTS governing the PROCEDURAL RIGHTS OF CRIMINAL DEFENDANTS, the Court has said repeatedly that DUE PROCESS requires courts to observe "that fundamental fairness essential to the very concept of jus-

tice."[1171] What is fair depends always on the circumstances.[1903] One absolute requirement is that the trial judge be impartial and disinterested. The Court struck down the practice of an Ohio town in which the mayor served as the justice of the peace and pocketed part of the fines assessed against defendants he convicted in court.[2077] When the judge might be biased against the defendant, even though the defendant himself was largely responsible for the judge's anger against him, fairness requires that someone else preside.[1273] Even the "probability of unfairness" is enough to require that a different judge hear the case.[1406] In other cases, the Court reversed convictions because a mob dominated the trial,[695, 1378] because PREJUDICIAL PUBLICITY poisoned the jurors' minds,[628] and even because the judge refused to remind the jury that the defendant was entitled to a PRESUMPTION OF INNOCENCE.[2001]

See also: CONTEMPT; IMPARTIALITY OF JUDGES AND HEARING OFFICERS; JURY AND JURORS, IMPARTIALITY OF; PUNISHMENT, CRIMINAL AND CIVIL.

trial, place of Art. III-§2[3] requires all federal criminal prosecutions to be held in the state where the crime was committed. However, this clause does not otherwise restrict the location of the trial. Under British law, criminal trials were held in the "vicinage," or neighborhood, of the crime, from which jurors would be drawn. The SIXTH AMENDMENT tightened the requirement, mandating a trial in the "district" within the state in which the crime occurred. What constitutes a district must be established by law. The term now means the federal judicial districts within which the U.S. DISTRICT COURTS are located in each state. Under the Vicinage Clause, an ACCUSED may not be tried in a district other than the one stated in the INDICTMENT to be the place where the crime occurred.[1786] Some crimes "occur" in more than one place: a conspiracy charge may be tried in any district in which an overt act occurred.[251] Mail fraud may be tried in the district to which the letter containing the fraudulent material was sent.[837] The Vicinage Clause does not prevent a judge from some other district from being assigned to conduct the trial in the district where the crime occurred.[1113] If a crime was committed in a federal territory or some place within the JURISDICTION of the United States other than a state, Congress has the sole power to determine where it may be tried[1034] and may even designate the place of trial after the crime has occurred.[459] Neither the Article III provision nor the Vicinage Clause of the Sixth Amendment applies to state prosecutions. However, DUE PROCESS may require a change of VENUE if pretrial PREJUDICIAL PUBLICITY would make the trial unfair.[991, 822]

trial, public   The SIXTH AMENDMENT entitles an ACCUSED to a public trial. Trials have been open to the public in every American jurisdiction, federal and state, since the beginning of the nation, and issues that would require the closing of a courtroom have rarely arisen. The right guarantees access to the courtroom by interested persons, including the press, but it does not carry with it an entitlement to film or televise a trial,[628] nor does it prohibit the judge from regulating the behavior of people in the courtroom, even by excluding disorderly and disruptive members of the audience.[1856] In 1979 the Court said that under rare circumstances the defendant may waive his or her right to public *pretrial* hearings, when the prosecutor and court agree.[723] But in 1980 the Court held that under the FIRST AMENDMENT "a criminal case must be open to the public," unless the judge articulates an "overriding interest" in excluding observers.[1727] Even when a witness—such as, for example, a juvenile victim of a sex offense—might be harmed by having to testify in front of outsiders, a state law may not absolutely require closure; rather, the judge must be permitted to determine whether the cir-

cumstances warrant closing the court for that particular testimony.[763]

trial, right to   The Constitution twice guarantees the right to TRIAL BY JURY in criminal prosecutions—both Art. III-§2[3] and the SIXTH AMENDMENT so declare. The SEVENTH AMENDMENT guarantees the right to a jury trial in civil SUITS AT COMMON LAW. But these three provisions do not embrace every type of dispute and do not stipulate whether every litigant with a legal dispute is entitled to a day in court, even without a jury. The issue has arisen in three major areas: WORKERS' COMPENSATION, disputes involving certain types of publicly created rights, and compulsory arbitration policies in certain regulated industries. The Supreme Court has consistently upheld the constitutionality of workers' compensation laws, which abolish a worker's right to sue the employer in court, in return for a no-fault recovery from a workers' compensation tribunal.[72] The findings of the administrative tribunals may constitutionally be made final, as long as there is some evidence of relationship between injury and work.[199] Likewise, the Court has long approved initial fact-finding by administrative agencies under antitrust, securities, and many other laws regulating trade and business practices as long as certain JURISDICTIONAL AND CONSTITUTIONAL FACTS may be reviewed independently in the courts.[494]

The Court has also distinguished between private rights, such as contract rights, and rights created under public law, such as BANKRUPTCY. Generally speaking, disputes over private rights must be heard in court; disputes over publicly created rights may be assigned to administrative tribunals, such as the ARTICLE I bankruptcy courts.[1500] But the Court has approved exceptions to even this policy. For example, it upheld the power of the Commodity Futures Trading Commission, a federal administrative agency, to decide certain kinds of claims that ordinarily would be brought in state courts. The Court reasoned that when Congress closely regulates a particular industry, it may require that all related claims be heard in a common forum, even though not a court.[443] Finally, the Court has recently upheld federal laws requiring that certain kinds of disputes arising in heavily regulated industries be committed to binding arbitration.[2039]

See also: ARTICLE III COURTS; JUDICIAL POWER; PRIVATE RIGHT–PUBLIC RIGHT DISTINCTION.

trial, speedy   The SIXTH AMENDMENT entitles the ACCUSED to a "speedy and public trial." The speedy trial requirement applies only when a person has been formally accused or arrested and held for formal charges.[1244] The government's slowness in investigating a crime or in presenting evidence to a GRAND JURY does not violate the requirement; the Sixth Amendment clock starts ticking only when the INDICTMENT has been handed down,[1218] unless prosecutorial bad faith can be shown to have prejudiced the defendant.[1197] Likewise, said the Court in 1986, delay in appealing the dismissal of an indictment is not a speedy trial violation, at least without a showing of bad faith by the prosecutor.[1189] But when a state does not even try to gain custody of the defendant, who is imprisoned elsewhere for an unrelated crime, so that no trial can possibly be held, the speedy trial right has been violated.[1890]

The speedy trial requirement prohibits prosecutors from leaving criminal charges hanging: the prosecutor may not move to release a suspect from custody with unfettered discretion at any later time to reinstate the charges.[1084] Nor may the trial court indefinitely postpone handing down a sentence.[1648] In general, the Court applies a BALANCING test to determine a speedy trial violation, looking to the length of and reason for the delay and prejudice to the defendant. A deliberate delay will count heavily against the prosecution. The absence of a witness might justify delay. Crowded dockets and prosecutorial negligence lie somewhere in between.[126] But once a court determines that the right to a speedy trial has been violated, the charges must be dismissed.[1972] In 1974 Congress enacted the Speedy Trial Act, laying upon prosecutors a strict timetable. Observing the timetable will prevent dismissal because of speedy trial concerns.

trial, televising of, *see:* **prejudicial publicity**

trial by jury   Art. III-§2[3] and the SIXTH AMENDMENT both guarantee a jury trial in most, but not all, federal criminal prosecutions. The Supreme Court has held that a jury is necessary when significant punishment may be meted out[551] or when the crime is nonpetty.[552] In 1968 the Court held the jury trial provisions applicable to the states; and in 1970 it generalized from its precedents to conclude that whenever imprisonment for more than six months is authorized, the crime is not petty and the defendant is entitled to a jury.[582] A crime may be nonpetty, even though carrying a sentence of six months or less, if large fines are at stake; but a traffic offense for which the maximum sentence is six months or less in jail, a one-thousand-dollar fine, suspension of a driver's license for ninety days, and mandatory driver's education training is petty and does not require a jury trial.[171] At one time the Court believed that a jury was required only when a defendant was formally charged with a crime; more recently it has declared that certain kinds of civil proceedings punitive by nature—for example, revocation of citizenship—require juries.[1061] Until the 1960s the Court consistently refused to recognize the right in criminal CONTEMPT proceedings, but it changed its mind in 1968. All but petty contempt charges must now be tried by a jury if the defendant wishes, whether in a state or federal proceeding.[174]

The right to a jury does not apply in juvenile delinquency proceedings, even if a sentence of more than six months might result.[1300]

In civil cases, the right to a jury trial is less universal. In federal SUITS AT COMMON LAW, either party may demand a jury trial if the amount in controversy is more than twenty dollars—an amount that demonstrates the dangers of fixing one generation's economic expectations on another's. In general, a suit at common law is a suit for DAMAGES or for certain other remedies, such as recovery of property. Suits for INJUNCTIONS are the major type of case for which a jury is not required, because at the time the Constitution was written injunctions were awarded in a legal proceeding other than a common-law suit.[1572] ADMIRALTY AND MARITIME cases likewise do not require a jury.[1572, 1757] When a new CAUSE OF ACTION or remedy is created, a jury trial is required as long as the right is "of the sort traditionally enforced" in common law courts. These might include a damage suit for racial discrimination in the rental of housing,[1607, 503] back pay awards against unions for failing to represent a member fairly, and a bankruptcy trustee's right to recover money fraudulently distributed from the bankrupt estate.[380, 792]

But when Congress enacts regulatory laws enforceable by fines assessed by ADMINISTRATIVE AGENCIES and collectible in federal court, no jury is required.[95] Sometimes this rule leads to odd results. For example, the Court said in 1987 that although a jury is necessary in determining under the Clean Water Act whether a person is *liable* to pay a fine, the *amount* of the fine may be set without a jury.[2076] When a case involves both legal and equitable remedies, the legal claims must be tried first before a jury.[139, 508, 1215] The Court has held in many cases that the Seventh Amendment does not outlaw various trial procedures, so that a judge may direct a verdict for the defendant on the ground that the plaintiff had insufficient evidence to prove his case[720] or may even reverse a jury's verdict because of insufficient evidence.[157] Unlike the jury trial provision in the SIXTH AMENDMENT, the Seventh Amendment does not apply to state courts.[2144, 1354] The parties may waive the right to a jury if they choose.[901]

See also: JURY AND JURORS, IMPARTIALITY OF; JURY DISCRIMINATION; JURY SIZE; JURY UNANIMITY; TRIAL, RIGHT TO.

tribal Indians, *see:* **Indians and Indian tribes**

troops, *see:* **armed forces**

trucking, *see:* **transportation**

tuition grants or vouchers   The states may not use public funds to pay the tuition of schoolchildren at private schools that discriminate in admission on the basis of race. In the aftermath of BROWN v. BOARD OF EDUCATION, some southern states permitted local school districts to close the public schools and even to transfer public school buildings to racially discriminatory private schools. In other cases the state paid tuition grants to white children withdrawn from public schools and sent to private schools that barred admission to blacks. The Court declared these tactics unconstitutional in 1964.[814] The Court also struck down, as a violation of the ESTABLISHMENT CLAUSE, tuition grants for attendance at religious schools by the children of poor parents.[441] The constitutionality of a general tuition voucher program, presently being pressed by many influential political leaders, has never been tested. Tuition vouchers paid on behalf of all school-age children might be upheld as a rational way to encourage the development of alternative means of education and as a spur to improvement of the public schools. But a system that tended to favor religious schools at the expense of public schools might well encounter fatal constitutional objections. The problem of tuition to racially discriminatory schools is now moot because the Court has ruled that private schools may not discriminate on racial grounds, whether or not they receive public revenue.[1774]

turban, *see:* **dress codes**

Twelfth Amendment   The Twelfth Amendment, proposed by Congress on December 9, 1803, and ratified on June 15, 1804, altered the ELECTORAL COLLEGE system for selecting the president. It was prompted by the impasse in the House of Representatives that required thirty-five ballots in 1804 to elect Thomas Jefferson over Aaron Burr. The election was thrown into the House because the original mechanism set out in Art. II-§1[3] did not permit presidential electors to distinguish their votes between presidential and vice-presidential candidates. The Twelfth Amendment separated balloting for each office. If no candidate gains a majority of electoral votes, the House, voting by state, must then choose the president, while the Senate chooses the vice president.

See also: PRESIDENT, ELECTION AND TERM OF; PRESIDENTIAL SUCCESSION.

Twentieth Amendment   Under Art. I-§4[1], Congress may fix the date of elections to Congress. Under Art. I-§4[2], Congress was to meet on the first Monday each December, unless Congress fixed some other date. Since Congress declared federal election day to be the first Tuesday after the first Monday in November, this clause meant that elected members of Congress might not begin their duties until thirteen months after they were elected. The Twentieth Amendment, proposed by Congress on March 2, 1932, and ratified on January 23, 1933, set the date for convening Congress on January 3 of each year. This provision effectively ended the "lame duck" Congresses, in which members defeated for election in November could

continue to vote until their successors took office later the following year. It was just such a lame duck Congress that gave President John Adams the votes to appoint his "midnight judges" and that led to MARBURY V. MADISON. Lame duck status now lasts from election day in November until the end of the congressional session, usually in December, but in no event later than January 2. The Twentieth Amendment also set January 20 as the date of the president's inauguration and made other changes to the rules of PRESIDENTIAL SUCCESSION.

See also: PRESIDENT, ELECTION AND TERM OF.

Twenty-fifth Amendment   The Twenty-fifth Amendment, proposed by Congress on July 6, 1965, and ratified on February 23, 1967, establishes rules of PRESIDENTIAL SUCCESSION and provides for the first time for the temporary or permanent disability of the president. It also establishes the office of ACTING PRESIDENT. It was proposed in reaction to the assassination of President John F. Kennedy in 1963.

See also: PRESIDENT, ELECTION AND TERM OF.

Twenty-first Amendment   The Twenty-first Amendment, proposed by Congress on February 20, 1933, and ratified on December 5, 1933, ended the national embarrassment of PROHIBITION by repealing the EIGHTEENTH AMENDMENT. It is the only amendment ever to have been ratified in state conventions rather than by the state legislatures. It did more than simply repeal the formal national ban on INTOXICATING BEVERAGES, because it left power in the states to continue a statewide regime of alcohol regulation and even prohibition, subject to certain COMMERCE POWER constraints.[326]

Twenty-fourth Amendment   The Twenty-fourth Amendment, proposed by Congress on August 27, 1962, and ratified on February 4, 1964, abolished the POLL TAX for all federal elections. In 1965, under this amendment, the Court struck down a law giving federal voters in Virginia the choice between paying a poll tax or filing a residence certificate six months before the election.[865] Two years later, the Court struck down on EQUAL PROTECTION grounds the requirement that state voters pay a poll tax.[867]

Twenty-second Amendment   The custom that presidents run for only two terms began with George Washington and endured until 1940, when President Franklin D. Roosevelt won a third term after the outbreak of World War II in Europe. The Twenty-second Amendment, proposed by Congress on March 21, 1947, two years after Roosevelt died, and ratified on February 27, 1951, incorporates Washington's precedent into the Constitution, limiting presidents to two full terms, or to no more than ten years if a vice president succeeded to the office with less than half the term of his predecessor remaining. By its terms, the amendment did not apply to the incumbent, Harry S. Truman, at the time of ratification. Truman chose not to run for a third term.

See also: PRESIDENTIAL SUCCESSION.

Twenty-seventh Amendment The Twenty-seventh Amendment is a constitutional oddity, proposed as the second of twelve articles in the original BILL OF RIGHTS in 1789 and ratified by three-quarters of the states 203 years later in 1992. It says that no pay raise for members of Congress may take effect until after "an election of Representatives shall have intervened," meaning that members of Congress may not vote themselves raises but may only raise the salaries of representatives and senators in the succeeding Congress. Ten of the twelve articles were ratified on December 5, 1791. But through the 1790s, only six states ratified the congressional pay raise amendment—Delaware, Maryland, North and South Carolina,

Vermont, and Virginia. Not until 1873 did another state, Ohio, ratify it. Wyoming chimed in 105 years later, in 1978. Then, as dissatisfaction against Congress mounted in the 1980s, more and more states climbed aboard the bandwagon. By May 1992 thirty-four states had ratified. During the first week in May four more states ratified. Michigan was the last, bringing the total to the requisite thirty-eight states. New Jersey ratified the amendment hours after Michigan; Illinois, a few days later. In mid-May the archivist of the United States, Don W. Wilson, certified that the amendment had finally been made part of the Constitution as of May 7, 1992.

See also: AMENDMENTS TO CONSTITUTION; EMOLUMENTS CLAUSE.

Twenty-sixth Amendment   The Twenty-sixth Amendment, proposed by Congress on March 23, 1971, and ratified on July 1, 1971, fixes the minimum voting age at eighteen in all state and federal elections. Proposed in part as a reaction to the drafting of young men who were not old enough to vote to serve in Vietnam, the Twenty-sixth Amendment was ratified in 107 days, more quickly than any other amendment.

See also: VOTING, RIGHT TO.

Twenty-third Amendment   The Twenty-third Amendment, proposed by Congress on June 17, 1960, and ratified on March 29, 1961, extends to residents of the District of Columbia the right to vote in presidential elections. The amendment deviates from the principle of allocating electoral votes by population. Even though the district has a population larger than thirteen of the fifty states, its votes in the ELECTORAL COLLEGE are limited to three, the number of electors possessed by the least populous state. The Twenty-third Amendment does not entitle the district to REPRESENTATION in either house of Congress.

See also: STATES AND STATEHOOD.

two-sovereignties doctrine Until 1964, a person could be convicted of a crime by one sovereign authority (for example, a state) on the basis of testimony he or she was compelled to give by another sovereign (for example, the federal government), despite the SIXTH AMENDMENT's guarantee of a right against SELF-INCRIMINATION.[841, 1407, 655] This peculiar result was explained by a doctrine that the dangers posed by a second sovereign are of no constitutional concern to the first one. Under the two-sovereignties doctrine, then, a state could grant a witness IMMUNITY FROM PROSECUTION and force his or her testimony, knowing that the witness could then be prosecuted under federal law. The Supreme Court repudiated this doctrine in two 1964 cases, *Murphy v. Waterfront Commission* and *Malloy v. Hogan,* holding that the right against self-incrimination extends to testimony that might tend to incriminate the witness under the laws of any JURISDICTION in the United States.

tyranny, *see:* **separation of powers**

U

unconstitutional conditions One hundred years ago Oliver Wendell Holmes, then chief justice of the Massachusetts Supreme Judicial Court, upheld the state's power to restrict a policeman's right to engage in political action: "The petitioner may have a constitutional right to talk politics, but he has no constitutional right to be a policeman." Holmes's classic aphorism suggests that if the state has no obligation to provide a benefit, such as a job or welfare, it may confer the benefit with strings attached—including the condition that the recipient waive a constitutional right. Holmes's logic would allow a state to deny welfare benefits to people who refuse to attend church, or terminate unemployment benefits if the recipient criticizes state officials. But as the Court recognized in 1926: "If the state may compel the surrender of one constitutional right as a condition of its favor, it may, in like manner, compel a surrender of all. It is inconceivable that guarantees embedded in the Constitution of the United States may thus be manipulated out of existence."[706] In many situations during the past half century, the Court has curtailed the assertion of such absolute government power by invoking a doctrine known as "unconstitutional conditions." For example, a school board may not

discharge a teacher for exercising his FIRST AMENDMENT right to free speech.[1625] A state may not refuse to pay unemployment benefits to a Seventh Day Adventist who rejects a job that requires her to sacrifice her religious faith by working on Saturday.[1857]

The doctrine of unconstitutional conditions does not preclude the government from imposing conditions reasonably related to the purpose of the benefit. In 1971, for example, the Court sustained a New York law that conditions welfare payments on the recipients' willingness to meet with caseworkers in their homes, rejecting the argument that mandatory home visits violate the FOURTH AMENDMENT's right to PRIVACY.[2266] And in 1987, against a claim that Congress may not tell the states what laws to pass, the Court upheld a federal law authorizing the secretary of transportation to withhold five percent of federal highway funds from any state that permitted persons under twenty-one years of age to purchase liquor.[1915] The Court held that "the condition imposed by Congress [raising the drinking age] is directly related to one of the main purposes for which highway funds are expended—safe interstate travel." In 1991 the Court upheld a Department of Health and Human Services regulation prohibiting family planning clinics receiving federal funds from discussing ABORTION with any clients.[1777]

But an unconstitutional condition unrelated to furthering the purpose of the benefit is invalid. For example, a city may tell its police officers how to dress for work but it may not hire or fire them for how they vote. A television station given public funds for programming may be restricted from using them to furnish its offices lavishly but may not be told to refrain from editorializing or endorsing candidates, activities that lie at the heart of the First Amendment.[641] A state may not condition a PROPERTY TAX exemption on the filing of an affidavit that the owner did not advocate forcible overthrow of the government: "To deny an exemption to claimants who engage in certain forms of speech is in effect to penalize them for such speech."[1930]

See also: PENALTY-SUBSIDY DISTINCTION; PUBLIC EMPLOYMENT.

unconstitutional laws In 1886 the Court said that an unconstitutional law "is not a law; it confers no rights; it creates no office; it is, in legal contemplation, as inoperative as though it had never been passed."[1503] The statement is true only in a narrow sense. A law has legal consequences until a court authoritatively declares it unconstitutional; to contest it you might have to stand trial and risk conviction and jail. In 1967 a narrowly divided Court ruled that a person who violates an injunction, even if it is unconstitutional, may be held in contempt for violating it. The proper course would have been to appeal the court's order. Said Justice Potter Stewart for the five-member majority: "respect for judicial process is a small price to pay for the civilizing hand of law."[2142] Moreover, a ruling in one state or federal jurisdiction that a law is unconstitutional does not automatically negate the law elsewhere, and even a Supreme Court ruling that the law conflicts with the Constitution does not automati-

cally void it. A ruling that the law is unconstitutional "as applied" in a particular case leaves the law available for proper application in another case. Even when the Court holds a law INVALID ON ITS FACE it does not disappear; if, as occasionally happens, the Court reverses itself, the law in effect springs back to life. For example, in 1923 the Supreme Court invalidated a District of Columbia minimum wage law as a violation of DUE PROCESS,[16] but in 1937 reversed itself.[2184] To regulate wages, was Congress obliged to reenact the law, or would the one struck down in 1923 be revived? The Court has not ruled directly on the issue, but under a widely accepted opinion of the attorney general, the law came back into effect automatically.

In more than two hundred years, the Court has struck down as unconstitutional 125 federal laws and 1,194 state and municipal laws and ordinances (through 1990). That is not the sum of cases involving unconstitutionality. It does not include all those cases in which the executive branch has been found to have acted unconstitutionally.

underinclusivity, see: **classifications, under- and overinclusive**

Union The Union was not formed, in legal theory, when the Constitution was ratified. The Preamble to the Constitution speaks of forming "a more perfect Union," not a new one. Until after the Civil War, however, the nature of national union was clouded by two warring theories. The DECLARATION OF INDEPENDENCE contained both. It declared the colonies "free and independent states." It also described the colonists as "one people" and called the country in which they lived "the United States of America." In the Kentucky and Virginia Resolutions of 1798–1799, James Madison and Thomas Jefferson held that the Union had been created by the sovereign *states.* According to this view, the states had created the central government and were alone competent to judge when it had breached the compact that had formed the Union. If the states chose to do so, they could, in Jefferson's word, "nullify" unauthorized acts of Congress. Opposing this view was that of the Federalists, who held that the Union had been called into being by the *people* of the United States, who divided power between the federal government and the states. The Federalists denied that the states could decree acts of the federal government unconstitutional; rather, the federal government was supreme within its sphere. In one form or another, the Madison-Jefferson *compact* theory was the basis for secessionist demands leading up to the Civil War and, like SLAVERY and the theory of secession, it perished in that war. Abraham Lincoln's assertion in his First Inaugural in 1861 that "the Union of these States is perpetual" had been upheld and has not been seriously challenged since. But that has not meant a collapse of the states into a central government; the constitutional theory of the United States has continued to require a union of states. As the Supreme Court said in a decision on Reconstruction policies in 1869: "The Constitution, in all its provisions, looks to an indestructible Union, composed of indestructible States."[2024]

See also: NULLIFICATION, INTERPOSITION, AND SECESSION.

unions, *see:* labor unions

United Nations, *see:* international law

United States The Constitution uses the name "United States of America" only once, in the Preamble. All other references are to the "United States," a name that had been used more than a decade earlier in the DECLARATION OF INDEPENDENCE. Although in ordinary usage the name "United States" refers to the nation as a whole, the Constitution also uses it in a more restricted sense, to distinguish a federal OFFICE or activity from a state one. Under the GUARANTEE CLAUSE, "United States" is used to signify Congress and the president, not the courts.[1208]

See also: SOVEREIGN IMMUNITY; references listed under "United States" in the Concordance.

United States circuits, *see:* Court of Appeals

United States courts, *see:* specific (named) courts

United States districts, *see:* district courts

unreasonable search and seizure, *see:* search and seizure

unusual punishments, *see:* punishment, cruel and unusual

unwritten Constitution, *see:* natural law; Ninth Amendment

use immunity, *see:* immunity from prosecution

use taxes A use tax is imposed by one state on a product purchased in another. States often impose use taxes, measured by the purchase price, to counterbalance the loss of revenues from consumers who buy goods out of state to avoid local sales taxes. Although out-of-state sellers have occasionally suggested that such use taxes are unconstitutional as burdens on INTERSTATE COMMERCE, the Court has refused to invalidate use taxes simply on this ground.[903] However, a use tax may not be imposed on goods from other states if there is absolutely no connection between the state in which the tax will be imposed and the out-of-state seller. For example, suppose you travel to another state and purchase a chair at a local furniture store. You pay sales tax in the state in which you purchased it. Back home, your state could not impose a use tax. Likewise, if you purchase goods through catalogues mailed to you from out of state, your state may not impose a use tax if the seller maintains no local sales offices.[1423] Nor may a state collect a use tax if the out-of-state seller solicits sales through local radio and newspaper advertising, even if the goods are delivered to purchasers in the seller's trucks.[1342] But when an out-of-state seller places orders through employees traveling in the state or through brokers with in-state offices, the use tax is constitutional.[1832]

Occasionally, the legitimacy of a use tax has been questioned on another basis. In a 1985 case, a Vermont law gave a use tax credit for sales taxes on out-of-state purchases of automobiles if the purchaser lived in Vermont and registered the car there. The law denied the credit to people who lived outside the state when they bought the car but later moved to Vermont. The Court invalidated the law under the EQUAL PROTECTION CLAUSE.[2221]

See also: TAXATION OF INTERSTATE COMMERCE.

useful arts, *see:* **Patent Clause**

utilities, regulation of   In the late nineteenth century, the Court used the FIFTH AMENDMENT to cripple the federal government's ability to regulate.[1899] Beginning early in the twentieth century, however, the Supreme Court began to change its mind and eventually made clear Congress's power to regulate utilities. In 1914

the Court upheld federal power over the transportation of oil and gas in pipelines.[1632] In 1927 it voided a state's regulation of the price of electricity to be sold to distributors out of state.[1672] In 1936 it upheld the federal government's power, through the Tennessee Valley Authority, to build dams and generate and sell electricity.[88] And in 1942, overturning earlier cases limiting federal power to regulate utility rates, the Court upheld the constitutional authority of the Federal Power Commission to set the wholesale price of natural gas piped from state to state.[649]

See also: COMMERCE CLAUSE; DORMANT COMMERCE CLAUSE; FAIR VALUE FALLACY; INTERSTATE COMMERCE; TAKING OF PROPERTY.

utilities, termination of service   Although electricity and other forms of power are now essential to civilized life, the government is not constitutionally obliged to provide these utilities to people who cannot afford them. Nor do private utility companies have any duty to provide a customer with a hearing before cutting off service for nonpayment. In 1974 the argument was pressed that when a state closely regulates private utility companies, the utility is performing a PUBLIC FUNCTION and must, as the state would be obliged to do if it were the supplier, give the customer a chance to explain before discontinuing service. The Court disagreed, holding that neither the act of supplying electricity nor the state's regulating of the electrical industry puts the utility into the shoes of the state.[997]

See also: ENTITLEMENTS; HEARING; STATE ACTION.

V

---

vacancies, *see:* recess appointments

vaccination   Since 1905, when the Court upheld a compulsory smallpox vaccination law,[1000] the power of the state to compel inoculations against contagious diseases has not been questioned. As the Court later put it: even "the right to practice religion freely does not include liberty to expose the community . . . to communicable disease."[1666]

vagrancy   Vagrancy laws were used for centuries to cleanse the streets, as the Court said in 1837, of "this moral pestilence of paupers, vagabonds, and possible convicts."[1469] Vagrancy laws were used by communities to imprison or banish beggars and the homeless. The Court first struck down a type of vagrancy statute in 1939, when it held as unconstitutionally vague a New Jersey statute that subjected "gangsters" loitering about the streets to fines and imprisonment. The law defined a "gangster" as any "person not engaged in any lawful occupation, known to be a member of a gang consisting of two or more persons" who had been convicted three times of being disorderly.[1121]

In 1972, in *Papachristou v. City of Jacksonville,* the Court invalidated a more general type of vagrancy law. Under a Jacksonville, Florida, ordinance, "vagrants" could be jailed if they met one of the following descriptions: "rogues and vagabonds . . . dissolute persons who go about begging . . . common night walkers . . . common railers and brawlers, persons wandering or strolling around from place to place without any lawful purpose or object, habitual loafers, disorderly persons . . . [and] persons able to work but habitually living upon the earnings of their wives or minor children." The descriptions were too vague to give adequate notice to violators about what activities could land them in jail. It also gave the police unfettered discretion to make arrests, without PROBABLE CAUSE as required by the FOURTH AMENDMENT, and it made criminal many wholly innocent activities, such as walking down the street at night. *Papachristou* spelled the end of blunderbuss vagrancy laws, and the states' inability to find more precise language is no doubt one reason that begging is now so widespread in many urban areas. The Court also has struck down similar laws that punished people for standing around in a "manner annoying to passersby"[412] and that permitted the police to demand "reliable" and "credible" identification of anyone who wanders along the streets.[1091] Not every form of street behavior, however, is constitutionally protected. For example, the Court has upheld laws that prohibit public drunkenness.[1655]

See also: VAGUENESS.

vagueness No society can be even minimally free if people do not know on what grounds they can be sent to jail. It would be no less tyrannical for the police to arrest the citizenry for violating secret laws than to arrest wholly arbitrarily, without any law at all. FUNDAMENTAL FAIRNESS requires that the law spell out what acts constitute criminal behavior; a vaguely worded law is as bad as no law at all. A statute prohibiting "all bad things that the legislature may constitutionally outlaw" is too vague to promote law-abiding behavior, either by the citizens or the police, and it would inhibit people from exercising their constitutional rights. It would also allow legislators to escape accountability by not specifying which actions they wish to forbid. In many decisions over the years, the Court has therefore invalidated under the DUE PROCESS Clauses of both the FIFTH and FOURTEENTH AMENDMENTS any law that "either forbids or requires the doing of an act in terms so vague that men of common intelligence must necessarily guess at its meaning and differ as to its application."[448] Moreover, a "vague law impermissibly delegates basic policy matters to policemen, judges, and juries for resolution on an ad hoc and subjective basis, with the attendant dangers of arbitrary and discriminatory applications."[797a]

In 1988 the Court held unconstitutionally vague the command that the jury could find as aggravating circumstances in DEATH PENALTY cases that the defendant had acted in an "especially heinous, atrocious or cruel" manner.[1275] But in 1990 it held the phrase no longer vague when the state appellate court said that it means the infliction of mental anguish or physical abuse on the victim.[2149]

There is no clear formula to determine when the language of a statute is "void for vagueness," but interference with FREEDOM OF SPEECH has been most frequently used. Many of the LOYALTY OATH cases were decided on that basis. The Court rejected an Arizona law, for example, that required teachers to take an oath

that they would "by precept and example promote respect for the flag."[102] A New Jersey ordinance stipulating that door-to-door canvassers could work only for "a recognized charitable [or] political campaign or cause" was struck down because no one could say what "recognized" meant.[972] A Massachusetts law prohibiting anyone from publicly treating the flag "contemptuously" was held invalid when a man was convicted for having sewn a small flag to his trousers.[1889] A Cincinnati ordinance that prohibited three or more people from congregating on the streets if they were "annoying" passersby was also overturned.[412]

In these types of cases, the Court holds the statute INVALID ON ITS FACE, striking down the entire law, even though the legislature might have been able to prohibit the particular conduct in which the defendant was engaged by using more precise language. For example, a law that says you may not "annoy" someone on the street will always be vague because no test could ever determine in advance what might or might not annoy a passerby. Therefore, the law is altogether invalid, even if a particular defendant was convicted under it for punching someone in the face, conduct that could have been prohibited under a more precisely worded statute.

In other types of cases, the law itself might be sustained, even though a conviction obtained under it might be overturned on the ground that the law as applied is too vague. For example, the Court upheld the court-martial of an Army captain for advising soldiers to disobey orders to go to Vietnam.[1570] He was convicted under articles of the Uniform Code of Military Justice, a law enacted by Congress that prohibits "conduct unbecoming an officer and a gentleman" and "disorders and neglects to the prejudice of good order and discipline." In the abstract, those articles are extremely vague, but the Court said they were not vague as applied to the captain because over the years military authorities had made it clear that whatever else "conduct unbecoming" might mean, it certainly includes counseling troops to disobey orders. In other words, the Army captain could not complain that he had no fair warning that his actions might result in a court-martial. But suppose that the Army decides to court-martial another officer for wearing a loud shirt on the base on his or her day off. A court might well conclude that the words "conduct unbecoming" are too vague in that instance to justify a conviction.

Some arguably vague laws are upheld because it may be impossible for a legislature to state the prohibition or the people subject to it in any clearer way. For instance, the Court sustained an ordinance requiring the police to investigate certain people having "connections with criminal elements."[1318] And the Court has consistently upheld OBSCENITY laws against a longstanding objection that the definitions of obscenity are too vague.[1566]

Outside the zone of constitutionally protected rights, the Court has acted more charitably toward vague statutes, especially those that penalize for economic activities, and especially when the particular persons tried under them can be expected to understand them. For example, the Court upheld a law requiring truckers to "avoid, so far as practicable" routes that are "congested."[212] It sustained a law prohibiting companies, with intent to hurt competitors, from selling goods at "unreasonably low prices"; in the particular case, a company was selling goods below cost and there was abundant proof that it wished to destroy its competition.[1427] And the Court let stand a law that required merchants to obtain a license to sell goods "designed or marketed for use" with unlawful drugs.[930] But it struck down a law aimed at war profiteering that prohibited making "any unjust or unreasonable rate or charge" and "excessive prices" for necessaries.[419]

See also: MORAL TURPITUDE; OVERBREADTH DOCTRINE.

venue "Venue" refers to the location of the court where a trial may be held. Art. III-§2[3] and the Sixth Amendment require that federal criminal trials be held in the particular district where the crime was committed. "District" refers to the geographic area in which a federal DISTRICT COURT sits. When a crime is committed in more than one district, the trial may be held in any one of them. A refusal to change when the defendant has been subjected to massive pretrial PREJUDICIAL PUBLICITY violates DUE PROCESS.[1728] One reason for changing venue is prejudicial publicity that might make it impossible for the defendant to get a fair trial. Federal and state law, not the Constitution, govern venue in civil cases.

See also: TRIAL, PLACE OF.

vessels, *see:* **admiralty and maritime jurisdiction; transportation**

vested rights The concept of vested rights was recognized early in our constitutional history in the seminal case MARBURY V. MADISON. Chief Justice John Marshall declared that because William Marbury had been duly commissioned a judge, he had a vested right to the office that not even the president could deprive him of: "The government of the United States has been emphatically termed a government of laws, and not of men. It will certainly cease to deserve this high appellation, if the laws furnish no remedy for the violation of a vested legal right." By "vested legal right," Marshall meant simply that when the law confers particular offices or benefits on particular people, the government may not legally divest them of those benefits. In two of his great opinions, Marshall extended the notion under the CONTRACT CLAUSE to interests in land and in corporate charters. In *Fletcher v. Peck* in 1810, he declared that Georgia could not revoke land grants once made. In *Dartmouth College v. Woodward,* he ruled that New Hampshire could not usurp the authority of a college board of trustees to transform a private college into a public one.

But owners do not, merely by virtue of ownership, have a vested right to do whatever they please with their possessions. Although the government is prohibited from confiscating property without providing JUST COMPENSATION, the states and the federal government may regulate property use to protect the public health, safety, and well-being. Moreover, because an ENTITLEMENT is legally vested only to the extent that the law says it is, many benefits of the modern welfare state may be rescinded. A legislature that funds unemployment or welfare benefits may also state the conditions under which they can be forfeited.

See also: ECONOMIC DUE PROCESS; HEARING; PROCESS THAT IS DUE; PROPERTY; TAKING OF PROPERTY.

'veterans' preference Many states grant preferences to veterans in obtaining public employment. In 1979 the Court upheld a Massachusetts "absolute lifetime" preference to veterans for state civil service jobs. Qualifying veterans are placed ahead of all nonveterans in the applicant pool. A nonveteran woman challenged the law as unconstitutional SEX DISCRIMINATION because ninety-eight percent of the veterans in the state were male. The Court rejected the challenge, holding that the law was not intended to discriminate against women, since the law "serves legitimate and worthy purposes," has a negative impact on many nonveteran men as well as women, and does benefit those women who are veterans.[1612] In 1986, the Court held that a state may not limit a veterans' preference on the civil service list only to those veterans who were residents of the state on a certain date and deny the benefit to veterans who moved to the state later. Any preference must be given equally to all veterans.[97]

See also: DURATIONAL RESIDENCY REQUIREMENT.

veto, legislative, *see:* **legislative veto**

veto, line-item, *see:* **line-item veto**

veto, pocket, *see:* **pocket veto**

veto power The "veto power" usually refers to the president's express power in Art. I-§7[2] to prevent bills enacted by Congress from becoming law. It is central to the system of CHECKS AND BALANCES within the federal government. Without it, presidents would be much less able to influence legislation and might be far less inclined to enforce laws of which they disapprove. The power is considerable: none of President George Bush's vetoes has been overridden, and in more than two hundred years Congress has managed to override fewer than seven percent of vetoed bills. The president may accept the bill or he may veto for any reason, although he must state his objections in a message to the house that originated the bill. Congress may override the president's veto by reenacting the bill in each house by a two-thirds majority. The Court has ruled that the override need be by only two-thirds of the members present in each house, as long as there is a quorum; thus, an override does not require two-thirds of the entire membership.[1366] Although some governors have the power under their state constitutions to veto particular portions of a bill, the president does not have a LINE-ITEM VETO. The president may also exercise a POCKET VETO by failing to sign a bill within ten days after Congress has adjourned.

See also: LEGISLATIVE VETO.

vice president "Not worth a pitcher full of warm spit" was how President Franklin D. Roosevelt's first vice president, John Nance Garner, characterized his office. The vice president has but two constitutional duties: under Art. I-§3[4] to preside over the SENATE and cast a vote only in the event of a tie, and under Art. II-§1[6], as amended by the TWENTIETH and TWENTY-FIFTH AMENDMENTS, to wait for the president to die, resign, or become disabled or removed from office. In practice, the vice president usually presides over the Senate only on ceremonial occasions, or when a vote is expected to be close. The vice president's agenda is usually determined by the needs of the president. In recent years, vice presidents have been dispatched on foreign missions and as stand-ins to rally the party faithful in speeches across the country. Some vice presidents have assumed administrative responsibilities, overseeing presidential task forces and coordinating federal programs. In recent years, Vice Presidents Walter Mondale and George Bush were both delegated extensive policy-making responsibilities.

See also: ELECTORAL COLLEGE; PRESIDENTIAL SUCCESSION.

vicinage, *see:* trial, place of

victim impact statements   In 1987 and 1989 the Court expressly disallowed prosecutors, during sentencing in a capital case, to offer evidence of the impact of the killing on the victim's survivors or to comment to a sentencing jury on the personal qualities of the victim.[198, 1911] The Court's concern was that so-called victim impact evidence violates the EIGHTH AMENDMENT's command against cruel and unusual punishment, because the evidence might permit a jury to decide "that defendants whose victims were assets to their community are more deserving of punishment than those whose victims are perceived to be less worthy." But in 1991 the Court abruptly overruled its previous decisions.[1580] Chief Justice William H. Rehnquist concluded that the Court had erred in supposing that evidence about the nature of the victim and the impact of the killing would lead "to the arbitrary imposition of the death penalty." Dissenting, Justice John Paul Stevens said that such evidence "serves no purpose other than to appeal to the sympathies or emotions of the jurors," noting that no one would allow the *defendant* to offer evidence

that, unknown to him at the time of a shooting in an armed robbery, a murdered convenience store clerk was immoral. "Evenhanded justice requires that the same constraint be imposed on the advocate of the death penalty."

See also: PUNISHMENT, CRUEL AND UNUSUAL; STARE DECISIS.

Vietnam War   In hindsight, Congress's 1964 GULF OF TONKIN RESOLUTION was a flimsy basis on which to rest presidential authority to wage war in Vietnam. It was not a declaration of war, although it authorized a military buildup to respond to attacks on U.S. vessels. Resisting the legality of orders to report for military service and challenging the war directly, many litigants during the Vietnam decade, roughly from 1965 to 1975, sought court rulings that the war was unconstitutional because undeclared. In every instance, the Supreme Court and most lower federal courts refused to hear the cases, principally on the grounds that the war presented nonjusticiable POLITICAL QUESTIONS and that SEPARATION OF POWERS precludes judicial involvement in issues that should be resolved through the political process.[96]

See also: WAR POWER; WAR POWERS RESOLUTION.

vindication of constitutional rights
Whether and to what extent an individual is entitled to relief when the government violates or threatens to violate a constitutional right depends on the circumstances. Some constitutional rights are almost impossible to vindicate in court because of STANDING requirements: when the government violates the Constitution in a way that affects all citizens equally, the courts will not entertain a constitutional challenge. The only real exception is for claims that the government is violating the ESTABLISHMENT CLAUSE by granting aid to religious institutions.

If the unconstitutional government action is directed toward a particular person, on the other hand, there is considerably more justification for challenging it. A defendant being prosecuted for violating an unconstitutional law can always defend by raising the issue of unconstitutionality. Sometimes it is possible to obtain a DECLARATORY JUDGMENT or an INJUNCTION before the government enforces a law or carries out a particular policy, if the law or policy is plainly unconstitutional. For example, a person challenging a PERMIT SYSTEM that gives absolute discretion to municipal officials to decide whether or not to let demonstrators march or hand out leaflets need not risk a prosecution but can go to court to enjoin operation of the system. But litigants disobey court orders at their peril. Even an unconstitutional injunction must be observed until a higher court overturns it on appeal.²¹⁴² Under the ABSTENTION DOCTRINE, a federal court may grant relief against an unconstitutional proceeding in a state court only in limited circumstances. For example, the federal courts will consider a challenge to the enforcement of allegedly unconstitutional state laws if the challenge was made before the prosecution was begun,⁵⁶¹ but will not entertain a challenge to a pending prosecution.²²⁸¹ Ordinarily, also, an individual may challenge the actions of ADMINISTRATIVE AGENCIES only after pursuing all possible appeals within the administrative body.

A criminal defendant may vindicate the constitutional right against SELF-INCRIMINATION and the right to be free of an unreasonable SEARCH AND SEIZURE by invoking the EXCLUSIONARY RULE, which requires unconstitutionally obtained evidence to be excluded from trial.

When a court's action is being challenged as unconstitutional, the litigant's only avenue of relief is through appeal within either the federal or state system and ultimately to the Supreme Court. Following some prosecutions, criminal defendants may file HABEAS CORPUS petitions in federal courts to challenge the constitutionality of their convictions in state courts. But not every constitutional error committed in court will necessarily result in a re-

versal of a conviction; the HARMLESS ERROR rule protects government from being held responsible in many instances.

Under federal CIVIL RIGHTS LEGISLATION, persons whose rights have been violated by unconstitutional actions of state officials may file suits for DAMAGES or injunctions. Under limited circumstances, an individual may sue federal officials for committing a CONSTITUTIONAL TORT.

See also: EXHAUSTION OF REMEDIES; IMPLIED CONSTITUTIONAL *RIGHT OF ACTION.*

Virginia Plan One of the major issues dividing the delegates to the CONSTITUTIONAL CONVENTION was the method by which the people should be represented in CONGRESS. Understandably, the small states wished all states to be represented equally; the large states advocated representation according to population. In the Virginia Plan, Edmund Randolph proposed that Congress should consist of two houses whose members would represent the states in proportion to their free populations. The lower house would be elected directly by the people; the upper house would be chosen by the lower house from a list of candidates supplied by each state legislature. This plan was bitterly opposed by the smaller states, since three states alone—Virginia, Pennsylvania, and Massachusetts—comprised nearly half the population of the country and could therefore have been expected to control Congress. The small states countered with the NEW JERSEY PLAN. Both were ultimately rejected in favor of the GREAT COMPROMISE that resulted in the present composition of Congress.

void-for-vagueness doctrine, *see:* **vagueness**

voir dire Old French for "to speak the truth," voir dire is the questioning of the jury panel to determine fitness to serve at a trial. Under the SIXTH AMENDMENT right to an impartial JURY, a prospective juror must be excluded if his or her "views would prevent or substantially impair the performance of his duties as a juror in accordance with his instructions and his oath."[2141] A potential juror may not be allowed to sit if he or she has formed an opinion about the case or has a particular bias against the parties or against the race or other characteristics of the parties. In cases raising the possibility of racial bias, the defendant is entitled to question members of the jury panel about their possible prejudice.[845] But special questioning about racial attitudes is not required solely because defendant and victim are of different races or ethnic groups;[1732] whether special questioning is necessary is for trial judges to decide case by case.[1758] Challenges on grounds of bias or of inability to abide by the juror's oath are known as "for cause" challenges, which the parties usually may exercise as often as necessary. In addition, both prosecution and defense are entitled to a certain number of PEREMPTORY CHALLENGES to keep someone off the jury for no reason at all. However, in *Batson v. Kentucky* the Court held that it is a violation of EQUAL PROTECTION for a prosecutor to systematically exclude blacks from a criminal jury through peremptory challenges. In addition, failure to *include*, no less than *exclude*, people with certain views may be unconstitutional. In 1968 the Court held that prospective jurors with doubts about the legitimacy of the death penalty may not be excluded from the jury, as long as they would consider imposing it in the appropriate case.[2240]

Volstead Act   The Volstead Act was the basic federal law embodying Prohibition. It was enacted over President Woodrow Wilson's veto in 1919 nine months after ratification of the EIGHTEENTH AMENDMENT. In 1920 the Court upheld the power of Congress to ban intrastate as well as interstate sale, possession, and use of intoxicating beverages.[1717] However, when Repeal came in 1933, the power of Congress to

enact Prohibition laws automatically lapsed and the Volstead Act became void.[368]

See also: INTOXICATING BEVERAGES; TWENTY-FIRST AMENDMENT.

voter qualifications   With the exception of the broad prohibitions against discrimination based on race, sex, wealth, and age, the Constitution does not set voter qualifications. Under Art. I-§2[1], anyone eligible to vote for the state legislative branch with the most members (state houses or state assemblies) must be allowed to vote in that state's elections for the U.S. HOUSE OF REPRESENTATIVES. But determining voter qualifications in state elections is a question for each state. Until relatively recently, many states used LITERACY TESTS to determine voter eligibility. Although it was never expressly condemned under the Constitution, the literacy test was outlawed by the VOTING RIGHTS ACT OF 1965. The only other general disqualifications are those of residency and conviction for a felony. Restriction of the polls to state residents who have properly registered is permissible, but in a number of cases during the past two decades, the Court has limited the power of the states to deny voting rights to residents who have not lived in the state for a requisite number of months.[583] The Court has expressly upheld the power of a state to deny the right to vote to convicted felons even after they have served their sentences.[1724] However, the justices unanimously struck down a provision of the Alabama constitution that denied the franchise to persons convicted of "any crime . . . involving MORAL TURPITUDE."[962] Justice William H. Rehnquist said that the provision was adopted expressly to disenfranchise blacks and that it continued to do so disproportionately to whites, violating the Equal Protection Clause.

See also: DURATIONAL RESIDENCY REQUIREMENTS; VOTING, RIGHT TO.

voting, right to   The right to vote is one of the fundamental political principles on which the nation was founded. The English kings' denial of that right was one of the chief justifications for revolution cited in the DECLARATION OF INDEPENDENCE. Nevertheless, the Constitution of 1787 does not expressly provide a right to vote, although in two places it sets out a rule and a principle that together amount to such a right. Art. I-§2[1] confers the right to vote for members of the HOUSE OF REPRESENTATIVES on anyone eligible to vote for the most numerous branch of the legislature in each state. Art. IV-§4 guarantees each state a "republican form of government," which presumably commands public elections for state legislators. The franchise has over the years gradually been extended to broader and broader classes of citizens, and the power of the states to restrict that franchise has been reduced. Indeed, more constitutional amendments concern suffrage than any other subject. Once hostile toward attempts to police restrictions on voting, the courts are now willing to "carefully and meticulously scrutinize" any infringement of voting rights.[1713]

Immediately after the American Revolution, most states limited voting to white males over twenty-one years of age with a certain amount of property. Many states also required the voter to swear a belief in God. Even in the free states, blacks were effectively denied the right to vote. At mid-nineteenth century, only Maine gave blacks and whites equal access to the polls; and in DRED SCOTT V. SANDFORD, the Supreme Court erased even that meager possibility in ruling that blacks simply could not be citizens.

After the Civil War, the trio of Civil Rights amendments opened up the possibility of voting for blacks. By giving Congress power to enforce its antislavery provisions, the THIRTEENTH AMENDMENT presumably enabled Congress to outlaw discriminatory state voting policies but, in fact, Section 2 of the FOURTEENTH AMENDMENT seemed to suggest that a state could disenfranchise its black citizens by agreeing to lower its representation in the U.S. House of Representatives. Despite widespread infringements on the right of blacks to vote, this provision was never enforced. In 1870, Republicans apparently saw the advantage to their party of enfranchising former slaves and succeeded in ratifying the FIFTEENTH AMENDMENT, which prohibits the federal government and the states from discriminating on the basis of "race, color, or previous condition of servitude."

Popular sentiment did not endorse the same policy for women. For about thirty years after the Declaration of Independence, women voted in New Jersey, but a state constitutional amendment in 1807 disenfranchised them; no other state had ever contemplated the possibility of women's suffrage. In 1838 Kentucky let women into the voting booths for school elections. Not until 1869, in the Wyoming Territory, did women win the general right to vote in all elections; even then, they did not gain the right to vote in a state until Wyoming joined the Union in 1890. Neither political nor legal strategies translated into action. During the next quarter century, only ten more states followed Wyoming's lead, and several restricted women's suffrage to certain elections only. The Court turned down a bid to read into the PRIVILEGES OR IMMUNITIES CLAUSE of the Fourteenth Amendment a general right to vote, holding that voting was a privilege of state but not national citizenship.[1358] Pressure for a constitutional amendment mounted during World War I, when large numbers of women went to work. With President Wilson's endorsement and the support of Republicans and some Democrats, the NINETEENTH AMENDMENT was ratified in 1920, a half-century after formal suffrage for blacks.

In 1961 voters in the District of Columbia, disenfranchised in federal elections since the District became the national capital, gained the right to vote in presidential elections with the ratification of the TWENTY-THIRD AMENDMENT.

In 1970, responding to cries about the unfairness of sending young men to war when they could not even vote for their national leaders, Congress enacted a bill lowering the voting age to eighteen in all elections. Later that year, the Court held that Congress had the constitutional authority to lower voting age for federal but not state elections.[1537] Fearing mass confusion from conflicting age limits when voters entered voting booths in which both state and federal candidates would be on the ballot, Congress proposed the TWENTY-SIXTH AMENDMENT, lowering the voting age to eighteen in all elections. It was ratified on July 1, 1971.

All but one of these constitutional extensions of suffrage were quickly and quietly accepted. In the seventy-two years since the Nineteenth Amendment was ratified, only one case asserting a violation of any of the later amendments has surfaced in the Supreme Court. When Virginia attempted in 1965 to hold on to its poll tax, the Court struck down the law.[865] Only the Fifteenth Amendment was widely disregarded from its inception; only recently has widespread enfranchisement of blacks been achieved.

The Court recognized by the early 1880s that state constitutions[1438] and laws[2270] are unconstitutional if they formally restrict the franchise to whites. For roughly the next eighty-five years, many states experimented with more subtle ways of denying black suffrage—sometimes through explicit laws written to take advantage of apparent loopholes in the Fifteenth Amendment, and more often through discriminatory administration of voter registration schemes. Between 1896 and 1904, when Louisiana adopted literacy, property, and poll tax qualifications, black registration fell from 130,334 to 1,342.

One of the earliest devices to be struck down was the GRANDFATHER CLAUSE, which permitted whites to avoid literacy requirements to which blacks were strictly held. The Court invalidated Oklahoma's grandfather clause in 1915.[830] The following year, Oklahoma enacted a more subtle grandfather clause that the Court only got around to invalidating in 1939.[1118]

The white primary laws proved equally recalcitrant. Throughout the one-party South in the first half of the twentieth century, the composition of elected posts was determined in the primaries, not in the general elections. The winner of the Democratic primary was sure to be elected in the general election. Texas passed a law restricting primaries to white voters, asserting that a primary is not an election and therefore the law did not violate the Fifteenth Amendment. In 1927 the Court invalidated the law on equal protection grounds.[1486] Texas responded by repealing the white primary law and enacting instead a law delegating to the executive committees of political parties the authority to determine who could vote in primaries. This time the state argued that private political parties could not violate the equal protection clause, since it applies only to STATE ACTION. The Court invalidated this scheme also, holding that the executive committee had become an agent of the state.[1484] Undaunted, Texas again amended the law, this time handing over the task of registering primary voters to the entire membership of the party. For a time, the Court was fooled by this subterfuge,[826] but in 1941 it held that a primary is an election,[406] and in 1944 finally declared that whenever a political party operates primaries with the active cooperation of the state, it is an agent of the state.[1885]

The white primaries were almost dead. The Court administered the coup de grâce in 1953, when it voided still another Texas system.[2012] The Jaybird Democratic Association, a purely private political organization that excluded blacks, held its own primary in May. The Jaybirds had no official connection with the Texas Democratic party, was not organized under state election laws, and did not use state funds or voting machinery. But for sixty years, with one exception, the winner of the Jaybird primary ran unopposed in the July Democratic primary and went on to win the November general election. This practice, too, the Court said, violates the Fifteenth Amendment.

In addition to these longstanding legislative discriminations, state executives carried on an even longer-running policy of administrative discrimination, centered mainly on LITERACY TESTS. Congress finally outlawed these tests in the 1975 amendments to the VOTING RIGHTS ACT.

Sporadically, the states and municipalities devised other, often unique methods of diluting the voting strength of blacks. The most famous example was the racial GERRYMANDERING of Tuskegee, Alabama. The town drew itself a district with twenty-eight sides to fence out the black residential sections. The Court invalidated the scheme in 1960 on equal protection grounds.[775] More recently, the Court upheld lower-court rulings that an at-large election system for a rural Georgia county with a majority of black citizens was intended to and did dilute their voting power.[1750]

The Court signaled in 1976 that it is mainly concerned with the division between black and white representation and will give less credence to the disenfranchisement claims of other groups. It upheld New York's redrawing of Brooklyn voting districts to guarantee black representation in the state legislature. To do so, the state had to split apart several white districts, including the thirty thousand–member Hasidic Jewish community. There was no single opinion to which a majority adhered, but the Court seemed to be saying that the redrawing, carried out to comply with the Voting Rights Act, was intended to benefit one group, not to harm the other. As whites, the Hasidic community as a group was "provided with fair representation," said Justice Byron R. White.[2094] Ultimately, the general enfranchisement of the black community came about not through constitutional rulings of the Supreme Court but through a powerful, even revolu-

tionary, piece of legislation, the Voting Rights Act.

In 1982, the Court noted that "the right to vote, per se, is not a constitutionally protected right," and upheld a rule permitting a vacant seat in the Puerto Rico legislature to be filled by someone from the political party of the member whose seat was prematurely vacated.[1747] In other words, there is no constitutional right that every legislator sitting in the legislature be *elected* by the voters; rather, the various amendments mean that whenever the voters do get to choose, the franchise must be equally open to all.

Aside from the general problem of racial discrimination, in the past thirty years the Court has pursued a somewhat uneven course of striking down laws that limit certain types of elections to "interested voters." In 1965, for example, the Court upset a Texas law denying the vote to a member of the armed forces who was a bona fide resident of the state.[349] In 1969 the Court struck down a New York law restricting the franchise in New York City school district elections to people who owned or leased property in the district or had children enrolled in a local school.[1097] In other decisions, the Court has invalidated laws limiting elections about municipal bonds to property owners.[398, 1624] Somewhat inconsistently, however, it has upheld policies restricting to landowners the right to vote in water storage and reclamation district elections, and it has even permitted the voting to be apportioned by the amount of property—"one acre, one vote" rather than ONE PERSON, ONE VOTE.[1788, 112]

The Court has also considered nonracial exclusions from party primaries. A closely divided Court upheld New York's "antiraiding" law requiring voters to affiliate with a party thirty days or more before a general election to be eligible to vote in that party's primary the following year.[1759] The effect was to force voters to remain affiliated with a party for as much as eleven months. But the Court overturned an

Illinois law barring anyone from voting in a party primary "if he has voted in the primary of any other party within the preceding 23 months" because the law in effect " 'locks' voters into a preexisting party affiliation from one election to the next, and the only way to break the 'lock' is to forego voting" for two years.[1101] In 1986 the Court invalidated a Connecticut law prohibiting anyone from voting in a party primary unless registered as a member of that party. The Court upheld the Republican party's right to welcome nonregistered independents to vote in its primaries.[1997]

Finally, the Court has specifically upheld the power of states to disenfranchise convicted felons, even after they have served their sentences.[1724] The Court based its conclusion on Section 2 of the FOURTEENTH AMENDMENT, which provides an exception for "participation in . . . crime" to the command that a state's denial of the right to vote must lead to a decrease in its congressional representation.

See also: ACCESS TO BALLOT; APPORTIONMENT OF POLITICAL DISTRICTS; CAMPAIGN FINANCING; DURATIONAL RESIDENCY REQUIREMENTS; ELECTORAL COLLEGE; GUARANTEE CLAUSE; ORDER, RESOLUTION, OR VOTE; POLL TAX; SEVENTEENTH AMENDMENT; VOTER QUALIFICATIONS.

Voting Rights Act of 1965

Despite the Court's willingness to disallow the infringement of the rights of black voters, it was costly, time-consuming, and ultimately ineffective to resort to lawsuits. In 1965, reacting to violence in southern voter registration drives, President Lyndon B. Johnson told Congress: "Every device of which human ingenuity is capable has been used to deny [the right to vote]. The Negro citizen may go to register only to be told that the day is wrong, or the hour is late, or the official in charge is absent. And if he persists and if he manages to present himself to the registrar, he may be disqualified because he did not spell out his middle name or because he abbreviated a word on the application. And if he manages to fill out an application, he is given a test. The registrar is the sole judge of whether he passes this test. He may be asked to recite the entire constitution, or explain the most complex provisions of state laws. And even a college degree cannot be used to prove that he can read and write. For the fact is that the only way to pass these barriers is to show a white skin."

Congress responded with the Voting Rights Act of 1965. In many ways it was the most radical CIVIL RIGHTS LEGISLATION ever enacted. Its provisions were triggered mostly in southern states and political subdivisions with less than fifty percent registration in 1964. The act suspended LITERACY TESTS, educational requirements, and other obstacles to voter registration, and required any state where tests were suspended to seek clearance either from the attorney general or a federal court before making any change that might abridge anyone's right to vote. Amendments in 1970, 1975, and 1982 extended the act to all the states. Various registration tests, including literacy tests, were abolished, other triggering years were added, and the clearance provisions were extended to 2007. The act has spawned dozens of cases interpreting its scope and reach, and few of them were purely constitutional.

However, in cases testing whether the act itself is constitutional, the Court issued significant rulings affirming a very broad power of Congress to enforce the provisions of the FIFTEENTH AMENDMENT.[1756, 1913] In essence, the Court has said that it will defer to Congress's judgment about the extent of the antidiscrimination policies of the Fourteenth and Fifteenth Amendments and that Congress may read them more broadly than the Court would.[1053] Many commentators have suggested that this is a rare exception to the general rule, espoused in MARBURY V. MADISON, that the Court alone may determine what the Constitution requires.

See also: VOTING, RIGHT TO; PURPOSE-IMPACT DISTINCTION.

vulgarity, *see:* offensive and indecent speech

W

wage and hours legislation, *see:* employment legislation

wage and price controls, *see:* price and wage controls

waiting period, *see:* durational residency requirements

waiver of constitutional rights, *see:* rights, waiver of

wall of separation, *see:* religious establishment

war, constitutional rights in; *see:* rights in wartime

war, declaration of   Art. I-§8[11] gives Congress exclusive power to "declare war." Despite the seeming definitiveness of the grant, only five of all the wars or military operations in which the United States has engaged have been declared officially by Congress: the War of 1812, the Mexican War (1846–48), the Spanish-American War (1898), World War I (1917–18), and World War II (1941–45). A sixth, the quick rout of the Iraqis that liberated Kuwait in 1991, was fought after Congress expressly authorized the president to commit troops to bat-

tle if Baghdad refused to withdraw. U.S. military forces have entered other major wars, however, including the Korean War (1950–53) and the Vietnam War (1964–73), without congressional declarations.

As the war power was originally conceived at the CONSTITUTIONAL CONVENTION, Congress was to have the sole power not merely to declare but to "make war." That provision was ultimately amended, narrowing Congress's role and enlarging the president's, both to ensure that the president would have the power, in Madison's words, "to repel sudden attacks" and to prevent Congress from interfering with the president's power to conduct the war as COMMANDER IN CHIEF once war had been declared.

In deploying troops, presidents have pointed to their power as commander in chief, their EXECUTIVE POWER, and DELEGATIONS of congressional authority to act. For example, in 1950, when he ordered U.S. troops to fight the North Koreans, President Harry S. Truman relied on a United Nations resolution, U.S. treaty obligations, and authority as commander in chief to protect American foreign interests. Because the Constitution divides war powers, giving Congress the power to declare war and the president the power to wage it, the issue ultimately has turned more on politics than constitutional law. Never in our history has the Supreme Court spurned a president's decision to send troops into battle. As early as 1827[1252] and on many occasions thereafter, the Court has sustained such decisions.

The first major test of the president's power to commit troops came in April 1861, when without seeking congressional approval, President Lincoln imposed a blockade of southern ports and seized several ships of neutral nations. Although Congress later ratified the blockade, the question remained whether the president had the independent power to initiate military action. Ruling 5–4 in the *Prize Cases,* the Court said it was not necessary for Congress to declare war because a state of war in fact existed: "If a war be made by invasion of a foreign nation, the President is not only authorized but bound to resist force, by force. He does not initiate the war, but is bound to accept the challenge without waiting for any special legislative authority. . . . The President was bound to meet [this greatest of civil wars] in the shape it presented itself, without waiting for Congress to baptize it with a name; and no name given to it by him or them could change the fact." In recent times, including during the Vietnam era, the Court has refused to consider challenges to the president's power to commit troops without congressional authority.

See also: GULF OF TONKIN RESOLUTION; WAR POWER; WAR POWERS RESOLUTION; WAR, STATE OF.

war, state of   In international law and under many federal laws, a "state of war" permits many emergency measures that would otherwise be unlawful, including the power of the president to commit troops and to seize enemy property. The Court has made it clear that a state of war does not depend on a formal declaration of war. It may exist before a formal declaration and after military action has ceased; likewise, a state of war may have ceased even though a formal peace treaty has not been signed.[1135] The Court is much more likely to scrutinize and even reject presidential actions or laws that touch on constitutional rights after a war has ended than during the war. As the Court noted even as it upheld a rent-control law in 1948: "We recognize the force of the argument that the effects of war under modern conditions may be felt in the economy for years and years, and that if the war power can be used in days of peace to treat all the wounds which war inflicts on our society, it may not only swallow up all other powers of Congress but largely obliterate the NINTH and TENTH AMENDMENTS as well."[1255]

See also: RIGHTS IN WARTIME; WAR POWER.

war crimes   During World War II, German saboteurs were caught in the United States. They were tried by a military tribunal and convicted for failing to wear insignia indicating their combatant status, even though no federal law required them to do so. The Court was unimpressed by the defendants' arguments that the lower court lacked jurisdiction because it had been convened by presidential order, followed rules devised solely for the occasion, and convicted them of a crime not specifically established by federal law. The Court said that the trial was permissible under a federal law authorizing military trials of acts "against the law of war."[1677] After World War II, the Court also upheld the conviction and death sentence of General Tomoyuki Yamashita, under whose command the Japanese forces in the Philippines committed innumerable atrocities. Yamashita asserted that he was being tried EX POST FACTO, since there was no law prohibiting aggressive acts of war. The Court said essentially that the decision to try war leaders is the exclusive prerogative of the president and the military.[2268]

war power   "War power" is a popular not a constitutional phrase, shorthand for a congeries of provisions that together endow the federal government with almost limitless power to wage hot wars and sweeping power to fight cold ones. Abraham Lincoln may have been the first to use the singular "war power" to refer to the various powers to combat an enemy; the Supreme Court adopted the language in 1875.[847] But relatively few constitutional decisions have emerged from the Supreme Court, and most of these have affirmed the power of one or the other or both branches of government. On relatively rare occasions has the Court been called upon to resolve tensions between Congress and the president.

Alexander Hamilton was the earliest advocate of the now-accepted view that the war power must be a broad national power. As he argued in *Federalist* 23: "The circumstances that endanger the safety of nations are infinite, and for this reason no constitutional shackles can wisely be imposed on the power to which the care of it is committed." The Constitution clearly entrusts that power to the federal government. Clauses 9 and 10 of Art. I-§10 prohibit the states from making treaties, keeping troops or ships in peacetime, or engaging in war unless invaded. Four clauses of Art. I-§8—11, 12, 13, and 14—assign to Congress the power to declare war and to raise, provide for, and govern the armed forces. Art. II appoints the president COMMANDER IN CHIEF. And Art. IV-§4 commits the federal government to protect the states against invasion.

The war power as a whole has been the constitutional basis for an astonishing array of federal policies not directly connected to military operations during war. The courts have sustained almost all war power policies that Congress and the president have pursued in tandem. Despite many challenges, the Supreme Court has never rejected a federal CONSCRIPTION law, even in peacetime. During the Vietnam era, Chief Justice Earl Warren noted in *United States v. O'Brien*, the draft card burning

case: "The power of Congress to classify and conscript manpower for military service is 'beyond question.'" Once enlisted or commissioned, members of the armed forces may claim fewer constitutional protections, despite the Court's occasional denials that the United States government may ignore the constitutional rights of soldiers and sailors.[1766] As the Court put it the year that American military involvement in Vietnam ended: "Congress is permitted to legislate both with greater breadth and with greater flexibility when prescribing the rules by which [military society] shall be governed than it is when prescribing rules for [civilian society]."[1570]

During the major declared wars—World War I and World War II—Congress enacted controls over every facet of the economy. In World War I, Congress delegated extensive power to the president to take over factories, railroads, and the telephone and telegraph system; to fix prices of foodstuffs; and to set coal prices and regulate coal production, among many other things. In World War II, there were even more sweeping controls over the national economy—consumer prices, including rents, were subject to regulation, as were commodity prices; many consumer goods were rationed. The president could seize war-related factories closed by strikes, censor radio communications, shift appropriated funds between federal departments and agencies, and recover "excess profits," or "renegotiate," under war production contracts. The constitutionality of most of these programs never reached the courts, but the Supreme Court took the opportunity to broadly uphold Congress's power to control profits when it compared the Renegotiation Act to the Selective Service Act: "The authority of Congress to authorize each of them sprang from its war powers. . . . Both acts were a form of mobilization. The language of the Constitution authorizing such measures is broad rather than restrictive

... [placing] emphasis upon the supporting as well as upon the raising of armies."[1163]

Even in peacetime, the war power has been used to support an array of federal programs, as the Court did when it upheld the Tennessee Valley Authority, authorized by the National Defense Act of 1916.[88] The Atomic Energy Act, highway construction projects, the national space program, and even federal financial support for education have all been justified, without serious legal challenge, by the war power.

The war power does not end when hostilities cease. As the Court has said: "[The war power] is not limited to victories in the field. . . . It carries with it inherently the power to guard against the immediate renewal of the conflict, and to remedy the evils which have arisen from its rise and progress."[1959] Though no formula describes the boundaries of Congress's power to act after the shooting stops, it is not limitless; the Court considers the issue case by case. For example, the Court sustained a post–World War I Prohibition Act, enacted after the Armistice was signed in 1918;[848] but it rejected a rent control law in the District of Columbia in 1924 on the grounds that the war emergency had ended.[379] By a 5–4 vote, it upheld the president's decision to deport certain enemy aliens even after World War II had ended based on his authority to deport during wartime.[1204]

The most serious debates about the war power have arisen over the degree to which the president may commit troops in the absence of a formal congressional declaration of war or otherwise act militarily under his power as commander in chief, without congressional authority, and the extent to which other constitutional provisions limit the reach of the war power. These subjects are treated in separate headings.

See also: ARMED FORCES; DELEGATION DOCTRINE; EXECUTIVE POWER; FOREIGN AFFAIRS POWER; IMPLIED AND INHERENT POWERS; MILITARY COURTS AND JUSTICE; PIRACY; RIGHTS IN WARTIME; STEEL SEIZURE CASE; WAR, DECLARATION OF; WAR POWERS RESOLUTION; WAR PRIZES; WAR, STATE OF.

War Powers Resolution   In 1973, over the veto of President Richard M. Nixon, who by then had been politically weakened by the spreading WATERGATE scandal, Congress passed the War Powers Resolution, by which it hoped to narrow the scope of presidential warmaking. The resolution says that the president may commit troops to battle in three situations only: (1) when Congress has declared war; (2) when Congress has specifically authorized troops to be deployed; or (3) when the United States has been attacked. If troops are deployed without a declaration of war, the president must report his actions to Congress within forty-eight hours and must withdraw the troops within sixty days unless Congress has either declared war or extended the period. At any time during the sixty days, Congress by concurrent resolution could order the troops withdrawn. This last provision, though never tested in court, seems clearly unconstitutional as a LEGISLATIVE VETO.[979] Whether the War Powers Resolution is otherwise constitutional has not yet been tested. Critics suggest that far from restricting the president, it may serve to give him a blank check to send troops into hostilities, for what constitutes an "attack" on the United States or its possessions is a large question, one that may forever be unanswered, at least in the courts.

In 1982 President Ronald Reagan ignored the resolution altogether in sending troops into Lebanon; Congress responded by authorizing troops to remain eighteen months. In 1986, ordering Navy and Air Force planes to drop bombs on Libya, President Reagan consulted leaders, but not Congress as a whole, only three hours before the bombs fell. In late December 1989 President George Bush sent troops into Panama after the newly proclaimed head of government, Manuel Noriega, declared his country "to be in a state of war" with the United States and after an off-duty U.S. soldier was killed at a roadblock. Although President Bush ignored the War Powers Resolution, most members of Congress said they supported the invasion. He ignored the War Powers Resolution again in 1990 when he sent massive numbers of troops to the Persian Gulf, although he ultimately secured congressional consent before beginning "Desert Storm," the brief war against Iraq to liberate Kuwait. In the give-and-take between Congress and the president the issue presumably will remain controversial.

war prizes War prizes are enemy properties captured during war, including military vessels, arms, and even possessions of civilian subjects. Property subject to capture and the manner of its disposition are exclusively for Congress to decide.[2035] During the Civil War and the world wars, Congress enacted several laws specifying property that could be confiscated. Property of enemy nations or enemy aliens is not subject to the limitations of the JUST COMPENSATION Clause in the FIFTH AMENDMENT, even if that property is within the United States.[259, 1341, 362, 855] Even property of friendly aliens may be seized.[1867] Federal law and treaties override international law of capture and prize, but in their absence the courts must apply international law to determine whether property may be seized.[2034]

warrant, *see:* **search warrant**

warrantless search, *see:* **search and seizure: with and without warrants**

warrants, execution of, *see:* **no-knock entry**

water rights disputes between states, *see:* **states, disputes between**

Watergate Two substantial constitutional issues bubbled to the surface of the boiling pot of controversy and crisis that constituted the Watergate scandal. The Supreme Court's answer to one mooted any test of the other.

On June 17, 1972, five men broke into Democratic headquarters in Washington, D.C. With the help of aggressive investigative reporting by Bob Woodward and Carl Bernstein of the *Washington Post* and the strict courtroom demeanor of the trial judge, John J. Sirica, the burglars were shown to be employees and agents of the Committee to Reelect the President. Responsibility for the break-in was ultimately traced to the highest officials of President Richard M. Nixon's campaign committee, including his former attorney general, John N. Mitchell.

At the burglars' trial in early 1973, following the November elections that gave President Nixon a landslide, they recanted their guilty pleas, asserting that they had been coerced into keeping quiet and even into committing perjury. A Senate investigating committee, headed by Senator Sam J. Ervin, was quickly formed. The nation sat astonished into the summer of 1973 as the daily televised hearings and the rapidly multiplying stories in the nation's newspapers produced mounting evidence of a White House campaign that included other unlawful break-ins, misuse of campaign funds, political spying, campaign law violations, and more. In the summer of 1973, it was revealed that the White House had secretly tape-recorded many of the president's conversations; but when a special prosecutor subpoenaed the tapes, the president resisted. The special prosecutor pressed the issue in court.

Simultaneously with the court case over the tapes, the Judiciary Committee of the HOUSE OF REPRESENTATIVES initiated impeachment proceedings. Both reached a climax in July 1974. The Supreme Court, hearing the case on an expedited basis, ruled 8–0 in *United States v.*

Nixon (Justice William H. Rehnquist having recused himself) that although under most circumstances the president has an EXECUTIVE PRIVILEGE to keep his documents confidential, the right of the trial court to the requested tapes was even more important because the president could point to no specific danger that might result and both prosecution and defense could show a particular need for them. That same month, the House Judiciary Committee reported to the full House three articles of impeachment, against a nine-month–long debate over whether the House could constitutionally impeach only for actual crimes or for political corruption, overreaching, and breach of trust. The House Committee voted to impeach on three counts: obstruction of justice, violation of citizens' constitutional rights, and refusal to hand over papers to the committee.

The Court's opinion left no room to maneuver. President Nixon capitulated and it soon became clear that he had indeed been engaged in a cover-up. Within three weeks of the Court decision, Nixon resigned, the first president ever to do so. The resignation mooted the impeachment proceedings; the full House never did vote on them.

Watergate also prompted the first use of the TWENTY-FIFTH AMENDMENT for presidential and vice presidential succession. In October 1973, Vice President Spiro T. Agnew resigned in a bribery scandal, allowing President Nixon to name Representative Gerald R. Ford the first person ever to be appointed vice president of the United States. Ford became president upon Nixon's resignation, the only person ever to serve both as vice president and president without having been elected to either office. President Ford raised a further constitutional controversy when, a month after taking office, he pardoned President Nixon of all crimes he may have committed.

See also: IMMUNITY FROM PROSECUTION; IMPEACHMENT OF GOVERNMENT OFFICIALS.

waterways, *see:* **bridges and waterways**

wealth classification and discrimination
There is no general constitutional rule against "wealth discrimination"—laws or regulations affecting rich and poor differently. Poverty is not an inborn characteristic; neither the EQUAL PROTECTION CLAUSE nor any other constitutional provision requires the government to waive all costs of programs or benefits or to provide funds so that the poor can obtain goods or services that would otherwise be beyond their means. In large part, the Court's reluctance to construct a rule of equality of rich and poor is due to the relativeness of the terms. To say that the government may not condition benefits on the race of the recipient is one thing. The rule is easy to state and to administer. The difference between rich and poor, however, is not absolute but relative. By what standard could the courts determine when a person is so poor that he or she is constitutionally entitled to a benefit the rest of us must pay for?

The Court on some occasions, however, has announced a rule against wealth discrimination when fundamental rights would be conditioned on making payments beyond a person's means. Thus the Court declared POLL TAXES unconstitutional on the ground that some people too poor to pay would be denied the franchise,[867] and it has struck down state laws that required indigent candidates to pay filing fees they could not afford.[272, 1202]

The Court has also created a partial constitutional right of ACCESS TO COURTS and legal process. It has struck down rules requiring defendants to supply costly transcripts when appealing their criminal convictions, holding that the state must pay the cost;[815, 1738] declared on SIXTH AMENDMENT grounds, in the well-known case *Gideon v. Wainwright,* that states must appoint counsel to criminal defendants who cannot afford to hire their own lawyers; held that indigent defendants are entitled to free counsel whenever the states guarantee a right to appeal a conviction;[569] and voided, on DUE PROCESS grounds, a Connecticut court rule that barred people from seeking divorces unless they could pay filing fees.[191] The Court also ordered the state to pay the cost of a blood test for a defendant in a noncriminal paternity suit[1172] and to provide a psychiatrist to an indigent defendant to help prepare an insanity defense.[24]

This right of access to courts does not hold for every charge the state cares to make, nor does it open every court to indigent parties. The Court has declined to require that costs be waived in appeals not legally required (in many states the APPELLATE COURT has discretion whether or not to hear an appeal).[1762] And in rejecting a claim that a fifty-dollar filing fee in bankruptcy cases is unconstitutional, the Court disavowed "an unlimited rule that an indigent at all times and in all cases has the right to relief without the payment of fees."[1098] Following the bankruptcy rather than the divorce ruling, the Court also sustained a twenty-five-dollar filing fee as a condition to an appeal when a state agency denied welfare benefits.[1542] And in a series of cases, the justices have refused to recognize a general right to the assistance of counsel in civil cases; for example, an indigent mother is not constitutionally entitled to a lawyer in a hearing to determine parental status.[1124]

In certain other limited areas, the Court has overturned laws because of their impact on the poor. In one line of cases, it has barred extra imprisonment beyond the maximum sentence for defendants who could not afford to pay monetary fines.[2212, 1998, 141] It has voided laws that require long waiting periods before indigents moving into a state can avail themselves of welfare benefits.[1850, 1312] And it rejected a Texas law that refused free public education to children of illegal aliens.[1641]

But the Court has rebuffed several major attempts to use poverty to force the government to provide benefits or satisfy important interests of the poor. For example, it has rejected a challenge to funding public education through property taxes raised by local school districts.[1791] Mexican-American parents in San Antonio, Texas, argued that this method of school funding violated equal protection because it meant that tax revenues in the poorer school districts would result in schools far inferior to those in much richer school districts. Speaking for a 5–4 majority, Justice Lewis F. Powell saw no merit in the wealth discrimination argument, because schoolchildren were not absolutely denied the right to an education (unlike defendants without transcripts, who were absolutely denied the right to an appeal) and because there was no reason to believe that the poor were clustered in only the poorer districts (many of the poor were in industrial districts with considerable school revenue from business taxes).

The Court has denied any constitutional right to the "necessities" of life, even food and shelter. For example, it sustained a Maryland program that limited the amount of welfare benefits to families.[511] And in upholding an Oregon policy that made it easy for landlords to evict tenants who failed to pay their rent, Justice Byron R. White declared for the 5–2 majority: "We do not denigrate the importance of decent, safe and sanitary housing. But the Constitution does not provide judicial remedies for every social and economic ill. We are unable to perceive in that document any constitutional guarantee of access to dwellings of a particular quality or any recognition of the right of a tenant to occupy the real property of his landlord beyond the term of his lease, without the payment of [rent]."[1168]

See also: COUNSEL, ASSISTANCE OF; COURTS, ACCESS TO; DURATIONAL RESIDENCY REQUIREMENTS; EQUAL PROTECTION OF THE LAWS; WELFARE BENEFITS, RIGHT TO.

weapons, *see:* **arms, right to keep and bear**

weights and measures Congress has the power under Art. I-§8[5] to "fix the standard of weights and measures." If it chose, Congress could enact a bill converting the nation to the metric system of centimeters and grams (or some other system) from the traditional English measures of inches and pounds.

welfare benefits, right to Welfare benefits are legislative choices, not constitutional commands. No provision in the Constitution requires the states or the federal government to extend any form of financial or other assistance to people too poor to afford necessities of life such as food, shelter, or medical care. Despite some hints that it might strike down as a violation of EQUAL PROTECTION laws that reduced or eliminated necessities,[1850] the Court in 1970 rejected the notion outright.[511] A Maryland program provided poor families with financial grants based on need but imposed a ceiling of $250 per month, regardless of family size or actual need. The ceiling was attacked as a violation of equal protection, because it invidiously discriminated against children in large, impoverished families who could not fend for themselves. Speaking for the 6–3 majority, Justice Potter Stewart said that the ceiling was reasonably aimed at encouraging employment and that a law is not unconstitutional "merely because the classifications made by its laws are imperfect. . . . The Constitution does not empower this Court to second-guess state officials charged with the difficult responsibility of allocating limited public welfare funds among the myriad of potential recipients."

Moreover, the government is free to choose among the types of benefits to be dispensed. For example, a state may decide to pay the expenses associated with childbirth or necessary operations, but refuse to fund abortions, whether nontherapeutic[1226] or medically necessary.[869] The government may also decide to distribute benefits to certain groups of needy people and exclude others. For example, more financial assistance may be provided to families with aged or infirm members than to families with children;[1009] survivors' benefits may be confined to widows and divorced wives and denied to the unmarried mothers of the children of deceased workers;[312] Social Security payments may be reduced if the recipient is receiving workers' compensation but need not be if private insurance is being paid.[1722]

Nevertheless, the Court has discerned in the Constitution certain limitations on the government's power to pick and choose among broad classes of welfare recipients. For example, it violates equal protection for states to deny welfare benefits to resident aliens,[791] and, in many cases, to determine eligibility for survivors' and other benefits by sex—reducing or refusing payments to husbands and fathers, for instance, but making them available to wives and mothers.[2178, 313, 2181] It violates the constitutional right to TRAVEL for states to refuse welfare payments to those citizens who have not yet lived in the state for at least one year.[1850]

Once having been provided, welfare benefits for a particular recipient may not be arbitrarily terminated. In a significant 1970 case, *Goldberg v. Kelly,* the Court held 6–3 that before a state may terminate welfare benefits, it must first prove at an evidentiary hearing that the recipient is ineligible. Said Justice William Brennan: "[T]ermination of aid pending resolution of the controversy over eligibility may deprive an *eligible* recipient of the very means by which to live while he waits."

See also: GOVERNMENT, AFFIRMATIVE OBLIGATIONS OF; SEX DISCRIMINATION; WEALTH DISCRIMINATION AND CLASSIFICATION.

well regulated militia, *see:* **militia**

wiretapping, *see:* **search and seizure: wiretapping and electronic surveillance**

witness, right to confront, *see:* **confrontation with witnesses**

witness immunity, *see:* **immunity from prosecution**

women's rights, *see:* **Brandeis brief; sex discrimination**

women's suffrage, *see:* **voting, right to**

workers' compensation   Workers' compensation is a no-fault insurance system through which employees receive payments to recover for job-related losses due to accident or illness. Now adopted in every state, workers' compensation programs developed in the early twentieth century to overcome serious deficiencies in the COMMON LAW negligence suit. At the close of the nineteenth century, workers could not recover in suits against their employers if the workers contributed to the accident themselves, if the accident was caused by the negligence of another employee, if the employees "assumed the risk" (for example, by working in a factory known to be dangerous), or if the employer was not at fault. Workers' compensation eliminated all these defenses but confined the worker's recovery to a specified schedule of benefits that was considerably lower than what a successful litigant might have recovered in a negligence action.

In a series of cases beginning in 1917, the Court upheld workers' compensation plans against claims that both employer and employee were being deprived of PROPERTY without DUE PROCESS of law.[1463, 1394, 72] Much more recently, the Court upheld a federal law imposing similar liability on coal mine operators for the disabilities of workers from black lung disease who had retired before the law was enacted.[2113] If a worker dies without survivors, the state may require the employer to pay the benefit to a special fund to rehabilitate disabled workers.[1852] The measure of compensation need not be limited to loss of wages; mandatory awards for such injuries as disfigurement are constitutional.[1462]

writ of assistance, *see:* **assistance, writ of**

writ of certiorari, *see:* **certiorari, writ of**

writ of error, *see:* **error, writ of**

writ of habeas corpus, *see:* **habeas corpus**

writ of mandamus, *see:* **mandamus, writ of**

writ of prohibition, *see:* **prohibition, writ of**

writings and discoveries   "Writings" and "discoveries" are the constitutional terms for the works of authors and inventors that Congress is empowered to protect under the Copyright and Patent Clause in Art. I-§8[8]. "Writings" embraces far more than novels or poems; it includes almost any form of creative expression, including painting, photography, screenplays, dramas, choreography, musical compositions, and sculpture. "Writings" does not, however, include an idea itself, and to be copyrightable a writing must have some degree of originality. In 1991, the Court denied copyright protection to a Kansas telephone company's "white pages," holding that a publisher of a competing telephone directory could reproduce the names, towns, and telephone numbers of the telephone company's subscribers because these were uncopyrightable facts and were not organized in any original way.[654] Similarly, "discoveries" means more—and less—than the ordinary connotation of the word. To be patentable, a discovery or invention must be embodied in some tangible form;[1771] for example, the recognition of a new physical law may not be patented.[712] An invention must be useful and "nonobvious," not a mere "gadget" that any "mechanic skilled in the art" could have created.[1873] But within this rather loose standard, Congress has broad power to determine what kinds of inventions are patentable. The Patent Act says that "any new and useful process, machine, manufacture, or composition of matter, or any new and useful improvement thereof" may be patented. Under this definition, the following kinds of things are patentable: a process for making products, such as steel; an apparatus to achieve a particular end, such as a motor and printing press; a particular product, such as a television, automobile, and telephone; and any useful rearrangement of elements, such as a metal alloy, not found in nature. The Court has held that even living organisms—for example, a "genetically engineered" bacterium that could "eat" oil spills—may be patented.[440]

See also: COPYRIGHT CLAUSE; PATENT CLAUSE.

writings, compelled disclosure of, *see:* **self-incrimination**

X

X-rated   The term "X-rated" comes from Hollywood, not the Constitution. It was one of the ratings devised by the Motion Picture Association of America to brand a movie unsuitable for children. In its usual connotation, the X-rated film was pornographic, or at least sexually explicit. In 1991 the rating system was changed; the equivalent today is NC-17. Film makers may voluntarily agree to submit to ratings, but it seems clear that the FIRST AMENDMENT would bar government at any level from requiring books or films to carry a "Surgeon General's warning" about their contents, although the Supreme Court did uphold a federal law requiring certain films produced by foreign governments to be labeled "political propaganda."[1310]

See also: BLACKLISTING; OBSCENITY AND PORNOGRAPHY.

Y

yarmulkes, *see:* **dress codes**

Yazoo land scandal   In 1795 the Georgia legislature sold to four land companies thirty-five million acres along the Yazoo River, comprising most of what today is Alabama and Mississippi, for two and one-half cents an acre. One of the land companies then resold much of the land to the New England Mississippi Company, which in turn parceled out the land to individual northern speculators. Within a year it became widely known that most of the Georgia legislators either had been bribed by the land companies or had been their partners. Georgia voters turned out most of these legislators in 1796, and their successors repealed the land grant law. Georgia then claimed that all Yazoo lands had reverted to the state with the repeal of the grant. Eventually the question reached the Supreme Court. In 1810, in *Fletcher v. Peck,* Chief Justice John Marshall held that the grant of land was a contract and that the state's attempt to rescind the deal violated the CONTRACT CLAUSE. This was the first time the Supreme Court held a state law unconstitutional. The motive of the legislators in voting for the land grants was not a reviewable issue, Marshall said. Good faith purchasers, those not party to the fraud, were entitled to keep their land. Marshall did not comment on how anyone could have been a good faith purchaser, since the extent of the corruption was widely known, and certainly by anyone sophisticated enough to have been investing in the Yazoo tracts.

yeas and nays   Yeas and nays are votes by members of Congress on pending bills or resolutions. In two places, Article I specifies that members' votes must be recorded. Art. I-§5[3] says that if one-fifth of the members demand it, the vote on a particular question before that house must be recorded in the JOURNAL OF PROCEEDINGS, today called the *Congressional Record.* Art. I-§7[2] says that whenever either house is voting to override a presidential VETO, the names of all members voting and how they each voted must be recorded.

yellow-dog contracts   A yellow-dog contract obligates workers, as a condition of employment, to resign from or pledge not to join a union. The term comes from an adage that the worker who signs one would have no more security than a yellow dog of unknown parentage. In the 1890s several states outlawed yellow-dog contracts, as did Congress in 1898, when it forbade their use by interstate railroads. In 1908 the Supreme Court struck down the federal law as a violation of "liberty of contract," in those days held to be protected by the Due Process Clause of the Fifth Amendment.[6] The Court also said that Congress could not regulate employment contracts since an employee's membership in organizations was not a part of interstate commerce. In 1915 the Court voided state laws against yellow-dog contracts, again on due process grounds, this time under the Fourteenth Amendment.[467]

However, by the 1930s, the Court began to backtrack. In finding in 1930 that union membership and interstate commerce are substantially connected in the railroad industry, it sustained the federal Railway Labor Act of 1926.[2017] In 1932 Congress enacted the Norris-LaGuardia Act, prohibiting federal courts from enforcing any yellow-dog contract. The Court readily upheld the provision under Congress's power to limit the jurisdiction of the lower federal courts.[1129] Finally, in the National Labor Relations Act of 1935, Congress directly outlawed yellow-dog contracts, and the Court sustained the prohibition in 1937.[1037] Today yellow-dog contracts are unlawful throughout the United States.

See also: LABOR AND LABOR LAWS; LABOR UNIONS.

Younger abstention doctrine, *see:* **abstention doctrine**

Z

Zenger, trial of John Peter Zenger was the protagonist of the most famous American libel trial, more than 250 years ago. Zenger was printer of the New York *Weekly Journal,* first published in 1733. A German immigrant with little English, he was the front for a number of New York lawyers bent on attacking the corrupt administration of William Cosby, the colonial governor. Articles in the *Weekly Journal* were anonymous; only Zenger's name appeared on the masthead. After a year of merciless criticism, Cosby ordered Zenger arrested on November 17, 1734, on four counts of SEDITIOUS LIBEL. For nine months, Zenger was imprisoned on the third floor of the colonial city hall. Cosby hoped that the lengthy confinement would prompt Zenger to identify the editorialists, grand juries having twice refused to indict James Alexander, the real editor and Cosby's leading opponent. But Zenger established a journalistic tradition by keeping his mouth shut, risking a death sentence if convicted. Equally remarkable was Zenger's wife, Anna Catherine Maulin, a native of Holland, who risked her own neck to keep the paper going during her husband's imprisonment. Finally, on August 4, 1734, Zenger was brought to trial before James DeLancey, a Cosby stooge who forbade Alexander to represent Zenger. So Alexander brought in the distinguished Philadelphia lawyer Andrew Hamilton.

Under the law then prevailing, a libel jury's only function was to determine whether the defendant actually uttered or wrote the words of which he stood accused. Whether they were in fact libelous was a question for the judge to decide. Hamilton stunned the court by admitting that Zenger had printed the offending issues, but argued, contrary to the law of the day, that truth was a defense to a charge of libel. Appealing to the jury, Hamilton said: "The question before the Court and you gentlemen of the jury is not of small nor private concern, it is not the cause of a poor printer, nor of New York alone, which you are now trying: No! It may in its consequence affect every freeman that lives under a British government on the main of America. It is the best cause. It is the cause of liberty; and I make no doubt but your upright conduct this day will . . . have laid a noble foundation for securing to ourselves, our posterity, and our neighbors that to which nature and the laws of our country have given us a right—the liberty—both of exposing and opposing arbitrary power (in these parts of the world, at least) by speaking and writing truth."

DeLancey, the judge, told the jury it had nothing left to decide and directed the twelve men to retire and return with a verdict of guilty. To general astonishment, the jury returned minutes later with the verdict "not guilty." Hamilton, for whom the phrase "Philadelphia lawyer" was coined, returned home with gun salutes from ships in the harbor. James Alexander published an account of the trial that circulated widely in England and America. Zenger's acquittal killed prosecutions for common law seditious libel, and was an important part of the intellectual background of the FIRST AMENDMENT. It also helped establish the principle in American law that truth is a defense to any libel action, although that principle was codified only in 1798 in the Sedition Act.

See also: ALIEN AND SEDITION ACTS; FREEDOM OF SPEECH.

zoning Zoning is the regulation of land use to further a community's safety, health, and well-being. Under zoning plans, municipalities and other governmental bodies determine where residences and businesses may be located, the height and density of buildings, the number of people who may live at one location, the types of business that may be carried on in particular places, and even the aesthetic appearance of land and buildings. Comprehensive zoning codes first began to appear at the end of the nineteenth century, although some well-known zoning laws had been enacted much earlier. In 1869, for example, Louisiana enacted a law granting a monopoly of the slaughtering trade to a state-chartered corporation, the Crescent City Live-Stock Landing and Slaughter-House Company. The law forced New Orleans butchers to conduct their business at the Crescent City facilities. The Supreme Court brushed off assertions that the law unconstitutionally deprived butchers of their PROPERTY, holding that regulating the place of slaughtering animals was among the most frequent exercises of the states' POLICE POWER.[1882]

The Supreme Court first directly upheld a comprehensive municipal zoning code in a 1926 case, *Village of Euclid v. Ambler Realty,* which concerned a suburb of Cleveland that had enacted a comprehensive plan creating zones within which property could be used only in certain ways. One zone was purely for residences; no businesses, retail stores, or even apartment houses were permitted. The owner of a tract of land asserted that it would have been worth ten thousand dollars had he been able to sell it for commercial uses, but since it was located in the residential zone, it was now worth only five thousand dollars. Arguing that the potential loss amounted to a deprivation of DUE PROCESS, he sought to enjoin the town from enforcing its zoning scheme.

The Supreme Court sustained the zoning plan against this blunderbuss attack, saying that zoning plans in general are within the states' police power. But the Court said that constitutionality of zoning in the abstract did not mean that any particular plan might be constitutional when actually put into operation. Indeed, two years later the Court struck down an attempt by Cambridge, Massachusetts, to block a parcel of land from being used for industrial purposes because a tiny piece of it fell within the residential zone. A SPECIAL MASTER appointed by the local courts had concluded that enforcing the zoning regulation would make the property worthless and that exempting the tract from the regulation would not harm the city's interests. To insist on enforcing the restriction without regard to the actual public safety, health, or welfare violates the FOURTEENTH AMENDMENT.[1442]

Modern zoning regulations raise three distinct types of problems: first, they may constitute an unconstitutional TAKING OF PROPERTY; second, they may abridge FREEDOM OF SPEECH by prohibiting the display of messages on signs; and third, they may violate the EQUAL PROTECTION CLAUSE by excluding certain kinds of people, usually the poor, from choice locations.

The Court has so far turned away claims of confiscation unless the regulation has denied owners complete use of their property. In the Grand Central Terminal case in 1978, for instance, the Court upheld New York City's Landmarks Preservation Law, under which a city commission denied Grand Central's owners permission to build an office tower because the new construction would be unaesthetic.[1585]

Zoning regulations aimed at unsightly billboards and the like have occasionally run afoul of the FIRST AMENDMENT. In a 1981 case, a San Diego ordinance banned all billboards except for signs advertising products sold on the premises, government signs, signs advertising homes for sale or lease, shopping mall signs, and temporary political campaign signs. The city sought "to eliminate hazards to pedestrians and motorists brought about by distracting sign displays" and "to preserve and improve the appearance of the city." The Court refrained from deciding whether an absolute ban would have been upheld; Justice Byron R. White focused, instead, on the city's discrimination among types of speech, holding that regulations dealing with the content of messages abridge free speech.[1320] In a 1984 case, the city of Los Angeles removed from utility poles a number of posters advertising a candidate for the city council. The city acted under an ordinance against posting signs on public property. Because the ordinance was content-neutral, aimed at eliminating "the visual assault on the citizens of Los Angeles presented by an accumulation of signs posted on public property," the Court upheld the ban.[401]

Because zoning ordinances frequently regulate the density of populations in residential areas, they sometimes conflict with constitutional values favoring family relations and the equal right of all to live within a town. To ease traffic and other congestion, a small village on Long Island, New York, consisting of two hundred families, prohibited groups of more than two unrelated persons from living together. The Court found no constitutional impediment to the ordinance, in part because the town did not try to prevent friends from visiting, only from staying with each other.[148] On the other hand, the Court, 5–4, struck down an ordinance of East Cleveland, Ohio, that narrowly zoned its residential area so that only closely related family members could live in the same house. A grandmother was convicted of violating the ordinance because she lived with her son and two grandsons who happened to be cousins. If the grandsons had been brothers, the ordinance would not have been violated. Justice Lewis F. Powell said that the zoning regulation violated SUBSTANTIVE DUE PROCESS: "The tradition of uncles, aunts, cousins, and especially grandparents sharing a household along with parents and children has [venerable] roots... deserving of constitutional recognition."[1379]

Although the Court seems to have limited this associational right to families, it has occasionally overturned zoning regulations that are not evenhanded. Under a Texas municipal zoning ordinance, operators of group homes for the mentally retarded must obtain building permits. The town denied a permit to a prospective operator, citing several concerns, including the safety of the residents and the fears of neighbors. But, said Justice Byron R. White, the town's denial was basically irrational, because similar types of uses, including hospitals, sanitariums, and nursing homes for convalescents and the aged, did not need a special permit.[407]

See also: JUST COMPENSATION.

The Supreme Court's 1991–92 Term

As the Supreme Court began its 1991–92 term, the drama of Anita Hill's accusations of sexual harrassment against Clarence Thomas, President Bush's nominee to replace the retired Justice Thurgood Marshall, largely eclipsed discussion about what the conservative jurist's impact on constitutional doctrine might be. On October 15, the Senate voted 52–48 to confirm, and Thomas promptly took his seat as the 105th justice in the nation's history. Since many of the cases the Court decided early in the term had been argued before Thomas joined the Court, his votes did not begin to appear until late in the winter when, for the most part, he voted with the most conservative bloc, often joining Justice Antonin Scalia in dissent.

At the same time, a new and wholly unforeseen voting bloc emerged—a moderate conservative group consisting of Justices Sandra Day O'Connor, Anthony M. Kennedy, and David Souter, who provided, most tellingly, the votes to sustain the essential core of Roe v. Wade.

The cases discussed in this section are exclusively those decided during the 1991–92 term of court—between October 1991 and June 29, 1992. For background on any of the topics in this section, see the corresponding topic in the main entries of this book.

abortion   To the surprise of many, although by the slimmest majority, the Supreme Court explicitly reaffirmed the "essential HOLDING" of Roe v. Wade in a case decided on June 29, the last day of the term.[38] An unusual PLURALITY OPINION jointly signed by Justices Sandra Day O'Connor, Anthony M. Kennedy, and David Souter restated the three parts of Roe that retain vitality: (1) before viability, a woman may choose to have an abortion "without undue interference from the state"; (2) the state may restrict abortions after viability, assuming that the law grants exceptions to preserve the mother's life and health; and (3) the state has "legitimate interests from the outset of the pregnancy in protecting the health of the woman and the life of the fetus." But the plurality swept away Roe's "trimester framework," in which the state's power to restrict abortion increased during each succeeding three-month period, and substituted an "undue burden" test by which a law will be struck down if its purpose is to place "a substantial obstacle in the path of a woman's choice." In the Pennsylvania law at issue, the majority upheld provisions requiring that the woman certify in writing that she has been warned of the risks both of abortion and childbirth, told the age of the fetus, and notified about the availability of printed material describing alternatives to abortions. Except for emergencies, no abortion may be performed less than twenty-four hours before she receives this "informed consent."

The Court reaffirmed previous cases in upholding a parental consent rule for girls under the age of eighteen with a "judicial bypass" procedure. It also upheld a requirement that abortion facilities maintain certain medical records and report certain information, including the names of referring physicians. But the Court struck down the requirement that no abortion could be performed unless the woman submitted a signed statement that she had notified her spouse. That provision posed an undue burden, the majority said, because "[f]or the great many women who are victims of abuse inflicted by their husbands, . . . a spousal notice requirement enables the husband to wield an effective veto over his wife's decision."

Four dissenters—Chief Justice William H. Rehnquist and Justices Byron R. White, Antonin Scalia, and Clarence Thomas—said that *Roe* was wrongly decided and should be overruled outright. Concurring with the majority, Justice Harry A. Blackmun, the author of *Roe*, noted that "just when so many expected the darkness to fall, the flame has grown bright" and praised the joint plurality opinion as "an act of personal courage and constitutional privilege." He plaintively concluded his concurrence by stating that the distance between the majority and the dissent "is but a single vote," and added: "I am 83 years old. I cannot remain on this Court forever."

See also: STARE DECISIS.

abstention   Under their DIVERSITY JURISDICTION, federal courts may hear claims based on state law when the parties are citizens of different states. Cases involving domestic relations have been a customary exception to this federal exercise of power to decide state ques-

tions. Spouses may not obtain DIVORCES or resolve ALIMONY or custody issues in federal courts. In a significant ruling that may open up the federal courts to many more such suits, the Supreme Court held that the federal courts need not abstain from hearing money DAMAGE suits involving family members. The mother of two daughters sued their father, her ex-husband, and his female companion for injuring the children. The Court allowed the suit, holding that the abstention doctrine of *Younger v. Harris* does not apply, since the federal court is not being called on to determine matters of marital or parental status, which must remain issues exclusively for state courts.[3]

access to ballot   Under an Illinois law, citizens wishing to organize a new political party were required to gather twenty-five thousand signatures from supporters for candidates for statewide office or from any large "political subdivision." But if the political subdivision contains separate districts, then supporters were required to collect twenty-five thousand signatures in each district. Candidates in the suburban part of Cook County, which includes the city of Chicago, wished to run on the Harold Washington Party (HWP) ticket, an established party in the city but not in the county as a whole. Partisans collected forty-four thousand signatures from Chicagoans for county board seats but fewer than eight thousand from suburbanites. The state supreme court disqualified the entire HWP slate because of insufficient signatures. It also construed a provision of the state election law to bar any candidate from running on the ballot under the name of an established political party, even if the party consented. The Court reversed, 7–1, holding that the state law unconstitutionally burdened the right to run for office because the signature requirement made it harder to establish a political party in a district than in any statewide race.[37] Moreover, statewide parties do not need to gather a minimum number of petitions from each district. Finally, while a state may prohibit the use of a party name by an unaffiliated group, it has no constitutional business denying a party label to those running with the party's blessings.

airport terminal, *see:* **public forum**

apportionment of political districts The 1990 census showed significant population changes requiring reapportionment of congressional districts among the states. Big winners included California, Florida, and Texas. One loser was Montana. Under the federal law governing apportionment of seats in the House of Representatives, Montana lost one of its two seats. The average population size of a congressional district is 572,466. With one district, Montana's population of 803,655 is 231,189 persons greater than the ideal district. With two districts, each would be smaller than the average by 170,638 persons. Montana claimed that the method of "equal proportions" prescribed by a federal law enacted in 1941 is unconstitutional.

Unlike previous apportionment cases involving how the states had determined the size of their own districts, this case turned on whether the basic federal law is constitutional. The Supreme Court held that it is.[49] Surveying in some detail the various mathematical methods by which districts may be allocated, the Court concluded that Congress has greater leeway than the states in determining a general rule for allocating seats, because the constitutional provision requiring that each state have at least one federal representative means that it would be illusory to require Congress to arrive at a "precise mathematical equality" for each district throughout the nation. There was no showing that Congress acted in bad faith in choosing one of several appropriate mathematical methods; independent scholars have sup-

ported it, and the Court refused to set it aside.

The Court also unanimously upheld the Census Bureau's decision to include overseas federal employees in their home states' count of citizens for purposes of allocating congressional seats.[20] The bureau's decision to allocate military personnel serving overseas to their "home of record" shifted a House seat from Massachusetts to Washington State. Massachusetts sued, asserting that established precedent requires voters to be allocated to their place of "usual residence," which, in the case of overseas personnel, should have been their foreign stations. The Court unanimously disagreed, holding that terms such as "usual residence," "inhabitant," and "usual place of abode" refer to the place of a person's *permanent* residence or domicile. Deciding to count those temporarily overseas as maintaining ties to the states from which they departed does not hinder but promotes the goal of equality of representation.

balancing In upholding several provisions of the Pennsylvania ABORTION law, the Court brought into sharper focus a balancing principle it has employed during the past several years to determine whether certain state regulations are constitutional that arguably interfere with a woman's right to an abortion. It phrased the test as one of "undue burden," and upheld all but one of the state requirements. The majority struck down a spousal notification procedure because it would effectively permit husbands to veto the procedure outright. But it saw no undue burden in other provisions, such as medical reporting and informed consent requirements, despite the greater burden that would be placed on many women and physicians by the costs, delays, and publicity that might ensue.

census, *see:* **apportionment of political districts**

cigarette advertising, *see:* **preemption**

civil commitment   Louisiana permits criminal defendants acquitted by reason of insanity to be committed to psychiatric hospitals. The law said that if it was later determined a patient so committed was no longer mentally ill, he could not be released unless he could prove he was dangerous neither to himself nor others. A state court refused to release one such patient because he had an "antisocial personality," had been in fights in the hospital, and a doctor testified that he would not "feel comfortable in certifying that [the patient] would not be a danger."

The Supreme Court, 5–4, reversed, holding that a person who is not mentally ill may not be held against his will, whatever his personality.[18] Since the patient was not convicted, the state may not punish him. Since he is not mentally ill, the state may not hold him. Although in limited circumstances the state may place a dangerous suspect in PREVENTIVE DETENTION, that rule does not save the Louisiana procedure, because Louisiana puts the burden on the defendant to prove he is not dangerous, rather than requiring the state to prove dangerousness by clear and convincing evidence. If the patient has committed criminal acts while in the hospital, it may prosecute him. Otherwise, it must release him. This decision does not negate the power of the states to commit defendants initially to mental hospitals immediately upon their acquittal by reason of insanity.

civil rights legislation, *see:* **implied right of action**

coercion, *see:* **prayer and Bible reading**

confrontation   At the trial of a defendant accused of sexual assault on a four-year-old girl, the state introduced HEARSAY evidence: the girl's mother and babysitter, a state investiga-

tor, and an emergency room nurse and doctor were all permitted to testify to what the girl had told them happened. The trial judge permitted the jury to hear such statements as "medical examination" exceptions to the hearsay rule, meaning that what a person says in the course of receiving medical care is trustworthy enough to be used in court even though the witness is not there personally to be cross-examined. The defendant asserted that under the SIXTH AMENDMENT right to confront witnesses against him, such evidence could be introduced only if the state produced the girl at trial or could show that she was unavailable.

The Court rejected the argument, holding that medical examination statements carry substantial independent weight unlikely to be duplicated by having the witness testify later in court.[51] At the same time, though, the Court majority rejected the assertion of the United States, arguing as AMICUS CURIAE that the Confrontation Clause applies only in those rare instances in which the hearsay was specifically made with the purpose of accusing the defendant. Chief Justice William H. Rehnquist said that not all hearsay is reliable and the Confrontation Clause applies to people whose testimony is adverse to defendants, not merely to those who specifically accuse the defendant.

constitutional torts, *see:* **exhaustion of remedies**

death penalty   A Florida judge accepted the recommendation of a state jury to condemn a convicted killer to death. The jury had been instructed that it could consider as an aggravating factor that "the crime . . . was especially wicked, evil, atrocious or cruel, and . . . was committed in a cold, calculated and premeditated manner." The jurors found that all these factors were present and that there were no mitigating factors in the killing. On appeal the Florida Supreme Court held that the first set of factors, relating to the heinousness of the crime, was not vague but that there was insufficient evidence to support the contention that the crime was committed in a cold manner. However, the state court held that the *jury's* error on this issue was harmless and affirmed the death penalty.

The Supreme Court reversed on the ground that the Florida procedure violated the EIGHTH AMENDMENT because though it permitted the trial *judge* to weigh the "coldness" of the criminal conduct, it did not require the higher courts to consider directly whether the judge's error in doing so was harmless. The Court remanded the case with instructions that the Florida courts decide whether the trial judge, beyond a REASONABLE DOUBT, would have imposed the sentence even without considering the coldness of the crime.[46]

The Court also held that in capital cases, the trial judge at VOIR DIRE may not refuse to ask potential jurors whether they would automatically vote to impose the death penalty, regardless of whatever facts developed during trial. Without knowing their answers, the defendant would not have the opportunity to object to their presence and thus to obtain a fair and impartial jury.[35] A judge's general question whether each juror would be "fair and impartial" is insufficient to determine their views on whether the death penalty should always be imposed if the defendant is convicted of murder.

When a prisoner seeks to have his death sentence overturned by filing successive HABEAS CORPUS petitions, he cannot succeed merely by showing that certain mitigating circumstances about his character were withheld from the sentencing jury. Psychological evidence does not relate to guilt or innocence, and only the offer of overlooked evidence relating to "actual innocence" is sufficient to entitle a federal court to hear a successive appeal. To succeed in such an appeal, the defendant must show that but for a constitutional error, such as exclusion of clear and convincing evidence that the defendant was innocent (for example, by showing that someone else later confessed to the crime), no reasonable juror would have imposed the death penalty.[44]

See also: FREEDOM OF ASSOCIATION; RETROACTIVITY.

demonstrators and demonstrations, *see:* **permit system**

diversity jurisdiction, *see:* abstention

Dormant Commerce Clause   Wyoming charged that Oklahoma violated the Dormant Commerce Clause through a law requiring that at least ten percent of the coal used in electrical generating plants in Oklahoma be mined in the state. The Court, 6–3, agreed that the law discriminates against Wyoming-mined coal.[55] Oklahoma had justified the law in part as an effort to keep in the state some of the money spent on coal. It also asserted, among other claims, that Wyoming had no standing to contest the law. The Court rejected this claim, agreeing that Wyoming had suffered an actual injury because the law had, in its effect, reduced the amount of tax revenue on local mining that Wyoming actually collected. The Court struck down the Oklahoma law, holding that it was nothing more "than protectionist and discriminatory, for the Act purports to exclude coal mined in other States based solely on its origin." Even though the amount of coal bought from Oklahoma mines was less than ten percent of the total, such a requirement does not avoid an unconstitutional discrimination merely because its extent is small.

The Court struck down an Alabama law imposing a special fee on hazardous wastes brought into the state for disposal. The fee did not apply to wastes deposited in hazardous waste facilities if they were generated within the state. Said an 8–1 majority: "No state may attempt to isolate itself from a problem common to the several states by raising barriers to the free flow of interstate trade."[9] Alabama sought to justify the fee by pointing to several local interests that could not be adequately served by nondiscriminatory alternatives, including conservation of natural resources and reducing the overall flow of wastes traveling on the state highways. But the state failed to explain why all these interests would not be served equally by imposing a fee on in-state wastes. Since there were ample nondiscriminatory means of serving the state's interest in the environment and health of its citizens, the special fee could not stand.

For similar reasons, the Court rejected a Michigan law that made it more difficult to dispose of wastes in any county if they were not generated there. Michigan argued that the law did not discriminate against interstate commerce, since it burdened the disposal of wastes generated within as well as outside the state. A 7–2 majority disagreed. A state may not engage in protectionist activity "by curtailing the movement of articles of commerce through subdivisions of the state, rather than through the state itself."[17]

double jeopardy   Federal narcotics agents raided and shut down a plant in Oklahoma used to manufacture unlawful drugs. The operator of the plant then ordered chemicals and equipment to begin a new operation in Missouri, but he was arrested before he could begin. He was tried and convicted in Missouri for attempted manufacture of an illegal drug. The conviction was based in part on his receipt of supplies in Missouri. Thereafter he was tried and convicted in Oklahoma for operating the manufacturing plant there. A federal appeals court reversed the Oklahoma conviction on the ground that it constituted double jeopardy. The Supreme Court disagreed and ordered the conviction reinstated. Although at the Missouri

trial proof was offered that the defendant had been operating illegally in Oklahoma, this was not a prosecution for that crime. There were two separate crimes, and each state was constitutionally entitled to try the defendant for the crimes against its own laws.[14]

entrapment   The federal Child Protection Act of 1984 prohibits the mailing or receipt in the mails of pictures of children engaged in sexual activities. Three months before the law was passed, a fifty-six-year-old Nebraska farmer ordered two magazines from a California adult bookstore. These contained pictures of nude teenage and preteenage boys, though not engaged in sexual activities. The receipt of these magazines did not then violate any law. Acting under the new law, federal postal inspectors checked into various adult mailing lists and found the farmer's name on one. For the next two and a half years, two federal agencies organized a sting operation and "through five fictitious organizations and a bogus pen pal" sought to induce the farmer to break the law by ordering further sexually explicit photographs of children. After dozens of mailings, one of the fictitious organizations sent a letter saying that there was "much hysterical nonsense" about pornography and that it had devised a way to put pornographic material into people's hands without government snooping. The farmer sent for a catalog and then ordered two pornographic magazines because, he later said at trial, his curiosity was piqued and he "wanted to see what the material was." Federal agents went to his home and arrested him. After a search they found only the original two magazines and the new magazines that they had sent him. There was no evidence that he collected or had received other child pornography.

In a 5–4 decision, the Supreme Court held that this conduct amounted to unlawful entrapment: "Government agents may not originate a criminal design, implant in an innocent person's mind the disposition to commit a criminal act, and then induce commission of the crime so that the Government may prosecute."²⁶ Particularly in this case, the government had no evidence of a predisposition to commit a crime, since the only original evidence—a name on a mailing list—pertained to conduct that was lawful at the time. Because of the government's abuse, the Court reversed the conviction outright.

equal protection, *see:* **property tax; venue**

exhaustion of remedies   A federal prisoner sued prison officials for money DAMAGES for their failure to pay attention to his medical needs in violation of the EIGHTH AMENDMENT's prohibition of cruel and unusual punishment, a CONSTITUTIONAL TORT. The lower courts held that his claim would have to be dismissed because he had failed to exhaust his administrative remedies by pursuing the internal grievance procedure of the Federal Bureau of Prisons. The Supreme Court held that the requirement that a litigant first exhaust all avenues of administrative relief applies only when the administrators are being asked to do something for the litigant or to refrain from doing something, because if they agree the dispute is effectively at an end.³¹ But no such principle guides a suit for damages, and the pursuit of internal appeals does not aid the courts in determining whether damages should be awarded for past wrongdoing.

extradition   In a case garnering considerable headlines and some international embarrassment for the United States, the Supreme Court upheld the power of the government to prosecute a foreign citizen kidnapped by American agents and brought to the United States for participating in a plot in Mexico to murder a U.S. drug enforcement agent. The defendant

insisted that he could not be tried because he had not been properly extradited under an extradition treaty between the United States and Mexico.

The Supreme Court ruled, 6–3, that since the extradition treaty was silent about abduction, it should not be read as prohibiting it.² Moreover, the Court had said as long ago as 1886 that kidnapped defendants could be tried in the state to which they were abducted. The Mexicans were on notice of this rule, and their failure to provide in the treaty for the possibility of kidnapping would not be held against the United States. The Court majority also rejected the proposition that because international law clearly condemns kidnapping there was no need to include a prohibition against it in the extradition treaty. Even if the kidnapping does violate international law, the question of returning the defendant is a decision for the president, not the courts.

Dissenting, Justice John Paul Stevens labeled the decision "shocking" and "monstrous." He accused the majority of misreading the treaty and noted that the earlier case dealt with a kidnapping by private individuals, not the government. The majority's decision, Stevens said, was tantamount to saying that because the treaty did not expressly prohibit torture or summary execution rather than extradition, the U.S. government could use these expedients in lieu of legal process. When the United States "flagrantly violates" international law by violating the territorial integrity of another country, the courts should not be permitted to retain jurisdiction over the abductee.

federalism, *see:* **Tenth Amendment**

fighting words   The Court's HATE SPEECH decision seems also to have narrowed the fifty-year-old fighting words doctrine. The Court held that a law is unconstitutional if it distinguishes among types of fighting words to ban.[41] The state may ban all or none. In earlier decisions involving LOWER-VALUE SPEECH, the Court has upheld the regulation of some types of advertising of harmful products on the ground that if the state has the power to ban the product altogether it can take the lesser step of merely banning advertising for it. But this COMMERCIAL SPEECH doctrine does not require the state to ban advertising for every type of harmful product if it decides to ban it for one type. Moreover, a ban on advertising touting a harmful product is not unconstitutional as a viewpoint-based restriction even though the state does not prohibit advertising that condemns the product. These doctrinal differences are difficult to reconcile with the Court's 1992 fighting words decision. Whether the constitutional doctrines governing commercial speech must now be adjusted remains to be seen.

freedom of association   The Court held, 8–1, that during a criminal sentencing proceeding at which the DEATH PENALTY might be imposed, introduction of evidence that the defendant belonged to a white supremacist prison gang violated his FREEDOM OF ASSOCIATION when the membership had no relevance to the sentencing proceeding. If the prosecutors had sought to show that the gang advocated the murder of inmates, drug use, and violent escapes, evidence of membership might have been relevant, but the mere statement that the defendant belonged to a "white racist prison gang that began in the 1960's in California in response to other gangs of racial minorities" had no probative value and tended to prejudice him solely because of his membership.[12]

freedom of speech, *see:* **fighting words; hate speech; permit system; solicitation; Son of Sam law**

garbage, *see:* **Dormant Commerce Clause**

garnishment and attachment, *see:* **immunity from suit**

government, affirmative obligations of   A city has no constitutional obligation to warn its employees about known hazards in the workplace, the Court unanimously ruled, rejecting a suit by the widow of a Texas town's sanitation department employee who died of asphyxia when he entered a manhole to unplug a sewer line. The city did not violate DUE PROCESS in failing to warn or train its employees or providing proper safety equipment, even though the city may have known about the hazards. Although a deliberate desire to harm might lead to a different result, there is no basis for concluding that the government has a constitutional duty to provide employees with a safe working environment, or even minimum levels of safety and security.[11]

grand jury   An Oklahoma investor was indicted by a federal grand jury for banking fraud. A federal district court dismissed the indictment because the government withheld from the grand jury certain information in its possession, including the investor's tax returns and general ledgers, that the investor claimed would have tended to show his innocence. The Court reversed, holding that neither the Constitution nor the federal appeals courts' general supervisory power over the trial courts requires the government to provide grand juries with information beyond that which it wishes to show. The grand jury "is an institution separate from the courts, over whose functioning the courts do not preside."[52]

habeas corpus   The Court decided six cases bearing on the right of habeas corpus during the 1991–92 term, an unusually high number. The results, however, were somewhat inconclusive. The justices tongue-lashed the judges of the United States Court of Appeals for the

Ninth Circuit for delaying decision in a DEATH PENALTY prisoner's second habeas petition. After being denied relief in his first appeal, a prisoner in Washington State filed another federal appeal to have his conviction set aside. The district court turned him down, but the appeals court issued a STAY OF EXECUTION and sat on the case after argument in June 1989. In the meantime the prisoner filed a third habeas petition, and the appeals court decided to delay decision on the second petition until the third one had been heard. It was also waiting for a report, not yet written, by its own Death Penalty Task Force. The Supreme Court said that none of these considerations justified a federal appeals court in stalling the decision in a death penalty case; whenever an appeals court issues a stay of execution it must "take all steps necessary to ensure a prompt resolution of the matter."[5]

The Court also refused to consider a fourth habeas petition of a death-row prisoner in California. Although all previous appeals had been rejected, the prisoner now contended that death by lethal gas is an unconstitutional cruel and unusual punishment. Overturning the Ninth Circuit's stay of execution, the Court said that the claim could have been made more than ten years earlier and that "[t]here is no good reason for this abusive delay, which has been compounded by last-minute attempts to manipulate the judicial process."[22]

In death penalty cases, successive habeas petitions will not be allowed unless there is clear and convincing evidence of "actual innocence." It is not enough simply to suggest that an error, even a constitutional error, was committed during the trial or sentencing procedure.[44] On the other hand, the Court set aside a death penalty in a habeas appeal because the state's standards for determining aggravating factors were unconstitutionally vague.[47]

In one of the most closely watched habeas cases during the term, the defendant, a Cuban immigrant, had pleaded no contest to first-degree manslaughter in Oregon. He later asserted that because he spoke no English his plea was not knowing and intelligent, since he had not understood a crucial element of the crime to which he was pleading. The state courts and a federal district court in a first habeas appeal denied him relief, holding that his interpreters had accurately explained the law and procedures. However, the court of appeals granted him a new hearing, holding that because the defendant's first lawyer had done a bad job, the state court proceedings had been defective in uncovering what really happened. Since the lawyer had merely been negligent and had not deliberately attempted to "bypass" the question in the first round of appeals, the appeals court said the defendant was entitled to demonstrate at an evidentiary hearing whether the translations really were adequate.

On appeal the Supreme Court reversed, holding that the "deliberate bypass" rule was too loose and permitted too many collateral appeals. The Court had earlier concluded that a defendant's failure to raise a federal claim during the original state proceeding bars later consideration of it unless good cause could be shown why it was not raised and actual prejudice to the defendant resulted. The Court now took the next step and held that the lawyer's failure "to properly develop such a claim" is also an unreviewable issue in a habeas appeal unless the "cause and prejudice" standard can be met. Merely because the lawyer had not deliberately refrained from raising an issue earlier is not enough to preserve it in for argument in a later appeal.[27]

Dissenting, Justice Sandra Day O'Connor protested that the defendant had "alleged a fact [a failure to explain] that, if true, would entitle him to the relief he seeks." By the Court's decision, the lawyer's failure blocked the defendant from ever demonstrating he had been dealt with unconstitutionally. She said the

Court's decision "changed the law of habeas corpus in a fundamental way." In essence, the Court's conclusion amounts to saying that most mistakes of a defendant's lawyer will be held against the client and may not be undone, even when the defendant later obtains a better lawyer who recognizes the first lawyer's negligence in failing to deal with violations of the defendant's constitutional rights.

The final habeas case of the term was billed as an opportunity for the new conservative majority to overturn *Brown v. Allen,* the landmark 1953 case that established the authority of federal courts to consider substantive errors made by state courts. However, although all the justices agreed that the particular facts of the case warranted a refusal to grant the defendant relief, there was no majority opinion; for the moment, *Brown* stands.[53]

See also: RETROACTIVITY.

hate speech   The Court dealt a potentially lethal blow to laws aimed at hate speech in holding that St. Paul, Minnesota, could not subject an ordinary BREACH OF PEACE or TRESPASS conviction to more serious penalties if the unlawful actions were motivated by racial or other prejudice.[41] Several youths were charged under the city's Bias-Motivated Crime Ordinance for burning a cross on a black family's lawn. The law prohibits anyone from displaying a symbol that he knows or has reason to know "arouses anger, alarm or resentment in others on the basis of race, color, creed, religion or gender." The trial court dismissed the charge on the ground that the law was unconstitutionally overbroad and content-based. The Minnesota Supreme Court reversed, holding that the phrase "arouses anger, alarm or resentment in others" was limited to FIGHTING WORDS, which the Supreme Court had for half a century said were unprotected by the FIRST AMENDMENT.

In *R.A.V. v. St. Paul,* the Court unanimously reversed, although only five justices agreed with Justice Antonin Scalia's reasoning in the majority opinion. Scalia held that the hate speech ordinance is unconstitutional because it "prohibits otherwise permitted speech solely on the basis of the subjects the speech addresses." The ordinance did not ban all fighting words, Scalia explained: "Displays containing abusive invective, no matter how vicious or severe, are permissible unless they are addressed to one of the specified disfavored topics." The law prohibited fighting words aimed at race, color, creed, religion, or gender. But people wishing "to use 'fighting words' in connection with other ideas—to express hostility, for example, on the basis of political affiliation, union membership, or homosexuality—are not covered."

This discrimination was one of two fatal flaws in the ordinance. The other was a form of "viewpoint discrimination." Although "odious racial epithets" were banned to all sides of any debate, some fighting words could be used by one side and not the other. A demonstrator "could hold up a sign saying, for example, that all 'anti-Catholic bigots' are misbegotten; but not that all 'papists' are, for that would insult and provoke violence 'on the basis of religion.'" Said Scalia: "St. Paul has no such authority to license one side of a debate to fight freestyle, while requiring the other to follow Marquis of Queensbury Rules." Scalia denounced the burning of a cross in someone's front yard as "reprehensible" conduct, but concluded that St. Paul has ample means of deterring it "without adding the First Amendment to the fire."

Concurring in the judgment but not in the majority opinion, Justice Byron R. White said that the Court need not have been so quick to rule in such a way as to make bias-related acts far more difficult to punish. The Court could have simply declared the ordinance overbroad because it punished some speech protected under the First Amendment. But since fighting words are not protected under the First Amendment, St. Paul could prohibit all or only some of them. A "ban on all fighting words or on a subset of the fighting words category would restrict only the social evil of hate speech, without creating the danger of driving viewpoints from the marketplace." More, White urged, the city surely met its burden in showing that the regulation was narrowly drawn to serve a compelling state interest in preserving "the basic human rights of members of groups that have historically been subject to discrimination."

immunities, intergovernmental The Court unanimously rejected a Kansas tax on the benefits received by federal military retirees living in the state but not on comparable benefits received by retired state and local government employees.[4] A discriminatory tax is justifiable only if there is a significant difference between the classes of retirees. Kansas asserted that the benefits for its own employees were a form of deferred compensation, whereas the benefits of military retirees was really "current pay for continued readiness to return to duty." The Court showed that the state's argument was flawed by an erroneous understanding of how the benefits are computed and a misapplication of the Court's earlier cases. It held that a state tax discriminating between federal and state benefits violates the doctrine of intergovernmental immunities. Concurring, Justice John Paul Stevens said he thought the Court had spoken too broadly; it could surely not be improper for a state to exempt its retired judges from certain taxes without thereby allowing all retired federal judges to make the same claim.

immunity from suit The Supreme Court unanimously held that a state trial judge was absolutely immune from a suit for money DAMAGES filed by a lawyer who accused the judge of ordering police to use excessive force to have the lawyer brought into the judge's courtroom. The lawyer, a Los Angeles county defender, was waiting in one courtroom for a case to be called when two police officers appeared and dragged him into the other courtroom at the insistence of a judge who was angered that many cases in his courtroom could not proceed because the lawyers were absent. The public defender accused the police of cursing him with "vulgar and offensive names" and of having "slammed" him into the second courtroom, all with the judge's approval. The trial court dismissed the case, but the U.S. Court of Appeals for the Ninth Circuit reinstated it, reasoning that the judge's actions were not taken in his "judicial capacity."

The Supreme Court held that the "direction to court officers to bring a person who is in the courthouse before him is a function normally performed by a judge." And even though excessive force is "not a function normally performed by a judge" the rule of judicial immunity embraces improper, erroneous, and unauthorized actions, as long as undertaken in a judicial capacity.[34]

The Court reached a somewhat different conclusion in holding that a state official may be sued in a "personal capacity," even though she is immune from suit for the same actions in an "official capacity." The official in question was elected to the post of auditor general of Pennsylvania. On assuming office, she fired several employees for having "bought" their jobs from her predecessor. They sued her in her personal capacity for violation of their federal rights, claiming they were fired because they supported her opponent politically. She urged dismissal on the ground that state officials are absolutely immune from suit for actions undertaken in their official capacities.

The Court disagreed. The difference, Justice Sandra Day O'Connor explained, is that a suit against a state official in her official capacity is really a suit against the state itself. Suits against the state are governed by a set of constitutional principles stemming from the ELEVENTH AMENDMENT that do not apply to state officials individually. State officials may be personally sued for violating someone's rights. But the defenses to such suits are different. To the extent the state is suable, it may not plead that its unconstitutional law or other action was undertaken in good faith. State officials, on the other hand, may mount a defense by showing that they acted in a good-faith belief that their actions were constitutional.[23]

In a third immunity case, a failed cattle partnership led one rancher to attach the cattle, a tractor, and other personal property of the other under a state law permitting anyone to obtain a court order for attachment by posting a bond and swearing that the property belonged to him. The issuing court had no discretion to refuse to issue an attachment order if the proper bond and affidavit were filed in court. As it turned out at a post-seizure hearing, the partner who attached the property was not entitled to it, and the court ordered its return. When the partner in possession refused, the rightful owner filed a federal suit against his former partner, the partner's lawyer, the county sheriff, and the deputies who had seized the cattle. The federal court held the seizure law unconstitutional but dismissed the suit against the sheriff and deputies on the ground that they were entitled to immunity from suit. It also held that the partner and lawyer had a "qualified immunity" from suit under the federal civil rights laws if they acted under a seizure law later found to be unconstitutional.

The Supreme Court disagreed. Private parties are not entitled to the immunity of public officials for proceeding on the assumption that a law is constitutional, if it later turns out that it was unconstitutional and their actions contributed to the constitutional violation.[54] The Court was careful to distinguish between qualified immunity and a good-faith defense. Private parties may be sued and forced to defend themselves, but they may have a valid defense if they can show that they proceeded with the good-faith belief that the law was constitutional. The Court did not decide the latter issue.

implied right of action   The Adoption Assistance and Child Welfare Act of 1980 provides federal funds to states that comply with federal standards in foster care and adoption programs. Suits were filed on behalf of juvenile beneficiaries against the Illinois Department of Children and Family Services, claiming that the state had violated the act by failing "to make reasonable efforts to prevent removal of children from their homes." The plaintiffs sued under federal civil rights laws, asserting that by violating the "reasonable efforts" provision, state officials had violated their civil rights. The plaintiffs also asserted that the federal adoption law gave them an implied right of action directly. The Supreme Court disagreed, holding that the law conferred enforcement power on the federal government but that private litigants had no implied right to enforce it because Congress had manifested no unambiguous intention to allow private suits.[48]

On the other hand, the Court held that when a private right of action is implied, all "appropriate remedies" are permissible unless Congress expressly says otherwise. The Court upheld a private money DAMAGE suit against a Georgia county school system for failing to take action against a high school teacher and coach who subjected a female student to a continuing course of sexual harassment in violation of federal law, even though the damage remedy was not specified in the law.[19]

in forma pauperis   For the first time, the Court expressly denied *in forma pauperis* status to two litigants for abusing the "integrity of [the Court's] process by filing frivolous petitions." One of the petitioners had filed seventy-three petitions in the Supreme Court during the past decade, thirty-four of them during the past two years. The Court emphasized that it was acting against only "extreme abuse of the system" and not against every weak or even nearly empty petition filed in the Court.[57]

insanity, *see:* **civil commitment**

jury discrimination   A 7–2 majority pushed still further the Court's recent line of decisions holding unconstitutional racially motivated peremptory challenges. The case involved criminal assault charges against three white people for beating a black couple in Georgia. When the defendants' lawyer indicated that to obtain a jury more likely to acquit he would strike black jurors from the jury panel solely on the basis of their race, the prosecutor sought a ruling that it would be unconstitutional to do so. The Georgia courts refused to give the order. The Supreme Court reversed, holding that it would violate the EQUAL PROTECTION Clause for either side in a criminal prosecution to use peremptory challenges in a racially biased manner.[21a]

kidnapping, *see:* **extradition**

leafleting, *see:* **public forum**

liberty, *see:* **civil commitment**

medication and surgery, forced   A prison doctor prescribed an antipsychotic drug for a Nevada defendant awaiting trial on murder and robbery charges, because he had complained of hearing voices and having trouble sleeping. However, just before trial, the defendant asked that the medication be suspended, because it would interfere with both his mental state and demeanor at trial, violating

his right to DUE PROCESS. The lower court denied the motion without explanation, although there was conflicting testimony about whether the defendant would be competent to stand trial if taken off the medicine. Some testimony indicated that the high dosage might tend to make him drowsy and confused. The state supreme court affirmed his subsequent conviction, holding that expert testimony made to the jury during trial was constitutionally adequate to explain the effect of the drug on the defendant's demeanor and testimony.

The Supreme Court reversed, holding that the forced medication violated his right to a fair trial because the state had failed to show that "treatment with antipsychotic medication was medically appropriate and, considering less intrusive alternatives, essential for the sake of [the defendant's] own safety or the safety of others."[42] The state has the burden of demonstrating that the drug was essential; the defendant need not "demonstrate how the trial would have proceeded differently if he had not been given" the drug. The Court declined to consider whether the state could compel medication if the defendant would be rendered incompetent to stand trial without it.

original jurisdiction, *see:* **Dormant Commerce Clause**

permit system   After right-wing extremists forced a halt to a small civil rights march through rural Forsyth County, Georgia, in early January 1987, a huge outpouring of sympathizers assembled "the largest civil rights demonstration in the South since the 1960s" the following weekend. Some twenty thousand people marched, including presidential candidates and U.S. senators. About a thousand counter-demonstrators lining the parade route were reined in by three thousand police and National Guardsmen. The total cost for police protection was $670,000; only a small part of the cost was borne by the county, which has a population of one thousand. A few days later, the county legislature enacted an ordinance requiring future demonstrators to obtain a permit and to pay up to one thousand dollars a day for use of public spaces. The county administrator was empowered to base the fee on the expenses of administering the ordinance and maintaining public order.

Two years later, the Nationalist Movement, a white supremacist group, decided to protest the federal holiday commemorating Martin Luther King, Jr., by holding a two-hour rally on the steps of the county courthouse. The county charged one hundred dollars for the permit. The group cancelled its plans and sued. The evidence showed that the county had no standard for determining how much to charge applicants. Some had been charged nothing for a permit, the Girl Scouts had been charged five dollars, and the organizers of a bike race paid twenty-five dollars. Some groups were even allowed to use the public spaces without obtaining any permit.

A sharply divided Court held the ordinance unconstitutional because it contained no "articulated standards" controlling the exercise of the administrator's discretion and because in actual operation the ordinance required that the content of a group's message be taken into account, the fee to "depend on the administrator's measure of the amount of hostility likely to be created by the speech based on its content."[16] The cap of one thousand dollars on the fee could not save it: "A tax based on the content of speech does not become more constitutional because it is a small tax." The dissenters objected that the Court was overlooking a series of decisions that had rejected flat taxes and approved nominal fees for such purposes. They contended that whether the ordinance was being discriminatorily applied had never been decided by the lower courts, to which the case should have been remanded.

political question In 1962, in *Baker v. Carr,* the Supreme Court rejected the contention that issues of legislative apportionment by the states are political questions that it is therefore barred from hearing. In 1992 the Court held that the political question doctrine likewise presents no barrier to its considering a challenge to a federal apportionment law.[49]

See also: APPORTIONMENT OF POLITICAL DISTRICTS.

prayer and Bible reading In a 5–4 decision, the Court adhered to the principle it enunciated thirty years earlier, holding that prayers offered as part of a public school ceremony are forbidden by the ESTABLISHMENT CLAUSE.[29] For many years, school authorities in Providence, Rhode Island, invited members of the clergy to offer prayers at middle and high school graduation ceremonies. The family of a fourteen-year-old graduate from a city middle school challenged the school's decision to invite a rabbi to give an invocation and benediction at the school's graduation in 1989. Suggesting that prayers on such occasions should be "nonsectarian," school officials gave the rabbi a copy of a pamphlet prepared by the National Conference of Christians and Jews entitled "Guidelines for Civic Occasions," which recommended that prayers be written with "inclusiveness and sensitivity." The lower courts refused to stay the prayers, but the graduate and her family attended the ceremony at which the prayers were read. They continued the suit, seeking a citywide injunction against prayers at future graduations, including the plaintiff's high school graduation a few years hence.

The Court held that the schools' graduation prayer practice is unconstitutional because "government involvement with religious activity . . . is pervasive, to the point of creating a state-sponsored and state-directed religious exercise in a public school." The dissenters objected to the Court's overturning two centuries of American historical experience with prayers recited at the beginning of innumerable state occasions, including the inaugurations of presidents. They saw no coercion in the school's offering a brief prayer, noting that graduates are under no compulsion to attend the ceremonies.

But, said Justice Anthony M. Kennedy, such an argument "lacks all persuasion. Law reaches past formalism. . . . Attendance may not be required by official decree, yet it is apparent that a student is not free to absent herself from the graduation exercise in any real sense of the term 'voluntary,' for absence would require forfeiture of those intangible benefits which have motivated the student through her youth and all her high school years," including the "time for family and those closest to the student to celebrate success." The state argued that it was appropriate to mark the ceremony with a recognition "that human achievements cannot be understood apart from their spiritual essence." The flaw in that argument, Kennedy said, is that it requires those who object to prayers to absent themselves from a major social occasion. The state agreed and said that it was appropriate for them to do so. But "[i]t is a tenet of the First Amendment that the State cannot require one of its citizens to forfeit his or her rights and benefits as the price of resisting conformance to state-sponsored religious practice."

preemption   In a case of potentially great significance to the future of the cigarette industry, the Supreme Court held that the Federal Cigarette Labeling and Advertising Act, passed by Congress in 1965 to require manufacturers to post warnings on cigarette packages about health hazards from smoking, does not preempt state laws permitting smokers to sue manufacturers for DAMAGES resulting from cancer and other diseases contracted from smoking.[10] The act, and a 1969 amendment, says: "No requirement or prohibition based on smoking and

health shall be imposed under State law with respect to the advertising or promotion of any cigarettes the packages of which are [lawfully] labeled."

The son of Rose Cipollone, a woman who had smoked for forty-two years and died of lung cancer, accused cigarette manufacturers of causing her death, asserting that the companies failed to warn smokers of the hazards, fraudulently misrepresented the hazards of smoking, and conspired to keep scientific information from public view. In a multipart decision with which different blocs of justices took issue, Justice John Paul Stevens held that the federal law preempts claims based on a failure of manufacturers to warn and their attempt to "neutralize" the impact of the federally required warnings. But federal law does not preempt claims based on express warranties, fraudulent misrepresentations, intentional fraud in concealing evidence of deleterious effects, and conspiracies among companies to misrepresent or conceal significant facts about health hazards—meaning that smokers and former smokers may file such suits in state courts across the country.

presumption, *see:* **proof, burden of**

prisoners' rights, *see:* **medication and surgery, forced**

proof, burden of   California law prohibits mentally incompetent defendants from being prosecuted for criminal acts. The law presumes that a defendant is competent; if a defendant claims otherwise, he must prove his incompetence by a preponderance of the evidence. A defendant who was found competent in a competency hearing was convicted of murder and sentenced to death. He challenged the constitutionality of the PRESUMPTION and the state's fastening on him the burden of proving his incompetence.

The Supreme Court upheld both the presumption and the burden of proof.[33] States may determine for themselves what procedures of the criminal law to follow. A procedure violates DUE PROCESS only if it "offends some principle of justice so rooted in the traditions and conscience of our people as to be ranked as fundamental." Even though a defendant has a constitutional right not to be tried while incompetent, to require the defendant to bear the burden of proof in a close case is not fundamentally unfair. "The Due Process Clause does not . . . require a State to adopt one procedure over another on the basis that it may produce results more favorable to the accused."

proof, standard of   The Court held that in a federal HABEAS CORPUS hearing, a prisoner fighting a death sentence is entitled to be resentenced only if he shows "by clear and convincing evidence that but for constitutional error at his [original] sentencing hearing, no reasonable juror would have found him eligible for the death penalty."[44]

property tax   In an 8–1 decision, the Court turned aside an EQUAL PROTECTION challenge to California's Proposition 13. Under Proposition 13, a 1978 amendment to the state constitution, the property tax on residences is set at one percent of a home's value, and the state may not increase the tax by more than two percent each year. For residences acquired before 1978 the value of the home is set at the amount the tax authorities assessed in 1975. For residences acquired later, the value is basically the purchase price. The huge inflation in property values since 1978 ensures that recently purchased homes will be taxed much more heavily than comparable residences purchased earlier. The plaintiff, who purchased a home in 1988 for $170,000, showed that she paid the same tax as the owner of a $2.1 million Malibu beachfront

home and five times the tax of comparable homes on her street. Nevertheless, said Justice Harry A. Blackmun, the California tax system does not violate the Equal Protection Clause because it is not "palpably arbitrary."[36a] The Court upheld California's justifications for Proposition 13—that it tended to preserve the stability of local neighborhoods by discouraging frequent sales and that a new buyer has a lesser interest in avoiding higher taxes than does an existing owner, who might be forced to sell in order to pay a sharply increased tax. Dissenting, Justice John Paul Stevens said that "[i]t is irrational to treat similarly situated persons differently on the basis of the date they joined the class of property owners."

public forum   In a case the Court itself denoted as "rare," a 5–3 majority held that a quintessential public forum, an area one hundred feet outside a polling booth, may be closed to electioneering on election day as a necessary means to ensure the integrity of the election process.[8]

In a ruling of potentially broader import, the Court held for the first time that at least some parts of airport terminals operated by public authorities are not public forums and thus may limit expressive activities conducted inside. The case arose when the Port Authority of New York and New Jersey, which operates John F. Kennedy International Airport, La-Guardia Airport, and Newark International Airport, banned the dissemination of all literature and the SOLICITATION of funds inside the terminals but permitted it on the sidewalks outside. The International Society for Krishna Consciousness, a religious group that raises funds by soliciting in public places, challenged the bans as unconstitutional.

Chief Justice William H. Rehnquist said that an airport terminal has no historical tradition of being dedicated to public activities; nor does it have as a principal purpose the "free ex-

THE SUPREME COURT'S 1991–92 TERM

change of ideas." Rather, it is designed "to process and serve air travelers efficiently." Since an airport terminal is not a public forum, restrictions on solicitation need only be reasonable, and a regulation that prohibits the disruptions caused by active solicitation is surely reasonable in preventing delays of even a few minutes and the potential for duress and fraud that can be practiced on the unwary, the physically handicapped, and children.[25]

However, in a COMPANION CASE testing the validity of the ban on the distribution of literature in the airport terminals, the Court came out the other way, holding the ban unconstitutional. Several justices who concurred in Rehnquist's conclusion that solicitation is not protected did not agree with his reasoning. They held that some parts of airport terminals are public forums and open to public discussion but that the ban on solicitation is reasonable in light of its purposes. However, the ban on the distribution and sale of literature is quite different, because it serves none of the purposes proffered to justify the ban on solicitation. It is not difficult to take a pamphlet out of someone's hands or to pass the offer by. As Justice Anthony M. Kennedy put it, "to prohibit distribution of literature for the mere reason that it is sold would leave organizations seeking to spread their message without funds to operate." A prohibition against sales of literature would prevent those "who lack access to more sophisticated media the opportunity to speak."[28]

See also: SOLICITATION; SPEECH, REGULATION OF CONTENT.

punishment, cruel and unusual　After an argument with an inmate, two Louisiana state penitentiary security officers placed him in handcuffs and shackles, and while one held him the other punched him in the mouth, eyes, chest, and stomach. A prison supervisor who watched the beating told the others "not to have too much fun." The prisoner suffered minor bruises and swelling, loosened teeth, and a cracked dental plate. He sued the three officers for violating his EIGHTH AMENDMENT right against cruel and unusual punishments.

The lower court agreed that the prison officials used force without need and ordered them to pay the prisoner eight hundred dollars. The U.S. Court of Appeals for the Fifth Circuit reversed, holding that to establish an Eighth Amendment violation, a prisoner must show "significant" injury resulting "directly and only from the use of force that was clearly excessive to the need." Moreover, the excessiveness must be "objectively unreasonable," and it must have constituted "an unnecessary and wanton infliction of pain." The court of appeals agreed that the force was objectively unreasonable because no force at all was called for, that the conduct was excessive, and that it inflicted wanton pain. But it held that because the prisoner's injuries were "minor," requiring no medical attention, there was no constitutional violation.

The Supreme Court reversed, holding that "[w]hen prison officials maliciously and sadistically use force to cause harm, contemporary standards of decency always are violated . . . whether or not significant injury is evident."[24] Although "not every malevolent touch by a prison guard gives rise to a federal cause of action," force that is more than minimal may. Dissenting, Justice Clarence Thomas said that "a use of force that causes only insignificant harm to a prisoner may be immoral, it may be tortious, it may be criminal, and it may even be remediable under other provisions of the Federal Constitution, but it is not 'cruel and unusual punishment,'" because what happened was not part of the prisoner's sentence, but an unauthorized act by guards.

religious establishment, *see:* **prayer and Bible reading**

rent control   Operators of mobile home parks in Escondido, California, complained that a local rent control ordinance, combined with a statewide law regulating the use of mobile home rental space, deprived them of the use of their property. They sued the state for JUST COMPENSATION. The operators rent out space, called "pads," in their parks to people living in mobile homes. Customarily, when a mobile home owner decides to move, the home stays in place when the buyer moves in. The state law prohibited the owners of the parks from refusing to rent space when mobile homes changed hands, unless the renter failed to pay rent or violated the rules of the park, or the park owner decided to change the use of his or her land altogether. The law was enacted to prevent new mobile home owners from losing the value of their investment by being put out, since the cost of moving a mobile home is significant. The state law does not limit the amount of rent that pad owners may charge, but in 1988 Escondido voters passed a proposition calling for rents to be set back to the 1986 level and prohibiting future increases without the sanction of the city council, which must approve proposed rent increases found to be "just, fair and reasonable." The operators charged that the ordinances deprived them of the complete use of their property. Their theory was that, in effect, the two laws gave mobile home owners a right to the property at a price below market value. The sellers of the mobile homes can realize a premium in value, but the owners of the park cannot.

The Court disagreed, holding that the laws do not take the owners' property but merely regulate its use and that many other forms of land regulation in effect transfer wealth from one group to another. Since the laws do not "compel a landowner to suffer the physical occupation of his property," there was no TAKING OF PROPERTY.[56]

residence, *see:* **apportionment of political districts**

retroactivity   A Mississippi couple was shot to death during an armed robbery of their home. One of the robbers, who did not fire the fatal shots, was convicted of felony murder and sentenced to death after the jury was instructed that it could consider certain aggravating factors, including that the crime was committed in a "heinous, atrocious or cruel" manner. The Mississippi judge did not define this phrase. After the defendant's appeals failed and his conviction became final, the Supreme Court decided in other cases that such phrases as Mississippi used to determine aggravation are unconstitutionally vague. The state argued that the defendant was not entitled to relief because the Court had issued a "new rule" that could not be applied retroactively.

The Court disagreed, holding that even though there were differences between the Mississippi sentencing process and those cases that led to the Court's vagueness rule, they were not sufficiently different from procedures condemned in other decisions handed down before the conviction. Moreover, just because the Mississippi aggravation standard was phrased in different words from cases predating the conviction, that did not constitute the application of a new rule. Mississippi lawmakers and the courts should have known that the law was defective.[47]

ripeness   A South Carolina ZONING law prohibited the construction of single-family homes on beachfront property. Before an owner's suit seeking compensation for the loss of his property values could be resolved, the state legislature amended the law to permit a state agency to issue "special permits." The state argued that the pending suit should be dismissed as "unripe" because the owner might after all be entitled to construct homes on the property. The Supreme Court held that the issue was justiciable and not barred under the ripeness doctrine because the state supreme court had decided the issue against the owner for *past* deprivation of the right to build. The Supreme Court said it could review the decision that the owner was entitled to no compensation for the years before the amendment was enacted. Only if the state court itself had concluded the matter was not yet ripe would the Supreme Court have refrained from hearing the case.

See also: TAKING OF PROPERTY.

schools, religion in, *see:* **prayer and Bible reading**

segregation and integration   The Court decided two cases dealing with school segregation. In the first, officials of the DeKalb County, Georgia, school system sought dismissal of a lawsuit, initiated in 1969, through which the federal courts had been supervising the dismantling of the formerly segregated secondary school systems. The U.S. district court agreed that the system had largely succeeded in achieving "unitary status," having complied in four of six respects with the plan to desegregate: student assignments, transportation, physical facilities, and extracurricular activities. The court agreed to end its continuing supervision over these factors, but it declined to terminate with respect to two other issues: faculty assignments and resource allocations. The U.S. Court of Appeals reversed, saying that the district court should have retained jurisdiction over all aspects of the school system until every part of the desegregation plan was fully implemented. The Supreme Court reversed again, holding that a district court may relinquish supervision over "discrete categories in which the school district has achieved compliance with a court-ordered desegregation plan."[21]

However, in a case arising out of the condition of the public university system in Mississippi, the Court took a harsher view of the state's progress in desegregating. Despite a suit filed in 1975 and a state plan to eliminate its prior de jure segregation, the student bodies at the formerly white universities were still largely white and the black student bodies were still largely black. The lower courts held that the states have no affirmative obligation to restrict student choice or otherwise achieve a particular racial balance in higher education as they do in secondary schools and that as long as the state's practices are racially neutral and implemented in good faith, they are constitutional.

The Supreme Court, 8–1, disagreed. Racial imbalance attributable to actions of the state that perpetuate its prior segregated school system is a product of unconstitutional policies that violate the EQUAL PROTECTION Clause. Among these policies that the Court identified are admissions policies requiring higher test scores for the white than the black universities, a refusal to consider high school grade performance, and the widespread duplication of programs at the various universities that lead to segregated campuses. The Court also took the lower courts to task for failing to consider the combined effects of the individual policies the state has adopted. It remanded the case and ordered the district court to consider, among other things, whether the state should maintain all of its current universities or whether one or more should be merged or closed.[15]

sentencing   Under federal sentencing laws, a U.S. DISTRICT COURT may impose a sentence below the statutory minimum, "[u]pon motion of the government," to reward a defendant who has substantially cooperated with the government in an ongoing criminal investigation or prosecution. Suppose a defendant cooperates but a prosecutor refuses to make a "substantial assistance" motion. May judges on their own sentence defendants below the minimum? The Supreme Court held that judges may act only upon the government's motion but that they may hold a hearing and grant a remedy "if they find that the refusal was based on an unconstitutional motive"—for example, because of the defendant's race or religion. But a mere allegation that a defendant has substantially cooperated is insufficient to trigger court review whenever the prosecutor chooses not to ask the court for leniency on the defendant's behalf.[50]

See also: DEATH PENALTY; FREEDOM OF ASSOCIATION; HABEAS CORPUS; PROOF, STANDARD OF.

separation of powers   Environmental organizations sued to prevent the United States Forest Service and the Bureau of Land Management from harvesting timber, asserting that doing so would violate several federal conservation laws. Congress responded to these suits by passing the Northwest Timber Compromise, requiring the federal agencies to undertake harvesting and imposing certain limitations on where timber could be cut. As part of the law, Congress specifically stated that the timber regulations satisfied the legal requirements that formed the basis of the specific suits filed by the environmental organizations. The groups challenged the law on the ground that it violated the doctrine of separation of powers, because it purported to tell the courts how to decide pending lawsuits. The Supreme Court disagreed, holding that Congress did not direct the courts on what facts to find or how to apply the old law but instead changed the law, substituting new legal standards under which the cases were to be decided. Since Congress may always change the law, there was no separation of powers problem.[43]

solicitation, *see:* **public forum**

Son of Sam law   The Supreme Court unanimously overturned New York State's so-called Son of Sam law, which barred convicted criminals from profiting from their crimes by selling publication or film rights to their stories. Under the law, any publisher or other entity contracting with either an accused or convicted person for the rights to tell the story was required to notify the state Crime Victims Board and turn over any income to the board that would otherwise have been payable to the criminal. The money was then to be held for the account of any victims of the crime. A victim had five years to file suit to collect damages from the fund. If no recovery was made and no suits were pending after five years, the board was required to pay over the money to the convicted criminal.

The case challenging the law grew out of the publication of *Wiseguy,* the book on which the film *Goodfellas* was based. The Crime Victim Board ordered Simon & Schuster, the book's publishers, to account for moneys paid to the protagonist, Henry Hill, and to remit to the board all amounts owing to Hill but unpaid. The publisher complied, then sued. The issue turned on whether the law imposed a "financial burden on speakers because of the content of their speech," a condition the Court has repeatedly held to be unconstitutional.

In *Simon & Schuster v. New York Crime Victims Board,* the Court agreed that the law did exactly that, since it applied to only one specified type of content—works about a person's own crimes. Although the state has a substantial interest in providing restitution to victims of crimes and barring criminals from profiting from their crimes, it may not do so in an unconstitutional manner, by compensating victims from income derived only from "storytelling" rather than from any of a criminal's other assets. The law was not narrowly tailored to achieve its objectives. It defined persons subject to the law quite broadly; it included "any person who has voluntarily and intelligently admitted the commission of a crime for which such person is not prosecuted." This definition, the Court said, would have permitted the state to escrow the royalty income of Martin Luther King, Jr., Malcolm X, Jesse Jackson, and Bertrand Russell. Moreover, it would also sweep up the earnings from the autobiography of a "prominent figure" who at the end of his career included a brief recollection of a childhood crime, even though the STATUTE OF LIMITATIONS had long since run. In short, the states may not single out "speech on a particular subject for a financial burden that it places on no other speech and no other income."

speech, regulation of content A Tennessee law prohibits anyone from soliciting votes or displaying or distributing campaign materials within one hundred feet of the entrance to a polling place on election day. The treasurer of a political campaign sued, charging that this "campaign-free zone" violated her FREEDOM OF SPEECH. The Tennessee Supreme Court held that although the state has a COMPELLING INTEREST in controlling vote solicitation within the building in which people vote, the law was overbroad in applying to the entrance to the building.

In upholding the entire law, Justice Harry A. Blackmun noted that it affected "three central concerns" of the FIRST AMENDMENT: "regulation of political speech, regulation of speech in a PUBLIC FORUM, and regulation based on the content of the speech." Since the law on its face was aimed at the content of political speech, it is constitutional only if necessary to serve a compelling state interest and narrowly drawn to achieve that end. Reciting a long history of voter fraud and intimidation that led to the establishment of private election booths, the Court found that the states have a compelling interest in ensuring the integrity of elections. Considering the alternative means of controlling fraud and intimidation (such as criminal laws against such conduct), the Court con-

cluded that none are as effective as the simple expedient of providing a zone within which electioneering must stop.[8]

See also: HATE SPEECH; PERMIT SYSTEM; SOLICITATION; SON OF SAM LAW.

standing In challenging the Census Bureau's decision to include overseas federal employees in the count of state residents for purposes of allocating seats in the House of Representatives, Massachusetts asserted both that the bureau unlawfully included the employees and that the data it used were inaccurate. The Court held that the plaintiffs had standing to challenge the constitutionality of the decision, since they could demonstrate that Massachusetts would have had an additional representative if the employees were excluded.[20] But the Court refused to permit them to challenge the accuracy of the data, because they had made no showing that any other set of data would have yielded an extra House seat. There can be no standing to sue without showing an injury in fact.

The Court also held that the Defenders of Wildlife, a conservation group, lacks standing to challenge a rule issued by the secretary of the interior stating that the Department of the Interior would apply the Endangered Species Act to federal activities only within the United States and not to activities beyond its borders.[31] The Defenders of Wildlife asserted that they were injured because the effect of the rule would be to permit certain species to become extinct at a faster rate. Recognizing the legal right to assert a "desire to use or observe an animal species, even for purely aesthetic purposes," the Court held that the claim was nevertheless barred because the conservation group could not show that its interest, or the particular interests of its members, was directly affected differently from everyone else. Standing requires a threat to a concrete, particular interest, not to a generalized interest shared by all.

See also: DORMANT COMMERCE CLAUSE; PROPERTY TAX.

stare decisis A major issue in *Planned Parenthood of Southeastern Pennsylvania v. Casey*, the Court's 1992 ABORTION decision, was whether stare decisis required the Court to adhere to *Roe v. Wade*, decided nineteen years earlier. The PLURALITY OPINION concluded that it did. The general principle of stare decisis is that the courts must respect what has already been decided, unless manifestly in error. In deciding whether to overrule *Roe*, the questions are whether *Roe*'s "central rule has been found unworkable"; whether it could be struck down without "serious inequity" to those who have relied on the right to an abortion or "significant damage" to the stability of society; and whether its underpinnings have become "somehow irrelevant or unjustifiable in dealing with the issue it addressed." The Court held that the answer to each of these questions must be no. "An entire generation has come of age free to assume *Roe*'s concept of liberty in defining the capacity of women to act in society, and to make reproductive decisions; no erosion of principle going to liberty or personal autonomy has left *Roe*'s central holding a doctrinal remnant."

Moreover, to overrule *Roe* with no reason other than a change in Court membership would seriously erode the Court's legitimacy, for it would be seen as compromising with "social and political pressures having, as such, no bearing on the principled choices the Court is obliged to make." Like the decision in 1954 in BROWN V. BOARD OF EDUCATION, *Roe* decided an "intensely divisive controversy"; only with the "most convincing justification," which is absent in the abortion controversy, could the Court overrule itself without appearing to "surrender to political pressure." In so doing, it would undermine the only basis of its constitu-tional authority and "the Nation's commitment to the rule of law."

state action The Court held that even though he is being tried by the state, a criminal defendant is a "state actor" when exercising peremptory challenges to determine the composition of the jury that will sit in judgment of him.[21a] Because the jury system exists solely through the state, and because the state through its courts gives legal effect to peremptory challenges, jury selection is inextricably a state function. Even though the state's interest is opposed to that of the defendant, "in exercising a peremptory challenge, a criminal defendant is wielding the power to choose a quintessential governmental body."

states and statehood, *see:* **Tenth Amendment**

taking of property A South Carolina law enacted in 1988 prohibited the prior purchaser of certain beachfront property from constructing single-family homes, even though there were such homes on adjacent property. A state court held that the law rendered the land valueless. Even so, the state argued that it was not bound to pay JUST COMPENSATION because the law was not a taking of property but a regulation of a "noxious use" of the property. The Supreme Court held that when the state renders property valueless, it cannot avoid paying compensation simply by saying that it was trying to stamp out some conduct it has decided is undesirable.[30] Rather, it must pay unless it can demonstrate that the regulation against building simply restated some prohibition against a use that was never "part of [the owner's] title to begin with."

See also: RENT CONTROL; RIPENESS.

taxation by states, *see:* **immunities, intergovernmental; property tax**

taxation of interstate commerce Despite some expectation to the contrary, the Court refused to back away from a 1967 precedent that prohibits the states from requiring mail-order houses to collect taxes on sales of products shipped to customers in states where the company has neither stores nor sales representatives. In 1967 the Court said that the collection of such taxes violates the DUE PROCESS Clause and unconstitutionally burdens INTERSTATE COMMERCE. In *Quill Corporation v. North Dakota,* the Court changed its mind about the due process issue, holding that any company "engaged in a continuous and widespread solicitation of business within a state" has availed itself sufficiently of the benefits of the economic market in the state to be subject to the state's taxing authority.

However, that conclusion did not alter the result, for the interstate commerce problem remains. The Court held that companies that do no more than take phone or mail orders from customers in a state in which the companies maintain no offices or other physical presence lack a "substantial nexus" with the state, so that any attempt to collect a tax is an unconstitutional burden on interstate commerce. Since the ultimate regulator of interstate commerce is Congress, the Court practically invited Congress to take action. If it chooses, Congress may enact laws authorizing the states to collect taxes from mail-order houses because under its COMMERCE POWER, it may determine in what ways the states may or may not impose upon interstate commerce.

The Court also upheld another interstate tax principle: that a state may tax a proportionate share of the total earnings of a company doing business both in and out of the state only if the company's activities are "unitary"—that is, all its business is the same, no matter where located. But if a company maintains separate and independent lines of business, the state may not tax the income of activities that are not carried on in the state.[1]

Tenth Amendment The Supreme Court has once again revived the Tenth Amendment, holding that it prohibits Congress from directly regulating the states. The case grew out of federal attempts to deal with the growing problem of disposing of low-level radioactive wastes. In a 1985 law, Congress established three mechanisms for cajoling the states into reaching a nationwide solution. The first was a set of monetary incentives for individual states to develop disposal sites. The second was a system of rules designed to permit states that act appropriately and quickly to deny access to their disposal sites for out-of-state wastes. The third was a rule that transferred ownership of wastes to a state itself if it failed by a certain date to dispose of wastes generated within its borders. Under this so-called "take title" provision, once ownership was transferred, the state became liable for any damages suffered by the previous owner for the state's failure to take possession and dispose of the waste.

In *New York v. United States,* the Court upheld the first two provisions; Congress has ample authority under both the COMMERCE POWER and the SPENDING POWER to cajole states into adopting certain policies. But the Court drew the line at the take title provision. "We have always understood," Justice Sandra Day O'Connor said, "that even where Congress has the authority under the Constitution to pass laws requiring or prohibiting certain acts, it lacks the power directly to compel the States to require or prohibit those acts." Congress may regulate interstate commerce directly, but it may not "regulate state governments' regulation of interstate commerce." This conclusion follows from the Tenth Amendment, which incorporates the principle that certain powers are "an attribute of state sovereignty" that may not be exercised by Congress. "States are not mere political subdivisions of the United States. . . . Whatever the outer limits of [their] sovereignty may be, one thing is clear: The Federal Government may not compel the

States to enact or administer a federal regulatory program." Congress may create national policies for disposing of radioactive wastes; it may preempt state legislation dealing with this concern; it may even "hold out incentives to the States as a means of encouraging them to adopt suggested regulatory schemes." But it may not "simply ... direct the states to provide for the disposal of the radioactive waste generated within their borders."

trial, competence to stand, *see:* **proof, burden of**

trial, fairness of, *see:* **medication and surgery, forced**

trial, speedy In 1980 a drug trafficker was indicted for conspiring to import cocaine. But when federal agents went to arrest him, they discovered he had already left the country. Several months later, an agent learned that he had been arrested on drug charges in Panama and asked Panamanian authorities to "expel" him to the United States. The Panamanians said they would do so when their own trial was finished, but when they eventually released him, he departed for Colombia. Nearly a year later, he reentered the United States, unaware that he was under indictment, and "passed unhindered through customs." Over the next six years he earned a college degree, married, found steady lawful work, and lived openly under his own name. The original agent made no real effort to trace him beyond Panama. Only because of a routine credit check conducted by the U.S. Marshal's Service to locate thousands of people subject to arrest warrants did his whereabouts become known. He was arrested six years after returning to the United States and more than eight years after being indicted. The defendant moved to dismiss the indictment on the ground that the government had violated his right to a speedy trial under the Sixth Amendment. The trial court held that since there was no showing that the delay had prejudiced him, the indictment must stand, even though the delay in seeking trial was entirely attributable to the government. The Supreme Court reversed and dismissed the case, holding that the government's failure to track him down was inexcusable neglect. It said that the longer the delay, the more inherent the prejudice to the defendant, because he would be unable to prepare a defense.[13]

venue Under Montana law, a plaintiff may sue a company incorporated in the state only in the county where its principal place of business is located. But a company doing business in the state and incorporated elsewhere may be sued in any county. In a challenge to the law on the ground that this venue provision violates the EQUAL PROTECTION Clause, the Court held that the law does not deprive foreign corporations of any fundamental right and does not draw a classification on any suspect ground, like race or religion; therefore, it must be upheld unless it fails "in rationally furthering legitimate state ends." Since parties to lawsuits frequently disagree about the best location of a trial, states always have a valid interest in striking an appropriate balance. Although the state is entitled to a wide range of choices, the defendant company asserted that since it had a principal place of business in the state, it should be treated just as the state treated home companies.

The Court held that it was reasonable for Montana to determine "that a corporate defendant's home office is generally of greater significance to the corporation's convenience in litigation than its other offices; that foreign corporations are unlikely to have their principal offices in Montana, and that Montana's domestic corporations will probably keep headquarters within the State." Since none of these assumptions is irrational, the state's venue rule must be upheld.[7]

voir dire, *see:* **death penalty**

voting, right to   The Court upheld a Hawaii law prohibiting voters from writing in the names of candidates on the general election ballot.[6] A voter protested that the law infringed on his FREEDOM OF ASSOCIATION and FREEDOM OF SPEECH, but the Court said that Hawaii's rule did not unreasonably interfere with anyone's ability to run for office because getting onto a ballot was relatively easy. Moreover, the rule served significant purposes. For example, it averted "divisive sore-loser candidacies" by barring someone losing in a primary from mounting a last-minute write-in campaign.

Voting Rights Act   When a black candidate was elected to an Alabama county commission that had authority to supervise maintenance and construction of country roads, the holdover commissioners changed the rules by which the commission operated, so that the newly elected black member who would otherwise have had considerable authority to spend public money on roads in his district was assigned instead to oversee maintenance of the county courthouse. He challenged the commission's rules as a racial discrimination that violated the Voting Rights Act because the rule changes were not cleared by the Justice Department under the act's procedures. The Court held that only rule changes affecting voting are governed by the act. The changes within the commission "affected only the allocation of power among governmental officials . . . [and] had no impact on the substantive question whether a particular office would be elective or the procedural question how an election would be conducted."[39]

zoning, *see:* **taking of property**

The Constitution of the United States

Note: Numbers in brackets have been added to identify paragraphs within sections; they are not part of the Constitution. Numbers in the Concordance following refer to Articles, Sections, and bracketed paragraph numbers. Thus, II-2[1] refers to Article II, Section 2, Paragraph 1. Phrases or sentences in brackets throughout have been repealed and are no longer operative.

[Preamble] We the People of the United States, in Order to form a more perfect Union, establish Justice, insure domestic Tranquility, provide for the common defence, promote the general Welfare, and secure the Blessings of Liberty to ourselves and our Posterity, do ordain and establish this Constitution for the United States of America.

ARTICLE I

Section 1. All legislative Powers herein granted shall be vested in a Congress of the United States, which shall consist of a Senate and House of Representatives.

Section 2. [1] The House of Representatives shall be composed of Members chosen every second Year by the People of the several States, and the Electors in each State shall have the Qualifications requisite for Electors of the most numerous Branch of the State Legislature.

[2] No Person shall be a Representative who shall not have attained to the Age of twenty five Years, and been seven Years a Citizen of the United States, and who shall not, when elected, be an Inhabitant of that State in which he shall be chosen.

[3] [Representatives and direct Taxes shall be apportioned among the several States which may be included within this Union, according to their respective Numbers, which shall be determined by adding to the whole Number of free Persons, including those bound to Service for a Term of Years, and excluding Indians not taxed, three fifths of all other Persons.] The actual Enumeration shall be made within three Years after the first Meeting of the Congress of the United States, and within every subsequent Term of ten Years, in such Manner as they shall by Law direct. The number of Representatives shall not exceed one for every thirty Thousand, but each State shall have at Least one Representative; and until such enumeration shall be made, the State of New Hampshire shall be entitled to chuse three, Massachusetts eight, Rhode-Island and Providence Plantations one, Connecticut five, New-York six, New Jersey four, Pennsylvania eight, Dela-

ware one, Maryland six, Virginia ten, North Carolina five, South Carolina five, and Georgia three.

[4] When vacancies happen in the Representation from any State, the Executive Authority thereof shall issue Writs of Election to fill such Vacancies.

[5] The House of Representatives shall chuse their Speaker and other Officers; and shall have the sole Power of Impeachment.

Section 3. [1] The Senate of the United States shall be composed of two Senators from each State, [chosen by the Legislature thereof,] for six Years; and each Senator shall have one Vote.

[2] Immediately after they shall be assembled in Consequence of the first Election, they shall be divided as equally as may be into three Classes. The Seats of the Senators of the first Class shall be vacated at the Expiration of the second Year, of the second Class at the Expiration of the fourth Year, and of the third Class at the Expiration of the sixth Year, so that one third may be chosen every second Year; [and if Vacancies happen by Resignation, or otherwise, during the Recess of the Legislature of any State, the Executive thereof may make temporary Appointments until the next Meeting of the Legislature, which shall then fill such Vacancies.]

[3] No Person shall be a Senator who shall not have attained to the Age of thirty Years, and been nine Years a Citizen of the United States, and who shall not, when elected, be an Inhabitant of that State for which he shall be chosen.

[4] The Vice President of the United States shall be President of the Senate, but shall have no Vote, unless they be equally divided.

[5] The Senate shall chuse their other Officers, and also a President pro tempore, in the Absence of the Vice President, or when he shall exercise the Office of President of the United States.

[6] The Senate shall have the sole Power to try all impeachments. When sitting for that Purpose, they shall be on Oath or Affirmation. When the President of the United States is tried, the Chief Justice shall preside: And no Person shall be convicted without the Concurrence of two thirds of the Members present.

[7] Judgment in Cases of Impeachment shall not extend further than to removal from Office, and disqualification to hold and enjoy any Office of honor, Trust or Profit under the United States: but the Party convicted shall nevertheless be liable and subject to Indictment, Trial, judgment and Punishment, according to Law.

Section 4 [1] The Times, Places and Manner of holding Elections for Senators and Representatives, shall be prescribed in each State by the Legislature thereof; but the Congress may at any time by Law make or alter such Regulations, except as to the Places of chusing Senators.

[2] The Congress shall assemble at least once in every Year, and such Meeting shall be [on the first Monday in December,] unless they shall by Law appoint a different Day.

Section 5. [1] Each House shall be the Judge of the Elections, Returns and Qualifications of its own Members, and a Majority of each shall constitute a Quorum to do Business; but a smaller Number may adjourn from day to day, and may be authorized to compel the Attendance of absent Members, in such Manner, and under such Penalties as each House may provide.

[2] Each House may determine the Rules of its Proceedings, punish its Members for disorderly Behaviour, and, with the Concurrence of two thirds, expel a Member.

[3] Each House shall keep a Journal of its Proceedings, and from time to time publish the same, excepting such Parts as may in their Judgment require Secrecy; and the Yeas and Nays of the Members of either House on any

question shall, at the Desire of one fifth of those Present, be entered on the Journal.

[4] Neither House, during the Session of Congress, shall, without the Consent of the other, adjourn for more than three days, nor to any other Place than that in which the two Houses shall be sitting.

Section 6. [1] The Senators and Representatives shall receive a Compensation for their Services, to be ascertained by Law, and paid out of the Treasury of the United States. They shall in all Cases, except Treason, Felony and Breach of the Peace, be privileged from Arrest during their Attendance at the Session of their respective Houses, and in going to and returning from the same; and for any Speech or Debate in either House, they shall not be questioned in any other Place.

[2] No Senator or Representative shall, during the Time for which he was elected, be appointed to any civil Office under the Authority of the United States, which shall have been created, or the Emoluments whereof shall have been encreased during such time; and no Person holding any Office under the United States, shall be a Member of either House during his Continuance in Office.

Section 7. [1] All Bills for raising Revenue shall originate in the House of Representatives; but the Senate may propose or concur with Amendments as on other Bills.

[2] Every Bill which shall have passed the House of Representatives and the Senate, shall, before it becomes a Law, be presented to the President of the United States; If he approve he shall sign it, but if not he shall return it, with his Objections to that House in which it shall have originated, who shall enter the Objections at large on their journal, and proceed to reconsider it. If after such Reconsideration two thirds of that House shall agree to pass the Bill, it shall be sent, together with the Objections, to the other House, by which it shall likewise be reconsidered, and if approved by two thirds of that House, it shall become a Law. But in all such Cases the Votes of both Houses shall be determined by yeas and Nays, and the Names of the Persons voting for and against the Bill shall be entered on the journal of each House respectively. If any Bill shall not be returned by the President within ten Days (Sundays excepted) after it shall have been presented to him, the Same shall be a Law, in like Manner as if he had signed it, unless the Congress by their Adjournment prevent its Return, in which Case it shall not be a Law.

[3] Every Order, Resolution, or Vote to which the Concurrence of the Senate and House of Representatives may be necessary (except on a question of Adjournment) shall be presented to the President of the United States; and before the Same shall take Effect, shall be approved by him, or being disapproved by him, shall be repassed by two thirds of the Senate and House of Representatives, according to the Rules and Limitations prescribed in the Case of a Bill.

Section 8. [1] The Congress shall have Power To lay and collect Taxes, Duties, Imposts and Excises, to pay the Debts and provide for the common Defence and general Welfare of the United States; but all Duties, Imposts and Excises shall be uniform throughout the United States;

[2] To borrow Money on the credit of the United States;

[3] To regulate Commerce with foreign Nations, and among the several States, and with the Indian Tribes;

[4] To establish an uniform Rule of Naturalization, and uniform Laws on the subject of Bankruptcies throughout the United States;

[5] To coin Money, regulate the Value thereof, and of foreign Coin, and fix the Standard of Weights and Measures;

[6] To provide for the Punishment of counterfeiting the Securities and current Coin of the United States;

[7] To establish Post Offices and post Roads;

[8] To promote the Progress of Science and useful Arts, by securing for limited Times to Authors and Inventors the exclusive Right to their respective Writings and Discoveries;

[9] To constitute Tribunals inferior to the supreme Court;

[10] To define and punish Piracies and Felonies committed on the high Seas, and Offenses against the Law of Nations;

[11] To declare War, grant Letters of Marque and Reprisal, and make Rules concerning Captures on Land and Water;

[12] To raise and support Armies, but no Appropriation of Money to that Use shall be for a longer Term than two Years;

[13] To provide and maintain a Navy;

[14] To make Rules for the Government and Regulation of the land and naval Forces;

[15] To provide for calling forth the Militia to execute the Laws of the Union, suppress Insurrections and repel Invasions;

[16] To provide for organizing, arming, and disciplining, the Militia, and for governing such Part of them as may be employed in the Service of the United States, reserving to the States respectively, the Appointment of the Officers, and the Authority of training the Militia according to the discipline prescribed by Congress;

[17] To exercise exclusive Legislation in all Cases whatsoever, over such District (not exceeding ten Miles square) as may, by Cession of particular States, and the Acceptance of Congress, become the Seat of the Government of the United States, and to exercise like Authority over all Places purchased by the Consent of the Legislature of the State in which the Same shall be, for the Erection of Forts, Magazines, Arsenals, dock-Yards and Other needful Buildings;—And

[18] To make all Laws which shall be necessary and proper for carrying into Execution the foregoing Powers, and all other Powers vested by this Constitution in the Government of the United States, or in any Department or Officer thereof.

Section 9. [1] The Migration or Importation of such Persons as any of the States now existing shall think proper to admit, shall not be prohibited by the Congress prior to the Year one thousand eight hundred and eight, but a Tax or duty may be imposed on such Importation, not exceeding ten dollars for each Person.

[2] The Privilege of the Writ of Habeas Corpus shall not be suspended, unless when in Cases of Rebellion or Invasion the public Safety may require it.

[3] No Bill of Attainder or ex post facto Law shall be passed.

[4] [No Capitation, or other direct, Tax shall be laid, unless in Proportion to the Census or Enumeration herein before directed to be taken.]

[5] No Tax or Duty shall be laid on Articles exported from any State.

[6] No Preference shall be given by any Regulation of Commerce or Revenue to the Ports of one State over those of another: nor shall Vessels bound to, or from, one State, be obliged to enter, clear, or pay Duties in another.

[7] No Money shall be drawn from the Treasury, but in Consequence of Appropriations made by Law; and a regular Statement and Account of the Receipts and Expenditures of all public Money shall be published from time to time.

[8] No Title of Nobility shall be granted by the United States: And no Person holding any Office of Profit or Trust under them, shall, without the Consent of the Congress, accept of any present, Emolument, Office, or Title, of any kind whatever, from any King, Prince, or foreign State.

Section 10. [1] No State shall enter into any Treaty, Alliance, or Confederation; grant Letters of Marque and Reprisal; coin Money; emit

Bills of Credit; make any Thing but gold and silver Coin a Tender in Payment of Debts; pass any Bill of Attainder, ex post facto Law, or Law impairing the Obligation of Contracts, or grant any Title of Nobility.

[2] No State shall, without the Consent of the Congress, lay any Imposts or Duties on Imports or Exports, except what may be absolutely necessary for executing it's inspection Laws: and the net Produce of all Duties and Imposts, laid by any State on Imports or Exports, shall be for the Use of the Treasury of the United States; and all such Laws shall be subject to the Revision and Controul of the Congress.

[3] No State shall, without the Consent of Congress, lay any Duty of Tonnage, keep Troops, or Ships of War in time of Peace, enter into any Agreement or Compact with another State, or with a foreign Power, or engage in War, unless actually invaded, or in such imminent Danger as will not admit of delay.

ARTICLE II

Section 1. [1] The executive Power shall be vested in a President of the United States of America. He shall hold his Office during the Term of four Years, and, together with the Vice President, chosen for the same Term, be elected, as follows

[2] Each State shall appoint, in such Manner as the Legislature thereof may direct, a Number of Electors, equal to the whole Number of Senators and Representatives to which the State may be entitled in the Congress: but no Senator or Representative, or Person holding an Office of Trust or Profit under the United States, shall be appointed an Elector.

[3] [The Electors shall meet in their respective States, and vote by Ballot for two Persons, of whom one at least shall not be an Inhabitant of the same State with themselves. And they shall make a List of all the Persons voted for, and of the Number of Votes for each; which List they shall sign and certify, and transmit sealed to the Seat of the Government of the United States, directed to the President of the Senate. The President of the Senate shall, in the Presence of the Senate and House of Representatives, open all the Certificates, and the Votes shall then be counted. The Person having the greatest Number of Votes shall be the President, if such Number be a Majority of the whole Number of Electors appointed; and if there be more than one who have such Majority, and have an equal Number of Votes, then the House of Representatives shall immediately chuse by Ballot one of them for President; and if no Person have a Majority, then from the five highest on the List the said House shall in like Manner chuse the President. But in chusing the President, the Votes shall be taken by States, the Representation from each State having one Vote; A quorum for this Purpose shall consist of a Member or Members from two thirds of the States, and a Majority of all the States shall be necessary to a Choice. In every Case, after the Choice of the President, the Person having the greatest Number of Votes of the Electors shall be the Vice President. But if there should remain two or more who have equal Votes, the Senate shall chuse from them by Ballot the Vice President.]

[4] The Congress may determine the Time of chusing the Electors, and the Day on which they shall give their Votes; which Day shall be the same throughout the United States.

[5] No Person except a natural born Citizen, or a Citizen of the United States, at the time of the Adoption of this Constitution, shall be eligible to the Office of the President; neither shall any person be eligible to that Office who shall not have attained to the Age of thirty five Years, and been fourteen Years a Resident within the United States.

[6] [In Case of the Removal of the President

from Office, or of his Death, Resignation, or Inability to discharge the Powers and Duties of the said Office, the Same shall devolve on the Vice President, and the Congress may by Law provide for the Case of Removal, Death, Resignation or Inability, both of the President and Vice President, declaring what Officer shall then act as President, and such Officer shall act accordingly, until the Disability be removed, or a President shall be elected.] The President shall, at stated Times, receive for his Services, a Compensation, which shall neither be increased nor diminished during the Period for which he shall have been elected, and he shall not receive within that Period any other Emolument from the United States, or any of them.

[7] Before he enter on the Execution of his Office, he shall take the following Oath or Affirmation: "I do solemnly swear (or affirm) that I will faithfully execute the Office of President of the United States, and will to the best of my Ability, preserve, protect and defend the Constitution of the United States."

Section 2. [1] The President shall be Commander in Chief of the Army and Navy of the United States, and of the Militia of the several States, when called into the actual Service of the United States; he may require the Opinion, in writing, of the principal Officer in each of the executive Departments, upon any Subject relating to the Duties of their respective Offices, and he shall have Power to grant Reprieves and Pardons for Offenses against the United States, except in Cases of Impeachment.

[2] He shall have Power, by and with the Advice and Consent of the Senate, to make Treaties, provided two thirds of the Senators present concur; and he shall nominate, and by and with the Advice and Consent of the Senate, shall appoint Ambassadors, other public Ministers and Consuls, Judges of the supreme Court, and all other Officers of the United States,

whose Appointments are herein otherwise provided for, and which shall be established by Law: but the Congress may by Law vest the Appointment of such inferior Officers, as they think proper, in the President alone, in the Courts of Law, or in the Heads of Departments.

[3] The President shall have Power to fill up all Vacancies that may happen during the Recess of the Senate, by granting Commissions which shall expire at the End of their next Session.

Section 3. He shall from time to time give to the Congress Information of the State of the Union, and recommend to their Consideration such Measures as he shall judge necessary and expedient; he may, on extraordinary Occasions, convene both Houses, or either of them, and in Case of Disagreement between them, with Respect to the Time of Adjournment, he may adjourn them to such Time as he shall think proper; he shall receive Ambassadors and other public Ministers; he shall take Care that the Laws be faithfully executed, and shall Commission all the Officers of the United States.

Section 4. The President, Vice President and all civil Officers of the United States, shall be removed from Office on Impeachment for, and Conviction of, Treason, Bribery, or other high Crimes and Misdemeanors.

ARTICLE III

Section 1. The judicial Power of the United States, shall be vested in one supreme Court, and in such inferior Courts as the Congress may from time to time ordain and establish. The Judges, both of the supreme and inferior Courts, shall hold their Offices during good Behaviour, and shall, at stated Times, receive for their Services, a Compensation, which shall not be diminished during their Continuance in Office.

Section 2. [1] The judicial Power shall extend to all Cases, in Law and Equity, arising under this Constitution, the Laws of the United States, and Treaties made, or which shall be made, under their Authority;—to all Cases affecting Ambassadors, other public Ministers and Consuls;—to all Cases of admiralty and maritime jurisdiction;—to Controversies to which the United States shall be a Party;—to Controversies between two or more States; [between a State and Citizens of another State;]—between Citizens of different States,—between Citizens of the same State claiming Lands under Grants of different States, [and between a State, or the Citizens thereof, and foreign States, Citizens or Subjects.]

[2] In all Cases affecting Ambassadors, other public Ministers and Consuls, and those in which a State shall be Party, the supreme Court shall have original jurisdiction. In all the other Cases before mentioned, the supreme Court shall have appellate jurisdiction, both as to Law and Fact, with such Exceptions, and under such Regulations as the Congress shall make.

[3] The Trial of all Crimes, except in Cases of Impeachment, shall be by jury; and such Trial shall be held in the State where the said Crimes shall have been committed; but when not committed within any State, the Trial shall be at such Place or Places as the Congress may by Law have directed.

Section 3. [1] Treason against the United States, shall consist only in levying War against them, or in adhering to their Enemies, giving them Aid and Comfort. No Person shall be convicted of Treason unless on the Testimony of two Witnesses to the same overt Act, or on Confession in open Court.

[2] The Congress shall have Power to declare the Punishment of Treason, but no Attainder of Treason shall work Corruption of Blood, or Forfeiture except during the Life of the Person attainted.

ARTICLE IV

Section 1. Full Faith and Credit shall be given in each State to the public Acts, Records, and judicial Proceedings of every other State; And the Congress may by general Laws prescribe the Manner in which such Acts, Records and Proceedings shall be proved, and the Effect thereof.

Section 2. [1] The Citizens of each State shall be entitled to all Privileges and Immunities of Citizens in the several States.

[2] A Person charged in any State with Treason, Felony, or other Crime, who shall flee from Justice, and be found in another State, shall on Demand of the executive Authority of the State from which he fled, be delivered up, to be removed to the State having Jurisdiction of the Crime.

[3] [No Person held to Service or Labour in one State, under the Laws thereof, escaping into another, shall, in Consequence of any Law or Regulation therein, be discharged from such Service or Labour, but shall be delivered up on Claim of the Party to whom such Service or Labour may be due.]

Section 3. [1] New States may be admitted by the Congress into this Union; but no new State shall be formed or erected within the Jurisdiction of any other State; nor any State be formed by the Junction of two or more States, or Parts of States, without the Consent of the Legislatures of the States concerned as well as of the Congress.

[2] The Congress shall have Power to dispose of and make all needful Rules and Regulations respecting the Territory or other Property belonging to the United States; and nothing in this Constitution shall be so construed as to Prejudice any Claims of the United States, or of any particular State.

Section 4. The United States shall guarantee to every State in this Union a Republican Form of Government, and shall protect each of them against Invasion; and on Application of the Legislature, or of the Executive (when the Legislature cannot be convened) against domestic Violence.

ARTICLE V

The Congress, whenever two thirds of both Houses shall deem it necessary, shall propose Amendments to this Constitution, or, on the Application of the Legislatures of two thirds of the several States, shall call a Convention for proposing Amendments, which, in either Case, shall be valid to all Intents and Purposes, as Part of this Constitution, when ratified by the Legislatures of three fourths of the several States, or by Conventions in three fourths thereof, as the one or the other Mode of Ratification may be proposed by the Congress; Provided that no Amendment which may be made prior to the Year One thousand eight hundred and eight shall in any Manner affect the first and fourth Clauses in the Ninth Section of the first Article; and that no State, without its Consent, shall be deprived of it's equal Suffrage in the Senate.

ARTICLE VI

[1] All Debts contracted and Engagements entered into, before the Adoption of this Constitution, shall be as valid against the United States under this Constitution, as under the Confederation.

[2] This Constitution, and the Laws of the United States which shall be made in Pursuance thereof; and all Treaties made, or which shall be made, under the Authority of the United States, shall be the supreme Law of the Land; and the Judges in every State shall be bound thereby, any Thing in the Constitution or Laws of any State to the Contrary notwithstanding.

[3] The Senators and Representatives before

mentioned, and the Members of the several State Legislatures, and all executive and judicial Officers, both of the United States and of the several States, shall be bound by Oath or Affirmation, to support this Constitution; but no religious Test shall ever be required as a Qualification to any Office or public Trust under the United States.

ARTICLE VII

[1] The Ratification of the Conventions of nine States, shall be sufficient for the Establishment of this Constitution between the States so ratifying the Same.

[2] done in Convention by the Unanimous Consent of the States present the Seventeenth Day of September in the Year of our Lord one thousand seven hundred and Eighty seven and of the Independence of the United States of America the Twelfth In Witness whereof We have hereunto subscribed our Names,

Gº. Washington—Presidᵗ.
and deputy from Virginia

New Hampshire	John Langdon
	Nicholas Gilman
Massachusetts	Nathaniel Gorham
	Rufus King
Connecticut	Wm. Sand. Johnson
	Roger Sherman
New York	Alexander Hamilton
New Jersey	Wil: Livingston
	David Brearley
	Wm. Paterson
	Jona: Dayton
Pennsylvania	B Franklin
	Thomas Mifflin
	Robt Morris
	Geo. Clymer
	Thos. FitzSimons
	Jared Ingersoll
	James Wilson
	Gouv Morris

Delaware	Geo: Read
	Gunning Bedford jun
	John Dickinson
	Richard Bassett
	Jaco: Broom
Maryland	James McHenry
	Dan of St Thos. Jenifer
	Danl Carroll
Virginia	John Blair-
	James Madison Jr.
North Carolina	Wm. Blount
	Richd. Dobbs Spaight
	Hu Williamson
South Carolina	J. Rutledge
	Charles Cotesworth Pinckney
	Charles Pinckney
	Pierce Butler
Georgia	William Few
	Abr Baldwin

Attest William Jackson Secretary

AMENDMENT I
(December 15, 1791)

Congress shall make no law respecting an establishment of religion, or prohibiting the free exercise thereof; or abridging the freedom of speech, or of the press, or the right of the people peaceably to assemble, and to petition the Government for a redress of grievances.

AMENDMENT II
(December 15, 1791)

A well regulated Militia, being necessary to the security of a free State, the right of the people to keep and bear Arms, shall not be infringed.

AMENDMENT III
(December 15, 1791)

No Soldier shall, in time of peace be quartered in any house, without the consent of the Owner, nor in time of war, but in a manner to be prescribed by law.

AMENDMENT IV
(December 15, 1791)

The right of the people to be secure in their persons, houses, papers, and effects, against unreasonable searches and seizures, shall not be violated, and no Warrants shall issue, but upon probable cause, supported by Oath or affirmation, and particularly describing the place to be searched, and the persons or things to be seized.

AMENDMENT V
(December 15, 1791)

No person shall be held to answer for a capital, or otherwise infamous crime, unless on a presentment or indictment of a Grand jury, except in cases arising in the land or naval forces, or in the Militia, when in actual service in time of War or public danger; nor shall any person be subject for the same offence to be twice put in jeopardy of life or limb, nor shall be compelled in any criminal case to be a witness against himself, nor be deprived of Life, liberty, or property, without due process of law; nor shall private property be taken for public use without just compensation.

AMENDMENT VI
(December 15, 1791)

In all criminal prosecutions, the accused shall enjoy the right to a speedy and public trial, by an impartial jury of the State and district wherein the crime shall have been committed; which district shall have been previously ascertained by law, and to be informed of the nature and cause of the accusation; to be confronted with the witnesses against him; to have compulsory process for obtaining witnesses in his favor, and to have the assistance of counsel for his defence.

AMENDMENT VII

(December 15, 1791)

In Suits at common law, where the value in controversy shall exceed twenty dollars, the right of trial by jury shall be preserved, and no fact tried by a jury shall be otherwise re-examined in any Court of the United States, than according to the rules of the common law.

AMENDMENT VIII

(December 15, 1791)

Excessive bail shall not be required, nor excessive fines imposed, nor cruel and unusual punishments inflicted.

AMENDMENT IX

(December 15, 1791)

The enumeration in the Constitution of certain rights shall not be construed to deny or disparage others retained by the people.

AMENDMENT X

(December 15, 1791)

The powers not delegated to the United States by the Constitution, nor prohibited by it to the States, are reserved to the States respectively, or to the people.

AMENDMENT XI

(February 7, 1795)

The Judicial power of the United States shall not be construed to extend to any suit in law or equity, commenced or prosecuted against one of the United States by Citizens of another State, or by Citizens or Subjects of any Foreign State.

AMENDMENT XII

(June 15, 1804)

The Electors shall meet in their respective states, and vote by ballot for President and Vice President, one of whom, at least, shall not be an inhabitant of the same state with themselves; they shall name in their ballots the person voted for as President, and in distinct ballots the person voted for as Vice-President, and they shall make distinct lists of all persons voted for as President, and of all persons voted for as Vice-President, and of the number of votes for each, which lists they shall sign and certify, and transmit sealed to the seat of the government of the United States, directed to the President of the Senate;—The President of the Senate shall, in the presence of the Senate and House of Representatives, open all the certificates and the votes shall then be counted;—The person having the greatest number of votes for President, shall be the President, if such number be a majority of the whole number of Electors appointed; and if no person have such majority, then from the persons having the highest numbers not exceeding three on the list of those voted for as President, the House of Representatives shall choose immediately, by ballot, the President. But in choosing the President, the votes shall be taken by states, the representation from each state having one vote; a quorum for this purpose shall consist of a member or members from two-thirds of the states, and a majority of all the states shall be necessary to a choice. [And if the House of Representatives shall not choose a President whenever the right of choice shall devolve upon them, before the fourth day of March next following, then the Vice-President shall act as President, as in the case of the death or other constitutional disability of the President—] The person having the greatest number of votes as Vice-President, shall be the Vice-President, if such number be a majority of the whole number of Electors appointed, and if no person have a majority, then from the two highest numbers on the list, the Senate shall choose the Vice-President; a quorum for the purpose shall consist of two-thirds of the whole number of Senators, and a majority of the whole number shall be necessary to a choice. But no person constitutionally ineligible to the office of President shall be eligible to that of Vice-President of the United States.

AMENDMENT XIII
(December 6, 1865)

Section 1. Neither slavery nor involuntary servitude, except as a punishment for crime whereof the party shall have been duly convicted, shall exist within the United States, or any place subject to their jurisdiction.

Section 2. Congress shall have power to enforce this article by appropriate legislation.

AMENDMENT XIV
(July 9, 1868)

Section 1. All persons born or naturalized in the United States and subject to the jurisdiction thereof, are citizens of the United States and of the State wherein they reside. No State shall make or enforce any law which shall abridge the privileges or immunities of citizens of the United States; nor shall any State deprive any person of life, liberty, or property, without due process of law; nor deny to any person within its jurisdiction the equal protection of the laws.

Section 2. Representatives shall be apportioned among the several States according to their respective numbers, counting the whole number of persons in each State, excluding Indians not taxed. But when the right to vote at any election for the choice of electors for President and Vice President of the United States, Representatives in Congress, the Executive and Judicial officers of a State, or the members of the Legislature thereof, is denied to any of the male inhabitants of such State, being twenty-one years of age, and citizens of the United States, or in any way abridged, except for participation in rebellion, or other crime, the basis of representation therein shall be reduced in the proportion which the number of such male citizens shall bear to the whole number of male citizens twenty-one years of age in such State.

Section 3. No person shall be a Senator or Representative in Congress, or elector of President and Vice President, or hold any office, civil or military, under the United States, or under any State, who, having previously taken an oath, as a member of Congress, or as an officer of the United States, or as a member of any State legislature, or as an executive or judicial officer of any State, to support the Constitution of the United States, shall have engaged in insurrection or rebellion against the same, or given aid or comfort to the enemies thereof. But Congress may by a vote of two-thirds of each House, remove such disability.

Section 4. The validity of the public debt of the United States, authorized by law, including debts incurred for payment of pensions and bounties for services in suppressing insurrection or rebellion, shall not be questioned. But neither the United States nor any State shall assume or pay any debt or obligation incurred in aid of insurrection or rebellion against the United States, or any claim for the loss or emancipation of any slave; but all such debts, obligations and claims shall be held illegal and void.

Section 5. The Congress shall have power to enforce, by appropriate legislation, the provisions of this article.

AMENDMENT XV
(February 3, 1870)

Section 1. The right of citizens of the United States to vote shall not be denied or abridged by the United States or by any State on account of race, color, or previous condition of servitude.

Section 2. The Congress shall have power to enforce this article by appropriate legislation.

AMENDMENT XVI
(February 3, 1913)

The Congress shall have power to lay and collect taxes on incomes, from whatever source derived, without apportionment among the several States, and without regard to any census or enumeration.

AMENDMENT XVII
(April 8, 1913)

[1] The Senate of the United States shall be composed of two Senators from each State, elected by the people thereof, for six years; and each Senator shall have one vote. The electors in each State shall have the qualifications requisite for electors of the most numerous branch of the State legislatures.

[2] When vacancies happen in the representation of any State in the Senate, the executive authority of such State shall issue writs of election to fill such vacancies: *Provided,* That the legislature of any State may empower the executive thereof to make temporary appointments until the people fill the vacancies by election as the legislature may direct.

[3] This amendment shall not be so construed as to affect the election or term of any Senator chosen before it becomes valid as part of the Constitution.

AMENDMENT XVIII
(January 16, 1919)

[**Section 1.** After one year from the ratification of this article the manufacture, sale, or transportation of intoxicating liquors within, the importation thereof into, or the exportation thereof from the United States and all territory subject to the jurisdiction thereof for beverage purposes is hereby prohibited.

Section 2. The Congress and the several States shall have concurrent power to enforce this article by appropriate legislation.

Section 3. This article shall be inoperative unless it shall have been ratified as an amendment to the Constitution by the legislatures of the several States, as provided in the Constitution, within seven years from the date of the submission hereof to the States by the Congress.]

AMENDMENT XIX
(August 18, 1920)

[1] The right of citizens of the United States to vote shall not be denied or abridged by the United States or by any State on account of sex.

[2] Congress shall have power to enforce this article by appropriate legislation.

AMENDMENT XX
(January 23, 1933)

Section 1. The terms of the President and Vice President shall end at noon on the 20th day of January, and the terms of Senators and Representatives at noon on the 3d day of January, of the years in which such terms would have ended if this article had not been ratified; and the terms of their successors shall then begin.

Section 2. The Congress shall assemble at least once in every year, and such meeting shall begin at noon on the 3d day of January, unless they shall by law appoint a different day.

Section 3. If, at the time fixed for the beginning of the term of the President, the President elect shall have died, the Vice President elect shall become President. If a President shall not have been chosen before the time fixed for the beginning of his term, or if the President elect shall have failed to qualify, then the Vice President elect shall act as President until a President shall have qualified; and the Congress may by law provide for the case wherein neither a President elect nor a Vice President elect shall have qualified, declaring who shall then act as President, or the manner in which one who is to act shall be selected, and such person shall act accordingly until a President or Vice President shall have qualified.

Section 4. The Congress may by law provide for the case of the death of any of the persons from whom the House of Representatives may choose a President whenever the right of choice shall have devolved upon them, and for the case of the death of any of the persons from whom the Senate may choose a Vice President whenever the right of choice shall have devolved upon them.

Section 5. Sections 1 and 2 shall take effect on the 15th day of October following the ratification of this article.

Section 6. This article shall be inoperative unless it shall have been ratified as an amendment to the Constitution by the legislatures of three fourths of the several States within seven years from the date of its submission.

Amendment XXI

(December 5, 1933)

Section 1. The eighteenth article of amendment to the Constitution of the United States is hereby repealed.

Section 2. The transportation or importation into any State, Territory, or possession of the United States for delivery or use therein of intoxicating liquors, in violation of the laws thereof, is hereby prohibited.

Section 3. This article shall be inoperative unless it shall have been ratified as an amendment to the Constitution by conventions in the several States, as provided in the Constitution, within seven years from the date of the submission hereof to the States by the Congress.

Amendment XXII

(February 27, 1951)

Section 1. No person shall be elected to the office of the President more than twice, and no person who has held the office of President, or acted as President, for more than two years of a term to which some other person was elected President shall be elected to the office of the President more than once. But this Article shall not apply to any person holding the office of President when this Article was proposed by the Congress, and shall not prevent any person who may be holding the office of President, or acting as President, during the term within which this Article becomes operative from holding the office of President or acting as President during the remainder of such term.

Section 2. This article shall be inoperative unless it shall have been ratified as an amendment to the Constitution by the legislatures of three fourths of the several States within seven years from the date of its submission to the States by the Congress.

Amendment XXIII

(March 29, 1961)

Section 1. [1] The District constituting the seat of Government of the United States shall appoint in such manner as the Congress may direct:

[2] A number of electors of President and Vice President equal to the whole number of Senators and Representatives in Congress to which the District would be entitled if it were a State, but in no event more than the least populous State; they shall be in addition to those appointed by the States, but they shall be considered, for the purposes of the election of President and Vice President, to be electors appointed by a State; and they shall meet in the

District and perform such duties as provided by the twelfth article of amendment.

Section 2. The Congress shall have power to enforce this article by appropriate legislation.

AMENDMENT XXIV

(January 23, 1964)

Section 1. The right of citizens of the United States to vote in any primary or other election for President or Vice President, for electors for President or Vice President, or for Senator or Representative in Congress, shall not be denied or abridged by the United States or any State by reason of failure to pay any poll tax or other tax.

Section 2. The Congress shall have power to enforce this article by appropriate legislation.

AMENDMENT XXV

(February 10, 1967)

Section 1. In case of the removal of the President from office or of his death or resignation, the Vice President shall become President.

Section 2. Whenever there is a vacancy in the office of the Vice President, the President shall nominate a Vice President who shall take office upon confirmation by a majority vote of both Houses of Congress.

Section 3. Whenever the President transmits to the President pro tempore of the Senate and the Speaker of the House of Representatives his written declaration that he is unable to discharge the powers and duties of his office, and until he transmits to them a written declaration to the contrary, such powers and duties shall be discharged by the Vice President as Acting President.

Section 4. [1] Whenever the Vice President and a majority of either the principal officers of the executive departments or of such other body as Congress may by law provide, transmit to the President pro tempore of the Senate and the Speaker of the House of Representatives their written declaration that the President is unable to discharge the powers and duties of his office, the Vice President shall immediately assume the powers and duties of the office as Acting President.

[2] Thereafter, when the President transmits to the President pro tempore of the Senate and the Speaker of the House of Representatives his written declaration that no inability exists, he shall resume the powers and duties of his office unless the Vice President and a majority of either the principal officers of the executive department or of such other body as Congress may by law provide, transmit within four days to the President pro tempore of the Senate and the Speaker of the House of Representatives their written declaration that the President is unable to discharge the powers and duties of his office. Thereupon Congress shall decide the issue, assembling within forty-eight hours for that purpose if not in session. If the Congress, within twenty-one days after receipt of the latter written declaration, or, if Congress is not in session, within twenty-one days after Congress is required to assemble, determines by two-thirds vote of both Houses that the President is unable to discharge the powers and duties of his office, the Vice President shall continue to discharge the same as Acting President; otherwise, the President shall resume the powers and duties of his office.

AMENDMENT XXVI
(July 1, 1971)

Section 1. The right of citizens of the United States, who are eighteen years of age or older, to vote shall not be denied or abridged by the United States or by any State on account of age.

Section 2. The Congress shall have power to enforce this article by appropriate legislation.

AMENDMENT XXVII
(May 7, 1992)

No law, varying the compensation for the services of the Senators and Representatives shall take effect, until an election of Representatives shall have intervened.

Concordance to the Constitution

Abridge the privileges or immunities of citizens of the United States, Am.14-1

Abridging the freedom of speech, Am.1

Absence of the Vice President, I-3[5]

Absent Members, I-5[1]

Absolutely necessary, I-10[2]

Account of the receipts and expenditures, I-9[7]

According to Law, I-3[7]

According to the rules of the common law, Am.7

According to their respective numbers, Am.14-2

Accusation, Am.6

Accused, Am.6

Act accordingly, Am.20-3

Act as President, Am.20-3

Acted as President, Am.22-1

Acting as President, Am.22-1

Acting President, Am.25-3, Am.25-4[1], Am.25-4[2]

Actual service in time of War, Am.5

Adhering to their Enemies, III-3[1]

Adjourn, I-5[4], II-3

Adjournment, I-7[2], I-7[3], II-3

Admiralty and maritime jurisdiction, III-2[1]

Admitted by the Congress into this Union, IV-3[1]

Adoption of this Constitution, II-1[5], VI-1

Advice and Consent, II-2[2]

Affirmation, I-3[6], II-1[7], VI-3, Am.4

Age, I-2[2], Am.26-1

Age of twenty five Years, I-2[2]

Age of thirty five Years, II-1[5]

Age of thirty Years, I-3[3]

Agreement or Compact with another State, I-10[3]

Aid and Comfort, III-3[1]

Aid of insurrection or rebellion, Am.14-4

Aid or comfort to the enemies, Am.14-3

All Cases, I-6[1]

All other Officers, II-2[2]

All persons, Am.12, Am.14-1

All such Cases, I-7[2]

Alliance, I-10[1]

Ambassadors, II-2[2], II-3, III-2[1], III-2[2]

Amendment, Am.17-3, Am.18-3, Am.20-6, Am.21-1, Am.21-3, Am.22-2, Am.23-1[2]

Amendments, V

America, *Preamble*, II-1[1], VII-2

Among the several States, I-8[3]

Any person, II-1[5], Am.5, Am.14-1, Am.22-1

Any State, I-2[4], I-3[2], I-9[5], I-10[2], III-2[2], IV-2[2], IV-3[1], VI-2, Am.14-1, Am.14-3, Am.14-4, Am.15-1, Am.17-2, Am.19-1, Am.21-2, Am.24-1, Am.26-1

Appellate jurisdiction, III-2[2]

Application of the Legislature, IV-4

Application of the Legislatures, V

Appoint, II-1[2], II-2[2], Am.20-2, Am.23-1[1]

Appointed by the States, Am.23-1[2]

Appointed to any civil Office, I-6[2]

Appointment of the Officers, I-8[16]

Appointments, I-3[2], II-2[2], Am.17-2

Apportioned, I-2[3]

Apportioned among the several States, Am.14-2

Classes, I-3[2]
Coin, I-8[5], I-8[6], I-10[1]
Coin Money, I-8[5], I-10[1]
Collect taxes on incomes, Am.16
Color, Am.15-1
Comfort, III-3[1], Am.14-3
Commander in Chief, II-2[1]
Commerce, I-9[6]
Commerce . . . among the several States, I-8[3]
Commerce . . . with the Indian Tribes, I-8[3]
Commerce with foreign Nations, I-8[3]
Commission all the Officers, II-3
Commissions, II-2[3]
Common defence, *Preamble,* I-8[1]
Common law, Am.7
Compact with another State, I-10[3]
Compel the Attendance of absent Members, I-5[1]
Compelled in any criminal case to be a witness against himself, Am.5
Compensation, I-6[1], II-1[6], III-1, Am.27
Compulsory process for obtaining witnesses, Am.6
Concurrence of the Senate and House of Representatives, I-7[3]
Concurrence of two thirds, I-5[2]
Concurrence of two thirds of the Members present, I-3[6]
Concurrent power, Am.18-2
Condition of servitude, Am.15-1
Confederation, I-10[1], VI-1
Confession, III-3[1]
Confirmation by a majority vote of both Houses of Congress, Am.25-2
Confronted with the witnesses against him, Am.6
Congress, I-1, I-4[1], I-4[2], I-5[4], I-7[2], I-8[1], I-8[16], I-8[17], I-9[1], I-10[2], II-1[2], II-1[4], II-1[6], II-2[2], II-3, III-1, III-2[2], III-2[3], III-3[2], IV-1, IV-3[1], IV-3[2], V, Am.1, Am.13-2, Am.14-2, Am.14-3, Am.14-5, Am.15-2, Am.16, Am.18-2, Am.18-3, Am.19-2, Am.20-2, Am.20-3, Am.20-4, Am.21-3, Am.22-1, Am.22-2, Am.23-1[1], Am.23-1[2], Am.23-2, Am.24-1, Am.24-2, Am.25-2, Am.25-4[1], Am.25-4[2], Am.26-2
Congress of the United States, I-1, I-2[3]
Congress shall assemble, I-4[2]
Congress shall have Power, I-8[1]
Connecticut, I-2[3]
Consent, I-5[4], I-8[17], I-9[8], I-10[2], I-10[3], II-2[2], IV-3[1], V, VII-2, Am.3
Consent of Congress, I-10[3]
Consent of the Congress, I-9[8], I-10[2]

Consent of the Legislatures, IV-3[1]
Consent of the other, I-5[4]
Consent of the Owner, Am.3
Constitute Tribunals inferior to the supreme Court, I-8[9]
Constitution, *Preamble,* I-8[18], II-1[5], II-1[7], III-2[1], IV-3[2], V, VI-1, VI-2, VI-3, VII-1, Am.9, Am.10, Am.14-3, Am.17-3, Am.18-3, Am.20-6, Am.21-1, Am.21-3, Am.22-2
Constitutional disability, Am.12
Constitutionally ineligible, Am.12
Construed, IV-3[2], Am.9, Am.11, Am.17-3
Consuls, II-2[2], III-2[1], III-2[2]
Continuance in Office, I-6[2]
Contracts, I-10[1]
Controul of the Congress, I-10[2]
Controversies between two or more States, III-2[1]
Controversies to which the United States shall be a Party, III-2[1]
Convene both Houses, II-3
Convention, VII-2
Convention for proposing Amendments, V
Conventions, V
Conventions in the several States, Am.21-3
Conventions of nine States, VII-1
Conviction, II-4
Corruption of Blood, III-3[2]
Counterfeiting, I-8[6]
Court, III-3[1]
Court of the United States, Am.7
Courts of Law, II-2[2]
Credit of the United States, I-8[2]
Crime, IV-2[2], Am.5, Am.6, Am.13-1, Am.14-2
Crimes, II-4, III-2[3]
Criminal case, Am.5
Criminal prosecutions, Am.6
Cruel and unusual punishments, Am.8

Danger, Am.5
Date of its submission, Am.20-6
Day on which they shall give their Votes, II-1[4]
Death, Am.12
Death of any of the persons, Am.20-4
Death or resignation, Am.25-1
Death, Resignation, or Inability to discharge the Powers and Duties, II-1[6]
Debate, I-6[1]
Debts, I-8[1], I-10[1], VI-1

Excessive fines, Am.8
Excises, I-8[1]
Exclusive Legislation, I-8[17]
Exclusive Right, I-8[8]
Execute the Laws of the Union, I-8[15]
Execution of his Office, II-1[7]
Executive, I-3[2], IV-4, VI-3
Executive and Judicial officers of a State, Am.14-2
Executive Authority, I-2[4]
Executive authority of such State, Am.17-2
Executive department, Am.25-4[2]
Executive Departments, II-2[1], Am.25-4[1]
Executive or judicial officer of any State, Am.14-3
Executive Power, II-1[1]
Exercise exclusive Legislation, I-8[17]
Expel a Member, I-5[2]
Expiration, I-3[2]
Expire at the End of their next Session, II-2[3]
Exportation, Am.18-1
Exported, I-9[5]
Exports, I-10[2]
Extraordinary Occasions, II-3

Fact, III-2[2]
Fact tried by a jury, Am.7
Failed to qualify, Am.20-3
Failure to pay any poll tax or other tax, Am.24-1
Faithfully execute the Office, II-1[7]
Faithfully executed, II-3
Felonies committed on the high Seas, I-8[10]
Felony, I-6[1], IV-2[2]
Fill up all Vacancies, II-2[3]
Fines, Am.8
First Election, I-3[2]
First Monday in December, I-4[2]
Five highest on the List, II-1[3]
Fix the Standard of Weights and Measures, I-8[5]
Flee from Justice, IV-2[2]
Foreign Coin, I-8[5]
Foreign Power, I-10[3]
Foreign State, I-9[8], Am.11
Foreign States, III-2[1]
Forfeiture, III-3[2]
Form of Government, IV-4
Forts, I-8[17]
Forty-eight hours, Am.25-4[2]
Four days, Am.25-4[2]
Four Years, II-1[1]

Fourteen Years, II-1[5]
Fourth day of March, Am.12
Free exercise, Am.1
Free Persons, I-2[3]
Free state, Am.2
Freedom of speech, Am.1
From time to time, II-3
Full Faith and Credit, IV-1

General Laws, IV-1
General Welfare, *Preamble,* I-8[1]
Georgia, I-2[3]
Going to and returning from, I-6[1]
Gold and silver Coin, I-10[1]
Good Behaviour, III-1
Government, I-8[14], I-8[17], I-8[18], II-1[3], IV-4, Am.1, Am.12, Am.23
Government and Regulation of the land and naval Forces, I-8[14]
Government of the United States, I-8[17], I-8[18], II-1[3], Am.12, Am.23-1, Am.23-1[1]
Grand jury, Am.5
Grant Letters of Marque and Reprisal, I-8[11]
Grievances, Am.1
Guarantee to every State, IV-4

Habeas Corpus, I-9[2]
Heads of Departments, II-2[2]
Held to answer, Am.5
High Crimes and Misdemeanors, II-4
High Seas, I-8[10]
Holding Elections, I-4[1]
Honor, Trust or Profit, I-3[7]
House, I-5[1], I-5[2], I-5[3], I-5[4], I-6[2], I-7[2], Am.3
House in which it shall have originated, I-7[2]
House of Representatives, I-1, I-2[1], I-2[5], I-7[1], I-7[2], I-7[3], II-1[3], Am.12, Am.20-4, Am.25-3
Houses, I-5[4], I-6[1], II-3, V, Am.4, Am.25-2

Illegal and void, Am.14-4
Imminent Danger, I-10[3]
Impairing the Obligation of Contracts, I-10[1]
Impartial jury, Am.6
Impeachment, I-2[5], I-3[7], II-2[1], II-4, III-2[3]
Impeachments, I-3[6]
Importation, Am.18-1
Importation of such Persons, I-9[1]
Imports, I-10[2]

Sign and certify, Am.12

Silver Coin, I-10[1]

Six years, Am.17-1

Slave, Am.14-4

Slavery, Am.13-1

Smaller Number may adjourn from day to day, I-5[1]

Soldier, Am.3

Sole Power to try all impeachments, I-3[6]

South Carolina, I-2[3]

Speaker, I-2[5]

Speaker of the House of Representatives, Am.25-3, Am.25-4[1], Am.25-4[2]

Speech, Am.1

Speech or Debate in either House, I-6[1]

Speedy and public trial, Am.6

Standard of Weights and Measures, I-8[5]

State, I-2[2], I-2[3], I-2[4], I-3[1], I-3[2], I-4[1], I-8[17], I-9[5], I-9[6], I-10[1], I-10[2], I-10[3], II-1[2], II-1[3], III-2[2], III-2[3], IV-1, IV-2[2], IV-2[3], IV-3[1], IV-3[2], IV-4, VI-2, VI-3, Am.2, Am.6, Am.14-1, Am.14-2, Am.14-3, Am.14-4, Am.17-1, Am.17-2, Am.19-1, Am.23-1[2], Am.26-1

State and district wherein the crime shall have been committed, Am.6

State Legislature, I-2[1], Am.14-3

State legislatures, Am.17-1

State of the Union, II-3

Statement and Account, I-9[7]

States, I-8[16], I-8[17], I-9[1], II-1[3], III-2[1], VII-1, VII-2, Am.10, Am.12, Am.18-3, Am.21-3, Am.22-2

Subject for the same offence, Am.5

Subject to Indictment, I-3[7]

Subject to the jurisdiction, Am.14-1, Am.18-1

Subject to their jurisdiction, Am.13-1

Subjects, III-2[1]

Subjects of any Foreign State, Am.11

Such other body as Congress may by law provide, Am.25-4[1], Am.25-4[2]

Suffrage, V

Suit in law or equity, Am.11

Suits at common law, Am.7

Sundays, I-7[3]

Support the Constitution, Am.14-3

Support this Constitution, VI-3

Suppress Insurrections, I-8[15]

Supreme and inferior Courts, III-1

Supreme Court, I-8[9], II-2[2], III-1, III-2[2]

Supreme Law of the Land, VI-2

Take Care that the Laws be faithfully executed, II-3

Taken for public use, Am.5

Tax, I-9[1], I-9[5], Am.24-1

Taxes, I-2[3]

Taxes, Duties, Imposts and Excises, I-8[1]

Taxes on incomes, Am.16

Temporary Appointments, I-3[2], Am.17-2

Ten Days, I-7[2]

Ten dollars, I-9[1]

Ten Miles square, I-8[17]

Ten Years, I-2[3]

Tender in Payment of Debts, I-10[1]

Term, Am.17-3, Am.22-1

Term of four Years, II-1[1]

Term of ten Years, I-2[3]

Term of the President, Am.20-3

Term within which this Article becomes operative, Am.22-1

Terms of Senators and Representatives, Am.20-1

Terms of the President and Vice President, Am.20-1

Terms of their successors, Am.20-1

Territory, IV-3[2], Am.18-1, Am.21-2

Testimony of two Witnesses, III-3[1]

Thirty Thousand, I-2[3]

Three Classes, I-3[2]

Three days, I-5[4]

Three fifths of all other Persons, I-2[3]

Three fourths, V

Three fourths of the several States, Am.20-6, Am.22-2

Three Years, I-2[3]

Time of Adjournment, II-3

Time of chusing the Electors, II-1[4]

Time of Peace, I-9[3], Am.3

Time of war, Am.3, Am.5

Times, Places and Manner of holding Elections, I-4[1]

Title, I-9[8]

Title of Nobility, I-10[1]

Training the Militia, I-8[16]

Tranquility, *Preamble*

Transmit sealed, Am.12

Transportation of intoxicating liquors, Am.18-1

Transportation or importation, Am.21-2

Treason, I-6[1], II-4, III-3[1], III-3[2], IV-2[2]

Treasury, I-6[1], I-9[7], I-10[2]

Treasury of the United States, I-6[1], I-9[7]

Treaties, III-2[1], VI-2

Treaty, I-10[1]

Trial, I-3[7], III-2[3]

Time Chart of the Justices of the Supreme Court

The following groupings of justices show the changes in membership of the Supreme Court since 1789. A new grouping is given for each year in which a new justice (shown in italics) joined the Court. Chief justices are shown in bold.

1789–90
John Jay
John Rutledge
William Cushing
James Wilson
John Blair

1790–91
John Jay
John Rutledge
William Cushing
James Wilson
John Blair
James Iredell (a new, sixth seat)

1791–93
John Jay
William Cushing
James Wilson
John Blair
James Iredell
Thomas Johnson

1793–95
John Jay
William Cushing
James Wilson
John Blair
James Iredell
William Paterson

1795–96
***John Rutledge** (recess appointment, unconfirmed)*
William Cushing
James Wilson
John Blair
James Iredell
William Paterson

1796–98
Oliver Ellsworth
William Cushing
James Wilson
James Iredell
William Paterson
Samuel Chase

1798–99
Oliver Ellsworth
William Cushing
James Iredell
William Paterson
Samuel Chase
Bushrod Washington

1799–1800
Oliver Ellsworth
William Cushing
William Paterson
Samuel Chase

Bushrod Washington
Alfred Moore

1801–04
John Marshall
William Cushing
William Paterson
Samuel Chase
Bushrod Washington
Alfred Moore

1804–06
John Marshall
William Cushing
William Paterson
Samuel Chase
Bushrod Washington
William Johnson

1806–07
John Marshall
William Cushing
Samuel Chase
Bushrod Washington
William Johnson
Henry Brockholst Livingston

1807–11
John Marshall
William Cushing
Samuel Chase
Bushrod Washington
William Johnson
Henry Brockholst Livingston
Thomas Todd (a new, seventh seat)

1811–23
John Marshall
Bushrod Washington
William Johnson
Thomas Todd
Henry Brockholst Livingston
Joseph Story
Gabriel Duvall

1823–26
John Marshall
Bushrod Washington
William Johnson
Thomas Todd
Joseph Story

Gabriel Duvall
Smith Thompson

1826–28
John Marshall
Bushrod Washington
William Johnson
Joseph Story
Gabriel Duvall
Smith Thompson
Robert Trimble

1829–30
John Marshall
Bushrod Washington
William Johnson
Joseph Story
Gabriel Duvall
Smith Thompson
John McLean

1830–35
John Marshall
William Johnson
Joseph Story
Gabriel Duvall
Smith Thompson
John McLean
Henry Baldwin

1835
John Marshall
Joseph Story
Gabriel Duvall
Smith Thompson
John McLean
Henry Baldwin
James M. Wayne

1836–37
Roger B. Taney
Joseph Story
Smith Thompson
John McLean
Henry Baldwin
James M. Wayne
Philip P. Barbour

1837–41
Roger B. Taney
Joseph Story

Smith Thompson
John McLean
Henry Baldwin
James M. Wayne
Philip P. Barbour
John Catron (a new, eighth seat)
John McKinley (a new, ninth seat)

1841–45
Roger B. Taney
Joseph Story
Smith Thompson
John McLean
Henry Baldwin
James M. Wayne
John Catron
John McKinley
Peter V. Daniel

1845–46
Roger B. Taney
John McLean
Henry Baldwin
James M. Wayne
John Catron
John McKinley
Peter V. Daniel
Samuel Nelson
Levi Woodbury

1846–51
Roger B. Taney
John McLean
James M. Wayne
John Catron
John McKinley
Peter V. Daniel
Samuel Nelson
Levi Woodbury
Robert C. Grier

1851–53
Roger B. Taney
John McLean
James M. Wayne
John Catron
John McKinley
Peter V. Daniel
Samuel Nelson

Robert C. Grier
Benjamin R. Curtis

1853–57
Roger B. Taney
John McLean
James M. Wayne
John Catron
Peter V. Daniel
Samuel Nelson
Robert C. Grier
Benjamin R. Curtis
John A. Campbell

1858–62
Roger B. Taney
John McLean
James M. Wayne
John Catron
Peter V. Daniel
Samuel Nelson
Robert C. Grier
John A. Campbell
Nathan A. Clifford

1862–63
Roger B. Taney
James M. Wayne
John Catron
Samuel Nelson
Robert C. Grier
Nathan A. Clifford
Noah H. Swayne
Samuel F. Miller
David Davis

1863–64
Roger B. Taney
James M. Wayne
John Catron
Samuel Nelson
Robert C. Grier
Nathan A. Clifford
Noah H. Swayne
Samuel F. Miller
David Davis
Stephen J. Field (a new, tenth seat)

1864–65
Salmon P. Chase
James M. Wayne

John Catron
Samuel Nelson
Robert C. Grier
Nathan A. Clifford
Noah H. Swayne
Samuel F. Miller
David Davis
Stephen J. Field

1865–67
Salmon P. Chase
James M. Wayne
Samuel Nelson
Robert C. Grier
Nathan A. Clifford
Noah H. Swayne
Samuel F. Miller
David Davis
Stephen J. Field
(Note: *Catron died in 1865 and Congress abolished his seat, reducing the number of justices to nine.*)

1867–70
Salmon P. Chase
Samuel Nelson
Robert C. Grier
Nathan A. Clifford
Noah H. Swayne
Samuel F. Miller
David Davis
Stephen J. Field
(Note: *Wayne died in 1867 and Congress abolished his seat, reducing the number of justices to eight.*)

1870–72
Salmon P. Chase
Samuel Nelson
Nathan A. Clifford
Noah H. Swayne
Samuel F. Miller
David Davis
Stephen J. Field
William Strong
Joseph P. Bradley (a new, ninth seat)

1872–74
Salmon P. Chase
Nathan A. Clifford
Noah H. Swayne
Samuel F. Miller

David Davis
Stephen J. Field
William Strong
Joseph P. Bradley
Ward Hunt

1874–77
Morrison R. Waite
Nathan A. Clifford
Noah H. Swayne
Samuel F. Miller
David Davis
Stephen J. Field
William Strong
Joseph P. Bradley
Ward Hunt

1877–80
Morrison R. Waite
Nathan A. Clifford
Noah H. Swayne
Samuel F. Miller
Stephen J. Field
William Strong
Joseph P. Bradley
Ward Hunt
John Marshall Harlan

1880–81
Morrison R. Waite
Nathan A. Clifford
Noah H. Swayne
Samuel F. Miller
Stephen J. Field
Joseph P. Bradley
Ward Hunt
John Marshall Harlan
William B. Woods

1881–82
Morrison R. Waite
Samuel F. Miller
Stephen J. Field
Joseph P. Bradley
Ward Hunt
John Marshall Harlan
William B. Woods
Stanley Matthews
Horace Gray

1882–88
Morrison R. Waite
Samuel F. Miller
Stephen J. Field
Joseph P. Bradley
John Marshall Harlan
William B. Woods
Stanley Matthews
Horace Gray
Samuel Blatchford

1888–89
Melville W. Fuller
Samuel F. Miller
Stephen J. Field
Joseph P. Bradley
John Marshall Harlan
Stanley Matthews
Horace Gray
Samuel Blatchford
Lucius Q. C. Lamar

1889–90
Melville W. Fuller
Samuel F. Miller
Stephen J. Field
Joseph P. Bradley
John Marshall Harlan
Horace Gray
Samuel Blatchford
Lucius Q. C. Lamar
David J. Brewer

1890–92
Melville W. Fuller
Stephen J. Field
Joseph P. Bradley
John Marshall Harlan
Horace Gray
Samuel Blatchford
Lucius Q. C. Lamar
David J. Brewer
Henry B. Brown

1892–93
Melville W. Fuller
Stephen J. Field
John Marshall Harlan
Horace Gray
Samuel Blatchford

Lucius Q. C. Lamar
David J. Brewer
Henry B. Brown
George Shiras

1893–94
Melville W. Fuller
Stephen J. Field
John Marshall Harlan
Horace Gray
Samuel Blatchford
David J. Brewer
Henry B. Brown
George Shiras
Howell E. Jackson

1894–95
Melville W. Fuller
Stephen J. Field
John Marshall Harlan
Horace Gray
David J. Brewer
Henry B. Brown
George Shiras
Howell E. Jackson
Edward D. White

1895–98
Melville W. Fuller
Stephen J. Field
John Marshall Harlan
Horace Gray
David J. Brewer
Henry B. Brown
George Shiras
Edward D. White
Rufus W. Peckham

1898–1902
Melville W. Fuller
John Marshall Harlan
Horace Gray
David J. Brewer
Henry B. Brown
George Shiras
Edward D. White
Rufus W. Peckham
Joseph McKenna

1902–03

Melville W. Fuller
John Marshall Harlan
David J. Brewer
Henry B. Brown
George Shiras
Edward D. White
Rufus W. Peckham
Joseph McKenna
Oliver Wendell Holmes

1903–06

Melville W. Fuller
John Marshall Harlan
David J. Brewer
Henry B. Brown
Edward D. White
Rufus W. Peckham
Joseph McKenna
Oliver Wendell Holmes
William R. Day

1906–09

Melville W. Fuller
John Marshall Harlan
David J. Brewer
Edward D. White
Rufus W. Peckham
Joseph McKenna
Oliver Wendell Holmes
William R. Day
William H. Moody

1909–10

Melville W. Fuller
John Marshall Harlan
David J. Brewer
Edward D. White
Joseph McKenna
Oliver Wendell Holmes
William R. Day
William H. Moody
Horace H. Lurton

1910–11

Edward D. White (elevated from associate justiceship)
John Marshall Harlan
Joseph McKenna
Oliver Wendell Holmes
William R. Day

Horace H. Lurton
Charles Evans Hughes
Willis Van Devanter
Joseph R. Lamar

1912–14

Edward D. White
Joseph McKenna
Oliver Wendell Holmes
William R. Day
Horace H. Lurton
Charles Evans Hughes
Willis Van Devanter
Joseph R. Lamar
Mahlon Pitney

1914–16

Edward D. White
Joseph McKenna
Oliver Wendell Holmes
William R. Day
Charles Evans Hughes
Willis Van Devanter
Joseph R. Lamar
Mahlon Pitney
James C. McReynolds

1916–21

Edward D. White
Joseph McKenna
Oliver Wendell Holmes
William R. Day
Willis Van Devanter
Mahlon Pitney
James C. McReynolds
Louis D. Brandeis
John J. Clarke

1921–22

William Howard Taft
Joseph McKenna
Oliver Wendell Holmes
William R. Day
Willis Van Devanter
Mahlon Pitney
James C. McReynolds
Louis D. Brandeis
John J. Clarke

1922–23
William Howard Taft
Joseph McKenna
Oliver Wendell Holmes
Willis Van Devanter
Mahlon Pitney
James C. McReynolds
Louis D. Brandeis
George Sutherland
Pierce Butler

1923–25
William Howard Taft
Joseph McKenna
Oliver Wendell Holmes
Willis Van Devanter
James C. McReynolds
Louis D. Brandeis
George Sutherland
Pierce Butler
Edward T. Sanford

1925–30
William Howard Taft
Oliver Wendell Holmes
Willis Van Devanter
James C. McReynolds
Louis D. Brandeis
George Sutherland
Pierce Butler
Edward T. Sanford
Harlan Fiske Stone

1930–32
Charles Evans Hughes
Oliver Wendell Holmes
Willis Van Devanter
James C. McReynolds
Louis D. Brandeis
George Sutherland
Pierce Butler
Harlan Fiske Stone
Owen J. Roberts

1932–37
Charles Evans Hughes
Willis Van Devanter
James C. McReynolds
Louis D. Brandeis
George Sutherland

Pierce Butler
Harlan Fiske Stone
Owen J. Roberts
Benjamin N. Cardozo

1937–38
Charles Evans Hughes
James C. McReynolds
Louis D. Brandeis
George Sutherland
Pierce Butler
Harlan Fiske Stone
Owen J. Roberts
Benjamin N. Cardozo
Hugo L. Black

1938–39
Charles Evans Hughes
James C. McReynolds
Louis D. Brandeis
Pierce Butler
Harlan Fiske Stone
Owen J. Roberts
Benjamin N. Cardozo
Hugo L. Black
Stanley F. Reed

1939–40
Charles Evans Hughes
James C. McReynolds
Pierce Butler
Harlan Fiske Stone
Owen J. Roberts
Hugo L. Black
Stanley F. Reed
Felix Frankfurter
William O. Douglas

1940–41
Charles Evans Hughes
James C. McReynolds
Harlan Fiske Stone
Owen J. Roberts
Hugo L. Black
Stanley F. Reed
Felix Frankfurter
William O. Douglas
Frank Murphy

1941–43
Harlan Fiske Stone *(elevated from associate justiceship)*
Owen J. Roberts
Hugo L. Black
Stanley F. Reed
Felix Frankfurter
William O. Douglas
Frank Murphy
James F. Byrnes
Robert H. Jackson

1943–45
Harlan Fiske Stone
Owen J. Roberts
Hugo L. Black
Stanley F. Reed
Felix Frankfurter
William O. Douglas
Frank Murphy
Robert H. Jackson
Wiley B. Rutledge

1945–46
Harlan Fiske Stone
Hugo L. Black
Stanley F. Reed
Felix Frankfurter
William O. Douglas
Frank Murphy
Robert H. Jackson
Wiley B. Rutledge
Harold H. Burton

1946–49
Fred M. Vinson
Hugo L. Black
Stanley F. Reed
Felix Frankfurter
William O. Douglas
Frank Murphy
Robert H. Jackson
Wiley B. Rutledge
Harold H. Burton

1949–53
Fred M. Vinson
Hugo L. Black
Stanley F. Reed
Felix Frankfurter
William O. Douglas

Robert H. Jackson
Harold H. Burton
Tom C. Clark
Sherman Minton

1953–55
Earl Warren
Hugo L. Black
Stanley F. Reed
Felix Frankfurter
William O. Douglas
Robert H. Jackson
Harold H. Burton
Tom C. Clark
Sherman Minton

1955–56
Earl Warren
Hugo L. Black
Stanley F. Reed
Felix Frankfurter
William O. Douglas
Harold H. Burton
Tom C. Clark
Sherman Minton
John Marshall Harlan

1956–57
Earl Warren
Hugo L. Black
Stanley F. Reed
Felix Frankfurter
William O. Douglas
Harold H. Burton
Tom C. Clark
John Marshall Harlan
William J. Brennan

1957–58
Earl Warren
Hugo L. Black
Felix Frankfurter
William O. Douglas
Harold H. Burton
Tom C. Clark
John Marshall Harlan
William J. Brennan
Charles E. Whittaker

1958–62

Earl Warren
Hugo L. Black
Felix Frankfurter
William O. Douglas
Tom C. Clark
John Marshall Harlan
William J. Brennan
Charles E. Whittaker
Potter Stewart

1962–65

Earl Warren
Hugo L. Black
William O. Douglas
Tom C. Clark
John Marshall Harlan
William J. Brennan
Potter Stewart
Byron R. White
Arthur Goldberg

1965–67

Earl Warren
Hugo L. Black
William O. Douglas
Tom C. Clark
John Marshall Harlan
William J. Brennan
Potter Stewart
Byron R. White
Abe Fortas

1967–69

Earl Warren
Hugo L. Black
William O. Douglas
John Marshall Harlan
William J. Brennan
Potter Stewart
Byron R. White
Abe Fortas
Thurgood Marshall

1969–70

Warren E. Burger
Hugo L. Black
William O. Douglas
John Marshall Harlan
William J. Brennan

Potter Stewart
Byron R. White
Abe Fortas
Thurgood Marshall

1970–71

Warren E. Burger
Hugo L. Black
William O. Douglas
John Marshall Harlan
William J. Brennan
Potter Stewart
Byron R. White
Thurgood Marshall
Harry A. Blackmun

1972–75

Warren E. Burger
William O. Douglas
William J. Brennan
Potter Stewart
Byron R. White
Thurgood Marshall
Harry A. Blackmun
Lewis F. Powell, Jr.
William H. Rehnquist

1975–81

Warren E. Burger
William J. Brennan
Potter Stewart
Byron R. White
Thurgood Marshall
Harry A. Blackmun
Lewis F. Powell, Jr.
William H. Rehnquist
John Paul Stevens

1981–86

Warren E. Burger
William J. Brennan
Byron R. White
Thurgood Marshall
Harry A. Blackmun
Lewis F. Powell, Jr.
William H. Rehnquist
John Paul Stevens
Sandra Day O'Connor

643

1986–87

William H. Rehnquist *(elevated from associate justiceship)*
William J. Brennan
Byron R. White
Thurgood Marshall
Harry A. Blackmun
Lewis F. Powell, Jr.
John Paul Stevens
Sandra Day O'Connor
Antonin Scalia

1988–90

William H. Rehnquist
William J. Brennan
Byron R. White
Thurgood Marshall
Harry A. Blackmun
John Paul Stevens
Sandra Day O'Connor
Antonin Scalia
Anthony M. Kennedy

1990–91

William H. Rehnquist
Byron R. White
Thurgood Marshall
Harry A. Blackmun
John Paul Stevens
Sandra Day O'Connor
Antonin Scalia
Anthony M. Kennedy
David H. Souter

1991–

William H. Rehnquist
Byron R. White
Harry A. Blackmun
John Paul Stevens
Sandra Day O'Connor
Antonin Scalia
Anthony M. Kennedy
David H. Souter
Clarence Thomas

Biographical Notes on the Justices of the Supreme Court

Dates following each name are years served on the Supreme Court. Chief justices are denoted immediately after dates of service by "CJ." Colleges and law schools attended, as applicable, and family status follow the dates of birth and death. Primary occupations or businesses and last official position before joining the Supreme Court then follow. After the confirmation vote is the date of confirmation. If a justice retired or resigned it is noted, but no notation is given if a justice died in office. Following the date of confirmation is the name of the succeeding justice.

BALDWIN, HENRY   1830–44

Born January 14, 1780, New Haven, CT; died April 21, 1844.

Yale College; studied law privately. Married twice, one child.

Lawyer; newspaper publisher; businessman. U.S. representative, Connecticut.

Nominated by President Jackson; confirmed 41–2, January 6, 1830; replaced by Robert C. Grier.

BARBOUR, PHILIP PENDLETON   1836–41

Born May 25, 1783, Orange County, VA; died February 25, 1841.

Attended one session at College of William and Mary; self-taught in law. Married, seven children.

Lawyer. Judge, U.S. District Court of Eastern Virginia.

Nominated by President Jackson; confirmed 30–11, March 15, 1836; replaced by Peter Vivian Daniel.

BLACK, HUGO LAFAYETTE   1937–71

Born February 27, 1886, Harlan, AL; died September 25, 1971.

Birmingham Medical College; University of Alabama Law School. Married twice, three children.

Lawyer. U.S. senator, Democrat–Alabama.

Nominated by President Franklin D. Roosevelt; confirmed 63–16, August 17, 1937; retired September 17, 1971; replaced by Lewis F. Powell, Jr.

BLACKMUN, HARRY ANDREW   1970–

Born November 12, 1908, Nashville, IL.

Harvard College; Harvard Law School. Married, three children.

Lawyer; law professor. Judge, U.S. Court of Appeals for the Eighth Circuit.

Nominated by President Nixon; confirmed 94–0, May 12, 1970.

BLAIR, JR., JOHN   1789–96

Born 1732, Williamsburg, VA; died August 31, 1800.

College of William and Mary; Middle Temple, London. Married.

Lawyer. Judge, Virginia Supreme Court of Appeals.

Nominated by President Washington; confirmed by voice vote, September 26, 1789; resigned January 27, 1796; replaced by Samuel Chase.

BLATCHFORD, SAMUEL   1882–93

Born March 9, 1820, New York, NY; died July 7, 1893.

Columbia College. Read law privately. Married.

Lawyer. Republican. Judge, Second Circuit of New York.
Nominated by President Arthur; confirmed by voice vote,
March 27, 1882; replaced by Edward D. White.

BRADLEY, JOSEPH P.   1870–92
Born March 14, 1813, Berne, NY; died January 22, 1892.
Rutgers University. Married, seven children.
Lawyer. Republican.
Nominated by President Grant; confirmed 46–9, March
21, 1870; replaced by George Shiras, Jr.

BRANDEIS, LOUIS DEMBITZ   1916–39
Born November 13, 1856, Louisville, KY; died October 5,
1941.
Harvard Law School. Married, two children.
Lawyer.
Nominated by President Wilson; confirmed 47–22, June 1,
1916; retired February 13, 1939; replaced by William O.
Douglas.

BRENNAN, JR., WILLIAM JOSEPH   1956–90
Born April 25, 1906, Newark, NJ.
University of Pennsylvania; Harvard Law School. Married twice, three children.
Lawyer. Democrat. Justice, New Jersey Supreme Court.
Recess appointment, President Eisenhower, October 16,
1956; nominated by President Eisenhower; confirmed
by voice vote, March 19, 1957; retired July 20, 1990;
replaced by David H. Souter.

BREWER, DAVID JOSIAH   1889–1910
Born June 20, 1837, Smyrna, Asia Minor; died March 28,
1910.
Wesleyan College; Yale University; Albany Law School.
Married twice.
Lawyer. Judge, federal circuit court for the Eighth Circuit.
Nominated by President Harrison; confirmed 53–11, December 18, 1889; replaced by Charles Evans Hughes.

BROWN, HENRY BILLINGS   1890–1906
Born March 2, 1836, South Lee, MA; died September 4,
1913.
Yale College; briefly at Yale and Harvard law schools.
Married twice.
Lawyer. Republican. Judge, U.S. District Court of Eastern
Michigan.

Nominated by President Harrison; confirmed by voice
vote, December 29, 1890; retired May 28, 1906; replaced
by William H. Moody.

BURGER, WARREN EARL   1969–86   CJ
Born September 17, 1907, St. Paul, MN.
University of Minnesota; St. Paul College of Law (Mitchell College). Married, two children.
Lawyer; law professor. Republican. Judge, U.S. Court of
Appeals for the District of Columbia Circuit.
Nominated chief justice by President Nixon to replace
Chief Justice Earl Warren; confirmed 74–3, June 9,
1969; retired September 26, 1986; replaced as chief justice by William H. Rehnquist.

BURTON, HAROLD HITZ   1945–58
Born June 22, 1888, Jamaica Plain, MA; died October, 28,
1964.
Bowdoin College; Harvard Law School. Married, four
children.
Lawyer. U.S. senator, Republican–Ohio.
Nominated by President Truman; confirmed by voice
vote, September 19, 1945; retired October, 13, 1958; replaced by Potter Stewart.

BUTLER, PIERCE   1922–39
Born March 17, 1866, Northfield, MN; died November 16,
1939.
Carleton College. Married, eight children.
Lawyer. County attorney, Ramsey County, Minnesota.
Nominated by President Harding; confirmed 61–8, December 21, 1922; replaced by Frank Murphy.

BYRNES, JAMES FRANCIS   1941–42
Born May 2, 1879, Charleston, SC; died April 9, 1972.
St. Patrick's parochial school; studied law privately. Married.
U.S. senator, Democrat–South Carolina.
Nominated by President Franklin D. Roosevelt; confirmed by voice vote, June 12, 1941; resigned October 3,
1942; replaced by Wiley B. Rutledge.

CAMPBELL, JOHN ARCHIBALD   1853–61
Born June 24, 1811, Washington, GA; died March 12, 1889.
Franklin College (University of Georgia); U.S. Military
Academy at West Point. Married, five children.
Lawyer. Alabama state representative, sessions 1837, 1843.

Nominated by President Pierce; confirmed by voice vote, March 25, 1853; resigned April 30, 1861; replaced by David Davis.

CARDOZO, BENJAMIN NATHAN   1932–38
Born May 24, 1870, New York, NY; died July 9, 1938.
Columbia College; Columbia Law School (no degree). Unmarried.
Lawyer. Chief judge, New York State Court of Appeals.
Nominated by President Hoover; confirmed by voice vote, February 24, 1932; replaced by Felix Frankfurter.

CATRON, JOHN   1837–65
Born c. 1786, PA; died May 30, 1865.
Self-educated. Married.
Businessman; lawyer. First chief justice of the Tennessee Supreme Court of Errors and Appeals.
Nominated by President Jackson to fill a newly created seat (later abolished by Congress); confirmed 28–15.

CHASE, SALMON PORTLAND   1864–73   CJ
Born January 13, 1808, Cornish, NH; died May 7, 1873.
Dartmouth College. Married three times, six children.
Lawyer. Republican. U.S. secretary of the treasury.
Nominated chief justice by President Lincoln; confirmed by voice vote, December 6, 1864; replaced by Morrison R. Waite.

CHASE, SAMUEL   1796–1811
Born April 17, 1741, Somerset County, MD; died June 19, 1811.
Tutored at home; studied law privately. Married twice, four children.
Businessman; lawyer. Federalist. Chief judge, General Court of Maryland.
Nominated by President Washington; confirmed by voice vote, January 27, 1796; replaced by Gabriel Duvall.

CLARK, TOM CAMPBELL   1949–67
Born September 23, 1899, Dallas, TX; died June 13, 1977.
University of Texas. Married, three children.
Lawyer. Democrat. U.S. attorney general.
Nominated by President Truman; confirmed 73–8, August 18, 1949; retired June 12, 1967; replaced by Thurgood Marshall.

CLARKE, JOHN HESSIN   1916–22
Born September 18, 1857, Lisbon, OH; died March 22, 1945.

Western Reserve University. Unmarried.
Lawyer. Judge, U.S. District Court for Northern District of Ohio.
Nominated by President Wilson; confirmed by voice vote, July 24, 1916; resigned September 18, 1922; replaced by George Sutherland.

CLIFFORD, NATHAN   1858–81
Born August 18, 1803, Rumney, NH; died July 25, 1881.
Studied law privately. Married, six children.
Lawyer. Democrat. Minister to Mexico.
Nominated by President Buchanan; confirmed 26–23, January 12, 1858; replaced by Horace Gray.

CURTIS, BENJAMIN ROBBINS   1851–57
Born November 4, 1809, Watertown, MA; died September 15, 1874.
Harvard College; Harvard Law School. Married three times, four children.
Lawyer. Whig. Massachusetts state representative.
Nominated by President Fillmore; confirmed by voice vote, December 29, 1851; resigned September 30, 1857; replaced by Nathan Clifford.

CUSHING, WILLIAM   1789–1810
Born March 1, 1732, Scituate, MA; died September 13, 1810.
Harvard College; studied law privately. Married.
Lawyer. Delegate to electoral college.
Nominated by President Washington; confirmed by voice vote, September 26, 1789; replaced by Joseph Story.

DANIEL, PETER VIVIAN   1841–60
Born April 24, 1784, Stafford County, VA; died May 31, 1860.
College of New Jersey (Princeton University). Studied law privately. Married twice, two children.
Lawyer. Democrat. Judge, U.S. District Court of Eastern Virginia.
Nominated by President Van Buren; confirmed 22–5, March 2, 1841; replaced by Samuel F. Miller.

DAVIS, DAVID   1862–77
Born March 9, 1815, Cecil County, MD; died June 26, 1886.
Kenyon College; Yale Law School. Married twice, two children.
Lawyer. Labor Reform. Judge, Illinois State Circuit.
Nominated by President Lincoln; confirmed by voice

vote, December 8, 1862; resigned March 4, 1877; replaced by John Marshall Harlan.

DAY, WILLIAM RUFUS 1903–22

Born April 17, 1849, Ravenna, OH; died July 9, 1923.

University of Michigan; University of Michigan Law School. Married, four children.

Lawyer. Republican. Judge, U.S. Court of Appeals for the Sixth Circuit.

Nominated by President Theodore Roosevelt; confirmed by voice vote, February 23, 1903; resigned November 13, 1922; replaced by Pierce Butler.

DOUGLAS, WILLIAM ORVILLE 1939–75

Born October 16, 1898, Maine, MN; died January 19, 1980.

Whitman College; Columbia Law School. Married four times, two children.

Lawyer; law professor. Chairman, Securities and Exchange Commission.

Nominated by President Franklin D. Roosevelt; confirmed 62–4, April 4, 1939; retired November 12, 1975; replaced by John Paul Stevens.

DUVALL, GABRIEL 1811–35

Born December 6, 1752, Prince Georges County, MD; died March 6, 1844.

Studied law privately. Married twice, one child.

First comptroller of the U.S. treasury.

Nominated by President Madison; confirmed by voice vote, November 18, 1811; resigned January 14, 1835; replaced by Philip Barbour.

ELLSWORTH, OLIVER 1796–1800 CJ

Born April 29, 1745, Windsor, CT; died November 26, 1807.

College of New Jersey (Princeton University). Married, seven children.

Lawyer; farmer. Federalist. U.S. senator, Connecticut.

Nominated chief justice by President Washington; confirmed 21–1, March 4, 1796; resigned September 30, 1800; replaced by John Marshall.

FIELD, STEPHEN JOHNSON 1863–97

Born November 4, 1816, Haddam, CT; died April 9, 1899.

Williams College; studied law privately. Married.

Lawyer. Justice, California Supreme Court.

Nominated by President Lincoln; confirmed by voice vote, March 10, 1863; retired December 1, 1897; replaced by Joseph McKenna.

FORTAS, ABE 1965–69

Born June 19, 1910, Memphis, TN; died April 5, 1982.

Southwestern College; Yale Law School. Married.

Lawyer; law professor. U.S. undersecretary of the interior.

Nominated by President Lyndon B. Johnson; confirmed by voice vote, August 11, 1965; resigned May 14, 1969; replaced by Harry A. Blackmun.

FRANKFURTER, FELIX 1939–62

Born November 15, 1882, Vienna, Austria; died February 22, 1965.

College of the City of New York; Harvard Law School. Married.

Lawyer; law professor. Chairman, War Labor Policies Board.

Nominated by President Franklin D. Roosevelt; confirmed by voice vote, January 17, 1939; retired August 28, 1962; replaced by Arthur Goldberg.

FULLER, MELVILLE WESTON 1888–1910 CJ

Born February 11, 1833, Augusta, ME; died July 4, 1910.

Bowdoin College; Harvard Law School. Married twice, eight children.

Lawyer. Democrat. Illinois state representative.

Nominated chief justice by President Cleveland; confirmed 41–20, July 20, 1888; replaced as chief justice by Edward D. White.

GOLDBERG, ARTHUR JOSEPH 1962–65

Born August 8, 1908, Chicago, IL.

Northwestern University. Married, two children.

Lawyer. U.S. secretary of labor.

Nominated by President Kennedy; confirmed by voice vote, September 25, 1962; resigned July 25, 1965; replaced by Abe Fortas.

GRAY, HORACE 1881–1902

Born March 24, 1828, Boston, MA; died September 15, 1902.

Harvard College; Harvard Law School. Married.

Lawyer. Free Soil Party. Chief justice, Massachusetts Supreme Court.

Nominated by President Arthur; confirmed 51–5, December 20, 1881; replaced by Oliver Wendell Holmes, Jr.

GRIER, ROBERT COOPER 1846–70

Born March 5, 1794, Cumberland County, PA; died September 25, 1870.

Dickinson College. Married.

Teacher; lawyer. Democrat. President judge, District Court of Allegheny County, PA.

Nominated by President Polk; confirmed by voice vote, August 4, 1846; retired January 31, 1870; replaced by William Strong.

HARLAN, JOHN MARSHALL   1877–1911

Born June 1, 1833, Boyle County, KY; died October 14, 1911.

Centre College; Transylvania University. Married, six children.

Lawyer. Republican. Member, Louisiana Reconstruction Commission.

Nominated by President Hayes; confirmed by voice vote, November 29, 1877; replaced by Mahlon Pitney.

HARLAN, JOHN MARSHALL   1955–71

Born May 20, 1899, Chicago, IL; died December 29, 1971.

Princeton University; Rhodes scholar, Balliol College, Oxford University; New York Law School. Married, one child.

Lawyer. Republican. Judge, U.S. Court of Appeals for the Second Circuit.

Nominated by President Eisenhower; confirmed 71–11, March 16, 1955; retired September 23, 1971; replaced by William H. Rehnquist.

HOLMES, JR., OLIVER WENDELL   1902–32

Born March 8, 1841, Boston, MA; died March 6, 1935.

Harvard College. Married.

Lawyer; law professor. Republican. Chief justice, Massachusetts Supreme Court.

Nominated by President Theodore Roosevelt; confirmed by voice vote, December 4, 1902; retired January 12, 1932; replaced by Benjamin N. Cardozo.

HUGHES, CHARLES EVANS   1910–16, 1930–41   CJ

Born April 11, 1862, Glens Falls, NY; died August 27, 1948.

Colgate University; Brown University; Columbia Law School. Married, three children.

Lawyer; law professor. Governor of New York.

Nominated by President Taft; confirmed by voice vote, May 2, 1910; resigned June 10, 1916; replaced by John H. Clarke; nominated chief justice by President Hoover; confirmed 52–26, February 13, 1930; retired July 1, 1941; replaced by Harlan F. Stone.

HUNT, WARD   1873–82

Born June 14, 1810, Utica, NY; died March 24, 1886.

Union College; studied law privately. Married twice, two children.

Lawyer. Republican. New York State commissioner of appeals.

Nominated by President Grant; confirmed by voice vote, December 11, 1872; retired January 27, 1882; replaced by Samuel Blatchford.

IREDELL, JAMES   1790–99

Born October 5, 1751, Lewes, England; died October 20, 1799.

Schooled in England; read law privately. Married, three children.

Lawyer. Member, North Carolina convention to ratify U.S. Constitution.

Nominated by President Washington; confirmed by voice vote, February 10, 1790; replaced by Alfred Moore.

JACKSON, HOWELL EDMUNDS   1893–95

Born April 8, 1832, Paris, TN; died August 8, 1895.

West Tennessee College; University of Virginia; Cumberland University. Married twice, seven children.

Lawyer. Whig. Judge, federal circuit court for the Sixth Circuit.

Nominated by President Harrison; confirmed by voice vote, February 18, 1893; replaced by Rufus W. Peckham.

JACKSON, ROBERT HOUGHWOUT   1941–54

Born February 13, 1892, Spring Creek, PA; died October 9, 1954.

Albany Law School; Chautauqua Institution. Married, two children.

Lawyer. Democrat. U.S. attorney general.

Nominated by President Franklin D. Roosevelt; confirmed by voice vote, July 7, 1941; replaced by John Marshall Harlan.

JAY, JOHN   1789–95   CJ

Born December 12, 1745, New York, NY; died May 17, 1829.

King's College (Columbia University). Married, seven children.

Lawyer. U.S. secretary of state.

Nominated chief justice by President Washington; confirmed by voice vote, September 26, 1789; resigned June 29, 1795; replaced by Oliver Ellsworth.

JOHNSON, THOMAS   1791–93

Born November 4, 1732, Calvert County, MD; died October 26, 1819.

Schooled at home; studied law privately. Married, eight children.

Lawyer; businessman. Chief judge, General Court of Maryland.

Nominated by President Washington; confirmed by voice vote, November 7, 1791; resigned February 1, 1793; replaced by William Paterson.

JOHNSON, WILLIAM   1804–34

Born December 17, 1771, Charleston, SC; died August 4, 1834.

College of New Jersey (Princeton University); studied law privately. Married, ten children.

Lawyer. Republican. Judge, New Jersey Court of Common Pleas.

Nominated by President Jefferson; confirmed by voice vote, March 24, 1804; replaced by James M. Wayne.

KENNEDY, ANTHONY MCLEOD   1988–

Born July 23, 1936, Sacramento, CA.

Stanford University; London School of Economics; Harvard Law School. Married, three children.

Lawyer; law professor. Judge, U.S. Court of Appeals for the Ninth Circuit.

Nominated by President Reagan; confirmed 97–0, February 3, 1988.

LAMAR, JOSEPH RUCKER   1910–16

Born October 14, 1857, Elbert County, GA; died January 2, 1916.

University of Georgia; Bethany College; Washington and Lee University. Married, three children.

Lawyer. Democrat. Justice, Georgia Supreme Court.

Nominated by President Taft; confirmed by voice vote, December 15, 1910; replaced by Louis D. Brandeis.

LAMAR, LUCIUS QUINTUS CINCINNATUS   1888–93

Born September 17, 1825, Eatonton, GA; died January 23, 1893.

Emory College. Married twice, four children.

Lawyer; professor of metaphysics. Democrat. U.S. secretary of the interior.

Nominated by President Cleveland; confirmed 32–28, January 16, 1888; replaced by Howell Edmunds Jackson.

LIVINGSTON, HENRY BROCKHOLST   1806–23

Born November 25, 1757, New York, NY; died March 18, 1823.

College of New Jersey (Princeton University); studied law privately. Married three times, eleven children.

Lawyer. Justice, New York State Supreme Court.

Nominated by President Jefferson; confirmed by voice vote, December 17, 1806; replaced by Smith Thompson.

LURTON, HORACE HARMON   1909–14

Born February 26, 1844, Newport, KY; died July 12, 1914.

University of Chicago; Cumberland University Law School. Married, four children.

Lawyer; banker; law professor; dean. Democrat. Judge, U.S. Court of Appeals for the Sixth Circuit.

Nominated by President Taft; confirmed by voice vote, December 20, 1909; replaced by James C. McReynolds.

MARSHALL, JOHN   1801–35   CJ

Born September 24, 1755, Germantown, VA; died July 6, 1835.

Home-educated; self-taught in law. Married, ten children.

Lawyer. U.S. secretary of state.

Nominated chief justice by President John Adams; confirmed by voice vote, January 27, 1801; replaced by Roger B. Taney.

MARSHALL, THURGOOD   1967–91

Born July 2, 1908, Baltimore, MD.

Lincoln University; Howard University Law School. Married twice, two children.

Lawyer. U.S. solicitor general.

Nominated by President Lyndon B. Johnson; confirmed 69–11, August 30, 1967; retired June 27, 1991; replaced by Clarence Thomas.

MATTHEWS, STANLEY   1881–89

Born July 21, 1824, Cincinnati, OH; died March 22, 1889.

Kenyon College. Married twice, eight children.

Lawyer. U.S. senator, Republican–Ohio.

Nominated by President Hayes (no action taken by Senate); renominated by President Garfield; confirmed 24–23, May 12, 1881; replaced by David J. Brewer.

MCKENNA, JOSEPH   1898–1925

Born August 10, 1843, Philadelphia, PA; died November 21, 1926.

Benicia Collegiate Institute. Married, three children.

Lawyer. Republican. U.S. attorney general.

Nominated by President McKinley; confirmed by voice

vote, January 21, 1898; retired January 5, 1925; replaced by Harlan F. Stone.

McKinley, John   1837–52

Born May 1, 1780, Culpeper County, VA; died July 19, 1852.

Self-taught in law. Married twice.

Lawyer. U.S. representative, Democrat–Alabama.

Nominated by President Van Buren; confirmed by voice vote, September 25, 1837; replaced by John A. Campbell.

McLean, John   1829–61

Born March 11, 1785, Morris County, NJ; died April 4, 1861.

Privately tutored; read law privately. Married twice, eight children.

Lawyer. Republican. U.S. postmaster general.

Nominated by President Jackson; confirmed by voice vote, January 7, 1829; replaced by Noah H. Swayne.

McReynolds, James Clark   1914–41

Born February 3, 1862, Elkton, KY; died August 24, 1946.

Vanderbilt University; University of Virginia Law School. Unmarried.

Lawyer; law professor. Democrat. U.S. attorney general.

Nominated by President Wilson; confirmed 44–6, August 29, 1914; retired January 31, 1941; replaced by Robert H. Jackson.

Miller, Samuel Freeman   1862–90

Born April 5, 1816, Richmond, KY; died October 13, 1890.

Transylvania University; studied law privately. Married twice, five children.

Medical doctor; lawyer. Republican. Justice of the peace and member of court, Knox County, Kentucky.

Nominated by President Lincoln; confirmed by voice vote, July 16, 1862; replaced by Henry B. Brown.

Minton, Sherman   1949–56

Born October 20, 1890, Georgetown, IN; died April 9, 1965.

Indiana University; Yale Law School. Married, three children.

Democrat. Judge, U.S. Court of Appeals for the Seventh Circuit.

Nominated by President Truman; confirmed 48–15, October 4, 1949; retired October 15, 1956; replaced by William J. Brennan, Jr.

Moody, William Henry   1906–10

Born December 23, 1853, Newbury, MA; died July 2, 1917.

Harvard College; Harvard Law School. Unmarried.

Lawyer. Republican. U.S. attorney general.

Nominated by President Theodore Roosevelt; confirmed by voice vote, December 12, 1906; retired November 20, 1910; replaced by Joseph R. Lamar.

Moore, Alfred   1799–1804

Born May 21, 1755, New Hanover County, NC; died October 15, 1810.

Studied law privately. Married.

Federalist. Judge, North Carolina Superior Court.

Nominated by President John Adams; confirmed by voice vote, December 10, 1799; resigned January 26, 1804; replaced by William Johnson.

Murphy, Francis William   1940–49

Born April 13, 1890, Harbor Beach, MI; died July 19, 1949.

University of Michigan; Lincoln's Inn, London; Trinity College, Dublin. Unmarried.

Lawyer. Democrat. U.S. attorney general.

Nominated by President Franklin D. Roosevelt; confirmed by voice vote, January 15, 1940; replaced by Tom C. Clark.

Nelson, Samuel   1845–72

Born November 10, 1792, Hebron, NY; died December 13, 1873.

Middlebury College. Married twice, four children.

Lawyer. Democrat. Chief justice, New York Supreme Court.

Nominated by President John Tyler; confirmed by voice vote, February 14, 1845; retired November 28, 1872; replaced by Ward Hunt.

O'Connor, Sandra Day   1981–

Born March 26, 1930, El Paso, TX.

Stanford University; Stanford Law School. Married, three children.

Lawyer. Judge, Arizona Court of Appeals.

Nominated by President Reagan; confirmed 99–0, September 21, 1981.

Paterson, William   1793–1806

Born December 24, 1745, County Antrim, Ireland; died September 9, 1806.

College of New Jersey (Princeton University); studied law privately. Married twice, three children.

Lawyer. Governor of New Jersey.

Nominated by President Washington; confirmed by voice vote, March 4, 1793; replaced by Henry B. Livingston.

PECKHAM, RUFUS WHEELER   1895–1909

Born November 8, 1838, Albany, NY; died October 24, 1909.

Albany Boys' Academy; studied privately. Married, two children.

Lawyer. Judge, New York Court of Appeals.

Nominated by President Cleveland; confirmed by voice vote, December 9, 1895; replaced by Horace Harmon Lurton.

PITNEY, MAHLON   1912–22

Born February 5, 1858, Morristown, NJ; died December 9, 1924.

College of New Jersey (Princeton University). Studied law privately. Married, three children.

Lawyer. Republican. Chancellor, New Jersey Court of Appeals.

Nominated by President Taft; confirmed 50–26, March 13, 1912; retired December 31, 1922; replaced by Edward T. Sanford.

POWELL, JR., LEWIS FRANKLIN   1971–87

Born September 19, 1907, Suffolk, VA.

Washington and Lee University; Washington and Lee Law School; Harvard Law School. Married, four children.

Lawyer. President, American Bar Association.

Nominated by President Nixon; confirmed 89–1, December 6, 1971; retired June 26, 1987; replaced by Anthony Kennedy.

REED, STANLEY FORMAN   1938–57

Born December 31, 1884, Minerva, KY; died April 2, 1980.

Kentucky Wesleyan College; Yale University; University of Virginia Law School; Columbia Law School; University of Paris. Married, two children.

Lawyer. Democrat. U.S. solicitor general.

Nominated by President Franklin D. Roosevelt; confirmed by voice vote, January 25, 1938; retired February 25, 1957; replaced by Charles E. Whittaker.

REHNQUIST, WILLIAM HUBBS   1971–   CJ

Born October 1, 1924, Milwaukee, WI.

Stanford University; Harvard University; Stanford Law School. Married, three children.

Lawyer. Republican. Assistant U.S. attorney general, Office of Legal Counsel.

Nominated by President Nixon; confirmed 68–26, December 10, 1971; nominated chief justice by President Reagan; confirmed 65–33, September 17, 1986; replaced as associate justice by Antonin Scalia.

ROBERTS, OWEN JOSEPHUS   1930–45

Born May 2, 1875, Germantown, PA; died May 17, 1955.

University of Pennsylvania; University of Pennsylvania Law School. Married.

Lawyer; law professor. Republican. Special U.S. attorney to investigate and prosecute the Teapot Dome Scandal.

Nominated by President Hoover; confirmed by voice vote, June 2, 1930; resigned July 31, 1945; replaced by Harold H. Burton.

RUTLEDGE, JOHN   1789–91

Born September, 1739, Charleston, SC; died July 18, 1800.

Privately tutored; studied law in England. Married, ten children.

Lawyer. Member, South Carolina convention to ratify U.S. Constitution.

Nominated by President Washington; confirmed by voice vote, September 26, 1789; resigned March 5, 1791; replaced by Thomas Johnson. (Later sworn in as chief justice August 12, 1795, but not confirmed.)

RUTLEDGE, WILEY BLOUNT   1943–49

Born July 20, 1894, Cloverport, KY; died September 10, 1949.

University of Wisconsin; University of Colorado. Married, three children.

Lawyer; law professor; dean. Judge, U.S. Court of Appeals for the District of Columbia Circuit.

Nominated by President Franklin D. Roosevelt; confirmed by voice vote, February 8, 1943; replaced by Sherman Minton.

SANFORD, EDWARD TERRY   1923–30

Born July 23, 1865, Knoxville, TN; died March 8, 1930.

University of Tennessee; Harvard College; Harvard Law School. Married, two children.

Lawyer. Judge, U.S. District Court for the Middle and Eastern Districts of Tennessee.

Nominated by President Harding; confirmed by voice vote, January 29, 1923; replaced by Owen J. Roberts.

SCALIA, ANTONIN   1986–

Born March 11, 1936, Trenton, NJ.

Georgetown University; Harvard Law School. Married, nine children.

Lawyer; law professor. Judge, U.S. Court of Appeals for the District of Columbia Circuit.

Nominated by President Reagan; confirmed 98–0, September 17, 1986.

SHIRAS, JR., GEORGE   1892–1903

Born January 26, 1832, Pittsburgh, PA; died August 2, 1924.

Ohio University; Yale University; studied law at Yale Law School and privately. Married, two children.

Lawyer. Republican.

Nominated by President Harrison; confirmed by voice vote, July 26, 1892; retired February 23, 1903; replaced by William R. Day.

STEVENS, JOHN PAUL   1975–

Born April 20, 1920, Chicago, IL.

University of Chicago; Northwestern University School of Law. Married twice, four children.

Lawyer; law professor. Republican. Judge, U.S. Court of Appeals for the Seventh Circuit.

Nominated by President Ford; confirmed 98–0, December 17, 1975.

STEWART, POTTER   1958–81

Born January 23, 1915, Jackson, MI; died December 7, 1985.

Yale College; Yale Law School; Cambridge University. Married, three children.

Lawyer. Republican. Judge, U.S. Court of Appeals for the Sixth Circuit.

Received recess appointment by President Eisenhower, October 14, 1958; nominated by President Eisenhower; confirmed 70–17, May 5, 1959; retired July 3, 1981; replaced by Sandra Day O'Connor.

STONE, HARLAN FISKE   1925–46   **CJ**

Born October 11, 1872, Chesterfield, NH; died April 22, 1946.

Amherst College; Columbia Law School. Married, two children.

Lawyer; law professor; dean. Republican. U.S. attorney general.

Nominated by President Coolidge; confirmed 71–6, February 5, 1925; nominated chief justice by President

Franklin D. Roosevelt; confirmed by voice vote, June 27, 1941; replaced by Fred M. Vinson.

STORY, JOSEPH   1811–45

Born September 18, 1779, Marblehead, MA; died September 10, 1845.

Harvard College; read law privately. Married twice, seven children.

Lawyer. U.S. representative, Republican-Democrat–Massachusetts.

Nominated by President Madison; confirmed by voice vote, November 18, 1811; replaced by Levi Woodbury.

STRONG, WILLIAM   1870–80

Born May 6, 1808, Somers, CT; died August 19, 1895.

Yale College. Married twice, seven children.

Lawyer. Republican. Justice, Pennsylvania Supreme Court.

Nominated by President Grant; confirmed by voice vote, February 18, 1870; retired December 14, 1880; replaced by William B. Woods.

SUTHERLAND, GEORGE   1922–38

Born March 25, 1862, Buckinghamshire, England; died July 18, 1942.

Brigham Young Academy; University of Michigan Law School. Married, three children.

Lawyer. Republican. U.S. counsel, Norway–United States arbitration, The Hague.

Nominated by President Harding; confirmed by voice vote, September 5, 1922; replaced by Stanley F. Reed.

SWAYNE, NOAH HAYNES   1862–81

Born December 7, 1804, Frederick County, VA; died June 8, 1884.

Studied law privately. Married, five children.

Lawyer. Republican. City councilman, Columbus, Ohio.

Nominated by President Lincoln; confirmed 38–1, January 24, 1862; retired January 24, 1881; replaced by Stanley Matthews.

TAFT, WILLIAM HOWARD   1921–30   **CJ**

Born September 15, 1857; died March 8, 1930.

Yale College; Cincinnati Law School. Married, three children.

Lawyer. Republican. U.S. president; joint chairman, National War Labor Board.

Nominated chief justice by President Harding; confirmed

by voice vote, June 30, 1921; retired February 3, 1930; replaced by Charles Evans Hughes.

TANEY, ROGER BROOKE   1836–64   CJ
Born March 17, 1777, Calvert County, MD; died October 12, 1864.
Dickinson College; read law privately. Married, seven children.
Lawyer. Federalist. U.S. secretary of the treasury.
Nominated chief justice by President Jackson; confirmed 29–15, March 15, 1836; replaced by Salmon P. Chase.

THOMAS, CLARENCE   1991–
Born June 28, 1948, Pin Point, GA.
Immaculate Conception Seminary; Holy Cross; Yale Law School. Married twice, one child.
Lawyer. Republican. Judge, U.S. Court of Appeals for the District of Columbia Circuit.
Nominated by President Bush; confirmed 52–48, October 15, 1991.

THOMPSON, SMITH   1823–43
Born c. January 17, 1768, Dutchess County, NY; died December 18, 1843.
College of New Jersey (Princeton University); studied law privately. Married twice.
Republican. U.S. secretary of the navy.
Nominated by President Monroe; confirmed by voice vote, December 19, 1823; replaced by Samuel Nelson.

TODD, THOMAS   1807–26
Born January 23, 1765, King and Queen County, VA; died, February 7, 1826.
Liberty Hall (Washington and Lee University); read law privately. Married twice, eight children.
Lawyer. Chief justice, Kentucky Court of Appeals.
Nominated by President Jefferson; confirmed by voice vote, March 3, 1807; replaced by Robert Trimble.

TRIMBLE, ROBERT   1826–28
Born November 17, 1776, Berkeley County, VA; died August 25, 1828.
Bourbon Academy; Kentucky Academy; read law privately. Married, ten children.
Lawyer. Judge, U.S. District Court of Kentucky.
Nominated by President John Quincy Adams; confirmed 27–5, May 9, 1826; replaced by John McLean.

VAN DEVANTER, WILLIS   1910–37
Born April 17, 1859, Marion, IN; died February 8, 1941.
Indiana Asbury University (DePauw); University of Cincinnati Law School. Married.
Lawyer. Republican. Judge, U.S. Court of Appeals for the Eighth Circuit.
Nominated by President Taft; confirmed by voice vote December 15, 1910; retired June 2, 1937; replaced by Hugo L. Black.

VINSON, FREDERICK MOORE   1946–53   CJ
Born January 22, 1890, Louisa, KY; died September 8, 1953.
Centre College. Married, two children.
Lawyer. U.S. secretary of the treasury.
Nominated chief justice by President Truman; confirmed by voice vote, June 20, 1946; replaced by Earl Warren.

WAITE, MORRISON REMICK   1874–88   CJ
Born November 29, 1816, Lyme, CT; died March 23, 1888.
Yale College. Married, five children.
Lawyer. Republican. President, Ohio constitutional convention.
Nominated chief justice by President Grant; confirmed 63–0, January 21, 1874; replaced by Melville W. Fuller.

WARREN, EARL   1953–69   CJ
Born March 19, 1891, Los Angeles, CA; died July 9, 1974.
University of California Law School. Married, six children.
Lawyer. Republican. Governor of California.
Nominated chief justice by President Eisenhower; confirmed by voice vote, March 1, 1954; retired June 23, 1969; replaced by Warren E. Burger.

WASHINGTON, BUSHROD   1798–1829
Born June 5, 1762, Westmoreland County, VA; died November 26, 1829.
College of William and Mary; read law privately. Married.
Lawyer. Member, Virginia convention to ratify U.S. Constitution.
Nominated by President John Adams; confirmed by voice vote, December 20, 1798; replaced by Henry Baldwin.

WAYNE, JAMES MOORE   1835–67
Born c. 1790, Savannah, GA; died July 5, 1867.
College of New Jersey (Princeton University); read law privately. Married, three children.

Lawyer. U.S. representative, Democrat–Georgia.

Nominated by President Jackson; confirmed by voice vote, January 9, 1835; replaced by Joseph Bradley.

WHITTAKER, CHARLES EVANS   1957–62

Born February 22, 1901, Troy, KS; died November 26, 1973.

University of Kansas City Law School. Married, three children.

Lawyer. Republican. Judge, U.S. Court of Appeals for the Eighth Circuit.

Nominated by President Eisenhower; confirmed by voice vote, March 19, 1957; retired March 31, 1962; replaced by Byron R. White.

WHITE, BYRON RAYMOND   1962–

Born June 8, 1917, Fort Collins, CO.

University of Colorado; Oxford University; Yale Law School. Married, two children.

Lawyer. Deputy U.S. attorney general.

Nominated by President Kennedy; confirmed by voice vote, April 11, 1962.

WHITE, EDWARD DOUGLASS   1894–1921   CJ

Born November 3, 1845, Parish of Lafourche, LA; died May 19, 1921.

Mount St. Mary's College; Georgetown College; studied law privately. Married.

Lawyer. U.S. senator, Democrat–Louisiana.

Nominated by President Cleveland; confirmed by voice vote, February 19, 1894; nominated chief justice by President Taft; confirmed by voice vote, December 12, 1910; replaced as chief justice by former President Taft.

WILSON, JAMES   1789–98

Born September 14, 1742, Caskardy, Scotland; died August 21, 1798.

University of St. Andrews, Scotland; read law privately. Married twice, seven children.

Lawyer; businessman. Member, Pennsylvania convention to ratify U.S. Constitution.

Nominated by President Washington; confirmed by voice vote, August 21, 1798; replaced by Bushrod Washington.

WOODBURY, LEVI   1846–51

Born December 22, 1789, Francestown, NH; died September 4, 1851.

Dartmouth College; Tapping Reeve Law School. Married, five children.

Lawyer. Democrat. U.S. secretary of the treasury.

Nominated by President Polk; confirmed by voice vote, January 3, 1846; replaced by Benjamin R. Curtis.

WOODS, WILLIAM BURNHAM   1880–87

Born August 3, 1824, Newark, OH; died May 14, 1887.

Western Reserve College; Yale College; studied law privately. Married, two children.

Lawyer. Republican. Judge, federal circuit court for the Fifth Circuit.

Nominated by President Hayes; confirmed 39–8, December 21, 1880; replaced by Lucius Q. C. Lamar.

Table of Cases

This table lists all Supreme Court cases from 1790 to 1991 discussed in this book. Cases decided during the 1991–92 term of the Supreme Court are listed in a separate table, beginning on p. 736. Cases decided by lower courts are noted in the Endnotes beginning on p. 742.

This table is arranged alphabetically. Cases with descriptive names—for example, the Steel Seizure Case—are cross-referenced to their formal names. Cases beginning with "Estate of," "Ex parte," "In re," "Matter of," and other merely descriptive labels are indexed by the names of the parties, as are cases beginning with "City of," "State of," "Village of," "United States," and the like.

Case numbers used throughout the text refer to the number preceding the name of each case in this table. The case name is followed by its citation in the *United States Reports*. For example, 410 U.S. 113 refers to volume 410 of the *U.S. Reports*, p. 113. (Until 1875, Supreme Court cases were cited also to the reporter who compiled them; for example, 5 U.S. (1 Cr.) 137 (1803), the citation to *Marbury v. Madison*, refers to volume one of William Cranch's compilations.) The most recent cases, those decided in 1991 and 1992, for which official citations have not yet been given, are cited instead by their location in the West Publishing Company's *Supreme Court Reporter* ("S.Ct."). Case citations are followed by the vote and by the justice who wrote the majority opinion (the name is in CAPITAL LETTERS). Justices who concurred or dissented are listed as indicated. The last page reference is to the length of all opinions in the *Reports* for each case.

Notation of concurrences or dissents is not intended to reflect the complexity of the voting coalitions in particular cases. In some cases, it is easy to determine the meaning of a 5–4 split: five justices were in the majority, and four dissented to the Court's judgment. But in many recent cases, it requires the considerable power of a tea leaf reader to discern who sided with whom and how, as the following notation of the justices' position in a 1991 case shows (the wording that follows is that of the Court itself):

BLACKMUN, J., announced the judgment of the Court and delivered the opinion of the Court with respect to Parts, I, II, III-B, III-C, IV-B (except for the final paragraph), IV-D, IV-E, and IV-F, in which REHNQUIST, C.J., and WHITE and STEVENS, JJ., joined. MARSHALL, J., filed an opinion concurring in part and dissenting in part. SCALIA, J., filed an opinion concurring in the judgment in part and dissenting in part, in which O'CONNOR and SOUTER, JJ., joined, and in all but Part III-C of which KENNEDY, J., joined. KENNEDY, J., filed an opinion concurring in the judgment in part and dissenting in part. [Lehnert v. Ferris Faculty Assn., 111 S.Ct. 1950 (1991)]

34. Alexander v. Holmes County Board of
    Education, 396 U.S. 19 (1969).
    9–0, PER CURIAM. 3pp.

35. Alexander v. Louisiana, 405 U.S. 625 (1972).
    7–0, WHITE. Concurrence: Douglas. Not
    voting: Powell, Rehnquist. 20pp.

36. Alfred Dunhill of London, Inc. v. Republic of
    Cuba, 425 U.S. 682 (1976).
    5–4, WHITE. Concurrences: Stevens, Powell.
    Dissents: Marshall, Brennan, Stewart,
    Blackmun. 55pp.

37. Allegheny County v. Greater Pittsburgh
    American Civil Liberties Union, 492 U.S.
    573 (1989).
    5–4 (various coalitions), BLACKMUN.
    Concurrences: O'Connor, Brennan, Stevens,
    Marshall, Kennedy. Dissents: Kennedy,
    Rehnquist, White, Scalia, Stevens, Brennan,
    Marshall. 107pp.

38. Allegheny Pittsburgh Coal v. Webster County,
    488 U.S. 336 (1989).
    9–0, REHNQUIST. 11pp.

39. Allgeyer v. Louisiana, 165 U.S. 578 (1897).
    9–0, PECKHAM. 15pp.

40. Allied Stores of Ohio, Inc. v. Bowers, 358 U.S.
    522 (1959).
    9–0, WHITTAKER. Concurrences: Brennan,
    Harlan. Not voting: Stewart. 12pp.

41. Allied Structural Steel Co. v. Spannaus, 438 U.S.
    234 (1978).
    6–3, STEWART. Dissents: Brennan, Marshall,
    White. 31pp.

42. Allstate Insurance Co. v. Hague, 449 U.S. 302
    (1981).
    5–3, BRENNAN. Concurrence: Stevens.
    Dissents: Powell, Burger, Rehnquist. Not
    voting: Stewart. 39pp.

43. Almeida-Sanchez v. U.S., 413 U.S. 266 (1973).
    5–4, STEWART. Concurrence: Powell.
    Dissents: White, Burger, Blackmun,
    Rehnquist. 34pp.

44. Amadeo v. Zant, 486 U.S. 214 (1988).
    9–0, MARSHALL. 15pp.

45. Amalgamated Food Employees v. Logan Valley
    Plaza, 391 U.S. 308 (1968).
    6–3, MARSHALL. Concurrence: Douglas.
    Dissents: Black, Harlan, White. 32pp.

46. Ambach v. Norwick, 441 U.S. 68 (1979).
    5–4, POWELL. Dissents: Blackmun, Brennan,
    Marshall, Stevens. 22pp.

47. Amerada Hess Corp. v. New Jersey Division of
    Taxation, 490 U.S. 66 (1989).
    8–0, BLACKMUN. Concurrence: Scalia. Not
    voting: O'Connor. 16pp.

48. American Booksellers Assn. v. Hudnut, 771 F.2d
    323 (7th Cir. 1985), aff'd, 475 U.S. 1001 (1986).
    PER CURIAM. 1p.

49. American Communications v. Douds, 339 U.S.
    382 (1950).
    6–3, VINSON. Dissents: Frankfurter, Jackson,
    Black. 72pp.

50. American Federation of Labor v. American Sash
    and Door Co., 335 U.S. 538 (1949).
    8–1, BLACK. Concurrences: Frankfurter,
    Rutledge. Dissent: Murphy. 5pp.

51. American Insurance Co. v. Canter, 26 U.S. (1
    Pet.) 511 (1828).
    7–0, MARSHALL. 36pp.

52. American Party of Texas v. White, 415 U.S. 767
    (1974).
    8–1, WHITE. Dissent: Douglas. 32pp.

53. American Power Co. v. Securities and Exchange
    Commission, 329 U.S. 90 (1946).
    4–2, MURPHY. Concurrences: Frankfurter,
    Rutledge. Dissents: Frankfurter, Rutledge.
    Not voting: Reed, Douglas, Jackson. 39pp.

54. American Publishing Co. v. Fisher, 166 U.S. 464
    (1897).
    9–0, BREWER. 5pp.

55. American Trucking Assns. v. Atchison, Topeka
    & Santa Fe Railway, 387 U.S. 397 (1967).
    6–3, FORTAS. Dissents: Black, Stewart,
    Harlan. 26pp.

56. American Trucking Assns. v. Smith, 496 U.S. 167
    (1990).
    5–4, O'CONNOR. Concurrence: Scalia.
    Dissents: Stevens, Brennan, Marshall,
    Blackmun. 58pp.

57. American Trucking Assns. v. Scheiner, 483 U.S.
    266 (1987).
    5–4, STEVENS. Dissents: O'Connor,
    Rehnquist, Powell, Scalia. 41pp.

58. Anastaplo, In re, 366 U.S. 82 (1961).
    5–4, HARLAN. Dissents: Black, Brennan,
    Warren, Douglas. 34pp.

84. Ashcraft v. Tennessee, 322 U.S. 143 (1944).
    6–3, BLACK. Dissents: Jackson, Roberts, Frankfurter. 31pp.

85. Ashe v. Swenson, 397 U.S. 436 (1970).
    8–1, STEWART. Concurrences: Black, Harlan, Brennan, Douglas, Marshall. Dissent: Burger. 35pp.

86. Ashton v. Cameron County District, 298 U.S. 513 (1936).
    5–4, McREYNOLDS. Dissents: Cardozo, Hughes, Brandeis, Stone. 31pp.

87. Ashton v. Kentucky, 384 U.S. 195 (1966).
    9–0, DOUGLAS. Concurrence: Harlan. 7pp.

88. Ashwander v. Tennessee Valley Authority, 297 U.S. 288 (1936).
    8–1, HUGHES. Concurrence: Brandeis. Dissent: McReynolds. 85pp.

89. Associated Enterprises v. Toltec Watershed Imp. District, 410 U.S. 743 (1973).
    6–3, PER CURIAM. Dissents: Douglas, Brennan, Marshall. 9pp.

90. Associated Press v. U.S., 326 U.S. 1 (1945).
    6–3, BLACK. Concurrences: Reed, Douglas, Rutledge, Frankfurter. Dissents: Stone, Roberts, Murphy. 59pp.

91. Associated Press v. Walker, 388 U.S. 130 (1967).
    7–2, 5–4, HARLAN. Concurrences: Warren, Black, Douglas, Brennan, White. Dissents: Black, Brennan, Douglas, White. 44pp.

92. Association of Data Processing Service Organizations v. Camp, 397 U.S. 150 (1970).
    7–2, DOUGLAS. Dissents: Brennan, White. 8pp.

93. Atherton Mills v. Johnston, 259 U.S. 13 (1922).
    9–0, TAFT. 3pp.

94. Atlantic Coast Line Railroad Co. v. City of Goldsboro, 232 U.S. 548 (1914).
    9–0, PITNEY. 15pp.

95. Atlas Roofing Co. v. OSHRC, 430 U.S. 442 (1977).
    8–0, WHITE. Not voting: Blackmun. 20pp.

96. Atlee v. Richardson, 411 U.S. 911 (1973).
    PER CURIAM. 1p.

97. Attorney General of New York v. Soto-Lopez, 476 U.S. 898 (1986).
    6–3, BRENNAN. Concurrences: Burger, White. Dissents: Stevens, O'Connor, Rehnquist. 28pp.

98. Austin v. Michigan State Chamber of Commerce, 494 U.S. 652 (1990).
    6–3, MARSHALL. Concurrences: Brennan, Stevens. Dissents: Scalia, Kennedy, O'Connor. 36pp.

99. Austin v. New Hampshire, 420 U.S. 656 (1975).
    7–1, MARSHALL. Dissent: Blackmun. Not voting: Douglas. 15pp.

100. Bacchus Imports, Ltd. v. Dias, 468 U.S. 263 (1984).
    6–3, WHITE. Dissents: Stevens, Rehnquist, O'Connor. 25pp.

101. Baender v. Barnett, 255 U.S. 224 (1921).
    9–0, VAN DEVANTER. 4pp.

102. Baggett v. Bullitt, 377 U.S. 360 (1964).
    7–2, WHITE. Dissents: Clark, Harlan. 24pp.

103. Bailey v. Alabama, 219 U.S. 219 (1911).
    7–2, HUGHES. Dissents: Holmes, Lurton. 31pp.

104. Bailey v. Drexel Furniture Co., 259 U.S. 20 (1922).
    8–1, TAFT. Dissent: Clarke. 24pp.

105. Baird v. State Bar of Arizona, 401 U.S. 1 (1971).
    5–4, BLACK. Concurrence: Stewart. Dissents: Blackmun, White, Harlan, Burger. 21pp.

106. Baiz, In re, 135 U.S. 403 (1890).
    9–0, FULLER. 29pp.

107. Bakelite Corp., Ex parte, 279 U.S. 438 (1929).
    9–0, VAN DEVANTER. 23pp.

108. Baker v. Carr, 369 U.S. 186 (1962).
    7–2, BRENNAN. Concurrences: Douglas, Clark, Stewart. Dissents: Frankfurter, Harlan. 62pp.

109. Baldwin v. Fish and Game Commission of Montana, 436 U.S. 371 (1978).
    6–3, BLACKMUN. Concurrence: Burger. Dissents: Brennan, White, Marshall. 35pp.

110. Baldwin v. G.A.F. Seelig, Inc., 294 U.S. 511 (1935).
    9–0, CARDOZO. 18pp.

111. Baldwin v. New York, 399 U.S. 66 (1970).
    7–2, WHITE. Concurrences: Black, Douglas. Dissents: Burger, Harlan. 12pp.

112. Ball v. James, 451 U.S. 355 (1981).
    5–4, STEWART. Concurrence: Powell. Dissents: White, Brennan, Marshall, Blackmun. 34pp.

113. Ballard, U.S. v., 322 U.S. 78 (1944).

6–3, BRENNAN. Concurrences: Douglas, Goldberg, Warren. Dissents: Black, Harlan, White. 121pp.

147. Bell v. Wolfish, 441 U.S. 520 (1979).
6–3, 5–4, REHNQUIST. Concurrence: Powell. Dissents: Marshall, Stevens, Brennan, Powell. 79pp.

148. Belle Terre, Village of, v. Boraas, 416 U.S. 1 (1974).
7–2, DOUGLAS. Dissents: Brennan, Marshall. 19pp.

149. Bellotti v. Baird (Bellotti II), 443 U.S. 622 (1979).
8–1, POWELL. Concurrences: Rehnquist, Stevens, Brennan, Marshall, Blackmun. Dissent: White. 35pp.

150. Bell's Gap R. Co. v. Pennsylvania, 134 U.S. 232 (1890).
9–0, BRADLEY. 8pp.

151. Belmont, U.S. v., 301 U.S. 324 (1937).
9–0, SUTHERLAND. Concurrences: Brandeis, Cardozo. 14pp.

152. Bendix Autolite Corp. v. Midwesco Enterprises, Inc., 486 U.S. 888 (1988).
8–1, KENNEDY. Concurrence: Scalia. Dissent: Rehnquist. 13pp.

153. Benton v. Maryland, 395 U.S. 784 (1969).
7–2, MARSHALL. Concurrence: White. Dissents: Harlan, Stewart. 28pp.

154. Berea College v. Kentucky, 211 U.S. 45 (1908).
7–2, BREWER. Concurrences: Holmes, Moody. Dissents: Harlan, Day. 25pp.

155. Berman v. Parker, 348 U.S. 26 (1954).
9–0, DOUGLAS. 11pp.

156. Bernal v. Fainter, 467 U.S. 216 (1984).
8–1, MARSHALL. Dissent: Rehnquist. 12pp.

157. Berry v. U.S., 312 U.S. 450 (1941).
9–0, BLACK. 7pp.

158. Bethel School District No. 403 v. Fraser, 478 U.S. 675 (1986).
7–2, BURGER. Concurrences: Brennan, Blackmun. Dissents: Marshall, Stevens. 21pp.

159. Betts v. Brady, 316 U.S. 455 (1942).
6–3, ROBERTS. Dissents: Black, Douglas, Murphy. 26pp.

160. Bi-Metallic Investment Co. v. State Board of Equalization, 239 U.S. 441 (1915).
9–0, HOLMES. 3pp.

161. Bibb v. Navajo Freight Lines, Inc., 359 U.S. 520 (1959).
9–0, DOUGLAS. Concurrences: Harlan, Stewart. 10pp.

162. Biddinger v. Commissioner of Police, 245 U.S. 128 (1917).
9–0, CLARKE. 8pp.

163. Biddle v. Perovich, 274 U.S. 480 (1927).
8–0, HOLMES. Not voting: Taft. 8pp.

164. Bigelow v. Virginia, 421 U.S. 809 (1975).
7–2, BLACKMUN. Dissents: Rehnquist, White. 27pp.

165. Bishop v. U.S., 350 U.S. 961 (1956).
9–0, PER CURIAM. 1p.

166. Bishop v. Wood, 426 U.S. 341 (1976).
5–4, STEVENS. Dissents: Brennan, Marshall, White, Blackmun. 22pp.

167. Biswell, U.S. v., 406 U.S. 311 (1972).
8–1, WHITE. Concurrence: Blackmun. Dissent: Douglas. 9pp.

168. Bivens v. Six Unknown Named Agents of the Federal Bureau of Narcotics, 403 U.S. 388 (1971).
6–3, BRENNAN. Concurrence: Harlan. Dissents: Burger, Black, Blackmun. 43pp.

169. Black & White Taxicab & Transfer Co. v. Brown & Yellow Taxicab & Transfer Co., 276 U.S. 518 (1928).
6–3, BUTLER. Dissents: Holmes, Brandeis, Stone. 19pp.

170. Blackledge v. Perry, 417 U.S. 21 (1974).
7–2, STEWART. Dissents: Rehnquist, Powell. 18pp.

171. Blanton v. City of North Las Vegas, 489 U.S. 538 (1989).
9–0, MARSHALL. 8pp.

172. Blau v. U.S., 340 U.S. 159 (1950).
8–0, BLACK. Not voting: Clark. 3pp.

173. Block v. Hirsh, 256 U.S. 135 (1921).
5–4, HOLMES. Dissents: McKenna, Taft, Van Devanter, McReynolds. 36pp.

174. Bloom v. Illinois, 391 U.S. 194 (1968).
7–2, WHITE. Concurrence: Fortas. Dissents: Harlan, Stewart. 22pp.

175. Blum v. Yaretsky, 457 U.S. 991 (1982).
7–2, REHNQUIST. Concurrence: White. Dissents: Brennan, Marshall. 39pp.

Dissents: White, Rehnquist, O'Connor.
35pp.

203. Boston Beer Co. v. Massachusetts, 97 U.S. 25 (1877).
9–0, BRADLEY. 9pp.

204. Bounds v. Smith, 430 U.S. 817 (1977).
6–3, MARSHALL. Concurrence: Powell.
Dissents: Burger, Stewart, Rehnquist. 25pp.

205. Bourjois, Inc. v. Chapman, 301 U.S. 183 (1937).
9–0, BRANDEIS. 8pp.

205a. Bowen v. Kendrick, 487 U.S. 589 (1988).
5–4, REHNQUIST. Concurrences:
O'Connor, Kennedy, Scalia. Dissents:
Blackmun, Brennan, Marshall, Stevens.
65pp.

206. Bowen v. Roy, 476 U.S. 693 (1986).
8–1, 5–4, BURGER. Concurrences: Blackmun,
Stevens, O'Connor, Brennan, Marshall.
Dissents: White, O'Connor, Brennan,
Marshall. 39pp.

207. Bowers v. Hardwick, 478 U.S. 186 (1986).
5–4, WHITE. Concurrences: Burger, Powell.
Dissents: Stevens, Blackmun, Brennan,
Marshall. 34pp.

208. Bowersock v. Smith, 243 U.S. 29 (1917).
9–0, WHITE. 7pp.

209. Bowles v. Willingham, 321 U.S. 503 (1944).
8–1, DOUGLAS. Concurrence: Rutledge.
Dissent: Roberts. 38pp.

210. Bowman v. Chicago & Northwestern Railway
Co., 125 U.S. 465 (1888).
6–3, MATTHEWS. Dissents: Waite, Harlan,
Gray. 60pp.

211. Bowsher v. Synar, 478 U.S. 714 (1986).
7–2, BURGER. Concurrences: Stevens,
Marshall. Dissents: Blackmun, White. 72pp.

212. Boyce Motor Lines, Inc. v. U.S., 342 U.S. 337 (1952).
6–3, CLARK. Dissents: Jackson, Black,
Frankfurter. 9pp.

213. Boyd v. U.S., 116 U.S. 616 (1886).
9–0, BRADLEY. Concurrence: Miller. 26pp.

213a. Boyd v. U.S., 142 U.S. 450 (1892).
9–0, HARLAN. 9pp.

214. Boyde v. California, 494 U.S. 370 (1990).
5–4, REHNQUIST. Dissents: Marshall,
Brennan, Blackmun, Stevens. 23pp.

215. Boyer, Ex parte, 109 U.S. 629 (1884).
9–0, BLATCHFORD. 4pp.

216. Boykin v. Alabama, 395 U.S. 238 (1969).
7–2, DOUGLAS. Dissents: Harlan, Black.
12pp.

217. Bradley v. Fisher, 80 U.S. (13 Wall.) 335 (1871).
7–2, FIELD. Dissents: Davis, Clifford. 23pp.

218. Bradley v. Public Utilities Commission, 289 U.S. 92 (1933).
9–0, BRANDEIS. 7pp.

219. Bradwell v. Illinois, 83 U.S. (16 Wall.) 130 (1873).
8–1, MILLER. Concurrences: Swayne, Field,
Bradley. Dissent: Chase. 13pp.

220. Brady v. Maryland, 373 U.S. 83 (1963).
7–2, DOUGLAS. Concurrence: White.
Dissents: Harlan, Black. 12pp.

221. Brady v. U.S., 397 U.S. 742 (1970).
9–0, WHITE. Concurrences: Brennan, Black.
17pp.

222. Brandenburg v. Ohio, 395 U.S. 444 (1969).
9–0, PER CURIAM. Concurrences: Black,
Douglas. 12pp.

223. Braniff Airways, Inc. v. Nebraska State Board of
Equalization & Assessment, 347 U.S. 590 (1954).
7–2, REED. Concurrences: Black, Douglas.
Dissents: Frankfurter, Jackson. 20pp.

224. Branti v. Finkel, 445 U.S. 507 (1980).
6–3, STEVENS. Dissents: Stewart, Powell,
Rehnquist. 28pp.

225. Branzburg v. Hayes, 408 U.S. 665 (1972).
5–4, WHITE. Concurrence: Powell. Dissents:
Douglas, Stewart, Brennan, Marshall. 87pp.

226. Braunfeld v. Brown, 366 U.S. 599 (1961).
6–3, WARREN. Concurrences: Harlan,
Brennan, Stewart, Frankfurter. Dissents:
Brennan, Stewart, Douglas. 17pp.

227. Breard v. Alexandria, 341 U.S. 622 (1951).
6–3, REED. Dissents: Vinson, Black, Douglas.
29pp.

228. Breed v. Jones, 421 U.S. 519 (1975).
9–0, BURGER. 23pp.

229. Breedlove v. Suttles, 302 U.S. 277 (1937).
9–0, BUTLER. 8pp.

230. Breithaupt v. Abram, 352 U.S. 432 (1957).
6–3, CLARK. Dissents: Warren, Douglas,
Black. 13pp.

231. Brewer v. Williams, 430 U.S. 387 (1977).

5–4, BROWN. Dissents: Field, Shiras, Gray, White. 38pp.

261. Brown, U.S. v., 381 U.S. 437 (1965).
5–4, WARREN. Dissents: White, Clark, Harlan, Stewart. 42pp.

262. Brown-Forman Distillers Corp. v. New York State Liquor Authority, 476 U.S. 573 (1986).
6–3, MARSHALL. Concurrence: Blackmun. Dissents: Stevens, White, Rehnquist. 30pp.

263. Browning-Ferris Industries v. Kelco Disposal, Inc., 492 U.S. 257 (1989).
7–2, BLACKMUN. Concurrences: Brennan, Marshall, O'Connor, Stevens. Dissents: O'Connor, Stevens. 45pp.

264. Brushaber v. Union Pacific Railroad Co., 240 U.S. 1 (1916).
9–0, WHITE. 26pp.

265. Bruton v. U.S., 391 U.S. 123 (1968).
6–2, BRENNAN. Concurrences: Black, Stewart. Dissents: White, Harlan. Not voting: Marshall. 22pp.

266. Bryan, U.S. v., 339 U.S. 323 (1950).
5–2, VINSON. Concurrence: Jackson. Dissents: Black, Frankfurter. Not voting: Douglas, Clark. 26pp.

267. Buchanan v. Warley, 245 U.S. 60 (1917).
9–0, DAY. 22pp.

268. Buck v. Bell, 274 U.S. 200 (1927).
8–1, HOLMES. Dissent: Butler. 8pp.

269. Buck v. Kuykendall, 267 U.S. 307 (1925).
8–1, BRANDEIS. Dissent: McReynolds. 10pp.

270. Buckley v. Valeo, 424 U.S. 1 (1976).
6–2, 5–3 (various coalitions), PER CURIAM. Dissents: Burger, White, Marshall, Rehnquist, Blackmun. 292pp.

271. Bullington v. Missouri, 451 U.S. 430 (1981).
5–4, BLACKMUN. Dissents: Powell, Burger, White, Rehnquist. 23pp.

272. Bullock v. Carter, 405 U.S. 134 (1972).
7–0, BURGER. Not voting: Rehnquist, Powell. 15pp.

273. Bumper v. North Carolina, 391 U.S. 543 (1968).
6–3, STEWART. Concurrence: Harlan. Dissents: Black, White, Douglas. 20pp.

274. Bunting v. Oregon, 243 U.S. 426 (1917).
5–3, McKENNA. Dissents: White, Van Devanter, McReynolds. 14pp.

275. Burbank, City of v. Lockheed Air Terminal, Inc., 411 U.S. 624 (1973).

5–4, DOUGLAS. Dissents: Rehnquist, Stewart, White, Marshall. 31pp.

276. Burch v. Louisiana, 441 U.S. 130 (1979).
6–3, REHNQUIST. Concurrences: Stevens, Brennan, Stewart, Marshall. Dissents: Brennan, Stewart, Marshall. 11pp.

277. Burdick v. U.S., 236 U.S. 79 (1915).
8–0, McKENNA. Not voting: McReynolds. 17pp.

278. Burford v. Sun Oil Co., 319 U.S. 315 (1943).
5–4, BLACK. Concurrence: Douglas. Dissents: Frankfurter, Stone, Roberts, Reed. 34pp.

279. Burke v. Barnes, 479 U.S. 361 (1987).
6–2, REHNQUIST. Dissents: Stevens, White. Not voting: Scalia. 6pp.

280. Burks v. U.S., 437 U.S. 1 (1978).
8–0, BURGER. Not voting: Blackmun. 17pp.

281. Burnham v. Superior Court, 495 U.S. 604 (1990).
9–0, SCALIA. Concurrences: White, Brennan, Marshall, Blackmun, O'Connor, Stevens. 35pp.

282. Burns v. Wilson, 346 U.S. 137 (1953).
7–2, VINSON. Concurrences: Frankfurter, Jackson, Minton. Dissents: Black, Douglas. 19pp.

283. Burns, U.S. v., 79 U.S. 246 (1871).
9–0, FIELD. 8pp.

284. Burrell v. McCray, 426 U.S. 471 (1976).
6–3, PER CURIAM. Concurrence: Stevens. Dissents: White, Brennan, Marshall. 5pp.

285. Burton v. Wilmington Parking Authority, 365 U.S. 715 (1961).
6–3, CLARK. Concurrence: Stewart. Dissents: Harlan, Frankfurter, Whittaker. 14pp.

286. Bush v. Lucas, 462 U.S. 367 (1983).
9–0, STEVENS. Concurrences: Marshall, Blackmun. 25pp.

287. Bush v. Orleans Parish School Board, 364 U.S. 500 (1960).
9–0, PER CURIAM. 2pp.

288. Butcher's Union Slaughter-House v. Crescent City Live-Stock Landing Co., 111 U.S. 746 (1884).
9–0, BRADLEY. 15pp.

289. Butler, U.S. v., 297 U.S. 1 (1936).
6–3, ROBERTS. Dissents: Stone, Brandeis, Cardozo. 87pp.

6–3, REHNQUIST. Concurrence: Stewart. Dissents: Douglas, Brennan, Marshall. 31pp.

323. California v. Trombetta, 467 U.S. 479 (1984).
9–0, MARSHALL. Concurrence: O'Connor. 13pp.

324. California v. U.S., 320 U.S. 577 (1944).
5–4, FRANKFURTER. Dissents: Roberts, Black, Douglas, Murphy. 14pp.

325. California Motor Transport Co. v. Trucking Unlimited, 404 U.S. 508 (1972).
7–0, DOUGLAS. Concurrences: Stewart, Brennan. Not voting: Powell, Rehnquist. 11pp.

326. California Retail Liquor Dealers Assn. v. Midcal Aluminum, Inc., 445 U.S. 97 (1980).
8–0, POWELL. Not voting: Brennan. 18pp.

327. California, U.S. v., 297 U.S. 175 (1936).
9–0, STONE. 15pp.

328. California, U.S. v., 332 U.S. 19 (1947).
7–2, BLACK. Dissents: Frankfurter, Reed. 24pp.

329. Callan v. Wilson, 127 U.S. 540 (1888).
9–0, HARLAN. 17pp.

330. Caltex, U.S. v., 344 U.S. 149 (1952).
7–2, VINSON. Dissents: Douglas, Black. 8pp.

331. Camara v. Municipal Court, 387 U.S. 523 (1967).
6–3, WHITE. Dissents: Clark, Harlan, Stewart. 18pp.

332. Caminetti v. U.S., 242 U.S. 470 (1917).
5–3, DAY. Dissents: McKenna, Clark, White. Not voting: McReynolds. 34pp.

333. Cantrell v. Forest City Publishing Co., 419 U.S. 245 (1974).
8–1, STEWART. Dissent: Douglas. 11pp.

334. Cantwell v. Connecticut, 310 U.S. 296 (1940).
9–0, ROBERTS. 14pp.

335. Capital Broadcasting Co. v. Kleindienst, 405 U.S. 1000 (1972).
PER CURIAM. 1p.

336. Capital Cities Cable, Inc. v. Crips, 467 U.S. 691 (1984).
9–0, BRENNAN. 26pp.

337. Capital City Dairy Co. v. Ohio, 183 U.S. 238 (1902).
9–0, WHITE. 12pp.

338. Capitol Greyhound Lines v. Brice, 339 U.S. 542 (1950).
7–2, BLACK. Dissents: Frankfurter, Jackson. 20pp.

339. Caplin & Drysdale v. U.S., 491 U.S. 617 (1989).
5–4, WHITE. Dissents: Blackmun, Brennan, Marshall, Stevens. 19pp.

340. Carella v. California, 491 U.S. 263 (1989).
9–0, PER CURIAM. Concurrences: Scalia, Brennan, Marshall, Blackmun. 11pp.

341. Carey v. Population Services International, 431 U.S. 678 (1977).
7–2, BRENNAN. Concurrences: White, Powell, Stevens. Dissents: Rehnquist, Burger. 40pp.

342. Carlesi v. New York, 233 U.S. 51 (1914).
9–0, WHITE. 9pp.

343. Carll, U.S. v., 105 U.S. 611 (1882).
9–0, GRAY. 3pp.

344. Carlson v. Green, 446 U.S. 14 (1980).
7–2, BRENNAN. Concurrences: Powell, Stewart. Dissents: Burger, Rehnquist. 40pp.

345. Carlson v. Landon, 342 U.S. 524 (1952).
5–4, REED. Dissents: Black, Frankfurter, Douglas, Burton. 46pp.

346. Carmack, U.S. v., 329 U.S. 230 (1946).
9–0, BURTON. Concurrence: Douglas. 19pp.

347. Carmichael v. Southern Coal & Coke Co., 301 U.S. 495 (1937).
5–4, STONE. Dissents: Sutherland, McReynolds, Van Devanter, Butler. 37pp.

348. Carolene Products Co., U.S. v., 304 U.S. 144 (1938).
6–1, STONE. Concurrences: Black, Butler. Dissent: McReynolds. Not voting: Cardozo, Reed. 12pp.

349. Carrington v. Rash, 380 U.S. 89 (1965).
8–1, STEWART. Dissent: Harlan. 13pp.

350. Carroll v. President & Commissioners of Princess Anne, 393 U.S. 175 (1968).
9–0, FORTAS. Concurrences: Black, Douglas. 11pp.

351. Carroll v. U.S., 267 U.S. 132 (1925).
7–2, TAFT. Concurrence: McKenna. Dissents: McReynolds, Sutherland. 44pp.

352. Carstairs v. Cochran, 193 U.S. 10 (1904).
9–0, BREWER. 8pp.

353. Carter v. Carter Coal Co., 298 U.S. 238 (1936).
5–4, 6–3, SUTHERLAND. Concurrence: Hughes. Dissents: Hughes, Cardozo, Brandeis, Stone. 103pp.

354. Carter v. Illinois, 329 U.S. 173 (1946).

387. Chicago & G.T. Railway Co. v. Wellmann, 143 U.S. 339 (1892).
9–0, BREWER. 8pp.

388. Chicago & Southern Airlines, Inc. v. Waterman Steamship Corp., 333 U.S. 103 (1948).
5–4, JACKSON. Dissents: Douglas, Black, Reed, Rutledge. 16pp.

389. Chicago Board of Trade v. Olsen, 262 U.S. 1 (1923).
7–2, TAFT. Dissents: McReynolds, Sutherland. 43pp.

390. Chicago, Burlington & Quincy Railway Co. v. Chicago, 166 U.S. 226 (1897).
7–1, HARLAN. Dissent: Brewer. Not voting: Fuller. 37pp.

391. Chicago, M. & S.P. Railway Co. v. Minnesota, 134 U.S. 418 (1890).
6–3, BLATCHFORD. Dissents: Bradley, Gray, Lamar. 16pp.

392. Chicago Teachers Union, Local No. 1 v. Hudson, 475 U.S. 292 (1986).
9–0, STEVENS. Concurrences: White, Burger. 20pp.

393. Chicot County Drainage District v. Baxter State Bank, 308 U.S. 371 (1940).
9–0, HUGHES. 8pp.

Child Labor Case, see Hammer v. Dagenhart
Child Labor Tax Case, see Bailey v. Drexel Furniture Co.

394. Chimel v. California, 395 U.S. 752 (1969).
7–2, STEWART. Concurrence: Harlan. Dissents: White, Black. 31pp.

Chinese Exclusion Case, see Chae Chan Ping v. U.S.

395. Chisholm v. Georgia, 2 U.S. (2 Dall.) 419 (1793).
6–0, IREDELL. 61pp.

396. Christoffel v. U.S., 338 U.S. 84 (1949).
5–4, MURPHY. Dissents: Jackson, Vinson, Reed, Burton. 12pp.

397. Cincinnati Soap Co. v. U.S., 301 U.S. 308 (1937).
9–0, SUTHERLAND. 16pp.

398. Cipriano v. Houma, 395 U.S. 701 (1969).
9–0, PER CURIAM. Concurrences: Black, Stewart, Harlan. 5pp.

399. Citizen Publishing Co. v. U.S., 394 U.S. 131 (1969).
7–1, DOUGLAS. Concurrence: Harlan. Dissent: Stewart. Not voting: Fortas. 15pp.

400. Citizens Against Rent Control v. City of Berkeley, 454 U.S. 290 (1980).
8–1, BURGER. Concurrences: Rehnquist, Marshall, Blackmun, O'Connor. Dissent: White. 22pp.

401. City Council of Los Angeles v. Taxpayers for Vincent, 466 U.S. 789 (1984).
6–3, STEVENS. Dissents: Brennan, Marshall, Blackmun. 43pp.

City of ———, see name of the city
Civil Rights Cases, see Singleton, U.S. v.

402. Civil Service Commission v. National Assn. of Letter Carriers, 413 U.S. 548 (1973).
6–3, WHITE. Dissents: Douglas, Brennan, Marshall. 53pp.

403. Clark v. Community for Creative Non-Violence, 468 U.S. 288 (1984).
7–2, WHITE. Concurrence: Burger. Dissents: Marshall, Brennan. 29pp.

404. Clark v. Jeter, 486 U.S. 456 (1988).
9–0, O'CONNOR. 9pp.

405. Clark v. Poor, 274 U.S. 554 (1927).
9–0, BRANDEIS. 5pp.

406. Classic, U.S. v., 313 U.S. 299 (1941).
6–3, STONE. Dissents: Douglas, Black, Murphy. 43pp.

407. Cleburne v. Cleburne Living Center, Inc., 473 U.S. 432 (1985).
6–3, WHITE. Concurrences: Stevens, Burger, Marshall, Brennan, Blackmun. Dissents: Marshall, Brennan, Blackmun. 46pp.

408. Cleveland Board of Education v. LaFleur, 414 U.S. 632 (1974).
7–2, STEWART. Concurrences: Douglas, Powell. Dissents: Rehnquist, Burger. 29pp.

409. Cleveland Board of Education v. Loudermill, 470 U.S. 532 (1985).
7–2, WHITE. Concurrences: Marshall, Brennan. Dissents: Brennan, Rehnquist. 31pp.

410. Clyatt v. U.S., 197 U.S. 207 (1905).
9–0, BREWER. Concurrences: McKenna, Harlan. 17pp.

411. Clyde Mallory Lines v. Alabama, 296 U.S. 261 (1935).
9–0, STONE. 8pp.

412. Coates v. City of Cincinnati, 402 U.S. 611 (1971).

440. Commissioner of Patents v. Chakrabarty, 447 U.S. 303 (1980).
5–4, BURGER. Dissents: Brennan, White, Marshall, Powell. 19pp.

441. Committee for Public Education & Religious Liberty v. Nyquist, 413 U.S. 756 (1973).
6–3, POWELL. Concurrences: Burger, Rehnquist. Dissents: Burger, White, Rehnquist. 58pp.

442. Committee for Public Education & Religious Liberty v. Regan, 444 U.S. 646 (1980).
6–3, WHITE. Concurrence: Stevens. Dissents: Blackmun, Brennan, Marshall. 26pp.

443. Commodity Futures Trading Commission v. Schor, 478 U.S. 833 (1986).
7–2, O'CONNOR. Dissents: Brennan, Marshall. 35pp.

444. Communications Association v. Douds, 339 U.S. 382 (1950).
4–2, 3–3 (various coalitions), VINSON. Concurrences: Frankfurter, Jackson. Dissents: Frankfurter, Jackson, Black. Not voting: Douglas, Clark, Minton. 72pp.

445. Communist Party v. Subversive Activities Control Board, 367 U.S. 1 (1961).
5–4, FRANKFURTER. Dissents: Warren, Black, Douglas, Brennan. 201pp.

446. Community Communications Co. v. City of Boulder, 455 U.S. 40 (1982).
6–3, BRENNAN. Concurrence: Stevens. Dissents: Rehnquist, Burger, O'Connor. 32pp.

447. Compco Corp. v. Day-Brite Lighting, Inc., 376 U.S. 234 (1964).
9–0, BLACK. Concurrence: Harlan. 6pp.

448. Connally v. General Construction Co., 269 U.S. 385 (1926).
9–0, SUTHERLAND. Concurrences: Holmes, Brandeis. 10pp.

449. Connally v. Georgia, 429 U.S. 245 (1977).
9–0, PER CURIAM. 7pp.

450. Connecticut v. Doehr, 111 S.Ct. 2105 (1991).
9–0, WHITE. Concurrences: Rehnquist, Blackmun, Scalia. 19pp.

451. Connecticut Board of Pardons v. Dumschat, 452 U.S. 458 (1981).
7–2, BURGER. Concurrences: Brennan, White. Dissents: Stevens, Marshall. 15pp.

452. Connecticut Mutual Life Insurance Co. v. Moore, 333 U.S. 541 (1948).
6–3, REED. Dissents: Frankfurter, Jackson, Douglas. 24pp.

453. Connick v. Myers, 461 U.S. 138 (1983).
5–4, WHITE. Dissents: Brennan, Marshall, Blackmun, Stevens. 32pp.

454. Consolidated Edison v. Public Service Commission, 447 U.S. 530 (1980).
7–2, POWELL. Concurrences: Marshall, Stevens. Dissents: Blackmun, Rehnquist. 27pp.

455. Constantine, U.S. v., 296 U.S. 287 (1935).
6–3, ROBERTS. Dissents: Cardozo, Brandeis, Stone. 13pp.

456. Continental Baking Co. v. Woodring, 286 U.S. 352 (1932).
9–0, HUGHES. 22pp.

457. Continental Illinois National Bank & Trust Co. v. Chicago, Rock Island & Pacific Ry, 294 U.S. 648 (1935).
8–0, SUTHERLAND. Not voting: Brandeis. 38pp.

458. Cook v. Hart, 146 U.S. 183 (1892).
9–0, BROWN. 13pp.

459. Cook v. U.S., 138 U.S. 157 (1891).
9–0, HARLAN. 29pp.

460. Cook v. U.S., 288 U.S. 102 (1933).
6–2, BRANDEIS. Dissents: Sutherland, Butler. Not voting: Van Devanter. 21pp.

461. Cooley v. Board of Wardens of the Port of Philadelphia, 53 U.S. (12 How.) 299 (1851).
7–2, CURTIS. Concurrence: Daniel. Dissents: McLean, Wayne. 22pp.

462. Coolidge v. New Hampshire, 403 U.S. 443 (1971).
9–0, 5–4, STEWART. Concurrences: Harlan, Blackmun, Burger, Black, White. Dissents: Burger, Black, White, Blackmun. 85pp.

463. Cooper v. Aaron, 358 U.S. 1 (1958).
9–0, PER CURIAM. Concurrence: Frankfurter. 26pp.

464. Cooper v. Newell, 173 U.S. 555 (1899).
9–0, FULLER. 18pp.

465. Cooper v. Pate, 378 U.S. 546 (1964).
9–0, PER CURIAM. 2pp.

466. Cooper, U.S. v., 4 U.S. (4 Dall.) 341 (1800).
6–0, CHASE. 2pp.

467. Coppage v. Kansas, 236 U.S. 1 (1915).

5–4, REHNQUIST. Concurrences:
O'Connor, Scalia. Dissents: Brennan,
Marshall, Blackmun, Stevens. 42pp.

498. CTS Corp. v. Dynamics Corp. of America, 481
U.S. 69 (1987).
6–3, POWELL. Concurrence: Scalia. Dissents:
White, Blackmun, Stevens. 32pp.

499. Culombe v. Connecticut, 367 U.S. 568 (1961).
6–3, FRANKFURTER. Concurrences:
Warren, Douglas, Black, Brennan. Dissents:
Harlan, Clark, Whittaker. 75pp.

500. Cummings v. Missouri, 71 U.S. (4 Wall.) 277
(1866).
5–4, FIELD. Dissents: Chase, Swayne, Davis,
Miller. 56pp.

501. Cupp v. Murphy, 412 U.S. 291 (1973).
7–2, STEWART. Concurrences: White,
Marshall, Blackmun, Burger, Powell,
Rehnquist. Dissents: Douglas, Brennan.
15pp.

502. Curran v. Arkansas, 56 U.S. (15 How.) 304 (1853).
6–3, CURTIS. Dissents: Catron, Daniel,
Nelson. 19pp.

503. Curtis v. Loether, 415 U.S. 189 (1974).
9–0, MARSHALL. 10pp.

504. Curtis Publishing Co. v. Butts, 388 U.S. 130
(1967).
5–4, HARLAN. Concurrences: Warren,
Black, Douglas, Brennan, White. Dissents:
Black, Brennan, Douglas, White. 45pp.

505. Curtiss-Wright Export Corp., U.S. v., 299 U.S.
304 (1936).
7–1, SUTHERLAND. Dissent: McReynolds.
Not voting: Stone. 30pp.

506. Cuyler v. Sullivan, 446 U.S. 335 (1980).
8–1, POWELL. Concurrences: Brennan,
Marshall. Dissent: Marshall. 24pp.

507. D.H. Overmyer Co., Inc. v. Frick Co., 405 U.S.
174 (1972).
7–0, BLACKMUN. Concurrences: Douglas,
Marshall. Not voting: Powell, Rehnquist.
17pp.

508. Dairy Queen v. Wood, 369 U.S. 469 (1962).
4–3, BLACK. Concurrences: Stewart, Harlan,
Douglas. Not voting: Frankfurter, White.
13pp.

509. Dameron v. Brodhead, 345 U.S. 322 (1953).
7–2, REED. Dissents: Douglas, Black. 8pp.

510. Dames & Moore v. Regan, 453 U.S. 654 (1981).
8–1, REHNQUIST. Concurrences: Stevens,
Powell. Dissent: Powell. 37pp.

511. Dandridge v. Williams, 397 U.S. 471 (1970).
6–3, STEWART. Concurrences: Black,
Burger, Harlan. Dissents: Douglas,
Marshall, Brennan. 58pp.

512. Dane v. Jackson, 256 U.S. 589 (1921).
9–0, CLARKE. 12pp.

513. Daniels v. Williams, 474 U.S. 327 (1986).
9–0, REHNQUIST. Concurrences: Marshall,
Blackmun, Stevens. 9pp.

514. Darby Lumber Co., U.S. v., 312 U.S. 100 (1941).
9–0, STONE. 26pp.

515. Darrington v. Bank of Alabama, 54 U.S. (13
How.) 12 (1851).
8–1, McLEAN. Dissent: Grier. 7pp.

516. Dartmouth College v. Woodward, 17 U.S. (4
Wheat.) 518 (1819).
6–1, MARSHALL. Concurrences: Johnson,
Livingston, Washington, Story. Dissent:
Duvall. 198pp.

516a. Darusmont, U.S. v., 449 U.S. 292 (1981).
9–0, PER CURIAM. 10pp.

517. Davidson v. Cannon, 474 U.S. 344 (1986).
6–3, REHNQUIST. Concurrence: Stevens.
Dissents: Brennan, Blackmun, Marshall.
15pp.

518. Davidson v. New Orleans, 96 U.S. 97 (1877).
9–0, MILLER. Concurrence: Bradley. 11pp.

519. Davis v. Bandemer, 478 U.S. 109 (1986).
9–0, 7–2, WHITE. Concurrences: Burger,
O'Connor, Rehnquist, Powell, Stevens.
Dissents: Powell, Stevens. 76pp.

520. Davis v. Beason, 133 U.S. 333 (1890).
9–0, FIELD. 16pp.

521. Davis v. Mann, 377 U.S. 678 (1964).
8–1, WARREN. Concurrences: Clark, Stewart.
Dissent: Harlan. 16pp.

521a. Davis v. Massachusetts, 167 U.S. 43 (1897).
9–0, WHITE. 6pp.

522. Davis v. Mississippi, 394 U.S. 721 (1969).
6–2, BRENNAN. Concurrence: Harlan.
Dissents: Stewart, Black. Not voting: Fortas.
10pp.

523. Davis v. Passman, 442 U.S. 228 (1979).
5–4, BRENNAN. Dissents: Burger, Powell,
Rehnquist, Stewart. 27pp.

554. Dixon v. Love, 431 U.S. 105 (1977).
9–0, BLACKMUN. Concurrences: Stevens, Marshall, Brennan. 13pp.

555. Doe v. Bolton, 410 U.S. 179 (1973).
7–2, BLACKMUN. Concurrences: Burger, Douglas, Stewart. Dissents: White, Rehnquist. 44pp.

556. Doe v. Braden, 57 U.S. (16 How.) 635 (1853).
9–0, TANEY. 25pp.

557. Doe v. McMillan, 412 U.S. 306 (1973).
9–0, 6–3, 5–4 (various coalitions), WHITE. Concurrences: Douglas, Brennan, Marshall, Burger, Blackmun, Rehnquist, Stewart. Dissents: Burger, Blackmun, Rehnquist, Stewart. 39pp.

558. Dohany v. Rogers, 281 U.S. 362 (1930).
9–0, STONE. 8pp.

559. Doherty & Co. v. Goodman, 294 U.S. 623 (1935).
9–0, McREYNOLDS. 6pp.

560. Dombrowski v. Eastland, 387 U.S. 82 (1967).
8–0, PER CURIAM. Not voting: Black. 4pp.

561. Dombrowski v. Pfister, 380 U.S. 479 (1965).
7–2, BRENNAN. Dissents: Harlan, Clark. 24pp.

562. Donovan v. Dewey, 452 U.S. 594 (1981).
8–1, MARSHALL. Concurrences: Stevens, Rehnquist. Dissent: Stewart. 21pp.

563. Dooley v. U.S., 182 U.S. 222 (1901).
5–4, BROWN. Dissents: White, Gray, Shiras, McKenna. 21pp.

564. Doran v. Salem Inn, Inc., 422 U.S. 922 (1975).
8–1, REHNQUIST. Concurrence: Douglas. Dissent: Douglas. 13pp.

565. Dorchy v. Kansas, 264 U.S. 286 (1924).
9–0, BRANDEIS. 6pp.

566. Doremus, U.S. v., 249 U.S. 86 (1919).
5–4, DAY. Dissents: White, McKenna, Van Devanter, McReynolds. 10pp.

567. Dorszynski v. U.S., 418 U.S. 424 (1974).
9–0, BURGER. Concurrences: Marshall, Douglas, Brennan, Stewart. 36pp.

568. Douglas v. Alabama, 380 U.S. 415 (1965).
9–0, BRENNAN. Concurrences: Harlan, Stewart. 9pp.

569. Douglas v. California, 372 U.S. 353 (1963).
6–3, DOUGLAS. Dissents: Harlan, Stewart, Clark. 14pp.

570. Douglas v. Green, 363 U.S. 192 (1960).
8–0, PER CURIAM. Not voting: Stewart. 2pp.

571. Dow v. Beidelman, 125 U.S. 680 (1888).
9–0, GRAY. 13pp.

572. Downes v. Bidwell, 182 U.S. 244 (1901).
5–4, WHITE. Concurrences: Brown, Gray, Shiras, McKenna. Dissents: Fuller, Harlan, Brewer, Peckham. 148pp.

573. Doyle v. Ohio, 426 U.S. 610 (1976).
6–3, POWELL. Dissents: Stevens, Blackmun, Rehnquist. 27pp.

574. Drake v. Zant, 449 U.S. 999 (1980).
5–4, PER CURIAM. Concurrence: Stevens. Dissents: Brennan, Marshall, Stewart, White. 5pp.

575. Draper v. U.S. 358 U.S. 307 (1959).
8–1, WHITTAKER. Dissent: Douglas. 11pp.

576. Draper v. Washington, 372 U.S. 487 (1963).
5–4, GOLDBERG. Dissents: White, Clark, Harlan, Stewart. 29pp.

577. Dred Scott v. Sanford, 60 U.S. (2 How.) 393 (1857).
7–2, TANEY. Concurrences: Wayne, Campbell, Grier, Nelson, Daniel, Catron. Dissents: McLean, Curtis. 240pp.

578. Duke v. U.S., 301 U.S. 492 (1937).
9–0, SUTHERLAND. 3pp.

579. Duke Power Co. v. Carolina Environmental Study Group, 438 U.S. 59 (1978).
9–0, BURGER. Concurrences: Stewart, Rehnquist, Stevens. 45pp.

580. Dun & Bradstreet, Inc. v. Greenmoss Builders, 472 U.S. 749 (1985).
5–4, POWELL. Concurrences: Burger, White. Dissents: Brennan, Marshall, Blackmun, Stevens. 47pp.

581. Duncan v. Kahanamoku, 327 U.S. 304 (1946).
6–2, BLACK. Concurrences: Murphy, Stone. Dissents: Frankfurter, Burton. Not voting: Jackson. 54pp.

582. Duncan v. Louisiana, 391 U.S. 145 (1968).
7–2, WHITE. Concurrences: Black, Douglas, Fortas. Dissents: Harlan, Stewart. 49pp.

583. Dunn v. Blumstein, 405 U.S. 330 (1972).
6–1, MARSHALL. Concurrence: Blackmun. Dissent: Burger. Not voting: Powell, Rehnquist. 34pp.

6–3, SCALIA. Concurrences: Brennan, Marshall, Blackmun, O'Connor. Dissents: Brennan, Marshall, Blackmun. 29pp.

615. Endo, Ex parte, 323 U.S. 283 (1944).
9–0, DOUGLAS. Concurrences: Murphy, Roberts. 28pp.

616. Energy Reserves Group, Inc. v. Kansas Power & Light Co., 459 U.S. 400 (1983).
9–0, BLACKMUN. Concurrences: Powell, Burger, Rehnquist. 22pp.

617. Engel v. Vitale, 370 U.S. 421 (1962).
6–1, BLACK. Concurrence: Douglas. Dissent: Stewart. Not voting: Frankfurter, White. 30pp.

618. Enmund v. Florida, 458 U.S. 782 (1982).
5–4, WHITE. Concurrence: Brennan. Dissents: O'Connor, Burger, Powell, Rehnquist. 50pp.

619. Epperson v. Arkansas, 393 U.S. 97 (1968).
9–0, FORTAS. 19pp.

620. Equal Employment Opportunity Commission v. Wyoming, 460 U.S. 226 (1983).
5–4, BRENNAN. Concurrence: Stevens. Dissents: Burger, Powell, Rehnquist, O'Connor. 50pp.

621. Erie Railroad v. Tompkins, 304 U.S. 64 (1938).
7–2, BRANDEIS. Concurrence: Reed. Dissents: Butler, McReynolds. 29pp.

622. Erznoznik v. City of Jacksonville, 422 U.S. 205 (1975).
6–3, POWELL. Concurrence: Douglas. Dissents: Burger, Rehnquist, White. 20pp.

623. Escanaba & Lake Michigan Transport Co. v. Chicago, 107 U.S. 678 (1883).
9–0, FIELD. 13pp.

624. Escobedo v. Illinois, 378 U.S. 478 (1964).
5–4, GOLDBERG. Dissents: White, Clark, Stewart, Harlan. 22pp.

625. Eskridge v. Washington State Board of Prison Terms of Paroles, 357 U.S. 214 (1958).
6–2, PER CURIAM. Dissents: Harlan, Whittaker. Not voting: Frankfurter. 3pp.

Estate of ———, see name of the party

626. Estelle v. Gamble, 429 U.S. 97 (1976).
8–1, MARSHALL. Concurrence: Blackmun. Dissent: Stevens. 21pp.

627. Estelle v. Williams, 425 U.S. 501 (1976).
7–2, BURGER. Concurrences: Powell, Stewart. Dissents: Brennan, Marshall. 35pp.

628. Estes v. Texas, 381 U.S. 532 (1964).
5–4, CLARK. Concurrences: Harlan, Warren, Douglas, Goldberg. Dissents: Stewart, Black, Brennan, White. 86pp.

629. Estin v. Estin, 334 U.S. 541 (1948).
7–2, DOUGLAS. Dissents: Frankfurter, Jackson. 14pp.

630. Eu v. San Francisco Democratic Committee, 489 U.S. 214 (1989).
8–0, MARSHALL. Concurrence: Stevens. Not voting: Rehnquist. 21pp.

631. Euclid, Village of v. Ambler Realty Co., 272 U.S. 365 (1926).
6–3, SUTHERLAND. Dissents: Van Devanter, McReynolds, Butler. 2pp.

632. Evans v. Gore, 253 U.S. 245 (1920).
7–2, VAN DEVANTER. Dissents: Holmes, Brandeis. 23pp.

633. Evans v. Newton, 382 U.S. 296 (1966).
6–3, DOUGLAS. Dissents: Black, Harlan, Stewart. 27pp.

634. Everson v. Board of Education, 330 U.S. 1 (1947).
5–4, BLACK. Dissents: Jackson, Rutledge, Frankfurter, Burton. 74pp.

635. Ewing v. Mytinger & Casselberry, 339 U.S. 594 (1950).
6–2, DOUGLAS. Concurrence: Burton. Dissents: Jackson, Frankfurter. Not voting: Clark. 11pp.

Ex parte ———, see name of the party

636. Examining Board v. Flores de Otero, 426 U.S. 572 (1976).
8–1, BLACKMUN. Dissent: Rehnquist. 38pp.

637. Exxon Corp. v. Eagerton, 462 U.S. 176 (1983).
9–0, MARSHALL. 21pp.

637a. Faretta v. California, 422 U.S. 806 (1975).
6–3, STEWART. Dissents: Burger, Blackmun, Rehnquist. 47pp.

638. Fauntleroy v. Lum, 210 U.S. 230 (1908).
5–4, HOLMES. Dissents: White, Harlan, McKenna, Day. 16pp.

639. Fay v. Noia, 372 U.S. 391 (1963).
6–3, BRENNAN. Dissents: Harlan, Clark, Stewart. 86pp.

640. Federal Baseball Club v. National League of Professional Baseball Clubs, 259 U.S. 200 (1922).
9–0, HOLMES. 10pp.

5–4, POWELL. Concurrence: Burger. Dissents: White, Brennan, Marshall, Rehnquist. 62pp.

668. First National Bank v. Fellows, 244 U.S. 416 (1917).
7–2, WHITE. Dissents: Van Devanter, Day. 16pp.

669. Fisher v. U.S. 425 U.S. 391 (1976).
9–0, WHITE. Concurrences: Brennan, Marshall. 44pp.

670. Fiske v. Kansas, 274 U.S. 380 (1927).
9–0, SANFORD. 7pp.

671. Fitzpatrick v. Bitzer, 427 U.S. 445 (1976).
9–0, REHNQUIST. Concurrences: Brennan, Stevens. 15pp.

672. Flagg Bros., Inc. v. Brooks, 436 U.S. 149 (1978).
6–3, REHNQUIST. Dissents: Marshall, Stevens, White. 31pp.

673. Flast v. Cohen, 392 U.S. 83 (1968).
8–1, WARREN. Concurrences: Douglas, Stewart, Fortas. Dissent: Harlan. 50pp.

674. Fleming v. Mohawk Wrecking & Lumber Co., 331 U.S. 111 (1947).
9–0, DOUGLAS. Concurrence: Jackson. 3pp.

675. Fleming v. Page, 50 U.S. (9 How.) 603 (1850).
8–1, TANEY. Dissent: McLean. 16pp.

676. Fleming v. Rhodes, 331 U.S. 100 (1947).
8–1, REED. Dissent: Frankfurter. 11pp.

677. Flemming v. Nestor, 363 U.S. 603 (1960).
5–4, HARLAN. Dissents: Black, Douglas, Brennan, Warren. 36pp.

678. Fletcher v. Peck, 10 U.S. (6 Cr.) 87 (1810).
6–1, MARSHALL. Dissent: Johnson. 39pp.

679. Flood v. Kuhn, 407 U.S. 258 (1972).
5–3, BLACKMUN. Concurrences: Burger, White. Dissents: Douglas, Marshall, Brennan. Not voting: Powell. 38pp.

680. Florida v. Bostick, 111 S.Ct. 2382 (1991).
6–3, O'CONNOR. Dissents: Marshall, Blackmun, Stevens. 14pp.

681. Florida v. Long, 487 U.S. 223 (1988).
8–1, 5–4, KENNEDY. Concurrences: Blackmun, Brennan, Marshall. Dissents: Blackmun, Brennan, Marshall, Stevens. 27pp.

682. Florida v. Riley, 488 U.S. 445 (1989).
5–4, WHITE. Concurrence: O'Connor. Dissents: Brennan, Marshall, Stevens, Blackmun. 24pp.

683. Florida East Coast Ry., U.S. v., 410 U.S. 224 (1973).
6–2, REHNQUIST. Dissents: Douglas, Stewart. Not voting: Powell. 33pp.

684. Florida Lime & Avocado Growers, Inc. v. Paul, 373 U.S. 132 (1963).
5–4, BRENNAN. Dissents: White, Black, Douglas, Clark. 46pp.

685. Florida Star v. B.J.F., 491 U.S. 524 (1989).
6–3, MARSHALL. Concurrence: Scalia. Dissents: White, Rehnquist, O'Connor. 30pp.

685a. Flower v. U.S., 407 U.S. 197 (1972).
6–3, PER CURIAM. Dissents: Blackmun, Rehnquist, Burger. 5pp.

686. Foley v. Connelie, 435 U.S. 291 (1978).
6–3, BURGER. Concurrences: Stewart, Blackmun. Dissents: Marshall, Brennan, Stevens. 21pp.

687. Fong Foo v. U.S., 369 U.S. 141 (1962).
7–1, PER CURIAM. Concurrence: Harlan. Dissent: Clark. Not voting: Whittaker. 6pp.

688. Fong Yue Ting v. U.S., 149 U.S. 698 (1893).
6–3, GRAY. Dissents: Brewer, Field, Fuller. 66pp.

689. Ford v. Georgia, 111 S.Ct. 850 (1991).
9–0, SOUTER. 9pp.

690. Ford v. Wainwright, 477 U.S. 399 (1986).
5–4, MARSHALL. Concurrences: Powell, O'Connor, White. Dissents: O'Connor, White, Rehnquist, Burger. 37pp.

691. Fortson v. Dorsey, 379 U.S. 433 (1965).
8–1, BRENNAN. Concurrence: Harlan. Dissent: Douglas. 55pp.

692. Fortson v. Morris, 385 U.S. 231 (1966).
5–4, BLACK. Dissents: Douglas, Warren, Brennan, Fortas. 20pp.

693. Foster v. Neilson, 27 U.S. (2 Pet.) 253 (1829).
7–0, MARSHALL. 65pp.

694. Fourteen Diamond Rings v. U.S., 183 U.S. 176 (1901).
5–4, FULLER. Concurrence: Brown. Dissents: Gray, Shiras, White, McKenna. 11pp.

695. Frank v. Mangum, 237 U.S. 309 (1915).
8–1, PITNEY. Dissents: Holmes. 41pp.

696. Franklin v. Gwinnett County Public Schools, 112 S.Ct. 1028 (1992).
9–0, WHITE. Concurrences: Scalia, Rehnquist, Thomas. 12pp.

724. Garcia v. San Antonio Metropolitan Transit Authority, 469 U.S. 528 (1985).
    5–4, BLACKMUN. Dissents: Powell, Burger, Rehnquist, O'Connor. 60pp.

725. Gardner v. Broderick, 392 U.S. 273 (1968).
    9–0, FORTAS. Concurrence: Black. 7pp.

726. Gardner v. California, 393 U.S. 367 (1969).
    6–3, DOUGLAS. Dissents: Harlan, Stewart, Black. 7pp.

727. Garland, Ex parte, 71 U.S. (4 Wall.) 333 (1867).
    5–4, WAYNE. Dissents: Miller, Chase, Swayne, Davis. 67pp.

728. Garner v. Board of Public Works, 341 U.S. 716 (1951).
    5–4, CLARK. Concurrences: Frankfurter, Burton. Dissents: Frankfurter, Burton, Douglas, Black. 16pp.

729. Garner v. U.S., 424 U.S. 648 (1976).
    9–0, POWELL. Concurrences: Marshall, Brennan. 21pp.

730. Garnett, In re, 141 U.S. 1 (1891).
    9–0, BRADLEY. 18pp.

731. Garrison v. Louisiana, 379 U.S. 64 (1964).
    9–0, BRENNAN. Concurrences: Black, Douglas. 15pp.

732. Garrity v. State of New Jersey, 385 U.S. 493 (1967).
    5–4, DOUGLAS. Dissents: Harlan, Clark, Stewart, White. 18pp.

733. Gault, In re, 387 U.S. 1 (1967).
    7–2, FORTAS. Concurrences: Black, White, Harlan. Dissents: Harlan, Stewart. 81pp.

734. Gayle v. Browder, 352 U.S. 903 (1956).
    PER CURIAM. 1p.

735. Geduldig v. Aiello, 417 U.S. 484 (1974).
    6–3, STEWART. Dissents: Brennan, Douglas, Marshall. 22pp.

736. Geer v. Connecticut, 161 U.S. 519 (1896).
    5–2, WHITE. Dissents: Field, Harlan. Not voting: Brewer, Peckham. 2pp.

737. Gelpcke v. Dubuque, 68 U.S. (1 Wall.) 175 (1864).
    8–1, SWAYNE. Dissent: Miller. Not voting: Taney. 46pp.

738. General Oil Co. v. Crain, 209 U.S. 211 (1908).
    8–1, McKENNA. Concurrences: Holmes, Harlan. Dissent: Moody. 26pp.

739. Gentile v. State Bar of California, 111 S.Ct. 2720 (1991).
    5–4, (various coalitions), KENNEDY. Concurrence: O'Connor. Dissents: Rehnquist, White, Scalia, Souter, O'Connor. 30pp.

740. Geofroy v. Riggs, 133 U.S. 258 (1890).
    9–0, FULLER. 15pp.

741. Georgia v. Stanton, 73 U.S. (6 Wall.) 50 (1867).
    8–0, NELSON. Concurrence: Chase. 28pp.

742. Gerende v. Board of Supervisors of Elections, 341 U.S. 56 (1951).
    9–0, PER CURIAM. Concurrence: Reed. 2pp.

743. Germaine, U.S. v., 99 U.S. 508 (1879).
    9–0, MILLER. 5pp.

744. German Alliance Ins. Co. v. Kansas, 233 U.S. 389 (1914).
    6–3, McKENNA. Dissents: Lamar, White, Van Devanter. 45pp.

745. Gerstein v. Pugh, 420 U.S. 103 (1975).
    9–0, POWELL. Concurrences: Stewart, Douglas, Brennan, Marshall. 25pp.

746. Gertz v. Robert Welch, Inc., 418 U.S. 323 (1974).
    5–4, POWELL. Concurrence: Blackmun. Dissents: Burger, Douglas, Brennan, White. 80pp.

747. Gibbons v. Ogden, 22 U.S. (9 Wheat.) 1 (1824).
    7–0, MARSHALL. 238pp.

748. Giboney v. Empire Storage & Ice Co., 336 U.S. 490 (1949).
    9–0, BLACK. 15pp.

749. Gibson v. Berryhill, 411 U.S. 564 (1973).
    9–0, WHITE. Concurrences: Burger, Marshall, Brennan. 18pp.

750. Gibson v. Florida Legislative Committee, 372 U.S. 539 (1963).
    5–4, GOLDBERG. Concurrences: Black, Douglas. Dissents: Harlan, Clark, Stewart, White. 45pp.

751. Gibson v. U.S., 166 U.S. 269 (1897).
    9–0, FULLER. 8pp.

752. Gideon v. Wainwright, 372 U.S. 335 (1963).
    9–0, BLACK. Concurrences: Clark, Harlan. 18pp.

753. Giglio v. U.S., 405 U.S. 150 (1972).
    7–0, BURGER. Not voting: Powell, Rehnquist. 5pp.

754. Gilbert v. California, 388 U.S. 263 (1967).
    9–0 (various other votes), BRENNAN. Concurrences: Warren, Black, Douglas,

783. Gordon v. U.S., 69 U.S. (2 Wall.) 561 (1865).
8–2, SUMMARY OPINION ONLY. Dissents: Miller, Field. 1p. (*see* Gordon v. U.S., 117 U.S. 697)

784. Gore v. U.S., 357 U.S. 386 (1958).
5–4, FRANKFURTER. Dissents: Warren, Douglas, Black, Brennan. 13pp.

785. Goss v. Lopez, 419 U.S. 565 (1975).
5–4, WHITE. Dissents: Powell, Burger, Blackmun, Rehnquist. 35pp.

786. Gouled v. U.S., 255 U.S. 298 (1921).
9–0, CLARKE. 16pp.

787. Gouveia, U.S. v., 467 U.S. 180 (1984).
8–1, REHNQUIST. Concurrences: Stevens, Brennan. Dissent: Marshall. 23pp.

788. Grace, U.S. v., 461 U.S. 171 (1983).
9–0, 7–2, WHITE. Concurrences: Marshall, Stevens. Dissents: Marshall, Stevens. 19pp.

789. Grady v. Corbin, 495 U.S. 508 (1990).
5–4, BRENNAN. Dissents: O'Connor, Scalia, Rehnquist, Kennedy. 37pp.

790. Graham v. John Deere Co. of Kansas City, 383 U.S. 1 (1966).
7–0, CLARK. Not voting: Stewart, Fortas. 37pp.

791. Graham v. Richardson, 403 U.S. 365 (1971).
9–0, BLACKMUN. Concurrence: Harlan. 18pp.

792. Granfinanciera, S.A. v. Nordberg, 492 U.S. 33 (1989).
6–3, BRENNAN. Concurrence: Scalia. Dissents: White, Blackmun, O'Connor. 62pp.

Granger Cases, *see* Munn v. Illinois

793. Gratiot, U.S. v., 39 U.S. (14 Pet.) 526 (1840).
9–0, THOMPSON. 14pp.

794. Gravel v. U.S., 408 U.S. 606 (1972).
5–4, WHITE. Dissents: Douglas, Brennan, Marshall, Stewart. 27pp.

795. Graves v. New York ex rel. O'Keefe, 306 U.S. 466 (1939).
7–2, STONE. Concurrences: Hughes, Frankfurter. Dissents: Butler, McReynolds. 27pp.

796. Gray v. Mississippi, 481 U.S. 648 (1987).
5–4, BLACKMUN. Concurrence: Powell. Dissents: Scalia, Rehnquist, White, O'Connor. 31pp.

797. Gray v. Sanders, 372 U.S. 368 (1963).
8–1, DOUGLAS. Concurrences: Stewart, Clark. Dissent: Harlan. 23pp.

797a. Grayned v. Rockford, 408 U.S. 104 (1972).
9–0, 8–1, MARSHALL. Concurrences: Blackmun, Douglas. Dissent: Douglas. 21pp.

798. Grayson, U.S. v., 438 U.S. 41 (1978).
6–3, BURGER. Dissents: Stewart, Brennan, Marshall. 18pp.

799. Great Northern Railway v. Minnesota, 278 U.S. 503 (1929).
9–0, SUTHERLAND. 7pp.

800. Green v. Chicago, B. & Q. Railway, 205 U.S. 530 (1907).
9–0, MOODY. 4pp.

801. Green v. County School Board of New Kentucky, 391 U.S. 430 (1968).
9–0, BRENNAN. 13pp.

802. Green v. U.S., 355 U.S. 184 (1957).
5–4, BLACK. Dissents: Frankfurter, Burton, Clark, Harlan. 36pp.

803. Greenbelt Cooperative Pub. Assn. v. Bresler, 398 U.S. 6 (1970).
9–0, STEWART. Concurrences: White, Black, Douglas. 18pp.

804. Greene v. Lindsey, 456 U.S. 444 (1982).
6–3, BRENNAN. Dissents: O'Connor, Burger, Rehnquist. 17pp.

805. Greene v. Massey, 437 U.S. 19 (1978).
9–0, BURGER. Concurrences: Powell, Rehnquist. 9pp.

806. Greene v. McElroy, 360 U.S. 474 (1959).
8–1, WARREN. Concurrences: Frankfurter, Harlan, Whittaker. Dissent: Clark. 51pp.

807. Greenholtz v. Inmates of Nebraska Penal and Correctional Complex, 442 U.S. 1 (1979).
5–4, BURGER. Concurrence: Powell. Dissents: Powell, Marshall, Brennan, Stevens. 41pp.

808. Greer v. Spock, 424 U.S. 828 (1976).
7–2, STEWART. Concurrences: Burger, Powell. Dissents: Brennan, Marshall. 45pp.

809. Gregg v. Georgia, 428 U.S. 153 (1976).
7–2, POWELL. Concurrences: White, Burger, Rehnquist, Blackmun. Dissents: Brennan, Marshall. 73pp.

810. Gregory v. Ashcroft, 111 S.Ct. 2395 (1991).
5–4, O'CONNOR. Concurrences: White,

Stevens. Dissents: White, Stevens, Blackmun, Marshall. 25pp.

811. Gregory v. Chicago, 394 U.S. 111 (1969).
9–0, WARREN. Concurrences: Douglas, Stewart, White, Black. 20pp.

812. Griffin v. Breckenridge, 403 U.S. 88 (1971).
9–0, STEWART. Concurrence: Harlan. 19pp.

813. Griffin v. California, 380 U.S. 609 (1965).
6–2, DOUGLAS. Concurrence: Harlan. Dissents: Stewart, White. Not voting: Warren. 15pp.

814. Griffin v. County School Board of Prince Edward County, 377 U.S. 218 (1964).
9–0, BLACK. 17pp.

815. Griffin v. Illinois, 351 U.S. 12 (1956).
5–4, BLACK. Concurrence: Frankfurter. Dissents: Burton, Minton, Reed, Harlan. 27pp.

816. Griffin v. Wisconsin, 483 U.S. 868 (1987).
5–4, SCALIA. Dissents: Blackmun, Marshall, Brennan, Stevens. 23pp.

817. Griffiths, In re, 413 U.S. 717 (1973).
7–2, POWELL. Dissents: Burger, Rehnquist. 16pp.

818. Grimaud, U.S. v., 220 U.S. 506 (1911).
9–0, LAMAR. 17pp.

819. Grisham v. Hagan, 361 U.S. 278 (1960).
7–2, CLARK. Dissents: Whittaker, Stewart. 3pp.

820. Griswold v. Connecticut, 381 U.S. 479 (1965).
7–2, DOUGLAS. Concurrences: Goldberg, Warren, Brennan. Dissents: Black, Stewart. 51pp.

821. Groban, In re, 352 U.S. 330 (1957).
5–4, REED. Concurrences: Frankfurter, Harlan. Dissents: Black, Warren, Douglas, Brennan. 24pp.

822. Groppi v. Wisconsin, 400 U.S. 505 (1971).
8–1, STEWART. Concurrences: Blackmun, Burger. Dissent: Black. 12pp.

823. Grosjean v. American Press Co., 297 U.S. 233 (1936).
9–0, SUTHERLAND. 17pp.

824. Grossman, Ex parte, 267 U.S. 87 (1925).
9–0, TAFT. 36pp.

825. Groves v. Slaughter, 40 U.S. (15 Pet.) 449 (1841).
5–2, THOMPSON. Concurrence: Baldwin.

Dissents: McKinley, Story. Not voting: Catron, Barbour. 69pp.

826. Grovey v. Townsend, 295 U.S. 45 (1935).
9–0, ROBERTS. 11pp.

827. Gruber, Ex parte, 269 U.S. 302 (1925).
9–0, SUTHERLAND. 2pp.

828. Guaranty Trust Co. v. York, 326 U.S. 99 (1945).
7–2, FRANKFURTER. Dissents: Rutledge, Murphy. 21pp.

829. Guest, U.S. v., 383 U.S. 745 (1966).
5–4, STEWART. Concurrences: Clark, Black, Fortas, Harlan, Brennan, Warren, Douglas. Dissents: Harlan, Brennan, Warren, Douglas. 42pp.

830. Guinn v. U.S., 238 U.S. 347 (1915).
8–0, WHITE. Not voting: McReynolds. 22pp.

831. Gulf Fisheries Co. v. MacInerney, 276 U.S. 124 (1928).
9–0, BRANDEIS. 4pp.

832. Gunter v. Atlantic Coast Line Railroad Co., 200 U.S. 273 (1906).
8–1, WHITE. Dissent: Brown. 21pp.

833. H.L. v. Matheson, 450 U.S. 398 (1981).
6–3, BURGER. Concurrences: Powell, Stewart, Stevens. Dissents: Marshall, Brennan, Blackmun. 57pp.

834. H.P. Hood & Sons v. DuMond, 336 U.S. 525 (1949).
5–4, JACKSON. Dissents: Frankfurter, Rutledge, Black, Murphy. 99pp.

835. Hadley v. Junior College District, 397 U.S. 50 (1970).
6–3, BLACK. Dissents: Burger, Harlan, Stewart. 22pp.

836. Hagar v. Reclamation District, 111 U.S. 701 (1884).
9–0, FIELD. 15pp.

837. Hagner v. U.S., 285 U.S. 427 (1932).
9–0, SUTHERLAND. 7pp.

838. Hague v. CIO, 307 U.S. 496 (1939).
5–2, ROBERTS. Concurrences: Black, Stone, Reed, Hughes. Dissents: McReynolds, Butler. Not voting: Frankfurter, Douglas. 37pp.

839. Haig v. Agee, 453 U.S. 280 (1981).
7–2, BURGER. Concurrence: Blackmun. Dissents: Brennan, Marshall. 41pp.

840. Hale v. Bimco Trading Co., 306 U.S. 375 (1939).
9–0, FRANKFURTER. 6pp.

841. Hale v. Henkel, 201 U.S. 43 (1906).
8–1, BROWN. Concurrences: Harlan, McKenna, Fuller. Dissent: Brewer. 47pp.

842. Haley v. Ohio, 332 U.S. 596 (1948).
5–4, DOUGLAS. Dissents: Burton, Vinson, Reed, Jackson. 30pp.

843. Hall v. Geiger-Jones Co., 242 U.S. 539 (1917).
8–1, McKENNA. Dissent: McReynolds. 21pp.

844. Halper, U.S. v., 490 U.S. 435 (1989).
9–0, BLACKMUN. Concurrence: Kennedy. 19pp.

845. Ham v. South Carolina, 409 U.S. 524 (1973).
7–2, REHNQUIST. Concurrences: Douglas, Marshall. Dissents: Douglas, Marshall. 11pp.

846. Hamilton v. Alabama, 368 U.S. 52 (1961).
9–0, DOUGLAS. 4pp.

847. Hamilton v. Dillin, 88 U.S. (21 Wall.) 73 (1875).
9–0, BRADLEY. 25pp.

848. Hamilton v. Kentucky Distilleries Co., 251 U.S. 146 (1919).
9–0, BRANDEIS. 23pp.

849. Hamling v. U.S., 418 U.S. 87 (1974).
5–4, REHNQUIST. Dissents: Douglas, Brennan, Stewart, Marshall. 66pp.

850. Hamm v. Rock Hill, 379 U.S. 306 (1964).
5–4, CLARK. Concurrences: Douglas, Goldberg. Dissents: Black, Harlan, Stewart, White. 23pp.

851. Hammer v. Dagenhart, 247 U.S. 251 (1918).
5–4, DAY. Dissents: Holmes, McKenna, Brandeis, Clarke. 31pp.

852. Hampton v. Mow Sun Wong, 426 U.S. 88 (1976).
5–4, STEVENS. Concurrences: Brennan, Marshall. Dissents: Rehnquist, Burger, White, Blackmun. 39pp.

853. Hampton v. U.S. 425 U.S. 484 (1976).
6–3, REHNQUIST. Concurrences: Powell, Blackmun. Dissents: Brennan, Stewart, Marshall. 17pp.

854. Hancock v. Train, 426 U.S. 167 (1976).
7–2, WHITE. Dissents: Stewart, Rehnquist. 33pp.

855. Handelsbureau La Mola v. Kennedy, 370 U.S. 940 (1962).
8–1, PER CURIAM. Dissent: Black. 4pp.

856. Hanfgarn v. Mark, 274 N.Y. 22, appeal dismissed, 302 U.S. 641 (1937).
9–0, PER CURIAM. 1p.

857. Hankerson v. North Carolina, 432 U.S. 233 (1977).
8–0, WHITE. Concurrences: Blackmun, Burger, Marshall, Powell. Not voting: Rehnquist. 16pp.

858. Hannah v. Plumer, 380 U.S. 460 (1965).
9–0, WARREN. Concurrences: Black, Harlan. 19pp.

859. Hannegan v. Esquire, Inc., 327 U.S. 146 (1946).
8–0, DOUGLAS. Concurrence: Frankfurter. Not voting: Jackson. 15pp.

860. Hanover National Bank v. Moyses, 186 U.S. 181 (1902).
9–0, FULLER. 12pp.

861. Hans v. Louisiana, 134 U.S. 1 (1890).
9–0, BRADLEY. Concurrence: Harlan. 21pp.

862. Hansberry v. Lee, 311 U.S. 32 (1940).
9–0, STONE. Concurrences: McReynolds, Roberts, Reed. 14pp.

863. Harisiades v. Shaughnessy, 342 U.S. 580 (1952).
6–2, JACKSON. Concurrence: Frankfurter. Dissents: Douglas, Black. Not voting: Clark. 22pp.

864. Harlow v. Fitzgerald, 457 U.S. 800 (1982).
8–1, POWELL. Concurrences: Brennan, Marshall, White, Blackmun, Rehnquist. Dissent: Burger. 30pp.

865. Harman v. Forssenius, 380 U.S. 528 (1965).
9–0, WARREN. 17pp.

866. Harmelin v. Michigan, 111 S.Ct. 2680 (1991).
5–4, SCALIA. Concurrences: Kennedy, O'Connor, Souter. Dissents: White, Blackmun, Stevens, Marshall. 40pp.

867. Harper v. Virginia State Board of Election, 383 U.S. 663 (1966).
6–3, DOUGLAS. Dissents: Black, Harlan, Stewart. 28pp.

868. Harper & Row v. Nation Enterprises, 471 U.S. 539 (1985).
6–3, O'CONNOR. Dissents: Brennan, White, Marshall. 66pp.

869. Harris v. McRae, 448 U.S. 297 (1980).
5–4, STEWART. Concurrence: White. Dissents: Brennan, Marshall, Blackmun, Stevens. 33pp.

870. Harris v. New York, 401 U.S. 222 (1971).
5–4, BURGER. Dissents: Black, Brennan, Douglas, Marshall. 11pp.

871. Harris v. Reed, 489 U.S. 255 (1989).

901. Henderson's Distilled Spirits, 81 U.S. (14 Wall.) 44 (1872).
  6–3, CLIFFORD. Dissents: Field, Chase, Miller. 26pp.

902. Hendrick v. Maryland, 235 U.S. 610 (1915).
  9–0, McREYNOLDS. 16pp.

903. Henneford v. Silas Mason Co., 300 U.S. 577 (1937).
  7–2, CARDOZO. Dissents: McReynolds, Butler. 12pp.

904. Henry v. Collins, 380 U.S. 356 (1965).
  9–0, PER CURIAM. 3pp.

905. Henry v. Mississippi, 379 U.S. 443 (1965).
  5–4, BRENNAN. Dissents: Black, Harlan, Clark, Stewart. 22pp.

906. Henry v. U.S., 361 U.S. 98 (1959).
  7–2, DOUGLAS. Concurrence: Black. Dissents: Clark, Warren. 9pp.

907. Henry L. Doherty & Co. v. Goodman, 294 U.S. 623 (1935).
  9–0, McREYNOLDS. 6pp.

908. Hepburn v. Ellzey, 6 U.S. (2 Cr.) 445 (1804).
  6–0, MARSHALL. 9pp.

909. Hepburn v. Griswold, 75 U.S. (8 Wall.) 603 (1869).
  5–3, CHASE. Dissents: Miller, Swayne, Davis. 37pp.

910. Herb v. Pitcairn, 324 U.S. 117 (1945).
  5–4, JACKSON. Dissents: Rutledge, Black, Douglas, Murphy. 21pp.

911. Herbert v. Lando, 441 U.S. 153 (1979).
  7–2, 6–3 (various coalitions), WHITE. Concurrence: Powell. Dissents: Brennan, Stewart, Marshall. 58pp.

912. Hernandez v. New York, 111 S.Ct. 1859 (1991).
  6–3, KENNEDY. Concurrences: O'Connor, Scalia. Dissents: Blackmun, Stevens, Marshall. 19pp.

913. Hernandez v. Texas, 347 U.S. 475 (1954).
  9–0, WARREN. 8pp.

914. Hess v. Indiana, 414 U.S. 105 (1973).
  6–3, PER CURIAM. Dissents: Rehnquist, Burger, Blackmun. 7pp.

915. Hess v. Pawloski, 274 U.S. 352 (1927).
  9–0, BUTLER. 6pp.

916. Hester v. U.S., 265 U.S. 57 (1924).
  9–0, HOLMES. 2pp.

917. Hewitt v. Helms, 459 U.S. 460 (1983).

5–4, REHNQUIST. Concurrence: Blackmun. Dissents: Blackmun, Stevens, Brennan, Marshall. 37pp.

918. Hiatt v. Brown, 339 U.S. 103 (1950).
  8–0, CLARK. Concurrence: Burton. Not voting: Douglas. 10pp.

919. Hicklin v. Orbeck, 437 U.S. 518 (1978).
  9–0, BRENNAN. 17pp.

920. Hicks v. Miranda, 422 U.S. 332 (1975).
  5–4, WHITE. Concurrence: Burger. Dissents: Stewart, Douglas, Brennan, Marshall. 26pp.

921. Hill v. Wallace, 259 U.S. 44 (1922).
  9–0, TAFT. Concurrence: Brandeis. 31pp.

922. Hinderlider v. La Plata River & Cherry Creek Ditch Co., 304 U.S. 92 (1938).
  8–0, BRANDEIS. Not voting: Cardozo. 20pp.

923. Hines v. Davidowitz, 312 U.S. 52 (1941).
  6–3, BLACK. Dissents: Stone, Hughes, McReynolds. 30pp.

924. Hipolite Egg Co. v. U.S., 220 U.S. 45 (1911).
  9–0, McKENNA. 16pp.

925. Hirabayashi v. U.S., 320 U.S. 81 (1943).
  9–0, STONE. Concurrences: Douglas, Murphy, Rutledge. 34pp.

926. Hodel v. Irving, 481 U.S. 704 (1987).
  9–0, O'CONNOR. Concurrences: Brennan, Marshall, Blackmun, Scalia, Rehnquist, Powell, Stevens, White. 31pp.

927. Hodel v. Virginia Surface Mining & Reclamation Assn., Inc., 452 U.S. 264 (1981).
  9–0, MARSHALL. Concurrences: Burger, Powell, Rehnquist. 44pp.

928. Hodges v. U.S., 203 U.S. 1 (1906).
  7–2, BREWER. Concurrence: Brown. Dissents: Harlan, Day. 38pp.

929. Hodgson v. Minnesota, 497 U.S. 417 (1990).
  9–0, 5–4 (various coalitions), STEVENS. Concurrences: O'Connor, Marshall, Brennan, Blackmun, Scalia, Kennedy. Dissents: Marshall, Brennan, Blackmun, Scalia, Kennedy, Rehnquist, White. 47pp.

930. Hoffman Estates v. Flipside, 455 U.S. 489 (1982).
  9–0, MARSHALL. Concurrence: White. 20pp.

931. Hoke v. U.S., 227 U.S. 308 (1913).
  9–0, McKENNA. 18pp.

932. Holden v. Hardy, 169 U.S. 366 (1898).
  7–2, BROWN. Dissents: Brewer, Peckham. 33pp.

963. Hurd v. Hodge, 334 U.S. 24 (1948).
     6–0, VINSON. Concurrence: Frankfurter.
     Not voting: Reed, Jackson, Rutledge. 13pp.
964. Hurtado v. California, 110 U.S. 516 (1884).
     9–0, MATTHEWS. 23pp.
965. Hustler Magazine v. Falwell, 485 U.S. 46 (1988).
     8–0, REHNQUIST. Concurrence: White.
     Not voting: Kennedy. 12pp.
966. Hutchinson v. Proxmire, 443 U.S. 111 (1979).
     7–2, BURGER. Concurrence: Stewart.
     Dissents: Stewart, Brennan. 26pp.
967. Hutchinson Ice Cream Co. v. Iowa, 242 U.S. 153
     (1916).
     9–0, BRANDEIS. 8pp.
968. Hutto v. Davis, 454 U.S. 370 (1982).
     6–3, PER CURIAM. Concurrence: Powell.
     Dissents: Brennan, Marshall, Stevens. 19pp.
969. Hutto v. Finney, 437 U.S. 678 (1978).
     8–1, STEVENS. Concurrences: Brennan,
     Powell. Dissents: Powell, White, Rehnquist.
     41pp.
970. Hyatt v. People ex rel. Corkran, 188 U.S. 691
     (1903).
     9–0, PECKHAM. 29pp.
971. Hylton v. U.S., 3 U.S. (3 Dall.) 171 (1796).
     6–0, CHASE. 14pp.
972. Hynes v. Mayor of Oradell, 425 U.S. 610 (1976).
     8–1, BURGER. Concurrences: Brennan,
     Marshall. Dissent: Rehnquist. 27pp.
973. Illinois v. City of Milwaukee, 406 U.S. 91 (1972).
     9–0, DOUGLAS. 18pp.
974. Illinois v. Gates, 462 U.S. 213 (1983).
     6–3, REHNQUIST. Concurrence: White.
     Dissents: Brennan, Marshall, Stevens. 83pp.
975. Illinois v. LaFayette, 462 U.S. 640 (1983).
     9–0, BURGER. Concurrences: Marshall,
     Brennan. 10pp.
976. Illinois v. Rodriguez, 497 U.S. 177 (1990).
     6–3, SCALIA. Dissents: Marshall, Brennan,
     Stevens. 14pp.
977. Illinois ex rel. McCollum v. Board of Education,
     Champaign County, 333 U.S. 203 (1948).
     8–1, BLACK. Concurrences: Rutledge,
     Burton, Jackson, Frankfurter. Dissent: Reed.
     54pp.
978. Imbler v. Pachtman, 424 U.S. 409 (1976).
     9–0, POWELL. Concurrences: White,
     Brennan, Marshall. 39pp.

979. Immigration & Naturalization Service v.
     Chadha, 462 U.S. 919 (1983).
     7–2, BURGER. Concurrence: Powell.
     Dissents: White, Rehnquist. 47pp.
In re ———, see name of the party
980. Ingraham v. Wright, 430 U.S. 651 (1977).
     5–4, POWELL. Dissents: White, Brennan,
     Marshall, Stevens. 52pp.
981. International Assn. of Machinists v. Street, 367
     U.S. 740 (1961).
     5–4, BRENNAN. Concurrences: Douglas,
     Whittaker. Dissents: Whittaker,
     Frankfurter, Harlan, Black. 41pp.
982. International Boxing Club, U.S. v., 348 U.S. 236
     (1955).
     7–2, WARREN. Concurrences: Burton, Reed.
     Dissents: Frankfurter, Minton. 17pp.
983. International Brotherhood, Electrical Workers
     501 v. National Labor Relations Board, 341
     U.S. 694 (1951).
     6–3, BURTON. Dissents: Douglas, Reed,
     Jackson. 12pp.
984. International Harvester Co. v. Kentucky, 234
     U.S. 579 (1914).
     9–0, DAY. 10pp.
985. International Shoe Co. v. Pinkus, 278 U.S. 261
     (1929).
     6–3, BUTLER. Dissents: McReynolds,
     Brandeis, Sanford. 8pp.
986. International Shoe Co. v. Washington, 326 U.S.
     310 (1945).
     9–0, STONE. 17pp.
987. Interstate Busses Corp. v. Blodgett, 276 U.S. 245
     (1928).
     9–0, STONE. 8pp.
988. Interstate Commerce Commission v. Illinois
     Central R.R. Co., 215 U.S. 452 (1910).
     8–1, WHITE. Dissent: Brewer. 28pp.
989. Interstate Commerce Commission v. Louisville
     & Nashville R.R., 227 U.S. 88 (1913).
     9–0, LAMAR. 11pp.
990. Iowa Mut. Ins. Co. v. LaPlante, 480 U.S. 9 (1987).
     8–1, MARSHALL. Concurrence: Stevens.
     Dissent: Stevens. 14pp.
991. Irvin v. Dowd, 366 U.S. 717 (1961).
     9–0, CLARK. Concurrence: Frankfurter. 14pp.
992. Irvine v. California, 347 U.S. 128 (1954).
     5–4, JACKSON. Concurrence: Clark.

7–2, WARREN. Concurrences: Clark, Harlan, Stewart, White. Dissents: Black, Douglas. 18pp.

1021. Johnson v. Robison, 415 U.S. 361 (1974).
8–1, BRENNAN. Dissent: Douglas. 30pp.

1022. Johnson v. U.S., 333 U.S. 10 (1948).
5–4, JACKSON. Dissents: Vinson, Black, Reed, Burton. 8pp.

1023. Johnson v. Virginia, 373 U.S. 61 (1963).
9–0, PER CURIAM. 2pp.

1024. Johnson v. Zerbst, 304 U.S. 458 (1938).
6–2, BLACK. Concurrence: Reed. Dissents: McReynolds, Butler. Not voting: Cardozo. 12pp.

1025. Johnson, U.S. v., 457 U.S. 537 (1982).
5–4, BLACKMUN. Concurrence: Brennan. Dissents: White, Burger, Rehnquist, O'Connor. 32pp.

1026. Johnson, U.S. v., 481 U.S. 681 (1987).
5–4, POWELL. Dissents: Scalia, Brennan, Marshall, Stevens. 23pp.

1027. Joint Anti-Fascist Refugee Committee v. McGrath, 341 U.S. 123 (1951).
5–3, BURTON. Concurrences: Black, Frankfurter, Douglas, Jackson. Dissents: Reed, Vinson, Minton. Not voting: Clark. 90pp.

1028. Jones v. Alfred H. Mayer Co., 392 U.S. 409 (1968).
7–2, STEWART. Concurrence: Douglas. Dissents: Harlan, White. 71pp.

1029. Jones v. City of Opelika, 316 U.S. 584 (1942).
5–4, REED. Dissents: Stone, Black, Douglas, Murphy. 41pp.

1030. Jones v. Helms, 452 U.S. 412 (1981).
9–0, STEVENS. Concurrences: White, Blackmun. 17pp.

1031. Jones v. North Carolina Prisoners' Union, 433 U.S. 119 (1977).
6–3, REHNQUIST. Concurrences: Burger, Stevens. Dissents: Stevens, Marshall, Brennan. 29pp.

1032. Jones v. Opelika, 316 U.S. 584 (1942).
5–4, REED. Dissents: Stone, Black, Douglas, Murphy. 41pp.

1033. Jones v. Opelika, 319 U.S. 103 (1943).
7–2, PER CURIAM. Dissents: Reed, Frankfurter. 2pp.

1034. Jones v. U.S., 137 U.S. 202 (1890).
9–0, GRAY. 23pp.

1035. Jones v. U.S., 463 U.S. 354 (1983).
5–4, POWELL. Dissents: Brennan, Marshall, Blackmun, Stevens. 34pp.

1036. Jones v. Wolf, 443 U.S. 595 (1979).
5–4, BLACKMUN. Dissents: Powell, Burger, Stewart, White. 27pp.

1037. Jones & Laughlin Steel Corp., U.S. v., 301 U.S. 1 (1937).
5–4, HUGHES. Dissents: McReynolds, Van Devanter, Sutherland, Butler. 102pp.

1038. Jones, U.S. v., 119 U.S. 477 (1886).
9–0, WAITE. 4pp.

1039. Jordan v. DeGeorge, 341 U.S. 223 (1951).
6–3, VINSON. Dissents: Jackson, Black, Frankfurter. 22pp.

1040. Jorn, U.S. v., 400 U.S. 470 (1971).
6–3, HARLAN. Concurrences: Burger, Black, Brennan. Dissents: Stewart, White, Blackmun. 24pp.

1041. Joseph Burstyn, Inc. v. Wilson, 343 U.S. 495 (1952).
9–0, CLARK. Concurrences: Reed, Frankfurter, Jackson, Burton. 46pp.

1042. Ju Toy, U.S. v., 198 U.S. 253 (1905).
6–3, HOLMES. Dissents: Brewer, Peckham, Day. 27pp.

Julliard v. Greenman, see Legal Tender Cases

1043. Jurek v. Texas, 428 U.S. 262 (1976).
7–2, STEVENS. Concurrences: Burger, White, Rehnquist, Blackmun. Dissents: Brennan, Marshall. 18pp.

1044. Kahn v. Shevin, 416 U.S. 351 (1974).
7–2, DOUGLAS. Dissents: Brennan, Marshall. 11pp.

1045. Kahriger, U.S. v., 345 U.S. 22 (1953).
6–3, REED. Concurrence: Jackson. Dissents: Frankfurter, Black, Douglas. 15pp.

1046. Kanapaux v. Ellisor, 419 U.S. 891 (1974).
9–0, PER CURIAM. 1p.

1047. Kansas v. Colorado, 206 U.S. 46 (1907).
8–0, BREWER. Concurrences: White, McKenna. Not voting: Moody. 73pp.

1048. Karo, U.S. v., 468 U.S. 705 (1984).
6–3, WHITE. Concurrences: O'Connor, Rehnquist, Stevens, Brennan, Marshall. Dissents: Stevens, Brennan, Marshall. 32pp.

1076. Kimball Laundry Co. v. U.S., 338 U.S. 1 (1949).
    5–4, FRANKFURTER. Concurrence: Rutledge. Dissents: Douglas, Vinson, Black, Reed. 24pp.

1077. Kimmish v. Ball, 129 U.S. 217 (1889).
    9–0, FIELD. 6pp.

1078. Kingsley International Pictures Corp. v. Regents of University of New York, 360 U.S. 684 (1959).
    9–0, STEWART. Concurrences: Black, Frankfurter, Douglas, Clark, Harlan, Whittaker. 25pp.

1079. Kinsella v. U.S. ex rel. Singleton, 361 U.S. 234 (1960).
    6–2, CLARK. Dissents: Harlan, Frankfurter. Not voting: Whittaker. 16pp.

1080. Kirby v. Illinois, 406 U.S. 682 (1972).
    5–4, STEWART. Concurrences: Burger, Powell. Dissents: Brennan, Douglas, Marshall, White. 24pp.

1081. Klaxon Co. v. Stentor Manufacturing Co., 313 U.S. 487 (1941).
    9–0, REED. 12pp.

1082. Klein, U.S. v., 80 U.S. (13 Wall.) 128 (1871).
    7–2, CHASE. Dissents: Miller, Bradley. 23pp.

1083. Kleppe v. New Mexico, 426 U.S. 529 (1976).
    9–0, MARSHALL. 18pp.

1084. Klopfer v. North Carolina, 386 U.S. 213 (1967).
    9–0, WARREN. Concurrences: Stewart, Harlan. 14pp.

1085. Knauff, U.S. ex rel. v. Shaughnessy, 338 U.S. 537 (1950).
    4–3, MINTON. Dissents: Jackson, Black, Frankfurter. Not voting: Douglas, Clark. 15pp.

1086. Knote v. U.S., 95 U.S. 149 (1877).
    9–0, FIELD. 8pp.

1087. Knotts, U.S. v., 460 U.S. 276 (1983).
    9–0, REHNQUIST. Concurrences: Brennan, Marshall, Blackmun, Stevens. 13pp.

1088. Knowlton v. Moore, 178 U.S. 41 (1900).
    5–3, WHITE. Dissents: Brewer, Harlan, McKenna. Not voting: Peckham. 71pp.

Knox v. Lee, *see* Legal Tender Cases

1089. Kohl v. U.S., 91 U.S. 367 (1875).
    8–1, STRONG. Dissent: Field. 13pp.

1090. Kokinda, U.S. v., 497 U.S. 720 (1990).
    5–4, O'CONNOR. Concurrence: Kennedy. Dissents: Brennan, Marshall, Stevens, Blackmun. 25pp.

1091. Kolender v. Lawson, 461 U.S. 352 (1983).
    7–2, O'CONNOR. Concurrence: Brennan. Dissents: White, Rehnquist. 23pp.

1092. Kollock, In re, 165 U.S. 526 (1897).
    9–0, FULLER. 12pp.

1093. Koningsberg v. State Bar of California, 366 U.S. 36 (1961).
    5–4, HARLAN. Dissents: Black, Warren, Douglas, Brennan. 46pp.

1094. Korematsu v. U.S., 323 U.S. 214 (1944).
    6–3, BLACK. Concurrence: Frankfurter. Dissents: Roberts, Murphy, Jackson. 35pp.

1095. Kotch v. Board of River Port Pilot Commissioners, 330 U.S. 552 (1947).
    5–4, BLACK. Dissents: Rutledge, Reed, Douglas, Murphy. 16pp.

1096. Kovacs v. Cooper, 336 U.S. 77 (1949).
    5–4, REED. Concurrences: Frankfurter, Jackson. Dissents: Black, Douglas, Rutledge, Murphy. 29pp.

1097. Kramer v. Union Free School District No. 15, 395 U.S. 621 (1969).
    6–3, WARREN. Dissents: Stewart, Black, Harlan. 21pp.

1098. Kras, U.S. v., 409 U.S. 434 (1973).
    5–4, BLACKMUN. Concurrence: Burger. Dissents: Douglas, Brennan, Stewart, Marshall. 30pp.

1099. Kulko v. Superior Court of California, 436 U.S. 84 (1978).
    6–3, MARSHALL. Dissents: Brennan, White, Powell. 19pp.

1100. Kurtz v. Moffitt, 115 U.S. 487 (1885).
    9–0, GRAY. 19pp.

1101. Kusper v. Pontikes, 414 U.S. 51 (1973).
    7–2, STEWART. Concurrence: Burger. Dissents: Blackmun, Rehnquist. 19pp.

1102. Kwock Jan Fat v. White, 253 U.S. 454 (1920).
    9–0, CLARKE. 12pp.

1103. Kwong Hai Chew v. Colding, 344 U.S. 590 (1953).
    8–1, BURTON. Dissent: Minton. 13pp.

1104. L. Cohen Grocery Co., U.S. v., 255 U.S. 81 (1921).
    8–0, WHITE. Concurrences: Pitney, Brandeis. Not voting: Day. 17pp.

694

9–0, HARLAN. Concurrences: Stewart, Warren, Black. 51pp.

1133. Leathers v. Medlock, 111 S.Ct. 1438 (1991).
7–2, O'CONNOR. Dissents: Marshall, Blackmun. 16pp.

1134. Lee v. Illinois, 476 U.S. 530 (1986).
5–4, BRENNAN. Dissents: Blackmun, Burger, Powell, Rehnquist. 28pp.

1135. Lee v. Madigan, 358 U.S. 228 (1959).
7–2, DOUGLAS. Dissents: Harlan, Clark. 13pp.

1136. Lee v. Washington, 390 U.S. 333 (1968).
9–0, PER CURIAM. Concurrences: Black, Harlan, Stewart. 2pp.

1137. Lee, U.S. v., 106 U.S. 196 (1882).
5–4, MILLER. Dissents: Gray, Waite, Bradley, Woods. 56pp.

1138. Lee, U.S. v., 455 U.S. 252 (1982).
9–0, BURGER. Concurrence: Stevens. 12pp.

1139. Lefkowitz, U.S. v., 285 U.S. 452 (1932).
9–0, BUTLER. 6pp.

1140. Lefkowitz v. Turley, 414 U.S. 70 (1973).
9–0, WHITE. Concurrences: Brennan, Douglas, Marshall. 16pp.

1141. Legal Tender Cases (Julliard v. Greenman), 110 U.S. 421 (1884).
8–1, GRAY. Dissent: Field. 50pp.

1142. Legal Tender Cases (Knox v. Lee), 79 U.S. (12 Wall.) 457 (1870).
5–4, STRONG. Concurrence: Bradley. Dissents: Chase, Nelson, Clifford, Field. 225pp.

Legislative Veto Case, *see* Immigration & Naturalization Service v. Chadha

1143. Lego v. Twomey, 404 U.S. 477 (1972).
4–3, WHITE. Dissents: Brennan, Douglas, Marshall. Not voting: Powell, Rehnquist. 19pp.

1144. Lehman v. City of Shaker Heights, 418 U.S. 298 (1974).
5–4, BLACKMUN. Concurrence: Douglas. Dissents: Brennan, Stewart, Marshall, Powell. 25pp.

1145. Lehmann v. U.S. ex rel. Carson, 353 U.S. 685 (1957).
7–2, WHITTAKER. Dissents: Black, Douglas. 7pp.

1146. Lehnert v. Ferris Faculty Assn., 111 S.Ct. 1950 (1991).

5–4, BLACKMUN. Concurrences: Marshall, Scalia, O'Connor, Souter, Kennedy. Dissents: Scalia, O'Connor, Souter, Kennedy. 33pp.

1147. Lehnhausen v. Lake Shore Auto Parts Co., 410 U.S. 356 (1973).
9–0, DOUGLAS. 10pp.

1148. Lehr v. Robertson, 463 U.S. 248 (1983).
6–3, STEVENS. Dissents: White, Marshall, Blackmun. 28pp.

1149. Leisy v. Hardin, 135 U.S. 100 (1890).
6–3, FULLER. Dissents: Gray, Harlan, Brewer. 61pp.

1150. Leiter Minerals v. U.S., 352 U.S. 220 (1957).
8–1, FRANKFURTER. Concurrence: Douglas. Dissent: Douglas. 12pp.

1151. Lemon v. Kurtzman, 403 U.S. 602 (1971).
8–1, 8–0 (various coalitions), BURGER. Concurrences: Douglas, Black, Marshall, Brennan, White. Dissent: White. Not voting (partially): Marshall. 40pp.

1152. Leon, U.S. v., 468 U.S. 897 (1984).
6–3, WHITE. Concurrence: Blackmun. Dissents: Brennan, Marshall, Stevens. 32pp.

1153. Lerner v. Casey, 357 U.S. 468 (1958).
5–4, HARLAN. Concurrence: Frankfurter. Dissents: Warren, Douglas, Black, Brennan. 12pp.

1154. Levitt v. Committee for Public Education & Religious Liberty, 413 U.S. 472 (1973).
8–1, BURGER. Concurrences: Douglas, Brennan, Marshall. Dissent: White. 11pp.

1155. Levitt, Ex parte, 302 U.S. 633 (1937).
9–0, PER CURIAM. 2pp.

1156. Levy v. Louisiana, 391 U.S. 68 (1968).
6–3, DOUGLAS. Dissents: Harlan, Black, Stewart. 5pp.

1157. Lewis v. BT Investment Managers, Inc., 447 U.S. 27 (1980).
9–0, BLACKMUN. 27pp.

1158. Lewis v. Jeffers, 497 U.S. 764 (1990).
5–4, O'CONNOR. Dissents: Brennan, Marshall, Blackmun, Stevens. 23pp.

1159. Lewis v. New Orleans, 408 U.S. 913 (1972).
6–3, PER CURIAM. Concurrence: Powell. Dissents: Burger, Blackmun, Rehnquist. 13pp.

1160. Lewis v. U.S., 445 U.S. 55 (1980).

5–4, REED. Concurrence: Frankfurter. Dissents: Burton, Douglas, Murphy, Rutledge. 23pp.

1192. Louisiana Power & Light Co. v. Thibodaux, 360 U.S. 25 (1959).
6–3, FRANKFURTER. Concurrence: Stewart. Dissents: Warren, Brennan, Douglas. 20pp.

1193. Louisiana Public Service Commission v. Texas & N.O.R. Co., 284 U.S. 125 (1931).
9–0, BUTLER. 11pp.

1194. Louisiana, U.S. v., 339 U.S. 699 (1950).
8–1, DOUGLAS. Dissent: Frankfurter. 8pp.

1195. Louisville & Nashville Railroad Co. v. Schmidt, 177 U.S. 230 (1900).
9–0, WHITE. 10pp.

1196. Louisville Joint Stock Land Bank v. Radford, 295 U.S. 555 (1935).
9–0, BRANDEIS. 47pp.

1197. Lovasco, U.S. v., 431 U.S. 783 (1977).
8–1, MARSHALL. Dissent: Stevens. 17pp.

1198. Lovell v. City of Griffin, 303 U.S. 444 (1938).
8–0, HUGHES. Not voting: Cardozo. 9pp.

1199. Lovett, U.S. v., 328 U.S. 303 (1946).
8–0, BLACK. Concurrences: Frankfurter, Reed. Not voting: Jackson. 28pp.

1200. Loving v. Virginia, 388 U.S. 1 (1967).
9–0, WARREN. Concurrence: Stewart. 12pp.

1201. Low v. Austin, 80 U.S. (13 Wall.) 29 (1873).
9–0, FIELD. 7pp.

1202. Lubin v. Panish, 415 U.S. 709 (1974).
9–0, BURGER. Concurrences: Douglas, Blackmun, Rehnquist. 15pp.

1203. Lucas v. Forty-Fourth General Assembly of Colorado, 377 U.S. 713 (1964).
6–3, WARREN. Dissents: Harlan, Stewart, Clark. 53pp.

1204. Ludecke v. Watkins, 335 U.S. 160 (1948).
5–4, FRANKFURTER. Dissents: Black, Douglas, Murphy, Rutledge. 27pp.

1205. Luftig v. McNamara, 373 F.2d 2664 (D.C.Cir.), cert. denied, 387 U.S. 945 (1967).
PER CURIAM. 1p.

1206. Lugar v. Edmondson Oil Co., Inc., 457 U.S. 922 (1982).
5–4, WHITE. Dissents: Burger, Powell, Rehnquist, O'Connor. 35pp.

1207. Lustig v. U.S., 338 U.S. 74 (1949).
5–4, FRANKFURTER. Concurrences: Black,

Murphy, Douglas, Rutledge. Dissents: Reed, Vinson, Jackson, Burton. 10pp.

1208. Luther v. Borden, 48 U.S. (7 How.) 1 (1849).
8–1, TANEY. Dissent: Woodbury. 47pp.

1209. Lynch v. Donnelly, 465 U.S. 668 (1984).
5–4, BURGER. Concurrence: O'Connor. Dissents: Brennan, Marshall, Blackmun, Stevens. 60pp.

1210. Lynch v. Household Finance Corp., 405 U.S. 538 (1972).
4–3, STEWART. Dissents: White, Burger, Blackmun. Not voting: Powell, Rehnquist. 24pp.

1211. Lynch v. U.S., 292 U.S. 571 (1934).
9–0, BRANDEIS. 19pp.

1212. Lyng v. Castillo, 477 U.S. 635 (1986).
6–3, STEVENS. Dissents: Brennan, White, Marshall. 13pp.

1213. Lyng v. Northwest Indian Cemetery Protective Assn., 485 U.S. 439 (1988).
5–3, O'CONNOR. Dissents: Brennan, Marshall, Blackmun. Not voting: Kennedy. 39pp.

1213a. Lyng v. Payne, 476 U.S. 926 (1986).
8–1, O'CONNOR. Dissent: Stevens. 26pp.

1214. Lynumn v. Illinois, 372 U.S. 528 (1963).
9–0, STEWART. 11pp.

1215. Lytle v. Household Manufacturing, Inc., 494 U.S. 545 (1990).
9–0, MARSHALL. Concurrences: O'Connor, Scalia. 9pp.

1216. Mabry v. Johnson, 467 U.S. 504 (1984).
9–0, STEVENS. 8pp.

1217. MacCollom, U.S. v., 426 U.S. 317 (1976).
5–4, REHNQUIST. Concurrence: Blackmun. Dissents: Brennan, Marshall, Stevens, White. 24pp.

1218. MacDonald, U.S. v., 456 U.S. 1 (1982).
6–3, BURGER. Concurrence: Stevens. Dissents: Marshall, Brennan, Blackmun. 24pp.

1219. Mackenzie v. Hare, 239 U.S. 299 (1915).
9–0, McKENNA. 14pp.

1220. Mackey v. Montrym, 443 U.S. 1 (1979).
5–4, BURGER. Dissents: Stewart, Brennan, Marshall, Stevens. 30pp.

1221. Mackey v. U.S., 401 U.S. 667 (1971).
7–2, WHITE. Concurrences: Brennan,

6–3, BLACK. Concurrence: Murphy. Dissents: Reed, Jackson, Roberts. 17pp.

1254. Martin v. Walton, 368 U.S. 25 (1961).
6–2, PER CURIAM. Concurrence: Warren. Dissents: Douglas, Black. Not voting: Whittaker. 5pp.

1255. Martin v. Wilks, 490 U.S. 755 (1989).
5–4, REHNQUIST. Dissents: Stevens, Brennan, Marshall, Blackmun. 39pp.

1256. Martinez v. California, 444 U.S. 277 (1980).
9–0, STEVENS. 9pp.

1257. Martinez-Fuerte, U.S. v., 428 U.S. 543 (1976).
7–2, POWELL. Dissents: Brennan, Marshall. 36pp.

1258. Maryland v. Buie, 494 U.S. 325 (1990).
7–2, WHITE. Concurrences: Stevens, Kennedy. Dissents: Brennan, Marshall. 18pp.

1259. Maryland v. Craig, 497 U.S. 836 (1990).
5–4, O'CONNOR. Dissents: Scalia, Brennan, Marshall, Stevens. 20pp.

1260. Maryland v. Garrison, 480 U.S. 79 (1987).
6–3, STEVENS. Dissents: Blackmun, Brennan, Marshall. 23pp.

1261. Maryland v. Louisiana, 451 U.S. 725 (1981).
7–1, WHITE. Concurrence: Burger. Dissent: Rehnquist. Not voting: Powell. 47pp.

1262. Maryland v. Wirtz, 392 U.S. 183 (1968).
6–2, HARLAN. Dissents: Douglas, Stewart. Not voting: Marshall. 23pp.

1263. Maryland Committee for Fair Representation v. Tawes, 377 U.S. 656 (1964).
7–2, WARREN. Concurrence: Clark. Dissents: Harlan, Stewart. 21pp.

1264. Massachusetts v. Missouri, 308 U.S. 1 (1939).
8–0, HUGHES. Not voting: Butler. 20pp.

1265. Massachusetts Board of Retirement v. Murgia, 427 U.S. 307 (1976).
8–1, PER CURIAM. Dissent: Marshall. 21pp.

1266. Massiah v. U.S., 377 U.S. 201 (1964).
6–3, STEWART. Dissents: White, Clark, Harlan. 13pp.

1267. Masson v. New Yorker Magazine, Inc., 111 S.Ct. 2419 (1991).
7–2, KENNEDY. Concurrences: White, Scalia. Dissents: White, Scalia. 21pp.

1268. Mathews v. Diaz, 426 U.S. 67 (1976).
9–0, STEVENS. 21pp.

1269. Mathews v. Eldridge, 424 U.S. 319 (1976).

6–2, POWELL. Dissents: Brennan, Marshall. Not voting: Stevens. 32pp.

1270. Mathews v. Lucas, 427 U.S. 495 (1976).
6–3, BLACKMUN. Dissents: Stevens, Brennan, Marshall. 29pp.

1271. Matlock, U.S. v., 415 U.S. 164 (1974).
6–3, WHITE. Dissents: Douglas, Brennan, Marshall. 25pp.

Matter of ———, see name of the party

1272. Mattox v. U.S., 156 U.S. 237 (1895).
6–3, BROWN. Dissents: Shiras, Gray, White. 24pp.

1273. Mayberry v. Pennsylvania, 400 U.S. 455 (1971).
9–0, DOUGLAS. Concurrences: Burger, Harlan, Black. 15pp.

1274. Mayer v. Chicago, 404 U.S. 189 (1971).
9–0, BRENNAN. Concurrences: Burger, Blackmun. 13pp.

1275. Maynard v. Cartwright, 486 U.S. 356 (1988).
9–0, WHITE. Concurrences: Brennan, Marshall. 10pp.

1276. Mayor of Baltimore v. Dawson, 350 U.S. 877 (1955).
9–0, PER CURIAM. 1p.

1277. McAllister v. U.S., 141 U.S. 174 (1891).
6–3, HARLAN. Dissents: Field, Gray, Brown, 28pp.

1278. McBratney, U.S. v., 104 U.S. 621 (1881).
9–0, GRAY. 4pp.

1279. McCabe v. Atchison, Topeka & Santa Fe R. Co., 235 U.S. 151 (1914).
9–0, HUGHES. Concurrences: White, Holmes, Lamar, McReynolds. 14pp.

1280. McCardle, Ex parte, 73 U.S. (6 Wall.) 318 (1867).
8–0, CHASE. 9pp.

1281. McCarthy v. Arndstein, 266 U.S. 34 (1924).
9–0, BRANDEIS. 9pp.

1282. McCleskey v. Kemp, 481 U.S. 279 (1987).
5–4, POWELL. Dissents: Brennan, Marshall, Blackmun, Stevens. 89pp.

1283. McCleskey v. Zant, 111 S.Ct. 1454 (1991).
6–3, POWELL. Dissents: Marshall, Blackmun, Stevens. 36pp.

1284. McCray v. Illinois, 386 U.S. 300 (1967).
5–4, STEWART. Dissents: Douglas, Warren, Brennan, Fortas. 17pp.

1285. McCray v. U.S., 195 U.S. 27 (1904).

1371. Mondou v. New York, New Haven & Hartford R.R. Co., 223 U.S. 1 (1912).
9–0, VAN DEVANTER. 59pp.

1372. Monell v. New York City Department of Social Services, 436 U.S. 658 (1978).
7–2, BRENNAN. Concurrences: Powell, Stevens. Dissents: Rehnquist, Burger. 67pp.

1373. Monitor Patriot Co. v. Roy, 401 U.S. 265 (1971).
7–2, STEWART. Concurrences: White, Black, Douglas. Dissents: Black, Douglas. 13pp.

1374. Monongahela Navigation Co. v. U.S., 148 U.S. 312 (1893).
7–0, BREWER. Not voting: Shiras, Jackson. 34pp.

1375. Monroe v. Pape, 365 U.S. 167 (1961).
8–1, DOUGLAS. Concurrences: Harlan, Stewart. Dissent: Frankfurter. 93pp.

1376. Montoya de Hernandez, U.S. v., 473 U.S. 531 (1985).
7–2, REHNQUIST. Concurrence: Stevens. Dissents: Brennan, Marshall. 36pp.

1377. Mooney v. Holohan, 294 U.S. 103 (1935).
9–0, PER CURIAM. 13pp.

1378. Moore v. Dempsey, 261 U.S. 86 (1923).
7–2, HOLMES. Dissents: McReynolds, Sutherland. 17pp.

1379. Moore v. East Cleveland, 431 U.S. 494 (1977).
5–4, POWELL. Concurrences: Brennan, Marshall, Stevens. Dissents: Burger, Stewart, Rehnquist, White. 58pp.

1379a. Moore v. Illinois, 55 U.S. (14 How.) 13 (1853).
8–1, GRIER. Dissent: McLean. 10pp.

1380. Moore v. Illinois, 408 U.S. 786 (1972).
9–0, 5–4, BLACKMUN. Concurrences: Marshall, Douglas, Stewart, Powell. Dissents: Marshall, Douglas, Stewart, Powell. 25pp.

1381. Moore v. Illinois, 434 U.S. 220 (1977).
9–0, POWELL. Concurrences: Rehnquist, Blackmun. 15pp.

1382. Moore v. Michigan, 355 U.S. 155 (1957).
5–4, BRENNAN. Dissents: Burton, Frankfurter, Clark, Harlan. 14pp.

1383. Moore v. Ogilvie, 394 U.S. 814 (1969).
7–2, DOUGLAS. Dissents: Stewart, Harlan. 9pp.

1384. Moose Lodge No. 107 v. Irvis, 407 U.S. 163 (1972).

6–3, REHNQUIST. Dissents: Douglas, Brennan, Marshall. 28pp.

1385. Moragne v. States Marine Lines, Inc., 398 U.S. 375 (1970).
8–0, HARLAN. Not voting: Blackmun. 35pp.

1386. Moran v. Burbine, 475 U.S. 412 (1986).
6–3, O'CONNOR. Dissents: Stevens, Brennan, Marshall. 57pp.

1387. Morgan's Louisiana & T.R. & S.S. Co. v. Louisiana, 118 U.S. 455 (1886).
9–0, MILLER. 13pp.

1388. Morissette v. U.S., 342 U.S. 246 (1952).
8–0, JACKSON. Concurrence: Douglas. Not voting: Minton. 31pp.

1389. Morrison v. Olson, 487 U.S. 654 (1988).
7–1, REHNQUIST. Dissent: Scalia. Not voting: Kennedy. 80pp.

1390. Morrissey v. Brewer, 408 U.S. 471 (1972).
8–1, BURGER. Concurrences: Brennan, Marshall. Dissent: Douglas. 30pp.

1391. Morton v. Mancari, 417 U.S. 535 (1974).
9–0, BLACKMUN. 21pp.

1392. Moses H. Cone Memorial Hospital v. Mercury Construction Corp., 460 U.S. 1 (1983).
6–3, BRENNAN. Dissents: Rehnquist, Burger, O'Connor. 36pp.

1393. Motes v. U.S., 178 U.S. 458 (1900).
9–0, HARLAN. 19pp.

1394. Mountain Timber Co. v. Washington, 243 U.S. 219 (1917).
5–4, PITNEY. Dissents: White, McKenna, Van Devanter, McReynolds. 28pp.

1395. Mt. Healthy City School District Board of Education v. Doyle, 429 U.S. 274 (1977).
9–0, REHNQUIST. 14pp.

1396. Mu'Min v. Virginia, 111 S.Ct. 1899 (1991).
5–4, REHNQUIST. Concurrence: O'Connor. Dissents: Marshall, Blackmun, Stevens, Kennedy. 21pp.

1397. Mugler v. Kansas, 123 U.S. 623 (1887).
8–1, HARLAN. Dissent: Field. 56pp.

1398. Mulford v. Smith, 307 U.S. 38 (1939).
7–2, ROBERTS. Dissents: Butler, McReynolds. 19pp.

1399. Mullane v. Central Hanover Bank & Trust Co., 339 U.S. 306 (1950).
7–1, JACKSON. Dissent: Burton. Not voting: Douglas. 15pp.

1400. Mullaney v. Wilbur, 421 U.S. 684 (1975).

5–4, HUGHES. Dissents: McReynolds, Van Devanter, Sutherland, Butler. 5pp.

1431. National Labor Relations Board v. Reliance Fuel Oil Co., 371 U.S. 224 (1963).
9–0, PER CURIAM. Concurrence: Black. 4pp.

1432. National Labor Relations Board v. Retail Clerks Local 1001, 447 U.S. 607 (1980).
6–3, POWELL. Concurrences: Blackmun, Stevens. Dissents: Brennan, White, Marshall. 18pp.

1433. National Labor Relations Board v. Virginia Electric & Power Co., 314 U.S. 469 (1941).
7–0, MURPHY. Not voting: Roberts, Jackson. 12pp.

1434. National League of Cities v. Usery, 426 U.S. 833 (1976).
5–4, REHNQUIST. Concurrence: Blackmun. Dissents: Brennan, White, Marshall, Stevens. 49pp.

1435. National Mutual Insurance Co. v. Tidewater Transfer Co., 337 U.S. 582 (1948).
5–4, JACKSON. Concurrences: Rutledge, Murphy. Dissents: Frankfurter, Reed, Vinson, Douglas. 64pp.

1436. National Treasury Employees Union v. Von Raab, 489 U.S. 656 (1989).
5–4, KENNEDY. Dissents: Marshall, Brennan, Stevens, Scalia. 32pp.

1437. Neagle, In re, 135 U.S. 1 (1890).
6–2, MILLER. Dissents: Lamar, Fuller. Not voting: Field. 99pp.

1438. Neal v. Delaware, 103 U.S. 370 (1881).
7–2, HARLAN. Dissents: Waite, Field. 39pp.

1439. Near v. Minnesota, 283 U.S. 697 (1931).
5–4, HUGHES. Dissents: Butler, Van Devanter, McReynolds, Sutherland. 42pp.

1440. Nebbia v. New York, 291 U.S. 502 (1934).
5–4, ROBERTS. Dissents: McReynolds, Van Devanter, Sutherland, Butler. 58pp.

1441. Nebraska Press Assn. v. Stuart, 427 U.S. 539 (1976).
9–0, BURGER. Concurrences: White, Powell, Brennan, Stewart, Marshall, Stevens. 79pp.

1442. Nectow v. Cambridge, 277 U.S. 183 (1928).
9–0, SUTHERLAND. 6pp.

1443. Neil v. Biggers, 409 U.S. 188 (1972).
8–0, 5–3, POWELL. Concurrences: Brennan, Douglas, Stewart. Dissents: Brennan,

Douglas, Stewart. Not voting: Marshall. 16pp.

1444. Nevada v. Hall, 440 U.S. 410 (1979).
6–3, STEVENS. Dissents: Blackmun, Burger, Rehnquist. 34pp.

1445. Nevada v. U.S., 463 U.S. 110 (1983).
9–0, REHNQUIST. Concurrence: Brennan. 36pp.

1446. New Energy Co. of Indiana v. Limbach, 486 U.S. 269 (1988).
9–0, SCALIA. 11pp.

1447. New Jersey v. Portash, 440 U.S. 450 (1979).
7–2, STEWART. Concurrences: Brennan, Marshall, Powell, Rehnquist. Dissents: Burger, Blackmun. 22pp.

1448. New Jersey v. T.L.O., 469 U.S. 325 (1985).
9–0, 6–3, WHITE. Concurrences: Powell, O'Connor, Blackmun, Brennan, Marshall, Stevens. Dissents: Brennan, Marshall, Stevens. 61pp.

1449. New Jersey v. Wilson, 11 U.S. (7 Cr.) 164 (1812).
7–0, MARSHALL. 4pp.

1450. New Jersey Steam Navigation Co. v. Merchants' Bank of Boston, 47 U.S. (6 How.) 344 (1847).
9–0, NELSON. Concurrences: Taney, McLean, Wayne. 93pp.

1451. New Mexico v. Mescalero Apache Tribe, 462 U.S. 324 (1983).
9–0, MARSHALL. 20pp.

1452. New Motor Vehicle Board v. Orrin W. Fox Co., 439 U.S. 96 (1978).
8–1, BRENNAN. Concurrences: Marshall, Blackmun, Powell. Dissent: Stevens. 32pp.

1453. New Negro Alliance v. Sanitary Grocery Co., 303 U.S. 552 (1938).
7–2, ROBERTS. Dissents: McReynolds, Butler. 12pp.

1454. New Orleans v. Dukes, 427 U.S. 297 (1976).
8–0, PER CURIAM. Concurrence: Marshall. Not voting: Stevens. 10pp.

1455. New Orleans City Park Improvement Assn. v. Detiege, 358 U.S. 54 (1958).
9–0, PER CURIAM. 1pp.

1456. New Rider v. Board of Education, 480 F.2d 693 (10th Cir. 1973), cert. denied, 414 U.S. 1097 (1973).
7–2. PER CURIAM. Dissents: Black, Douglas. 1p.

Stevens, Blackmun, Powell. Dissents: Burger, Rehnquist. 136pp.

1484. Nixon v. Condon, 286 U.S. 73 (1932).
5–4, CARDOZO. Dissents: McReynolds, Van Devanter, Sutherland, Butler. 33pp.

1485. Nixon v. Fitzgerald, 457 U.S. 731 (1982).
5–4, POWELL. Concurrence: Burger. Dissents: White, Brennan, Marshall, Blackmun. 69pp.

1486. Nixon v. Herndon, 273 U.S. 536 (1927).
9–0, HOLMES. 6pp.

1487. Nixon, U.S. v., 418 U.S. 683 (1974).
8–0, BURGER. Not voting: Rehnquist. 34pp.

1488. Noble v. Oklahoma City, 297 U.S. 481 (1936).
9–0, ROBERTS. 15pp.

1489. Nollan v. California Coastal Commission, 483 U.S. 825 (1987).
5–4, SCALIA. Dissents: Brennan, Marshall, Blackmun, Stevens. 43pp.

1490. Norman v. Baltimore & Ohio Railroad Co., 294 U.S. 240 (1935).
5–4, HUGHES. Dissents: McReynolds, Van Devanter, Sutherland, Butler. 4pp.

1491. Norris v. Alabama, 294 U.S. 587 (1935).
8–0, HUGHES. Not voting: McReynolds. 13pp.

1492. North American Co. v. Securities and Exchange Commission, 327 U.S. 686 (1946).
6–0, MURPHY. Not voting: Reed, Douglas, Jackson. 25pp.

1493. North American Cold Storage Co. v. Chicago, 211 U.S. 306 (1908).
8–1, PECKHAM. Dissent: Brewer. 15pp.

1494. North Carolina v. Butler, 441 U.S. 369 (1979).
6–3, STEWART. Concurrence: Blackmun. Dissents: Brennan, Marshall, Stevens. 11pp.

1495. North Carolina v. Pearce, 395 U.S. 711 (1969).
7–2, STEWART. Concurrences: Douglas, Marshall, Harlan, Black, White. Dissents: Harlan, Black. 41pp.

1496. North Carolina State Board of Education v. Swann, 402 U.S. 43 (1971).
9–0, BURGER. 4pp.

1497. North Dakota v. U.S., 460 U.S. 300 (1983).
7–2, BLACKMUN. Concurrences: O'Connor, Rehnquist. Dissents: O'Connor, Rehnquist. 24pp.

1498. North Georgia Finishing v. Di-Chem, 419 U.S. 601 (1975).
6–3, WHITE. Concurrences: Stewart, Powell. Dissents: Blackmun, Rehnquist, Burger. 20pp.

1499. North v. Russell, 427 U.S. 328 (1976).
7–2, BURGER. Concurrence: Brennan. Dissents: Stewart, Marshall. 19pp.

1500. Northern Pipeline Construction Co. v. Marathon Pipe Line Co., 458 U.S. 50 (1982).
6–3, BRENNAN. Concurrences: Rehnquist, O'Connor. Dissents: Burger, White, Powell. 69pp.

1501. Northern States Portland Cement Co. v. Minnesota, 358 U.S. 450 (1959).
6–3, CLARK. Concurrence: Harlan. Dissents: Whittaker, Frankfurter, Stewart. 28pp.

1502. Northwest Airlines v. Minnesota, 322 U.S. 292 (1944).
5–4, FRANKFURTER. Concurrences: Black, Jackson. Dissents: Stone, Roberts, Reed, Rutledge. 35pp.

1503. Norton v. Shelby County, 118 U.S. 425 (1886).
9–0, FIELD. 30pp.

1504. Noto v. U.S., 367 U.S. 290 (1961).
9–0, HARLAN. Concurrences: Brennan, Warren, Black, Douglas. 13pp.

1505. O'Bannon v. Town Court Nursing Center, 447 U.S. 773 (1980).
8–1, STEVENS. Concurrence: Blackmun. Dissent: Brennan. 34pp.

1506. O'Brien v. Brown, 409 U.S. 1 (1972).
6–3, PER CURIAM. Concurrence: Brennan. Dissents: White, Douglas, Marshall. 16pp.

1507. O'Brien v. Skinner, 414 U.S. 524 (1974).
7–2, BURGER. Concurrences: Marshall, Douglas, Brennan. Dissents: Blackmun, Rehnquist. 14pp.

1508. O'Brien, U.S. v., 391 U.S. 367 (1968).
8–1, WARREN. Concurrence: Harlan. Dissent: Douglas. 24pp.

1509. O'Callahan v. Parker, 395 U.S. 258 (1969).
6–3, DOUGLAS. Dissents: Harlan, Stewart, White. 27pp.

1510. O'Connor v. Donaldson, 422 U.S. 563 (1975).
9–0, STEWART. Concurrence: Burger. 27pp.

1511. O'Connor v. Ortega, 480 U.S. 709 (1987).
5–4, O'CONNOR. Concurrence: Scalia.

Marshall, Harlan, Stewart, Burger, Blackmun. 185pp.

1538. Organization for a Better Austin v. Keefe, 402 U.S. 415 (1971).
8–1, BURGER. Dissent: Harlan. 9pp.

1539. Orozco v. Texas, 394 U.S. 324 (1969).
6–2, BLACK. Concurrence: Harlan. Dissents: White, Stewart. Not voting: Fortas. 8pp.

1540. Orr v. Orr, 440 U.S. 268 (1979).
6–3, BRENNAN. Concurrences: Blackmun, Stevens. Dissents: Powell, Rehnquist, Burger. 33pp.

1541. Ortega, U.S. v., 24 U.S. (11 Wheat.) 467 (1826).
9–0, WASHINGTON. 3pp.

1542. Ortwein v. Schwab, 410 U.S. 656 (1973).
5–4, PER CURIAM. Dissents: Stewart, Douglas, Brennan, Marshall. 11pp.

1543. Osborn v. United States Bank, 22 U.S. (9 Wheat.) 738 (1824).
6–1, MARSHALL. Dissent: Johnson. 166pp.

1544. Ott v. Mississippi Valley Barge Line Co., 336 U.S. 169 (1949).
8–1, DOUGLAS. Dissent: Jackson. 7pp.

1545. Owen v. City of Independence, 445 U.S. 622 (1980).
5–4, BRENNAN. Dissents: Powell, Burger, Stewart, Rehnquist. 62pp.

1546. Oyama v. California, 332 U.S. 633 (1948).
6–3, VINSON. Concurrences: Black, Douglas, Murphy, Rutledge. Dissents: Reed, Jackson, Burton. 56pp.

1547. Oyler v. Boles, 368 U.S. 448 (1962).
5–4, CLARK. Concurrence: Harlan. Dissents: Warren, Douglas, Black, Brennan. 16pp.

1548. Ozawa v. U.S., 260 U.S. 178 (1922).
9–0, SUTHERLAND. 21pp.

1549. Pace v. Alabama, 106 U.S. 583 (1883).
9–0, FIELD. 3pp.

1550. Pacific Gas & Electric Co. v. Public Utilities Commission of California, 475 U.S. 1 (1986).
5–3, POWELL. Concurrences: Burger, Marshall. Dissents: Rehnquist, White, Stevens. Not voting: Blackmun.

1551. Pacific Gas & Electric Co. v. State Energy Resources Conservation & Develop. Comm., 461 U.S. 190 (1983).
9–0, WHITE. Concurrences: Blackmun, Stevens. 40pp.

1552. Pacific Mutual Life Insurance Co. v. Haslip, 111 S.Ct. 1032 (1991).
7–1, BLACKMUN. Concurrences: Scalia, Kennedy. Dissent: O'Connor. Not voting: Souter. 36pp.

1553. Pacific Railroad, U.S. v., 120 U.S. 227 (1887).
9–0, FIELD. 14pp.

1554. Pacific States Telephone & Telegraph Co. v. Oregon, 223 U.S. 151 (1912).
9–0, WHITE. 16pp.

1555. Packet Co. v. Keokuk, 95 U.S. 80 (1877).
9–0, STRONG. 10pp.

1556. Palermo v. U.S., 360 U.S. 343 (1959).
9–0, FRANKFURTER. Concurrences: Brennan, Warren, Black, Douglas. 23pp.

1557. Palko v. Connecticut, 302 U.S. 319 (1937).
8–1, CARDOZO. Dissent: Butler. 10pp.

1558. Palmer v. Thompson, 403 U.S. 217 (1971).
5–4, BLACK. Concurrences: Burger, Blackmun. Dissents: Douglas, White, Brennan, Marshall. 57pp.

1559. Palmer, U.S. v., 16 U.S. (3 Wheat.) 610 (1817).
7–0, MARSHALL. 35pp.

1560. Palmore v. Sidoti, 466 U.S. 429 (1984).
9–0, BURGER. 6pp.

1561. Panama Canal Co. v. Grace Line, Inc., 356 U.S. 309 (1958).
9–0, DOUGLAS. 11pp.

1562. Panama Refining Co. v. Ryan, 293 U.S. 388 (1935).
8–1, HUGHES. Dissent: Cardozo. 61pp.

1563. Papachristou v. City of Jacksonville, 405 U.S. 156 (1972).
7–0, DOUGLAS. Not voting: Powell, Rehnquist. 16pp.

1564. Papish v. Board of Curators of University of Missouri, 410 U.S. 667 (1973).
6–3, PER CURIAM. Dissents: Burger, Rehnquist, Blackmun. 11pp.

1565. Parham v. J.R., 442 U.S. 584 (1979).
6–3, BURGER. Concurrences: Stewart, Brennan, Marshall, Stevens. Dissents: Brennan, Marshall, Stevens. 55pp.

1566. Paris Adult Theatre I v. Slaton, 413 U.S. 49 (1973).
6–3, BURGER. Dissents: Douglas, Brennan, Stewart, Marshall. 24pp.

1567. Park, U.S. v., 421 U.S. 658 (1975).

1596. Pennsylvania Coal Co. v. Mahon, 260 U.S. 393 (1922).
   8–1, HOLMES. Dissent: Brandeis. 30pp.

1597. Pennsylvania ex rel. Herman v. Claudy, 350 U.S. 116 (1956).
   9–0, BLACK. 8pp.

1598. Pennsylvania Fire Insurance Co. v. Gold Issue Mining & Milling Co., 243 U.S. 93 (1917).
   9–0, HOLMES. 5pp.

1599. Penry v. Lynaugh, 492 U.S. 302 (1989).
   9–0, 5–4 (various coalitions), O'CONNOR. Concurrences: Brennan, Marshall, Stevens, Blackmun, Scalia, Rehnquist, White, Kennedy. Dissents: Brennan, Marshall, Stevens, Blackmun, Scalia, Rehnquist, White, Kennedy. 58pp.

   Pentagon Papers Case, see New York Times Co. v. U.S.

1600. Perez v. Brownell, 356 U.S. 44 (1958).
   5–4, FRANKFURTER. Dissents: Warren, Black, Douglas, Whittaker. 42pp.

1601. Perez v. Campbell, 402 U.S. 637 (1971).
   5–4, WHITE. Concurrences: Blackmun, Burger, Harlan, Stewart. Dissents: Blackmun, Burger, Harlan, Stewart. 36pp.

1602. Perez v. Ledesma, 401 U.S. 82 (1971).
   5–4, BLACK. Concurrences: Stewart, Blackmun, Brennan, White, Marshall. Dissents: Douglas, Brennan, White, Marshall. 55pp.

1603. Perez v. U.S., 402 U.S. 146 (1971).
   8–1, DOUGLAS. Dissent: Stewart. 12pp.

1604. Perez, U.S. v., 22 U.S. (9 Wheat.) 579 (1824).
   7–0, STORY. 2pp.

1605. Perkins v. Elg, 307 U.S. 325 (1939).
   8–0, HUGHES. Not voting: Douglas. 26pp.

1606. Permoli v. Municipality No. 1, New Orleans, 44 U.S. (3 How.) 589 (1845).
   9–0, CATRON. 22pp.

1607. Pernell v. Southall Realty, 416 U.S. 363 (1974).
   9–0, MARSHALL. Concurrences: Burger, Douglas. 22pp.

1608. Perpich v. Dept. of Defense, 496 U.S. 334 (1990).
   9–0, STEVENS. 13pp.

1609. Perry Education Assn. v. Perry Local Educators' Assn., 460 U.S. 37 (1983).
   5–4, WHITE. Dissents: Brennan, Marshall, Powell, Stevens. 35pp.

1610. Perry v. Sindermann, 408 U.S. 593 (1972).
   5–3, STEWART. Concurrence: Burger. Dissents: Marshall, Brennan, Douglas. Not voting: Powell. 13pp.

1611. Perry v. U.S., 294 U.S. 330 (1935).
   5–4, HUGHES. Concurrence: Stone. Dissents: McReynolds, Van Devanter, Sutherland, Butler. 32pp.

1612. Personnel Administrator of Massachusetts v. Feeney, 442 U.S. 256 (1979).
   7–2, STEWART. Concurrences: Stevens, White. Dissents: Marshall, Brennan. 33pp.

1613. Peters v. Hobby, 349 U.S. 331 (1955).
   7–2, WARREN. Concurrences: Black, Douglas. Dissents: Reed, Burton. 27pp.

1614. Peters v. Kiff, 407 U.S. 493 (1972).
   6–3, MARSHALL. Concurrences: White, Brennan, Powell. Dissents: Burger, Blackmun, Rehnquist. 21pp.

1615. Peterson v. City of Greenville, 373 U.S. 244 (1963).
   8–1, WARREN. Concurrence: Harlan. Dissent: Harlan. 5pp.

1616. Peterson, Ex parte, 253 U.S. 300 (1920).
   6–3, BRANDEIS. Dissents: McKenna, Pitney, McReynolds. 20pp.

1617. Petit v. Minnesota, 177 U.S. 164 (1900).
   9–0, FULLER. 5pp.

1618. Petty v. Tennessee-Missouri Commission, 359 U.S. 275 (1959).
   6–3, DOUGLAS. Concurrences: Black, Clark, Stewart. Dissents: Frankfurter, Harlan, Whittaker. 15pp.

1619. Philadelphia Co. v. Stimson, 223 U.S. 605 (1912).
   9–0, HUGHES. 34pp.

1620. Philadelphia Newspapers, Inc. v. Hepps, 475 U.S. 767 (1986).
   5–4, O'CONNOR. Concurrences: Brennan, Blackmun. Dissents: Stevens, Burger, White, Rehnquist. 24pp.

1621. Philadelphia v. New Jersey, 437 U.S. 617 (1978).
   7–2, STEWART. Dissents: Rehnquist, Burger. 17pp.

1622. Phillips Chemical Co. v. Dumas School District, 361 U.S. 376 (1960).
   9–0, WARREN. Concurrence: Frankfurter. 12pp.

1623. Phillips Petroleum Co. v. Shutts, 472 U.S. 797 (1985).

1651. Poulos v. New Hampshire, 345 U.S. 395 (1953).
7–2, REED. Concurrence: Frankfurter. Dissents: Black, Douglas. 32pp.

1652. Powell v. Alabama, 287 U.S. 45 (1932).
7–2, SUTHERLAND. Dissents: Butler, McReynolds. 32pp.

1653. Powell v. McCormack, 395 U.S. 486 (1969).
8–1, WARREN. Dissent: Stewart. 89pp.

1654. Powell v. Pennsylvania, 127 U.S. 678 (1888).
9–0, HARLAN. 10pp.

1655. Powell v. Texas, 392 U.S. 514 (1968).
5–4, MARSHALL. Concurrences: Black, Harlan, White. Dissents: Fortas, Brennan, Douglas, Stewart. 56pp.

1656. Powers v. Ohio, 111 S.Ct. 1364 (1991).
7–2, KENNEDY. Dissents: Scalia, Rehnquist. 19pp.

1657. Powers v. U.S., 223 U.S. 303 (1912).
9–0, DAY. 14pp.

1658. Presbyterian Church in the U.S. v. Mary Elizabeth Blue Hull Mem. Presbyterian Church, 393 U.S. 440 (1969).
9–0, BRENNAN. Concurrence: Harlan. 13pp.

1659. Press-Enterprise Co. v. Superior Court of California I, 464 U.S. 501 (1984).
9–0, BURGER. Concurrences: Blackmun, Stevens, Marshall. 22pp.

1660. Press-Enterprise Co. v. Superior Court of California II, 478 U.S. 1 (1986).
7–2, BURGER. Dissents: Stevens, Rehnquist. 29pp.

1661. Presser v. Illinois, 116 U.S. 252 (1886).
9–0, WOODS. 18pp.

1662. Price, U.S. v., 116 U.S. 43 (1885).
9–0, WAITE. 2pp.

1663. Price, U.S. v., 383 U.S. 787 (1966).
9–0, FORTAS. Concurrence: Black. 33pp.

1664. Prigg v. Pennsylvania, 41 U.S. (16 Pet.) 539 (1842).
9–0, STORY. Concurrences: Taney, Thompson, Wayne, Daniel. 135pp.

1665. Primus, In re, 436 U.S. 412 (1978).
8–1, POWELL. Concurrences: Blackmun, Marshall. Dissent: Rehnquist. 34pp.

1666. Prince v. Massachusetts, 321 U.S. 158 (1944).
5–4, RUTLEDGE. Dissents: Jackson, Roberts, Frankfurter, Murphy. 19pp.

1667. Prize Cases, 67 U.S. (2 Bl.) 635 (1862).
5–4, GRIER. Dissents: Nelson, Taney, Catron, Clifford. 65pp.

1668. Procunier v. Martinez, 416 U.S. 396 (1974).
9–0, POWELL. Concurrences: Marshall, Brennan, Douglas. 33pp.

1669. Pruneyard Shopping Center v. Robins, 447 U.S. 74 (1980).
9–0, REHNQUIST. Concurrences: Blackmun, Marshall, White, Powell. 28pp.

1670. Ptasynski, U.S. v., 462 U.S. 74 (1983).
9–0, POWELL. 13pp.

1671. Public Clearing House v. Coyne, 194 U.S. 497 (1904).
8–1, BROWN. Concurrences: Brewer, White, Holmes. Dissent: Peckham. 20pp.

1672. Public Utilities Commission v. Attleboro Co., 273 U.S. 83 (1927).
8–1, SANFORD. Dissent: Brandeis. 10pp.

1673. Public Utilities Commission v. Pollak, 343 U.S. 451 (1952).
6–2, BURTON. Dissents: Black, Douglas. Not voting: Frankfurter. 19pp.

1674. Puerto Rico v. Branstad, 483 U.S. 219 (1987).
9–0, MARSHALL. Concurrences: O'Connor, Powell, Scalia. 12pp.

1675. Pulley v. Harris, 465 U.S. 37 (1984).
7–2, WHITE. Concurrence: Stevens. Dissents: Brennan, Marshall. 37pp.

1676. Quaker City Cab Co. v. Pennsylvania, 277 U.S. 389 (1928).
6–3, BUTLER. Dissents: Holmes, Brandeis, Stone. 24pp.

1677. Quirin, Ex parte, 317 U.S. 1 (1942).
8–0, PER CURIAM. Not voting: Murphy. 11pp.

1678. R.J. Reynolds Tobacco Co. v. Durham County, 479 U.S. 130 (1986).
9–0, BLACKMUN. 27pp.

1679. R.M.J., In re, 455 U.S. 191 (1982).
9–0, POWELL. 17pp.

1680. Rabe v. Washington, 405 U.S. 313 (1972).
9–0, PER CURIAM. Concurrences: Burger, Rehnquist. 5pp.

1681. Radovich v. National Football League, 352 U.S. 445 (1957).
6–3, CLARK. Dissents: Frankfurter, Harlan, Brennan. 12pp.

1682. Rahrer, In re, 140 U.S. 545 (1891).
9–0, FULLER. Concurrences: Harlan, Gray, Brewer. 21pp.

1683. Railroad Commission v. Pullman Co., 312 U.S. 496 (1941).
    8–0, FRANKFURTER. Not voting: Roberts. 7pp.
1684. Railroad Commission Cases, 116 U.S. 307 (1886).
    6–2, WAITE. Dissents: Harlan, Field. Not voting: Blatchford. 42pp.
1685. Railroad Retirement Board v. Alton Railroad Co., 295 U.S. 330 (1935).
    5–4, ROBERTS. Dissents: Hughes, Brandeis, Stone, Cardozo. 63pp.
1686. Railway Employees' Dept. v. Hanson, 351 U.S. 225 (1956).
    9–0, DOUGLAS. Concurrence: Frankfurter. 17pp.
1687. Railway Express Agency v. New York, 336 U.S. 106 (1949).
    9–0, DOUGLAS. Concurrence: Jackson. 5pp.
1688. Railway Labor Executives' Association v. Gibbons, 455 U.S. 457 (1982).
    9–0, REHNQUIST. Concurrences: Mashall, Brennan. 21pp.
1689. Rakas v. Illinois, 439 U.S. 128 (1978).
    5–4, REHNQUIST. Concurrences: Powell, Burger. Dissents: White, Brennan, Marshall, Stevens. 42pp.
1690. Ramah Navajo School Board v. Bureau of Revenue of New Mexico, 458 U.S. 832 (1982).
    6–3, MARSHALL. Dissents: Rehnquist, White, Stevens. 26pp.
1691. Ramsey, U.S. v., 431 U.S. 606 (1977).
    6–3, REHNQUIST. Concurrence: Powell. Dissents: Stevens, Brennan, Marshall. 27pp.
1692. Rands, U.S. v., 389 U.S. 121 (1967).
    8–0, WHITE. Not voting: Marshall. 8pp.
1693. Rankin v. McPherson, 483 U.S. 378 (1987).
    5–4, MARSHALL. Concurrence: Powell. Dissents: Scalia, Rehnquist, White, O'Connor. 24pp.
1694. Rapier, In re, 143 U.S. 110 (1892).
    9–0, FULLER. 26pp.
1695. Rawlings v. Kentucky, 448 U.S. 98 (1980).
    5–4, REHNQUIST. Concurrences: Blackmun, White, Stewart. Dissents: White, Stewart, Marshall, Brennan. 24pp.
1696. Ray v. Blair, 343 U.S. 214 (1952).
    7–2, REED. Dissents: Jackson, Douglas. 22pp.

1697. Rea v. U.S., 350 U.S. 214 (1956).
    5–4, DOUGLAS. Dissents: Harlan, Reed, Burton, Minton. 7pp.
1698. Reading Railroad v. Pennsylvania, 82 U.S. (15 Wall.) 232 (1873).
    7–2, STRONG. Dissents: Swayne, Davis. 52pp.
1699. Reagan v. Farmers' Loan & Trust Co., 154 U.S. 362 (1894).
    9–0, BREWER. 51pp.
1700. Red Lion Broadcasting Co. v. Federal Communications Commission, 395 U.S. 367 (1969).
    8–0, WHITE. Not voting: Douglas. 35pp.
1701. Reed v. Reed, 404 U.S. 71 (1971).
    9–0, BURGER. 7pp.
1702. Reese, U.S. v., 92 U.S. 214 (1875).
    7–2, WAITE. Dissents: Clifford, Hunt. 43pp.
1703. Reeves, Inc. v. Stake, 447 U.S. 429 (1980).
    5–4, BLACKMUN. Dissents: Powell, Brennan, White, Stevens. 25pp.
1704. Regan v. Taxation with Representation of Washington, 461 U.S. 540 (1983).
    9–0, REHNQUIST. Concurrences: Blackmun, Brennan, Marshall. 15pp.
1705. Regents of the University of California v. Bakke, 438 U.S. 265 (1978).
    5–4 (two four-justice pluralities dissenting from each other), POWELL (swing vote). One concurring and dissenting coalition: Brennan, White, Marshall, Blackmun. The other concurring and dissenting coalition: Stevens, Burger, Stewart, Rehnquist. 157pp.
1706. Reid v. Covert, 354 U.S. 1 (1957).
    6–2, BLACK. Concurrences: Frankfurter, Harlan. Dissents: Clark, Burton. Not voting: Whittaker. 90pp.
1707. Reidel, U.S. v., 402 U.S. 351 (1971).
    7–2, WHITE. Concurrences: Harlan, Marshall. Dissents: Black, Douglas. 9pp.
1708. Reitman v. Mulkey, 387 U.S. 369 (1967).
    5–4, WHITE. Concurrence: Douglas. Dissents: Harlan, Black, Clark, Stewart. 28pp.
1709. Rendell-Baker v. Kohn, 457 U.S. 830 (1982).
    7–2, BURGER. Concurrence: White. Dissents: Marshall, Brennan. 22pp.
1710. Renne v. Geary, 111 S.Ct. 2331 (1991).
    6–3, KENNEDY. Concurrences: Stevens,

Scalia. Dissents: White, Marshall, Blackmun. 24pp.

1711. Renton, City of, v. Playtime Theatres, Inc., 475 U.S. 41 (1986).
7–2, REHNQUIST. Concurrence: Blackmun. Dissents: Brennan, Marshall. 25pp.

1712. Republic Steel Corp., U.S. v., 362 U.S. 482 (1960).
5–4, DOUGLAS. Dissents: Harlan, Frankfurter, Whittaker, Stewart. 29pp.

1713. Reynolds v. Sims, 377 U.S. 533 (1964).
8–1, WARREN. Concurrences: Clark, Stewart. Dissent: Harlan. 99pp.

1714. Reynolds v. U.S., 98 U.S. 145 (1879).
9–0, WAITE. Concurrence: Field. 24pp.

1715. Reynolds, U.S. v., 345 U.S. 1 (1953).
6–3, VINSON. Dissents: Black, Frankfurter, Jackson. 12pp.

1716. Rhode Island v. Massachusetts, 37 U.S. (12 Pet.) 657 (1838).
7–1, BALDWIN. Concurrence: Barbour. Dissent: Taney. Not voting: Story. 98pp.

1717. Rhode Island v. Palmer, 253 U.S. 350 (1920).
7–2, VAN DEVANTER. Concurrences: McReynolds, White. Dissents: McKenna, Clarke. 57pp.

1718. Rhodes v. Chapman, 452 U.S. 337 (1981).
8–1, POWELL. Concurrences: Brennan, Blackmun, Stevens. Dissent: Marshall. 41pp.

1719. Rice v. Rehner, 463 U.S. 713 (1983).
6–3, O'CONNOR. Dissents: Blackmun, Brennan, Marshall. 32pp.

1720. Rice v. Rice, 336 U.S. 674 (1949).
5–4, PER CURIAM. Dissents: Jackson, Black, Douglas, Rutledge. 7pp.

1721. Rice v. Santa Fe Elevator Corp., 331 U.S. 218 (1947).
7–2, DOUGLAS. Dissents: Frankfurter, Rutledge. 30pp.

1722. Richardson v. Belcher, 404 U.S. 78 (1971).
6–3, STEWART. Dissents: Douglas, Marshall, Brennan. 19pp.

1723. Richardson v. Perales, 402 U.S. 389 (1971).
6–3, BLACKMUN. Dissents: Douglas, Black, Brennan. 26pp.

1724. Richardson v. Ramirez, 418 U.S. 24 (1974).
6–3, REHNQUIST. Dissents: Douglas, Marshall, Brennan. 62pp.

1725. Richardson, U.S. v., 418 U.S. 166 (1974).

5–4, BURGER. Concurrence: Powell. Dissents: Douglas, Stewart, Marshall, Brennan. 42pp.

1726. Richmond v. J.A. Croson Company, 488 U.S. 469 (1989).
6–3, O'CONNOR. Concurrences: Stevens, Kennedy, Scalia. Dissents: Marshall, Brennan, Blackmun. 92pp.

1727. Richmond Newspapers, Inc. v. Virginia, 448 U.S. 555 (1980).
8–1, BURGER. Concurrences: White, Stevens, Brennan, Marshall, Stewart, Blackmun. Dissent: Rehnquist. 52pp.

1728. Rideau v. Louisiana, 373 U.S. 723 (1963).
7–2, STEWART. Dissents: Clark, Harlan. 11pp.

1729. Riley v. National Federation of the Blind of North Carolina, 487 U.S. 781 (1988).
6–3, BRENNAN. Concurrences: Scalia, Stevens. Dissents: Stevens, Rehnquist, O'Connor. 34pp.

1730. Rinaldi v. Yeager, 384 U.S. 305 (1966).
8–1, STEWART. Dissent: Harlan. 7pp.

1731. Rio Grande Dam & Irrigation Co., U.S. v., 174 U.S. 690 (1899).
7–0, BREWER. Not voting: Gray, McKenna. 21pp.

1732. Ristaino v. Ross, 424 U.S. 589 (1976).
7–2, POWELL. Concurrence: White. Dissents: Marshall, Brennan. 11pp.

1733. Rivera v. Minnich, 483 U.S. 574 (1987).
8–1, STEVENS. Concurrence: O'Connor. Dissent: Brennan. 13pp.

1734. Rizzo v. Goode, 423 U.S. 362 (1976).
6–3, REHNQUIST. Dissents: Blackmun, Brennan, Marshall. 25pp.

1735. Robbins v. Shelby Taxing District, 120 U.S. 489 (1887).
6–3, BRADLEY. Dissents: White, Field, Gray. 14pp.

1736. Robel, U.S. v., 389 U.S. 258 (1967).
7–2, WARREN. Concurrence: Brennan. Dissents: White, Harlan. 32pp.

1737. Robert Mitchell Furniture Co. v. Selden Breck Construction Co., 257 U.S. 213 (1921).
9–0, HOLMES. 4pp.

1738. Roberts v. LaVallee, 389 U.S. 40 (1967).
8–1, PER CURIAM. Dissent: Harlan. 5pp.

1768. Roudebush v. Hartke, 405 U.S. 15 (1972).
5–2, STEWART. Dissents: Douglas, Brennan. Not voting: Powell, Rehnquist. 19pp.

1769. Rowan v. United States Post Office Department, 397 U.S. 728 (1970).
9–0, BURGER. Concurrences: Brennan, Douglas. 14pp.

1770. Royal Arcanum v. Green, 237 U.S. 531 (1915).
9–0, WHITE. 16pp.

1771. Rubber-Tip Pencil Co. v. Howard, 87 U.S. (20 Wall.) 498 (1874).
9–0, WAITE. 9pp.

1772. Ruffalo, In re, 390 U.S. 544 (1968).
8–0, DOUGLAS. Concurrences: Black, Harlan, White, Marshall. Not voting: Stewart. 13pp.

1773. Rummel v. Estelle, 445 U.S. 263 (1980).
5–4, REHNQUIST. Concurrence: Stewart. Dissents: Powell, Brennan, Marshall, Stevens. 45pp.

1774. Runyon v. McCrary, 427 U.S. 160 (1976).
7–2, STEWART. Concurrences: Powell, Stevens. Dissents: White, Rehnquist. 55pp.

1775. Rush v. Savchuk, 444 U.S. 320 (1980).
7–2, MARSHALL. Dissents: Brennan, Stevens. 15pp.

1776. Russell v. U.S., 369 U.S. 749 (1962).
4–2, STEWART. Concurrence: Douglas. Dissents: Harlan, Clark. Not voting: Frankfurter, White, Brennan. 46pp.

1776a. Russell v. U.S., 471 U.S. 858 (1985).
9–0, STEVENS. 5pp.

1777. Rust v. Sullivan, 111 S.Ct. 1759 (1991).
5–4, REHNQUIST. Dissents: Blackmun, Marshall, Stevens, O'Connor. 31pp.

1778. Rutan v. Republican Party of Illinois, 497 U.S. 62 (1990).
5–4, BRENNAN. Concurrence: Stevens. Dissents: Scalia, Rehnquist, Kennedy, O'Connor. 30pp.

1779. Rutkin v. U.S., 343 U.S. 130 (1952).
5–4, BURTON. Dissents: Black, Reed, Frankfurter, Douglas. 17pp.

1780. Sable Communications, Inc. v. Federal Communications Commission, 492 U.S. 115 (1989).
6–3, WHITE. Concurrences: Scalia, Brennan, Marshall, Stevens. Dissents: Brennan, Marshall, Stevens. 21pp.

1781. Saffle v. Parks, 494 U.S. 484 (1990).
5–4, KENNEDY. Dissents: Brennan, Marshall, Blackmun, Stevens. 17pp.

1782. Sage Stores Co. v. Kansas, 323 U.S. 32 (1944).
9–0, REED. Concurrences: Black, Douglas. 5pp.

1783. Saia v. New York, 334 U.S. 558 (1948).
5–4, DOUGLAS. Dissents: Frankfurter, Reed, Burton, Jackson. 15pp.

1784. Saint Francis College v. Al-Khazraji, 481 U.S. 604 (1987).
9–0, WHITE. Concurrence: Brennan. 11pp.

1785. Salerno, U.S. v., 481 U.S. 739 (1987).
6–3, REHNQUIST. Dissents: Marshall, Brennan, Stevens. 31pp.

1786. Salinger v. Loisel, 265 U.S. 224 (1924).
9–0, VAN DEVANTER. 15pp.

1787. Salve Regina College v. Russell, 111 S.Ct. 1217 (1991).
6–3, BLACKMUN. Dissents: Rehnquist, White, Stevens. 11pp.

1788. Salyer Land Co. v. Tulare Lake Basin Water Storage District, 410 U.S. 719 (1973).
6–3, REHNQUIST. Dissents: Douglas, Brennan, Marshall. 24pp.

1789. Samuels v. Mackell, 401 U.S. 66 (1971).
9–0, BLACK. Concurrences: Douglas, Brennan, White, Marshall, Stewart, Harlan. 10pp.

1790. Samuels v. McCurdy, 267 U.S. 188 (1925).
8–1, TAFT. Dissent: Butler. 16pp.

1791. San Antonio School District v. Rodriguez, 411 U.S. 1 (1973).
5–4, POWELL. Concurrence: Stewart. Dissents: Brennan, White, Douglas, Marshall. 132pp.

1792. San Diego Building Trades Council v. Garmon, 359 U.S. 236 (1959).
9–0, FRANKFURTER. Concurrences: Harlan, Clark, Whittaker, Stewart. 19pp.

1793. San Diego Land & Town Co. v. Jasper, 189 U.S. 439 (1903).
9–0, HOLMES. 9pp.

1794. San Francisco Arts & Athletics v. U.S. Olympic Committee, 483 U.S. 522 (1987).
5–4, POWELL. Concurrences: O'Connor, Blackmun. Dissents: O'Connor, Blackmun, Brennan, Marshall. 52pp.

1795. Sanabria v. U.S., 437 U.S. 54 (1978).

5–4, BLACKMUN. Dissents: Powell, Brennan, Marshall, Stevens. 26pp.

1828. Schwimmer, U.S. v., 279 U.S. 644 (1929).
6–3, BUTLER. Dissents: Holmes, Sanford, Brandeis. 11pp.

1829. Scott v. Illinois, 440 U.S. 367 (1979).
5–4, REHNQUIST. Concurrence: Powell. Dissents: Brennan, Marshall, Stevens, Blackmun. 23pp.

1830. SCRAP, U.S. v., 412 U.S. 669 (1973).
8–0, 5–3 (various coalitions), STEWART. Concurrences: Douglas, Marshall, Burger, White, Rehnquist, Blackmun, Brennan. Dissents: Douglas, White, Burger, Rehnquist, Marshall. Not voting: Powell. 66pp.

1831. Screws v. U.S., 325 U.S. 91 (1945).
5–4, DOUGLAS. Concurrence: Rutledge. Dissents: Murphy, Roberts, Frankfurter, Jackson. 70pp.

1832. Scripto v. Carson, 362 U.S. 207 (1960).
8–1, CLARK. Dissent: Whittaker. 7pp.

1833. Seaboard Air Line Ry. v. Blackwell, 244 U.S. 310 (1917).
6–3, McKENNA. Dissents: White, Pitney, Brandeis. 6pp.

1834. Seagram & Sons v. Hostetter, 384 U.S. 35 (1966).
9–0, STEWART. 24pp.

1835. Searight v. Stokes, 44 U.S. (3 How.) 151 (1845).
8–1, TANEY. Dissent: McLean. 36pp.

1835a. Sears, Roebuck & Co. v. Stiffel Co., 376 U.S. 225 (1964).
9–0, BLACK. Concurrence: Harlan. 9pp.

1836. Seattle Times Co. v. Rhinehart, 467 U.S. 20 (1984).
9–0, POWELL. Concurrences: Brennan, Marshall. 19pp.

Second Employers' Liability Cases, *see* Mondou v. New York, New Haven & Hartford R.R. Co.

1837. Secretary of State of Maryland v. Joseph H. Munson Co., 467 U.S. 947 (1984).
5–4, BLACKMUN. Concurrence: Stevens. Dissents: Rehnquist, Burger, Powell, O'Connor. 39pp.

1838. Securities and Exchange Commission v. Sloan, 436 U.S. 103 (1978).
9–0, REHNQUIST. Concurrences: Brennan, Marshall, Blackmun. 25pp.

1839. See v. City of Seattle, 387 U.S. 541 (1967).
6–3, WHITE. Dissents: Clark, Harlan, Stewart. 6pp.

1840. Seeger, U.S. v., 380 U.S. 163 (1965).
9–0, CLARK. Concurrence: Douglas. 30pp.

1841. Segura v. U.S., 468 U.S. 796 (1984).
5–4, BURGER. Concurrence: O'Connor. Dissents: Stevens, Brennan, Marshall, Blackmun. 44pp.

1842. Selective Draft Law Cases, 245 U.S. 366 (1918).
9–0, WHITE. 25pp.

1843. Senn v. Tile Layers Protective Union, 301 U.S. 468 (1937).
5–4, BRANDEIS. Dissents: Butler, Van Devanter, McReynolds, Sutherland. 24pp.

1844. Serbian Eastern Orthodox Diocese for the U.S. & Canada v. Milivojevich, 426 U.S. 696 (1976).
7–2, BRENNAN. Concurrences: Burger, White. Dissents: Rehnquist, Stevens. 39pp.

1845. Service v. Dulles, 354 U.S. 363 (1957).
8–0, HARLAN. Not voting: Clark. 26pp.

1846. Sgro v. U.S., 287 U.S. 206 (1932).
7–2, HUGHES. Concurrence: McReynolds. Dissents: Stone, Cardozo. 11pp.

1847. Shaare Tefila Congregation v. Cobb, 481 U.S. 615 (1987).
9–0, WHITE. 3pp.

1848. Shadwick v. City of Tampa, 407 U.S. 345 (1972).
9–0, POWELL. 10pp.

1849. Shapero v. Kentucky Bar Assn., 486 U.S. 466 (1988).
6–3, 5–4, BRENNAN. Concurrences: White, Stevens. Dissents: White, Stevens, O'Connor, Rehnquist, Scalia. 25pp.

1850. Shapiro v. Thompson, 394 U.S. 618 (1969).
6–3, BRENNAN. Concurrence: Stewart. Dissents: Warren, Black, Harlan. 60pp.

1851. Shaughnessy v. U.S. ex rel. Mezei, 345 U.S. 206 (1953).
5–4, CLARK. Dissents: Black, Jackson, Frankfurter, Douglas. 23pp.

1852. Sheehan Co. v. Shuler, 265 U.S. 371 (1924).
9–0, SANFORD. 8pp.

1853. Sheldon v. Sill, 49 U.S. (8 How.) 441 (1850).
9–0, GRIER. 10pp.

1854. Shelley v. Kraemer, 334 U.S. 1 (1948).
6–0, VINSON. Not voting: Reed, Jackson, Rutledge. 22pp.

8–1, REED. Concurrence: Frankfurter. Dissent: Roberts. 22pp.

1886. Smith v. Bennett, 365 U.S. 708 (1961).
9–0, CLARK. 7pp.

1887. Smith v. California, 361 U.S. 147 (1959).
8–1, BRENNAN. Concurrences: Black, Frankfurter, Douglas, Harlan. Dissent: Harlan. 26pp.

1888. Smith v. Collin, 439 U.S. 916 (1978).
7–2, PER CURIAM. Dissents: Blackmun, White. 4pp.

1889. Smith v. Goguen, 415 U.S. 566 (1974).
6–3, POWELL. Concurrence: White. Dissents: Blackmun, Burger, Rehnquist. 39pp.

1890. Smith v. Hooey, 393 U.S. 374 (1969).
9–0, STEWART. Concurrences: Black, Harlan, White. 11pp.

1891. Smith v. Illinois, 390 U.S. 129 (1968).
8–1, STEWART. Concurrences: White, Marshall. Dissent: Harlan. 7pp.

1892. Smith v. Kansas Title & Trust Co., 255 U.S. 180 (1921).
6–2, DAY. Dissents: Holmes, McReynolds. Not voting: Brandeis. 36pp.

1893. Smith v. Maryland, 442 U.S. 735 (1979).
6–3, BLACKMUN. Dissents: Stewart, Marshall, Brennan. 17pp.

1894. Smith v. Organization of Foster Families for Equality and Reform, 431 U.S. 816 (1977).
9–0, BRENNAN. Concurrences: Stewart, Burger, Rehnquist. 47pp.

1895. Smith v. Phillips, 455 U.S. 209 (1982).
6–3, REHNQUIST. Concurrence: O'Connor. Dissents: Marshall, Brennan, Stevens. 36pp.

1896. Smith v. St. Louis and Southwestern Ry. Co. of Texas, 181 U.S. 248 (1901).
6–3, McKENNA. Dissents: Harlan, Brown, White. 16pp.

1897. Smith, U.S. v., 18 U.S. (5 Wheat.) 153 (1820).
8–1, STORY. Dissent: Livingstone. 31pp.

1898. Smith, U.S. v., 286 U.S. 6 (1932).
9–0, BRANDEIS. 44pp.

1899. Smyth v. Ames, 169 U.S. 466 (1898).
9–0, HARLAN. 85pp.

1900. Snepp v. U.S., 444 U.S. 507 (1980).
6–3, PER CURIAM. Dissents: Stevens, Brennan, Marshall. 20pp.

1901. Sniadach v. Family Finance Corp., 395 U.S. 337 (1969).
8–1, DOUGLAS. Concurrence: Harlan. Dissent: Black. 15pp.

1902. Snowden v. Hughes, 321 U.S. 1 (1944).
7–2, STONE. Concurrences: Rutledge, Frankfurter. Dissents: Douglas, Murphy. 19pp.

1903. Snyder v. Massachusetts, 291 U.S. 97 (1934).
5–4, CARDOZO. Dissents: Roberts, Brandeis, Sutherland, Butler. 42pp.

1904. Sokolow, U.S. v., 490 U.S. 1 (1989).
7–2, REHNQUIST. Dissents: Marshall, Brennan. 17pp.

1905. Solem v. Helm, 463 U.S. 277 (1983).
5–4, POWELL. Dissents: Burger, White, Rehnquist, O'Connor. 51pp.

1906. Soliah v. Heskin, 222 U.S. 522 (1912).
9–0, LAMAR. 3pp.

1907. Solorio v. U.S., 483 U.S. 435 (1987).
6–3, REHNQUIST. Concurrence: Stevens. Dissents: Marshall, Brennan, Blackmun. 33pp.

1908. Sonzinsky v. U.S., 300 U.S. 506 (1937).
9–0, STONE. 9pp.

1909. Sosna v. Iowa, 419 U.S. 393 (1975).
6–3, REHNQUIST. Dissents: White, Marshall, Brennan. 35pp.

1910. South Carolina v. Baker, 485 U.S. 505 (1988).
7–1, BRENNAN. Concurrences: Stevens, Scalia, Rehnquist. Dissent: O'Connor. Not voting: Kennedy. 29pp.

1911. South Carolina v. Gathers, 490 U.S. 805 (1989).
6–3, BRENNAN. Concurrence: White. Dissents: Rehnquist, O'Connor, Scalia. 41pp.

1912. South Carolina v. Georgia, 93 U.S. 4 (1876).
9–0, STRONG. 11pp.

1913. South Carolina v. Katzenbach, 383 U.S. 301 (1966).
8–1, WARREN. Concurrence: Black. Dissent: Black. 61pp.

1914. South Carolina State Highway Dept. v. Barnwell Bros., Inc., 303 U.S. 177 (1938).
7–0, STONE. Not voting: Cardozo, Reed. 20pp.

1915. South Dakota v. Dole, 483 U.S. 203 (1987).
7–2, REHNQUIST. Dissents: Brennan, O'Connor. 16pp.

1916. South Dakota v. Opperman, 428 U.S. 364 (1976).

2008. Tennessee Valley Authority v. Hill, 437 U.S. 153 (1978).
6–3, BURGER. Dissents: Powell, Blackmun, Rehnquist. 61pp.

2009. Tenney v. Brandhove, 341 U.S. 367 (1951).
8–1, FRANKFURTER. Concurrence: Black. Dissent: Douglas. 16pp.

2010. Terlinden v. Ames, 184 U.S. 270 (1902).
9–0, FULLER. 21pp.

2011. Terminiello v. Chicago, 337 U.S. 1 (1949).
5–4, DOUGLAS. Dissents: Vinson, Frankfurter, Jackson, Burton. 37pp.

2012. Terry v. Adams, 345 U.S. 461 (1953).
8–1, BLACK. Concurrences: Clark, Warren, Reed, Jackson. Dissent: Minton. 34pp.

2013. Terry v. Ohio, 392 U.S. 1 (1968).
8–1, WARREN. Concurrences: Black, Harlan, White. Dissent: Douglas. 33pp.

2014. Terry, Ex parte, 128 U.S. 289 (1888).
9–0, HARLAN. 26pp.

Test Oath Cases, see Garland, Ex parte

2015. Testa v. Katt, 330 U.S. 386 (1947).
9–0, BLACK. 9pp.

2016. Texaco v. Short, 454 U.S. 516 (1982).
5–4, STEVENS. Dissents: Brennan, White, Marshall, Powell. 39pp.

2017. Texas & N.O.R. Co. v. Brotherhood of Railway Clerks, 281 U.S. 548 (1930).
8–0, HUGHES. Not voting: McReynolds. 24pp.

2018. Texas Monthly, Inc. v. Bullock, 489 U.S. 1 (1989).
6–3, BRENNAN. Concurrences: White, Blackmun, O'Connor. Dissents: Scalia, Rehnquist, Kennedy. 45pp.

2019. Texas v. Brown, 460 U.S. 730 (1983).
9–0, REHNQUIST. Concurrences: White, Powell, Blackmun, Stevens, Brennan, Marshall. 22pp.

2020. Texas v. Florida, 306 U.S. 398 (1939).
7–2, STONE. Dissents: Frankfurter, Black. 37pp.

2021. Texas v. Johnson, 491 U.S. 397 (1989).
5–4, BRENNAN. Concurrence: Kennedy. Dissents: Rehnquist, White, O'Connor, Stevens. 43pp.

2022. Texas v. New Jersey, 379 U.S. 674 (1965).
8–1, BLACK. Dissent: Stewart. 10pp.

2023. Texas v. New Mexico, 482 U.S. 124 (1987).
8–0, WHITE. Not voting: Stevens. 12pp.

2024. Texas v. White, 74 U.S. (7 Wall.) 700 (1869).
5–3, CHASE. Dissents: Grier, Swayne, Miller. 43pp.

2025. Texas, U.S. v., 339 U.S. 707 (1950).
4–3, DOUGLAS. Dissents: Reed, Minton, Frankfurter. Not voting: Clark, Jackson. 18pp.

2026. The Antelope, 23 U.S. (10 Wheat.) 66 (1825).
7–0, MARSHALL. 67pp.

2027. The Brig Aurora, 11 U.S. (7 Cr.) 382 (1813).
6–0, JOHNSON. Not voting: Todd. 8pp.

2028. The Daniel Ball, 77 U.S. (10 Wall.) 557 (1870).
9–0, FIELD. 10pp.

2029. The Eagle, 75 U.S. (8 Wall.) 15 (1868).
8–0, NELSON. 8pp.

2030. The Genessee Chief v. Fitzhugh, 53 U.S. (12 How.) 443 (1851).
8–1, TANEY. Dissent: Daniel. 23pp.

2031. The Laura v. Bridgeport Steam-Boat Co., 114 U.S. 411 (1885).
9–0, HARLAN. 7pp.

2032. The Lottawanna, 88 U.S. (21 Wall.) 558 (1874).
7–2, BRADLEY. Dissents: Clifford, Field. 52pp.

2033. The Magnolia, 61 U.S. (20 How.) 296 (1857).
6–3, GRIER. Concurrence: McLean. Dissents: Catron, Daniel, Campbell. 47pp.

2034. The Paquette Habana, 175 U.S. 677 (1900).
6–3, GRAY. Dissents: Fuller, Harlan, McKenna. 44pp.

2035. The Siren, 80 U.S. (13 Wall.) 389 (1871).
9–0, SWAYNE. 8pp.

2036. The Steamboat Thomas Jefferson, 23 U.S. (10 Wheat.) 428 (1825).
7–0, STORY. 3pp.

2037. Thind, U.S. v., 261 U.S. 204 (1923).
9–0, SUTHERLAND. 12pp.

2038. Thomas v. Collins, 323 U.S. 516 (1945).
5–4, RUTLEDGE. Concurrences: Douglas, Black, Murphy, Jackson. Dissents: Roberts, Stone, Reed, Frankfurter. 42pp.

2039. Thomas v. Union Carbide Agricultural Products Co., 473 U.S. 568 (1985).
9–0, O'CONNOR. Concurrences: Brennan, Marshall, Blackmun, Stevens. 38pp.

2068. Trade-Mark Cases, 100 U.S. 82 (1879).
9–0, MILLER. 18pp.

2069. Travis v. Yale & Towne Mfg. Co., 252 U.S. 60 (1920).
9–0, PITNEY. Concurrence: McReynolds. 23pp.

2070. Triangle Improvement Council v. Ritchie, 402 U.S. 497 (1971).
5–4, PER CURIAM. Concurrence: Harlan. Dissents: Douglas, Black, Brennan, Marshall. 12pp.

2071. Trimble v. Gordon, 430 U.S. 762 (1977).
5–4, POWELL. Dissents: Burger, Stewart, Blackmun, Rehnquist. 24pp.

2072. Trop v. Dulles, 356 U.S. 86 (1958).
5–4, WARREN. Concurrences: Black, Douglas, Brennan. Dissents: Frankfurter, Burton, Clark, Harlan. 43pp.

2073. Truax v. Corrigan, 257 U.S. 312 (1921).
5–4, TAFT. Dissents: Holmes, Pitney, Clarke, Brandeis. 65pp.

2074. Truax v. Raich, 239 U.S. 33 (1915).
8–1, HUGHES. Dissent: McReynolds. 11pp.

2075. Tucker, U.S. v., 404 U.S. 443 (1972).
5–2, STEWART. Dissents: Blackmun, Burger. Not voting: Powell, Rehnquist. 10pp.

2076. Tull v. U.S., 481 U.S. 412 (1987).
7–2, BRENNAN. Concurrences: Scalia, Stevens. Dissents: Scalia, Stevens. 16pp.

2077. Tumey v. Ohio, 273 U.S. 510 (1927).
9–0, TAFT. 26pp.

2078. Turner v. Bank of North America, 4 U.S. (4 Dall.) 8 (1799).
6–0, ELLSWORTH. 3pp.

2079. Turner v. Louisiana, 379 U.S. 466 (1965).
8–1, STEWART. Dissent: Clark. 10pp.

2080. Turner v. Maryland, 107 U.S. 38 (1883).
9–0, BLATCHFORD. 22pp.

2081. Turner v. Memphis, 369 U.S. 350 (1962).
8–0, PER CURIAM. Not voting: Whittaker. 4pp.

2082. Turner v. Safley, 482 U.S. 78 (1987).
5–4, O'CONNOR. Concurrences: Stevens, Brennan, Marshall, Blackmun. Dissents: Stevens, Brennan, Marshall, Blackmun. 39pp.

2083. Turner v. U.S., 396 U.S. 398 (1970).
7–2, WHITE. Concurrence: Marshall. Dissents: Black, Douglas. 36pp.

2084. Turpin v. Lemon, 187 U.S. 51 (1902).
9–0, FULLER. 10pp.

2085. Twelve 200-Foot Reels of Super 8mm Film, U.S. v., 413 U.S. 123 (1973).
5–4, BURGER. Dissents: Douglas, Brennan, Stewart, Marshall. 16pp.

2086. Twining v. New Jersey, 211 U.S. 78 (1908).
8–1, MOODY. Dissent: Harlan. 37pp.

2087. Tyler Pipe Industries, Inc. v. Washington Dept. of Revenue, 483 U.S. 232 (1987).
8–0, 6–2, STEVENS. Concurrences: O'Connor, Scalia, Rehnquist. Dissents: Scalia, Rehnquist. Not voting: Powell. 34pp.

2088. Ullman v. U.S., 350 U.S. 422 (1956).
6–3, FRANKFURTER. Concurrence: Reed. Dissents: Douglas, Black, Reed. 33pp.

2089. Underhill v. Hernandez, 168 U.S. 250 (1897).
9–0, FULLER. 5pp.

2090. Uniformed Sanitation Men Assn. v. Commissioner of Sanitation, 392 U.S. 280 (1968).
9–0, FORTAS. Concurrence: Black. 4pp.

2091. Union Bridge Co. v. U.S., 204 U.S. 364 (1907).
6–2, HARLAN. Dissents: Brewer, Peckham. Not voting: Moody. 40pp.

2092. Union Refrigerator Transit Co. v. Kentucky, 199 U.S. 194 (1905).
7–2, BROWN. Concurrence: White. Dissents: Holmes, Fuller. 18pp.

2093. United Building & Construction Trades Council v. Mayor of Camden, 465 U.S. 208 (1984).
8–1, REHNQUIST. Dissent: Blackmun. 28pp.

2094. United Jewish Organizations v. Carey, 430 U.S. 144 (1977).
8–1, WHITE. Concurrences: Brennan, Stewart, Powell. Dissent: Burger. 44pp.

2095. United Mine Workers v. Gibbs, 383 U.S. 715 (1966).
8–0, BRENNAN. Concurrences: Harlan, Clark. Not voting: Warren. 29pp.

2096. United Mine Workers v. Illinois State Bar Assn., 389 U.S. 217 (1967).
8–1, BLACK. Concurrence: Stewart. Dissent: Harlan. 18pp.

2097. United Mine Workers, U.S. v., 330 U.S. 258 (1947).
5–4, VINSON. Concurrences: Black, Frankfurter, Douglas, Jackson. Dissents:

2122. Vendo Co. v. Lektro-Vend Corp., 433 U.S. 623 (1977).
5–4, REHNQUIST. Concurrences: Blackmun, Burger. Dissents: Stevens, Brennan, White, Marshall. 44pp.

2123. Ventresca, U.S. v., 380 U.S. 102 (1965).
7–2, GOLDBERG. Dissents: Douglas, Warren. 22pp.

2124. Verdugo-Urquidez, U.S. v., 494 U.S. 259 (1990).
6–3, REHNQUIST. Concurrences: Kennedy, Stevens. Dissents: Brennan, Marshall, Blackmun. 40pp.

2125. Vermont Yankee Nuclear Power Corp. v. Natural Resources Defense Council, 435 U.S. 519 (1978).
7–0, REHNQUIST. Not voting: Blackmun, Powell. 40pp.

Village of ———, see name of the village

2126. Villamonte-Marquez, U.S. v., 462 U.S. 579 (1983).
6–3, REHNQUIST. Dissents: Brennan, Marshall, Stevens. 32pp.

2127. Virginia v. Tennessee, 148 U.S. 503 (1893).
9–0, FIELD. 26pp.

2128. Virginia v. West Virginia, 220 U.S. 1 (1911).
9–0, HOLMES. 36pp.

2129. Virginia v. West Virginia, 246 U.S. 565 (1918).
9–0, WHITE. 42pp.

2130. Virginia, Ex parte, 100 U.S. 339 (1879).
7–2, STRONG. Dissents: Field, Clifford. 32pp.

2131. Virginia State Board of Pharmacy v. Virginia Citizens Consumer Council, 425 U.S. 748 (1976).
8–1, BLACKMUN. Concurrences: Burger, Stewart. Dissent: Rehnquist. 42pp.

2132. Virginian Railway v. System No. 40 Federation, 300 U.S. 515 (1937).
9–0, STONE. 49pp.

2133. Vitek v. Jones, 445 U.S. 480 (1980).
5–4, WHITE. Concurrence: Powell. Dissents: Stewart, Burger, Rehnquist, Blackmun. 27pp.

2134. Vlandis v. Kline, 412 U.S. 441 (1973).
6–3, STEWART. Concurrences: Marshall, Brennan, White. Dissents: Burger, Rehnquist, Douglas. 28pp.

2135. Voight v. Wright, 141 U.S. 62 (1891).
8–0, BRADLEY. Not voting: Brown. 6pp.

2136. W.S. Kirkpatrick & Co., Inc. v. Environmental Tectonics Corp. Intl., 493 U.S. 400 (1990).
9–0, SCALIA. 11pp.

2137. W.T. Grant Co., U.S. v., 345 U.S. 629 (1953).
7–2, CLARK. Dissents: Douglas, Black. 10pp.

2138. Wabash, St. Louis & P. Ry. Co. v. Illinois, 118 U.S. 557 (1886).
6–3, MILLER. Dissents: Bradley, Gray, White. 39pp.

2139. Wade, U.S. v., 388 U.S. 218 (1967).
5–4 (various coalitions), BRENNAN. Concurrence: Clark. Dissents: Warren, Douglas, Fortas, Black, White, Stewart, Harlan. 45pp.

2140. Wainwright v. Sykes, 433 U.S. 72 (1977).
7–2, REHNQUIST. Concurrences: Burger, Stevens, White. Dissents: Brennan, Marshall. 47pp.

2141. Wainwright v. Witt, 469 U.S. 412 (1985).
7–2, REHNQUIST. Concurrence: Stevens. Dissents: Brennan, Marshall. 52pp.

2142. Walker v. Birmingham, 388 U.S. 307 (1967).
5–4, STEWART. Dissents: Warren, Douglas, Brennan, Fortas. 43pp.

2143. Walker v. New Mexico & Southern Pacific Railroad Co., 165 U.S. 593 (1897).
9–0, BREWER. 13pp.

2144. Walker v. Sauvinet, 92 U.S. 90 (1875).
7–2, WAITE. Dissents: Field, Clifford. 4pp.

2145. Wallace v. Adams, 204 U.S. 415 (1907).
9–0, BREWER. 11pp.

2146. Wallace v. Jaffree, 472 U.S. 38 (1985).
6–3, STEVENS. Concurrences: Powell, O'Connor. Dissents: Burger, White, Rehnquist. 76pp.

2147. Wallach v. Van Riswick, 92 U.S. 202 (1875).
9–0, STRONG. 12pp.

2148. Walters v. National Association of Radiation Survivors, 473 U.S. 305 (1985).
6–3, REHNQUIST. Concurrences: O'Connor, Blackmun. Dissents: Brennan, Marshall, Stevens. 67pp.

2149. Walton v. Arizona, 110 S.Ct. 3047 (1990).
5–4, WHITE. Concurrence: Scalia. Dissents: Brennan, Marshall, Blackmun, Stevens. 46pp.

2150. Walz v. Tax Commission of the City of New York, 397 U.S. 664 (1970).

2180. Welton v. Missouri, 91 U.S. 275 (1876).
9–0, FIELD. 8pp.

2181. Wengler v. Druggists Mutual Insurance Co.,
446 U.S. 142 (1980).
8–1, WHITE. Concurrence: Stevens. Dissent:
Rehnquist. 14pp.

2182. Wesberry v. Sanders, 376 U.S. 1 (1964).
6–3, BLACK. Concurrence: Clark. Dissents:
Clark, Harlan, Stewart. 49pp.

2183. West v. Kansas Gas Co., 221 U.S. 229 (1911).
6–3, McKENNA. Dissents: Holmes, Lurton,
Hughes. 15pp.

2184. West Coast Hotel Co. v. Parrish, 300 U.S. 379
(1937).
5–4, HUGHES. Dissents: Sutherland, Van
Devanter, McReynolds, Butler. 35pp.

2185. West River Bridge Co. v. Dix, 47 U.S. (6 How.)
507 (1848).
8–1, DANIEL. Dissent: Wayne. 43pp.

2186. West Virginia State Board of Education v.
Barnette, 319 U.S. 624 (1943).
6–3, JACKSON. Concurrences: Black,
Douglas, Murphy. Dissents: Frankfurter,
Roberts, Reed. 48pp.

2187. Westbrook v. Balkcom, 449 U.S. 999 (1980).
5–4, PER CURIAM. Dissents: Brennan,
Marshall, Stewart, White. 5pp.

2188. Westside Community Board of Education v.
Mergens, 496 U.S. 226 (1990).
8–1, O'CONNOR. Concurrences: Kennedy,
Scalia, Marshall, Brennan. Dissent: Stevens.
66pp.

2189. Whalen v. Roe, 429 U.S. 589 (1977).
9–0, STEVENS. Concurrences: Brennan,
Stewart. 21pp.

2189a. Wheat v. U.S., 486 U.S. 153 (1988).
5–4, REHNQUIST. Dissents: Marshall,
Brennan, Stevens, Blackmun. 20pp.

2190. Wheeler v. Jackson, 137 U.S. 245 (1890).
9–0, HARLAN. 14pp.

2191. Wheeler, U.S. v., 435 U.S. 313 (1978).
8–0, STEWART. Not voting: Brennan. 20pp.

2192. White Mountain Apache Tribe v. Bracker, 448
U.S. 136 (1980).
6–3, MARSHALL. Concurrence: Powell.
Dissents: Stevens, Stewart, Rehnquist. 24pp.

2193. White v. Maryland, 373 U.S. 59 (1963).
9–0, PER CURIAM. 2pp.

2194. White v. Massachusetts Council of Construction
Employers, Inc., 460 U.S. 204 (1983).
7–2, REHNQUIST. Concurrences: Blackmun,
White. Dissents: Blackmun, White. 22pp.

2195. White v. Regester, 412 U.S. 755 (1973).
6–3, WHITE. Concurrences: Brennan,
Douglas, Marshall. Dissents: Brennan,
Douglas, Marshall. 16pp.

2196. White v. Weiser, 412 U.S. 783 (1973).
9–0, WHITE. Concurrences: Powell, Burger,
Rehnquist, Marshall. 17pp.

2197. White, U.S. v., 322 U.S. 694 (1944).
9–0, MURPHY. Concurrences: Roberts,
Frankfurter, Jackson. 12pp.

2198. Whiteley v. Warden, Wyoming State
Penitentiary, 401 U.S. 560 (1971).
6–3, HARLAN. Dissents: Black, Burger,
Blackmun. 15pp.

2199. Whitney v. California, 274 U.S. 357 (1927).
9–0, SANFORD. Concurrence: Brandeis.
24pp.

2200. WHYY v. Glassboro, 393 U.S. 117 (1968).
8–1, PER CURIAM. Dissent: Black. 4pp.

2201. Wickard v. Filburn, 317 U.S. 111 (1942).
9–0, JACKSON. 23pp.

2202. Widmar v. Vincent, 454 U.S. 263 (1981).
8–1, POWELL. Concurrence: Stevens.
Dissent: White. 27pp.

2203. Wieman v. Updegraff, 344 U.S. 183 (1952).
8–0, CLARK. Concurrences: Black, Douglas,
Frankfurter, Burton. Not voting: Jackson.
15pp.

2204. Wiener v. U.S., 357 U.S. 349 (1958).
9–0, FRANKFURTER. 8pp.

2205. Wilcox v. McConnel, 38 U.S. (13 Pet.) 498 (1839).
9–0, BARBOUR. 21pp.

2206. Wilkerson v. Utah, 99 U.S. 130 (1878).
9–0, CLIFFORD. 8pp.

2207. Wilkinson v. Jones, 800 F.2d 989 (10th Cir.), aff'd,
480 U.S. 926 (1986).
PER CURIAM. 1p.

2208. Will, U.S. v., 449 U.S. 200 (1980).
8–0, BURGER. Not voting: Blackmun. 31pp.

2209. Williams v. Bruffy, 96 U.S. 176 (1877).
9–0, FIELD. 17pp.

2210. Williams v. Florida, 399 U.S. 78 (1970).
6–3, WHITE. Concurrences: Burger, Harlan,
Stewart, Black, Douglas. Dissents: Black,
Douglas, Marshall. 40pp.

2243. WMCA, Inc. v. Lomenzo, 377 U.S. 633 (1964).
6–3, WARREN. Dissents: Harlan, Stewart, Clark. 23pp.

2244. Wolf v. Colorado, 338 U.S. 25 (1949).
6–3, FRANKFURTER. Concurrence: Black. Dissents: Rutledge, Murphy, Douglas. 22pp.

2245. Wolff v. McDonnell, 418 U.S. 539 (1974).
6–3, WHITE. Concurrences: Douglas, Marshall, Brennan. Dissents: Douglas, Marshall, Brennan. 63pp.

2246. Wolman v. Walter, 433 U.S. 229 (1977).
7–2 (Parts I, V, VII, VIII), 6–3 (Parts III, IV, VI), 5–4 (Part II), BLACKMUN. Concurrences and dissents: Burger, Rehnquist, Stewart, White, Brennan, Marshall, Powell, Stevens. 38pp.

2247. Wolston v. Reader's Digest Assn., 443 U.S. 157 (1979).
8–1, REHNQUIST. Concurrences: Blackmun, Marshall. Dissent: Brennan. 16pp.

2248. Women's Sportswear Mfg. Assn., U.S. v., 336 U.S. 460 (1949).
9–0, JACKSON. 5pp.

2249. Wong Kim Ark, U.S. v., 169 U.S. 649 (1898).
6–2, GRAY. Dissents: Fuller, Harlan. Not voting: McKenna. 84pp.

2250. Wong Sun v. U.S., 371 U.S. 471 (1963).
5–4, BRENNAN. Concurrence: Douglas. Dissents: Clark, Harlan, Stewart, White. 34pp.

2251. Wong Yang Sung v. McGrath, 339 U.S. 33 (1950).
8–1, JACKSON. Dissent: Reed. 23pp.

2252. Wood v. Georgia, 370 U.S. 375 (1962).
7–2, WARREN. Dissents: Harlan, Clark. 29pp.

2253. Woodruff v. Parham, 75 U.S. (8 Wall.) 123 (1869).
8–1, MILLER. Dissent: Nelson. 25pp.

2254. Woodruff v. Trapnall, 51 U.S. (10 How.) 190 (1851).
5–4, McLEAN. Dissents: Catron, Daniel, Nelson, Grier. 29pp.

2255. Woods v. Cloyd W. Miller Co., 333 U.S. 138 (1948).
9–0, DOUGLAS. Concurrences: Frankfurter, Jackson. 10pp.

2256. Woods v. Stone, 333 U.S. 472 (1948).
8–1, JACKSON. Concurrence: Frankfurter. Dissent: Douglas. 11pp.

2257. Woodson v. North Carolina, 428 U.S. 280 (1976).
5–4, STEWART. Concurrences: Brennan, Marshall. Dissents: White, Burger, Rehnquist, Blackmun. 45pp.

2258. Wooley v. Maynard, 430 U.S. 705 (1977).
6–3, BURGER. Dissents: White, Blackmun, Rehnquist. 18pp.

2259. Worcester v. State of Georgia, 31 U.S. (6 Pet.) 515 (1832).
6–1, MARSHALL. Concurrence: McLean. Dissent: Baldwin. 83pp.

2260. World-Wide Volkswagen Corp. v. Woodson, 444 U.S. 286 (1980).
6–3, WHITE. Dissents: Marshall, Blackmun, Brennan. 34pp.

2261. Wright v. Union Central Insurance Co., 304 U.S. 502 (1938).
8–0, REED. Not voting: Cardozo. 17pp.

2262. Wright v. United States, 302 U.S. 583 (1938).
7–2, HUGHES. Dissents: Stone, Brandeis. 27pp.

2263. Wright v. Vinton Branch of Mountain Trust Bank of Roanoke, 300 U.S. 440 (1937).
9–0, BRANDEIS. 31pp.

2264. Wrightwood Dairy Co., U.S. v., 315 U.S. 110 (1942).
8–0, STONE. Not voting: Roberts. 17pp.

2265. Wygant v. Jackson Board of Education, 476 U.S. 267 (1986).
5–4, POWELL. Concurrences: O'Connor, White. Dissents: Marshall, Brennan, Blackmun, Stevens. 54pp.

2266. Wyman v. James, 400 U.S. 309 (1971).
6–3, BLACKMUN. Concurrence: White. Dissents: Douglas, Marshall, Brennan. 39pp.

2267. Yakus v. U.S., 321 U.S. 414 (1944).
6–3, STONE. Dissents: Rutledge, Roberts, Murphy. 76pp.

2268. Yamashita, In re, 327 U.S. 1 (1946).
7–2, STONE. Dissents: Rutledge, Murphy. 82pp.

2269. Yamataya v. Fisher, 189 U.S. 86 (1903).
7–2, HARLAN. Dissents: Brewer, Peckham. 17pp.

2270. Yarbrough, Ex parte, 110 U.S. 651 (1884).
9–0, MILLER. 16pp.

2271. Yaselli v. Goff, 275 U.S. 503 (1927).
9–0, PER CURIAM. 1p.

2272. Yates v. U.S., 354 U.S. 298 (1957).

Table of Cases, 1991–92

Cases listed in this table are exclusively those decided by the Supreme Court during its 1991–92 term. All citations are to the West Publishing Company's *Supreme Court Reporter*. For information about citations and the information digested in this table, see the discussion on p. 656 of the principal Table of Cases.

1. Allied-Signal, Inc. v. Director, Division of Taxation, 112 S.Ct. 2251 (1992).
   5–4, KENNEDY. Dissents: O'Connor, Rehnquist, Blackmun, Thomas. 17pp.
2. Alvarez-Machain, U.S. v., 112 S.Ct. 2188 (1992).
   6–3, REHNQUIST. Dissents: Stevens, Blackmun, O'Connor. 19pp.
3. Ankenbrandt v. Richards, 112 S.Ct. 2206 (1992).
   9–0, WHITE. Concurrences: Blackmun, Stevens, Thomas. 17pp.
4. Barker v. Kansas, 112 S.Ct. 1619 (1992).
   9–0, WHITE. Concurrences: Stevens, Thomas. 8pp.
5. Blodget, In re, 112 S.Ct. 674 (1992).
   9–0, PER CURIAM. Concurrences: Stevens, Blackmun. 5pp.
6. Burdick v. Takushi, 112 S.Ct. 2059 (1992).
   6–3, WHITE. Dissents: Kennedy, Blackmun, Stevens. 14pp.
7. Burlington Northern Railroad Co. v. Ford, 112 S.Ct. 2184 (1992).
   9–0, SOUTER. 5pp.

8. Burson v. Freeman, 112 S.Ct. 1846 (1992).
   5–3, BLACKMUN. Concurrences: Kennedy, Scalia. Dissents: Stevens, O'Connor, Souter. Not voting: Thomas. 22pp.
9. Chemical Waste Management, Inc. v. Hunt, 112 S.Ct. 2009 (1992).
   8–1, WHITE. Dissent: Rehnquist. 11pp.
10. Cipollone v. Liggett Group, Inc., 112 S.Ct. 2608 (1992).
    9–0, 7–2, 6–3 (various coalitions), STEVENS. Concurrences: Blackmun, Kennedy, Souter, Scalia, Thomas. Dissents: Blackmun, Kennedy, Souter, Scalia, Thomas. 28pp.
11. Collins v. City of Harker Heights, 112 S.Ct. 1061 (1992).
    9–0, STEVENS. 11pp.
12. Dawson v. Delaware, 112 S.Ct. 1093 (1992).
    8–1, REHNQUIST. Concurrence: Blackmun. Dissent: Thomas. 13pp.
13. Doggett v. U.S., 112 S.Ct. 2686 (1992).
    5–4, SOUTER. Dissents: O'Connor, Thomas, Rehnquist, Scalia. 13pp.
14. Felix, U.S. v., 112 S.Ct. 1377 (1992).
    9–0, REHNQUIST. Concurrences: Stevens, Blackmun. 10pp.
15. Fordice, U.S. v., 112 S.Ct. 2727 (1992).
    8–1, WHITE. Concurrences: O'Connor, Thomas, Scalia. Dissent: Scalia. 25pp.
16. Forsyth County v. Nationalist Movement, 112 S.Ct. 2395 (1992).

40. Quill Corporation v. North Dakota, 112 S.Ct. 1904 (1992).

    8–1, STEVENS. Concurrences: White, Scalia, Kennedy, Thomas. Dissents: White. 21pp.

41. R.A.V. v. St. Paul, 112 S.Ct. 2538 (1992).

    9–0, SCALIA. Concurrences: White, Blackmun, O'Connor, Stevens. 29pp.

42. Riggins v. Nevada, 112 S.Ct. 1810 (1992).

    7–2, O'CONNOR. Concurrence: Kennedy. Dissents: Thomas, Scalia. 17pp.

43. Robertson v. Seattle Audubon Society, 112 S.Ct. 1407 (1992).

    9–0, THOMAS. 9pp.

44. Sawyer v. Whitley, 112 S.Ct. 2514 (1992).

    9–0, REHNQUIST. Concurrences: Blackmun, Stevens, O'Connor. 23pp.

45. Simon & Schuster, Inc. v. New York State Crime Victims Board, 112 S.Ct. 501 (1992).

    8–0, O'CONNOR. Concurrences: Blackmun, Kennedy. Not voting: Thomas. 15pp.

46. Sochor v. Florida, 112 S.Ct. 2114 (1992).

    9–0, 8–1, 7–2, 6–3, 5–4 (various coalitions), SOUTER. Concurrences: O'Connor, Rehnquist, White, Thomas, Stevens, Blackmun, Scalia. Dissents: Rehnquist, White, Thomas, Stevens, Blackmun, Scalia. 17pp.

47. Stringer v. Black, 112 S.Ct. 1130 (1992).

    6–3, KENNEDY. Dissents: Souter, Scalia, Thomas. 17pp.

48. Suter v. Artist M., 112 S.Ct. 1360 (1992).

    7–2, REHNQUIST. Dissents: Blackmun, Stevens. 18pp.

49. United States Dept. of Commerce v. Montana, 112 S.Ct. 1415 (1992).

    9–0, STEVENS. 16pp.

50. Wade, U.S. v., 112 S.Ct. 1840 (1992).

    9–0, SOUTER. 5pp.

51. White v. Illinois, 112 S.Ct. 736 (1992).

    9–0, REHNQUIST. Concurrences: Thomas, Scalia. 13pp.

52. Williams, U.S. v., 112 S.Ct. 1735 (1992).

    5–4, SCALIA. Dissents: Stevens, Blackmun, O'Connor, Thomas. 20pp.

53. Wright v. West, 112 S.Ct. 2482 (1992).

    9–0 (various coalitions), THOMAS. Concurrences: O'Connor, Blackmun, Stevens, White, Kennedy, Souter. 18pp.

54. Wyatt v. Cole, 112 S.Ct. 1827 (1992).

    6–3, O'CONNOR. Concurrences: Kennedy, Scalia. Dissents: Rehnquist, Souter, Thomas. 14pp.

55. Wyoming v. Oklahoma, 112 S.Ct. 789.

    6–3, WHITE. Dissents: Scalia, Rehnquist, Thomas. 24pp.

56. Yee v. City of Escondido, 112 S.Ct. 1522 (1992).

    9–0, O'CONNOR. Concurrences: Blackmun, Souter. 14pp.

57. Zatko v. California, 112 S.Ct. 355 (1991).

    7–2, PER CURIAM. Dissents: Stevens, Blackmun. Not voting: Thomas. 4pp.

Further Reading

The following thirteen sets of books proved indispensable in writing this one. The reader who wishes more detailed discussion of the constitutional themes discussed here, or excerpts from most of the leading cases, should consult the following works: Johnny H. Killian and Leland H. Beck, eds., *The Constitution of the United States: Analysis and Interpretation* (Washington, D.C.: Government Printing Office, 1987) and Johnny H. Killian and George A. Costello, eds., *1990 Supplement* (Washington, D.C.: Government Printing Office, 1991). This annotation prepared and periodically updated by the Congressional Research Service of the Library of Congress is the most exhaustive one-volume work on the subject. The most comprehensive multivolume work accessible to the lay reader is Philip B. Kurland and Ralph Lerner, *The Founders' Constitution* (Chicago: Univ. of Chicago Press, 5 vols., 1987). Leading treatises include Laurence H. Tribe, *American Constitutional Law* (Mineola, NY: Foundation, 2nd ed., 1988); John E. Nowak and Ronald D. Rotunda, *Constitutional Law* (St. Paul: West, 4th ed., 1991); Wayne R. LaFave and Jerold H. Israel, *Criminal Procedure* (St. Paul: West, 2nd ed., 1992). Casebooks to which I am greatly indebted are Gerald Gunther, *Constitutional Law* (Westbury, NY: Foundation, 1991, with annual supplements); William B. Lockhart, Yale Kamisar, Jesse H. Choper, Steven H. Shiffrin, *Constitutional Law: Cases, Comments, Questions* (St. Paul: West, 7th ed., 1991); and David M. O'Brien, *Constitutional Law and Politics* (New York: Norton, 1991), in two volumes with annual supplements: *Struggles for Power and Governmental Accountability* (vol. 1) and *Civil Rights and Civil Liberties* (vol. 2). The O'Brien volumes are chock-full of inter-esting summaries and sidelights on the Court and many of its decisions. I have also profited from William W. Van Alstyne, *First Amendment: Cases and Materials* (Westbury, NY: Foundation, 1991); Stephen G. Breyer and Richard B. Stewart, *Administrative Law and Regulatory Policy* (Boston: Little, Brown, 2nd ed., 1985); and Paul A. Freund, Arthur E. Sutherland, Mark DeWolfe Howe, and Ernest J. Brown, eds., *Constitutional Law: Cases and Other Problems* (Boston: Little, Brown, 2nd ed., 1961). Finally, much information about the modern Supreme Court and its workings is contained in Elder Witt, *Congressional Quarterly's Guide to the U.S. Supreme Court* (Washington, D.C.: Congressional Quarterly, 1990).

A comprehensive and sensitive history of the Supreme Court's treatment of the Constitution is told in David P. Currie, *The Constitution in the Supreme Court: The First Hundred Years* (Chicago: Univ. of Chicago Press, 1985) and *The Constitution in the Supreme Court: The Second Century, 1888–1986* (Chicago: Univ. of Chicago Press, 1990). More general narratives of the course of constitutional law include my own *The Enduring Constitution* (St. Paul: West, 1987) and Page Smith, *The Constitution; A Documentary and Narrative History* (New York: Morrow Quill, 1980). A highly readable account of the Constitution's popular reception during the past two centuries is Michael Kammen, *A Machine That Would Go of Itself: The Constitution in American Culture* (New York: Knopf, 1986).

The following are suggestions for further reading about selected topics on constitutional history and law:

Historical and intellectual origins of the Constitution. Gordon S. Wood, *The Creation of the American Repub-

lic, 1776–1787 (New York: Norton, 1969); Jack N. Rakove, *The Beginnings of National Politics: An Interpretive History of the Continental Congress* (Baltimore: Johns Hopkins Univ. Press, 1979); Bernard Bailyn, *The Ideological Origins of the American Revolution* (Cambridge: Harvard Univ. Press, 1967); Jackson Turner Main, *The Anti-Federalists: Critics of the Constitution, 1781–1788* (Chapel Hill: Univ. of North Carolina Press, 1961); Forrest McDonald, *Novus Ordo Seclorum: The Intellectual Origins of the Constitution* (Lawrence: Univ. Press of Kansas, 1985); Thomas L. Pangle, *The Spirit of Modern Republicanism: The Moral Vision of the American Founders and the Philosophy of Locke* (Chicago: Univ. of Chicago Press, 1988); Leonard W. Levy and Dennis J. Mahoney, eds., *The Framing and Ratification of the Constitution* (New York: Macmillan, 1987); Leonard W. Levy, *Essays on the Making of the Constitution* (New York: Oxford Univ. Press, 1969); Max Farrand, *The Framing of the Constitution of the United States* (New Haven: Yale Univ. Press, 1913); Clinton Rossiter, *1787: The Grand Convention* (New York: Macmillan, 1966); Catherine Drinker Bowen, *Miracle at Philadelphia* (Boston: Little, Brown, 1966); Mitchell and Louise Broadus, *A Biography of the Constitution of the United States* (New York: Oxford Univ. Press, 1964); Daniel A. Farber and Suzanna Sherry, *A History of the American Constitution* (St. Paul: West, 1990); Max Farrand, ed., *The Records of the Federal Convention of 1787* (New Haven: Yale Univ. Press, rev. ed. in 3 vols., 1937); James H. Hutson, ed., *Supplement to Max Farrand's The Records of the Federal Convention of 1787* (New Haven: Yale Univ. Press, 1987).

Constitutional intent and interpretation. Alexander Hamilton, James Madison, John Jay, *The Federalist Papers* (New York: New American Library, Clinton Rossiter, ed., 1961); Jack N. Rakove, *Interpreting the Constitution: The Debate over Original Intent* (Boston: Northeastern Univ. Press, 1990); Leonard W. Levy, *Original Intent and the Framers' Constitution* (New York: Macmillan, 1988); John H. Garvey and T. Alexander Aleinikoff, eds., *Modern Constitutional Theory: A Reader* (St. Paul: West, 2nd ed., 1991); Harry H. Wellington, *Interpreting the Constitution: The Supreme Court and the Process of Adjudication* (New Haven: Yale Univ. Press, 1990); Leonard W. Levy, *The Establishment Clause: Religion and the First Amendment* (New York: Macmillan, 1986); John Hart Ely, *Democracy and Distrust: A Theory of Judicial Review* (Cambridge: Harvard Univ. Press, 1980); Michael J. Perry, *The Constitution, Courts, and Human Rights* (New Haven: Yale Univ. Press, 1982); Mark Tushnet, *Red, White, and Blue: A Critical Analysis of Constitutional Law* (Cambridge: Harvard Univ. Press, 1988); Philip Bobbitt,

Constitutional Fate: Theory of the Constitution (New York: Oxford Univ. Press, 1982); Sotirios A. Barber, *On What the Constitution Means* (Baltimore: Johns Hopkins Univ. Press, 1984); Robert H. Bork, *The Tempting of America: The Political Seductions of the Law* (New York: Simon & Schuster, 1990); J. Roland Pennock and John W. Chapman, eds., *Constitutionalism* (New York: New York Univ. Press, 1979).

Constitutional history. Leonard W. Levy, *Judgments: Essays on American Constitutional History* (Chicago: Quadrangle, 1972); C. Vann Woodward, *The Strange Career of Jim Crow* (New York: Oxford Univ. Press, 3rd rev. ed., 1974); William M. Wiecek, *The Sources of Antislavery Constitutionalism in America, 1760–1848* (Ithaca: Cornell Univ. Press, 1977); Harold M. Hyman and William M. Wiecek, *Equal Justice Under Law: Constitutional Development: 1835–1875* (New York: Harper & Row, 1982); Harold M. Hyman, *A More Perfect Union: The Impact of the Civil War and Reconstruction on the Constitution* (Boston: Houghton Mifflin, 1975); Paul L. Murphy, *The Constitution in Crisis Times* (New York: Harper & Row, 1972); Louis Fisher, *Constitutional Conflicts between Congress and the President* (Princeton: Princeton Univ. Press, 1985); Arthur E. Sutherland, *Constitutionalism in America* (New York: Blaisdell, 1965).

The First Amendment. Leonard W. Levy, *Emergence of a Free Press* (New York: Oxford Univ. Press, 1985); Zechariah Chafee, Jr., *Free Speech in the United States* (Cambridge: Harvard Univ. Press, 1941); Harry Kalven, Jr., *A Worthy Tradition*, Jamie Kalven, ed., (New York: Harper & Row, 1988).

The Supreme Court. Charles Warren, *The Supreme Court in United States History* (Boston: Little, Brown, rev. ed., 2 vols., 1926); Robert H. Jackson; *The Struggle for Judicial Supremacy* (New York: Vintage, 1941); Paul A. Freund, *The Supreme Court of the United States: Its Business, Purposes, and Performance* (Chicago: Northwestern Univ. Press, 1949); Charles L. Black, *The People and the Court* (New York: Macmillan, 1960); Robert G. McCloskey, *The American Supreme Court* (Chicago: Univ. of Chicago Press, 1960); Alexander M. Bickel, *The Least Dangerous Branch: The Supreme Court at the Bar of Politics* (Indianapolis: Bobbs-Merrill, 1962); Alexander M. Bickel, *The Supreme Court and the Idea of Progress* (New Haven: Yale Univ. Press, 1978); Walter F. Murphy, *Elements of Judicial Strategy* (Chicago: Univ. of Chicago Press, 1964); Leo Pfeffer, *This Honorable Court: A History of the United States Supreme Court* (Boston: Beacon, 1965); James F. Simon, *In His Own Image: The Supreme Court in Richard Nixon's America* (New York:

McKay, 1973); Bob Woodward and Scott Armstrong, *The Brethren* (New York: Simon & Schuster, 1980); Bernard Schwartz, *Super Chief: Earl Warren and His Supreme Court: A Judicial Biography* (New York: New York Univ. Press, 1983); Laurence H. Tribe, *God Save This Honorable Court* (New York: Random House, 1985); David M. O'Brien, *Storm Center: The Supreme Court in American Politics* (New York: Norton, 1986); Archibald Cox, *The Court and the Constitution* (Boston: Houghton Mifflin, 1987); William H. Rehnquist, *The Supreme Court: How It Was, How It Is* (New York: Morrow, 1987).

Stories about constitutional cases. Peter Irons, *The Courage of Their Convictions: Sixteen Americans Who Fought Their Way to the Supreme Court* (New York: Penguin, 1990); John A. Garraty, ed., *Quarrels That Have Shaped the Constitution* (New York: Harper Colophon, 1966); Richard Kluger, *Simple Justice: Brown v. Board of Education and Black America's Struggle for Equality* (New York: Knopf, 1976); Anthony Lewis, *Gideon's Trumpet* (New York: Vintage, 1964); Alan F. Westin, ed., *The Anatomy of a Constitutional Law Case* (New York: Macmillan, 1958); Vincent C. Hopkins, *Dred Scott's Case* (New York: Atheneum, 1971); C. Peter Magrath, *Yazoo: The Case of Fletcher v. Peck* (New York: Norton, 1966); Gerald Gunther, *John Marshall's Defense of McCulloch v. Maryland* (Stanford: Stanford Univ. Press, 1969); Jethro K. Lieberman, *Milestones! 200 Years of American Law* (St. Paul: West, 1976).

Finding the Court's cases and analysis. The full text of Supreme Court decisions appears in *U.S. Law Week,* published by the Bureau of National Affairs in Washington, D.C. Every year the *Harvard Law Review* in its November issue publishes statistics on the Court's last completed term and analyzes many of its most significant decisions. *Preview of United States Supreme Court Cases,* a monthly publication of the American Bar Association, 541 North Fairbanks Court, Chicago, IL 60611-3314, discusses in short compass the major issues presented by significant cases pending before the Court.

Endnotes

SOME THOUGHTS ON INTERPRETING THE CONSTITUTION

Page

12 George M. Dallas quoted in W. Hickey, *The Constitution of the United States of America,* 4th ed. (Philadelphia, 1851), iii.

13 Madison on Framers and Ratifiers: Quoted in Jack
N. Rakove, "Mr. Meese, Meet Mr. Madison," *Atlantic,* December 1986, 79.

14 The Commerce Clause gives Congress power to
outlaw arson: *Russell v. United States,* 471 U.S. 858
(1985).

14 Jefferson's behavior in holding slaves: In fact,
Dumas Malone, Jefferson's biographer, writes that
Jefferson "deplored" slavery. In an 1814 letter, Jefferson wrote: "My opinion has ever been that, until
more can be done for [the slaves], we should endeavor, with those whom fortune has thrown into
our hands, to feed and clothe them well, protect
them from ill usage, require such reasonable labor
only as is performed voluntarily by freemen, and be
led by no repugnancies to abdicate them, and our
duties to them." Jefferson did emancipate some of
his slaves during his lifetime and, says Malone,
"when he freed a particular slave, that individual
was prepared for freedom in his opinion, and had a
good place to go." Dumas Malone, *Jefferson and the
Ordeal of Liberty* (Boston: Little, Brown, 1962), 207,
208.

15 Chief Justice Marshall on Congress's power to punish violations of its laws: *McCulloch v. Maryland,* 17
U.S. (4 Wheat.) 315 (1819).

17 The Court held the Seventh Amendment applicable: *Pernell v. Southall Realty,* 416 U.S. 363 (1974).

17 The Occupational Safety & Health Administration
seeks to impose monetary fines: *Atlas Roofing Co. v.
Occupational Safety and Health Review Commission,* 430
U.S. 442 (1977).

18 Justice Holmes on experience and the Constitution:
Missouri v. Holland, 252 U.S. 416 (1920).

HOW THE SUPREME COURT HEARS AND DECIDES CASES

20 Washington journalist on the Supreme Court: Alex
Heard, "Heard v. U.S.," *New Republic,* April 28, 1986,
12.

20 Statistics for the Supreme Court's 1990–91 term are
from the compilations in 105 *Harvard Law Review*
419 (November 1991).

A

28 Outrageous ballot schemes: Among the worst offenders is New York State, which generates "more
than half the election law litigation in the nation."
Among the technical violations that will keep a
voter's signature from being counted toward the
total required nominating petitions: signers who
give post office rather than legal voting addresses;
corrections of the address by campaign staff in the
absence of initials from the person collecting the
signature in the first place; and signatures, otherwise fine, collected by people who don't live in the

voters' districts. *New York Times*, February 5, 1992, A22, lead editorial.

34 Small bureaucracy that carried on the real work of the government: As Merrill Jensen noted: "The creation of a responsible staff of civil servants by the Confederation government is an almost unknown story. These men carried on the work of the departments of war, foreign affairs, finance, and the post office in season and out. The best example of this was Joseph Nourse of Virginia who became register of the treasury in 1779, a post which he held until 1829 when he retired because of old age. He kept books and prepared innumerable reports for Robert Morris, the board of treasury, Alexander Hamilton, and the secretaries of the treasuries who followed him. If it had not been for Nourse and men like him, with years of practical experience in the day-to-day affairs of government behind them, the Washington administration would have been badly hampered." Merrill Jensen, *The New Nation: A History of the United States during the Confederation 1781–1789* (Boston: Northeastern Univ. Press, 1981), 360.

41 Advisory opinions and justices responding to President Washington: See Henry M. Hart, Jr., and Herbert Wechsler, *The Federal Courts and the Federal System* (Brooklyn: Foundation, 1953), 95; and *Hayburn's Case*, 2 U.S. (2 Dall.) 409 (1792).

41 Jay's letter to Jefferson on the "lines of separation": See Henry P. Johnston, *Correspondence and Public Papers of John Jay* (New York: Da Capo, 1971; originally published, 1891), 486–9.

41 Jay's informal advice to President Washington on circuit riding is noted in Henry M. Hart, Jr., and Herbert Wechsler, *The Federal Courts and the Federal System* (Brooklyn: Foundation, 1953), 75–7.

48 In one egregious case: In *Shaughnessy v. United States ex rel. Mezei*, 345 U.S. 206 (1953), the Court said, in effect, that as far as the Constitution is concerned, an alien could be imprisoned for life without explanation or a hearing. In fact, he was held for three years and then quietly let back into the country.

50 Some ten thousand amendments: Different commentators give different figures. Walter Dellinger, in *The Encyclopedia of the Constitution*, 47, says five thousand. Gilbert Y. Steiner, in *Constitutional Inequality: The Political Fortunes of the Equal Rights Amendment* (Washington: Brookings Institution, 1985), 29, estimates ten thousand. According to H.

Ames, *The Proposed Amendments to the Constitution during the First Century of Its History* (H.Doc. 353, pt. 2, 54th Cong., 2d Sess., 1897), Congress considered 1,736 amendments from 1789 to 1889. From 1890 to 1926, another 1,316 amendments were introduced (*Proposed Amendments to the Constitution of the United States*, Sen. Doc. No. 93, 69th Congress, 1st Session, 1926). From 1926 through 1962, 2,340 more proposals were recorded (*Proposed Amendments to the Constitution of the United States of America*, Sen. Doc. No. 163, 87th Cong., 2d Sess., 1962).

53 Madison on states' warfare against each other: Quoted in Max Farrand, *The Framing of the Constitution* (New Haven: Yale Univ. Press, 1913), 7.

58 Long line of opinions of the attorneys general: See, for example, *3 Opinions of the Attorney General* 188 (1837).

60 Frankfurter on the "political thicket": Strictly speaking in *Colegrove v. Green*, 328 U.S. 549 (1946), Justice Frankfurter could muster only three votes for the proposition that the case presented a nonjusticiable political question, although the Court nevertheless declined to hear the case.

64 Citywide ban on all handguns: *Quilici v. Morton Grove*, 695 F.2d 261 (7th Cir. 1982), cert. denied, 464 U.S. 863 (1983).

B

75 Thomas Jefferson to James Madison: Quoted in Gordon S. Wood, *The Creation of the American Republic, 1776–1787* (New York: Norton, 1969), 537.

C

93 Mandatory appeals after 1988: Act to Improve the Administration of Justice of 1988; the various Judiciary Acts are summarized in David M. O'Brien, *Constitutional Law and Politics* (New York: Norton, 1991), 1:102–4.

93 Virtue of the people: Gordon S. Wood, *The Creation of the American Republic, 1776–1787* (New York: Norton, 1969), 95ff.

95 Earl Warren's biographers, on his fashioning a unanimous vote in *Brown v. Board:* See, in particular, Richard Kluger, *Simple Justice: The History of Brown*

Page

v. *Board of Education and Black America's Struggle for Equality* (New York: Random House, 1976).

96 In nearly one hundred cases since 1961: a Westlaw search for "chilling effect" turned up ninety-seven cases between 1961 and 1992.

96 Article by Paul Freund: "The Supreme Court and Civil Liberties," 4 *Vanderbilt Law Review* 533, 539 (1951).

99 Children born on the high seas: *Lam Mow v. Nagle*, 24 F.2d 316 (9th Cir. 1928).

100 Member of Congress as holding a civil office: Federal law prohibits military officers from holding civil office. Department of Defense regulations define civil office as an "office, not military in nature, that involves the exercise of powers of or authority of civil government. It may be either an elective or appointed office under the United States." Department of Defense Directive 1344.10, September 23, 1969, ¶III.D.

101 Generally accepted opinion on meaning of civil office: A. Hinds, *Precedents of the House of Representatives* (Washington, DC: 1907), 1:§493; C. Cannon, *Precedents of the House of Representatives* (Washington, DC: 1936), 6:§§63–4.

101 Equal rights under the law: 42 *United States Code* §1981.

101 Federal law guaranteeing property rights of citizens: 42 *United States Code* §1982.

102 Jefferson and civil liberties: Leonard W. Levy, *Jefferson and Civil Liberties: The Darker Side* (Cambridge: Harvard Univ. Press, 1963), chap. 3.

104 Criminal provisions of federal civil rights laws: 18 *United States Code* §§241, 242.

115 On delegates' accepting without debate the wording of the Commerce Clause (and others): Max Farrand, *The Records of the Federal Convention of 1787* (New Haven: Yale Univ. Press, rev. ed., 1937), 2: 308.

115 Necessary and Proper Clause accepted without debate: They debated a motion by Madison and Pinckney to insert the words "and establish all offices" between "laws" and "necessary," but the motion was defeated as adding unnecessary surplusage. The clause was then accepted without debate.

125 Consensus on meaning of age and citizenship requirements: S. Rept. No. 904, 74th Cong., 1st Sess. (1935), in 79 *Congressional Record* 9841-42, 9561-53

(1935); A. Hinds, *Precedents of the House of Representatives* (Washington, DC: 1907), 1:§§418, 429.

129 Jefferson quoted on demi-gods: Max Farrand, *The Framing of the Constitution* (New Haven: Yale Univ. Press, 1913), 39.

130 William H. Rehnquist, "The Notion of a Living Constitution," in *Views from the Bench: The Judiciary and the Constitution*, ed. by Mark Cannon and David O'Brien (Chatham, NJ: Chatham House, 1985), 191.

130 Karl N. Llewellyn wrote: "The Constitution as an Institution," 34 *Columbia Law Review* 40 (1934).

131 Greatest act of prestidigitation: Page Smith, *The Constitution: A Documentary and Narrative History* (New York: Morrow Quill, 1980), 527.

131 King of America: Daniel A. Farber and Suzanna Sherry, *A History of the American Constitution* (St. Paul: West, 1990), 27.

132 Begetting fatal altercations: Madison's notes for May 28, 1787, quoted in Max Farrand, *The Records of the Federal Convention of 1787* (New Haven: Yale Univ. Press, rev. ed., 1937), 1:11.

132 Madison on Morris: Max Farrand, *The Framing of the Constitution* (New Haven: Yale Univ. Press, 1913), 181.

132 Madison, Morris, and Wilson quoted in Max Farrand, *The Framing of the Constitution* (New Haven: Yale Univ. Press, 1913), 61–2.

132 Madison on Franklin's observation of the rising sun: Max Farrand, *The Framing of the Constitution* (New Haven: Yale Univ. Press, 1913), 194.

133 As Judge Richard Posner has written: "What Am I? A Potted Plant?" *New Republic*, Sept. 28, 1987, 23.

133 Critics of Marshall's decision in *Marbury*: Quoted in Charles Warren, *The Supreme Court in United States History* (Boston: Little, Brown, 1922), 1:256–7.

139 Gouverneur Morris on Council of Revision: Max Farrand, *The Records of the Federal Convention of 1787* (New Haven: Yale Univ. Press, rev. ed., 1937), 2:75.

143 Roosevelt on horse-and-buggy days: Arthur M. Schlesinger, Jr., *The Politics of Upheaval* (Boston: Houghton Mifflin, 1966), 285–6.

143 Jackson on the Court's narrowing and expanding: Robert H. Jackson, *The Struggle for Judicial Supremacy* (New York: Vintage, 1941), xii–xiii.

143 Chief Justice Hughes's letter: Documents on the court-packing plan are reprinted in *Reorganization of the Federal Judiciary—Adverse Report of the Committee on the Judiciary*, Senate Report No. 711, 75th Cong., 1st Sess. (1937).

D

156 Madison on direct taxation: Quotation is taken from Johnny H. Killian and Leland E. Beck, eds., *The Constitution of the United States of America: Analysis and Interpretation* (Washington, DC: Government Printing Office, 1982), 384, n. 2, citing in turn Madison, *The Debates in the Federal Convention of 1787*, G. Hunt and J. Scott, eds. (Westport, CT: Greenwood, 1970), 435.

159 Charles Evans Hughes on dissenting opinions: *The Supreme Court of the United States* (New York: Columbia Univ. Press, 1928), 68.

167 The war came: Abraham Lincoln, Second Inaugural, 1865.

167 Sumptuary law: Mason quoted in Max Farrand, *The Records of the Federal Convention of 1787* (New Haven: Yale Univ. Press, rev. ed., 1937), 2:344.

168 New York police may not search open field with warrant: *New York Times*, April 3, 1992, A1.

E

182 Abscam cases: *United States v. Kelly*, 707 F.2d 1460 (D.C.Cir. 1983).

187 Leonard W. Levy has persuasively argued, on meaning of Establishment Clause: Leonard W. Levy, *The Establishment Clause: Religion and the First Amendment* (New York: Macmillan, 1986).

188 As one commentary summed up these rules: Wayne R. LaFave and Jerold H. Israel, *Criminal Procedure* (St. Paul: West, 2nd ed., 1992), 1016.

F

196 Fair value theory branded a fallacy: See Robert L. Hale, *Freedom Through Law: Public Control of Private Governing Power* (New York: Columbia Univ. Press, 1952), 462.

204 Madison's unaccepted constitutional amendment: Quoted in Johnny H. Killian and Leland E. Beck, eds., *The Constitution of the United States of America: Analysis and Interpretation* (Washington, DC: Government Printing Office, 1982), 951, from 1 *Annals of Congress* 755 (August 17, 1789).

211- Although dismissing the indictment in 1876 for an-
212 other reason: Actually, the Court's rejection of the defendants' assertion in *United States v. Cruikshank*, 92 U.S. 542 (1876), was dictum, since the Court found a technical defect in the indictment: the government had failed to say that the people were assembling to discuss federal issues. But the Court's acceptance of freedom of assembly is plain enough. The right of peaceable assembly has now been incorporated in the Fourteenth Amendment, so the technical difficulty in 1876 would no longer apply.

217 Tumultuous petitioning: William W. Van Alstyne, *First Amendment Cases and Materials* (Westbury, NY: Foundation, 1991), 26, n. 57.

221 Levy on the Framers' being sharply divided: Leonard W. Levy, *Emergence of a Free Press* (New York: Oxford Univ. Press, 1985), 281.

227 Early influential decision by Justice Bushrod Washington: *Corfield v. Coryell*, 6 Fed.Cas. 546 (No. 3230) (C.C.E.D.Pa. 1823).

G

236 The Supreme Court steadfastly refused to hear such cases: See, for example, *Luftig v. McNamara*, 373 F.2d 2664 (D.C.Cir.), cert. denied, 387 U.S. 945 (1967).

H

240 Reagan on the pursuit of happiness: Robert Pear, "Reagan Seems to Mix Supreme Court Cases," *New York Times*, June 12, 1986, A21.

240 Happiness amendment: See discussion in Jethro K. Lieberman, *The Litigious Society* (New York: Basic Books, 1981), 185.

241 On the Stanford rules, see Gerald Gunther, *Constitutional Law* (Westbury, NY: Foundation, 1991), 1135; generally, James Weinstein, "A Constitutional Roadmap to the Regulation of Campus Hate Speech," 38 *Wayne Law Review* 163 (1991); Charles R. Lawrence, "If He Hollers Let Him Go: On Regulating Racist Speech on Campus," 1990 *Duke Law Journal* 431; Nadine Strossen, "Regulating Racist Speech on Campus: A Modest Proposal?" 1990 *Duke Law Journal* 484; Kenneth Karst, "Boundaries and Reasons: Freedom of Expression and the Subordination of Groups," 1990 *Illinois Law Review* 95; Mari J. Matsuda, "Public Response to Racist Speech: Considering the Victim's Story," 87 *Michigan Law Review* 2320 (1989); Richard Delgado, "Words that Wound: A Tort Action for Racial Insults, Epithets,

Page

and Name-Calling," 17 *Harvard Civil Rights–Civil Liberties Law Review* 133 (1982).

244 Chase impeachment: Proponents quoted in Johnny H. Killian and Leland E. Beck, eds., *The Constitution of the United States of America: Analysis and Interpretation* (Washington, DC: Government Printing Office, 1982), 606.

I

258 Madison declared this amendment to be "the most valuable of the whole list": Quoted in Johnny H. Killian and Leland E. Beck, eds., *The Constitution of the United States of America: Analysis and Interpretation* (Washington, DC: Government Printing Office, 1982), 951, from 1 *Annals of Congress* 755 (August 17, 1789).

261 Extraordinary improprieties: 38 *Federal Register* 29466 (1973).

262 Cherokee treaty as brazen sham: See Glen Fleischmann, *The Cherokee Removal, 1838* (New York: Franklin Watts, 1971).

267 On institutional litigation, see Jethro K. Lieberman, *The Litigious Society* (New York: Basic Books, 1981), chap. 5.

268 On interpretivism, see excerpts from many of the leading articles and books in John H. Garvey and T. Alexander Aleinikoff, *Modern Constitutional Theory: A Reader* (St. Paul: West, 1991), chap. 2. These writings include: Michael J. Perry, *The Constitution, the Courts, and Human Rights* (New York: Oxford Univ. Press, 1982); and Perry, "The Authority of Text, Tradition and Reason: A Theory of Constitutional 'Interpretation,' " 58 *Southern California Law Review* 551 (1985); Thomas C. Grey, "Do We Have an Unwritten Constitution?" 27 *Stanford Law Review* 703 (1975); and Grey, "The Constitution as Scripture," 37 *Stanford Law Review* 1 (1985); Paul Brest, "The Misconceived Quest for the Original Understanding," 60 *Boston University Law Review* 204 (1980); Hans Linde, "Judges, Critics and the Realist Tradition," 82 *Yale Law Journal* 227 (1972); Robert Bork, "Neutral Principles and Some First Amendment Problems," 47 *Indiana Law Journal* 1 (1971); John Hart Ely, *Democracy and Distrust* (Cambridge: Harvard Univ. Press, 1980); Harry H. Wellington, "History and Morals in Constitutional Adjudication," 97 *Harvard Law Review* 326 (1983); Ira C. Lupu, "Constitutional Theory

and the Search for the Workable Premise," 8 *University of Dayton Law Review* 579 (1983); William Van Alstyne, "Interpreting *This* Constitution: The Unhelpful Contributions of Special Theories of Judicial Review," 35 *University of Florida Law Review* 209 (1983); Mark Tushnet, "Following the Rules Laid Down: A Critique of Interpretivism and Neutral Principles," 96 *Harvard Law Review* 781 (1983); Philip Bobbitt, *Constitutional Fate: Theory of the Constitution* (New York: Oxford Univ. Press, 1982); Henry P. Monaghan, "Our Perfect Constitution," 56 *New York University Law Review* 353 (1981); Suzanna Sherry, "The Founders' Unwritten Constitution," 54 *University of Chicago Law Review* 1127 (1987).

J

275 John J. McCloy's statement: Kai Bird, *The Chairman* (New York: Simon & Schuster, 1992), 149–50.

277 Vacated Fred Korematsu's conviction: *Korematsu v. U.S.,* 584 F.Supp. 1406 (N.D.Cal. 1984).

277 Charge against Hirabayashi vacated: 627 F.Supp. 1445 (W.D. Wash. 1986).

281 One English judge in 1701: *City of London v. Wood,* 12 Mod. Rep. 669, 687–88 (1701); quoted in Daniel A. Farber and Suzanna Sherry, *A History of the American Constitution* (St. Paul: West, 1990), 67.

281 Otis and Adams: Quoted in Daniel A. Farber and Suzanna Sherry, *A History of the American Constitution* (St. Paul: West, 1990), 67–8.

281 Francis Mercer said: Max Farrand, *The Records of the Federal Convention of 1787* (New Haven: Yale Univ. Press, rev. ed., 1937), 2:298.

282 Chief Justice Hughes's speech: May 3, 1907.

283 Meese's theory of constitutional interpretation: The Third Circuit upheld the act's constitutionality: *Ameron, Inc. v. U.S. Army Corps of Engineers,* 787 F.2d 875 (3d Cir. 1986). The hearings are in *Constitutionality of GAO's Bid Protest Function: Hearings Before the Subcommittee on Legislation and National Security of the House Committee on Government Operations,* 99th Cong., 1st Sess. (1985). The story is told in Murray Waas and Jeffrey Toobin, "Meese's Power Grab," *New Republic,* May 19, 1986, 15.

291 The Supreme Court declined to hear a challenge by Pawnee Indian children to a short-hair rule: *New Rider v. Board of Education,* 480 F.2d 693 (10th Cir. 1973), cert. denied, 414 U.S. 1097 (1973).

L

296 Frankfurter on judges making law retail: Quoted in O'Brien, 1:73.

308 Doubtful that Congress could grant line-item veto: See Laurence Tribe, *American Constitutional Law* (Mineola, NY: Foundation, 2nd ed., 1988), 265–8.

310 On why these activities are only supposedly unethical, see discussion in Jethro K. Lieberman, *Crisis at the Bar: Lawyers' Unethical Ethics and What to Do about It* (New York: Norton, 1978).

312 The story of Jefferson's Louisiana Purchase is told in Dumas Malone, *Jefferson the President: First Term 1801–1805* (Boston: Little, Brown, 1970), chaps. 16–17.

314 Woolf on oaths: Virginia Woolf, *Orlando* (New York: Penguin, 1942), 105.

M

316 "All other records paled into insignificance": Max Farrand, *The Records of the Federal Convention of 1787* (New Haven: Yale Univ. Press, rev. ed., 1937), 1:xv.

316 Crosskey's two-volume work: William W. Crosskey, *Politics and the Constitution in the History of the United States* (Chicago: Univ. of Chicago Press, 1953). A third volume, *Political Background of the Federal Convention* (with Jeffrey Williams), was published by the University of Chicago Press in 1980.

316 Hutson concluded that Madison's notes are a "faithful account": James H. Hutson, "The Creation of the Constitution: The Integrity of the Documentary Record," 65 *Texas Law Review* 1, 29 (1986).

317 Madison's notes are "far from a verbatim record": James H. Hutson, "The Creation of the Constitution: The Integrity of the Documentary Record," 65 *Texas Law Review* 1, 32 (1986).

318 Professor Black has suggested: Charles L. Black, Jr., *Decision According to Law* (New York: Norton, 1981), 18.

322 The story of *Marbury v. Madison* is told in more detail in Jethro K. Lieberman, *Milestones! 200 Years of American Law* (St. Paul: West, 1976), chap. 4.

330 Thirty-four years after the Carolene Products Co. lost major lawsuits to ship "filled milk" in interstate commerce, it succeeded under another name, the Milnot Co., in overturning the ban on due process grounds. This was not really a return to economic due process, however, because of the peculiar circumstances it managed to show. In the intervening years, scientists had learned of the dangers of cholesterol in dairy products, and many other products almost identical to Milnot's filled milk were regularly being sold in interstate commerce because they did not technically violate the law. But a federal district court concluded that it was essentially irrational to permit the others and exclude Milnot's milk. See *Milnot Co. v. Richardson*, 350 F.Supp. 221 (S.D.Ill. 1972). Thereafter the Food and Drug Administration concluded that it would no longer enforce the Filled Milk Act.

N

340 On the "unwritten Constitution": See, for example, Thomas C. Grey, "Do We Have an Unwritten Constitution?" 27 *Stanford Law Review* 703 (1975).

340-341 Hamilton on the rights of mankind: Quoted in Daniel A. Farber and Suzanna Sherry, *A History of the American Constitution* (St. Paul: West, 1990), 68.

343 Wechsler's speech is reprinted in Herbert Wechsler, "Toward Neutral Principles of Constitutional Law," 73 *Harvard Law Review* 1, 11, 16 (1959).

344 For a later assessment of neutral principles, see Kent Greenawalt, "The Enduring Significance of Neutral Principles," 78 *Columbia Law Review* 982 (1978).

345 Historians of the period: See, especially, Leonard W. Levy, *Original Intent and the Framers' Constitution* (New York: Macmillan, 1988), chap. 13.

346 "Created in us by the decrees of Providence": John Dickinson, 1766, quoted by Levy, *Original Intent and the Framers' Constitution*, 275.

346 Repository for natural rights: Leonard W. Levy, *Original Intent and the Framers' Constitution*, 278.

346 1,200 lower court cases: According to a computer study cited in Raoul Berger, "The Ninth Amendment," 61 *Cornell Law Review* 1, n. 2 (1980).

346 Charles L. Black, *Decision According to Law* (New York: Norton, 1981), 18.

350 Senator Eastland quoted in *Look* magazine, April 3, 1956, 24.

O

354 Tendency to corrupt test: *Regina v. Hicklin*, L.R. 3 Q.B. 360 (1868).

354 Judge Woolsey's decision to allow Joyce's *Ulysses* to

Page

circulate in America: *United States v. One Book Called "Ulysses,"* 5 F.Supp. 182 (S.D.N.Y. 1933), *aff'd,* 72 F.2d 705 (2d Cir. 1934).

354 Walt Disney movie and southern schoolchildren: *New York Times,* June 27, 1969, 1; noted in Henry J. Abraham, *Freedom and the Court* (New York: Oxford Univ. Press, 4th ed., 1982), 188–9.

364 Meese's speech on the jurisprudence of original intention is reprinted, along with many other valuable essays concurring and dissenting, in Jack N. Rakove, ed., *Interpreting the Constitution: The Debate Over Original Intention* (Boston: Northeastern Univ. Press, 1990), 13.

364 Historians disagree: H. Jefferson Powell, "The Original Understanding of Original Intent," 98 *Harvard Law Review* 885 (1985); Charles A. Lofgren, "The Original Understanding of Original Intent?" 5 *Constitutional Commentary* 77 (1988), both reprinted in Rakove, 53, 117.

364 Madison's position on original intent: Jack N. Rakove, ed., *Interpreting the Constitution* (Boston: Northeastern Univ. Press, 1990), 183.

364 Madison's notes are "far from a verbatim record": James H. Hutson, "The Creation of the Constitution: The Integrity of the Documentary Record," 65 *Texas Law Review* 1, 29, 32, 34 (1986).

364 Constitutional historians: See, for example, Leonard W. Levy, *Original Intent and the Framers' Constitution* (New York: Macmillan, 1988).

366 Meaning of other public ministers quoted: 7 *Opinions of the Attorneys General* 168 (1855).

367 According to one count: See the listing in Johnny H. Killian and George A. Costello, eds., *The Constitution of the United States of America: Analysis and Interpretation, 1990 Supplement* (Washington, DC: Congressional Research Service, Library of Congress, 1991), 266. The list through 1990 reaches 196 overruled cases, and since then the Court has overruled a few others.

P

377 Corporation as person: The story is told in Hugh Davis Graham, *Everyman's Constitution—Historical Essays on the Fourteenth Amendment, the "Conspiracy Theory," and American Constitutionalism* (Madison: Univ. of Wisconsin Press, 1968).

394 Locke on royal prerogative: Second Treatise, §§159–61.

397 Dispute between Hamilton and Madison on neutrality proclamation: See Edward S. Corwin, *The President's Control of Foreign Relations* (Princeton: Princeton Univ. Press, 1917), chap. 1.

397 Theodore Roosevelt on his powers as president: *Autobiography* (New York: Macmillan, 1931), 38.

398 Washington with little to do: Forrest McDonald, *The Presidency of George Washington* (Lawrence: Univ. of Kansas Press, 1973), 26.

407 Famous article co-authored by Brandeis: Samuel Warren and Louis D. Brandeis, "The Right to Privacy," 4 *Harvard Law Review* 193 (1890).

413 Cardozo on the blundering constable: *People v. DeFore,* 242 N.Y. 13, 150 N.E. 585 (1926).

415 Professor Reich's law review article on entitlements: "The New Property," 73 *Yale Law Journal* 733 (1964).

424 Prosecutors are rarely disciplined for participating in fraud and perjury: See Jethro K. Lieberman, *How the Government Breaks the Law* (New York: Stein & Day, 1972), 35–48.

424 Defining harm in a general way: See Jethro K. Lieberman, "The Relativity of Injury," 7 *Philosophy and Public Affairs* 60 (1977); "Toward a Theory of Injury," in *Pernicious Ideas and Costly Consequences: The Intellectual Roots of the Tort Crisis* (Washington, DC: National Legal Center for the Public Interest, 1990), 99. See also Joel Feinberg's magisterial four-volume *The Moral Limits of the Criminal Law* (New York: Oxford Univ. Press)—*Harm to Others,* 1984; *Offense to Others,* 1985; *Harm to Self,* 1986; *Harmless Wrongdoing,* 1988.

425 Holmes on free speech rights of policemen: *McAuliffe v. Mayor of New Bedford,* 155 Mass. 216, 29 N.E. 517 (1892).

427 Holmes on laws limiting speech in public parks: *Massachusetts v. Davis,* 162 Mass. 510, 39 N.E. 113 (1895), *aff'd,* 167 U.S. 43 (1897).

R

442 Lower courts concluded: *Griffin's Case,* 11 Fed.Cas. 7, No. 5815 (C.C.D.Va. 1869).

454 Popular uprising in Rhode Island: For a history of the rebellion, see Marvin E. Gettleman, *The Dorr Rebellion* (New York: Random House, 1973).

462 Holmes on policeman's right to talk politics: *McAuliffe v. Mayor of New Bedford*, 155 Mass. 216, 220, 29 N.E. 517, 518 (1892).

464 Thomas Paine wrote: *Common Sense*, ed. Isaac Kramnick (New York: Penguin, 1982), 98.

S

484 Lemuel Shaw's opinion: *Roberts v. City of Boston*, 59 Mass. 198 (1849).

497 Heap of inconsistencies: Justice Antonin Scalia, dissenting in *United States v. Johnson*, 481 U.S. 681 (1987), offered the following example of the intersection of various laws consenting to suit against the United States and the doctrine barring suits by military personnel: "A serviceman is told by his superior officer to deliver some papers to the local United States Courthouse. As he nears his destination, a wheel on his government vehicle breaks, causing the vehicle to injure him, his daughter (whose class happens to be touring the Courthouse that day) and a United States marshal on duty. Under our case law and federal statute, the serviceman may not sue the Government; the guard may not sue the Government; the daughter may not sue the Government for the loss of her father's companionship, but may sue the Government for her own injuries. The serviceman and her guard may sue the manufacturer of the vehicle, as may the daughter, both for her own injuries and for the loss of her father's companionship. The manufacturer may assert contributory negligence as a defense in any of the suits. Moreover, the manufacturer may implead the Government in the daughter's suit and in the guard's suit, even though the guard was compensated under a statute that contains an exclusivity provision. But the manufacturer may not implead the Government in the serviceman's suit, even though the serviceman was compensated under a statute that does not contain an exclusivity provision." 481 U.S. 681, 701–702 (citations are omitted).

497 James Wilson on sovereignty: See Gordon S. Wood, *The Creation of the American Republic, 1776–1787* (New York: Norton, 1969), 530, 532.

503 Congressional standing: *Kennedy v. Sampson*, 511 F.2d 430 (D.C.Cir. 1974) (standing to sue for violation of the Pocket Veto Clause).

523 The description of the Supreme Court is taken from Jethro K. Lieberman, *The Enduring Constitution* (New York: Harper & Row, 1987), 120–1. The quotations are from *Congressional Quarterly's Guide to the Supreme Court* (Washington, DC: Congressional Quarterly, 1979), 772.

524 Leading commentator has argued: Charles L. Black, Jr., *Decision According to Law* (New York: Norton, 1981), 43.

T

538 Franklin on sheep not making insurrection: Quoted in William M. Wiecek, *The Sources of Antislavery Constitutionalism in America, 1760–1848* (Ithaca, NY: Cornell Univ. Press, 1977), 57.

542 Professor Tribe on interstate trucking case: Laurence H. Tribe, *American Constitutional Law* (Mineola, NY: Foundation, 2nd ed., 1988), 422.

U

552 Holmes on a policeman's right to talk politics: *McAuliffe v. Mayor of New Bedford*, 155 Mass. 216, 29 N.E. 517 (1892).

553 Opinion of the attorney general: 39 *Opinions of the Attorney General* (1937).

553 Court has struck down 125 federal laws: Johnny H. Killian and George A. Costello, eds., *The Constitution of the United States of America: Analysis and Interpretation, 1990 Supplement* (Washington, DC: Congressional Research Service, Library of Congress, 1991), 242, 259, 263.

V

563 Presumably commands public elections for state legislators: The Court has ruled that the Guarantee Clause is nonjusticiable. But it is hard to understand what a "republican form of government" would be if the people could not vote. For a general argument about the constitutional bases of voting, see John Hart Ely, *Democracy and Distrust* (Cambridge: Harvard Univ. Press, 1980), 117.

564 Louisiana black registration fell: The figures are from C. Vann Woodward, *The Strange Career*

Page

of Jim Crow (New York: Oxford Univ. Press, 1974), 85.

W

567 Madison on "sudden attacks": Max Farrand, *The Records of the Federal Convention of 1787* (New Haven: Yale Univ. Press, rev. ed., 1937), 2:318.

569 Lincoln's use of the phrase "war power": Message to Congress of July 4, 1861, reprinted in *Abraham Lincoln: Speeches and Writings 1859–1865* (New York: Library of America, 1989), 250.

Y

578 The story of the Yazoo land scandal is told in C. Peter Magrath, *Yazoo: The Case of Fletcher v. Peck* (New York: Norton, 1966).

Z

581 The story of the Zenger trial is told in James Alexander, *A Brief Narrative of the Case and Trial of John Peter Zenger,* ed. Stanley N. Katz (Cambridge: Harvard Univ. Press, 2nd ed., 1972).

Acknowledgments

The proximate cause of this book was my deep unhappiness with the impoverished state of indexing in America. Let me be candid. Most publishers do not seem to care that people might actually wish to use their books for reference. Pathetic is not too strong a word to use in connection with the indexing to the great constitutional casebooks, the treatises, and even the masterly annotated Constitution produced by the Congressional Research Service of the Library of Congress. To escape such criticism, this book omits an index, but only because it tries to be one, body and soul.

Along the way I have accumulated considerable debts to the following people for their assistance: Susan Karp and Scott Odierno, my students in 1990–91, for help in assembling the topics and stuffing nearly 1,500 folders with relevant material; Mary-Jane Oltarziewski, also my student in 1990–91, for heroically beginning the Table of Cases; Tracy A. Smith for heroically finishing and painstakingly checking it, for preparing the section on the justices of the Supreme Court, and for helping above and beyond the call of duty on many other aspects of production; Paul Mastrangelo, of the New York Law School library staff, for his always cheerful and prompt reactions to my obscure requests; Fernando Cruz, for clerical assistance large and small; Erika S. Fine for showing me how to use some of the more arcane features of Westlaw; my colleague Professor Ruti Teitel for a draft of the entry "Rebellion"; New York Law School and Dean James F. Simon for providing two summer research grants without which this book would not likely have been completed on schedule; Charlotte Leon Mayerson, my editor at Random House, for her acute editorial red pencil that cut without distorting and for her prodding that got me from A to Z; Random House production editors Judy Kaplan Johnson and Lila M. Gardner, copyeditor Carole Cook, and proofreaders Mary Louise Byrd, Sharon Goldstein, and Karen Osborne for labors that must have produced many an over-the-counter headache; Gerry Uram and Seth Lieberman for their usual efficient courier services; and my wife, Jo Shifrin, who could always be coaxed into late-night sessions to check numbing case numbers and to cross-check entries.

Finally to update the record, and because I promised to note their progress, Jessica and Seth have both graduated from college and no longer pledge to read my books, someday.

The usual apology for the errors that remain is, in this case, no mere cliché. This is a first edition of a work embracing close to a thousand topics, every one of which has students more expert than I. So I conjoin my apology with the entreaty that those who spot omissions or errors of fact and judgment alert me to them to the end of perfecting someday a revised edition.

Hastings-on-Hudson, NY   J.K.L.

ABOUT THE AUTHOR

JETHRO K. LIEBERMAN is professor of law and director of the writing program at New York Law School, where he has served on the faculty since 1985. He is a graduate of Yale College and Harvard Law School and has had a long career as a writer and journalist. He was the founding editor of *Business Week*'s Legal Affairs Department, serving in that position from 1973 to 1982. Mr. Lieberman is the author of twenty-one published books, including *The Litigious Society* and *The Enduring Constitution*, both of which won the American Bar Association's highest writing honor, the Silver Gavel Award (in 1982 and 1988). He lives with his wife in Hastings-on-Hudson, New York.

The Evolving Constitution

If you would like to obtain annual supplements to this volume, with complete summaries of the constitutional decisions of the U.S. Supreme Court during future terms, please fill in the form below and mail it to:

Dialogue Press, Inc.
Box 45, 1678 Shattuck Avenue
Berkeley, California 94709

☐ Yes, I would like to obtain annual supplements to *The Evolving Constitution*. Please notify me when the next supplement is ready.

Name: _____

Street: _____

City: _____

State: _____ Zip: _____